The intellectual and cultural changes that took place from the Renaissance to contemporary times are dramatically illustrated by the ADORATION OF THE SACRED LAMB from the Ghent altarpiece by Jan van Eyck (c. 1380–1441) and AROUND THE FISH by Paul Klee (1879–1940). In the altarpiece, Van Eyck endeavored to paint each detail in nature as he saw it. Klee, on the other hand, sought new relationships between objects and the inner essence of individual things not apparent to the eye. (Altarpiece from Art Reference Bureau. Klee painting from Museum of Modern Art, Abby Aldrich Rockefeller Fund)

THE LIPPINCOTT HISTORY SERIES

under the editorship of Robert F. Byrnes, Indiana University

THE

RENAISSANCE

J. RUSSELL MAJOR
Emory University

J. B. LIPPINCOTT COMPANY

WESTERN WORLD

TO THE PRESENT

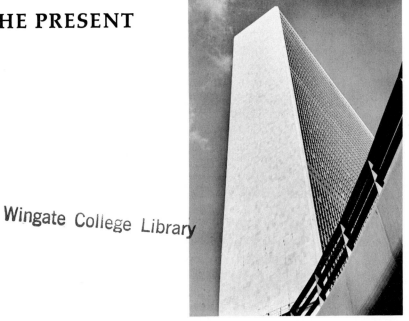

PHILADELPHIA AND NEW YORK

TO

Blair Louise
Randon Leigh
Clara Jean
Russell

Preface

THIS BOOK is a history of the Western world from the Renaissance to the present. The term Western world refers to that portion of the earth which subscribed to most of the basic tenets of Western civilization during a given period. As a result, the subject matter gradually expands beyond the boundaries of Europe, in keeping with the gradual expansion of European civilization, until the text becomes a history of the entire world. This organization should enable the reader to become acquainted not only with European history since the Renaissance but also with contemporary developments in many parts of the globe.

Although analytical history has not been neglected, a special effort has been made to delineate the characters and motives of the leading personages of the past as well as to describe the political and social institutions through which they worked. In the sections on cultural history, more attention has been given to the dominant style of a period than to the works of individual artists and writers, and in the sections on intellectual history as much space has been devoted to describing the climate of opinion of an era as to explaining the ideas of a few famous thinkers. It is hoped that this approach will enable the reader to achieve a better understanding of the various historical epochs. Difficult subjects have not been omitted, but an effort has been made to clarify them for the non-specialist. For example, the scientific revolutions of the seventeenth and twentieth centuries have been explained and interpreted in non-technical terms.

Another characteristic of this book is that it presents an interpretation of the history of the Western world. This interpretation has been influenced by recent works which have shown that the Renaissance was dominated by a reconstructed aristocracy, not by the middle class; that the seventeenth century was characterized by political, social, and economic crises; and that the era between 1750 and 1850 witnessed democratic revolutions in Europe and America. On the other hand, the somewhat unusual treatment of the scientific and aesthetic revolutions of the twentieth century was suggested as much by an understanding of the earlier periods as by specific studies on these subjects.

Although historians will disagree with some aspects of the overall interpretation, an interpretative work should be of greater interest than one that merely assembles the basic facts. However, the author has tried not to weight the facts too heavily in the direction of his interpretation so that those who disagree with him will have ammunition available to defend a contrary point of view.

As a part of this interpretation, reference is made throughout the book to certain great themes of Western civilization. These include the themes of population growth, urbanization, the evolution of social classes, the changing nature and function of the state, the relationship between science, thought, and religion, the rise and decline of naturalism in art and literature, and the expansion of Western civilization to other parts of the world.

The author of any book covering so large a span of history must depend heavily on the advice of others. To my colleagues in the history department of Emory University I am indebted for their suggestions of what to read and what interpretations to accept concerning many areas of history that were largely unfamiliar to me. Of their number, I wish to thank especially Professors Joseph J. Mathews and Douglas A. Unfug for the guidance they have given me on nineteenth- and twentieth-century European history.

Three historians who have never been connected with Emory have contributed heavily to this book. The first was the late Professor E. Harris Harbison under whom I studied at Princeton. His ability to interpret, synthesize, and express complex problems in a clear, simple style has provided a model which I have tried to emulate. To the late Professor Sidney Painter of The Johns Hopkins University I also owe a heavy debt. We were collaborating on a two-volume history of Western civilization when his untimely death brought that project to an abrupt end and caused me to undertake the present, less ambitious work alone. I did, however, have the benefit of Professor Painter's criticisms of a number of chapters. Finally, to Professor Robert F. Byrnes of the University of Indiana I wish to express my appreciation for his careful reading and well-advised criticism of the entire manuscript.

To my wife I also owe a great debt. She has read and re-read the entire work and to her has fallen the brunt of the task of transferring my illegible handwritten manuscript to typed pages. To the various departmental secretaries who have assisted in the latter chore when their other duties permitted, I also wish to give my thanks. Alex Fraser, Thomas Abrams, and John Bernheim, of J. B. Lippincott Company, have improved the clarity and style of the book, prepared the chronological tables, and given editorial help of unusual intelligence. Lastly, I wish to thank my four children for their forbearance during the years I have spent writing this text. Monographs are often created during academic leaves of absence, but a book of this sort must of necessity be the product of evening, weekend, and summer work that has deprived me of their society more than otherwise would have been the case. To them this work is affectionately dedicated.

Emory University　　　　　　　　　　　　　　　　J. Russell Major
September, 1965

Contents

Contents

Contents

xi

Contents

Contents

Contents

PART I

INTRODUCTION

EUROPE AS A WHOLE	WESTERN EUROPE	EASTERN EUROPE
	1225-1274, St. Thomas Aquinas	
	1260-1327, Meister Eckhart	
c.1300-c.1450, Decline of the Church; revival of nominalism; economic depression; social strife; population decline (Black Death, c.1347-c.1350); weakening of medieval monarchy	1300-1349, William of Ockham 1302, *Unam Sanctam;* Estates-General meets in France 1305, Clement V elected pope, later establishes papacy at Avignon	
	1324, *Defensor Pacis* of Marsiglio of Padua	
	1330-1384, John Wyclif	
	1337-1453, Hundred Years War	
	1351, Statute of Laborers	
		1354, Ottoman Turks begin expansion into Balkans 1370-1415, John Hus
	1378-1417, The Great Schism c.1380, Groote founds *Devotia Moderna*	
		1396, Moslems defeat Christians at Nicopolis
	1414-1417, General Council meets at Constance	
		1419-1436, Hussite Wars
		1453, Ottoman Turks capture Constantinople

THIS is the story of our modern civilization. Some of the characteristics of this civilization had appeared in Western Europe by the fourteenth century; others did not appear until the eighteenth century. Always there were some Western European countries that lagged far behind the others. In the fifteenth century this nascent civilization began to expand southward along the African coast, westward across the Atlantic, and eastward around Africa to southern Asia. Later, the Russians were brought within its boundaries, and through them Western civilization expanded across northern Asia to the Pacific. Today, only a tiny minority of the world's inhabitants remain altogether outside its scope. At the close of the nineteenth century, some characteristics of this civilization began to change; others became more pronounced. At the present time, Western civilization is undergoing its most serious crisis. Whatever the outcome, the civilization that began to emerge in Western Europe in the fourteenth and fifteenth centuries has already accomplished far more than any of its predecessors.

Obviously, the story of a civilization that has no real beginning and may or may not be coming to an end is a very complicated one. Before beginning its study, we should enquire into the nature and purpose of history, the geographical setting in which modern Western civilization emerged, and the people who brought it into being. We should also survey the great medieval civilization whose decline opened the way for our modern Western civilization.

3

1/ History, Geography, and People

THE NATURE AND PURPOSE OF HISTORY

HISTORY is the story of the past. In the broadest sense of the word it includes everything that has happened before you picked up this book. There is a history of art, a history of literature, a history of business administration, a history of science, and a history of every other activity in which man has ever engaged. History, in short, is by no means limited to a narrative of political events. Indeed, the study of natural science itself is often largely historical: the geologist studies the earth as it has changed in time, and the biologist studies the various species as they have evolved through time. However, for the purposes of this book the term history is applied only to the activities of man.

Why study the past? We live in the present, and our aspirations can be achieved only in the future. Henry Ford admirably summarized this point of view when he declared that "history is bunk." With a little reflection, however, the debunkers will recognize that history is one of the most important social sciences as well as one of the most important humanistic studies.

4

HISTORY AS A SOCIAL SCIENCE

The average man of twenty-five can learn and think as rapidly as the average man of fifty because the mental processes do not speed up with increased age. This fact suggests that it would be justifiable to give a new college graduate hired by the Ford Motor Company as high a position as that once held by the aging Henry Ford and to start the West Point graduate on his military career with the rank of general. That is, it would be justifiable if Henry Ford and the army officer with thirty years of service did not have more experience than the new college or West Point graduate. Experience is the knowledge of how to deal with various situations, a knowledge achieved by dealing with similar situations in the past. It is, in short, a form of historical knowledge. Those with experience merit positions superior to new college graduates because they know history, their own personal history.

If experience—the knowledge of one's own history—is of value, a knowledge of other people's experiences must also be of value. History is useful because it enables us to draw on the experiences of others both in our own time and in past generations. The human being is the only creature capable of thinking historically except in the most basic sense, and this is one of the most important reasons for his triumph over other animals.

Man, or something closely related to man, has been able to fabricate instruments for at least a million and a half years, but at first human experiences could be exchanged only by word of mouth. About twenty thousand years ago, man learned to convey experiences by drawing pictures on the walls of caves, and about four thousand years ago he developed the alphabet. With the invention of writing, man's capacity to learn from history increased rapidly because he no longer had to depend on oral tradition. About five hundred years ago, Europeans began to print with movable type. This invention multiplied many times over his capacity to record and publicize events, and hundreds of inventions since that time have added to this ability. Thus, man's capacity to learn from the past has increased very rapidly during the last few thousand years. This is one reason why, after making very slow progress towards civilization during the first 1,500,000 years of his existence, man has been moving forward at a rapidly accelerating rate during the last one-half of one per cent of his life on this earth.

Some uninformed people believe that in our scientific era the study of history is declining, but the reverse is true. As late as 1880 there were only eleven professors of history in American colleges. The typical college had no historian at all, and professors of philosophy, theology, and literature taught the few history courses that were offered. Today there are thousands of history professors in the United States, and a single institution, with one or two thousand students, usually employs as many historians as there were in the country in 1880.

5

One reason for the rapid growth of the profession is that the need to know history is greater now than ever before. In the second century before Christ, the Greek historian Polybius declared that "History offers the best training for those who are to take part in public affairs." This advice was repeated by thousands of scholars after his day, but since only kings and nobles governed, it was often stipulated that only kings and nobles need study history. This situation was changed by the growth of democracy. Having won the right to participate in public affairs by voting, every adult has become morally obligated to learn the lessons of the past so that he can exercise his suffrage more intelligently.

The knowledge we get from history is used in the same way as the knowledge we get from our own experiences. In our lives we are never confronted with two identical situations, just as history never repeats itself. But we do meet similar situations, and the experience we get trying to handle one situation may help us handle another that is comparable. In the same manner, if we know how a problem was met in the past, we can approach a similar current problem more intelligently. For example, the American refusal to join the League of Nations after World War I contributed to the failure of the League to cope with aggressors. As a result, the United States joined the United Nations after World War II and thereby definitely furthered the cause of world peace.

Unfortunately, some historians have tried to use history to serve their own ends. Medieval Christians wrote history to explain what they conceived to be the unfolding of the divine plan. Marxist historians write history describing the struggle between the social classes in the hope of convincing the reader of the inevitable triumph of communism. To inculcate patriotism, nationalistic historians have painted their own countries in glowing terms and have belittled the achievements of other peoples. A few conservatives have made Franklin D. Roosevelt responsible for the Japanese attack on Pearl Harbor in 1941, while some liberals have tried to blame the assassination of President Kennedy on the extremely conservative leadership of Dallas, although the assassin was a Communist sympathizer who had spent very little of his life in that city.

History written to prove a point may be very interesting and have the merit of provoking thought, but it is also very dangerous because it perverts the truth. To avoid this danger, many scholars have tried to write "scientific" history. They have gathered all the surviving information about a particular event, have tried to evaluate each item objectively, and, then, in the words of Leopold von Ranke (1795-1886), have simply stated "what has actually happened."

Some historians have argued that history can never be written scientifically because much of the data has been lost and because it is difficult for anyone to be completely objective when he selects his material and organizes it into a coherent pattern. There is considerable truth in these criticisms, but they are not wholly fair. Although a vast amount of data has been lost, the historian often knows more about a past event than the participants. Some of General Eisenhower's thoughts and actions during the Normandy landing in World War II have not been recorded, but historians know more about what the Germans were doing than he did at the time, and they certainly know far more about the significant actions in both armies than the average participant knew. A historian may not escape bias altogether when he selects and organizes his data; but if he tries to be objective, he will come nearer to the truth than if he does not, just as the man who is capable of self-examination profits more from his own experiences than one who is self-righteous. Scientific history, then, is a worthy and useful ideal, though one that will never be realized fully.

Even when two historians try to write scientific history about the same subject, they often arrive at different conclusions. The judgment of men varies; what seems important to one may seem unimportant to another. When historians make no effort to be scientific, however, their conclusions differ more often and more widely. One historian's explanation of a past event, when it differs from the explanation of another historian, is said to be his *interpretation*. There are different interpretations of the nature of the Renaissance, the causes of World War I, and almost every other important event. The inability of historians to agree always with one another does not negate the value of history. Indeed, in some respects it makes history more valuable because it stimulates one's capacity to think historically by showing more clearly the different ways in which historical problems can be approached.

One of the greatest debates among historians is over the question of how far man can guide the course of human history. To Communist historians economic factors determine the course of events and individual men are only the pawns of this great historical force. Other historians have argued for the overwhelming importance of ideas, culture, political institutions, climate and soil, and a host of other things. In opposition to these interpretations, there are historians who believe that man is the master of his destiny and can create and alter economic and political institutions, ideas, culture, and, with the aid of modern science, even climate and soil, to meet his needs. The truth probably lies somewhere between those who emphasize the role of historical forces and those who emphasize the role of man. In this text, an effort is made to analyze the forces in a given epoch and then to give a predominantly chronological account of how these forces affected man and how man altered and directed these forces.

As suggested above, the forces were different in different epochs. Since the late seventeenth century, it has been customary to divide the past into three epochs or periods—the ancient, the medieval, and the modern. Actually, there were more than three periods, although historians have reached no agreement concerning exactly what they were. This text is concerned with what has traditionally been called modern history, the history of Western man from the Renaissance to the present. Modern history is divided, however, into a number of epochs around a century in length in which the majority of the people had a common set of ideas, principles, and aesthetic values. The common quality of an epoch is called its "climate of opinion." There were, of course, many people who were at odds with the climate of opinion of their time, but their attitudes can be treated only in histories that are more specialized than this one.

HISTORY AS ONE OF THE HUMANITIES

Thus far, we have treated history only as a social science, that is, the scientific study of society undertaken to obtain practical knowledge. It is also one of the humanities. Many scholars have regarded history as a form of literature, and there is no reason why it cannot be as well written as a novel. Then, too, a knowledge of history can make other activities more enjoyable. If one learns the history of the Renaissance, for example, he can understand and enjoy the art and literature of that period more fully. If he is fortunate enough to travel abroad, old castles and churches will have more meaning for him. He will understand the people of the various countries and have more sympathy for their ways. To visit Paris or Florence without a knowledge of history is to lose three-fourths of the pleasure of the journey. History, like the other humanities, provides a deeper, richer, more meaningful life.

At one time, it was necessary for over 90 per cent of the population to work seventy or eighty hours a week so that the remainder could have a little leisure. The invention of labor-saving machines, however, has enabled man to supply his needs by working fewer hours. Nearly everyone now has as much leisure as the kings and nobles of the past. The growth of democracy made it necessary for the average citizen to obtain a knowledge of history that only princes needed in the past; at the same time, the growth of leisure has made it possible for him to study the subject for his own enjoyment.

History is also one of the humanities in the broadest sense of the term, in that it helps one to understand people. The Scottish philosopher David Hume (1711-1776), who was skeptical about so many things, thought that it was possible to use history "to discover the constant and universal principles of human nature . . ." Although most historians now doubt whether there are any "constant and universal principles of human nature," it remains true that the study of history can help us to understand human beings better. The novelist writes about the people of his imagination. He may have excellent insight, but he is under no obligation to depict the normal, and his work will be colored throughout by his own individuality. The historian, on the other hand, writes about real people who face actual problems, and the requirement that he strive for objectivity makes it necessary for him to strip his own peculiarities and prejudices from his work as much as possible.

The function of history as a social science and as one of the humanities has been recognized for over two thousand years, but few have expressed the delights of "the great adventure" better than Niccolò Machiavelli (1469-1527), who was a diplomat, government official, military theorist, political scientist, poet, and dramatist as well as a historian. After losing his government post, Machiavelli retired to his farm for the rest of his life. There, he took up the study of history. In a letter of December 10, 1513, he tells how he occupies his mornings managing his little estate. "Then," he writes,

> I move on down the road to the inn, talk with passers-by, ask news of the places they come from, hear this and that, and note the various tastes and fancies of mankind. This brings me to lunch-time, when I and my family eat such food this poor house and my slender patrimony affords. When I have eaten, I go back to the inn, where I usually find the landlord, a butcher, a miller, and a couple of brick-makers. With these I act the rustic for the rest of the day, playing at *cricca* and *tricche-trach*, which lead to a thousand squabbles and countless slanging matches—our fights are usually over a farthing, but we can be heard shouting nonetheless from San Casciano. So, trapped among this vermin I rub the mould off my wits and work off the sense of being so cruelly treated by Fate—content to be driven along this road if only to watch for her to show some sign of shame.
>
> When evening comes, I return home and go into my study. On the threshold I strip off the muddy, sweaty clothes of everyday, and put on the robes of court and palace, and in this graver dress I enter the antique courts of the ancients where, being welcomed by them, I taste the food that alone is mine, for which I was born. And there I make bold to speak to them and ask the motives of their actions. And they, in their humanity, reply to me. And for the space of four hours I forget the world, remember no vexation, fear poverty no more, tremble no more at death: I am wholly absorbed in them. And as Dante says that there can be no understanding without the memory retaining what it has heard, I have written down what I have gained from their conversation, and composed a small work *De principatibus,* where I dive as deep as I can into ideas about this subject, discussing the nature of princely rule, what forms it takes, how these are acquired, how they are maintained, why they are lost.[1]

We shall meet Machiavelli again, but meanwhile put on the robes of court and palace, enter the antique courts of the ancients, and make bold to speak to them and ask the motives of their actions.

THE INFLUENCE OF GEOGRAPHY AND CLIMATE

The planet we call the earth is probably between three and a half and four and a half billion years old. Its climate and surface have undergone great changes during its long history, but in the last five hundred years there have been no significant variations. They may therefore be treated as constant factors during the modern period. The earth's surface consists of

[1] Quoted in John R. Hale, *Machiavelli and Renaissance Italy* (London: The English Universities Press, 1961), pp. 148-49.

nearly two hundred million square miles, almost three-fourths of which is water. Even the continents are only large islands, and within them there are many seas, lakes, and rivers.

It is customary to divide the land mass of our planet into seven continents and numerous smaller islands that vary in size from a few square feet to many thousands of square miles. Actually, there are only four land masses with over a million square miles. One of these, the Eurasian-African, contains nearly 60 per cent of the earth's land. Another, the two Americas, contains nearly 30 per cent, while the remaining two, Australia and Antarctica, have only a few million square miles apiece. Migrations from Eurasia-Africa to the Americas and Australia took place thousands of years ago, but during the period of recorded history contacts between these land masses were of minor importance until the close of the fifteenth century. As a result, it was possible for advanced civilizations to develop on the Eurasian-African land mass without influencing or being influenced by other people until modern times.

Europe itself is really only a peninsula slightly larger than the United States, thrusting westward from Asia. The Ural Mountains provide the traditional dividing line between the two continents, although they are too low to be much of a barrier and people have always been able to move through them with relative ease. Europe does not actually touch Africa, but the Iberian, Italian, and Greek peninsulas jut out into the Mediterranean so far that it has always been easy to reach the north African coast. As a result, there has been a constant interplay among the inhabitants of these three continents.

Generally speaking, southern Europe is mountainous, but great plains stretch across northern and eastern Europe. There are, however, important exceptions to this rule. In the south, navigable rivers such as the Danube, the Po, and the Rhône have cut wide valleys through the mountain ranges, and much of the Iberian Peninsula consists of a high plateau. Nevertheless, there are many rugged mountain ranges in southern Europe. The Sierra Nevada and the Pyrénées rise over 11,000 feet above sea level, the Alps over 15,000 feet, and the Caucasus Mountains over 18,000 feet. In northern and eastern Europe, the great plains are divided by the Central Russian Highland, and most of the Scandinavian Peninsula is mountainous.

Europe is farther north than other thickly inhabited portions of the earth. Rome and Madrid are at about the same latitude as New York City and Peking, and London and Berlin are as far north as parts of Labrador. Its location, however, does not prevent Western Europe from having a very attractive climate because of the influence of neighboring bodies of water. An ocean current from the Gulf of Mexico flows across the Atlantic and warms the coastal belt of Europe as far north as the Arctic Circle, where in Norway the winters are no colder than in New York City. Winds from the Sahara Desert blow across the Mediterranean Sea and warm the south-

PHYSICAL MAP OF EUROPE

SCALE OF MILES
0   100   200   300   400   500

ern shores of the continent where the Gulf Stream does not reach. In crossing the Mediterranean, these winds pick up enough moisture to ensure an adequate amount of rainfall, and the prevailing winds that follow the Gulf Stream perform a similar service for the coastal region. As a result, southern and western Europe have mild climates devoid of extremes of cold and heat, and there is ample rainfall in the various seasons to support forest vegetation except in parts of the Iberian Peninsula.

The climate of eastern Europe, on the other hand, is more typical of a northern continent. The land mass is too wide and too far removed from the Atlantic Ocean and the southern seas to profit from their warming influence or their moisture. The winters are quite cold and much of the region suffers from a lack of rainfall, although there is little desert. This difference in climate helps to explain why the Mediterranean and Atlantic regions were the great centers of Western civilization until the twentieth century, when technological developments enabled the eastern Europeans to overcome some of their geographical disadvantages.

In spite of its relatively small size, the peninsular character of the continent gives it fifty thousand miles of coast line with numerous harbors. No other continent is nearly so fortunate in this respect. Since water travel was faster and cheaper than land travel until the invention of the railroad, Europe was in an advantageous position for trade. For centuries, the Mediterranean Sea was the center of commerce; when the art of sailing on the rough Atlantic was learned, that ocean became an even greater traverse of trade. On a planet whose surface is predominantly water, mastery of the sea meant probable mastery of the world, until our time when technological advances have made control of the air even more important.

The soils of Europe vary widely from one region to another. In the Mediterranean area the top soil is often too thin and sandy to permit the cultivation of many crops, and the inhabitants devote much of their energy to raising grapes, olives, and citrus fruit. The southern and central portions of the great European plain to the north have a deep, rich, loamy soil that permits the intensive cultivation of wheat, rye, potatoes, sugar beets, and similar crops, but the northern part of the great plain is often sandy and marshy.

Some individual European countries like Spain and Italy lack minerals, but the continent as a whole is well endowed in this respect. Sweden, Russia, Germany, and France contain valuable deposits of iron ore, while coal is plentiful in Great Britain, Germany, Poland, Russia, Belgium, and France. High mountains and abundant rainfall provide for hydroelectric power, and oil has been found in Rumania and elsewhere. Electricity and oil have become important only in recent years, but the favorable climate, soil, and mineral resources of most of Western Europe and its peninsular character have contributed greatly to the importance of this relatively small portion of the earth.

RACES AND PEOPLES

Mankind is a single biological species, but it has become customary to classify individual people according to race, just as dogs are classified according to breed. There has never been any agreement on what the races are. Most often color has been taken as the determining characteristic, but the form of the head hair, the shape of the skull, and other bodily features have been used. Each criterion leads to somewhat different results. If the head hair method of classification is used, the white inhabitants of Europe are grouped with the nearly black Australian aborigines.

Color may not be the best basis for classification, but it is the oldest and the most used in popular parlance. Some scholars who have accepted it have argued that there are five races: the Caucasian or white, the Mongolian or yellow, the Negro or black, the Malayan or brown, and the American or red. Several of these races, such as the Mongolian and American, are obviously related, and there are many mixed races. Nevertheless, if this classification is accepted, virtually all Europeans are Caucasians.

The Europeans have been subdivided into the Nordic people in the north, who are frequently tall, blond, blue-eyed, and fair-skinned; the Mediterranean people in the south, who are short, black-haired, brown-eyed, and dark-skinned; and the Alpine people in the center, whose traits are somewhere in between. It is impossible to draw lines on a map showing where these sub-races live, and if one travels from southern Italy northward to Sweden, he notes that the changes in the inhabitants' complexions are not sudden but gradual, because of frequent intermarriage between neighboring peoples. Therefore, although the average Swede looks quite different from the average southern Italian, the Europeans as a whole have become too intermixed for any sort of racial classification to be very useful.

For this reason, many scholars have preferred to classify the inhabitants of the world according to the language they speak. There are now three or four thousand languages, as well as numerous dialects. Many of these languages are related to one another, and this relation can be ascertained from the presence of the same words and from other linguistic similarities. Occasionally, the actual historical development of a language can be traced. For example, the Latin language used in the Roman Empire was clearly the parent of the Romance languages: French, Spanish, Portuguese, Italian, and Rumanian. German, Dutch, English, and the Scandinavian languages also have a common ancestor, as do the Slavonic languages spoken in eastern Europe. In a remarkable feat of linguistic analysis, it has been shown that the Romantic, Germanic, and Slavonic languages had a common ancestor that is usually called Indo-European.

The Indo-European language probably originated along the eastern shores of the Baltic Sea and spread over nearly all of Europe and part of

Asia. As time passed, it broke up into dialects that became languages. These languages in turn became the parents of other languages. Thus, the Indo-European language gave birth to Latin, which in turn became the parent of the Romance languages. Not only are the Romantic, Slavonic, and Germanic languages descended from Indo-European, but also Greek and Celtic, which are still spoken in parts of Europe, as well as Iranian, Indic, and their descendants, which are spoken in Iran, India, and other places in the Middle East.

The Indo-European linguistic family is by far the most important in Europe, but three others have been identified. The Finno-Ugrian linguistic family probably orginated in the Ural Mountain area. It is spoken by the Finns, Lapps, and Estonians in northern Europe, by some of the inhabitants of the Soviet Union, and by the Magyars in the Danube Basin. The Magyars conquered Hungary near the close of the ninth century where their presence separated the southern Slavs from the eastern and western Slavs to the north. A Caucasian linguistic family consists of Georgian and various dialects spoken in the Caucasus Mountains as well as several extinct languages. Finally, the inhabitants of the western Pyrénées speak Basque, a language of unknown linguistic origin and unrelated to any other that is used today.

There is obviously no necessary relation between language and race. The ancient Indo-Europeans probably spread their language largely by their migrations, but when they conquered another people, they intermarried with them at the same time that they gave them their language. Language, however, is one of the most important aspects of culture. This makes the fact that nearly all Europeans speak an Indo-European language very significant to Western civilization.

Within the Indo-European linguistic family, nearly all the major contributions in modern history have been made by members of the Romantic, Germanic, and Slavonic branches of the family. Educated persons within each of these three families have long been conscious of their relationship, and such movements as Pan-Slavism have had an important influence on history. Each of the major language groups has influenced the others. English, for example, belongs to the Germanic branch of the Indo-European linguistic family, but it has been heavily influenced by French as a result of the Norman Conquest in 1066. Contacts between the Germanic- and Romantic-speaking peoples have been constant for several thousand years, as have the contacts between the Germanic- and the Slavonic-speaking peoples.

Those who spoke the Romance languages inhabited southern Europe; those who spoke the Germanic languages, northern Europe; and those who spoke the Slavonic languages, eastern Europe, when the medieval civilizations began to wane in the early fourteenth century. For a long time, the story of Western civilization was essentially the story of the Romantic- and Germanic-speaking peoples who inhabited southern and western Europe where the climate was mild, the rainfall generally adequate, and the sea a major avenue of trade. Only gradually did the Slavs assume the important place they hold today in Western civilization.

THEMES IN WESTERN CIVILIZATION

The civilization that originated in the western half of the European continent had several outstanding features. The origin and development of these features and the changing climates of opinion of the various epochs of modern history are the principal themes of this book.

The most striking characteristic of Western civilization is its material progress and high standard of living. In preceding civilizations, including that of the Middle Ages, over nine-tenths of the population had to engage in agriculture so that the remainder could be administrators, merchants, artisans, and professional people. Even the wealthy had fewer comforts than the skilled laborer in the United States now possesses, and most of the people barely maintained their existence. Disease and malnutrition, if not actual famine, often decimated the population, and life expectancy at birth was less than thirty years. Men lived longer than women because the hazards of war were less serious than the hazards of childbirth.

Today one-tenth of the population of a Western nation can produce more food than the remainder can eat, enabling 90 per cent to engage in industry and in other occupations that have added greatly to the material wealth of the people. Science and technology have increased the productivity of labor and have conquered many diseases. Life expectancy at birth is now over seventy years, and the population has increased many times over.

These changes have produced a social revolution. Five hundred years ago the typical man lived in a village and worked on a farm. A town of 20,000 inhabitants was considered a metropolis, and there were no European cities with 100,000 residents. Today the typical man lives in a metropolitan area and engages in industry, marketing, or some related enterprise. In a highly industrialized country like England, 40 per cent of the inhabitants live in cities of over 100,000 inhabitants and 70 per cent in cities of over 20,000. The shift from agriculture to industry and from country to city has broken the power of the landed aristocracy and led to the rise of the urban middle class and the laboring class that competes with it for control of the government. Serfs and slaves have ceased to be part of the social order.

The political achievements of Western civilization are nearly as striking as its economic and social achievements. Medieval government was primarily in the hands of the king, nobility, and clergy; modern government is secular and democratic, and both men and women have an equal voice. The medieval citizen was loyal to his town, province, and ruling dynasty;

the modern citizen is loyal to a nation-state. Medieval liberty entailed different rights and privileges for each of the social classes; modern liberty entails equal rights for all citizens. Medieval government did little beyond protecting citizens from physical harm and administering justice; modern government assists the individual in many ways. Medieval war and diplomacy functioned without the benefit of standing armies or permanent diplomatic corps; modern war is conducted by large, well-trained, well-equipped armies, and diplomacy by resident ambassadors with a large number of specialized assistants. Medieval man based his hope for peace on the idea of Christian unity; modern man looks to an international organization for collective security.

Medieval civilization was almost entirely restricted to part of one small continent. During its formative period modern Western civilization spread to eastern Europe; it also established settlements in the Americas and along portions of the African and Asian coasts. As Western civilization reached its maturity, the entire world was brought wholly or partly within its sway. No other civilization has ever been so widespread or come so near to obliterating its rivals. As a result, the early chapters of this book deal only with Western Europe while the last two chapters deal with the recent history of the entire world.

The achievements of Western civilization were largely made possible by revolutionary progress in science and technology. During the Middle Ages the Western Europeans borrowed most of their scientific ideas from the ancient Greeks and Romans and were indebted to the Chinese and other Asiatics for some of their most significant technological developments. Since the scientific revolution in the seventeenth century, however, Western civilization has excelled all other civilizations, ancient and modern, in science and technology. Scientific and technological development and its relation to society and thought is one of the major themes of Western civilization.

It is more difficult to claim superiority for Western civilization in philosophy, religion, and the arts, but significant changes took place in these fields that must be considered. During the Middle Ages nearly all the inhabitants of Western Europe were Roman Catholics; philosophy and theology were allies. The sixteenth-century Protestant movement led to a multiplication of Christian sects, and the scientific revolution that followed caused most philosophers to abandon theology for science as a supporting discipline. There has been no steady movement from a religious to a secular society, for Western civilization has experienced several great religious revivals and a higher percentage of the population of the United States are church members today than in the eighteenth century. Nevertheless, modern Western society has been predominantly materialistic and secular.

The arts, too, have fluctuated rather than moved in a continuous direction. The greatest Western contributions have been in the direction of naturalism in art and materialism in literature—that is, the depicting of man, nature, and society as they really are. There have, however, been periods when artists have sought an idealized beauty or distorted the human body to achieve an emotional effect and when authors have preferred the "truth" of feeling to the "truth" of observation and intellect.

Perhaps the most significant concept in Western civilization has been the idea of progress and the perfectibility of man. This idea was born in the eighteenth century when most intellectuals began to believe that man was molded by his environment and could be made happier and better by more suitable surroundings. A great reforming impetus was given to Western civilization that is still characteristic of both the capitalistic and Communistic countries.

The essential features of modern Western civilization did not emerge suddenly. Instead, they developed gradually through a number of epochs, and it is necessary to understand the climate of opinion of each of these periods. The first epoch was the Renaissance, when artists learned to paint nature as it really appeared to be, when a multiplicity of religions developed, and when the expansion of Western civilization beyond Europe began. The second epoch was the Seventeenth-Century Crisis, when the progress made during the Renaissance was brought to a close in many spheres and when Western civilization threatened to become stagnant. A scientific revolution, however, ushered in the Age of the Egalitarian Revolutions, in which great material progress began to be made and the ideas of progress and human perfectibility were born. The early revolutions of this period were undertaken in the name of liberty, equality, and the right of self-government. Later revolutions also stressed the right of each nationality to have its own independent state. Significant reforms were achieved during this period, but the Triumph of Western Civilization was delayed until after 1850. Between then and the close of World War I, the boundaries between states were established approximately in accordance with nationality, democratic forms of government with equality before the law became the rule, material progress continued at an accelerated rate, and nearly all the inhabitants of the world were brought within the sway of Western civilization.

Today we live in a new epoch when Western civilization is once more in a state of crisis. Recent scientific discoveries have facilitated astounding material progress, but they have also undermined the idea of the omnipotence of the environment upon which the concepts of democracy, equality, reform, and human perfectibility have been based. Totalitarian governments have curtailed the liberty of many people more severely than ever before, and the possibility of an atomic holocaust is always before us. Amid these disturbing developments, however, there are many signs that the progress of civilization will continue, if we, like our seventeenth-century forebears, have the wisdom and the fortitude to meet the crisis.

2/ The Decline of Medieval Civilization

D URING the first quarter of the fourteenth century, medieval civilization reached its height. For three centuries, there had been almost
uninterrupted progress. The popes had freed themselves from secular rulers and had won recognition as the religious and moral leaders of the
Western world. The clergy had been reformed and reformed again. Gothic
cathedrals had been built in numerous cities, and their tall spires towered
over the other buildings to proclaim the power and wealth of the Roman
Catholic Church and the devotion of the people. Political order had been
established; the tiny urban population that had survived the decline of the
Roman Empire had been greatly augmented; and the middle class had
grown in numbers, wealth, and power. At the same time, the nobility had
continued to prosper in spite of the emancipation of most of the serfs. It
was an age of optimism, of hope for the future in both this world and the
next, a fact clearly indicated by the smiling faces on many of the statues
adorning the cathedrals.

A smiling angel. RHEIMS CATHEDRAL.
(Courtesy of New York Public Library)

A century later all of this had changed. The political, intellectual, ecclesiastical, and social order had collapsed. A severe depression had halted three centuries of economic progress, and intense suffering, death, and decay had become the dominant theme of many artists. Seldom has history provided as dramatic a reversal of fortune. But it was only after the rich and deeply rooted medieval civilization had suffered a painful death that a new civilization could arise.

THE MEDIEVAL CIVILIZATION

THE CHURCH

The Middle Ages have been called "the Age of Faith." This title probably overemphasizes the religious motivation of the typical medieval man, for the records upon which the historian must base his judgments were generally made and preserved by members of the clergy. If most of the secular records of our contemporary era were destroyed and future generations were compelled to judge us primarily by the writings of our theologians and the art of our churches, they would arrive at some very strange conclusions. Yet the very fact that the medieval church was the custodian, not only of spiritual and ethical values but also of most of the knowledge and culture of the period, enabled it to exercise a greater influence than it had exercised before or has obtained since.

The head of this Church was the bishop of Rome, the pope or father of all Christians in Western Europe. In the early days, the primacy of the popes had not always been accepted, although their position as leaders of the church in the capital of the Roman Empire had assured them an influence greater than that exercised by other bishops, with the possible exception of those at Alexandria, Antioch, and Constantinople. However, during the seventh century, Alexandria and Antioch had been conquered by the Moslems, and in 1054 the Christians of eastern Europe had broken with those of the West and had established the Greek Orthodox Church with its seat at Constantinople. The Roman popes had thereby been left without a serious rival in Western Europe, where they had gradually persuaded the leading clergymen in other cities to recognize their authority. In achieving this primacy, the popes had been greatly aided by the fact that theirs was the only church in the West that could claim to have been founded by an apostle. Indeed, it was generally accepted in the Middle Ages that Peter had been the first bishop of Rome, that Jesus had given him the keys to the Kingdom of Heaven, and that his successors to the Roman see held comparable powers.

Below the pope were the archbishops and bishops, and still lower were the priests of the individual parishes. Each member of the hierarchy, except the priest, had many officials to aid him in his spiritual and secular duties. This was especially true of the pope, who was not only the head of the Church but also the ruler of a territorial state in central Italy. His *curia* or court consisted of the bishops of the six neighboring dioceses and the principal parish priests and deacons of Rome. These dignitaries, who were known as cardinals, numbered among their duties that of electing the pope when the incumbent died, although they in turn were appointed by the pope. At this time, the cardinals generally resided in Rome and personally performed the spiritual duties of their offices as well as acted in various administrative capacities in the papal government. During the late Middle Ages, the current practice was introduced of appointing some non-Italian cardinals who, although they continued to reside in their native countries, held titular churches in Rome as symbols of their membership in the clergy of that city.

The growing complexity of the papal government led the members of the papal curia to specialize in different functions. Gradually, four departments or bureaus, each headed by a cardinal, came into being. One department, the chancery, handled correspondence and decrees; a second handled absolutions; a third finance, for the papacy drew revenue from all parts of the Roman Catholic world as well as from the papal states; and a fourth served as a judicial tribunal. At this time, all ecclesiastics, including those who had not yet become priests, claimed the privilege of being tried by the church courts, irrespective of the nature of their crime. Cases of a spiritual kind, such as those concerning marriage, church doctrine, oaths, and usury, were also subject to ecclesiastical jurisdiction, regardless of the status of the persons involved. Most of the cases originated in

20

the lower church courts located throughout the Western world, with the papal court serving as the highest court of appeal, but a few cases originated in the papal court itself. A successful pope had to be an able administrator trained in canon law, and similar requirements were placed upon many other clergymen in high posts both at Rome and in the dioceses, where the bishops were compelled to devote much of their time to the secular responsibilities of their offices.

The most devout members of the Church often preferred to join one of the monastic orders, in which they lived according to a rule and enjoyed a life of mystical contemplation and prayer. Others, equally religious but desiring more active lives, became Dominicans or Franciscans and went among the people as begging friars to preach and teach. But even the monks and friars, who could own nothing, were unable to escape the growing secularization of the Church; their very holiness led the faithful to give wealth to their orders, as corporations, and with wealth came worldly responsibilities. Thus, the seeds of decay were being sown at the very moment when the Church appeared to be at the height of its power.

Nevertheless, Roman Catholic doctrine assigned to the clergy such an important role that its position seemed secure. Like all orthodox Christians, the medieval Catholic believed that God created Adam and Eve with free will but that they had been driven out of the Garden of Eden for their disobedience. From that time neither they nor their descendants had been capable of doing good. Sin and death had been brought into the world, and the fires of hell were justly man's ultimate end. This end was certain until Jesus, who was both man and God, willingly suffered death on the cross to atone for the deeds of man. By His act, such a treasure of merit was stored up that henceforth sinful man had an opportunity to be saved. It was on the question of how this merit or grace was awarded to man that Catholic and Protestant were later to quarrel. Catholics held that varying amounts of grace were awarded to everyone at birth, enough to give a degree of free will and some power to love God but not so much that it could not be resisted. He who resisted was, of course, damned as before, but he who cooperated and, properly prepared, received additional grace through the sacraments would be saved.

These sacraments were seven in number. Individual Christians did not normally take all of them, for only priests underwent the sacrament of *ordination* and only the laity were permitted the sacrament of *marriage*. Of special importance to everyone were *baptism*, which cleansed original and prebaptismal sins and gave birth to a new nature; the *Eucharist* or Mass, in which the bread and wine were literally transformed into the body and blood of Christ and He was once more sacrificed; and *penance*, in which the contrite believer confessed his sins, was absolved, and submitted to penalties prescribed by the priest. Upon death, the penitent sinner was sent to purgatory where he suffered for a length of time that varied in accordance with the sins that he had not expiated. Since baptism was the only sacrament that could be performed by anyone other than a priest, the sacramental system provided the Church with a powerful weapon. By excommunicating someone—that is, by denying him the sacraments—the Church could imperil his soul. At the same time, the sacramental system made both God, through the gift of grace, and man, through his cooperation, necessary for salvation. Some latitude was left to the individual theologian concerning how much emphasis to place on man's will and how much to place on God's. One fifteenth-century theologian explained the paradox between free will and predestination as follows:

> However faithfully and carefully a farmer may sow his field, the sweat of his brow counts for nothing unless God from heaven bless his work. But after the seed is sown he does not expect a blessing from heaven alone; he expects it because he has a fertile farm, because he has the seed, the beasts of burden and agricultural implements, because he has his limbs, and strength and willingness to endure. In a word, what he is and has is altogether due to the beneficence of God; for in the last analysis both we and all our possessions are from God. But although God is the source of all things, still he wishes the farmer to labor through these agencies,—and this to such an extent that although God himself does it all, no blessing, no fruit will attend a lazy, snoring farmer.[1]

MEDIEVAL PHILOSOPHY

The Christian edifice described above owed a great debt to the medieval philosophers. For the most part, these philosophers believed that human reason was of great assistance to religious faith and not contradictory to it. The marriage between faith and reason was facilitated by the philosophers' conception of what was "real" and by their method of argument. If we, today, were asked what is real, we would say those things we can touch, taste, smell, see, or hear. Not so the typical medieval philosopher, who derived his conception of reality from Plato, Aristotle, and other thinkers of the ancient world. Until the thirteenth century, Plato's conception of reality, based on his theory of ideas, dominated medieval philosophy. There are many cats, Plato would have argued, but what is important is not their differences as detected by the senses but rather the essence or character common to all cats beneath their varying and changing appearances. This common character he called the "idea," and it is the idea or universal character common to all cats that is real. As one modern philosopher explains it: ". . . the word 'cat' means a certain ideal cat, '*the* cat,' created by God, and unique. Particular cats partake of the nature of *the* cat, but more or less imperfectly; it is only owing to this imperfection that there can be many of them. *The* cat is real; particular cats are only apparent."[2] Furthermore, ideas to Plato were not isolated entities but rather part of a

[1] Quoted by Albert Hyma, *The Christian Renaissance* (New York: The Century Co., 1924), p. 256.
[2] Bertrand Russell, *A History of Western Philosophy* (New York: Simon and Schuster, 1945), pp. 121-122.

system at the top of which was the highest idea of all, the universal of universals, the good, or, to the medieval Christian, God. Thus, to the *realists*, as the advocates of the Platonic system were called, reality lay only in the universal. Since the universals can be apprehended only by reason, the realists put great emphasis on reason and relegated the senses to a minor role. Later followers of Plato, called *Neoplatonists*, rejected matter still further and longed for the escape of the soul from the body and its return to the Godhead. From Plato and the Neoplatonists important elements of asceticism, mysticism, and otherworldliness were introduced into medieval Christian thought, elements that had been largely lacking among the Jews and early Christians.

Aristotle agreed with Plato that the ideas or universals were real, but he thought that Plato went too far when he argued that they existed irrespective of material things, that is, that the idea of the cat could exist without any cats in the material world. Aristotle insisted that ideas or universals could exist only in particular things, that *the* cat can exist only in individual cats. The universals were supreme, but a place had been found for the material things of this world. His position gradually supplanted Plato's during the thirteenth century.

A third possibility was that the ideas were only names and that only the individual things in the material world were real. This was the position of the *nominalists*, but they did not become important until the fourteenth century. Thus, the Platonist believed that reality lay only in the universal, the Aristotelian that reality lay only in the universals but that the universals exist only in the particular, and the nominalist that reality exists only in the particular.

The predominance of the Platonic conception of ideas during the formative period of Christian thought had a profound effect. It freed man from the necessity of accepting his sensorial experiences as true and provided a way of interpreting the Bible other than by relying on the literal word. When it was pointed out that the bread and wine had the same sensible appearances after the miracle of the Mass as before, it could be argued that the essence, the real substance, had been transformed into the body and blood of Christ and that only the "accidents," the nonessential sensible appearances, remained unaltered. If the idea was real, the physical aspects were unimportant.

In interpreting the Bible and other writings, the medieval man constantly sought for the idea behind the story, for hidden meanings behind the words. He thought in terms of allegories and felt no obligation to believe only the literal word. Thus Saint Augustine accepted Christianity only after Saint Ambrose had explained that he did not have to take literally all the Biblical narratives. Dante, the great medieval poet, explained the method of literary interpretation in the following manner:

> It should be known that writings may be taken and should be expounded chiefly in four senses. The first is called the literal, and it is the one that ex-

tends no further than the letter as it stands; the second is called the allegorical, and is the one that hides itself under the mantle of these tales, and is a truth hidden under beauteous fiction. . . . The third sense is called moral, and this is the one that lecturers should go intently noting throughout the Scriptures for their own behoof and that of their disciples. . . . The fourth sense is called the anagogical, that is to say "above the sense"; and this is when a scripture is spiritually expounded which even in the literal sense, by the very things it signifies, signifies again some portion of the supernal things of eternal glory.

Thus: "When Israel came out of Egypt, the house of Jacob out of a barbarous people, Judea became his sanctification, Israel his power." For should we consider the *letter* only, the exit of the children of Israel from Egypt in the time of Moses is what is signified to us; if the *allegory,* our redemption accomplished through Christ is signified to us; if the *moral* sense, the conversion of the mind from the grief and misery of sin to the state of grace is signified to us; if the *anagogical,* the exit of the holy soul from the slavery of this corruption to the liberty of eternal glory is signified.[3]

Using this method of interpreting the Bible, popes, church councils, and theologians gradually developed the great Roman Catholic tradition with its rituals and its dogmas. Without it, the veneration of saints would have smacked of polytheism, and some of the sacraments could not have been accepted; without the conception of the universals, the statues in the churches would have been idols rather than instructional devices reminding the generally illiterate congregations of the saints, martyrs, and the suffering on the cross. To the literalist, the story of the flood was but an account of how Noah and his family were saved, but to Pope Boniface VIII it was taken as proof that there was but one Church headed by the pope, outside of which there was no salvation. During his quarrel with Philip IV of France, he declared in the bull *Unam Sanctam* that:

There was one ark of Noah, indeed, at the time of the flood, symbolizing one church; and this being finished in one cubit had, namely, one Noah as helmsman and commander. And, with the exception of this ark, all things existing upon the earth were, as we read, destroyed.

Neither observation nor experiment was essential to this method of discovering truth. Instead, the medieval philosopher developed a system of logical analysis known as the scholastic method. Saint Thomas Aquinas (1225-1274), the greatest of the scholastic philosophers, often analyzed a major problem by dividing it into a series of subsidiary articles or propositions beginning with the word *whether.* Under each article, he listed the authorities who opposed it and those who favored it. Then he stated his own position in favor of the article and supported it by argument. Finally, he refuted or reinterpreted the authorities whom he had listed as opposing the article. Since the authorities cited included the Bible and the church fathers as well as Aristotle and other thinkers of the classical era, this method actually involved explaining by use of logic seemingly contradictory state-

[3] Quoted by John H. Randall, Jr., *The Making of the Modern Mind* (Boston: Houghton Mifflin, 1940 ed.), p. 97.

ments on dogma. Thus, logic was used to understand and explain dogma, and the Middle Ages were an age of reason as well as an age of faith. Many religious truths, such as the existence of God, were held to be demonstrable by reason. To Aquinas, those that were not demonstrable, such as the doctrine of the Trinity, were not contrary to reason. Rather, they were beyond our understanding, for since divine and natural law, faith and reason, had a common originator—God—they could not contradict each other.

One of Saint Thomas' greatest achievements was to reconcile Aristotle with the Christian tradition. So successful was he that the Platonic influence that had prevailed for so long had faded by the closing years of the thirteenth century, and Aristotle was almost everywhere ascendant among those who believed that faith and reason were compatible.

SCIENCE AND ART

The emphasis on deductive reasoning by the Neoplatonists precluded many noteworthy developments in the experimental sciences until the thirteenth century. Instead of employing observation and experiments to study a particular thing to find out *how* it worked, the medieval man preferred to study the natural world to obtain a knowledge of God's purpose, for had He not created it for man's edification? Was it not rational and ordered like God's mind, and might it not yield answers to fundamental questions on the nature, purpose, and destiny of man? This approach was especially characteristic of the earlier, Neoplatonic period of the Middle Ages, when behind every object and event was thought to be an idea with spiritual and moral significance. As a scholar has recently expressed it:

> In the most literal sense the men of the age found "sermons in stones and books in running brooks." They believed that the universe was a vast rebus to be solved, a cryptogram to be decoded. All that is red became to them a reminder of the blood of Christ; all that is wooden, a memento of the true cross; every spring evoked a recollection of their rebirth through baptism. . . . The pelican, which was believed to nourish its young with its own blood, was the analogue of Christ, who feeds mankind with his blood. In such a world there was no thought of hiding behind a clump of reeds actually to observe the habits of a pelican. There would have been no point to it. Once one had grasped the spiritual meaning of the pelican, one lost interest in individual pelicans. The world was indeed a world of shadows and reflections where the knowledge of things was barren, for the things themselves were not actually real.[4]

The growing influence of Aristotle and Aquinas, with their insistence that the universals existed only in regard to the particulars, was paralleled by a growing interest in experimental science and nature, but the most significant advances in the natural sciences were made by friars of the

[4] Francis N. Estey, "Science in the Late Middle Ages," *Social Education,* XV (1951), p. 226.

West portal of the Cathedral of Chartres. The statues on the portal were carved around the middle of the twelfth century before the Gothic style was fully developed. The figure of Christ over the center door is surrounded by a winged man, a lion, a bull, and an eagle—symbols representing the four Evangelists, Matthew, Mark, Luke, and John. Note the unnaturally elongated statues around the doorways which seem so unreal when viewed separately and yet superb when seen in context with the entire portal. (Bettmann Archive)

Franciscan order, who, unlike the majority of their contemporaries, saw little cause to use deductive reasoning to buttress their faith and turned more and more from abstract thought to observed fact.

The emphasis on deductive reasoning had an equally profound effect on art, largely because art in the Middle Ages centered around the cathedral. The bishops and canons, who planned and arranged the stained glass and statues for the cathedrals, were well versed in scholastic thought. These officials associated closely with the architects, who were men of acknowledged position and perhaps of some education. The craftsmen who did the actual work were without academic training and did not have the social status later attained by artists, but the control exercised over them from above and the teachings they absorbed from the Church led them to capture something of the scholastic spirit. Since they were a migratory group going from one building project to another as their specialized talents were demanded, new architectural styles spread with relative rapidity in Western Europe.

Two styles were dominant in the high Middle Ages. The first, the Ro-

26

West portal of the Cathedral of Amiens. The statues on this Gothic portal were probably carved between 1225 and 1236. Observe that the unity of the larger whole is maintained, but that the individual statues have more natural proportions than those on the west portal of Chartres (opposite page) and seem capable of movement. Note also the logical arrangement of the statues with registers or lines on the tympanum above the portal. (Ewing Galloway)

manesque, was characterized by the abstract, monumental style of the churches. Details were everywhere subordinated to the larger whole in accordance to the philosophical conceptions of the realists. The exterior of the churches, especially near the doors, was generally ornamented with sculpture, but these statues were elongated to conform to the walls and were so much a part of the architectural element that they were incapable of movement. This denial of man's natural proportions gave the Romanesque style an emotional, religious quality. Symbolism was frequently employed and the overall effect was one of unity. Reality clearly lay in the universal concept, not in the individual statues and ornamentation. The axis of the interior of the Romanesque church was horizontal so that when he entered the nave the worshiper's eyes were directed toward the altar. The windows were small, and the light that penetrated was not sufficient to brighten the interior, even though there were colorful paintings on the walls. The whole effect was one of majestic but somber dignity in which the presence of the Deity could be felt.

Detail of west portal of the Cathedral of Amiens. This forceful, lifelike statue of God is a triumph of Gothic naturalism; yet it remains part of the larger whole (p.27). (Courtesy of New York Public Library)

In the middle of the twelfth century, a new style of architecture began to emerge in northern France that has since become known as Gothic. The statues on the façades of the Gothic cathedrals were more naturalistic than those on the Romanesque and became increasingly so as time progressed. Figures assumed lifelike proportions and gradually freed themselves physically from the architecture so that they seemed capable of movement. The deeply religious expressions began to be replaced by more secular ones, and the Virgin Mary was seen to smile as she held her child. Yet, in spite of the growing naturalism, the statues remained a part of the

28

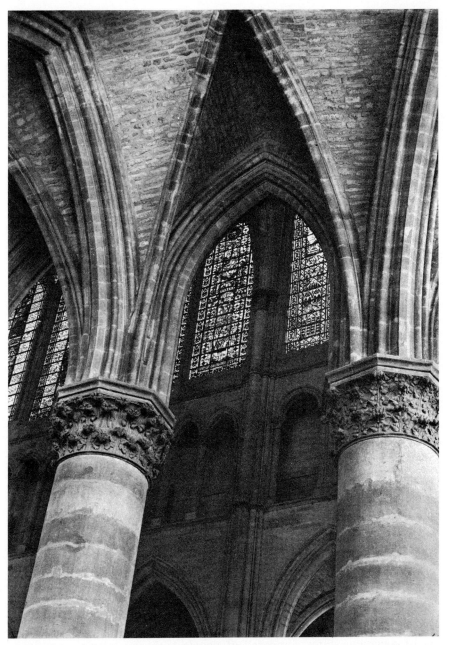

Cathedral of Rheims (interior). The pointed arches and long panels of stained glass carry the observer's eyes upward as he enters a Gothic cathedral. (Courtesy of New York Public Library)

larger whole, for reality was still thought to reside in the universals, even though there was a growing realization that the universal existed only with respect to the individual things that composed it. Scholastic thought also imposed a more logical arrangement of the statues than before. The number of statues and motifs increased, but the same order and clarity prevailed as in the writing of Saint Thomas Aquinas. The tympanums, or sculptured surfaces over the portals, for example, were clearly divided into three registers or lines to prevent confusion of detail. But the most striking distinction between the Gothic and the Romanesque church is that the observer, on entering the former, finds his eyes carried upward toward the light filtering through vast panels of colored glass, rather than towards the altar. Light, the most immaterial of all substances, was widely regarded as the nearest analogy to God. This effect was accomplished by heightening the nave and replacing more and more of the wall with stained glass. Technical devices, such as the pointed arch and the flying buttresses that have become synonymous with the Gothic cathedral, were used to give the structure greater strength.

As stained glass replaced the walls, there was less and less space for painters to practice their art, and they were gradually forced to divert their talents to the illumination of manuscripts. In Italy, however, where there was more sunlight than in northern Europe, stained glass rarely replaced walls and painting continued to be an important part of ecclesiastical art.

The Church was as important a center for music as for the other arts. The late twelfth and thirteenth centuries, which saw the development of the Gothic cathedral, witnessed a movement to organize music into rhythmic modes that were sung simultaneously, one above the other. This introduction of polyphony did not lead to confusion. Just as the numerous statues on the façades of the cathedrals did not destroy the unity of the larger whole, so the music remained coherent and symmetrical. Secular music, including the songs of the troubadours of Provence and their counterparts to the north, joined the trend towards polyphony during the second half of the thirteenth century. Thus, the scholastic spirit imposed unity and order on the arts.

THE IDEA OF CHRISTENDOM

The scholastic philosophers also applied their system of thought to the state and society. Instead of seeing in the political system of Europe a number of sovereign states composed of people with equal rights, privileges, and social status, as we do today, they thought in terms of a hierarchy of social classes, each with its own mission, and of a hierarchy of political units that became more important as they became larger and more inclusive. Thus Dante, the great Italian, who so often reflected scholastic conceptions in his poetry and in his political theory, could write that just "as Nature fashions the thumb for one purpose, the whole hand for another, then the arm for a purpose differing from both, and the entire man for one differing from all, so she creates for one end the individual, for another the family, for another the village, for still another end the city, for another the kingdom, and finally for an ultimate end, by means of His art which is Nature, the Eternal God brings into being the human race in its totality." [5] Furthermore:

> The human race . . . is ordered for the best, when according to the utmost of its power it becomes like unto God. But the human race is most like unto God when it is most one, for the principle of unity dwells in Him above. . . . But the human race is most one when all are united together, a state which is manifestly impossible unless humanity as a whole becomes subject to one Prince, and consequently comes most into accordance with that divine intention which . . . is the good, nay, is the best disposition of mankind.[6]

The idea of a universal empire, of a Christian commonwealth, was generally accepted by theorists as both logical and desirable, although they sometimes disagreed violently over the respective roles of the emperor and the pope. The idea of a Christian empire was also justified by medieval historians, who believed that the Roman Empire had never died and was preserved in their day as the Holy Roman Empire. On this point, there was a wide difference between theory and fact. Charlemagne, who was crowned emperor in 800, and his son were the only medieval emperors who ruled nearly all the Christians in western and central Europe, and after the latter's death in 840 the Empire was divided. The title of emperor was maintained, but outside of the Holy Roman Empire it carried no power and little prestige, except that its bearer and his ambassadors were given precedence in diplomatic matters. Even within the Empire, the powers of the emperor waned, and after the death of Frederick II in 1250, incumbents generally used the prestige and what remained of the power of their office to strengthen the position of their dynasty rather than to govern the Empire effectively.

By the dawn of the thirteenth century, what there was of international leadership in Christendom was exercised by the pope. Innocent III (1198-1216) clearly conceived of Christendom as a single community over which he was determined to have both moral and political leadership. "No king can reign rightly," he wrote, "unless he devoutly serves Christ's vicar. . . . The priesthood is the sun, and monarchy the moon. Kings rule over their respective kingdoms, but Peter rules over the whole earth. . . . The Lord gave Peter the rule not only over the universal Church, but also over the whole world." [7] Certainly no pope ever exercised

[5] *The De Monarchia of Dante Alighieri*, trans. Aurelia Henry (Boston: Houghton Mifflin, 1904), p. 9.

[6] *Ibid.*, pp. 26-27.

[7] Quoted by Joseph R. Strayer and Dana C. Munro, *The Middle Ages* (New York: Appleton-Century-Crofts, 4th ed., 1959), p. 307.

31

such wide authority, but several were remarkably influential in the political affairs of Europe. Innocent was able to force King Philip Augustus of France to take back a discarded wife, King John of England to recognize an archbishop he did not want, and King Alfonso of León to break off a marriage with a cousin. He decided a disputed succession to the throne of Hungary, received the homage as papal vassals of the rulers of Aragon, Portugal, England, Denmark, Hungary, Bulgaria, Poland, and Serbia, and intervened in every great question in European politics. His successors were hardly less influential, and near the close of the thirteenth century the papacy appeared to be near the peak of its prestige and influence.

THE MEDIEVAL STATE

At the very time, however, that the popes were replacing the emperors as the leaders of Christendom, strong kings were emerging, especially in Western Europe. These kings were neither able nor willing to compete with the pope for supremacy in Christendom, but they refused to tolerate foreign, including papal, interference within their own kingdoms. The question ceased to be whether the pope or the emperor should rule Christendom and became one of whether Christendom itself would be more than a vague name applied to a group of separate, warring, secular states.

By 1300, the Western European monarchies had become hereditary, and the disputes over royal succession that had characterized the Empire and the eastern European states had been reduced. Towns and nobles had been persuaded or forced to recognize the basic royal prerogatives, and rudimentary administrative and judicial systems had developed. The *curia regis,* or royal court, that had aided the king in the earlier period had become specialized and, like the papal administration, had been divided into departments or bureaus. Some became law courts for civil, criminal, or financial matters. One, the chancery, handled correspondence, edicts, and ordinances, and another, the council, advised the king on all matters. The king's council varied widely in composition. It usually included a group of professional advisers and administrators who remained at the king's side wherever he went and a group of great nobles and ecclesiastics whose duties and interests often kept them on their feudal estates or dioceses but who attended the meetings of the council when they were at court or when they were specially summoned by the king to treat with matters of unusual importance.

These enlarged meetings of the council led to the development of representative institutions, for the less important members of the clergy and nobility, as well as the burghers of the towns, gradually acquired so much collective importance that the kings found their participation advisable. Since the members of these influential classes could not all appear in person, in several countries the crown began to select a few individuals from each class to attend, even though these individuals could speak only for themselves. By the early thirteenth century, cathedral chapters and other groups of the less important clergy, the minor nobility, and the towns began to be required to choose deputies to participate in assemblies. They gave their deputies instructions and powers to act in their name, just as today individuals and corporations give proxies and powers of attorney to lawyers and other persons to act for them. This procedure was probably begun by the papacy, but by the fourteenth century the more advanced European states had adopted it, and the Parliament of England, the *cortes* of the Spanish kingdom, the Estates-General of France, and similar institutions in other countries were beginning to play significant roles.

In England, a two-house legislature eventually emerged. One, the House of Lords, consisted of the great nobles and ecclesiastics who were summoned individually; the second, the House of Commons, consisted of the deputies of the knightly or gentry class and of the towns. On the continent, the elected deputies sometimes deliberated together, as they did in England, and sometimes in separate chambers. In a few places, the great nobles and the lesser nobles sat separately, and here and there even the peasants were permitted to send deputies. The variety of assemblies was infinite, but perhaps the most typical assembly was in France, where each class in society was thought to form an *estate*. The first estate included the clergy, the second the nobility, and the third the remainder of the free inhabitants, of whom the burghers of the towns and the royal officials were by far the most important. Those who attended the large assemblies from each of these estates sometimes deliberated together and sometimes apart.

There were a number of reasons why a king might want to summon the deputies of the various estates to meet with his council. Legally, he was a constitutional ruler, limited in theory by divine law, natural law (the universal principles of justice and morality established by God and discoverable by human reason), and customary law (the immemorial customs of the people of a particular locality). It was through divine power that his office was given a particular sanctity when he was anointed at his coronation; it was through the use of reason that Aquinas and others proved that monarchy was the most natural and most just form of government; and it was through custom that the king's right to the crown and his relations to his subjects were determined. On the advice and consent of his subjects, divine, natural, and customary laws could be defined and applied, although theoretically these laws could not be changed. Furthermore, a free man's most cherished right was to his property, and no king could legally tax him without his consent. Everything, indeed, that concerned the free man closely was subject to his approval; "what touches all should be approved by all," a statement taken from Roman law, was a favorite maxim of the age. Thus, a monarch could define and apply the law, tax, and take other important or unusual actions only with the con-

In the early fourteenth century, France numbered about 13,500,000 inhabitants, only slightly less than the Holy Roman Empire, which included Germany, Switzerland, Austria, Bohemia (western Czechoslovakia), northern Italy, and most of the Low Countries. England had only about 3,700,000 inhabitants, but its kings, who controlled a large part of France, had created one of the most centralized states of the period. The Iberian Peninsula had about 9,500,000 inhabitants. It was governed by the Christian kings of (1) Portugal, (2) Castile and León, (3) Aragon, Valencia, and Catalonia, and (4) Navarre, and by the Moorish ruler of the little kingdom of Granada. Most of northern Italy was in the Empire, but the Venetian Republic (1,500,000) was independent. Other Italian states included Naples (2,000,000), Sicily (600,000), and the Papal States (1,500,000). Norway, Sweden, and Denmark contributed little to medieval civilization. Poland and Hungary performed great service in protecting Western Europe against assault from the east but were less important in other respects than France and England. The remainder of the European continent included several kingdoms whose inhabitants belonged to the Greek Orthodox branch of Christianity and who were not part of Western medieval civilization; it also included the heathen state of Lithuania and the Golden Horde.

sent of his subjects, and this consent was best obtained by summoning representative assemblies.

These assemblies were also useful because they gave the king an excellent opportunity to persuade his subjects to accept and support his policies in an age before radio, television, and printing press. At the same time, the instructions the deputies brought from their various localities provided the government with valuable information on local conditions. In short, the representative assembly was a useful tool because it enabled the king to rule legally, by persuasion, at a time when he had neither the army nor the bureaucracy to rule by force.

The reason for the inability of a king to rule by force may be readily realized when we consider how the provinces were governed. The typical medieval king kept only a small part of his kingdom directly under his control. This part, known as the royal domain, was administered by officials whom he generally appointed and could often remove. Within the royal domain, his position was relatively secure, and from here he derived much of his financial and military support. The remainder of the kingdom was divided into fiefs and administered by dukes, counts, earls, and other great nobles. Each recipient of a fief became a vassal and, in a ceremonial act known as homage, swore to be faithful to his lord. These great nobles set aside part of their fiefs as their domain and divided the remainder among lesser nobles who in turn became their vassals. Each lesser noble might subdivide his fief in a similar manner until at length the basic unit of the feudal system became the manor, a village with surrounding farms, generally governed by a lord who was called a knight or seigneur.

A vassal was obligated to give aid and counsel to his lord. Specifically, he was expected to obey the lord's summons to his court to give advice, to serve with his retainers in military campaigns for a specified period, usually forty days, without pay, to give financial assistance when the lord had to incur certain heavy financial expenses, as he did when his eldest son was knighted, his eldest daughter was married, or he was held for ransom. In return, the lord protected his vassal and, through the fief, provided for his support.

In theory, this system, which was called *feudalism*, should have been effective. In time of danger, the king would summon his vassals, who in turn would summon theirs, for military duty. Or on more pacific matters, the king could call on the great nobles to advise him in the governance of the kingdom, and the great nobles could call on the lesser nobles to help them administer their duchies and counties.

In practice, feudalism had serious flaws. Many nobles owned more than one fief and were vassals of several lords. If these lords quarreled, as they frequently did, the vassal had to choose which oath to honor. Indeed, the whole system was held together primarily by a sense of personal loyalty, for the lord exercised very little control over the internal affairs of his vassals' fiefs. Even the king was frequently unable to send royal officials into the great fiefs or to exercise any authority there except with the acquiescence of the duke or count concerned. In the first generation, the vassal was usually loyal, but fiefs became hereditary and succeeding generations tended to look upon them as private rights rather than public trusts. Ties of personal loyalty weakened, although homage was rendered on the father's death. Only a strong monarch, under favorable circumstances, could operate effectively within the system.

To strengthen their position, some kings and great nobles gave their vassals fiefs in money rather than in land; that is, in return for homage and the usual feudal obligations, they promised an annual money payment. If the vassal proved disloyal, the payments could be stopped more easily than a fief could be recovered. However, few kings had enough cash to provide for a large number of money fiefs, and their power over the nobility, apparently secure in many places in 1300, could easily deteriorate.

Towns had virtually disappeared in most of Europe during the early Middle Ages, but, with a revival of trade in the late tenth and early eleventh centuries, merchants began to travel again in significant numbers. For protection they usually halted at night at the seat of a bishop, called a city, or at the castle of a noble, called a bourg. Blacksmiths, cobblers, and other artisans soon gathered in these localities to serve the merchants' needs, and the merchants themselves began to establish permanent residences there and to employ others to brave the dangers and inconveniences of travel. The merchants took the lead in persuading or forcing the bishop, noble, or even king to grant the new communities charters that provided for varying degrees of municipal self-government. These charters often granted the towns the right to elect their own officials, establish and enforce their own laws, collect taxes, and provide for their own defense when they outgrew the protecting arm of the castle. Thus, within the royal domain and the great fiefs, there were units of government that partly or almost wholly escaped the authority of the lord.

THE MEDIEVAL SOCIETY AND ECONOMY

The medieval economy was predominantly agricultural. About 90 per cent of the population lived in the country, where the basic economic unit was not the individual farm but the manor. At the heart of the typical manor was the village, consisting of from fifteen or twenty to several hundred families. In dry climates or where the soil was poor, the arable land was usually divided into two fields. In alternate years, one field was sown in wheat, and the other was permitted to lie fallow in order to recover its fertility. Where the soil was richer and the rainfall abundant, the arable land was usually divided into three fields, two of which were planted and the third permitted to lie fallow. Although agricultural plan-

36

ning was a village responsibility, the inhabitants did not work together in a common labor force; rather, the fields were divided into long, narrow strips, and the various heads of families usually cultivated several strips in each field. Some strips were set aside for the support of the parish priest and others, perhaps a third, for the lord of the manor. This system was most uneconomical, for not only was one third or one half of the arable land left fallow each year, but also a part of the cultivated fields had to be devoted to roads and paths leading to the individual strips. Seed was scattered instead of sown in rows, a wasteful practice which, along with the poor agricultural methods of the day, made it necessary to plant about two bushels of seed per acre in order to produce eight or ten bushels of wheat. Animals belonging to the various inhabitants of the village grazed together on the wastelands, or the fallow field, and on the cultivated fields after harvest. Under these circumstances, scientific breeding was impossible. Lack of feed was also a problem, and most species of livestock weighed less than half what they do today. It is not surprising that nine people had to work on the farm to provide food for one in the town, while today one farmer can easily supply nine of his city brethren.

The lord of the manor usually dwelt in a house a little removed from the village. If he were merely a knight, the manor house might contain little more than a large hall, which served as a living room, dining room, and kitchen, and one or two bedrooms. If he were an important noble who derived income from many other manors as well, he might have a stone castle surrounded by a moat filled with water or perched on a steep hill to make its walls difficult to assail by possible enemies. Even the castle, however, was far from a comfortable habitation, and the advantages a straightbacked, carved wooden chair had over the villager's wooden bench were slight. Indeed, the greatest material advantage of being lord of the manor was a more plentiful diet. The lord escaped manual labor, but he had the hazardous duties of defending the manor in time of danger and accompanying his own lord in battle.

Many of the inhabitants of the villages were still serfs, who were bound to the soil and could not marry without the lord's permission. They worked on the lord's land without compensation for about three days a week, and after their death their heirs were forced to pay a heavy duty before they could have the house and land they had farmed. Other inhabitants were free tenants who could come and go as they pleased and had to perform very little forced labor. The serf and often the free tenant paid a tallage or tax to the lord, and both were expected to use the lord's mill and wine press, to pay other fees, and to perform certain services without pay, such as repairing roads and bridges. Only the free tenants had any legal rights against the lord of the manor, but the unfortunate position of the other inhabitants was partly mitigated by the important role played by the custom of the manor, which defined the rights and obligations of the in-

*Nottingham Castle, England. Engraving from painting by T. Hine.
(Charles Phelps Cushing)*

habitants. Disputes concerning these rights or between peasants were generally settled in the manorial court presided over by the lord or, in his absence, his bailiff.

Legally, the inhabitants of the towns were in a much more fortunate position. Serfdom was nonexistent, urban law courts handled most judicial cases, and the citizens were not subject to labor services, although the town itself paid a fixed money rent to the lord in return for these concessions. Furthermore, many burghers were members of associations called guilds that were designed to advance their interests and to protect their rights. The oldest and the most important of the guilds were those of the merchants. The merchants, who had taken the lead in the effort to win concessions from the lord of the town in the early years, sought to control the town once a charter had been won. To protect themselves from exploitation by the merchants, to prevent competition from outside the town, and to regulate production within the town, the artisans organized themselves into craft guilds. A given town might have one craft guild for cobblers, another for tanners, and still others for fishmongers, weavers, and other trades, although in every town some occupations were not organized into guilds and some towns had no guilds at all. The craft guild was equally important as a social, religious, and welfare organization in which the members played together, prayed together, and cared for the sick members as well as the widows and orphans. A master in a craft guild usually owned a house, the first floor of which was used as his

38

Blois, France. This engraving of Blois was made in the sixteenth century. Its characteristics, however, were similar to other towns from the
revival of urban life in the high Middle Ages until the eighteenth century or later. During this long period towns were protected by walls with
occasional towers. Highway and bridge entrances were strongly fortified
as in the upper and lower parts of the engraving. There were only a few
streets that were wide enough for carriages to pass; houses were clus-
tered, separated by narrow alleys, and churches towered over other buildings.

shop, the upper floor as a dwelling place for his family, and the garret as
a sleeping place for several apprentices who were working with him learning his trade. In addition, there might be one or more journeymen who
had completed their apprenticeship and were working for a daily wage
until they could afford to set themselves up as masters.

It would be a grievous error to exaggerate the pleasures of medieval
urban life. The town had to be walled for protection. Since walls were expensive to construct, all the space within their circumference had to be
used. Parks were nonexistent, houses sometimes had to be built on bridges
or against the walls, and streets were so narrow that carriages could
rarely pass. Paving was often inadequate, and sewerage virtually unknown.
Most inhabitants had livestock; and pigs, horses, chickens, and children
wallowed together in the muddy streets where the sun could penetrate
between the closely adjoining rooftops only a few hours a day. Under these
conditions, disease was rife and the life expectancy of the city dweller remained considerably lower than that of the peasant until the dawn of the

nineteenth century. It was partly for this reason that towns were small by modern standards. In Western Europe, perhaps only Paris and four or five Italian cities had over 50,000 inhabitants in 1300.

In spite of economic and social conditions that were far from ideal by modern standards, the medieval civilization was at its height in the thirteenth century, and there was general satisfaction with the political and social structure as well as hope for continued economic progress. Then the monarchies opened an attack on the papacy.

THE ATTACK ON THE PAPACY

The fourteenth and early fifteenth centuries witnessed a threefold attack on the papacy that removed the pope as the leader of Christendom and nearly transformed the papal monarchy into a republic. The attack was begun by the secular monarchs.

THE MONARCHICAL ATTACK

The monarchical attack on the papacy grew out of the special privileges claimed by the clergy. These privileges, which included exemption from royal taxation and the right to be tried by ecclesiastical courts, had long been acknowledged, but the growing secularization of the upper clergy had cost the Church much of its popularity. At the same time, the increased education of the laity had freed the monarchs from a narrow dependence on the clergy for administrative personnel. Under these circumstances, it is not surprising that some strong kings believed that they had both the need and the ability to challenge papal leadership.

The immediate occasion for the dispute was a war between Edward I (1272-1307) of England and Philip IV (1285-1314) of France. Both rulers demanded financial assistance from the clergy in their respective countries to further their military designs. In the past, the clergy had been subjected to taxation to support the Crusades and occasionally, with papal permission, for less worthy purposes. From the Church's point of view it was ridiculous for French ecclesiastics to finance the slaughter of English Christians and for English ecclesiastics to finance the slaughter of French Christians. Furthermore, neither monarch asked for papal permission before acting. Under these circumstances, it is not surprising that in 1296 Pope Boniface VIII (1294-1303) issued the bull *Clericis Laicos,* in which he threatened with excommunication all persons who taxed the clergy without papal consent. Philip rallied public opinion to his side and counterattacked by prohibiting the export of gold and silver from France, a severe blow to papal revenue. Edward reacted by denying the nontax-paying clergy protection from would-be despoilers. In 1297, Boniface VIII, beset with troubles elsewhere, was forced to permit clerical taxation for the defense of a kingdom.

A few years later, when Philip arrested a bishop, Boniface felt strong enough to renew the attack. Threatened by the revived papal claims, Philip and his advisers went to unusual lengths to rally popular support and to discredit their adversary. The task of discrediting Boniface was not difficult. Though an able canon lawyer, he was an irascible old man who had made many enemies at Rome and elsewhere. Unpleasant rumors were being circulated about him, even before the French government began its campaign. As a part of this campaign, Philip summoned the Estates-General to Paris and won the support of a majority of the members, including the clergy. Undaunted, Boniface issued the bull *Unam Sanctam,* in which he declared that subjection to the Roman pontiff was absolutely necessary to salvation for every human creature. The French government countered by demanding a church council to try the Pope for heresy, simony, adultery, and a host of other crimes; then, in an amazingly bold action, one of Philip's ministers kidnapped Boniface at Anagni, Italy. The aged pope was quickly rescued by local inhabitants but died soon after from shock at the indignity.

The outcome of this critical issue now depended on the new pope. If Boniface's actions had aroused criticism, the affair at Anagni had shocked the European conscience. Hence, a capable and determined successor to Boniface might have been able to rally enough support to restore papal prestige. But in 1305, the College of Cardinals elected Clement V, who had been archbishop of Bordeaux and probably owed his position to French influence. Whatever his reasons—gratitude for his new position, loyalty to France, the wish to avoid further scandals—Clement bowed to Philip's desires. The king, he declared, had shown praiseworthy zeal in accusing Boniface, his ministers were pardoned, and he was permitted to confiscate the wealth of the Knights Templar, a crusading order of knighthood that had grown very rich. He was also allowed to tax the French clergy without further papal interference.

Clement had intended to go to Rome, but that faction-ridden city did not seem safe at the moment and his health was poor. Moreover, there was need to remain near France during the period of delicate negotiations with Philip. He therefore established his headquarters at Avignon, a small city then in the Empire but just across the Rhône River from France. Here he and his successors remained until 1377, in spite of several more or less serious attempts to return to Rome. An immense papal palace was constructed to house the papal court, and Avignon became the new capital of the Church.

There may have been sound administrative reasons for the popes to remain at Avignon, but few actions could have been more damaging to their prestige. The circumstances surrounding Clement's election, the proximity of Avignon to France, and the fact that the next six popes, and 113 of the 134 cardinals they appointed, were French, all suggested French domination of the papacy. The English and other opponents of

France came to regard the Pope as a tool of the French king and to regard the Church dues paid to the papacy as little more than subsidies to an enemy state.

Unhappily, these dues became more and more onerous. Frequent rebellions in the papal states, where the nobility and townsmen desired more independence, not only cut off most of the revenue from that source, but also necessitated the maintenance of an army there to keep a semblance of control. The situation worsened when Pope John XXII (1316-1334) entered into a quarrel with the Emperor that was costly in both prestige and money. To pay for these charges, ecclesiastical offices were sold. When no more offices were available, the would-be purchaser was permitted to buy an "expectancy" that entitled him to the next vacant post. Once in office, the ecclesiastic was expected to pay "annates," the first year's income from his post. Heavy income taxes were imposed thereafter, so that the clergy itself complained vigorously at papal exactions. The laity too was persuaded to contribute, and nearly every type of religious benefit was sold. Avignon, to the Italian poet Petrarch, was "the fountain of anguish, the dwelling-place of wrath, the school of errors, the temple of heresy, once Rome, now the false guilt-laden Babylon, the forge of lies, the horrible prison, the hell on earth." So critical did the European public become that the period of the Avignon papacy became known as the Babylonian Captivity. It mattered little that the popes after Clement V followed policies independent of the French kings or that the Church needed substantial revenue in order to fulfill its many responsibilities. The most vocal elements of the population were thoroughly aroused, and Edward III (1327-1377) of England seized the opportunity to get Parliament to outlaw papal appointments to ecclesiastical positions and to limit papal jurisdiction.

The popes never intended to remain permanently at Avignon. One actually returned to Rome, only to abandon that city three years later because of dissension there. Another, Gregory XI, renewed the effort, only to die in Rome in 1378 a few months after his arrival. The cardinals who had followed Gregory XI to Rome assembled and named an Italian, Urban VI, as his successor. Whether they acted under compulsion from a mob demanding a Roman, or at least an Italian, pope or whether they chose freely cannot be determined. What is certain is that when Urban began to make drastic reforms that included a reduction in the cardinals' revenue, they fled from Rome, charged that Urban's election was invalid because it had been held under duress, and elected a new pope, Clement VII. Clement and the French cardinals settled once more at Avignon, and Urban appointed new cardinals and remained at Rome. The period of the Great Schism had begun. Until 1409, there were two popes, and during the five years after 1409, there were three. Each had his own cardinals and bureaucracy, and each administration vied with its rivals for prestige and support. As the expenses of two papal courts were greater than for one, unpopular financial practices had to be continued. At the same time, the secular monarchs found themselves in the enviable position of being able to demand concessions in return for recognition, although France and its allies usually supported the Avignon popes and England and its allies usually supported the Roman pontiff. Never had the prestige of the popes sunk so low; it was widely believed that until the Church was re-united no one could enter the Kingdom of Heaven. The demand for reforms grew steadily stronger.

THE INTELLECTUAL ATTACK

At the same time that the kings were attacking the authority of the pope, a group of theologians was beginning to undermine the position of the papacy and the intellectual order upon which so much of Catholic dogma rested. Some of the most devastating attacks came from realists who turned the doctrine of the universals against the position of the pope and even the dogma of the Mass. Far more serious in the long run, however, was the revival, in the fourteenth century, of nominalism.

The nominalists, as we have seen, believed that individual things were real and that knowledge of this world could be derived only from information received from the senses. The universals, they argued, were only names invented by men to stand for groups of individual things. There were individual men, but "man" in the collective sense did not exist. There were individual Christians and individual Christian states, but "Christendom" was merely a convenient word. Thus, the medieval hierarchy of values was reversed, and the individual was placed before society and the state before Christendom. The revival of nominalism benefited the natural sciences by leading men to investigate individual things and may be related to profound changes in art and literature. But it also represented a serious challenge both to Catholic theology and to the position of the papacy.

The essence of this challenge was that the nominalist, by rejecting the Platonic system of ideas, reduced the role of reason by which these ideas were apprehended and made the will the dominant power of the soul and the controlling force of man's actions. God ceased to be thought of as the infinite wisdom that created a rational and ordered universe because, being infinitely wise, He could have created no other kind. Rather, God came to be thought of as an omnipotent will that could have created man and the universe in any manner He saw fit. Such a God could not be known by petty human reason, and the basic tenets of the Christian faith could not be proved. Thus, faith, instead of being supported by reason, was divorced from it; theology and philosophy gradually diverged, and man was taught that he could know nothing of the ultimate, but must

43

obey God's will without question and without understanding. It was wrong to kill, not because murder was contrary to the rational and beneficent order of the universe and to the general principles of morality, but because God had commanded: "Thou shalt not kill."

And where was the will of God to be found? The first and most important source was the Bible, but the nominalists' rejection of the reality of ideas and general concepts caused them to reject the allegorical, moral, and anagogical methods of interpretation advocated by Dante and the realists and to insist on a literal interpretation. To the nominalist, the story of how Moses led the children of Israel out of Egypt meant what it said and nothing more. The ark was not taken to symbolize one church or the presence of Noah as helmsman to indicate the necessity for one man, the pope, to be its head. Thus, one prop after another that upheld Catholic theology and the ecclesiastical hierarchy was withdrawn. Many, indeed most, nominalists continued to accept on faith what they had formerly accepted as reasonable, but there were some who insisted that only those parts of the dogma that could be literally found in the Bible should be accepted, that true Christians should model their lives after Christians of the first century, and that the imitation of Christ was the highest ideal. The position of the pope, the bishops, and monasticism was challenged, as were some of the sacraments. Even the miracle of the Mass became suspect: did the words of Jesus at the Last Supper literally promise that future miracles would be performed by a priesthood that did not exist in its present privileged position in the New Testament? And a nominalist who had lost his faith might be troubled by the fact that the bread and wine had the same appearance and taste after the Mass as before. What had been the "accidents" to the realists became reality itself to those who rejected as false all knowledge not conveyed to them by their senses.

One must not exaggerate the immediate influence of the revival of nominalism. Many theologians, especially in the Dominican order, preferred to continue to follow the teaching of Aquinas, the *via antiqua,* or old way. Among the nominalists, the advocates of the *via moderna,* or new way, there were many who accepted so much on faith that neither hierarchy nor dogma was challenged, although they did reject the medieval synthesis of faith and reason. Other nominalists did not carry their philosophy to its logical conclusion—a complete rejection of human reason and a pure materialism. Indeed, nominalists generally employed the scholastic method in attacking the realists. Nevertheless, there were those who criticized both hierarchy and dogma in the fourteenth century, and as time went on the breach between faith and reason became wider. In the modern world, philosophy has come to rely more on science than on theology.

The first and most brilliant of the fourteenth-century nominalists was William of Ockham, who was born in a village of that name in Surrey, England, between 1290 and 1300. He studied at Oxford, became a monk of

44

the Franciscan order and then a teacher at Oxford, where his razor-sharp, empirical mind quickly led to charges that his lectures were unorthodox. He was summoned to Avignon in 1324 and stayed there for some years while his writings were being investigated. Instead of remaining discreetly quiet under these dangerous circumstances, he joined the general of the Franciscan order in insisting that their vows of absolute poverty be literally followed after the manner of Jesus and their founder, Saint Francis of Assisi. Few actions could have more angered John XXII, one of the ablest and most secular-minded of the Avignon popes. He had no desire to have the apostolic poverty of the Franciscan friars contrasted with his papal palaces, and he had already lent his support to the less literal-minded Franciscans who did not wish to see their rule strictly applied. Ockham recognized the dangers of his position and in 1328 fled to the Emperor, who was then engaged in one of his periodic quarrels with the pope. For years he employed his brilliant talents trying to prove that the emperor was completely independent of the pope, that the Bible was the highest spiritual authority, and that a general council of the Church was superior to the pope, although he taught that the general council, like the pope, could err. By the time of his death in 1349, nominalism had been firmly implanted in the Franciscan order, and there were signs of a growing conviction among the faithful that a general council of the Church was needed to reform the Avignon papacy.

More radical but equally penetrating was the *Defensor Pacis*, which was written primarily by Marsiglio of Padua (c. 1290-1343) in 1324. To Marsiglio, the great enemy was not a corrupted ecclesiastical hierarchy, as it was to Ockham, but rather the influence wielded by the clergy in secular affairs. Faith and divine law, he thought, came from God, but human law came from the people. The clergy was only one of many classes in society and, like all other classes, was under the authority of the state. The clergyman's duty was to care for the soul just as the physician cared for the body. Like the physician, the clergyman could advise, instruct, and admonish, but not coerce. The Church was composed of all Christians, priest and layman alike, and the ultimate authority on matters of doctrine was a general council representing the entire Christian community. Papal pretensions were completely rejected, and far-reaching claims for popular sovereignty were made.

As the years passed and the Avignon papacy was followed by the period of the Great Schism when Rome, too, boasted a pope, the desire for reform became stronger. Scholars of unquestioned orthodoxy took up the demand for a general council to heal the schism and to reform the Church in its head and members. The universities, even the University of Paris, one of the most conservative in matters of theology, took up the cry. By the dawn of the fifteenth century, the voice of a few antipapal intellectuals like William of Ockham and Marsiglio of Padua had been swelled into the voice of a European conscience demanding action.

THE POPULAR ATTACK

The monarchs had found it to their advantage to stir up public opinion against the popes in order to strengthen their own position. The intellectuals had begun to undermine the doctrinal and hierarchical structure of the Church and to provide the theoretical framework for a general council to heal the schism and to institute reforms. Under these circumstances, it is not surprising that the monarchical and intellectual onslaughts were followed by a popular attack on the papacy.

The popular attack took two forms, the one heretical and the other a reform movement within the Church itself. The distinction between the heretics and the reformers should not be overemphasized, however, since at first the doctrinal position of both groups was often quite similar. The real difference was that the heretic was excommunicated because he refused to obey the ecclesiastical authorities when they sought to check his zeal, while the reformer was not actually excommunicated, either because the authorities were too intelligent, too sympathetic, or too indifferent to halt his efforts or because he himself bowed before the will of the authorized spokesmen of the Church. Only after he was excommunicated did the teachings of the heretic become decidedly more radical than those of the reformer.

The popular attack on the papacy and the whole ecclesiastical hierarchy was characterized by mysticism, Biblical literalism, and a growing tendency to reject the subtleties of scholastic theology in favor of simple piety. A mystic is one who seeks union with God. To achieve this union, the mystic follows either a negative or a positive approach. The type of union sought by the negative mystic is one of essence, in which his soul merges completely with God. For a moment, God and the mystic become one. The mystic as a conscious person in the material world ceases to exist. This type of religious experience is usually achieved by contemplating the divine, especially the passion of Jesus. Frequently, the negative mystic subjects himself to long periods of self-denial and self-examination preparatory to the desired union with God. This period, during which the mystic is usually tormented by doubts concerning the possibility of salvation, has received the picturesque name of "the dark night of the soul." The negative mystic, to be successful, has to abandon all self-will. He often rejects the active life in favor of a life of mystical contemplation and ecstatic experiences in a monastery. The state of mind cultivated by the negative mystic is common to some oriental religions and entered Christian thought through Neoplatonism. Although most negative mystics were strictly orthodox and devout, their religious approach was full of dangers to the Church because neither the priesthood nor the sacraments were essential to the achievement of their greatest desire, the mystical union with God.

There were many negative mystics throughout the Middle Ages, es-

46

pecially among the Italians, but in the fourteenth century the center of the movement shifted and there was a genuine flowering of mysticism in the Rhine Valley. This flowering was due largely to the efforts of Meister Eckhart (1260-1327), a highly-educated Dominican who had been deeply influenced by the writings of earlier Neoplatonic mystics. Although Eckhart wrote several Latin works, he exerted his greatest influence through a series of sermons delivered in German to the inhabitants of Cologne, Strasbourg, and other Rhineland cities. He was never intentionally guilty of heresy, but two years after his death some of his writings were condemned by the pope. By then, however, he had kindled a flame that could not be extinguished, and his followers among both the laity and the clergy formed a loosely-organized association known as the Friends of God to help each other seek spiritual solace through mystical experience.

Under the leadership of Johann Tauler (c. 1300-1361), the Friends of God began to stress the necessity of preparing the soul for the union with God by leading Christian lives. Thus, a practical lay piety was encouraged, although emphasis on the denial of self-will and the desire for mystical experiences continued.

This movement towards lay piety was furthered by the Dutch preacher Gerard Groote (1340-1384), a well educated man but secular-minded until his religious interests were awakened in his mid-thirties. In search of a solution to his spiritual problems, he visited a noted Flemish mystic, Jan Ruysbroeck (1293-1381), who had recently built a priory in the lovely vale of Groenendael to the south of Brussels. Ruysbroeck had been deeply influenced by the writings of the Friends of God, but his mysticism also had a more positive, active element. Instead of seeking only a mystical union with God through contemplation, he taught the value of a mystical relationship in which man felt the spirit of God within him. Out of love of God, he sought to do His will, just as a piece of iron, penetrated by fire, did the work of fire.

Groote did not immediately adopt Ruysbroeck's more positive program but retired to a Carthusian monastery where he spent two years in contemplation, without becoming a priest. At length, in 1379, five years before his death, he emerged from the cloister and spent his remaining years leading an active life as a lay preacher. Theological subtleties meant nothing to him, for he regarded the arguments of the realist and nominalist alike as a waste of time. Rather, he emphasized the value of an inner spiritual life and the necessity of transforming it into a life of action. He interpreted the Bible literally, and he taught that man's duty was to imitate the lives of Christ and the early Christians as closely as possible. He quickly won a number of followers who became known as the *Devotia Moderna* or New Devotion.

Although Groote was technically orthodox, he and his lay preachers incurred the enmity of the local clergy because their earnestness and piety contrasted so sharply with the behavior of many ordained priests. By their very example, they were a living rebuke to the existing situation in the Church. This growing enmity led Groote to suggest on his deathbed that those of his followers most fitted for a monastic life join the Augustinian order, so that they could carry on their work unmolested and at the same time provide protection for the lay members of the society. As a result, a monastery was established at Windesheim in 1386 and a convent at Diepenveen some years later.

For those members of the New Devotion who chose to remain outside the monasteries, houses were established where they could live pious lives without taking formal monastic vows. The Brethren and Sisters of the Common Life, as the lay members of the New Devotion were called, were not allowed to own property and were expected to live a communal existence in prayer and meditation, copying and translating the Bible and other religious books. Many became popular lay preachers, but the most important work carried on by the Brethren was in the field of education. In some cities, they founded their own schools, in others they furnished faculty members for existing institutions, but wherever the spirit of the Brethren prevailed, piety was stressed more than theology and virtue more than ritual. Excellent instruction in secular subjects was provided and eventually came to include Greek as well as Latin. So popular did these schools become that children came from hundreds of miles to attend, and several had over a thousand students. A firm basis was laid for a dynamic reform movement in the Netherlands and western Germany.

The monastic members of the New Devotion also turned their energy to religious writings and church reform. By 1500, the congregation included over a hundred reformed priories in the Netherlands and Germany. However, perhaps the movement's greatest contribution to religion was a little devotional book entitled *The Imitation of Christ*, one of the most widely read pieces of Christian literature. The devotional classic was compiled by a Windesheim monk named Thomas à Kempis (1380-1471), who used notes left by Groote and others. The work lacked structural unity, consisting as it did of a series of prayers, meditations, and admonitions. Dogma was ignored and church rituals were rarely mentioned. Instead, stress was placed on morality and piety, and man was depicted as a pilgrim on earth, imprisoned by the flesh but longing to return to the Godhead in imitation of Christ.

Groote and his followers remained within the fold of the Catholic Church. A different fate awaited John Wyclif (c. 1330-1384) and John Hus (1370-1415), who were also motivated by a desire to reform the Church. Wyclif was a retiring, scholarly professor at Oxford until he was pressed into royal service in the 1370's to defend the crown's right to tax the English clergy and to deny the pope a similar privilege. This service he performed with so much enthusiasm that his writings were soon condemned by the Church and later by the anticlerical but still orthodox English government. Like Marsiglio of Padua and William of Ockham, he placed the secular government over the Church in the temporal sphere, after which he proceeded to argue that the clergy should be reformed by stripping it of its property. The Church, he maintained, consisted of those predestined to be saved, a definition that included part of the laity and excluded, in his opinion, much of the clergy. Furthermore, sacraments administered by a priest not in a state of grace were not efficacious. The Bible was the only source of God's law and should be interpreted literally. To this end, sincerity of purpose was more valuable than a theological education. Wyclif and his followers began to translate the Bible into English to be used by priests and laymen who did not read Latin. His Biblical literalism and his general philosophical position led him to challenge other Catholic doctrines. These included the doctrine of the Mass, for Wyclif argued that the bread and wine were still present after the consecration. Soon he had a wide following, known as the Lollards, among the Oxford faculty, the gentry, and the lower classes. As the movement grew more radical, however, and became involved in demands for social reform, his following among the aristocracy declined. The government's decision less than two decades after his death to impose the death sentence on those who adhered to his heretical teachings led to further desertions. In the end, Lollardy was driven underground and to what extent it secretly survived among the lower classes in England cannot be determined. It had lasted long enough, however, to discredit further the ecclesiastical hierarchy in the popular mind and to cultivate the seeds, already planted in Bohemia, of a more serious movement against the Church.

There was a bitter quarrel at the university in Prague in the late fourteenth and early fifteenth centuries between the German and the Czech members of the faculty, in which the Czechs were frequently outvoted. The disagreement stemmed partly from a nascent Czech nationalism that reacted vigorously against German influences and partly from opposite philosophical and ecclesiastical positions. The Czechs were realists; the Germans were nominalists. The Czechs were loud in their demands for clerical reform; the Germans were not. Students of both nationalities joined in the dispute, and several brawls occurred. Under such circumstances Wyclif's writings were eagerly devoured by Czech scholars and preachers, among whom was the energetic and earnest John Hus.

Hus adopted most of Wyclif's ideas, but he did reject some of the Englishman's more radical doctrines, including his interpretation of the Mass. Most Czechs supported him, but the Germans rallied to the orthodox Catholic position. In 1409, when the Bohemian king decided to support the Czechs, several thousand German professors and students departed for Leipzig where they founded a new university. The German exodus left the Czechs in control of the university in Prague, and they quickly took advantage of their position to elect Hus rector. At this point the archbishop of Prague excommunicated Hus and had Wyclif's books burned, but in 1412 the fiery Czech left Prague and went to southern Bohemia where he continued his writing and preaching. In spite of the opposition of some Czech conservatives, the new movement found many adherents. Thus, to the problem of the Great Schism and the acknowledged need for church reform was added that of a widespread heresy supported and protected by a king.

THE CONCILIAR MOVEMENT

The Great Schism, the need for church reform, and the spread of heresy led the theologians of the conservative University of Paris to adopt the view, called the conciliar theory, that a general council of the Church was superior to the pope. It also led some kings to recognize the need for action and to withdraw their support from this or that rival pope. At length, a majority of the cardinals in both the Avignon and Roman camps summoned a general council of the Church to meet at Pisa in 1409. There, both popes were declared deposed and a new pope was elected. Unfortunately, neither the Roman nor the Avignon pontiffs would accept the decrees of the council; as a result, there were now three prelates who claimed to be the successor of Saint Peter. To make matters worse, the pope elected at Pisa died soon thereafter, and his successor, John XXIII (1410-1415),[8] chosen because his military power was thought necessary to deal with the tumultuous situation in Italy, had the morals as well as the training of a professional soldier. Since John XXIII proved to be as anxious to avoid conciliar checks on his authority as any of his predecessors, the reformers soon found it necessary to persuade Emperor Sigismund to bring pressure on him to summon a general council to meet at Constance in 1414.

At Constance, the delegates undertook to heal the schism, to reform the Church "in head and members," and to extirpate heresy. The first task proved to be the easiest. Both John XXIII and the Avignon pope were deposed, and the Roman pope avoided a similar fate by abdicating. Martin V (1417-1431) was chosen to the see of Saint Peter and gradually brought the schism to an end by winning recognition from the followers of the deposed popes.

Heresy proved a more difficult problem. The council summoned Hus from Bohemia, but he consented more with the hope of converting the council to his views than with the intention of submitting to the authority of the leaders of the Church. When he refused to recant, he was turned over to the secular authority to be burned. The cruelty of this act served only to inflame his followers, and when the king died in 1419, his brother,

[8] The Avignon popes and the other popes, as John XXIII, who were chosen in an irregular manner are not recognized by the Catholic Church. Therefore, the pope who was elected in 1958 took the name of John XXIII rather than John XXIV.

Emperor Sigismund, laid claim to the Bohemian crown with the obvious intention of extirpating heresy. A bloody war broke out in which the brilliant Hussite general, John Ziska (1360-1424), repeatedly defeated the forces of the Emperor and the crusaders who had answered the call of the Pope to aid his pious endeavor. Permanent victory might well have been won by the Hussites had they not become divided into two factions. One of these followed the relatively moderate teachings of Hus, and the other endorsed the most radical statements of Wyclif. Finally, in the 1430's, the moderates made peace with the orthodox Catholics in return for the special privilege of giving the wine as well as the bread of the communion to the laity, a significant concession because it seemed to remove part of the special status of the clergy. Then the Utraquists, as the moderates were called, joined with the Catholics to crush the radicals. In the end, heresy was driven underground, the Utraquists and Catholics quarreled, and Bohemia was in ruins.

The third goal of the delegates at Constance, reform, proved even more elusive. A few minor reforms were decreed, but a thorough reformation was postponed in the belief that it could be instituted at a later date. In this belief the delegates were wrong. Although they stated that their authority came directly from Christ and that everyone including the pope was bound to obey their decrees, they had no means to enforce their claim for supremacy once they had elected a pope and returned to their homes. Martin V and his successor, Eugenius IV (1431-1447), proved to be able and reasonably conscientious popes, but both quickly found that the secular problems of the papacy necessitated the continuation of many of the unpopular fiscal exactions that had caused so much discontent. Furthermore, both popes were dedicated to the idea of papal supremacy over the Church and did all they could to weaken the claims of the council. The delegates at Constance had wisely established a time schedule for future councils in the hope of ensuring a thorough reformation of the Church, but at each scheduled meeting they found their efforts thwarted by papal intransigence and by their own inability to agree. In 1449, the last of this series of councils came to an end. The popes had reasserted their sovereignty over the Church, and reform had been indefinitely postponed.

The popes' victory had been achieved largely through their policy of winning support from the secular monarchs. Since the kings had initially supported the conciliarists, the popes could gain their support only by permitting them to assume more control over the Church in their respective countries. The power of the kings to make ecclesiastical appointments and to extract revenue from the clergy in their respective states increased while papal revenue from the various kingdoms was sharply reduced. Thus the popes, in defeating the conciliar movement, were defeated in turn by the secular monarchs. More and more they became Italian princes. Instead of asserting their authority in temporal matters throughout Catholic Europe, they devoted their energies to consolidating their power in the papal states and to fighting wars against the petty Italian rulers.

THE MONARCHICAL FAILURE

One might think that the monarchs' gradual triumph over the papacy between 1300 and 1450 was part of a steady consolidation of the various territorial states. In fact, history was no kinder to the kings than to the popes, and their authority sank during this period nearly as low as that of their rivals. It was papal weakness, not monarchical strength, that led to the latter's victory during the first half of the fifteenth century. The kings of the twelfth and thirteenth centuries had on the whole been able monarchs, but those of the next 150 years were for the most part either weak incompetents or, when nature endowed them with a modest amount of energy and ability, knights-errant who plunged their countries into bloody, destructive wars. Plagues, economic depression, social unrest, and intellectual revolt added greatly to the disasters precipitated by weak rulers and by wars. Together, these factors mark a partial break in the advance of European civilization that had begun during the Middle Ages around the year 1000.

FRANCE AND THE HUNDRED YEARS WAR

Medieval civilization at its height was centered in France. The culture of France was dominant in England, the northern part of the Iberian Peninsula, and parts of the Empire. The fate of France, then, was intertwined with the entire medieval civilization. For this reason, the Hundred Years War, which saw plundering troops ravage the French countryside disrupting the economy, was a tragedy that affected nearly all of Western Europe.

The origins of the war were feudal and dynastic. The Plantagenets were independent kings of England, but they were also dukes of Aquitaine, a large duchy in southwestern France which they held as vassals of the French kings, whose officials infringed on their rights just as they did on those of less powerful nobles. This situation had led to bloody quarrels between the two royal families even before 1316 when, for the first time in over three centuries, a Capetian king failed to provide a son to take his place on the throne of France. The daughters of the last king were passed over in favor of his brother. When this brother died in 1322 with no male heirs, the process was repeated. Then, in 1328, when the third and last brother died, again without leaving a son, the throne was given to a cousin, Philip VI (1328-1350) of the house of Valois. Precedent had established the inability of a woman to rule, but could a man claim the throne through a woman? This question was eventually raised by Edward III (1327-1377) of England when a quarrel arose over Aquitaine. Through his mother, he was more closely related to the last Capetians than Philip VI, and he hoped that by claiming the French throne he could make Aquitaine independent by severing its feudal ties with the Paris government, as well as pick up some additional territory. He did not, on the other hand, entertain serious hope of becoming king of France.

Edward sought allies in the Empire, and Philip sought an alliance with Scotland. Both found support in Flanders, a country largely situated in what is now Belgium. The count, who was Philip's vassal, assisted him, while the burghers, who depended on England for their wool trade, turned to Edward. Eventually, part of the Iberian Peninsula was drawn into the conflict, so that a feudal, dynastic quarrel plunged most of Western Europe into war.

The first phase of the war (1337-1360) was marked by great English victories at Crécy and Poitiers that were largely made possible by the longbow, a new weapon to the continent that could be shot three times as rapidly as the crossbow and had a greater range. At Crécy, against the well-aimed English arrows, the armored and undisciplined French cavalry was helpless. Calais fell to the English in 1347, and Philip died three years later, to be succeeded by John the Good (1350-1364). As a knight-errant, John was indeed good, but not as a king. Defeated at Poitiers in 1356, John gallantly refused to flee from the field. He was captured and held for a ransom that had to be paid by subjects who were already being driven to open revolt by heavy taxation, inefficient government, military defeats, and pillaging troops. Uprisings at Paris and among the peasants were suppressed, and peace was made at Brétigny in 1360. Edward was given Aquitaine, Calais, the surrounding territories, and a large ransom. When a hostage who had been given in return for John's release escaped before the terms of the treaty had been fulfilled, John, good knight-errant to the last, returned to captivity in accordance with the chivalrous code and died in England in 1364.

John's oldest son, Charles V (1364-1380), was more an administrator than a soldier. He strengthened royal control over taxation and improved the army before the war was renewed in 1369. This time, instead of fighting pitched battles as in the past, when the English longbowmen had invariably outmatched their feudal army, the French, under the command of their able constable, Bertrand du Guesclin, adopted guerrilla tactics and fell on troop detachments and isolated garrisons when the opportunity presented itself. The new tactics were successful, and by the time of Charles' death in 1380 only the regions around Bordeaux and Calais remained in English hands.

A generation of nominal peace between the two countries followed, not because of the wisdom of the monarchs but because internal difficulties reduced them to impotence. Richard II of England was only a child when he inherited the throne from his grandfather, Edward III, in 1377. The barons took advantage of his youth, and when, on reaching manhood, he tried to restore the position of the crown, he went too far and was deposed in 1399 by Henry IV (1399-1413) of the house of Lancaster.

France suffered even more, for Charles VI (1380-1422) began his reign as a minor and from early manhood suffered intermittent attacks of insanity. The great nobles sought to control the government for their own ends. Charles' uncle, Philip the Bold, Duke of Burgundy, got French support to make good his claims to Flanders and adjacent territories. His brother, the Duke of Orléans, sought to check the Burgundian influence for his own advantage but was assassinated for his efforts, and a bloody civil war followed. The English once more intervened, this time as allies of the Burgundian faction, and Henry V (1413-1422) won a famous victory at Agincourt in 1415. By the terms of the Treaty of Troyes, 1420, Henry received recognition from Charles VI as his heir and the hand of his daughter in marriage. Charles' son and namesake was declared illegitimate, a not incredible charge in view of his mother's notorious immorality.

At that point, it looked as though the youthful Henry V might wear both crowns, but Henry died suddenly in 1422, several months before his insane father-in-law. His ten-month-old son, Henry VI (1422-1461), was proclaimed king of England and France, with Burgundian support. The Orléanist faction refused to accept this situation and recognized Charles' son as King Charles VII (1422-1461).

The war continued. The Atlantic coastal provinces and the region north of the Loire River supported the English and their Burgundian allies, and for a time the forces of the infant Henry seemed more than a match for those of the weak and indecisive Charles. But as he grew older Henry fell prey to the attacks of insanity that had plagued his Valois grandfather, while Charles gradually found able supporters who guided him, sometimes in spite of himself, towards victory.

The most famous of those who took up the cause of Charles was the illiterate peasant girl Joan of Arc (1412-1431), a devout mystic who began to have visions when she was thirteen and a few years later followed the command of celestial voices to offer her services to Charles and France. The story of how she persuaded a few rough soldiers to take her to Charles at Chinon, of how she gave new heart to the French troops, raised the siege of Orléans, and was finally captured by the English, tried, and burned for witchcraft is too well known to be detailed here. It is enough to say that she gave a seemingly lost cause the inspiration needed to turn the tide. Once victory seemed possible, support for Charles swelled. The Duke of Burgundy deserted the English for the French in 1435. Once united, the far greater strength of France began to tell, and by 1453 the English were driven from the continent except for the toehold they were able to keep at Calais.

Victory had finally come, but France lay in ruins. More serious still was the detrimental effect of the war on society and government. The crown emerged with a small army and a system of taxation to support it, but the army was untrustworthy and the taxes fell mainly on the peasants, who were least able to pay them. To get the support of the wealthier classes during the war, the crown had been forced to relinquish nearly all claim to tax the nobility, the clergy, royal officials, and even some towns. The clergy and the towns were eventually persuaded to contribute something, but from this time until the Revolution of 1789 the poorest classes were heavily taxed and the wealthiest classes contributed very little. Furthermore, the war had made communications with southern France so difficult that autonomous administrative and judicial systems had been established there. Similar privileges were given to most of the territories recaptured from the English.

Thus, the war contributed heavily towards making France a decentralized state with several highly privileged classes.

OTHER KINGS AND OTHER WARS

The French were able to inflict little direct damage on England during the Hundred Years War; but their Scottish allies conducted several invasions into the northern counties, and with their aid, the Welsh, led by the able Owen Glendower, made a gallant attempt to throw off the English yoke between 1402 and 1409. However, the greatest damage suffered by England during the period of the Hundred Years War was inflicted by the English themselves. Most of the rulers were knights-errant like Henry V or incompetents like Henry VI. Four of the nine kings who came to the throne between 1307 and 1485 were minors. During their minority, the great nobles were able to seize control of the government and had to be forcibly dispossessed when the kings reached manhood. Revolts were frequent. The violence in English public life during this period is best illustrated by the fact that four kings were deposed and murdered, one was killed in battle, and only four contrived to die natural deaths. The mass of the English people did not participate in these episodes, but their suffering caused several serious uprisings among the peasants and the poorer classes in the towns. The kings did retain the ability to tax the upper classes, although in the process Parliament was firmly established as an institution for giving consent. Equally significant, there was very little tendency for semisovereign provincial institutions to develop as they did in France.

The Hundred Years War spread to the south of the Pyrénées, where at this time there were the four Christian kingdoms of Aragon, Castile, Navarre, and Portugal as well as the Moslem kingdom of Granada. Both England and France supported rival claimants to the throne of Castile.

Portugal fought a successful war with Castile, and both of these Iberian states carried on an intermittent, indecisive war with the Moslems, and both suffered from revolts and private warfare. In Castile, for example, six of the nine kings who ruled between 1284 and 1474 were troubled by rival claimants to the throne and by civil wars. The other three were minors who could not prevent struggles for control of the government. Aragon, which had traditionally looked to the Mediterranean, became embroiled in many conflicts there, including a successful bid for Naples at the expense of a younger branch of the French royal family.

Italy too was divided into a number of states at this time and suffered from constant warfare. The papal states virtually disintegrated. Rome itself fell prey to the rivalry of several noble factions, and for a brief time a republic was actually established. Other towns became virtually independent of the popes but were torn by internal struggles for power. It is not surprising that the popes preferred the relative security of Avignon. At one time, Naples threatened to engulf southern and central Italy, and an ambitious, warlike Milan had similar designs on the north. Lesser towns conquered their still smaller neighbors. Although the Italian battlefields may have been less bloody than those of France, the general picture of the Italian Peninsula was one of constant wars and rebellions.

The authority of the emperor was already low in the Empire, but continued Italian ambitions and renewed papal interference weakened it further. The incompetent, quixotic adventurers who usually wore the crown made matters worse, and rival claims to the throne led to many quarrels. During the later stages of the Great Schism, the imperial crown could also boast three claimants. For a time, it looked as though the Empire might break up into a number of states ruled by the princes and dukes, with the abler emperors setting the example by consolidating their position in their hereditary lands. But even the princes were not able to stabilize the situation, for in their territories the clergy, nobles, and towns joined together to form provincial estates. Through the control over taxation that they exercised in their assemblies, these three classes could block the more ambitious moves of the princes, but at the same time they were able to undertake few constructive measures themselves. The disorder became so great that cities had to join together to form the Rhine League, the Swabian League, and the more famous Hanseatic League, to secure their walls and to protect their trade. The Swiss cantons, still nominally a part of the Empire, carried on intermittent warfare with their Habsburg overlords that was punctuated by frequent conflicts among themselves. Bohemia and the surrounding lands were devastated by the Hussite wars.

Thus, medieval civilization, from England to Bohemia, suffered for over a century from the depredations of undisciplined troops and the misrule of incompetent, irresponsible kings.

56

The Decline of Medieval Civilization

At this same time, the periphery of medieval civilization contracted. The preceding centuries had been periods of expansion. The Germans had advanced at the expense of the Slavs, and Roman Catholicism had pressed eastward into Poland and Hungary and northward into Scandinavia, carrying with it much of the medieval civilization. The Scandinavian people themselves had established settlements in Iceland and Greenland and had visited the New World. The Spanish had driven relentlessly southward from a tiny foothold in the Pyrénées to engulf most of the Iberian Peninsula; only the Kingdom of Granada survived of the once powerful Moorish state. The Crusades had led to the temporary conquest of Jerusalem and the establishment of Latin states and trading posts in the eastern Mediterranean. The formation of the great Mongol Empire in the thirteenth century, which extended from the Black Sea to the Pacific Ocean, had made it possible for merchants and priests to travel safely to China, and by the early fourteenth century a chain of Christian missions had been established from Constantinople to Peking.

This tide of events, which seemed to presage the modern expansion of Europe, was brought to an end by a series of events after 1300. The religious and economic ties with the Far East came to an end when the breakup of the Mongol Empire into a host of quarreling states made travel dangerous. To the west, the Scandinavians ceased their voyages to North America and abandoned their settlements in Greenland. To the south, the Iberian kingdoms made no further advances after 1340.

From the southeast, the Ottoman Turks, an Asiatic Moslem tribe that had settled south of the Black Sea in Anatolia, began to extend their conquests into the Balkans in 1354. Within a generation, they conquered Bulgaria and unsuccessfully besieged Constantinople. A crusade was preached in the West with all the ardor of the past, but the Christian knights proved no match for their Moslem enemies and were completely defeated at Nicopolis in 1396. Constantinople was temporarily saved, but in 1453 it fell before the heavy cannon of Mohammed II (1451-1481), who then proceeded to drive the Genoese out of their Black Sea trading posts and the Venetians from the Aegean Islands and part of the Adriatic coast. Western influence was once more excluded from the eastern Mediterranean. Still not content, Mohammed expanded his empire in the Balkans to the Danube River. Syria, Arabia, and Egypt were overrun in the early sixteenth century, and in 1526 Suleiman the Magnificent (1520-1566) defeated the Hungarians at Mohács and incorporated most of their kingdom into his empire. Three years later, he expanded his influence along the coast of North Africa as far as Algeria and even made an unsuccessful attempt to take Vienna.

Most of the territorial gains the Europeans had made during the medieval period of expansion had been lost, and there seemed little reason to believe that the Christian states could do more than hold their own during the coming years.

THE PLAGUES

Incompetent kings and internal wars help to account for the contraction of Christendom during the fourteenth and fifteenth centuries, but a series of violent plagues and a severe depression were also important factors. The bubonic plague, or Black Death as it has come to be called, was a disease carried by fleas on rats. It apparently began in central Asia and moved eastward into China and westward along the trade routes, entering Europe in 1347 during a period of famine when the poor had little natural resistance to combat the disease. In three years, the plague spread to nearly every country in Christendom, decimating the villages and towns in its path. "Such obvious symptoms," a modern historian writes, "as gangrenous inflammation of the throat and lungs, violent pains in the chest, vomiting and spitting of blood, pestilential odor from bodies and breath, tumors in the groin and axillae and on the neck, constipation or diarrhea, and purple spots (caused by subcutaneous hemorrhages) marked the victims. Frequent stabs of pain gave rise to the conviction that the stricken were being shot with arrows by some invisible demon." [9] Sickness came three days after exposure, and a Thuringian chronicle recorded that the infected slept for "three days and nights and, when they awoke, they immediately began to struggle with death, until they gave up the ghost."

Most estimates suggest that about one-third of the population of Europe was wiped out, the losses among the poor being heavier than among the rich. Some localities suffered heavily, others lightly, but even after the plague had spent its force around 1350, it returned again and again during the next century. The little town of Givry in Burgundy had about 1,600 inhabitants when the plague arrived in 1348, but between August 5 and November 19 there were 615 deaths. The city of Florence had 110,000 inhabitants in 1338, and only 45,000 to 50,000 in 1351. Partial recovery followed in most localities, only to be halted by the return of the plague, so that the north German cities were at least 20 per cent smaller at the end of the fifteenth century than they were at the beginning of the fourteenth. Zurich had 12,375 inhabitants in 1350 and 4,713 in 1468. Catalonia, a country in the northeastern part of the Iberian Peninsula, recovered rapidly from the first onslaught and boasted 95,000 homesteads in 1365, but in 1497 it had only 59,000. England had 3,700,000 inhabitants when the Black Death struck in 1348, but only 2,100,000 in the early fifteenth century. As high a percentage of the population lost their lives as is usually predicted if Europe were subjected to the twentieth-century form of holocaust, the nuclear war. When the plague struck a city, it

[9] Charles F. Mullett, *The Bubonic Plague and England* (Lexington: University of Kentucky Press, 1956), p. 14.

58

moved rapidly, often taking a proportion of the inhabitants equal to that killed at Hiroshima or Nagasaki.

It is difficult to evaluate the impact of the Black Death on European civilization. The modern world has not yet had to suffer so acutely either from disease or war. Today, when epidemics strike, the suffering can be attributed to natural causes and mitigated by medical and social services. The fourteenth-century man, on the other hand, often thought in terms of an angry God or of vengeful demons. To the horror of death was added the fear of the supernatural and inexpiable. A Flemish chronicler thought he knew what happened because his information came from the papal court at Avignon:

> This year, 1347, in the month of September, there began a terrible mortality and plague, as I saw in the copy of a letter from a canon and precentor of St. Donatien at Bruges, who was then at the Roman Court with a cardinal, his master; which letter he had sent to his fellows at Bruges in view of the terrible news. He wrote how, in the East, hard by Greater India, in a certain province, certain horrors and unheard-of tempests overwhelmed the whole province for the space of three days. On the first day there was a rain of frogs, serpents, lizards, scorpions, and many venomous beasts of that sort. On the second, thunder was heard, and lightning and sheets of fire fell upon the earth, mingled with hailstones of marvelous size, which slew almost all, from the greatest even to the least. On the third day there fell fire from heaven and stinking smoke, which slew all that were left of men and beasts, and burned up all the cities and towns in those parts. By these tempests the whole province was infected; and it is conjectured that from this infection, through the foul blast of wind that came from the south, the whole seashore and surrounding lands were infected, and are waxing more and more venomous from day to day; and now, as some suspect, it cometh round the seacoasts, by God's will, after the following fashion. For, in January of the year 1348, three galleys touched at Genoa, driven by a fierce blast from the East, horribly infected and laden with divers spices and other weighty goods. When the men of Genoa learned this, and saw how suddenly and irremediably they infected other folk, they were driven forth from that port by fiery arrows and divers engines of war; for no man dared touch them; nor could any man deal with them in merchandise, but he would die forthwith. Thus, they were scattered from port to port, till at length one of these aforesaid three galleys came to Marseilles; at whose coming all who took no precautions were infected and died forthwith.[10]

Before the unknown horror, brave men became panic-stricken and men of responsibility deserted their charges. Magistrates fled from stricken cities, physicians refused to attend the sick, clergymen to administer the sacraments, and notaries to write the wills of the dying. Few had the courage to expose themselves by burying the dead. "Neither kinsfolk nor friends nor priests nor friars went with the corpses, nor was the funeral office sung," wrote a Sienese chronicler, "and I, Angelo da Tura, buried five of mine own children in one grave with mine own hands, and so did

[10] Quoted by G. Coulton, *The Black Death* (New York: McBride and Co., 1930), pp. 12-14.

many others likewise; and, beyond this, some of them were so ill covered that the dogs drew them forth and ate many bodies about the city."

THE DEPRESSION AND SOCIAL STRIFE

As though war and plagues were not enough, three hundred years of economic advance came to an end in the early fourteenth century. The causes of this economic decline are not fully known, but the fact that there were signs of it in some places before the Black Death or the wars suggests that the economic system itself was at fault. Agriculture was perhaps the immediate source of the difficulty. During the years of prosperity, the rapidly growing population had been fed by bringing more land under cultivation and by the spread of the three-field system, which permitted the annual use of two-thirds rather than only one-half of the arable land. By 1300, in the more thickly populated portions of Europe, there was no new land suitable for farming, and there were indications of lower yields per acre because of land exhaustion or the use of marginal fields. New technological advances were necessary if food was to be found for a population that increased rapidly unless checked by war or disease. But the medieval European failed to meet the challenge; no new ways were found to improve agriculture, and there was widespread famine in 1315-17. At Ypres, a town of 20,000 inhabitants, 2,794 corpses were buried between May and October 1316. Other localities also suffered, and whenever the population again exceeded the number of persons who could be supported by the agricultural system or when there was a poor harvest, hunger and privation once more acted as a cruel check. There were widespread famines in 1333-34, 1337-42, and in 1345-47.

In addition to greater agricultural productivity, new markets and new industrial techniques were necessary to ensure the continued growth of the towns. However, instead of expanding geographically to embrace new markets abroad, Europe contracted, thereby losing some old markets as well as the chance of developing new ones. Certainly the greatest potential market of all lay in the European masses themselves. But as long as the feudal-agrarian society was predominant, industry had to cater to the limited market provided by the noble, the prelate, and the burgher. The workers in the towns could afford to buy little besides food. Because of their limited purchasing power, the peasants, who still made up over four-fifths of the population, had to rely on the manor to supply their needs. Not until mass production technology enabled industrialists to produce goods at lower prices and the social and economic structure provided for more than a luxury market could Europe move significantly beyond the peak reached at the dawn of the fourteenth century. Material progress seemed doomed; there could be depressions and recoveries, but not advances significantly beyond the earlier peak. Like the Chinese and Arab civilizations in certain periods of their history, Europe had become stagnant. Not until the eighteenth century did technological progress and social change permit new advances comparable to those achieved during the high Middle Ages.

The wars and plagues also had their economic effect. Certainly the Black Death, which in a few months carried off over half the population of some towns, was significant, although economically less catastrophic than one might think. If it sharply reduced the number of consumers and accounted for much of the decline in trade that surviving statistics suggest, it also reduced even more substantially the number of producers, since the poorly fed workers were more susceptible to disease than the well-to-do burghers. As a result, there was a temporary shortage of workers that forced employers to pay higher wages until the population increased once more, and the quantity of goods per person—that is, the standard of living —was not reduced.

More serious for the urban economy, perhaps, were the wars that disrupted trade and led several kings to repudiate the debts which they had incurred to put armies in the field. When, for example, Edward III of England failed to meet his financial obligations in 1343, two great Florentine merchant-banking houses were bankrupted and other firms were adversely affected. Thus, the Hundred Years War between England and France damaged the Italian economy and contributed to the depression.

The cessation of economic progress led to social strife in the towns. The merchants, who had hitherto played the dominant role in municipal government, now sought to use their political power to support their economic position. Their interests frequently clashed with those of the craft guilds, because the latter, faced with declining markets, sought to raise protective tariff walls around their towns to prevent outside competition, to make more stringent economic regulations within the towns, and to halt, forcibly in some instances, the manufacture of cloth in neighboring villages. The merchants, of course, tried to block these efforts because they depended on interurban, indeed, international trade. They were assisted by the handful of industrialists who were circumventing the guild system by arranging for peasants to make cloth in neighboring villages. Revolt often seemed the only recourse for the craft guilds, and there were frequent uprisings in the Low Countries and northern Italy where the economy had been furthest advanced and where, therefore, the depression caused the most unrest.

Within the craft guilds themselves, there were bitter quarrels. During the period of medieval expansion, it had been relatively easy for a boy to learn a trade as an apprentice, work a few years as a journeyman, saving his wages the while, and finally set himself up as a master while he was still in his twenties. However, when markets were reduced in the late Middle Ages, fewer guildmasters were needed. Those who had already achieved that position found means to make it more difficult for others to advance so that the available masterships would be reserved for their own children. As a result, artisans without family connections found the avenue of advancement cut off and the journeymen became a permanent wage-earning proletariat who were willing to revolt if need be to secure higher pay. Thus, there was a three-way struggle, often violent, between the merchant, the guildmaster, and the journeyman for control of the towns. Especially in the Low Countries, a noble or a king continually intervened on one side or the other.

Rural agitation was equally severe, for the noble was badly hurt by the economic decline and sought to make good his losses at the expense of the peasant. The Black Death and the wars created a labor shortage in the country as in the towns. This shortage forced the price of agricultural labor up, but the nobles tried to circumvent this natural rise by every means in their power. Prior to the catastrophes, they had usually found it to their advantage to free their serfs and to commute their labor services into a money rent, but they now tried to halt this movement in order to avoid paying high wages. The emancipation movement slowed, but did not cease entirely because concessions were still sometimes granted to prevent serfs from fleeing. The nobles who had already freed their serfs tried to hold down wages through collective action. In England, they caused Parliament to pass the Statute of Laborers in 1351, which froze wages at the level reached before the Black Death, but the law could not be enforced and wages continued to rise. In desperation, many nobles began to lease their land to ambitious farmers. On thus ceasing to exploit the soil directly, they broke their close ties with the villages and weakened the manorial system. Whatever action they took, the nobles clashed with the peasants whose interests opposed theirs. There were serious uprisings in England and France that merged with urban revolts and in the former country with religious discontent.

One reason for the nobles' intransigent attitude was that, when the urban population diminished and the famines ceased, there was no longer an adequate market for agricultural goods. Grain prices fell faster than other prices, and the nobles could not have paid the higher wages demanded even if they had been willing. Some were financially ruined; others were killed in the numerous wars. Thus, these were years of trial for the noble as well as the peasant, for the merchant as well as the guildmaster and the journeyman. The old order had ceased to work and no one fully understood why.

THE EUROPEAN PSYCHOLOGY

During the late Middle Ages, Europeans lived in the midst of wars, plagues, and social unrest. The Church, long divided, was still in need of reform; the intellectual synthesis that had helped to support it was under attack from many quarters, and heresy was spreading. The old authorities —whether king, noble, or pope—were discredited in many eyes; old customs no longer sufficed, and old institutions no longer worked. No one understood what was happening, and no one had a bold, original program to propose for the future. Indeed, the idea of earthly progress, of economic, social, and moral betterment had scarcely been born. The optimism that had characterized the thirteenth century yielded to a profound pessimism. "I, man of sadness, born in an eclipse of darkness, and thick fogs of lamentation," wrote one chronicler, and his autobiographical sketch could have applied to the age as a whole.

Because the world seemed to be disintegrating, an emotional instability replaced the serenity of the earlier age. Men laughed and cried at the slightest provocation; they were alternately cruel and merciful, generous and grasping, devout and immoral, loyal and treacherous. This tendency towards opposite extremes resulted from the general insecurity of the age and has been called "the violent tenor of life" by the great Dutch historian Johan Huizinga. Some sought to restore the old system by glorifying its customs and values to the point of absurdity. It was in this period, when the archer frequently triumphed over the knight and when artillery was making its appearance, that the various orders of chivalry were founded. Never had the chivalrous ideal been so zealously cultivated in literature and at court, although perhaps not on the battlefield. Honor, glory, and the conventions of courtly love were celebrated with religious fervor, and the crusading ideal was never stronger, although the numerous expeditions sent to the East were dismal failures. Huizinga saw in these aspirations an attempt to create a dream world into which men could escape from the grim actuality of the present.

The same tendency towards extremism may be found in the religious life of the period. Fasting and mortification of the flesh were practiced by some to a degree unknown before, but there were instances of equally extreme forms of licentiousness. Mysticism and religious emotionalism flourished in many forms, yet there were those who sought the assistance of the devil. Gilles de Rais (1404?-1440), patron of the arts, one-time companion of Joan of Arc, and Marshal of France, sold himself to the devil in return for knowledge, power, and wealth. In the diabolical rituals performed in his castle, he and his cohorts sacrificed scores of children. Others sought contact with the underworld, and their crimes lent a small degree of justification for an increase in the number of trials for witchcraft. However, the vast majority of those who were condemned for witchcraft suffered because their fellow men could imagine only two reasons for the disasters of the period: either an angry God was punishing them for their sins or their neighbors had turned the demons of the underworld loose upon them.

Perhaps the temper of the age can be seen best through its abnormal preoccupation with death and decay. In sculpture, in painting, and in stained glass, the human body was often depicted as it would appear after death, with the flesh falling off the bones and the worms doing their frightful work. It was probably at Paris that a new artistic motif first appeared, the Dance of Death. That crowded city did not have enough cemetery space to bury its many dead. After a corpse had rested for a brief period in the Cemetery of the Innocents in the heart of the city, it was dug up to make room for another. The bones were piled in the charnel houses, without distinction of rank, for all to see, a lesson in the frailty of earthly glory and a suggestion that even death brought no repose. This scene in the daily life of the Parisian inspired an artist to paint along the cemetery's cloister walls a series of persons fully clothed in all the dignity of their earthly station but each figure accompanied by its own future corpse, leading it onward to the dance of the dead. Had this macabre theme been confined to the cloister wall of the Cemetery of the Innocents, it would have had little significance. But it was reproduced in many churches, it influenced such great writers as François Villon, it was acted out at the court of the dukes of Burgundy, and it was depicted in a book as early as 1485. The motif had a meaning for the age that it is difficult for us to understand.

Thus, the medieval civilization was dying and seemed almost conscious of its fate. The experience was painful, especially in France and the western portions of the Empire where the roots of that civilization were deepest. In dying, it would give birth to something new.

PART II

THE RENAISSANCE

EUROPE AS A WHOLE	NORTHERN EUROPE	SOUTHERN EUROPE
		1265-1321, Dante **1266-1337,** Giotto **c.1300,** Italians improve business techniques **1304-1374,** Petrarch
	1380-1441, Van Eyck	
	1390-1453, John Dunstable	**1385-1402,** Giangaleazzo and the rise of Milan
		c.1400-c.1430, Birth of civic humanism and discovery of laws of perspective in Florence
1417-1431, Pope Martin V	**1417-1431,** Pope Martin V **1419-1467,** Philip the Good, Duke of Burgundy **1422-1461,** Charles VII and the reorganization of France **c.1450,** Gutenberg uses movable type	**1417-1431,** Pope Martin V
	1450-1516, Hieronymous Bosch	**1444-1510,** Botticelli
		1452-1519, Leonardo da Vinci
	1459-1525, Jacob Fugger	**1460,** Portuguese reach Sierra Leona
	1461-1483, Reigns of Louis XI of France and Edward IV of England	
	1471-1528, Albrecht Dürer	**1469-1492,** Lorenzo de Medici governs Florence
		1474-1504/16, Reigns of Isabella and Ferdinand of Spain

EUROPE AS A WHOLE	NORTHERN EUROPE	SOUTHERN EUROPE
c.1475-c.1625, Economic revival; reconstruction of aristocracy; shift in major commercial centers from Italy to Atlantic begins	**1475-1528,** Mathias Grunewald	**1475-1564,** Michelangelo
		1478, Revival of Inquisition in Spain
		1483-1520, Raphael
	1485-1509, Reign of Henry VII of England	
		1487, Dias rounds Cape of Good Hope
		1490, Savonarola begins to preach in Florence
		1492, Voyage of Columbus; fall of Granada
1492-1503, Pope Alexander VI	**1492-1503,** Pope Alexander VI	**1492-1503,** Pope Alexander VI
1494-1559, Habsburg-Valois wars		**1494,** French invasion of Italy; Treaty of Tordesillas
		1498, Da Gama discovers water route to India
	1499-1500, Erasmus' first visit to England	
1503-1513, Pope Julius II	**1503-1513,** Pope Julius II	**1503-1513,** Pope Julius II
	1509-1547, Reign of Henry VIII of England	
		1513, Machiavelli writes *The Prince*
	1515, Sir Thomas More begins *Utopia*	
	1515-1547, Reign of Francis I of France	
	1517, Luther attacks sale of indulgences	**1519-1522,** Magellan expedition
1519-1556, Reign of Emperor Charles V	**1519-1556,** Reign of Emperor Charles V	**1519-1556,** Reign of Emperor Charles V
	1533, Rabelais publishes *Pantagruel*	
	1534, Henry VIII breaks with Rome	
	1536, Calvin publishes *Institutes of the Christian Religion*	
1540, Loyola founds Society of Jesus		
1545-1563, Council of Trent		
	1553, Calvin becomes virtual ruler of Geneva	
	1555, Peace of Augsburg	
		1556-1598, Reign of Philip II of Spain
	1558-1603, Reign of Elizabeth I of England	
	1559, John Knox introduces Calvinism into Scotland	
	1563, Church of England is established	
		1567-1594, Palestrini

THE word *renaissance* means *rebirth,* but whether this term may be correctly applied to the period between the mid-fourteenth and mid-seventeenth centuries is a matter of endless dispute among historians. The greatest proponent of the idea that there was a rebirth during this period was Jakob Burckhardt, a Swiss historian who published in 1860 *The Civilization of the Renaissance in Italy.* To Burckhardt, a new civilization developed in Italy that had as its central characteristic "the discovery of the world and of man." By the discovery of the world, Burckhardt meant not only travel and exploration but also an interest in the natural sciences and the beauty of the landscape. By the discovery of man, he meant the conscious development of individualism and of the human personality. He attributed this awakening of the human spirit to the political situation in Italy that allowed its inhabitants to develop their individuality by struggling for political power unchecked by pope, emperor, or hereditary ruler. Once they had thrown off the medieval veil, "woven of faith, illusion, and childish prepossession," the genius of the Italian people asserted itself, and, guided by classical culture, they became "the first-born among the sons of modern Europe."

Burckhardt's study had an immense impact. Some of his followers said the same thing in more words; others put the emphasis on different factors but arrived at the same conclusions. Economic historians preferred to attribute the development of individualism to the capitalists' quest for wealth; social historians stressed the structure of society. Neither hesitated to see the great art of the age as the product of its wealth or its urban society. From Italy, it was agreed, the new civilization spread to the rest of Europe and marked the beginning of the modern world.

For more than a generation the Burckhardtian interpretation has been under attack. Some scholars now deny that Italy was far ahead of the rest of Europe. Others claim that nearly every characteristic which Burckhardt attributed to the Renaissance also existed in the Middle Ages. Some are willing to concede that there were more humanists or more artists in the Renaissance than in the preceding period, but they will go no further than to say that the Renaissance marked a continued growth of earlier developments. Others argue that the chief characteristic of the period was the decline of the medieval civilization; the natural sciences and the economy, they say, reached a higher peak in the early fourteenth century than they achieved again until the mid-sixteenth. Ardent Catholics cannot be expected to hail as progressive an age that saw the breakup of the medieval synthesis and the advent of Protestantism.

There is some truth to each of these positions, but they cannot all be totally right. The view taken in these pages is that the period called the Renaissance formed a distinct epoch of history which differed not only from the medieval civilization but also from the modern civilization that followed. It was born amid the wars, plagues, and economic stagnation of the fourteenth century and died amid the wars, plagues, and economic

67

stagnation of the seventeenth century. In those human activities, such as art, in which the human spirit can with relative ease free itself from the past, the distinctive character of the Renaissance is readily apparent. For the first time, artists discovered the laws of perspective and learned to paint pictures that were the mirrors of nature. In other activities, such as government, in which one generation automatically accepts basic institutions from its predecessors and passes these on to its successors, there was considerable continuity between the Renaissance and the epochs on either side of it, and changes are more difficult to detect. Nevertheless, many countries underwent a period of administrative and institutional reorganization that led to a restoration of internal order after years of civil war and brigandage. Through dynastic marriages, the groundwork was laid for the formation of several new states, and new diplomatic techniques were developed to deal with the changing international situation.

The Renaissance witnessed an economic revival after the depression of the late Middle Ages. This revival was accompanied by the discovery of a water route to India and of the American continents. Modern Western civilization began to expand beyond the peninsular continent at the very moment when it started to take form. Neither the economic revival nor the wealth won by the discoveries enabled the middle class to become ascendant; instead, the aristocracy was reconstituted and remained dominant almost everywhere.

An increased interest in classical Latin and Greek affected the intellectual climate of the period. Finally, a great religious revival led to a dispute that split the medieval Catholic Church and resulted in the religious diversity of modern times.

3/ The Renaissance State

THE catastrophes of the fourteenth and early fifteenth centuries were so severe that the usually incompetent kings of the age were unable to prevent the decline, if not the actual disintegration, of the medieval state. But eventually, out of this chaos, able men came to power and created the Renaissance state. These rulers restored internal order and gave new direction to the economic, social, religious, and cultural development of their people.

In some countries, such as England and France, the kings accomplished their restorative mission by making old institutions work. In others, they created new states through their marriages. However, behind the façade of the royal court, the various lands that they had brought together kept their old institutions and a surprising degree of autonomy.

In the Empire, where monarchical authority had disintegrated more completely, the greatest innovations took place. There, the prince, the bishop, and the town each sought to form territorial states by increasing their authority over their feudal dependents and expanding their juris-diction at the expense of their weaker neighbors. In the Germanic part of the Empire, the princes built their authority in part on existing institutions, as in the kingdoms to the west, and the towns were fortunate if they could maintain their semi-independent status. In northern Italy, which was still a part of the Empire, the towns were wealthier and more populous. Here, largely isolated from the rest of Europe, unhindered by the presence of great nobles, and far removed from the waning authority of the emperor, the most important towns expanded their boundaries to become territorial states often ruled by new men who became dukes. It was in this micro-cosm that new power situations emerged and modern diplomacy was born.

THE ITALIAN MICROCOSM

GENERAL CHARACTERISTICS

Northern Italy remained technically a part of the Empire throughout the Renaissance, but between the mid-thirteenth and the early sixteenth centuries, the emperors were rarely in a position to intervene effectively, and the numerous towns in the Po Valley of Lombardy and the hills of Tuscany to the south emerged as autonomous city-states, each ruling over the surrounding countryside. In these two provinces, there had been no great feudal nobles in the late Middle Ages, and the lesser nobles, unable to dominate the towns from their rural fortresses, had succumbed to the attraction of the city where they now resided in fortified houses having tall towers reminiscent of feudal keeps. Here they had intermarried with wealthy merchant families to form a class known as the *grandi* and to en-gage in trade.

Beneath the *grandi* were the wealthy members of important guilds dealing in foreign trade, then the members of the lesser guilds, and finally the day laborers, who were not members of any guild and had no voting rights. These four classes, especially during the economic contraction of the fourteenth century, became engaged in an internal struggle for power in which family and party ties frequently cut across economic lines. Gen-erally, the wealthy merchants and the members of the lesser guilds united under a popularly elected "captain of the people" to take control of the government from the *grandi*. Quarrels between the merchants and the lesser guilds then necessitated the captains' continuance in office for longer periods than intended and slowly enabled them to make their position hereditary.

After rising to power with the aid of the people, the captains sought to make their position legitimate by purchasing the office of vicar from the emperor. This office lessened their dependence on the people and gave them a pretext to extend their authority over the smaller neighboring towns. Those who were most successful in strengthening their authority returned to the emperor with money for higher titles. In this manner, a Visconti became Duke of Milan in 1395, a Gonzaga was made Marquis of Mantua in 1432, and an Este won from the pope the title of Duke of Ferrara in 1471. Thus, the fifteenth century witnessed the emergence of a new class of great nobles in northern Italy who ruled over small territorial states as the none-too-obedient vassals of the pope or emperor.

Much has been written about the tyrannical behavior of these rulers. However, although violence and deceit were among their weapons, they had come to power through popular vote and been ennobled by imperial or papal decree. Even in expanding their states, they were careful to keep a cloak of legitimacy over their machinations. Sometimes a faction in a neighboring town was persuaded to invite one of them to take control, although military force often had to be applied against rival factions before the actual occupation could take place. Sometimes they purchased territories. But whatever the means, the transfer of control was authorized by the town council or a popular assembly, although not always a free one. When a newly acquired town came under the control of a duke and his council, it kept its municipal institutions and its municipal autonomy. During periods of ducal weakness, it often reasserted its independence.

MILAN

There is no need to relate the history of each of these new states, since many of them were soon swallowed up by their more powerful neighbors, but Milan, Venice, and Florence were so important that they must be considered. Milan escaped the fourteenth-century depression because of its favorable location in a rich agricultural district on the main north-south, east-west highways. Neither the international merchants nor the day laborers were particularly important, however, and the struggle for power was between the *grandi,* who still held prosperous estates in the countryside, and the guilds. In 1277, the former emerged victorious under the leadership of Archbishop Otto Visconti, and from that time until 1447 the city was almost continuously under the domination of his family. The boundaries of the city-state were constantly extended in spite of the Visconti practice of dividing its territory between the various sons.

One of the ablest of the Viscontis, Giangaleazzo (1385-1402), managed to reunite the family possessions; take Verona, Vicenza, and Padua; and advance into Tuscany where he threatened Florence. In the process, he won recognition for his house. The emperor conferred on him the title of Duke of Milan, and one of his daughters married into the French royal family, an act that was later to give France a claim to the duchy. With such family ties and such wealthy and expanding territories, it looked as though Giangaleazzo might unite northern Italy and thereby alter the course of Italian history. This possibility suddenly came to an end in 1402 when Giangaleazzo died of the plague.

71

Like so many others of his day, Giangaleazzo had looked on his territory more as a family patrimony than as a territorial state and had arranged for his possessions to be divided between his two sons. Quickly the brothers quarreled, and many of the cities within the duchy that had been allowed to keep their own institutions re-established their independence. The process of disintegration was reversed when Filippo Maria (1402-1447) became the unchallenged head of his family after the assassination of his brother. His aggressive policy drove Venice and Florence into an alliance to check his ambitions. Both sides employed professional soldiers, as had long been the custom, but since these troops were notoriously unreliable, Filippo Maria married his natural daughter to his peasant-born mercenary commander, Francesco Sforza (1450-1466). He thereby gave Francesco a claim to be his successor, since he had no legitimate children. This claim, backed by military power, enabled Francesco to establish his dynasty on the ducal throne in 1450. His successors were much less able. Family quarrels weakened the dynasty, and finally, in 1492, Francesco's son, Ludovico il Moro, called on France for aid against a growing number of enemies. The French agreed, and their invasion of Italy in 1494 ushered in the Italian and Habsburg-Valois wars.[1]

VENICE

The history of Venice was quite different from that of Milan and the other towns of the Lombard plains. The city's location on islands just east of the mainland freed it from foreign threats during the medieval period and enabled it to devote its energies to the expansion of trade with the eastern Mediterranean. Moreover, the absence of mainland territories meant that there were no feudal nobles to absorb. As a result, power fell into the hands of a merchant oligarchy that after 1297 was limited to the two-hundred families which made up the grand council. This council served as the basic electoral body for the senate, the cabinet, and the *doge* or duke, who served only for life in spite of earlier efforts to make the office hereditary. In addition, there was a council of ten that met in secrecy to deal with conspiracies and in time of crisis became the principal organ of government. So able and so public-spirited was the ruling oligarchy that the excluded classes rarely protested; assassinations were exceptional, and revolts virtually unknown.

In spite of this relatively tranquil domestic history, the Venetians were constantly beset with problems from abroad. Hardly had they won control of the eastern Mediterranean in 1381 from their Italian rival, Genoa, than the Ottoman Empire arose as a far more serious menace. At the same time, the consolidation of the Italian mainland under the Visconti and others posed another serious threat. It was from the mainland that the Venetians drew their food supply and through the mainland that much of their trade

[1] See pages 117-119.

passed to northern Europe. So long as this territory remained in the hands of a number of small city-states, Venetian security was not threatened, but once it fell under the control of the powerful duchy of Milan, Venice was compelled to take action. For this reason, before the French invasion in 1494, Venice had acquired the adjacent mainland cities as well as other territories around the Adriatic Sea.

FLORENCE

Both the nobles and the mercantile-banking families were powerful in Florence, the latter group having close business ties with the papal states and with the countries north of the Alps. There were also the minor guilds and a large day-labor population that was employed especially by the weaving industry. The result was a four-way struggle for power during the fourteenth century in which each group achieved a dominant position at one time or another. On several occasions, one-man rule was almost established, but each time the city's republican traditions triumphed. By the last decade of the century, control had passed into the hands of a faction of the merchant oligarchy led by the Albizzi family. It was during this period, when Milan threatened to conquer Florence and the other Tuscan towns, that the artistic and literary innovations took place in Florence that are usually considered as marking the dawn of Renaissance culture. It was also during this period, which saw the eventual defeat of Milan and the Florentine conquest of Pisa, that the city definitely established itself as a territorial state. A blundering, unsuccessful war against Lucca, however, led to the fall of the Albizzi in 1434 and the beginning of the Medici era during which Florentine culture reached its height.

The Medici were of rural extraction. Around 1200, they left their mountain farm and settled in Florence, where less than a century later they were found among the merchant oligarchy. In spite of their growing wealth, however, they carefully cultivated a reputation for favoring the members of the lesser guilds and the workers, and in time of crisis they were able to draw support from these groups. The first member of the family to direct Florentine affairs for a long period was Cosimo (1434-1464), a man of exceptional business insight who furthered the banking and trading interests of his family. He provided excellent political and diplomatic leadership for the city, acted as a patron of the arts and letters, and was, at the same time, a sincere Christian who retired periodically to a monastery for contemplation and prayer. Cosimo was succeeded by his son, Piero (1464-1469), who, in spite of a severe gout that made him a semi-invalid was able to retain control of Florence and to pass his position of leadership on to his son, Lorenzo the Magnificent (1469-1492). Although Lorenzo lost part of the family fortune through neglect and did not scruple to make up his losses from the city treasury, he inherited all the political and diplomatic gifts of his grandfather. He was also a poet of considerable talent and carried on the family tradition of patronizing the arts. Under Lorenzo, Renaissance Florence reached its peak, but two years after his death, his son's incompetence and the French invasion brought the Medici domination of the city to a temporary end.

The Medici used indirect methods to control Florence. They kept the republican institutions intact and during the fifteenth century never sought to make themselves dukes after the example of the Visconti in Milan. The violence that characterized so many other Renaissance regimes was largely absent, and their power rested on popularity more than on fear. Cosimo, a somewhat retiring man and a poor public speaker, rarely accepted an important public post but kept control through the influence he wielded over those chosen for office.

The absence of a duke meant that there was no ducal council or other administrative organs to govern the territories outside the city, and the Florentine municipal institutions could not perform this function. When a

74

The Palace of the Priors (now the Palazzo Vecchio or Old Palace), Florence. Begun in 1299, this castlelike structure served as an office building and residence for the municipal officials, who were called priors. Its tower and other military features were intended to protect the officials from the turbulent populace. (Courtesy of Italian State Tourist Office)

town was annexed, Florence appointed a chief executive and a garrison commander but otherwise left its local institutions intact. This method was unsatisfactory because the inhabitants of the conquered towns felt no loyalty to the state and were excluded from participation in Florentine municipal government. Lorenzo, especially, did his best to correct this weakness through personal contact and special favors. At Pisa, he revived the university and tried to improve the port. There and elsewhere he bought estates where he frequently resided in order to become acquainted with the local inhabitants. His ancestors had married into the leading Florentine families, and the alliances thus achieved had been a fundamental factor in the family's control of the city, but Lorenzo married into a princely Roman house. With his increasing prestige, he was able to get ecclesiastical benefices for his son, Giovanni, from the time he was eight and a cardinal's hat for him when he was only fourteen. These benefices were strategically located throughout Tuscany and strengthened the family's control of the region.

Although this remarkable regime collapsed in 1494 when the French invaded Italy, the illegitimate great-grandson of Lorenzo was established as duke of Florence in 1530 after several republican and Medici eras. Seven years later, he was murdered and the ducal throne passed to Cosimo, a member of a younger branch of the family. Cosimo added Siena to his domain and made himself Grand Duke of Tuscany. Thus, Florence eventually lost its republican institutions, just as Milan and other Italian cities had, but these institutions were still functioning during the great age of Florentine culture that will be discussed later.

THE PAPAL STATES

Unlike most of the new city-states to the north, the papacy already had relatively extensive territories and long established institutions when the Renaissance began. As a result, the problem confronting the popes was less to create a new system than to make the old system work. Nevertheless, there was a marked difference between the pontificate of Martin V (1417-1431), the first of the popes to rule after the Great Schism, and that of his predecessors before the Avignon papacy. The earlier popes had been able to direct most of their attention to the spiritual and temporal affairs of Europe. But the concessions that Martin was forced to grant the monarchs in return for their support against the conciliar movement, the revenue he was compelled to abandon at the Council of Constance, and the general weakness of papal power had reduced papal revenues to one-third of their former amount. Since the only remaining way of raising enough money to carry on the legitimate activities of the Church was to extract more from the papal states, Martin and his immediate successors had to be Italian princes first and spiritual leaders of the Catholic world second.

Even this prospect could not have seemed very promising to Martin when he arrived at Rome in 1420. The city was without commerce or industry, its 10,000 inhabitants were extremely poor, and even the churches were in ruins. Outside the city, and especially in the central and eastern provinces, most of the towns had fallen into the hands of individual lords who were trying to create little independent states for themselves after the manner of the Visconti in Milan. Most of them had already received legal recognition from the Avignon popes, with the title of vicar, in return for their vague acknowledgment that they were not completely sovereign. Even these territories were threatened by Naples, Milan, and other states.

Fortunately, Martin was able and efficient, thrifty to the point of stinginess, and accomplished in the rare art of combining moderation with determination. He drew his support from the only resource he had, his family. As a Colonna, he was a member of one of the most powerful clans in Rome and had numerous nephews and more distant relatives whom he could appoint to key posts, as well as female relatives who could be almost equally useful when married to important persons. With their aid, he raised a mercenary army and enforced his will on those who would not recognize his authority; those who willingly acknowledged him were given legal confirmation in positions that they had often seized by treachery and force. Martin's methods were those of any other factional leader who relied on his family and friends, but by his death the papal states had been largely restored and the churches of Rome were beginning to be rebuilt.

However suitable Martin's techniques might have been for a secular prince, they had one serious disadvantage in an elective monarchy. Martin's relatives were unwilling to give his successor, Eugenius IV (1431-1447), the same loyalty that they had given him, so that the new pope's first task was to dispossess the Colonna. This process was repeated again and again throughout the Renaissance, for the desire to reward their families as well as to find trustworthy servants led the popes to repeat the errors of their predecessors, and nepotism became one of the greatest political and moral problems of the age.

Three of the next four popes were humanists and began the patronage of art and letters that soon won for Rome the cultural leadership which had been held by Florence. Not until the election of Francesco della Rovere, who took the name of Sixtus IV (1471-1484), did the throne of Saint Peter begin to sink to the depths popularly associated with the Renaissance papacy. Six of the cardinals whom he appointed were his nephews or cousins, and the remainder were so lacking in moral stature that years passed before they elected a sincerely religious man to the highest office in the Church. Not content with showering as many as eight bishoprics on a nephew who had taken orders, he sought to carve a lordship out of the papal states for one who had not. When he found his designs blocked by Lorenzo de' Medici, he became at least indirectly involved in a plot with members of the Pazzi family to murder the Florentine leader. A professional soldier was employed to assassinate Lorenzo and his brother, but he withdrew when he learned that the crime was to take place in the cathedral at Florence during Mass. Two priests were found who were less squeamish. But they were also less competent, and Lorenzo managed to escape, leaving his younger brother dead upon the cathedral pavement.

The next pope, Innocent VIII (1484-1492), added weakness to the immorality that was coming to be expected of Renaissance popes. He sought to provide for his illegitimate children, whom he readily acknowledged, as well as his nephews. Under him, the sale of religious benefits reached new heights. "The Lord desireth not the death of a sinner," one of his officials declared, "but rather that he may live and pay." His successor was the Borgia pope, Alexander VI (1492-1503), an able but immoral man who sought to create a powerful duchy in the papal states for his son, Cesare, and might have succeeded had he lived a little longer. He was followed by Julius II (1503-1513), an outstanding soldier and diplomat, a capable organizer, an intelligent patron of the arts, and one of the greatest monarchs of his age. With ruthless determination, Julius crushed Cesare and the other rebellious lords and became the principal creator of the papal monarchy. Well might the kindly and indolent son of Lorenzo de' Medici, Leo X (1513-1521), anticipate a peaceful reign after such a pope. But it was during Leo's pontificate that a German monk named Martin Luther led a revolt that created unprecedented problems for the Church.

NAPLES

A strong and prosperous kingdom developed around Naples and Sicily during the twelfth century. In 1268, a member of the French royal family won the crown, but he was driven out of Sicily fourteen years later and the throne was given to the king of Aragon. During the generations that followed, the descendants of the king of Aragon continued to rule in Sicily and those of the French claimant continued to rule in Naples, while the barons on both sides took advantage of this division in the kingdom to usurp royal authority. Finally, Alfonso the Magnanimous (1435-1458), king of Aragon and Sicily, seized Naples and made it the center of his empire. Although Alfonso himself was a patron of the arts, the Neopolitans contributed little to Renaissance culture, and the country had importance only because of its military strength relative to other Italian states. On Alfonso's death, Sicily and Aragon went to his brother, John, and Naples was won by his illegitimate son, Ferrante, who reigned until Charles VIII revived the French claims to the throne and occupied Naples in 1494.

THE ORIGINS OF MODERN DIPLOMACY

The decline of the Empire in northern Italy and the emergence of a number of city-states provided the necessary environment for the development of a more modern diplomatic system. The concentrated population and relatively high per-capita income in this region gave a city-state the

78

financial means to launch an attack on its neighbor. Since a marching army could usually reach the neighboring capital in a few days, it could strike with little warning; and since the neighbor's territory was small, the invader could conquer and hold it all. Thus survival in Italy depended on alertness. It was this need for alertness that gave birth to the modern diplomatic system.

This situation developed in Italy only after the pope and the emperor had both lost their power to keep order. North of the Alps, where the monarchies were large and their resources disorganized, neighboring states at war could wrest only a few provinces from each other. Over a century of warfare did not enable the English to conquer France, even though their king, as duke of Aquitaine, received considerable help from the French themselves. Florence, on the other hand, was able to conquer all of the republic of Pisa, and Milan was able to incorporate nearly all the city-states in Lombardy.

Under the old system, there had been no need for ambassadors to reside permanently in a foreign country. When it was necessary to establish diplomatic contact, an ambassador might be sent, but he returned home when his mission was completed. His mission, at least so he liked to believe, was to make peace, confirm friendships, arrange for dynastic marriages, and the like, but not to spy on the host country and plot its ruin. An ambassador had diplomatic immunity in regard to acts he had committed *before* his embassy began, but while on his mission he was subject to arrest by the host prince for fraud, violence, espionage, and many other crimes. In an age that thought in terms of the supremacy of the law and the idea of Christendom, an ambassador was expected to pay the penalty for his misdeeds and not merely be sent home, as he is today regardless of the nature of his crimes.

Perhaps the little state of Mantua was the first to send a resident diplomatic agent abroad. His destination was the imperial court, where the emperor was his master's ally and hope for protection from stronger, ambitious neighbors. This was in 1341, but Giangaleazzo Visconti (1385-1402) was the first to make widespread use of permanent resident agents. As lord of Milan, he was probably the first Italian prince to have sufficient income for sustained diplomatic action, and his agents were not used for national preservation, as in the case of Mantua, but for national aggrandizement. Their mission was to divide his enemies, to find supporters in the cities marked for conquest, to spy, to deceive, and, if need be, to betray. They were not accorded the rank of ambassadors because their activities might make it necessary to disavow them, but their efforts were largely responsible for the rapid Milanese expansion in which many towns surrendered their independence without a battle.

The capacity of one Italian city-state to conquer another also led to the development of the idea of a balance of power, although not until many of the smaller cities had been conquered by the five major Italian states:

79

Venice, Florence, Milan, the papal states, and Naples. Each of these powers was too jealous and fearful of the others to permit them to expand at the expense of the remaining smaller states. Under such circumstances, the idea of a balance of power came into being. The essential characteristic of this concept was that no state or alliance of states was permitted to become so strong that it could threaten the territorial sovereignty of another state. If it tried to increase its power, it was checked, by force if necessary. In this manner, a precarious peace was usually preserved and existing boundaries were maintained. Thus, when Florence decided that its ally Venice was becoming too strong, it withdrew from the alliance and formed a new one with that country's ancient enemy, Milan, thereby checking Venetian ambitions.

Wars and threats of wars continued as the balance of power began to operate in Italy. This situation, in conjunction with the possibility of French intervention and the growing Turkish threat after the fall of Constantinople in 1453, led the Italian states to rationalize the system further. By the terms of the Treaty of Lodi of 1454 and the League of Venice which followed, the signatories renounced the right to make any agreement prejudicial to each others' interests and agreed, if war threatened, that all the signatories should be consulted immediately. Permanent peace and the status quo were to be guaranteed in this manner through the joint action of the Italian states. To facilitate the working of the new alliance, resident ambassadors were exchanged between the member-states. Embassies were established, resident secretaries were appointed, and couriers were employed to carry frequent dispatches.

Unfortunately, the concert of Italy established in 1454 did not bring peace. During the next four decades, there were six brief wars and many threats of war as one power after another violated the spirit of the concert. The tension remained constant, although diplomatic action quickly terminated each conflict. Under these circumstances, there was a change in the conception of the responsibility and duty of the ambassador. No longer was peace regarded as his essential mission. Rather, in the closing years of the fifteenth century a Venetian diplomat wrote in a manual prepared to guide others in his profession: "The first duty of an ambassador is exactly the same as that of any other servant of a government, that is, to do, say, advise and think whatever may best serve the preservation and aggrandizement of his own state." No longer was the ambassador subject to a higher law; instead, he had become "a man sent to lie abroad for his country's good." Responsibility to the individual sovereign state had replaced the moral order suggested by the idea of Christendom.

MACHIAVELLI

No man has been more closely associated with the political theory that justifies every action taken to preserve and enhance the state than

Machiavelli at the age of about 45 from a portrait in Warwick Castle, England, by Hanneman. (Courtesy of New York Public Library)

Niccolò Machiavelli (1469-1527). A member of the minor Florentine nobility, Machiavelli served the republic between 1498 and 1512 as a diplomat and chancery official during a period when the Medici were living in exile. When this family was restored to power in 1512, he was dismissed from his post, arrested, and tortured for suspicion of treason to the new regime. When he was finally released, Machiavelli retired to his nearby family estate and stayed there for most of his remaining years, living on a meager income. There, bitter at his treatment and thoroughly cynical, he wrote *The Prince,* a study of how power could be won and retained. As his enforced retirement continued, he turned more to history for instruction and amusement. Out of this new interest came *The Discourses,* a study of republics suggested by Livy's history of Rome.

The two books were different in tone, for time had partly healed his bitterness and scholarly research had helped to mature his judgment. But in certain fundamental respects they are alike. In neither can be found the concept of a universal monarchy that had inspired Dante or of a moral law higher than the good of one's country. Instead, Machiavelli pictures quarreling, irresponsible states in which selfish and unprincipled men seek power through violence and fraud. "I believe it to be most true," he wrote in *The Discourses,* "that it seldom happens that men rise from low condition to high rank without employing either force or fraud, unless that rank should be attained either by gift or inheritance. Nor do I believe that force alone will ever be found to suffice, whilst it will often be the case that cunning alone serves the purpose. . . ." And in *The Prince* he declared that "how we live is so far removed from how we ought to live, that he who abandons what is done for what ought to be done, will rather learn to bring about his own ruin than his preservation. A man who wishes to make a profession of goodness in everything must necessarily come to grief among so many who are not good. Therefore it is necessary for a prince, who wishes to maintain himself, to learn how not to be good, and to use this knowledge and not use it, according to the necessity of the case."

Thus, Machiavelli taught that the end—power within the state—justifies the means. Citing the deeds of the Romans and of those political figures who had been successful in his own day, he condoned the separation of political from private morality, arguing that it was right for an ambassador to lie or a prince to deceive for his own or his country's good. Such ideas were condemned in Machiavelli's own day and for several centuries thereafter, but they have led some modern scholars to admire what they describe as his objectivity and realism. Some Italian nationalists have also praised him because in the closing chapter of *The Prince* he added—it now seems as an afterthought—the suggestion that a ruler who followed his program could drive the French and Spanish invaders from the land.

It should not be assumed that Machiavelli condoned private immorality. Except in regard to women, his personal ethics were puritanical. Moreover, he attributed the difficulties in which Florence and Italy found themselves to a loss of morality and civic virtue among the people. He preferred a republican form of government and hoped for the temporary emergence of a prince who would discipline the body politic and provide a new code of laws under which people could live virtuously in republican simplicity. Yet in the idea that man could make laws and that the proper laws and institutions could mold a people's character, he was once more breaking with the medieval tradition.

There is another side to Machiavelli that has been too seldom stressed; he recognized that the strength of a Renaissance state, whether monarchy or republic, rested ultimately upon the people. The prince might be obliged to imitate "the fox and the lion," but it was wise for him "to seem merciful, faithful, humane, sincere, religious, and also to be so." He must avoid making himself hated or despised. For the "prince who possesses a strong city and does not make himself hated, cannot be assaulted." Hence, "the best fortress is to be found in the love of the people, for although you may have fortresses they will not save you if you are hated by the people." Popular approval was especially important because, Machiavelli argued, the citizen-soldier was far superior to the hired mercenary, a conviction that he held so strongly that he wrote *The Art of War* to prove his point.

In addition to advising rulers to seek popularity by practicing the traditional virtues as much as possible and always appearing to have them, Machiavelli cautioned them to remember "that they begin to lose their state from the moment when they begin to disregard the laws and ancient customs under which the people have lived contented for some time." When they acquired new provinces, they were "to make no alteration either in their laws or in their taxes." In more difficult cases, he advised the new ruler to take up residence in the captive province. The ruler should take the life of no one unless the justification and reason for it are obvious, "but above all he must abstain from taking the property of others, for," he added cynically, "men forget more easily the death of their father than the loss of their patrimony."

Modern as Machiavelli seems to be in separating morality from politics, he was far from conceiving of the modern, omnipotent state. Many of his ideas concerning monarchies were derived from his knowledge of France, whose laws and institutions he never tired of praising. To understand Machiavelli's admiration for that country, we must examine the French monarchy and the other monarchies to the north.

THE RENAISSANCE MONARCHIES IN THE NORTH

GENERAL CHARACTERISTICS

No two Renaissance monarchies were exactly alike, but they all had certain characteristics in common. The most pronounced of these was their dynastic structure and motivation. Foreign and domestic policies centered upon the question of marriages, for it was by marriage that additional territories were acquired. Wars of conquest were undertaken to secure a claimed inheritance, not natural boundaries, national unity, or the people's prosperity. The internal expansion of a monarchy also depended on dynastic factors, for when a great noble died without heirs, his fiefs reverted to the crown; it was the chance extinction of several great noble houses in France that made possible the rise of the French monarchy. On the other hand, the state was still sometimes regarded as a private patrimony that kings divided among their sons. Even when the eldest was given sovereignty over all the lands, large fiefs with special privileges were often granted to younger children, which became threats to the monarchy. Thus, it was through marriages and children that states prospered or declined.

A second characteristic of the Renaissance monarchy was its decentralization. When two rulers married, each continued to rule his own state. Even if they were succeeded by a common heir, he governed each of his states through its own institutions. In the same way, when a great noble had no heirs and his fief reverted to the crown, the privileges of the inhabitants were confirmed, their customs, laws, and institutions remained the same, and the most discernible difference was that a royal governor resided in the ducal palace and performed his duties in the king's name.

A third characteristic of the Renaissance monarchy was its inherent weakness. Neither its bureaucracy nor its army was adequate. Around 1505, there were approximately 12,000 royal officials in France: one official for each 1,250 inhabitants or one for each 14.4 square miles. In 1934, by contrast, France had one official for each 70 inhabitants and 56 for each 14.4 square miles, while in 1964 the United States had one official for each twenty inhabitants. The number of royal officials increased during the sixteenth century, but at no time could they have intervened in the actions of the people as effectively as they do in the modern democracies.

Moreover, the king could not always control the few royal officials that he had. Some local officials, especially the provincial governors, were great nobles who ingratiated themselves with the people of their government 'by defending their privileges against the interests of the crown, only to use their popularity to lead their people in revolt when the occasion arose. Lesser officials often purchased their offices and could not ordinarily be removed unless their money was refunded, a concession that few monarchs were prepared to make. In England, there were important officials who were not paid for their services and who for this reason often performed them negligently.

To guide and control this motley array of local officials, the kings relied primarily on their chancelleries, until the second quarter of the sixteenth century when their secretaries became more prominent, but these officials were pitifully few in number. If there were today only 1,800 bureaucrats in Washington, D. C., the President would have a staff of about the same size in proportion to the population of the United States as Henry III of France had in 1587. Furthermore, Henry III's bureaucrats had no telephones, typewriters, or mimeograph machines. Technological as well as bureaucratic limitations prevented a government from issuing specific regulations or supervising their enforcement. Only broad statements of general policy could be decreed, leaving local officials a wide latitude of interpretation and enforcement.

The royal armies were as inadequate as the royal bureaucracy. No ruler outside of Italy could muster the strength to conquer a neighbor of equal size or to suppress a revolt actively supported by a majority of his subjects. Some kings limited their peacetime establishments to their palace guards and a few frontier garrisons, and none of them habitually kept more than 10,000 or 15,000 men under arms. To put 50,000 men in the field in time of war required an exceptional effort by the greatest states. Even with immensely superior twentieth-century training and equipment and with modern facilities of transportation and communication, a force of 50,000 men could hardly have subjected one of the more populous Renaissance states. Furthermore, the subjects themselves were well armed. The great nobles in every country could still put armies in the field. The towns had militia that fought bravely behind their fortified walls and cannon that kept the royal artillery too far away to be effective. Indeed, the art of fortifi-

EUROPE IN 1526

BOUNDARY OF THE
HOLY ROMAN EMPIRE

LANDS RULED BY
THE HABSBURGS

OTTOMAN EMPIRE

SCALE OF MILES

0   100   200   300   400

cation developed more rapidly during the last half of the fifteenth century than the art of making cannon, with the result that sieges became more difficult than before. Though a king could usually defeat any noble and capture any single town in his kingdom, it was cheaper and easier to avoid offending his subjects, and attacking a large number of nobles or towns was clearly impossible.

Besides the smallness of the royal army and the presence of armed nobles and towns, there was a third check to limit the king's capacity to make war on his subjects: he could not count on the obedience and loyalty of his own troops. The cavalry was composed almost entirely of the local nobility and captained by members of the leading families of the provinces. The infantry militia was composed of the lower classes from the towns and villages. Such an army was only a slight improvement on the feudal levies of the Middle Ages and often followed its noble commanders in revolt. The mercenaries, so numerous in time of war, were no more trustworthy. They obeyed the orders of the officers who paid them, not those of the king, and until the latter half of the seventeenth century it was a commonplace occurrence for them to change sides or to go home on the eve of a battle. Armies were only beginning to wear uniforms, live in garrisons, submit to the discipline of dismounted drill, and, above all, to be paid directly by the king rather than by an officer who had contracted to raise the troops.

A fourth characteristic of the Renaissance monarchy was that it depended on popular support. Since kings had neither the army nor the administrative organs to compel obedience, they were obeyed only when they could get the bulk of the more important elements of the population to support their cause. In this, they were generally successful. With few exceptions, they were able men who knew how to use their position. For a number of reasons, their subjects were disposed to follow them. They were the restorers of order after a long period of warfare when undisciplined bands of soldiers roamed the countryside pillaging and murdering at will. There was no safe, logical alternative to the king's rule, however much town and noble might be opposed to further increases in royal power. Most of the monarchs of the day accurately sensed the feelings of the people and were ready to recognize, support, and protect their privileges, even against their own officials. They kept in intimate contact with the people by traveling from one part of their kingdom to another, receiving everyone without the barriers of rigid formality. Indeed, there was a degree of intimacy between the kings and their people that surprised the ambassadors of republican Venice. In 1561, one of them attributed the devotion of the French people to the crown to the "familiarity which exists between the monarch and his subjects, all of whom he treats as his companions. No one is excluded from his presence. Lackeys and people of lowest condition dare to enter the king's private office in order to see everything that happens and to hear all that is said. If one wishes to

The Estates-General at Orléans in 1560-61. The King, Queen Mother, princes, cardinals, and high royal officials are seated on the platform while the deputies of the three Estates are crowded together in two groups separated by a table with four secretaries. A clergyman is standing before the table speaking for his Estate. (From a contemporary engraving by J. Tortorel)

speak of something important, he must have the patience to find a place where there are not a great many people and then talk in a low voice in order not to be heard. This great familiarity, it is true, makes subjects insolent, but at the same time it makes them faithful and devoted to their kings." Even the birth of a prince was a public affair, and when a midwife complained that the crowd of people gathered to witness the birth of the future Louis XIII of France got in her way, the king said, "Be quiet, woman, this child belongs to everybody. Everybody must rejoice in him."

If popular support was to be won by familiarity with one's subjects, it was also to be won by display. When the occasion demanded—a royal marriage, a tournament, the opening of the Estates-General, or the triumphant entry into a city—kings and courts regaled themselves in all their ceremonial robes and provided the people with a form of theatrical entertainment that also served to impress them with royal magnificence and power. The printing press was used to disseminate accounts of such occasions nearly two centuries before it was extensively used for the routine affairs of government.

A more tangible way of winning support was also available to the Renaissance monarch. He controlled a vast system of patronage. Most of the highest offices of the church lay at his disposal, and the wealthiest bishoprics and abbeys went to his faithful supporters. Government positions, one of the most lucrative of all forms of employment during the period, found their way into the same hands. Fiefs, patents of nobility, pensions, and nearly every type of privilege lay at the disposal of the monarch. He who served the crown loyally could hope for untold riches. He who did not could hope for few rewards.

A final way of winning popular support was through the use of representative institutions. These institutions had been created by the medieval kings to strengthen their authority, but with the decline of royal power during the fourteenth century there had been a tendency in many countries for local and provincial assemblies to spring up in their place. With the revival of royal authority during the Renaissance, the kings again made use of national representative institutions to explain their policies to their subjects and to extend their influence into fields of activity ordinarily denied to them. Thus, Henry VIII declared to the English House of Commons in 1543 that "We at no time stand so highly in our estate royal as in time of Parliament, wherein we as head and you as members are conjoined and knit together in one body politic." A generation later, Henry III declared to the Estates-General of France "that holding the estates is a remedy . . . to reaffirm the legitimate authority of the sovereign rather than to disturb or diminish it."

BURGUNDY

For several generations, the wealthiest and most brilliant court north of the Alps, perhaps in all of Europe, was the court of the Burgundian dukes. Although these dukes were vassals of the king of France, they tried to build a new state. In this they resembled the Visconti of Milan, but they used different methods. With the death of the last Capetian duke in 1361, the duchy of Burgundy had reverted to the crown. Several years later, King John bestowed it on his son, Philip the Bold, as a reward for his gallantry in the battle of Poitiers, which had been fought in 1356 before Philip had reached his fifteenth birthday.

The duchy was a generous gift, but it did not have the wealth to provide for the greatness that Burgundy was later to achieve nor was it sufficiently independent of France. It was stipulated that royal decrees would be executed there and that appeals from the ducal court to those at Paris would be permitted. Instead, dynastic marriages formed the basis of Burgundian wealth and power. In 1369, Philip married Margaret of Flanders, heiress to Franche-Comté, which adjoined the duchy but was situated in the Empire, and to the counties of Rethel, Nevers, Artois, and Flanders in France. The last was especially important because of its location in what became known as the Netherlands, where the towns rivaled in wealth those of northern Italy.

Philip immediately began to extend his influence into the prospective inheritance by helping his father-in-law curb the independent spirit

TERRITORIES OF THE DUKES OF BURGUNDY,
DUCHIES AND COUNTIES OF FRANCE

ROYAL DOMAIN IN 1461		APPANAGES OF VALOIS PRINCES	
BURGUNDIAN TERRITORIES ADDED TO THE ROYAL DOMAIN BY LOUIS XI		OTHER FIEFS HELD OF THE FRENCH CROWN	
OTHER TERRITORIES ADDED TO THE ROYAL DOMAIN BY LOUIS XI		BOUNDARY BETWEEN FRANCE AND THE EMPIRE	
ADDITIONS TO ROYAL DOMAIN BY CHARLES VIII AND FRANCIS I		B.	BISHOPRIC
POSSESSIONS OF THE HOUSE OF BURGUNDY INDEPENDENT AFTER DEATH OF CHARLES THE BOLD		C.	COUNTY
BURGUNDIAN TERRITORIES TO THE HOUSE OF HABSBURG AFTER THE DEATH OF CHARLES THE BOLD		D.	DUCHY
TERRITORIES RETAINED BY BURGUNDY-NEVERS AFTER THE DEATH OF CHARLES THE BOLD		V.	VISCOUNTY

of the towns in Flanders and by taking the nobles there into his own service. At the same time, he played a key role in the French government and called on Paris for aid when his father-in-law died in 1382, to safeguard his inheritance. Once well entrenched in Flanders, Philip sought to expand his family's lands. He purchased a county for his eldest son, marriage brought another son the duchy of Brabant, and his daughters were married to neighboring princes in the Empire to ensure friendly neighbors to the east. Having no more children, Philip tried to strengthen his position to the west by seeking marriage alliances between his grandchildren and leading French nobles.

Philip was a loyal, if self-interested, French prince. His son, John the Fearless (1404-1419), was less squeamish. He continued his father's expansive policy in the Netherlands, but his principal ambition was to control France by taking advantage of Charles VI's madness. This he tried to do first by seeking popular support in France by posing as a reformer, then by having the Duke of Orléans, his principal rival, murdered, and finally, when that too failed to bring the desired results, by allying himself with the English. He met a fitting end on the bridge of Montereau when he was murdered by the Orléanists in circumstances which implicated the future Charles VII.

This murder broke the tie between Burgundy and France. The new duke, Philip the Good (1419-1467), swore to avenge his father's death and allied himself with England. In 1435, Charles finally persuaded him to break this foreign alliance so that the Hundred Years War could be brought to a successful conclusion, but the two men were too distrustful of each other to renew the close relationship that had existed between their grandparents. Philip ceased to think of himself as a French prince and devoted his energy to transforming the duchies and counties that he had inherited from his father and other relatives into a territorial state. This was a difficult task because he held each of his territories as vassal either of the king of France or of the emperor and ruled each only as its local count or duke. The inhabitants recognized no common tie, they spoke two languages and many dialects, had diverse economic interests, and were separated from one another by intervening states.

The first step taken by the Burgundian dukes in the creation of a new state was to win popular support. They recognized the privileges and institutions of each new territory that they acquired and used the provincial estates to obtain consent to taxation. A few towns caused difficulties because of internal dissensions, but the dukes tried to reconcile differences and to promote economic development. Their strongest support came from the nobility, for whom they found employment in their army, at court, and as governors and other officials in the provinces. To bolster loyalty to the dynasty, Philip the Good created the Golden Fleece, the most colorful of all the orders of knighthood. Gradually, the great nobles began to feel more loyalty to the dynasty than to their provinces. The towns were more reserved, but they did come to prefer this dynasty to any other.

Their second step was to create central institutions to govern their various lands. Philip the Bold had been content to establish one council for his Burgundian territories and another for those in the Netherlands. This division of the two widely separated groups of ducal territories was continued, but Philip the Good took special pains to create additional central institutions in the Netherlands. A council was formed to look after political affairs, a *parlement* was established as the highest court of justice, a ducal army was organized, and ducal coins were made to provide a common currency. In addition, an Estates-General was created to which the estates of their various duchies and counties sent deputies. This institution gave the dukes an opportunity to appear before their subjects, explain their policies, and ask for common action. Even though the estates of the individual duchies and counties jealously preserved control over taxation, the deliberations of the Estates-General taught the deputies to think to some extent in terms of a common nationality.

Logically, the third step would have been for the Burgundian dukes to break their feudal ties with the king of France and the emperor, but this Philip the Good did not attempt to do, although he was anything but an obedient vassal. When he died in 1467, he owned the duchy and county of Burgundy, adjacent territories in France, most of what are now the Benelux countries, and the northern tip of France. From five to seven million people inhabited these territories, over twice the number then living in England. In addition, his illegitimate children ruled several ecclesiastical states that were enclaves in his territories. To his only legitimate son, Charles the Bold (1467-1477), went a truly royal inheritance.

To enlarge and transform this inheritance into a kingdom became Charles's obsession. There was a remote historical precedent for such a state. When the grandsons of Charlemagne had divided his empire into three parts, one part had become France, a second part had become Germany, and the third had become the land lying between these two countries. It included the Netherlands, Burgundy, Alsace and Lorraine, Provence, Switzerland, and northern Italy. This kingdom had been swallowed up by its neighbors, but Charles now sought to recreate it. Louis XI of France and the emperor tried to thwart his efforts, but he moved boldly forward to annex Alsace and Lorraine through purchase and through conquest. At one point, the emperor almost recognized him as king, but in the end Charles fell in battle against the Swiss and the dispossessed Duke of Lorraine, leaving only a daughter, who, because of her sex, could not hope to fulfill his dream. Through her, however, he was to have a great-grandson, Emperor Charles V, who ruled more territory than any other European since the days of Rome. Belgium and the Netherlands are today living witnesses of the deeds of the Burgundian dukes.

THE FORMATION OF THE RENAISSANCE MONARCHY IN FRANCE

The Renaissance monarchy in France began to take form during the last years of the Hundred Years War when Charles VII (1422-1461) was king. The character of this prince is an enigma. As a youth, he was weak, indolent, and extravagant, lacking self-confidence and determination. As his armies began to win victories over the English, however, a modest degree of confidence, energy, and wisdom came to him, and it is difficult to decide whether he or his ministers were responsible for the actions of the government.

Charles's original intention was to give the central institutions of his state jurisdiction over the lands reconquered from the English as well as those territories that had profited from the war to become semi-independent; and with the recapture of Paris in 1436, the various royal courts and institutions were reunited and returned to their former location. But as the English were slowly driven back, the difficulties of governing the already large and ever-expanding French kingdom increased and the demands for local autonomy continued. The result was a change in policy out of which the Renaissance monarchy in France was born.

Around 1440, Charles and his advisers abandoned the medieval doctrine that the sovereign courts and essential services of the administration were indivisible organisms which exercised their authority over the whole kingdom. Instead, in their hour of strength, they began to create sovereign provincial institutions, a step that had previously been taken only in periods of royal weakness and abandoned as soon as possible thereafter. *Parlements* (sovereign law courts) were established once more at Toulouse in 1443 for Languedoc and at Bordeaux for the southwestern provinces when that city was recaptured from the English in 1451. Sovereign financial courts were established in the more distant provinces. The Estates-General ceased to be convoked after 1440 except in emergencies, and Charles adopted the practice of going directly to the provincial estates that had long functioned in many parts of the kingdom.

This last decision should not be interpreted as indicating a fear of large representative assemblies but rather that the Estates-General was no longer useful to the crown. For nearly two decades it had been regularly convoked and the deputies, who had always been loyal to the king, had voted most of the funds requested. But the people were so provincially minded that even after the Estates-General had consented to a tax they had insisted that each of the provincial estates give its approval before the money was collected. Where there were no provincial estates, the towns often claimed the same privilege. Rarely did one of the provincial estates or towns agree to give its full share of the amount voted by the Estates-General. Thus, the Estates-General had in effect served only as a forum where the crown could explain its need for financial assistance and rally popular support. Once victory over the English seemed assured, popular support was no longer so essential, and Charles VII began to go directly to the provincial estates and the towns for taxes.

Charles would undoubtedly have preferred to win approval for taxation in one large assembly, as did his English rival, who was thus able to avoid separate negotiations with many small assemblies. Indeed, it was far more difficult for Charles to control the deliberations of the provincial estates and the towns than to control those of the Estates-General. When the representatives of the kingdom met, they were in his power. Persuaded by the royal councillors, impressed by the royal majesty, surrounded by the palace guard, and far from their homes, they rarely mustered sufficient courage to resist the king's desires.

In the provincial estates and municipal assemblies, the reverse was true. The king was not present, and in his place stood one or more royal commissioners who inspired little awe among the local leaders. There was no council to guide the deliberations, and the initiative was seized by the members of the assembly, who treated and bargained with their monarch instead of following his lead. Secure in a fortified town or castle, surrounded by their friends, and far from the royal army, they did not hesitate to change the form of a tax, reduce the amount of the levy, or even refuse to vote anything at all. If they granted money, they were likely to request concessions in the same breath. Thus, it was the provincial estates and the privileged towns that were the true checks on royal taxation. Once the English were defeated, Charles's power and prestige were so great that he could persuade the stronger provincial estates, like those of Languedoc, to be more cooperative. In northern and parts of central France, where the provincial estates were weaker, he ceased to convoke them regularly to gain consent to taxation. Taxing these provinces without their formal consent caused little disturbance because the end of the war enabled Charles to reduce taxes by over one-third.

Charles did not, however, abandon the popular nature of the monarchy. When the occasion demanded, he continued to summon large groups of advisers to national assemblies and to convoke the provincial estates in those places where they had ceased to meet regularly. When provinces were recaptured from the English, their privileges were confirmed and their institutions were permitted to continue, although the inhabitants of the Bordeaux region temporarily lost these concessions when they revolted shortly after their conquest and asked the English to return.

Members of the clergy continued to hold special assemblies. One such meeting issued the Pragmatic Sanction of Bourges, in which many sources of papal revenue from France were abolished and the right of the chapters and monasteries to elect their bishops and abbots free from papal interference was confirmed. This act, which was part of the antipapal reaction during the conciliar period, laid the foundation of the Gallican Church, an institution which made the French Church almost independent of that of Rome except in matters of doctrine. Later kings revised the Pragmatic

Sanction with papal approval so that they could have more voice in ecclesiastical appointments, although Charles had reserved some rights for the crown in this regard.

An example of how the provincial and local estates were consulted when the occasion demanded, even in places where they were not regularly convoked to give consent to taxation, may be found in the measures taken to codify customary law. France at this time had no single written law code; instead, each of the provinces, bailiwicks, and other localities had its own oral customs and traditions. Rather than trying to unify them, Charles ordered assemblies to meet in each jurisdiction to establish definitely its customary law and to put it in writing. Once this had been done, it was virtually impossible to develop a common law code for the entire country by any means other than revolution.

Thus, Charles established or confirmed both the popular, consultative function of the French monarchy and its administrative decentralization. He also took steps to organize a permanent army, supported by a permanent system of taxation. In ordinances issued in 1445 and 1446, he created a cavalry force of 12,000 men including noncombatants, and several years later he organized a somewhat smaller infantry militia that was eventually abandoned. This military force proved useful in driving out the English in the closing years of the war and in destroying the marauding bands that had been pillaging France since the struggle had begun. However, since it was commanded by nobles who awarded subordinate positions to their supporters and since the troops kept in close contact with friends and relatives during the annual six-months leave period granted during peacetime, this army was not strictly reliable from the king's point of view.

A number of great feudal vassals remained, and among the most troublesome of these in the last years of Charles's reign was his own son, Louis. Louis had joined a coalition of rebellious nobles in 1440. Seven years later, when he was sent to Dauphiné, he set himself up as an independent ruler and undermined French foreign policy at every opportunity. He became deeply interested in Italian affairs and married Charlotte of Savoy over his father's protests. Finally, Charles forcibly dispossessed his errant son, only to have him flee for protection to Burgundy where he continued his intrigues and even invited the English to invade France once more. Such was the man who came to the throne in 1461 when Charles VII died thoroughly convinced that his son was trying to poison him.

LOUIS XI AND HIS SUCCESSORS

Louis XI (1461-1483) was a lean-faced, long-nosed man with a poor physique and a skin disease which became so severe that he imagined himself to be a leper. His nervous energy kept him constantly on the move

Louis XI. Portrait in Château de Saint-Roch, France. (Giraudon)

and ever eager to chat with his subjects. His religion was of a superstitious and practical sort, and he relied on holy hermits, sacred relics, and the saintly inhabitants of Paradise, on whose churches he lavished gifts, to cure his illnesses and to protect him from his enemies. He trusted no one and was unworthy of trust himself. Rather than earn loyalty, he tried to buy it with extravagant gifts that were a financial drain on the monarchy, and few kings were so frequently betrayed. He cared nothing for tradition, honor, chivalry, or display, all so dear to his age. Mercy and gratitude were virtues unknown to him. Yet, with all his faults and eccentricities, this strange man had an abundance of energy and a highly original mind, stimulated by years of indirect contact with Renaissance Italy.

Soon after he came to the throne, Louis quarreled with Charles the Bold of Burgundy. Thereafter, most of his efforts were directed towards destroying this powerful vassal who, as we have seen, was attempting to construct an independent state. Louis sought support against Charles by lavishing gifts of money, titles, and land on his retainers at home, whether noble or non-noble, and by buying allies abroad. When Edward IV invaded France on Charles's behalf, Louis offered him 75,000 crowns down and 50,000 crowns annually to return to England and remain there, a proposition that the practical English king was happy to accept. The emperor did not disdain to receive a pension, and some Rhineland princes followed his example. The Swiss, whose soldiers Louis admired, were treated generously, and in the end the inhabitants of the upper Rhine River Valley, influenced by Louis' gifts and motivated by fear of Charles's expansive policies, united under the Duke of Lorraine to defeat and kill Charles in 1477. Louis was wild with joy, but his elation did not prevent him from refusing to consider Lorraine's claim to inherit Provence several years later.

Since Charles had only an unmarried daughter, Mary, Louis could claim that all the Burgundian lands held from the crown of France reverted to him. In addition, he sought Hainaut and Franche-Comté, although they were fiefs of the Empire. Through his impatience and blundering, however, he drove Mary into marriage with the Habsburg emperor's son, Maximilian of Austria, who won the lion's share of the Burgundian state. Louis got little more than the duchy of Burgundy, although Franche-Comté and Artois were temporarily brought within the French sphere of influence.

Other fiefs reverted to the crown with less effort on Louis' part. Anjou, Bar, Guyenne, Maine, and Provence escheated when their feudal lords died without male heirs. To acquire more land by this process, Louis compelled the Duke of Orléans to marry his deformed daughter knowing, he cynically wrote a subordinate, that "their children will not cost them much to keep." Louis correctly predicted a childless couple, but when his own son failed to provide an heir, the Duke of Orléans ascended the throne as Louis XII.

Nevertheless, by the end of Louis XI's eventful reign, only the Bourbons in central France, the Foix in the south, and the dukes of Brittany remained of the once numerous great feudal dynasties. The extinction of the other dynasties did not lead to a centralized government, however, for Louis always confirmed the privileges of the inhabitants of the escheated fiefs and preserved their institutions. In the cases of Burgundy and Provence, the feudal law courts were eventually transformed into sovereign *parlements*.

Louis kept the regalian powers of the dukes in his own hands, but these powers were exercised through noble governors whom he appointed. Also, he seems to have granted the ducal lands to his supporters, since the income from the royal domain remained very small throughout his reign. Louis was equally famous for his social and economic policies, and it is certain that he had some highly original ideas. He talked of taxing the nobility and permitting them to engage in trade without loss of privilege, as they could in Italy, of a common law code, and of a single system of weights and measures for the kingdom, but he did little to implement these ideas. He is often credited with favoring the towns and with making the kingdom more prosperous. It is certain that he frequently convened the deputies of the towns to hear their opinions, for no king enjoyed consulting his subjects more than Louis XI, but his economic policy was directed as much toward weakening Burgundy as towards making France more prosperous. The privilege that he granted Lyons of holding fairs may have caused that town to prosper, but his interference in other areas may have been less helpful. A slow economic recovery had begun soon after the Hundred Years War, and the slight improvement in Louis' reign may not have been the result of his own activities. Nevertheless, he was one of the few kings of his age to use economics as a weapon of policy. He constantly interfered in the towns. Although he favored the bourgeois patricians at the expense of the lower classes, the urban population as a whole seemed as happy at his death as the nobility.

One reason for Louis' unpopularity was the heavy taxes he levied to support an enlarged army and to finance the gifts lavished on those at home and abroad whose support he wanted. The *taille*, a tax that fell principally on the peasants, was increased from 1,055,000 *livres* in 1461 to 4,600,000 *livres* twenty years later. Even this was not sufficient, and Louis forced churches, towns, and individuals to loan him money. "Go tomorrow to Paris, and find money in the magic box," he told an official, "and let there be no lack." This meant that once more the burghers of the capital were to contribute to royal policy.

A reaction inevitably set in after Louis XI's death. His thirteen-year-old son, Charles VIII (1483-1498), was too young to rule, but his daughter, Anne of Beaujeu, was a woman of remarkable ability. Her wily father had dubbed her "the least foolish woman in the world," and in fact she was a far better statesman than he. At first, Anne and her husband moved with the popular tide. In conjunction with other nobles, they convoked the Estates-General at Tours in 1484 where administrative reforms were promised, the army was reduced, and other economies were put into effect so that the *taille* could be cut to about one-third the amount Louis had levied during the closing years of his reign. In the meantime, the Beaujeus gradually won the support of part of the great nobles so that they could defeat the remainder and restore royal authority. Instead of returning to Louis XI's devious methods, they governed in accordance with the traditions of Charles VII.

The most important event of the Beaujeu regime was the death of the Duke of Brittany. The hand of his young daughter and heir, Anne, was immediately sought by many, because the duchy was the most independent that remained in France and its strategic location next to England gave its possessor added influence in European affairs. Maximilian of Austria at first seemed successful, but the Beaujeus seized Anne and married her to Charles VIII. When Charles died without issue, his successor, Louis XII, persuaded the pope to annul his marriage so that he could marry Anne, and the daughter of this union was married to Francis I, Louis' cousin and successor. In this manner, Brittany was finally joined to the crown of France, although, in keeping with the principles of the Renaissance monarchy, it was permitted to keep its own institutions.

Charles VIII was weak of mind and body. When he assumed control of the government on reaching manhood, he surrendered Franche-Comté and Artois to the Habsburgs and territories in the Pyrénées to Spain in return for their promise of neutrality when he embarked in 1494 on an expedition to make good an old claim to the throne of Naples. In this manner, a series of Italian wars began that lasted until 1559.

Later kings might be driven to take unusual measures to raise money; but they had neither the persistence nor the desire to alter the nature of the monarchy, and it continued to develop along the lines established by Charles VII. Louis XII was especially willing to create provincial sovereign courts and to respect the privileges of his subjects. He made every effort to keep taxes low in spite of his involvement in the Italian wars and was given the proud title of "the father of his people."

Francis I (1515-1547) was a large, handsome man whose four expensive hobbies—war, château-building, hunting, and women—made him popular with the nobility but increased the burden of taxation borne by his subjects. His son, Henry II (1547-1559), was more reserved but was strong enough to keep control of affairs in spite of his limited intellect. During these reigns, most of the extensive Bourbon lands in central France returned to the crown, and the house of Foix-Albret, which had extensive lands on both sides of the Pyrénées, was weakened by the Spanish conquest of the southern part of its kingdom of Navarre. The great feudal dependencies had ceased to exist, but, as will be shown later, a new aristocracy was emerging to check the authority of the crown.

Neither Francis nor Henry had the intellectual qualities, the administrative interests, or the perseverence to change the nature of the monarchy. Financial necessity led to the beginning of a system of public credit in which the crown borrowed money through the big cities, whose record of repayment was much better than the kings'. The government itself continued to be directed through the councils, although large consultative assemblies became less frequent and four secretaries of state began to emerge to handle the more administrative or bureaucratic aspects of government. A theory of royal absolutism appeared, but it seems to have provided reading material only for the lawyers, the bulk of the people remaining loyal to the more popular traditions of the Renaissance monarchy.

EDWARD IV OF ENGLAND

The origins of the Renaissance monarchy in England cannot be dated as exactly as they can in France. At one time, it was assumed that the innovations associated with the Renaissance monarchy began with the Tudor dynasty in 1485, but more recently some historians have tried to push the date back to the reign of Edward IV (1461-1483) and others to move it forward to the 1530's.

In 1455, the Duke of York took advantage of the insanity of Henry VI of the house of Lancaster to revive his family's very strong claim to the throne, a claim that rested on his direct descent from Edward III. A factional struggle known as the Wars of the Roses followed in which the duke

THE ENGLISH SUCCESSION

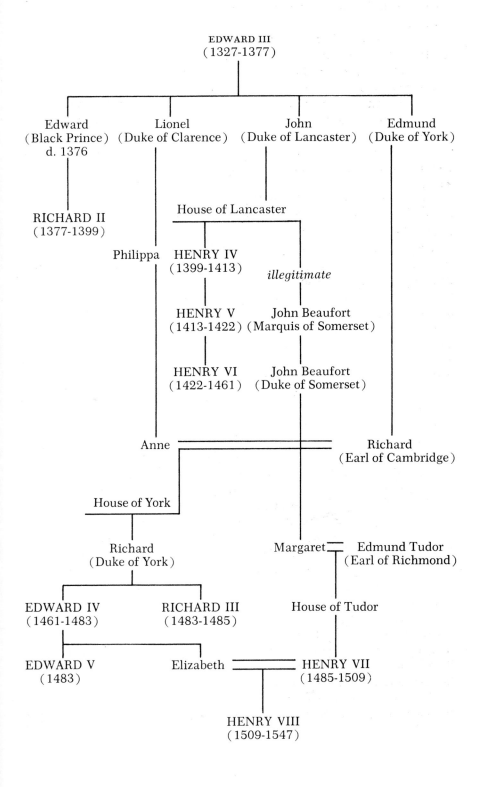

EDWARD III
(1327-1377)

Edward
(Black Prince)
d. 1376

Lionel
(Duke of Clarence)

John
(Duke of Lancaster)

Edmund
(Duke of York)

RICHARD II
(1377-1399)

House of Lancaster

Philippa

HENRY IV
(1399-1413)

illegitimate

HENRY V
(1413-1422)

John Beaufort
(Marquis of Somerset)

HENRY VI
(1422-1461)

John Beaufort
(Duke of Somerset)

Anne

Richard
(Earl of Cambridge)

House of York

Richard
(Duke of York)

Margaret

Edmund Tudor
(Earl of Richmond)

EDWARD IV
(1461-1483)

RICHARD III
(1483-1485)

House of Tudor

EDWARD V
(1483)

Elizabeth

HENRY VII
(1485-1509)

HENRY VIII
(1509-1547)

was killed but his son, Edward IV (1461-1483), managed to win the throne in 1461.

Edward was a tall, handsome man with genuine gifts as a soldier and administrator. He was also somewhat indolent and very dissolute but strong-willed and determined to be king in fact as well as in name. In this desire, he soon clashed with Richard Neville, Earl of Warwick, who was to become known as "the kingmaker." The Nevilles had long been a powerful clan in northern England, and judicious marriage alliances had recently increased their lands elsewhere. From these extensive estates, they had drawn the wealth and retainers to put Edward on the throne, and now Warwick as the head of his house expected to direct the government.

For a time all went well, for Edward appeared content to amuse himself and Warwick was both popular and able. But trouble began in 1464 when Edward announced that he had secretly married Elizabeth Wydeville at a time when Warwick was arranging for him to marry a French princess in order to ensure friendship with the traditional enemy. Edward then antagonized Warwick further by proceeding to shower lands and titles on Elizabeth's relatives rather than the Neville faction. Since Elizabeth had five brothers, seven sisters, and two sons by a previous marriage, in addition to a grasping father, a new group of magnates began to appear. Finally, in 1470, Warwick rebelled, drove Edward from England, and put Henry VI back on the throne. The following year Edward returned with Burgundian help and regained the crown after defeating and killing Warwick in battle. Henry VI and his son were murdered, leaving Edward so securely on the throne that the year 1471 has sometimes been taken as the beginning of the Renaissance monarchy in England.

There were three respects in which the situation after 1471 was essentially different. In the first place, most people were tired of wars, which threatened life and property, and were willing to support any strong king. In the second place, many of the great nobles had been killed or executed during the Wars of the Roses so that Warwick has been called "the last of the barons"—that is, the last of the great lords who could make or break kings. In the third place, it was now Edward who had the great estates. When he had become king, he had confiscated the lands of Henry VI's supporters; when he defeated Warwick, he took the lands belonging to the Nevilles and their adherents. These estates, with those of the crown and the York family, gave Edward almost enough money to support the government, even though he turned Warwick's own estates over to his two brothers who had married the earl's daughters. Thus, after 1471 the English monarchy was more powerful than in preceding periods and English public opinion was more willing to tolerate infringements on traditional liberties in return for peace and order.

Because he possessed greater power, Edward could use the old institutions more effectively than his predecessors had. Those institutions that were particularly serviceable became more prominent, while others decayed through disuse. The council became the most important instrument of government because the king could now choose its members more freely and most of those he selected were able men who owed their importance to him alone and not to their personal wealth and titles. Indeed, the council became so busy that, although its theoretical unity was maintained, it was informally divided into the Privy Council, which accompanied the king wherever he went and dealt largely with political matters, and the Star Chamber, which remained at the palace of Westminster just outside of London and dealt largely with judicial matters. The judicial role of the council was particularly important. The regular courts were often reluctant to render a decision against a great lord or one of his retainers, but the council, backed by a strong king, could render justice to the powerless suitor.

The king's household also grew in importance and performed a large part of the routine administrative chores. The king's secretary, once a minor clerk, became a trusted and important official, but in this period the chancellor remained the most important person in the administration and his Chancery Court handled new types of civil cases that the common law did not cover. Local justice and administration were in the hands of the justices of the peace, who were unpaid officials drawn from the gentry.

The government had been so centralized during the Middle Ages that the people had begun to think of themselves as Englishmen rather than as inhabitants of this or that province. As a result, the decentralizing tendencies found in France were absent, even during the troublous period before the reign of Edward IV, but to ensure order in the more distant part of his realm Edward now decentralized the work of his council. A Council of Wales and the Marches was created in 1471 to administer the royal estates and look after judicial and military matters in that region, and the troublesome Scottish border area was turned over to his brother, Richard. When Richard became king, his work was assumed by the Council in the North, but these two councils marked the limit of decentralization in England. The other confiscated fiefs were governed through the regular royal bureaucracy, a procedure that was markedly different from the French practice. The one innovation was the creation of an efficient system of administering the royal estates that brought the crown a large revenue. When Louis XI began to pay Edward 50,000 crowns annually for not invading France, Edward was able to govern without the aid of Parliamentary taxation, and there were growing signs that Parliament might die through lack of use.

Unfortunately, the promising start of the Yorkist dynasty was halted by Edward's death in 1483 at the age of forty. Immediately, there was a struggle between his brother, Richard, and his wife's relatives, the Wydevilles, for control of the government of the twelve-year-old Edward V. Richard won, and for a time remained faithful to his charge; but when he learned, or professed to learn, that the Wydeville marriage was illegal, he declared that his nephews were illegitimate, locked them up in the Tower of London where they were eventually murdered, and seized the crown for himself as his brother's legal heir. By these acts, he lost popular support, and Henry Tudor of the house of Lancaster defeated and killed him in the battle of Bosworth Field in 1485.

HENRY VII

Henry VII (1485-1509) had very little royal blood in his veins,[2] and there were others far closer to the throne than he; but the laws of heredity were not yet firmly established, and Henry had the only army in the field. He made himself king by right of conquest, declaring that God had given him victory in battle and had thereby sanctioned his claim to the throne. To Parliament he owed nothing, because he was king before he summoned that body. He married Edward IV's daughter, not to strengthen his claim to the throne but to win support from the Yorkist faction. Nevertheless, many Yorkists remained dissatisfied, and the first fourteen years of Henry's reign were spent in suppressing their rebellions. Not until 1500 did the new dynasty seem reasonably secure, and even thereafter the Tudor sovereigns availed themselves of every excuse to do away with those of royal blood.

Henry was a hard working, able, colorless man who won the respect, but not the love, of his subjects. He made few administrative innovations but preferred to continue the policies of his Yorkist predecessors. The council sitting in the Star Chamber became increasingly important in ensuring law and order. Parliament was less fortunate since Henry had little need to convoke that body after the first twelve years of his reign. Of this fact he was very proud because Parliamentary sessions were expensive. He exacted every penny from every source that was due him but was careful not to levy taxes without Parliamentary consent. So long as this concession was made, the English people were content. When he died in 1509, Henry left his son a full treasury and a throne made secure by popular support rather than military force, for there was no army worthy of the name.

HENRY VIII

Few reigns ever began more auspiciously than that of Henry VIII. He was a handsome, athletic young man with above average intelligence and a better education than most princes. He spoke Latin, French, and Spanish and knew some Italian. He loved music and was intrigued by the new learning that had begun to emerge from Italy. But great as were the accomplishments of this teen-age ruler, a keen observer could early have noted the selfish, cruel, tyrannical side of his character. One of his first acts was to

[2] See genealogical table, page 99.

Henry VIII, a portrait by Hans Holbein the Younger, who had been appointed Court Painter by the King. (National Portrait Gallery, London)

execute two of his father's unpopular financial officials on trumped-up charges of treason in order to increase his own popularity. He fought a needless though popular war with France and returned home content to bask in glory and pursue his many pleasures.

Unhappily, someone had to formulate policy and attend to the details of government. For this task Henry chose Thomas Wolsey. The son of a butcher and cattle dealer, Wolsey had graduated from Oxford with distinction and had entered the clergy because it was the profession most open for advancement to a man of low birth. By 1515, he was both Archbishop of York and Chancellor of England. To these posts he added every lucrative or powerful administrative position and ecclesiastical benefice that he could lay his hands on. Soon he was the wealthiest, most powerful, and most hated man in the kingdom. But Henry upheld him, knowing that he could dispose of his overbearing minister when he ceased to be useful.

Wolsey was a man of considerable ability, but the goals he set for himself were overly ambitious and sometimes misguided as well. Through his office as chancellor, he managed to get control of the various secular branches of government and proceeded to anger the most influential classes in the country. He antagonized the gentry by trying to protect the rights of the poor farmer and alienated the well-to-do by insisting on a new tax called a subsidy and based on a fair assessment of income from land and wages. When his autocratic methods made Parliament recalcitrant, he demanded loans from the wealthy which the government had no intention of repaying.

In bringing more and more judicial cases to the courts of the Chancery and the Star Chamber, Wolsey made a genuine contribution to the development of English law. The common law, which had taken its form in a feudal, agrarian society, no longer met the needs of the day and was almost as likely to prevent justice as to ensure it. The so-called prerogative courts, on the other hand, which included the Chancery and the Star Chamber, depended on the judge's sense of justice, often influenced by his knowledge of Roman law. That they were popular with many is indicated by the number of people who chose to plead before them. However, the use of these courts angered the common law lawyers, who were usually untrained in Roman law and feared its growing application. The nobility and the gentry also disliked the prerogative courts, because they often gave decisions in favor of the poor. Wolsey's policy of favoring the prerogative courts may deserve praise, but it had the effect of offending the most powerful elements of the population at a time when the government depended on popular support.

Even this restricted praise cannot be given to his ecclesiastical policy. The Church of England did not exist at this time. The archdioceses of Canterbury and York were completely separate, and some monasteries were exempt from episcopal authority. To control all the monasteries, Wolsey won from Rome the office of papal legate. With the power of the Pope behind him, he overrode the clergy in assemblies, known as Convocation, interfered with ecclesiastical courts, seized numerous benefices for himself, and refused to fill vacancies so that he could appropriate the income assigned to support the incumbents. When he did fill a post, it was with a favorite or a foreigner who never visited England. Though he professed to act in the name of reform, he himself was a pluralist in that he held more than one benefice, a nonresident in that he never visited his archdiocese of York until after he had fallen from royal favor, and a violator of the concept of priesthood in that he loved wealth, pomp, and power and fathered several children. Yet this man had the smaller monasteries investigated, and dissolved those that were found wanting. By these means and others, Wolsey destroyed the power of the English clergy, broke their will to resist, and conditioned them to accepting the authority of the crown and its officers.

As a diplomat, Wolsey fancied himself without peer, but it was his failures in diplomacy that brought his downfall. During most of his period in office, he took England in and out of foreign coalitions in the vain hope that he might be elected pope. Then, in the spring of 1527, Henry gave

Wolsey a new assignment. He ordered him to obtain from the Pope an annulment of his marriage to Catherine of Aragon.

Henry wanted an heir to secure a peaceful succession to the throne, but of Catherine's many children only a daughter, Mary, survived. Only once, some four hundred years before, had a woman ascended the English throne, and her claim had been repulsed during a long period of civil war. Neither Henry nor his subjects wanted the experience repeated, but a new wife was needed to provide a male heir, for Catherine could have no more children. A second motive that drove the king to rid himself of his wife was that he had fallen in love with a lady of his court, Anne Boleyn. Anne, remembering well that her sister had surrendered to the king only to be cast aside when he had tired of her, insisted on marriage. Whether the desire for an heir or the desire for Anne was uppermost in Henry's mind will never be known, but together they led to the downfall of Wolsey and the break with Rome.

Henry's request for an annulment was not unusual. Two Renaissance French kings put aside their wives with the papal blessing. As Catherine had been the wife of his deceased fourteen-year-old brother, Henry could argue that his marriage to her was contrary to canon law, for Leviticus 20:21 declared that a man who takes his brother's wife shall be childless. Unhappily for Henry, Catherine was the aunt of Emperor Charles V, whose power in Italy was such that the Pope dared not grant his request. In October, 1529, when the last hope of securing the annulment by cooperating with the papacy ended, Wolsey was dismissed and Henry began to rid himself of his wife by establishing a new church under his control.

During the three years after Wolsey's fall, Henry tried to achieve his goal by summoning Parliament to give vent to its anti-clerical temper. He hoped that this tactic would strengthen his control over the Anglican clergy and frighten the Pope into the concession that had been refused when friendship was offered. But the Pope continued to fear the Emperor more than the king, and Henry was driven to take more extreme steps. He was now to act through a new minister, Thomas Cromwell (1485?-1540), who became his principal adviser in 1532.

Cromwell was a blacksmith's son who had been an adventurer, a merchant, a member of Parliament, and finally a servant of the crown. He had extraordinary administrative abilities and a great capacity for work, two traits which enabled him to make such significant changes during his eight years as leading minister that they have been called "the Tudor revolution in government." Parliament was readily persuaded to declare that England was an empire from whose ecclesiastical courts no appeals could be made to Rome and that the king was the supreme head of the Church of England. Thereafter, Henry could marry and annul a marriage as often as he pleased. In all, he was to have six wives; two he beheaded on charges of adultery, two he cast aside, one died of natural causes, and one had the good fortune to outlive him.

As supreme head of the Church, Henry did not claim the right to perform the duties of the priest, but matters of doctrine, ecclesiastical appointments, and clerical discipline were subject to his authority. In the name of clerical discipline, the monasteries were inspected, found wanting, and suppressed, their vast lands going to the royal coffers. Had Henry and his successors been less improvident, these estates and those already held by the crown might have freed them from asking Parliament for taxes, but in the end most of the lands fell into the hands of the gentry, merchants, and well-to-do farmers who became the basis of the English aristocracy.

During the dangerous period when he was breaking with Rome, Henry had displayed some Protestant leanings in the hope of receiving support from that quarter. The Archbishop of Canterbury, Thomas Cranmer, who had received papal approval of his appointment just before Catherine was put aside, was regarded as a Lutheran. He introduced a translation of the Bible into England and prepared the beautiful *Book of Common Prayer* that contained supplications and responses to be sung or spoken during church services. However, in spite of their criticism of papal interference and clerical abuses, the vast majority of the English people remained loyal to the Catholic religion. In recognition of this fact, Henry got Parliament to pass the Six Acts in 1539 reaffirming the principal Catholic doctrines.

As noted earlier, Henry often used Parliament to implement his religious policies. One of the principal characteristics of the Tudor revolution in government was the important role played by this institution. There had been signs since the reign of Edward IV that Parliament was becoming less useful to the crown. The meeting in 1529 was only the second in seventeen years. But the close cooperation between king and Parliament in passing the legislation breaking with Rome and establishing the Church of England altered the situation.

For this change, Cromwell deserves much of the credit. He found that by preparing statutes in advance for submission and by having royal officials participate in the debates, he could usually get the unprepared deputies to adhere to the royal will. This was especially true because the speaker of the house, a royal nominee, had control over the business to be discussed and because some of the deputies owed their election to royal influence. Statutes issued with the approval of Parliament carried more weight than proclamations issued on royal authority alone and were therefore more enforceable, both legally and morally. For this reason, the idea emerged in Tudor England that sovereignty rested with king and Parliament, who were "conjoined and knit together in one body politic," and although throughout the period the king dominated Parliament, the time was to come when the reverse would be true.

Cromwell also made many improvements in the administrative machinery of the government. From his time forward, the king's secretary, an office that Cromwell held, had greater administrative importance than the office of chancellor. He incorporated Wales into England, and the Welsh counties began to send deputies to Parliament. This was one of the few instances in which one state actually merged with another during the Renaissance. The explanation for this unusual event was that Wales had long been associated with England and the Tudors were popular there because of their Welsh ancestry. Unfortunately for Cromwell, he was more favorable to the Protestants than to the king, and when he chose a Protestant bride for Henry whom his royal master did not like, he was made Earl of Essex as a reward for his great services and beheaded a few months later for his unpardonable mistake. By the time of Cromwell's death, the Renaissance monarchy in England had assumed its essential characteristics, although the country was still Catholic in ritual and dogma.

THE SPANISH KINGDOMS

The architects of the Renaissance monarchy in the Spanish kingdoms were Ferdinand (1479-1516) and Isabella (1474-1504). At the time when the young couple were married in 1469, Ferdinand was heir to Aragon, Catalonia, and Valencia, a loosely associated group of states ruled by his father, and Isabella had a claim to the throne of the integrated kingdoms of Castile and León. This marriage led eventually to the creation of a single Spanish state, but neither geography, economic factors, nor tradition pointed to this result, nor did the young bride and groom think beyond the typical dynastic arrangement.

Castile was a backward, lawless kingdom situated on the high arid plateau of the central portion of the Iberian Peninsula. The climate was not conducive to agriculture, and the lack of good roads and Mediterranean seaports limited trade. Sheep raising was the most lucrative occupation, although lack of rainfall made annual migrations necessary. Many of the practices associated with stockraising in the American southwest in the nineteenth century first appeared on the high Castilian plains. Since Castile had been a frontier kingdom during the period of the reconquest from the Moors, the inhabitants had become accustomed to living in walled towns for protection. The merchants and minor nobles (*hidalgos*) lived together in the towns and, as the same classes did in Italy, dominated the municipal governments and the surrounding countryside. The period of the reconquest had also given rise to a group of powerful nobles who lived in castles, to three large crusading orders, and to an unusually influential clergy. The nobles and the Church owned most of the land and were uncommonly successful in exploiting the peasants.

Aragon, Valencia, and Catalonia were much smaller but had used their location on the Mediterranean coast to develop a highly profitable trade and a large colonial empire that included Sicily, Sardinia, and the Balearics as well as claims to Naples. Catalonia especially, with its once great city of Barcelona, had mercantile traditions, and the language and customs of its inhabitants were much more closely related to the language and customs of southern France than to those of Castile. The nobles were also powerful in these states and formed a closely knit group that vigorously defended their well established privileges against the king. They were more orderly than their Castilian counterparts, but, being better organized, they were more difficult to reduce to the royal will.

Indeed, Castile had much less in common with these states than with Portugal, whose language was more closely akin to Castilian than to Catalan. Geography also intended Portugal and Castile to be one country, for the rivers of the central Iberian plateau flowed to the west and with them went the roads and the trade routes. The Portuguese king sought Isabella's hand and also her niece's, who had a better claim to the throne than she. Had these two states united, the great Spanish and Portuguese colonial empires would have merged. Instead, when Isabella married Ferdinand, Castile and Portugal became colonial rivals. More serious, the marriage between Ferdinand and Isabella committed Castile to supporting the extensive Aragonese Mediterranean empire. This commitment was to involve Castile in European wars which so exhausted that country that the decline of the Renaissance also marked the decline of Spanish greatness.

If history did not decree the marriage of Ferdinand and Isabella, in a sense their personalities did; for where one was strong, the other was weak. Isabella was a pious, intolerant woman, so ambitious and determined that she usurped the Castilian throne from her niece on the apparently false charge that she was illegitimate. Ferdinand was more cosmopolitan and tolerant, though equally determined to achieve his goals and devious and deceitful in his methods. Isabella loved pomp and display, but Ferdinand was too parsimonious ever to have risked his money on Columbus' desperate gamble. As evidenced by the marriage contract and by their subsequent behavior, neither foresaw nor intended the ultimate union of Aragon and Castile. By the terms of the agreement, Ferdinand was to govern his kingdoms alone. Since he also had claims to the Castilian throne, he was given some voice in the government of Castile, although Isabella was to have the major role. Because Castile was the more important state, the usual procedure was reversed; Ferdinand provided his wife with a dowry and promised not to leave Castile without her permission. As a result, there was not to be even a personal union of the two states.

When Isabella died in 1504, she left Castile to their daughter, Joanna the Mad, and Ferdinand was forced to withdraw to Aragon, where he married again with the hope of having male heirs. It was only his failure to do so that enabled Joanna and her descendants to inherit his kingdoms and to bring them and Castile under the same sovereign.

Institutional unity was equally absent. Each state kept its own council, law courts, cortes (parliaments), taxes, and other customs and institutions. No system for the extradition of criminals was established until much later, and the tariffs between the states were allowed to continue.

Isabella even declared in her will that since the colonization of the New World had been made "at the expense of my kingdoms and settled with nationals of these kingdoms, it is right that all their trade and traffic should belong to my kingdoms of Castile and León and be conducted from them; and everything brought from the Indies should go to them and be for them." As a result, Ferdinand's subjects, so experienced in seafaring, trade, and the government of colonies, were excluded from the New World to the benefit of the land-oriented Castilians. When Ferdinand made good a claim to the kingdom of Navarre in 1512 by conquering all of it south of the Pyrénées, it too was permitted to keep its separate customs and institutions.

More surprising still, when the Moorish kingdom of Granada was conquered in 1492, the inhabitants were promised that they could keep their laws, customs, language, dress, and even their religion. In the end, Isabella's intolerance was too strong and so much pressure was placed on the Moors to be converted that they rebelled. When defeated, they were given a choice between conversion and leaving the country. Those who chose to remain, known as the Moriscos, were placed under the watchful eye of the Inquisition, and attempts were made to stamp out their language, dress, and laws. This persecution led to a serious revolt in 1569-71 and a final expulsion of Moriscos in 1609-14 that left Spain racially and religiously united in its intolerance and poverty. Elsewhere, the federal structure of the crown was maintained. When, in 1580, the great-grandson of Ferdinand and Isabella, Philip II, fell heir to the throne of Portugal, the Portuguese were permitted to keep their separate identity in every respect. Thus, through dynastic marriages and the conquest of Granada, the Iberian Peninsula became united during the Renaissance, but it was a union in the person of the sovereign and not one of laws or institutions.

Since Castile was the largest and most lawless of their kingdoms, Ferdinand and Isabella devoted most of their energies to reforming its government. The Cortes was summoned, and it gave support to the royal demand that crown lands granted to undeserving nobles during the earlier period of royal weakness be restored and that the castles of the lawless be destroyed. The *Hermandad,* or league of cities, was revived, and its urban militia was used to police the countryside. Eventually, a kind of national guard was formed to take its place. Military tactics were altered under the inspired leadership of Gonzalo de Córdoba. Reliance was placed on infantry armed with pikes and short swords and supported by troops with arquebuses. These regiments were grouped in hollow squares and fought so effectively that for over a century they were without rival in Europe. The towns were brought under surveillance by the appointment of *corregidores* to sit with the municipal council in every city. Ferdinand became the commander of each of the three crusading orders, an arrangement that brought them under royal control and diverted their great revenues into the coffers of the crown.

As in England, the central government was essentially conciliar, and lawyers and secretaries began to play a more important role than the great nobles. The administration of justice was decentralized, as in France, with supreme courts being established in several different cities. Bulls were won from the popes that gave the crown almost complete control over clerical appointments and led to the formation of a national church, as in France. However, the Spanish sovereigns, acting through the great Cardinal Ximenes de Cisneros (1437-1517), used their authority to obtain not only the submission of the clergy but also its reform.

Most controversial of all was the revival of the Inquisition in 1478, for the avowed purpose of rooting out heresy among the converted Jews. Unlike the medieval Inquisition, which had been subject to the bishop's authority, control over this later Inquisition was given to the crown and the confiscations it ordered went to the royal treasury. The judicial procedures followed by the Inquisition were no worse, and perhaps not so bad, as those used in the administration of secular justice, but the power exercised by the crown has led some historians to believe that this second Inquisition was used against the king's enemies and to line the royal purse. Whether or not this charge is true, it is certain that Ferdinand extended the Inquisition, over popular protests, into Aragon and that it became the one institution common to all the Spanish kingdoms.

Many of these changes served to increase royal revenue, but in themselves they would not have been sufficient to support Ferdinand's aggressive policies. Few new taxes were created, but the growth of the economy and more efficient and honest collection led to a thirty-fold increase in revenue. The Cortes was frequently asked to give its consent to levies, but the nobles and clergy, who did not have to pay taxes, lost interest and gradually ceased to attend, leaving the deputies of the towns to confront the royal demands alone. Thus, Castile was transformed into a well-organized state resting on popular support and capable of serving as a base from which future monarchs could strengthen their position in Aragon and play a leading role in European affairs.

GERMANY

During this period, the Emperor was little more able to assert his prerogatives in Germany than in the Italian territories of the Empire, and the restoration of authority after about 1450 was accomplished by the great nobles or princes, who adopted practices similar to those of the Renaissance monarchs in western Europe. The first task of the princes was to give their people the sense of belonging to a single state. This was a difficult task because the lands of one noble were often separated by the lands of another lord or by a town. The nobles overcame this difficulty by creating assemblies in which the three estates of all their possessions were compelled to participate. It was through constant attendance of these sessions that the inhabitants gradually became conscious of common problems and a common destiny. In fact, the members of the estates often outdid the prince who had assembled them in recognizing the existence of the state. They sometimes tried, for example, to prevent the prince from dividing his territory among his children as if it were his private property. Their efforts and the growing influence of Roman law, which distinguished between public authority and private property, ultimately led most princely families to adopt primogeniture. Thus, by interaction the princes and the estates created the territorial state.

Since the prince and the estates were roughly equal in power throughout the Renaissance, German historians have usually characterized this period as a dualism in which the assembly voted taxes that fell on the nobility and the towns, as well as the peasants, in return for the redress of its grievances. With the money obtained, the princes restored order, forced the towns and minor nobles in their territory to acknowledge their authority, and sometimes gained control of adjoining towns and minor nobles over whom they had no claim. The princes' work of territorial consolidation was never completed, however, for nearly two thousand minor nobles managed to retain their independence. Because they acknowledged no overlord other than the emperor, they became known as imperial knights. Sixty-six cities were equally fortunate and continued to be self-governing communes similar to those in Italy. The presence of strong princely states, however, prevented the towns from expanding to form territorial states, as they had done south of the Alps. Nevertheless, the dominant political fact in Germany from the latter part of the fifteenth century was the territorial state ruled by the prince, whose formal title might be elector, duke, margrave, or even archbishop or bishop. Like the larger monarchies, these states were administered through councils and household officials.

The duchy of Bavaria, located in southern Germany, typified the princely state. It was among the oldest duchies in Germany, having been formed in the eighth century. In 1180, it fell into the hands of the Wittelsbach family, who ruled it until 1918. Like many other German princely families, the Wittelsbach family divided the territory among the sons. In 1255, the duchy was separated into Upper and Lower Bavaria. Further divisions followed although the chance extinction of one of the lines of the family occasionally reunited portions of the duchy. Wars between brothers and cousins over conflicting claims were frequent, and these family quarrels, coupled with the division of the duchy, weakened ducal authority. The result was that by the close of the fourteenth century the three estates of each of the territories into which the duchy was divided had won the privilege of appointing committees to supervise taxation and were able to influence administration, legislation, and diplomacy. The right of the estates of one territory to conclude unions with those of other territories was recognized by the emperor in 1422, a privilege which enabled them to collaborate with other estates against ducal authority. They frequently sought to prevent quarrels between the Wittelsbach dukes since they saw little reason to be taxed, pillaged, or murdered because of family disputes.

The chance extinction of several branches of the family and the use of force to make good his claims finally enabled Albert IV to reunite the duchy in 1505. At the same time, the estates of various Bavarian territories joined together on their own initiative, an exceptional act because some effort on the part of the prince was usually necessary to get the estates of different territories to unite. A territorial state with about 10,800 square miles and nearly a million inhabitants emerged, in which the power of the prince was balanced by the power of the estates. To prevent future divisions of the duchy, Albert persuaded his brother to accept the principle of primogeniture. Quarrels between members of the Wittelsbach family did not cease entirely, and disputes between the dukes and the estates were frequent, especially over the question of taxation, but a semblance of order was maintained. Munich, the capital, became a regional cultural center, and Bavaria itself became one of the most important German states.

Since political authority was concentrated at the level of the territorial state, the Empire could become strong only if the princes were willing to lend it strength or if the emperor was able to gain support from beyond the Empire. Both approaches were attempted during the Renaissance.

Distress over the declining position of the Empire in European affairs, the desire to prevent quarrels between the princes, the fear of the imperial knights and towns that they might be absorbed in the territorial states, and the popular sentiment in favor of the Empire led to efforts at reform, especially between 1495 and 1524. The *Reichstag* (parliament of the Empire) began to meet more regularly, and its composition and procedures became more definitely established. It consisted of three houses. One of these was composed of the seven electors who had the right of choosing the emperor; a second of the territorial princes; and the third of the free imperial cities. The clergy as such were not represented; but three of the electors were archbishops, and some of the princes were ecclesiastics.

Together, the electors and princes easily dominated the towns and, for that matter, the emperor as well. Hence, the Reichstag was essentially their tool. In 1495, the Reichstag established an imperial tribunal, an imperial army, and a tax to support both of these institutions. But the more powerful territorial rulers refused to permit appeals from their courts to the imperial tribunal, and in effect the territorial states and free cities contributed what they pleased. As a result, revenues were not adequate to support the tribunal properly or to finance an army of sufficient size. Perhaps the princes would have been more willing to build a strong imperial army if the emperor had cooperated with the Imperial Governing Council which they created, but the emperor opposed this institution because it was dominated by the electors and princes rather than by men of his choice. Without the Council, the princes feared a large imperial army, which the

Emperor Charles V at the age of 48, a portrait by Titian. (Bruckmann-Art Reference Bureau)

emperor could use against them. Therefore, the efforts at reform were disappointing, although the work of the Reichstag and the Imperial Tribunal was of sufficient importance to prevent the further disintegration of the Empire. To make the Empire a reality, the emperor would have to find additional sources of power; for a time, it appeared that one of the emperors, Charles V, had acquired the necessary strength.

CHARLES V

Members of the Habsburg family held the imperial title continuously from 1438 to 1740, but it was not until the marriage of Maximilian (1493-1519) with Mary, the daughter of Charles the Bold of Burgundy, that the family acquired enough land and power to surpass several other princely houses. Not content with this glittering success, Maximilian's son married Joanna the Mad, heir of Ferdinand and Isabella. The child of that union, who became Emperor Charles V, therefore inherited not only the Habsburg and Burgundian lands in the Empire and in France but also the Spanish kingdoms with their possessions in the Mediterranean and the New World. Through dynastic marriages, the Habsburgs had created one of the largest empires ever to be ruled by a European prince.

The man called upon to rule this gigantic empire had no more than average intelligence and somewhat less than average good looks. Charles V was a mediocre student and a poor linguist, and his lower jaw protruded so far forward that he had difficulty chewing. His father died when Charles was six, and his mother was insane. He loved to read about the deeds of his Burgundian ancestors, and his earliest dreams were those of the knight-errant and crusader. But he had the good fortune to be raised by his aunt, Margaret of Austria, regent of the Netherlands, an able statesman and intelligent patron of the arts. Moreover, this unprepossessing man was imbued with a love for his house and his church that was to give him a dignity and a steadfast courage which, despite his modest endowments, raised him far above such contemporaries as the more intelligent Henry VIII of England and the more colorful Francis I of France.

Charles was only fifteen when he assumed the government of the Netherlands, sixteen when he became king of Spain, and nineteen when he was elected emperor. Fortunately, he had capable advisers during these early years of responsibility, the most influential of whom was his brilliant chancellor, the Italian-born Gattinara, who taught him to believe that his position as emperor gave him the political and moral leadership of the world. At a time when territorial states were everywhere being formed, Charles sought to revive the medieval concept of Christendom. This ambition blended with his dynastic and religious loyalties. As an emperor, he sought to restore imperial authority in the Empire and peace in Europe. As a dynastic prince, he felt bound to win and hold the territories he had inherited and to acquire more for his descendants by dynastic marriages. As a Christian monarch, he saw himself as "God's standard-bearer," charged with the mission of fighting the Turks abroad and stamping out heresy at home. That these aims were often conflicting or self-defeating he did not fully realize. He never felt himself to be an aggressor against a fellow Christian prince, but his dynastic claims often conflicted with theirs. He even sought the duchy of Burgundy where his ancestors were buried, although it had belonged to France since the death of Charles the Bold. His plans to improve the already powerful position of his house through marriages alarmed his rivals still more. He established a claim to the Portuguese throne for his son by marrying a Portuguese princess, and he hoped that this son would absorb England for the following generation through his marriage to Henry VIII's daughter, Mary. His brother, Ferdinand, aided

CHARLES V AND HIS INHERITANCE

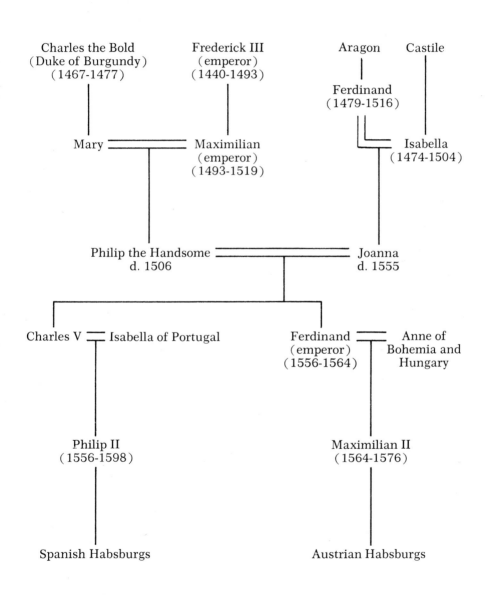

BURGUNDIAN INHERITANCE   HABSBURG INHERITANCE   SPANISH INHERITANCE

Charles the Bold
(Duke of Burgundy)
(1467-1477)

Frederick III
(emperor)
(1440-1493)

Aragon   Castile

Ferdinand
(1479-1516)

Mary ══════ Maximilian
(emperor)
(1493-1519)

Isabella
(1474-1504)

Philip the Handsome ══════ Joanna
d. 1506   d. 1555

Charles V ══ Isabella of Portugal

Ferdinand ══ Anne of
(emperor)   Bohemia and
(1556-1564)   Hungary

Philip II
(1556-1598)

Maximilian II
(1564-1576)

Spanish Habsburgs

Austrian Habsburgs

by marriage ties, was elected king of both Bohemia and Hungary. His dynastic policies provided some justification for the already belligerent attitude of the French and explain why the popes, fearful for their independence, thwarted "God's standard-bearer" as much as they dared. At the same time, his desire to restore his authority in the Empire made the German Catholic princes lukewarm to his proposals to conquer the Protestant princes, for the Catholic rulers feared that their turn would be next.

These dreams of a united Christendom and of a crusade, dreams that were in a sense medieval revivals, Charles sought to realize by using the techniques of the Renaissance monarchs. Dynasticism was his most important weapon, and decentralization was the principal characteristic of his empire. No imperial institutions of lasting importance were created, and imperial unity continued to rest on a common loyalty to the person of the emperor. Charles sought advice from whomever he chose and used the secretariat inherited from Ferdinand to handle the administrative correspondence relating to the Spanish kingdoms and their dependencies, and the Burgundian secretariat to handle affairs north of the Alps. Each individual state kept its own customs, laws, and institutions and was governed much as it had been before Charles became its lord. Members of his family served as governors or regents of the Netherlands, the Empire, and the Spanish kingdoms, and great nobles represented him in his Italian lands and other less important territories.

Since there was neither an imperial army, nor an imperial bureaucracy, nor an imperial treasury, Charles's government depended on popular support. He sought to enlist support through patronage, which he granted himself so that the grantee's loyalty would be to him and not to the subordinate officials who usually dispensed the royal favors. In this way, he won the support of most of the great nobles and of many lawyers for whom the Empire offered opportunities for employment. His efforts to combat the Turks in the Mediterranean fired the historic crusading ardor of the Spanish, and he won the support of a handful of wealthy merchant-bankers by granting them special concessions. Most of the people remained attached to their local customs and institutions, which Charles nearly always respected. Even when his territories in the Netherlands refused to establish an army for their common defense, he was careful not to press matters far enough to lead to a revolt. At first, the Spanish were troublesome because they regarded Charles as a foreign prince who taxed them to support policies in which they had no interest, but after a serious revolt of the towns had been suppressed in 1520-21, he gradually won their loyalty, and in the end Spain became the heart of his territories.

Nevertheless, wars and rebellions were his constant lot. He never had a capital but wandered from place to place. He visited the Empire nine times, Spain six times, France four times, Africa twice, and England twice, and he began and ended his reign in the Netherlands. He usually spent at least several months in each of his territories in order to become acquainted with its problems, but before he could fully solve them he was usually summoned to another territory where war or rebellion was threatening or to a diplomatic mission in France or England. Had he been able to devote all his resources to defeating the Turks or the French or to ridding the Empire of its Protestants, he might have succeeded, but in the end even Charles saw that his dreams were not to be realized. In 1555-56, he relinquished his various thrones and retired to Spain where he spent his two remaining years in a monastery.

The imperial idea had failed. To his devoted son, Philip II, he gave the Spanish kingdoms, including their possessions in Italy and the New World, as well as the inheritance from his Burgundian ancestors. To his brother Ferdinand went the Habsburg inheritance and the imperial crown. In thus dividing his territories, Charles made one serious mistake. By denying the Burgundian inheritance to Ferdinand, he left him too weak to dominate the Empire, and by giving it to his son he involved him in wars and rebellions that exhausted Spain's strength. Economic considerations have been cited to explain this division, but a deeper explanation is that the Burgundian territories had been the home of Charles's most admired ancestors and of his own youth. He never thought of giving them to anyone but his son.

THE ITALIAN AND THE HABSBURG-VALOIS WARS

In 1494, the long period of Italian isolation came to an end. The victorious completion of the Hundred Years War and the disappearance of most of the great feudal dynasties left France free to engage in foreign adventures. In like manner, his marriage to Isabella and the restoration of her authority in Castile gave Ferdinand of Aragon sufficient strength to press his claims in the Italian Peninsula. From the modern point of view, the struggle between the French and Spanish for Italy was senseless. Italy was outside the natural boundaries of either state and was inhabited by people of a different nationality. But the Renaissance monarchs used different criteria to judge when to make war. They asked whether they had a dynastic claim to the coveted state that would quiet their consciences and help them to obtain some support from the inhabitants. They wanted to know how much revenue the conquest would bring them, and their councillors mentally divided their own share of the spoils. The desire for glory was still a mainspring of their actions, and only a handful of scholars thought that glory could be won by providing one's subjects with peace, justice, and prosperity. In an age when great states were being built through marriages, it is not surprising that the French kings gave little thought to the fact that Naples was far removed from the borders of France and inhabited by Italians. Were not Burgundy and the Netherlands separated by many miles and inhabited by people of different tongues, yet one prince had successfully ruled them both? Nor did the French kings think to encroach on the Empire instead, for here they had no dynastic claims and Naples was then a richer prize than Alsace or Lorraine.

The immediate cause of the war was the formation of an alliance between Florence and Naples to despoil Milan. To remove this threat, Milan's Ludovico Sforza appealed to Charles VIII of France to make good his dynastic claim to Naples. Charles required little urging. In the hope of securing their neutrality, he returned Franche-Comté and Artois to the Habsburgs and several Pyrénéan territories to Spain, concessions that were detrimental to French national interests from the modern point of view, and in 1494 he swept into Italy with 30,000 men. Since no Italian state could hope to stand against such a force, this first French invasion was little else than a triumphant march to Naples. However, Ferdinand of Aragon felt that his kingdom of Sicily was threatened, and he too had claims on Naples. With the aid of Italian allies, he drove the French back almost as rapidly as they had come.

For a few years there was peace, but in 1499 Louis XII decided to make good his claim to the duchy of Milan. He too was initially successful, and he too finally had to fight Ferdinand. The Italian states were deeply involved, first on one side and then on the other, and Emperor Maximilian and England occasionally participated. In the end, Louis was defeated, but Francis I quickly renewed the attack upon coming to the throne in 1515. At first he was victorious, but when Charles V began to rule, his numerous possessions turned the tide. Francis was defeated and captured at Pavia in 1525 but was released in return for promising to abandon Italy and to surrender the duchy of Burgundy. Once released, Francis repudiated the treaty, and the war was renewed with varying fortunes. At times, Francis allied himself with the Turks and the Protestant princes in Germany against Charles, while the troops of the devout Emperor sacked Rome.

There is no need to follow the armies back and forth through Europe in this seemingly endless struggle. Finally, too exhausted financially to sustain the war and increasingly concerned by the growth of Protestantism, Philip II of Spain and Henry II of France made peace at Cateau-Cambrésis in 1559. The Habsburgs were confirmed in their dominance of Italy, but the French got Calais, which had been taken by the Duke of Guise from the English in 1558, and won Metz, Toul, and Verdun near their eastern frontier.

A far-reaching consequence of this long struggle between the Habsburgs and the Valois kings of France was that the war in Italy brought the northern monarchies into closer contact with the Italian Renaissance and facilitated its spread to other parts of Europe. The soldier himself rarely absorbs much of an alien culture, but the kings and great nobles who fought in Italy brought historians, humanists, and artists back to their native countries. Such contacts had already been established and would undoubtedly have continued, but the wars seem to have increased their frequency. War necessitated constant negotiations, and the northern states adopted Italian diplomatic techniques. Resident ambassadors were exchanged, and intermarriage between the northern royal and Italian ducal houses became more common. Two Medicis became queens of France, and this led to still further contacts. Italians began to frequent the northern courts where some of them were absorbed into the local nobility and others received important appointments in the Church. Italy became an essential part of the itinerary of every traveling aristocrat and the most popular place of study for the artist and scholar.

CONCLUSIONS

The Italian states contributed little or nothing to the constitutional and administrative practices of the kingdoms to the north. Indeed, the tendency was for the Italian states to become more like those elsewhere. These Italian states had been new creations, and there was an element of illegitimacy in their conquests and in the origins of their reigning families. Most of the northern monarchies, on the other hand, had been founded long before this period, and they expanded through dynastic marriages rather than through conquest alone. However, these differences should not be exaggerated. The northern Italian states threw a cloak of legitimacy over their conquests, and their dynasties sought confirmation for their titles from the emperor or the pope. What had been upstart states ruled by upstart families in the early Renaissance seemed to be as time-tested and as legitimate as other states by the mid-sixteenth century. Moreover, some of the ruling families of the north had, in the beginning, acquired their thrones by force, and many now used force to back their dynastic claims. Ultimately, the Italian ruling class ceased to be burghers and took on the trappings of monarchy in their ducal courts; otherwise, their etiquette and manners could not have been absorbed into the court life of the north.

One notable difference remained, however. Since the states of northern Italy were formed by the expansion of individual cities, the municipal governments became the territorial governments and representative institutions were not established as they had been in the north. The Italian monarchies and older duchies, on the other hand, were similar to those north of the Alps, and representative assemblies were frequently summoned in Sicily and Savoy.

North and south, the Renaissance states had major characteristics in common that distinguish them from the modern state. Almost everywhere, they were decentralized, weak by modern standards, and dependent on popular support. In explaining how power could be won and kept, Machiavelli drew his examples from all of Western Europe and rarely felt it necessary to distinguish between the Italian prince and the northern king, except to concede that in the beginning the former had less legitimacy.

On both sides of the Alps, the Renaissance state differed also from the medieval state. The princes and states of northern Italy were obviously new creations, but even among the northern monarchies there were important differences that separated the Renaissance from the preceding period. The medieval state had also been dynastic, legitimate, decentralized, and dependent on popular support. But medieval decentralization had derived largely from the activities of great feudal nobles and their vassals. Renaissance decentralization was essentially bureaucratic. Thus, in the Middle Ages, Brittany was governed by its duke. In the Renaissance, it was ruled by a royal governor and subordinate officials; there were several types of sovereign courts to administer justice and provincial estates to negotiate with the crown. It was not the individual rights of the duke of Brittany that were stressed in regard to the crown, but the collective privileges of the duchy.

A combination of time and degree also separated the medieval period from the Renaissance. The thirteenth-century monarchs had been strong; those of the fourteenth and early fifteenth centuries had been weak. The kings of the late fifteenth and sixteenth centuries were again men of ability. A Henry VI breaks the continuity between Edward I and Henry VIII. Furthermore, the Renaissance monarchs were able to do bigger things than their predecessors. They created some new states and restored order in others, thereby facilitating an economic revival. But they did more: as will be shown in the following chapters, they encouraged exploration and trade with lands on the Atlantic, Pacific, and Indian oceans; they created a new aristocracy, became the greatest patrons of arts and letters of their age, and were the most important single factor in determining the religion of their subjects.

4/ The Economic Revival, the Discoveries, and the Aristocracy

T HE restoration of order by the Renaissance monarchs during the closing years of the fifteenth century made possible an economic recovery that, despite occasional slumps, was to last in most European countries until around 1620 or 1630. By encouraging voyages that led to the discovery of a water route to India and of the American continents, these monarchs also took the first step in spreading the European civilization to every part of the world.

Nevertheless, during the Renaissance an observer from another planet could not have predicted confidently that the European civilization would ultimately triumph over its rivals. During most of the period, the Moslem civilization seemed more dynamic. The armies of the Ottoman Turks overran the Balkans and almost took Vienna, while other Moslems conquered India and spread their religion in the East Indies. The Arab merchant was without peer, and the Arab mariner knew more about world geography than anyone else before the discoveries. Yet, in spite of its great military and missionary vitality, the Moslem world soon entered a period of decadence, perhaps because it no longer had the intellectual vigor to meet and profit by new developments.

The Ming dynasty won control of China during the late fourteenth century and between 1405 and 1433 dispatched seven great fleets that visited the East Indies and crossed the Indian Ocean to Arabia and Africa in search of trade, geographical knowledge, and tribute. In science and technology, the Chinese had long been ahead of the West. They knew of the compass, printing press, gunpowder, and paper money, inventions so important to the sailor, the scholar, the soldier, and the merchant, centuries before these articles appeared in the West. But the Chinese were so scornful of other civilizations that they learned nothing from them, and they were so immersed in their own past that they lost their intellectual vitality and ceased to accept new ideas. The great Chinese naval expeditions of 1405-1433 bore no lasting results, although centuries were to elapse before a European king could send as large a fleet so far from home.

Thus, the Chinese consciously turned their backs on the rest of the world in one of the most critical periods in history while the less mature West, spurred on by the dynamic energy, the inquiring minds, and the acquisitive spirit of a few individuals, became at least the equal of any other civilization by the end of the Renaissance. After a period of crisis during the seventeenth century, the West moved forward to spread its knowledge and its values to every corner of the world.

THE ECONOMIC REVIVAL

CAUSES

The most obvious cause of the economic revival that began in the West in the last quarter of the fifteenth century was the restoration of order by the Renaissance monarchs. Only when robber barons, brigands, and pillaging troops had been suppressed could trade flow freely and peasants reap their harvest unmolested. Once in power, the monarchs stimulated trade, industry, mining, and voyages of discovery by providing incentives for those willing to risk their money and their lives in such ventures. They rarely had the capital to invest significant amounts in such enterprises, but they could grant monopolies to the manufacturer who introduced a new industry, mining privileges to those who dug for copper and silver, and titles, governorships, and a share of the profits to explorers who discovered new lands beyond the seas and new routes to the wealth of the East. Essentially, then, their role was to give legality and protection to the acts of men with new ideas, with capital to invest in hazardous ventures, or with the courage to face the unknown. If the monopolies that they granted were often detrimental to industry, their contribution to the discoveries cannot be denied. If their wars interfered with trade, the armies that they equipped and the taxes that they collected gave a few favored individuals the opportunity to make large profits. If they bankrupted many great banking families by not paying the debts that they incurred to fight their wars and build their palaces, those who were repaid profited heavily from high rates of interest. On balance, the Renaissance monarchs affected the economy beneficially, although their motives were usually selfish and their economic policies shortsighted by modern standards.

Another cause of the economic revival was the growth in population that provided the labor to cultivate fields which had been abandoned after the Black Death and to work in the mines and industries. The principal reason for the population upswing after a century of decline was a reduction in the number and severity of the plagues, although the restoration of order by the monarchs played a significant role. An increase in population was naturally accompanied by an increase in production and trade.

Finally, the discovery and adoption of new techniques in business, industry, and mining increased the efficiency of the merchant and the banker as well as the productivity of labor. Many of these techniques had been discovered during the late Middle Ages but did not come into general use until the sixteenth century. Indeed, it may be that the period of economic decline in the late Middle Ages stimulated the search for technological improvements to compensate for the scarcity of labor and forced businessmen to adopt more efficient procedures in order to survive. If this is true, the adverse conditions of the late Middle Ages actually contributed to the daring and creative spirit so characteristic of the Renaissance.

BUSINESS TECHNIQUES

The economic contraction of the late Middle Ages led to an increase in the number of guilds as small producers sought to ensure an equitable division of what remained of the market. At this level, innovations were discouraged, but the great banking and merchant guilds were less restrictive, and it was at their level that many important innovations took place during the Renaissance.

In the Middle Ages, the typical large-scale business enterprise had been a centralized family partnership. After the bankruptcies of the mid-fourteenth century, however, most family concerns were decentralized. At the same time, these family concerns began more and more to diversify their economic activity so that failure in one area would not bring bankruptcy in another. The Medici firm, for example, was both decentralized and diversified. It did not consist of a single partnership but of one partnership for the home office at Florence, one for each of the three industrial establishments at Florence, and one for each of the branch offices abroad. Each partnership was a legal entity with its own capital and books. One branch, therefore, could not be sued for what another branch did, and the bankruptcy of one did not mean the failure of all. The Medicis contributed over half the capital to each partnership in order to maintain control. The branch managers were members or friends of the family who contributed part of the capital and enjoyed a larger share of the profits than their investment would warrant because they received no salary. When the partnership was dissolved after several years, the profits were divided, and a new partnership was formed. This system necessitated detailed and accurate business records and resulted in the increased use of double-entry bookkeeping with one column for credits and one for debits.

Many Italian firms not only traded in different types of articles to reduce risks but also engaged in industry and mining to produce goods to sell and in banking to facilitate the exchange of currency. The Medicis had one silk-manufacturing and two cloth-manufacturing partnerships in Florence as well as a controlling share in the company exploiting the papal alum mine at Tolfa. The economic sophistication of the period is suggested by the establishment of a cartel arrangement between the Medicis and the King of Naples, who had the only other important alum mines in Europe, in order to force prices to rise. The pope cooperated by threatening to excommunicate anyone who bought Turkish alum, but alum was so important in the manufacture of dye that other sources were found and some Turkish alum was imported in spite of papal threats. The arrangement was terminated in 1478 when the pope and the Medicis quarreled bitterly over other matters.

To prevent ruin when a consignment of goods was lost at sea, merchants purchased insurance or divided their cargo among a number of ships so that the loss of one ship would not be catastrophic.

Banking, credit, and foreign exchange facilities were also developed. Since it was expensive and dangerous to transfer large quantities of gold and silver across Europe, the bill of exchange was invented to facilitate business transactions. If a merchant in Bruges wanted to purchase goods in Florence, he could go to the branch office of the Medici bank and purchase a bill of exchange payable in Florence several months later. At the appointed date, he or his agent in Florence could go to the Medici bank in that city and get the designated sum. Because some Florentine businessman probably wanted to make purchases in Bruges with a bill of exchange, the one would approximately cancel the other and very little gold or silver would actually have to be transferred, just as the checks we send to another part of the country today rarely necessitate the actual movement of money. These bills of exchange were also used by travelers much as we use travelers' checks today and, for that matter, by the papacy itself to transfer the fees and contributions of the faithful to Rome.

The role of the bank as a place to deposit money was much less important than it is today, but it did exist. The Medicis, for example, permitted outsiders to deposit money in their bank that was withdrawable at a specific time, not on demand. In return, they paid from 8 to 12 per cent interest. Credit was provided by pawnshops and by retail banks that sold goods on the installment plan. Their interest rates were quite high, and various ways were found to escape prosecution for usury in these and other transactions. One of the most common devices was for the debtor to promise repayment in an impossibly short time and then to pay a specified sum for failure to meet the terms of the agreement.

Although bills of exchange, double-entry bookkeeping, insurance, and the various types of banking facilities all existed in the commercially advanced Italian cities by 1300, they spread very slowly to other parts of Europe. Not until these economic instruments were generally adopted during the Renaissance did they contribute to economic revival north of the Alps.

NEW DEVELOPMENTS IN INDUSTRY AND MINING

No new sources of power were developed during the Renaissance, although some experiments were made with the use of steam. Water and wind power had long been known in Europe. During the Renaissance, however, the use of water power was increased, and in the late fifteenth century the windmill was greatly improved through the invention of a turret that could be turned in the direction necessary to make the maximum use of the available wind, a highly desirable innovation because wind direction varied greatly in Europe.

Several inventions increased the productive capacity of workers in the important textile industry. A method was developed by which the spindle used in spinning could be rotated by a treadle operated with the foot, leaving the worker's hands free to manipulate the fibers. Treadles were also employed in operating the looms used in weaving. After the cloth was made, it had to be fulled, that is, cleaned and thickened. At one time, this operation was performed by tramping on the cloth in troughs, but gradually the watermill, which had been known as early as the twelfth century, replaced human power in this laborious work.

Knitting was scarcely known before the dawn of the Renaissance, and the growing demand for knitted goods, such as silk stockings, led to the invention of a stocking frame in the late sixteenth century that could make from 1,000 to 1,500 stitches per minute, as compared with 100 by hand-knitters. At one time, raw silk had to be imported from the East, but silkworms were brought to Italy and cultivated in such large numbers that the production of silk fabrics became one of the principal Italian industries during the sixteenth century. France and other countries sought to introduce silk manufacture to compete with the Italians.

More striking were the developments in mining and metallurgy. In the Middle Ages, surface ores had been mined, but by the fourteenth century they were nearly exhausted and the mining industry declined sharply. The early Renaissance saw the development of better methods for making shafts and draining mines so that it became possible to get ores from below the surface. In southern and eastern Germany, Bohemia, and Hungary, a mining boom developed. By 1525, as many as 100,000 persons may have been employed in the mining and metallurgy industry in the Empire, and the production of silver, copper, and zinc increased many times over. Methods were developed to extract silver located in copper ore and to smelt, cast, roll, and forge metals efficiently. Water power was used extensively in the various metallurgical processes, and illustrated books were published describing the miners' work. Around the middle of the sixteenth century, the center of mining activity shifted to England where there were rich deposits of coal. So much was mined that the period 1540-1640 has been called the first Industrial Revolution.

THE CLOCK AND THE PRINTING PRESS

The inventions and technological improvements described in the preceding paragraphs increased the productive capacity of the individual worker and thereby improved the standard of living, but the practice of installing clocks in churches and the invention of the printing press were far more significant. Although methods of telling time with sundials, water clocks, and hour glasses had been known for several thousand years, mechanical clocks did not make their appearance in European churches until the fourteenth century and did not become commonplace until the early Renaissance. Thereafter, on the hour, and often on the quarter hour, these clocks struck, telling the local inhabitants the time of day or night. People's lives began to be regulated by a concept of exact, astronomical time rather than by dawn, noon, and sunset, which were subject to seasonal variation and were the basis for the timing of church services. Since mechanical clocks were driven by weights, they were large and stationary, but around 1500 spring-driven watches were invented. These were bigger and more spherically shaped than modern pocket watches and probably gained or lost about fifteen minutes a day, but they marked the beginning of an effort to provide a personal timepiece for the well-to-do. Although the scheduling of human activities by the clock did not reach modern proportions during the Renaissance, the groundwork was laid for this unique and time-saving characteristic of modern Western civilization.

Important as was the growing concept of time, the invention of movable type for printing was of greater immediate and long-range significance. By the sixth century, the Chinese were making prints by pressing linen paper against inked wooden blocks. It took hundreds of years for knowledge of this process to reach Europe, but by the early fifteenth century wood engravings and block-printed books were being made. In itself, this process was not very important because each page had to be carved separately and block-printed books were therefore expensive. It did lead to valuable experimentation, however, for around 1450 Johann Gutenberg of Mainz began to make individual metal letters instead of wooden blocks.

Since these letters were interchangeable and could be used over and over again, the process was relatively inexpensive and books could be produced rapidly in large numbers. The success of this invention was immediate. By 1501, there were printing presses in about 110 European cities and towns.

Before the invention of movable type, it had often taken centuries for knowledge of a new mechanical device to spread from one part of Europe to another, and the work of the philosopher, theologian, poet, and artist could benefit only a few. Once movable type and the related technique of engraving had been invented, knowledge, culture, and one form of art could be made available, rapidly and inexpensively, to a large number of people. The tempo of progress and change was greatly accelerated.

THE DISCOVERIES

PRINCE HENRY THE NAVIGATOR

When the sons of John I (1385-1433) of Portugal expressed a desire to win knighthood, their father offered to hold a great tournament. The young princes refused to earn their spurs by playing at war and persuaded him to attack the Moorish town of Ceuta, located on the northern tip of Morocco. The expedition was far more successful than most of its kind. Ceuta fell in a day. Among those knighted in the mosque was the twenty-one-year-old son of the king, Henry, known to history as the Navigator. By this typical act of medieval knight-errantry, Portugal unknowingly took the first step toward the discovery of a water route to Asia and the creation of a colonial empire.

At Ceuta, Prince Henry apparently talked to Moorish merchants who had traveled back and forth across north Africa and south of the Sahara Desert to Tombouctou. Possibly as a result of these conversations, he determined to explore the African coast south of Cape Bojador, from which no European had ever returned. According to a contemporary chronicler, he had these objectives in mind: to satisfy his curiosity, to establish profitable trade relations with inhabitants, to defeat the Moors in alliance with any Christian rulers who might be found, to convert the natives, and to fulfill the prediction in his horoscope that he would "engage in great and noble conquests, and above all . . . attempt the discovery of things which were hidden from other men."

These motives may be taken as typical of those who engaged in the great voyages of discovery in the fifteenth and sixteenth centuries. Nearly all of them sought wealth. Prince Henry, for example, expected to find gold, as did many of his successors. Others hoped to make their fortune by trading in spices, ivory, silk, slaves, and other valuable commodities, by discovering rich fisheries, or by creating fiefs for themselves in some distant land. Religious zeal was an equally strong motive, especially among the inhabitants of the Iberian Peninsula, whose history prior to the conquest of Granada in 1492 had been marked by frequent crusades against the neighboring Moors. Regardless of the faults in their personal lives, the early explorers were devout men who believed that it was their duty to convert or humble the infidel. Prince Henry, for example, was the head of a crusading order and led attacks on the north African coasts whenever he could persuade his royal kinsmen to provide the money. Curiosity was another motive for the explorations of the fifteenth and sixteenth centuries. Sometimes it was stimulated by reading of the adventures of Marco Polo or some other traveler; sometimes it was aroused by the tales of those who had already gone to sea. No motive was stronger, however, than the desire for fame. Prince Henry believed that the stars had decreed that he should do great deeds. The desire for fame and glory possessed Hernando Cortés, the conqueror of Mexico, who was proud that Alexander the Great could boast no exploits as bold as his. The same desire possessed one Bernal Díaz, a soldier-historian who accompanied Cortés and whose only claim to nobility was that he had fought in over twice as many battles as Julius Caesar.

These motives were not peculiar to the Renaissance. They had all existed in the Middle Ages, including the desire for glory. However, the growth of literacy and the advent of printing during the Renaissance may have enabled more people than ever before to read of the deeds of past heroes and to be inspired by them. Certainly, these developments spread the news of the discoveries more rapidly than could have been the case during the Middle Ages and spurred others to follow those who had taken the lead.

The timing of the Spanish interest in the discoveries was related to the conquest of Granada in 1492. From that time onward, there were no longer Moors on the peninsula from whom the Spanish could win wealth by plundering, fame by killing, or salvation by converting. After Granada had been divided into fiefs by the victors, it was necessary to look elsewhere for these opportunities.

Prince Henry, of course, had accomplished his work before Granada was captured or printing came to Portugal, but these were developments that later helped to turn the efforts of one man into the goal of many thousands. Prince Henry did not participate personally in the numerous expeditions that he sent out during the forty-five years that remained to him after the capture of Ceuta but stayed in Portugal to direct his ambitious enterprise. He built a small castle at Sagres on the southern tip of his country where he gathered around him geographers, astronomers, and explorers, men of any type, whether Italians, Jews, or Spanish Moors, who could aid him in his expeditions. His were to be no haphazard explorations; they were the product of calculation and planning. He shrouded his activities in secrecy, and his maps and records have disappeared; but it is probable that he possessed most of the knowledge concerning the world available to

This map was printed by Henricus Martellus around 1489 and probably depicts the world as Columbus visualized it when he set sail three years later—in 1492. The Mediterranean coastline is fairly accurate as is the western coast of Africa, thanks to Portuguese explorations. Asia, however, is shown in accordance with the conceptions of Ptolemy and Marco Polo. The existence of the American continents was not anticipated. (British Museum)

the Europe of his day, and the events themselves give proof of his accomplishments.

From the days of the Greeks, scholars had known that the world was round, but most ancient geographers had underestimated its size. Ptolemy, the best known of these geographers, believed that Africa bent eastward and joined southeastern Asia, making the Indian Ocean an inland sea. Other scholars disagreed with Ptolemy and thought that Africa was a short continent and the Indian Ocean an open sea. If the latter view were correct, it would be possible to sail around Africa and reach India. Whether, or at what point, this became Prince Henry's ambition is impossible to say, but ultimately India became the goal of Portuguese exploration.

The late medieval man's knowledge of the world may be indicated by maps prepared in 1375 by a Jew of Majorca whose son entered Prince Henry's service. The Mediterranean region, including north Africa, was accurately depicted, and northern Europe was fairly well-known, but central and southern Africa were matters for conjecture. Prince Henry believed that a wealthy Christian kingdom ruled by Prester John was located somewhere in central or southern Africa, and he hoped to persuade this legendary ruler to assist him against the Moors. Asia was fairly well depicted, thanks to ancient and medieval travelers of whom Marco Polo was only the most famous. Japan and southeastern Asia were poorly drawn, and Australia and the New World were unsuspected. The Viking explorations of North America were unknown in most of Europe, and while the Atlantic was believed to contain many islands, it was also believed to extend to Asia, whose shores were thought to be much closer to Europe than they really are.

By this time, the Europeans knew how to make accurate maps, and the compass had developed from a magnetized needle floating on a straw in a bowl of water to its present form. However, when Prince Henry began his explorations, there was so much difficulty in determining longitude that sailors never liked to lose sight of land. During the fifteenth century, a method of determining latitude was developed by measuring the height of the North Star. Since the North Star cannot be seen in southern latitudes, a more complicated system had to be worked out, based on the height of the sun at midday. Speed was estimated by throwing a knotted rope overboard and observing how fast it ran out to the rear. Longitude continued to be a problem until the eighteenth century, but by knowing the direction in which his ship was moving and by estimating its speed, a good navigator could plot his course and have at least a vague idea of his general location.

Naval architecture also improved considerably. The quiet Mediterranean had been ideal for oared galleys, but in the rough Atlantic the sail was necessary. The early European sailing ships were clumsy affairs, and the Portuguese development of the highly maneuverable and efficient caravel was a necessary preliminary to the discoveries. Although artillery had

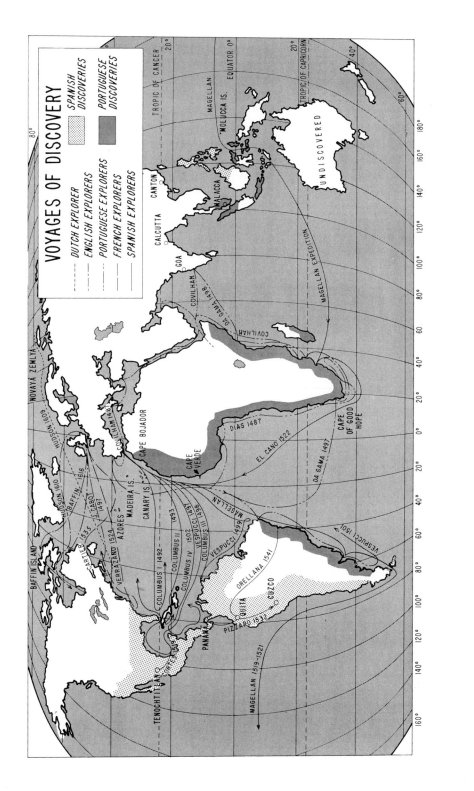

VOYAGES OF DISCOVERY

| | SPANISH DISCOVERIES |
| | PORTUGUESE DISCOVERIES |

DUTCH EXPLORER
ENGLISH EXPLORERS
PORTUGUESE EXPLORERS
FRENCH EXPLORERS
SPANISH EXPLORERS

80°

TROPIC OF CANCER   20°
MAGELLAN
MOLUCCA IS.
EQUATOR   0°
TROPIC OF CAPRICORN
20°
40°
60°

CANTON
MALACCA
CALCUTTA
GOA
COVILHAM
COVILHAM
DA GAMA 1498
CAPE OF GOOD HOPE
MAGELLAN EXPEDITION
UNDISCOVERED

NOVAYA ZEMLYA
HUDSON 1609
COVILHAM 1487
CAPE BOJADOR
DIAS 1487
CAPE VERDE
EL CANO 1522
DA GAMA 1497

BAFFIN ISLAND
HUDSON 1610
BAFFIN 1616
CABOT 1497
MADEIRA IS.
CANARY IS.
AZORES
VERRAZANO 1524
CARTIER 1535
COLUMBUS I 1492
COLUMBUS II 1493
COLUMBUS IV 1502
COLUMBUS III 1498
VESPUCCI 1497
VESPUCCI 1499
MAGELLAN
VESPUCCI 1501

TENOCHTITLAN
CORTES 1519
PANAMA
QUITO
ORELLANA 1541
CUZCO
PIZZARO 1532
MAGELLAN 1519-1521

160° 140° 120° 100° 80° 60° 40° 20° 0° 20° 40° 60° 80° 100° 120° 140° 160° 180°

been used on ships since the fourteenth century, it was of minor importance in naval warfare until the Portuguese placed their cannon on either side of their caravels. This arrangement gradually changed the naval engagement from a hand-to-hand battle between soldiers on two adjoining ships into an artillery duel. By the time the Portuguese actually reached the Indian Ocean, they were superior to the Moslem traders there in navigation, naval architecture, and naval warfare, although a hundred years earlier several other civilizations had surpassed the Europeans in naval technology and, indeed, had contributed much to European progress in this field. Only after it had achieved naval technological superiority could the European civilization have expanded.

These improvements were only gradual, however, and at first Portuguese progress was slow because the sailors feared that the southern seas were too hot to navigate and that the tropical sun would change them to Negroes. Prince Henry successfully colonized the Madeira Islands and the Azores, and in 1434 an expedition finally passed beyond Cape Bojador. In 1441, one of his captains reached Cape Blanco and returned with gold dust and Negro slaves. The prospect of profit encouraged the Portuguese to redouble their efforts, and in 1460, the year of Prince Henry's death, they reached Sierra Leone.

JOHN II AND VASCO DA GAMA

Prince Henry had acted as a private individual, but since he was childless, the right to exploit his discoveries was inherited by his nephew, King Alfonso V (1438-1481). Alfonso was less active in explorations than his uncle, but this situation was dramatically reversed in 1481 when John II (1481-1495) came to the throne. John had long taken an interest in exploration and had exercised the royal monopoly in African trade and exploration before his father's death. Expeditions in 1482 and 1484 boldly pressed on to and beyond the mouth of the Congo River. Heartened, John decided on an ambitious scheme to reach the wealthy Indian trade. In 1487, he dispatched two expeditions, one by sea and one by land. The sea expedition, under the command of Bartholomeu Dias, was told to try to sail around Africa. When already far down the African coast, Dias' vessels got caught in a gale that drove them southward out of sight of land for thirteen days. When he regained the African coast, Dias discovered that he had already passed the African cape and was in the Indian Ocean. A rebellious crew would permit him to go no farther, but when he returned to Portugal the happy king called his discovery the Cape of Good Hope, for it now seemed certain that Africa did not curve around to eastern Asia and that India could be reached by sea.

The second expedition, consisting of Pero de Covilham and one companion, was to take the land route to India to learn about trading condi-

Vasco da Gama. From a contemporary portrait, artist unknown, in Lisbon. (Courtesy of National Maritime Museum)

tions there and to try to establish contact with the mysterious Christian kingdom of Prester John, somewhere in Africa. Covilham crossed north Africa to Cairo, made his way down the Red Sea, and then on to Calcutta. When he returned to Cairo, he learned that his companion, who was to have gone to Ethiopia in search of Prester John, had died. Covilham wrote to King John, telling him how the Moslems took advantage of the monsoon winds, which blew from the west in the spring and summer and from the east during the remainder of the year, to carry on their Indian Ocean trade, information that later proved most useful. Then, after a side trip to Mecca and Medina disguised as a Moslem, the Arabic-speaking Covilham made his way southward to Abyssinia, where he found the kingdom of Prester John. This last success must have brought with it disappointment, because the Abyssinian king had neither great wealth nor enough military strength to help the Portuguese fight the Moslems, but the inhabitants were indeed members of the Coptic Christian Church which had been cut off from the rest of Christendom since the Arab conquest of north Africa centuries before. For some reason, the king refused to let Covilham leave, and upon his arrival in 1520 the Portuguese ambassador found the intrepid traveler living with a native wife and children.

Internal difficulties and the need to design sturdier vessels to navigate near the stormy Cape of Good Hope prevented the Portuguese from following up Dias' expedition immediately. John II died in 1495, and it was his cousin, King Manuel the Fortunate (1495-1521) who dispatched Vasco da Gama (1469?-1524) with a small fleet in 1497. To avoid unfavorable winds, Da Gama swung far out into the Atlantic and then proceeded around the Cape of Good Hope and up the eastern coast of Africa, where he found a pilot who brought him safely to Calcutta in 1498. The water route to India had been found, but still to be determined was how the Portuguese could profit from their discovery.

THE PORTUGUESE EMPIRE

Several difficulties still stood in the way of the development of Portuguese trade. The Europeans needed spices to preserve meat for winter consumption: pepper from India, cinnamon from Ceylon, nutmeg and cloves from the East Indies, and ginger from China. They also wanted Indian cotton cloth, Chinese silk, and precious stones. But in exchange for the treasures of the East, Europeans had little to offer. The cultured Oriental scorned European manufactures as inferior to his own. Furthermore, the Portuguese arrived in the Indian Ocean during a period of Moslem expansion. While the Ottoman Turks were taking Constantinople and pressing up the Danube River Valley, other Moslems were slowly conquering India and converting the inhabitants of the Malay Peninsula and the East Indies. Trade was everywhere in Moslem hands except along the China coast, which the Chinese themselves controlled.

Under these circumstances, the Portuguese had no chance of competing with the Arabs, who were then bringing Oriental goods from India to Alexandria and other eastern Mediterranean ports, where Italian merchants bought them for resale throughout Europe at prices little higher than if they had been transported by water around Africa. To be successful, the Portuguese had to establish control of the Indian Ocean and cut off Arab trade, a fantastic ambition for a little nation of one million people located thousands of miles from the scene of the conflict. Yet for years, under the leadership of such outstanding colonial governors as Affonso de Albuquerque (1453-1515), they were on the verge of success. In battle after battle, they defeated larger Moslem fleets. Secure naval bases were established in strategic locations to refit their vessels, protect their business, and halt rival traders. Goa, an important island city, became their principal post in India. Ormuz was seized in the mouth of the Persian Gulf to block Arab trade in those waters, and an unsuccessful effort was made to take Aden to deny the Arabs use of the Red Sea. Malacca, the gateway between the Indian Ocean and the Far East, was taken in 1511. Pressing northward, the Portuguese reached Canton in 1513 but later decided to establish their permanent Chinese trading headquarters on the island city of Macao. Pressing eastward, they opened trading relations with the clove-producing Molucca Islands. Smaller colonies were established elsewhere as far off as Japan.

The Portuguese made no effort to occupy the mainland except for a few strategic ports, and even here easily defended offshore islands were preferred. Theirs was a trading empire, dependent on superior naval technology, and only adventurers and missionaries like Saint Francis Xavier penetrated far into the interior. The Indian Ocean was too large to be policed by the small number of Portuguese ships, and some Arab commerce continued. The Portuguese were, however, successful in deflecting a major portion of Oriental trade around Africa to Portugal and in causing concern among the Venetians, who saw the supply of spices coming into Alexandria diminish. For a brief period, the empire prospered, but in the end the strain was too much and other nations profited more from the farsighted and heroic efforts of the Portuguese.

Meanwhile, the Portuguese had not been neglecting the Atlantic. Voyages to Iceland, Greenland, and conceivably beyond had taken place, and Prince Henry the Navigator had established successful colonies in the Cape Verde Islands and in the Azores, far out in the Atlantic. Other voyages had been dispatched still farther to the west in search of various legendary islands. What they found, if anything, is not known, and although Portuguese historians are especially insistent that their countrymen had a pre-Columbian knowledge of Brazil, there is no positive evidence that land was discovered there before 1499. But because of Portuguese Atlantic explorations, it was not surprising that Christopher Columbus should turn first to John II when he sought support for a daring scheme.

COLUMBUS

Columbus was born in Genoa in 1451. His father was a wool-weaver, but his own interests turned toward the sea at an early age. In 1476, when sailing in a Genoese ship, he was wrecked off the Portuguese coast. He managed to swim ashore and found employment with his brother in Lisbon as a chart-maker. He traveled as far north as Iceland, as far west as the Azores, and southward along the African coast. He also established important connections by marrying a Portuguese noblewoman with whom he lived for a time in the Madeira Islands. With such experience and family connections, he hopefully asked King John II in 1484 to finance an attempt to reach Japan and the East by sailing westward across the Atlantic. The idea was not original with Columbus; what was new was a series of miscalculations that led him to believe that Japan was less than three thousand nautical miles from Europe, a much shorter distance than Da Gama traveled out of sight of land several years later when he rounded the Cape of Good Hope. John and his advisers were evidently better geographers than the boastful and demanding Columbus. They rejected his proposals, but sent two Portuguese captains to sail west of the Azores in search of more Atlantic islands.

Columbus next turned to the court of Ferdinand and Isabella in Spain, where the royal geographers were equally insistent that the distance to the East was greater than Columbus supposed—too great indeed to make the voyage feasible. But Isabella was a gambler, and Columbus had a powerful friend at court. On August 3, 1492, he sailed in three vessels from

Palos. Instead of going directly across the Atlantic, he headed for the Canary Islands, where the prevailing winds from the east carried him rapidly over the unknown waters. One of the Bahamas was sighted on October 12, just in time to quiet the growing fears of the crew. His success had been due to his choice of the southern route where the winds were favorable. Had he sailed from the Azores as the Portuguese did, he would have failed as they had so often done, because the winds are from the west in that part of the Atlantic. After discovering Cuba and establishing a temporary settlement on Santo Domingo (Hispaniola), Columbus took advantage of the favorable winds of the northern route to return by the Azores, never doubting that he had discovered islands in the vicinity of Japan, for he had gone a little farther west than he thought necessary to reach that country.

John II correctly believed that Columbus had only discovered some more Atlantic islands, but the more credulous Ferdinand and Isabella hailed him as their "Admiral of the Ocean Sea, Viceroy and Governor of the Islands that he hath discovered in the Indies." The Indians and the small amount of gold that he had found quelled any doubts, and he was given a fleet of seventeen vessels and fifteen hundred men to return to Hispaniola and establish a permanent colony to serve as a base for a renewed search for Japan and India.

At the same time, negotiations with Portugal were undertaken to settle the conflicting Portuguese and Spanish claims. By the Treaty of Tordesillas, 1494, Isabella and her descendants were given a right to all heathen lands to the west of a line drawn from pole to pole 360 leagues west of the Cape Verde Islands, and the Portuguese king was to have similar privileges to the east. Once more, John had seemingly turned his superior geographical knowledge to good advantage. He had gotten nearly the whole of the south Atlantic with the true water route to India as well as Brazil, while the Spanish were apparently limited to some Atlantic islands inhabited by savages.

For a generation, it appeared as though the Portuguese had gotten the best of the bargain. Columbus found a few more West Indian islands on his second voyage but could not discover China and India. His third and fourth voyages revealed the continental outline from Central America to Venezuela, but he persisted in his belief that this was the Malay Peninsula and that a strait leading to India lay farther to the south. His effort to rule a colony was such a conspicuous failure that he was relieved of his position as governor. He died wealthy but in relative obscurity in 1506.

MAGELLAN AND THE SOUTHERN PASSAGE

One reason for Columbus' growing obscurity was that in 1499, at a time when the wealth of the East continued to elude him, Vasco da Gama completed a voyage around Africa to India. Furthermore, from the beginning, expert geographers had been skeptical of his claims to have reached the East, and each new voyage added proof to their conviction. In 1497 and 1498, John Cabot, an Italian in the service of Henry VII of England, made voyages on the north Atlantic from Greenland and Labrador as far south as New England. His exploits revealed the existence of a vast coastline in this region at the same time that Columbus was sailing along the Venezuelan coast in his third voyage. The Portuguese visited Brazil in 1500, and other voyages began to reveal land in the intervening gaps. Recognition that a New World had been discovered became more general with the publication in 1507 of a number of letters by the Florentine Amerigo Vespucci (1451-1512). Vespucci made a number of voyages between 1497 and 1505 in which he saw much of the Central and South American coastlines and became convinced that a long continent sheltered the East from Atlantic exploration. His letters were so widely read that the New World which Columbus had unwittingly discovered was given his name.

Deflected by a long land barrier in the Atlantic between Europe and Asia, those who wanted to compete with the Portuguese for the wealth of the East set out to find a way around or through the undesirable land mass. A Portuguese noble named Ferdinand Magellan (1480?-1521), who had spent some time in the East visiting Malacca and probably the Moluccas, arrived at the conclusion that the East could be reached by sailing around South America. He could not hope that his own government would support his proposal because the African route was quite satisfactory and the southern part of South America probably lay within the area assigned to Spain by the Treaty of Tordesillas. He therefore turned to the Spanish, who were enviously watching the Portuguese profits and bewailing the meager returns that they had thus far received from Columbus' discoveries. Magellan's plan was based on sound geographical reasoning, but he made one serious mistake. He thought that his destination, the Moluccas and other spice islands, was close to the American continent. This view may seem surprising, since both the Pacific islands and America had been visited, but before the discovery of a way to determine longitude, it was not possible to determine the distance between two points in an east-west direction without actually sailing between them.

Magellan set sail with five ships and high expectations in September, 1519. On reaching Brazil, he followed the coast southward, looking for a waterway that led to the Pacific. Finally, after spending a severe winter in Patagonia, losing one ship, and quelling a serious mutiny, he discovered and successfully navigated the treacherous strait which bears his name. But instead of having the anticipated short voyage to the Moluccas, Magellan wandered across the vast uncharted Pacific for more than four months, dieting on leather and ship rats before he finally reached the Philippine Islands. There he became involved in a quarrel between two native chiefs and was killed.

This representation of the VITTORIA, *first ship to circumnavigate the world, is from Ortelius' Atlas of 1592. The* VITTORIA *is typical of those ships used by Magellan and other explorers during the first half of the sixteenth century. (Courtesy of Mariners Museum, Newport News, Virginia)*

The command now fell on Sebastian del Cano, who made his way to the Moluccas, picked up a cargo of cloves, and eluded the Portuguese in a long voyage across the Indian Ocean, around Africa, and back to Spain. The world had been circumnavigated and a new route had been found to the East, but the voyage had taken three years and only one of five ships had returned.

Undaunted by these difficulties, the Spanish sent a larger expedition to the Moluccas in 1525. This time the attempt was a dismal failure, and in 1529 Charles V sold his claims to the islands to the Portuguese. One reason for his decision was that the prevailing winds in the Pacific were to the west and therefore made the outward journey relatively easy but a return home by the same route impossible. The only known alternate route was to duplicate the Magellan expedition and continue around the world, a hazardous undertaking both because of the distance involved and because of the unfriendly attitude of the Portuguese. Only the discovery in the 1560's that favorable winds for a return voyage could be found by sailing far to the north before turning toward the American continent made possible the successful Spanish colonization of the Philippines. But before that time the Spanish had learned of the value of the New World and were content to devote the greater part of their energies to its exploitation.

THE SEARCH FOR A NORTHEAST PASSAGE

There were two remaining hopes of finding additional water routes to India: there might be a northwest passage around or through the North American continent, and there might be a northeast passage around the Eurasian land mass. Neither would seem a very good prospect to us today, but in the Renaissance the vast extent of the polar icecap was not suspected. Balboa's discovery in 1513 that the New World was only a few miles wide at Panama suggested that the continent was narrow and that one or more waterways could be found through it. The Eurasian solution was attractive because the Arctic coastline was thought to recede southward soon after Scandinavia was passed, leaving a clear passage to the China coast. Either route would be much shorter than that used by the Portuguese.

At first, the English preferred to search for the northeast passage, and a company was formed to finance an expedition. In 1553, Sir Hugh Willoughby set sail with three ships, but the vessels became separated. Sir Hugh with two ships attempted to winter on the Norwegian Arctic coast, where he and his crew died of cold and starvation. The third ship under Richard Chancellor reached a point during the summer where there was "no night at all, but a continual light and brightnesse of the sunne shining clearly upon the huge and mighty sea." Then, bearing southward, he made his way into the White Sea where he found the small village of Archangel. Here he learned for the first time of the rising state of Muscovy. On receiving an invitation from the czar, he journeyed overland to Moscow, where he wintered more comfortably than Willoughby and his companions.

At this time, Russia was shut off from the West by Poland, and its few trading contacts with the other European states were through the auspices of the Hanseatic League. Since the czar was then quarreling with the League, he welcomed an opportunity to establish trading relations with England. When Chancellor returned home, the Muscovy Company was formed to exploit this opportunity, but at the same time the English continued to search for a northeast passage. Their expeditions and several sponsored by the Dutch failed to get more than a few miles past the island of Novaya Zemlya, and the effort to find a commercially feasible northeast passage ceased by the close of the first decade of the seventeenth century.

THE SEARCH FOR A NORTHWEST PASSAGE

The search for a northwest passage covered a longer period and was more persistent. Both the English and the Portuguese explored the Labrador coast around 1500 in the hope of finding a waterway to the East, but Da Gama's success caused the Portuguese to abandon the effort. The French, however, joined in the contest, and in 1524 Giovanni da Verrazzano explored the coast from North Carolina to Newfoundland on the orders of Francis I, only to reach the conclusion that any passage must be farther to the north. Ten years later, Jacques Cartier renewed the search along the Labrador coast without success. On one of his voyages, however, Cartier went up the St. Lawrence River as far as the present city of Montreal, thereby laying the groundwork for further French exploration and colonization in this region.

The English became interested in finding a northwest passage during the last quarter of the sixteenth century. In 1576, Martin Frobisher explored the southern coast of Baffin Island. He entered Frobisher Bay feeling certain that the land on his right was Asia, that the land on his left was North America, and that the waters ahead led to China, a conclusion that would have been correct only if he had been sailing southward through the Bering Strait many thousands of miles away. Unfortunately, Eskimos captured five of his crew, leaving him so undermanned that he had to return home without discovering his error. His optimistic report and the belief that he had found gold led to the formation of the Company of Cathay, in which Queen Elizabeth herself invested. In 1577 Frobisher was sent back to find more gold and to proceed on to the Pacific. Needless to say, the second objective was forgotten and the intrepid Elizabethan returned laden with rocks that proved to be worthless.

John Davis made three voyages during the 1580's and succeeded in pushing up the strait which bears his name as far as the 72nd parallel of latitude, only to be halted by ice. For a time, the English were too occupied by a war with Spain to renew the effort, but in 1607 the Muscovy Company employed Henry Hudson to sail over the North Pole to China in the belief that there was an ice-free passage to the east of Greenland, a theory revived by the British Admiralty and Royal Society in 1773. The assignment was impossible, but Hudson did manage to get within nine degrees of the Pole near Spitsbergen. In 1608, he sought a northeast passage, but could not get beyond Novaya Zemlya.

With this failure, the Muscovy Company abandoned the effort, but Hudson remained as determined as ever to find a northern route to China. He entered the service of the Dutch East India Company, and after another vain attempt to find a northeast passage, he crossed the Atlantic and explored Delaware Bay and the Hudson River as far north as the site of Albany in the belief that his friend Captain John Smith was correct when he reported that there was a sea north of Virginia leading into the Pacific. This hope was doomed, but Hudson's efforts were the basis of the Dutch claim for New York. In 1610, Hudson went once more to the north, this time under English auspices. He passed through Hudson Strait and into Hudson Bay confident that the spacious sea extending south before him led to China. Unfortunately, it was already late in the season and he could not explore beyond James Bay before winter set in. By spring the crew was mutinous. Hudson, his young son, and the sick and faithful members of the crew were set adrift in a small open boat never to be seen again. The remainder of the sailors took the ship back to England where they escaped punishment, perhaps because of the hopeful news they brought.

Further explorations revealed that there was no passage to the East out of Hudson Bay. In 1616, William Baffin pushed up Baffin Bay between Greenland and the island that bears his name as far as the 78th parallel before being halted by ice. Turning eastward, he saw Lancaster Sound through which lay the only passage to the Pacific, but, losing hope because of the everpresent ice that separated the ship from shore, he returned home. Two minor attempts were made to find a passage in 1631, but enough geographical knowledge had been obtained to prove that there was no commercially feasible passage. A long and heroic search had come to a temporary end. The difficulties that the Renaissance explorers faced were fully revealed when it took Roald Amundsen from June 16, 1903, to August 31, 1906, to complete the first successful voyage from Europe to Nome, Alaska, through the northwest passage.

THE CONQUISTADORES

The long search for routes to the East bore more fruit than the repeated failures to find a passage suggest. Trade was established with Russia through Archangel, whales were found in the North Atlantic, and rich fisheries were revealed off the Newfoundland banks. The possibilities of getting timber suitable for masts in Newfoundland, fur from the Canadian and Hudson Bay Indians, brazilwood for dye from Brazil, and sugar and tobacco in the West Indies led many to appreciate the New World for itself. Because of the backward state of the Indian civilizations, however, these opportunities could not be exploited by establishing trading stations as the Portuguese had done in the East. Instead, it was necessary for the Europeans to found colonies and exploit the natural resources of America themselves. The English and French made unsuccessful efforts to establish settlements during the sixteenth century, and the Portuguese early began a small but successful colony in Brazil. But it was the search for gold and silver that led to most of the early exploration of the interior of the New World and to the establishment of the first large

European colonies. Since precious metals were found almost entirely in the region pre-empted by Spain, it was the Spanish who played the leading role in exploration and colonization during the Renaissance.

Within two decades after the discovery of America, the Spanish had successfully colonized Santo Domingo, Jamaica, Cuba, and Puerto Rico, where the raising of livestock, tobacco, and sugar was soon to become profitable. A little gold had been found, as well as some pearls, off the Venezuelan coast. The docile, backward Indians of the West Indies were rapidly exterminated by disease, war, and brutality, and by 1508 the estimated 250,000 Indians on Santo Domingo at the time of Columbus' arrival had been reduced to 60,000. Missionary protests became so strong that the crown decreed in 1512 that the Indians were free men who were to be converted to Christianity by persuasion, not force. Nevertheless, the *encomienda* system, in which Indian settlements were assigned to support individual Spaniards just as in Europe the manor had supported the knight, was widespread. Negro slaves from Africa, who were hardier than the Indians, were brought in to replace the aborigines and, in the end, dominated the ethnic makeup of most of the islands. Thus, a base was established for further exploration and colonization, just as Columbus had intended, but the colonies themselves did not yet pay for the expense they caused.

In 1509, settlers were sent to the Panama isthmus and to a point a little to the west on the Colombia coast. Warlike Indians, armed with poisoned arrows, forced the Spanish to abandon the Panama settlement. In the Colombia settlement, the situation became so desperate that a stowaway named Vasco Nuñez de Balboa, who was escaping his creditors in Santo Domingo, was able to seize power, move the colony to a better site at Darien, and send the royal-appointed governor back to Spain.

Balboa was the first of the *Conquistadores*, brutal men who had often learned the art of war fighting the Moors and the French but also courageous men who were not intimidated by the odds against them. Motivated by a desire for wealth, position, and adventure, they thought nothing of flaunting the authority of their distant king in expectation that the successful accomplishment of some bold and profitable enterprise would bring royal recognition. Balboa was more statesmanlike than most of his kind. He treated the Indians with a stern justice that won their cooperation in getting food and gold for the colony. From them, he learned of the Pacific, which he discovered in 1513 and on which he was preparing to sail westward in search of the wealth of the East when he was arrested and executed on orders of the crown-appointed Pedrarias. Pedrarias, a savage man who treated the Indians with great brutality, founded the city of Panama and extended his authority as far as Nicaragua.

Meanwhile, the Spanish had been hearing frequent reports from the Indians of the wealthy Aztec empire to the north. In 1519, the Cuban governor dispatched his secretary, Hernando Cortés (1485-1547), with

600 men to investigate, but Cortés immediately repudiated this tie and landed on the Mexican coast at Vera Cruz determined to create an independent position for himself. After dramatically burning his ships behind him, he pressed up the tall mountain passes into the interior.

The Aztecs were nomadic Indians from the north who had settled in 1325 on an island in a shallow lake in central Mexico. Here they had built the city of Tenochtitlán (Mexico City) and gradually conquered the surrounding cities and tribes to create an empire more populous than Castile. Their civilization, which had been adopted from their predecessors, was in some respects very advanced. They had an accurate solar calendar, a form of picture writing, a well-developed agriculture, and a complex social structure. Their capital of Tenochtitlán was probably as large as any city in Europe, and the Spanish themselves marveled at its stone temples and palaces, its clean streets, and its aqueduct that brought water from the neighboring hills. Yet these people had never invented the wheel, had no beast of burden, no money, and worked with stone tools. Without horses, steel weapons, and armor, they were no match for the Spanish, who had brought only thirteen muskets and a few small cannons with them. Even the numerical odds against the Spanish were not as heavy as it might seem because many Indians of other tribes hated their Aztec masters, who exacted tribute from them and sacrificed many of their number to their gods. Cortés won considerable assistance by exploiting this situation; nevertheless, his own ability and audacity were key factors in his final conquest of Tenochtitlán in 1521.

Once in control of the Aztec capital, Cortés tore down its heathen temples and palaces and built a new city. *Encomiendas* were established to support the individual Spanish warriors, Cortés assigning 23,000 heads of households to himself. Since the Indians had practiced communal farming and had been accustomed to paying tribute to the Aztecs, they docilely accepted the new arrangement. The Aztecs were rich in gold and silver, and Cortés was able to send enough treasure to Spain to be given the post of governor and captain-general of New Spain, as his conquest was called.

So great was the wealth found by Cortés in New Spain that every tale, however strange, was now believed. Many expeditions wandered across the southern part of what is now the United States, looking for the Seven Cities of Cibola, Golden Quivira, and a water passage connecting the Atlantic and the Pacific. While such efforts were doomed from the start, they added greatly to geographical knowledge and spread Spanish authority and culture throughout the southern half of the North American continent.

Equally romantic tales were spread concerning the southern continent, and one of them proved to be true. Amid the peaks of the Andes, on a plateau from 9,000 to 13,000 feet above sea level, stretched the 2,000-mile-long Inca empire. The Incas had no picture writing, but their culture was in most respects a little more sophisticated than Aztec culture. Human sacrifice had ceased, the social welfare of the people was more stressed, and the llama was used as a small beast of burden. Communication in their highly centralized monarchy was facilitated by a surprisingly good system of roads and bridges. Nevertheless, like Aztec culture, theirs was essentially Stone Age, and without steel they were no match for the Spanish.

Under the leadership of the sixty-one-year-old Francisco Pizarro (1470?-1541), the illiterate son of a peasant, about six hundred Spaniards launched an attack on the Inca empire in 1531. Fortunately for them, a struggle for the Inca crown was taking place at that time. Pizarro treacherously captured the victor, held him for a ransom set at a room full of golden dishes, and, when this sum was collected, strangled him. Pizarro had no virtue save courage and no wisdom save cunning. He soon quarreled with other members of his party, and a fratricidal struggle followed in which Pizarro was murdered in 1541. Order was not restored until the middle of the century. By this time, however, the Spanish had extended their authority over most of the western half of South America.

Meanwhile, Jiménez de Quesada conquered the relatively advanced Chibchas Indians who inhabited the plateau region of modern Colombia. He too found gold and precious stones to reward his tremendous effort.

The wealth found among the Incas and Chibchas encouraged even wilder rumors, and expedition after expedition set out to search for the lost city of the Incas and the fabulous El Dorado, the man of gold. El Dorado was thought to reside in the fabled city of Manoa somewhere in modern Venezuela. For a century, one attempt after another was made to find him. These expeditions were usually led by Spaniards, but German bankers were interested in the region and the famous Englishman Sir Walter Raleigh led several attempts, the last in 1617. Their great efforts led only to more geographical knowledge, for not even a small cache of gold or silver was found.

Meanwhile, Francisco de Orellana had crossed the Andes and floated down the Amazon River in 1541 in hopes of finding a rich government for himself. A few years earlier, other Spanish settlers had founded Buenos Aires and Asunción on the Rio de la Plata (River of Silver), where they were stimulated to further efforts by rumors of a silver empire deeper in the interior and of a lost city of the Caesars somewhere across the pampas. Thus, the quest for wealth and fame and the search for adventure had led the Conquistadores to explore the better part of two continents within two generations after Columbus had sighted the New World. Their achievements were without equal in European history, but by the middle of the sixteenth century their age was coming to an end and the crown was turning their conquests into a more law-abiding empire governed by great nobles and lawyers more obedient to its will.

THE IMPACT OF THE DISCOVERIES

GENERAL CONSIDERATIONS

The discoveries rank among the most influential events in history, but a distinction must be made between their influence during the Renaissance and their influence during later periods. Thus, although the discovery of the New World and the increased contact with Asian civilizations broadened the intellectual horizons and quickened the adventurous spirit of many Europeans, these contacts did not exercise a profound influence on European thought, literature, and art until the late seventeenth century.

The discoveries were also the first step in the expansion of European civilization to every point on the globe, but only in the late eighteenth and nineteenth centuries were the advanced Asian civilizations deeply affected. During the Renaissance, the Chinese regarded Europeans as barbarous. Asian Indians and Arabs considered them uncouth but dangerous interlopers who could not be ignored but who need not be imitated. Only the more primitive societies were rapidly changed. The backward American Indians of the West Indies and elsewhere were exterminated, and the Europeans simply transported themselves and their society, institutions, and culture into the regions these people had inhabited. The more advanced Indians of Mexico and Peru managed to survive the European onslaught, although in greatly reduced numbers, and it was only among them that Western civilization began to make significant inroads during the Renaissance.

The immediate impact of the discoveries on Europe was primarily economic. Such unknown or rare articles as potatoes, tobacco, corn, cocoa, chocolate, sugar, rice, coffee, and cotton began to be imported from the New World. The quantities involved were not great, however, during the Renaissance. During this period, the economic impact resulted primarily from the establishment of a water route to the Orient and from the influx of precious metals discovered in the New World.

THE INFLUENCE OF THE WATER ROUTE TO THE EAST

The eastern Mediterranean had been the cradle of civilization, and the sea as a whole had been the avenue of trade for the Roman world. Italy, jutting out into the center of this traffic, had profited most, but the entire region had been prosperous in comparison with the land-based states far removed from its shores. In 1500, Italian merchants were still buying spices in Egypt and Syria which the Arabs had brought from the Orient through the Red Sea and Persian Gulf. These spices and Italian manufactured goods were still being delivered throughout Europe, primarily under Italian auspices. Italian business and industrial techniques were acknowledged to be superior in nearly every respect, and despite the depression during the late Middle Ages, the people of Italy remained the most prosperous in Europe.

However, there were signs by 1500 that the days of Italian supremacy might be numbered. Other countries were adopting their business and industrial techniques. English wool cloth was making inroads into their markets. The south German banking firms were challenging their predominance in finance, making large sums in the revived mining industry, and profiting from the trade routes that went from Italy over the Alpine passes and through their streets to various points in northern Europe. In Augsburg, the taxable wealth of the inhabitants increased thirteenfold between 1470 and 1550. But it was when the Portuguese got control of the spice trade from the East that Italy received its most severe blow. Around 1500, the Venetians usually purchased about 1,750 tons of spices annually from eastern merchants for distribution in Europe, but in July, 1504, the Portuguese delivered 1,000 tons in Antwerp. By 1509, Venice did not have enough spices to justify sending galleys to England and Flanders, and although its spice trade revived somewhat for a time, the discovery of a water route had led to serious losses. Fortunately, Italian silks, glassware, and other luxury goods remained popular, and Italian bankers and merchants were so skillful that they remained fairly prosperous until the seventeenth century. Other Mediterranean countries also held their own because their olives, wines, and other products were in demand, but weak spots in the Mediterranean economy were constantly appearing and it became increasingly clear that the greatest progress was being made by the Atlantic powers.

Favored by their geographical position, those Atlantic seaboard countries and cities that were willing to permit economic freedom began to make significant progress during the Age of Discovery. England and the Netherlands moved forward rapidly, and Antwerp became the banking and commercial capital of Europe. Here foreign merchants were welcome, and the guild regulations rarely interfered with industry. Innovations and experiments were the order of the day, and businessmen were willing to risk losses in the hope of making fortunes. Here the Portuguese brought spices from the East to be exchanged for copper and silver from Germany and for cloth from many localities to take to India and Africa. Here the English brought their cloth to be sold and the French their wines, while the Baltic countries sent wheat to be exchanged for other products. Here the Habsburgs and others borrowed money at rates that varied between 11 and 31 per cent. The population of the city quickly swelled to 100,000 people whose search for homes created a real estate boom. Antwerp began to occupy a position comparable to London in the nineteenth century and New York in the twentieth.

In the neighboring cities of Flanders, where foreign merchants were restricted and the guilds sought to regulate industry, the cities declined, as did those of the Hanseatic League, where conservative, traditional policies

Antwerp and its harbor in the mid-sixteenth century from a contemporary engraving by Peter Schenk. (Courtesy of Mariners Museum, Newport News, Virginia)

were also followed. In spite of these depressed areas, the Atlantic was nearly the equal of the Mediterranean by the end of the Renaissance and, with the growth of the colonies in the New World, was to become the principal waterway of the eighteenth century, while the Mediterranean sank to secondary status as a carrier of trade. Thus, the center of European commerce slowly began to shift from Italy and the Mediterranean to the west.

THE PRICE REVOLUTION

The improvement of banking and credit facilities and their increased use outside of Italy stimulated a rise in prices, but by far the most important cause of their upward turn was the increase in the quantity of precious metals. Columbus had brought back some gold on his first voyage, and the south German and Hungarian mines had begun to yield silver a few years earlier, but the great increase began with the conquest of Mexico and Peru. After the Spaniards had seized all the precious metals in the possession of the Indians, they began to operate the silver mines themselves and produced far more than ever before. In the five-year period 1521-1525, 134,170 pesos of silver were brought to Spain; in 1526-1530, 1,038,437 pesos; in 1546-1550, 5,508,711 pesos; and in 1591-1595, a peak of 35,184,863 pesos was reached. Since money consisted of gold and silver at this time, paper money being unknown in Europe, the great increase in the quantity of precious metals had a decided inflationary effect. Prices in Spain were about four times as high in 1600 as they had been a century before.

The Spanish, in accordance with the economic theory of the day, made every effort to prevent the export of the gold and silver to foreign countries. At the same time, they attempted to carry on all the trade with the colonies. Both policies proved impossible. The farflung responsibilities of the Habsburgs made it necessary for them to support large armies abroad, and precious metals flowed out of Spain for this purpose. Furthermore, the Spanish proved unable to supply their colonies with all the goods they desired. In the end, foreigners had to be permitted to bring their less expensive wares to Seville for the Spanish and New World markets, but they could find little but money to take home in exchange. As a result, the precious metals from the New World slowly moved to other parts of Europe, causing prices to rise about two and one-half times in terms of silver, or four or five times in terms of money since most countries debased their currency by putting more base metal in their gold and silver coins.

It has often been pointed out that this inflationary period stimulated the economic revival and the growth of capitalism because prices rose much more rapidly than wages in every country except Spain, where there was a scarcity of labor. The resulting increase in profits gave the merchants and industrialists greater profit incentive as well as more capital to invest in large-scale economic enterprises. The upper bourgeoisie greatly improved its economic position, while the position of the wage laborer declined. The inflationary period of the Renaissance, therefore, had a significant economic effect, although it was only one factor in an economic revival that had already begun.

Capitalism had also existed before the price revolution, and a full-grown capitalistic spirit did not come until later. By *capitalism* is meant a system of private enterprise in which large sums are used in industrial, commercial, and banking enterprises designed to produce further profits for investment. The owner of capital and the worker are widely separated functionally, economically, and socially. A master in a cobbler's guild would not be a capitalist because of his small investment and his close contact with his journeymen and apprentices, but the Medici bank would be a capitalistic enterprise. By this definition, it becomes apparent that capitalism had existed in the Middle Ages but that it became increasingly important during the price revolution.

By the term *capitalistic spirit* is meant something more than the pursuit of material gain, a goal that is probably inherent in every human being, although it is often suppressed by religious teaching and social mores. Rather, the capitalistic spirit involves the belief that the quest for wealth is both justifiable and socially desirable, an idea that did not become common even in the most advanced economies until the eighteenth century. The hard-headed Italian businessman Francesco Datini might write, "In the name of God and of profit" on the first page of his business ledgers, but in his will he was careful to set aside 1,500 florins "about which my executors are well-informed" to be distributed by them upon the advice of doctors of theology and canon law "for the good of Francesco's soul." What more proof is needed to show that his lifelong pursuit of gain, probably involving usury and unethical practices, was troubling his conscience.

THE FUGGERS

Perhaps no family illustrates better the origins of the economic revival and the growth of capitalistic enterprises than the Fuggers. The first Fugger about whom anything is known was Hans, who left a small village where he had worked as a weaver about 1380 and migrated to Augsburg to ply his trade. Soon he had enough capital to import raw cotton from Venice and to export the finished cloth. He left two sons, both of whom were given coats of arms signifying the growing prominence of the family. One son eventually went bankrupt, but Jacob I, the second son, died in 1469 after a prosperous career in which he traded in Venetian spices, silk, and woolen cloth as well as cotton. He left a widow with eleven young children, but she was able to operate the business successfully until the three sons who survived were old enough to manage the company themselves.

It was to the youngest of seven brothers, Jacob II, known as the Rich, that the family owed its rise to a dominant financial position. He was born in 1459 and was intended for the priesthood, but he reluctantly abandoned his clerical studies when the death of four of his older brothers made it necessary for him to help carry on the family business. He worked for a few years in Venice to learn accounting and other Italian commercial practices. When he returned to Augsburg, his recognized ability soon won for him the acknowledged position as leader of the family partnership. This position was strengthened on the death of his two brothers in 1506 and 1510, for although he admitted his nephews to the partnership, he ruled them with an iron hand.

Jacob II and his brothers owed their great wealth to their decision to transfer more and more capital from trade to mining. They made loans to the Habsburg Duke of Tyrol that were guaranteed by his copper and silver mines. Soon they became engaged in mining in Hungary as well and nearly succeeded in getting a monopoly on copper mining, smelting, and rolling. The close ties with the Habsburgs continued, and Charles V borrowed 543,-000 gold gulden from them to bribe the electors to name him emperor. Jacob Fugger never hesitated to remind his imperial majesty of this favor when he desired further concessions. As bankers, the Fuggers handled part of the Habsburg loans, financial transfers, and exchange, as well as the transfer of papal money from Germany to Rome. They held a mortgage on the crown estates in Spain and participated to a small degree in the Spanish and Portuguese voyages of trade and exploration. Their branch at Antwerp was so active that it contributed considerably to the rise of that city, and their active agents in the important commercial centers of Europe wrote regular newsletters to Augsburg to keep them acquainted with the affairs of the business world.

The results were fantastic. In 1494, the three brothers had a capital of 54,385 gold gulden; by 1517, it had become 269,091, a handsome increase of 15 per cent per annum; and by 1527, two years after Jacob's death, it had passed the two million mark as a result of profits that averaged about 50 per cent per annum. The peak of the family fortune was achieved in 1546, when its capital reached 5,000,000. The bulk of this money was invested in banking, merchant, and mining enterprises, but Jacob bought several estates belonging to nobles at a total cost of 92,000 gulden and became a count. The purchase of landed estates by wealthy burghers was commonplace during the Renaissance and, except in the south German and northern Italian cities where the status of merchant bore no stigma, was usually accompanied by the abandonment of trade, residence in the country, and gradual acceptance by the local nobility. Jacob, however, who loved business too much ever to leave it, owned a fine palace in Augsburg and, with his brothers, constructed a model development in his native city of 106 dwellings to house his "fellow citizens who live righteously, but are beset by poverty."

This development still stands today as a reminder of the Fuggers' bourgeois status, but if Jacob was so proud to be a citizen of Augsburg, why did he purchase landed estates when they netted him little more than 3 per cent on his investment? The answer seems to lie partly in the prestige they brought him, a valuable asset in his business dealings throughout Europe, and partly in their greater security. If land yielded smaller returns than banking, it was also a safer investment because it was not dependent on the financial solvency of the Renaissance monarchs. Once more, Jacob's foresight becomes evident. The Spanish Habsburgs defaulted in their payments in 1557, 1575, and 1607, causing the Fuggers to lose a total of 9,000,000 gulden and in the end ruining their business. However, Jacob's heirs were able to retire to their estates and live comfortably as imperial counts.

THE RECONSTRUCTION OF THE ARISTOCRACY

For a long time, most historians thought that the economic revival during the Renaissance and the impact of the discoveries led to the triumph of the middle class. The Renaissance monarchs and the middle class, it was assumed, governed the various states to their mutual advantage. Nothing, it now seems, was further from the truth. The Medicis, Fuggers, and other successful members of the middle class joined the aristocracy, and the aristocrats, both old and new, managed to dominate society just as they had done in the Middle Ages, although the techniques they used were somewhat different.

THE NUMERICAL RECONSTRUCTION

Wars, rebellions, plagues, and natural attrition reduced the ranks of the nobility in Western Europe during the late Middle Ages, and the first one or two Renaissance monarchs in each country further decimated their number. Although these kings were not hostile to the nobility as a whole, they were strongly opposed to any usurpation of their royal prerogatives or any violation of their laws. Their opponents included those great nobles who wanted to establish independent or semi-independent principalities for themselves and those minor nobles who had become robber barons, earning a comfortable, though hazardous, livelihood by pillaging merchants, travelers, and peasants. Once order was restored, however, the Renaissance monarchs, who had neither an adequate army nor an adequate bureaucracy, found it advisable to win the support of their more powerful subjects by making them great nobles. Titles were also given to those who had served them faithfully and to their relatives and favorites. The ranks of the lesser nobility were replenished by merchants, lawyers, and even peasants who bought noble estates and began to live nobly. By the dawn of the sixteenth century a new aristocracy was emerging, composed of both the descendants of the feudal nobility and newly ennobled members of other classes.

In England, the aristocracy was divided legally into the peerage, whose members sat in the House of Lords, and the gentry, who were styled knights, esquires, and gentlemen. Economically and socially, no exact distinction can be made between the two, because both drew their income primarily from landed estates and mixed socially at court and in the counties. Younger sons of peers usually joined the ranks of the gentry, since only the eldest son inherited the father's title. On the other hand, the more fortunate members of the gentry could aspire to receiving a title from the king. The two groups of the aristocracy often intermarried, and both had coats of arms. Earls had greater prestige than gentlemen and their estates were usually much larger, but they were more the leaders of a class than members of a different order in society.

When Henry VII died, there was only one duke, one marquis, and a few minor peers left in the kingdom. Henry VIII created only seven new peers during the first two decades of his reign, but between 1530 and his death in 1547 he created eighteen more. Edward and Mary added fifteen during their brief reigns, so that by the time Elizabeth came to the throne in 1558 a group of Tudor peers had come into being to replace those of the Middle Ages. Some of the new peers were members or friends of the royal family, but most of them were elevated either as a reward for faithful service to the crown or to ensure future loyalty. Usually, they had belonged to the gentry, but a few, like Thomas Cromwell, advanced from the lower walks of life to an earldom; and frequently one generation was enough for a family to reach the ranks of the gentry, and a second to win a place in the peerage.

No royal act was necessary to join the ranks of the gentry; it was sufficient to buy an estate, get a coat of arms, and adopt the manners and mores of the country gentleman. For a generation or so, the new owner might be regarded as a parvenu, but in the end he was accepted. Because the estate of a gentleman was left to his eldest son, younger sons often went to sea or to the towns where they became merchants and lawyers. If successful, they or their descendants frequently bought new estates and became country gentlemen once more. As a result, the lower ranks of the gentry blurred with the more successful members of the legal and mercantile professions just as its upper ranks blurred with the peerage. Aristocratic as England most assuredly was, there was considerable social mobility during the Renaissance. Nearly everyone accepted the hierarchical conception of society, but this hierarchy depended more on the present status of the individual than on birth.

In France, the social and economic equivalent of the English gentry were the seigneurs, or lords of the manor, who were classified as nobles. Above them was a middle nobility consisting of counts, marquises, and others, who may be equated with the lesser members of the English House of Lords. Above them were the dukes and peers of the realm, and still higher were the relatives of the royal family who were referred to as princes of the blood.

Elevation to the middle and higher nobility depended on the favor of the kings, and their criteria for advancement were much the same as the Tudors', except that the percentage of those who won advancement through distinguished service was smaller while the percentage of those who moved forward with little claim for reward other than the friendship of the king was larger. At the beginning of the sixteenth century, there were only five lay peers in France, but between 1515 and 1600 twenty-eight new peerages were created. Elevation to the ranks of the middle nobility was even more generously granted, and in his fifteen-year reign Henry III alone created fifty-five counties, marquisates, duchies, and principalities. These titles were not empty dignities; they gave their holders special privileges and their feudal courts great importance. Indeed, the privileges granted to the younger sons of the kings in the lands set aside for their support were comparable to those that King John gave to the first Valois Duke of Burgundy. France was fortunate that none of these sons had children, or new Charles the Bolds might have arisen to plague the crown.

Movement into the lower nobility could come through royal action, but by far the most frequent method was for the merchant or lawyer to purchase a fief and adopt the manners and ways of the rural seigneur. The process might have been a little more difficult than in England because the transition involved a change in legal status, but it was nevertheless commonplace. Indeed, if there had not been a considerable amount of social mobility, the nobility would have slowly disappeared through normal attrition. In the county of Forez, there were 215 noble families in the thirteenth century, only five of which survived until the Revolution of 1789. Here, and presumably elsewhere, the average duration of a noble line was from three to six generations.

A nobility of royal officeholders also emerged in France during the late Middle Ages and Renaissance, for long service in the upper bureaucracy and higher law courts brought ennoblement. Thus, there was a functional as well as a hierarchical division within the ranks of the French nobility, while in England no distinction was made between the gentleman who held office and the one who lived on his estates. However, this difference should not be exaggerated, for many members of the seigneurial nobility became royal officials, while nearly all the officeholding nobility purchased estates. Intermarriage was frequent, and it was not until the close of the Renaissance that a sharp distinction developed between the two types of nobles, one becoming known as nobles of the sword and the other as nobles of the robe.

The Spanish kings also tried to win support by creating great nobles. When Ferdinand and Isabella came to the throne, there were only seven dukes in Castile, but during their reign the number was increased to fifteen, and under Charles V to a still higher figure. The lesser nobles, or *hidalgos,* were quite numerous in Castile, where they made up one-seventh of the population. Because they already resided in the towns in many instances, there was less movement back and forth between the urban and rural population except near a few important trading centers such as Seville, where the merchants often bought estates in the surrounding countryside.

The emperor was in a less fortunate position than the rulers in the west. When a ducal line became extinct, he was usually forced to recognize a member of a collateral line as successor, rather than claiming that the duchy had reverted to the crown. As a result, the principalities remained intact, and except in the north Italian parts of the Empire, few new territorial princes were created. However, within the German principalities the more prominent nobles were elevated to higher ranks. There was no distinction between nobles who lived on their estates and those who served in the bureaucracy, as there was in France, but movement from the bourgeoisie to the nobility by the purchase of estates appears to have been more difficult than elsewhere because of the nobles' opposition to new-comers.

In Italy, new duchies were created, such as Milan and Florence, while older ones continued to exist. In each, there was an upper nobility that spent considerable time at court and a lower nobility that inhabited the towns and countryside. Social mobility was greater than elsewhere, for merchants and even peasants could become dukes, nobles could engage in trade, and burghers could find means to become nobles if they de-sired.

Thus, the Renaissance saw the numerical restoration of the greater and lesser nobility through the survival of some persons born to these ranks and through the advancement of those belonging to lesser posi-tions in society. More significant, the nobility also regained its power dur-ing this period.

THE ECONOMIC POSITION OF THE ARISTOCRACY

At one time, it was believed that the aristocracy declined economi-cally during the Renaissance because prices rose faster than incomes from landed estates. Prices in general did increase four- or five-fold, but the rapid growth in population caused food prices to rise even faster than other prices. The critical question was who profited most, the peasants or the lord of the manor, and this depended on how the land was held. Where the feudal dues were still paid in kind, the lord could profit by selling the goods received at inflated prices. If payment was in money, as was cus-tomary except in the more backward regions, his profits depended on how much land he held. If he owned a large demesne, he could exploit it him-self or divide it among peasant farmers. These peasants worked as share-croppers or as tenants with short-term leases that were periodically raised as the land-hungry farmers drove up the price of land rents faster than prices in general.

Only where the noble's demesne was small and the peasants paid him fixed monetary rent was he in trouble. But even here he could hope to increase his income by better management of his demesne or by getting more land. Following the Black Death, a large amount of land ceased to be cultivated, but it and other wastelands were now brought under cultiva-tion. By building dikes, the Netherlands managed to claim 110,000 acres from the North Sea between 1565 and 1615. In England, some aristocrats took possession of the village pastures that had been held in common, but these enclosures were much less frequent than the literature of the day suggests, and most kings tried to protect the peasants. Some nobles pur-chased peasant holdings and other rights, and when church lands were put on sale during the Reformation, they bought as much as they could. This last opportunity was not limited to Protestant countries. In Catholic France and in some other places, church land was sold—theoretically, at least, to help to pay for wars against the religious minority. As a result, many nobles, especially those east of the Elbe River, prospered from their estates as never before. Here, and to a lesser extent elsewhere, the lord of the manor was becoming a landlord or estate manager, and the old reciprocal relation of mutual service and responsibility between noble and peasant declined.

Some nobles sought additional income from business enterprises. Except in Italy, there was a strong taboo against nobles engaging in small-scale industry and trade, but mining, glassmaking, international trade, colonization, and other large-scale enterprises were acceptable. Some of the most aggressive businessmen in Tudor England were peers of the realm, and, though much less frequently, the continental nobility followed their example. Other nobles looked to royal favor for advancement. At the disposal of the king were appointments in the Church, the army, and the bureaucracy. Perhaps the most rapid of all ways to wealth was through court influence, and those who wanted to increase or recoup their fortunes were often inclined to make use of it.

It is true that some nobles were so improvident or so incompetent that their fortunes sank. Other noble families became extinct either because they had no children or because they had so many that they ruined their eldest son's chances by providing too generously for their other offspring. On the continent, younger sons generally had some legal rights to the family estate, and in England, where primogeniture was more fully practiced, fond fathers often gave them generous cash settlements. But when a noble had to sell his estate, a fellow noble was given a chance to add to his lands. Or if the buyer was a merchant, then a new noble family was about to rise. It is therefore probable that in the Renaissance the nobility as a whole became more wealthy, a conclusion that is supported by the numerous châteaux and manor houses that they built and by the more elegant way of life that they adopted.

The burghers' desire to purchase an estate and join the ranks of the aristocracy weakened the middle class by depriving it of its ablest members. By putting the profits of business into agriculture rather than reinvesting it in urban activities, the burghers slowed the expansion of trade and industry. Once in the country, the burgher quickly adopted the manners and mores of the class he was joining; as a parvenu, he dared not do otherwise. Indeed, the Renaissance, far from marking a general rise of the middle class, saw its decline in some localities. The position of many towns in central Europe and most towns in eastern Europe actually deteriorated. In Italy and Spain, the nobility often replaced the middle class as the controlling force in municipal government, while in France royal officials and lawyers often won election to municipal office.

155

This drawing (c. 1485-88) by Leonardo da Vinci shows workmen raising a large cannon into position. Leonardo's interests as an artist and as an engineer are reflected both by the human figures in motion and by the crane, which facilitates their work. The drawing is in Windsor Castle, England. (By gracious permission of Her Majesty Queen Elizabeth the Second)

THE MILITARY POWER OF THE ARISTOCRACY

It has been suggested that the aristocracy declined militarily during the Renaissance because of the invention of gunpowder, the weakening of the lord-vassal relation, and the establishment of permanent royal armies. Each of these arguments is subject to question. It was not until near the middle of the sixteenth century that firearms became superior to the bow, and by then the armor of the knight was so strengthened that only a direct hit at a fairly close range was fatal. Although cannons, throwing solid metal balls, could certainly batter down the walls of a medieval castle, new methods of fortification were quickly developed. Walls were lowered and made thicker, angular bastions were built that projected out from the walls to provide flanking fire, and moats were dug deeper to prevent the walls from being mined. While the assailants were trying to batter down the wall, the garrison built dirt embankments immediately to the rear, so that if a break were made in the outer wall, there would be a new one to take its place. So great were the improvements in the knowledge of fortification that pitched battles were rare after 1525 and siege warfare replaced the war of movement that had characterized the fifteenth century. From the early sixteenth century until near the close of the eighteenth century, there were many instances of cities and fortresses withstanding the assault of large armies for months. The cannon did not make the castle obsolete; it only made modernization necessary.

Yet when the noble decided to rebuild his home, he did not turn to the new style of fortification; he sought comfort instead. Glass windows were placed in the interior courtyard to admit more light, and moats became ponds surrounded by flowers. The towers and turrets were maintained only for decorative purposes and to indicate the noble status of the owner, and finally disappeared altogether. By the middle of the sixteenth century, the castle had been replaced, not by the fortress but by the pleasure palace or manor house where the owner could live comfortably and entertain his friends. After the Renaissance monarchs had restored order, the nobles had no further need to fortify their homes against marauding bands or antagonistic neighbors, and they had other means to check any aggressive designs the king might have.

The medieval lord-vassal relation declined slowly during the Renaissance, although throughout the period kings summoned the feudal levy in time of emergency and great nobles called on their vassals for support when they revolted. But beside the lord-vassal relation there emerged a patron-client relation that has sometimes been referred to as "the new feudalism." A member of the lesser nobility, ambitious for advancement, often entered the service of a great lord. He might begin with a minor post in the lord's household or as a man-at-arms in the royal troops he commanded, but, if he proved able and loyal, he could aspire to an important household position, the captaincy of a château, or, through the favor of

This seventeenth-century drawing shows the low-walled angular bastions that could withstand long sieges. Within the enclosure a palace and gardens are designed. Most palace architects, however, had long since abandoned any pretense of providing for defense against assault. (Bettmann Archive)

his patron, a position at court or in the royal bureaucracy. Other nobles preferred to reside at home but dispatched their sons to their patron's château to serve as pages and to receive their education. The patron in return either provided for the pages when they reached manhood or used his influence with the king to get them positions in the Church, the army, or the bureaucracy. When a patron summoned his clients to accompany him into battle, on a journey to court, or for some other service, he expected them to come clad in his livery, or at least his device, and with a suitable number of followers according to their rank. If a client was wanted for some crime, the patron was expected to use every means possible to prevent his being punished.

This system was often formalized by a written oath called an indenture, in which the client swore to serve his patron faithfully. In the early Renaissance, the patron sometimes paid his client a regular salary, but by the sixteenth century the more common practice was for the patron to reward his client by using his influence on his behalf and to pay him only when unusual services were performed. In some respects, the new feudalism was more dangerous to the crown than the old. Under the old system,

This view of the Château Chenonceau in the Loire Valley of France shows the transition from the medieval keep to the Renaissance palace. In the center the old keep still stands with its machicolation just below the windows. Through these openings the defenders poured hot liquids and shot projectiles at those who attempted to scale the walls. On the left is a pleasure palace built in the early sixteenth century. Note that the towers and machicolation have become ornaments showing the noble status of the owner. (Bettmann Archive)

the lord was limited in the number of his vassals by the number of his fiefs or, in the case of the money fief, by the size of his treasury. Under the new feudalism, neither fiefs nor specific payments were required, and the number of clients a lord had was limited only by his prestige, influence, and the popularity of his cause.

A few kings opposed the new feudalism because of the patron's obligations to protect his turbulent clients from justice, and it was largely to mitigate this evil that the Tudors employed the Star Chamber rather than local justice officials, who were more easily cowed by the great patrons. Nevertheless, the kings found that if they made the great patrons their own clients, they could, through them, maintain their influence throughout the aristocracy. The result was that the king awarded favors to the great nobles, who shared them with their clients, and in time of war the king relied on his clients and his clients' clients just as his predecessors had relied on their vassals and their vassals' vassals.

The system worked very well so long as the king was strong, but when there was a minority or a weak ruler, and one faction was given all the royal patronage, the other factions were very likely to revolt. At such times, the new feudalism became extremely dangerous, because the great nobles who commanded the royal companies often appointed their clients and vassals to key subordinate positions. This tie, taken with the normal loyalty and obedience of a soldier to his captain, caused royal troops to follow their noble commanders into rebellion on many occasions.

The nobles were therefore able to maintain their military power, not only because they had their vassals, their clients, and the economic capability to hire some mercenary troops, but also because they exercised considerable authority in the royal army itself.

THE POLITICAL POWER OF THE ARISTOCRACY

It has been suggested that the aristocracy declined politically during the Renaissance because kings gave key governmental posts to the lesser nobility and to men of bourgeois extraction, but this argument is open to debate. Although the early Renaissance monarchs included few great nobles in their councils, by 1550 this practice was changing and in England, France, and other countries great nobles were among the most important advisers of the king. When great fiefs had escheated to the crown and when additional territories were won through dynastic marriages, leading nobles were named to govern them in the king's name. The practice of having governors soon spread to the older portions of the royal domain, thereby putting the responsibility for local government largely in the hands of the nobles. In England and many of the German states, the gentry and lesser nobility held many administrative posts. English justices of the peace, chosen from the gentry, were charged with every type of law enforcement in the various localities, and the German nobles, especially those east of the Elbe, performed similar duties on their estates. In France, a specially created officeholding nobility held most of the key legal and administrative positions at Paris and in the country. Their partial separation from the seigneurial nobility weakened the aristocracy as a whole, but when these two classes cooperated, their position could not be challenged.

Collectively, the great nobles with their important posts and their numerous clients throughout the various branches of government were the dominant force in the Renaissance monarchy. In practice, they were jealous of each other and stood united against the crown only if their privileges were threatened. Furthermore, they had to contend with their own clients and the collective power of the lesser nobility. A great noble who could not or would not reward a client was likely to lose his services to another lord. To prevent this from happening, patrons sometimes rebelled in the hope that the king would buy their submission with money and offices for themselves and their clients. Thus the client, usually of the lesser nobility, could influence the actions of his patron just as his patron could influence the policy of the greatest patron of them all, the king.

Azay-le-Rideau, perhaps the most beautiful of the early sixteenth-century pleasure palaces in the Loire Valley. (Ewing Galloway)

More serious was the power wielded by the lesser nobility through representative assemblies, which they generally dominated in spite of the presence of the clergy and towns. In England, the gentry made up the bulk of the House of Commons because most of the towns were persuaded to choose their deputies from their number. Slowly, the Commons grew in importance, and from the middle of the sixteenth century it was often able to maintain its position when its opinion conflicted with the crown or the House of Lords. In the Empire, the nobles played an important role in the estates of the various principalities. In those parts of France where the king looked to the provincial estates to vote taxes to support the government and the governor looked in the same direction for his salary, the three estates had a weapon that could be used to win consideration for their interests. The Castilian nobles displayed so little interest in the cortes that they gradually ceased to be summoned as a class, but they were nevertheless successful in shifting most of the burden of taxation to the non-noble classes. Furthermore, the minor nobles usually represented the

During the Renaissance, aristocratic fashions constantly changed just as do the styles worn by the average American today. Note that all the styles represented here seem to stress that the wearer did no manual labor. (Charles Phelps Cushing)

towns in the cortes just as the English gentry did their municipalities.

Thus, the Renaissance witnessed the reconstruction of the aristocracy on a somewhat different basis in the economic, military, and political spheres. It is now necessary to consider how well the members of this aristocracy were educated for their self-appointed task and what ideas and social mores governed their conduct.

THE EDUCATION OF THE ARISTOCRACY

During the late Middle Ages and early Renaissance, the typical minor noble's son was sent to the château of a great noble patron to serve as a page and to receive an education. The process began when the lad was about seven and ended when he was about twenty. The aims of this education were eminently practical, answering the needs of the day. The academic training consisted primarily of learning to read and write, for illiteracy had become rare among the nobility. The social graces were emphasized, including music, dancing, poetry, and the art of courtly love, as well as riding and hunting. Honor, courage, loyalty, truth, and courtesy were the moral traits sought, and the art of warfare was stressed as pre-professional training, for the ultimate goal was knighthood.

With the restoration of order by the Renaissance monarchs, warfare ceased to be so exclusive an occupation for the noble and greater demands were placed on administrative and judicial competence. In view of these demands, the aristocracy was compelled to put more stress on academic matters or to abdicate its role in government. Jean de Lannoy, an important noble in the French-speaking part of Flanders, heralded the new age when he wrote a letter in 1465 directing the method to be used in the

1586

1586

1625

1633

education of his newborn son and prospective heir. Instead of receiving all his training in a noble household, Lannoy said that his son was to be sent to one of the Latin schools at Louvain, Cologne, or Paris where he was to learn Latin and participate in the school disputations. At the same time, he was to study German from a priest who was to accompany him. Books on ethics, economics, and especially politics were recommended. Lannoy's reason for this change in emphasis was that:

> Those who have learned and retained much, and who have the greatest desire to learn and know, attain great good, honor, and riches. . . . This has often caused me deep displeasure not for envy of them, but, because of my simplicity and slight knowledge and because I was never put to school. I therefore know and can know nothing. I realize that this chance is for me lost and gone, never to be recovered, for I do not see or expect any remedy as to Latin or other studies. No day passes that I do not regret this, and especially when I find myself in the council of the king or of the Duke of Burgundy, and I know not nor dare not to speak my opinion after the learned, eloquent legists and ystoryens who have spoken before me. For I do not know the order or manner of speaking and can say nothing, but "Master John or Master Peter has spoken well, and I am of his opinion." Whence I have often felt deep shame and humiliation in my heart.[1]

This theme was repeated many times during the Renaissance.

The English aristocrats clearly followed Lannoy's precepts. By the middle of the sixteenth century, they were sending their sons to such schools as Eton and Winchester and to the universities of Oxford and Cambridge in such numbers that there were complaints that those studying for the clergy and the sons of the poor were being crowded out. Others studied at the Inns of Court where English lawyers were trained, not with the idea of practicing law, but rather to be better qualified to serve as justices of the peace and in other administrative positions. Thirty-three per cent of the deputies serving in the House of Commons in 1563 had received some

[1] Quoted by Jack H. Hexter, *Reappraisals in History* (London: Longmans, Green and Co., 1961), p. 63.

education at the universities, the Inns of Court, or both. By 1584, the percentage had increased to forty-eight, and by 1593 to fifty-four. Other aristocrats studied with tutors and often traveled abroad under their guidance. Thus, the English aristocracy responded to the needs of the day with surprising energy, and its education, ability, and conscientiousness enabled it to dominate the country well into the nineteenth century.

The education of the French aristocracy seems to have suffered because of the growing division between the seigneurial and officeholding nobility. The aristocrat who wanted to be a judge or to hold a local administrative post went to the university to study law, but one who looked forward to a life in the army or on his estate was frequently educated as a page in a great noble's household as before. By combining the roles of soldier, estate manager, justice of the peace, and member of Parliament, the English had secured a well-educated aristocracy. By separating them, the French achieved a well-educated aristocratic bureaucracy and a relatively poorly educated seigneurial nobility, although there were individual exceptions to this rule. But in England, France, Spain, and the Empire, the Renaissance aristocracy was better educated than its medieval predecessor to meet the responsibilities that its pre-eminent position in society demanded, and kings found it less necessary than during the Middle Ages to appoint ecclesiastics to posts requiring a good education.

The changing pattern of aristocratic education is reflected by the change in what nobles read. The early publications of the printing press stressed the romances of chivalry more than any other subject except religious literature, and the tales of King Arthur's Round Table remained popular throughout the Renaissance. By the mid-sixteenth century, however, many nobles were also reading the classics, though often in translation, and books on history and politics were increasing in popularity. The Italian courts, once bourgeois but now aristocratic, adopted the romances of chivalry, making them more acceptable to their tastes by recasting them in romantic poetry.

Many monarchs took an interest in education and gathered around them the more talented members of the aristocracy and a few professional scholars and artists. The most famous of these courtly societies were in Italy, and it was here that Count Baldassare Castiglione (1478-1529) wrote *The Courtier,* which was to become a guide for aristocratic manners and education. Castiglione wrote that the courtier should be trained in arms but that he should also have a liberal education. Classical languages and literature should be studied, but this was not enough, for the ideal courtier should be able to write both prose and poetry and should also be a musician and something of an artist. The code of the knight was to be replaced by that of the gentleman; specifically, good manners were to be stressed rather than courtly love. Gravity, moderation, and self-control were highly desirable, and loudness and conspicuousness were to be avoided. Thus, the Renaissance aristocrat was to become a gentleman of universal attainments. Castiglione suggested that these objectives could be obtained by those who were not of noble birth, but he was too much a man of his age not to argue for the value of ancestry.

Castiglione's book was translated into many languages and frequently reprinted. Few could achieve the ideals he set, but many strove to do so and a surprisingly large number succeeded. The appearance of courtly society should not be interpreted as marking the beginning of the foppish courtier, for the Renaissance courtier was a man of responsibility and solid worth. One has only to think of Sir Walter Raleigh (1552-1618), that tall, handsome Englishman who was supposed to have won Queen Elizabeth's attention by spreading his velvet cloak over a mud puddle that she wanted to cross. This one-time student at Oxford was not only an accomplished courtier, poet, and historian; he was also a soldier, sailor, and explorer and one of the foremost advocates of the English colonization of America. He was too proud, haughty, and overdressed to meet Castiglione's dictum on these scores and such traits were to make many enemies, but men of his sterling qualities were not uncommon among the reconstructed aristocracy of the Renaissance.

5/ The Cultural
and Religious Renaissance

HISTORIANS of the medieval era devote much of their time to proving that humanism in literature and naturalism in art existed in the Middle Ages and that the period known as the Renaissance did not see a rebirth but only the continued growth of what had begun earlier. They have offered considerable evidence to support their point of view, but one basic fact remains undisputed. The intellectuals of the fifteenth and sixteenth centuries *thought* that they were doing something new, and they themselves first used the word "Renaissance" to describe their era. To them, the ancient world was a golden age of literature and art and the Middle Ages were a period of barbarism and darkness. To them, there began with Giotto and Petrarch an artistic and literary Renaissance in which sound learning and naturalistic art once more came into being. Cola di Rienzi sought a political rebirth in the restoration of the Roman republic, and Machiavelli dreamed of a rebirth of the civic virtues of the earlier age.

Of the several ideas of rebirth, the concept of a *spiritual* rebirth was the oldest and strongest. This concept was to be found in the Bible and in the teachings of the primitive Christians. It had reappeared during the Middle Ages and again during the Renaissance, when it was constantly charged that scholastic philosophy had destroyed religious piety and corrupted the Christian religion. Momentarily optimistic about the revival of piety, Erasmus wrote Pope Leo X in 1517 that: "This our age,—which bids fair to be an age of gold, if ever such there was,—wherein I see, under your happy auspices and by your holy counsels, three of the chief blessings of humanity are about to be restored to her. I mean, first that truly Christian piety, which has in many ways fallen into decay, secondly, learning of the best sort . . . , hitherto partly neglected and partly corrupted, and thirdly, the public and lasting concord of Christendom, the source and parent of Piety and Erudition." [1]

The idea of a rebirth in every artistic and cultural discipline except music appeared first in Italy. During the high Middle Ages, the Italians had lagged behind the north in every field except economics. Latin humanism, several vernacular literary forms, scholastic philosophy, Aristotelian thought, and Gothic art were not introduced into Italy from the north until near the close of the thirteenth century. This sudden impact of so much that was new gave the Italians a sense of breaking with the medieval world as they had known it in their own country, while in the north, where these forms and ideas had been maturing slowly for several centuries, there was little consciousness of change.

The fact that the Italians thought that they were witnessing a rebirth was of immense psychological importance. The medieval man had not been conscious of belonging to a historical epoch different from that of Rome and therefore had interpreted everything Roman in the light of his own age. Classical works of art had been invested with Christian meaning. Hector had been regarded as a medieval knight and Alexander the Great as a medieval king. Elements of classical culture had been absorbed into the medieval civilization, but only with changed forms and meanings. On the other hand, the Italian, now conscious of a gap that separated him from the ancient world, could study it as a different civilization, understand its values, and consciously adopt them. Therefore, the belated interest in classical antiquity in Italy led to more profound changes than elsewhere. Furthermore, the consciousness of doing something new stimulated a spirit of inquiry and created a willingness to experiment with new ideas and artistic forms, for except in literature the Italians turned to antiquity for inspiration rather than for models to imitate. As a result, after several centuries of study and experimentation the Italians produced a new culture, which in turn influenced the people north of the Alps.

Meanwhile, the north had been seeking beauty—in literature, architecture, and music—and the correct imitation of nature in painting and sculp-

[1] Quoted by Johan Huizinga, *Men and Ideas* (New York: Meridian Books, 1959), trans. by James S. Holmes and Hans von Marle, p. 277.

ture through the use of details. This attempt during the fourteenth and fifteenth centuries to make each little detail seem real may be compared with the growing acceptance of nominalism, which taught that reality lay in the individual thing. At first, the Italians had also sought naturalism through the perfect rendition of details, but under the impact of their study of the classical form and of a revival of Platonism, with its concept of the universals, they came to prefer symmetry and harmony to detail. It was this concept that they exported to the north.

During this same period, there were many who desired a religious renascence, although they were far from agreement on what the nature of this rebirth should be. Some hoped for the acceptance of "the philosophy of Christ," others for the imitation of the lives of the primitive Christians or a change in theology and ritual to conform to the Bible and early church fathers, while still others sought to reinvigorate medieval Catholic Christianity. Out of the conflict that ensued, a reformed Catholic Church and numerous Protestant churches emerged.

LITERATURE AND THOUGHT

THE FLOWERING OF ITALIAN LITERATURE

The Italians were slow in developing a vernacular literature. In the second half of the thirteenth century, when they finally began to make literary use of their own language, they adopted the poetic forms of the well-developed Provençal lyric, so popular in southeastern France, to their own Tuscan dialect. At the same time, they replaced the French chivalric theme with a mystical one in which the beautiful woman was not courted as an earthly being but as a symbol of the divine.

Among this group of Florentine innovators was Dante Alighieri (1265-1321). Of a noble though not wealthy family, Dante rose high in the service of his city only to be exiled in 1302 when the faction to which he belonged was overthrown. For the remainder of his life, he wandered about northern Italy, seeking consolation for his earthly disappointments by describing his spiritual life in such works as the *Divine Comedy*. As a writer, he has seldom been surpassed. He borrowed his poetic form from France, and the intellectual content of his works was purely medieval. Although he obviously observed nature with care and had a rare gift for delineating character, both description and characterization were kept subservient to mood and allegory. He constantly declared his love for Beatrice in his literary works, but he scarcely knew her in real life and in the *Divine Comedy* she was the personification of divine revelation. While Dante was the first great Italian poet, he contributed little that was new; rather, he superbly adapted the medieval literature of the north to the Italian scene and to his own religious experience.

Dante, from the portrait by Giotto in the chapel of the Podesta in the Bargello at Florence. (Courtesy of New York Public Library)

The originator of the literary innovations of the Renaissance was Francesco Petrarca (1304-1374), or Petrarch. Petrarch's father was a Florentine lawyer who was exiled from his native city at the same time as Dante but who soon managed to find a position at the papal court at Avignon. There was no room for the wandering family in the city itself, and young Petrarch was raised a few miles away in the beautiful Provence countryside. Here he acquired his love of nature and became acquainted with the conventions of Provençal poetry. He studied law at the universities of Montpellier and Bologna, where he achieved a profound dislike for scholastic philosophy, Aristotle, and the legal profession, which he abandoned to devote his life to literature. Since before the invention of printing and the establishment of copyright laws it was impossible for a writer to make a living from his books, Petrarch took minor orders to be eligible for ecclesiastical preferment. He never became a priest, however, for though he was sincerely religious, he was a vain dandy, proud of his good looks and of his feminine conquests and anxious only to achieve fame by writing. In this, he was conspicuously successful. During his later life, prelates, princes, and towns competed for the privilege of having him as their guest. "The greatest kings of this age have loved and courted me," he declared. "With some of them I was on such terms that they seemed in a certain sense my guests rather than I theirs."

His greatest works by modern standards were his Italian sonnets, in which he told of his love for Laura. In style and inspiration, he borrowed heavily from the medieval Provençal and southern Italian poets. Most of his poetry, like that of the troubadours, consisted of pleadings for a lady's love and lamentations that it was not obtainable. Each little contact with Laura was described with minute detail; the theft of her glove was worth three sonnets. Indeed, she was so idolized that some scholars have doubted whether she actually existed, but she was idolized only as a woman and not as divine revelation as was Dante's Beatrice.

Petrarch's inherent romanticism and love of nature led him to turn to pastoral themes. He also felt compelled to reveal his innermost thoughts in a confessional autobiography. But he influenced his age most by insisting that it was not enough to imitate the literary style and form of the classical writers; their languages should also be used. Petrarch himself never managed to learn Greek, but he developed the finest Latin style of his age and wrote an epic in that language of which he was unjustifiably proud.

In his effort to restore an interest in classical literature Petrarch was aided by his friend Giovanni Boccaccio (1313-1375). Boccaccio's father was a Florentine traveling salesman, and his mother was a Parisian. He was born out of wedlock, and his youth was a rather haphazard one in which his father tried to make him a merchant and then a lawyer. With such a background, it is not surprising that Boccaccio had an abundance of witty, off-color stories to tell. Much of his youth was spent at Naples, where he successfully courted a woman whom he called his Fiammetta (Little Flame). The affair was devoid of the idealized qualities that characterized Dante's and Petrarch's relations with Beatrice and Laura. Boccaccio described the physical relationship in great detail and his later lamentations were merely those of a discarded lover. Although he wrote some verse, Boccaccio's greatest contribution was to raise prose to the highest level that it had yet attained. His *Decameron* consisted of a series of short stories told by ten young people to amuse themselves in a rural retreat while the plague was taking its toll in Florence. In these stories, the morals of the clergy were depicted in a most unfavorable light, and woman was pictured as a sensual being, ever ready to deceive her husband for the benefit of her lover. For this she was not condemned; rather, her unsuspecting husband was ridiculed. The secular subject matter of these stories was no innovation; few, if any, of the stories originated with Boccaccio. His contribution was to tell them better than they had been told before.

Boccaccio's role as an innovator really began when he repented his carefree younger days and, under the guidance of Petrarch, began to write works on classical antiquity in Latin in the hope of teaching moral lessons as well as a better style. Even here, there was much of the medieval in his outlook, and he made full use of the allegorical method to interpret classical myths. He wrote, for example, that

these fables have a plural meaning. The first meaning may be derived from the "bark" of such figments, and is called *literal;* the others are called *allegorical.* In order that I may be more easily understood, let me give an example. Perseus, son of Jupiter, according to a poetic figment, killed Gorgon and fled victorious to heaven. But if, instead of reading this myth according to the manner in which it is written, and instead of taking it merely in its *historical* meaning, the reader seeks for the *moral* significance, the myth shows the victory of the prudent man over vice, and the way leading to virtue. If we wish to interpret the whole *allegorically,* the myth designates the rise of the pious mind to heavenly things, and its contempt for earthly matters. Furthermore, it could analogically be said that the myth symbolizes Christ's ascent to his Father, after his overcoming the "prince of the world" (the devil).[2]

Perseus would hardly have recognized himself, but others followed Boccaccio's lead and the constant use of classical stories in the literature and art of the Renaissance resulted in part from the belief that they contained moral lessons.

The decision of Petrarch, Boccaccio, and others to study classical antiquity in search of cultural inspiration and moral guidance brought to an end the brief flowering of Italian vernacular literature and marked the beginnings of Italian Renaissance humanism.

THE ORIGINS OF RENAISSANCE HUMANISM

To the man of the Renaissance, a humanist was someone who studied the classics. Classical studies had lagged in Italy during the Middle Ages, and it was only with Petrarch that humanism became a significant movement on the peninsula. Many efforts have been made to associate the new interest in the literature of antiquity with the nature of Italian society, in which noble and burgher lived together in towns. One authority has recently declared that

> neither the chivalric nor the clerical literary traditions of the Middle Ages could furnish an adequate foundation for a new urban culture. The upper-class laymen of the Italian cities had lost contact with the feudal and chivalric mores that had produced the secular literature of medieval France, while at the same time they lacked the professional training and the special interests of the clerical schoolmen. But if medieval traditions proved inadequate the Italians had only to turn to a more distant past to find a congenial inspiration in the culture of a society very much like their own. The literature of Roman and Greek antiquity was the product of a wealthy, aristocratic, secular, and predominantly urban society, in which the citizen's life was set in the framework of a nonfeudal state, a society, in short, in which the upper classes of the Italian city-states could easily imagine themselves at home.[3]

Although this argument is persuasive, the nature of Italian society was probably not a major cause for the growing interest in classical antiquity. People frequently like to read about social classes different from their own.

[2] Quoted by Guiseppe Toffanin, *History of Humanism* (New York: Las Americas Publishing Company, 1954), trans. by Elio Gianturco, p. 131.

[3] Wallace K. Ferguson, *Europe in Transition, 1300-1520* (Boston: Houghton Mifflin Co., 1962), p. 290.

There had been one classical revival under the Carolingian empire and a second one during the twelfth century that was still strong in some circles in France during Petrarch's lifetime. It is true that nearly all the leaders in the northern movement were clerics, since few laymen knew Latin, but classical stories must have reached many people in the north, for they appeared widely there in painting and sculpture. Furthermore, the medieval chivalric epics were very popular among the Italian masses to whom they were sung by street singers. These people were much further removed from Charlemagne and Roland than the urban patricians, who were in the process of turning themselves into princes and courtiers in many cities at the time that humanism was beginning in Italy. Petrarch himself chose to reside more in the Milan of the Visconti than in republican Florence. Indeed, by insisting on the use of Latin, the humanists cut themselves off from the bulk of the bourgeois public, for it has been estimated that in early fourteenth-century Florence 10,000 children were learning to read and write in Italian while only 550 to 600 were studying Latin.

It is therefore difficult to escape the conclusion that the decision of Petrarch and his fellow humanists to turn to the classics was a matter of personal taste. Here they could find style, form, and eloquence, traits so lacking in most medieval literature but so prized by the ancients. Furthermore, they were naturally attracted to ancient Rome where their ancestors had played such important roles and had left so many buildings as reminders of their greatness. Just as the royal courts in the north found a dream world in the romances of chivalry,[4] so now the Italian humanists found a dream world for themselves in their own classical heritage. From it, they hoped to derive moral guidance as well as cultural inspiration.

When humanism was transplanted south of the Alps, it underwent certain changes. Classical Latin was more nearly related to Italian than to any other language; hence, it was easier for the Italians to achieve mastery in its use. The Italians alone were conscious of the gap that separated them from the ancient world, and this consciousness enabled them to recapture more of the classical spirit. As a result, they quickly became more erudite and skillful than the northern humanists.

Furthermore, the Italian humanists were able to win a larger place for themselves in the educational system than were their northern counterparts, and they therefore exercised a wider influence. There had been a strong medieval tradition for the teaching of rhetoric to prospective notaries, secretaries, and others to enable them to compose better speeches, letters, and documents. The humanists were soon able to win acceptance for the idea that to speak and write correctly it was necessary to imitate the ancients. This idea led to a very rapid increase in the number of students of the classics; gradually, classical training became one of the principal ingredients of elementary and secondary education. At the university level, the humanists took over the few existing chairs of grammar and

[4] See page 63.

rhetoric. The former included the study of poetry, and the latter the writing of prose as well as public speaking. History and sometimes moral philosophy were also taught by the holders of these chairs because historical writings were among the types of prose studied and because the classics in general were thought to provide moral guidance. The only new chairs created, largely as a result of humanistic activity, were in Greek. Thus, the humanistic movement in Italy "seems to have originated from a fusion between the novel interest in classical studies imported from France toward the end of the thirteenth century and the much earlier traditions of medieval Italian rhetoric." [5]

THE CONTRIBUTIONS OF THE ITALIAN HUMANISTS

The tie between humanism and the teaching of grammar and rhetoric helped to determine the contributions of the early humanists. These men have often been criticized for not contributing more to the natural sciences but it would have been nearly as surprising for them to have done so as for a modern professor of English to make a discovery in physics. Medicine and other scientific subjects continued to be taught by specialists who were falling more and more under the influence of the Aristotelian science that was introduced from the north around 1300. Theology and philosophy had been neglected in Italian universities. When chairs were finally established in these disciplines during the fourteenth century, the occupants naturally adopted the scholasticism of the north. Thus humanism, Aristotelianism, and scholasticism all arrived in Italy at about the same time, and each operated in its separate sphere, making few direct contributions to the others. Indeed, there was considerable departmental bickering. The humanists never tired of complaining about their colleagues' Latin style, while their colleagues charged them with pursuing eloquence devoid of intellectual content.

Within their sphere of activity, the humanists made significant contributions. A few, like Petrarch, devoted their lives to creative writing, but most of them combined their interest in classical scholarship with careers as teachers or as secretaries for the various princes, prelates, and towns. While serving in these capacities, they made every effort to discover and publish classical manuscripts. Their role in this respect has been minimized by medievalists, who have correctly pointed out that the manuscripts discovered by the humanists were copies made during the Middle Ages and deposited in monastic libraries. However, there was a vast difference between one or two copies of a Latin text, lying in some remote corner of Switzerland or Germany, and numerous copies in the newly established public and private libraries in Italy. With the invention of the printing press, the humanists ceased to copy manuscripts and be-

[5] Paul O. Kristeller, *Renaissance Thought* (New York: Harper and Row, 1961), p. 108.

came their editors, thereby spreading classical culture still further. In this manner, they virtually discovered Lucretius and Tacitus as well as many of the writings of Cicero. Through contacts with Byzantine scholars, they obtained copies of Greek manuscripts and translated them into Latin. This work had actually been begun during the Middle Ages, but it had been limited largely to Aristotle's works and Greek scientific writings. Now, Greek history and literature were made available to Western students for the first time. Through their efforts, the texts were provided that made it possible for classical learning to become the basic ingredient of European education until the dawn of the twentieth century.

To produce good texts, it was necessary to prepare dictionaries of the classical languages and to study grammar, spelling, and word usage. This work led to the development of the new discipline of philology. Scholars learned to differentiate between the Latin written during different centuries, just as we can readily tell Shakespearean English from modern English. Armed with his knowledge of philology, Lorenzo Valla (1405-1457) proved that several documents which the popes had used to claim territorial sovereignty in Italy and leadership within the Christian church were forgeries prepared in the eighth century. He subjected the New Testament to textual criticism and speculated on whether the Apostles' Creed had been written by the Apostles. As secretary to Pope Nicholas V, himself a humanist and the founder of the Vatican library, Valla was immune to punishment for his questioning mind. His efforts and those of other humanists gradually restored Latin to its classical form, for during the Middle Ages so·many changes had been introduced that medieval Latin is sometimes taught as a separate language today. These changes made for such great clarity and precision that Latin continued to be used for most scholarly and scientific works until the close of the seventeenth century.

However, the early humanists did not produce a good Latin literature of their own because their admiration for the classical writers led them to imitate rather than to create. Most of their works were filled with classical allusions and quotations that served little purpose beyond displaying their knowledge. Their efforts at eloquence were too obvious to escape notice and caused most of their writings to be two or three times as long as they should have been. Nevertheless, their critical studies led to the establishment of rules to govern various types of literary production. Plays were to have five acts, and epics were to begin in the middle of the story and the hero was always to emerge victorious. These and other rules that no author dared to disregard imposed a sense of style and form that was sadly lacking in most medieval theatrical and literary efforts. Eventually, the vernacular languages and literature were subjected to the same searching study as the classical, although it was not until the seventeenth century that good dictionaries became available and fairly precise standards of spelling and grammar were established. Before then, one spelled English or French as he pleased, a delightful privilege for the author but one that has made the task of the reader, whether Renaissance or modern, more difficult.

History, as a form of prose, came under the scrutiny of the humanists, and here also they made significant contributions. Medieval historians had written from a universal point of view which included the belief that the Holy Roman Empire was a continuation of the Roman Empire and which prevented the development of national and communal histories except in the context of universal history. Historical events were sometimes attributed to divine intervention, and legends were uncritically accepted. Historians often believed that their countries were founded by classical heroes, especially by Trojans fleeing from the fall of Troy, and Giovanni Villani (1280-1348) began his *Florentine Chronicle* with the Biblical story of the tower of Babel. Stories such as the one of Romulus and Remus, the legendary founders of Rome who were said to have been suckled by a she-wolf, were uncritically accepted.

Their admiration of classical antiquity led Petrarch and his fellow humanists to divide history into two periods: the golden age of Greece and Rome, and the dark ages that followed. In spite of a growing belief that an intellectual awakening had occurred, they included their own time in the dark ages; not until the seventeenth century was the age of the Renaissance regarded as the beginning of a third period of history. The new periodization of history gave historians a perspective that freed them from viewing the ancient and medieval civilizations as projections of their own society into the past. Released from the obligation of treating their subject as a part of universal history, the Italian humanists began to write patriotic accounts of their cities from their emergence as semi-independent jurisdictions after the decline of the Roman Empire. Histories of the individual states north of the Alps came to be written in the same manner around 1500, and it ceased to be necessary to begin an account of one's city with the Tower of Babel or of one's country with the fall of Troy.

The humanists modeled their work on that of the classical historians. As a result, their histories were narrowly political like those that they imitated. Economic and social factors were ignored, and literary and artistic matters were dealt with in separate works. Unfortunate as this was, the adoption of the classical model caused humanist historians to explain events as a result of human motives and human actions rather than divine intervention. If an occurrence could not be explained through the deeds of man, then fate, chance, or, less happily, astrological data were sometimes invoked, but rarely the vengeance of an angry God. Their knowledge of philology enabled them to be much more critical in the use of materials, and some documents once widely accepted were discarded as forgeries. Since history was regarded as a form of literature, great emphasis was placed on style. It was also regarded as a subject of practical value that taught political, moral, and ethical lessons. Thus, history was secularized and began to yield principles for political and moral philosophy.

HUMANISM AND CHRISTIANITY

The humanists' emphasis on classical studies, taken with the immoral behavior of some leading figures of the period, should not lead one to believe that the Renaissance was essentially pagan. Violence, corruption, and greed were equally rife during the Middle Ages whenever there was a breakdown of political authority. The humanists themselves were often vain, jealous, and quarrelsome, but many of them saw in the wisdom of the ancients the source and inspiration for a more moral and Christian way of life, as well as for better literary style and form.

The humanists did not attack the scholastic philosophers because of their religion, but because they believed that scholasticism subverted true religious feeling. The scholastics had organized Christianity topically and discussed rationally problems concerning grace, the existence of God, and immortality. To the humanist, this was barren intellectualism in a poor Latin style. Instead, they stressed morality and piety as found in the early Church fathers and the Bible. In spite of strong worldly inclinations, Petrarch always regarded Saint Augustine as his greatest teacher, but, significantly, it was the personal nature of the *Confessions* that attracted him more than the philosophical *City of God*. He and other early humanists praised the idea of withdrawing from the world and devoting their lives to study and contemplation. In one of his most famous works, *The Ascent of Mont Ventoux*, Petrarch tells how he was admiring the view from a mountain top when he opened Augustine's *Confessions* and read: "And men go to admire the high mountains, the vast floods of the sea, the huge streams of the rivers, the circumference of the ocean, and the revolutions of the stars—and desert themselves." "I was stunned," Petrarch wrote, ". . . and closed the book, angry with myself that I still admired earthly things." "How often," he continued as he descended, "do you think, did I turn back and look up to the summit of the mountain today while I was walking down? It seemed to me hardly higher than a cubit compared to the height of human contemplation, were the latter not plunged into the filth of earthly sordidness." [6]

In a similar manner, Petrarch rejected the scientists' study of nature, for even if their discoveries were true "they would not contribute anything whatsoever to the blessed life. What is the use—I beseech you—of knowing the nature of quadrupeds, fowls, fishes, and serpents and not knowing

[6] Ernst Cassirer, Paul O. Kristeller, and John H. Randall, Jr., eds., *The Renaissance Philosophy of Man* (Chicago: University of Chicago Press, 1948), pp. 44, 45.

or even neglecting man's nature, the purpose for which we are born, and whence and whereto we travel."

Petrarch believed that he found the scorn of wealth and the glorification of the contemplative life in Cicero and other Roman writers. However, by giving the moral code an anchor in classical antiquity, as well as in theology, the humanists obviously weakened the Christian position. This situation became especially evident when the humanists began to understand the classical writers better. Cicero, they discovered shortly before 1400, had not been an advocate of the contemplative life but an active and courageous defender of republican Rome against the threats of dictatorship. When Milan seemed on the verge of conquering Florence several years later, the Florentine humanists began to see themselves as modern Ciceros defending their native city from despotism, and hence an active, civic humanism was born. This civic humanism was not anti-Christian, but it marked the growing tendency of scholars to devote their lives to active, secular affairs.

Thus, the early Italian humanists enriched Christianity by discovering, translating, and publishing the writings of the early Christian fathers, altered Christianity by emphasizing virtue rather than theology, and weakened Christianity by finding a new basis for the moral code and by leading the intellectual to engage in secular activities.

THE PHILOSOPHY OF MAN

As classical scholars interested in literary form and style, the humanists used their control over primary and secondary education to train students in classical studies. Many of these students then specialized in law, theology, philosophy, natural science, and other subjects at the universities. As a result, from about 1450 many scholars trained by the humanists were able to combine their early classical education with their work in their chosen disciplines. Scientists, philosophers, and government officials drew more heavily on the ancients than before and wrote in the clear but overly eloquent humanistic style. Every discipline profited to some extent by this relationship, and the modern idea of the value of a liberal education emerged, although the word *humanism* was not coined until 1808.

This broadened concept of humanism had as its focal point anything to do with man. Petrarch himself had early displayed a keen interest in man, and there was a notable increase in the number of biographies and portraits during the Renaissance. But it was only when humanism was combined with Platonic or Aristotelian thought that a fully developed philosophy of man came into being.

The first important figure in this movement was Marsilio Ficino (1433-1499), who became such an able Greek scholar at an early age that Cosimo de Medici provided him with a villa and a library of Greek manuscripts that would enable him to study Platonic and Neoplatonic thought. Other scholars joined Ficino in his work, and the little group became known as the Platonic Academy, although no formal academic courses were taught.

The preference for Plato among all the ancient philosophers was due in part to the superiority of his literary style over that of Aristotle, who was known only from his lecture notes, and in part to the more idealistic and mystical nature of Platonic thought. From his Platonic studies, Ficino developed the doctrine that love of the physical beauty of this world was but the first of a series of steps leading to the love of the spiritual beauty of God, a doctrine that awakened a warm response among the artistically inclined men of the Renaissance. Man, with his physical, mortal body and spiritual, immortal soul occupied the mid-point in a chain linking the material world with the spiritual God, and it was from this central position that he achieved his dignity.

One of the most important participants in the Platonic Academy was Giovanni Pico, Count of Mirandola (1463-1494). Pico combined the usual humanistic education in the Latin and Greek writers with a knowledge of Hebrew and Arabic, as well as training in scholastic philosophy. His avowed goal was to reconcile Plato, Aristotle, and the Hebraic and oriental religions with Christianity. Unhappily, he died before he could complete his synthesis, but when he was twenty-four he announced that he was ready to defend in debate nine hundred theses explaining his position. The debate never took place because of papal interference, but the introduction to the theses entitled *Oration on the Dignity of Man* became the finest statement of the Renaissance philosophy of man. Man, according to Pico, had been created with complete free will. When "he came into life the Father conferred the seeds of all kinds and the germs of every way of life. Whatever seeds each man cultivates will grow to maturity and bear in him their own fruit. If they be vegetative, he will be like a plant. If sensitive, he will become brutish. If rational, he will grow into a heavenly being. If intellectual, he will be an angel and the son of God." [7]

There was a strong tendency in Pico to reject this world and to desire a mystical union with God, but his basic position that the dignity of man rested upon his unique capacity to make of himself what he would was very popular among Renaissance humanists. Man was a spiritual individual, but this belief should not be confused with the rampant individualism of the nineteenth century. Neither Pico nor his fellow humanists sought to justify the rights of the individual at the expense of society. Indeed, the whole concept of civic humanism involved social responsibility; and if many men in the Renaissance behaved as though they were laws unto themselves, their actions were not justified by the Renaissance philosophy of man.

[7] *Ibid.,* p. 225.

THE SPREAD OF HUMANISM

Between 1350 and 1450, while the Italian humanists were slowly making a place for themselves in the political system and in the schools, medieval interest in classical literature was waning north of the Alps. Intellectual interest in the universities was centered on the increasingly barren quarrels between the moderate realists and the nominalists, quarrels that in some instances became so bitter that faculties were split into two sections, each with its own dean, teachers, and classrooms.

During the second half of the fifteenth century, communication between Italy and the north increased. The restoration of order by the Renaissance monarchs promoted trade between the two areas and made it possible for more scholars from the north to study in Italy. The Italian wars that began with the French invasion in 1494 opened the eyes of the northerner to the more cultured and sophisticated way of life south of the Alps. Kings and great nobles brought back Italian scholars and artists in their train, and many Italians were given important positions at court and in the Church in the various northern states. Humanist historians were employed to write the histories of England, France, and other countries. The invention of printing enabled scholars in other parts of Europe to profit by the works of the Italians. Almost overnight, scholars appeared in Germany, the Netherlands, France, and England who were the equal of the Italians, and for a generation after 1494 humanism was the leading intellectual movement in Western Europe.

A few northern humanists were indifferent to religion, but the great majority looked to Italy for religious as well as scholarly inspiration. They saw that Italian philological techniques could lead to a better understanding of the Bible and the early Church fathers by providing more accurate editions and translations. At this point, agreement ceased. Some scholastic philosophers welcomed the New Learning in the expectation that it would buttress their position, although most of them recoiled when they recognized its antiphilosophical tendencies. Religious mystics were attracted by Pico, Ficino, and their fellow Platonists, but they often rejected their doctrine of the dignity of man. Others were repelled by religious mysticism but stimulated by the idea of free will and the prospect of a new moral code based on the philosophy of Christ.

Rudolf Agricola (1444-1485) remained loyal to Aristotle and his scholastic interpreters in spite of a love of eloquence that had been instilled in him during ten years of study in Italy. He had a mastery of Latin and Greek and did much to introduce the humanistic approach to the study of these languages in the Empire. Through his pupils, the New Learning reached the well-attended schools of the Brethren of the Common Life.

Johann Reuchlin (1455-1522) was inspired by Pico to study Hebrew in the belief that it would enhance his understanding of the Bible. He published a Hebrew grammar in 1506 and became the leading Christian authority on Jewish literature. His efforts aroused the ire of the conservatives in Germany who wanted to destroy all Jewish literature because it was not Christian. A bitter controversy ensued. Reuchlin was tried for heresy but was eventually acquitted, and Hebraic studies continued to expand especially in the north.

France produced a number of humanistic scholars, the most famous of whom was Jacques Lefèvre d'Etaples (1450?-1536), a professor of philosophy at the University of Paris. Lefèvre studied in Italy, where he came under the influence of Ficino, Pico, and other members of the Platonic Academy at Florence. In spite of strong mystical leanings, he continued to regard Aristotle as the leading authority on the physical world and prepared a new translation of his works. His greatest interest, however, was to achieve a better understanding of the Bible. He translated Saint Paul's Epistles from Greek into Latin and most of the Bible into French. He opposed scholasticism and other dogmatic theologies, and his study of the writings of Saint Paul and his own mystical nature led him to adopt a position quite similar to Luther's,[8] even though he remained loyal to the Catholic Church.

Spain was as receptive to the new intellectual currents as other countries. Italian tutors were often employed in the great noble families and Queen Isabella herself set the example by studying Latin. Cardinal Ximenes furthered the cause of humanism by establishing a university at Alcalá, where Latin, Greek, Hebrew, and Aramaic were taught. Under his direction, members of the university faculty published the Polyglot Bible in which the text was printed both in the original languages and in the official Latin version (the Vulgate) to facilitate textual comparisons.

John Colet (1466?-1519), the ascetic dean of Saint Paul's Cathedral in London, came under the influence of Ficino and other Platonists when he traveled in Italy. On his return to England, he began to study Saint Paul's Epistles by seeking to understand the whole in the light of early Christian conditions, rather than searching for allegorical meanings in individual passages. His work confirmed his conviction of the depravity of man and underlined the decaying position of scholasticism.

The leading member of Colet's circle was Sir Thomas More (1478-1535), a lawyer who succeeded Cardinal Wolsey as Chancellor of England and a Greek and Latin scholar with few peers. His activities as a lawyer and government official gave More a deeper insight into social problems than most humanists possessed. In his *Utopia,* he satirized the pride and greed in English society and at the same time pointed out that the Utopians were able to live virtuous lives without the aid of Christianity. What More intended to prove by this paradox is difficult to say, but he was always a devout Christian and in the end suffered martyrdom for his faith.

[8] See pages 208-216.

Erasmus, from a contemporary wood engraving by Hans Holbein the Younger. (Courtesy of New York Public Library)

ERASMUS

Unquestionably the most famous humanist of the age was Erasmus of Rotterdam (1469?-1536). Erasmus was educated in the schools of the Brethren of the Common Life, where he acquired the rudiments of a classical education and a deep sympathy for the piety and morality of his teachers but not for their mystical leanings. After the death of his father, his guardians provided for his future by securing his admission to an Augustinian monastery. Here Erasmus continued his studies but found the life of a monk increasingly distasteful. He secured a leave of absence to study at the University of Paris in 1495, only to find himself repelled by scholastic philosophy and unattracted by the religious Platonism of Lefèvre d'Etaples. He derived more pleasure from his association with a small group of secular-minded humanists in that city, and when he made his first trip to England in 1499, he seemed bent on becoming a man of letters.

While in England, Erasmus came under the influence of the deeply religious Colet and More. Although he rejected Colet's mysticism and his belief in the depravity of man, he was deeply influenced by Colet's efforts to recapture the true meaning of Saint Paul. Slowly, the classics ceased to be an end in themselves to Erasmus and became the means of understanding "the philosophy of Christ." Like so many Italian humanists, he believed in the dignity of man. Man had free will and could rise above his earthly appetite with the proper education and guidance. Scholastic philosophy and the medieval theologians merely confused the issue and shut man off from the true source of inspiration, the Bible and the writings of the early Church fathers. Prescribed religious observances and Church rituals, such as fasting, confessions, indulgences, pilgrimages, and the veneration of saints and relics, were of little value at best and actually harmful if they caused one to rely on them rather than to lead a good life. "We kiss the shoes of the saints and their dirty handkerchiefs," Erasmus declared, "and we leave their books, their most holy and efficacious relics, neglected."

Erasmus therefore turned his back on the medieval contributions to religion and sought inspiration directly from Biblical antiquity. "I should wish," he wrote, "that this simple and pure Christ might be deeply impressed upon the minds of men, and that I deem best attainable in this way, that we, supported by our knowledge of the original languages, should philosophize *at the sources* themselves." Erasmus did indeed return to the sources, although it meant years of additional study of Greek. Eventually, a new Greek edition of the New Testament appeared from his pen which became the basis of various translations into the vernacular, including that of Martin Luther. Once the word of God was correctly established and made available to the common man, Erasmus fervently believed, the philosophy of Christ as found in the Golden Rule and the Sermon on the Mount would become known and followed by all. Ploughmen would sing the Scriptures at the plow, weavers would keep time with them at their looms, and travelers would rehearse them to escape the tedium of their voyages. Piety and charity would become the rule.

Other scholarly works, such as a multi-volume edition of Saint Jerome, were highly regarded in his day, but Erasmus has become known chiefly for his more popular writings, such as the *Praise of Folly*. In these popular works, his superb Latin style, his wit, and his urbanity were fully employed, but even in these writings we find the same message. Like many other educators, Erasmus believed that, once men understood what was good, they would do it.

THE REVIVAL OF VERNACULAR LITERATURE

At the very time that Renaissance humanism was spreading north of the Alps, the Italians themselves were beginning to write their creative works in the vernacular once more.[9] Perhaps they realized that the imitation of Ciceronian Latin was stifling their own creative impulses. Perhaps the fact that Lorenzo de Medici had a personal preference for Italian was enough to set the new mode. Whatever the reasons, the Italians began to apply what they had learned about style and form from their classical studies to the writing of literature in their own tongue. To write acceptably in the vernacular, a classical education was still regarded as necessary, for, as one humanist said, "Let no one believe that he could express himself eloquently, nay even tolerably, in the *volgare* without previous genuine and perfect familiarity with Latin letters."

The revived use of Italian began at Florence, where Lorenzo himself produced good poetry. This renewal of Florentine literary leadership in the

[9] See page 171.

vernacular led to the acceptance of the Tuscan dialect as the literary language of Italy. The poetic achievements of the fourteenth century were not equaled in spite of the commendable efforts of Lodovico Ariosto (1474-1533), who capitalized on the growing interest in the romances of chivalry to produce the epic *Orlando Furioso*, a modified tale of Charlemagne's heroic general, Roland. Historical writings in Italian reached a high standard of excellence with Niccolò Machiavelli taking the lead here as in political thought.[10] Machiavelli was also a playwright of exceptional gifts and a ready wit. His naughty comedy, *Mandragola*, still enjoys wide popularity.

Latin remained the literary language of the Europeans north of the Alps for about a generation, but from the 1520's more and more authors began to use the vernacular. Italian and classical models influenced them greatly, and in several countries there were difficulties over which of several dialects would become the literary language. Germany produced no great literary figures during the sixteenth century and the honor of being the principal contributor to the formation of a single German language fell to Martin Luther, whose German translation of the Bible went through 377 editions during his lifetime. Portuguese literature reached its height during the Renaissance and Castilian writers developed such skill that they contributed towards making their dialect the basis for modern Spanish, although the golden age of Spanish literature was to come only at the close of the Renaissance.

The French language developed so rapidly during the sixteenth century that some claimed that it was equal to Latin and Italian. François Rabelais (1494?-1553), monk, priest, and finally physician, was the greatest figure in French Renaissance prose. He is best known for his meandering story of two giants, Gargantua and Pantagruel. This story, half burlesque and half satire on contemporary society, was used by Rabelais to dramatize his humanistic belief that man is essentially good. The rule of the fictitious abbey of Thélème, where men and women came and went as they pleased, needed only to be, "Do what thou wilt," for "men who are free, well-bred, well-educated, conversant with genteel folk, have by nature an instinct and spur which impels them to virtuous actions and restrains them from vice; and this they call honor." It is by a vigorous life of action, not by monastic withdrawal or philosophical speculation, that man fulfills himself.

During a brief flowering of English literature in the second half of the fourteenth century, the writings of Geoffrey Chaucer (1340?-1400) had done much to establish the East Midland dialect as the parent of modern English, but Chaucer had no worthy successors until the literary revival that took place during the reign of Elizabeth I (1558-1603). Perhaps the greatest poet of this period was Edmund Spenser (1552?-1599), a university-educated scholar who was thoroughly acquainted with classical and Italian literature. His most ambitious work was *The Faerie Queene*, an allegorical poem intended to honor his queen and "to fashion a gentleman

[10] See page 9.

or noble person in virtuous discipline." Following Ficino, he found in the love of earthly beauty the first step towards the love of the spiritual beauty of God.

William Shakespeare (1564-1616) had far less education than Spenser, but he knew the principal stories of Roman and Italian literature from translations. These he borrowed whenever he saw fit, but mystical and philosophical systems like Platonism escaped his notice. As a poet and dramatist, he was without equal, but his genius lay more in the use of words and the delineation of character than in abstract thought. Yet by having his heroes create their own tragic dilemmas and fall through their own sins and mistakes, Shakespeare joined those humanists who believed that the dignity of man lay in his freedom to choose.

ART AND MUSIC

GOTHIC NATURALISM

The Renaissance Italians were convinced that the fourteenth century witnessed a rebirth of painting as well as of literature but they character-ized this rebirth as an imitation of nature rather than of classical an-tiquity. They believed that it was nature which the ancient artists them-selves had taken as their model. "Hence the painter will produce pictures of small merit," Leonardo da Vinci wrote

> if he takes for his standard the pictures of others, but if he will study from natural objects he will bear good fruit. As was seen in the painters after the Romans who always imitated each other and so their art constantly declined from age to age. After these came Giotto, the Florentine, who—not content with imitating the works of Cimabue, his master—being born in the moun-tains and in a solitude inhabited only by goats and such beasts, and being guided by nature to his art, began by drawing on the rocks the movements of the goats of which he was keeper. And thus he began to draw all the animals which were to be found in the country, and in such wise that after much study he excelled not only all the masters of his time but all those of many bygone ages.[11]

The tradition that Giotto began a rebirth of painting by trying to depict nature accurately is therefore as old as the Renaissance itself, but unhap-pily for the primacy of the Italians, the desire to imitate nature had been born nearly a century before Giotto drew goats on rocks. No less an au-thority than Saint Thomas Aquinas had already declared that: "Art is imitation of nature. Works of art are successful to the extent that they achieve a likeness of nature."

But it is one thing to try to imitate nature and another thing to do it

[11] Elizabeth G. Holt, ed., *A Documentary History of Art* (Garden City: Double-day Anchor Books, 1957), I, p. 286.

Duccio di Buoninsegna (c. 1255-1319). THE CALLING OF THE APOSTLES PETER AND ANDREW. *The subject of this painting provided a splendid opportunity for a seascape with two fishermen, but faithful to medieval Byzantine tradition, the artist used a background of gold and was content to depict the "idea" of a sea and the "idea" of fish. He was interested in telling a story, not in painting nature as it appears to the eye. Indeed, this painting was one of ninety-two panels of an altarpiece in Siena relating the life of Christ. (National Gallery of Art, Washington, D.C., Samuel H. Kress Collection)*

successfully. Well-established traditions had to be broken and new techniques developed. Medieval painting had been a church art that was designed to teach, for as Pope Gregory the Great had said near the close of the sixth century: "Painting can do for the illiterate what writing does for those who can read." But to write with pictures, it was necessary to remove all unnecessary details, in order not to distract the viewer's attention from the main theme, and to draw each individual Biblical person in a conventional manner so that he could be identified by laymen. Since to tell a story several actions had to be related, three or four different events were often put in the same painting or even in the same work of sculpture. To convey the meaning better, gestures were exaggerated, and to excite an emotional response, further violence was done to nature. Thus, a medieval painting was more comparable to a newspaper comic strip than to a Renaissance work of art. Moreover, nature is three-dimensional, but the painter works in a two-dimensional medium. It was necessary to learn how to give a sense of perspective through the use of varying proportions and of light and shadow. This feat is so difficult that it was never accomplished before the Renaissance. About 1235, Villard de Honnecourt portrayed a lion that he proudly declared "was drawn from life," but his lion was strictly a two-dimensional animal. In another respect, too, Honnecourt's lion was not "drawn from life." He seemed to be more an idealized lion in general than an individual lion; reality had not yet broken its connection with the universal and become associated only with the particular.

The story of how art became more like nature is the story of how artists came to depict *single* scenes as they are in nature, without idealized persons but with the necessary details arranged to give the viewer a sense of perspective.

Some progress towards the representation of nature had been made in Gothic sculpture north of the Alps during the thirteenth century. Sculpture, unlike painting, is a three-dimensional art, and fewer technical difficulties had to be overcome. Flowers and leaves assumed their natural form; statues began to break away from the cathedral walls where they had been little more than bas-reliefs and to assume more lifelike proportions that seemed capable of movement. Saints and the Virgin Mary with her Child became less like the participants in a Bible story carved in such a manner as to create a religious response and became more like human beings with human emotions. Nevertheless, most statues remained somewhat idealized and continued to be a part of the cathedral, just as in the prevailing philosophy of moderate realism reality was thought to lie only in the universals, although these universals exist only in regard to the particular. As for Gothic paintings, these became more lifelike than their predecessors but remained more idealized and conventional than Gothic sculpture and lacked perspective.

Gothic art was introduced into Italy near the close of the thirteenth century about the same time as humanism. It met a long-felt need. The Byzantine and Romanesque styles that had dominated the Italian scene were specifically designed to emphasize otherworldliness even to the point of keeping details to a minimum and using gold backgrounds, the most ethereal of colors. The figures themselves were drawn to provoke an emotional response in the viewer but were so idealized as to be devoid of human personality or feeling. The Italians, however, had been deeply influenced by Saint Francis of Assisi and his friars, who had emphasized the human side of the Bible stories rather than the philosophical. They therefore welcomed Gothic art because of its more natural and human ele-

Giotto, THE FLIGHT TO EGYPT. *Although this is essentially a two-dimensional picture in respect to landscapes, note the solid, three-dimensional figures. Giotto gives his figures weight and volume, which are lacking in the work of his contemporary, Duccio (see p. 185). The painting is at Cappella dell' Arena, Padua. (Alinari-Art Reference Bureau)*

ments, and Giotto (c. 1266-1337) was but the first great Italian painter to adopt the new style from the north.

This is not to deny that Giotto made original contributions. It was he who discovered how to make people look round, solid, and statuelike in spite of his two-dimensional medium. He did not know the laws of perspective, but he was able to give some sense of depth. The Biblical and religious scenes that he drew on the walls of churches in Assisi, Padua, and Florence have an emotional appeal, but at the same time his characters could move, gesture, and display their feelings. So successful was Giotto that the Gothic style became common in Italy during the fourteenth century, and his technique of painting three-dimensional figures was copied by artists in the north. Gothic sculpture was also adopted in Italy and reached a peak in grace, beauty, and charm in the carvings that Lorenzo Ghiberti (1378-1455) made on the bronze doors of the Baptistery of Florence.

Thus during the fourteenth century the Gothic international style prevailed in Western Europe, and it is against this background that the artistic revolution that began about 1400 in both Italy and the Netherlands must be considered.

THE IMITATION OF NATURE IN THE NORTH

In seeking to solve the problem of how to depict nature accurately, the painters of the Netherlands and Italy followed different courses. In the north, the advent of the Gothic architecture removed painting from the cathedrals because the walls formerly used for this purpose were replaced by stained glass. Painters therefore devoted most of their efforts to the illumination of manuscripts of devotional and secular literature. Since the amount of manuscript space available for a scene was very limited, painters had to draw each object with the greatest care. Gradually, they achieved a mastery in rendering detail that they utilized when they began to be called upon to paint wooden panels to be placed behind altars. The custom of having altarpieces, which began in the north around 1400, was a boon to the illuminators because it gave them a large, important medium to work with.

The first illuminator to achieve fame for his altarpieces was Jan van Eyck (1380?-1441). He continued to pay attention to detail; indeed, he was among the first to use oil paint. He also developed a technique in which he put on several coats of paint to eliminate all brush marks and to give his work a bright and glittering quality. The results were truly astonishing. Portraits were rendered so accurately that they seemed alive. Each hair of a fur robe or a dog could be distinguished just as it can with the naked eye, and even velvet nap stood out when examined with a magnifying glass. The tiniest jewels in a crown glittered. Horses were solid, three-dimensional animals; each tree looked like an individual tree; and a lawn consisted of innumerable blades of grass rather than a patch of green. Towns and castles were real, with each window drawn regardless of how tiny it was in the distance. Each detail was painted as it could be found in nature. Yet in spite of his genius, Van Eyck failed in one important respect: he did not fully understand the laws of perspective. To find room for all the details that he wanted to include, he sometimes made his horizons too high, as in the Ghent altarpiece, and while he knew that distant objects should be made smaller, he determined the amount of the reduction by empirical methods only.

Van Eyck sometimes permitted a fairly good landscape to be seen through an open window, but he always centered the viewer's attention on the scene inside the building. Perhaps the first painter to produce a land-

Conrad Witz, CHRIST WALKING ON THE WAVES. *This Renaissance artist used this Biblical story as an excuse to paint a beautiful landscape actually located at Geneva. A comparison of this work with that of Duccio's (p. 185) will show how far removed Renaissance naturalistic art was from medieval art. (Marburg-Art Reference Bureau)*

scape that was the dominating element of the picture was Conrad Witz (1400?-1446?). In an altarpiece intended to show Christ walking on the waters of Lake Genesareth, he set the scene of the event on his native Lake Geneva. The lake, with the beautiful Swiss landscape beyond, holds the viewer's attention more than Christ and the realistic-looking fishermen. Furthermore, Witz noted that when one gazes into water immediately before him, he sees the lake bottom, but when he looks further away, he sees the reflection of the surrounding hills and buildings. Two centuries were to elapse before scientists formulated a physical law explaining this phenomenon that had been observed and depicted by a highly perceptive artist.

The efforts of Van Eyck and Witz to imitate nature through the perfect rendering of details were a continuation of the efforts of the fourteenth-century Gothic illuminators, though in their success these two painters lost some of the grace and flowing curves of their predecessors. They also depicted scenes in a more unconventional, unstylized manner. Van Eyck had displayed little emotion, and Witz had turned a religious subject into a secular scene. Some northern artists followed their lead, but many tried to combine their technical achievements with traditional ways. The German Stefan Lochner (1410?-1451) could render exact detail and give a sense of depth. In his famous "Madonna in a Rose Garden," however, he preferred to keep the gold background of the earlier period, although he used his knowledge of how to paint a three-dimensional head to give the Madonna a revealing inner consciousness so characteristic of the negative mystics of the Cologne region. Roger van der Weyden (c. 1400-1464) and Hugo van der Goes (1440-1482) accepted the technical innovations but imparted to their paintings a religious and emotional intensity lacking in the works of Van Eyck and Witz.

THE IMITATION OF NATURE IN ITALY

The Italian painters never equalled the mastery of detail attained in the north. Even when Gothic cathedrals were finally built in Italy, the use of stained glass was less extensive than in the north, leaving ample wall space for paintings. For this reason, there was less need in Italy to learn the art of manuscript illumination in order to find employment and therefore less opportunity to learn the mastery of details. Furthermore, since a fresco method was used in wall painting, the colors had to be applied to wet plaster, and the artist had to work so rapidly that there was no time for the perfection of details. Although wooden panels for altarpieces and for homes were painted in Italy during the fourteenth century and thereafter, the Italians were slow to adopt the oil painting techniques of the north and tended to paint panels as they did frescoes. As a result, although many Italian artists attempted to paint details, they never approached the mastery of the northerners, and they had to find a way to make their paintings look natural by using their own larger, more monumental figures.

The artist who first accomplished this feat was the youthful Masaccio (1401-1428), whose "Holy Trinity" on the walls of the church of Santa Maria Novella of Florence began an artistic revolution. A friend of Masaccio, the architect Brunelleschi, had discovered the mathematical laws of perspective by which the sizes of objects recede into the background, and Masaccio used this discovery to "hollow out" the church wall, creating a chapel which the viewer feels that he can walk into. His large, three-dimensional, statuelike figures, his use of light and shadow, and the absence of unnecessary detail gave the painting an austere but simple grandeur. Gone were the grace, refinement, and gently flowing curves of the Gothic international style. Nature had been recaptured, and a new style of painting had been born.

The new style was accepted, modified, or largely rejected by other Italian painters during the remainder of the fifteenth century. Fra Angel-

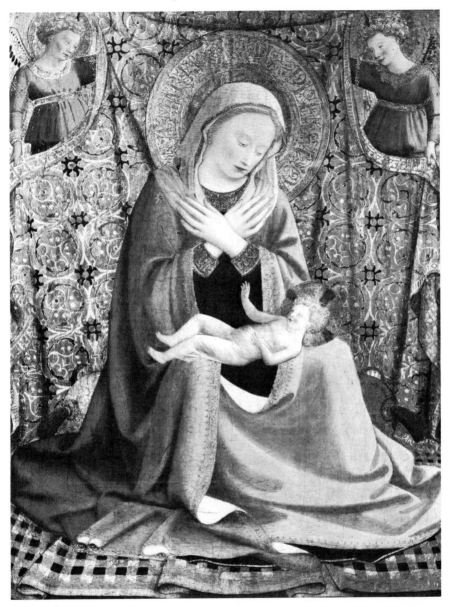

Fra Angelico, MADONNA OF HUMILITY. (*National Gallery of Art, Washington, Mellon Collection*)

ico (1387-1455) kept Masaccio's simplicity, and he understood the new laws of perspective, but his deeply religious nature led him to emphasize the stories from the Bible when he painted the walls of the monastery of San Marco in Florence. Paolo Uccello (1397-1475) was enamored of the new laws of perspective and made his horses and riders so three-dimensional that they looked more like hobby horses on a stage than knights on the field of battle. On the other hand, Benozzo Gozzoli (1420-1497) covered the chapel of the Medici palace with an ornate and courtly pageantry depicting the journey of the three magi to Bethlehem through a landscape that was anything but real. Perhaps the greatest successor to Masaccio in the naturalist style was Piero della Francesca (1416?-1492), who was his equal in the use of perspective and his superior in the use of light. As the fifteenth century drew to a close, the Italian painters began to feel that they had mastered the art of depicting nature in their two-dimensional medium and began to search for deeper meanings and greater harmony. In this quest, part of their inspiration came from the Platonic Academy at Florence.

THE IDEALIZATION OF NATURE IN ITALY

The early artists had been artisans who were members of a craft guild. As such, they had not been considered the social equals of the wealthy patricians or even of the humanists. They had possessed little formal education, and their subjects for painting had usually been selected by a patron who wanted scenes represented in a conventional manner. During the fifteenth century, however, their genius came to be recognized, and they began to be welcomed in the homes of patricians and to engage in conversations with humanists and philosophers. As a result, they became acquainted with the intellectual currents of the day and boldly sought to incorporate them into their art.

During the latter part of the fifteenth century, Platonism became fashionable in Florence, and its teaching, as interpreted by Ficino, that love of the physical beauty of the world was but the first of a series of steps leading to love of the spiritual beauty of God, captivated the artists. They became convinced that the more beauty they conferred on the human body in their paintings, the more God-like it became. Nature, instead of being copied, was to be improved upon. This conviction led them to study anatomy more carefully and to seek to correct the defects in their art. The nude became a subject for art in its own right for the first time since the classical era, and Venus, the goddess of beauty, was painted as often as Mary, the Mother of God.

The first important painter who sought to improve on nature was Sandro Botticelli (1444-1510). In his early works he had depicted nature as he had seen it, but by 1478 he had come under the influence of the Platonic Academy and had begun a series of paintings on classical subjects that were thought to contain Christian truths. In his "Birth of Venus" he recreated the myth of how Venus had risen from the sea to bring beauty into the world. Neither the sea nor the shell on which Venus was riding was realistic, and she herself was too graceful, too light, too pure, too beautiful, to be of this world.

Sandro Botticelli, THE BIRTH OF VENUS. *Uffizi Palace, Florence. (Alinari-Art Reference Bureau)*

Other painters followed in Botticelli's footsteps, including the three greatest names in the high Italian Renaissance (c.1490-1520), although the methods they used to depict the divine quality in man differed. The first of the three, Leonardo da Vinci (1452-1519), was one of the most versatile geniuses of all time. Engineer, inventor, musician, scientist, and sculptor, but above all painter, Leonardo was one of the keenest observers of nature that the Renaissance produced. He studied the flight of birds and the anatomy of man, performing over thirty dissections of the human body to see how it functioned. "The summit of art," he thought, "is to draw well the body of a nude man and a nude woman," but there was enough of the desire to idealize nature in his artistic theory for him to tell a student: "On winter evenings, all the drawings from the nude which you have made in the summer should be brought together, and you should make a choice from among them of the best limbs and bodies, and practice these and learn them by heart."

Nevertheless, in the "Last Supper," painted on the walls of the refectory of a monastery in Milan, he gave the disciples little of the idealized beauty sought by Botticelli. He had almost no contact with the Platonists and was primarily interested in man's psychological makeup. Previous paintings of the last supper had shown Jesus giving out the Sacrament with Judas seated alone on the opposite side of the table, but Leonardo chose the moment when Jesus said: "One of you shall betray me." The gestures and facial expressions of the disciples are penetrating studies of human nature, and the tourist today often amuses himself by trying to inter-

Raphael Sanzio, MADONNA DEL GRANDUCA. *Pitti Palace, Florence. (Alinari-Art Reference Bureau)*

pret them. The famous "Mona Lisa" was also a study of human personality. Was she smiling or was she sad? From each angle, she assumes a different mood and a different meaning. Leonardo had done more than a camera could do.

The second great artist of the high Renaissance was Raphael Sanzio (1483-1520), who, like Botticelli, sought a beauty greater than could be found in nature. His slightly idealized Madonnas achieved a wide popularity, and he managed to impart harmony, grace, and movement without the windy, ethereal effect that characterized the "Birth of Venus" by the earlier painter.

The third of the great trio was Michelangelo Buonarroti (1475-1564), a versatile genius like Leonardo who addressed his talents to architecture and poetry as well as painting and sculpture. During his youthful years at the Medici palace, he was deeply influenced by the Platonists and sought beauty as a steppingstone to God. In one sonnet he wrote:

> *For every beauty that we look on here*
> *Brings, to wise souls, in recollection clear*
> *The merciable fount whence all things flow;*
> *Nor other pledge nor other fruit have we*
> *Of heaven on earth. Who loves thee faithfully*
> *To God ascends, and makes death precious so.*[12]

Beauty to Michelangelo was not to be found in the ordinary human form but in the great muscular figures that he created, such as the huge statue of David in Florence or the statue of the beautiful young Virgin in the Pietà in Saint Peter's. Equally powerful and dramatic were his frescoes on the ceiling of the Sistine Chapel at Rome. Here he removed all unnecessary details so that the viewer would concentrate on the figures in each scene. Gradually, his religious intensity increased under the impact of the Catholic Reformation, and he abandoned the Renaissance style to become a precursor of Mannerism (see pp. 353-354).

Other skillful painters abounded during the high Renaissance, especially at Venice where oil painting was imported from the north about 1475 and canvases began to be used soon thereafter. Painters like Giovanni Bellini (c. 1430-1516) and Giorgione da Castelfranco (1477-1510) excelled in the use of light and color, and the long-lived Titian (1477?-1576) achieved fame as a portrait painter, a form of art that had become increasingly popular during the Renaissance. So great had been the Italian achievement that from about 1500 artists from the north began to come to Italy to study. Those who could not make the trip learned something of the techniques used in the south from the newly developed systems of reproducing art through woodcuts and engravings.

[12] Quoted by Nesca A. Robb, *Neoplatonism of the Italian Renaissance* (London: George Allen and Unwin, 1935), p. 268.

THE NORTHERN PAINTERS OF THE HIGH RENAISSANCE

The Italian masters had surpassed those of the north in the knowledge of perspective; they had discovered its mathematical laws, while their rivals relied on an empirical approach which involved the use of so many details that harmony and sometimes movement were lost. Through their study of anatomy, the Italians had also developed theories of proportion —that is, of the mathematical relation between the size of one part of the body and another in various circumstances. This had enabled them to beautify and idealize the human form. There was some truth in Michelangelo's criticism of northern painting: "In Flanders they paint, before all things, to render exactly and deceptively the outward appearance of things. The painters choose, by preference, subjects provoking transports of piety, like the figures of saints or of prophets. But most of the time they paint what are called landscapes with plenty of figures. Though the eye is agreeably impressed, these pictures have neither art nor reason; neither symmetry nor proportion; neither choice of values nor grandeur. In short, this art is without power and without distinction; it aims at rendering minutely many things at the same time, of which a single one would have sufficed to call forth a man's whole application." [13]

On the other hand, the purpose of the northern painters differed from that of Michelangelo and other Italian artists who were influenced by Platonism. The former, as Michelangelo charged, wanted to provoke piety and tears, to make their audience long for heaven and fear hell. They rejected the Platonists' belief that human beauty was a step towards the divine and that religious truths could be found in the myths of classical mythology. Most of them therefore adopted the Italian techniques when it suited their purpose and assimilated these to their own artistic heritage.

Of the great northern artists of this period, no one studied the Italians more closely than Albrecht Dürer (1471-1528), the son of a Nuremberg goldsmith. Dürer visited Italy twice and became so interested in the theory of proportions that he published a book on the subject. In his woodcuts, engravings, and paintings, he showed a mastery of detail characteristic of the north, but he constantly sought better ways to fit these details more harmoniously into his compositions. Although he searched for the ideal of beauty by studying the human form with a care unprecedented in the north, he did not reject the use of other details. Christian rather than classical subjects nearly always claimed his attention, except in his early years. In one visit to Italy, he complained that "here I am a lord, at home a parasite," but well before his death he had won enough recognition in his homeland to enjoy a privileged status.

In the altarpiece painted for the monastic hospital at Isenheim, the south German painter popularly called Matthias Grünewald (c. 1475-1582) told the story of the suffering on the cross and the triumphant resurrection

---

[13] Quoted by Johan Huizinga, *The Waning of the Middle Ages* (London: Edward Arnold and Company, 1924), p. 244.

Grünewald. Detail from the Isenheim altarpiece in the Unterlinden Museum, Colmar. The risen Christ is being transformed into the spirit. His legs are still material, but His head has become pure light. The intended effect of the painting was to assure the inmates of the monastic hospital at Isenheim that they too may be saved from their sufferings. (Art Reference Bureau)

more dramatically than it had ever been told before. The painting consisted of nine panels swung on hinges so that different scenes could be displayed on Sundays, week days, and special holidays. On week days the crucifixion scene showed a huge Christ and several smaller figures. The tortured fingers of Christ pointing towards heaven, His mouth opened in the last agony, His ribs protruding, His feet twisted, and His body bleeding from countless thorns reminded the hospital inmates that their suffering could not compare with His. Grünewald did not hesitate to exaggerate the size of Christ and to remove the need for a landscape that might distract the viewer's attention by painting a strangely black and ghostly night. On Sundays and during the Easter holiday, the annunciation was shown on the left panel and Mary holding the infant Jesus was shown on the central panel. Both panels were filled with the richness of color and the wealth of detail of the northern school. The right panel (reproduced above) showed the resurrection.

Hieronymus Bosch. Detail from a triptych in the Gemaldegalerie, Vienna, THE TORMENTS OF HELL. (*Bruckmann-Art Reference Bureau*)

Hieronymus Bosch (c. 1450-1516) revealed another side of religious experience in the north. Bosch lived in the Dutch town of Hertogenbosch, where he came under the influence of the Brethren of the Common Life, whose practical piety he sought to emulate. Sometimes he painted parables teaching moral lessons or portrayed the seven deadly sins as reminders to his viewers. Sometimes he sought to show the contrast between good and evil by drawing Christ carrying the cross, but he so exaggerated the wicked features of the tormentors that they hold the viewer's attention at the expense of the good Christ. Sometimes, as in the "Hay Wagon," he painted the fall from Eden on the left panel, man's sinful life on earth on the central panel, and a hell on the right panel that was full of strange and unearthly animals torturing the wicked. No Calvinist preacher ever described fire and brimstone more vividly.

Through paintings, we can detect the difference between the nature of the religious spirit in Italy and the north a few years before Luther began his attack on Rome. Some of the Italian techniques had been adopted, but the fundamental distinctions remained.

SCULPTURE

Sculpture is a three-dimensional medium and therefore the accurate representation of nature presented fewer technical problems than it did in

Scenes from the life of Christ on choir screen at Chartres. (Courtesy of New York Public Library)

painting. By the close of the thirteenth century, statues in the north had been sufficiently freed from the architectural element to permit full movement, draperies flowed in a natural manner, and in a few instances the human form was partially visible beneath the garments. During the fourteenth century and thereafter, many sculptors began to make exquisite little statues of silver, ivory, or wood to adorn private chapels. These statues, which were completely divorced from the architectural element, were lifelike in every respect; no detail was too small to claim the sculptor's attention. Sometimes little scenes were carved in which a half-dozen or more statues depicted a Bible story. The marble retable representing the seven joys of the Virgin that was made for the church at Brou shortly after 1500 and the scenes from the life of Christ that were begun on the choir screen at the cathedral at Chartres at about the same time are superb examples of the minute and painstaking work of these craftsmen.

199

Donatello, ST. GEORGE *(detail). Unlike the sculptor of the choir screen of Chartres (p. 199), Donatello achieves a forceful naturalism without excessive use of detail. (Anderson-Art Reference Bureau)*

In sculpture, as in the paintings of Van Eyck and his fellow artists, reality was achieved through the use of detail, although this technique led to a certain lack of harmony in the whole.

The northern sculptors displayed the same unflagging zeal for detail when they attempted larger works. The statues of the prophets that Claus

200

Michelangelo Buonarroti, PIETA, *Rome. (Courtesy of Italian State Tourist Office)*

Sluter made near Dijon for the Burgundian dukes between 1380 and 1400 seem almost alive because they appear to move and have such natural beards and lined brows. Even the embalming stitches may be seen in the sepulchral monument of Louis XII of France which was made more than a century later. Some funeral statues depicted the state of the deceased after death by showing worms crawling over the body and skin rotting from the bones. Nature, to the man of the north, was not always beautiful, but in his art it was always natural.

During the fourteenth century, the Italian sculptors followed the course

201

set in the north, but at the same time that Masaccio was starting a new style in painting at Florence, Donatello (1386?-1466) began to break with the traditional style in sculpture. Part of his inspiration came from the study of anatomy. He reduced the number of details in his statues and gave them a heavy, solid, determined air. If Donatello breathed life into his statues by giving them weight, mass, and energy, Michelangelo, as we have seen, went further and sought to give his statues an idealized beauty that surpassed human nature. Only slowly did their discoveries penetrate the north, and once more a difference in aesthetic temperament and in the use of details may be detected between Italy and the rest of Europe.

The giving of a lifelike quality to sculpture was not an unmitigated blessing because it meant that the statue ceased to be an integral part of the cathedral and became an artistic work prepared in a workshop for a niche in the interior or exterior of a building. As a result, the Renaissance church looks like a museum for statues. The growth of naturalism had destroyed the unity of the arts in the Gothic cathedral just as the growth of nominalism had destroyed medieval intellectual unity.

ARCHITECTURE

The northern architect of the late Middle Ages and early Renaissance displayed the same fondness for details as the painter and sculptor. The basic structure of Gothic architecture continued to be used, but spires were added to the square towers, complicated tracery was put in the windows, the number of ribs on the vaults was multiplied, and everywhere there was an increase in ornamentation. In France, the new style became known as the Flamboyant; and in England, where such superb buildings as Henry VII's Chapel in Westminster Abbey and Saint George's Chapel at Windsor were constructed, it was called the Perpendicular.

During the fourteenth century, the Italians followed the example set by the north, and buildings like the Doges' palace in Venice were constructed in the highly decorated manner. Once more, it was a Florentine of the early fifteenth century who created the new style.

Filippo Brunelleschi (1377-1446) studied Roman ruins with Donatello and discovered the laws of perspective that Masaccio used so effectively. On his return to Florence, he began to adapt the classical style to the architecture of his day. Exact copying was not possible because the Roman temple had not been designed to hold a congregation and because the convenience of the owner had to be considered when palaces were constructed. As a result, the basic structure of his buildings was not consistently classical, but it differed from what had gone before. Horizontal lines were stressed in his churches rather than the vertical; windows and arches were rounded instead of pointed; classical pilasters were introduced to replace Gothic decorations; and classical columns were used for the interior of palace courtyards and for small churches.

These innovations were very popular, but the architects wanted to go

SAN FRANCESCO, *Rimini. The facade of this church was begun by Leone Battista Alberti (1404-72) in 1446. The rounded arches and columns reflect a classical influence that contrasts sharply with the Gothic facades of Amiens (p. 27) and Rheims (p. 29). (Alinari-Art Reference Bureau)*

further; and when Pope Julius II decided to tear down the old basilica of Saint Peter, a church closely modeled after the classical style was planned. In the end, the design had to be altered, but only after the architects had studied the ancients so thoroughly that henceforth, although buildings were rarely constructed in the classical model, they were given the classical spirit of harmony and symmetry. These basic characteristics were incorporated in the Saint Peter's that was finally built, although Baroque manifestations were added at a later date.

The new style slowly spread to the north. At first, classical ornamentation was used to decorate Flamboyant buildings, but gradually the desire for harmony and symmetry prevailed.

MUSIC

Music displayed much the same tendencies as the other arts during the late Middle Ages and early Renaissance except that in this case the innovations occurred in the north. Simplicity and coherence were abandoned in favor of infinite variations and attention to detail. The new developments were given theoretical sanction in a musical treatise called the *Ars Nova* written by a Frenchman, Philippe de Vitry (1291-1361), at about the same time that Petrarch was reviving interest in the classical style. Composers, however, had no classical models to guide their efforts, and it was left to an Englishman, John Dunstable (c.1390-1453), and to a group of Netherland composers led by Guillaume Dufay (c.1400-1474) to organize the multiplicity of variations and details into a more coherent whole, just as the Italian artists of the same period were doing in their mediums. The different kinds of musical instruments, which had been increased to give a greater variety of sounds, were now coordinated more effectively. To the canon, a musical composition in which each voice had sung the same melody but no two voices had ever sung the same phrase, Dufay gave a semblance of unity by having the second voice repeat the same phrase, although occasionally backwards. The system was further complicated by the developing practice of having a chorus, rather than individual voices, sing the same words, but on the whole, words and music were better intergrated than before. Like the Italian artists, the composers were conscious of doing something new, and one of them declared in 1477 that "there is no music worth hearing save only in the last forty years."

Netherlandish music reached its peak in Josquin des Prez (1450-1521). By this time, composers had ceased to write for the instruments and each voice separately and had begun to think of all the parts of their composition as a whole. The result was greater symmetry and harmony. A slow decline followed Des Prez's death, although the willingness to experiment remained. One of his pupils tried to copy the sounds of nature and produced surprisingly realistic imitations of the battle of Marignano, the noises of the city, and the singing of the birds.

During this period kings, noblemen, and wealthy burghers often became musical patrons. Their interest led to an increase in the quantity of secular music and to a larger number of compositions for the vernacular languages. At first, the Italian princes had often imported composers from the Netherlands to take charge of their court music, and it was not until around 1600 that musical supremacy passed to the south. That it finally did so was largely due to Giovanni Palestrina (1526?-1594), who spent his active years in Rome in the service of the popes. Unlike his contemporaries, he devoted nearly all his energies to church music. His genius enabled him to bring to the complexities of the contrapuntal style the same grace, harmony, unity, and restraint that the great painters of the high Renaissance had given to the mass of details that had appeared in their medium. Music, like painting, had become much more complicated since 1300, but in both fields discipline had been imposed by 1575, although the unity of the arts that had existed in the Gothic cathedral had been lost. Painting, sculpture, architecture, and music were going their separate ways.

The growing complexity of music had caused the monk and troubadour to be replaced at church and at court by professional musicians and singers, just as the triumphs of art had raised the artist in status from craftsman to professional. By 1480, there were sixty-three salaried singers in the cathedral of Antwerp, and many would-be composers were beginning their training as choir boys. There were those who regretted the professionalization of music at the expense of general participation. The amateur who likes to sing might find himself in accord with that devout member of the New Devotion, Thomas à Kempis, when he said: "If you cannot sing like the nightingale and the lark, then sing like the crows and the frogs, which sing as God meant them to."

CONCLUSIONS

By the early sixteenth century, the intellectual and aesthetic outlook of European civilization had changed drastically from what it had been two hundred years before. Kings, nobles, and wealthy merchants had joined the leaders of the Church as patrons of the arts and letters and had brought secular tastes into fields long dominated by religious concerns. These tastes, however, were not pagan. The classicism that had come to dominate the arts and letters had been fused with the Christian tradition. In the process, Christianity itself was being changed. The humanists had found a secular basis for the moral code that they hoped would lend support to Christian ethical teachings, and they had come to believe that man had the capacity to make of himself what he would.

The artists had made revolutionary technical discoveries. Some used their newly-found skill to recapture the physical beauty of the world, believing that physical beauty led them toward the spiritual beauty of God. Other artists strove for a grim realism, to teach their public the promise of a future life, the evils of sin, and the pains of hell.

The medieval synthesis, with its scholastic philosophy and its Gothic art, was being rejected, and even the tongue of the Church was being rivaled by the rapidly developing vernacular languages. It was not that Europe was becoming less religious. It was, perhaps, more religious in 1517 than it had ever been before.

THE RELIGIOUS RENAISSANCE

The cultural and artistic rebirths were accompanied by a spiritual rebirth that reached more people than the other two movements combined. It is more difficult to tell when and how the religious Renaissance began. The devout have always sought a spiritual rebirth, and throughout Christian history, periods of spiritual apathy and moral decline have alternated with periods of religious revival. The great Franciscan and Dominican reform movements of the thirteenth century had been followed by the religious decline of the Avignon papacy; by the time humanism had become a full-grown movement in Italy and artists had discovered how to imitate nature, a new religious crest was reached with the members of the New Devotion, the leaders of the conciliar movement, and radical reformers like Wyclif and Hus. A new trough followed after the healing of the Great Schism, but only a very shallow one, for the New Devotion became stronger and the growing humanistic movement supported the demands for reform. Also, neither the conciliar movement, Lollardy, nor the Hussites had passed from the scene. As the fifteenth century drew to a close, it was obvious that a revival was once more in progress; and in the sixteenth century, a religious tidal wave struck Europe that had few, if any, equals.

The New Devotion spread its teaching throughout the Netherlands and into most of Germany. In the Spanish kingdoms, where religious fervor had always been strong, Cardinal Ximenes de Cisneros (1437-1517) had reformed the Spanish church, even before Luther began his attack on the indulgences in 1517,[14] and had reinvigorated scholastic thought. The piety of the New Devotion and the Erasmian spirit had flowed in from abroad, and those who wished to minimize the role of the sacraments took the mystics' way. In the Carmelite nun, St. Teresa (1515-1582), Spain produced a great mystic who so vividly described her ecstatic experiences that her country's art and literature were deeply affected.

Italy, the birthplace of so much of the cultural Renaissance, played a leading role in the religious revival. Between the mid-fourteenth and mid-sixteenth century, about eighty-two Italians were canonized, far more than in any other country. The Neoplatonic philosopher Ficino called out for reform, and humanists there as elsewhere sought a better understanding of the Bible and the early Church fathers. The Dominican friar, Girolamo Savonarola (1452-1498), showed the same willingness to defy the pope in the name of religion that Luther later displayed. His fiery sermons and his prophecies, which he claimed to be from God, brought him a wide following in Florence. The inhabitants of that city, who had done so much to inaugurate the cultural Renaissance, were persuaded to burn their immoral books and their works of art. Pico della Mirandola and Michelangelo were deeply influenced. But Savonarola made as many enemies as he did friends. In 1497 he was excommunicated by the pope, and the following year he was put to death by his fellow citizens.

More orthodox was the Oratory of Divine Love, begun in Italy a little before 1500. It consisted of clergymen and laymen who sought personal sanctification through private devotions and charitable deeds. From its members came some of the outstanding sixteenth-century religious leaders.

The religious orders took on new life in the early sixteenth century. Considerable progress was made in reforming the old orders, and some new orders were started. The Theatines were founded in 1524, through the

14 See pages 211-212.

efforts of several members of the Oratory of Divine Love, in order to re-vitalize the pastoral work of the clergy. Four years later the Franciscans established a new branch, the Capuchins, who insisted that the rule of St. Francis be applied in all its severity. In general, the new monastic move-ment stressed the need for its members to work actively in society, preaching, teaching, and caring for the sick, instead of withdrawing from the world to contemplate and pray.

The New Devotion exercised some influence in France, and the French themselves produced several notable reformers; but in 1517, the religious revival was less strong there than in Spain, Italy, Germany, or the Nether-lands. In England it had scarcely begun.

One of the greatest problems of the reformers was that they could not agree on what the nature of the new Church should be. There were those who wanted to revitalize the medieval Church and its scholastic philoso-phy, although there was no agreement on whether they should take the realist or the nominalist way.[15] There were those who, like the members of the New Devotion, stressed piety more than theology and virtue more than ritual, who hated sin and had a deep, abiding fear of hell. There were those who, like Erasmus, sought to combine the moral lessons of classical antiq-uity with the teachings of Christ and believed that man owed his dignity to his free will. Finally, there were those who wanted literally to recreate the Church of the early Christians. With so much diversity of opinion, it was impossible to predict which way the Catholic Church would go, if it moved at all.

One of the most important aspects of the religious reform movement was the hold that it won on the laity and the lower clergy. The members of the upper clergy, who so often owed their positions to family ties rather than religious commitments, were far less deeply affected. The papacy escaped the reforming zeal altogether, although the two Medici popes, Leo X (1513-1521) and Clement VII (1523-1534) were cultured gentlemen who mildly encouraged others to reform, rather than evil men as some of their predecessors had been.

In Germany, the reform movement among the laity and lower clergy was very strong, but the ecclesiastical hierarchy as a whole was too indif-ferent to use its authority to institute the desired changes. In Spain and to a lesser extent in Italy, the hierarchy, exclusive of the popes, had done enough to give the reformers hope for further progress. In France and England, there were still too few reformers to be dangerous. In Germany, then, where the religious revival was so strong and the hierarchy so indif-ferent, there was the greatest danger that an exasperated reformer would take the path to heresy and lead a revolt against the universal church.

Yet no one doubted that these dissensions would somehow be held in check and that the Church, united, would weather the storm as so often before. No one had more confidence that this would be the case than Mar-

[15] See pages 43-45.

tin Luther when, about midday on October 31, 1517, he walked through the little town of Wittenberg to nail ninety-five theses on the door of the castle church.

LUTHER'S EARLY LIFE

Martin Luther (1483-1546) lived his entire life in the agricultural and mining section of what is now the eastern part of Germany. His father was of peasant extraction, but by virtue of hard work he had managed to become a successful copper miner and smelter. The young Luther was therefore exposed to the coarseness and superstition of the typical peasant. He never doubted that there were witches and demons, and he described his bouts with the devil throughout his life. His father was financially able to provide him with an excellent education, and in 1505 he received his Master's degree from the nearby University of Erfurt, where he stood second in a class of seventeen. His father planned for him to study law, but on his way back to Erfurt that same year, Luther was caught in a thunderstorm and thrown to the ground by a bolt of lightning. Thoroughly frightened, he vowed to Saint Anne to become a monk if he survived; several weeks later, he entered the Augustinian monastery at Erfurt, where he was ordained a priest in 1507.

Luther's vow was not taken so much in fear of death as in fear of hell. In his youth, he had been exposed to the simple piety of the Brethren of the Common Life, and everywhere he had seen paintings showing the horrible fate of those who were not saved. In his undergraduate days at Erfurt and later in his theological studies there, he had been trained in the nominalist or *via moderna* tradition. He had been taught that God was a god of justice who punished the wicked and that man, largely through his own efforts, could merit salvation by loving God and doing His will. But Luther could not love this God of the nominalists, this God of sheer, arbitrary will. At times, the pressures of work kept his mind off his spiritual problems, but he suffered from recurring fits of depression in which he continually asked himself: "How can I be saved?" One such period of depression had occurred a little before the vow in the thunderstorm, and in deciding to become a monk, he had adopted what was then regarded as the surest means of escaping the flames of hell.

For a time the monastery seemed to be the answer, but Luther went through another crisis the first time he said Mass. He confessed his sins frequently, he fasted for three days at a time, and he nearly froze from sleeping without blankets. "I was a good monk," he later declared, "and I kept the rule of my order so strictly that I may say that if ever a monk got to heaven by his monkery it was I." But he still could not convince himself that he would be saved. When he was sent to Rome on a mission in 1510, he took advantage of the opportunity to visit the numerous sacred shrines in the Eternal City, but the pilgrim's way brought no more com-

Martin Luther. Engraved from a portrait in Windsor Castle by Hans Holbein the Younger. (Courtesy of the New York Public Library)

fort than the ascetic's. At length, he came under the guidance of Johann von Staupitz, vicar-general of the Augustinian order, a learned, kindly man who followed the mystical way of the Friends of God. Luther never managed to have a comforting vision, although it may have been the mystics who taught him that man could not be saved by his own will. In desperation, Staupitz decided that his charge should take his Doctorate in theology and obtained for him the chair of the Bible at the new university at Wittenberg, the capital of electoral Saxony. By teaching, the brilliant but overly emotional young monk was to learn.

LUTHER'S THEOLOGY

Luther commenced his Biblical lectures during the summer of 1513, and about the same time he began to solve his problem through the study of the Psalms and especially St. Paul. St. Paul's phrase, "righteousness of God," [16] which he had been taught by the nominalists meant the punitive righteousness by which God punishes those who have not loved and obeyed Him, Luther now came to interpret as meaning the forgiving righteousness with which the merciful God justifies, that is, saves man by giving him faith.

[16] Romans I: 17.

209

Man by himself can do nothing. He is a sinner and deserves only damnation, but if God in His mercy gives him faith, he cannot help believing and is saved. Thus, the principal point in Luther's theology was that man is justified by faith alone.

It is on this point that Luther broke with so much of Catholic theology, for his insistence that a man could be saved only by faith given him directly by God removed the need for the complex apparatus through which Catholics believed that man, in cooperation with God, earned salvation. Gone were pilgrimages, the veneration of saints and relics, the monastic life, the celibacy of the clergy, and the other means through which men had sought to lead more holy lives to earn salvation. Gone also was most of the sacramental system through which Catholics believed that God imparted grace to help man towards faith and virtue. To Luther, grace was not a substance, but simply an act of forgiveness and restoration to divine favor. Somewhat inconsistently, Luther kept the sacraments of baptism and the Lord's Supper, because they seemed so firmly implanted in the Bible, but he altered the nature of the latter by declaring that there was no miracle of the Mass in which the priest changed the bread and wine into the body and blood of Christ. Rather, God became present in the elements, and their efficacy depended primarily on the faith of the recipient.

Luther's insistence that man could do nothing to save himself raised the question of why he should lead a moral life. To this, Luther replied that so long as a man was in doubt about his salvation, he was in bondage to his own fears, but once he had received inward assurance of a future life through faith, he was freed from his anxiety and given strength to serve God and his neighbor. The Catholic believed that man was saved by faith and works; Luther taught that man was saved by faith alone but that faith led inevitably to good works.

With the abandonment of nearly all the sacraments including ordination, the clergy ceased to be a separate class in society. Indeed, Luther's doctrine that salvation was a direct gift from God made religion an individual affair, and every man became his own "priest." Luther did recognize the need for trained pastors, but in the early days of the Lutheran movement, they were selected by the congregation, for to him the Church was a community of all true believers.

But in what were Christians to believe? To this, Luther answered, the Bible. He himself preferred some parts of the Bible to others, but the Bible as a whole contained the true word of God. The traditions of the Catholic Church, the authority of the pope, and the rulings of the Church councils he repudiated one by one. Whenever he was challenged, he sought support from the Scriptures. The Scriptures, he insisted, must be interpreted literally, although he himself sometimes took surprising liberties. Gone were the allegorical, moral, and anagogical interpretations of the medieval Christians, and with them went further justifications for

Catholic traditions. When asked by his opponents how he could be so sure that he alone knew how to interpret the Bible, Luther had no ready answer, but impelled by the inward certainty that his own interpretations were correct, he did not waver.

Soon Luther's interpretations were challenged by his own followers, and he made the unhappy discovery that by abandoning the Catholic institutional system he had lost the power to control the movement. His only means of enforcing his views was to turn for help to the territorial princes who favored his position, and from that time the state exercised ultimate control over the Lutheran movement.

These ideas did not spring full-grown from Luther's mind. They were formed gradually as a result of his studies and through the ever-changing demands that were placed upon him as the leader of a revolutionary movement. The basic outlines of his thought had been formed, however, when word reached him that indulgences were being sold in neighboring territories.

FROM PROTEST TO REBELLION

An indulgence is a remission, granted on the authorization of the pope, of temporal punishment in purgatory for sins for which insufficient penance had been done while on earth. The idea of an indulgence grew from the belief that accumulated merits, derived from the perfect lives of Jesus and the saints, could be transferred to individual sinners by the pope, who, as the successor of St. Peter, held the keys to the Kingdom of Heaven. There was nothing abusive about indulgences in themselves, and they had long been granted to contrite persons who had been forgiven for their sins in return for pious acts such as going on crusades and pilgrimages. Unfortunately, a gift of money to the Church came to be considered one of the acceptable pious acts, and the Renaissance papacy could not resist making the most of this situation. In the actual distribution of indulgences in 1517, those in charge often neglected to mention the niceties of contrition and confession and in effect promised freedom from suffering in purgatory in return for a cash payment. Indeed, the indulgence salesmen even promised that the souls of those already dead would be released upon the purchase of indulgences for them by relatives or friends; they recited this little ditty:

> *As soon as coin in coffer rings,*
> *The soul from purgatory springs.*

Half the money raised by the sale of indulgences in 1517 was to go to the building of the new St. Peter's at Rome and half to the recently elected Archbishop of Mainz to enable him to buy a dispensation from the pope authorizing him to hold that post as well as the archbishopric of Magdeburg and other offices. It was not, however, the abusive manner in which the indulgences were sold that disturbed Luther so much as the theological ideas behind them.

When Luther nailed his theses attacking the indulgences on the church door, he intended only to provoke an academic debate, but his statement was soon translated into German, printed, and widely circulated. Many jumped to his support, and the revenue from the indulgences dropped. Complaints were sent to Rome, and several efforts were made to silence him. Matters grew increasingly serious as Luther declared that the pope and Church council could err and dramatically threw down the gauntlet in December, 1520, by publicly burning a papal bull condemning his teachings as heretical. The following spring Luther appeared before a meeting of the *Reichstag* at Worms where, in the presence of Emperor Charles V, he was called upon to repudiate his errors. Though sweating from fear, he held his ground, replying that: "Unless I am convicted by Scripture and plain reason—I do not accept the authority of popes and councils, for they have contradicted each other—my conscience is captive to the Word of God. I cannot and I will not recant anything, for to go against conscience is neither right nor safe. God help me. Amen." [17]

In the deliberations that followed, the youthful emperor took an equally dramatic stand in favor of the traditional faith. "I am descended from a long line of Christian emperors of this noble German nation, and of the Catholic kings of Spain, the archdukes of Austria, and the dukes of Burgundy. They were all faithful to the death to the Church of Rome, and they defended the Catholic faith and the honor of God. I have resolved to follow in their steps. A single friar who goes counter to all Christianity for a thousand years must be wrong. Therefore I am resolved to stake my lands, my friends, my body, my blood, my life, and my soul." [18] But, man of honor that he was, Charles permitted Luther to depart unmolested because he had given him a safe conduct. The electors of Saxony and the Palatinate sided with Luther, but the remaining electors stood by Charles, and Luther was placed under the ban of the Empire. The new religion was not to conquer the old without a struggle.

During the years that followed, Lutheranism won many converts in southern Germany and became the dominant religion in northern Germany and the Scandinavian countries. It won a following, especially among the nobility, in Poland, Bohemia, Austria, and Hungary. In Western Europe, Lutheranism gained only isolated support, but other Protestant denominations soon arose there to compete with the Catholics. By the time of Luther's death in 1546, the religious unity of Christendom had been brought to an end. The Empire was religiously divided, and there were important Protestant minorities in other states.

[17] Quoted by Roland H. Bainton, *Here I Stand. A Life of Martin Luther* (New York: Mentor Books, 1955), p. 144.

[18] *Ibid.*, p. 145.

REASONS FOR THE SPREAD OF PROTESTANTISM

The rapid spread of Lutheranism and other Protestant denominations was in marked contrast with the limited successes achieved by previous religious leaders like Wyclif and Hus who had also broken with Rome. Many reasons have been given to explain Luther's success.

Luther had nearly every quality essential to a revolutionary leader. His courage and intense conviction enabled him to take his stand against pope and emperor, and his intellectual and argumentative powers often convinced the skeptical. Although many of his sermons and pamphlets now seem unnecessarily violent and vindictive, they made as many friends as enemies. His literary style was superior, and he had genuine gifts as a writer of hymns. Indeed, he was the first person to make congregational singing an important part of the church service. However, it would be hasty to assume that he was a better leader than Wyclif or Hus, whose theological positions were quite similar to his own.

Luther did have one great advantage that had been denied to his predecessors—the printing press. Their ability to influence people had been limited by the relatively few who could hear their sermons or read the handful of manuscripts that they and their supporters could copy, but the printing press enabled Luther to make the entire Empire his audience. He made special use of small pamphlets from six to eight pages in length that could be sold for very little; some 350,000 copies of these were printed between 1517 and 1520. Woodcuts on the title pages suggested the contents to the illiterate and attracted the attention of those who could read. Quickly they enabled Luther to gain so wide a following that he could have been halted only by the use of a large army.

Another advantage possessed by Luther was that the unusual political situation in Germany gave him time to consolidate his position. The semi-independent status of the Elector Frederick of Saxony enabled him to protect Luther from the wrath of the Church and the secular authorities. Frederick's position was especially strong at the time because Emperor Maximilian was dying when the indulgence question arose; in the interregnum that followed, the pope was more anxious to persuade Frederick to help block the election of Charles V to the imperial throne than he was to get him to punish a rebellious monk. More than three years elapsed after Luther had posted the ninety-five theses before he was excommunicated or placed under the ban of the Empire.

By that time, the Lutheran movement had become so strong that only a large military force could have stamped it out. Charles was in no position to act because war broke out with France that same year and lasted almost continuously until 1544. The Turks besieged Vienna in 1529, and that war continued to sap the imperial strength until 1545. It was not until the following year that Charles was able to take military action against the Protestants. Although he won some initial successes, neither the pope nor the Catholic German princes would give him their wholehearted support for fear that while he was defeating the Protestants he would also make himself political master of the Empire. Finally, renewed French intervention brought an end to Charles's hopes, and he abdicated, leaving to his brother Ferdinand the task of making a religious settlement. By the terms of the Peace of Augsburg, 1555, the individual princes and imperial cities were given the right to decide whether their subjects would be Lutheran or Catholic and those who objected were to be permitted to emigrate. Church lands seized by the Lutherans prior to 1552 were to be retained, but in the future, bishops who became Protestants were to forfeit their lands rather than turn them into secular principalities as they had done before. Protestant sects other than the Lutherans were not recognized, but the existence of a Lutheran church in the Empire was not seriously threatened again until the Thirty Years War (1618-1648).

The printing press and the advantageous political situation in the Empire gave Luther the time and the means to gather converts, but less obvious factors may also have contributed to his extraordinary success. Most of those who objected only to the abuses in the Catholic Church stayed in its fold to work for reform, but the existence of abuses lowered the respect in which the ecclesiastical hierarchy was held and thereby lessened its capacity to combat Protestantism. In addition, the abuses provided Luther and his supporters with propaganda that they never tired of using. Still, bad as they were, the abuses were not so important a factor in the Protestant revolt as might be imagined.

In some respects, the issue of abuses became entangled with the nascent nationalism of the age. At this time, nationalism was a negative force opposing outside interference, more than a positive force drawing different provinces together. The pope, as the head of the one remaining international institution, was constantly under attack. His right to fill many clerical vacancies and to grant indulgences, his claim to receive annates and various other revenues, and his ecclesiastical courts, which served as final courts of appeal in ecclesiastical cases, including divorces, were everywhere unpopular. It was well known that papal favors could usually be purchased, and it was widely believed that the constant flow of money to Rome was hurting local economies. Strong monarchies like those of France, England, and the Spanish kingdoms had been able to reduce papal influence, especially during the conciliar movement, but the emperor had lacked the power to do so effectively. Nowhere was the influence of Rome greater than in the Empire.

This situation provoked the ire of Ulrich von Hutten (1488-1523), an imperial knight whose humanistic studies had led him to Tacitus' (55-118?) description of the early Germans as brave, loyal, and liberty-loving. History, as Hutten saw it, had witnessed a constant struggle between the Latins, represented by the Roman Empire in ancient times and the popes of his day, and the Germans. The Lutheran movement was for him an effort to throw off foreign domination. He enlisted the help of some other imperial knights, including Franz von Sickingen, a mercenary soldier who possessed an army. In 1522, they attempted to secularize the lands of the Archbishop of Trier but were defeated the following year. Their failure, taken with Charles V's decision at the meeting of the *Reichstag* at Worms to remain loyal to Rome, removed the possibility of the Lutheran movement's merging fully with nationalistic forces to create an independent German church.

It has often been suggested that economic and social factors helped the Protestant cause. Although the peasants in southern and central Germany were, as a whole, becoming more prosperous, higher taxes and increased exactions by the nobility were taking a large part of their gains. They looked to the emperor for support against the great nobles and boldly coupled their economic demands with requests for such Lutheran reforms as the election of ministers by their congregations. Although Luther recognized some justice in their position, he was furious at their efforts to use religion to justify their worldly aspirations and argued that the Bible defended serfdom. By 1524, the peasant movement had become a revolt. In some towns, the lower classes supported the peasants, as did a few of the more radical Protestant ministers, but Luther was violently opposed. Although he was himself of peasant descent, he wrote the virulent pamphlet, *Against the Murdering Hordes of Peasants,* in which he urged the princes to "knock down, strangle, and stab . . . Such wonderful times are these that a prince can merit heaven better with bloodshed than another with prayer." His advice was hardly necessary. The poorly led peasants were easily defeated, and an estimated 100,000 were slaughtered in the blood bath that followed. Belatedly, Luther called for mercy, but most of the German masses had been permanently alienated.

Many, especially the Marxists, have sought to associate Protestantism with the rise of the middle class. Catholicism, they argued, was an ascetic religion ideally suited for a medieval, feudal, agrarian society, but the growth of a bourgeois capitalistic economy created a need for a new religion that would justify worldly pursuits and business practices such as the charging of interest. Unhappily for the advocates of this point of view, Luther was more conservative in his social and economic outlook than most Catholics and bitterly attacked the pope for permitting usury. No Protestant leader was willing to make more concessions to the capitalists than they already enjoyed in Italy; and Italy, where the middle class was more highly developed than anywhere else in Europe, remained overwhelmingly Catholic.

Indeed, a higher percentage of the nobility joined the Protestant churches than of any other social class. Some nobles may have hoped to get the lands of the Catholic Church or to persuade the Protestants to support their political ambitions, but the risk in abandoning Catholicism was so great during the early stages that it is doubtful whether many, other than the religiously committed, were initially willing to brave the dangers. Only after the territorial prince adopted the new religion or a Protestant military leader had achieved considerable strength would many have been tempted to change their faith for economic or political reasons alone.

The territorial prince and the magistrates of imperial cities undoubtedly played major roles in the spread of Protestantism. The desire to be rid of papal influence and to increase their authority over the local clergy, as well as the desire for the wealth of the Church, commonly prompted rulers to abandon Catholicism. It was a dangerous step to take, however, and most of the German princes and magistrates who turned to Protestantism appear to have done so primarily for religious reasons. In England, where Henry VIII was obviously motivated almost entirely by secular considerations, religious doctrine was not initially changed to a significant degree. Once a ruler decided to become a Protestant, many of his subjects followed his example. Only the most devout put their religious faith ahead of their desire for law and order, which they thought necessitated unquestioned obedience.

The humanists may have paved the way for Protestantism by their study of philology, by their criticism of scholastic thought, and by their de-emphasis of Catholic dogma and ritual, but here the parallel ceases. The humanists taught a moral code that they found common to Christianity and the writers of classical antiquity. The Protestants taught a religious faith that was exemplified by the incarnation, the crucifixion, and the resurrection. The humanists emphasized that the dignity of man lay in his free will. The Protestants emphasized the depravity of man and insisted that he could do nothing of himself to merit salvation. When Luther began his attack on Rome, many humanists watched hopefully, but as soon as they recognized the character of the new movement, nearly all of the best known of their number decided to remain within the Catholic Church although some young humanistically trained scholars joined the Protestants. When, in 1524, Erasmus finally entered the fray, it was to decry Luther's denial of free will, but he could have added the Protestant overemphasis on theology and the Protestant willingness to destroy the unity of the Church to his list of grievances.

The aesthetic aspects of the Renaissance were rejected by the Protestants. They regarded most church art as a form of idolatry and secular art as a vain conceit. Only hymn singing received their blessing. Thus, the Renaissance and Protestantism were contrary movements in many respects. They were alike only in that they had several common enemies and each in its own way fostered the development of individualism, the Renaissance by its emphasis on the dignity of man and Protestantism by its emphasis on the direct relationship between man and God.

Therefore, Protestantism was obviously a religious movement. Most of Luther's early support came from those like himself who had been taught by sermons and pictures to fear the flames of hell and who felt unable to merit salvation through their own efforts. To such people, the Protestant doctrine of salvation by faith alone brought a measure of hope. They were most numerous in the north; in Italy, where the religious intensity was less, Luther met with little response.

THE ANABAPTISTS

Luther, as we have seen, did not carry all of his ideas to their logical conclusion. Although he spoke of the priesthood of all believers and insisted that the clergy was not a special class in society, the ministers of his church wore distinctive garments and looked to the state for salary and support. He attacked the sacramental system, but kept the sacraments of baptism and Holy Communion. He believed in the literal interpretation of the Bible but did not attempt to reconstruct society along the lines followed by the primitive Christians. These conservative tendencies angered the radicals who sought a more literal revival of primitive Christianity. They were known collectively as the Anabaptists, although their beliefs varied considerably.

In general, the Anabaptists taught that the church was a community of saints who had experienced spiritual regeneration. Like the Catholics, they believed that salvation was a combined product of man's own efforts and of grace, but, to them, grace was not imparted by means of a sacramental system but was a direct gift that took the form of an inner, half-mystical experience. Only after one had testified that he had had such an experience was he baptized. Baptism was therefore regarded as a sign of spiritual regeneration and was given only to adults. Because these early Baptists had already received infant baptism in the Catholic Church, they were called Anabaptists (those who practice rebaptism). Holy Communion was interpreted as a commemorative service only.

The Anabaptists usually practiced strict democracy. Pastors were elected by the congregations and wore no distinctive garments. Those who were not pastors shared in the responsibility of helping their fellow believers and serving as missionaries to nonbelievers. Most Anabaptists believed in a strict separation of church and state, a belief which they carried to the point of not holding political offices. They therefore had neither the means nor the desire to compel others to believe as they did, and although the heretic and the unholy were excommunicated, it was a spiritual punishment only. They alone of the early Protestants believed in freedom of conscience and condemned religious persecution.

Some of the leaders of the Anabaptists were highly educated men, but most of their members were drawn from the lower classes who were attracted by the emotional and democratic aspects of the doctrine. They were usually pacifists who practiced a high moral code, but their emphasis on Biblical literalism led a few groups to extremes. Some believed that the end of the world was at hand and that the thousand-year rule of the saints was about to begin, as predicted in Revelation 20. Others believed that the early Christians practiced community ownership of property and followed their example. A few emphasized the more violent passages of the Old Testament and sought to establish the Kingdom of God on earth by forceful means, or else found in the early chapters of the Bible a justification for polygamy.

Such occasional practices made the Anabaptists hated and feared, but their complete denial of a sacramental system was enough to lead to their persecution by the Catholics and the other Protestant denominations. They were stamped out in most of Germany, but a few survived in eastern Europe and in the Netherlands where Menno Simons (1496-1559) organized them into the Mennonite Church. The Mennonites influenced the Quakers, Independents, and Baptists of the English-speaking world.

CALVIN AND THE SWISS REFORMATION

Luther had hardly begun his revolt against papal authority in Wittenberg before several Swiss towns began to follow his example by severing their ties with the pope. The first important Swiss reformer was Ulrich Zwingli (1484-1531), a humanistically trained priest who had begun to demand political and moral reforms before Luther broke with Rome. By the close of 1524, he had successfully established the Protestant religion in the canton of Zurich through peaceful persuasion. Bern, Basel, and several other German- and Italian-speaking cantons soon followed Zurich's example. Unfortunately, a doctrinal dispute arose between Luther and Zwingli that centered around the interpretation of the Last Supper. To Zwingli, it was only a commemorative service in which Christ was spiritually, but not physically, present. After an unsuccessful attempt at Marburg in 1529 to bring the two reformers into agreement, it became obvious that the Protestant movement would not unite in one church but divide into many warring sects. The belligerent Zwingli persuaded Zurich to provoke a quarrel with neighboring Catholic cantons, but he was defeated and killed in 1531. Zurich, Bern, and Basel remained Protestant, but the Zwinglian church was eventually absorbed into the Calvinist church that developed in Geneva.

John Calvin (1509-1564) was born in the French town of Noyon. At the age of fourteen he was sent to the University of Paris to study for the priesthood. In 1528, his father, who had quarreled with some local church officials, directed him to study law, but after his parent's death three years later, Calvin determined on an academic career as a humanist. About 1534, he became a Protestant and withdrew to the upper Rhineland, where in Basel he published the first edition of the *Institutes of the Christian Religion* in 1536, a masterful synthesis of Protestant thought. That same year he settled in Geneva and thereafter devoted his life, except

John Calvin by Hans Holbein. (Courtesy Free Library of Philadelphia)

for a three-year exile between 1538 and 1541, to making that city a city of God."

Geneva was a banking-commercial city of about 17,000 inhabitants. The duke of Savoy, the local bishop, and the town council had shared in its government, but just before Calvin's arrival, there had been a successful revolt in which the duke and the bishop had been removed from authority and Geneva had become an independent Protestant city-state. Contrary to what has often been thought, Calvin did not establish a theocracy in Geneva. Ultimate authority, even in matters of doctrine, always rested with the secular government, and candidates for the ministry had to receive its approval. The maintenance of church discipline was placed in the hands of twelve elders who were members of the governing assemblies of the city. These elders and the ministers of the city, who were five in number in 1541, met weekly in the Consistory to consider minor cases of un-Christian conduct, but serious offenses remained the responsibility of the city officials. Thus, Calvin ruled only through his influence, and it was not until after 1553 that his influence became decisive.

Calvin believed in a more complete separation of church and state than the Lutherans or the Anglicans. Much of the actual government of the church was in the hands of the Consistory in Geneva or in synods in larger states where the elders and the ministers shared control. This made it necessary for the sovereign authority to deal with assemblies which were partly representative in character, rather than with bishops whom it appointed and through whom it could control the lower clergy. Calvin, like other Protestants, preached obedience to the secular authority except when its commands were contrary to the will of God. Even in that case, he counseled passive disobedience and reminded his followers of the story of Daniel in the lion's den. Nevertheless, as a lawyer he knew that authority in the Renaissance monarchy was shared by the king with the estates and other magistrates. If a king became tyrannical, he hinted that the estates or magistrates were justified in resisting, but not ordinary citizens. Although a similar doctrine was developed by the Lutherans, the aggressive character of the Calvinist movement, coupled with its lack of an ecclesiastical hierarchy, made it the most feared of the Protestant sects.

In most respects, Calvin's doctrines were similar to those of Luther, although his conception of God and the rigorous logic of his lawyer-trained mind led to some differences that were never resolved. Calvin accepted Luther's doctrine of justification by faith alone, but the absolute sovereignty of God was his central belief. God is "the Arbiter and Governor of all things, who, in His own wisdom, has, from the remotest eternity, decreed what He would do, and now, by His own power, executes what He has decreed." He "has once and for all determined, both whom He would admit to salvation, and whom He would condemn to destruction." God has foreordained what man will do; some, the elect, He has arbitrarily saved through the gift of faith, and the remainder He has doomed to hell, although there had been nothing that they could have done by their own efforts to merit salvation. If this seemed unjust, it must be remembered that "the will of God is the highest rule of justice, so that what He wills must be considered just, for this very reason, because He wills it." No other theologian had ever stated the doctrine of predestination more strongly.

There was no infallible way of determining who were among the elect and who were not, but those who seemed to be carrying out God's purpose could take it as a hopeful sign. Thus, the doctrine of predestination gave to its Calvinist adherents a powerful motive to do God's work in order to convince themselves that they would be saved, and the advances of Protestantism after 1546 were due mostly to their efforts.

God's purpose and God's laws can be found in the Bible. Although Calvin used the New Testament more frequently, his conception of God was closer to that of the arbitrary deity of the Old Testament. One part of the Bible was as important as another, and any seeming conflict was to be resolved. The elect, by the gift of grace, will carry out God's will, and the damned should be made to conform as far as possible to the Christian way of life in order to do honor to God. Therefore, every effort was exerted to make the citizens of Geneva live according to "the Word of God."

ESTABLISHED CHURCHES AROUND 1600

LUTHERAN	GREEK ORTHODOX	MINORITIES OR SECTS UNDER THE TERRITORIAL CHURCHES:
CALVINIST	MOSLEM	
ANGLICAN		R ROMAN CATHOLIC S SOCINIANS
CATHOLIC		C CALVINISTS B ANABAPTISTS
		L LUTHERANS

Minute regulations were enforced governing every aspect of life, and the inhabitants were constantly spied upon to ensure compliance. Children were sometimes questioned concerning their parents. Citizens were punished for attending the theater and for not attending sermons. Dancing and card playing were outlawed, and the criticism of ministers was forbidden. More serious crimes were punished by banishment or death, and between 1542 and 1546 fifty-eight persons were executed in Geneva for heresy, blasphemy, adultery, and witchcraft. Among those convicted of adultery were Calvin's sister-in-law and his stepdaughter. Gradually, as the incorrigibles left the city or were put to death and their place was taken by austere persons from all over Europe, the quality of the inhabitants began to change. In 1556, John Knox (1505-1572) reported that Geneva was "the most perfect school of Christ that ever was on earth since the days of the apostles."

From this "school of Christ" missionaries were sent all over Europe. John Knox, a former Scottish priest who had been converted to Protestantism, visited Geneva and was so impressed that when he returned to Scotland in 1559 he introduced Calvinism. Local circumstances aided his cause. Mary, the inexperienced young queen, was neither able nor moral. She was considered a foreigner by many because of her long residence in France, and the very year that Knox returned, French troops were sent to stamp out the nascent Protestant movement. Most of these troops were withdrawn in 1560, leaving the inexperienced Mary to cope with her thoroughly aroused subjects. Parliament broke the ties with Rome and adopted a strongly Calvinistic confession of faith. By the time Mary was forced to flee to England in 1568, the Protestant triumph in Scotland was virtually complete.

Calvin also lived to see his version of Protestantism adopted by large numbers in France, the Netherlands, Germany, Poland, and Hungary, while in Switzerland itself most of Zwingli's followers were drawing towards his camp. Soon, even England was to feel the impact of his thought.

THE CHURCH OF ENGLAND

The religious revival of the late fifteenth century had not spread to England and there was little in its art or literature to suggest the preoccupation with death and the fear of hell that characterized so much of northern Europe. Only a handful of persons were prepared to risk martyrdom by opposing Henry VIII's ecclesiastical break with Rome or his later insistence that Catholic ritual and dogma be maintained. During the brief reign of his young son, Edward VI (1547-1553), however, a number of continental reformers settled in England, where several of them were given university professorships. Under their influence and with the support of the leading nobles in the government and the Archbishop of Canterbury, Thomas Cranmer (1489-1556), England moved steadily towards the Protestant camp.

This trend was arrested in 1553, when Edward's death brought Mary (1553-1558), Henry VIII's daughter by Catherine of Aragon, to the throne. Mary was a devout Catholic who immediately tried to restore Catholicism to England. Although the majority still preferred the Catholic religion, their aversion to papal interference was as strong as ever, and the powerful aristocracy had no intention of restoring the monastic lands that had been confiscated during her father's reign. Mass was once more said, and Parliament was finally persuaded to repeal Henry VIII's laws leading to the break with Rome, but Mary's every act brought increased opposition. About two thousand clergymen were deprived of their posts, for the most part because they had married during her brother's reign. More unpopular still was the burning of 273 men and women for heresy, including Cranmer and four other bishops. To make matters worse, Mary aroused the nationalistic prejudices of her subjects by marrying Philip II of Spain. Mary rejected the Spanish advice of moderation in dealing with the religious situation in England, but she honored the Spanish appeal for assistance on the continent when the Habsburg-Valois wars were renewed in 1556. The result of English involvement in this war was the loss in 1558 of Calais, the last remaining English possession on the continent. Heartbroken, the pathetic, misguided queen died that same year, leaving England Catholic in name but less Catholic in spirit than when her ill-starred reign had begun.

Her successor was her half-sister, Elizabeth I (1558-1603), a tall, red-haired woman of twenty-five whose early years of adversity had already made her an experienced politician. From the age of three when her mother, Anne Boleyn, had been executed for adultery, until Mary's death, Elizabeth had been beset with difficulties. The Protestants who had plotted against her predecessor had sought to tie her to their cause, and at times her very life was in danger. She was intelligent, determined, and courageous, and yet often dilatory in making decisions and inclined to change her mind once she had made them. As often as not, however, her very procrastination redounded to her benefit, and to this day it is impossible to tell whether her various negotiations for a foreign marriage were carried on entirely to secure temporary diplomatic advantages or whether her delay in rejecting proposals resulted from her inability to make up her mind. She was stingy and deceitful, imperious and majestic. The glorious events of her reign were partly due to fortuitous circumstances and the host of able men produced in that half century of English history but equally due to her own ability and character and her choice of the right people to advise and serve her. Of these, the most important was Sir William Cecil, Lord Burghley, who was her principal adviser until his death in 1598.

It has often been assumed that Elizabeth, as Anne Boleyn's daughter, had no choice but to lead England back to Protestantism, but this assumption is not valid. The pope was willing to grant her a dispensation, and Philip II offered to make her his wife. England at the time was at war with France, and Spain was the only English ally. The domestic situation, however, pointed towards a restoration of Protestantism. During her brief reign, Mary had succeeded in discrediting the religion she loved; and while the majority were still Catholic, many were lukewarm in their faith and anxious to avoid foreign influence, whether from the pope or from another Spanish marriage. Above all, those who held monastic land would never feel secure in their gains while a Catholic reigned. Therefore, Elizabeth determined to throw in her lot with the belligerent Protestant minority led by some eight hundred returning exiles, who had spent Mary's reign drinking from the fountains of Protestantism at Geneva, Strassburg, Zurich, and other cities. But she moved with her customary caution, and only after she had made peace with France in 1559 did she risk antagonizing the Spanish by breaking with Rome. The following year, when the French withdrew from Scotland and that country moved into the Protestant ranks, her religious settlement was confirmed.

Elizabeth herself would probably have preferred to return to the church of her father, for she loved the pomp and ceremony of that service, but she was dependent upon the more extreme Protestants for support. The Thirty-Nine Articles which were passed by Parliament in 1563 establishing the Anglican Church were Protestant in dogma, although many phrases were left ambiguous to blur the differences between the Lutheran and Calvinist interpretations. The liturgy was similar to that of the Catholics except that it was in English. Elizabeth was declared to be the "supreme governor" of the church, which she administered through a hierarchy of archbishops and bishops. On the whole, the new church was a successful compromise. The Catholic bishops refused to accept it, but most of the lower clergy were satisfied, while the mass of the people, though still Catholic in sentiment, were content to see so much of the ceremony of the ancient church preserved and did not trouble themselves about the niceties of dogma. Always tolerant in such matters, Elizabeth winked at the continuance of Mass in the remoter parts of her kingdom.

In the long run, the extreme Protestants became a more serious threat than the Catholics. An ill-defined group known as the Puritans wanted to "purify" the Anglican Church of its papal rites and ecclesiastical hierarchy and return to the simple rituals of the early Christians. They caused Elizabeth considerable trouble in Parliament with their demands, and they were always anxious to embroil England on the continent in defense of their fellow Protestants.

The constant attacks of the Puritans led Richard Hooker (1553-1600) to begin to publish his *Ecclesiastical Polity* in 1594, in which he rejected the radicals' contention that the Bible should be the sole guide to church organization and ritual. Hooker argued that the traditions of the church and human reason must also be considered and that only those forms and ceremonies which were bad in themselves ought to be rejected. Although his defense became a landmark in the history of the Anglican Church, it did not convince the Puritans.

Some Anglicans were more conservative than Hooker, and instead of defending episcopacy on the grounds that it was administratively convenient, as he had done, they claimed for the clergy a special status by reviving the doctrine of apostolic succession. The Church, they argued, "is a society of believers under bishops and pastors, succeeding those on whom the Holy Ghost came down, and (by receiving ordination of those that had that power before them, that is of the bishops of the church, the continued successors of the Apostles) lawfully called to these offices." [19] This conception of the clergy, which differed from that of the Roman Catholics only in its refusal to give a special status to the pope, became a tenet of the High Church faction in the Anglican communion.

THE CATHOLIC REFORMATION

As we have seen, a religious revival had begun within the Catholic Church itself long before the time of Luther. Accordingly, many reformers continued to remain in the Church, choosing to correct its faults from within rather than join one of the new Protestant sects. To succeed, it was necessary to capture the highest positions in the Church. This was a very difficult task, for kings at this time chose prelates from among their friends and supporters rather than from the devout. The popes had long named their own relatives and those of the kings to the College of Cardinals where the popes themselves were elected. Under such circumstances, the clergy was dominated by secular-minded men with little to recommend them for their posts except their aristocratic birth. Even when the system produced a good bishop, his hands were often tied because so many clergymen in his diocese had been exempted from his jurisdiction that he had little authority. The Archbishop of Lyon could appoint priests in only 21 of the 392 parishes in his diocese. Lyon was an extreme case, but the Bishop of Paris' control over only 215 of 469 parishes in his diocese was probably typical. There was often open conflict between the bishops and the clergy of their cathedral chapters, and the monasteries in their jurisdiction were usually exempt from their control. Moreover, large sums were necessary to carry on the legitimate activities of the Church; if the financial abuses were corrected, new sources of revenue would have to be found. Finally, to fortify the faithful against heresy, it would be necessary to define Catholic dogma clearly and carefully, and yet Catholics themselves were not always agreed on doctrine. Whether, and at what time, the reformers could have overcome these difficulties if Luther

[19] Quoted by Arthur C. McGiffert, *Protestant Thought Before Kant* (New York: Harper Torchbooks, 1961), p. 139.

had not created a rival church in the heart of Christendom is difficult to say, but the Protestant threat certainly strengthened the hands of the reformers and enabled them to carry the Catholic Church to new heights within several generations.

The situation became so desperate that even the members of the College of Cardinals recognized the necessity of reform. When Clement VII died in 1534, they chose the sincere Paul III (1534-1549) to be his successor. Neither Paul nor most of his successors escaped the practice of nepotism, so close were family ties in the Renaissance, nor could they avoid the fact that the papacy was a political state whose worldly interests often conflicted with the program of reform. Nevertheless, Paul reduced the financial abuses at Rome, appointed devout men to the College of Cardinals, accepted the Society of Jesus as a new religious order, and summoned a general council of the Church to meet at Trent. He sometimes procrastinated and compromised, but by his death in 1549, the reform movement was definitely under way. Of the instruments of the Catholic revival none were more important than the Society of Jesus.

LOYOLA AND THE JESUITS

The founder of the Society of Jesus, or the Jesuits as they are more commonly called, was Ignatius Loyola (1491?-1556), a Spanish nobleman who read the romances of chivalry and dreamed of distinguishing himself with feats of arms. War with France gave him his opportunity, but in 1521, while he was courageously defending the town of Pamplona, he was struck in the leg. Pamplona fell, but the victorious French permitted their wounded opponent to retire to his family's castle to recover. There followed a period of intense suffering. His leg had been badly set and had to be rebroken. Once more the physicians failed, and part of the bone had to be sawed off, leaving the thirty-year-old soldier lame.

While he was recovering from this ordeal, Loyola hunted for some romances of chivalry but could find only lives of the saints and a life of Christ. Disappointed, he started to read, but slowly his interest grew and he began to imagine himself a soldier of Christ fighting for the faith, with a new lady, the Virgin Mary, replacing the high-born damsel whom he had formerly served. When he had recovered sufficiently, he set out for the abbey of Montserrat, where young soldiers prayed all night before receiving knighthood. At sunrise, Loyola did not gird himself in armor but left his weapons before the image of the Virgin Mary and in a pilgrim's garb set out for Manresa, where he lived alone in a cave. Here in weeks of lonely prayer and meditation he ate little; his hair and beard and nails grew long.

Out of this experience, Loyola wrote the *Spiritual Exercises* to serve as a guide to his devotions and later for those who chose to follow his way. The book was divided into four parts to provide one "exercise" for

Pope Paul III by Titian. Presented to the pontiff in 1543, the portrait is now in the Naples Museum. (Courtesy of Free Library of Philadelphia)

each week. The first week was devoted to the contemplation of sin, the second to the life of Christ, the third to the passion, and the fourth to the resurrection. Loyola's mysticism was of a positive, active variety, and the goal of the *Spiritual Exercises* was to enable the practitioner to renounce his own desires and follow the will of God. Far from agreeing with Luther and Calvin that man could play no role in the drama of salvation, he believed in free will as far as Catholic doctrine would allow and saw himself entering the lists under the banner of God in His constant struggle with Satan.

Always ready to choose the most difficult and romantic course, Loyola set out for Palestine to convert the Moslems, but after visiting the shrines, he returned to Spain and began to study. While at the university, he tried to save souls, but his enthusiasm outran his knowledge of doctrine and he was arrested by the Inquisition on several occasions. Always his sincerity and willingness to accept correction won for him an early release. In 1528, he enrolled at the University of Paris, where he became the leader of a little group that included the great missionary Francis Xavier. Six years later, Loyola and six companions visited a chapel in the Montmartre, which was then a village outside Paris, and took a vow to go to Jerusalem to convert the infidel. If this proved impossible, they agreed to put themselves at the pope's disposal. War with the Turks prevented the attainment of the first objective, but in 1540 Pope Paul III issued a bull creating the Society of Jesus. Soon it became the most effective tool of the Catholic Reformation.

A number of factors explain the effectiveness of the Jesuits. First, they

227

were a highly centralized, efficient, military-like organization whose members took special vows of obedience. Second, they placed more emphasis on the quality of their members than on the quantity. Priests were well educated in both scholastic philosophy and humanistic studies. Third, everything was directed towards making their work effective. They were not shut up in monasteries and wore no distinctive garb but dressed in accordance with the demands of their individual assignments. No fasts, scourging, or ascetic practices were imposed by Jesuit rule, because Loyola had found from his own experience that when physically weakened he could do less work. Begging he also came to oppose because it took time. Fourth, the Jesuits sought to reach the laity through education, the hearing of confessions, and missionary activity. Their schools and universities became the finest in Europe. Although the humanistic disciplines were stressed, efforts were also made to tie Catholic youths closer to the Church. As confessors, the Jesuits gained control of consciences. Instead of emphasizing the difficulties in achieving salvation, they were instructed to send no one away dejected. This practice led to charges of laxity, but it was nonetheless effective. They were especially pleased to become confessors of princes because this office enabled them to influence political affairs to the benefit of Catholicism. They avoided controversial, dogmatic questions and preached simple sermons that stressed morality. As missionaries to the New World and the Far East, they found no task too dangerous or too difficult. No other group so perfectly blended the piety of the religious Renaissance with the morality, classical learning, and belief in free will so characteristic of Christian humanism.

THE COUNCIL OF TRENT

If the Jesuits were the principal educators and missionaries of the Catholic revival, those who participated in the Council of Trent did the most to define the course it was to take. Pope Paul III, as we have seen, ordered the council to meet at Trent in 1545. It recessed in 1547, and further meetings were held in 1551-1552 and 1562-1563. Paul and his successors hesitated to call each of these sessions.

Charles V and later his brother, Emperor Ferdinand I, were anxious to use the council to reach a compromise with the Protestants, while many bishops hoped that it would result in further checks on papal authority. In the end, however, the councils were convened and the popes were victorious. Tradition and the Bible as interpreted by the Church were declared to be the source of doctrine, and the various tenets of the faith were defined more carefully than before. Many reforms were agreed upon. Bishops were told to reside in their dioceses but were given greater authority to act. Seminaries were established to train priests, and the pope, kings, and bishops were encouraged to appoint better men to ecclesiastical positions.

Yet the most important work of the council was negative. It rejected any concessions that could conceivably have brought a reunion with the more moderate Protestants and any institutional checks that would have permitted the council or the bishops to limit the authority of the pope. Few countries permitted the nondoctrinal decrees of the council to be published. Nevertheless, the work of reform was carried on by a number of popes, one of whom, Pius V (1566-1572), became a saint. Devoted priests appeared in every country, and the number of saints in the late sixteenth and early seventeenth centuries exceeds the number in most other periods. Their efforts brought new fervor to the Catholic laity. The Inquisition was revived in several countries to root out heresy, and an Index of forbidden books was published to prevent Catholics from reading works that might lead them into error. Revived, reformed, and vigorous, the Catholic Church stood ready to meet the challenge of Protestantism when the Council of Trent came to an end in 1563, and it soon had an opportunity to regain some of its losses.

THE RESULTS OF THE RELIGIOUS RENAISSANCE

The reformers had triumphed. From the middle of the sixteenth century, religion permeated every aspect of life. Diplomacy, political theory, statecraft, historiography, and a host of other fields were affected, while the art of the Renaissance was transformed into a style more in keeping with the fervor of the Catholic Church. Educational institutions put more emphasis on religious subjects. The New Learning of the Renaissance was blended with Catholicism by the Jesuits or studied primarily as a tool for understanding the Bible by the Protestants. The secular trend that had begun with the revival of trade and urban life around the year 1000 was reversed.

Yet for such a victory a price had to be paid. The religious unity of Latin Europe had been destroyed. The religious Renaissance had been like a storm cloud hovering over a continental divide. When the storm broke, the rain that fell on one side of the divide formed into the channel of Catholic reform, while the rain that fell on the other side formed into the many streams of the Protestant reform. Both currents came from the same source, but they flowed to the sea in opposite directions, never perhaps to join again.

This religious division helped inaugurate a period of foreign and civil war that provoked constitutional crises in nearly every country. It led to religious intolerance, persecution, and censorship. Only after generations of conflict that began around 1560 did a reaction begin, and this reaction, in paving the way for religious toleration and intellectual freedom, also paved the way for skepticism and a standard of conduct in economic activities that was divorced from the ordinary code of Christian ethics. These developments will be among those discussed in the following chapters.

PART **III**

THE SEVENTEENTH-CENTURY CRISIS, C. 1560-1715

EUROPE AS A WHOLE	WESTERN EUROPE	EASTERN EUROPE
543, Copernicus and Vesalius publish studies that begin scientific revolution		
	1556-1598, Reign of Philip II of Spain	
1560-c.1650, Religious differences intensify conflicts		
1560-c.1715, Continual warfare in Europe; national armies become larger and more efficient; costs of government increase; constitutional crises beset every major country		
	1562, Wars of Religion begin in France	
		1566, Death of Suleiman the Magnificent and beginning of Ottoman decline
	1568, Revolt begins in Netherlands	
		1572, End of Jagellon dynasty in Poland; Polish monarchy becomes elective
	1576, Bodin's *Republic*	
	1588, Defeat of the Armada	
	1589-1610, Reign of Henry IV of France	
	c.1592, Shakespeare emerges as playwright	
		c.1595-c.1700, Gentry gain control of Poland; peasants there and in Russia reduced to serfdom
	1598, Edict of Nantes	

EUROPE AS A WHOLE	WESTERN EUROPE	EASTERN EUROPE
	1603-1625, Reign of James I	
	1605, *Don Quixote* published	
	1607, English found Jamestown	
	1608, French found Quebec	
	1611, King James version of the Bible completed	
		1613, Election of Michael Romanov as tsar ends "Tin of Troubles" in Russia
1618-1648, Thirty Years War	**1618,** Revolt in Bohemia	
	1624, Cardinal Richelieu becomes chief minister of Louis XIII	
c.1625-c.1715, Economic stagnation; population growth ceases	**1630,** Gustavus Adolphus intervenes in Thirty Years War	
1632, Galileo publishes *Dialogue Concerning the Two Systems of the World*	**1635,** France enters Thirty Years War	
1636, Descartes publishes *Discourse on Method*		
	1640-1688, Reign of Frederick William (The Great Elector)	
	1642, English Civil War begins	
	1643-1661, Mazarin chief minister in France	
1648, Treaty of Westphalia	**1648,** Treaty of Westphalia	
	1648-1653, The Fronde	
	1649-1660, The Puritan Regime in England	
c.1650, Religious issues become secondary in international affairs, but wars continue		**1656,** Mohammed Kiuprili made grand vizier and beg to revive Ottoman Empire
	1659, Treaty of Pyrénées; France replaces Spain as greatest power in Europe	
	1660, Stuart restoration	
	1661-1715, Personal reign of Louis XIV	
	1667-1684, Louis XIV extends boundaries of France; series of alliances formed against France	**1667,** Russia annexes eastern Ukraine
		1674, John Sobieski elected king of Poland
		1682-1725, Reign of Peter th Great
		1685-1691, Europeans occup Balkans
1687, Newton's *Principia*		
	1688-1697, War of the League of Augsburg	
	1688, The Glorious Revolution in England	
	1690, Locke publishes *Two Treatises on Civil Government*	
	1697-1718, Reign of Charles XII of Sweden	**1697,** Peter the Great dispatc embassies to Europe; Russ contacts with West increa
	1700-1721, The Great Northern War	
	1701-1713, The War of Spanish Succession	
	1713, Treaty of Utrecht	

THE age of the Renaissance was followed by a period of crisis out of which our modern civilization was born. This crisis, which began in the latter part of the sixteenth century, was caused largely by the religious revival and the accompanying diversity of religious beliefs. It was characterized by change and revolt in nearly every sphere of human activity: diplomatic practices and alliances were altered, subjects rebelled against their king, artists against the idea that their work should conform to nature or to classical antiquity, and scientists against Aristotelian thought. In this age of revolt, economic progress ceased, and wars, plagues, and famines killed millions. But out of these rebellions and catastrophes powerful, stable states emerged in many parts of Europe, and the basis was laid for new scientific, philosophic, and artistic syntheses.

233

6/ War, Depression, and Colonization

THE Habsburg-Valois wars were followed by a series of religious revolts in many countries in which other Catholic and Protestant powers intervened on behalf of their coreligionists. By the middle of the seventeenth century, the religious factor had dwindled in importance, but the wars continued. These wars led to the development of large, well-trained armies in many states, armies that were able to bring the contraction of eastern Europe to an end. For the first time since the Crusades, the European powers expanded their civilization on land by force of arms. Russia began to adopt Western civilization, partly to survive the attack from the west, and territory was won back from the Ottoman Turks. Meanwhile, the expansion by water that had begun during the Renaissance when the Europeans won naval superiority over their foes continued. Colonial empires were established in the Americas, and the number of trading stations was increased in Africa and Asia. Economic progress, however, ceased, social classes became less mobile, hunger and disease became widespread,

234

and the population ceased to grow. Once more, Europe threatened to become as stagnant as the civilizations of the East.

THE WARS

THE COSTS OF WARFARE

Revolt broke out in France in 1562 and in the Netherlands a few years later. Other states intervened. One war followed another, and between 1562 and 1721 there were only four years in which all of Europe was at peace. Three factors made these conflicts more serious than those of the Renaissance. First, men fought with greater ferocity when they fought in the name of religion, and for a century nearly all these struggles pitted one faith against another. Second, the armies and navies grew rapidly in size, and with increased size came increased destructive capacity. Third, the larger, better armed military forces greatly increased the financial burden that had to be imposed upon the people.

There were no permanent, standing, peacetime armies in 1600 worthy of the name. Palace guards and frontier garrisons made up the regular force of every Christian nation. Even France could not boast of a peacetime army of 15,000 men. When war came, kings relied on mercenary troops, volunteers, and a militia that was little better than the old feudal levies. Henry IV of France mustered only 40,000 men when he planned to attack the Habsburgs in 1610, and few battles involved half that number at this time. However, as the century progressed, the armies got larger and larger. By 1700, France had an army of about 400,000 men. Even the Elector of Brandenburg increased his forces from 2,500 to 27,000 men during the two decades following 1640. The navies of the maritime powers grew at a similar rate.

At first, the larger the armies became, the wider the area of destruction they left in their path. Instead of isolated towns and villages, whole provinces were laid waste. Fortunately for the noncombatants, the growth in the size of the armies was paralleled by improved discipline after the middle of the seventeenth century. Kings asserted more control over the conduct of their troops. Inspectors were sent to watch the activities of the army; soldiers were put into uniforms, and in some instances housed in barracks instead of being quartered on the inhabitants. Even supply services were improved so that soldiers would not have to live off the country. As a result, after 1650 the destruction in wars did not increase in proportion to the size of the armies.

On the other hand, it cost more to clothe, equip, and supply a soldier than to have him provide for his own needs, and he was better armed than ever before. Flintlocks and bayonets replaced muskets and pikes near the end of the century. The increased cost per soldier and the growing size

Firing a mortar in the seventeenth century (copper engraving). (Bett-mann Archive)

of the armies added a tremendous burden to the royal treasuries. Constitutional crises were provoked in many nations. Rulers like those of France or Brandenburg-Prussia who found the means to raise the necessary sums became more powerful. Those who could not, like the kings of Spain and Poland, saw their international position deteriorate. From the standpoint of the ordinary citizen, the depredations of the marauding soldier were not much worse than the exactions of the tax collector; heavy taxation led to more than one revolt.

REFORMATION DIPLOMACY

The diversity of religious beliefs following the Reformation had a profound effect on diplomacy. The dynastic marriage had been the most essential aspect of the Renaissance system. It had been used to bind allies together, to turn enemies into friends, and to provide the bases for territorial claims. These alliances and ordinary diplomatic negotiations had been facilitated everywhere by resident ambassadors who had been exchanged by nearly all the states.

The advent of Protestantism was a severe blow to this system, because for generations marriage between members of different religions was regarded as unthinkable. Who would give the hand of his daughter to a heretic and doom to damnation his grandchildren, who were sure to be raised in the faith of their father? If a father insisted, as he surely would, that his daughter have the right to be accompanied by her own priests or ministers and to worship as she pleased at her husband's court, negotiations were likely to be terminated at once. Who could imagine a Protestant rite being celebrated at the court of Philip II of Spain or the Catholic Mass in a Protestant capital? In a few cases, the kings themselves might have been willing, but their subjects would never have consented. Marriages between members of Catholic and Protestant royal families ceased, and the Habsburgs, who had won their vast lands through the judicious choice of mates, began to marry each other, primarily to renew the ties between the Spanish and Austrian branches of the family but also because the other choices had become limited. Philip II's fourth wife was his niece, and his heir was the product of that union, while marriage between first cousins was not uncommon.

Somewhat similar difficulties beset the resident ambassadors, for they too wanted freedom of worship. Furthermore, they ceased to be of use to their masters, unless they became deeply involved in intrigues. One of their principal duties had been to report information gathered from friends at court, but the division in religion cut off ambassadors from such contacts. It would have been as foolish for an ambitious English official to befriend the Spanish ambassador as it would be today for a government employee in Washington to be seen in the company of members of the Soviet embassy. "It is impossible for me to find out anything certain at present here," the Spanish ambassador wrote early in Elizabeth of England's reign. "Nobody wants to talk to me; people flee from me as if I were the devil."

Unhappily, his statement was not quite true, for disgruntled English Catholics poured out their ills to him and gave a completely false idea of the temper of the English people. English Catholics who fled to the continent reinforced these reports, and together they gave the impression that England was ready to revolt as soon as a foreign army appeared to signal an uprising. The reverse was equally true, and the Protestants in England and elsewhere formed their ideas about public opinion in Catholic countries from the distorted reports of their ambassadors and of their coreligionists who had fled from Catholic states. According to these refugees, the fires of the Inquisition burned ever more brightly. As fear and hatred increased, Spanish ambassadors began to plot rebellions and even assassinations in their host countries.

Under such circumstances an iron curtain gradually descended between nations with different religious ideologies, just as today economic ideologies have divided one world into two. Ancient allies like Spain and England, or France and Scotland, became enemies. Spain and the Italian states ceased to be represented at Protestant courts; of the Catholic powers, only France was privileged by the presence of an English ambassador. For over eight decades, there was no general meeting of the representatives of the great powers. Intrigue and war became the order of the day as Catholic and Protestant alike plotted to rescue their enslaved coreligionists in foreign countries and to expand their own doctrines by any means they could.

PHILIP II

The principal figure in the Catholic camp was Philip II (1556-1598). As King of Spain, he had the finest army in Europe; as lord of the Netherlands, part of Italy, and vast lands in the New World, he possessed a larger treasury than any other king in Europe. However, with his far-flung empire came responsibilities that used up his tremendous resources and brought him to bankruptcy on several occasions. Spain was ascendant in Europe throughout his reign, but never to the extent that it could arbitrarily impose its will on any country except neighboring Portugal.

Philip, with his blue eyes and blond hair, was more German in appearance than Spanish, but in most respects his character reflected his Iberian ancestors more than his German or Burgundian ones. Certainly, he preferred Spain to any of his other lands. He went to Spain as soon as he could after his father's abdication and, except to visit Portugal, remained there until his death. He was by nature reserved, and he carefully cultivated the art of hiding his emotions. Both the triumphs and the disappointments of his life he treated as the inexplicable unfolding of God's will. Deeply religious, he mixed his faith with his public acts and his private life.

On a barren hillside some thirty miles north of Madrid he constructed the palace of Escorial. It was an extraordinary palace that provided insufficient space for even a modest court but contained a monastery and a large church that was to serve as the final resting place of the Spanish Habsburgs and their Bourbon successors. No other royal family today boasts so large and well-filled a mausoleum. Philip himself buried seventeen members of his family there before he had passed his sixtieth year, statistics that bespeak the personal tragedies of his life.

Of the four wives and many children who preceded Philip to the grave, none brought him greater grief than Don Carlos, the heir to his many thrones. As he grew older, Don Carlos began to show increasing signs of insanity. At last, convinced that his son would never be fit to rule, Philip summoned several members of his council and, swords in hand, they went late one night to Don Carlos' room, where they seized his pistols and nailed up the doors and windows. Within six months, the young prince was dead, many said on Philip's order. Such charges can neither be proved nor disproved, but if he was guilty of his son's death, Philip's act should be taken more as evidence of his high sense of duty than as a sign of morbid cruelty, for we know that he was devoted to his other children.

This sense of obligation characterized his every act. He worked tirelessly to enhance the prestige of his dynasty, to strengthen the position of the Catholic faith, and to render justice to his people. Unfortunately, he had no more than average intelligence and was either inherently unable or unwilling to delegate authority. As a result, he became bogged down in the endless details of government, while his officials and generals in various parts of the world awaited his decisions before they could act.

Part of Philip's attention had to be devoted to the Turkish threat, and one of the most glorious moments of his reign was the victory of his fleet in the great naval battle of Lepanto in 1571, but Spain and her allies failed to follow up their success and the Turks quickly recovered their former position. More successful was his effort in 1580 to make good a dynastic claim to the Portuguese throne. It took several battles on land and sea before his most serious rival, aided by the English and French, could be defeated. In keeping with the practices of the Renaissance monarchs, Philip promised to respect the rights and privileges of his new subjects and to govern through Portuguese officials. The work of Ferdinand and Isabella had been completed. The Iberian Peninsula was united under one sovereign as were all the permanent settlements in the New World and the trading posts along the African coast, the shores of the Indian Ocean, and in the Far East.

THE REVOLT OF THE NETHERLANDS

As the years passed, however, Philip had to use more and more of his resources to retain his position in Western Europe. In 1568, a revolt broke out in the Netherlands that ended in the independence of the northern half of the territory. Habsburg power there had rested primarily on the aristocracy, and Charles V and his Burgundian ancestors had been careful to cater to its wishes. Perhaps unconsciously, Philip II departed from this policy. He never resided there after 1559, thereby making himself an alien prince. His absence deprived the aristocracy of the opportunity to influence his imperial policies, and he almost never appointed its members to lucrative positions in other parts of his empire. His natural sister, Margaret of Parma, served as his regent in the Netherlands. If he had left her to her own devices, she might have kept the loyalty of the nobility by seeking their advice and by appointing them to posts in the Netherlands itself. Philip, however, insisted on making major policy decisions himself, and for advisers he gave Margaret lawyers and technicians, rather than great Netherlander nobles. He guarded all patronage with special jealousy, leaving Margaret without adequate means to win support.

This situation was worsened by the spread of Protestantism. Philip in-

239

sisted on repression, and the persecution that followed, so foreign to the Erasmian spirit of the inhabitants, alienated many people. To make matters even worse, the Spanish king reorganized the ecclesiastical jurisdictions to strengthen the position of the crown, to enable the Church to correct the abuses within its midst, and to combat Protestantism. To the six former bishops, he added fourteen new ones with three archbishops. These new bishops were to be trained theologians of good moral character, and they were endowed with much of the land of the abbeys. This well-intentioned move angered the great nobles because the higher qualifications stipulated largely removed the Church as a career for their younger sons, and it frightened the Protestants who feared its success. The result was that the Protestants, the lower classes in the towns who had economic grievances, and the great nobles were slowly driven together. They soon found a great leader in William I, Prince of Orange.

William of Orange was thirty-five when he assumed the leadership of the revolt in 1568. He had only moderate ability as a soldier, but his good looks, attractive personality, and great diplomatic talents made him an ideal leader to weld together the resistance to Philip II. To his personal virtues, it should be added that he came from a distinguished family and held more extensive lands than anyone else in the Netherlands—a fact which did not prevent him from being perpetually in debt because of his generosity and extravagance. He even advocated religious toleration, although this advanced position may have been the product of his religious indifference. Although he had been raised as a Lutheran, he became a Catholic to secure favor at the court of Charles V. In 1566, he was still attending Mass, but in 1567 he returned to the Lutheran church, and by 1571 he had become a Calvinist to ensure his influence with the most warlike of the rebels.

William had difficulty in getting the Catholics, who made up the majority of the population, to cooperate with the Protestants, many of whom insisted on burning abbeys and plundering churches. No religious statue, painting, or stained glass was safe from the iconoclastic tendencies of the adherents of the new religion. Jealousy between the various provinces and among the nobles added to his difficulties, and William might not have been able to organize any sort of general movement if Philip II had not sent the ruthless Duke of Alva (1508?-1583) to the Netherlands with Spanish troops. Alva vigorously suppressed the Calvinists, executed several great nobles, and levied a 10 per cent sales tax without the permission of the Estates-General. The result was that Catholic and Protestant, noble and merchant, were driven into each other's arms. William could not compete with Alva in the field, but with the aid of Dutch sailors, known as the sea beggars, he was more than able to hold his own on the sea. This was of great military significance because parts of the provinces of Holland and Zeeland could be protected from infantry assault by opening the dikes. It was here that William established the center of his resistance, and from here he could not be dislodged.

Alva was recalled, the sales tax was repealed, but the Spanish were still unable to quell the revolt. In 1576, the seventeen provinces signed the Pacification of Ghent, in which they agreed to drive the Spanish out. For a brief moment, it looked as though they might be successful, but Philip found in his nephew, the Duke of Parma (1545-1592), a worthy opponent for William of Orange. Parma was a far better general than William and his equal as a diplomat. He played upon the fears of the nobility and upper middle class, who were alarmed at the way in which the lower classes were taking control of the towns and provinces. Above all, Parma pointed out to the Catholics how the Calvinists persecuted their coreligionists in the provinces that they controlled. Meanwhile, Calvinist mobs continued to pillage Catholic churches and to seize more and more Catholic towns despite anything that William could do. Their bigotry cost the Netherlands its unity because it enabled the diplomatic Parma to detach from the union the southern provinces where the Catholics were predominant. He then made use of his military talents to conquer the adjoining areas. His success was so great that William of Orange was in serious difficulty when he was assassinated in 1584. The great prince died before the independence of the northern provinces was assured, but his contributions justify his title of father of his country.

THE ARMADA

William's death proved to be a doubtful blessing to Philip, since the English sent troops to prevent a Spanish victory. Philip, who usually acted with prudence, was gradually driven to gamble on an invasion of England to restore Catholicism there and to ensure victory in the Netherlands. At the same time, he became more deeply involved in France. In 1584, the brother of Henry III had died, leaving the Calvinist, Henry of Navarre, heir to the throne. If France became Protestant, the Catholic cause would be lost north of the Alps and the Pyrénées. To prevent this possibility, Philip began to give financial support to the ultra-Catholic faction led by the Duke of Guise. As 1588 approached, Philip evolved a master plan. The combined Spanish and Portuguese fleets were to sail up the English Channel, establish contact with Parma's army, and invade England, while Guise caused so much trouble that the French could not intervene.[1] The English Catholics were to rise as soon as Parma landed, and together they were to make Philip king.

From the start, well-informed observers like Parma knew that there was no chance of success, but driven on by his desire to advance the cause of his religion and his dynasty, the usually cautious Philip overrode all

[1] See pages 296-297.

opposition. The Duke of Medina Sidonia, whom he appointed to command the armada, pleaded to be excused. "My health is not equal to such a voyage," he wrote Philip, "for I know by experience of the little I have been at sea that I am always seasick and always catch cold." His protests were to no avail, and on May 9, 1588, the Spanish fleet began its departure from Lisbon "sailing," as one experienced naval officer put it, "in the confident hope of a miracle."

The reasons for the Spanish pessimism became apparent as soon as the battle started in the English Channel. The English ships compared favorably in size and were faster and more maneuverable. As a result, the Spanish were unable to grapple and board the English vessels so that the superior fighting qualities of their soldiers could have effect. The battle became a running artillery duel in which the English kept out of range of the Spanish guns, taking advantage of their more rapid-firing, longer-ranged cannons. When they ran out of ammunition and food, they were supplied from shore. The Spanish, on the other hand, were too far from home to be resupplied, and when their food and munitions were exhausted, they had no choice except to return home by sailing around the British Isles. Storms took their toll, and thousands died from lack of food and water. Parma never put to sea because he knew that his troops would be sunk by the small Netherlander vessels before they could reach the protective guns of the armada, which could not come close to shore because of the shallow water. The only part of Philip's master plan that worked was the one that could hardly have failed: France did not intervene.

This battle is of interest because it was the first large naval battle in the Atlantic, although to keep one's perspective it should be remembered that the Chinese had sent a fleet nearly twice as large to Arabia about 150 years before. The English victory was not decisive. They sent an equally unsuccessful expedition against Portugal the following year, and the war dragged on until 1604, when peace was made without altering the status quo. Five years later, the Spanish temporarily abandoned their effort to reconquer the northern provinces of the Netherlands and concluded a twelve-year truce. Only in France did Philip achieve some success. He was unable to prevent Henry of Navarre from coming to the throne, but he and the French Catholics had taken such a strong stand that Henry had had to become a Catholic. Thus, the triumph of Catholicism was assured in France, but the survival of Protestantism in England and part of the Netherlands pointed to the tremendous problems that confronted the Catholic revival.

Philip did not live to see the final failure of his efforts against the English and the Netherlands. After a long and painful illness, he died in September, 1598, in the sparsely furnished little room in the Escorial where he had spent so much of his life laboring for a cause that he felt was right. This room, more fitting for a monk than for the most powerful king in Europe, may still be seen with its opening through which the devout king gazed out upon the altar of the great monastic church on whose construction he had lavished so much care.

THE THIRTY YEARS WAR: FERDINAND II

Europe had expected that the struggle between Catholic and Protestant would be renewed in 1621 when the truce between Spain and the northern provinces of the Netherlands came to an end, but it began in the Empire several years earlier and gradually most of Europe became involved. Since Charles V, backed by the power of Spain, had been unable either to strengthen his authority at the expense of the territorial princes or to wipe out Protestantism, it was natural that his immediate successors preferred to leave the constitutional and religious issues alone. Ferdinand I (1556-1564) and Maximilian II (1564-1576) devoted most of their energy to fighting the Turks, while Rudolf II (1576-1612) preferred to dabble in astrology and to search for the philosopher's stone to turn base metals into gold. During their reigns, however, the Catholic revival was gathering momentum, and it remained only for Ferdinand II (1619-1637) to put the new Catholic fervor into action.

The red-haired, red-faced, good-natured Ferdinand was not a great man, but he possessed more virtues than most kings. He was both a devoted husband and father and a conscientious ruler interested in the welfare of his people. It was said—with exaggeration no doubt—that when he was Duke of Styria, he knew the names of all his subjects and that he provided free legal service for the poorest of their number. Above all else, however, he was a Habsburg: he was dedicated to the twofold task of restoring the authority of the emperor in the Empire and of re-establishing Catholicism in central Europe.

In his desire to restore the authority of the emperor, he could count on the support of Spain. Spain was only awaiting the end of a twelve-year truce made in 1609 to renew its efforts to reconquer the rebellious provinces in the Netherlands. Because of Dutch naval strength, the Spanish would have to send their troops to the Netherlands by way of Italy, the Alpine passes, and the Rhine River Valley. A strong emperor meant greater imperial authority in the Rhineland and with it more ease in moving troops. Indeed, Ferdinand had already promised Alsace to his Spanish cousins in return for supporting his candidacy to the imperial throne, and he was to promise more in return for military assistance.

Ferdinand could rely on the forces of the Catholic Reformation in his efforts to roll back the tide of Protestantism. The Catholic revival had already recouped a few losses in southern Germany, and Ferdinand himself had stamped out Protestantism in his duchies. Unfortunately, his allies were at cross purposes. The Spanish emphasized the need to increase imperial authority because it was essential to their reconquest of the Netherlands, but the German Catholic princes were only willing to help Ferdinand against the Protestants and strongly opposed any increase in imperial power that might curb their own independence.

More serious still was the interest of foreign powers in Germany. Would France permit Spain to take Alsace, the rest of the Rhineland, and the Netherlands, thereby drawing a tight net around its borders? Would Denmark and Sweden sit quietly by while the Habsburgs extended their power to the Baltic Sea and suppressed their fellow Lutherans? Or would they intervene to maintain their security and, perhaps, to add to their lands in northern Germany? Germany was in central Europe, and the German problem could not be settled without the intervention of surrounding states. It was not enough for Ferdinand to win the allies necessary to defeat the German Protestant princes. He ought to have been less ambitious or else prepared to fight both France and the leading Protestant states. It was not, however, left to him to decide to break the peace. The first step was taken by his rebellious subjects in Bohemia. Gradually and inevitably, the struggle spread to the rest of Germany and then to Europe.

The majority of the inhabitants of Bohemia were Lutheran, Calvinist, or members of one of the Hussite sects, although the Catholic minority supported by the Habsburgs was growing in strength. In addition, the Bohemian nobles were opposed to the encroachment by Habsburg officials on their power. This dissatisfaction with the religious and political policies of the Habsburgs, taken with the certainty that Ferdinand would push them further when he came to power, led to the revolt. On May 23, 1618, a year before Ferdinand was named emperor, the Bohemian leaders unceremoniously threw two imperial officials out of a window in the palace at Prague. They fell seventy feet, but escaped with their lives, either because of the intercession of the Virgin Mary, as Catholic propagandists confidently asserted, or because they landed in a dung hill, as Protestants claimed. In any case, civil war was now inevitable and a European conflict almost certain.

The rebels quickly seized control of Bohemia, won assistance from Transylvania, elected as king the Calvinist Elector Frederick of the Palatinate, and marched on Vienna. Ferdinand had neither money nor troops, but he had to regain Bohemia. That wealthy country furnished half the imperial revenue, and its king held one of the seven electoral votes that determined who would be emperor. Since three votes already belonged to Protestant princes, the loss of Bohemia might mean the choice of a Protestant instead of a Catholic Habsburg in an imperial election.

Ferdinand turned to Maximilian (1597-1651) of Bavaria and Spain for assistance. Maximilian was an able prince who had consolidated his hold over his duchy and had organized a Catholic League. Furthermore, he had the rare good fortune to have an army under an able, loyal commander. To him, Ferdinand promised the Upper Palatinate and Frederick's title of elector. To Spain, he offered the control of Frederick's Rhineland possessions. With these allies, Ferdinand quickly reconquered Bohemia. Catholicism and imperial authority were ruthlessly restored. The once elective monarchy was made an hereditary Habsburg dominion. By 1623, Ferdinand and his Catholic allies had also occupied Frederick's hereditary lands. Southern Germany was theirs, but the Protestant princes in northern Germany had become alarmed, and foreign powers determined to intervene before the Habsburgs could consolidate their position. France took steps to cut the Spanish supply route through the Alps, and the Danes, financed in part by the English, the Dutch, and the French, marched into Germany with 30,000 men.

WALLENSTEIN

Meanwhile, Ferdinand had come to realize that he could not achieve his objectives if he had to depend solely on allies. He therefore accepted the offer of a Bohemian nobleman named Albrecht von Wallenstein (1583-1634) to raise an imperial army. Born a Lutheran, Wallenstein had become a Catholic to qualify for imperial favor. Certainly religion was not the motivating force in this tall, thin, forbidding man. It was to the stars that he turned for guidance when he doubted the conclusions reached by his own brilliant but undisciplined mind. He was born under the conjunction of Saturn and Jupiter. The great astronomer Kepler informed him when he cast his horoscope that he had "a restless, exacting mind, impatient of old methods and forever striving for the new and the untried, secretive, melancholy, suspicious, contemptuous of his fellow men and their conventions. He would be avaricious, deceitful, greedy for power, loving no one and by no one beloved, changeable in his humours, quarrelsome, friendless and cruel." [2] Seldom have the stars spoken more truly.

The first step the wily Wallenstein took toward greatness was to marry a wealthy widow who conveniently died soon thereafter, leaving him her estates and the freedom to espouse the daughter of one of Ferdinand's councillors. To wealth and influence he added a businessman's instinct for organization and profit. He managed his estates so well that he came to control a quarter of the land in Bohemia and was able to offer to raise, quarter, and provision 50,000 men at his own expense, leaving to Ferdinand only the responsibility of their pay. The emperor recognized the danger of giving too much power to this powerful subject but the alternative was continued dependence on the Spanish and Bavarians. He therefore accepted Wallenstein's offer and was rewarded with quick victories by the Bavarian and imperial forces over the Danes. Much of northern Germany was occupied, and the ascendant Wallenstein was given Mecklenburg as a reward for his services, the former ruler of this Baltic duchy having made

[2] Cicely V. Wedgwood, *The Thirty Years War* (London: Jonathan Cape, 1944), pp. 171-172.

the mistake of siding with the Danes. Internal developments caused France and England to withdraw, and by the end of 1626 it looked as though the war might come to an end.

The fate of Germany rested upon Ferdinand's next step. He could accept Wallenstein's advice and use his great power to create a more centralized Germany, or he could satisfy the Catholic Reformation's demand for the restoration of the Church lands seized by the Protestants since the Peace of Augsburg in 1555. To choose the former course would alienate Maximilian and other Catholic princes who were opposed to any increase in imperial power. To choose the latter would frighten the remaining Protestant princes, some of whom had thus far been neutral. Ferdinand lacked the strength to take both courses simultaneously. He hesitated but finally chose Catholicism and political disunity. By the Edict of Restitution in 1629, he ordered the restoration of the former ecclesiastical territories to the Catholics, and to placate Maximilian, he dismissed Wallenstein. By placing his reliance on Maximilian and the Catholic League, Ferdinand had condemned Germany to more than two centuries of political disunity.

THE SWEDISH INTERVENTION

The folly of his choice was soon revealed. On July 4, 1630, Gustavus Adolphus (1611-1632) landed in Germany with a well-trained, well-disciplined army. The Swedish king was a tall, broad-shouldered man with a big appetite but simple tastes. From childhood he had been trained to be a king. When he was six, he began to accompany the army on campaigns; when he was ten, he began to sit at the council table and give his opinions; and when he was in his teens, he received ambassadors unaided. Now thirty-six, Gustavus had already given evidence of being one of the greatest men of his age. In his nineteen years as king, he had proved himself to be as able an administrator as Maximilian of Bavaria and as careful a military organizer as Wallenstein. He was now about to show that he was a gifted diplomat, a devout Protestant, and at the same time one of the greatest field commanders of his age.

His tactics deserve special comment. He abandoned the current emphasis on mass battle formations in order to achieve greater mobility and firepower. Cavalry and infantry were deployed in a series of alternating small squares so that they could turn easily in any direction. Light artillery was substituted for heavy artillery because it could be advanced rapidly, fired from the front lines in battle, and withdraw quickly if necessary. Musketeers were organized in files five deep. The first file was taught to fire and step back to reload. Then the second file fired and stepped back to reload, and then the third and the fourth and the fifth, by which time the first file was ready to fire again. Thus, continuous fire emerged from the Swedish lines.

246

The one important advantage that Gustavus Adolphus lacked was money, for Sweden was a poor country. When the French offered financial assistance, he therefore accepted but was careful never to let French wishes interfere with his policy. During his brief, glorious career in Germany, he was clearly his own master.

Many considerations led Gustavus Adolphus to enter the war. First, he dared not permit the Habsburgs to consolidate their hold on the southern shores of the Baltic Sea. Sooner or later, they were sure to use the ports of this area as a jumping off place to attack Sweden. Their ally, the Catholic Sigismund of Poland, had a good claim to the Swedish throne.[3] All he needed was imperial assistance to seek to depose Gustavus Adolphus and re-establish Catholicism in the northern kingdom. But if Sweden seized the southern shores of the Baltic, no invasion was possible. "It is better," the Swedish estates declared when they learned of the situation, "that we tether our horses to the enemy's fence, than he to ours." Second, the Swedes had long desired to turn the Baltic into a Swedish lake, and northern Germany would have to become theirs to make this dream a reality. Already a large part of the royal revenue came from Baltic commerce. Third, Gustavus Adolphus, a sincere Lutheran, was genuinely distressed to see the plight of his coreligionists in Germany.

The Swedish invasion completely altered the situation in the Empire. After a great victory in the battle of Breitenfeld, Gustavus Adolphus was free to march where he pleased. Ferdinand had no choice but to recall Wallenstein. The two generals fought an indecisive battle at Nuremberg, and Gustavus Adolphus withdrew to the north. Once more they clashed at Lützen, and this time the Swedes were victorious, but at the cost of their king's life.

The death of Gustavus Adolphus gave the Catholics new hope, but the rivalry between Maximilian and Wallenstein weakened their cause. The Bohemian, who had never forgiven Maximilian and Ferdinand for his first dismissal, plotted with the Swedes and French. Some think that he wanted to create a great middle European empire in which Catholic and Protestant could live in peace. Others see him as a Czech patriot who sought to revive the Bohemian state with himself as king. More probably he was motivated only by his selfish, restless ambition. Whatever Wallenstein's plans, Ferdinand knew that he could not be trusted. He was declared guilty of treason and was murdered, defenseless in his bedroom, by a disloyal contingent of his own troops.

Ferdinand was freed from one peril, and in September, 1634, six months later, he was relieved of another. The imperial forces defeated the Swedes at Nördlingen. The northern kingdom was no longer a serious threat, and one by one the German Protestant princes made peace in return for the abandonment of the Edict of Restitution. Ferdinand kept the gains he had made before 1627, and he now had the united support of the German

[3] See pages 253-254.

princes. Their support was an important asset, because nine days before the terms of the peace were published, France had declared war in order to check the power of Spain.

THE FRENCH INTERVENTION AND THE TREATY OF WESTPHALIA

The conflict entered a new phase. Spain, Austria, and the other German states were pitted against the French, the Dutch, and what was left of the Swedes. Religion had become a secondary issue, and the old struggle between the Habsburgs and the French, now ruled by the Bourbons rather than the Valois, held the center of the stage. There were no decisive battles, with the possible exception of Rocroi in 1643 where the young Duke of Enghein—later Prince of Condé—won a victory over the Spanish. Peace negotiations were begun in 1643, but they proceeded slowly. Not until 1648 was the Treaty of Westphalia signed by most of the conflicting powers, France and Spain alone continuing the struggle. Finally, with the Treaty of Pyrénées in 1659, even this conflict was brought to an end. The Habsburgs had lost the first round of their struggle with the Bourbons.

The results of the war and the two peace treaties were highly significant. France replaced Spain as the greatest power in Europe. With Sweden, France had blocked the Habsburg efforts to strengthen their authority in the Empire. At Westphalia, the right of the individual states within the Empire to make war and conclude alliances was recognized. In theory as well as in fact, the most important of these states became virtually autonomous, and German unity was postponed for more than two centuries. The Empire was further dismembered by the recognition of the independence of Switzerland and the seven northern provinces of the Netherlands. Two new powers emerged in northern Germany. Sweden received part of Pomerania and the bishoprics of Bremen and Verden; Brandenburg-Prussia added the rest of Pomerania and several secularized bishoprics to its possessions. In southern Germany, the Bavarian rulers were permitted to keep the Upper Palatinate and the title of elector, but the Lower Palatinate was restored to Frederick's son and an eighth electorate was created for him. France received most of Alsace by the Treaty of Westphalia, and by the Treaty of Pyrénées parts of Flanders and Artois in the Spanish Netherlands and lands in the Pyrénées. The religious settlement at Westphalia confirmed the predominance of Catholicism in southern Germany and of Protestantism in northern Germany. The principle accepted by the Peace of Augsburg of 1555 that Catholic and Lutheran princes could determine the religion practiced in their territory was maintained, and this privilege was extended to include the Calvinists as well. The Austrian Habsburgs had failed in their efforts to increase their authority in the Empire and to eradicate Protestantism, but they emerged from the war stronger than before. In Bohemia, they had stamped out Protestantism, broken the

power of the old nobility, and declared the crown hereditary in the male
line of their family. With Bohemia now firmly in their grasp and with
their large group of adjoining territories, they were ready to expand to the
east in the Balkans, to the south in Italy, or to interfere once more in the
Empire.

The real losers in the war were the German people. Over 300,000 had
been killed in battle. Millions of civilians had died of malnutrition and
disease, and wandering, undisciplined troops had robbed, burned, and
looted almost at will. Most authorities believe that the population of the
Empire dropped from about 21,000,000 to 13,500,000 between 1618 and
1648. Even if they exaggerate, the Thirty Years War remains one of the
most terrible in history.

THE ASCENDANCY OF FRANCE

The treaties of Westphalia and the Pyrénées mark the beginning of the ascendancy of France. When Louis XIV assumed personal control over his government in 1661, he found himself at the head of the most populous and one of the wealthiest countries in Europe. He exercised more power in France than any other important sovereign did in his own kingdom, and he had the best diplomats, the finest generals, and the largest army in Europe. Italy and the Empire were too disunited to check his ambitions. Spain was in a state of economic decline and, after 1665, had an incompetent king. England's internal situation prevented that country from playing an active role on the continent. Even a peace-loving ruler would have been tempted to take advantage of such a situation.

By this time, the religious issue had been reduced to secondary importance in international affairs. Ambassadors were once more exchanged between Catholic and Protestant states, and dynastic marriages were occasionally arranged between members of different religions. Except for the greater use of financial gifts to kings and foreign statesmen in return for their diplomatic support, there was little to differentiate the principles of Louis XIV's foreign policy from those of the Renaissance monarchs prior to the bitterness engendered by the Reformation. Neither the modern nationalistic concept that all Frenchmen ought to be under one flag nor the idea that France should achieve its natural boundary of the Rhine River ever crossed his mind. The motivating forces behind his foreign policy were pride and glory. To be a great king, he had to expand his kingdom and revenge every slight, but at the same time he wanted to convince himself and others that the wars he fought were just. He therefore sought to incorporate Franche-Comté, Lorraine, and the Spanish Netherlands into France on the grounds that he had claims, usually of a dynastic nature, to them. These territories also interested him because they were strategically important to the defense of Paris and at the same time stepping-stones to further inroads into the Empire.

The first of Louis XIV's many wars began in 1667, when he sent his armies into the Spanish Netherlands to seize some lands to which his wife had a dubious claim. His armies, led by the great generals Condé and Turenne, were successful, but their victories upset the balance of power, and the English, Swedes, and Dutch formed an alliance to halt the French. Louis quickly made peace, contenting himself with a slice of the Spanish Netherlands.

Louis now saw that he could not expand as long as other nations united to maintain the balance of power. He therefore isolated the Spanish and Dutch, drawing England and Sweden to his side by subsidizing their rulers. With confidence, he sent his armies northward once more in the hope of taking the Spanish Netherlands and destroying Dutch com-

EXPANSION OF FRANCE

——	BOUNDARY OF FRANCE IN 1618	1659 TREATY OF THE PYRENEES
	ACQUIRED IN PEACE OF WESTPHALIA, 1648	1668 TREATY OF AIX-LA-CHAPELLE
	METZ, TOUL AND VERDUN WERE OCCUPIED IN 1552 AND FULLY ANNEXED IN 1648	1678 TREATY OF NIMWEGEN

1713 TREATY OF UTRECHT

FULLY ANNEXED 1766

ACQUIRED IN 1791 BY REVOLUTION AND PLEBISCITE

SCALE OF MILES 0   50   100   200

mercial supremacy. Once more his armies were victorious, but England detached itself from France, and the emperor came to the rescue of the Dutch and Spanish to preserve the balance of power. When peace was restored in 1678, France received Franche-Comté and additional Spanish territories along its northern border.

During the peaceful interlude that followed, Louis appropriated one territory after another in Alsace and Lorraine. Once more there was the inevitable reaction on the part of the other European powers. In 1686, Sweden, Spain, the Dutch, the emperor, and many German states formed the League of Augsburg against the French, and several years later England joined the alliance. In part because he felt threatened and in part because he had a dynastic claim to some lands east of the Rhine River, Louis decided to strike first by marching into Germany. The War of the League of Augsburg which followed lasted until 1697, when the exhausted European powers agreed on peace. This time Louis added nothing to his territories, and both he and his bankrupt country were anxious to have a period of peace. In 1701, however, the War of Spanish Succession began.

A war over Spain had long been anticipated. Since 1665 that once mighty nation had been ruled by a pitiful cripple who could have no children. At first, there were three rival heirs to the Spanish throne, one French, one Austrian, and one Bavarian. To have permitted either the Austrian or the French prince to inherit would have upset the balance of power. Consequently, most of the great powers agreed to divide the Spanish possessions in Italy between the French and Austrian claimants and to give the remainder of the Spanish empire to the Bavarian. But the Bavarian prince died, and Spanish patriots brought pressure to bear on their king to leave his entire domain to either a Bourbon or a Habsburg to prevent the division of their far-flung empire. He agreed, and prepared a will giving Louis' grandson, Philip, everything, but if the Bourbons refused to accept this inheritance, all was to go to the Habsburg archduke, Charles.

Louis was thus left with the choice of claiming the whole inheritance for his grandson or letting it fall to Charles. After some hesitation, he chose the former course. Inevitably, a grand alliance of Austria, England, the Dutch, and other powers was formed to prevent this great increase in French power, for few statesmen were willing to count on Louis' promise that the thrones of France and Spain would never be united. This time Louis' armies were defeated more often than not. His great ministers and generals had died, and his system of government had not produced equally great men to take their place. On the other hand, England and Austria had found in John Churchill, Duke of Marlborough, and Eugene of Savoy commanders second to none. They won great victories at Blenheim, Ramillies, and Oudenarde. Only by heroic efforts did France stave off defeat. By 1713 the European powers were exhausted. In the Treaty of Utrecht, England received Newfoundland, Nova Scotia, and the Hudson Bay Territory from France, and Gibraltar from Spain. Austria got Naples, Sardinia, Milan, and the Spanish Netherlands. France got nothing, but Philip was permitted to keep what remained of the Spanish empire. The balance of power had been preserved, for the English and Austrian gains offset any advantage the Bourbons had won. Only Spain and the people of Europe had lost. Everywhere there was a cry for peace, and even the kings began to hear.

THE STRUGGLE FOR BALTIC SUPREMACY

The struggle between the Habsburgs and the Bourbons in Western Europe has usually received more attention from historians than any other European wars of that time, but of equal or greater importance were the struggles that took place during this same period for supremacy in the Baltic Sea region and the Danube Basin.

Denmark was the most powerful nation in the Baltic region at the close of the Middle Ages. Its kings ruled over what is now Norway, Sweden, Denmark, and Finland. The tie was a loose one, however, and in 1520, when the Danish monarch tried to assert his authority in Sweden, that country revolted. A young noble named Gustavus Vasa (1523-1560) was made king of an independent Swedish state, and a few years later Lutheranism became the established church.

Near the end of the sixteenth century, Sigismund, a grandson of Gustavus Vasa, became a Catholic and was elected King of Poland. Later, he inherited the Swedish throne and attempted to restore Catholicism. As a result, he was deposed by his uncle, and a long series of wars began between Poland and Sweden. The dynastic struggle between the two branches of the Vasa dynasty had important results because it led to further Swedish acquisition of territory on the Baltic shore. Soon, Swedish statesmen began to conceive of a Baltic empire stretching around the entire sea. The variety of nationalities in the region made little difference at this time, and the sea itself was no barrier since transportation by water was easier than by land in the absence of good roads. The Swedes were able to cut Russia off from the Baltic, and in 1629, when Gustavus Adolphus was about to enter the Thirty Years War, his chief minister could claim that they held all the Baltic ports except those on the southern shores between Danzig and Denmark. At the Peace of Westphalia, Sweden closed part of this gap by getting most of Pomerania.

By this time, Sweden had become so powerful that the other Baltic states were tempted to join together to prevent the Swedes from acquiring more territory. In 1655, Charles X of Sweden (1654-1660) renewed the quarrel with Poland. Brandenburg-Prussia offered him assistance, but after an important Swedish victory at Warsaw, Russia, Denmark, and the Empire declared war and Brandenburg-Prussia deserted the alliance. Undaunted, the Swedish king turned on the Danes and lay siege to Copenhagen. The Dutch now intervened to prevent the Swedes from getting control of the entrance to the Baltic. Only the death of Charles made Sweden accept peace, but by the treaties of Oliva and Copenhagen in 1660, Sweden added the southern part of the Scandinavian Peninsula to its territory. Of equal importance, the Elector of Brandenburg was recognized as holding Prussia in full sovereignty.

Several of the Baltic states became involved in the Habsburg-Bourbon wars, but the decisive struggle for control of the sea did not take place until the Great Northern War, 1700-1721. In 1697, when the fifteen-year-old Charles XII (1697-1718) ascended the Swedish throne, his neighbors decided to take advantage of his youth. Frederick IV of Denmark, Augustus the Strong of Saxony and Poland, and Peter the Great of Russia formed an alliance for this purpose. The youthful Charles saw that his only salvation lay in defeating his opponents in turn. He quickly marched on Copenhagen and forced the Danes to capitulate. Next, he turned on the Russians. Peter the Great had invaded Livonia in the hope of securing access to the sea. Charles met him at Narva in November, 1700, and, although outnumbered four to one, put the Russians to flight. The eighteen-year-old king then turned on Poland, deposed Augustus, and set up a puppet king.

Charles was now master of northern Europe. His courage as a soldier and skill as a general were unsurpassed. Both the French and the English sought his assistance in the War of Spanish Succession, but he had already conquered too vast a territory to be held by the armies of one small nation. When he learned that Peter the Great was reorganizing and training an army to renew the struggle, he led his troops against Moscow in the fall of 1707. Not daring to fight a pitched battle, the Russians attacked the Swedish supply lines, retreating at the same time and burning all before them. Charles turned south in hope of joining with a rebel cossack, Mazeppa, but the Russians managed to burn Mazeppa's capital first. Finally, Peter gave battle at Pultava in June, 1709. This time he outnumbered the Swedes only two to one, but his opponents had lost almost all their artillery. Although Charles planned the attack boldly, he had been wounded in the foot and could not lead his troops in person. His generals made mistakes, while the Russian troops made good use of the training that they had received since their defeat at Narva. The Russians were left in control of the field.

After his defeat, Charles fled to the Ottoman Empire to persuade the Turks to attack the Russians from the south while the Swedes invaded from the west. Although the Turks managed to surround Peter, they permitted the Russian king to buy his freedom by giving them Azov, a region that he had recently conquered from them. Charles was furious, but he did not abandon hope. Twice more he persuaded the Turks to declare war, and both times intrigues at the sultan's court brought his efforts to naught. Finally, his hosts asked him to leave, but he obstinately refused. When they sent an army to see that he complied, he barricaded the mansion that had been assigned to him and defended it for eight hours with a handful of men. At length, the Turks fired the building and captured their unwanted guest when he tripped over his spurs in an effort to renew the battle outdoors.

In 1714, Charles returned to Sweden, as determined as ever to preserve the Swedish empire even though Brandenburg-Prussia and Hanover had now joined his enemies. He raised a new army and was besieging Fried-richshall, Norway, in 1718, when he was felled by a bullet probably fired by an assassin employed by his brother-in-law, who had designs on the Swedish throne. Thus ended one of the most amazing careers in history. Western scholars usually characterize Charles as a "wild warrior king" who was at home only in battle, but Swedish scholars rank him second only to Gustavus Adolphus. To them he was a brilliant general and a far-sighted sovereign who loved peace but fought gloriously against over-whelming odds to preserve Sweden's Baltic empire.

The death of Charles left Sweden no alternative but to sue for peace. By the treaties of Stockholm and Nystadt, 1720-1721, Brandenburg-Prussia won the rest of Pomerania, and Russia took Livonia, Estonia, Ingria, and part of Karelia from the Swedes. Peter the Great had secured access to the sea and had made Russia a great European power, but Sweden's Baltic empire was brought to an end. Sweden's rise to power had been swift, but its greatness was due to the ability of its kings, the courage of its people, and the disorganization of its enemies. When finally pitted against such men as Peter the Great, who controlled thirteen million subjects, a nation of only a million inhabitants was doomed to defeat.

THE STRUGGLE FOR THE DANUBE BASIN

The Ottoman Empire began to decline after the death of Suleiman the Magnificent in 1566. At first, its deterioration was hardly perceptible, but from the close of the sixteenth century it was rapid. This decline may be partly explained by the economic stagnation of the Mediterranean region as a whole during the seventeenth century[4] and by the Turkish failure to keep pace with the technological developments of the West. Equally im-portant, however, was a change in the character and ability of the sultans themselves. The Empire had been built by a line of ten able sultans, but Suleiman was succeeded by his son, Selim the Sot, a nickname that ac-curately described his character. Of the twenty-six sultans who followed Selim, only one was capable of leading an army in battle.

The inability of Selim and his immediate successors may be explained by chance, but there was a more tangible reason for the incompetence of later sultans. Until the beginning of the seventeenth century, it had been customary for a sultan to murder his brothers and other near relatives when he came to the throne. This cruel practice had the advantage of pre-venting the princely rebellions that plagued so many Christian kingdoms. The "law of fratricide" was abandoned, however, in a wave of reaction following Mohammed III's murder of nineteen brothers and an unde-termined number of pregnant women in his father's harem when he came to the throne in 1595. As an alternate means of preventing princely re-

[4] See pages 260-262.

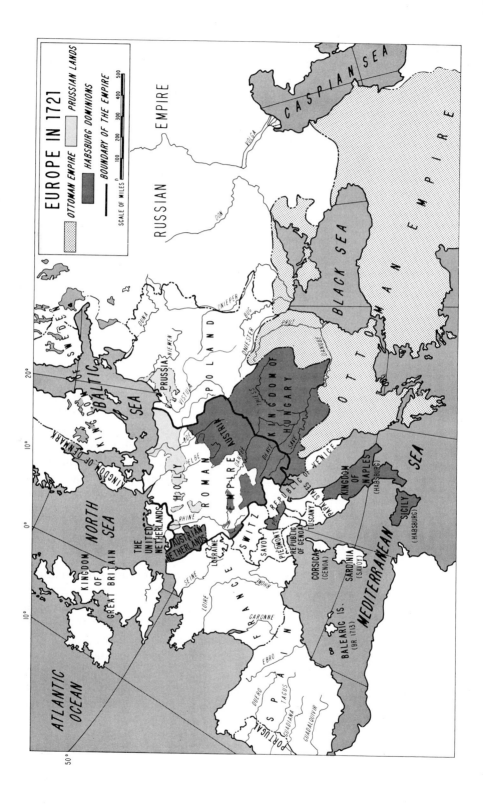

EUROPE IN 1721

OTTOMAN EMPIRE   PRUSSIAN LANDS

HABSBURG DOMINIONS

BOUNDARY OF THE EMPIRE

SCALE OF MILES   0   100   200   300   400   500

ATLANTIC OCEAN

RUSSIAN EMPIRE

CASPIAN SEA

SWEDEN

KINGDOM OF DENMARK

BALTIC SEA

NORTH SEA

KINGDOM OF GREAT BRITAIN

THE UNITED NETHERLANDS

AUSTRIAN NETHERLANDS

PRUSSIA

POLAND

HOLY ROMAN EMPIRE

AUSTRIA

KINGDOM OF HUNGARY

OTTOMAN EMPIRE

BLACK SEA

LORRAINE

SWITZ.

FRANCE

SAVOY

PIEDMONT

REPUBLIC OF GENOA

REPUBLIC OF VENICE

PAPAL STATES

TUSCANY?

KINGDOM OF NAPLES (HABSBURG)

SICILY (HABSBURG)

MEDITERRANEAN SEA

CORSICA (GENOA)

SARDINIA (SAVOY)

BALEARIC IS. (BR 1713)

SPAIN

PORTUGAL

RHINE

SEINE

LOIRE

GARONNE

RHONE

EBRO

DUERO

TAGUS

GUADIANA

GUADALQUIVIR

ELBE

ODER

VISTULA

NIEMEN

DUNA

DNIEPER

BUG

DNIESTER

PRUTH

DANUBE

THEISS

SAVE

DRAVE

DON

VOLGA

50°

10°   0°   10°   20°

bellions, it was decided to confine the sultan's sons in a special harem that was little more than a prison. Liberty of movement was not allowed, and the young princes were given no training or experience in the art of government. Under such circumstances they spent their lives unless they were called upon to rule. Only three of the last twenty-three sultans spent less than ten years in the harem before coming to the throne, and six spent over forty years in this manner. It is not surprising that most of the sultans were highly neurotic, subject to harem influence, and completely unfit to rule.

When the sultans ceased to be able or willing to rule, the Empire began to disintegrate. Their military power had rested largely on a standing army known as the Janissaries. The Janissary corps had been founded upon a system of conscripting Christian children in the Balkans and raising them as fanatical Moslems. Cut off from their parents and forbidden to marry, their only loyalty had been to the sultan. This rule of celibacy was now relaxed, and the Janissaries began to admit their own children into their ranks. The levies on Christian children ceased, and instead of being a small, highly trained army of devout Moslems completely loyal to the sultan, the Janissaries became a large, motley force more interested in plotting palace revolutions to secure some advantage than in fighting for the Empire. Thus, the Ottoman army became less effective at the very time that the Christians were enlarging and disciplining their forces.

The removal of the strong army of the sultan also left royal officials free to plot, bribe, and intrigue. Inefficient and dishonest government led to fiscal difficulties and eventually to unrest among the subject peoples. The only periods of greatness that remained to the Ottoman Empire occurred when an able man was appointed grand vizier (prime minister), and this seldom happened.

During the century following the death of Suleiman, the European states were too involved with internal revolts and wars among themselves to take advantage of the growing Ottoman weakness. Even the great naval victory of the Spanish and Venetians at Lepanto in 1571 was not followed up. Only after the close of the Thirty Years War were the Christian nations free to turn to the Ottoman question. By then, the Turks were once more ready to meet any challenge.

The cause of this revival was the Kiuprili dynasty. Its first important member, Mohammed Kiuprili, had found employment in the sultan's palace as a butcher but gradually rose to become chief cook, steward, falconer, provincial governor, and finally, in 1656, grand vizier. Even though Mohammed owed his rise partly to harem influence, once he came to power he brutally punished corrupt, inefficient, and disloyal officials. Thousands were executed at his order, but when he died five years later, he left to his son and successor, Ahmed Kiuprili, a chastened Empire. Ahmed continued to make administrative reforms, at the same time governing justly and leniently in the name of his worthless sultan. Although he managed to take Crete from Venice, and Podolia from the Poles, Ahmed was less successful as a soldier than as an administrator. His troops were often an unequal match for the improved armies of the Christian kingdoms. The Austrians completely defeated him at St. Gothard in 1664, and the Poles, under their able general, John Sobieski, defeated him on several occasions.

The post of grand vizier was next given to Ahmed's cruel, corrupt, ambitious brother-in-law, Kara Mustapha. In 1683, when Kara Mustapha lay siege to Vienna with a huge army, the emperor fled, leaving a garrison to defend the city. The fate of the Danube Basin hung in the balance. A victory for the Turks would bring them into the heart of Germany; a Turkish defeat would pave the way for the expansion of the Christian kingdoms into the Balkans. At the critical moment when the supplies of the garrison were nearly exhausted and their walls were undermined, John Sobieski, now King of Poland, arrived from that country with 20,-000 men.

Sobieski assumed command of the imperial army already on the scene and maneuvered his weary troops up the difficult terrain leading to the top of a mountain overlooking the city. When he saw the Turkish army before him, he felt sure of victory. "This man is badly encamped. He knows nothing of war," he declared, and he led his troops in four columns down the other side of the mountain and onto the Turkish trenches. They were outnumbered about 200,000 to 70,000, but superior leadership and training more than compensated. The Turks were driven back, slowly at first, then in rapid retreat. Even the famed Janissaries were cut to pieces. Kara Mustapha escaped, but the exultant Sobieski was able to write of the victory to his beloved wife "from the tents of the Vizier." The battle was one of the most important in history. For centuries, the Moslems had threatened Europe. Now the military superiority of the Europeans was clearly proven. For the next 270 years, it was the Christian who expanded at the expense of the Moslem.

The Poles and Austrians were quick to follow up their advantages, and they were soon joined by the Venetians and Russians. Budapest fell in 1685; Belgrade was taken; Serbia, Transylvania, Bulgaria, Greece, and Albania were occupied. The Turks executed Kara Mustapha, deposed the sultan, and sent him back to the harem prison, but it was the appointment of Zadé Kiuprili, brother of Ahmed, as grand vizier that staved off complete defeat. He proved as capable as the other members of his family and was able to retake Bulgaria and Serbia before his death in 1691. The Turkish revival was helped considerably by internal difficulties in Poland, and by Austria's participation in the War of the League of Augsburg with Louis XIV. The war dragged on. Finally, in 1697, the Austrian commander, Eugene of Savoy, won a great victory at Zenta, and peace was made at Karlowitz in 1699. The Habsburgs took Hungary, Transylvania, and Croatia, thereby compensating themselves for their failure to unite Germany during the Thirty Years War by winning a vast Danubian empire. The Poles regained Podolia, the Venetians received parts of Greece and the Dalamatian coast, and the Russians an outlet on the Black Sea at Azov. In alliance with Charles XII of Sweden, the Turks regained Azov from Peter the Great in 1711,[5] but European pressure on the Turks continued until the Ottoman Empire ceased to exist.

THE AFTERMATH

The wars of the seventeenth century saw the European states assume the great power. and secondary power positions that they were to occupy until the 1860's. Once-mighty Spain was henceforth only a minor state, the Holy Roman Empire little more than a name, and the Ottoman Empire a territory to be divided. The Dutch and Swedes had enjoyed brief moments of greatness, but they, too, sank to the status of secondary powers. Those states—Great Britain, France, Austria, Russia, and Brandenburg-Prussia—that emerged as great powers during the course of the century maintained that position. Even the last half of the nineteenth century saw only the addition of Italy and Germany (created around Brandenburg-Prussia) to the number of great powers.

The cost had been tremendous. Every nation was in financial difficulty. The War of Spanish Succession had increased the French debt sevenfold in spite of extraordinary tax measures. After the termination of the conflict, the interest on the debt and the cost of government were so great that there was an annual deficit of 45,000,000 livres—a far larger sum than the entire royal revenue in 1610. Other nations fared little better, and only the British government was in a position to borrow. The loss of life and the destruction of property had been great, and social unrest had increased. Constitutional crises had been provoked in many countries and new ones were sure to come unless the European statesmen could find some means to preserve peace for a few decades so that the state and society, indeed the entire European edifice, would not fall apart.

THE ECONOMIC CRISIS AND ITS SOCIAL EFFECTS

The economic progress that had started in the late fifteenth century began to decelerate around 1560. Between 1620 and 1630, it halted, at a point somewhat in advance of the peak that had been reached around 1300, just before the fourteenth-century decline had begun. For the remainder of the seventeenth century, an economic depression that led to social unrest gripped most of Europe.

[5] See page 255.

THE CESSATION OF ECONOMIC PROGRESS

The Mediterranean states were especially hard hit. Northern Italy, once wealthy and industrialized, was transformed into an economically depressed area that depended primarily on agriculture. During the course of the seventeenth century, the output of the Venetian woolen industry dropped from 20,000 to 2,000 cloths annually. The number of firms in the woolen industry in Milan dropped from sixty or seventy to one during the same period. The silk, building, and metallurgical industries also suffered heavily. Plagues in 1630 and in 1657 reduced the population of the large Italian cities by one-third. By the end of the century, the cities had been repopulated, but the depressed economy offered few opportunities for employment. Part of Italy's difficulty was caused by increased competition from the northern nations that had begun to copy Italian banking, trading, and industrial techniques and to develop their own merchant fleets; another cause was a general decline of the Mediterranean economy that affected other states from the Ottoman Empire to Spain.

An economic depression fastened upon most of northern Europe as well. Germany and Poland suffered heavily, Baltic Sea trade declined drastically, and the French economy did not maintain its earlier rate of progress but fluctuated violently. Russia, Sweden, and Switzerland probably moved forward. The most conspicuous progress, however, was made by the English and Dutch, although these maritime peoples also underwent some economic difficulties. Even the possession of Atlantic seaports did not guarantee economic success, for Spain's trade with its overseas colonies declined drastically.

There were four causes for the cessation of economic progress during the seventeenth century. The first was the bankruptcy of both the Habsburgs and the Valois at the close of the long wars between the two houses. The Renaissance capitalists had derived much of their income from handling royal finances, from supplying royal armies, courts, and bureaucracies, and from mining, industrial, and commercial privileges granted them by the monarchs. In return, they had been expected to loan money to the ever-needy rulers to pay for their wars and other activities. Since interest rates were high, these loans were another source of capitalistic profit. Then, in 1557, Spain repudiated part of its debt and France stopped interest and amortization payments. The following years witnessed an international financial crisis. Kings, merchants, and bankers suffered heavily. Hardly had recovery begun when Spain once more defaulted. The defeat of the Armada provoked a third crisis. Even the Fuggers, who owed so much of their economic rise to the Habsburgs, were forced into bankruptcy in 1607 by the failure of that family and others to pay their debts.

Wars were a second cause of the cessation of economic progress. During the first half of the sixteenth century, most of the fighting had taken place in Italy, to the serious detriment of the Italian economy. Later, as we have seen, the center of armed conflict moved to other parts of Europe. Civil wars broke out in France, the Low Countries, the Empire, and England. The Habsburgs fought the Bourbons; others struggled for control of the Baltic or for the Danube Basin. These wars destroyed considerable property, made the transfer of goods difficult, turned many workers into penniless refugees if not corpses, and led to higher taxes. Increased taxation reduced the poor to abject misery and deprived the well-to-do of capital that could have been used for new commercial and industrial enterprises.

Lack of capital was a third cause. Rich merchants often desired social prestige more than they did wealth. To join the aristocracy, they purchased estates, offices, or titles, rather than invest in new industrial and trading enterprises. The use of capital for nonproductive investments became more serious around 1630, when the Spanish silver mines in the New World were exhausted. For more than a century, precious metals had poured into Europe, bringing a rapid rise in prices. This currency inflation had favored the interests of the capitalists, for prices had far outstripped rising labor costs, leaving a large excess of capital to invest. However, when the importation of precious metals was reduced, prices leveled off and even declined. Wages, which had lagged far behind the rise in prices during the Renaissance, continued to move slowly upward during the last two-thirds of the seventeenth century, further reducing the merchants' profits. The result was still less money to invest in business enterprises.

The fourth cause of economic decline was a technological failure. Banking and credit facilities were not improved to make borrowing easier and to achieve a more flexible currency. Transportation facilities, especially on land, were not sufficiently developed. Labor-saving machines were not invented, nor were new sources of power found. A long period of cold weather began at the close of the sixteenth century. This fact, coupled with a failure to improve agricultural techniques, prevented the farmers from providing food for an enlarged urban population and from earning enough income to purchase goods produced in the cities. Until these problems were solved, Europe could move no further. It could only hope to hold its own.

THE EFFECT ON SOCIETY

The cessation of economic progress had a profound effect. During the Renaissance, an increase in population had been made possible by bringing more land into cultivation and by minor agricultural improvements. This increase had been absorbed by the newly established farms and by the towns whose expanding trade and industry created a demand for additional laborers. Now these opportunities were closing, but the population continued to increase. In 1500, most European nations still suffered from a scarcity of labor; a century later, the English had to introduce a Poor Law to provide for the growing number of the needy. In 1696, a statistician estimated that one-sixth of the population of England lived on alms and that half of the population was too poverty-stricken to contribute to the poor or to the church. Yet at the same time he argued that the per capita wealth of England after taxation was greater than that of Holland or France. It was certainly higher than in the other European countries.

Excess population led to untold misery. Surviving records show clearly that during the seventeenth century the number of births and deaths varied with the size of the crop and the severity of the winter. A crop failure brought undernourishment, and undernourishment brought fewer births and more deaths from disease and cold. Deaths from actual famine were not rare, and even cases of cannibalism were reported. In some years, there were crop failures throughout most of Europe. In other years, one province in a kingdom might be in want while another had an abundance of food, but inadequate land transportation made it difficult to move grain from one locality to another and the poor did not have the money to pay the high prices asked for what was moved. The sudden deaths caused by plagues and wars were almost a mercy, for when the population of a province was decimated by one or the other, those who survived would have food and jobs until the population increased and again outstripped the food supply.

This situation caused the population of the various European countries to fluctuate violently. Germany probably lost 40 per cent of its population during the Thirty Years War, but within three or four generations the number of its inhabitants was as great as before. The population of France continued to grow slowly during the first half of the seventeenth century except for the famine years of 1629-1630. Poor harvests led to drops in 1648-1651, 1660-1661, 1693-1694, and 1709-1710. During the intervening years, losses were largely recouped; nevertheless, there was an over-all decline of from 20,000,000 to 19,000,000 people during the last half of the seventeenth century. The number of inhabitants in Europe as a whole was only slightly greater in 1700 than in 1600.

Under these conditions, life expectancy at birth was less than twenty years. A third of the children died during their first year. Less than half reached adulthood, and a man of forty was thought to be old. All classes suffered from wars and poor medical care, but malnutrition, hunger, and disease made their greatest inroads among the poor. In one French town, the workers lost 60 per cent of their children before they were fifteen, while the bourgeoisie lost only 40 per cent, a ratio that was probably typical. Poor sanitary conditions and the difficulty of obtaining food during times of scarcity made the death rate in cities higher than in the country. As late as 1742-1743, the number of burials in London stood at 25,000, as opposed to 15,000 baptisms. Only the continual influx of the excess population of the rural areas made possible the continued growth of urban centers.

The cessation of economic progress caused the social classes to become more stratified. Higher taxes and reduced economic opportunities made it difficult for members of the middle class to find the means of joining the aristocracy, as they had so often done during the Renaissance. Those who managed to buy estates now often found their claims to nobility challenged by needy governments anxious to prevent their wealthiest citizens from claiming the tax exemptions traditionally held by the nobility in many countries. Letters of ennoblement could usually be purchased from the bankrupt kings, but this took still more money.

One of the most popular methods of joining the aristocracy had been through the purchase of an office, but even here opportunities for advancement became limited because some offices were made hereditary and others were filled by the younger sons of those who already held important positions. Thus, the landed and officeholding nobility tended to become castes, and powerful ones at that, for from England to Russia one or both of these types of nobles ruled in conjunction with the crown. In some countries, as in France, the king was an important partner; in others, as in Poland, he was not. Only in the Netherlands, Switzerland, and a few Italian city states was the middle class of greater importance than the aristocracy.

Other social classes also suffered during the last two-thirds of the seventeenth century. Any increase in the real wages of workers was negated by higher taxes. The failure of trade and population to continue to expand made it increasingly difficult for journeymen to become masters. The guilds generally gave the few openings that occurred to the children of their members. More stable grain prices reduced the peasants' profits, and the lower classes as a whole suffered from the growth of taxation. As in the fourteenth century, once again the European economy was threatened with the stagnation that had arrested so many other civilizations.

THE MERCANTILISTS

Under these conditions, as in other periods of social-economic distress, the state intervened in the hope of stimulating prosperity. Unfortunately, the economic theory of the period was based on three fundamental errors. First, economists confused precious metals with wealth. They put a greater value on gold and silver than on the goods that these metals bought. Since few European nations possessed natural deposits of precious metals, each country felt it necessary to export more goods than it imported on the assumption that the difference would be made up by money payments. Thus, every effort was made to export the very goods necessary to sustain the lives and provide for the material well-being of the people, in return for precious metals that were of little value except as a medium of exchange. The economists who advocated this theory later received the name of *mercantilists*, and their doctrines had considerable influence over the statesmen of the period.

The second error of the mercantilists was closely related to the first.

They believed that there was a fixed quantity of economic resources in the world, an understandable position during a period of stagnation. Hence, one country could increase its wealth only at the expense of another. This static conception of economic life led to fierce competition among nations. Each sought to increase its exports and to decrease its imports in order to add to its stock of precious metals. France, for example, sought to limit imports from Italy, but at the same time to sell more to the Italians. The Italian states adopted a similar attitude towards France. The result, of course, was the establishment of regulations that severely limited international trade to the profit of no one. When economic measures to gain a competitive advantage failed, states sometimes resorted to war. Both England and France sought to lessen the prosperity of the Dutch to their own advantage by means of armed attack. No one saw that the well-being of one European nation depended in part on the well-being of the others.

The third error of the mercantilists was their failure to recognize the relationship between the quantity of food available and the size of the population. No effort was made to limit the number of births. Indeed, there were frequent attempts to increase the population in the belief that a larger labor force meant greater production and that greater production meant more goods to export in return for gold and silver. Then, too, a large labor force made for low wages and low wages reduced costs, thereby encouraging exports. "We have hardly Poor enough," wrote one mercantilist, "to do what is necessary to make us subsist." Or again, "the surest Wealth consists of a Multitude of laborious Poor." Thus, most of the mercantilists advocated an increased population at a time when there was insufficient food, and low wages when half the people lived in poverty.

The various European nations followed the ideas of the mercantilists to a greater or lesser degree, but none went further than France under the inspiration of Jean Baptiste Colbert (1619-1683). In 1661, the industrious Colbert rose to the position of chief economic adviser to Louis XIV. In this capacity, he sought to increase the wealth and power of France by rigid adherence to the mercantilist doctrines. To increase exports, he attempted to improve the quality of French manufactured goods. Rules were established for training apprentices to ensure that each new master would be competent in his trade, and regulations were made governing the quality of the various types of goods produced. Even the width of a piece of cloth and the number of threads it contained were determined by the state. The guilds were pressed into service to enforce these rules, and government inspectors were appointed. To increase production, special privileges, including tax exemptions, loans, and local monopolies, were granted to those who established new industries. To ensure a large supply of cheap labor, Colbert sought to increase the population by giving temporary tax exemptions to men who married before they were twenty and to fathers of ten or more children. Idleness was discouraged and children as young as six were made to work in industry.

Colbert, from a painting by Lefebvre in Versailles. (Bulloz-Art Reference Bureau)

To decrease imports, tariffs were raised on foreign manufactured goods, but raw materials to be manufactured and sold abroad were allowed to pass into France free of duty. Colonies that produced things not available in the mother country were encouraged, in order to remove the need to pay for foreign imports. Shipping was also stressed; Colbert had no desire to pay Dutch or English vessels for transporting French goods abroad. Trading companies were established, and roads and canals were improved to facilitate the transportation of goods.

The French economy improved during the early years of Colbert's administration, but this improvement resulted more from a temporary restoration of peace and order than from his economic program. His use of guilds to enforce industrial regulations strengthened them at a time when they had begun to die out. Their continued existence slowed the development of large industrial enterprises. His attempts to regulate trade were often equally hurtful. It is not surprising that the Dutch and English, who put less emphasis on mercantilism than the French did and let their guilds slowly disappear, prospered more. The return of war during the last quarter of the century brought dire results, and in 1683 Colbert died with the knowledge that he had failed to improve the economic position of France.

The activities of Colbert and his imitators in other countries should not be interpreted to mean that the seventeenth-century state was socialistic. Although the state encouraged business and invested in industrial and commercial enterprises, it did not seek to own the means of production. Nor was the system designed to improve the lot of the workers, although it was an accepted principle that a high tariff protected labor. The mercantilists were traders, industrialists, and royal ministers who favored commercial development. Their solution to the economic crisis was that of the businessmen of their day. Like the businessmen of the twentieth century, they prized economic liberty but were willing to accept state aid and a degree of state regulation during a depression. Even Colbert was a staunch advocate of economic freedom up to a point, and he frequently said that "liberty is the soul of trade." His efforts to establish economic liberty, however, were limited largely to the removal of tolls and provincial barriers to permit the free flow of goods within France. He and other mercantilists dared go no further because they believed that the majority would suffer if men were allowed to indulge their selfish desires. An intellectual revolution was necessary to convince lawmakers that the selfish initiative of the individual was of benefit to mankind.

THE COLONIAL EMPIRES

The establishment and expansion of European colonies in other parts of the world was related to the economic difficulties of the seventeenth century and to the mercantilist doctrines that became so important during this period. Other factors, however, were more important in determining the characteristics of the new outposts of European civilization. Among them were the state of civilization achieved by the non-European people in the region contacted, the geographical and climatic conditions of the settlement, and the institutions, traditions, and religion of the colonial power at the time that the colony was established.

Broadly speaking, the colonies may be divided into two types: those that were essentially trading posts, and those that comprised large areas of land. The former type included the settlements established in Asia, where there were highly civilized and thickly populated native states that could not be conquered, and in Africa, where the climate was unfavorable and where slaves and the products that Europeans wanted could be obtained without controlling the interior. In many of these regions, European civilization did not penetrate deeply until the last hundred years.

The second type of colony was established in the Americas, where the Europeans found it necessary to occupy the territory to obtain the products that they wanted. In many regions, the climate was suitable for those who wanted to emigrate for religious or economic reasons, and nowhere were the natives capable of resisting the European advances effectively. Invariably, the Europeans tried to continue their old way of life in the New World, but the problems of a frontier society, character of the native population of the region, and geographical and climatic conditions forced some modifications. With these changes, which were often minor, the civilization of the western peninsula of the Eurasian continent gradually expanded through the Americas.

THE LATIN AMERICAN COLONIES

Shortly after Columbus returned from his first voyage, the pope gave all the newly discovered heathen lands to the Spanish and Portuguese monarchs. These rulers agreed that a line drawn from pole to pole 360 leagues west of the Cape Verde Islands should divide their claims, a division that gave Brazil to Portugal and the remainder of the Americas to Spain. At first, neither ruler sought to exercise directly his claim to ownership. The Portuguese concentrated on developing their trade with Asia to the neglect of Brazil, and the Spanish sovereigns left the development of their lands to the initiative of private individuals, such as Columbus, Cortés, and Pizarro. It was not until the reign of Philip II that a determined effort was made to impose royal authority.

During the Renaissance, the Spanish sovereigns tried to exercise their authority over the colonies through councils, just as they used conciliar government at home. When colonial affairs became too burdensome for the regular royal council, a Council of the Indies was established to serve as the supreme administrative and legal authority, and a less important institution was located in Seville to serve as a clearinghouse for trade, immigration, and other economic matters.

In a similar manner, the Habsburgs borrowed from their experience in governing far-flung territories in Europe when they established viceroyalties in the New World. At first, there were two viceroyalties: one, New Spain, for the territories in North America, and a second, Peru, for the lands in South America. During the eighteenth century, the latter was subdivided into the viceroyalties of New Granada, La Plata, and Peru. At the head of each viceroyalty was a viceroy who resided in the colonial capital and exercised every aspect of royal authority as directed by the king and the Council of the Indies. The viceroy was a great noble sent out from Spain to govern for a limited number of years. Because he was far removed from the mother country, it was difficult for the home government to watch or control his actions. To provide for closer supervision, he was given legal and administrative advisers whom he had to consult, and at the end of his term of office an inquest was held to determine whether he was guilty of wrongdoing. Even with these precautions, however, there was a wide difference between the theory of the empire as propounded in Spain and its actual functioning in the New World.

The viceroyalties were divided into judicial and administrative subdivisions that were often virtually autonomous. At the base of the administrative pyramid was the town. As in early Renaissance Spain, the towns were at first semi-independent political units that dominated the surrounding countryside. During the reign of Philip II, the practice developed of having town councillors purchase their offices. This practice, taken with the growing authority of royal officials, led to a gradual decline of municipal government that paralleled the increasing decadence of the towns in the mother country during the late sixteenth and seventeenth centuries.

The *Conquistadores* were eager to transpose the manorial system to the New World by reducing the natives to peasants or serfs and exalting themselves into feudal overlords. The establishment of the *encomienda*[6] system was an important step in this direction, but the crown made every effort to prevent these grants from becoming hereditary. The holder of an *encomendero* was obligated to perform military service, but he was not permitted to have judicial and administrative authority comparable to that exercised by the lord of a medieval manor. After two or three generations, the *encomiendas* usually reverted to the crown and were administered by salaried royal officials.

The decline of the *encomienda* was due to a number of factors. The crown was understandably reluctant to see the feudal system transferred to the New World, where the distance from the center of royal power was so great that control would be difficult. Priests, inspired by the zeal of the Catholic Reformation, looked on the Spanish empire as an instrument to facilitate the conversion of the natives, not as an instrument of economic exploitation through the *encomienda* system. They made every effort to protect the Indians, to convert them to Christianity by instruction and persuasion, and even to train a native priesthood. Devout sovereigns like Isabella and Philip II listened to their arguments and furthered their proposals in every practical way. Finally, the economic value of the *encomiendas* declined steadily because of the diminution of the native population and the ability of those who survived to acquire European skills and to move to the towns to work for wages. By the seventeenth century, the *encomiendas* were generally replaced by large estates owned by Spanish settlers in which Indians provided labor in return for the land they cultivated for their own support, small farms owned by natives or those of

[6] See pages 142-143.

mixed blood, and crown lands containing many Indian communities that were supervised by paid royal officials and forced to contribute some male inhabitants for several weeks each year to labor on public works or in the silver mines.

The failure of the early Spanish settlers to establish the feudal and manorial system did not prevent them from transplanting other aspects of their economic system. European mining techniques were employed to extract gold, silver, tin, copper, nitrates, and other minerals, to the enrichment of the local Spanish miners and of the crown, which claimed a fifth of the produce. Where the climate and soil were suitable, European products such as sugar, bananas, olives, coffee, and rice were planted, and native products such as potatoes and corn continued to be grown. Other localities were found to resemble the high, arid plains of Castile where stockraising had long been a prominent occupation. Here, horses, sheep, and cattle were introduced with quick success, and soon the cowboy with his lasso was so much a part of the scene that in America today one is apt to regard the ranch as a contribution of the New World rather than the Old. The price of beef dropped so rapidly that soon cattle were valued primarily for hides.

The Spanish monarchs made every effort to regulate trade. All ships except those specially licensed were directed to sail in convoys from Seville and to dock only at Havana, Veracruz, or Portobelo on the Panama Isthmus. Since there were only two convoys a year, this regulation injured trade. Furthermore, Spain itself could not produce quality manufactured goods in the quantity or at the price desired by the colonists. As a result, smuggling became commonplace, and the crown was unable to enforce the trading monopoly with the New World that it had given to the Seville merchants.

During the late sixteenth century, a severe economic depression began in the Spanish colonies that lasted for over a hundred years. A cause of the depression was the alarming decline of the native population. One authority has estimated that the number of inhabitants in central Mexico dropped from about 11,000,000 in 1519 to 2,500,000 in 1597, primarily because of disease that reached epidemic proportions in the 1540's and 1570's. At first, the decline had little effect on the economy, since the Spanish cattle ranches required fewer laborers than the native farms which they replaced, but as the century ended, a scarcity of labor developed and even the all-important mining industry suffered. Thus, the prolonged European depression had its counterpart in the New World.

When a colony was first established, all the inhabitants were either Spaniards or Indians. As generations passed, however, a much more complex social pattern developed. Those Spaniards who had been born in Spain remained at the top of the social ladder. Many were of noble birth and had come to the New World with the idea of making a fortune and returning to Spain. They held the principal offices. Next came the *creoles,* the white inhabitants who had been born in the colonies. Although they were often educated, intelligent, and well-to-do, the members of this class were usually assigned posts of only secondary importance in the government. Then came the *mestizos,* who were of mixed white and Indian ancestry, and the *mulattoes,* who were part white and part Negro. These people were usually artisans or minor officials, although a few achieved prominence during the colonial era. Lower yet in the social scale were the Indians, who still made up about four-fifths of the population of Spanish America as late as 1660, the freed Negroes, and those of mixed Indian and Negro blood. Finally, there were Negro slaves.

In general, where there had been a large and advanced Indian population at the time of the discoveries, as in Mexico and Peru, the natives and *mestizos* remained the largest ethnic group. In tropical climates where the Indians had been primitive, as in the West Indies, the natives were gradually exterminated by disease, war, and brutality. Negro slaves were imported to provide a labor force, and the Negroid and *mulatto* population became large. Where the climate was temperate and the number of natives small, as in Argentina and Chile, the dominant ethnic group was Spanish. Nevertheless, most of the races and racial mixtures mentioned above were represented in all the colonies. Although the Spaniard was less color-conscious than the Englishman, he was nevertheless inordinately proud of his family and looked with scorn on those whom he thought beneath him. As colonial society became more established and the economic depression curtailed opportunities for advancement, a rigid caste system replaced the relatively mobile social situation that had characterized the age of discovery.

The Spanish brought with them their religion and culture. Archdioceses and dioceses were established throughout their colonies, and few villages did not boast a church. The regular clergy was especially active, and numerous missions were established to convert the Indians. Native beliefs and ceremonies were often grafted onto the Christian, but the missionaries' accomplishments were nevertheless remarkable. Although they generally neglected the Negro, they did much to protect and educate the Indian. Thus, at an early date, the clergy achieved a powerful position in the colonies, a position that was, on the whole, beneficial until a later age, when they became overly anxious to defend the status quo.

Education was not neglected. By the time of Charles V's abdication in 1556, three universities had been established in the Spanish colonies, and three more were started during the seventeenth century. Children of the wealthy were often sent to Spain to be educated, but most colonials studied law, medicine, and theology in the New World. Unfortunately, the colonials, like the Spanish, failed to keep abreast of the rapidly changing intellectual climate of the seventeenth century and by the eighteenth century had been left far behind. A printing press was established in Mexico City in the 1530's, and others soon followed elsewhere. A respectable quantity of prose and poetry was produced, for the most part dealing with the exploits of the *Conquistadores* or with religious subjects.

Spanish art and architecture were also brought to America, where natives became skilled in carving and painting works of art for the Church.

The Portuguese monarchy first tried to settle Brazil by granting great feudal estates to nobles who were to establish settlements at their own expense, but this experiment was shortlived, and in 1549 a royal governor-general was appointed to act as a viceroy. A little later a council comparable to the Council of the Indies was established in Portugal, and the huge colony was subdivided into provinces, each with a governor who was subordinate to the governor-general.

Geographical conditions in Brazil favored the cultivation of sugar and therefore encouraged the development of large estates worked by slaves. Since the Indians of the region were too primitive for agricultural labor, a type of work that they had reserved to women, the Portuguese imported Negro slaves from Africa. Other crops were raised, such as coffee and tobacco, and during the late seventeenth and eighteenth centuries, some gold and diamonds were mined. By 1700, there were about 750,000 civilized inhabitants in the colony, the majority of whom were Negroes and *mulattoes*. The Catholic Church was as firmly established as in Spanish America, but Brazil lagged behind in education, and there was no university in the colony. The European civilization in a somewhat modified form was nevertheless spreading into the interior of Brazil as it was in the Spanish colonies.

THE FRENCH COLONIES IN AMERICA

The pope's decision to divide the heathen lands of the world between the Spanish and Portuguese sovereigns was not respected by other would-be colonizers, either Catholic or Protestant. During the sixteenth century, the French attempted to establish colonies in Brazil, Florida, and Canada, only to be driven out by the Portuguese and Spanish in the first two instances and by cold, hunger, and hardship in the last. The violent struggle that broke out between Catholics and Protestants in France prevented serious colonizing efforts after 1564 until Henry IV became firmly seated on the throne in 1598.[7]

In 1605, the French founded a successful colony in Nova Scotia. Three years later the energetic Samuel de Champlain (1567?-1635) pressed up the St. Lawrence River to Quebec, where he established a settlement that was to be the center of the fur trade for years to come. French colonial activities were carried out by chartered companies, as were the English, but the government usually furnished part of the capital and named some or all of the directors of the company.

The relative lack of interest among French merchants in colonial enterprises accounts in part for the slow development of Canada, but

[7] See pages 295-297.

other factors were more important. The French usually formed a single company for both trade and colonization. Company officials inevitably emphasized trade rather than colonization, since trade yielded quick profits while colonies were not likely to bring returns for decades. When a colony was finally established, few Frenchmen were willing to emigrate. The chartered company possessed a trading monopoly with its colonies that enabled it to charge the colonials high prices for European goods. Company directors and others were given large seigneuries that they tried to settle by making grants on semi-feudal terms, but few peasants were willing to exchange feudal obligations in France for feudal obligations in a harsh New World. Furthermore, after the death of Henry IV, the crown adopted the policy of allowing only Catholics to settle in the colonies. This policy removed the religious motive for emigration that inspired so many Englishmen to leave their homes.

As a result, there were less than 2,000 white colonists in Canada in 1660, and the regular military establishment consisted of about thirty soldiers. Furthermore, the French had incurred the enmity of the powerful Iroquois confederacy soon after their arrival in Canada, and for decades settlers had to work in the fields with their guns beside them. As late as 1660, the Iroquois nearly succeeded in destroying the colony. The Dutch and the English were a still more serious threat, and in 1629 the latter actually captured Quebec and held it for several years. Except for the Iroquois, most of the Indians of the region were friendly and the missionary activities of the Jesuits led to many baptisms, but the French, unlike the Spanish, made little effort to civilize the Indians in other respects and Christianity remained a thin veneer. Under these circumstances, it is remarkable that the French accomplished as much as they did.

Their successes came largely from their willingness and exceptional capacity to live in the forest and associate with the Indians. This practice was furthered by frequent intermarriages with the Indians, a policy that was officially encouraged to populate the colony. As a result, Frenchmen and halfbreeds were soon wandering over the St. Lawrence and Great Lakes region in search of furs. In 1663, Louis XIV made New France (Canada) a royal colony and sent sufficient troops to dispose of the Iroquois threat temporarily. Able officials, such as Count Frontenac (1620-1698), who served as governor from 1672 to 1682 and again from 1689 to 1698, were sent there. Traders and explorers pushed further and further into the interior. In 1673, Father Marquette (1637-1675), a Jesuit priest, explored the Mississippi River as far south as Arkansas in hopes that it would empty into the Gulf of California and thereby provide a water route from the Great Lakes region to the Pacific. Nine years later Robert de La Salle (1643-1687) descended the Mississippi to its mouth. A vast empire, extending westward and then southward from Nova Scotia to Louisiana and held together by the St. Lawrence, Great Lakes, Ohio, and Mississippi waterways, appeared within the French grasp. The English colonies could be bottled up along

AREA OF
EXPLORATION
AND
SETTLEMENT

DUTCH

ENGLISH

SPANISH

FRENCH

SCALE OF MILES
0 100 200 300 400 500

ONTARIO

ERIE

HURON

MICHIGAN

SUPERIOR

MISSOURI

N. PLATTE

ARKANSAS

RED

SNAKE

GREEN

PEGOS

RIO GRANDE

MISSISSIPPI

GULF OF MEXICO

70°

80°

90°

100°

110°

120°

40°

30°

the Atlantic coast, leaving the French free to exploit the western portion of the continent. Frontenac and others wanted to seize this opportunity, but Louis XIV's military commitments prevented him from providing the necessary support. A colony was established in Louisiana, but the French continental empire remained a vast, precariously-held land, occupied by primitive Indians, slightly more civilized halfbreeds, and a handful of Frenchmen. It was not even possible to prevent the English Hudson's Bay Company from developing a large trade in furs in the far north.

More valuable from the contemporary French point of view were the colonies that France began to establish on Martinique, Guadeloupe, and other West Indian Islands in 1625. Here, tobacco and sugar were grown with the aid of Negro slave labor, and substantial profits were quickly realized. An important consideration to the mercantilist theorists was that these islands provided commodities that France would otherwise have been forced to purchase from economic competitors. For this reason, a vast continental empire was neglected in favor of a few tiny islands, and in the end it was the less venturesome English colonists who took hold of most of North America.

THE ENGLISH COLONIES IN AMERICA

The English made unsuccessful attempts to establish colonies in New-foundland and off the North Carolina coast during the sixteenth century, but it was only after 1600 that they made a successful entry into the race for colonies that the Spanish had begun more than a century before. Like the Spanish, they were motivated by a desire for profit and adventure, but in another respect their motives were different. The Spanish and other Catholics were also impelled by an intense desire to spread Christianity among the Indians. The English and other Protestants who engaged in colonial activity, such as the Dutch, gave only lip service to the missionary ideal and rarely attempted to convert the Indians. The Spanish tried to baptize and civilize the Indians, and the French tried to baptize them, but the English simply drove them westward as their colonies expanded. This is not to say that the English settlers were irreligious; many actually came to the New World in search of religious freedom for themselves, a quest that was not open to the non-Catholic Spaniard and Frenchman. Rather, the religious motivation of the Englishman was to worship as he chose, and of the Spaniard to convert the natives to his beliefs.

The costs of starting a colony were greater than the English crown wished to bear. As a result, many of the early English colonies were founded by joint stock companies. The Virginia Company of London was incorporated in 1606 and given a royal charter in 1609. Shares were distributed to those who emigrated to Virginia at their own expense or contributed sums for others to do so, one share being granted for each person transported. Once the colony became firmly established, land was distributed among the shareholders according to the number of shares they held. The directors of the company resided in London but appointed a governor and a council for the colony. Beginning in 1619, the colonists were permitted to elect a colonial legislature whose consent was necessary for making laws and levying taxes. England became the only European country to transplant representative institutions to the New World, although such assemblies still existed in all the colonizing powers and played a far more important role in at least one, the Netherlands, than in England itself. This significant development, which was probably due primarily to the fortunate insight of one or more influential members of the company in London, caused the governmental system in the colonies to resemble the system in England, where king, lords, and commons had their colonial counterparts in governor, council, and house of burgesses.

The Massachusetts Bay Company, which played a leading role in settling New England, was organized in a manner similar to the Virginia Company, except that the headquarters of the company were established in Boston rather than London, an arrangement that gave the colonists greater control over their own affairs.

Other colonies owed their origins to the efforts of private individuals who were given extensive tracts of land. These proprietors appointed the governors and councils of their colonies, but permitted the formation of representative assemblies. English activities in Barbados and other West Indian islands resulted largely from the efforts of proprietors, while on the mainland the efforts of Lord Baltimore led to the establishment of a colony in Maryland in 1634. In 1663, the Carolinas were given to eight proprietors, and when the Dutch colony of New Netherland was captured the following year, the Duke of York was made proprietor. To the south, William Penn became the proprietor of Pennsylvania in 1681.

While the English kings rarely became financially involved in the foundation of a colony, nearly all the colonies eventually fell into their hands. Financial difficulties and internal disputes between the leaders of the Virginia Company led the king to revoke its charter in 1624 and turn the youthful settlement into a royal colony. Thereafter, governor and council were appointed by the king. From the standpoint of the colonists, this change made little difference, since their institutions remained the same. Nearly all the other colonies eventually came under the control of the crown without a significant change in the system of government.

Even after the king had assumed control over most of the colonies, no special royal institutions for their administration were established in England until near the close of the seventeenth century. The king was content to exercise his authority in a negative fashion through the veto right his governor exercised over the colonial legislatures and through the privy council's power to disallow acts of the governors, legislatures, and other officials. Positive action by the government in London was largely limited to the regulation of trade; the internal affairs of the colonists were left in

275

their own hands. Thus, the English colonial system was more decentralized than that of other powers, and more freedom of action was left to the settlers.

Companies and proprietors frequently made careful plans to guide the economic activities of their colonies, but their plans usually proved impractical. Virginia, it had been hoped, would supply precious metals in the same abundance as Latin America. In addition to mining, the wine, naval stores, and silk industries were to be developed to free the mother country from having to import such products from foreign nations. Such dreams were quickly dispelled, and Virginia became a tobacco-producing colony in spite of the conviction of King James I that smoking was bad for both health and morals. Georgia, the last English colony to be established on the mainland, was envisioned as a buffer of small farms owned by white freemen ready to halt Spanish efforts to expand northward from Florida, but in the end, plantations worked by slave labor became as characteristic as in the other southern colonies. Proprietors frequently planned to transplant the manorial system in the New World, but to get settlers they soon found that they had to be content with a small quit rent.

The independent spirit displayed by the early English colonists and their willingness to accommodate their economic program to climatic conditions did not prevent them from carrying as much of their social life and culture to America as they could. In Puritan New England, people lived in small towns so that they could participate in church and communal life. Even in Virginia, where separate farm houses became characteristic, settlers were not so far apart that social contacts ceased. In contrast to the bold excursions of the French settlers into the hinterland, the westward movement of the English was slow and orderly. The primitive Indians whom they encountered were either exterminated or driven westward, and the only large non-European ethnic group in their midst were Negroes brought from Africa to work in the tobacco fields of the southern colonies and the sugar islands of the West Indies.

The colonies north of Virginia were founded largely for religious reasons, and here the church, whether Puritan, Baptist, Catholic, or Quaker, played an important role. Elsewhere, the Anglican Church was preferred by the leading settlers, but the failure to appoint bishops to the New World, as the Spanish Catholics had done, increased the difficulty in obtaining an ordained ministry large enough to care for the spiritual needs of the colonists. Public schools became a New England characteristic at an early date. Elsewhere, churches, ministers, and private individuals made some effort to provide schools, although many inhabitants remained unlettered. Higher education was not neglected; Harvard was founded in 1636, William and Mary in 1693, Yale in 1701, and other colleges at later dates.

From the beginning, the same social structure existed in the colonies as in England, except for the almost complete absence of noblemen and the presence of Negro slaves and indentured servants who had bound themselves out to work for a specified number of years to pay for their passage. In the few cities, there were wealthy merchants, shopkeepers, and laborers, while the countryside boasted a gentry class, small farmers, and agricultural laborers.

The English, like the French, at first regarded their small West Indian sugar-producing islands more highly than their mainland colonies. As late as 1640 the island population was as great as that of the mainland, but the future lay with the latter, and the willingness of the English to settle in large numbers on the continent was a decisive factor in their struggle with the French during the eighteenth century.

AFRICA

Although European expansion and discovery were first directed along the African coast, the inhabitants of that vast continent were little influenced by Western civilization until the latter part of the nineteenth century. One reason for this long delay was that geographical conditions and native opposition made the African continent difficult to penetrate. Another was that the Europeans did not need to establish colonies to get the slaves, ivory, gold dust, and other products that they wanted. Coastal trading stations were sufficient.

The Sahara Desert made it difficult to enter central Africa from the north, and mountains that run parallel to the sea made access to the interior difficult from a large portion of the east and west coasts. Desert or disease-infested jungle added to the hazards of some regions, while the dearth of good harbors and navigable rivers increased the difficulties of penetrating the interior.

Northern Africa was in the hands of the Moslems, who possessed an advanced culture of their own and still had the military power to repel assaults from Europe. Immediately south of the Sahara, a wide belt across the continent was suitable for horse and camel. Here, Arabs brought their religion and culture when they penetrated the region in search of trade. A number of strong, relatively advanced native states developed under their influence, such as the Songhai empire with its fabled city of Tombouctou that boasted a university long before Columbus made his historic voyages. Only the west African coast from Senegal to Angola and the southern tip of the continent were significantly affected by the Europeans during this period.

The west African coast was brought within the European orbit primarily by the slave trade, although gold dust and ivory were also sought. First the Portuguese and then the French, English, Dutch, and others established small posts along the coast. They sold from fifteen to twenty million Negroes into slavery during the two centuries following 1640 to work the plantations of the New World, an amazing number when one considers that at no time did the total population of Negro Africa exceed seventy-five million. These slaves were purchased from coastal tribes that proved all too willing to raid their neighbors for slaves in return for firearms, rum, and a few of the more useful products of the West. The Dahomey and Ashanti empires, whose slave-hunting expeditions brought misery to the region, owed their rise in part to this contact with Europe.

It is true that the Portuguese brought corn, sweet potatoes, pineapples, and tobacco to Africa and that natives far in the interior were soon cultivating these new agricultural products. Only in the Congo, however, did the Portuguese exercise much of a civilizing influence, and even here their work ended in failure. Here, the intelligent Bantu tribes welcomed European ways. Their king was converted to Christianity and took the name of Dom Affonso I (1506-1543). Affonso learned to read and write in Portuguese and sent some of his subjects to Lisbon to be educated. His court aped that of Portugal in its ceremony and dress, and titles like duke and marquis were given to leading subjects. European craftsmen, including two German printers who brought a printing press with them in 1492, joined Catholic priests in their civilizing mission. A stone cathedral was constructed in the capital city of Mbanza Congo, rechristened São Salvador, and schools were built in many towns. Unfortunately, the Portuguese lacked the resources and, after a few decades, the will to provide adequate guidance. In the end, they quarreled with the Congolese, and their victory in a battle in 1665 was followed by the speedy decline of the native kingdom. By 1800, little trace of it remained.

The southern tip of Africa was one of the few points along the coast where the climate was attractive and the interior could be easily penetrated. At Cape Town in 1652, the Dutch East India Company established a port of call to supply their passing ships with meat and fresh vegetables. Although the primitive Bushmen and Hottentots could offer no effective resistance, the colony grew slowly during the seventeenth and eighteenth centuries, largely because of the illiberal policies of the company. At a time when the Europeanization of the Americas was moving forward at a rapid rate, the Europeanization of Africa was scarcely moving forward at all.

CONTACTS WITH THE EAST

European civilization did not penetrate more deeply into Asia than it did into Africa during the seventeenth century. The inhabitants of this continent were too highly civilized to accept an alien culture until it was demonstrably superior in important respects to their own, a situation that did not exist until the last hundred years. Furthermore, the Europeans who went to the East were primarily interested in trade and did not want to divert time and money from trade to conquest. Contact with the natives was therefore largely limited to the inhabitants of coastal cities.

The Portuguese had made considerable strides towards establishing a commercial empire in the East during the first three-quarters of the sixteenth century, but thereafter signs of decay began to appear. They lacked the necessary population to support so large an enterprise. Since few Portuguese women went to the East, marriage with the natives was encouraged. The resulting half-castes became an important element in the Portuguese commercial efforts, but they lacked the initiative and seamanship qualities of their fathers, and the efficiency of the Portuguese navy declined. At the same time, the Portuguese lost their lead in naval architecture. The result was that, whereas they had lost only 7 per cent of their ships on voyages to the East prior to 1580, 31 per cent failed to return in the generation that followed.

The religious intolerance of the Portuguese limited the effectiveness of their missionary efforts and prevented them from establishing a firm understanding with the Hindu states in southern India, or even with the Nestorians, an Asiatic Christian sect whom they regarded as heretics. Without significant native support, the Portuguese were unable to resist the Moslems when they pressed down into southern India, conquering the Hindu states and threatening the Portuguese trading settlements.

When Philip II won the Portuguese throne in 1580, it was widely felt that the power of Spain would be used to save the Portuguese empire. Unfortunately, Philip brought more enemies than he did troops. His rebellious Dutch subjects felt free to make inroads into the Portuguese empire now that he was its master and their one-time profitable trade with Lisbon was curtailed. The entrance of England into the war with Spain also brought their ships into the East. At first, individual English and Dutch merchants tried to break the Spanish-Portuguese monopoly of the spice trade, but it soon became apparent that only large, well-financed groups could hope for success. In 1600, the English East India Company was formed to exploit this possibility, and two years later the larger Dutch East India Company was established.

The Dutch East India Company was a joint-stock company owned and operated by merchants and run for profit. The missionary fervor that had characterized the Spanish and Portuguese efforts was almost entirely absent. Since exploration had sometimes yielded returns, the Dutch sent ships north of Japan to the Kuriles and eastward to Tasmania, New Zealand, and the Fijis, but since these islands did not seem to offer much opportunity for trade, they were not settled. Instead, the Dutch concentrated their attention on winning a monopoly of the East Indian spice trade. The Portuguese were driven out, and other nationalities, including their former English allies, were ruthlessly excluded. A number of settlements were established on the various islands, the principal one at Batavia on the northern coast of Java. This city became the capital of the Dutch empire and the center of its trade, but here as elsewhere the Dutch resisted any temptation to conquer the hinterland. Some involvement in the rivalries between native states and chieftains could not be avoided, however, and native groups were gradually taken under their protection. A Dutch resident was sent to each of these protectorates to administer justice to any Europeans who might be there and to see that the natives produced and turned over the desired amount of spices to the company. Native customs and law were left alone. As a result, the Dutch disrupted native trade and influenced political developments but did not significantly alter native society, religion, or culture.

The initial capitalization of the English East India Company was only about one-tenth of that of the Dutch. As a result, the English were unable to compete successfully for the profitable spice trade and turned their attention to India. Here they persuaded the powerful Moslem emperor to rent them a warehouse on the eastern coast at Surat. In 1639, the company established a post on the western coast at Madras that included six square miles of land. Bombay was added in 1662 as part of the dowry that a Portuguese princess brought Charles II, but when the company tried to throw off its subservience to the Moslem emperor in the 1680's, its forces were defeated and continued trade was permitted only in return for the payment of about £17,000 per year. Nevertheless, the company established a base at Calcutta near the close of the century. Although it was unable to pay any dividends between 1692 and 1700, it was able to expand after the Moslem empire in India began to decline following the death of its last great sultan in 1707.

The French also became interested in the Indian trade and established bases at Pondichéry and several other places. With the decline of the Moslem empire during the eighteenth century, it was they, not the Portuguese, who competed with the English for control of the vast subcontinent.

Meanwhile, the eastern trade was becoming more diversified. The desire for spices had originally motivated this trade, but after 1650 trade in coffee, tea, raw silk, and especially Indian cottons became important. Within fifty years, the sale of Asiatic coffee in Europe increased from 40,000 pounds per year to over 3,000,000 per year. Coffeehouses became popular social and literary institutions in such fashionable cities as London, Paris, and Amsterdam. Cotton cloth was even more important; the English alone increased their importations from less than 100,000 pieces in 1650 to 2,000,000 a generation later. The European woolen industry was injured, but mercantilist efforts to limit the influx of cottons were to no avail.

The increased imports from the East found no counterpart in exports from the West, because the Europeans still had few products that were desired by the highly developed Oriental peoples. Since their purchases had to be paid for with gold and silver, the constant drain of precious metals led to cries from many mercantilists, but the one-sided trade continued.

As the seventeenth century drew to a close, the New World was becoming Europeanized and was exchanging its goods with the parent nations. The Asiatic people, however, remained unwilling to buy European products or to adopt European institutions or culture. Indeed, Chinese porcelain, lacquer, and garden designs were beginning to influence European aesthetic tastes, and glowing accounts of Chinese morals, philosophy, and institutions were having a disturbing effect on European intellectuals. A base may have been established for the Europeanization of the world, but in Asia the process itself had hardly begun.

7/ The Constitutional Crisis

THE Renaissance monarchy, as we have seen, was a conglomeration of kingdoms that had been linked together by dynastic marriages and of feudal duchies that had reverted to the crown. As a result, the inhabitants of its various territories had different laws, customs, institutions, and privileges; and tariff barriers limited trade between territories. Weakened by this decentralization, monarchical authority was even more seriously limited by the absence of large loyal armies and adequate bureaucracies. Thus, the power a king could wield depended largely on popular support. After 1560, this support began to be withdrawn in many countries and a constitutional crisis ensued.

At first, the Renaissance monarchs had been successful in winning popular support, but the Protestant Reformation presented them with a new and difficult problem. For over a thousand years, there had been only one Church in central and western Europe. Now there were many, but instead of accepting this situation, nearly every ruler tried to bring about a return to religious conformity by persuasion or persecution.

Catholic monarchs insisted on religious conformity for two reasons. First, they believed that those who espoused the new religion were certain of damnation. To permit Protestants to preach was to expose their subjects to the sufferings of hell. Just as the state of our day seeks to prolong the earthly life of its citizens by eradicating disease, so the monarchs of the Reformation era sought to ensure the eternal life of their people by eradicating heresy. Second, Catholic monarchs looked upon the Church as one of the principal props of the crown. The clergy paid taxes to support the government, served as some of the principal officers of the state, and taught the people to respect and obey their kings. Clerical offices were among the most lucrative rewards that monarchs had to bestow on their faithful servants and friends.

At first, Protestants taught obedience to the secular decrees of their Catholic rulers. They did so in part from religious conviction and in part because they had more hope of converting monarchs to their point of view than of overthrowing the state. When they failed and were persecuted for their beliefs, they revised their doctrines to justify rebellion. This was particularly true in those countries with a large number of noble converts. The nobility was still the warrior class, and in their seigneuries they were more accustomed to command than to obey. It is not surprising that they often chose to raise their standards in rebellion rather than submit to persecution by the government.

When the Protestants were able to persuade or compel the crown to adopt their religious beliefs, the Catholics were persecuted. It was then the priest who became the advocate of rebellion and even assassination, and there were many uprisings in the name of the Roman Church. Sometimes members of two Protestant sects fought to control the state, and both Catholics and Protestants were guilty of plotting with foreign powers to overthrow an unfriendly government at home. Members of outlawed religions were as subversive as the Communists are today and were regarded with equal horror by those in power. Well might a French chancellor say in 1560: "The division of languages [nationalities] does not separate kingdoms, but that of religion and laws divides a nation in two. From this comes the old proverb, one faith, one law, one king."

The economic developments of the sixteenth and seventeenth centuries also made for unrest. The price revolution had a profound effect. The cost of governing increased more rapidly than the income from the crown lands and the regular royal levies. Some monarchs sought to meet growing deficits by borrowing, but eventually the loans had to be repaid. Other monarchs debased the currency, but this led prices to rise still more rapidly. In the end, every ruler had to increase taxation or seek additional income by resurrecting forgotten feudal dues, inflicting heavy fines for failure to obey laws that for centuries had not been enforced, selling monopolies, and demanding forced loans and gifts. These activities brought the kings into conflict with their subjects, and constitutional crises ensued.

The increased financial demands of the crown were not the only problems raised by the price revolution. Those individuals whose incomes did not keep pace with rising costs also suffered, and they blamed many of their difficulties on the government or on each other. Even the merchants —the very group who profited most—were often discontented. They fretted at the numerous regulations that restricted their profits. They were angered especially by the monopolies granted by the crown, because these monopolies restricted economic enterprise.

The economic depression that began in the second fifth of the seventeenth century made matters worse. Wars led the kings to demand higher and higher taxes, but many subjects had less money to spare. Opportunities to rise from one social class to another diminished. Journeymen found it difficult to become masters in the craft guilds, merchants were less frequently able to join the ranks of the aristocracy, and peasants often revolted.

Thus, the spirit of cooperation between crown and subject that had characterized the Renaissance came to an end. Kings found it necessary to stretch their prerogatives and to centralize their states to further their quest for religious unity and an adequate revenue. Subjects of different religious views sought with equal fervor to impose their religion on the crown. They opposed the centralizing efforts of the government, increases in taxation, and royal economic regulations, but at the same time they blamed the kings for their economic difficulties. The more the kings were thwarted in their design, the more power they sought to ensure compliance with their regulations. The more power they won, the greater became the opposition of the people. The result was that in the late sixteenth and seventeenth centuries there were revolts in every important European country. Depending on the outcome of these revolts, monarchical or parliamentary governments were established and the old dynastic state either yielded to a centralized state, remained intact, or disintegrated into its component provinces, duchies, and counties.

THE CONSTITUTIONAL CRISIS IN ENGLAND

THE EARLY STUARTS

The constitutional crisis did not begin in England until the seventeenth century, but the outcome of the struggle for power had far-reaching results. Henry VIII had been able to disengage England from Rome with a minimum of difficulty. One daughter, Mary, had made England Catholic again, and another daughter, Elizabeth, had returned her country to the Protestant fold. These sudden changes provoked only minor uprisings and posed no major constitutional problems except in the relationship between church and state. The ease with which the Tudor monarchs changed the official religion may be accounted for by the fact that the great religious revival which had sparked both the Catholic and the Protestant reformations on the continent made little headway in England until near the close of the sixteenth century. There were few devout enough to court martyrdom or to plot the overthrow of the dynasty. The memory of the Wars of the Roses and later the threat of a Spanish invasion bound most Englishmen too closely to their sovereigns to permit rebellion, whatever the justification. Then, too, the Tudors had known when and how to lead public opinion and when to acquiesce in the desires of their subjects. Above all else, they had known how to control Parliament. This happy combination of experience and circumstance came to an end when Queen Elizabeth—the last of the Tudors—died in 1603. The English crown passed to her cousin, James Stuart, King of Scotland for thirty-six of his thirty-seven years.

In some ways, James seemed well-qualified for his new responsibilities. He had managed to restore royal power in Scotland without provoking a major rebellion and without using undue force. He was better educated than most kings and was among the more acute political theorists of his day. He was a peace-loving man who bent his efforts towards preventing war in Europe. These very virtues, however, contributed to his undoing. His success in Scotland made him overconfident and arrogant. His love of political theory and scholarly disputations led him to define the royal prerogatives at a time when they should have been left vague enough to be stretched in case of need. He never lost an opportunity to lecture Parliament about his powers in terms that seemed extreme even for his day. He was equally careless with the religious susceptibilities of his subjects and was always ready to lecture them on theology and church organization. This combination of learning and lack of tact led one continental statesman to refer to him as "the wisest fool in Christendom." To make matters worse, James was a foreigner who spoke English with an accent and who pampered more than one worthless Scottish favorite at English expense.

The second Stuart monarch, Charles, was more attractive than his father. He was a devout Anglican and, after the first few years of his marriage, a devoted husband. No king was ever more anxious to protect his poorer subjects. He upheld the craftsman against the manufacturer, the wage-earner against the employer, and the peasant against the gentry who wanted to enclose the land. Unfortunately, these virtues were overshadowed by his autocratic, uncompromising character and by policies that antagonized the most powerful classes in the kingdom. He and his father would have experienced difficulties even if certain events had not been taking place that were largely beyond their control.

The first difficulty arose from increasing dissent within the Anglican Church. Many persons, led by the archbishops and bishops, wanted to keep the rituals and ceremonies of the Catholic Church. They believed that inward devotion could not exist without "the beauty of holiness." These prelates won the support of the crown, but their program brought them into conflict with the Puritans. The Puritans wanted to purify the Anglican Church by reducing the amount of ritual and emphasizing the Calvinist theology and code of behavior. Some Puritans were content to work for mild reforms within the existing organization of the Church, but others, who were generally classified as Presbyterians, wanted to abolish the offices of archbishop and bishop and turn the control of the churches over to committees of laymen and clergymen. The split between Anglican and Puritan was widened by James, who took a strong stand in support of the prelates because his experience with the presbyterian form of church government in Scotland led him to believe that "Presbytery agreeth as well with a monarch as God and the devil. Then Jack and Tom, and Will and Dick shall meet at their pleasure, censure me and my council and all our proceedings." He swore to make the Puritans conform or "harry them out of the land." Those clergymen who refused to accept the Anglican Prayer Book were deprived of their livings.

The division between Anglican and Puritan became wider during the reign of Charles I (1625-1649). Charles gave full backing to the efforts of his Archbishop of Canterbury, William Laud (1573-1645), to secure complete conformity with the Anglican doctrine and ceremony. To many Puritans, it seemed as though Charles's insistence on ritual was but the first step towards the restoration of Catholicism.

The Thirty Years War led to more difficulties. At times, it looked as though the Spanish and Austrian Habsburgs would be able to restore Catholicism in northern Germany and the Netherlands. Among Protestant princes expelled from their lands was Frederick of the Palatinate, James's son-in-law. James had no stomach for a military crusade to rescue his relatives and save Protestantism. Rather, he sought to accomplish these ends through a dynastic alliance between Charles and a Spanish princess. This plan was unpopular in England because it was recognized that a Catholic marriage would mean priests at court to care for the princess' religious needs and a relaxation of laws against English Catholics. Marriage negotiations continued for years, and only when the Spanish finally rejected Charles did James intervene on the continent. His efforts, and those of Charles after his death, were ineffectual, and the prestige of the dynasty declined still further. Charles worsened the situation by choosing a French princess as his bride. The much feared Catholic influence entered the court, and detested English Catholics were more leniently treated than the Puritans. These developments reinforced the fear that the king himself might become a Catholic.

The third development largely outside the control of the Stuarts was the price revolution. The rise in prices in the last half of the sixteenth and early seventeenth centuries increased the costs of government more rapidly than the ordinary revenue of the crown. Even frugal Queen Elizabeth had been unable to keep a balanced budget. The Stuarts showed less wisdom in their expenditures, though, in justice, it should be pointed out that it took more to support an entire royal family than an unmarried queen. The result was that the Stuarts had either to make increased demands on Parliament or to find additional income by some other means.

At first, James turned to Parliament, but members of the Commons were unsympathetic and had little understanding of his difficulties. He was unable to win the cooperation that his predecessors had received, in part because he did not understand how to manipulate the debates. The Tudors had seen to it that a large number of their ablest councillors had seats in the Commons where they presented the royal program. The councillors took the initiative in the deliberations. With the help of the speaker of the House, who was also a royal appointee, they were usually able to guide the king's program through the chamber and at the same time to prevent undesired proposals from being passed. In the face of such leadership, it was difficult for the opposition to operate effectively in a large unwieldy assembly of four or five hundred deputies. Unfortunately, the Stuarts did not understand the Tudor techniques of controlling Parliament, and few of their councillors sought seats in the Commons. At the same time, the practice of using committees developed. A small committee could study, plan, debate, and prepare measures as effectively as the royal councillors. There were too many committees for the councillors to attend, and the speaker exercised little direct control over their activities. The leaders of the opposition to the Stuarts were quick to realize the advantages of committees, and they used them to put forward their policies. Gradually, they won the initiative from the crown in the Commons. Parliamentary opposition blocked the union between England and Scotland so desired by James. It pressed for stronger anti-Catholic laws. It demanded intervention in the continental struggle between Catholic and Protestant, but refused to vote sufficient funds to ensure military success. When the English armies met defeat, it sought to impeach the king's chief minister.

The growing opposition in Parliament drove the Stuarts to actions that were unpopular at best and of questionable constitutionality at worst. The increased disabilities placed on Catholics were relaxed on royal order. Feudal rights of the crown were revived or increased, tariffs were raised without the consent of Parliament, forced loans were demanded, titles were sold, and monopolies were granted in order to raise money. Thus, the Stuarts answered the attack by the Commons on their authority by stretching their own powers beyond the limits allowed by the constitutional ideas of the time.

In 1628, the two factions reached a temporary agreement. Parliament voted a grant, and in return Charles accepted the Petition of Right. This petition prohibited taxation without consent, billeting soldiers in private houses, declaring martial law in time of peace, and arbitrary arrests. But the truce was short-lived, and in January, 1629, members of the Commons held their unwilling speaker in his chair while they passed resolutions declaring that whoever introduced religious innovations or voluntarily paid taxes without the consent of Parliament was an enemy of the kingdom. This action left Charles no choice but to arrest the leaders of Parliament and to dissolve that assembly.

During the next eleven years, Charles governed without Parliament. By withdrawing from the continental war and reducing his expenditures, he managed to raise enough money to support his government. This he did by stretching his prerogatives still further. In addition to the various forms of unparliamentary taxation practiced before, he extended ship-money, a tax that had hitherto been levied only on the seaboard towns to support the navy, to the entire kingdom. Meanwhile, the headstrong king continued to anger the Puritans by his support of the high-church Anglican policy of Archbishop Laud and by his leniency towards Catholics, the landowners by his desire to protect the peasants from enclosures, and the middle class by his efforts to set minimum wages. Only an opportunity to organize was needed for the opponents of the Stuarts to throw the island into turmoil. This opportunity was provided by a revolt in Scotland.

THE PURITAN REVOLUTION

In 1637, Charles ordered the Scots to accept a new prayer book based on Laud's high-church ideas. The Scottish people were far more strongly Presbyterian than the English, and when the bishop of Edinburgh tried to use the new service, an angry woman threw a stool at him. This action touched off a riot and led to a Solemn League and Covenant to resist religious innovations. The rebels abolished episcopacy and seized Edinburgh Castle.

This uprising drove Charles to convoke Parliament in 1640 in the hope of getting money for an army, but once in session, the House of Commons showed little disposition to vote taxes until its grievances had been heard. The deputies abolished the courts of the Star Chamber[1] and of the High Commission, which had exercised the ecclesiastical jurisdiction of the crown, and passed acts requiring that Parliament be held every three years and that the king's chief minister be executed. Charles fearfully acquiesced but later was goaded by his wife into entering the Commons with a band of followers to arrest five members. "The birds," Charles discovered, "had flown," but with this action civil war began.

The war that followed was not a class struggle. An analysis of the members of the Commons who sided with the king and those who stood by Parliament shows that the country gentleman, the lawyer, and the merchant could be found nearly as often in one camp as in the other. The division between Englishmen was along personal, constitutional, and religious, not social, lines. Those who had received royal favors, their clients, and their relatives tended to side with the king. Those who felt wronged by the king or who were denied his bounty often joined the op-

[1] See pages 101-104.

288

position. Those who thought that the king had exceeded his prerogatives leaned towards the side of Parliament. Those who believed that Parliament had been guilty of encroaching on the powers of the crown tended to remain loyal to the king. Most of the Puritans and religious radicals were to be found in the Parliamentary camp while the majority of the high church Anglicans and Catholics stood by the crown. Perhaps a majority of Englishmen never took sides, preferring to avoid the hazards of a war in which both sides were partly in the wrong.

At first, the opposing forces were about evenly divided, but the intervention of Scotland on the side of Parliament and the formation of a well-trained army under a Puritan gentleman named Oliver Cromwell (1599-1658) turned the tide against the king. The defeat of the royalist army in the battle of Naseby in 1645 left Charles no recourse but to surrender.

The victors then quarreled. The Presbyterian wing of the Puritan movement, supported by the Scots, sought to set up a constitutional monarchy with Charles at its head and their creed as the established church of England. In this, they were opposed by the army, which was more radical than Parliament. Many soldiers wanted a republic and still more were Independents, a left-wing branch of Puritanism. The Independents favored religious toleration for all except the Catholics and Anglicans and opposed Presbyterianism as the established church. Added to these political and religious grievances, Parliament refused to pay the troops.

Charles saw his chance. He tried to play the army against Parliament and the Scots against the English, until all but the staunchest royalists had lost faith in him. Finally, Cromwell, in disgust, put an end to the farce by defeating the Scottish army, purging Parliament of ninety-six Presbyterian members, and seizing, trying, and executing the faithless Charles. The monarchy was terminated and the House of Lords was abolished. The problem was to find an alternative form of government.

OLIVER CROMWELL

Cromwell was more responsible for the overthrow of the Stuarts than any other man, and as the commander of a large, well-trained army, he had the power to establish a dictatorship. However, he was no ordinary military conqueror who sought civil power, and the real tragedy of his career was that he was forced to assume a political role in order to protect the ideals for which he and his men had fought. Although he was one of the greatest military commanders in history, he had little political imagination. He stumbled from one expedient to another in search of some form of government which a majority of Englishmen would support, but the painful truth was that the opponents of the Stuarts could agree on no alternative to Stuart rule.

At first, Cromwell left civil affairs in the hands of the Rump—the unpurged members of Parliament—and an appointed council. He turned

Oliver Cromwell from a contemporary portrait. (Courtesy of Free Library of Philadelphia)

to Ireland, where he suppressed a rebellion with great cruelty, and then to Scotland, where he put down a Stuart uprising. The mercantile element in Parliament brought England into a war with the Dutch and passed measures designed to help big-city merchants. At the same time, Parliament was lax in the payment of troops, and some of its members were accused of accepting bribes. To ensure their continuance in power, they even decided to fill vacant seats by nomination instead of election. Cromwell could stand it no longer. In April, 1653, he ordered his troops to disperse the Rump. As the members of Parliament departed, the general shouted: "It's you that have forced me to do this, for I have sought the Lord night and day that he would slay me rather than put me upon the doing of this work." With the arrogant certainty of one who is convinced that he is doing God's will, Cromwell had now destroyed both king and Parliament.

God was less helpful in revealing to Cromwell what alternate form of government should be established. The doughty general was unwilling to indulge in naked military rule. At length, he was persuaded that the best way to secure a new Parliament composed of righteous men was to appoint its members upon the advice of the Independent preachers. The religious fanaticism of this Parliament is best illustrated by the name of one of its members, Praise-God Barebones. Within five months, this group of extremists had so angered Cromwell by their impractical policies that he turned them out as he had done their predecessors.

A still more radical departure in government was needed. This the army provided by drawing up the Instrument of Government, the only written constitution England has ever had. By its terms, Cromwell was made Lord Protector for life and a new Parliament was ordered. Cromwell had nearly as much difficulty with this Parliament as with its predecessors, for he understood the techniques of controlling deliberative assemblies no better than the Stuarts. But he was now chief executive, and in this capacity he terminated the indecisive Dutch War and sought to form a grand alliance of Protestant states against the Catholics. England joined France in its war against Spain and won Dunkirk and Jamaica as a result. In dealing with internal affairs, Cromwell was less successful. His wars made high taxes necessary. Many people were restive under his rule, and the first Parliament under the Protectorate had to be dissolved for attacking his powers. This action was followed by another uprising. To keep order, Cromwell felt it necessary to divide England into twelve districts, each administered by a major-general with an army at his disposal. Blue laws were strictly enforced. Theaters were closed, Sunday became a day for prayer, and recreation was forbidden. Calvin's Geneva was imposed on Merry England, and unwillingly Cromwell became a virtual military dictator.

When Cromwell summoned Parliament in 1656, he found that the deputies were restive. They wanted to return to the old constitutional rule of king, lords, and commons, but they were still not ready to accept another Stuart. They created a new House of Lords, and offered Cromwell the title of king. The great general hesitated. To become king was to end his uncertain legal position; to tie himself and the things that he stood for with the past was to give greater assurance of a stable future. Yet, he finally refused. Perhaps he feared that his republican officers would turn the army against him. Perhaps he thought that a royal title without royal blood had no meaning—that he would be a dictator still. Whatever the reason for his refusal, his struggle to find an alternative to royal government was about to end. On September 3, 1658, he died, leaving as his successor a son too weak to control the quarreling generals and a jealous Parliament. Early in 1660, one of his commanders seized London and brought an end to the confusion by summoning a special Parliament to invite Charles II (1660-1685), the son of the murdered king, to return to the throne.

THE RESTORATION

No specific limitations on royal power were extracted from Charles in return for the monarchical restoration. The new king did issue the Declaration of Breda promising to let Parliament determine the religious settlement and the disposition of lands lost by the royalists during the Puritan regime. These problems were difficult to solve without causing dissatisfaction, and Charles may well have been happy to escape the responsibility. He promised to punish no one for the late rebellion except those designated by Parliament and to pay and disband the army. The first concession cost him little, for he was not a vindictive man, and the second was to his advantage since the continued existence of the Puritan army would have endangered his regime. These provisions did enhance the importance of Parliament, but they did not increase its constitutional powers. Of greater significance was the fact that the laws passed by Parliament and approved by Charles I between 1640 and 1642 remained in effect. Thus, there was no longer a Star Chamber to compete with the Common Law courts or to help regulate the activities of the justices of the peace. More than ever, the crown was at the mercy of the landed gentry for the functioning of local government. Yet when all is said, Charles II was not much weaker than his predecessors, for he kept the remainder of the royal powers intact.

In some ways, the reaction against the Puritan regime made Charles stronger. Never did the Anglican Church support the divine right theory with more fervor. The new Parliament was strongly royalist and sought only to restore the spirit of cooperation with the crown that had characterized the Tudor era. Its members had so little desire to limit monarchical authority that they voted the king taxes for life that they thought would yield enough to support the government. Thus, they abandoned their strongest weapon against the monarchy. In return, Charles surrendered the feudal exactions that had caused so much difficulty between his ancestors and their subjects. Perhaps the greatest advantage Charles had over his predecessors was that the effort to establish an alternative to royal absolutism had failed. The Puritan interlude was a bitter memory to most Englishmen. They were not likely to experiment again in the future. All Charles had to do was to uphold the Anglican Church to keep enough popular support to remain securely on the throne. Charles himself was so surprised at the popular acclaim that greeted him on his arrival in England that he remarked: "It must have been my own fault that I did not come before, for I find no one but declares he is glad to see me."

On the whole, Charles was admirably suited to the task of restoring monarchical authority. He was a tall, healthy man with a good sense of humor and a gracious manner. Whereas his predecessors had been headstrong and tactless, he knew when to yield and how to say no without angering. His many mistresses led even his intimate acquaintances to believe that he was too fond of pleasure to make the necessary effort to establish an absolute monarchy. Charles bowed to the desire of the new royalist, Anglican Parliament to repress Puritanism and Catholicism and ensure nominal conformity with the Anglican Church. Later, he sought to free both Puritans and Catholics from these restrictions, but quickly backed down before the protests of Parliament. When it became apparent that the grant which Parliament had voted him for life was insufficient to support the government, he managed to avoid a direct conflict with his subjects by getting the necessary funds without much additional taxation. He sold Dunkirk to the French, married a Portuguese princess who brought a large dowry, and made a secret treaty with Louis XIV in which he promised to support the French in a war against the Dutch.[2] He also promised that he and his brother James would embrace Catholicism openly. In return, Louis gave him large sums. Charles did not carry out his promise to accept Catholicism until he was on his deathbed, but James did not hesitate. This fact led to the eventual break between Charles and Parliament, for James was heir to the throne.

The first step was taken by Parliament in 1673 when the Test Act was passed requiring all officeholders to take the communion of the Anglican Church. This forced James, who had acknowledged his conversion to Catholicism, to abandon his government post. Parliament was not content with this victory and sought to enact a bill excluding James from the throne. Here Charles stood firm. Those who rallied to the support of the crown became known as Tories and those who supported the exclusion bill were called Whigs. In 1681, Charles blocked the Whig efforts to exclude his brother by dissolving Parliament, and it met no more during his reign. Some Whig leaders became involved in an anti-Stuart plot, but they were either forced into exile or executed. Town charters were revoked, and new ones were issued that subordinated municipal government and elections to royal control. Louis XIV gave financial support, and James was reinstated in office. When Charles died in 1685, it looked as though he had reestablished royal power in England.

James II (1685-1688), the new king, was of a different stamp. In both physical appearance and personal integrity, he was superior to his brother, but whereas Charles's greatest ambition had been to hold his throne, James's undying hope was to restore Catholicism to England. This desire proved his undoing. A rebellion in 1685 gave him an excuse to raise an army, which he kept under arms after order had been restored. To it and to various governmental posts he illegally apppointed Catholics, whom he also named to key positions at Oxford University. In 1687, he issued a declaration giving religious liberty to Catholics and Puritans alike. There was little doubt that his generosity towards the left-wing Protestants was motivated by his desire to gain their support for his pro-Catholic policy. When seven bishops refused to have this declaration read in their churches, they were brought to trial. By this action, James alienated his strongest supporters, the Anglican clergy and the Tories. Only the expectation that the Protestant daughters of the aging king would succeed him prevented revolution. Even this hope was dashed in 1688. After years of childlessness, James's second wife, a Catholic, gave birth to a son. The baby prince automatically replaced Mary, wife of William III of Orange and James's eldest daughter by an earlier Protestant marriage, as heir to the throne. A Catholic succession seemed assured.

[2] See page 252.

THE GLORIOUS REVOLUTION

Neither Whig nor Tory could stomach this possibility. To remove the scruples of the believers in divine right, a story was manufactured that the baby had been smuggled into the queen's bedroom in a warming pan, this despite the fact that about sixty persons had been present at the royal birth. More significant, Whig and Tory united in inviting William and Mary to come to England. Too late, James realized his errors; support for his policies was so completely lacking that he fled to France. A special Parliament was called that named William (1689-1702) and Mary (1689-1694) joint sovereigns. A revolution had been accomplished without the loss of a single life.

This Glorious Revolution marked the beginning of a chain of events that led to the establishment of a parliamentary monarchy in England during the nineteenth century. At first, it seemed as though William and Mary would wield the authority legally exercised by their predecessors. A Bill of Rights was passed in 1689, but it was designed to outlaw specifically the constitutional violations that James was accused of committing, not to impose new limitations on the crown. It re-emphasized the role of Parliament in legislation and taxation, authorized freedom of election and freedom of debate in Parliament, prohibited excessive bail, and insisted on trial by jury. Only the outlawing of a standing army without the consent of Parliament was new. It is true that the revolutionary settlement weakened the divine-right theory of kingship by violating the laws of heredity, but this doctrine remained popular until it became apparent that the Protestant Stuart line would become extinct. An Act of Settlement was passed in 1701 providing that the throne would go to Sophia of Hanover and her issue, although there were nearer Catholic heirs. This act had an effect on political thought, but there had been many changes in the English ruling families before. Of greater significance were the practical developments.

William wanted the crown almost as much to ensure English support for the Dutch in their wars against the French as for its own sake. To get the necessary money from Parliament, he permitted the Commons to exercise greater control over how it was to be spent. To get the necessary army, he submitted to further Parliamentary influence. To get support for his diplomacy, he soon found it advisable to consult the leaders of the Commons. More than ever before, it became necessary for royal councillors to be influential in Parliament. At the same time, the gentry continued to strengthen its control over local government.

However, it would be erroneous to regard the Glorious Revolution and its immediate aftermath as giving the gentry and Parliament complete control over the government. What Parliament had won was the unquestioned right to participate in the affairs of state. English kings could no longer hope to govern alone, and Queen Anne (1702-1714) was the last sovereign to veto a bill. On the other hand, Parliament was equally incapable of functioning without the crown until political parties became firmly established and ministerial responsibility to the Commons generally accepted. Meanwhile, king and Parliament were dependent on each other.

THE CONSTITUTIONAL CRISIS IN FRANCE

THE WARS OF RELIGION

The Wars of Religion broke out in France in 1562. During the following years, the country was frequently threatened with dismemberment by the ambitious great nobles and their foreign allies, although the idea of monarchy itself was never seriously challenged as it was in England. The cause of the wars lay primarily in the growth of a disaffected Protestant minority and the struggle for power between various noble factions. Rivalry between royal officials and the burghers for control of the towns and economic discontent among the lower classes, occasioned by heavy taxation and rising prices, were also factors.

In 1555, Calvin started sending large numbers of pastors from Geneva into France to spread his religious doctrines, and by 1562 about 5 per cent of the population had been converted. This rapid growth was in itself frightening to the Catholics, but even more serious from their standpoint was the conversion of a number of nobles, including members of the powerful Bourbon and Montmorency families and their numerous clients. These nobles soon added to their power by becoming protectors of the Calvinist churches from whom they drew both money and manpower.

In normal times, a judicious and liberal distribution of royal patronage might have sufficed to maintain the loyalty of those nobles, including most of the Bourbons, whose conversion to Calvinism resulted from political expediency, but the Habsburg-Valois wars had left the monarchy in a state of virtual bankruptcy that could be remedied only by rigid economy and higher taxes. Furthermore, the few gifts that could be made were not distributed fairly because the three weak-willed sons of Henry II who ruled in turn between 1559 and 1589 favored one faction and then another.

For three years, peace was maintained through the efforts of the queen mother, Catherine de Medici (1519-1589), a woman with a gift for intrigue but not for statesmanship. She understood neither the depth and power of religious conviction nor the economic difficulties that beset the nation. Her policy consisted of trying to keep the support of the three great noble factions by promising future favors, while she attempted to quell popular discontent, improve the financial position of the crown, and make a religious settlement. She and her advisers hoped to achieve the first two of these goals by reviving the Estates-General and the third by holding a meeting of leading Catholic and Protestant clergymen to resolve their religious differences.

It was hoped that the Estates-General would provide a forum in which the government could promise the reforms requested by the people. In return, it was anticipated that the deputies would vote additional funds when they learned of the financial difficulties of the crown. Unfortunately, the French monarchs were even less adept at manipulating parliamentary debates than the early Stuarts, and in two meetings of the Estates-General held in 1560 and 1561 the deputies of the nobility and the third estate refused to vote funds, although the crown issued a great reforming ordinance at their request. The French kings tried on several later occasions to get the Estates-General to agree to increased taxation, but without success. Finally, they abandoned their efforts to make use of the institution, just as Charles VII had done. The people voiced little opposition to the crown's failure to use the Estates-General, because their country was so large that they had difficulty thinking in terms of France as a whole. Few saw that they must check the authority of the crown at Paris if they were going to preserve their privileges. Instead, they sought to resist at the local level. As a result of this provincialism, the constitutional struggle in France was between the central authority of a king and the local authority of the great nobles and towns, and not between crown and parliament as in England.

The meeting between the Catholic and Protestant theologians was as disappointing as the Estates-General. No agreement could be reached on a common religious doctrine. Distrust between Catholics and Protestants deepened. Finally, in 1562, an armed conflict broke out that has become known as the Wars of Religion, although religion was only one of the issues at stake. In addition to the struggle for supremacy between Catholics and Huguenots, as Calvin's followers in France were called, the wars saw a concerted effort by each of the great nobles to establish control over a province, and by the bourgeoisie of the towns to free themselves from the authority of local royal officials. There were advocates of provincial liberty in both the Huguenot and Catholic forces, and the religious and the constitutional struggles became intermixed. Both sides sought foreign aid, and Spain especially became involved in French affairs.[3] The nobles who supported the Huguenots were either sincerely attached to the new religion or else convinced that it offered the best vehicle for their ambition. The nobles who put themselves at the head of a Catholic League were also motivated by religious convictions or secular designs. Similarly, the towns were divided between Catholics and Huguenots. In the end, about an equal number of nobles chose each camp, but the overwhelming majority of the towns remained strongly Catholic. The peasants continued to be loyal to the Roman Church except in those localities where their lords saw to it that they were converted. The result was that the Huguenots were too weak to win control of France but too strong to be eradicated.

The wars were fought with great cruelty. Towns were sacked, women

[3] See pages 241-242.

and children were slaughtered, and assassinations were frequent. In towns or provinces where one religion became ascendant, its adherents expelled or exterminated its rivals. Royal power steadily declined as the series of weak kings vainly tried to restore order, usually in alliance with the Catholic faction. One province after another fell under the control of a great noble. The Bourbons won much of southwest France and imposed Calvinism. The Duke of Guise was especially strong in the northeast, where he maintained Catholicism. Several secular-minded Catholic nobles found themselves in control of provinces in which the Huguenots were so numerous that they sought to keep peace between the warring factions, but they paid no more deference to the king than did Guise or Bourbon. By 1588, the position of Henry III (1574-1589), the last surviving son of Henry II, had become so desperate that he treacherously assassinated the Duke of Guise and sought to regain control of his kingdom in alliance with the Bourbon Huguenot leader, Henry of Navarre. The alliance was short-lived, for in 1589 an ultra-Catholic assassinated Henry III. As the nearest male relative, Navarre became the legal ruler.

HENRY IV

Henry of Navarre, or Henry IV (1589-1610) as he now became, was one of the greatest French kings. He did not owe his success to originality, for he took few actions during his reign that had not been attempted before. It was his personality and capacity for leadership that made him one of France's greatest kings. He had a quick wit and a good sense of humor that endeared him to his companions. He was an enthusiastic hunter and equally persistent in his quest of the ladies of his court. Above all else, he was a gallant soldier. Just as the Battle of Ivry began, he put a plume of three white feathers in his helmet and, turning to his men, cried, "If you lose your ensigns, cornet, or banners, lose not the sight of my white plume, which you will always find in the road to honour and victory." Indeed, he possessed both the most admirable virtues and the most attractive faults of his class. For this, he was admired and beloved by his fellow nobles.

It took more, however, than a pleasant personality to cool the passions of the day. Henry was fortunate in having as an adviser the Duke of Sully (1560-1641), a staunch, dour, egotistical Protestant who provided the bureaucratic efficiency and steadfastness of purpose that his master lacked. Together, they made an admirable team capable of bringing peace and prosperity to the war-weary country.

Only his fellow Protestants and a few liberal Catholics recognized Henry as king in 1589. To most of the French people, he was a heretic. After four years of vain efforts to recapture the kingdom, Henry became a Catholic. He was not a devout man and had already changed his religion several times for political convenience. The return to Catholicism cost him little. He is supposed to have remarked, "Paris is worth a Mass." The conversion did bring him Paris and many other cities, for now most Catholics rallied to his cause. Henry, in turn, was loyal to the Catholic Church throughout the remainder of his life. Few kings cooperated more firmly with the pope or the local clergy, and by his death the old alliance between throne and altar was as strong as ever.

Indeed, many Protestants became disgruntled at the favor their former leader showed to the Catholics, and in 1598, Henry had to issue the Edict of Nantes to ensure their loyalty. This edict did not bring religious toleration; no country was ready for that. But it did give the Huguenots the right to worship in certain towns and in the houses of important nobles. Public offices were opened to them, and they were given the right to fortify some localities for their protection.

The process of bringing the great nobles back to loyalty proved more expensive. Some were defeated, but most of them had to be bribed to render submission. Royal officials had also acquired the habit of behaving in an independent manner during the wars, and some of them served a noble patron more faithfully than the king. Henry won their allegiance by making their offices hereditary in return for an annual payment. He took measures to strengthen his influence in towns that had proved particularly rebellious by reducing the number of municipal officials and exercising some control over their appointment. By the turn of the century, he had regained command of his kingdom.

Henry did not neglect economic considerations. With the aid of Sully, he reduced governmental waste and corruption. This made possible a reduction in taxation. Roads and canals were built or improved, agriculture and manufacturing were encouraged, and trade was increased. By 1610, when Henry was assassinated by a fanatical Catholic, prosperity had returned to France.

LOUIS XIII AND RICHELIEU

Although Henry had restored peace and plenty, he had not destroyed the ability of the nobles and Protestants to revolt. His sudden death made his ten-year-old son, Louis XIII (1610-1643), king, and his wife, regent. The great nobles were quick to seize this opportunity to demand concessions. The Protestant forces grew restive under the Catholic policy of the government. Revolt followed revolt. The best that the crown could do was to buy the cooperation of the rebels, but this practice led to further revolts. By 1617, Louis was old enough to take a personal hand in the government. At first, he threw himself into a struggle against the Huguenots in southern France, but the early successes of the Habsburgs in the Thirty Years War saw him pause. Should he continue to fight for religious conformity and internal order in France, or should he intervene in the war to prevent the Habsburgs from strengthening their control over the small Italian and German states near the borders of France?

Louis was a strong man in many ways. Once he had determined on a course of action, he seldom wavered, but he lacked the acuteness to foresee the implications of making this or that choice. His education was faulty—as a child he had not been above offering to make his tutor a bishop in return for shorter assignments—and he disliked administrative work. Like most French kings, he neglected his wife, but unlike his father and successor, he was equally indifferent to the ladies of the court. It was the chase and war that he craved. He needed a minister to plan the long-range program of his government and to handle administrative details. In 1624, he had the good fortune to find Cardinal Richelieu (1585-1642). For nearly two decades, the king and the minister worked together.

The cardinal was quick to perceive the alternatives that faced the king. Louis could destroy the Huguenots, do away with the provincial estates, weaken the nobility, reform the administration, lower taxes, in short, create a modern, centralized, well-ordered state; but to do so meant that no time or money could be spent in the quest for glory abroad. Spain would be permitted to strengthen its hold over the Italian and German border states, thereby sealing a ring around France. The alternative was to abandon the hope of domestic reorganization and intervene in the Thirty Years War to prevent the Habsburg noose from being drawn too tightly. Richelieu recognized clearly that the crown did not have the resources to undertake both policies at once. "If the king," he wrote, "decides on war, it is necessary to give up all thought of repose, economy, and the interior regulation of the kingdom. If, on the other hand, he wishes peace, it is necessary to give up thought of Italy. . . ."

To Richelieu the choice was clear, and Louis decided as his minister wished. France intervened first in Italy, then in Germany itself. The preference for foreign adventures over domestic reform was continued throughout the remainder of the century. One result was the expansion of France towards the Rhine River. Another was that the monarchy became more burdensome without becoming much more efficient. The masses suffered rather than benefited, and the French kings paid for their policy with the French Revolution.

War meant the creation of a larger army. The peacetime force under Henry IV had been about 15,000 men, but by 1633 the French army had been expanded to 210,000. A navy was also developed. Richelieu sought to improve the discipline and supply of the troops, but he could accomplish little. More serious, the loyalty of the common soldier was still to his commander, not the king. As a result, a general like Condé or Turenne could turn his army on the king almost as easily as on the enemy.

The costs of supporting the military force were immense. Taxes were more than doubled during Louis' reign, but borrowing money and the creation of offices to sell was still necessary. The lower classes on whom the bulk of the burden fell became restive, nor were the nobles or the Huguenots above taking advantage of the government's preoccupation with for-

Cardinal Richelieu, by Philippe de Champaigne. (Bulloz-Art Reference Bureau)

eign affairs. There were numerous uprisings, but soon the rebels learned that it was better not to court the displeasure of the cardinal and his king. When the nobles rebelled, Louis defeated them on the field of battle and beheaded their leaders, instead of buying their submission as his predecessors had done. When the Huguenots rebelled, he captured their strong-holds and defeated their armies. At the same time, he refrained from making noble or Huguenot enemies of the crown. The former was needed to serve in the armies and the latter to work in trade, industry, and agriculture. As a result, Louis and Richelieu left the nobles their privileges, sought means to improve their economic status, and even tried to protect them from themselves by outlawing private wars and duels. Richelieu's uncle had been ambushed and slain by a neighboring noble. His father had had to flee to Poland after getting revenge, and his older brother had been killed in a duel. Such family tragedies weighed heavily upon him, but he was unable to change the customs of his class. Dueling continued unabated for over a century.

Louis and Richelieu were more successful in their dealings with the Huguenots. They took away their armies and their forts, but left them the right to worship in those places guaranteed them in the Edict of Nantes. In return, the Huguenots caused no further trouble to the crown. Near the end of his life, Richelieu was able to boast that he had brought both noble and Huguenot into obedience to the king.

The cardinal had less to say about the reforms that had to be postponed. One of his leading subordinates, Michel de Marillac (1563-1632), did lay plans to abolish the sale of government offices and to unify the royal administration. He advocated the reduction and equalization of taxes and the abolition of the provincial estates. He never tired of arguing that the principal attribute of good government "is to consider the subjects' welfare and the good regulation of the state which can be accomplished only through peace." Richelieu may not have been unsympathetic to parts of this program, but he felt that peace was too great a price to pay. Marillac continued to press for the adoption of his program. For a brief moment, it looked as though Louis might side with him. Courtiers swarmed in his antechamber hoping to win his favor, but at the last moment Louis announced his decision to retain the cardinal and Marillac was disgraced.

MAZARIN

Richelieu died in 1642 and Louis XIII followed him to the grave a few months later, leaving to others the task of completing their work. The great cardinal was replaced by an Italian adventurer named Mazarin (1602-1661), who was also a prince of the Church. Louis was followed by his five-year-old son, Louis XIV (1643-1715). A regency was once more necessary, and as usual the office fell on the queen-mother, Anne of Austria. Mazarin quickly made approaches to Anne and became her lover, if not her husband. This assured his position, and from then until his death in 1661 he directed the affairs of state.

Strangely enough, the Italian Mazarin and the Habsburg Anne pursued the anti-Habsburg policy of Richelieu. Intervention in Germany was continued until victory was won. At the Peace of Westphalia, France received Metz, Toul, Verdun, and parts of Alsace. The possibility of having to face a united Germany was removed for two centuries. The war with Spain was continued until 1659, when by the Treaty of the Pyrénées France received lands along both its southern and northern borders. Richelieu's dream had been realized. France had clearly replaced Spain as the dominant power in Europe. There was no longer danger that the Habsburgs would be able to draw an iron ring around the country.

The cost, however, had been terrific. Reform had once more been postponed, taxes were high, and the people complained. One serious revolt, known as the Fronde, took place between 1648 and 1653. Many of its causes were similar to those of the Wars of Religion—economic distress, the desire of the great nobles to control the central government or to create semi-independent principalities in the provinces, and heavy taxation. There were two differences, however. First, religion was no longer a factor. The Huguenots remained content with the liberty of cult left them by Richelieu. Second, royal officials played a major role. For centuries, many government posts had been sold to raise revenue. Thus, public office had become a property right, and its possessor could not normally be removed unless he was financially reimbursed, a feat no king could or would perform. As a result, the crown exercised little control over its officials. Henry IV agreed to make offices hereditary in return for a fee. This action temporarily gave the king the support of the bureaucracy because this privilege was dependent on his pleasure. However, as people became more accustomed to the sale and inheritance of public office, officials felt less threatened. Soon they found courage to ignore royal directives, if not actively to resist the authority of the king. The crown had spent centuries trying to tame the old feudal nobility; now it was faced with a new hereditary nobility of officeholders.

To correct injustices committed by local officials and to ensure greater efficiency in government, the crown had adopted the practice during the sixteenth century of sending inspectors known as intendants out from Paris for limited periods of time. The intendants did not buy their offices and they therefore had to obey the king or risk dismissal. Gradually, the intendants expanded their activities; from being temporary inspectors in a few provinces, they became permanent administrators in all the provinces. Exactly when this change took place is not known. Richelieu still spoke of the intendant as a temporary inspector, but by the time of the Fronde they had become important enough to threaten the position of the local royal officials who had purchased their offices. The local officials resisted, and in this they were supported by the members of the principal law courts at Paris. Thus, the Fronde consisted of three revolts: one by the lower and middle classes against heavy taxation, a second by the nobles to increase their political power, and a third by the officeholders

Cardinal Mazarin, by Philippe de Champaigne. (Bulloz-Art Reference Bureau)

to protect their position from various activities of the crown, including the use of intendants.

No important segment of the population actively supported Mazarin. He had to rely on those who sought personal rewards. Even the army was of little help. It followed the lead of its commanders, and its commanders sided with the rebels as often as not. Twice Mazarin was forced into exile. Only the rivalries between the great nobles and their difficulty in agreeing on a common program with the royal officials saved the cardinal. Finally, he was able to return to power, but only after much suffering had been inflicted on the people by the forces of the opposing sides. One result of the Fronde was that the French became willing to accept a much stronger, more centralized government under their king in order to prevent future civil wars. Another result was that the youthful Louis XIV determined to take whatever steps were necessary to avoid further disorders.

LOUIS XIV

During his youth, Louis was content to leave the government in Mazarin's hands, but when the latter died in 1661, the twenty-two-year-old king declared that henceforth he would be his own prime minister. From that day until his death over a half century later, he directed the affairs of state and dispensed the crown's patronage to ensure that power rested with him personally and not with a chief minister. Louis' character changed as he matured from a youthful, untried king to Europe's most powerful ruler. At first, he was a pleasure-loving monarch whose many mistresses caused comment in an age not readily surprised by such activities. As he grew older, he became more devout, his court became more moral, and he even married his last mistress, although secretly. One aspect of Louis' character, however, never changed—his love of glory. Magnificence, generosity, and military conquests had long been considered the true marks of greatness. The seventeenth century added another criterion—the passion for system and order. Louis sought to achieve each of these attributes of greatness.

Louis was only of medium height and could scarcely have been called handsome, but he possessed a natural dignity and a commanding appearance that left no one in doubt that he was every inch a king. He was not well educated and possessed little imagination, but he had both the determination to master the details of government and the ability to direct the administration of the kingdom. He was unfailingly courteous and usually honest and straightforward, although he was a master of dissimulation when there was need. Had it not been for his desire for glory, he could have been a great king by modern standards rather than by the standards of his day.

It was the desire for system and order, for unity and obedience, that first claimed Louis' attention. He believed with a political theorist of his day "that the king alone is sovereign in his kingdom and that sovereignty is no more divisible than the point in geometry." All power had to be gathered in his hands. He denied the great nobles a significant role in the government, but to win their loyalty he brought them to court and treated them to a series of entertainments. He heaped on them titles, honorary positions, and pensions. To their younger sons went the richest ecclesiastical benefices. When court life became dull, there was usually a war on which king and noble could embark in search of honor and glory. No noble could hope for advancement without winning favor at court, and royal generosity was a heavy financial drain on France. Louis finally tamed the French nobility, but in doing so he became their captive. From the time of his reign, the fortunes of king and great noble were so closely bound together that they could not be separated. Their alliance led to their mutual destruction in the Revolution.

By enticing the great nobles to court, Louis broke their tie with the

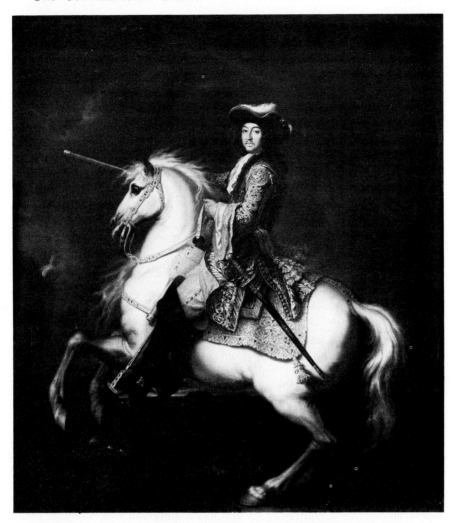

Louis XIV, by Van der Meulen. (Bulloz-Art Reference Bureau)

lesser nobles who remained in the provinces. They became to all intents two separate classes, and the duke or prince could no longer count on a host of clients ready to revolt at his call. Louis curbed the authority of the local royal officials who purchased or inherited their offices and of the elected town officials by expanding the duties of the intendant. The old bureaucracy was left its offices, the towns kept their officials, and the nobles retained their privileges, but the administration of the provinces was actually carried on largely by the intendants, and the chief royal advisers were drawn from the lesser nobility and the middle class. As long as the crown could prevent the intendants from escaping its control, its directives were certain to carry weight throughout the kingdom.

305

To prevent the army from rebelling under the lead of its commanders, Louis saw to it that, for every colonel drawn from a great noble family, there was an experienced lieutenant-colonel drawn from one of the lesser noble families who owed his advancement to royal favor. Troops were raised and paid in the name of their king, not their captain. Uniforms came into frequent use for the first time, and some barracks were built to house the troops. Inspectors were sent out from the royal council to make certain that regulations were complied with. These measures made for obedient officers and disciplined soldiers. No longer would an army follow its commander into revolt against the king, and the crown had an effective force that could be used for military conquest and the suppression of rebellions.

To celebrate the glories of his reign, Louis became a patron of arts and letters. His taste was not always good, and the controls he established limited the development of the artists' individuality; but his palaces were decorated in a magnificent manner with paintings celebrating the conquests of Alexander, Caesar, and Louis. Historians were not above drawing similar parallels, though in his youth Louis had insulted their profession by having Mézeray's *History of France* read at night to put him to sleep. The censor was not neglected. His task was to see to it that unfavorable comments were not published in France. Louis became the most admired and emulated monarch in Europe. French culture spread everywhere.

The finest example of Louis' desire for magnificence may be found in the palace at Versailles. It was large, so large that it took 35,000 people more than three decades to build it. The interior was magnificently furnished with mosaics, paintings, and mirrors. Surrounding the palace were acres of gardens, lakes, and fountains. The cost in lives and money was staggering, but Louis pushed the work to completion, for here was a palace suitable for the greatest of kings. Louis insisted on the most elaborate court etiquette. From the time he arose in the morning until the time he went to bed at night, he was attended by the leading nobles of the realm. A prince might be permitted to hand him his shirt, but a mere count could hope to do no more than watch the royal toilette. The elaborate etiquette would have bored all but the most devoted adherent of the cult of kings, but Louis manfully followed the pattern of life which he thought led to greatness. Indeed, the palace did not have the most elementary comforts by modern standards. It was totally lacking in plumbing; perfume was the accepted substitute for the bath. Nevertheless, the splendor of Versailles did much to impress the Europeans of the day, and before long even the petty German princes were imitating the ways of the "Grand Monarch."

To support so much magnificence a sound fiscal system and a good economy were necessary. In this respect, Louis' minister, Colbert, was invaluable. Colbert cut the cost of collecting taxes, reduced graft and corruption, and adopted an accurate system of bookkeeping. He tried with slight success to equalize taxation between the various provinces. Industry

The Hall of Mirrors, Palace of Versailles. (Bettmann Archive)

and agriculture were encouraged, and efforts were made to create free trade between the interior provinces of the kingdom.[4]

Colbert's fiscal measures were wise and some of his economic measures were helpful, but in the long run Louis' policies destroyed any beneficial effects of Colbert's. In 1685, Louis revoked the Edict of Nantes because his growing interest in religion made toleration impossible. The Huguenots were compelled to choose between conversion to Catholicism, persecution, and flight from the country. About 200,000 chose the last course, and France lost some of its most valuable workers, although this loss was less serious than has sometimes been supposed.

Far more harmful were Louis' wars. He fought many, as we have seen, and before his death he realized that they had cost too much in money, in blood, and in reforms postponed. He was further saddened by the death of his son and heir and two grandsons. His throne was to pass to his great-grandson, and in 1715 the dying monarch called this sickly lad to him and said, "My child, you will soon be the king of a great realm. Never forget your obligations towards God; remember that you owe him all that you are. Try to preserve peace with your neighbors. I have been too fond of war. Do not imitate me in that, nor in the too great expenditures I have made. Lighten the burdens of your people as soon as you can, and do that which I have had the misfortune not to accomplish myself." A few days

[4] See pages 264-266.

The Palace of Versailles as seen from the garden. (Bettmann Archive)

later, Louis XIV, the Grand Monarch, died after a reign of seventy-two years. He, Richelieu, and Mazarin had broken the power of Spain. They had expanded France a long way towards its present boundaries, but they had bankrupted their people. They had created an absolute monarchy, but they had failed to make the type of reforms necessary to ensure loyalty to the crown.

THE CONSTITUTIONAL CRISIS IN WESTERN AND CENTRAL EUROPE

THE DECLINE OF SPAIN

In spite of some reverses during the last decade of his reign, few Europeans doubted that Philip II left Spain the most powerful country in the world when he died in 1598. His son inherited not only Aragon, Castile, Portugal, Navarre, and Catalonia in the Iberian Peninsula, but also Sardinia, Sicily, Naples, Milan, and Franche-Comté in Europe and vast territories in the Americas and Asia. The Spanish army was considered the best in Europe, and the gold and silver mines of the New World provided part of its necessary financial support. Nevertheless, within fifty years, as we have seen, France replaced Spain as the dominant European power, and within a hundred years, the War of Spanish Succession was fought to determine how to divide this once-mighty empire.

The Constitutional Crisis

There were three principal causes for this decline. The first was the dynastic, decentralized nature of the monarchy, which prevented the sovereign from getting the maximum support from his various kingdoms. The second was a demographic and economic decline, and the third was an overly ambitious foreign policy, occasioned in part by excessive commitments in many parts of the world.

The kingdoms on the Iberian Peninsula had been brought together by a series of fortuitous dynastic marriages beginning with that of Ferdinand and Isabella, but at the outbreak of the Thirty Years War the only common bond between them lay in the person of their sovereign. Each kingdom had its own institutions, laws, customs, and system of taxation. Tariff walls still limited trade between the various states, and the Portuguese and Catalonians stood ready to protest against the appointment of a Castilian, or other outsider, to a government position in their respective lands.

From the beginning, the Spanish monarchs had found Castile the most valuable and cooperative of their kingdoms. Castilian soldiers made up most of their army, Castilian *Conquistadores* had won an empire in the New World, and the Castilian taxpayer bore the brunt of the costs of imperial policies. Of a total revenue of 15,648,000 ducats in 1610, only 700,-000 came from Aragon, Catalonia, Valencia, and Navarre. Portugal and the Italian territories barely paid for the costs of governing them, but the Castilians contributed 5,100,000 ducats in the excise tax alone, and about 2,000,000 more came to the crown as its share of the precious metals imported from Castilian lands in the New World.

If the Castilians bore the brunt of the costs of the empire, their aristocracy reaped nearly all the rewards. By the reign of Philip III (1598-1621), the Spanish monarchs had ceased to be itinerant and had established their court in their palaces in and around Madrid. Here the great Castilian nobles flocked and vied with one another for positions in the army, the church, the bureaucracy, or the court, for themselves, their relatives, and their clients. The aristocracy of the other kingdoms felt itself cut off from a monarch it almost never saw and from whom it received neither honors nor rewards. Even ecclesiastical positions and military commands in these kingdoms were frequently given to Castilians. Posts in the bureaucracy were reserved for the native aristocracy, but they were too few to satisfy the demand. There were less than a dozen positions in the royal central administration of Catalonia, for example, to satisfy about 500 competing aristocrats, and the 488 who were unsuccessful felt their ties with their sovereign correspondingly diminished. As a result, the power of the Spanish monarch rested upon the contribution of the Castilians, while the subjects of his other states neither contributed to the empire nor benefited from the association. For this reason, the demographic and economic situation in Castile was of the utmost importance for the continuation of Spanish leadership in Europe.

Unfortunately, Castile was hit harder by the seventeenth-century decline in population than most of the rest of Europe. About 6.5 million of the 8.5 million inhabitants of the peninsula had resided in Castile around 1550. During the sixteenth century, however, there was a migration from northern Castile, where the army had drawn most of its recruits, to such cities in the south as Seville, the center of the trans-Atlantic trade. Perhaps as many as 150,000 Castilians emigrated to the New World before 1550, and thousands of others followed their example thereafter. Others fell in wars, while intolerance cost still more lives. Between 1609 and 1614, about 275,000 Moriscos (baptized Moors) were expelled from Spain because it was believed that they conformed only outwardly to the Christian religion. Of these, some 90,000 had resided in Castile. Plagues in 1599-1600 and 1647-1650 took severe tolls; it has been suggested that plagues reduced the population of Castile 25 per cent during the seventeenth century, a disastrous reduction when one considers that even before the first of these epidemics the number of inhabitants was only about a third that of France, Spain's greatest rival.

The causes of Castile's economic decline are not fully known. One factor was that prices rose more rapidly than elsewhere, largely because the influx of precious metals from the New World inevitably had more severe repercussions here than in other parts of Europe. The high cost of Castilian goods opened the way for the importation of foreign products that had an unfortunate effect on local industry. Agriculture also declined because of the unfavorable climate and poor soil in most of the peninsula. To find pastures, sheep had to be driven back and forth across the country from one season to another, to the detriment of the farmers' crops.

Also important, but difficult to explain, was a general scientific and technological failure that was clearly in evidence by 1600. Castilians, who were once in the forefront of Europe, began to lag in banking, manufacturing, and agricultural techniques. Their ships and artillery were surpassed by those of the Dutch and English, and they lacked skilled engineers for military and civilian pursuits. This failure of the Castilians to keep pace with other Europeans has been attributed to the growing influence of the Catholic Church during the reign of Philip II. The ecclesiastical hierarchy, it has been argued, distrusted foreign ideas after the advent of Protestantism on the grounds that these ideas were often heretical. Whatever the reason, the scientific and intellectual life in Castile became stagnant during the course of the seventeenth century and remained so until our day.

The profits from overseas trade also declined. A peak in the trade with both the New World and the Philippine Islands was reached around 1620. By 1640, a precipitous decline had set in. To make matters worse, an increasingly high percentage of the goods that were shipped had been manufactured in foreign countries. More and more foreign bankers and merchants profited from Spanish markets. Reduced profits for subjects meant reduced taxes to the monarch. Royal revenues were also seriously curtailed by a decline in the production of silver in the New World. Prior to 1610 the crown's share had been about two million ducats per year, or nearly 15 per cent of its total revenue. Between 1621 and 1640, the yield was only about half that amount; and thereafter it was reduced to a trickle. Thus, Castile entered upon a period of economic decline at the very moment when unprecedented demands were being made on its resources by the Thirty Years War.

PHILIP IV AND OLIVAREZ

Philip IV (1621-1665) was an amiable, easygoing youth who was content to entrust the government to the Duke of Olivarez (1587-1645), a man possessed by the desire to reassert Spanish dominance in Europe. Since additional money was needed to achieve this goal, Olivarez reduced waste, improved administrative efficiency, and increased taxes in Castile. It was quickly apparent that these measures would not be sufficient, and in 1624, he drew up a secret memorandum for the king, recommending that the dynastic, decentralized monarchy of the Spanish kingdoms be transformed into a united kingdom with a common set of laws, taxes, and opportunities. "The most important task that confronts your Majesty," he declared, "is to make yourself King of Spain; by which I mean, Sir, that your Majesty should not rest content with the titles of King of Portugal, King of Aragon, King of Valencia, and Count of Barcelona, but that your Majesty should labour and plan, with careful and secret consideration, to reduce all these realms of which Spain is now composed, to the fashion and laws of Castile, without any difference." Thus, the Iberian Peninsula was to be Castilianized; the inhabitants of the other kingdoms were to contribute their share in money and manpower to the costs of empire. In return, they were to have an equal opportunity to hold office.

Unfortunately, Olivarez was afraid to publicize his plans because the Castilian nobles were as opposed to sharing their officeholding monopoly as the inhabitants of the other kingdoms were to losing their local privileges. He was able to reveal enough of his plan to win some support from the *cortes* (estates) of Aragon and Valencia, but Catalonia refused to contribute its share to the costs of empire. With the formal entrance of France into the war in 1635, the situation became desperate. Olivarez redoubled his attempts to involve all the Spanish kingdoms directly in the war, but his efforts were repaid by revolts in Catalonia and Portugal in 1640, where the inhabitants felt little loyalty to the empire, and by an uprising in Naples a few years later. In the end, Portugal made good its bid for independence, although during the period of Spanish rule it had lost nearly all of its Asiatic possessions to the Dutch. The uprisings in Catalonia and Naples were suppressed, but both were permitted to keep their former privileges and the Spanish empire remained a conglomeration of separate kingdoms. Failure to take united action had removed whatever chance there had been of maintaining Spanish dominance, and the Treaty of the Pyrénées, 1659, inaugurated a period of French supremacy.

During the years that followed, Spain fell further behind the rest of

Europe. The well-intentioned but stupid Charles II (1665-1700) suffered from half a dozen infirmities that grew in part from the practice of frequent intermarriages between the Austrian and Spanish branches of the Habsburg family. After several generations of alliances between first cousins, Philip IV married his niece, thus making the pathetic Charles first cousin to his own mother. It was soon obvious that he could neither procreate nor rule. Other monarchs impatiently awaited his death so that they could divide his territories, while factional strife prevented concerted action by the Spanish themselves. The result, as we have seen, was the War of Spanish Succession, which ended in the loss of what remained of Spanish lands in Italy and the Low Countries and in the establishment of a Bourbon on the Spanish throne.

THE NETHERLANDS DIVIDED

The provinces of the Netherlands, which the Burgundian dukes had begun to draw together into a territorial state during the late Middle Ages, revolted against Philip II in 1568. The northern provinces were able to establish their independence, while the southern provinces remained under Habsburg rule. The boundary between the two Netherland states that emerged was not based on religious or ethnic lines. Many Protestants resided in the south and many Catholics in the north at the time of the break, and those who spoke the same Dutch dialect often found themselves divided between the two states. Only in the southern part of the Spanish Netherlands was French the native language of the people, although French became the language of the upper classes in the entire state. Instead, the boundary was determined by military and geographical factors. The rebels had wisely taken their initial stand in the northwest, where the wide rivers, lakes, and marshes prevented the Spanish from employing their splendid infantry to full advantage, and during the course of the war they had been able to conquer the northwestern provinces that were far removed from the center of Spanish power. The terrain of the southern provinces, on the other hand, was suitable for the Spanish troops, and the rebels were never able to challenge them seriously in this region.

The task of statebuilding in the southern provinces was less difficult because Habsburg institutions remained and a member of that family or a viceroy resided there to exercise royal authority. By expulsion and conversion, these provinces once more became almost entirely Catholic, but their economic importance was never fully restored. Although the medieval cities of Flanders had begun to decline long before the revolt began, the prosperity of the region as a whole had been maintained through the rise of Antwerp, which had become the principal banking and commercial center of Europe. Now Antwerp declined precipitously. The fortunes of war had given the Dutch the mouth of the Scheldt River through which ships had to pass to reach Antwerp's wharves, and the business-minded

Dutch successfully kept the river closed, leaving the merchants of Antwerp little recourse but to move to the northern state where many of them settled in Amsterdam. By the eighteenth century, agriculture had become more important than trade and industry in the southern Netherlands, or Belgium as these provinces were eventually called.

The situation was almost the reverse in the northern provinces, for most of the seventeenth century was a golden age of unprecedented economic progress for this area. The prosperity of the Dutch was due in part to the decline of Antwerp, but equally important was the quality of their trading ships. The inhabitants of the western provinces of Holland and Zeeland had long been engaged in fishing, and as a result of their experience, they had learned to build ships that could haul larger cargoes with fewer sailors than those of any other nation. Their shipping rates were therefore the lowest in Europe, and about half of the international carrying trade fell into their hands in spite of mercantilistic laws of other states designed to protect their merchant marines. Amsterdam became the trading and banking capital of Europe. Its population jumped to 100,000, and neighboring seaports also grew rapidly. With the growth of cities, technologically advanced agricultural methods were developed to feed the people, so that prosperity spread to the surrounding countryside, although the more distant eastern provinces remained relatively backward.

Another factor which stimulated economic growth and made the new state one of the intellectual centers of Europe was its relative tolerance. Although bigoted Calvinist ministers were influential enough to make conformity a requirement for officeholding and to prevent public worship in other churches, the Erasmian spirit was still so strong that actual persecution was exceptional. As late as 1650, about half the population was still Catholic, while Jews and the more radical Protestant sects were tolerated and printing presses willingly published the views of original, unorthodox thinkers. The country became a haven for those who were persecuted elsewhere, and it profited from their talents.

The Dutch were less fortunate in solving their political-constitutional problems, although they kept most of the basic institutional structure of the Burgundian state. When they deposed Philip II in 1581, it became necessary to establish a new form of government. This step was more difficult than might be imagined because at this time monarchies were almost universal and the only republics were those dominated by a single city. It is therefore not surprising that for a time the Dutch considered electing a ruler. In the end, however, they established the first territorial republic in modern Europe.

The provincialism which had so often plagued the Burgundian dukes and the Habsburgs did not die, and the government that emerged was quite decentralized. Each province retained its sovereignty. Each had its provincial estates, its army, and its elected stadholder or governor. The federal government consisted of an Estates-General composed of deputies elected by the provincial estates, a small council of state, and a few officials, including an admiral and a general. The Estates-General was a congress of ambassadors more than a true representative assembly. Its members had to refer back to the provincial estates for instruction just as the deputies of the United Nations today must ask for directives on how to vote. The adverse vote of a single province could usually stop action. When taxes were voted, the provincial estates could still block their collection, or for that matter any other action taken by the Estates-General.

This system would have been unsatisfactory even if the seven provinces had had similar interests, but they did not. Holland and Zeeland were wealthy maritime provinces controlled by the burgher aristocracy of the great cities. Friesland was controlled by the peasantry and the remaining provinces by the nobility. Agricultural interests were pitted against commercial interests, the nobility against the burghers. Religious disputes added to the difficulty. The rural areas were controlled by orthodox Calvinists, but the wealthy burghers of the great towns preferred some relaxation of the doctrine of predestination and favored more beauty in their churches. These differences led to quarrels that colored the history of the republic.

Only the combination of dangers abroad and able leadership at home from several generations of the Orange family kept the republic from falling apart. The descendants of William of Orange usually held the office of stadholder in most of the provinces, and at times it seemed possible that they would be able to make themselves kings. This was especially true during those periods in which there was a serious threat from abroad, as there was from Spain during the early years or from France during the last quarter of the seventeenth century.

On the other hand, between 1650 and 1672, when there was no serious foreign threat and the Prince of Orange was only a boy, the provinces went their separate ways and republicanism flourished more than ever. William III took advantage of the aggressive attitude of Louis XIV to regain the position of his family in 1672, but after he became King of England in 1688, he left the Dutch largely to their own devices. Not until 1747 was the Orange dynasty restored to its former position, and in 1815 a member of the family was recognized as king of a reunited Netherlands. Although the great republican experiment had finally failed, its achievements had nonetheless been remarkable. Not only had it survived the threat of provincialism at home and aggression from abroad, but it had also facilitated the creation of a great colonial empire and had seen the Dutch people take a leading role in the intellectual and artistic endeavors of Europe.

THE EMPIRE

The Thirty Years War solved one constitutional problem in central Europe. The Holy Roman Empire was not to grow into a unified territorial state, but neither was it to disappear entirely. The institutions of the Empire continued to function and in some instances actually increased in importance. The Reichstag became permanent in 1663, although representatives of the princes rather than the princes themselves usually attended. The threat from France, and to a lesser extent from the Ottoman Turks, led to the enlargement of the imperial army. The 51 remaining imperial free cities, the 1,500 imperial knights, and the smaller princely states continued to use either the imperial tribunal or a special court established by the emperor at Vienna. Sometimes these courts actually intervened in disputes between a prince and his subjects. Only the larger principalities became virtually independent states.

It is difficult to make generalizations about the struggle that took place between the princes and their estates, but a few facts seem clear. The Thirty Years War had wrecked the economy and decimated the population, while the persistence of a general European depression in the seventeenth century made rapid recovery impossible. The result was a weakening of the towns and the nobility. This in itself strengthened the princes, and they were further aided by a slow increase in religious toleration. Years of religious strife and the need to welcome every prospective immigrant to repopulate their states led many princes to ask few questions about the church affiliations of their subjects. Once persecution ceased, subjects were more willing to be loyal to a prince of a different faith, and the religious factor in the constitutional crisis was removed.

Some princes were able to profit from their greater strength and levy taxes without the consent of the estates. Under these circumstances, the estates were rarely convoked and gradually died through disuse. Other princes were less provident, less intelligent, or less fortunate and needed such heavy taxes that they dared not act without the consent of the estates. The result, in these instances, was the continuation of the balance of power between the prince and the estates that had characterized the Renaissance monarchy. The princes emerged victorious in the constitutional struggle in Bavaria, Brandenburg-Prussia, and Holstein, while the estates held their own in Saxony, Mecklenburg, and Wurttemberg. It is not possible to deal with all these conflicts, and only the activities of the Hohenzollern family in the north and the Habsburgs in the southeast will be considered, for only these two families were able to create states that played leading roles in European history.

THE HOHENZOLLERNS

The Hohenzollern lands were widely scattered. Their core was the electorate of Brandenburg, a poor, backward, sparsely populated region that had come into the family in 1417. In 1609, the Hohenzollerns inherited the duchies of Cleves and Mark in the rich Rhine Valley, and the death of a childless cousin ten years later brought them the duchy of Prussia. Prussia had once been ruled by the Teutonic Knights, a crusading order, but in 1525 the grandmaster had become a Lutheran, secularized the lands of the order, and won recognition as hereditary duke from his overlord, the King of Poland. Each of these territories had its own privileges, local loyalties, and assemblies of the estates; they were in no way connected except through the person of the elector. Within a century of the time they received their inheritance, the Hohenzollern princes created centralized institutions over the local ones, broke the power of the estates, added more territories, and became sovereign kings.

Most of this work was done by Frederick William, the Great Elector (1640-1688). Tall and dignified, Frederick William was only twenty when he succeeded his father, but experience had already taught him much. The Thirty Years War had so damaged his father's domains that Frederick had not enjoyed the usual luxurious upbringing of a prince. Once he had had to flee from Wallenstein's troops, and valuable years had been spent in Holland where he learned a great deal from the practical Dutch. These experiences had taught him tolerance, fortitude, and deceitfulness. They had made him determined to strengthen his domain in order that neither his dynasty nor his people would suffer the same indignities in the future.

His timid father had pursued a pro-Austrian policy during his last years, and the Swedes had retaliated by occupying part of his lands. Frederick William saw no alternative but to secure their withdrawal by signing an armistice. At the same time, he began his lifelong task of building an efficient, loyal army, starting with only 2,500 men. As his financial resources increased, he enlarged his force. By 1648, he had 8,000 men, a sufficient force to make good his claim to part of Pomerania and several secularized bishoprics in the Peace of Westphalia.

The years immediately following the war were devoted to the work of restoration, but in 1655 the Elector once more became involved in conflict. First, he assisted the Swedes in an attack on Poland; then, he assisted the Poles in their efforts to drive out the Swedes. The upshot of this devious policy was his recognition as independent Duke of Prussia by both Poland and Sweden.[5] To pursue this warlike, treacherous policy, Frederick William needed a still larger army. This meant higher taxes and a quarrel with the estates.

The first clash occurred in Brandenburg in 1653, for Frederick William anticipated the future needs of the army. He sought an excise tax to finance additional troops but was blocked by the estates. Since the opposition was led by the nobility, who were the strongest estate, it was with the nobility that he had to compromise. He confirmed their former privileges, gave them almost unlimited control over their peasants, and exempted them from taxation. In return, the nobles agreed to permit the levy on the other inhabitants. Later, similar compromises were reached with the nobles in Cleves, Mark, and Prussia. The towns and peasants were too weak to resist.

[5] See page 254.

The results of these compromises were far-reaching. Frederick William got the army that he felt was necessary to protect and expand his domains. In 1678, he was able to put 45,000 men into the field. At the same time, the nobles profited. They were poorer than those in western Europe, and the army and the new bureaucracy provided welcome employment for their younger sons. Equally important, they were permitted to transform their feudal fiefs into landed estates. Instead of collecting rents from peasant farmers, the nobles appropriated the land, reduced the peasants to serf laborers, and raised grain for export to the more thickly inhabited parts of Europe. The process of debasing the free peasants into serfs had been going on for a long time, but the action of the Great Elector speeded their reduction. Similar developments took place elsewhere in the northern and eastern parts of the Empire. The result was that this region, like England, became marked by large landed estates farmed by the lesser nobility or gentry. An important difference, however, was that in England the agricultural laborer remained a free man.

Frederick William was not content with the creation of an army in each of his territories. He wanted to bring these forces together under a single command in spite of the strong feeling in each territory that its troops ought not be used to defend the others. To secure this objective, he created a general staff to exercise military command and a war commissariat to collect taxes and to recruit, supply, and quarter troops from all his domains. Not only did this make for greater efficiency, but the policy of creating national institutions over local ones weakened the provincialism of the people in the long run and taught them a common loyalty to the Hohenzollern state.

The Great Elector did not stop here. Other institutions were centralized, a postal service was created, agricultural experiments were encouraged, and Frisian, Swiss, Jewish, and Huguenot immigrants were settled in the depopulated land. At one time, one-sixth of the population of Berlin were Huguenot refugees from the intolerance of Louis XIV. By his death in 1688, Frederick William had laid a firm foundation for future Hohenzollern greatness.

Frederick William's successor was a less able man, but he pushed the dynasty forward by winning the title of king in Prussia in return for joining the Austrians in the War of Spanish Succession. He also had a sincere interest in culture and was the founder of the Berlin Academy. The Great Northern War brought Swedish Pomerania to the Hohenzollerns, leaving little doubt that a new great power had been born.

THE AUSTRIAN HABSBURGS

The unsuccessful efforts of the Austrian Habsburgs to consolidate their control over the Holy Roman Empire and to inherit the possessions of their Spanish cousins have already been described, but one should not be left with the impression that this dynasty was in a state of decline. The Aus-

EXPANSION OF
BRANDENBURG-PRUSSIA

ACQUIRED BY HOHENZOLLERN
FAMILY IN FIFTEENTH CENTURY

ACQUIRED 1614-1648

ACQUIRED DURING EIGHTEENTH CENTURY

ACQUIRED DURING NAPOLEONIC WARS

BOUNDARIES OF THE EMPIRE

SCALE OF MILES

0   25 50   100   200   300

NORTH SEA

BLACK SEA

DENMARK

DUCHY OF PRUSSIA 1618

1722

DANZIG 1793

FROM POLAND IN FIRST PARTITION

FARTHER POMERANIA 1648

WEST PRUSSIA 1772

TO RUSSIA 1815

SILESIA 1742

RÜGEN 1815

1815

1720

HITHER POMERANIA

BRANDENBURG

MAGDEBURG 1648

HALBERSTADT 1648

FROM SAXONY, 1815

BOHEMIA

AUSTRIA

EAST FRIESLAND 1744

MINDEN 1648

RAVENSBURG 1614

MARK 1614

LINGEN 1707

CLEVES 1614

UPPER GELDERLAND 1713

GERMAN PRINCIPALITIES

FRANCE

trians gained more in the seventeenth and early eighteenth centuries than any other European power. They consolidated their hold over Bohemia, took Hungary, Transylvania, and adjacent territories from the Ottoman Empire, and annexed the Spanish Netherlands, Milan, Naples, and Sardinia.

The problem of creating a unified government for these far-flung estates was greater than that faced by the Hohenzollerns. Perhaps it was for this reason that the Habsburgs did not press centralization as far as Frederick William did in Brandenburg-Prussia. For the most part, they confirmed the privileges of their new provinces and let them keep their estates. Their efforts to create loyalty to their dynasty consisted largely of establishing national institutions over local ones. A permanent army was created in 1680, sections were formed in the chancellery at Vienna to deal with each major territory, and the great Hungarian nobles and those in other localities were tamed by bringing them to Vienna to enjoy the gay life of the court. There was even talk of creating an Estates-General for the entire empire to tie the component parts together, but provincialism proved too strong to make this plan feasible. Since the nobility was already so powerful in the Danubian part of their lands, the Habsburgs tried to purchase their loyalty by letting them increase their control over the peasants. The result was the growth of serfdom, as in Brandenburg-Prussia. To prevent rebellion, the Habsburgs even permitted the Hungarian Protestants a degree of toleration.

Most of the Habsburg crowns were elective. It was therefore necessary to take special action to ensure the future unity of the state. The Bohemians were forced to recognize the Habsburgs as their hereditary monarchs after their reconquest in 1620, and the Hungarians were persuaded to fix the succession in the male Habsburg line in 1687. In 1713, Emperor Charles VI, who had no son, issued a Pragmatic Sanction which decreed that his territories were forever indivisible and that the female line could inherit in default of the male. Much of his reign was spent in winning internal and foreign recognition of this decree, but in the process the concept of a great Danubian empire emerged whose capital, Vienna, rivaled the Paris of Louis XIV. Its art, its music, its Baroque splendor have left their traces through countless wars to the present time.

THE CONSTITUTIONAL CRISIS IN EASTERN EUROPE

POLAND

There were two important Slavic kingdoms in eastern Europe during the seventeenth century. One of them, Poland, had been predominantly Roman Catholic and Western in its orientation during the late Middle Ages and the Renaissance. The other, Russia, had not then been incorporated into the European civilization. By the eighteenth century, Russia had become a great European power (see page 323), and Poland was regarded as an anachronism.

During the late Middle Ages, the Poles had not managed their affairs very differently from other central and east Europeans. They had a king who was theoretically elected but who was always chosen from the reigning dynasty, a diet (estates-general), a small army, and the usual mixture of great and lesser nobles, townsmen, and peasants. Under this system of government and as a result of a dynastic union with the Lithuanian royal family in 1386, Poland in 1500 was second only to Russia in size and included more people than any European nation except France. At times, the Polish empire stretched from the Baltic to the Black Sea. At the close of the Middle Ages, it had looked as though the great nobles might become virtually independent rulers, like their counterparts in the Holy Roman Empire, but this was never to be the case. On the contrary, the anachronistic character of eighteenth-century Poland derived from the fact that it was the gentry, rather than the king, as in France, or the great nobles, as in the Empire, who triumphed in the seventeenth-century struggle for power.

The gentry did not achieve its success by staging a great rebellion, although this class was not indisposed to an occasional insurrection. No great religious issues divided king and subject, for although the population included Catholics, Greek Orthodox, and Protestants, the sixteenth-century Poles were more tolerant than other people. The price revolution did not hurt the landed gentry, for like their counterparts in east Germany the members of this class prospered by taking all the land, reducing the peasants to serfdom, and raising grain for export. No growing centralization threatened them. Indeed, the reverse was true, for they usurped more and more authority from the central government.

There were several reasons for the decline of the monarchy. One was the failure of the Jagellon dynasty to produce a male heir. With the death of Sigismund II in 1572, the dynasty came to an end, and the monarchy became elective in the broadest sense of the word. The Polish gentry, fifty thousand strong, met on the outskirts of Warsaw and chose a French prince as their king. Next they elected a Transylvanian. Swedes, Saxons, and even a few Poles followed. Quickly the crown became a prize for which foreigners intrigued, bribed, and fought. The new king often had a heavy debt to pay both to his foreign backers and to his domestic supporters. The members of the gentry were careful to see that their part in the election was not forgotten. Beginning in 1573, they made each successful candidate sign a *pacta conventa*, or charter, confirming their privileges and agreeing to limit his control over the army and legislation. He was not even to marry without the consent of the diet, an assembly that was to meet every two years. With each election, the gentry increased its demands. As the *pacta conventa* grew longer, monarchical authority waned.

Another factor in the decline of royal authority was the exposed position of Poland. There were no Pyrénées or Alps to protect its borders, and only small areas were sheltered by the sea. As a result, a frontier of several thousand miles had to be defended against Russian, Cossack, Turk, German, and Swede. War had to be the chief concern of each king. To secure the money and manpower necessary for the common defense, the king could not turn primarily to the towns, which had always been rather small and which declined rapidly during the seventeenth-century depression, but had to rely heavily on the gentry, who often exacted further concessions in return for their help.

Moreover, the very size of Poland told against any form of centralized government. Transportation was too slow to permit a careful watch on distant officials. Indeed, since public servants were appointed for life, the king could not remove them even if they proved disobedient. He also lacked the funds to increase the size of the bureaucracy or to develop an adequate army; during the seventeenth century, Poland was almost alone among the nations of Europe in lacking these two concomitants of statehood.

The diet did not replace the king as the controlling force in the government. Like the Dutch estates-general, it was really no more than a congress of ambassadors who voted as their electorate directed. The tradition had developed prior to the seventeenth century that agreement had to be unanimous before any action could be taken. Gradually, the Poles talked more and more of their liberties, and at the same time the crown's ability to limit irresponsible action declined. In 1652, a single individual prevented a measure from being accepted. This action established the precedent that a negative vote automatically dissolved the assembly and nullified all its previous acts. Of the fifty-five diets held between then and 1764, forty-eight were "exploded" in this fashion. The Polish diet had become as ineffectual as the Polish king.

Government passed to the local authorities. In a few cases, the local authority was a great noble with an estate as large as that of some of the German territorial princes, but for the most part, power passed to the gentry, who made up 8 per cent of the population. As the military class of the nation, the gentry was usually capable of holding its own against the handful of great nobles. With its dietines, or provincial estates, the members of this class had the organization to make their wishes respected. It was through the dietines that they elected and controlled their deputies to the national diet. It was through them that they slowly usurped the functions of the central government. Even taxation came into their hands.

The members of the gentry made use of their position to reduce the peasants to serfdom. In the hope of controlling prices, they put numerous regulations on trade. In 1643, the profits of Polish merchants were limited to 7 per cent, foreign merchants to 5 per cent, and Jews to 3 per cent. The towns declined further as a result, and by 1765 a royal commission reported that "every street [was] an open field, every square a desert." The burgher, like the free peasant, had disappeared. The few inhabitants who remained in the towns were Jews, who stayed because they were treated almost as badly elsewhere in Europe.

With an inadequate army, bureaucracy, and system of taxation, with no wealthy, cultured burghers or sturdy, free peasants, Poland fell prey to foreign powers. Time and again during the seventeenth century the Swedes marched back and forth across the land. Brandenburg took the duchy of Prussia in full sovereignty in 1657; Russia took the eastern Ukraine and other territories in 1667; and the Turks seized Podolia in 1672. When it began to look as though the country would be swallowed up by its enemies, the Poles found a warrior-king in John Sobieski.

Sobieski's ancestors came from the gentry but had recently attained the status of great nobles. In his youth, he was a curious mixture of a pleasure-loving reprobate and an energetic, heroic soldier. He was capable of the most generous self-sacrifice and the most consummate greed. In 1665, he married a widow of French extraction whom he had long loved. She was an ambitious woman who was able to impart to her husband her own strength of purpose. She urged him to win the Polish crown, convert the elective monarchy into a hereditary one, reform the government—in short, make Poland once more a great power. It is true that she was pro-French and guilty of encouraging her husband's greed, but this couple offered Poland its last real chance of survival.

The first task proved the easiest. The fame won by Sobieski as a soldier led to his election as king in 1674. For years he continued his wars, mainly against the Turks, whom he defeated in battle after battle. The relief of Vienna in 1683 was only his most famous exploit.[6] By 1690, the way was prepared for the recognition of his eldest son as heir apparent and for genuine constitutional reform. The emperor had even given his sister as bride to the prospective king, but the youth felt no gratitude towards his father. He intrigued with the enemies of the crown and finally fled to Austria. It was clear that such a man could never rule. Sobieski's health was broken, he was in constant pain, his dreams—and he was above all else a dreamer—had come to nothing. He died in 1696 a broken man.

Poland died more slowly than its king. For a time, the Swedes, Russians, Prussians, and other powers tried to rule the whole country through a puppet king rather than annex parts of it. This policy changed in 1772, when the Russians, Prussians, and Austrians agreed to divide a third of Poland's territory. The Poles were incapable of resisting their powerful neighbors, and when they tried to reform their government thereafter, these same powers divided the remainder of their country in two more partitions. Poland ceased to exist because the gentry had been so jealous of their liberties that they had ruined the other social classes and had refused to permit a more modern state to develop until it was too late.

[6] See pages 258-259.

The Constitutional Crisis

Until the latter part of the seventeenth century, Russia seemed even less likely to survive as an independent state than Poland. Like Poland, Russia was a huge country with no natural boundaries along either its eastern or western frontiers. Throughout the Middle Ages, European Russia had been invaded time and again by hordes that swept across the Asiatic plains, over the low Ural Mountains that separate the two continents, and onto the flat plains north of the Black Sea, where they spread in all directions. At the same time, the excellent network of rivers flowing northward into the Baltic Sea and southward into the Black Sea provided highways through which invaders from the north and cultural influences from the south penetrated into the center of the country. The western borders were equally indefensible, and several times during the early seventeenth century Russian independence was threatened by the Poles and Swedes. Thus, Russia lay in the heartland of the Eurasian continent on a crossroads of north-south and east-west movements that prevented the country from belonging wholly to either the East or the West.

A relatively advanced state began to develop along the Dnieper River in the ninth century. Its capital, Kiev, became an important trading city. Cultural contacts were established with the Byzantine empire, and the inhabitants became converts of the Greek Orthodox Church. This promising beginning was cut short by the Mongol invasion in 1240. The various principalities into which Kievan Russia had become divided were overrun, and contacts with the Byzantine civilization were sharply reduced. The Russians were thus isolated from the more advanced culture to the south, while the intellectual manifestations of the Renaissance failed to reach them.

For a time it seemed possible that the future of Russia might lie with the city-state of Novgorod, situated in the northwest, far from the center of Mongol power. Novgorod had trading connections with the West, but its relatively exposed position made it subject to repeated attacks by the Scandinavians, Germans, and Lithuanians. Although the inhabitants managed to repel these assaults, they were seriously weakened by the constant wars. The southwestern portion of the former Kievan state was less fortunate, for after a long struggle the region was conquered by Lithuania. After Lithuania joined Poland in a dynastic union in 1386, Polish influence became strong. The result was that linguistic and ethnic divisions that had already begun to appear among the Russian people were solidified. European Russia became divided into White Russia and the Ukraine, which fell to Poland-Lithuania, and Great Russia to the north and east, which remained under Mongol control. In the end, it was the principality of Muscovy located in the Great Russian part of the former Kievan state that succeeded in providing the nucleus for the future Russian empire.

Around the middle of the fourteenth century, Muscovy consisted of only six hundred square miles, but under a series of able princes the little state managed to expand its territory. The most important of these rulers was Ivan III (1462-1505), called the Great, who occupies a place in Russian history comparable to that occupied by the Renaissance monarchs in the West. He threw off what remained of the Mongol yoke and, through purchase, inheritance, and especially conquest, won the surrounding states, the most important of which was once-mighty Novgorod itself. In 1472, he married the niece of the last Byzantine emperor. This marriage led the Muscovite rulers to adopt the title of tsar or caesar and to imitate the coronation ceremony and court ritual of the Byzantines. More important, it provided a theoretical and moral claim to justify the emergence of a monarchy that was actually based on military force.

Once Muscovy became stronger than its neighbors, the very network of north-south rivers and east-west plains that had made invasion so easy facilitated rapid expansion in every direction except the west. Here, for a century, strong Polish and Swedish states checked the Muscovite advance. Ivan III's grandson, Ivan IV (1533-1584), called the Terrible, won control of the entire course of the Volga River by conquering several Mongol states, and the penetration into Siberia was begun. Turning to the west, he won an outlet on the Baltic Sea only to lose it to the Swedes some years later. The latter part of his reign was marred by attacks of insanity. The mad king murdered all who opposed him; the great nobles received most of his wrath, but even his son and heir fell by his own hand.

The death of Ivan IV's weak and childless son in 1598 brought the dynasty to an end. There followed a confused fifteen-year period known as the Time of Troubles. The *Zemsky Sobor* or estates-general elected Boris Godunov, one of the great nobles, tsar, but he died a few years later. First one and then another pretender laid claim to the throne, each claiming to be a tsar's son. Both received foreign help, and one even managed to seize and hold the throne for a brief period. For a time, it looked as though a Polish prince would become king and form a dynastic union of the two Slavic kingdoms. Finally, the wars and murders led to a reaction, and in 1613, the *Zemsky Sobor* elected a young noble, Michael Romanov, tsar. Michael (1613-1645), unlike Sobieski, was able to establish his dynasty on the throne where it remained until the Revolution of 1917. During his reign, an expedition crossed Siberia reaching the Pacific in 1637, and during that of his son, Alexis I (1645-1676), part of the Ukraine, including Kiev, was won back from Poland.

THE EVOLUTION OF RUSSIAN SOCIETY

Meanwhile, Russian society had been changing. In its early days, Muscovy, like the other little states into which European Russia was divided during the period of Mongol suzerainty, was ruled by a prince in conjunction with a council of *boyars*, a class of nobles who held land with no obligation to serve the prince. The prince, the *boyars,* and the Church owned nearly all the land. Local administration and justice were in the hands of these landowners or their agents. The peasants who worked in the fields during this period were usually freemen, but wars, famines, plagues, and other catastrophes gradually increased their dependence on the landlord. In return for a loan of money, food, or tools, they promised to pay dues and perform labor services. Once in debt, they were not permitted to leave the soil until after the autumn harvest, and then only if their obligations had been fulfilled.

As the Muscovite state expanded, the conquered lands became the property of the tsar, who assigned them to his principal assistants in return for their support. Thus, a service gentry came into being that, as the state grew, became the most powerful class in the kingdom, just as a reconstituted aristocracy in the West became the most powerful class in the Renaissance monarchy.

The triumph of the service gentry spelled disaster for the peasants who worked the land. Their right to leave the soil even if their debts had been paid was removed around 1600. Many fled to the vast unoccupied stretches along the ever-expanding frontier, where they established free democratic, warlike societies. Such fugitive peasants became known as cossacks. Their departure, added to the wars and famines during the Time of Troubles, led to a scarcity of labor in central Russia. The gentry redoubled its efforts to keep the remaining peasants on the soil. For a time, if a peasant escaped and eluded capture for a specified number of years, he became legally free, but in 1649 this time limit was abolished and the peasants on the land of the service gentry became perpetual serfs. No limits were placed on the services rendered by the serfs, and since the landowners were charged with justice and law enforcement on their estates, the serfs were at their mercy. By the close of the seventeenth century, they could even be bought and sold. Their position was far worse than the serfs in the medieval West; they were little better than slaves. Only the peasants on the estates kept by the tsar for his own support enjoyed a more favorable position. These estates were located for the most part to the north and east of Moscow, where there had been less need to grant estates to a service gentry to facilitate the expansion or defense of the empire.

By the middle of the seventeenth century, Russian society had become stratified. There was an aristocracy consisting of the *boyars* and the service gentry and an agricultural population consisting of crown peasants and serfs. Stratification had also developed in the towns, where the artisans were sharply separated from the merchants. Even among the *boyars,* the existence of a rigid hierarchy compelled the tsar to make his important appointments in accordance with the standing of each individual family rather than on merit. As a result, social mobility was reduced during the seventeenth century crisis in Russia just as it had been in the West.

RUSSIAN INSTITUTIONS

The Muscovite rulers claimed to be divinely ordained, absolute monarchs. Moscow, they argued, was a third Rome, the now-conquered Constantinople having been the second. In assuming the title of tsar, they claimed to be the successors of the caesars. But with all their imperial titles and ceremonies, their government was popular and consultative like the Renaissance monarchies in the West. Important decisions had to be consented to by a council of *boyars* known as the *Duma*. The need to reach other influential classes was also recognized, and in 1550 Ivan IV summoned the first full meeting of the *Zemsky Sobor* to give its approval to some projected reforms. This institution, which in many ways resembled the estates-generals in the West, consisted initially of appointed members of the clergy, *boyars*, and service gentry, but townsmen were later added, and on at least one occasion the crown peasants participated.

Ivan IV had seen in the *Zemsky Sobor* an instrument for learning the grievances of the people and persuading the influential elements of the population to support his program, for no ruler in this age had the army or the bureaucracy to make innovations that the bulk of his more vocal subjects opposed. After the disappearance of the old reigning dynasty, however, it became necessary for the *Zemsky Sobor* to elect a new tsar on several occasions. The Romanovs themselves owed their throne to a choice made by this institution. As a result, Michael Romanov consulted it frequently when he was tsar and invariably won its consent for the taxes he levied. In this manner, the tsar and the *Zemsky Sobor* came to share in the government of the empire as the king and the estates had in the West during the Renaissance.

The usual departments of government were established in Moscow, and governors were appointed to administer the individual provinces. These governors quickly escaped from the control of the central bureaucracy and acted as they pleased. A degree of local self-government also developed during the sixteenth century. Positions in the judiciary, police, and municipalities were often elective, and local assemblies called *zemstvos* were organized to deal with judicial, financial, and administrative matters. Thus, some of the popular and decentralized aspects of the Renaissance monarchies had parallel developments in Russia.

There was one important exception to this rule. The Western state was created by dynastic marriages and the reverting of great feudal duchies to the crown. Under these circumstances, each former kingdom and duchy kept its own laws, institutions, and special privileges. The Russian state, on the other hand, was created primarily by military conquest, and the laws and institutions of Muscovy were imposed on the entire empire. Local variations disappeared, and a common legal and institutional structure emerged. Only England, thanks to the Norman conquest, could boast equal uniformity in these respects.

RELIGION AND CULTURE

The contrast between Russia and the West was more striking in the areas of religion and culture. Byzantine culture had penetrated into the region during the Kievan period, and the inhabitants had been converted to the Greek Orthodox religion. During the Mongol period, contact with Constantinople had been reduced, leaving native elements free to re-emerge. By the sixteenth century, culture and social life reflected both native Russian and Greek-Byzantine characteristics. Men wore beards, and gentlewomen were veiled and secluded. Drunkenness and coarse humor were accepted without question. Education was rare, and the art of cultivated conversation unappreciated. There was no national literature comparable to that found in the West and little art outside the churches. Able craftsmen were scarce, and science was in a primitive state. Neither Arabic numerals nor the Western calendar had been adopted, and church ritual and literature had been corrupted. In short, Russia was centuries behind both the Western and the Greek Orthodox worlds in nearly every aspect of civilization.

The defeat of the Mongols and the rapid expansion of the Muscovite state made possible renewed contacts with Constantinople and the West. Western ideas began to creep in through neighboring Poland and were carried to Moscow itself by English merchants during the reign of Ivan IV.[7] Germans and other foreigners began to settle in Moscow, where they were restricted to a quarter in the city. Of more immediate importance, contacts with the better-educated Greek Orthodox clergy in the Ottoman Empire were increased, and the head of the Muscovite Church was recognized as a patriarch by the Orthodox prelates in other parts of the world. This enabled him to strengthen his hold over the clergy in his own country and led to an attempt to bring Russian ritual into line with the Orthodox ceremony elsewhere. A large part of the lower clergy resisted these foreign innovations, but the tsar and the ecclesiastical hierarchy attempted to impose them by force. The struggle began in the reign of Alexis (1645-1676), the second Romanov monarch.

Alexis was more cultivated than most of his predecessors, but he was too weak and kindly to compel his subjects to adopt the ways of the West. It is surprising that he permitted his desire to reform the Greek Orthodox Church to be pushed to the point that it led to schism. Many errors had crept into Russian religious books; poor translations and editing had even led the name of Jesus to be misspelled. Time had caused the Russian ritual to vary from the Greek Orthodox. Under the leadership of the patriarch and with Alexis' approval, orders were issued to print correct editions of the Bible and other religious works and to adopt the Greek ritual. To the Old Believers, as the fundamentalists were called, these innovations altered the basis of their religion. They had accepted the old throughout their lives

[7] See page 139.

without question and lacked the education to recognize the reasons for change. They resisted, and the quarrel between the state and ecclesiastical hierarchy on one hand and the Old Believers on the other continued for years. No amount of persecution could make the Old Believers abandon their beliefs, but in the end their lack of ecclesiastical organization caused them to break up into sects, some of which still exist today.

Happily for Alexis, the Old Believers did not become deeply involved in the social uprisings during his reign, and neither the religious nor the social rebels used the *Zemsky Sobor* as an institution around which to rally discontent. Russia had had its Reformation that ended in schism, but unlike that of the West, it had taken place in response to the demands of the ecclesiastical hierarchy, rather than demands from segments of the lower clergy and the people. The issues at stake had been primarily ritualistic rather than dogmatic, and the support of the Old Believers had come from the small merchants and surviving peasantry rather than the gentry. The resistance to established authority had therefore been less dangerous than in the Protestant movement, which had won many noble converts, and the Russian state survived with relative ease. The *Zemsky Sobor* was rarely convoked after 1653, and the Russian Church itself was so weakened by the loss of many of its most devout members that it succumbed to state control before the end of the century.

Under Alexis, the Russian Church had reintegrated with the Greek Orthodox and the penetration of Western ideas into a few circles had continued, but it remained for his son, Peter the Great (1689-1725), to bring Russia into the mainstream of European politics.

PETER THE GREAT

Peter was only four when his father died, and in the tumultuous years that followed, his life was in danger several times. Once, drunken soldiers spent three days in the royal palace murdering officials whom they opposed; at another time, he fled the palace in his nightshirt to escape assassination. Such an atmosphere was hardly conducive to a normal academic education, but Peter did manage to frequent the foreign quarter of Moscow. There he became acquainted with the West—with its tobacco, its mechanical gadgets, and its free association of men and women. There he found his first mistress, Anna Mons, and his lifetime love, the ship. There he came to realize that Russia must modernize or risk losing its independence.

At seventeen, Peter seized control of the government from his older sister who had ruled during his minority, but he was still an overgrown boy more interested in playing soldier or sailor than in governing. Already, some of his later characteristics were plainly in evidence—his great size, his tremendous energy, his love for doing things with his hands, and his utter ruthlessness. He always insisted on beginning at the bottom and working his way up through the ranks. He served as an able seaman, a

328

common soldier, a carpenter, a mechanic, a barber, a dentist. Promotion was rapid, but it was granted only after he had mastered a vocation. In 1697, when he dispatched an embassy of 250 to learn about the West and to form an alliance against the Turks, Peter joined the group incognito. He worked as a carpenter in Holland; in England, he is reported to have ruined his landlord's prize holly hedge "by trundling his wheelbarrow through it." He returned to Moscow in 1698, firmly determined to Westernize his own mammoth kingdom.

Some of Peter's reforms smacked of the ridiculous. Westerners wore no beards; therefore, Russian beards must be removed. He personally shaved his courtiers, but many of his subjects resisted; to shave, they felt, was to deface the image of God, for had not man been created in His likeness? The religious taboo was so strong that the practical tsar had to content himself

329

Peter the Great (Brown Brothers)

with levying a tax on beards. He encouraged smoking, but taxed tobacco. He practiced the art of dentistry, to the discomfiture of his courtiers and did not hesitate to direct a choir. When he ordered the extermination of the rebellious Moscow guard, it was said that this furious man personally assumed the role of executioner. Yet it was all done for a purpose. He was determined that blind adherence to the past must cease and that every member of the gentry must learn to serve the state. He insisted that they start at the bottom, in either the army, navy, or administration, and work their way up just as he himself had done. Birth and family influence meant nothing. Ability was the only criterion. He also insisted that the gentry receive an elementary school education. When many failed to observe the edict, Peter decreed that a diploma must be produced before a member of the gentry could marry. Russians were sent to the West to be educated. Skilled workers and military, naval, and administrative experts were imported from abroad.

When Charles XII of Sweden completely defeated the numerically superior Russian army at Narva, Peter instigated military reforms.[8] Peasant and burgher were subjected to conscription for twenty-five years. They were given flintlocks and bayonets in place of the outmoded muskets and pikes. Artillery was improved, discipline enforced, and the army enlarged. By the time of his death, Peter had a force of 210,000 men without counting the irregulars, a substantial army for a nation of only 13,000,000 inhabitants. He was equally the father of the Russian navy. Perhaps Peter's most remarkable achievement was that he effected these improvements without foreign loans, or even loans from local capitalists, who were

[8] See page 254.

350

nonexistent. The ruthless, energetic tsar extracted the necessary money from his subjects in the form of higher taxes and greater services. Governmental income was five and a half times as high in 1724 as it had been in 1680. Just as the Russian Communists have in this century built a mighty industrial power through oppressive measures, so Peter built a mighty military force and laid the foundations for future industrial growth by driving his subjects ruthlessly.

He reorganized the central government along Western lines. What remained of the consultative, self-governing aspects of the old monarchy disappeared. The *Zemsky Sobor* was not summoned, and the *boyar duma* was ignored. Peter did not, however, follow Louis XIV's practice of excluding the nobility from the government. Instead, he insisted that they serve the state and what little distinction remained between the old *boyar* families and the service gentry was obliterated. A senate was created to supervise administrative, financial, and judicial affairs, and ministries were established for war, finance, commerce, foreign affairs, and other branches of government. A group of ministers, called a college, headed each of these agencies rather than a single official because the restless monarch trusted the wisdom of several men more than one alone. Peter divided the country into forty-three provinces, each administered by a governor responsible to him, and he sent out inspectors to see that he was obeyed. Industry and mining were encouraged, and by the time of his death, the Russians were probably producing more pig iron than the English.

The Greek Orthodox Church was brought more directly under the control of the state. Peter abolished the office of patriarch and substituted a Holy Synod, or church council, composed of leading ecclesiastics, and a lay chief procurator whom he appointed to guide its work. No longer was there a patriarch to rival the tsar in importance. The calendar was altered to conform to the Western practice of beginning the new year on January 1 and of numbering the years from the birth of Christ rather than from the creation of the world, as had been the Russian practice. Arabic numerals were introduced, and the alphabet was simplified. A newspaper was established with, of course, the energetic tsar editing the first issue. Peter corresponded with leading Western scholars and laid plans for an academy of science, but death denied him the glory of attending the first session. In November, 1724, when he saw a shipwreck, he characteristically jumped into the cold northern water to assist in the rescue. Sickness resulted, and death followed several months later.

Peter had often been troubled about what might happen to his reforms after his death, for a majority in every class resisted his innovations. To ensure continual contact with the West, he had wrested the eastern shores of the Baltic from the Swedes. Here he built St. Petersburg, a new capital, that could be reached far more easily from the West than landlocked Moscow. The cost in money and lives was tremendous, but Peter drove the work towards completion. He organized the social life of the court along Western lines. Even his own manners improved somewhat, and by 1712 a courtier could report that at a private dinner with the Prussian royal family Peter neither belched nor picked his teeth "at least as far as I heard or saw."

Perhaps the most important step that Peter took to ensure the continuation of Western influence in Russia was to introduce the practice of marrying royal princes to Western princesses. Thereafter, nearly every tsar had a German wife, and thus the German influence became strong in upper-class circles. Peter himself had been married to the daughter of a Russian nobleman in his youth in accordance with the earlier practice, but he put her in a convent soon after he began to govern personally. Perhaps realizing that under the circumstances he could not hope to find a suitable Western princess for himself, he eventually married his mistress, Catherine. Catherine was a Lithuanian of low origin who had already given him three children, but she proved a fit companion for the restless monarch.

The most immediate threat to continued Westernization came from Peter's son, Alexis. Alexis was the direct opposite of his father. He was cultivated, but lazy. Father and son soon quarreled, and Alexis joined the enemies of Westernization. Matters became worse and Alexis fled to Austria in 1716. Peter saw that if he permitted Alexis to succeed him, his work would be undone. He coaxed Alexis back to Russia with promises of forgiveness, but once he got his hands on his son, he had him tortured to learn of his plans and accomplices. Alexis was tried and condemned to death, but before Peter announced his final decision, Alexis died; officially from apoplexy, more probably from violence. Even Peter lacked the courage to execute his son publicly.

It is difficult to evaluate Peter's work. By his energy and ruthlessness he modernized Russia to the extent that it was strong enough to escape the fate of Poland and the Ottoman Empire, but the deeper aspects of Western culture never penetrated below the aristocracy, and the masses of the Russian people were forced down lower than ever. They remained in ignorance, now separated culturally as well as economically and socially from their superiors.

CONCLUSIONS

More than a century of constitutional crises had come to an end. In France, Brandenburg-Prussia, Austria, and Russia the kings had become more powerful. In England, the Netherlands, and Poland they had lost some or all of their power. There are no easy explanations to account for these divergent developments. English historians have often insisted that they owe their parliamentary government largely to the diversity of religion that led to rebellions against the crown; but the revolts of the Huguenots caused a reaction in favor of royal authority in France, and Protestant subjects did not prevent a monarchical triumph in Brandenburg-Prussia. Some historians emphasize the long history of the English Parliament, which provided an alternative to royal absolutism; but the Dutch Estates-General and the Polish Diet, relatively recent creations, were even more successful against the crown, and an institution as ancient as the cortes of Castile was reduced to impotence. Actually, these and other factors were influential; each weighted the probable results on one side or the other. But two things seem evident: chance and the actions of men must be emphasized. The failure of a dynasty to produce an heir could have far-reaching results. Or again, the initial triumph of the rebels in England may be explained largely by the stupidity of Charles I and ability of the dedicated Cromwell, while Mazarin's astuteness had much to do with the Bourbons' victory over the poorly led Fronde at the same time.

Likewise, no simple explanation can be advanced to show why England, France, Russia, and Brandenburg-Prussia became relatively centralized while the Empire, the Netherlands, and Poland witnessed the triumph of local authorities. Smallness made for greater unity; yet Russia and France became more centralized, while the Netherlands disintegrated. A unity of traditions was significant; yet the Holy Roman Empire became more decentralized, while the Hohenzollerns welded together several separate states to form Brandenburg-Prussia. The great dynastic state of Charles V was partitioned; yet the Austrians were able to create a new one that was quite large. It has often been suggested that the middle class wanted national unity, but the Netherlands, where this class was stronger than elsewhere in Europe, became a decentralized state. Once more, it was a combination of factors, including chance and the actions of men, that explain the evolution of the European states. All that is certain is that strong states, with large armies and bureaucracies supported by heavy taxes, did appear on the European continent. These states were capable of suppressing internal rebellions and of devouring countries that remained weak. Unless some means could be found to curb their appetites, individual rights and liberties would perish and wars would become still more destructive. These were two of the fundamental problems that the men of the seventeenth century left for their successors to solve.

8/ Science, Thought, and Art

THE emergence of several strong, independent, warlike states was as much of a threat to the existence of European civilization as it was a promise of future development. Moreover, the cessation of economic progress, the inadequate food supply, and the growth of rigid class distinctions indicated that Europe might be entering a period of stagnation comparable to that found in the East. In science, however, there was great progress; by the close of the seventeenth century, new discoveries had destroyed the scientific premises of the ancient and medieval world, influenced other forms of intellectual activity, and affected aesthetic standards.

THE SCIENTIFIC REVOLUTION

ASTRONOMY AND PHYSICS

The year 1543 may be taken as the beginning of the scientific revolution, for it was then that Copernicus published *The Revolutions of the Heavenly Bodies* and Vesalius, *On the Structure of the Human Body.*

334

Within a century and a half, man's conception of himself and the universe he inhabited was altered, and the scholastic method of reasoning was replaced by new scientific methods.

Nicholas Copernicus was born in the Polish city of Torun in 1473. Since his father, who was a merchant of German extraction, died when he was ten, he was raised by his uncle, the Bishop of Ermland. The bishop found an ecclesiastical position for his nephew and arranged for him to be educated in Italy between 1496 and 1506. While in Italy, Copernicus studied the generally accepted astronomical system of Ptolemy. This system depicted the universe as consisting of the earth and ten spheres: the moon, Mercury, Venus, the sun, Mars, Jupiter, Saturn, the Firmament (fixed stars), the Crystalline Heaven which imparted motion to the spheres around the earth, and finally the motionless Empyrean Heaven where God dwelt with the elect. These spheres were generally believed to be solid and transparent, and the planets to be of a nonearthly weightless substance fitted into the spheres and revolving with them around the motionless earth. Beyond the Empyrean Heaven there was nothing. Thus, the universe was considered to be a finite entity with the stationary earth as its center.

The difficulty with the Ptolemaic system was that the planets and stars did not revolve exactly as predicted. The more observations the medieval astronomers made, the more it became apparent that something was wrong. To accommodate these discrepancies, the astronomers modified the system by suggesting that there were sub- and off-center spheres. Finally, the number of the various types of spheres reached eighty, but still mathematical calculations did not coincide with observed data. Astrologers could blame their errors on faulty astronomy and thereby repel the inference that no relation existed between the planets and fate. The calendar was known to be in error, but it was difficult to decide what corrections to make.

Copernicus became interested in these problems. He knew that an ancient astronomer, Aristarchus, had argued that the earth and the other planets revolved around the sun and that the earth also revolved daily on its axis. He determined to make mathematical calculations based on these theories, to see if they would bring better results. He kept the idea of the sub- and off-center spheres and never doubted that the planets' paths around the sun were circular because his Platonic background led him to believe that the circle was the most perfect of geometric figures. Consequently, his calculations yielded predictions that were no more accurate than the modified Ptolemaic system. His calculations were simpler, however, and the number of sub- and off-center spheres could now be reduced to thirty-four.

As might be expected, the few theologians who took note of Copernicus' system were inclined to reject it. Luther scornfully remarked that "this fool wishes to reverse the entire science of astronomy; but sacred Scripture tells us that Joshua commanded the sun to stand still, and not

335

the earth." More serious was the critical attitude of other scientists. Copernicus had anticipated some of their objections. The earth could rotate on its axis from west to east, he pointed out, without causing a constant, high-velocity wind from east to west if the air revolved at the same speed and in the same direction. Also, the earth could move in an orbit around the sun without causing the stars to seem to change their location provided that the distance traveled by the earth was such a tiny fraction of the distance to the stars that the actual change in position could not be measured. His theory that vast distances separated the planets did not lead Copernicus to believe that the universe was infinite, although his supporters would soon advance that view. Only where his theory ran counter to the Aristotelian conception of gravity and motion was Copernicus unable to provide his critics with satisfactory answers.

To the Aristotelians, gravity was the natural tendency of heavy bodies to move towards the center of the universe. In situations in which gravity was not a factor, an object remained at rest unless a force was applied against it. If a force were constantly applied, the object moved at a constant, not an accelerated, speed. If the force were removed, the object stopped. As long as these theories were accepted, the Ptolemaic system caused fewer difficulties than the Copernican. If, as Aristotle said, a rock naturally fell towards the center of the universe, the Copernican astronomer had to explain why it actually moved towards the earth rather than the sun. Also, to Aristotle, a constant force had to be applied either to the earth to keep it moving around the sun or to the sun and planets to keep them moving around the earth. The former was the more difficult to believe because the earth was known to be very large and heavy while the sun and planets were thought to be composed of an unearthly, weightless substance that could be easily moved by the angels or some other supernatural force. Thus, a new theory of gravity and a new theory of motion had to be developed before the Copernican system could win acceptance. This was doubly true because the Aristotelians were still firmly entrenched in the university chairs of science and philosophy.

Furthermore, the Copernican system demanded that a man deny his senses, which daily told him that the sun went around the earth, in return for some mathematical calculations which made possible no better astronomical predictions than the Ptolemaic method. It is not surprising that for more than a century there were scientists who denied the validity of the Copernican system.

The debate led to a three-sided quarrel concerning the proper scientific method. The Aristotelians preferred to analyze the nature of things. They used little mathematics and few experiments but sought to construct their system by logical arguments leading from a few basic premises. Their goal was more to explain *why* things happen than to describe *how* they happen. A second school, led by such men as the Danish astronomer Tycho Brahe (1546-1601) and the English philosopher Francis Bacon

(1561-1626) favored the inductive method. They argued that the scientist should amass all the data possible through experiment and observation. Once assembled, these data would point to the correct conclusion. Tycho Brahe, for example, made observations on the motion of the planets that were as numerous and as accurate as they could have been before the invention of the telescope. His plot of the periodic changes in the location of the heavenly bodies led him to believe that Mercury and Venus revolved around the sun, but that the sun and the other planets revolved in turn around the earth. He never reduced his system to a mathematical statement, but it did follow *observed* fact more closely than Copernicus' system.

The mathematical, deductive approach was the third system advocated at this time. It had received unintentional assistance from the Renaissance humanists who had preferred Plato to Aristotle, for Plato himself had been deeply influenced by a Greek mathematician of the sixth century B.C. named Pythagoras. Pythagoras had noted that the sound produced by plucking a stretched string varied with its length. This relationship between the pitch and the length of the string, which was subject to geometrical representation and mathematical measurement, led him to believe that all the important elements in the universe were subject to mathematical demonstration and that certain numbers had a peculiar mystical significance. Plato accepted this point of view and depicted nature in terms of straight lines, circles, triangles, and other geometric figures that were more perfect than the objects actually observed. Under his influence, Greek science became more mathematical than experimental, and the renewed emphasis on his thought had a similar effect in the late Renaissance. Among the chief supporters of the deductive-mathematical approach of Plato and Pythagoras were Copernicus himself and Johannes Kepler. Galileo Galilei, the third of the great trio of mathematicians, chose Archimedes as his model because that ancient scientist had applied mathematics to practical problems in physics and suggested the method that Galileo was to make his own.

Kepler (1571-1630) was an ardent Platonist who believed that simple mathematical laws were the basis of all natural phenomena. Using the data collected by his master, Brahe, he showed that planets follow elliptical orbits around the sun. He also found that they moved more rapidly as they neared the sun and that a mathematical law could express the relationship between the size of their orbits and the time that it took them to go all the way around them. His discoveries removed one of the objections to a sun-centered solar system, for his planetary tables were more accurate than those provided by the advocates of any other system.

Kepler offered no satisfactory answer to the problem of gravity, and the best explanation that he could offer for the force that moved the planets was to suggest that it came from the sun. Other developments, however, were gradually undermining the Aristotelian conception of motion and gravity. A new star that was so bright that it could be seen in daylight appeared in 1572 only to disappear again in 1574. Obviously, the region of the fixed stars was not permanent and unchanging as the Aristotelians taught. A few years later, a new comet was seen passing through the region on the far side of the moon that Aristotelians said was composed of the impenetrable, transparent spheres in which the revolving planets were located. Clearly the Aristotelians were wrong, but if the planets did not get their capacity to move in fixed orbits from the spheres, where did they get their power of motion and what force held them to a prescribed path? The next great contribution towards providing an answer to these questions and winning acceptance for the Copernican theory was made by Galileo Galilei (1564-1642).

GALILEO

Galileo was born in Pisa of a noble Florentine family. He served as professor of mathematics at both Pisa and Padua and later held a post in the court of the Grand Duke of Tuscany. His scientific successes were due to his ability to make what some historians have called "thought experiments." Taking a particular problem, such as the law that governs falling bodies, he would strip it of all complicating factors, such as the effect of air resistance, and then speculate on what would happen. Would a heavy object fall faster in a vacuum than a lighter one as the Aristotelians argued, or would they fall together at the same speed? Galileo drew lines to represent the various forces involved and by the use of geometry reduced them to a mathematical formula. In this manner he showed that $s = \dfrac{gt^2}{2}$ where s is the distance of the fall, t is the time of fall, and g is a constant. This discovery undermined the Aristotelians in two respects. It showed that there was no relation between the weight of a body and the speed at which it fell, and that if a uniform force (g) was applied to an object, it would move at an accelerated speed rather than at a constant speed as the Aristotelians had argued. This meant that if a force were constantly being applied to the planets, they would rotate faster and faster around their orbits. Since this was obviously not the case, the force which had originally set the planets in motion was no longer being applied. Neither the angels nor any other supernatural power was needed to keep the planets in motion, for as our modern law of inertia states, a body in motion continues to move in a straight line until something stops it or alters its course. Galileo, himself, did not fully state the law of inertia, and its implication that the universe could function without the active interference of a God was not generally accepted by scientists until the eighteenth century, but Aristotelian science had received a mortal blow.

Galileo also contributed to the development of the scientific method.

338

He had not needed to perform any experiments to arrive at the law of falling bodies, and, contrary to legend, he probably never dropped a light and a heavy object from the Leaning Tower of Pisa. Mathematical proof was preferred because with mathematics alone could he remove the extraneous parts of the problem and express his law simply. Bacon and the advocates of induction insisted that such factors as air resistance be considered at the same time, and the problem was thereby made too complex to find a formula readily. An Aristotelian did drop two weights from the tower at Pisa and went away claiming that Aristotle had been right, that the heavier object had landed first. Other factors must have intervened to cause the experiment to go awry. With mathematics, Galileo thought, there could be no mistakes. Therefore, he confidently reduced the universe to mass and motion. Both could be expressed in geometric terms. "Philosophy," he wrote, "is written in the great book which ever lies before our eyes—I mean the universe—but we cannot understand it if we do not first learn the language and grasp the symbols, in which it is written. The book is written in the mathematical language, and the symbols are triangles, circles, and other geometrical figures, without whose help it is impossible to comprehend a single word of it; without which one wanders in vain through a dark labyrinth."

He was drawn to the system of Copernicus and Kepler because they made use of geometric reasoning. "I cannot sufficiently admire," he wrote, "the eminence of those men's wits, that have received and held it to be true, and with the sprightliness of their judgments offered such violence to their own senses, as that they have been able to prefer that which their reason dictated to them, to that which sensible experiments represented most manifestly to the contrary. . . . I cannot find any bounds for my admiration, how that reason was able in Aristarchus and Copernicus, to commit such a rape on their senses, as in spite thereof to make herself mistress of their credulity."

Galileo's preference for mathematical calculations to knowledge derived only from his senses does not mean that he never made use of observation. Indeed, he was the first to use a telescope in astronomical work. He studied the moon and found that it was composed of the same substances as the earth and that it produced no light of its own, but only reflected rays from the sun. He turned his telescope on the sun itself and saw that it had spots. The sun was not a perfect substance, then, and since the spots moved, the sun rotated on its axis in the same direction as the planets moved in their orbits. He found the four satellites of Jupiter and saw that they revolved around the planet. These discoveries confirmed his belief in the heliocentric system and suggested that other heavenly bodies had the same properties as the earth.

In 1632, he published his *Dialogue Concerning the Two Chief Systems of World*. He wrote in Italian to reach a wide audience and doubtless hoped to defeat forever the defenders of Ptolemy. He showed how the rotation of the earth on its axis produced the apparent rotation of the heavens, why an object dropped from a tower will land directly below because it moved eastward with the rotation of the earth at the same speed as the tower, how gravitation prevented objects from being thrown off the whirling earth, and how the stars' great distance from the earth prevented man from being able to see their changed position as the earth moved around the sun. One by one, Galileo answered the objections that had been offered to the Copernican system; at the same time, he pointed out problems that made the continual acceptance of the Ptolemaic system absurd. His work was a success, but he was summoned before the Inquisition at Rome for teaching a doctrine "contrary to Holy Scripture" and was compelled to recant. His book was placed on the Index where it remained until 1822, but it was too late to halt the new astronomy and physics.

The Copernican system with its new theory of motion and its mathematical, deductive method was now enthusiastically accepted by most scientists, although the problem of gravity was not fully solved. As early as 1600, William Gilbert (1540-1603) had published a study in which he argued that gravity was a universal magnetic attraction. The earth, he believed, was a gigantic magnet that attracted the moon, and the moon in turn was a magnet that attracted the earth. When he discovered that a spherical magnet revolved on its axis when placed in a magnetic field, he offered this as an explanation of why the earth and other heavenly bodies rotated on their axes. Kepler accepted many of Gilbert's ideas, and the view that gravity was a universal property became widely accepted. Christian Huygens (1629-1695) explained how the force of gravity, which pulled the planets towards the sun, was counterbalanced by a centrifugal force tending to cause them to leave their orbits on a tangent. It remained, however, for Sir Isaac Newton to discover the law of gravitation. With this discovery, he provided the capstone to the scientific revolution in astronomy and physics. In so doing, however, he ushered in a new era. For this reason, his work will be discussed in the following chapter.

The triumphs achieved by the mathematical method redoubled efforts in the field of mathematics itself, and during the seventeenth century, analytic geometry and calculus were discovered, logarithms and the slide rule were invented, and arithmetical and algebraic symbols were improved and came into common use. The need for accurate measuring instruments led to the invention of the barometer, thermometer, pendulum clock, microscope, telescope, and air pump. These and other discoveries had a profound effect. They influenced philosophy, religion, art, and political thought. As a contemporary wrote, the "geometric spirit is not so exclusively bound to geometry that it could not be separated from it and applied to other fields. A work on ethics, politics, criticism, or even eloquence, other things being equal, is merely so much more beautiful and perfect if it is written in the geometric spirit."

ANATOMY AND PHYSICAL CHEMISTRY

The scientific revolution of the seventeenth century was marked by the waning influence of the ancients, not only in the fields of astronomy and physics, but also in anatomy. Galen, the most revered of the ancient authorities, had taught that one kind of blood flowed from the liver through the veins to all parts of the body, while another kind of blood flowed from the heart through the arteries. The role of the heart as a pump was not recognized, and neither type of blood was thought to return to its original source. It seems strange that such views were still held, since medieval and Renaissance surgeons practiced both human and animal dissection. Their respect for Galen was so great, however, that, when a dissection did not conform with what the ancient master had led them to expect, they assumed that they were wrong. Dissection was thus used to demonstrate known truths rather than to discover new ones.

What the anatomists needed, of course, was accurate observation and a willingness to believe what they saw. Developments in art and scholarship during the Renaissance helped to meet both of these needs. Renaissance artists had studied human anatomy very carefully to make their paintings lifelike and had learned how to depict the smallest details accurately. Although most artists confined their observations to the visible portions of the human body, a few, like Leonardo da Vinci, practiced human dissection and made excellent drawings of what they saw. Later, woodcuts and engravings were used to make anatomical drawings available to many scholars.

Meanwhile, the humanists were giving wider circulation to a greater number of classical authors, and these writings led to the realization that the ancients had often disagreed with one another. Aristotle, for example, gave a more prominent role to the heart in the movement of the blood than Galen had. Gradually, the anatomists found courage to disagree with Galen, just as reading Aristarchus had stimulated Copernicus to challenge Ptolemy.

Andreas Vesalius (1514-1564), a university professor at Padua, was the first anatomist to make an important contribution based on the skill of the artist and the more reliable view of ancient thought derived from the humanists. In 1543, he published *On the Structure of the Human Body,* in which he illustrated the human body section by section and layer by layer. In a few instances, he disagreed with Galen, although on the whole his study fell within the ancient tradition. His greatest contribution was to show that anatomy must be studied by careful dissection and experiment. His work caused an empirical, inductive method in anatomy to replace the commentaries by the ancients just as Copernicus and his successors had substituted a mathematical, deductive method in the fields of astronomy and physics.

William Harvey (1578-1657), an Englishman, took the most important

William Harvey, from a contemporary engraving. (Courtesy of Free Library of Philadelphia)

step in the development of a more modern conception of anatomy by showing how the blood circulated. In 1628, after long years of study at the University of Padua, where Copernicus, Galileo, and Vesalius had found so much inspiration, Harvey published his treatise *On the Motion of the Heart and Blood,* in which he showed how blood was pumped by the heart through the arteries and back again through the veins. The only important omission was his failure to explain how the blood passed from the arteries to the veins, a link that was supplied a generation later when capillaries were found with the aid of a microscope. These discoveries led to the view that the human body, indeed all forms of animal life, was essentially mechanical. Its parts functioned like a well-ordered machine, just as the parts of the universe moved in a previously determined mechanical pattern.

Physical chemistry underwent a similar revolution, although fewer immediate benefits resulted from the overthrow of classical modes of thought. To Aristotle and to most other ancient and medieval authorities, there were four elements—earth, water, air, and fire. This view of the nature of terrestrial substances was challenged during the seventeenth century by Robert Boyle (1627-1691) and a number of scholars who had become enamored of the atomic or corpuscular theory that had been held by Democritus and several other ancient scholars. According to this theory, all substances were composed of solid, tiny atoms or corpuscles, and the

342

different appearances of things were caused by the way in which these invisible atoms were joined together by chance to make visible objects. One important difference between the seventeenth-century corpuscular theorists and their ancient counterparts was that the former believed that the atoms acted in accordance with rational, mechanical laws. Since the atom had extension—the capacity to occupy space—and motion, the whole universe, composed as it was of atoms, must have extension and motion, both mechanical properties subject to mathematical demonstration. Because he advanced this theory, Boyle's name must be added to those of Copernicus, Galileo, Harvey, and others who contributed to the idea of a mechanistic universe.

THE SCIENTIFIC SOCIETIES

During the high Middle Ages, the universities had been the principal seats of learning. During the Renaissance, on the other hand, the literary activities of the humanists were carried on largely outside the universities. At first, scientific inquiry received a better welcome, and so many of the early figures in the scientific revolution were connected with the University of Padua that this institution has a respectable claim to being the birthplace of the movement. The universities as a whole, however, remained strongholds of scholastic thought until near the end of the seventeenth century, and the advocates of the new science had to find new institutions for the extension of knowledge.

At first, those who were interested in science were content to meet in private homes to discuss their common problems and to rely on letters to keep in touch with more distant investigators. Later, during the course of the seventeenth century, scientific societies were formed in which scholars met to exchange ideas and discoveries. The first such group was the *Accademia dei Lincei* of Rome, of which Galileo was a member. *The Royal Society of London for the Promotion of Natural Knowledge* received its charter in 1662, and the French *Académie Royale des Sciences* was formed under the auspices of Colbert shortly thereafter. Soon, every nation had its scientific society; even Russia established one the year after Peter the Great's death. These societies not only stimulated discoveries; they also became centers for gathering and disseminating information through public lectures and through their scientific journals.

Although some of the members of these societies were professional scientists who were supported by patrons or had independent incomes, many were clergymen, physicians, and country gentlemen who combined their interest in science with the practice of other professions. Their presence sometimes lent an air of dilettantism to the proceedings, but their efforts should not be scorned. At this time, only a small amount of knowledge was necessary to make one an authority in a given field and elaborate equipment was not needed for scientific experiments. Many men with original minds, working a few hours each week in their homes, were able to make significant contributions. They and the societies to which they belonged did much to make Europe scientific-minded.

THE INTELLECTUAL REVOLUTION

The revolution in science was paralleled by an equally momentous revolution in philosophy. The sixteenth century had been marked by a conflict between authorities. The Protestant had insisted on his interpretation of the Bible against the authority of the Roman Catholic Church, noble and burgher had pitted their traditional rights and privileges against the growing exactions of the crown, the humanists had revived Plato and hurled him against the Aristotelians. It is not surprising that mild, thoughtful men began to doubt whether any knowledge was certain and whether even certain knowledge justified the persecution and slaughter of dissidents.

MONTAIGNE

The dawning skepticism was admirably personified by the French gentleman, Michel de Montaigne (1533-1592). The France of Montaigne's adult life was torn by the Wars of Religion, but he took no part. He preferred to devote his time to writing his *Essays*, which were first published in 1580, twelve years before his death. He had seen men kill and be killed for their beliefs, and he could not understand how they could be so sure that they were right. He was certain only that "the conviction of wisdom is the plague of man." He had no faith in miracles; it was more likely that those who reported them were lying. He put little emphasis on customs and traditions because he knew that they varied from place to place. He had little faith in reason, for philosophers could reach no agreement. "Should it be true what the Epicureans say, namely, 'That we have no knowledge if the senses represent things falsely'; and also true what the Stoics say, 'That the senses represent things so falsely, that they cannot furnish us with any manner of knowledge,' we shall arrive at the conclusion, to the cost of these two great Dogmatic Schools, that there is no such thing as knowledge." Empiricism, that is, knowledge derived from the senses, he also rejected, for "any man may provide himself with as many examples as he pleases . . . [of how] they play us false." A dog's senses, for example, are more acute than a man's, but a man, he wrote hopefully, has greater knowledge than a dog.

Montaigne's strength was the gentle, humorous way in which he could question the most accepted beliefs without causing anger. His weakness was that he had no real convictions to offer in place of those that he attacked. He could only advise moderation, toleration, and, above all,

Michel de Montaigne, from a contemporary portrait. (Giraudon)

self-examination. Most men of his day wanted to find something more tangible before they abandoned their old beliefs. They discovered it in the mathematical sciences.

DESCARTES

The man most responsible for cementing science to philosophy was René Descartes. Descartes was born in France in 1596 just as the Wars of Religion were coming to an end. After having received a good education from the Jesuits, he served for a brief time with the army of Maximilian of Bavaria in the Thirty Years War. In 1629, he settled in Holland, where he spent most of the remainder of his life. Here, in 1637, he published his *Discourse on Method* and other works in which he explained his new philosophy.

The starting point with Descartes was doubt. Like Montaigne, he asked: "What do I know?" Like Montaigne also, his initial answer was negative. "I found myself embarrassed with so many doubts and errors that it seemed to me the effort to instruct myself had no effect other than the increasing discovery of my own ignorance." Nevertheless, he determined to discard all that was not certain and then construct a new philosophical system on what remained. Philosophy was cast aside because even the greatest philosophers disagreed. The senses were also rejected, because they often deceived. They were not even trustworthy enough to prove the existence of the world or our bodies. Finally, Descartes wrote that "While I wanted to think everything false, it must necessarily be that I who thought was something; and remarking that this truth, *I think, therefore I am*, was so solid and so certain that all the most extravagant supposi-

345

Rene Descartes, by Franz Hals. (Giraudon)

tions of the sceptics were incapable of upsetting it, I judged that I could receive it without scruple as the first principle of the philosophy that I sought." Thus, he took the mind before the senses. Indeed, he divorced the world of ideas from the world of matter. The latter, according to the latest scientific discoveries, consisted only of extension and motion, both easily measurable by the new mathematics. "I thence concluded that I was a substance whose whole essence or nature consists in thinking, and which, that it may exist, has need of no place, nor is dependent on any material thing; so that 'I,' that is to say, the mind by which I am what I am, is wholly distinct from the body, and is even more easily known than the latter, and is such, that although the latter were not, it would still continue to be all that it is."

The mind was thus left free to speculate, to theorize, to engage in "thought experiments" without careful observations. Descartes believed that many of our ideas were *innate*—that is, were born in us. Other ideas come from the outside, but through the action of the mind upon the senses, not of the senses upon the mind. "In truth we perceive no object such as it is by sense alone (but only by our reason exercised upon sensible objects)." Finally, he recognized the existence of ideas "invented by me," that is, those created by his method of thought.

The method advocated by Descartes was mathematical and deductive. He was an excellent mathematician and had invented analytic geometry while still very young. He started with a simple, obvious truth, "I think, therefore I am," and built upward and outward until he produced a new system of thought, just as the mathematician started with the proposition that the shortest distance between two points was a straight line and from there proved a series of theorems and corollaries, proceeding from the simple to the more complex, until first triangles, rectangles, and circles, and finally pyramids, cubes, and spheres could be solved.

What Descartes actually demonstrated with his method was less important than the method itself. He developed a proof for the existence of God, but others had done so more convincingly. He strongly supported the Copernican theory, and in an effort to reconcile it with the Biblical statement that the earth stood still, he argued that the universe was composed of vortices, whirling masses of transparent fluid. The earth is at rest in the center of one vortex, just as there is no motion in the center of a whirlpool, but the moon is in the whirling mass and is carried around the earth. So also are the other planets in the centers of vortices that carry their satellites around them, but the sun is at the center of a huge vortex and the smaller vortices around each planet are carried around it. Thus, the earth remains still in regard to the vortex that surrounds it, but at the same time it is carried around the sun. Both the Bible and Copernicus were correct. This ingenious system was also used by Descartes to explain gravity, the sun spots, and other natural phenomena. It dealt with cause more than the Newtonian system and was widely accepted for several generations, but it was unchecked by actual observation.

Descartes and the Cartesians, as his followers were called, dominated philosophic thought on the continent for the remainder of the seventeenth century. Even great thinkers like Spinoza (1632-1677), who were not formally members of the school and who were more interested in ethics than mathematics, carefully followed deductive, geometric reasoning, complete with definitions, axioms, and theorems.

The impact of the scientific and philosophical revolutions cannot be overestimated. The ancient authorities—Aristotle, Plato, Ptolemy, and Galen—were discredited. Philosophy was divorced from theology and found a new ally in the natural sciences. The scholastic method of reasoning was abandoned in favor of mathematical, deductive arguments. Nature was no longer studied to learn God's will, but to discover its laws. It is true that something had been lost. Man had thought that reason justified his religion, but with each new discovery, religious faith was shaken. Gradually, he was left with a choice of accepting his religious beliefs on faith alone or abandoning many of them. Man had believed that he had been created to enjoy the earth, an earth that was in the center of a small finite universe. Now he learned that his earth was but a tiny planet hurtling around a sun that was itself but a speck in a boundless universe. His dignity had received a terrible blow, but he pressed forward with more optimism than he had known for centuries. Had he not learned that the universe was a mechanical device governed by natural laws? Save for God and man's soul, did it not consist only of mass and movement? Could not the laws governing its actions be discovered by the new scientific method? It was an affirmative answer to these questions that Descartes gave when he made his proud boast: "Give me extension and motion and I will construct the universe."

POLITICAL THOUGHT

Political thought underwent a remarkable period of development during the constitutional crises of the seventeenth century. This development may be attributed to the desire of the supporters of the crown and of the opposition to justify their positions and to the influence of the mathematical, deductive method of the natural sciences.

During the Middle Ages and the Renaissance, society and institutions had been erroneously regarded as permanent and unchanging. Theoretically, there had been no need to alter old laws or to make new laws for new circumstances. Everyone, including kings, was regarded as being under divine law (the law of God), natural law (the law of right reason and universal justice), fundamental law (the law regulating the succession to the throne and other basic constitutional matters), and customary law (the law of property, family, social, and feudal relations).

The king was essentially an executive. He was responsible for the administration of the government, for diplomacy, and for the army. In addition, he was the supreme judge, and justice was administered in his name, but neither he nor anyone else had in theory the right to make laws on fundamental matters. Granted, judicial interpretations and administrative decrees often had the effect of legislating, and kings, especially in conjunction with their estates-general, issued statutes and ordinances on almost every conceivable matter. Nevertheless, the idea of the supremacy of the law was so strong that these actions effected the necessary changes only when there were few important disputes within the body politic. They were altogether inadequate for the revolutionary period that was inaugurated with the Reformation. Kings had to claim new powers to meet the emergency, but nobles and burghers defended their privileges with vigor. The clergy, whether Catholic or Protestant, preached rebellion when the king's interpretation of divine law differed from their own. The result was a constitutional crisis in every major European country.

The monarchs' supporters studied precedents to prove that royal prerogative could be stretched to cover the new circumstances, and they spoke of the divine nature of the kingly estate. The opposition countered with an equally imposing list of precedents to justify its position. To these historical arguments, they added that there had been a contract between the king and the people in which the king had promised to rule justly and the people had sworn to obey him as long as he did so. If the king broke the contract, the people were justified in rebelling.

BODIN AND SOVEREIGNTY

At first, no important theorists saw that kings needed additional power to cope with the situation but that there were limits on how much more authority could be granted to the king without endangering liberty. Then, in 1576, a French lawyer named Jean Bodin (1530-1596) published the *Six Bookes of a Commonweale*. Bodin recognized more clearly than most of his contemporaries that he lived in an age of change. He had been among the first to associate the rise in prices with the influx of precious metals from the New World. He had sought an explanation for the historical process and had written a book with the engaging title *The Method for the Easy Comprehension of History*. In this work, he speculated on the possible relationship between such numbers as the square and cubes of 7 and 9 and historical events. Above all else, he considered the part played by environmental forces, especially geography, climate, and the conjunction of the planets.

Next, Bodin turned to the state to learn what it was and how it was constructed. Especially, he wanted to find a way to strengthen the ruler's power to cope with change without making him a tyrant. His solution lay in a new concept of sovereignty. Sovereignty, he said, was the supreme and perpetual right to make law, not divine, natural, or fundamental law, but customary law and other regulations such as are made by modern legislatures. By definition, the sovereign power could have no earthly superior, and subjects were required to obey all decrees that were not contrary to divine and natural law. In this manner, the king was given the authority to make the necessary regulations to compensate for change. At the same time, he remained subject to the laws of God, right reason and justice, and the constitution. To protect property, Bodin argued that it was a natural right. Hence, the king had no power to tax without the consent of his subjects. Bodin left no doubt on this score. Immediately after the publication of the *Six Bookes of the Commonweale*, he served as deputy in the Estates-General of 1576, where he not only insisted on the right of consent, but also played a leading role in a move not to grant additional taxes.

Bodin's argument that the sovereign authority could make laws received wide acceptance, but his belief that this authority ought to be wielded by a hereditary monarch was often disputed. Rebels cited precedents to show that sovereignty rested with the parliaments, estates, or the corporate body of the people. Royalists, on the other hand, felt the need for order as one civil war followed another. They forgot Bodin's refusal to permit the sovereign to tax and emphasized the divine right of kings. Kings, they argued, were so closely related to God that even if their religion differed from their subjects', rebellion was not justified. "Kings," wrote James I of England, "are not only God's lieutenants upon earth, and sit on God's throne, but even by God himself they are called Gods." In this manner, the late medieval-Renaissance theory of the dual authority of the king and the estates, with the presumption of a degree of cooperation between the two, gave way before the idea that the king and the estates naturally conflict and that one or the other was sovereign.

349

THE DEDUCTIVE THEORISTS: HOBBES AND LOCKE

About the middle of the seventeenth century, the arguments support-ing the sovereignty of either king or parliament began to change. Histori-cal precedents had been used so long by both sides in the debate that they no longer carried much weight. The divine right theory was hardly satisfactory although it remained popular among monarchists until the eighteenth century. A new theory based on more certain grounds was needed, and the mathematical, deductive method that had yielded such gratifying results for the scientists was employed. Most theorists now abandoned history and the Bible in favor of deduction. The deductive process in political theory involved beginning with a basic assumption that was supposed to be self-evident and building outward and upward by use of reason until certain conclusions were reached. To the deductive theorists, the basic assumption was that man had once existed in a state of nature without any government. Depending on how they thought man fared under these conditions, they explained why he joined with others and made a social contract establishing the state. Again, it was the nature of the contract that determined the powers of the ruler and the rights, if any, of the subjects.

The first great deductive theorist was Thomas Hobbes (1588-1679). He was born in the year of the Spanish Armada and was forced into exile during the Puritan Revolution. All his life, he tells us, was spent in fear, and he determined to fashion a political theory that would justify a strong state to prevent further disorder. He had been employed as a tutor in a noble household and had traveled widely on the continent with his charge, meeting many scientists and learning the principles of the new method. In 1651, he published the *Leviathan* to support the Stuart cause.

To Hobbes, men in a state of nature were so nearly equal in mind and body that "the weakest has strength enough to kill the strongest." Every man in his selfish egotism was at war with every other man. For self-protection, it was necessary to join together and form a state. "A *com-monwealth* is said to be *instituted,* when a *multitude* of men do agree, and *covenant, every one, with everyone,* that to whatsoever *man,* or *assembly of men,* shall be given by the major part, the *right* to *present* the person of them all, that is to say, to be their *representative;* every one, as well he that *voted for it,* as he that *voted against it,* shall *authorize* all the actions and judgments, of that man, or assembly of men, in the same man-ner, as if they were his own, to the end, to live peaceable amongst themselves, and be protected against other men.

"From this institution of a commonwealth are derived all the *rights,* and *faculties* of him, or them, on whom sovereign power is conferred by the consent of the people assembled."

Two things should be noticed about this contract. In the first place, the sovereign power was not a party to it. Hence, the sovereign could

John Locke. (Courtesy of Free Library of Philadelphia)

not break the contract, and there could be no justification for rebellion on this score. Second, sovereign power could be given either to a man (the king) or an assembly of men (the Parliament). Hobbes's theory really justified the existing state, not merely monarchical rule. For this reason, and because the Stuarts preferred the divine right theory, the *Leviathan* was not popular among royalists. Eventually, it was used to justify the absolute authority of Parliament.

The great defender of constitutional monarchy was John Locke (1632-1704). In 1690, he published the *Two Treatises on Civil Government* which he had prepared just before the Glorious Revolution as an attack on James II. In the first treatise, he attacked the divine right theory and in the second he offered a deductive theory attacking Hobbes. To Locke, the state of nature was not so black, for it had "a law of Nature to govern it, which obliges every one, and reason, which is that law, teaches all mankind who will but consult it, that being all equal and independent, no one ought to harm another in his life, health, liberty or possessions . . . [for men are] all the workmanship of one omnipotent and infinitely wise Maker. . . ." Among the natural rights that man has in a state of nature was the right to own the things with which he has "mixed his labor." Hence, life, liberty, and property were protected by the law of nature.

The difficulty was that there was no organization in the state of nature to enforce this law. Every man had to protect his own interests. To escape this inconvenience and to preserve "himself, his liberty and property," man bound himself to other men to form a community, each giving his consent and agreeing to accept the will of the majority. This community then established executive, legislative, and judicial authorities. If one or all of these authorities infringed on the life, liberty, or property of the people, the community could get rid of it. The community itself was not dissolved; instead, it now acted to create a new government. Life, liberty, and property were always protected since they were natural rights that existed before the formation of the community. Neither king nor Parliament could deprive a subject of them without consent. When James II threatened the life, liberty, and property of Englishmen, they deposed him and established William and Mary to rule with Parliament in his stead. Locke was often vague and sometimes inconsistent, but he exercised a powerful influence throughout the eighteenth century because he expressed the desire to avoid arbitrary government and to safeguard liberty and property.

THE ARTS

Art, music, and literature passed through three stylistic stages between the Renaissance and the early eighteenth century. As might be expected, these changes were closely related to the political, religious, intellectual, and scientific developments during the period. The Renaissance had seen the classical principles of harmony and balance re-established in the arts, although in the process the unity of the Gothic had been destroyed, and painting, sculpture, and architecture had gone their separate ways. Artists had learned to depict the third dimension; details had been subjected to the larger whole; and beautiful landscapes had replaced the gold backgrounds of the typical two-dimensional medieval paintings. Under the influence of the Platonic revival, artists of the high Italian Renaissance like Raphael had sought a physical beauty superior to that ordinarily found in nature because they thought that it would be a step towards the spiritual beauty of God. So great were their triumphs that there seemed nothing for future artists to learn. Then, beginning in Italy in the early sixteenth century, there was a marked change in aesthetic tastes that brought the Renaissance to an end.

THE MANNERIST REVOLT

The psychological origins of the Mannerist revolt are to be found in the religious revival, with its renewed emphasis on spiritual values, and in the political turmoil that accompanied the Italian wars and the religious revolts. Both added new dimensions to life. The secular gaiety and optimism of the Renaissance were challenged by a growing consciousness

Tintoretto (Jacopo Roliusti) (1518-94), CHRIST AT THE SEA OF GALILEE. *The elongated figure of Christ and the dramatic background clearly denote the Mannerist style. Compare with the Renaissance naturalism of Witz (p. 189) and the medieval Byzantine style of Duccio (p. 185) in their paintings of similar scenes. (National Gallery of Art, Washington, Samuel H. Kress Collection)*

of human suffering. Doubt and uncertainty about this life and the next often accompanied a longing for spiritual experience. The contemplation of a beautiful painting no longer illuminated the divine, and Raphael's Madonnas began to seem superficial. Under such circumstances, artists abandoned the Renaissance style and sought new ways of expressing the changing spirit of their age. They ignored the rules of proportion so admired in the earlier age and made elongated, twisted figures to convey suffering, unresolved tensions, and religious ecstasy. They abandoned the third dimension and in its place made backgrounds intended to dramatize the emotional scene shown in the foreground. The unusual, the bizarre, and the irrational were stressed.

The change to the new mood may be seen in the late works of Michelangelo Buonarroti (1475-1564). Michelangelo began, as we have seen, as a typical artist of the high Renaissance.[1] As a young man, he sought balance, proportion, and beauty of form. He differed from his contemporaries only in his ability and in his love of the heroic, a love that led him to carve and paint huge, muscular figures. Gradually, the religious intensity of the Catholic Reformation caused this thoughtful, emotional man to change his style. Beauty, uniformity, proportion, and space were aban-

[1] See page 195.

353

Michelangelo Buonarroti, LAST JUDGMENT, *Sistine Chapel, Rome. A muscular Christ, in the upper center of the painting, arises to guide mankind while angels below sound the trumpets of doom. On His right the saved rise up to Heaven; on His left demons pull the damned down to Hell. To the left, at His foot, St. Bartholomew holds a layer of skin torn from a human body. On it is the tortured face of Michelangelo. (Alinari-Art Reference Bureau)*

doned. In their place, he created in the Sistine Chapel a "Last Judgment" that was "a picture of bewilderment and despair, a cry for redemption from the chaos which suddenly threatens to swallow up the world of the Renaissance." [2] His last sculptures bore only a partial resemblance to hu-

[2] Arnold Hauser, *The Social History of Art* (New York: Vintage, 1957), II, p. 115.

Michelangelo, PIETA, Florence. This work was done about 1548-55, a full half-century after the Roman PIETA (p. 201). A comparison of the two versions of PIETA shows the difference between the Renaissance and Mannerist styles. In place of the beautiful Mary holding the body of Christ, here His lifeless body is supported by Joseph of Arimathea. On Joseph's face Michelangelo carved his own features. (The figure of Mary Magdalen and the trunk of Christ were polished by a later sculptor.) (Brogi-Art Reference Bureau)

man figures. However, their very de-emphasis of the natural gave these last sculptures an emotional, religious quality that has never been surpassed.

Perhaps the greatest painter of the Mannerist style was the Crete-born, Venetian-trained El Greco (1548?-1614?). El Greco settled in Toledo, where he soon became a favorite artist among the devout Spaniards. He achieved a powerful, emotional, religious effect by painting elongated, curved figures that dominated the foreground. His backgrounds were not the pretty landscapes of the Renaissance; they often lacked depth, and when he made a genuine effort to create a third dimension, he did so in a manner that stressed the supernatural, the weird, and the emotional. Nature was used to help create the mood. It was assigned no value in its own right.

The preference for the emotional in lieu of balance, proportion, and order was also reflected in literature. The knightly romance was revived, for the adventures of knights and the trials of kings were more dramatic than the activities of ordinary men. The epic poem, featuring the adventures of heroes of high station, flourished once more. The theater became more popular, for it provided one of the most suitable media for expressing the dramatic and the emotional. Murders and battles took place on stage, ghosts and witches abounded. The tragic, the pathetic, and the horrible were united with the buffooneries of clowns and valets. Truth and fantasy were interwoven as never before. We have only to think of John Webster's (1580?-1625?) *The Tragedy of the Duchess of Malfi;* of Christopher Marlowe's (1564-1593) *Tamburlaine the Great, Doctor Faustus,* and *The Jew of Malta;* or of any one of a number of William Shakespeare's (1564-1616) later plays, such as *Hamlet, Macbeth, Othello,* and *King Lear,* to recognize both the greatness and the melodramatic qualities of the manneristic stage. Lope de Vega (1562-1635), the great Spanish playwright, wrote at this time in much the same vein.

Nowhere in literature, however, was the Manneristic style more apparent than in Miguel de Cervantes' (1547-1616) *Don Quixote.* Too often, *Don Quixote* has been interpreted only as a satire on chivalry. Every school child has laughed at this story of a knight who tilted with windmills, but it should be remembered that there were similarities between the careers of Don Quixote and his creator. Cervantes was a poor Spanish nobleman who served as a common soldier in the armies of his king. He fought in Italy, was badly wounded at Lepanto in the great victory over the Turks, and spent five years as a prisoner of the North African pirates. Like Spain, he had answered the call of chivalry, dynastic loyalty, and the Church; like Spain, the quest of an ideal had left him broken and ruined. In *Don Quixote,* Cervantes depicted the clash between the idealistic and the real, the romantic and the rational. He never really decided which side he favored but wavered back and forth between the two extremes. His own aspirations and dreams were those of the knight, while his common sense drew him towards Don Quixote's practical squire,

El Greco, ST. MARTIN AND THE BEGGAR. (*National Gallery of Art, Washington, Widener Collection*)

Sancho Panza. It has been said that in literature "Before Cervantes there had been only good and bad characters, deliverers and traitors, saints and blasphemers," [3] but in Don Quixote we have the saint and the fool in one and the same person. The result is an emotional and psychological study that rivals the best of Mannerist art. Like Mannerist art, the book is unbalanced and lacks uniformity and proportion. Many of the details related are unnecessary, tensions are created only to be left unresolved, and it is even carelessly written. Yet Don Quixote emerges, even in his most ridiculous acts, as a man of dignity and pathos.

Manneristic music possessed many of the traits found in the other arts. Here, too, the stylistic unity, proportion, harmony, and restraint of the Renaissance were abandoned. Music, like painting, became emotional. Composers sought to convey violent pain or extreme joy. They loved the monumental, the dramatic, the elaborate. In place of an even flow of beats, they substituted rhythmic extremes, and there was an extraordinary desire for dissonance. Vocal music was preferred to instrumental music, and passionate arias were much admired.

THE BAROQUE SYNTHESIS

The second stylistic stage of this period was the Baroque. It originated in Italy shortly before 1600 and spread to the rest of Europe just as the Renaissance and Mannerist styles had done. The artists of this period sought to reconcile the classical traditions of Renaissance art with the spiritual dimensions of the religious revival. In this search, they found allies among the Jesuits, who, as we have seen, were seeking to reconcile the classical learning of the Renaissance with the teachings of their Church and the religious inspiration of their founder. The Jesuits were the first to build their churches in the Baroque style, and so closely were the two movements associated that the Baroque has sometimes been called Jesuit art. The Catholic reform movement, as a whole, soon adopted the Baroque style. The Protestants were also frequently influenced.

The Baroque artists were more conscious of science than their predecessors had been. The theory that the universe was infinite caused them to try to impart a sense of infinite space to their works, and the theory that the earth moved without any visible aid around the sun caused them to make paintings, even statues, that seemed to float without visible support. Knowing that the earth did not stand still, they sought to convey a sense of movement.

The artists also tried to combine painting, sculpture, and architecture into a single artistic expression. Their churches and their palaces ceased to be buildings that merely contained paintings and statues, as they had been in the Renaissance. Instead, the three forms of art were blended into a larger whole for the first time since the decline of the Gothic style.

[3] *Ibid.,* II, p. 147.

Façade of IL GESÙ, *Rome, the first Baroque church, was built around 1575 by the Jesuits, who did so much to blend the Renaissance with the religious revival. Classical—and Renaissance—elements such as columns and pilasters abound; yet a certain austerity prevails. Classical rules are frequently violated by such devices as double columns and double pilasters; yet the unity of the whole is maintained. (Alinari-Art Reference Bureau)*

Painters and sculptors emphasized the material by abandoning the elongated, twisted figures of the Mannerists and by representing the human form in its natural proportions. A sense of wealth and grandeur was imparted by the monumental size of their works and by the use of rich, sensuous pigments and brightly colored marble. In this respect, no painter achieved greater success than Peter Paul Rubens (1577-1640), who spent most of his career at the court of the Spanish Netherlands. He loved to paint ponderous bodies in violent motion. A wild hunting scene, a triumphant royal entry, or a tale from classical mythology gave him the type of subject that he most enjoyed. He was particularly famous for the flesh of his voluptuous nudes, which were enhanced by his use of light and shadow. A host of Dutch artists painted landscapes, still lifes, and portraits with a naturalness never before achieved.

The spiritual dimension was achieved in various ways. Some artists, like the Dutchman Rembrandt van Rijn (1606-1669), tried to communicate spiritual meaning through their portrait studies. By the use of somber backgrounds and by an interplay of light and shadows on the faces of his subjects, Rembrandt gave them a thoughtful, introspective character that reflected man's spiritual nature. Others tried to achieve the spiritual by denying the material, or at least by disguising the true nature of the artistic medium. Figures in paint and marble were made to float on clouds, and stone draperies were carved that seemed to blow in the wind. Wood and stucco were colored to simulate marble, and ceilings were painted that seemed to be continuations of the walls of churches or openings into heaven.

The scientific concept of infinite space was conveyed through a new type of perspective. Renaissance depth had been cone shaped; it caused the observer to restrict his field of vision as he looked further into the background of a painting. Baroque perspective was nearly the reverse. After an initial period of contracted vision, the observer was suddenly permitted to expand his vision in every direction to give a sense of the infinite. The Renaissance painter had preferred line to color so that the objects he drew were clearly defined. Baroque painters put more emphasis on color, and objects were blurred in order to have no exact beginning or ending. As a result, the observer received the impression of something moving, yet immeasurable and infinite. The exterior façades and the interior ceilings of most Renaissance buildings had been relatively flat, but Baroque architects often used columns to give the exterior of their buildings greater depth and to blur the point where the façade actually began. Rounded and domed ceilings were often employed to give a similar effect in the interior. Sometimes exterior walls were made to curve in and out to give a sense of movement, while clouds and blue sky were painted in every ceiling to give a sense of opening out into infinite space. Gushing water added both sound and movement, and Rome, the city of the Baroque, was also Rome, the city of fountains.

The greatest figure of the Baroque was Lorenzo Bernini (1598-1680). Both as a sculptor and as an architect, Bernini was without equal, and a description of several of his most famous works will do much to indicate the nature of the Baroque synthesis. When asked to design a square in front of the basilica of St. Peter's in Rome, he planned a giant ellipse comparable to the shape of the planetary orbits. It was bounded by a gallery supported by four huge columns through which the pilgrims going to the sacred shrine passed. As they approached, each view they caught of the basilica from the colonnade seemed more grand, for the columns channeled their vision along a fixed path until it broke forth in every direction onto the square and basilica after passing the last columns. If the pilgrim stood in the middle of the square that seemed to open its arms and engulf all mankind, he was not confronted with a solid row of buildings but with a series of columns casting shadows in the midst of the natural light that penetrated. The whole effect suggested endless space.

The interior of the basilica provided more problems for Bernini to solve. A gigantic dome had been placed over the tomb of St. Peter and in the vast space between the two there was only an altar. To fill the gap

Lorenzo Bernini, BALDACCHINO, *St. Peter's, Rome.* (*Alinari-Art Reference Bureau*)

Bernini determined to place a baldachin. A baldachin is a canopy of cloth used to cover the sacrament in religious processions, but the canopy that Bernini prepared to cover the altar of St. Peter's was supported by four tall twisted columns that carry the observer's eyes upward in a rhythmical movement. The canopy at the top was made of bronze that seemed to blow back and forth in response to gentle breezes like the flimsiest cloth.

The reliquary constructed by Bernini to hold the chair that St. Peter

Lorenzo Bernini, ST. PETER'S CHAIR, *St. Peter's Cathedral, Rome.*
(*Alinari-Art Reference Bureau*)

was believed to have used provides another example of the Baroque synthesis. The lower half of the composition represented the Church of this
world and the upper half represented the spiritual world that was to
come. The former was accomplished by making statues of the Church
fathers; the latter, by a large window with a dove at the center representing
the Holy Ghost. The natural light from the window mixed with sculptured
shafts of golden light radiating out in every direction. A sense of
movement from the material to the spiritual was provided by clouds that

362

Lorenzo Bernini, ST. THERESA IN ECSTASY, *Santa Maria della Vittoria.*
(*Alinari-Art Reference Bureau*)

billowed upward from beneath the reliquary which was shaped like an
armchair. The reliquary itself seemed to be supported more by the clouds
than by the Church fathers. All was movement. Angels and cherubs alike
were animated.

Bernini's greatest work was not for the basilica of St. Peter but for the

363

little Roman church of Santa Maria della Vittoria, where he combined painting, sculpture, and architecture to provide a visual representation of the vision of St. Theresa. In her writings, the Spanish mystic had told how a beautiful angel had stabbed her with a golden spear and left her "completely afire with the great love of God. The pain was so sharp that it made me utter several moans; and so excessive was the sweetness caused me by the intense pain that one can never wish to lose it." In Bernini's conception, the angel and the saint swooning in ecstasy are seen floating on a cloud that is being carried upward by a breeze that is ruffling her garments. A hidden window sheds light upon the scene, but the efforts of nature are augmented by shafts of golden light supplied by the sculptor. Some unsympathetic observers have referred to the work as an immoral bedroom scene, but to the Baroque, sacred and profane love, the spiritual and the material, were joined together in a new synthesis.

Bernini's pupil, Giovanni Battista Gaulli (1639-1709), carried his master's teachings into painting. With his brush, Gaulli caused the ceiling of a chapel in the church of II Gesù in Rome to open into heaven where the cherubs and the elect soar upward on billowing clouds and the fallen angels and the damned tumble earthward in despair. Architectural and sculptural elements were integrated with the painting. Some of the damned were statues on the wall, some were paintings on the ceiling. The effect is too theatrical for many, but the work involved a superb knowledge of perspective and was a splendid synthesis of the arts.

In Baroque music, as in Baroque art, the violent emotions of the Mannerists were curbed and an effort was made to combine an intensity of feeling with a sense of harmony. Dissonance was restrained and polyphony declined in favor of balance and melody. The imposition of logic and unity did not detract from the grandeur and power of the music of the period. Indeed, the Baroque opened a new musical age whose most glorious contribution was the opera.

The Italian Claudio Monteverdi (1567-1643) was the first great operatic composer. His musical career began at the ducal court of Mantua and ended at Venice, where for thirty years he held the important post of choirmaster at St. Mark's Cathedral. Much of his voluminous musical output was Mannerist, but his *Orfeo*, the first great opera, was essentially Baroque.

The opera, like Baroque art, was overly theatrical, but it too marked the achievement of a new synthesis. Voice and instrumental music, acting, elaborate stage settings, and glittering costumes were merged into an aesthetic whole. Success was immediate, and the opera quickly spread to all of Europe.

Literature also saw a movement away from the emotional disunity of the Manneristic style under the influence of a renewed interest in classicism and the growing popularity of the salon. The salon was a fashionable assemblage of statesmen, great nobles, and their wives, who met with writers

Giovanni Battista Gaulli, THE WORSHIP OF THE HOLY NAME OF JESUS, *Il Gesù, Rome. (Alinari-Art Reference Bureau)*

and artists to discuss literature, painting, sculpture, and music and to practice the art of polite conversation. Among the most famous of the early salons was that of Catherine de Vivonne, Marquise de Rambouillet. In 1613, the Marquise, who was part Italian, withdrew from the French court, which she regarded as uncouth, and began to receive her cultivated friends in her Paris home. Her salon also served as her bedroom, and madame received her guests, seated on her bed but separated from them by a railing. Under these conditions, the violence and crudity of the early period had to be abandoned. The delicate analysis of sentiments, the elegant, and the witty were preferred. The salon served to educate a select element of the great nobility and their wives before the royal court was ready to take the lead. The salon led to the pageant of Versailles.

On the whole, the literature of the Baroque was inferior to that of the preceding periods in Italy, Spain, and England, but the last country did produce John Milton (1608-1674) and his Baroque masterpiece *Paradise Lost*. Gone were the excessive emotionalism, disunity, and unresolved tensions of the Mannerists. In their place, was a dignified, harmonious epic, but one in which none of the grandeur and power of the original story was lost.

THE LATE BAROQUE

The third stylistic stage of the period was the late Baroque. The earlier post-Gothic styles had originated in Italy; the late Baroque began in the France of Louis XIV. France clearly replaced Italy as the cultural leader of Europe at the same time that it became the most powerful nation on the continent. In many respects, the late Baroque was a continuation of the Baroque itself, but it marked the triumph of the rational concepts of the classical period and of the new mathematical, deductive science. Simplicity, balance, and harmony became the norm; the emotional and sensuous were reduced to secondary importance.

The nature of the new style is best shown by the rules of the French Academy of Painting and Sculpture. This academy taught that the artists of antiquity should be imitated and that the teachings of the new sciences should be followed. The scientists, as we have seen, had a marked preference for the rational, mathematical, and deductive over material gathered by the senses. Descartes had scorned the empirical and preferred innate ideas to those derived from the senses. Translated into art, this preference meant that nature was to be consulted with caution only. For this reason, artists made sketches and models to help in the arrangement of the figures. Live models and nature were rarely employed, for they were subject to imperfections that would have to be corrected. Correct drawing was the highest merit because it made for definite shapes and forms that were essentially geometric. Color, because it is sensuous, was of secondary importance and not to be exaggerated. Gone were the thick, bright paints of Rubens and the interplay between light and shadow that had given a sense of the infinite in the Baroque. In the new style, objects were clear; a definite line distinguished one from another. The Baroque conception of grandeur and power was preserved in that only noble subjects were supposed to be painted—those from the classical poets, the his-

Nicolas Poussin (1594-1665), FUNERAL OF PHOCION, *Louvre, Paris. This French-born artist spent most of his adult life in Rome, where he developed a style that was greatly admired by the French Academy of Painting and Sculpture, the rules of which conformed to his precepts. (Agrari-Art Reference Bureau)*

torians, or perhaps a version of Louis XIV crossing the Rhine. Violent emotions were to be avoided, and good taste was always to be used.

The mathematical conceptions of the era were also revealed in the formal garden of Versailles. Galileo had said that the universe "is written in the mathematical language, and the symbols are triangles, circles, and other geometrical figures, without whose help it is impossible to comprehend a single word of it; without which one wanders in vain through a dark labyrinth." Trees at Versailles were trimmed to form arches, shrubs were clipped to make pyramids and cones, flowers were planted to depict geometric patterns. Nature was corrected to conform to man's conception of the universe. In the Cartesian era, the gardener was no more willing to copy nature than the artist.

Literature was also subjected to a classical, Cartesian influence. The polished, clever, and correct were admired more than the elaborate, emotional, and imaginative. This preference for style over originality was admirably expressed by Alexander Pope when he wrote:

> *True wit is Nature to advantage dressed,*
> *What oft was thought but ne'er so well expressed.*

Comedies were to be clever. Characters might be exaggerated a little, but they were nevertheless to be real. The vulgarity and buffoonery of an earlier day were frowned upon. Tragedy was also changed; murder and vio-

THE GARDEN AT VERSAILLES. *Painting by J. B. Martin in Versailles Museum.* (*Bettmann Archive*)

lence were removed from the stage, and a strict connection between scenes was required. Plots were not to be complicated, and miraculous endings were avoided. Reason and social concepts such as duty, loyalty, and honor were usually depicted as triumphing over passion, just as the philosopher taught the superiority of the mind over the senses. Even poetry was denied sensuous beauty; it lived on pure reason, on balance and correct form.

The literary style of the late Baroque may have stifled the originality of all but exceptional geniuses like Molière (1622-1673) and Racine (1639-1699), but its overall effect was good. Interests in correct usage led to a marked improvement in various languages. The French Academy set itself to the task of "purifying the language of the filth which it has gathered either in the mouths of the people, or in the mob of the Palais de Justice, or in the impurities of chicane, or by the bad usage of ignorant courtiers, or by the abuse of writers and preachers who say the right thing in the wrong way." The result was a two-volume dictionary, published in 1687-1691, which standardized vocabulary and spelling. Many words were dropped from the language, and to this day an unabridged French dictionary has fewer entries than a similar dictionary in English. Meanwhile, men like John Dryden (1631-1700) and Alexander Pope (1688-1744) had done much to discipline their native English literature. It was only with the late Baroque era that the vulgar, or vernacular, languages became as precise and clear as Latin. The language of the Romans no longer had to be used by those who needed to express complex philosophical and scientific ideas, and by the dawn of the eighteenth century it was nearly abandoned as a normal medium of expression.

Music, too, submitted to the classical and the mathematical. Descartes, Galileo, and others believed that music depended on mathematical prin-

Garden of the Tuileries in 1680. The geometric design of this garden, then on the outskirts of Paris, is immediately apparent. (Bettmann Archive)

ciples. To the German philosopher, Leibnitz, music was "the arithmetic of a mind unconscious that it is reckoning." Rational explanations were sought for pleasant sounds. As a result, still more of the emotional content of Manneristic music was removed. Instrumental music, because it was more subject to control, dominated vocal music, which had a more personal quality. Rhythm became more mechanical, tonality became fully established, and chord progressions and dissonance treatment were regularized. The technique of writing musical scores was improved and served to standardize musical performances, just as the new dictionaries standardized the vulgar languages. Superb instruments were constructed that challenged the creative genius of the composers. Indeed, the late Baroque marked the culmination of a century of rapid development, and in Bach and Handel a high point in musical history was reached.

Johann Sebastian Bach (1685-1750) was born at Eisenach near the heart of the Luther country. Both a composer and a performer, Bach was appointed organist or director of chamber music in several German churches and courts. In 1723, he became cantor at Leipzig, where he remained until his retirement in 1745, five years before his death. His position with various churches and his own devout nature caused most of his work to have a religious theme. His output was tremendous; yet his genius was such that even the most complicated pieces were organized with mathematical exactness. In him, the complex polyphony of the earlier period was reconciled with the simple monody usually preferred by the Baroque. Perhaps his most famous composition was the *Passion According to St. Matthew*.

George Frederick Handel (1685-1759) was born in Germany and

369

trained in Italy but spent most of his life in England, where he directed an opera company. Unlike Bach, Handel was a temperamental man who successfully sought international fame. He did much to popularize opera and oratorio in England. Although he frequently made use of religious subjects, he was essentially a humanist. Though differing from Bach in temperament and interests, Handel was equally capable of composing complicated pieces that were both balanced and clear. Polyphony was one of his most effective tools.

Thus art, literature, and music returned to the classical ideal after the Mannerist revolt, just as many states emerged stronger after the constitutional crisis. Yet, just as the monarchy of Louis XIV differed from that of Francis I, so the classicism in the art, literature, and music of the late Baroque differed from that of the late Renaissance. Part of the difference was due to the scientific and philosophical revolution, part to the accumulated experience available in the later epoch, and part to the diverse genius of great men.

PART IV

THE AGE OF THE
EGALITARIAN REVOLUTIONS

AMERICA	WESTERN EUROPE	EASTERN EUROPE
		1682-1725, Reign of Peter the Great of Russia
	1690, Locke's *Essay Concerning Human Understanding*	
c.1715-c.1775, Development of colonies and of trade with mother countries	**c.1715-c.1800,** Era of the Enlightenment; orthodox Christianity weakened; growth of Deism; economic revival; agricultural improvements; increase in population	
	1733, Voltaire's *Letters on the English*	**1733-1735,** War of Polish Succession
	1738, Conversion of John Wesley	
	1740, War of Austrian Succession begins	
	1740-1786, Reign of Frederick the Great	
		1741-1762, Reign of Elizabeth of Russia
	1748, Montesquieu's *Spirit of Laws*	
	1751-1772, Diderot's *Encyclopedia*	
	1754-1762, Period of Rousseau's greatest works	
	1756-1761, Pitt the elder Secretary of State	
	1756-1763, Seven Years War	
	c.1760, Industrial Revolution begins	
		1762-1796, Reign of Catherine the Great of Russia
		1772, First partition of Poland

AMERICA	WESTERN EUROPE	EASTERN EUROPE
1773, Boston Tea Party		
1774, First Continental Congress	1774-1792, Reign of Louis XVI	
1775-1783, American War of Independence		
1776, Declaration of Independence	1776, Adam Smith's *Wealth of Nations*	
	c.1780, Kant becomes increasingly influential	
	1783-1801, Pitt the younger's first ministry	
1789, U.S. Constitution adopted	1789, French Revolution begins; meeting of Estates-General; fall of Bastille; Declaration of the Rights of Man	1789-1807, Reign of Selim III of Turkey
	1789-1791, National Assembly	
	1792, First French Republic	
	1792-1795, The National Convention	
1793, Invention of cotton gin; cotton and slavery more important to South	1794, Fall of Robespierre	1793, Second partition of Poland
	1795, The Directory	1795, Third partition of Poland
	1799-1804, The Consulate	
1801-1835, John Marshall Chief Justice of Supreme Court		1801-1825, Reign of Alexander I of Russia
1803, Louisiana Purchase		
	1804-1814,The First Empire	
	1806, Holy Roman Empire abolished	
	1808, Goethe publishes first part of *Faust*	
	1809-1848, Metternich foreign minister of Austria	
1812, War with Great Britain begins		1812, Napoleon invades Russia
	1813, Battle of Leipzig	
	1814, Bourbon restoration	
	1814-1815, Congress of Vienna	
	1815, Battle of Waterloo	1815, Alexander I of Russia becomes king of Poland
	c.1815-1850, Age of Romanticism; conservatism is dominant; great powers suppress nationalism and liberalism	
1816-1825, Spanish colonies in Latin America win independence; political instability follows		
c.1820, Brazil becomes independent monarchy		
		1822-1829, Greek war for independence
1823, Monroe Doctrine		
	1824-1830, Reign of Charles X of France	
1829-1837, Jackson President		1829, Treaty of Adrianople; Greece becomes independent and Serbia autonomous
	1830-1831, Revolutions in France, Belgium, Italy, and Germany	
	1832, Reform Bill in England	
	1833, Slaves in British Empire freed	
	1837-1901, Reign of Victoria	
1846-1848, Mexican War	1848, Revolutions in France, Germany, Austria, and Italy	
	1852, Louis Napoleon becomes Napoleon III	

THE Renaissance had witnessed the triumph of naturalism in art, and the seventeenth-century crisis had seen the scientific revolution. In both ages, European civilization had expanded, literacy had increased, the printing press had disseminated more information, and the vernacular languages had developed, although classical languages enjoyed an important role in education. Earlier ideas and characteristics, however, remained dominant in most fields, and fundamental problems remained unsolved. People still thought in terms of a hierarchy of social classes, each with its special rights, privileges, and obligations, rather than in terms of natural rights and natural laws that applied equally to all persons. Their loyalties were to their towns, provinces, and ruling dynasties rather than to nation-states or their fellow citizens. For their utopias, they still looked back to the glory of Greece and Rome rather than forward to an era of greatness. Their goal was stability, not progress. The food supply limited the population; and until the productivity of farmers increased, the percentage of the population engaged in manufacturing could not increase. This situation was a factor in halting economic growth in the early fourteenth century and the Renaissance economic revival in the early seventeenth century. Until the problem was solved, the European civilization would continue to undergo the same long periods of stagnation that have beset other civilizations.

This situation changed in the eighteenth and nineteenth centuries. The scientific revolution was followed by a period of agricultural experimentation that greatly increased the food supply and made urbanization and industrialization possible to an extent hitherto unknown. Increased productivity led to a rise in the standard of living and enabled the middle class to replace the landed aristocracy as the leaders of the various nations.

Equally important, the growing belief that the mind of man was devoid of ideas at birth gave rise to the theory that all men were created equal and were capable of being molded by their environment. The hierarchical conception of society was discredited, and the idea that social and moral progress could be achieved by creating the proper environment gradually replaced the older desire for stability and order. At first, the proper environment was thought to be one in which everyone could exercise his natural rights and obey governmental regulations that were made in accordance with natural law. Gradually, the concept was expanded to include democracy and the right of each nationality to govern itself. To secure this environment, there were numerous revolts, and the period that began near the close of the seventeenth century when the new ideas began to germinate and ended with the Revolution of 1848 may be thought of as the age of the egalitarian revolutions.

373

9/ The Era of the Enlightenment, I

THE seventeenth century had been a century of crisis. For a time, it had seemed possible that the progress of the European civilization would cease and that this civilization would become static like those in other parts of the world. Amidst all the wars and revolutions during the latter part of the century, however, scientific and philosophical progress was taking place, new procedures were being developed in banking and agriculture, and efforts were being made to prevent the sufferings of wars. These developments were carried forward at an accelerated rate during the eighteenth century. The spirit of humanitarianism and cosmopolitanism became more common, and men began to advocate that progress and human perfection were not only possible but inevitable. With this spirit of optimism, the modern European civilization was born. The new age called itself the Enlightenment. For nearly two centuries, its ideals, in one form or another, dominated European thought, and so much material progress was achieved that, by comparison, the inhabitants of the most advanced non-European civilizations were reduced to the role of backward peoples.

SCIENCE AND PHILOSOPHY

NEWTON AND LOCKE

The new optimism was based on the scientific discoveries of Sir Isaac Newton and the philosophical works of John Locke. Great as had been the contributions of Galileo and Descartes during the first half of the seventeenth century, the new mathematical science was beset by one dangerous threat and embarrassed by one notable failure. The threat was the tendency to make glittering hypotheses and then to fail to check them by experiment, or even to hold to them after empirical evidence pointed to the contrary. The "thought experiments" of Galileo were a powerful weapon in the hands of a natural scientist of genius, but they could prove dangerous in the hands of less able men—and philosophers. A safer, scientific method was needed. The failure of the mathematical scientists lay in their inability to discover the law regulating and controlling the universe. The planets and the earth were believed to have common properties and to be governed by common forces, but these properties and forces must be found and reduced to a mathematical formula. It was for Sir Isaac Newton to find a compromise between the mathematical method of Galileo and the need to observe and experiment. It was for Sir Isaac Newton to discover the law governing the universe.

Newton was born in England in 1642 and graduated from Cambridge early in 1665. In the two years that followed, he invented calculus, discovered the law of the composition of light, and formulated the law of gravitation, all by the time he was twenty-four. Although Newton did not publish his findings immediately, he lived long enough to see his ideas accepted by the scientific world. Few men have been so honored in their lifetime. He was knighted in 1705, and served as president of the Royal Society for twenty-four years. He died in 1727 and was buried in Westminster Abbey.

Great as Newton's genius was, he was indebted to his predecessors. "If I have seen farther [than other men]," he wrote, "it is because I have stood upon the shoulders of giants." These giants included not only Copernicus, Galileo, and the mathematical scientists, but also Bacon, Boyle, and the empirical scientists who were more highly regarded in England than on the continent. Newton combined the best features of each when he formulated his own scientific method. He shared with Galileo the belief in the simplicity of nature and the desire to explain phenomena mathematically, but he recognized that nature could not be reduced to geometry, for geometry was only a tool for finding out about nature. Although he formulated his law of gravitation mathematically, he insisted that one begin with direct observations rather than general assumptions and that every hypothesis be verified by experiments.

Newton published his greatest work, *Mathematical Principles of Natural Philosophy*, in 1687. In it, he explained a mathematical method for measuring the force exerted by objects moving at different speeds and

Sir Isaac Newton at the age of 60. Portrait by Sir Godfrey Kneller. (National Portrait Gallery)

in different directions and orbits. He then showed that these rules not only applied to the earth, but also to the entire universe. He studied the motion of the satellites of Jupiter and Saturn, of the planets, and finally of the moon, whose gravity caused tides just as the earth's gravity held the moon in its orbit. Even Galileo had attributed tides to the shaking of the earth as it rotated on its axis and moved around the sun. Now all seemed clear. Newton had produced a mechanical universe and explained it in mathematical terms. He was soon regarded as the greatest genius that had ever lived. As one eighteenth-century scientist put it, "There is but one universe and it can happen to but one man in the world's history to be the interpreter of its laws." Or as Alexander Pope wrote:

> *Nature and Nature's laws lay hid in night;*
> *God said, Let Newton be! and all was light.*

So important were Newton's scientific discoveries that his method was widely adopted in England. Soon, his followers were criticizing the continental Cartesians for failing to prove their hypotheses by actual observation. Especially did the vortices theory come under attack.[1] "If," Roger Cotes wrote in his preface to the second edition of Newton's *Principles*, "they could explain the phenomena ever so accurately by their hypotheses, we could not yet say that they have discovered true philosophy, and the true causes of the celestial motions, unless they could either demonstrate that those causes do actually exist, or, at least, that no other do exist." We

[1] See page 347.

must not seek the laws of nature, he wrote, "from uncertain conjectures, but learn them from observations and experiments. He who thinks to find the true principles of physics and the laws of natural things by the force alone of his own mind, and the internal light of his reason, must either suppose that the world exists by necessity, and by the same necessity follows the laws proposed; or, if the order of Nature was established by the will of God, that himself, a miserable reptile, can tell what was fittest to be done."

Popularizers expounded the new science to the public. One explained Newton to those "who have not studied mathematics," another did so in verse for those who were poetically inclined, and still another wrote a special treatment for ladies. "Very few people read Newton," Voltaire said, "because it is necessary to be learned to understand him. But *everybody talks about him.*" By mid-eighteenth century, the Cartesians had been routed, and the inductive, experimental method had become more important than the deductive, mathematical one.

The victory of induction was greatly aided by John Locke. In 1690, he published *An Essay Concerning Human Understanding.* The *Essay* was a vigorous attack on the Cartesians. Like Descartes, Locke sought to prove his existence. "As for our own existence, we perceive it so plainly and so certainly that it neither needs nor is capable of any proof. For nothing can be more evident to us than our own existence. *I think, I reason, I feel pleasure and pain:* can any of these be more evident to me than my own existence. If I doubt of all other things, that very doubt makes me perceive my own existence, and will not suffer me to doubt of that. For if I know *I feel pain,* it is evident I have as certain perception of mine own existence as the existence of the pain I feel; or if I know I doubt, I have as certain perception of the existence of the thing doubting, as of that thought which I call doubt. Experience, then, convinces us that we have an intuitive knowledge of our own existence, and an internal infallible perception that we are. In every act of *sensation, reasoning, or thinking,* we are conscious to ourselves of our own being, and in this matter, come not short of the highest degree of certainty." [2]

To Descartes' "I think, therefore I am," Locke had added the senses. Man's capacity to reason was accepted, but it followed sensation just as Newton's mathematics was but a tool of induction. There was no room for thought completely independent of sensation. There could, therefore, be no innate ideas. "Let us then suppose," Locke wrote, "the mind to be, as we say, white paper, void of all characters, without any ideas; how comes it to be furnished? Whence comes it by that vast store, which the busy and boundless fancy of man has painted on it with an almost endless variety? Whence has it all the materials of reason and knowledge? To this I answer, in one word, from *experience.* In that all our knowledge is founded, and from that it ultimately derives itself. Our observation, employed

[2] Book IV, Chapter 9. The italics are added.

377

either about external sensible objects, or about the internal operations of our minds, perceived and reflected by ourselves, is that which supplies our understandings with all the materials of thinking. These two are the fountains of knowledge, from whence all the ideas we have, or can naturally have, do spring." [3] Descartes and, for that matter, nearly all philosophers from the time of Plato were reversed. The mind did not act on the senses; instead, the senses acted on the mind. Man was not master of his environment. Environment was the master of man.

THE EXPERIMENTAL SCIENCES

The results of the acceptance of Newton and Locke were far-reaching. Mathematics and the mathematical sciences became less important. By 1754, a leading authority could "dare almost assert that in less than a century we shall not have three great geometers left in Europe." Fortunately, he proved to be incorrect, but there were no developments in mathematics, or for that matter in astronomy and physics, comparable to those of the preceding period. On the other hand, the inductive sciences, those in which great masses of data must be collected by observation and experiment before satisfactory conclusions can be reached, flourished. Chemistry was at last firmly established on a scientific basis. In 1766, air began to be broken into its component parts; first hydrogen and then oxygen and other gases were discovered. The Aristotelian concept of the four elements, earth, air, fire, and water, was forever discredited. Antoine Lavoisier (1743-1794) became the true father of modern chemistry. In a useful life that was tragically cut short during the French Revolution by the guillotine, he explained combustion and respiration and formulated the law that matter could be neither created nor destroyed. In his numerous experiments, he made full use of quantitative analysis, and this branch of chemistry is especially indebted to him.

Biology was also scientifically studied and systematized. As early as 1694, the sexuality of plants was discovered, when pollen was correctly identified as the male and the ovary as the female element. The Swede Carl Linnaeus (1707-1778) studied both plant and animal life. He developed our modern system of classification according to family or related groups. The cat and the related lion were grouped together as felines in the still larger category of mammals. A French scientist, George, Count of Buffon (1707-1788), made use of his post of keeper of the royal garden to observe plants and animals. The result was his thirty-six volume *Natural History*, in which he made many pertinent and some foolish observations. He recognized the relationship between man and the ape and considered the possibility of evolution, only to reject it. Other scientists were still more insistent that man was merely an animal. To the most advanced thinkers, he lost his once proud position as the only creature capable of

[3] Book II, Chapter 1. The italics are added.

reasoning and endowed with a soul. Like other animals, he was governed by his instincts and his environment.

The study of medicine also improved, in spite of some prejudice against human dissection. The practice of inoculation against smallpox was imported from the East at the beginning of the eighteenth century, but since it involved taking the disease from someone who had a mild case and giving it to others, the practice sometimes proved dangerous. It was left to an English country doctor, Edward Jenner (1749-1823), to conquer the "severest scourge of the human race." Jenner noted that those who had contracted cowpox from their cattle did not later catch smallpox. He experimented with the cowpox vaccine and discovered that it rendered the patient immune to smallpox. As cowpox was not dangerous, the vaccine could be safely used. Smallpox became the first dread disease to be eradicated, and the techniques used in inoculation and vaccination were later applied to other diseases. Man's life span began to increase.

Geography and geology also profited by the switch from the deductive-mathematical method to the inductive. Formerly, exploration had been a by-product of the search for wealth and trade or for heathens to convert. Now it became a subject for scientific investigation in its own right. The Pacific was explored from the Arctic to the Antarctic by James Cook (1728-1779) in a series of voyages. Russians penetrated into unknown parts of Siberia and Alaska. Frenchmen, Spaniards, Englishmen, and finally Americans explored the interior of the American continent. In their work, they made use of improved methods of surveying. Cartography became highly developed, and in 1744 a detailed, accurate map of France began to be published. The French Academy of Science sent out two expeditions to measure a degree of latitude at the equator and one near the Arctic Circle. The latter was found to be larger, proving that the earth was not a sphere but flattened at the poles.

Buffon abandoned biology long enough to speculate on the history of the earth. He suggested that it had once been a part of the sun but had broken off, solidified, and cooled. The oldest mountains and valleys were formed during the cooling process and hollows were left in the interior. When the earth had cooled sufficiently, the vapor around it condensed, forming a great ocean from nine to twelve thousand feet above the present sea level. This, Buffon believed, explained the fossils and other evidence that Europe had once been under water. When the sea receded, plant and animal life appeared and the continents separated. Although Buffon lacked evidence to prove his ideas, his theory is significant because he recognized that the earth's surface was not permanent and unchanging and that our planet was much older than had formerly been thought. Buffon reckoned its age at about 75,000 years, a far cry from the truth but a notable improvement over the estimates of Biblical scholars who set the date of creation at 4004 B.C. Buffon's work touched off a lively controversy on whether a vast ocean had once covered the earth and determined its structure or whether the heat in its interior had been the controlling force. Victory was won by the latter school. Equally important, by the close of the century, earthquakes, tidal waves, and volcanic eruptions could no longer be explained as punishments visited by an angry God on the wickedness of man. They had come to be considered natural phenomena to be explained by natural causes.

Never had science attracted so much interest. It seemed as though nature were at last ready to unfold all its secrets. "One would say," wrote a contemporary, "that Nature acted like those virgins who long preserved their most precious possession, and then allowed themselves to be ravished in a moment of that they had preserved with such care, and defended with such constancy." No elaborate terminology was needed to read or write scientific articles; the ordinary language of men would do. No expensive equipment was required; all that one had to do was to observe the insects, flowers, or rocks in his backyard. Real originality of mind was not essential; the gathering of facts was the simplest of all scientific processes. Here was a game at which all could play. The dabbler and even the charlatan could mix with the genuine scientific genius. Scientific societies and journals encouraged and disseminated new findings, botanical and zoological gardens were established, and museums were opened. Prince, noble, statesman, even philosopher and humanist, investigated nature. Montesquieu, an authority on comparative government, studied geology; Rousseau, a political theorist, anatomy; Diderot, an encyclopedist, physiology; Franklin, a publisher, electricity; and Leibnitz, a philosopher, physics; while Jefferson, a statesman, made contributions in a number of fields; and Voltaire, a man of letters, was primarily responsible for bringing Newton and Locke to his fellow countrymen. Science invaded the salon and more than one royal princess turned to physics or biology. Voltaire's mistress found time to write on gravitation, while another lady, interested in anatomy, kept corpses in her boudoir.

THE PHILOSOPHERS

The acceptance of the inductive method encouraged the development of the natural sciences but discouraged the creation of the philosophical systems so beloved by the deductive seventeenth century. Since it is a product of reflection, a comprehensive, consistent system of philosophy is best expounded by the deductive method. Locke himself used deduction to prove the advantages of the inductive method and was alarmingly unaware of his inconsistency. Thereafter, the Enlightenment saw few important efforts to create systems, and those who called themselves philosophers were primarily literary figures who wrote about religion, morals, economics, and government.

The most famous of the philosophers was François Marie Arouet (1694-1778), better known as Voltaire. His father was a lawyer, but his mother came from a minor noble family. He received a good education

Voltaire, by Jean Antoine Houdon. (National Gallery of Art, Washington, D.C.)

and at seventeen determined to become a man of letters. To this proposal his practical father retorted: "That's the position of a man who wishes to be useless to society, a burden to his parents, and to die of hunger." Seldom has a parent been more in error. Voltaire's writings and business transactions brought him wealth, while the role he played in popularizing the ideas of the Enlightenment made him one of the founders of modern civilization.

Although the elder Arouet sought to control his difficult son by having him study law, the young man did not abandon his literary interests. His clever, mordant wit was already in evidence, and in 1717 he was briefly imprisoned without trial for attacking the Duke of Orléans. His literary reputation was firmly established by the time he was twenty-four, but he overreached himself by insulting the powerful Chevalier of Rohan. Rohan had Voltaire beaten by servants, and when the abused author issued a challenge to a duel, Rohan had him placed in the Bastille. Thus Voltaire, the injured party, was the one punished by the law. He had the good fortune to get his sentence quickly changed to exile to England, where he not unnaturally became an admirer of British rights and liberties. He returned to France and in 1733 published *Letters on the English,* a work which did much to popularize Newton, Locke, and the British way of life on the continent. Once more, he was forced to leave Paris; he returned only to have to flee again. After spending several years with Frederick the Great of Prussia, he bought an estate conveniently near the safety of the Swiss border. There he remained until a few months before his death, when he returned to Paris in triumph after an absence of twenty-eight years.

Voltaire was a vain, quarrelsome man, but he often employed his satirical wit in good causes. He hated religious intolerance and saw in the multitude of religious sects in England one of the principal causes of the relative freedom that prevailed there. "If there were only one religion in England," he wrote, "we should have to fear despotism; if there were two, they would cut each other's throats; but there are thirty, and they live in peace and happiness." When a French Protestant, Jean Calas, was tortured and executed on the charge that he had murdered his son to prevent his conversion to Catholicism, Voltaire made every effort to win his rehabilitation. In the end, he succeeded; Calas' family was paid an indemnity, the questionable legal procedures of the French courts were exposed, and a celebrated blow was struck for religious liberty. "If you wish to be like Jesus Christ," he advised, "be martyrs, not executioners."

Other forms of freedom were equally dear to Voltaire. To explain his position, he harked back to his happy years in England. "Here is what English law had at last attained to," he wrote in his *Philosophical Dictionary.*

> It has restored each man to all the rights of nature of which he has been deprived in most monarchies. These rights are: full liberty of his person, of his goods; freedom to speak to the nation by the pen; freedom not to be tried under any criminal charge except by a jury formed of independent men; freedom not to be tried in any case except according to the precise terms of the law; freedom to profess peacefully any religion he wishes, on condition of renouncing those employments open only to Anglicans. These are called prerogatives. And, in fact, it is a very great and happy prerogative to be sure on going to bed that you will awake the next morning with the same fortune you possessed the evening before; that you will not be torn from the arms of your wife or your children, in the middle of the night, to be lodged in a dungeon or exiled to a desert; that, on opening your eyes from sleep, you have the right to publish all you think; that, if you are accused, either of acting or speaking or writing ill, you will be judged only according to law. This prerogative extends to everyone landing in England. A foreigner there enjoys the same liberty of property or person, and, if he is accused, can require that half of his jurors shall be foreigners.[4]

Wars and social injustices also aroused Voltaire's ire. His passion for social justice conflicted with the complacent optimism of most early eighteenth-century intellectuals, whose thinking had been colored by the scientific, philosophical, and artistic triumphs of the preceding period. Most of these intellectuals were men of means or in the pay of some patron, so that they escaped the economic privations so characteristic of the age; and as men of letters, they were not expected to participate in wars. The German philosopher Leibnitz went to considerable pains to show that God permitted evil to exist only because He knew that it helped make a better world. The English poet Alexander Pope admirably summed up this optimistic creed when he wrote:

> *One truth is clear: whatever is, is right.*

To Voltaire, the one clear truth was that there could be no significant reforms as long as this complacent attitude existed, and in a short novel

---

[4] Quoted in George R. Havens, *The Age of Ideas* (New York: Collier Books, 1962), pp. 223-224.

Jean Jacques Rousseau by Maurice de la Tour. (Bulloz-Art Reference Bureau)

called *Candide* he ridiculed the optimists. This work was printed at least thirteen times in 1759 alone and has remained popular until this day. It did much to confirm the idea that changes were necessary and to turn the typical intellectual into a reformer.

Jean Jacques Rousseau (1712-1778) occupied a position second only to Voltaire's. Rousseau was born in Geneva. His mother died in childbirth, and his father, a watchmaker, was too erratic to provide him with a normal childhood. He quit school at the age of twelve; and after serving as an apprentice in various trades for four years, he fled from his native city. After a period of wandering, he settled in Paris in 1741 and soon established a relationship with a servant girl who provided him with five children, each of whom he turned over to a foundling hospital to be raised. In Paris, Rousseau became acquainted with other philosophers, but it was not until 1750, when he won the prize in an essay contest sponsored by the Academy of Dijon, that he achieved fame. Four years later, he published an elaboration of this essay entitled a *Discourse on the Origin of Inequality*. He argued that man was naturally good but had been corrupted by society. The theory was by no means original, but Rousseau went on to imply that the remedy was to abandon civilization. "The savage man when he has dined is at peace with all nature and the friend of all his fellow creatures." The development of private property had led to inequality and hence greed, ambition, and strife. Voltaire was quick to see the danger of this approach. He wrote: "I have received your new book against the human race, and thank you for it. Never was such a cleverness used in the design of making us all stupid. One longs, in reading your book, to walk on all fours. But as

Denis Diderot by Van Loo. (Bulloz-Art Reference Bureau)

I have lost that habit for more than sixty years, I feel unhappily the impossibility of resuming it. Nor can I embark in search of the savages of Canada, because the maladies to which I am condemned render a European surgeon necessary to me; because war is going on in those regions; and because the example of our actions has made the savages nearly as bad as ourselves."

Actually, Rousseau aimed at a simpler, less artificial society, not the destruction of civilization. He began to preach the cultivation of the heart rather than of the mind, for he believed that the heart was a better guide to conduct. "I do not deduce these rules," he has the Savoyard Vicar say in *Émile,* "from the principles of a high philosophy, but I find them in the depths of my heart, written by Nature in ineffaceable characters." Man should cultivate his own nature, follow his own feelings, let his emotions be his guide rather than the conventions of society. Only in this manner would man be truly virtuous. By his emphasis on emotion and feeling, Rousseau became one of the leading members of a cult of sensibility that was very popular during the later stages of the Enlightenment and that eventually contributed to romanticism; in his emphasis on virtue, he was a typical product of his age, and through his admiration of the "noble savage," he did much to undermine the complex social structure of the old regime.

The publication most influential in broadcasting the ideas of the Enlightenment was not by a single man but by many. It was the *Encyclopedia,* whose seventeen volumes of text and eleven volumes of plates were

This illustration from Diderot's ENCYLOPEDIA *depicts child labor being used in the manufacture of paper. The children are working on rags in the process between the fermentation and maceration phases of paper-making. Before the limp, sour rags are thrown into the mill, the boys cut them up by hand. Since the boys—no girls are employed—are of varying size, platforms are provided so that the children can reach their work (fig. 3). The boys cut up the rags with a scythe blade, which requires frequent trips to the sharpener (fig. 4). (Courtesy New York Public Library)*

published between 1751 and 1772. Its chief editor was Denis Diderot (1713-1784), a man of humbler origins than Voltaire and of a humbler position throughout his life. Nevertheless, Diderot had a more creative mind and cleverly turned the *Encyclopedia* into a powerful weapon for reform. "The aim of an Encyclopedia," he wrote, "is to assemble the knowledge scattered over the face of the earth; to explain its general plan to the men with whom we live, and to transmit it to those who will come after us, so that the labors of past centuries may not be useless to future times; so that our descendants, by becoming better informed, may in consequence be happier and more virtuous; and so that we may not die without having deserved well of the human race." The goal was typical of the Enlightenment and the inductive method was both advocated and used. Although neither the government nor the Church was directly attacked, article after article contained criticisms that did not escape the censor. Other encyclopedias followed, including the still popular *Encyclopaedia Britannica,* which first appeared in three volumes between 1768 and 1771.

The encyclopedia was only one of the weapons used by the philosophers. Novels became important for the first time. Earlier, fiction had been thought to be of little value; now it was seized upon as a means of preaching social and moral reform and of penetrating the psychological nature of man. Newspapers, pamphlets, magazines, and the theater were used to spread ideas. The salon in France and the coffee shop in England provided popular gathering places for the devotees of the new learning. The universities, on the other hand, failed to open their doors to the new learning except in Germany, and many philosophers actually received their education from the Jesuits, whom they later bitterly attacked.

RELIGION, THE SOCIAL SCIENCES, AND AESTHETICS

The shift from the predominantly deductive, mathematical approach of Galileo and Descartes to the predominantly inductive, empirical approach of Newton and Locke led to a profound change in the social sciences. Nature ceased to be thought of as a mathematical pattern or man as the unquestioned master of his environment. Gradually, the efforts of Voltaire, Rousseau, Diderot, and others caused most of the intellectuals to become reformers, and by the last third of the eighteenth century, a large percentage of the literate public in Western Europe had become disciples of the Enlightenment. Some intellectuals and many of the privileged members of society continued to defend the status quo, but their position will be considered at a later point. The following sections concern the mainstream of eighteenth-century thought.

RELIGION

Scientific and philosophical developments had a profound effect on religious thought. Although religion was not abandoned during the Enlightenment, its nature and purpose were radically changed by the intellectuals. During the Reformation era, the religious controversy centered around the manner in which grace was awarded. Was it awarded through sacraments controlled by the Church, or through God's direct action upon the individual? In the seventeenth century, religious disputes centered more around the respective roles of grace and free will in the process of salvation. The conflict was especially bitter within French Catholicism and the English and Dutch Protestant churches. Now, during the Enlightenment, there was another change. The very existence of grace, revelation, and the trinity was debated. Even immortality and the existence of God were questioned.

This new approach to religion was partly a reaction against religious wars and persecution and against the greed, hypocrisy, and complacency exhibited by large sections of both the Catholic and Protestant clergies after the Reformation fervor had passed. Enlightened philosophers never tired of pointing out that Christianity had been named for the Prince of Peace, while the clergy advocated violence in His name. However, the principal cause for the different approach was the new scientific method. Religion, like everything else, was to be tested by the new technique.

Newton himself was a devout man who spent much of his later life writing *Two Notable Corruptions of Scripture* and *Observations on the Prophecies of Daniel and the Apocalypse of St. John*. In these works, he denied that the Bible taught the doctrine of the trinity; nevertheless, he argued that the harmony and order found in nature must have been established by a God. There were occasional irregularities in the world machine, and these necessitated the continual interference of God to correct them. The Diety's hand had not yet been withdrawn from the universe.

Locke, the co-founder of the new method, also turned his attention to religion. "By what has been before said of reason," he wrote, "we may be able to make some guess at the distinction of things into those that are according to, above, and contrary to reason. According to reason are such propositions whose truths we can discover by examining and tracing those ideas we have from sensation and reflection; and by natural deduction find to be true or probable. Above reason are such propositions whose truth or probability we cannot by reason derive from those principles. Contrary to reason are such propositions as are inconsistent with, or irreconcilable to our clear and distinct ideas. Thus, the existence of one God is according to reason; the existence of more than one God contrary to reason; the resurrection of the dead above reason." [5] He had found a place in natural religion for the resurrection and other miracles, but would other philosophers be as generous now that the practice had begun of trying religion before the bar of reason?

They were not. The Bible was subjected to textual criticism, and it was claimed that there were 30,000 variant readings in the Greek text of the New Testament. Its divine inspiration was questioned by those who pointed out that the prophecies in the Old Testament had not been fulfilled exactly in the New. Rational explanations were offered for Biblical miracles, or else they were treated as allegories. Astronomers found scientific explanations for the natural irregularities emphasized by Newton. The universe became a perpetual machine that needed a creator, but no longer needed a repairman. The hand of God was withdrawn from the world.

A telling blow against the belief in miracles was delivered by the Scottish philosopher David Hume (1711-1776). "No testimony," he wrote, "is sufficient to establish a miracle, unless the testimony be of such a kind, that its falsehood would be more miraculous, than the fact, which it endeavors to establish. . . . A miracle can never be proved, so as to be the foundation of a system of religion. . . . Suppose all the historians who treat of England should agree [that Queen Elizabeth died, and after being buried a month returned to her throne and governed England again]. I should not doubt of her pretended death, and of those other public circumstances that followed it: I should only assert it to have been pretended, and that it neither was, nor possibly could be real. . . . I would still reply,

[5] Quoted in John H. Randall, *The Making of the Modern Mind* (New York: Houghton Mifflin, 1940), p. 288.

that the knavery and folly of men are such common phenomena, that I should rather believe the most extraordinary events to arise from their concurrence, than admit of so signal a violation of the laws of nature. But should this miracle be ascribed to any new system of religion; men, in all ages, have been so much imposed on by ridiculous stories of that kind, that this very circumstance would be a full proof of a cheat, and sufficient, with all men of sense, not only to make them reject the fact, but even to reject it without farther examination. . . . As the violations of truth are more common in the testimony concerning religious miracles, than in that concerning any other matter; . . . this must make us form a general resolution, never to lend any attention to it, with whatever specious pretence it may be covered." [6]

An increasing knowledge of religions in other parts of the world, made possible by the geographical discoveries of the sixteenth and seventeenth centuries, also weakened the position of orthodox Christianity. Similarities between Christian beliefs and those of other faiths were noted, giving support to those who argued that a simple universal creed could be deduced by the comparative study of religion. Alexander Pope gave expression to this hope when he wrote:

> *Father of all! in every age,*
> *In every clime adored,*
> *By saint, by savage, and by sage,*
> *Jehovah, Jove, or Lord! . . .*
> *Yet not to earth's contracted span*
> *Thy goodness let me bound,*
> *Or think thee Lord alone of man,*
> *When thousand worlds are round.*

Geography and environment alone determined in what church one was raised. Voltaire has a Moslem heroine declare:

> *Custom and law alone, applied in early youth,*
> *Have caused me to believe Islam to be the truth.*
> *I see it all. The bent of children's education*
> *Makes their belief and thoughts those cherished*
> *   by their nation.*
> *Were I an Indian, a false god I should fear.*
> *A Christian girl in France, a faithful Moslem here.* [7]

Would the attacks on religion never stop? For a time, it looked as though heaven would be completely dismantled, but finally a group of intellectuals took a stand in favor of deism. The deists believed in the existence of God, for only a diety could have created the universe and made its laws. As Voltaire put it: "In the opinion that there is a God, there are difficulties; but in the contrary opinion there are absurdities." They believed

[6] *Ibid.*, p. 293.

[7] Quoted in Preserved Smith, *A History of Modern Culture* (New York: Henry Holt, 1934), II, p. 501.

in immortality, but admitted that there was only circumstantial proof. Where, except in a life after death, could the good be rewarded and the wicked punished for those deeds which escaped earthly justice? However, the doctrines of original sin and the atonement, indeed theology as a whole, were abandoned. Jesus was just a good man. Like him, man ought to lead a good life on earth. Deists also thought that there were certain moral principles common to all people. By following them, and not the rituals and dogmas of the established churches, one achieved immortality. As Pope so aptly put it:

> *For modes of faith let graceless bigots fight;*
> *He can't be wrong whose life is in the right.*

Or, in the words of a future American president, John Adams: "The design of Christianity is not to make good riddle-solvers or good mystery-mongers, but good men, good magistrates, and good subjects." His countryman Benjamin Franklin summarized the beliefs of his fellow deists when he wrote: "I never doubted the existence of a Deity; that he made the world, and governed it by his Providence; that the most acceptable service of God was the doing good to man; that our souls are immortal; and that all crime will be punished and virtue rewarded, either here or hereafter. These I esteemed the essentials of every religion." But could even these essentials be proved? A few bold spirits began to say no. For the first time in centuries, there were avowed skeptics and atheists in Europe.

A NEW BASE FOR SOCIETY

But if the Church and its doctrines crumbled, a new edifice would have to be found upon which to base society. For the time being, the masses required religion; some form of compulsion was needed to make the ignorant behave. Voltaire showed his contempt for both religion and the people when he told Frederick the Great of Prussia: "As long as there are fools and knaves, there will be religion. Ours is the most ridiculous, the most absurd, and the most bloody that has ever infected the world. Your Majesty will do the human race an eternal service in extirpating this infamous superstition, I do not say among the rabble, who are not worthy of being enlightened and who are apt for every yoke; I say among the well-bred, among those who think, among those who wish to think. Their number is not very great." [8]

But what of those who thought? The intellectuals began to plan a new society based on Locke's philosophy and on a new definition of natural law and natural rights. Man, Locke had taught, was devoid of knowledge at birth. He had no innate ideas nor was he subject to original sin. His thoughts, his very character, must therefore be molded by environment— by the experiences that he received through his senses from surrounding

[8] *Ibid.*

objects. To construct a social environment favorable to the development of knowledge, character, and happiness required an understanding of the relation between social experience and human nature, and to learn about man and the society in which he lived, it was necessary to gather facts on both the contemporary world and the past. Unfortunately, facts were not then readily available. There were few collections of documents for the historian to use, and the science of statistics was only being born. Systematic censuses were rare before the close of the eighteenth century. Only by the most painstaking effort could sufficient data be collected for the satisfactory use of the inductive method.

For the most part, the philosophers of the eighteenth century were not given to painstaking research. They were gentlemen or men of letters more accustomed to the salon than to governmental archives. They unquestioningly assumed that human nature was everywhere the same and that their limited observations would yield its secrets. "My aim has been much less to accumulate a vast quantity of facts, which are always self-contradictory," Voltaire wrote, "than to select the most important and best documented facts in order to guide the reader so that he may judge for himself concerning the extinction, revival, and progress of the human spirit. . . ." When a Swedish historian pointed to errors that Voltaire had made in his *History of Charles XII*, the redoubtable Frenchman fired back: "A historian has many duties. Allow me to remind you here of two which are of some importance. The first is not to slander; the second is not to bore. I can excuse you for neglect of the first because few will read your work; I cannot, however, forgive you for neglecting the second, for I was forced to read you." The philosophers of the Enlightenment wrote of man and society using limited and selected facts—facts chosen, usually unconsciously, to support their preconceived notions. These notions were based on their concept of natural law and natural rights.

The concept of natural law is almost as old as political thought itself. In the classical period, it had usually been connected with principles of morality and justice or with nature per se. In the Middle Ages, natural law was divorced from the physical universe and merged with God's laws. Then, during the scientific revolution of the seventeenth century, there was a return to the earlier concept. It became generally accepted that there was a body of principles that would exist even in the absence of God. It was difficult to reconcile the existence of these principles, which could neither be seen nor touched, with the theory that all ideas were derived from the senses. Voltaire sought to show that no conflict existed. "I agree with Locke," he wrote, "that there is really no innate idea; it clearly follows that there is no proposition of morality innate in our soul; but from the fact that we were not born with beards, does it follow that we were not born, we inhabitants of this continent, to be bearded at a certain age? We are not born with the strength to walk, but whoever is born with two feet will some day walk. Similarly, no one is born with the idea that it is necessary to be just; but God has so formed the organs of man that all at a certain age agree to this truth." [9] God endowed bees with the instinct to work together, "and He endowed man with certain inalienable feelings; and these are the eternal bonds and the first laws of human society." "It would be very singular that all nature and all the stars should obey eternal laws, and that there should be one little animal five feet tall which, despite these laws, could always act as suited its own caprice." Hence, there must be natural laws for man and society just as there were natural laws governing the universe.

The concept of natural rights was closely associated with that of natural laws. Natural rights were thought to be unalienable privileges that ought not to be denied to any individual regardless of his station in life, even with his own consent. These privileges included equality before the law; freedom of worship, of speech, and of the press; and the right to assemble, to own property, and to pursue happiness. They were admirably summarized by Thomas Jefferson in the second paragraph of the American Declaration of Independence: "We hold these truths to be self-evident, that all men are created equal; that they are endowed by their Creator with certain unalienable rights; that among these, are life, liberty, and the pursuit of happiness." They were reiterated by the French Declaration of the Rights of Man in 1789, which held that "Men are born and remain free and equal."

Both Locke's inductive philosophy and the new approach to natural laws and natural rights had far-reaching implications. If man was molded by his environment, there was no justification for a hereditary aristocracy. Furthermore, his material well-being, his happiness, his character itself, could be improved by subjecting him to the proper influences. The proper influences were, of course, those found in a society in which natural rights and natural laws were observed. Since no country in the mid-eighteenth century observed these laws fully, the ideal environment could be achieved only by instituting changes. It was in the desire to institute these changes that the age of the egalitarian revolutions was born. But before discussing the revolutions, it is necessary to relate these new ideas to economic and political thought and to the philosophers' conception of man's future on this earth.

ECONOMIC THOUGHT

Economists gradually abandoned the mercantilist doctrines during the Enlightenment. Psychologically, the principal cause for the change was that agriculture, trade, and industry revived soon after the close of the static seventeenth century. The businessman ceased to rely as much on the state for aid; instead, he criticized laws which hampered his economic

---

[9] Quoted in Ernst Cassirer, *The Philosophy of the Enlightenment* (Boston: Beacon Press), 1953, p. 244.

freedom. The world's resources no longer seemed static; there was enough for everyone to increase his share if only he were free to do so. This situation gave rise to three changes in economic doctrine. First, man's self-interest came to be regarded as advantageous to society; second, production, not trade, came to be considered the source of wealth; and third, natural laws were accepted as applicable to economic activity.

The belief that self-interest was useful to society was a revolt from mercantilist and orthodox Christian doctrines. It was brought about largely by a Dutch doctor named Bernard de Mandeville (1670-1733) and by later developments in Protestant thought. Mandeville was educated at Leyden and visited England to learn the language. He liked that country so well that he determined to stay. In 1714, he published *The Fable of the Bees*, a short poem accompanied by a long prose commentary. The poem told of a beehive plagued with every vice, but these very vices made for prosperity. Quarrelsomeness gave employment to lawyers, thieves made locksmiths necessary, and the love of luxury employed the merchant.

> *Thus Vice nurs'd Ingenuity,*
> *Which join'd with Time and Industry,*
> *Had carry'd Life's Conveniences,*
> *Its real Pleasures, Comforts, Ease,*
> *To such a Height, the very Poor*
> *Liv'd better than the Rich before,*
> *And nothing could be added more.*

But Jove reformed the wicked, prosperous hive. There was no longer need for lawyers, or locksmiths, or dealers in luxury goods. Trade and manufacturers declined, the population decreased, and enemy hives were emboldened to attack. The bees fought courageously, but their eventual victory was costly and they withdrew to "a hollow Tree" where they were "Blest with Content and Honesty," but not with their former opulent society. Mandeville's *Fable* created a sensation. For a time, some philosophers argued that man was motivated by benevolence, but in the end Mandeville's view was accepted. The belief that man naturally follows his self-interest is as old as the story of Adam and Eve, but the theory that self-interest benefits society was a radical departure from Christian ethics. The capitalists' pursuit of gain had finally become justifiable.

Ironically, the Protestant Reformation helped to pave the way for the justification of the acquisitive spirit, although Luther had been very conservative in his economic thinking and Calvin had been no more willing to countenance usury and other aspects of capitalism than many Catholics had. Protestants, more than Catholics, were willing to leave to the state the responsibility of enforcing ethical standards. When the secular forces favoring capitalism became ascendant, legal limitations on usury and other business practices gradually came to an end. Furthermore, within the Protestant denominations themselves, the laymen exercised considerable influence and eventually saw to it that church doctrine in economic matters was ignored or else interpreted as they wished. At first, the Church of England was able to withstand the demands for greater leniency, but the Puritan Revolution destroyed its power of resistance. Thereafter, ecclesiastical restrictions on business activity in England were removed, and economic thought was divorced from Christian ethics. "Trade is one thing and religion is another," became the slogan of more than one convert to the new creed of selfishness.

Some Puritans went even further. They conceived it a Christian duty to try to acquire wealth, and a sign of salvation if success were attained by their efforts. The Puritan was a staunch believer in predestination. Only those chosen by God could be saved, but how could one tell if he were among the elect? By the beginning of the Enlightenment, some answered that success at one's "calling" or occupation could be taken as a sign of election. Even material success could be attained only with the aid of God. This belief gave additional drive to the acquisition of wealth. Some came to believe that it was wrong not to seek material gain. "If God shows you a way in which you may lawfully get more than in another way (without wrong to your soul or to any other)," one Puritan wrote, "if you refuse this, and choose the less gainful way, you cross one of the ends of your Calling, and you refuse to be God's steward, and to accept his gifts, and use them for him when he requireth it." There were those, however, who forgot that they were to acquire wealth for the service of God rather than for their own use. At this point they ceased to be orthodox Puritans and became devotees of the acquisitive spirit in the fullest sense of the word. Thus, Christian ethics had undergone a drastic change since the fourteenth-century when a schoolman had written that "He who has enough to satisfy his wants and nevertheless ceaselessly labors to acquire riches, either in order to obtain a higher social position, or that subsequently he may have enough to live without labor, or that his sons may become men of wealth and importance—all such are incited by a damnable avarice, sensuality, or pride."

Catholic economic thought did not change as greatly, because the independent position of the priest enabled him to resist the desires of the laity to a greater degree. Nevertheless, even the Church of Rome showed some disposition to accommodate itself to the new trend, and self-interest became widely accepted as a positive asset to human society. Pope admirably summarized the new thinking when he wrote:

> *Thus God and Nature formed the general frame,*
> *And bade self-love and social be the same.*

The emphasis on production as the source of wealth and the belief in natural economic laws were contributions of an Irishman named Richard Cantillon (1680?-1734) and a group of economists known as the Physiocrats. Cantillon's support of the Stuart cause made necessary his flight to France, where he became a successful banker and wrote an essay on trade. The first paragraph of his essay marked a sharp shift from the

393

mercantilist doctrine that precious metals were the principal embodiment of wealth. "Land," wrote Cantillon, "is the source or material from which one extracts riches; human labor is the form which produces it: and wealth in itself is nothing but the food, conveniences, and comforts of life." Precious metals were only mediums of exchange that in themselves had no value, and nations without gold and silver mines no longer had to seek a favorable balance of trade. Only by mixing labor with the land could they achieve wealth. Industry made no direct contribution, for the ultimate source of its products was the land, and trade served only to exchange goods. The intrinsic value of an article depended on the land and labor which entered into its production, but Cantillon recognized that the market price depended "on the humors and fancies of men and their consumption," that is, on the natural economic law of supply and demand.

Cantillon's *Essay* greatly influenced the Marquis of Mirabeau (1715-1789). In 1756, Mirabeau published *The Friend of Man*, in which he argued that "the state is a tree; the roots are agriculture; the branches are industry; the leaves are commerce and the arts." This further popularized the idea that agriculture was the root of prosperity. Mirabeau came into contact with François Quesnay (1694-1774), a court physician and economic theorist. With some other kindred spirits, they formed a group known as the Physiocrats, who continued to stress the importance of agriculture. They were so sincere in this that they insisted that all taxes be abolished except for one on land, for land was the ultimate source of wealth and therefore of all taxes, this despite the fact that most of them were landowners.

The Physiocrats were equally convinced that there was a harmonious natural order in economic life. They believed that if the state removed all trade restrictions and permitted the natural economic laws to function freely, the nation would prosper. Man had a natural right to take his property where he pleased. If he were permitted to do so, he would act according to his self-interest and this would benefit society. It was the Physiocrats who popularized the phrase laissez-faire (noninterference) that was to become the watchword of the new economic liberalism.

ADAM SMITH

The new economic thought, with its emphasis on the benefits of laissez-faire, received a tremendous impetus from Adam Smith (1723-1790), who was professor of moral philosophy at the University of Edinburgh. In 1776, he published *An Inquiry into the Nature and Causes of the Wealth of Nations*, a book which for a century was to be the starting point for economic studies. Contributing little that was new, Smith combined the economic thought of the Physiocrats and other contemporaries into a single system. The result was a well-organized, well-written, reasonably complete study of the various aspects of economics.

Smith assumed the existence of an economic order in nature that required a system of natural liberty for its beneficent operation. Avoiding the extreme agrarian bias of the Physiocrats, he argued that wealth was produced by labor in both agriculture and industry. To increase its wealth, a nation must increase its productivity. To increase its productivity, it must achieve a division of labor. "In a tribe of hunters or shepherds a particular person makes bows and arrows, for example, with more readiness and dexterity than any other. He frequently exchanges them for cattle or for venison with his companions; and he finds at last that he can in this manner get more cattle and venison, than if he himself went to the field to catch them." Soon his natural dexterity is improved by practice, he invents better tools to aid his work, and by specialization he no longer has to waste time moving from one job to another. He produces more and better bows and arrows. These he uses to barter for goods produced by others who have also come to specialize. The further the division of labor is extended, the greater the quantity of goods produced. Foreign trade is beneficial because it extends the division of trade to include several nations. The discovery of America was important because "by opening a new and inexhaustible market to all the commodities of Europe, it gave occasion to new divisions of labour."

Arguing that any form of tariff or trade restriction was hurtful because it limited the division of labor and hence production, Smith discredited the mercantilists and other advocates of a protective tariff.

> To give the monopoly of the home-market, he wrote, to the produce of domestic industry, in any particular art of manufacture, is in some measure to direct private people in what manner they ought to employ their capitals, and must, in almost all cases, be either a useless or a hurtful regulation. If the produce of domestic can be brought there as cheap as that of foreign industry, the regulation is evidently useless. If it cannot, it must generally be hurtful. It is the maxim of every prudent master of a family, never to attempt to make at home what it will cost him more to make than to buy. The taylor does not attempt to make his own shoes, but buys them of the shoemaker. The shoemaker does not attempt to make his own clothes, but employs a taylor. The farmer attempts to make neither the one nor the other, but employs those different artificers. All of them find it for their interest to employ their whole industry in a way in which they have some advantage over their neighbors, and to purchase with a part of its produce, or what is the same thing, with the price of a part of it, whatever else they have occasion for.
>
> What is prudence in the conduct of every private family, can scarce be folly in that of a great kingdom. If a foreign country can supply us with a commodity cheaper than we ourselves can make it, better buy it of them with some part of the produce of our own industry, employed in a way in which we have some advantage. (*The Wealth of Nations*, Bk. IV, Ch. 2)

In a similar manner, Smith explained the functioning of economic laws in the fields of banking and currency, using a combination of the deductive method and examples taken from history and his own experience. He was no doctrinaire liberal and would admit a few exceptions to free trade, but the tenor of his work was to show that the natural economic order should be freed from government interference, that man should be permitted to pursue his economic self-interest, and that every nation should produce what it could produce most profitably and exchange freely with other nations. In this manner, the wealth of the world would increase to the benefit of all mankind.

HUMANITARIANISM AND COSMOPOLITANISM

The desire of the advocates of laissez-faire to better the lot of man was only one aspect of a general humanitarian and cosmopolitan movement during the Enlightenment. If nature decreed that man had natural rights to life, liberty, and property, society must be altered to ensure proper enforcement of these rights. Furthermore, these natural rights were not regarded as the exclusive property of the aristocracy. They also belonged to the lower classes in one's own country, the people of other European countries, and the inhabitants of the backward, un-Christian parts of the world. Rights ceased to be associated only with the privileged few; they became the property of all mankind.

The slave trade had been accepted without question at the beginning of the eighteenth century. Even the God-fearing Puritan had been blissfully unaware that there was anything wrong with seizing African Negroes and transporting them in overcrowded ships to perpetual bondage in America, but by 1750 the English Parliament was ready to take steps to remedy the worst abuses and within another fifty years the horror of slavery had become almost universally recognized. Leaders in the new republic of the United States abolished the importation of slaves and sought vainly for means to free those already in their land.

A demand for religious toleration succeeded in mitigating persecution, although legal equality between the various faiths in a country was rarely established. The retreat of superstition before the onslaught of science gradually brought to an end execution for witchcraft. Although the desire for equality was growing, in no country were the rich and poor treated alike. A great noble could have a commoner beaten and escape punishment, but a poor man was often sent to the galleys or executed for petty thievery. The law, reformers argued, should be applied equally without regard for rank. Punishment should accord with the seriousness of the crime. The whole concept of capital punishment was attacked, and efforts were made to limit the number of crimes for which it was imposed. Torture was strongly condemned, and other attempts were made to protect the rights of the accused. It was even suggested that the criminal should be treated as a sick man rather than as an enemy of society and that laws should be designed to prevent crime rather than to punish criminals. Imprisonment for debt was decried, and there were demands that the insane be treated with kindness. Even animals found protectors. Prior to 1789, the reformers accomplished few of their practical objectives, but they did succeed in arousing the European conscience.

The emphasis on the right of all men throughout the world to life, liberty, and property led to the growth of cosmopolitanism. The philosophers regarded dynastic and patriotic duties as secondary to their obligation to mankind. "Patriotism," said a learned Englishman, "is the last refuge of a scoundrel." Wars were regarded as contrary to human nature and a violation of the natural rights of others. Voltaire attacked war with his usual biting sarcasm. "Truly that is a noble art which desolates countries, destroys habitations, and causes the death of from forty to a hundred thousand men a year! . . . The most amazing part of this infernal enterprise is that each murderous chief causes his colors to be blessed, and solemnly invokes God before he goes to exterminate his neighbors!" The intellectual's desire for peace and the concept of one world were never stronger.

Some philosophers thought that perpetual peace could be achieved only through education and reason. If man would learn what was moral, he would desist from his immoral actions. Other philosophers sought to implement peace by preparing specific plans. Scattered references made by Henry IV and Sully to a "grand design" to secure peace were brought together and published in 1745. The two Frenchmen advocated a redivision of Europe to ensure the proper functioning of the balance of power and to recognize nationalistic differences. They wanted a general council and a court of arbitration to settle disputes and advocated the use of force to ensure order. In 1713, the Abbot of Saint-Pierre (1658-1743) published a three-volume work entitled *Project for Perpetual Peace*, in which he abandoned the insistence on a balance of power but maintained the idea of a general council and a court of arbitration. He strengthened the proposed league of nations by giving it an army supported by contributions from the member-states. The league was to act directly on the people. Whoever assisted a ruler who was at war with the international organization was to be executed or imprisoned for life. Whoever did not support such a ruler was to be rewarded. Rousseau, Kant, and other philosophers prepared additional plans, and the intellectual groundwork was laid for a future international organization.

THE IDEA OF PROGRESS AND THE PERFECTIBILITY OF MAN

The belief that man was molded by his environment and that the universe was regulated by a natural, benevolent order gave rise to a glorious dream. The philosophers began to suggest that, in the future, man's lot on earth would be more pleasant and that his very character would improve. For the average American, so accustomed to the idea that civilization has advanced and that it will continue to advance, it is difficult to believe that the concept of progress is relatively new. Prior to the eighteenth century, the historical process was thought to move in circles or else to stand still. Utopias were placed in the remote past or on some distant island. With the Enlightenment, they began to be placed in the future.

Three steps had to be taken before the idea of progress and the perfectibility of man could be accepted. First, belief in the superiority of the ancient classical civilization had to be destroyed. So long as man looked to the past for his model, he would never look to the future for his dreams. Admiration for the scientific and philosophical achievements of the seventeenth century enabled men to take this first step. In 1687, Charles Perrault read a poem before the French Academy entitled *The Age of Louis the Great*. His verses were bad, but his ideas were provocative. "Within the last twenty or thirty years," he argued, "more discoveries have been made in natural science than were made throughout the whole period of learned antiquity." Classical literature was not above reproach and even the *Iliad* could be improved upon. Knowledge, he believed, was cumulative, and therefore the men of the present knew more than those of the past. Perrault's thesis may have pleased Louis XIV, but it infuriated the classicists, or Ancients, as they came to be called. The defenders of Perrault were called Moderns. For a generation, in England as well as in France, a bitter debate raged between the Ancients and the Moderns. The eventual victory of the Moderns was of great significance. For the first time, man began to hope that the future might be more glorious than the past, but he was not yet certain.

A second step had to be taken. God, as an intervening force, had to be removed from the world. So long as man believed in a supernatural power that could drown the world in another flood or destroy it with fire and brimstone, so long as he thought that his fate was subject to an arbitrary force, he could not be sure of the future. As we have seen, the scientists and philosophers of the Enlightenment were removing this fear. To them, God was not a father capable of punishing His wicked children. He was only a creator who had made the universe and set it in motion. He had not condemned man for the sin of Adam. He had left him free to be molded by his environment. He had decreed neither continued sin nor eventual destruction but had left man's fate to be determined by man's actions.

The third step was to demonstrate that continued progress and man's perfectibility were assured. Economists argued that, if the natural economic laws were allowed to operate freely, the resulting worldwide division of labor would greatly increase the wealth of mankind. Philosophers argued that, if education, laws, and institutions were properly altered, man's moral character would improve under the influence of an improved environment. In the final analysis, however, the Enlightenment turned to history for evidence that progress and perfectibility were assured. The study of the past showed clearly that there had been great material progress. Future scientific discoveries were certain to lead to new comforts, and the printing press guaranteed that knowledge, once obtained, would never again be lost. But what of the moral character of man? Here history was less conclusive. Few philosophers felt that there had been much moral improvement, but many were convinced that they had only to apply the inductive method to the study of man and society to determine the type of environment that would assure man's progress toward perfection.

POLITICAL THOUGHT

How did the philosophers plan to implement their dreams? They themselves suggested three different methods. At first many of them, including the Physiocrats, believed that the natural rights of man could be best established and preserved by an enlightened prince. A monarch, guided by scholars, could quickly destroy the old order and build the new. It would take years to accomplish the task if a more democratic approach were used and the people were first indoctrinated with the ideas of the Enlightenment. China, with its emperor and bureaucracy of philosophers who were appointed after taking an examination, was often held up as a model. It may seem strange to us that intelligent men would look to an enlightened despot to establish freedom of thought, expression, and religion and to abolish torture and war, but for centuries it had been customary to appeal to the throne for reform and most eighteenth-century monarchs knew more about the new ideas than the great mass of their people. They usually took their duties seriously and were in agreement with Frederick the Great of Prussia that a king "is only the first servant of the state."

A second method was to establish constitutional guarantees. The exponents of this method admired the British system of government and studied Locke with enthusiasm. The most important theorist to be influenced by Locke was the Baron of Montesquieu (1689-1755), who published *The Spirit of Laws* in 1748. The very title of the work pointed to the assumption that there were universal principles underlying states and societies. He opened the book with a very brief description of the state of nature and natural laws, but he quickly abandoned this typical approach and turned to a comparative study of past and present constitutions and societies. In an age that advocated the inductive method, Montesquieu was one of the few to use it extensively. The result was that in a very long book he reached no clear-cut conclusions. His real goal had been to find the constitutional and sociological conditions upon which freedom depended, but his study convinced him that there was no system suitable for all people. Differences in climate, soil, and religion, in constitutional traditions and customs, made it unlikely that a solution satisfactory in one country would be satisfactory in another. He did express an admiration for the English constitution because he believed that it ensured liberty

399

by dividing authority between executive and legislative branches of the government, each of which served as a check on the other. His arguments were so persuasive that not only did he convince the English that this was the true nature of their government, but in the end both the Americans and the French tried to establish liberty by accepting his interpretation. Actually, Montesquieu never intended that his conception of the British constitution be set up in France. He really advocated a return to the decentralized government of the days before Louis XIV, with its provincial estates and law courts, with its emphasis on custom and privilege. In this, he ran counter to the dominant intellectual trend of his age, which moved more in the direction of egalitarianism than aristocracy.

Democracy was a third method for establishing the ideal society. Its foremost advocate was Jean Jacques Rousseau (1712-1778). In *The Social Contract*, Rousseau used the deductive method to expound his political theory and drew few illustrations from actual events. To him, man was neither good nor bad, happy nor unhappy, in a state of nature. He had no natural rights, no moral qualities, not even a language. In short, his social institutions were those of the most primitive savage, and he was guided by instinct rather than reason. It was only with the formation of the community that man achieved rights, and it therefore followed that man had no rights against the community. "The fundamental problem is to find a form of association which defends and protects with the whole common force the person and goods of each associate, and in which each, while uniting himself with all, may still obey only himself, and remain as free as before." This, Rousseau thought, could be best done by each man giving himself absolutely to the community, retaining no rights for himself. But, "each man, in giving himself to all, gives himself to none; and as there is no associate over which he does not acquire the same right as he gives others over himself, he gains the equivalent of everything he loses, and an increase of force for the preservation of what he has." To Rousseau, the social contract need consist only of these terms: "Each of us puts his person and all his power in common under the supreme direction of the general will, collectively, and we receive each member as an indivisible part of the whole. This passage from the state of nature to the civil state produces a very remarkable change in man, by substituting justice for instinct in his conduct, and giving to his actions the morality they had formerly lacked."

But how is this "general will" which directs society, this concept which by very definition "is always right and always tends to the public advantage," expressed? Rousseau was not completely clear, but his basic premise was that it was approximated by the majority vote of all the citizens of the community. Rousseau advocated a democracy in which every man surrendered his power to do as he pleased, but through his vote won the right to exercise some power in determining what all the members of the community did. The individual was left no protection from the will of

The Petit-Trianon, Versailles. In 1762 Louis XV began to construct this little palace for Madame de Pompadour as a retreat from the formality of the great château of Versailles. (Bettmann Archive)

the majority, but Rousseau's faith in man was such that he did not see in this a threat to liberty.

Rousseau did not believe in the use of representatives. Each citizen must act for himself in the popular assembly. As a result, his system was practical only in a small city-state like Geneva, where he was born. However, his followers were less insistent on this point and were willing to accept representative government. Thus, the philosophers found three possible ways to realize their dreams: they could rely on the enlightened despot, the constitutional liberties of Locke and Montesquieu, or the democracy of Rousseau. One and all were to be tried, but their dreams were not to come true.

AESTHETICS

The scientific and philosophical investigations of Newton and Locke had a profound influence on aesthetics. In no form of art was this more clear than in gardening. The trees and shrubs of the seventeenth century had been trimmed to geometric designs, for it had been thought that the book of the universe was written in a mathematical language. Now man had come to believe that the senses acted on the mind, not the mind on the senses. Trees and hedges were allowed to assume their normal shapes and wandering streams replaced straight canals. Paths with little bridges meandered through the gardens, artificial grottoes were constructed, and

The hamlet at Versailles where Marie Antoinette and the great ladies of the court dressed as shepherdesses. The trees were no longer made to conform to geometric patterns as they had been in the gardens of Versailles (p. 368) and the Tuileries, and nature dominated the architectural element. (Bettmann Archive)

rocks were arranged in a fantastic manner. Temples of love, Chinese pagodas, even rustic villages were included to arouse the proper feelings. Always the garden dominated the architectural element, for nature controlled the works of man. One has only to walk from the formal gardens around the palace of Versailles to the hamlet where Marie Antoinette and the court played shepherds in the last quarter of the century to realize that a new age had been born. In aesthetics, rationalism had been abandoned in return for sensuous experience.

The new style, the Rococo, owed its name to the *rocailles,* or rock piles, in the gardens. It marked a change from the Baroque emphasis on grandeur and power to an emphasis on grace and charm, and from heavy masses in movement to slower, gentler action. The small intimate palace was preferred to crowded Versailles, and the number of country houses multiplied. Columns vanished and the white walls of the rooms were covered with interlaced designs colored in gold. Furniture was characterized by its delicate contours, and chairs had gracefully curved arms and legs. They were lighter and more decorative than before.

Artists again put more emphasis on color than on line. They abandoned heroic subjects and in their place drew scenes from court and everyday life. Some painters, like William Hogarth (1697-1764), reflected the Enlightenment's interest in morality. Hogarth painted series of pictures tell-

William Hogarth, GIN LANE. *(Bettmann Archive)*

ing the story of how idleness and sin led to crime and death. Their very titles, "The Rake's Progress," "The Idle Apprentice," "The Four Stages of Cruelty," "Gin Lane," and "Beer Street," reflect their content. Reproduced as engravings, they sold by the thousands. Other painters, such as François Boucher (1703-1770) and Jean Honoré Fragonard (1732-1806), delighted in depicting the gay naughtiness of the aristocracy.

Drama was neglected, serious poetry languished, the novel became increasingly sentimental, but wit and satire were universally admired. The grand opera declined, and the light, amusing *opéra comique* took its place. Orchestras performed less in the great halls of palaces and more in con-

Jean Honoré Fragonard, THE SWING. *A comparison with Poussin's* FU-
NERAL OF PHOCION (*p. 367*) *reveals the changes that occurred between
the late seventeenth and late eighteenth centuries in respect to color,
linear drawing, and subject matter. (National Gallery of Art, Washington, Samuel H. Kress Collection)*

cert halls and drawing rooms. There were those who argued that music
was not "a science of harmony and of measurements" but "an artistic expression of sentiments." Thus, while the philosophers were undermining
the political and social structure, taste was being dominated by the light,
the gay, the amusing, and the sentimental.

THE ECONOMIC REVIVAL

The economic stagnation that had gripped the seventeenth century came to an end in Western Europe soon after the War of Spanish Succession (1713). At first, the revival was slow, involving experiments in banking and currency and a mild upturn in commerce and agriculture. By mid-century, it had gathered momentum and industrial production was increasing. By 1801, an industrial revolution was taking place in England, and the number of paupers had been reduced from about 25 per cent of the population in 1688 to a mere 10 per cent. The Mediterranean countries were less affected by these changes, and the Atlantic seaboard moved far ahead economically for the first time.

The causes of the economic revival are difficult to determine precisely, but they nearly all go back to the inventive genius of the late seventeenth- and early eighteenth-century mind. "The age is running mad after innovation," said England's literary dictator, Dr. Johnson; "all the business of the world is to be done in a new way. . . ." The men of this period were met by the challenge of economic stagnation, with its problems of overpopulation, famine, misery, and social stratification. Instead of resigning themselves to these problems, as the Asiatic peoples were doing, they undertook to solve them.

Many statesmen recognized that wars had been a major cause of economic decline during the seventeenth century; they therefore found means to preserve Western Europe to a considerable degree from plundering armies between 1713 and 1792.[10] Farmers and inventors contributed to the economic revival by making improvements in agriculture, transportation, and industry. Bankers began to take steps that eventually provided adequate credit for government and industry and a currency independent of the supply of precious metals.

BANKING AND CURRENCY

An important step was taken towards solving credit and currency problems when the Bank of England was formed in 1694. Earlier banks had been banks of deposit and exchange designed only to store or transfer the trader's money and to exchange foreign currencies. The Bank of England, however, was a loan bank. It was formed by William Paterson and others to help finance the war with France by loaning the government £1,200,000 at 8 per cent interest. Later, additional loans were made and the interest was lowered. In return, the bank was empowered to issue notes, discount bills, and make loans. No other bank was permitted to have over six partners, a ruling that gave the Bank of England a monopoly on large banking transactions. It confined its activities to the government, to big

[10] See page 418.

firms like the East India Company, and to small private banks. The notes it issued backed by its credit were easily negotiable and provided the first adequate paper substitute for gold and silver currency. Only with the acceptance of paper notes could the Europeans get enough currency for their needs. The chronic scarcity of money, which had become a serious problem when gold and silver mining declined in the seventeenth century, was ended, and both the government and businessmen could get loans more easily to carry on their activities. Indeed, the ability of the English government to borrow more than its continental rivals was one reason for its triumph in the struggle for colonies.

Unfortunately, the limits of the use of paper notes were not thoroughly understood. At first, bankrupt governments and speculators were inclined to overstep the bounds of discretion. The most famous of these miscalculations was that of John Law (1671-1729). Law devised a scheme for paying the French national debt and greatly increasing French commerce. In 1716, he was given a charter for a bank which had the authority to issue notes secured by Louisiana land and in 1718 by the crown. These notes were issued in part to pay royal debts, but in return they were accepted by the government in the payment of taxes. The scheme might have worked if it had not been carried too far. The total value of Law's notes was about twice that of the metallic currency then in circulation. This led to a price rise in Paris of 88 per cent and touched off speculation that brought about the collapse of his second enterprise, the Company of the West. This company had been given a monopoly on the trade with Louisiana, the sale of tobacco in France, and the beaver trade with Canada. Unfortunately, the demand for the company's stock was so great that by December, 1719, it was selling at ten times its par value. Soon, wiser speculators realized that the price of the stock was fantastically high in relation to the company's earnings. They began to sell and the bubble burst. Both Law's bank and company failed, and many lost their fortunes. This experience led the French to regard banks and paper notes with suspicion for the rest of the century. The British underwent a similar speculative boom and bust, but the Bank of England survived. These experiences did not prevent banks and paper notes from coming into use in other European countries, and these two institutions did much to relieve the credit and currency shortage. After about 1750, the production of precious metals in the New World was increased once more, and aided in the solution of the monetary problem.

TRADE, INDUSTRY, AND TRANSPORTATION

European countries in the eighteenth century carried on foreign trade with three different areas: Europe, the New World, and India and southeast Asia. The most important area from the standpoint of bulk was the intra-European trade. Wheat and timber from the Baltic Sea region continued in demand, as did wines from France, wool from Spain, and silk from the Mediterranean countries. However, the quantity of trade in this area increased only slightly. The great growth in trade was with the other areas, especially with the New World.

The improved banking and monetary system undoubtedly facilitated the growth of this trade, but more important was the development of colonies. During the course of the eighteenth century, the number of Europeans in the New World increased rapidly, and with the aid of an ever-growing number of African slaves, the colonists produced crops that could not be grown in Europe. Sometimes traders followed a triangular route, going first to the west African coast, where they exchanged cheap textiles and other products for slaves. The slaves were then taken to the West Indies, where they were sold for sugar, tobacco, indigo, and like produce needed by the mother country. Other shipowners preferred to voyage directly back and forth between the mother country and the colonies, hoping to make two trips instead of one per year. The West Indian and southern colonies were at first universally considered more valuable than those to the north because they furnished raw materials not grown in Europe. By 1763, however, British industrialists realized that the more populous northern colonies offered better markets for their goods. At the same time, colonial wheat began to seem more valuable, for England was becoming a grain importer rather than a grain exporter. Asian trade was much less valuable than that with the West Indies, but there was still a ready market for Asian tea, spices, and cheap textiles.

The international rivalry to secure profit from commerce was fierce. The Spanish and Portuguese managed to carry on considerable trade with their vast colonial empires, despite legal and illegal operations by the British.[11] The Dutch remained important in the intra-European carrying trade, and their East India Company continued to yield profits. However, they were not strong enough to hold their own against larger nations, and they lacked the natural resources to supply the industrial needs of colonies. It was England and France that became the great competitors for trade, and their rivalry sparked several wars.

For a long time it seemed as though the French would surpass the English. They managed to increase their exports by three and a half times between 1720 and 1774, while the British only doubled theirs during the same period. Other Western European countries, with the exception of the Dutch, shared in the growth of trade. Even Spain became more prosperous, and Russia more than tripled its foreign trade between 1725 and 1762. Perhaps the most remarkable thing about the increase in trade is that it was accomplished in spite of mercantilist restrictions. Not until near the end of the century did governments begin to implement the free trade ideas of the Physiocrats and Adam Smith, but by the time Smith published his *Wealth of Nations* the advantages of a world-wide division of labor were already apparent.

Although trade among the various Western European countries also

[11] See page 269.

increased, it is difficult to measure the extent. Certainly, the increase was facilitated by improved transportation, and here the ingenuity and energy of the age was once more in evidence. Canal building began in earnest around 1750 after it had been discovered that canal freight rates could sometimes be reduced to one-sixth the amount charged by land transport.

The growing markets made it advisable for European countries to produce more for exchange. Large establishments remained rare, however, and only in the fields of mining, metallurgy, glass making, and ship-building did any companies employ over a thousand persons. In France, and to a lesser extent in England, the number of firms employing over a hundred persons grew. England had experienced a period of rapid growth in coal and iron production in the late Tudor and early Stuart periods and now France began to catch up. Production of pig and bar iron stood at about 45,000 tons per year in both countries in 1700, but by 1789 France was producing 230,000 tons to England's 101,000. Although England maintained its lead in coal, the French managed to increase their production sevenfold. Spain and parts of the Empire also enjoyed considerable growth. On the whole, however, the eighteenth century was a period of industrial progress, not industrial revolution. The master with his journeymen and apprentices accounted for the bulk of production in most fields. The increased demand simply meant more employment. The domestic system continued to be important, and family enterprises and partnerships remained the preferred types of industrial and commercial organizations. Joint stock companies were organized only for the few large-scale enterprises, such as the Dutch and British East India companies.

There were, however, signs of change. With the improvement in transportation, it was becoming possible to move coal, iron, and raw materials to the same locality; with the invention of labor-saving devices, it was becoming advantageous to bring workers together in a factory; with the availability of capital from loan banks and trading profits, large-scale enterprises could be undertaken. All that was needed was a new source of power—perhaps from steam—to launch an industrial revolution.

THE AGRICULTURAL REVOLUTION

In an economic context, the word "revolution" does not denote the sudden change that it denotes in a political context. While it eventually alters the nature of society, an economic revolution takes place gradually, over a number of years. In this sense, an agricultural revolution began in the eighteenth century; by employing the experimental method advocated by the Enlightenment, farmers began to increase their productivity so much that for the first time a large percentage of the population could live in cities and work in factories.

For centuries farmers had been content to employ the techniques of their fathers, but after 1700 a new approach to agriculture and animal husbandry was adopted, especially in England although the English had had some Italian and Dutch precursors. One reason for the new approach was that agriculture and animal husbandry, like chemistry and biology, throve under the application of experimental science. New knowledge about plants and animals, far more than new machines, led to agricultural improvements. Another reason was that the revived love of nature prompted more landowners to reside on their estates rather than at court or in towns. As a result, they took more interest in their land. It became fashionable for the aristocracy to carry on agricultural experiments. Viscount Townshend (1674-1738), in the words of a contemporary, "quitted all the power and lustre of a Court for the amusements of agriculture." George III of England was equally interested and in 1770 opened a Parliament designated to deal with colonial trade problems with: "My Lords and Gentlemen: It is with much concern that I find myself obliged to open the session of Parliament with acquainting you that the distemper among the horned cattle has lately broke out in this Kingdom." The growing influence of the Physiocrats points to the popularity of farming in France, and agricultural societies flourished everywhere. A third incentive for the change in method was a desire for profit. The new agriculture yielded bigger crops and hence more income. This was especially true after about 1760 when there was a rise in the price of farm products.

Increased food production was brought about by cultivating more land, getting bigger yields per acre, and improving livestock. The old open field system in which a field was left fallow every two or three years was abandoned. Turnips, alfalfa, or clover were planted instead. These crops not only restored the soil more rapidly than if it were left idle, but also provided food for livestock. Furthermore, improved agricultural techniques made it possible to cultivate land that had formerly been considered useless. In 1696, it was estimated that 10,000,000 acres in England were waste. In the eighteenth century, much of this land was brought into use. The demise of strip farming that accompanied the abandonment of the open field system also increased the land available for crops. The roads and innumerable footpaths leading to the individual strips could now be used. The result was that wheat acreage in England increased by one-third, and there were turnips, alfalfa, and clover besides.

At the same time that more land was being brought under cultivation, yields per acre were increased. Fertilizer in the form of animal manure and a mixture of clay and lime came into use and proved invaluable. An Englishman, Jethro Tull (1674-1741), discovered that yields could be increased by thoroughly pulverizing the soil to allow air and moisture to reach the roots of plants. He substituted a drill that planted seeds in rows for the older method of scattering grain by hand, an innovation that greatly reduced the quantity of seed needed and enabled the farmer to use the horse hoe that Tull had also invented to kill weeds and keep the soil broken up. Vegetables were planted in greater quantities than ever before and yielded more food per acre than grain. Most important of all was the introduction of the potato. This plant was probably brought to Europe from South America during the sixteenth century, but it was only after 1700 that its cultivation became widespread. At last a nourishing food had been found that could be easily grown in large quantities in a small area and stored for winter consumption. The potato became a basic ingredient in the European diet.

Substantial improvements were made in animal husbandry. In the old open field system, animals had been allowed to mix indiscriminately on the wasteland and the commons, making scientific breeding impossible. However, when a farm was enclosed, an enterprising owner could breed his animals intelligently. Robert Bakewell (1725-1795) was especially noted for his successful experiments along this line. Furthermore, the alfalfa, turnips, and clover that were being planted in lieu of leaving the land fallow provided a much improved diet for animals. Formerly, lack of fodder had forced many farmers to kill their beasts during winter, and those that survived were thin and unhealthy. As a result of breeding and adequate food the year around, the weight of the beasts sold in London's Smithfield market doubled between 1710 and 1795. Increased food also made possible a larger number of animals. For the first time, meat became a significant part of a workingman's diet.

Before the new agricultural and stock-raising methods could be adopted, a change in the system of land tenure was necessary. The open field strips and the cooperative farming of the village community had to be abandoned. In England, the manorial lord and the yeomen often enclosed the land by common consent, each receiving a consolidated farm whose acreage depended on the size of their former holdings and their claims to the commons. If agreement could not be reached, the lord could petition Parliament to pass an enclosure act. Since both houses were dominated by the aristocracy, a sympathetic ear could be anticipated. Between 1700 and 1760, an average of four enclosure acts per year were passed by Parliament, between 1760 and 1792, an average of forty, and between 1798 and 1815, an average of eighty. Those yeomen who did not receive enough land to live on were gradually forced to sell their holdings and become laborers in the town or country. As a result, England slowly became a land of large estates. By 1873, over half the country was owned by 2,250 persons whose estates averaged 7,300 acres. Some landlords divided their estates into farms of from 100 to 500 acres and leased them to tenant farmers; others managed them themselves using paid wage-laborers. In this manner, agriculture fell into the hands of people with enough capital and knowledge to take advantage of the new techniques. The quantity of food increased prodigiously. There continued to be owners of small farms, however, and the population of rural areas increased until the introduction of machinery during the middle third of the nineteenth century.

In eastern Europe, as we have seen, the powerful nobility had already seized most of the land and were exploiting it with serf labor. In France and western Germany, there was less demand for enclosures. The nobility owned only a fifth of the land directly and part of the remainder was held by the clergy and middle class, but a third was in the hands of peasants who paid feudal dues to their overlords. For the noble to insist on enclosures meant the loss of manorial revenue and services because the peasants would then become complete owners of their own farms. Most nobles were therefore content to leave things as they were or to try to find means to increase their manorial revenue. It is true that the Physiocrats advocated the new farming techniques and that after 1750 the French government began to take a more kindly view of enclosures, but it was only in the Paris Basin and the maritime provinces, where the market for agricultural produce was large, that much progress was made.

There were, therefore, three systems of agriculture in Europe by 1789: the English system, in which large estates were worked by tenant farmers or paid laborers; the east European system, in which large farms were worked by serf labor; and the west European system, in which small farms were worked by peasant proprietors. Scientific farming was most difficult, and quarrels between lord and peasant were most frequent, under the west Europeon system, with results that will be described later.

POPULATION GROWTH AND SOCIAL CHANGE

The increased production of food made it possible for Europe to support a larger, better nourished population, and the growth of trade and industry provided employment for additional millions. Great plagues like those that swept through Europe during the fourteenth and seventeenth centuries did not recur, and man's life span began to increase. In one region north of Paris, a historian has discovered that 20 per cent more adults lived to the age of sixty between 1771 and 1790 than in the seventeenth century. The birth rate may have grown slightly as a result of earlier marriages and better nourishment. The inevitable result was an increase in population. At first, the rate of growth was quite slow; but as the economic opportunities and food supply increased, it picked up speed. Between 1715 and 1790, the European population increased from about 130 million to 175 million. Russia replaced France as the most populous European nation, the number of its inhabitants increasing from about 13 to 30 million. France enjoyed an increase from 19 to 26 million; Spain grew from 5 to 9 million; Brandenburg-Prussia from 1.5 to 5.5 million, and England from 6 to 9 million. At the same time, several million Europeans emigrated to overseas colonies. The numerical growth of Western civilization had definitely begun.

The economic revival had a profound effect on social classes. The growth of trade and industry in Western Europe caused the middle class to become larger and wealthier. This class was more indoctrinated with the ideas of the Enlightenment than any other, and it naturally sought political power to put its economic and social reform program into effect. The position of the landed aristocracy was less certain. Except in the handful of small republics, the members of this class dominated every country from England to Russia. As a rule, then, they were defenders of the old regime. However, agricultural innovations and even commercial adventures had brought many of them wealth. Some accepted much of the Enlightenment and advocated a degree of change, but not as much as the more radical middle class. The day laborers in town and country had grievances because wages had generally lagged behind the rise in prices. They had no constructive program of their own, but their discontent made them willing tools of the reformers.

10/ The Era of the Enlightenment, II

T HE years between the Treaty of Utrecht in 1713 and the outbreak of the French Revolution in 1789 may be divided into two periods. The first period witnessed a cooperative effort by the kings and the aristocracy to preserve the governmental and social institutions inherited from the seventeenth century. Their success may be attributed to the fact that the old causes of rebellions were largely removed and new ones had not yet gathered strength. Religious intolerance remained, but it was not intense enough to precipitate a revolt. Taxes were heavy, but they did not become more burdensome because the great powers cooperated to maintain a precarious peace. The aristocracy was sometimes disgruntled, but it remained loyal because the kings respected its privileges.

Three developments in the decades immediately following 1740 led to a renewal of strife between the kings and the privileged members of society. The first was a series of three world wars in which the governments of the defeated states were discredited, and the victors and vanquished alike

413

had to reform their administrations and seek additional revenue that could come only from the aristocracy. The second was the gradual acceptance of the ideas of the philosophers by a large part of the literate population, and the third was the economic revival and the attendant growth in importance of the middle class.

In general, the kings were the first to try to change the existing order. Some acted to get additional revenue or to make their governments more efficient; others acted because they themselves had become disciples of the philosophers. Often the mixture of these motives lay behind their deeds. The result was a struggle in which the middle and lower classes usually sided with the aristocracy because they mistakenly assumed that any opponent of the crown was a defender of their interests.

THE ARISTOCRATIC VS. THE EGALITARIAN FORCES

THE ARISTOCRACY

In 1740, the aristocracy was ascendant in every European country and in the more developed colonies in other parts of the world. Strong seventeenth-century rulers, like Peter the Great of Russia and Louis XIV of France, had changed the nature of the aristocracies in their respective countries and had compelled them to be obedient, but after their determined hands were removed, the aristocracy reasserted itself. In other countries, such as Poland and England, where the aristocracy had already triumphed in the struggle with the crown, it held a dominant position from the beginning of the century.

The economic base of the aristocracy varied from country to country. In eastern Europe and most of the Americas, the aristocracy derived its income almost entirely from land, although a small part of the Russian aristocracy was interested in mining and industry, and wealthy merchants in such important colonial cities as Boston, New York, Philadelphia, and Charleston claimed a status comparable to that of the large landowners. In England and France, the aristocracy was also essentially a landed class. In England, the situation was complicated by the willingness of noblemen and gentry to invest in large-scale business enterprises. In France, the most aggressive part of the aristocracy were the hereditary officeholders, but since these officeholders were also the owners of landed estates, the difference between them and the "nobility of the sword" was gradually becoming less distinct. In Holland, the northern Italian city-states, and the largely self-governing Swiss and free imperial German cities, the aristocracy consisted primarily of wealthy merchant families that had become so entrenched that they could no longer be thought of as belonging to the middle class.

In eastern Europe and the American colonies, the aristocrats derived much of their power from their control over the serfs or slaves who worked their estates. In these countries and also those in Western Europe, they held most of the offices in national and rural government. In the cities, a small group of merchant patricians had a monopoly on governmental positions to the exclusion of the less established burghers and artisans. Many countries had parliaments or estates-general that were dominated by the aristocracy. Where such institutions did not exist, as in Prussia and France, or where important subjects were excluded from the national assembly, there were often local assemblies in which they could exert their influence. Everywhere the aristocracy held most of the important ecclesiastical positions.

The aristocrats did not regard themselves as the enemies of liberty; instead, they saw themselves as a bulwark against despotism. They stood between the king and the common people to prevent the former from wielding unjust, arbitrary authority and the latter from behaving with license. To them, as to Montesquieu, however, liberty meant the free exercise of the traditional rights and privileges belonging to the members of a particular class or locality without infringement by an arbitrary power, whether wielded by a king or the common people. They did not think in terms of equal rights for all men but of particular rights for this or that class.

To perform their self-assigned task, the aristocrats felt it necessary to put great emphasis on heredity. If a king were allowed to ennoble as many commoners as he liked or to appoint men of any station in life to government positions, he could undermine the aristocracy. Many seventeenth-century monarchs had actually followed this practice to some extent, although society as a whole had been more static at that time than in the Renaissance.

Eighteenth-century monarchs were either more sympathetic towards the aristocrats or else lacked the will or power to check their wishes. In eastern Europe, the aristocratic monopoly on position and prestige was almost complete; no other class could offer serious competition. Even in Western Europe, where the economic revival was slowly strengthening the middle class, the lines between it and the aristocracy became more tightly drawn. In England and its colonies, the aristocracy began to entail its estates so that future generations would not sell them. This practice ensured the continued enjoyment of a high social position by established families, but since the number of estates in England itself was limited, it reduced the opportunity for wealthy merchants to rise in society by becoming landowners. An effort was even made to prevent the king from creating new nobles.

In France, the bureaucracy had long been largely hereditary, and non-nobles found it increasingly difficult to purchase the few vacancies that did occur. The officer corps became increasingly a private preserve of the nobility. The tendency to stress nobility of long standing may be seen in ecclesiastical appointments. Under Louis XIV, 53 per cent of the bishops were from families that had been noble for two hundred years or more. By 1790, 80 per cent could claim that distinction. In England, the percentage of bishops who were from noble or gentry families increased from 36 to 63 during approximately the same period.

THE MIDDLE CLASS

Where the middle class was weak, as in eastern Europe, it had no choice but to accept the superior position of the aristocracy, but in western Europe the economic revival brought increasing wealth to many of their number. At first they had no egalitarian tendencies; in the past, they had had little difficulty in joining the aristocracy when they could afford to purchase estates or offices, and they asked nothing better than to continue to do so. Their wealth, their intelligence, and their social graces so exceeded those of a large part of the aristocracy that it was doubly galling to be assigned to a subordinate social position.

It was only when they found the path to the aristocracy closed to them that the members of the middle class began to talk of equality, and even then they thought more in terms of their equality with the noblemen than in terms of the peasants' or artisans' equality with themselves. Slowly, motivated by wounded self-esteem, many merchants, doctors, lawyers, and other business and professional people began to accept the more egalitarian ideas of the Enlightenment. If man was, indeed, molded by his environment, an aristocracy of birth could not be justified. If there were natural rights, they were the same for all men. If there were natural laws, they should bind noble and merchant alike. The councils, estates, law courts, and other corporate groups that the aristocracy had seen as the bulwarks of constitutional liberties, the middle class began to see as instruments for the prevention of natural liberties. This transition was slow, and until the beginning of the French Revolution in 1789, the middle class usually supported the aristocracy in its struggle against the crown.

THE KINGS AND THE CONDUCT OF WAR

One of the most effective contributions to egalitarianism was made by the monarchs themselves. Many were enlightened despots who tried to break the power of the estates, law courts, and other corporate groups and to establish greater equality among their subjects. Some were motivated by a sincere desire to realize the dreams of the philosophers; others were driven to undertake reforms because the three world wars between 1740 and 1783 compelled them to reduce class and local privileges in order to govern more effectively and to raise the money necessary to carry on the struggle.

It seems strange that the most peaceful period in the century was between 1713 and 1740, before the philosophy of the Enlightenment had won much acceptance, and that the wars thereafter were often conducted by men who espoused such enlightened principles as humanitarianism and cosmopolitanism. However, eighteenth-century warfare was the most humane the world had yet seen, a happy circumstance that may be attributed more to the economic and social situation than to the influence of the philosophers. Armies and navies became increasingly expensive because the cost of equipment rose and the size of the military establishments increased. Between 1740 and 1784, the French standing army grew from 190,000 to 300,000 men, the British from 18,000 to 58,000, the Austrian from 108,000 to 282,000, and the Russian from 130,000 to 290,-000, while the maritime powers increased their navies at a similar rate.

These statistics help to explain the conduct of war during the eighteenth century. In the first place, the productive part of the population had to be left unmolested so that it could pay taxes. Officers were drawn primarily from the nobility, while seamen and privates were usually vagabonds, drunkards, and unemployed persons who were seized in taverns and elsewhere and compelled to serve. Prussia and Russia conscripted some peasants, but on the whole, economically productive people were not directly affected by war. Except for the officers, troops were not expected to show any loyalty to the causes for which they fought. Indeed, they were often recruited abroad to reduce still further the disrupting effects of war on the economy. The British hired German troops to fight in the American Revolution, and Frederick the Great forcibly enlisted prisoners of war in his own army. To camp near a large woods, to conduct a night march, to send out a foraging party, or to grant sailors shore leave was to invite wholesale desertion. Sailors had to be kept aboard ship and soldiers had to march in close order by day and carry their supplies with them. As a result, armies could not travel more than five days' march from their base of supplies, military objectives had to be limited, and wars tended to degenerate into sieges.

In the second place, armies were so expensive that generals hesitated to risk pitched battles. The current military doctrine was not to destroy the enemy forces but to secure every possible advantage by maneuver. Even Frederick the Great could not escape this type of warfare, and he owed his military victories primarily to his skillful maneuvers and his well-trained officer corps.

Civilian suffering was curtailed by the limited objectives of eighteenth-century warfare, by the careful discipline required from officers to prevent desertion, and by the absence of the fanaticism that had accompanied the religious wars of the previous period. The rules of warfare that were accepted by the various participants were also a factor, and unless one was so unfortunate as to be caught in a besieged city, he could hope to escape most of the horrors of war—except taxes. It was largely to collect more taxes that many kings attempted to curtail the privileges of the aristocracy, provinces, towns, and other special groups.

THE WARS

In the eighteenth century, France lost the dominant position it had held on the continent during the reign of Louis XIV, but a balance of power had been so carefully created by the Treaty of Utrecht that no other country was able to assume France's role, although all the major states increased their territory. In the colonial sphere, Great Britain achieved such gains in the Seven Years War that its rivals seized the opportunity created by some rebellious colonies to weaken the country's position in North America. These events took place after a brief experiment in collective security.

AN EXPERIMENT IN COLLECTIVE SECURITY, 1713-1740

Between 1713 and 1740, Western Europe enjoyed a period of relative peace. People were tired of war, and the new rulers of Austria, France, and Great Britain were peaceful men who had neither the money nor the desire to provoke conflicts. The Treaty of Utrecht had established a balance of power that made it dangerous for a state to seek additional territory. Furthermore, the great powers had learned to cooperate whenever an aggressor appeared.

There were, of course, threats to peace. The Great Northern War was not brought to an end until 1721;[1] both Austria and Venice tried to annex portions of the crumbling Ottoman Empire; and the Stuarts plotted to oust the Hanoverian George I from the English throne. Spain was the most discontented power. The European part of its empire had been dismembered as a result of the War of Spanish Succession, and its queen was anxious to get lands in Italy for her sons to rule. Sardinia was seized from Austria in 1717, and Sicily was attacked the following year.

The great powers proved equal to these challenges. Great Britain, France, Austria, and the Dutch formed a quadruple alliance in 1718. The British defeated a Spanish fleet, Austrian troops invaded Sicily, and France sent an army across the Spanish border. By 1720 Spain had no choice but to surrender. International cooperation had quickly restored peace, and the only territorial change resulting from Spanish aggression was that Austria gave Sardinia to Savoy in return for Sicily.

Cooperation to repel aggression quickly became cooperation to preserve peace. Between 1722 and 1725, representatives of the quadruple alliance, with representatives from Spain and some minor German states, deliberated at Cambrai on several problems. In 1727, Spain tried to seize Gibraltar from the British, but the island kingdom refrained from reprisals and sent representatives to Soissons to meet with those of other states in an effort to restore peace. The congress remained in session for two years, and once more the great powers managed to bring an end to conflict.

[1] See pages 254-255.

The peace of Europe was again threatened when the Polish king died in 1733. France and Spain supported one candidate to the elective throne, and Austria and Russia supported another. With the great powers thus divided, a long war seemed inevitable, but for a third time peace was quickly restored through diplomacy. The Austro-Russian candidate was recognized as king, but France was guaranteed eventual possession of Lorraine and a son of Philip V of Spain was given Naples and Sicily. Trouble was brewing, however, which the nascent system of collective security could not control. In 1739, war broke out between England and Spain, and in the following year, Brandenburg-Prussia, Bavaria, and France attacked Austria.

THE WAR OF AUSTRIAN SUCCESSION

Why did this early system of international cooperation fail? One reason was the intense commercial rivalry between England, Spain, and France. The economy of Spain was incapable of supplying the needs of its vast colonial empire in the New World, and its elaborate system of mercantilistic restrictions hampered commerce. This situation encouraged British smugglers to develop a huge illicit trade. Inevitably, the Spanish retaliated by searching British ships in their territorial waters for smuggled goods. English merchants were outraged. Sir Robert Walpole, the peace-loving prime minister, was unable to control his countrymen, and England declared war. France's equally peace-loving minister, Cardinal Fleury, determined to intervene. From one-half to seven-ninths of the goods legally exported to the Spanish colonies came from France. To permit England to compel Spain to open its ports would upset the balance of power in the Caribbean and lead eventually to the loss of the French West Indies as well. A purely commercial and colonial war between three of the leading maritime powers began.

Cardinal Fleury had decided to intervene only because continental Europe was at peace and the leading continental powers were friendly to France. Two deaths in 1740 brutally upset his calculations and provided a second reason for the collapse of international cooperation. One death was that of Emperor Charles VI. Charles had devoted the better part of his reign to getting the various parts of his Danubian empire and the other European states to recognize the Pragmatic Sanction naming his daughter, Maria Theresa, as his sole heir.[2] If the European rulers had upheld their agreements, Charles's death would have been no threat to peace. Unfortunately, Frederick William of Brandenburg-Prussia died the same year, and his able, ambitious son, Frederick the Great, decided to expand his domain. With little or no justification, he sent his armies into Silesia. Charles of Bavaria laid claim to much of the remaining Habsburg territory and had himself elected emperor. For the first time in three centuries, a Habsburg did not sit on the imperial throne. Other powers also laid claim to Austrian

[2] See pages 319, 435-436.

territory, and Spain renewed its attempts to expand in Italy. Court intrigue soon caused France to declare war on its hereditary enemy, despite Cardinal Fleury's desire to concentrate on the maritime war. A worldwide conflict known as the War of Austrian Succession began. It looked as though nothing could save the twenty-three-year-old Maria Theresa.

Help came to Maria Theresa from two directions. She won the support of her Hungarian subjects by promising to respect their local autonomy, and she concluded an alliance with Great Britain. The English decision to intervene in the continental war was based on the fear that the French would achieve a preponderance of power on the continent. French dominance would not only have jeopardized Hanover, which belonged to the English king, but would also have been a threat to the British Isles.

In a series of brilliant victories, Frederick the Great took Silesia and held it against Austrian counterattacks. The French took the Austrian Netherlands and seized Madras in India from the British. In the New World, however, the British navy won several victories in the West Indies and the New England colonists captured the important French fortress of Louisburg that controlled the entrance into the Saint Lawrence River. By 1748, the European nations were too exhausted to continue hostilities. The peace terms called for a restoration of all conquests, except that Brandenburg-Prussia was allowed to keep the valuable province of Silesia, and Parma and Piacenza were given to a younger son of Philip V of Spain.

THE SEVEN YEARS WAR

Maria Theresa was unwilling to accept the loss of Silesia, and with the aid of her able minister, Prince Kaunitz, she plotted to separate Prussia from its principal ally, France. In 1756, the two schemers brought about a diplomatic revolution. France was persuaded to abandon its traditional hostility towards Austria and to join with Russia and several lesser powers in an effort to despoil Frederick the Great. Great Britain completed the reversal of alliances by giving aid to Prussia. The resulting Seven Years War was the most costly since the days of Louis XIV. The French forced a British army to surrender, but time and again Frederick the Great was able to defeat invading Austrian, Russian, and French forces. Slowly, his strength waned before such overwhelming odds. Only the timely death of Empress Elizabeth of Russia saved him. Her successor, Peter III, had a strong admiration for the Hohenzollern and withdrew his forces. Maria Theresa and her remaining allies realized that their cause was now hopeless. Conquests in Europe were returned and peace was restored.

The Seven Years War was also fought in other parts of the world, and here the results were of the utmost significance. The peace treaties that had ended the War of Austrian Succession had been no more than armed truces for the colonists. The French in India begrudged the return of Ma-

THE WORLD IN 1763

POSSESSIONS
SPANISH
BRITISH
DUTCH
FRENCH
PORTUGUESE

ARCTIC OCEAN

PACIFIC OCEAN

ATLANTIC OCEAN

INDIAN OCEAN

UNKNOWN

RUSSIAN

HUDSON BAY CO. (BR.)

PITTSBURGH 1758

SAN FRANCISCO 1769

VICEROYALTY OF NEW SPAIN

BERMUDA (BR.)

BRITISH, FRENCH SPANISH, DANISH DUTCH ISLANDS

NEW GRANADA

PERU

BRAZIL

LA PLATA

FALKLAND IS.

CAPE HORN

TROPIC OF CANCER

EQUATOR

TROPIC OF CAPRICORN

ANTARCTIC CIRCLE

ARCTIC CIRCLE

GIBRALTAR (BR.)

EUROPE

OTTOMAN EMPIRE

RUSSIAN EMPIRE

RUSSIAN SETTLEMENTS AND FORTS

UNKNOWN

CHINESE EMPIRE

JAPAN

NAGASAKI

CANTON

MACAO (PORT.)

PHILLIPINES (SP.)

PERSIA

INDIA

BOMBAY (BR.)

GOA (PORT.)

MADRAS (BR.)

PONDICHERY (FR.)

CEYLON (DUTCH)

DUTCH EAST INDIES

GAMBIA

GUINEA

DUTCH

CAPE OF GOOD HOPE

ASCENSION (BR.)

ST HELENA (BR.)

MAURITIUS (FR.)

BOURBON (FR.)

UNKNOWN

UNKNOWN

UNKNOWN

dras to Britain. Under the leadership of the able Joseph Dupleix (1697-1763), they abandoned the old policy of trade with the Indians and began to interfere in the quarrels between the native princes. In this way, Dupleix sought to supplement the profits of trade with taxes and tribute from the local population. By taking over the hinterland, he also hoped to deal a death blow to the trade of the British East India Company. The British under Robert Clive (1725-1774) retaliated by adopting a similar program. When a small war broke out between local Indian rulers, the English and French took different sides, and the conflict quickly merged into the Seven Years War. At the outset, the French outnumbered the British in India, but they had foolishly recalled Dupleix and could find no other leader to match Clive. Lack of funds to pay the troops and poor naval support also contributed to their defeat. By the terms of the Treaty of Paris in 1763, France almost completely withdrew from India, leaving the British free to encroach slowly on the native states until all the vast subcontinent was theirs.

The struggle ended much the same way in North America, where from the beginning the British had the advantage of numbers. By 1775, about a million Englishmen inhabited a series of colonies extending along the Atlantic seaboard from Nova Scotia to Georgia. Each colony was jealous of its liberties and unwilling to accept direction from higher authority in a united effort against the French. Most of the English colonists were farmers, but here and there trade and industry were important. French North America consisted of the Saint Lawrence and Mississippi River valleys. Only 60,000 white men inhabited the entire region, for the French had been less willing than the English to leave their homeland. Fur trading was the most profitable occupation, and since there was little agriculture, it was doubtful that enough food could be produced to feed an army. Only their superior leadership in the early years permitted the French to prolong the war.

Hostilities began in North America in 1754, months before the formal declaration of war. In that year, the Virginia governor sent young George Washington (1732-1799) into the disputed Ohio Valley with a small army. Washington found the French well entrenched in newly-built Fort Duquesne at the forks of the Ohio River where Pittsburgh now stands. The Virginia army was defeated and forced to withdraw, but the following year the mother country came to the rescue and sent General Braddock with regular troops to capture Fort Duquesne. Braddock was ambushed and defeated by the French and Indians. The outbreak of war in Europe did not initially weaken the French, and their able commander, the Marquis of Montcalm, succeeded in clearing the British from the Great Lakes region. Fortunately for the island kingdom, it found in William Pitt the elder (1708-1778) a leader capable of reversing the course of the war.

Pitt was a great orator and a global strategist who believed that Britain's future depended on the destruction of France as a colonial and com-

422

William Pitt, the Elder, at the age of 58, in a portrait by R. Brompton. (National Portrait Gallery, London)

mercial power. At first, he was disliked by the king, but he won the support of the merchant classes by his booming oratory and his defense of their interests. By 1757, numerous British defeats left the king no recourse but to charge him with the conduct of the war. Pitt gave Frederick the Great enough support to keep France and its allies occupied on the continent while he threw the main British effort into the colonial war. His policy was successful. In 1758, Louisburg and Fort Duquesne were captured, and in 1759, Wolfe defeated Montcalm on the Plains of Abraham outside Quebec. Both generals were killed, but Canada fell into the hands of the British. At the peace conference, France ceded Canada and the lands east of the Mississippi River to the British except for New Orleans. Spain, which had belatedly entered the war on the side of France, surrendered Florida to the victor but was compensated for this loss by getting the Louisiana territory from its ally. Of France's vast American empire, little of value except its West Indian islands remained. The balance of power in North America had been upset, and Britain had become the greatest colonial power.

THE AMERICAN REVOLUTION

The next great colonial war was different in two significant ways. First, the British had so completely upset the balance of power in the New World that all the maritime states now united against them. This time they had no continental allies to divert French and Spanish strength and were forced to meet the undivided power of their enemies in their struggle to hold their empire. Secondly, the colonial population that had previously supported the mother country was now in revolt. Indeed, it was the revolutionary activity of the Americans that touched off the new colonial war.

One of the underlying causes of the revolt of the American colonies was their growing confidence and strength. The Seven Years War had removed the threat of French encroachment, and the colonial population had grown from 200,000 in 1700 to 2,200,000 in 1770. England itself had only four times as many people. Nothing seemed to stand in the way of continued expansion and increased prosperity—nothing, that is, except the crown, which provided a second cause of the Revolution. The Seven Years War had created a huge public debt and English landowners had to pay over 15 per cent of their income in taxes. Why should not the colonists be asked to assume part of the burden, especially since the war had been fought partly for their protection? To the tax-conscious Englishman, there was no logical reply to this argument. The period 1763-1775 saw one effort after another by the mother country to raise revenue from the colonies. Each new measure was resisted by the colonists. Finally, the dispute became a quarrel, and the quarrel a revolt.

Prior to 1763, Parliament had passed many measures affecting the colonies, but these measures had caused little difficulty. The colonists had smuggled to avoid tariffs and had traded with the French West Indies when forbidden to do so. After the Seven Years War, Great Britain decided to enforce its regulations. Between 1763 and 1765, it forbade colonists to settle west of the Alleghenies; determined to enforce a Sugar Act putting a tariff on sugar, molasses, and several other articles; required that stamps be purchased and used on newspapers and legal documents; and prohibited the colonies from issuing paper money. Each of these measures struck at special colonial interests, but each seemed justified in British eyes. Halting the westward movement was designed to prevent further Indian trouble, but it was a severe blow to colonial land speculators. The Sugar and Stamp acts were designed to raise revenue to help pay for the troops stationed in the colonies for their protection. Although it actually cut duties on molasses in half, the Sugar Act provided for rigid enforcement that hurt trade. The Stamp Act struck at lawyers and editors, the most vocal elements of the population, and the Currency Act was designed to prevent American debtors from paying their English creditors in depreciated colonial paper money.

British efforts to induce the colonies to abandon their special privileges and contribute to the costs of empire may be compared with Olivarez's attempt to persuade the non-Castilian Spanish kingdoms to contribute towards the costs of the Thirty Years War.[3] The levies demanded by the British amounted to about one shilling per person, an insignificant sum when compared with the twenty-six shillings per head paid in England. In no colony would the total taxes per inhabitant have been a tenth that paid by the average Englishman. Nevertheless, the colonies resisted just as the Catalonians had done, because their traditional privileges had been in-

[3] See page 311.

fringed upon. Their colonial legislatures were no more willing to permit internal taxation by Parliament than the provincial estates of France had been willing to accept taxation by the Estates-General.[4] "A Parliament of Great Britain," John Adams declared, "can have no more right to tax the colonies than a Parliament of Paris."

Delegates from nine colonies met in New York in October, 1765, to protest against taxation "without their own consent." Radical groups like the Sons of Liberty stirred up discontent, and colonists agreed not to buy British goods until the objectionable acts were repealed. They admitted the right of Parliament to regulate trade but denied it the right to tax them. The difficulty was that most trade regulation took the form of tariffs, and tariffs gave revenue. Here was a fine distinction that gave rise to further quarrels. Parliament obligingly repealed the Stamp Act but passed the Townshend Acts putting import duties on glass, lead, paper, and tea. Again the colonists boycotted British goods. Again Parliament gave in and removed all the duties except the one on tea. Between 1770 and 1772, relations between the mother country and the colonies improved a little, but in December, 1773, a group of Massachusetts citizens disguised themselves as Indians, boarded some tea ships in Boston harbor, and tossed the tea overboard. Parliament retaliated with the Coercive Acts, which closed the port of Boston until the tea had been paid for, and unilaterally altered the Massachusetts charter. The governor's powers were increased, and town meetings were forbidden without the governor's permission.

Eleven colonies responded to Massachusetts' call for aid and sent delegates to Philadelphia, where the First Continental Congress opened in September, 1774. There was talk of compromise. There was talk of more boycotts of British goods. But before any action was taken, news reached the delegates that on April 19, 1775, British troops sent to destroy military stores in Lexington and Concord had been fired upon. War had finally come.

The British had the advantage of numbers and wealth. They had an army and a large navy, but these advantages were offset by the necessity of operating three thousand miles from home in a vast country with few roads. Moreover, their victory in the Seven Years War put them at a disadvantage: if the colonists made a determined fight, other colonial powers were almost certain to seize the opportunity to restore the balance of power in the New World. The greatest handicaps of the colonists were that their thirteen colonial legislatures would not cooperate and that only a part of the population gave active assistance to their cause. Conservatives feared the radicalism of the revolutionaries, and new immigrants usually remained loyal to the mother country. In North Carolina, the backwoods farmers declared for the king when they learned that the hated tidewater aristocracy had joined the rebellion. New York furnished more troops for the British than for the colonial cause, while the British subjects in Canada, the

[4] See pages 92-93.

West Indies, and Florida did not join in the revolt at all. Most of the inhabitants of the thirteen rebellious colonies tried to continue their normal lives without involvement on one side or the other, although when compared with the lack of popular participation in the European wars at this time, the American revolutionaries showed considerable enthusiasm for their cause.

For a time, the colonists maintained the fiction that they were fighting the royal ministers, not the king, but when it became apparent that there could be no compromise, they decided to separate from the crown. The task of justifying a declaration of independence was assigned to Thomas Jefferson (1743-1826). Following John Locke, the Virginian based his argument on natural law and natural rights. He proclaimed that man had been created "with certain unalienable rights; that among these are life, liberty, and the pursuit of happiness; that, to secure these rights, governments are instituted among men, deriving their just powers from the consent of the governed; that whenever any form of government becomes destructive of these ends, it is the right of the people to alter or to abolish it and to institute a new government. . . ." George III had violated these natural rights. Therefore, "these united colonies are, and of a right ought to be, free and independent states."

This stirring cry for liberty was heard throughout Europe. Enlightened reformers saw in the American example a way to escape the misgovernment of their rulers. Statesmen saw in the rebellion an opportunity to wreck the British colonial empire. When the new republic defeated and captured a British army at Saratoga in October, 1777, the French could desist no longer. They declared war on their old enemy; Spain followed suit in hope of recovering Gibraltar and Florida; and the Dutch also joined the war. It was only a matter of time before the British had to sue for peace. By the terms of the Treaty of Paris in 1783, the independence of the United States was recognized, with the Mississippi as its western boundary. Spain regained Florida, but France received little for its efforts besides a greatly increased debt. France had only weakened, not destroyed, the British empire, and in a decade the struggle was renewed.

The colonists had halted the effort to curb their provincialism by subordinating their institutions to king and Parliament. In doing so, they had checked the growth of a colonial aristocracy; for the sixty thousand or more loyalists who left the rebellious colonies to go to Canada or England had been among the staunchest supporters of the idea of social gradations, and some of them had even dreamed of establishing a colonial nobility. Many aristocrats had fought in the patriot cause and remained to lead the new nation, but they had become allied with the more democratic elements of the population in the war. When victory was achieved, the new federal and state governments that were established did much to guarantee equal rights and liberties for all. By showing that the people could create a government that could provide liberty and equality, the American Revolution had a profound effect on the minds of disaffected Europeans.

THE EUROPEAN STATES

The philosophers had failed to persuade the European monarchs that the blessings and virtues of peace were superior to the glories and profits of war, but a more important question was whether the kings would support domestic reform or a privileged aristocracy would block every effort at democratic change.

GREAT BRITAIN

Great Britain was the first home of the Enlightenment and the center of the new agriculture, trade, and industry. In spite of these two liberating forces, the British strongly opposed both the American and the French revolutionary movements and avoided serious reform at home. This paradox may be partly explained by the American rejection of Parliamentary authority and by long-lived British opposition to French dominance on the continent, whether under a monarchical or a republican regime. But part of the explanation also lay in the structure of British politics.

Although the Glorious Revolution had blocked the efforts of James II to create an absolute monarchy, it had not reduced the king to a ceremonial figurehead. Instead, it marked a return to the dualism that had characterized the Renaissance monarchy, in which the king and the aristocracy ruled together. The king could not govern without the aristocracy, who controlled Parliament and monopolized the key posts in national and local government. The aristocracy, on the other hand, was so divided into factions that the king could win a large following by using his power to reward. The rewards at his disposal included not only titles and ecclesiastical positions, but also posts in the government and royal household, many of which required little work for a good salary. The cost of the last-mentioned sinecures was met by a civil list voted the king at the beginning of his reign. Although Parliament had no control over this fund, it was expected to make good the deficit if the king overspent, as he frequently did.

The Tudors had governed with Parliament by seating members of their council in the Lords and the Commons, where they took the initiative in legislation. The growing use of committees, however, enabled the members of the two houses to take control and led to the revolution in 1642.[5] The Hanoverian kings could not hope to return to the Tudor system of government. If they and their advisers were to govern the kingdom, they had to find new ways to control the deliberations of Parliament. This they managed to do because of the structure of eighteenth-century politics.

The most important unit of local government was the county, and the county was under the control of the justices of the peace. These justices were usually country gentlemen who compared in social and economic

[5] See page 287.

427

status with the lesser nobility on the continent. Although they had no special privileges before the law and did not escape taxation, they were as able as their French equivalents to preserve the prestige of their families. *Primogeniture* ensured that the entire estate was inherited by the eldest son, and *entail* prohibited future generations from transferring family property. Younger sons had no alternative but to enter a profession, usually the army, law, or the clergy, or to join the ranks of the middle class. Although family position was preserved by the eldest son, the distinction between the gentry and the middle class was less sharp in England than on the continent. The justices of the peace met in quarter-sessions four times a year, where they not only dispensed justice, but also discussed national and local problems and often decided on candidates for Parliament.

The lord lieutenant, who controlled the appointments of the justices of the peace and distributed royal patronage in the country, was another important local official. For a gentleman to win a lucrative government post, a promotion in the church for his brothers, or the prestige that accompanied election to Parliament, it was well to be on friendly terms with the lord lieutenant. The lord lieutenant, of course, had to have the support of the crown, for it was in the king's name that appointments were made. Therefore, the king could influence the lord lieutenants, and the lord lieutenants, with the aid of royal patronage, could influence local government and the Commons.

The lord lieutenants were either great peers or important ministers. An English peer, like a continental noble, had special privileges. With his title came the right to sit in the House of Lords, and it was only before that august body that he could be tried. Since the title was inherited by the eldest son and younger sons were left to join the ranks of the gentry or to enter the professions, there was a close blood tie between the peerage and the gentry. As landowners, the two groups shared the same economic interests. They were not separate classes, nor were they divided into political parties. The terms *Whig* and *Tory*, which had come into being during the rule of the later Stuarts, were almost meaningless. There were no party platforms, no party conventions, and no real party candidates. What mattered was family and faction.

England was small, and power was held by a few. In 1726, there were only 179 peers, some of whom were too old, too young, or too stupid to take a part in politics. The active few were acquainted with one another and with the leading gentry of their counties. They were divided into factions by family rivalries and conflicting ambitions. It was the struggle between these factions that shaped the political history of England during the eighteenth century.

Some deputies to the Commons were chosen by the counties, but most were elected by the boroughs. Past history, rather than population, determined which boroughs could elect deputies and which could not. New industrial centers like Manchester and Birmingham were legally still villages and had no representation; on the other hand, some boroughs had dwindled in size to such an extent that only a half-dozen persons could vote for their two members of Parliament. This situation was ideal for patronage, but few patrons could count absolutely on a borough. Even the Duke of Newcastle, the greatest patron of all, who held estates in twelve counties and the lord lieutenancy of three, controlled only seven boroughs. Elsewhere, he competed with others to get his candidates elected. The large cities and a few of the small boroughs sometimes insisted on making a free choice of deputies, but the majority of those who went to Parliament were bound to someone or in pursuit of their own interests. Since middle-class representation was so slight and since a large number of deputies profited from the patronage system, it is not surprising that the reform movement was weak in Parliament.

Everything depended on whom the king chose to be his ministers and to exercise his patronage, for it was through patronage that Parliament was controlled. Only when there was a catastrophe could public opinion force the change of a minister. George I (1714-1727) and George II (1727-1760) relied on Sir Robert Walpole (1676-1745) to serve as prime minister and the Duke of Newcastle (1693-1768) to handle patronage. Walpole stood for peace, largely because an aggressive foreign policy meant higher land taxes. He believed in commerce but was unwilling to win trade and empire by war. He came to power in 1721 and maintained peace until 1739 when public clamor carried Britain into war with Spain. Three years later, he was forced out of office by the desertion of Newcastle and others who favored surrendering to the popular demand for a more vigorous prosecution of the war. George I did not attend cabinet meetings during this period, partly because he knew no English, but he continued to consult his ministers and his consent remained necessary before they could take any action. Nevertheless, the withdrawal of the king was an important step towards the development of a modern cabinet system because the task of handling crown patronage and managing Parliament was left to the king's ministers.

Meanwhile, the middle class was being greatly strengthened by the growth of trade and industry, and in William Pitt the elder it found a spokesman. Pitt did not belong to the old landowning aristocracy. His family fortune dated back only to his grandfather, who was an East Indian merchant. With such forebears, it is not surprising that Pitt caught the vision of empire. He argued that Britain need only destroy France's fleet and seize its trading bases to achieve wealth and power. He had the fiery eloquence to make his plan of plunder seem a moral duty and he was idolized by the London merchants. Pitt's rivals distrusted his ideas. War was expensive and success was dangerous, for if Britain became too powerful its friends would become enemies. Nevertheless, the initial failures in the Seven Years War brought Pitt to power in 1757. He directed the war effort and Newcastle handled the patronage. Pitt, as we have seen, quickly turned defeat into a series of brilliant victories. Canada and India were taken during the next three years. There was one battle, however, that Pitt could not win. In 1760, George II died, and his grandson, George III, soon dismissed the great minister.

George III (1760-1820) has too often been depicted as a stupid tyrant whose determination to restore monarchical authority nearly drove his British subjects into rebellion and led the thirteen colonies to sever ties with the mother country. There is some truth in this picture. George III was stupid, just as his two predecessors had been, but he was no tyrant. He was a man of high moral character and a believer in constitutional principles. His fault was that he tried to govern by wielding royal patronage himself as Louis XIV had done, rather than by leaving his ministers relatively free to act in his name.

The British people were also changing. The ideas of the Enlightenment were winning some acceptance; newspapers were reaching a wide public; and the commercial and industrial middle class was stronger. Fed by Adam Smith, the advocates of free trade attacked the principles of mercantilism. Slavery and the slave trade were widely condemned, and exponents of religious toleration decried the fact that only Anglicans could attend the universities or hold public office. Although there was general satisfaction with British institutions, there were growing demands to reduce the patronage system by reforming the electoral procedure and by abolishing a number of offices.

Perhaps the bitterest controversy centered on John Wilkes (1727-1797), the son of a wealthy distiller. In 1763, Wilkes was imprisoned for criticizing George III in his journal, this despite the fact that as a member of Parliament he claimed immunity from arrest. The royal attack on freedom of speech and parliamentary privilege was not without precedent; but Wilkes won his case in the courts. He was, however, expelled from Parliament on charges of writing immoral literature. Again and again, he was re-elected by his constituency, but he was consistently denied his seat until 1774. The episode underscored the need for parliamentary reform, and the more radical members of the middle class were insistent on change. A few Englishmen identified their own cause with that of the American colonists, and others became alarmed at the incompetent prosecution of the war. In 1780, the House of Commons resolved that "the influence of the crown has increased, is increasing, and ought to be diminished." Two years later, a number of lucrative, useless offices were abolished in order to reduce patronage, but the triumph of the anti-royal faction was short-lived in spite of the Franco-American victory in the war. After some hesitation, George III made the son and namesake of the great William Pitt prime minister in order to restore the influence of the crown.

William Pitt the younger (1759-1806) was only twenty-four years old when he was called to office in 1783. Like his father, he had the support of the merchant and industrial classes, and his mild advocacy of reform won him the backing of most of the supporters of the Enlightenment.

His foe was the agrarian aristocracy, but as long as the king stood by him he had nothing to fear. He persuaded the king to create a host of new peers to swamp the House of Lords and made full use of patronage to control the Commons. He did much to make Adam Smith's ideas of free trade a reality, for England removed one trade restriction after another. He dabbled with the ideas of stopping the slave trade and reforming the electoral procedure for Parliament. Then, for a few months in the winter of 1787-1788, he was in trouble. George III mistook a tree in Windsor Park for the King of Prussia. Without royal support, no minister could govern, but George temporarily recovered his sanity, and it was he and Pitt who faced the onslaught of the French Revolution and Napoleon. Although England may have been near revolt in the 1770's, the American victory in the Revolutionary War discredited liberal ideas in England and Pitt united the country again before there was bloodshed.

THE EMPIRE

Voltaire is supposed to have quipped that the Holy Roman Empire was neither holy, nor Roman, nor an empire. There was some truth in his barb, for although there continued to be an emperor, an imperial court of justice, an army, and a Reichstag that exercised some control over the smaller territories, the larger principalities drifted apart. Three of the electors, Hanover (Great Britain), Saxony (Poland), and Brandenburg (Prussia), ruled kingdoms outside the Empire, and less than a third of the Habsburg territories were within its boundaries. Foreign influence remained strong. The kings of Denmark, Sweden, and Russia ruled duchies in the Empire, and France had allies there. The independence of the smaller German states was preserved by the principle of the balance of power, not by their own military strength. Their rulers mimicked the French court and contributed little to the evolution of the European civilization. It will therefore suffice to treat only with Brandenburg-Prussia and the Habsburg empire.

PRUSSIA

Prussia had the rare good fortune to be ruled by two able kings during the eighteenth century. The first was the simple, straightforward, hard-working Frederick William I (1713-1740). Frederick William had a violent temper and caned his family and his subjects alike, but he had a sincere interest in the welfare of both. No one worked harder in the service of the state. "Salvation," he wrote, "is of the Lord, but everything else is my affair."

His great interest was the army, and during his reign he increased its size from 40,000 to 83,000 men. Incompetent officers were weeded out, and troops were well equipped and carefully trained. Frederick William participated in drills and maneuvers and was the first European monarch to wear a uniform regularly. His fondness for his troops was so great that he hated to see them sacrificed in battle. He especially loved his Potsdam Giants, a regiment composed of men over six feet tall. As a result, his reign was among the most peaceful in Prussian history.

An army cost money. Frederick William raised the necessary funds by increasing taxes and by practicing rigid economies. He carefully operated the royal domain to make it contribute larger sums, forced the peasants to surrender 40 per cent of their net incomes, and even taxed the nobles' land in some provinces. He was thoroughly convinced that "50,000 soldiers are worth more than 100,000 ministers." He dismissed two-thirds of the court officials when he came to the throne and reduced the costs of his household and administration to less than one-fourth the former figure. Nonessential expenditure was everywhere curtailed, and the court lived in Spartan simplicity. Frederick William was more willing than his predecessors or his successors to appoint members of the middle class to office, and he watched his noble and non-noble officials carefully to make certain that they were honest and efficient. He would not tolerate laziness. A Saxon minister reported that: "Every day His Majesty gives new proofs of his justice. Walking recently at Potsdam at six in the morning, he saw a post-coach arrive with several passengers who knocked for a long time at the post-house which was still closed. The King, seeing that no one opened the door, joined them in knocking and even knocked in some window-panes. The master of the post then opened the door and scolded the travelers, for no one recognized the King. But His Majesty let himself be known by giving the official some good blows of his cane and drove him from his house and his job after apologizing to the travelers for his laziness. Examples of this sort, of which I could relate several others, make everybody alert and exact." [6]

Nowhere did Frederick William's stern justice display itself more clearly than in his treatment of Frederick, his eldest son. As a youth, Frederick seemed the opposite of his father. He loved music, poetry, and philosophy. His father regarded cultural pursuits as a waste of time. He had little interest in religion; his father was a devout Calvinist. Frederick was especially alienated by his father's stinginess and by his arbitrary treatment of him. He determined to flee, but his plans were discovered. Frederick William was furious. He contemplated imposing the death penalty on his son, but was persuaded to imprison him for a year instead. He did make Frederick witness the execution of a young friend and accomplice. When Frederick was released, he was given an opportunity to redeem himself by hard work in military and administrative posts. He labored to become an expert in the various aspects of government, and only in the evenings did he find time to resume his cultural pursuits. Although he became one of the best educated monarchs in Europe, he never again allowed his

---

[6] Quoted in Sidney B. Fay, *The Rise of Brandenburg-Prussia to 1786* (New York: Holt, 1937), p. 103.

cultural interests to interfere with his work. In 1740, his father could die happily, "being sure of such a worthy son and successor."

In some respects, Frederick the Great (1740-1786) was one of the finest examples of the enlightened despot. His love of learning and his devotion to duty brought him the plaudits of the philosophers. He privately accepted the contract theory of the state and made no effort to defend his powers on the basis of divine right. A good monarch, he believed, provided the best government, but he must perform certain services.

> These services consisted in the maintenance of the laws; a strict execution of justice; an employment of his whole powers to prevent any corruption of manners; and defending the state against its enemies. It is the duty of this magistrate to pay attention to agriculture; it should be his care that provisions for the nation should be in abundance, and that commerce and industry should be encouraged. He is a perpetual sentinal, who must watch the acts and the conduct of the enemies of the state. . . . If he be the first general, the first minister of the realm, it is not that he should remain the shadow of authority, but that he should fulfill the duties of such titles. He is only the first servant of the state. . . .

So Frederick the Great conscientiously set out to be "the first servant of the state." He displayed little administrative imagination and made few changes in governmental organization. His brilliance lay more in his mastery of the details of the system that he inherited. He began work at 6 A.M. daily and did not stop until evening, when he turned to cultural pursuits. Even Sundays brought no day of rest, for Frederick was not an orthodox Christian. He carried on a prodigious correspondence with his ministers and traveled around the country talking to citizens and officials. Inefficiency was quickly punished, and the graft and corruption that characterized the governments of other European states was scarcely known. The honesty and efficiency of the Prussian bureaucracy became the marvel of Europe. It is true that an able, dedicated king was needed to make the system work, but the Hohenzollern family produced more than its share of men of this type.

Frederick reorganized the judicial system and prepared a single code of laws for his domains. Torture was abolished except in treason and murder cases. Complete religious toleration was granted, and a degree of freedom of speech and the press was permitted. Although Frederick recognized the evils of serfdom, he was too dependent on the nobility for their service in the army and bureaucracy to do much about correcting these evils. Indeed, he accepted the hierarchical conception of society and did not reduce the various privileges of the different classes of society into a single code of rights held by all citizens. The noble continued to serve as both administrator and judge on his estate, and serious conflict between the crown and the aristocracy was avoided. Frederick sought to encourage industry and trade, but he was too wedded to mercantilism to accept the more advanced economic ideas of his day. He did, however, remove many internal tolls to make trade easier.

433

Frederick the Great from a contemporary portrait. (Courtesy Free Library of Philadelphia)

Frederick took considerable interest in his army and economized in other departments of government in order to enlarge it. Unlike his father, however, he had no objection to using it. He began his reign by seizing Silesia from Austria and managed to preserve his conquest in a series of brilliant campaigns during the War of Austrian Succession and the Seven Years War. When the latter conflict ended in 1763, his country was exhausted. From that time until his death in 1786, he sought to preserve the peace but at the same time to prevent Austrian expansion into Germany. In 1772, he acted in conjunction with Austria and Russia to partition a large part of Poland. Frederick got the smallest but most valuable share, the Polish territory between Prussia and Brandenburg. His scattered lands were now more nearly united and more easily defended. The Poles were too weak to resist, nor could they defend themselves when in 1793 and 1795 the great powers divided the remainder of their territory. The partitions of Poland greatly increased Prussian strength. A poor backward state surrounded by powerful neighbors had become a great European power. The population had increased from 750,000 in 1648 to 5,000,000 in 1786, and the army had grown from 8,000 to 200,000 during these years. In spite

434

of this, Frederick left his successor a full treasury at a time when kings of more prosperous countries were bankrupt. These achievements had been the result of the ability and determination of the Hohenzollern kings. Their very success suggests that great men more than natural advantages determine the course of history.

THE HABSBURG MONARCHY

Between 1683 and 1714, the Habsburgs conquered extensive territories in the Danube Basin from the Turks and replaced Spain in Italy and the Netherlands. Thereafter, their military fortunes fluctuated. They won northern Serbia, including Belgrade, from the Turks in 1718, but lost it again in 1739. Naples and Sicily were turned over to the Spanish Bourbons in 1738, and Frederick the Great took Silesia in 1740. These losses were compensated for by the annexation of a third of Poland in 1772 and 1795.

In terms of population increase and cultural achievement, the Habsburg lands made great progress during the eighteenth century. Vienna became a beautiful Baroque city filled with magnificent palaces and churches. Gluck, Mozart, Haydn, and Beethoven made it the music capital of Europe. Emperor Charles VI composed an opera, and his daughters danced in the ballet. Over two hundred thousand people crowded the streets of this city that had been besieged by the Turks only a few decades before, and the surrounding provinces grew proportionately. By the close of the century, over twenty-five million people inhabited Habsburg lands. The most rapid growth was in Hungary, where the Turkish withdrawal left large unoccupied territories. The population sprang from 2,500,000 to 8,000,000 between 1720 and 1787. Only part of this growth was supplied by the native Magyars. So many of the colonists were Germans, Slavs, and Rumanians that the Magyars were reduced from 90 to 40 per cent of the population. They became a minority in their ancient kingdom, just as the Germans were a minority in the remainder of the Habsburg lands.

This situation pointed to the great weakness of the Habsburg empire. It had neither linguistic, racial, religious, nor cultural unity, although Baroque architecture ornamented every city. Equally serious, it lacked administrative centralization, common laws, and internal free trade. During the eighteenth century, the Habsburgs tried to draw together this sprawling and disjointed empire.

Charles VI (1711-1740) spent the better part of his reign winning international and internal recognition for the Pragmatic Sanction. This Sanction declared that his territories were indivisible and that the female line could inherit in default of the male. Most of his subjects readily agreed, but the Hungarians insisted that he and his successors swear at their coronation to rule Hungary according to its own laws. Included was the right of the nobility to be exempt from taxation. Thus the separate status of Hungary with respect to the rest of the Habsburg empire dates back to the earliest efforts to transform the conglomeration of kingdoms and duchies into something that resembled a state.

Charles left his twenty-three-year-old daughter, Maria Theresa (1740-1780), the legal right to be his successor, but he also left her an inadequate army and an empty treasury with which to enforce her claim. The result, as we have seen, was the War of Austrian Succession in which Prussia, Bavaria, France, and other states forgot their promises and tried to despoil the defenseless girl. Although many persons in Vienna itself favored her enemies, Maria Theresa proved equal to the situation. She dramatically appeared before the Hungarian diet and, making full use of her youth, beauty, and sex, won the support of her most rebellious subjects. The Hungarian nobility, however, were not so gallant as to forget to extract a promise from her that she would respect their privileges. Their assistance was sufficient to hold her empire together, but not enough to regain Silesia. When peace came in 1748, she determined to make the reforms necessary to strengthen her empire against the Prussian foe.

The old Austrian and Bohemian chancelleries were abolished. In their place, departments of foreign affairs, commerce, war, justice, and internal affairs were established with jurisdiction over both territories. Justice was separated from administration, and a supreme court was created. Local government was also reorganized. In the past, provincial estates dominated by the nobility had not only voted taxes but also controlled local administration. Only a fraction of the money assessed ever reached Vienna. Maria Theresa recognized that sound finance was the basis of a strong state. The nobility and clergy were subjected to property and income taxes, and the provincial estates voted additional levies for ten years. The estates also lost their administrative duties. In their place, ten provinces were created, each administered by royal officials. For the first time, the crown came into direct contact with the peasants. The Habsburg monarchy was becoming more bureaucratic and less decentralized. The Austrian Netherlands, Milan, and Hungary, however, were exempted from these changes. In these regions, particularism was too strong to be easily abolished, but Maria Theresa did make progress in this direction. The lure of the court and imperial favors drew many great nobles to Vienna. Their loyalty to the Habsburgs slowly grew, and through their influence, Maria Theresa was able to control her more distant lands.

Maria Theresa was not an enlightened despot in the sense that she admired or studied the philosophers. She forbade the teaching of English in the universities "because of the dangerous character of this language in respect to its corrupting religious and ethical principles." Her administrative reforms were far-reaching, but they were also necessary for survival. At heart, Maria Theresa was a conservative. Although her morality and sense of justice did lead her to suppress the Inquisition in Milan and to restrict the use of torture, she would not upset the social order. Indeed, she neglected the education of her sixteen children, and her devotion to Catholicism led her to persecute Jews and Protestants. It is surprising and ironic that her son, Joseph II, was the purest example of the enlightened despot produced during the eighteenth century.

At an early age, Joseph became an ardent admirer of the Enlightenment and an imitator of Frederick the Great. He was not a practical reformer like the Prussian but a doctrinaire idealist. Tradition and custom meant nothing to him, and he held the nobility in contempt. Everything was to be swept away that stood in the path of reason. In 1765, he became emperor of the Holy Roman Empire and co-regent of the Habsburg lands, but Maria Theresa kept final authority until her death in 1780. Held in check, he grew restless. "The work piles up daily," he wrote, "and nothing is done. I labor unceasingly all morning, and until five or six in the afternoon, with fifteen minutes out while I eat a solitary lunch, but there is no result. The petty objections, the intrigues, of which I have so long been the victim, hinder and obstruct me, and with delay everything is going to the devil."

Finally, in 1780 his mother's death freed him to carry out his dream of leading his people along the path to happiness and progress. "I have made Philosophy the lawmaker of my empire," he declared; "her logical applications are going to transform Austria." For ten years no institution was safe. A revolution was imposed on the Habsburg empire from above.

Joseph hoped to replace the large noble estates worked by serf labor with small peasant farms. In 1781, he took the first step towards this goal by permitting the serf to marry whomever he pleased, to leave the manor when he wished, and to learn whatever trade he desired. By this act, Joseph freed the serf, but those who remained on the manor continued to perform unpaid labor service on the noble's estate and to pay dues in cash and in kind. A few years later, he gave the peasants hereditary right to their holdings, and in 1789, he tried to increase the reward for their labors. Before this time, they had retained only 27 per cent of their earnings; 10 per cent had gone to the Church, 29 per cent to the lord, and 34 per cent to the state. Now the peasants were to keep 70 per cent; the lord and the state were to share the remaining 30 per cent; and the Church was to rely on voluntary contributions.

Joseph was an admirer of the Physiocrats. He abandoned economic restraints and let natural economic laws operate. Internal trade barriers were removed, subsidies to industries were restricted, and monopolies terminated. Guild restrictions were abolished, and nobles were permitted to engage in trade without loss of status. Joseph even tried to introduce the physiocratic single-tax system, but he failed to follow their teachings on one point. He raised tariff barriers to limit imports from abroad and other nations inevitably retaliated by raising duties on Habsburg goods. Their products were barred from passage on the Elbe, the Oder, and the Danube rivers.

To render justice to the mass of his people Joseph issued a new penal code that abolished the death penalty and made everybody, whether noble or peasant, equal before the law. Witchcraft ceased to be a crime, and marriage between Christian and non-Christian was permitted. He advocated a national secular system of education from the primary schools through the university, but his plans never materialized. German became the language of instruction, of the law courts, and of the administration. Magyar and the numerous Slav tongues were not officially tolerated.

Some of Joseph's far-reaching reforms concerned religion. As a true man of the Enlightenment, he gave religious toleration and citizenship to all his subjects whether Protestant, Greek Orthodox, or Jew. He established control over the Catholic Church in his country and refused to permit papal decrees to be published without permission. He closed a third of the Austrian monasteries and cut the number of monks and nuns from 65,000 to 27,000. This act provided a large endowment for hospitals, schools, and charitable institutions. He remained a nominal Catholic, but had no use for "superstitions" or for spending money on lavish rituals. Fifteen Saints Days were abolished because he thought that the people had too many holidays; they were to work as hard as their royal master. Marriage became a civil contract, and divorce was permitted. In all, this energetic, reforming monarch issued 6,000 decrees and 11,000 new laws.

Joseph relentlessly pursued his policy of centralization and of liberalization from the past. Those who opposed him he regarded as knaves or fools. "I lack servants of every sort," he complained, "either for planning or for executing my designs. To be frank, I have found scarcely one person who is filled. with a genuine zeal for the good of the country." No one seemed to value his efforts. The very peasants whom he had freed rebelled because they did not understand what he was trying to do and objected to their remaining disabilities. The Jews, relieved at last from centuries of persecution and restrictions, were unhappy to find themselves subject to military conscription like other citizens and to see their children's education secularized. Less surprising was the opposition of the nobility, the clergy, and other privileged groups. The Hungarians and Belgians, who had previously enjoyed a special status in the empire, revolted; in January, 1790, a group of rebels met in Brussels to proclaim the independence of the United States of Belgium. A new republic had been created to check the activities of a reforming monarch.

Joseph saw that he was defeated, and on February 20 of that same year, he died at the age of forty-nine. He had lost his chance for personal happiness when his beloved wife had passed away more than a quarter of a century before. His impatience and his contempt for tradition had prevented him from bringing enlightenment and progress to his people. He wrote his own tragic epitaph: "Here lies Joseph II, who was unfortunate in everything that he undertook."

Joseph was succeeded by his brother, Leopold II (1790-1792), who had achieved a reputation as an enlightened ruler during the twenty-five years

438

that he had governed Tuscany. Leopold was, however, a more practical man and knew that the weak position of the middle class in most of his domains left him no choice but to govern with the aid of the aristocracy and through the historic provinces, estates, and other constituted bodies. Indeed, the aristocratic reaction against the egalitarian reforms had become so strong that Joseph II had begun to retreat just before his death. Leopold went further in restoring the old order and dared not resist the reaction to the point of provoking revolt. Joseph's attempt to let the peasants keep 70 per cent of their earnings had to be abandoned. The peasants continued to labor on the lord's estate without compensation and to pay dues in cash or kind, but their status as free men who could go where they wished and marry whom they pleased was preserved.

RUSSIA

Peter the Great (1682-1725) was not survived by a son, and the Russians had no rule prescribing hereditary succession. During the next seven reigns the palace guard determined who was to rule. This guard was composed of the gentry whom Peter had compelled to serve the state. Its members exercised a powerful influence in the army, whose officers, of course, belonged to their class. When a tsar died or was murdered for displeasing the gentry, the guard chose a successor who seemed likely to make concessions to their class. The army acquiesced, and no one dared protest. Hereditary right entailed no more than a marriage or blood tie with the Romanov dynasty. Of the eight immediate successors to Peter, one was a baby, one a boy, one an idiot, one a fool, and four were women. Two of these women had no blood ties with the royal family, but came into prominence through marriage with the reigning tsar. The result was that the gentry gradually won relief from the requirement that they serve the state and at the same time increased their control over the serfs. In the criminal code of 1754, serfs were listed as the property of the gentry.

Peter's immediate successor was Catherine I (1725-1727), a Lithuanian servant girl who had been his mistress for years before becoming his wife. Because she had accompanied her lover on campaigns, she was known to the guards, and this was enough to put her on the throne of the tsars. Other rulers followed in quick succession. Some died young; some were deposed or murdered. The first reign of more than ten years was that of Peter's daughter. Elizabeth (1741-1762) was an easygoing, immoral, extravagant woman whose wardrobe was said to include 15,000 dresses; fortunately for the taxpayers, she neglected to pay for most of them. She may have married a cossack peasant who gained admission to court as a choir boy. With all her faults, her reign was not as unfortunate as most. The German influence at court was reduced, but at the same time Peter's Westernization program was continued. Education was improved, and the first Russian university was established at Moscow in 1755. Elizabeth's gravest mistake was to challenge Prussia in the Baltic by entering the Seven Years War. Russian troops fought well, but the war brought more hardships for the people.

Elizabeth was succeeded by her nephew, Peter III (1762), who, as son of the Duke of Holstein-Gottorp, had been raised as a German Lutheran prince. Part of his program was justifiable, but he quickly alienated everyone. The army was angered by his decision to make peace with Frederick the Great and send troops to fight Denmark on behalf of his petty German duchy. The palace guard was put in Prussian-style uniforms and subjected to strict military discipline. It seemed likely that Peter planned the destruction of this force. The clergy was infuriated by his scoffing at the ritual of the Orthodox Church and his determination to make all religions equal by law. He even dared to secularize church lands. Meanwhile, Catherine, his German wife, had learned Russian, become a member of the Orthodox Church, and courted the favor of the guard. She knew that her husband planned to divorce her and to marry his mistress. The setting was perfect for another palace revolution. After a reign of less than six months, Peter was murdered, and Catherine II (1762-1796) was seated on her husband's throne.

Two facts must be borne in mind when one considers Catherine's policies as empress. First, she owed her throne to the palace guards. If she angered them or the gentry class to which they belonged, she knew that she would quickly be deposed. Second, she was a woman of intelligence and wide reading. She had delved deeply into the writings of the philosophers and numbered Voltaire and Diderot among her correspondents. Frequently, her enlightened ideas and the desires of the gentry were at cross purposes. Always a practical woman, she gave in to their wishes.

At first, Catherine may have hoped that she could persuade the gentry to accept some reforms. She summoned an assembly elected by all the elements of the population except the clergy and the serfs, to discuss the preparation of a new law code. To guide the deliberations, Catherine prepared an *Instruction* in which serfdom, capital punishment, and torture were called into question and equality before the law was advocated. The assembly sat for a year and a half and undoubtedly provided Catherine with much useful information, but it was soon apparent that the gentry was unwilling to make any sacrifices for the benefit of the serf. Indeed, what changes Catherine did introduce during her long reign benefited this privileged class.

She reorganized local government by dividing the country into fifty provinces that in turn were subdivided into districts. Most of the provincial officials were appointed, but those at the district level were usually elected by the gentry. This class was organized in each district as a corporate group with special privileges comparable to the estates or orders in the West. Before, the gentry had been powerful, but it had lacked specific legal rights separating it from the rest of the population. The rights now granted

Catherine the Great. (Sovfoto)

included exemption from personal taxation and corporal punishment, and trial by peers. The gentry was given the exclusive privilege of purchasing villages and of owning factories and mines, and it shared with the townsmen the right to engage in trade. Towns were granted charters as in the West, and an effort was made to give a special status to the burghers. In 1767, Catherine deprived a serf of the right to appeal to the state against his master, and after a serious peasant uprising led by a cossack, Pugachev, had been suppressed, she abandoned any further thought of rural reform. Indeed, serfdom was extended into the newer parts of the empire, and in her desire to hold the support of the gentry, Catherine gave them huge tracts of crown land. As a result of this last concession, 800,000 relatively well-treated peasants on the royal estates were reduced to serfdom.

Catherine was enough of a laissez-faire economist to establish internal free trade, abolish state monopolies, and build canals. The quantity of trade increased, especially with other European countries. Nevertheless, the urban population was small even by the standards of the time, and those members of the land-owning gentry who engaged in trade profited most from these economic reforms.

Catherine encouraged the Westernization of aristocratic society and brought Russia further into the European intellectual tradition. She also expanded the boundaries of her adopted country. She annexed about half of Poland in the three partitions and also expanded in the south at the expense of the Turks. By the terms of the Treaty of Kuchuk-Kainarji in 1774, Russia was given some additional provinces, the privilege of navigating in Turkish waters, and the right to protect Greek Orthodox Christians in the Ottoman Empire. Catherine even dreamed of setting up an independent state at Constantinople with her grandson, appropriately named Constantine, as ruler. She was one of the great territorial builders of the Russian Empire, and her policy in regard to the Ottoman Empire foreshadowed later Russian moves.

Catherine was succeeded upon her death by her son, Paul I (1796-1801). Paul had been rigorously excluded from participating in the government by his mother who feared that he might seek the throne to which he would have been entitled had the Russians possessed any normal law of succession. As a result, he had neither practical experience nor a realistic view of what a tsar could and could not safely do. He was further handicapped by being eccentric, if not actually mad. Many of his actions were just, but few of them were wise. He sought to help the serf at a time when power resided with the gentry. He reduced the price of salt, established grain reserves for the relief of the poor in time of famine, and sought to improve the caliber of the clergy. But he also opposed the importation of luxury goods, abused his army officers, and limited to three days a week the amount of labor that a serf could perform free for the gentry. In short, he offended the gentry. In 1801, he was strangled in another palace revolution, and his son, Alexander I, who had agreed to his deposition, if not his murder, came to the throne.

THE LESSER STATES

Many of the smaller states were ruled by enlightened despots during the latter part of the eighteenth century. Leopold I (1745-1790) of Tuscany administered his domain honestly and efficiently. He abolished serfdom, encouraged trade and industry, reformed the penal code, and drove out the Inquisition. Pope Benedict XIV (1740-1758) was influenced by the Enlightenment and, like the secular monarchs, encouraged agriculture and trade. Another pope, Clement XIV (1769-1774), dissolved the Jesuits. This order had come under attack by philosophers everywhere because of its militant Catholicism. Kings feared it because some of its members had once advocated tyrannicide; merchants despised it because other members had engaged in trade. France, Spain, Portugal, and Austria had already expelled the order, and the pope had little choice but to follow the wishes of the Catholic sovereigns.

Spain was partly rejuvenated by the Bourbons during the eighteenth century. Since Aragon, Valencia, and Catalonia had supported the claims of the Austrian Archduke Charles in the War of Spanish Succession, Philip V (1700-1746) had an excellent excuse to deprive them of their special privileges; and the dynastic, decentralized monarchy that Ferdinand and Isabella had created by their marriage became a relatively centralized state. The laws and administrative institutions of Castile were established in the other kingdoms, and Castilian became the official language. The government of Castile itself, however, was changed in spite of its loyal support of the Bourbon cause during the war. The old conciliar system of government was partly replaced by French-style ministries, and intendants were appointed to administer the various provinces. Olivarez' dream had become true; the king of Castile had truly become the king of all Spain.

The Treaty of Utrecht also freed Spain from the responsibility of ruling territories in Italy and the Netherlands, but Philip's Italian wife embroiled the country in several wars in an attempt to get thrones for her sons. These efforts were partly successful, but at the cost of delaying a Spanish recovery. It was not until her son, Charles III (1759-1788), came to the throne that the worst administrative abuses were removed, the military forces strengthened, and trade, industry, and agriculture improved. Although a good Catholic, Charles banished the Jesuits and limited the authority of the Inquisition. He respected the privileges of the aristocracy and thereby avoided conflict on this score, but in spite of his accomplishments his death was followed by renewed difficulties for the unhappy country.

Portugal found no enlightened despot, but the long ministry of the Marquis of Pombal (1699-1782) served the same purpose. Pombal was bolder and more ruthless than most of the monarchs of his day. He weakened the nobility, attacked the Church, and at the same time encouraged trade, industry, and agriculture. He took an interest in education and did much to breathe life into the once-proud Portuguese empire, but in the end he lost the support of the crown and was exiled. During the last quarter of the century, the clergy and nobility began to recover their former position.

The Swedish nobility profited by the death of Charles XII in 1718 and the defeat in the Great Northern War to seize control of the government. The king was reduced to the status of a puppet, and the diet and council became the principal organs of government. However, the nobility soon became divided into pro-French and pro-Russian factions that quarreled continually. This division paved the way for Gustavus III (1771-1792) to reassert royal authority. Gustavus became one of the most enlightened monarchs of his age. "The one object I have in view . . ." he boldly proclaimed, "is the re-establishment of liberty. That and only that can make you happy." For two decades, Europe was treated with the sight of a king establishing freedom of religion, thought, and the press. He reorganized the code of justice and abolished torture. Tariffs were reduced, tolls were abolished, and trade and agriculture were encouraged. Gustavus also exercised a profound cultural influence. He was a great orator, a good playwright, and a believer in better education for his subjects. Inevitably, the nobles reacted strongly against their loss of power, and in 1792 a group of conspirators took advantage of the disguises worn at a masquerade ball to assassinate him. His successor, however, was able to hold the unruly nobility in check.

The able John Frederick Struensee tried to introduce similar reforms into Denmark in the name of his king, Christian VII, but an aristocratic reaction led to his execution in 1772 after a year in power. Even Poland went through a brief period of reform after the first partition, but its powerful neighbors desired to annex more of its territory and refused to permit constitutional changes that might strengthen Polish capacity to resist. The result was the division of the remainder of the country in 1793 and 1795 among Russia, Prussia, and Austria.

In the Netherlands and Switzerland, the aristocracy consisted primarily of bourgeois patrician families who controlled the towns to the exclusion of the lesser inhabitants. Their preferred position was inherited, and the newly rich merchant was not readily welcomed into their midst. Indeed, they differed from the aristocracies of other countries only in that they usually resided in towns and drew their income from business. As might be expected, there were quarrels between this aristocracy and the other urban classes.

In the Netherlands, this quarrel was complicated by the position of the house of Orange. At first the regents, as the Dutch bourgeois aristocracy was called, sought to reduce the power of the Orangists, but when they were faced with the growth of more democratic forces, that were encouraged by the French, they divided. The more liberal members joined the democrats who called themselves the patriot party, while the more conservative were forced into the camp of their traditional enemy, the house of Orange. William V (1766-1795), Prince of Orange, was closely allied with the British and Prussian royal families. The former provided financial support, and in 1787 the latter sent an army into the Netherlands to restore his position and, with it, the position of the aristocracy.

In Switzerland, there was neither a king nor a house of Orange to vie with the urban aristocracy. This situation, coupled with the beginnings of that prosperity now associated with this mountainous region, reduced social strife to a minimum. Only in Geneva, which was not then a part of the Confederation, was there serious difficulty. In 1768, the bulk of the middle-class inhabitants broke the stranglehold that the patricians held on the government, only to lose their gains in 1782 to an aristocratic resurgence.

As the fateful year 1789 dawned, a hereditary aristocracy was nearly everywhere ascendant in Europe. Most countries had been ruled by enlightened despots or ministers, but many of these rulers had limited their activities to administrative and judicial reforms, and those that had tried to reduce the powers of the aristocracy had in the long run suffered defeat. Indeed, the new republic of the United States was the only country in the Western world where the aristocracy had definitely been defeated and even there the Constitution of 1789 offered greater protection for the propertied classes than the confederacy of the thirteen states had provided before.

The aristocracy saw itself as the champion of liberty against the threats of the crown and the populace, but liberty meant the traditional rights and privileges of the various social classes, rights and privileges that were safeguarded by parliaments, estates, and other long-standing institutions. This aristocratic conception of liberty was in accord with the popular cry for no taxation without representation and for freedom of speech and fair trials. Noble and egalitarian alike desired the life, liberty, and property demanded by Locke and Montesquieu. They divided on the question of whether all men are born equal and molded by their environment, or whether their character and worth are determined by the position to which they are born in society. This division of opinion became apparent in most countries only after the populace had joined forces with the aristocracy to defeat the crown's effort to reduce the distinctions between the different provinces and social classes. At this point, the aristocratic resurgence was followed by a democratic revolt. To investigate this change we must turn to France.

FRANCE

The economic revival was greater in France than in most continental countries, and the philosophers achieved a wide following there, but a third force for change was lacking. France produced no enlightened despots and no rulers who were willing to back an enlightened minister long enough to ensure reform. Revolution was the ultimate price the monarchy had to pay for this failure.

LOUIS XV AND LOUIS XVI

When Louis XIV died in 1715, he left his five-year-old great-grandson and namesake as his heir, a public debt greater than the entire amount of money in circulation, and a discontented, critical people. The time seemed right for a violent reaction, comparable to the Fronde, against monarchical authority. It is a tribute to the effectiveness of the work of Louis XIV and the regency of the Duke of Orléans (1674-1723) that there were no revolts.

Orléans was a good-natured, kindly man with above average intelligence who made a sincere effort to govern well. He saw that reform was necessary and was more willing to experiment than any of his successors. He weathered the demands for drastic changes by pretending to favor a revival of the Estates-General and by associating the great nobles with the government. Within three years, they had so discredited themselves that he was able to return to the earlier system of ruling through professional administrators. He checked the militant Catholicism of the previous reign, made efforts to improve the system of taxation, and lent support to Law's unsuccessful scheme for solving the crown's fiscal and currency problems.[7]

[7] See page 406.

Louis XV by Van Loo. (Bulloz-Art Reference Bureau)

Unfortunately, Orléans was also an obscene, immoral drunkard whose personal behavior did much to change the character of the court from the pious bigotry of the latter part of Louis XIV's reign to the gay, irresponsible immorality so characteristic of eighteenth-century Versailles.

Orléans died in 1723. After a brief interlude in which the incompetent Duke of Bourbon headed the state, the youthful Louis XV named his seventy-three-year-old tutor, Cardinal Fleury (1653-1743), first minister. Until he died at the age of ninety, Fleury directed the government. He saw that the country needed a period of peace and repose in which to recover from the wars of Louis XIV. Happily, the English minister, Walpole, was in agreement, and the two statesmen acted together to keep Europe at peace until 1740. During this respite, trade and commerce doubled, industry was encouraged, and roads and canals were built. Some legal reforms were made, and through rigid economy the budget was balanced in 1738, the only time in the century. Fleury was cautious and unspectacular, but he gave France its best government for many years. It is regrettable that he returned to the policy of religious persecution.

At the death of Cardinal Fleury in 1743, the thirty-year-old Louis announced that henceforth he would be his own first minister. When his great-grandfather had said this, he had meant it, but Louis XV did not. His intentions were good; but after a few months, affairs of state began to bore him. He did retain an interest in diplomacy, but his devious nature had led him to correspond with his agents without the knowledge of his foreign minister. Louis did not intend to be deceitful. He merely lacked the courage to face determined opposition and found it easier to undermine a minister by going behind his back. There were often two foreign policies: one official, the other secret and royal. Neither was successful. Louis was not stupid. He was a handsome man of average intelligence,

446

Louis XVI by Duplessis. (Bulloz-Art Reference Bureau)

but he had little energy and was perpetually bored. His kindly, dull wife could not hold his interest, although she bore him ten children in less than twelve years. One mistress followed another, and there were many lesser affairs. The post of *maitresse en titre* became the most coveted one in the kingdom, for unlike his predecessor, Louis XV permitted the current object of his interests to influence affairs of state. Fathers sought the post for their daughters, husbands for their wives, politicians for their friends. The court became a center of intrigue. To be a friend of a rising star was to be assured of high public office. To offend a mistress like the Marquise of Pompadour (1721-1764) or Madame du Barry (1746?-1793) was to risk dismissal. These women encouraged Louis' spendthrift ways, but more important their prominent position at Versailles brought the monarchy into disrepute. Louis, who had been called "the well beloved" in his youth, became the most despised of kings. He sensed the growing disillusionment of his people as France barely held its own during the War of Austrian Succession and lost an empire during the Seven Years War, as taxes became more oppressive and public debts mounted, as soldiers were unpaid in the field, people went hungry in the streets, and court life at Versailles remained gay, extravagant, and frivolous. "Things will last my time at any rate," he remarked, and he may have said the equally prophetic, "After me the deluge."

When Louis died in 1774, there was still time to reform, if an enlightened despot could be found. Unfortunately, Louis' successor was his nineteen-year-old grandson, Louis XVI (1774-1792). No one could have been less qualified for such a role. He was a fat, stupid, plain man who could summon the energy to hunt and make locks, but not to stay awake in a meeting of his council. His worst fault was lack of confidence. He had great difficulty in arriving at any decision, and when he finally issued an order, it was easy to persuade him to countermand it. Even his virtues—kindness, simplicity, modesty—were not those of a dynamic, reforming king who had to injure a few before he could help the many.

Louis' wife was the pretty, attractive, shallow Marie Antoinette, a poorly educated daughter of Maria Theresa. Marie Antoinette was not vicious and perhaps not immoral. At first, she had aimed to please, but finding her husband shy and dull, she began to indulge herself in the gay court life, in masques and balls, in expensive jewels and costly clothes, in gambling and flirtations. She used her influence over Louis to interfere in the government and helped destroy what little hope there was for real reform. "What business have you to interfere with the placing of ministers," her brother Joseph II warned. "You behave more like a Pompadour or a Du Barry than a great Princess." Politics made her enemies and she was certainly indiscreet, though she may have committed no indiscretions. Soon she was gossiped about in the streets. Untold harm was done to the monarchy, for the one person at Versailles who was expected to be faithful to her marriage vows was the queen.

THE STRUCTURE OF SOCIETY

In justice to Louis XV and Louis XVI, it was no easy task to reform France after the image of the philosophers. They were not dictators who could impose their will; every town, every province, and every social class had its special rights and privileges, protected by law. These rights and privileges were not designed to protect individual liberty. This was the complaint of the philosophers. The king could issue *lettres de cachet* imprisoning persons without trial, although he rarely did so. The press was censored, religious liberty was denied, and torture and inhuman punishments were inflicted. The guilds regulated industry, trade was not permitted to flow freely even within the country, and the occupations one could engage in depended largely upon birth.

The French social structure was designed instead to protect the family and the privileges of the various orders and estates into which society was divided. The father controlled the actions of his children. He chose their marital partners and their professions. If a child disobeyed, he could use the state to enforce his authority. Many of the arbitrary imprisonments were the result of the request of a father for assistance in disciplining a wayward son. To perpetuate the family, the eldest male child inherited more property than his younger brothers. Children of the nobility were designated for the army, for the Church, or for living on the ancestral estate. Those of the middle class were usually groomed for their father's trade or profession. Freedom of choice was everywhere denied. Nevertheless, each person had his rightful place in society, his privileges as well as his obligations. Even the few remaining serfs had some rights.

There were three legal divisions or estates into which the French population was divided. The first estate, or clergy, consisted of about 100,000 priests, monks, and nuns. The members of this estate derived their revenue from their ownership of between 6 and 10 per cent of the land of France, from the manorial dues derived from the manors over which they held lordships, and from the tithes, fees, and gifts of the faithful. Their responsibilities were numerous. Not only did they look after the spiritual welfare of the people, but they bore most of the burden of education and poor relief. The privileges of the clergy were also great. As the first order of society, they enjoyed pre-eminence over the other estates. They were legally organized as a corporation. Since 1561, they had sent deputies to periodic assemblies that voted the direct taxes, or "free gifts" as they were called, to be contributed by their estate for the support of the government. These assemblies did not hesitate to couple petitions of grievance with their vote of funds. The clergy had agents to look after their welfare when their assembly was not in session. The ordinary ecclesiastical organization of archdioceses and dioceses gave additional strength and cohesion to the order. They even had their own law courts, and, of course, they wore distinctive garments.

449

Internal division was the great weakness of the clergy. Nearly all the bishops and abbots were of noble origin. Many of them enjoyed large incomes, and inevitably they supported the existing society and government. At the opposite extreme were the curés and vicars of the villages who were usually of peasant extraction. Even after it was increased in 1786, their annual income was little better than that of the peasants they served. Between these two extremes were the curés of the towns and the members of the chapters. They were usually of middle-class extraction, but their incomes fell far below that of the wealthy prelates. The members of the lesser clergy were influenced to some extent by the Enlightenment and were not anxious to preserve the status quo. As early as 1763, they showed an inclination to challenge the authority of the bishops.

The second estate was the nobility. It consisted of about 400,000 persons, including women and children, who alone were allowed to carry a sword and wear other distinctive garments. They were exempt from most direct taxes but had no national assembly in which to voice their views. They owned about a fifth of the land and most of the manors, from which they derived feudal dues. There were several types of nobles, but the differ-

450

ences between them, unlike the differences between members of the clergy, became less pronounced during the course of the century. The nobles of the sword enjoyed the greatest prestige. They claimed erroneously to be descended from the German invaders who had conquered the country from the Romans. Though few could in fact trace their ancestry back to the Hundred Years War, the idea that they were a distinct and courageous race led them to separate from the rest of the population. As seigneurs, they still held certain police and judicial powers in their manors. They alone could hunt, fish, have a private pew in the church, and keep a gallows, although the right to inflict capital punishment had long been denied them. The wealthiest and most distinguished members of this class resided at Versailles where they participated in the intrigues and gaiety of the court. The great majority remained at home, where some lived comfortably and others had difficulty making a living from their estates.

The nobles of the robe were the second segment of the second estate. Their function was to serve on the law and financial courts. At one time it had been relatively easy for a wealthy member of the middle class to enter their ranks, but when Henry IV made these offices hereditary, the nobility of the robe became a caste. Its leaders in the *parlements* were the staunchest defenders of privileges.

The members of a third type of nobility were of middle-class origin. These were bankers, tax collectors, and public functionaries whose positions were not inherited but who were often ennobled because of their essential services to the crown. They were very rich and intermarried with the nobles of the sword and of the robe who were willing to forget differences in birth in return for wealth. Although they were advocates of reform, in the last analysis their economic interests bound them to the old regime.

The fusion of the three functional types of nobility did not prevent other differences from arising. Some nobles were rich and lived at court or in elegant châteaux. Some were so poor that they were little better off than peasants. Some adopted the new economic ideas. They enclosed their land, farmed in accordance with scientific methods, speculated on the stock exchange or in real estate, and derived profits from mining, smelting, glassmaking, or sugar plantations in the West Indies. These nobles welcomed changes and dreamed of reviving the Estates-General so that they could participate in the government as the English lords did in Parliament. A few, like Lafayette (1757-1834), who joined the American colonists in their war for independence, were deeply influenced by the ideas of the Enlightenment. Most nobles, however, remained conservative. They were willing to make a few concessions, but none that would seriously weaken their economic position or destroy their privileged status.

The third estate consisted of an even more bewildering variety of people. At the top of the ladder were the financiers, the merchants who en-

451

gaged in wholesale trade, and the industrialists—men whose wealth gave them power. As a rule, they were not averse to reform, but they did not wish to overthrow the monarchy because they had too much at stake in the existing regime. Professional people—lawyers, doctors, writers,—came next. They were favorably inclined towards the ideas of the Enlightenment and advocated radical changes. Members of the legal profession were particularly disgruntled because their ordinary advancement to important judgeships was blocked by the hereditary nobility of the robe. The craft guildmasters, journeymen, and apprentices, who made up another group within the third estate, were also discontented, but for different reasons. They were anxious to preserve those privileges that protected them from the competition of the wholesale merchants and capitalists. With the day laborers of the cities, whose wages lagged behind the rising prices, they formed a powerful force for mob action.

The third estate also included nearly all the inhabitants of the manor. The peasants owned a third of the land but made up over three-fourths of the population. They were divided into several economic groups. A few were prosperous because they owned or rented large tracts of land. Many more were small farmers who often had to lease some land in order to support their families. Still less fortunate were the sharecroppers, who surrendered a large part of their produce to the landowners. Finally, there were the agricultural laborers who owned or rented little or no land and worked for the lord of the manor or well-to-do peasant farmers. The few serfs were far more fortunate than those in eastern Europe. They were protected from their masters by royal justice, and, after 1799, the lord was not permitted to pursue them if they fled.

The peasants labored under several difficulties. They paid far more than their share of taxes and were almost alone in being forced to serve in the army and to work on the roads without pay. In addition to their obligations to the crown, they owed certain obligations and dues to the lord of the manor for their own land. They paid him a large fee when their land passed from their hands into those of another whether because of death or sale. They were compelled to grind their grain at the lord's mill, to bake their bread at his oven, and to press their grapes at his wine press. For each of these services a fee was extracted. They paid an annual quit rent in cash or in kind based on the amount of land that they held. The peasants were even denied the right to hunt, fish, or keep rabbits or pigeons, for these privileges were reserved for the lord. Actually, the peasants did not surrender more than 15 per cent of the income from their land to the lord, far less than went to the crown in taxes. However, since they regarded the land as their own, they saw no reason to pay anything at all. They were bitter at not even being permitted to protect their crops from rabbits, pigeons, and other wildlife. As a result, the French peasants resented the injustices of their position although they were much better off than their counterparts in central or eastern Europe.

The Era of the Enlightenment, II

THE CROWN AND THE ARISTOCRACY

During the last half of the eighteenth century tension between the crown and the aristocracy increased. First the king, then the nobility, and finally various elements within the third estate tried to alter the French government.

Neither Louis XV nor Louis XVI really wanted to change the system of government or the structure of society. Occasionally, they appointed a minister with a zeal for reform, but they never gave such a man their support for long. Royal attempts to make changes grew out of financial necessity. While the wars of the period increased the expenses of government, the poor could pay no more taxes and the government could not borrow indefinitely. Only by assessing the rich and the privileged, could the crown hope for a balanced budget.

The first major effort in this direction was undertaken by the finance minister, Machault (1701-1794), to meet the debts that had been incurred in the War of Austrian Succession. In 1749, he persuaded the king to issue an edict levying a perpetual 5 per cent income tax to be paid by everyone. Immediately, the nobility, the clergy, the provincial estates, and the law courts began to protest. The king capitulated, but the Seven Years War reduced royal finances to such a state that it was necessary for him to renew the quarrel. Gradually, the dispute became centered on the relations between the *parlements* and the crown.

There were thirteen theoretically equal *parlements*, or supreme law courts, in France. Although each exercised final jurisdiction over a different area, the *parlement* at Paris was by far the most important because of its location and huge jurisdiction. The *parlements* had the power to obstruct the royal program because only those measures registered by them could be enforced. Thus the judges had a veto over royal legislation and taxation. Only by a personal appearance before the court could the king override their opposition. The *parlements*, controlled as they were by the nobles of the robe, became the spokesmen of the aristocracy. Judges used their power to block reforms, to interfere with legislation, and to attack the militant pro-Jesuit wing of the Catholic clergy. Sometimes Louis XV tried to conciliate the judges, even to the extent of suppressing the Jesuits. On other occasions, he tried to destroy their power by exiling them to small towns or by reducing their jurisdiction. Although the *parlements* defended privilege, their stand was popular with the people, who mistakenly assumed that any opponent of the hated king was their friend.

During the first two years of his reign, it looked as though Louis XVI might support the program of the Enlightenment. In spite of the opposition of the court and aristocracy, he stood by Turgot (1727-1781), a reforming minister who had achieved an enviable reputation as intendant of Limoges. Turgot tried to balance the budget by reducing expenditures, including those of the queen and the court, and by better tax collection.

He abolished the requirement that made peasants liable for working from six to thirty days on roads without pay and levied a tax on all landowners for the upkeep of the highways. He believed that there were natural economic laws, and to permit them to function properly, he established free trade in grain in the interior of France and did away with guild restrictions. These measures were unpopular with the privileged groups, from the queen, through the *parlements,* and down to the guild artisans. The weak-willed Louis was prevailed upon to dismiss his minister in 1776, and most of the reforms were abandoned.

Shortly thereafter, France decided to enter the American war for independence, and the financial situation worsened. Louis found in a Swiss Calvinist banker named Necker (1732-1804) a minister who could use his connections to borrow money, but Necker too insisted on royal economy. For this crime and a few mild reforms, the court persuaded the king to dismiss him. Another minister of finance, Calonne (1734-1802), continued the practice of making good the government deficit by borrowing, but by 1786 royal credit was exhausted. Since the poor could pay no more taxes, the aristocracy had to be persuaded to assume a large part of the burden if bankruptcy were to be avoided.

Even though the nobility as a whole had greater purchasing power at this time than during the seventeenth century, most of them felt that their incomes were inadequate. During the eighteenth century, the variety and quality of goods that one must own to maintain his position in society increased. Middle-class wealth grew so rapidly that the aristocracy had trouble maintaining its superiority. Some nobles, as we have seen, sought to tap the new sources of income by engaging in mining or investing in trade or industry. Most of them, however, had neither the surplus wealth nor the inclination to become involved in such enterprises. They preferred to put renewed emphasis on their manorial rights. Forgotten dues were revived, and accepted dues were increased. Registers were prepared listing the exact amount owed by each peasant, and invariably the sum was greater than that paid before. Rents were raised 98 per cent between 1740 and 1789, while prices went up only 65 per cent. Some nobles won edicts from the king authorizing them to appropriate part of the common lands and to enclose their fields. Yet the middle class continued to make gains.

As their relative economic position became weaker, the nobles made greater efforts to prevent the ennoblement of commoners. At the same time, they tried to win control of the government. By 1786 they dominated the Church, the *parlements* and other law courts, and the surviving provincial estates. Nearly all army and naval officers were drawn from their ranks, and most high government officials were members of their class. Even the intendants, the backbone of Louis XIV's provincial administration, were now noblemen with marriage ties and property interests in

454

their jurisdictions. Thus, when Calonne proposed to tax the nobility, he was striking at a powerful class that felt no disposition to make sacrifices itself except in return for further concessions from the crown. Out of the resulting conflict between the king and the aristocracy the French Revolution was born.

11/ The French Revolution and Napoleon

FROM the standpoint of the broad sweep of history, the holocaust of the French Revolution emerges as part of a larger, middle-class revolutionary movement that embraced most of the Western world. This revolutionary movement began with several small uprisings in Europe and the revolt of thirteen British colonies in North America and continued intermittently until the middle of the nineteenth century. Its underlying causes were the ideas of the Enlightenment and the social changes produced by the economic revival that began in the eighteenth century. At times, this revolutionary movement merged with an aristocratic reaction against monarchical efforts to reform and with a nationalistic spirit that ran counter to the cosmopolitanism of the Enlightenment, but by 1918, the middle class was triumphant and liberty, equality, and fraternity, the three ideals of the French revolutionaries, were ascendant in most of Europe and America.

Many of those who lived in the revolutionary era were conscious of the international character of the movement. Nevertheless, if one approaches the French Revolution from the standpoint of the day-by-day course of events, no single class appeared to be struggling for power, no single set of ideas sought mastery of the human mind, and no single goal inspired the participants.

Many members of the middle class did play leading roles, but they were assisted by the liberal nobles, the lesser clergy, the lower classes in the towns, and the peasants. These groups did not agree on what the most important objectives should be. The peasants, for example, sought the abolition of the tithe, manorial dues, and the *taille*, but they neither understood nor were interested in the ideas of the Enlightenment. The lower classes in the towns thought in terms of their pressing economic needs, not their natural rights. They were ready to follow any demagogue who promised to alleviate their misery. Peasant and worker opposed the middle-class emphasis on private property and laissez-faire. The former usually wanted to keep their collective rights on the land, and the latter remained loyal to the guilds and advocates of price control. The lesser clergy accepted most of the political and social ideas of the Enlightenment, but the majority in this group remained loyal to the religious teachings of their Church and obedient to the authority of Rome. Neither the members of the middle class nor the liberal nobles could agree among themselves on how far the reform program should be pushed or what the exact nature of the French constitution should be. No individual, no party, no class had a concrete program with a definite idea of how it was to be achieved. One uprising followed another, with few common characteristics beyond dissatisfaction with the existing regime. No leader emerged to give firm direction to the forces of change until Napoleon came to power in 1799. Earlier, a contemporary's statement that "we live in a time of great events but little men" had been all too true.

THE CONSTITUTIONAL MONARCHY

THE BEGINNING OF THE REVOLUTION

The French Revolution began with Calonne's decision in 1786 that fundamental changes would have to be made in the old regime.[1] He was faced with the painful fact that governmental income was about 500,000,-000 livres and expenditures were 630,000,000 livres. In the past, the deficit had been made good by borrowing, but now credit was exhausted. Economy would help, but not enough to balance the budget. The expenses of the court of Versailles, that center of extravagance, were only 6 per cent of the total cost of the government. The basic reason for the deficit was that over half the money collected in taxes went to service the national

[1] See pages 454-455.

debt. Additional revenue was obviously needed, but the peasants were already overtaxed. Clearly, the aristocracy would have to contribute more. To achieve this goal, Calonne proposed a land tax which was to be paid by everyone and assessed by provincial assemblies elected by taxpayers without regard to their social status. He hoped to encourage internal trade by removing some sales taxes and by permitting the free circulation of grain throughout France. Since Calonne was too much a realist to expect the aristocracy to welcome his proposals, he persuaded the king to summon a carefully selected aristocratic assembly of 144 notables, in the hope that they would support these revolutionary changes when they learned of the crown's predicament.

The notables met in a stormy session from February to May, 1787. Though willing to accept parts of the program, they balked at paying the land tax, demanding concessions in return. These concessions included the right to examine royal financial accounts and to control local administration through provincial assemblies. Cooperation between the crown and the aristocracy ceased, and Calonne was forced from office. His successor, Brienne, did no better. Finally, the government decided to take its rejected proposals directly to the *parlement* of Paris to be registered. The *parlement* accepted the edicts to free the grain trade and to create provincial assemblies but declared that only the Estates-General had the right to grant new taxes. The American revolutionaries' cry against taxation without representation was heard in the capital of France. The crown sought to break *parlement's* resistance by exiling several judges, but the remainder made a strong protest against arbitrary arrest. The provincial *parlements* lent their support to the *parlement* of Paris, as did the clergy, who voted only a seventh of their usual sum when they assembled. The army and the intendants refused to cooperate with the crown, and the middle and lower classes proved willing allies of the rebellious aristocracy. Riots occurred throughout France, and the newly formed provincial estates joined the resistance. Faced with well-organized opposition by all three estates and the imminent threat of bankruptcy, Louis capitulated. The *parlement* of Paris was restored to its former position in answer to the demands of the aristocracy, and the Estates-General was summoned to meet on May 1, 1789, after a lapse of 175 years.

At this point, the aristocracy reached the height of its influence. Its stand for consent to taxation and for individual liberty was so popular that it won wide support from the third estate. However, its triumph was momentary, for the third estate wanted legal equality as well as liberty. This the aristocrats were not prepared to concede. Some were willing to accept equality in taxation, but they insisted on maintaining their lesser immunities, their hereditary rights, and their privileged social status. Above all, they refused to share political power with the third estate.

The immediate issues over which the aristocracy and the third estate split concerned the composition and procedures of the Estates-General.

The third estate demanded that the Estates-General consist of a single chamber, in which half the deputies would be from their order. The other half were to be divided equally between the clergy and nobility. Since the parish clergy and liberal nobles were sure to support them, they would control the deliberations. The aristocracy opposed this move and demanded that the Estates-General be divided into three houses, one for the deputies of each estate, as had been done in 1614. A pamphlet war ensued in which each side bombarded the other with its proposals. The third estate's demands were eloquently expressed by the liberal clergyman, Abbé Sieyès, when he queried: "What is the Third Estate? Everything. What has it been until now? Nothing. What does it ask? To be something."

Since, from the government's point of view, the purpose of the Estates-General was to vote taxes that would fall on the aristocracy, it ought to have supported the demands of the third estate. This stand, along with a program of reform, might have saved the monarchy, for there were still no avowed republicans in France. However, Louis and Necker, who was recalled, took no definite action beyond giving the third estate double the representation of the other orders. Nearly every male citizen participated in the elections, but the method of voting was so complex that the deputies who were elected did not represent the people as a whole. Each order chose its own deputies, and within the third estate there was an elaborate system of indirect suffrage that favored the inhabitants of the principal towns in each jurisdiction at the expense of the peasantry. The result was that over two-thirds of those who were elected to represent the third estate were lawyers, many of whom held public office. Only 13 per cent were merchants, industrialists, or financiers, and none were peasants. The parish priests were much more successful; although the cathedral chapters and monasteries sent deputies to the local electoral assemblies, the priests attended in person. Their victory was important, because they were usually more sympathetic to the popular cause than the aristocratic members of the chapters or the monks.

The electoral assemblies of each estate prepared lists of grievances called *cahiers* for their deputies to submit to the king. These *cahiers* reveal that the political program of the Enlightenment had won general acceptance but that there was considerable disagreement on what form society should take. All three estates wanted to limit royal authority by having an Estates-General that met regularly to vote taxes and to legislate, and provincial estates to handle administrative matters. Individual liberty and freedom of expression were generally desired, except in matters of religion where the clergy, especially, opposed the removal of disabilities against the Protestants. Governmental waste and inefficiency were universally decried. Yet, with all these criticisms of the existing regime, the fact that France ought to have a king with considerable executive power was not called into question. Provincial loyalties were still strong, but where they caused inconvenience, a willingness was revealed to think in national terms. A uniform system of weights and measures and a national law code were often requested to replace the great variety of local practices, and belief in free trade was at least carried to the point of requesting that tariff barriers between provinces be removed.

It was the question of social status that divided the three estates. The nobles showed a willingness to consider abandoning their special privileges in regard to taxation, but they refused to consider anything that smacked of the civil equality demanded by the third estate. Following Montesquieu, many nobles dreamed of a return to the Renaissance monarchy, when the crown had rarely interfered with their privileges. Others looked across the channel to England, where the aristocracy was socially respected and where it governed in conjunction with the king. The third estate, on the other hand, was opposed to the idea of hereditary privileges and accepted the basic principle of the Enlightenment that all men are equal at birth and are molded by their environment. Though still monarchists, they admired the new American republic, and a few showed the direct influence of Rousseau. Thus, a battle line between aristocracy and egalitarianism was gradually drawn, the one taking its theoretical support from the traditional belief in the importance of heredity and the other from the new concept that man himself and his environment determined personal worth.

THE ESTATES-GENERAL AND THE NATIONAL ASSEMBLY

When the Estates-General opened at Versailles on May 5, 1789, the government still had no plan of action. Seeing this, the deputies took matters in their own hands. The clergy and nobility organized themselves into separate chambers, but the third estate refused to do anything until joined by the other estates. Nothing was accomplished until the lesser clergy, whose sympathies were with the third estate, began to desert their order. Emboldened, the third estate declared that its chamber, being composed of the representatives of the great majority of the French people, represented France as a whole and would henceforth be called the National Assembly. The king scheduled a joint meeting with the three estates to deal with the situation and closed the third estate's assembly hall to enable workmen to make the necessary arrangements. When, on June 20, the deputies found themselves barred from their meeting place, they assumed that the king planned to dissolve the Estates-General. Amid anger and excitement, they assembled on a neighboring tennis court and swore "never to separate but to meet in any place that circumstances may require, until the constitution of the kingdom shall be laid and established on secure foundations."

Three days later in the joint meeting of the three estates, Louis recognized the right of the Estates-General to vote taxes and to allocate funds. He promised other reforms, including guarantees of personal liberty and freedom of the press, but he insisted that the social privileges of the

THE TENNIS COURT OATH, *by Jacques-Louis David. (Bulloz-Art Reference Bureau)*

aristocracy be preserved and that the three estates deliberate separately on matters of importance. From the standpoint of the crown these concessions were great, but wherever a choice had to be made between the desires of the aristocracy and those of the third estate the king had chosen the former. The thoroughly aroused deputies of the third estate remained in the assembly hall with part of the lesser clergy after the king had left and the joint session had ended. When ordered to depart, one deputy cried out: "We will not leave except by force of the bayonet." On learning of this opposition, Louis, hesitant as usual, remarked, "Oh, well, the devil with it—let them stay." The royal surrender left the other deputies little choice. Within a few days, the remainder of the clergy and the nobility joined the third estate, and the National Assembly began to prepare a new constitution for France.

The court aristocracy, however, had no intention of giving in so easily, and Louis was as incapable of withstanding pressure from them as from the third estate. On June 26, he was persuaded to order troops to move into the vicinity of Paris and Versailles; Necker was dismissed on July 11; and a conservative ministry was appointed. Force was clearly to supplant persuasion.

The members of the National Assembly did not know which way to turn. Happily for them, first the inhabitants of the towns, then those of the countryside, intervened. The causes of their intervention were misery and fear. A crop failure had brought high food prices, but the urban populace blamed the inflation on aristocratic hoarders and grain merchants who withheld supplies to force prices higher. Workers' wages had gone up only 22 per cent, compared with a 65 per cent rise in the cost of living during the previous half century. To make matters worse, unemployment was unusually high because of a temporary industrial depression. Rumors spread that the aristocracy was conspiring to prevent the National Assembly from improving the situation, and the actions of the court did little to dispel this impression.

News of troop movements and of the dismissal of Necker were all that was needed to stir up the small shopkeepers, artisans, and workers of Paris. These people were virtually unrepresented in the National Assembly, but hunger and fear led them to make common cause with the threatened deputies at Versailles, some of whom may have instigated their actions. Mobs roamed the Paris streets, and on July 14 the Bastille was seized. This old Paris fortress was not primarily a prison as popular legend has depicted it. Only seven prisoners were there in 1789; two of these were mental cases, one was confined at the request of his family, and four were being prosecuted for forgery. The mobs attacked the Bastille because it was a symbol of monarchical authority and because they thought that it contained the arms that they would need to repel an expected attack by royal troops. The aristocratic municipal government was overthrown, and a more democratic one was substituted. A national guard composed of local citizens was created for protection, and the liberal Lafayette became its first commander. Provincial towns followed suit when news from the capital reached them. Revolutionary committees and local militia were everywhere organized. Royal authority was reduced to nil, and even the commands of the National Assembly were frequently ignored.

The peasants were bitterly opposed to recent attempts by the aristocracy to increase its manorial income, and like the poorer inhabitants of the towns, they suffered from a lack of food. The news from the capital reached them quickly by way of the provincial towns. They became frightened. There were widespread rumors of an aristocratic conspiracy designed to prevent the king from abolishing manorial obligations and restoring enclosed commons. How else could the inaction of the National Assembly be explained? Naive peasants were convinced that the king would not have convoked the assembly had he not intended to redress their grievances. Fear of the aristocracy, fear of troops, and, especially, fear of brigands spread through much of France. In some places, peasants fled on receiving rumors of approaching forces. In others, they rose up, burned châteaux, and destroyed the records of their manorial obligations. The countryside, like the towns, ceased to obey centralized authority. France was rapidly falling into anarchy.

Louis was not the man to face such a situation resolutely. He did muster courage to refuse to flee from the country with his brother and some conservative nobles. Instead, he gave in again, removed the troops, and recalled Necker. Once more, he had capitulated before a show of force, but there were limits to how many surrenders he could make and still retain his crown.

THE WORK OF THE NATIONAL ASSEMBLY

Louis' actions temporarily placated the National Assembly and led to a partial restoration of order in the towns, but they failed to satisfy the peasants. Soon the more liberal deputies realized that drastic measures were needed. On the night of August 3, they met secretly and determined, wrote a deputy, "to use a *kind of magic* . . . [to secure the obliteration of] the privileges of classes, provinces, towns, and corporations." The "magic" consisted of having one liberal noble after another get up in the assembly the following evening and renounce, in return for compensation, the fees due him from the peasants for the use of his land and, without compensation, the labor services that were also a part of his manorial rights. This action generated tremendous enthusiasm. Some of the less liberal nobles were so carried away that they followed suit. Provinces and towns also renounced their privileges. By the time the meeting adjourned at two in the morning of August 5, all obligations, including serfdom and manorial fees, had been abolished. Ecclesiastical tithes also passed into oblivion. In one night, the National Assembly had destroyed the old social order with its system of special rights and privileges. In its place was substituted the concept that Frenchmen, from whatever class or province, constituted a single nation. To implement this concept, a Declaration of the Rights of Man was issued on August 26 in which it was declared that: "Men are born and remain free and equal in rights." Liberty, property, and the essential freedoms were guaranteed and sovereignty was declared to rest "essentially in the nation." The ideas of the Enlightenment seemed about to be realized. The liberals were triumphant.

But their victory was neither complete nor secure. The oft-rumored aristocratic conspiracy became a fact. Conservative nobles were not reconciled to their losses on the night of August 4, nor were all the clergy happy about the abolition of the tithe. Even some members of the middle class who owned fiefs began to wonder whether events had not gone too far. The king again summoned troops to Versailles, and the court did not hide its chagrin at the course of events.

Meanwhile, the National Assembly was dividing on more and more issues. Some deputies wanted a legislature with a Lords and Commons like England. Others stood for a single chamber that would represent the entire nation. Some were willing to give the king a veto, others were not. More serious still, the king did not specifically accept the decrees of the assembly. "I will never consent," he wrote concerning the night of August 4, "to the spoliation of my clergy or of my nobility. I will not sanction decrees by which they are despoiled." He was no more enthusiastic about efforts to deny him veto power over the National Assembly's acts. For over a month, the fate of France was in the balance.

Gradually, the more democratic deputies realized that they must again use force to ensure the gains won on the night of August 4, and they determined to bring the king to Paris where he would be free from the influence of the aristocracy. The continued misery of the people played into their hands. Food was scarce and expensive—more so than before—for the disturbances in the provinces had slowed the movement of goods. Unemployment was worse because some free-spending nobles had fled and the uncertain future caused some businessmen to curtail their operations. On October 5, six or seven thousand Parisians, mostly women, marched on Versailles to demand bread. Lafayette and the national guard did nothing to halt the demonstration until late afternoon, when they too began to move toward the court. The king considered flight but changed his mind. At dawn the following day, the mob broke into the palace and killed several members of the royal guard. Lafayette restored order and took the royal family back to Paris with him. The National Assembly followed the king to the capital minus its more conservative members, who departed in disgust. From that time, both king and deputies were even more subject to the pressures of the Paris populace.

For nearly three years, however, it seemed possible that the revolution might be consolidated without bloodshed. The march on Versailles had induced Louis to accept the Declaration of the Rights of Man and the decrees of the night of August 4. The National Assembly set about preparing a new constitution whose provisions were usually put into effect as soon as they were decided upon. Local government was completely reorganized. In the interest of the new national feeling, the old provinces were abolished. In their place, a logical, consistent system of local government was established. France was divided into eighty-three departments named after local rivers or mountains. Each department was subdivided into districts, cantons, and communes. These units were almost completely self-governing, a fact which made the task of the central government far more difficult. Gone were the intendants, the *parlements*, the provincial estates, and the hereditary officeholders. In their place were elected officials, judges, and members of departmental assemblies.

The central government was equally uprooted. Most authority was placed in a Legislative Assembly, which controlled legislation, taxation, and expenditures. The Legislative Assembly, however, was not to be elected until after the National Assembly had completed the reorganization of France. The king was given a suspensive veto, but not the right to make war, peace, or treaties without the Legislative Assembly's consent. His powers were more restricted than those of the president under the new Constitution of the United States, except that as a hereditary monarch he did not have to stand election.

The bourgeois influence on the Revolution was reflected by the abolition of titles and coats of arms. Strikes, trade unions, and other collective organizations were forbidden. At the same time, those who did not pay taxes in an amount equal to three days' wages were denied the right to vote. At least 2,000,000 of the 6,000,000 males over twenty-five were thereby disfranchised. The "active" citizens, those not completely disfranchised, could vote only for electors who actually named the deputies, and the property qualification to be an elector was so high that less than 50,000 persons had the means to qualify. The aristocracy of birth had been destroyed. In its place, was an aristocracy of wealth.

The National Assembly was faced with the same financial problems that had beset Louis XVI. The government was hopelessly in debt. There was widespread resistance to paying the old unpopular taxes; yet additional funds had to be found to balance the budget. The first step of the Assembly was to substitute an income tax to be paid by everyone for the *taille* and other taxes. The second was to confiscate Church property and use it to back an issue of paper money known as the *assignats*. The decision to confiscate Church property entailed a new relationship between church and state. Most of the monasteries were closed, and the support of the secular clergy was undertaken by the government. The old dioceses were abolished, and a new diocese was created for each department. Bishops and priests were to be like government officials. Since the pope was denied any role in the formation of the Civil Constitution of the Clergy or in ecclesiastical appointments, he was left no choice but to condemn the measure. Ecclesiastical reforms had certainly been desirable, but by going so far the National Assembly had involved itself in a struggle with the Church. It had become impossible for an orthodox Catholic to accept the Revolution.

Over half the secular clergy, including some priests who had formerly supported the liberals, were discharged when they refused to take the oath accepting the new order. Since many citizens continued to prefer the nonjuring priests, these priests were outlawed. The Revolution that was to restore to man his natural rights now persecuted the faith of a majority of Frenchmen. "Can then," a group of conservatives asked, "an entire century of philosophy but have led us back to the religious intolerance of the sixteenth century, and by the very road of liberty itself?"

No one was more upset by the turn of events than Louis himself. On June 20, 1791, he escaped from Paris with his family but was recaptured at Varennes near the borders of the Empire. This left the National Assembly in the position of having created a constitutional monarchy but having a thoroughly discredited, disloyal monarch. It had accomplished a great deal in spite of tremendous odds, but there were already grave doubts about how long the monarchy would last when on October 1, 1791, the recently elected Legislative Assembly assumed authority under the terms of the new constitution.

465

THE LEGISLATIVE ASSEMBLY

The Legislative Assembly was much more radical than the National Assembly. The clergy and nobility no longer had the right of separate representation, and only the most liberal of their number had any hope of being elected. The result was that the constitutional monarchists, the liberals in the old assembly, were the conservatives in the new. They held 264 of the 745 seats, but had no outstanding leaders and steadily lost strength.

On the left there were about 136 deputies who, having lost all faith in Louis XVI, sought to establish a republic. They had two advantages which more than compensated for their small numbers. First, in the Jacobin Club they had an organization that included many Parisian municipal leaders and had branches throughout France. Here, public affairs were debated, and plans of action determined upon, the Paris club serving as a sort of party headquarters. No other faction in the Legislative Assembly was so well organized or had such close contact with the Parisian populace. Second, in George Danton (1759-1794) and Maximilien Robespierre (1758-1794) they had competent leaders. Danton was a powerful, ugly man with great oratorical ability. He had been a successful lawyer before the Revolution and was now taking advantage of the opportunity to achieve wealth and political power. Most of his following came from the liberal element of the middle class. Robespierre had also been a lawyer, but, unlike Danton, he was an idealist more than an opportunist. As a fanatical follower of Rousseau, he dreamed of establishing "a republic of virtue." Wealth he scorned as a corrupting influence. Humanity he worshipped, but when the Revolution was in danger, he was willing to exterminate his opponents with the utmost ruthlessness.

As neither Danton nor Robespierre was a member of the Legislative Assembly, leadership in that body fell to some able orators largely from the department of the Gironde in southwestern France. The Girondists, led by the lawyers Brissot and Vergniaud, favored a federal republic, while Danton and Robespierre stood for more centralized control from Paris. These and other differences of opinion, accompanied by personal rivalries, later divided the republican movement, but for the time being the left stood united in its desire to overthrow the constitutional monarchy.

In the center of the Legislative Assembly were the remainder of the deputies who had neither strong monarchical nor strong republican convictions. They were capable of being swayed by either the right or the left, but were important because they held the balance of power.

At first, the constitutional monarchists were in control. They believed that if the leftward progress of the Revolution was not halted, property would be threatened. Louis the king was essential to them as a symbol of stability and authority. He had therefore been restored after his flight, but was kept carefully guarded in Paris. It was France's relations with the rest of Europe that now led to his downfall.

George Danton. Portrait by Charpentier in Versailles. (Bulloz-Art Reference Bureau)

The early European reactions to the Revolution were divided. Advocates of the Enlightenment were enthusiastic. A few of the more revolutionary spirits migrated to Paris, where they were welcomed by the still cosmopolitan-minded French leaders. Others began to agitate for similar reforms in their own countries. The inhabitants of the papal state of Avignon asked to be united with France. Foreign statesmen were relieved to find France too divided to be a threat, and many conservatives were momentarily indifferent. It is true that both Catherine of Russia and Gustavus III of Sweden quickly advised intervention; but the former was occupied with Turkish and Polish affairs, and Gustavus was not likely to take action alone.

Only after the attempted flight of the royal family did the Habsburg, Leopold II, give serious thought to intervening to save his sister, Marie Antoinette, and her husband's throne. By that time, the treatment meted out to the French clergy by the National Assembly and the annexation of Avignon had antagonized the pope and the most loyal supporters of the Church. German princes who owned land in the French province of Alsace had been angered by the loss of their manorial rights and revenues. French emigrants, including Louis XVI's brothers, had spread hatred and fear of the Revolution abroad, where occasional democratic disturbances gave credence to their claim that monarchy and aristocracy were everywhere threatened. Under these circumstances, moderates became conservatives and conservatives became reactionaries.

In August, 1791, Leopold II issued the Declaration of Pillnitz in conjunction with Frederick William II of Prussia. This document declared the monarch's intention of protecting the French royal family if other

Maximilien Robespierre from a contemporary drawing in Versailles. (Bulloz-Art Reference Bureau)

European powers agreed. By this and other threats, Leopold hoped to curb French revolutionary ardor and to save Marie Antoinette. However, he and the other monarchs were actually so suspicious of one another and so preoccupied with the partition of Poland that plans for joint intervention were difficult to implement. Only with the accession in 1792 of the less cautious but more conservative Habsburg, Francis II, did Austria and Prussia begin to move to restore Louis XVI to his former position and incidentally to despoil France of some of its territory. It was the French, however, who actually started the series of wars that was to last almost continuously until 1815.

The French reactionaries wanted war because they hoped that it would lead to a restoration of the old regime. The constitutional monarchists wanted war because they saw that their power was slipping and hoped to inspire loyalty to king and constitution by a series of victories. The Girondists wanted a war that would sweep them to power on a wave of popular enthusiasm and spread the Revolution to other parts of Europe. "The time has come," Brissot declared, "for a new crusade, a crusade of universal freedom." An almost united France opened hostilities in the spring of 1792.

The French fared badly in the initial fighting. Marie Antoinette was correctly suspected of treasonable correspondence with her Habsburg kinsmen, and Louis unwisely vetoed several measures. The result was that on August 10 radical republican leaders organized a mob attack on the royal palace. Louis fled to the Legislative Assembly for protection, but that body itself was at the mercy of the Paris populace. It consented to the calling of a National Convention elected by universal manhood suffrage to draw up a new constitution. In early September, it was further cowed when the Paris populace massacred over a thousand priests and political prisoners.

468

Two weeks later the French army halted the Prussians at Valmy, thereby temporarily removing the foreign threat before the National Convention opened on September 21.

THE FIRST REPUBLIC

THE NATIONAL CONVENTION

Just as the Legislative Assembly had proved more radical than the National Assembly, so the National Convention was more radical than its predecessor. Louis' actions had discredited the monarchy, and the September massacres had frightened those with monarchical sympathies. As a result, nine-tenths of the eligible voters did not cast ballots; only republicans voted, and only republicans were elected. However, the republicans themselves divided into factions. In part, the division was a result of personal rivalries and jealousies, but there were also some significant differences in policy. The Girondists, who were now the most conservative element in the assembly, were for the most part well-to-do members of the middle class who favored the laissez-faire doctrines of the physiocrats. They disliked the anti-capitalistic temper displayed by the Parisian populace and favored a federal republic in which the capital city would play a small role.

The left was composed of the followers of Danton and Robespierre. They won control of the Jacobin Club and derived much of their power from the support that they received from the Parisian populace. This populace consisted of petty bourgeoisie, artisans, and wage earners who were often referred to as the *sansculottes* because they wore the long trousers of the workingman rather than the knee breeches and stockings of the aristocracy and middle class. Their economic outlook reflected the guild system, with its minute regulations to protect everyone, more than the capitalistic, laissez-faire concepts of the bourgeoisie. They controlled the sections into which the city of Paris was divided and had a powerful voice in the municipal government itself. Both Danton and Robespierre were middle class in their outlook, but the latter had a deep sympathy for the *sansculottes* and came to favor price and wage legislation as well as drastic actions to ensure an adequate supply of food. Between the two extremes was the great body of deputies who first gave their support to the Girondists but gradually fell in behind the Jacobins.

All factions agreed on the abolition of the monarchy and the establishment of a republic. However, a lively dispute developed over the fate of the king. Finally, the Jacobins got a slim majority to support the demand for Louis' immediate execution. On January 21, 1793, he faced the guillotine with more courage than he had faced the numerous decisions of his tumultuous reign. However, the rivalry between the Girondists and Jacobins increased. Each planned to use force against the other, but the Jacobins had more influence with the *sansculottes* because they were willing to accept a program of economic controls to combat rising prices and food shortages. On June 2, thousands of men surrounded the assembly hall of the Convention and demanded the arrest of twenty-nine Girondist deputies. The Girondists, like the priests, the nobles, and the constitutional monarchists before them, were proscribed by the revolution that they had helped create, leaving the Jacobins undisputedly in power.

For a time, it seemed that the Jacobin triumph would be short-lived. Most of the Girondist deputies escaped to the provinces, where they raised the standard of rebellion. Often, they joined with royalists in their efforts to dislodge the Jacobins. The most serious rebellion had begun several months earlier in the Vendée area in western France. There the peasants were devoutly Catholic and loyal to their priests, who had refused to accept the Civil Constitution of the Clergy. Under the leadership of the local nobility, who had treated them with unusual kindness, they seized control of the region. By the beginning of July, over sixty departments were in the hands of the counterrevolution and Paris itself was threatened.

The foreign war also began to take a turn for the worse when Great Britain, Spain, Portugal, and the Dutch decided to join the Austrians and Prussians. This decision was a result of the changing attitude of the French people towards the war and a realization on the part of the other European rulers that the new republic was a serious threat to the established order and the balance of power.

In 1790, the French National Assembly had renounced wars of conquest, but slowly the cosmopolitan, pacifist concept of the philosophers gave way before the idea of engaging in a crusade to help other peoples regain their natural rights. On November 19, 1792, the National Convention declared "in the name of the French nation that it will bring fraternity and aid to all peoples that wish to recover their liberty . . ." The immediate result of the changed French attitude towards war was near disaster. Except for Austria and Prussia, most European powers had been willing to let the French work out their internal difficulties in peace, but when the revolutionaries offered to aid others to overthrow their governments, they came to be considered dangerous to the European social order. The execution of Louis XVI sent a thrill of horror throughout Europe. Finally, the French upset the balance of power and threatened the English and Dutch by occupying the Austrian Netherlands. The inevitable result was the formation of a powerful coalition which recaptured the Austrian Netherlands and invaded France.

Meanwhile, economic problems beset the republic. The urban workers had won little from their revolutionary efforts because prices had continued to rise faster than wages. Grain was scarcer than ever because of wartime dislocation and uncertainty. The inflation made the creditor element of the middle class unhappy. The *assignats* had depreciated to less than a third of their face value, and government securities had also fared badly. Only extraordinary action could save the republic.

THE COMMITTEE OF PUBLIC SAFETY

In April, 1793, the Convention established a Committee of Public Safety with almost unlimited executive authority to save the republic. A *levée en masse* was decreed on August 23, 1793, which called on everyone to join in the war effort. "Young men will go to the front; married men will forge arms and transport food, women will make tents, clothes, and serve in hospitals; children will tear rags into lint; old men will be carried to public places to incite the courage of the warriors, the hatred of kings and unity in the republic." Lazare Carnot and Prieur de la Côte-d'Or of the Committee of Public Safety directed the industrial and military effort. Guns, powder, and uniforms were made in huge quantities. The army was enlarged and reorganized, incompetent generals were punished or removed, and commissioners were sent out from Paris to ensure the obedience of military and provincial administrators. The Vendéans were defeated in October, the allies were driven across the Rhine by December, and the Austrian Netherlands were reconquered by June, 1794. In less than a year, an army of 650,000 men had been built, an internal rebellion had been suppressed, and a coalition more formidable than any faced by the old monarchy had been defeated.

It would be incorrect to give all the credit for these astounding victories to the *levée en masse*. The *levée* was important because it marked the first step away from the older idea that only the unproductive members of society should engage in battle and towards the modern concept of total war. It was also important because the patriotic citizen replaced the riffraff and mercenaries who had filled the ranks of the old army. Patriotism on the part of some, however, was not enough to win battles, especially when others were so opposed to the government that they were rebelling or cooperating with the invading forces. Equally important were the contributions of the old royal army itself.

After their defeat in the Seven Years War, the French had begun to reform the army. Military schools had been established to train young officers, weapons and equipment had been standardized to simplify supply problems, generals had been told to be offensive-minded and to attack in mass to seize key objectives. With the overthrow of the monarchy, many of the senior officers, who were generally attached to the court, fled, but the army itself remained. Well-trained junior officers and noncommissioned officers were rapidly promoted to take their place. Ability became the only criterion for command. It was this army that won the initial battles and instructed the recruits raised by the *levée en masse*. It became the nucleus of the best-led, best-trained, most patriotic army in Europe.

Economic and social problems proved more difficult to solve. Under the older system of warfare, in which only the nonproductive portion of the population was involved, there had been little need to interfere with normal economic activities, but the *levée en masse* made economic controls necessary to ensure supplies and prevent injustices. The urban workers were especially insistent that a maximum be set on prices. In September, 1793, the middle-class Convention gave in but put a ceiling on wages as well. Foreign trade and the stock exchange were also regulated and rationing became necessary. When there was a lack of supplies, forced requisitions were authorized.

Unfortunately, the danger to the republic led the Jacobins and their supporters, once their position was more secure, to stamp out the remaining signs of opposition ruthlessly. Only in this way could loyalty to their program be instilled. "The mainspring of popular government in a revolution," Robespierre said, "is at once virtue and terror; virtue without which terror is baleful, terror without which virtue is powerless." The suppression of the internal revolt was therefore followed by a Reign of Terror in which supposed enemies of the republic were executed with little or no trial. Between November, 1793, and July, 1794, over 13,000 persons were put to death, mostly in the rebellious departments and in Paris. The fiction has developed that the Terror pitted the lower classes against the aristocracy and that only aristocrats were executed. Actually, it was an intra-class struggle between the minority who accepted the Jacobin government and the majority who did not. Only 8 per cent of those executed were nobles and 6 per cent clergy. A fourth were members of the middle class and over half were workers and peasants. Similarly, over half of those who emigrated from France to escape the Revolution were members of the third estate. The majority of the nobles remained quietly at home throughout the troubled period.

Having devoured its enemies, the Revolution began to devour more of its own children as various factions struggled for power. In March, 1794, Hébert and his fellow leaders of the Paris populace were seized and executed. The Hébertists were the extreme radicals of the period, and their death marked an end of the steady movement to the left. Two weeks later, Danton and his supporters suffered a like fate. Danton had been corrupt, but he had opposed the fanaticism of his fellow Jacobins. With a degree of sincerity he could declare that it was "Better a hundred times to be guillotined than to guillotine." Robespierre and other devotees of Rousseau were left in control of the republic.

What kind of republic did they create? Above all, it was a dictatorship. Only a small minority of the population supported the regime. Censorship and terroristic methods had to be used temporarily, but Robespierre hoped to persuade his countrymen eventually to become virtuous and patriotic. Schools were to indoctrinate children in the new values of the republic. Plays were to damn royalty and exalt the republic. Literature and art were to perform the same services. Even the deck of cards was made to conform; the kings and queens were removed to make room for "liberties" and "equalities." Dances and songs celebrated the virtues of equality, and the first national anthem, the "Marseillaise," glorified patriotism. The names of towns, streets, and individuals were changed to commemorate the heroes of the new regime. The aristocratic "monsieur" and "madame" were dropped in favor of the democratic "citizen" and "citizeness." The old calendar with its Christian emphasis was abandoned and the birth of the republic replaced the birth of Christ as the year one. The worship of the Supreme Being was encouraged and an elaborate ritual was developed for the new devotion. Even dress was influenced. Patriots abandoned powdered hair, knee breeches, and stockings and wore the long trousers of the workingman. Women, adopting the costumes of republican Rome, wore flowing robes. There were a few exceptions. Robespierre himself preferred the dress of the old regime, but in the long run the Jacobins brought about a revolution in style.

Robespierre's regime, however, was as short-lived as its predecessors. In less than four months after the execution of Danton, he too was guillotined. It has been suggested that Robespierre fell because he sought economic justice for the poor. As early as March, 1794, he had moved to try 300,000 suspects by special commissions and, if they were found guilty, to divide their property among the "worthy" poor. Certainly, this measure was unpopular with the bulk of the middle class, who had thus far obtained most of the confiscated land of the Church and the emigrants, but actually Robespierre, like his predecessors, fell because he lost the struggle for power. On July 26, he indicated in a speech that there were still unvirtuous men in the government and that a new purge was necessary. His frightened enemies determined to strike first, and he and his followers were executed before they had time to organize their defense.

Robespierre's enemies had not intended to change the nature of the government, but a popular reaction set in that led to a gradual relaxation of the Jacobin regime. Well-to-do citizens asserted control over the Paris populace. Freedom of the press and religion were restored, the surviving Girondists resumed their places in the Convention, the Jacobin Club was closed, its leaders were punished, and the Committee of Public Safety was deprived of its great powers. Plans for a redistribution of property and price fixing were abandoned, the stock market was reopened, and a return was made to a laissez-faire economy. These changes are generally referred to as the Thermidorean Reaction because they took place in the month of Thermidor in the revolutionary calendar. In August, 1795, a new constitution was put into effect that reflected the turn towards a more conservative republicanism.

THE DIRECTORY

The government established by the Constitution of 1795 was known as the Directory. It marked a middle-class victory over the urban populace. Suffrage was granted to men who paid direct taxes or who had served in the army, but important offices were limited to those who owned or rented large amounts of land. A bicameral legislature and a five-man directory to execute the laws were created in the hope that by dividing authority a return to dictatorship could be avoided. The lower house, or Council of Five Hundred, was to propose laws, and the upper house, or Council of Ancients, was to accept or reject them. Executive authority was vested in five directors chosen by the Ancients, not by the people.

The members of the Convention recognized that they were unpopular and feared a royalist reaction. They therefore stipulated that two-thirds of the new legislators be chosen from their number. This last measure aroused much opposition. Royalist and moderate elements in Paris revolted in October, but they were quickly dispersed by artillery commanded by a young general named Napoleon Bonaparte. From that time, it was clear that the army would play a key role in any change in government.

The Directory lasted for four years. It has been charged with immorality, corruption, and inefficiency; yet when all is considered, it was less objectionable than many other French regimes. Most of the government leaders were sincere but moderate republicans who on the whole governed successfully.

The Directory tempered its laissez-faire liberalism with a degree of economic regulation. Food was requisitioned when necessary, and foreign trade and foreign exchange were controlled. Research and inventions were encouraged to help industry. The *assignats*, which had depreciated to a fraction of their former value immediately after the fall of Robespierre, were eventually abandoned and a return was made to sound metallic currency. Government expenses were substantially cut in 1797, the tax structure was modified, and part of the national debt was in effect repudiated.

THE GRAND NATION

The Directory was also moderately successful in war and diplomacy, and it was largely under its auspices that most of Western Europe was remodeled along French Republican lines. The ideas of the Enlightenment had found some adherents in every country in the Western world, and in several countries, there had been uprisings prior to 1789. Once the revolution had succeeded in France, a propaganda offensive began to win adherents in other states. The newspaper, the pamphlet, and the theater were put to use, and sympathetic foreigners were welcomed in France. In some localities, such as Geneva and Ireland, there were relatively democratic uprisings. In Hungary and Poland, where the middle class was weak, there were aristocratic rebellions in which little was said about the rights of the serfs. These and other revolts contributed to the success of the French revolutionary movement by diverting the conservative powers; they all ended in failure, however, except where the French army offered effective assistance.

Foreign sympathizers of the Revolution commonly waited until the French armies invaded before they took any action, but a few of the more adventurous advocates of change went to Paris, where with kindred spirits from their own country they organized "clubs" to foment revolutionary activity. When the French invaded a state, they themselves organized more clubs, which they attended along with sympathetic natives. These clubs were similar to the French Jacobins and were to play a key role in the expansion of France and of the Revolution. It was largely to them that the French turned when they wanted to annex a territory or establish a new republic.

The National Convention had adopted a policy of expanding France to its "natural frontiers" and of assisting foreign revolutionaries to overthrow their governments. These natural frontiers were thought to be the Alps, the Rhine, the Pyrénées, and the sea. The last two had already been achieved and little effort was required to gain control of the western slopes of the Alps; thus the Rhine became the great French objective. Louis XIV and other monarchs had tried to expand in that direction, not to achieve natural boundaries, since this concept was unknown to them, but to make good dynastic claims, to protect the approaches to Paris, and to satisfy their desire for glory. Some historians and pamphleteers had mentioned the idea of natural frontiers prior to 1792, but the republic was the first government that tried to realize the concept.

Since the French republicans could not justify the annexation of territory west of the Rhine by appealing to dynastic claims, they adopted the idea of self-determination, which consorted well with their concept of the sovereignty of the people. When they occupied a territory, they used the clubs to persuade the native "patriots," that is, revolutionaries, to elect assemblies that would ask to be incorporated. Nonpatriots were regarded as reactionaries and were therefore excluded. Once a territory was incorporated into France as a result of this procedure, it was divided into departments, the manorial system was abolished, and social equality was decreed. In short, the political and social order became indistinguishable from that of France itself.

The natural frontiers had been achieved by the time the Directory came to power, but the new regime was primarily responsible for establishing a number of sister republics beyond the Alps and the Rhine. In this undertaking, it was greatly aided by the victories won by the commander of their Italian army, Napoleon Bonaparte. Beyond their natural frontiers, as well as within them, French troops were welcomed by groups of patriots who proceeded to organize republics under the protection of their bayonets. The French system served as a model, although the inhabitants of each new state took into some account native conditions and customs. The privileges of the various provinces and social classes were abolished, unified states were created, and everyone was made equal before the law. Out went the old manorial system and any surviving relics of human bondage. In this manner, the Dutch provinces became the centralized Batavian Republic, the Swiss cantons were less successfully amalgamated into the Helvetian Republic, and the Italian states became the Cisalpine, the Ligurian, the Roman, and the Parthenopean republics. Thus, the Grand Nation, as it was called, surrounded itself with sister republics that acted as buffers against the surviving monarchies, as regions for economic exploitation by the French middle class, and as instruments to spread the creed of liberty, equality, and fraternity.

NAPOLEON

THE RISE OF NAPOLEON

The Directory collapsed in 1799, more because of its enemies than because of its failures. The government was in the unhappy position of being attacked from both right and left. In 1796, a semicommunistic uprising led by Gracchus Babeuf was suppressed, and the following year the conservatives attempted to win power. In 1798-99, the voters reacted against some initial successes achieved by a second coalition against the overmighty republic by giving the Jacobins victories in the elections. Two radical measures were then passed; one called for a compulsory loan from the rich and the other for taking hostages from the families of emigrants to ensure their good behavior. The Jacobin dictatorship seemed about to be revived. Conservative republicans led by Abbé Sieyès wanted to establish a government that would prevent this eventuality and also prevent a return of the royalists. They needed a general like Napoleon Bonaparte to implement their designs.

Napoleon was born in Corsica in 1769 shortly after the island had become a French possession. He was the second son of a minor noble of Florentine descent who possessed little wealth to forward the interests of his numerous children. When he was nine, Napoleon was sent to France to study in one of the new military schools to become an officer. At sixteen, he became a sublieutenant in the artillery, the one branch of the service in the old monarchy where ability meant nearly as much as family influence. In the normal course of events, he could hope to be a captain in twelve years, but the times were not normal. In nine years, he became a general, and in fourteen, ruler of the greatest empire since Charlemagne.

Napoleon I at the age of thirty-five from a portrait by Jacques-Louis David. (Courtesy New York Public Library)

When the Revolution began in 1789, there was little reason to suspect such a future. The young lieutenant, with his short stature, Italian accent, and lean purse, was not highly regarded by his fellow officers. Left alone, he devoted his time to studying military tactics and reading the philosophers, including Voltaire, Rousseau, and Adam Smith. His dream was to liberate Corsica from French rule or at least to write a history of his native island. It was the downfall of the monarchy, the flight of many senior officers, and the European war that gave him his opportunity. In 1792, he was a captain; in 1793, he distinguished himself as artillery commander in the siege of Toulon; and in 1794, he was promoted to brigadier general by the Committee of Public Safety, although he was not yet twenty-five. The fall of Robespierre led to his temporary imprisonment, but he was soon released. In 1795, as we have seen, he defended the Convention from the irate Parisians. In 1796, he was given command of the French armies in Italy where, after a series of great victories, he crossed the Alps and dictated peace within a hundred miles of Vienna. England remained France's only opponent, but the island kingdom was safe from attack so long as it controlled the seas. Unable to make a direct assault, Napoleon determined to weaken his foe by seizing the approaches to India. Once more, his army was successful. Egypt and Palestine were overrun, but the British navy under Admiral Nelson defeated the French fleet in the Battle of the Nile. With his supplies cut off, eventual defeat was certain, and Napoleon decided to abandon his army before it was compelled to surrender. In 1799, at the age of thirty, he returned to Paris.

Within two weeks after his arrival in Paris, Napoleon joined Sieyès and the conservative republicans in their conspiracy. On November 9, a

477

Jacobin plot was "discovered," the legislature was persuaded to move to neighboring Saint Cloud for greater security, and Napoleon was given command of the army in the area. Sieyès and two other directors then resigned, and the bicameral legislature was requested to name three consuls, including Sieyès and Napoleon, to draw up a new constitution. The conservative Ancients made little trouble, but when Napoleon appeared before the Five Hundred, some Jacobins yelled: "Down with the tyrant! Down with the dictator! Outlaw him!" Troops had to be called to clear the assembly hall. The thirty who remained accepted the Consulate.

THE CONSULATE, THE CHURCH, AND THE CODE NAPOLEON

The constitution of the Consulate maintained the republican form, but in reality Napoleon as first consul directly controlled the executive authority and wielded overwhelming influence over the legislature. He was given the right to appoint the council of state, which recommended legislation. A tribunate was established with powers to discuss the legislation but not to vote, and a legislative chamber was created to vote on the proposed legislation but not to discuss it. The independence of the tribunate and the legislative chamber was further limited by a system of indirect suffrage through which the people in each community selected a group of electors. These electors named those who stood for the department, and the departmental electors named those who were eligible to be chosen by a senate to sit in the tribunate and legislative chamber. The senate, as might be supposed, was appointed in the first instance by the consuls. Thus, the elective and deliberative aspects of a republican form of government were preserved, but power was centered in the hands of Napoleon. To emphasize the popular nature of the new constitution, it was submitted to the people for approval. The official count recorded 3,011,107 in favor and 1,567 opposed.

The greatest internal problem that Napoleon faced on coming to power was to make his regime permanent and stable. Since 1789, governments had toppled so rapidly that many people hopefully or fearfully expected his to fall as well. It was clearly necessary to reduce opposition and to win additional support.

The most important single group who opposed the Revolution and, with it, the regime, were the orthodox Catholics. He therefore made a Concordat with the pope in 1801. By its terms, Catholicism was recognized as the religion of a majority of Frenchmen. The curés were to be named by the archbishops and bishops, and the archbishops and bishops were to be nominated by the first consul and consecrated by the pope. The Church was to give up claim to its confiscated lands, but the salary of the clergy was to be paid by the state. The government maintained the right to make necessary police regulations with regard to the Church, and papal decrees were not to be published in France without permission. Thus, Napoleon removed the threat of one of the staunchest allies of royalism. At the same time, he was careful not to offend anti-Catholic republican sentiment. Religious freedom was maintained, and Protestant ministers were also paid by the state. The purchasers of Church land were confirmed in their possessions, and the Catholic clergy was not restored to its former duty of keeping the official records of birth, marriage, and death or to its former role in education. France had become the most secularized Catholic country in Europe.

Napoleon also sought to satisfy those who wanted unity, order, and efficiency in government. The National Assembly had broken the power of the provincial estates, nobles, and intendants, but had replaced them with largely self-governing, departmental assemblies that did much as they pleased. Napoleon substituted for these assemblies prefects, sub-prefects, and mayors appointed and controlled from Paris. Tax collection was also placed under control of the Paris administration, and careful checks were made to prevent graft. France's government became the most centralized and efficient in Europe.

The handling of the public debt was simplified by the issuance of bonds carrying 5 per cent interest to replace the various existing obligations. In 1800, a Bank of France was created under private control but closely connected with the government. It issued paper bank notes, lent money to the government, and served as a place of deposit for state funds. These measures, plus strict economy, led to a balanced budget in 1801, but constant warfare kept public finances in a precarious state in spite of large sums levied on tributary states.

Administrative centralization put a premium on able officials, and Napoleon was constantly plagued by their lack. As a result, he ignored political background and appointed both ex-Jacobins and ex-royalists to important posts. He sought to develop a high esprit de corps in the civil as well as the military services and ordered that salaries, promotions, and retirement pay be generous. Still, the supply of competent officials was inadequate. Only by major educational reforms could the French government hope to secure an adequate staff for its great civil and military commitments.

Napoleon tackled this problem without hesitation. He established centralized lay control over education and directed that schools teach loyalty to his regime and useful professions. Primary education was neglected, but secondary and professional schools were improved. The emphasis on professional studies is reflected by the fact that at one time 25 per cent of the students in higher education studied law and 24 per cent medicine. France emerged with a better than average educational system, but it fell far short of solving Napoleon's personnel problems.

Legal unity followed administrative and educational centralization. Before the Revolution, each district had had its own code of laws, and the centuries-old desire of legal authorities to create a single set of laws for all of France had never been realized. Previous revolutionary governments had made efforts to prepare such a code, but it remained for Napoleon to bring the work to completion. The Code Napoleon preserved most of the social and economic gains of the middle class. It "affirmed the equality of all citizens before the law, the right of the individual to choose his profession, the supremacy of the lay state, and the freedom of the individual conscience." [2] Wives, however, were subordinated to the authority of their husbands and children to their fathers. Thus, the emphasis on the family, so characteristic in old France, was restored and passed on to the nineteenth century. Property rights and the interests of the employer were carefully protected by outlawing trade unions and strikes. This measure brought Napoleon some middle-class support, but the workers had to be content with such civil rights as the privilege of public trial by jury. Whatever its faults, the Code was a tremendous improvement over what had existed before, and it was to exercise a profound influence on other countries.

ECONOMIC AND SOCIAL POLICIES

Napoleon's economic policies were also intended to further the interests of the middle class. He was enough of a Physiocrat to rate agriculture, then industry, and finally commerce in that order of importance. He left agriculture and industry alone except to encourage several new crops, ensure cheap credit, and make beneficial trade treaties. His commercial policy, however, was no more intelligent than that of the mercantilists. Under the best of circumstances, French overseas trade was in jeopardy because its arch-enemy, England, controlled the seas, but Napoleon's protectionist policy made matters worse. At no time did overseas trade under his regime reach the point it had attained under Louis XVI. Internal trade fared better and was stimulated by the building of roads and canals.

Napoleon knew that his Code and his economic policy were not enough to win middle-class support. Ambitious, able men wanted equality before the law, but they also wanted the opportunity to rise above their fellows. Hence, he determined to create a new aristocracy, an aristocracy based on merit. The nobility of the old regime was recognized, and Napoleon hoped for a fusion of the old and the new aristocracy that would strengthen and dignify his regime. Military and civil promotions were rapid for those who had ability, and the highest officials were given titles and permanent pensions. By 1815, there were four princes, thirty-one dukes, about 400 counts, and over 2,500 barons and knights. In addition, Napoleon created the Legion of Honor to reward those who had rendered special services. Such measures offended the egalitarian spirit of many republicans, but the abler members of the middle class had always longed for the opportunity to join the aristocracy. The failure of the nobility to welcome them under

[2] Geoffrey Bruun, *Europe and the French Imperium* (New York: Harper, 1938), p. 27.

the old regime had led to grave difficulties; now, Napoleon's willingness to give them such baubles won for him their loyalty and service.

The creation of a titled aristocracy followed a return to monarchical government. In 1802, Napoleon was made consul for life, and in 1804 he had himself proclaimed hereditary emperor, both to satisfy his ego and to stabilize the regime. The pope attended the coronation ceremony, but the little Corsican was careful to place the crown on his own head. The step was ratified in a plebiscite by a vote officially tabulated as 3,572,329 for and 2,569 against. The emperor soon turned to the problem of providing his realm with an heir. Since his first wife, Josephine, had borne him no children, he divorced her and in 1810 married Marie Louise, daughter of Emperor Francis I. A Bonaparte had married a Habsburg, a child of the Revolution had been united with the niece of Marie Antoinette. When a son was born to this union, a year later, the future of the empire seemed assured.

An emperor and an aristocracy must have a court. Napoleon established one. The new court lacked the gaiety and charm that had distinguished the Bourbon court. Napoleon was too nervous, too impulsive, too active, to permit the cultivation of a sense of grace or ease. Surprisingly enough, he was awkward, a fault that revealed itself when he was on horseback and in the ballroom. He disliked the aristocratic sport of hunting, although he occasionally shot at his wife's tame birds in the garden. He had no interest in art and the best he could do at polite conversation was to tell a lady of her husband's amorous escapades. The ceremony of the court could be revived, but not the spirit of the salon.

The failure of the court pointed to the failure of Napoleon's policy of amalgamation. The old and new aristocracy never really fused. The conservative forces in France remained divided between loyalty to the Bourbons and loyalty to the Bonapartes throughout the nineteenth century. This fact made possible the eventual triumph of the republic.

NAPOLEON'S VICTORIES

When Napoleon became consul in 1799, France was at war with the Second Coalition. The First Coalition, which had been formed in 1792, had been terminated in 1797 when Austria withdrew from the conflict, leaving the English to fight on alone. The Second Coalition, which had been formed near the close of the following year, had included Russia as well as Great Britain and Austria. The French armies had suffered some initial defeats, especially at the hands of the Russians, but by the time Napoleon had overthrown the Directory, France had recovered its position and Russia had withdrawn from the coalition. Austria withdrew in 1801, after being defeated in several major battles, and in 1802 the war came to an end as a result of a treaty made between the English and French at Amiens. After a decade of war, peace had been restored to Europe.

Unhappily, this treaty proved to be only a truce. The following year

Napoleon led France into a new war with Great Britain because he believed that the English would never accept his domination of the Low Countries and his other ambitious policies. It seemed expedient to destroy the island kingdom while his continental enemies nursed the bruises of the previous conflict. The British, led by their able minister, William Pitt, were willing to renew the struggle because of Napoleon's continental predominance and his growing interest in building a navy and a colonial empire. Unfortunately for the French, Napoleon's interference in Germany and Italy caused Austria, Russia, and Sweden to join Great Britain in a Third Coalition.

At first, Napoleon toyed with the idea of a cross-channel invasion. Then, suddenly, in 1805 he marched into central Europe where he defeated the Austrians at Ulm and the combined Russian and Austrian armies at Austerlitz. Austria was forced to withdraw from the war, but Prussia took its place. At Jena and Auerstädt, the army that Frederick the Great had so often led to victory was crushed. Russia was defeated at Friedland, and peace was made at Tilsit in 1807. Napoleon next turned on Portugal because of its refusal to stop trading with Great Britain, his one remaining enemy. To reach Portugal, the French armies had to cross Spain. Both countries quickly fell within the French orbit. The Portuguese royal family fled to Brazil, and the Spanish king abdicated, leaving Napoleon temporary master of western and central Europe.

Napoleon undoubtedly owed his great victories in part to the jealous quarrels between the members of the coalitions that had opposed him; nevertheless, as a military commander he had few equals. His strategy and tactics were those that he had learned at officers' school in the 1780's, but he applied brilliantly what he had learned of the value of mass and mobility. His troops marched rapidly, supplies were kept to a minimum because he lived off the country, and when he reached the battlefield, he usually had the larger army. He also made better use of artillery than his opponents, and he was ably assisted by a group of subordinate officers who owed their position to ability rather than family position.

THE GRAND EMPIRE

Meanwhile, Napoleon had been busy creating a new European order. A lover of the romantic in spite of his great military and administrative ability, he thought of himself as a second Charlemagne and determined to create a new empire. First, the map of Europe had to be redrawn. He had already destroyed the numerous tiny Italian states, including that of the pope. A third of the peninsula was incorporated into France, and the remainder was divided between a new kingdom of Italy and the kingdom of Naples. Germany was treated with equal violence. The old Holy Roman Empire was abolished in 1806. The ecclesiastical states, imperial cities, and free knights of the Empire suffered a like fate. Their lands were divided among larger states such as Bavaria and Württemberg, given to France, or united to form the new kingdom of Westphalia. Prussia and Austria were forced to disgorge part of their recent gains at the expense of the Poles to make way for the creation of a Grand Duchy of Warsaw.

The death of the old European order was followed by the birth of the new, of the "Grand Empire," as Napoleon called it. The Grand Empire consisted of three parts. The inner core was the French empire, which extended to the Rhine on the east and included the western half of the Italian peninsula from Rome northward. Then came the dependent states, which had often been republics under the Directory but were now made kingdoms under the rule of Napoleon's relatives. His brothers, Joseph, Louis, and Jerome, were made kings of Spain, Holland, and Westphalia. His brother-in-law, Murat, was given the throne of Naples. His stepchild, Eugène de Beauharnais, served as viceroy of the kingdom of Italy. One of his marshals, Bernadotte, was chosen crown prince of Sweden. Other dependent states included the Swiss republic, the new Grand Duchy of Warsaw, and the Confederation of the Rhine. This Confederation encompassed nearly all of Germany not incorporated into France, except Prussia and Austria. Most of the member-states of the Confederation had been enlarged at the expense of the old ecclesiastical territories, imperial cities, and free barons. Four of them—Saxony, Bavaria, Württemberg, and Westphalia—were elevated to kingdoms, and the new lands and titles ensured Napoleon a degree of loyalty from their rulers. Napoleon named himself protector of the Confederation, thereby extending his influence to the borders of eastern Europe.

The third part of the Grand Empire was composed of allied states. These were powers that had been defeated by Napoleon and were now forced to accept his anti-British program. Included were Prussia, or the half of it that remained, and Austria. Prussia's army was limited to 42,000 men, its wealth was stripped to pay a large indemnity, and its ports were closed to British goods. Austria was denuded of its Italian, Adriatic, and Low Country provinces and denied any connection with its historic ally, England. Francis II abandoned his title of Holy Roman Emperor and assumed the less pretentious title of Francis I, Emperor of Austria. A third defeated power, Russia, was more fortunate than the other states that had tried to curb the little Corsican. Although its armies had been defeated, its lands had not yet been invaded. In the Treaty of Tilsit, 1807, Napoleon had not been in a position to demand more from Russia than recognition of the "Grand Empire" and adherence to a boycott against British goods. Only one major European power, Great Britain, remained completely outside the Napoleonic sphere.

The internal organization of the Grand Empire varied outside its inner core, but Napoleon regarded himself as the head of the whole. "Europe cannot be at rest except under a single head who will have kings for his officers, who will distribute his kingdom to his lieutenants." When his

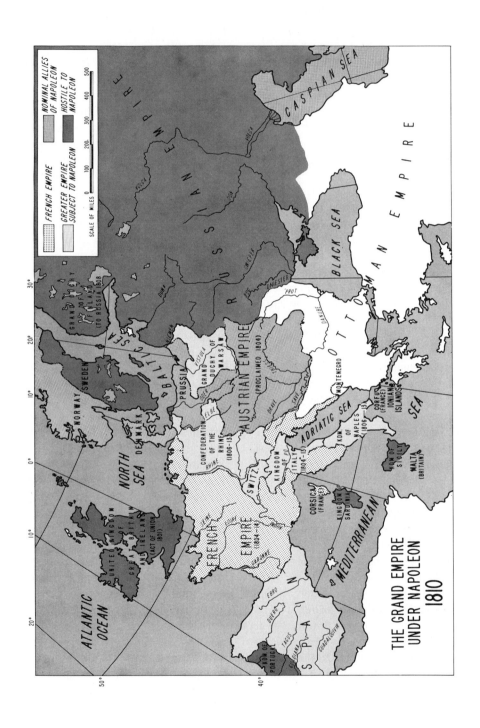

THE GRAND EMPIRE
UNDER NAPOLEON
1810

FRENCH EMPIRE
GREATER EMPIRE
SUBJECT TO NAPOLEON
NOMINAL ALLIES
OF NAPOLEON
HOSTILE TO
NAPOLEON

SCALE OF MILES
0 100 200 300 400 500

ATLANTIC
OCEAN

UNITED
KINGDOM
OF
GREAT BRITAIN
AND IRELAND
(ACT OF UNION
1801)

NORTH
SEA

NORWAY

SWEDEN

DENMARK

GRAND DUCHY
OF
FINLAND
(TO RUSSIA 1808)

BALTIC
SEA

PRUSSIA

GRAND
DUCHY OF
WARSAW

R U S S I A N   E M P I R E

VOLGA

VOLGA

DON

DNIEPER

CONFEDERATION
OF THE
RHINE
(1806-13)

ELBE

ODER

AUSTRIAN EMPIRE
(PROCLAIMED 1804)

VISTULA

DNIESTER

PRUT

CASPIAN
SEA

FRENCH
EMPIRE
(1804-?)

SEINE

LOIRE

GARONNE

EBRO

DUERO

TAGUS

GUADIANA

GUADALQUIVIR

KINGDOM
OF
PORTUGAL

S P A I N

SWITZ.

RHINE

KINGDOM
OF
ITALY
(1804-13)

PO

TICINO

ADIGE

SAVE

DRAVE

TISZA

DANUBE

ADRIATIC
SEA

MONTENEGRO

KINGDOM
OF NAPLES
(1806-)

CORSICA
(FRANCE)

KINGDOM OF
SARDINIA

KINGDOM
OF
SICILY

MALTA
(BRITAIN)

MEDITERRANEAN   SEA

CORFU
(FRANCE)
IONIAN
ISLANDS

O T T O M A N   E M P I R E

BLACK   SEA

50°

40°

20°

10°

0°

10°

20°

30°

brother Louis disobeyed his instructions, he was removed from his throne and Holland was incorporated into France. Rulers less closely related to the clannish Napoleon could expect less gentle treatment.

Napoleon insisted on obedience partly because a united front was necessary against the British threat and partly because his natural egotism demanded adherence to his every wish. Nevertheless, he was a child of the Enlightenment and his opportunities had been created by the Revolution. He was a sincere cosmopolitan with a passion for unity, order, and simplicity. He disliked the complexities, diversities, and inequalities of the old regime, and despite his own arbitrary actions, he believed in the supremacy of law. He sought universal acceptance of the ideas of civil equality, religious tolerance, freedom of economic action, and other reforms embodied in the Code Napoleon. "What the peoples of Germany impatiently demand," he told his brother when he became King of Westphalia, "is that men who are not nobles, but who do have ability, should have an equal right to your favor and your employment, and that every kind of serfdom, or of feudal powers between the sovereign and the lowest class of his subjects, should be entirely done away with. The benefits of the Code Napoleon, public trial and the introduction of juries, will be so many distinctive features of your monarchy. . . . What people will want to return under the arbitrary Prussian rule, once it has tasted the benefits of a wise and liberal administration? The peoples of Germany, as of France, Italy and Spain, want equality and liberal ideas. For some years now I have managed the affairs of Europe, and I am convinced that the cackling of the privileged classes was everywhere disliked. Be a constitutional king. Even if reason and the enlightenment of the age were not sufficient cause, it would be good policy for one in your position." [3] In part, Napoleon's program was designed to win the support of the unprivileged, but his belief in his system was at times doctrinaire. When Murat pointed out that some of the provisions of the Code were unpopular in Naples, Napoleon wrote: "I cannot, as protector of the constitution, consent to any modification of the Napoleonic code."

In the inner core and the dependent states the old order was destroyed, with its three estates, each having its special rights and privileges. Nobles lost their special tax and officeholding privileges. Ecclesiastics lost their special courts, churches their property, and guilds their monopolies. Equality of opportunity, a free choice of profession, and religious tolerance were decreed. Provinces, towns, and fiefs ceased to be governing units; all were subjected to a centralized administration and a single law of the land. The manorial system was abolished, but in Italy and the area east of the Rhine, the peasants were expected to compensate their former lords. In Poland, the most distant part of the Grand Empire, the serfs were freed, but Napoleon did not give them land since he needed the support of

[3] Quoted in Robert R. Palmer, *A History of the Modern World* (New York: Knopf, 1956), pp. 392-93.

the Polish nobility. The passion for simplicity led to the introduction of the metric system of weights and measures and the decimal system of money. Great Britain was almost alone in maintaining its archaic, inconvenient bushels and pecks, pints and quarts, shillings and pounds.

THE DOWNFALL OF NAPOLEON AND THE PEACE SETTLEMENT

THE FAILURE OF THE CONTINENTAL SYSTEM

Although Napoleon hoped that his Grand Empire would last for centuries, it collapsed almost as rapidly as it had been formed. One cause for its downfall was the survival of Great Britain. The island kingdom was always ready to raise and subsidize coalitions against its ancient enemy. At the same time, it was invulnerable to military attack as long as it ruled the sea. In 1803, Napoleon began to build a fleet to seize control of the English Channel, but two years later the British under Lord Nelson defeated it at Trafalgar. Napoleon then sought to accomplish Britain's ruin by means of the Continental System.

The Continental System was established in November, 1806, and December, 1807, by the Berlin and Milan decrees, which declared that the British Isles were in a state of blockade. Inhabitants of the Grand Empire were forbidden to buy British goods, and British citizens were to be arrested if found on the continent. Even neutral vessels coming from British ports were to be denied admittance. These economic measures, Napoleon thought, would accomplish what military measures had not. He expected the boycott of British goods to cause a depression in the island kingdom. The depression would lead to social disturbances and unemployment, and the result would be bankruptcy when custom revenue declined. Britain would no longer be able to intervene on the continent. At the same time, the removal of British competition would increase French sales on the continent.

For several reasons, the Continental System did not humble Great Britain. The bureaucracy of the Grand Empire was neither large enough nor efficient enough to enforce the decrees, even if it had desired. Smuggling increased, the allied states made only token efforts to implement the blockade, and Napoleon himself sometimes issued permits to import needed British products. Britain was hurt, but the opening of Latin American ports to British commerce after the French occupation of Spain and Portugal partially compensated. At the same time, Great Britain tightened its blockade of French ports. British and colonial goods became scarce, and French custom revenue declined. Most important, the scarcity and high prices caused by the Continental System contributed to the growing discontent in the dependent and allied states.

It had always been obvious that the old Europe would oppose the Grand Empire as much as it dared. A noble dispossessed of his privileges, a bishop stripped of his lands, an industrialist or guildsman deprived of his monopolies could hardly be expected to support the new order. The allied states were only waiting for an opportunity to throw off the Napoleonic yoke, and even the dependent rulers who owed much to Napoleon were willing to betray him if it were to their advantage. However, Great Britain and the conservative forces needed additional support to overthrow the Grand Empire. Strangely enough, they received this support from liberalism and nationalism, the very forces that had done so much to strengthen the French Revolution.

At first, the European liberals were receptive to the Revolution. There were always some members of the middle class who welcomed the French army because of the economic freedom and social equality that the invaders brought with them. Intellectuals had hailed the spread of the Enlightenment, and the peasants had been satisfied with the abolition of the manorial system. Slowly, however, these attitudes began to change. Napoleon's substitution of satellite kingdoms for satellite republics offended the doctrinaire republicans. His rigorous censorship of the press and his occasional arbitrary actions offended the devotees of liberty. His practice of demanding military and financial support from all who came within his power caused dismay. His Continental System brought financial losses to the merchant and scarce, high-priced goods to the consumer. His other economic policies favored French merchants at the expense of merchants in the dependent states. Finally, the arrogant behavior of French occupational troops antagonized the local inhabitants, who had originally admired the French but were now quick to defend their own customs. By about 1810, former liberals needed only the creed of nationalism to turn them into rebels against the Grand Empire and only the assurance that the newly-won reforms would be preserved to turn them into allies of their former rulers.

We have seen that between 1792 and 1794, under the stress of foreign invasion, Frenchmen had abandoned the cosmopolitan spirit of the age for a feeling of solidarity and national brotherhood. This feeling, which had contributed so much to the success of the French revolutionary armies, was now turned against France itself.

Nationalism in one sense has always been a factor in history. People usually recoil from the outsider, especially if that outsider adopts policies unfavorable to their interests or occupies their land with troops. But in the past, this negative nationalism, this dislike of foreigners, had rarely become a positive force uniting a people. Provincialism had divided those with the same cultural and racial background, and higher loyalties had been largely reserved for the reigning dynasty or the universal Church. The Enlightenment had rejected the barriers of provincialism and the claims of the Church; it had proclaimed that there were principles of morality and law common to all, that the brotherhood of man was not a romantic dream but a scientific fact and a rational principle.

In some countries, such as Spain, the nationalistic reaction against the French was largely of the older type. The ideas of the Enlightenment had not penetrated deeply into that country, and there were few who welcomed the French as the bearers of civil equality or religious freedom. The great majority were motivated by a dislike of the foreigner and a loyalty to the Church that Napoleon abused and to the dynasty that he dethroned.

In other countries, such as Germany, the reaction to the French led to a rejection of the Enlightenment in favor of a new type of nationalism. French cultural influence had spread deeply into Germany during the eighteenth century, and the courts of its petty princes had been modeled after Versailles. Its aristocracy had adopted the French language and French ways, and even Frederick the Great had preferred to write in the tongue of the Bourbons. Nowhere had cosmopolitanism been stronger. Goethe, the greatest of the German poets, had declared in his youth: "It is the privilege and duty of the philosopher and of the poet to belong to no nation and to no time, but rather to be a contemporary of all times."

Even before the arrival of French armies, there had been signs that the Germans were about to revolt against the Enlightenment. Johann Herder (1744-1803) had taught that literature should be natural and spontaneous. It was artificial and shallow for a German to imitate classical authors or the French, for every people (*Volk*) had its own peculiar spirit (*Geist*). There were no universal truths, no universal criteria. A good poem should reflect the spirit of the people (*Volksgeist*) and not follow the rules of the French Academy. A good law should reflect the traditions and customs of the people. There were no universal principles of morality and justice that it must follow. Herder made no effort to show that the German *Geist* was better than that of other peoples. He declared only that it had an equal claim to respect.

There was, however, but one step between a claim to equality and a claim to superiority. The French practice of destroying foreign social and political institutions in the name of universal reason and justice came to be considered an effort to impose their *Geist* on others. The Germans rose in defense of their past. They began to talk more of their traditional ways and less of their natural rights. They made fun of those who aped the French, and in Johann Fichte (1762-1814) they found a philosopher who boldly proclaimed their superiority. At first, Fichte had accepted the Enlightenment and the French Revolution, but the French occupation of

Germany had made him conscious of the differences between Frenchman and German. The German, he argued, had his own inner moral spirit. He should remain true to the folklore of his people. It was his debt to the past; it was his contribution to the future. The tie between past and future generations was so close that "man sees in his country the realization of his earthly immortality." Thus, the irrational, particularistic forces of nationalism came to replace in Germany the rational universalism of the Enlightenment.

THE REFORM MOVEMENT IN AUSTRIA AND PRUSSIA

But the Germans had no national state. Germany was merely a geographical expression denoting a territory that began in the west somewhere in the Rhineland and ended in the east somewhere in the Slavic world. Patriots first looked to their former emperors, the Habsburgs, to lead a national movement against the French. In 1808, they began to win some response. The Habsburgs created a militia that included all men between the ages of eighteen and forty-five, the army was carefully trained, and a patriotic spirit began to influence the masses. The war was renewed, but the legions of Napoleon were victorious. Vienna was taken and the Tyrolese innkeeper, Andreas Hofer, who had raised the standards of rebellion in Bavarian territory, was captured and executed. Still, Austria was not destroyed. It merely awaited a new opportunity.

Prussia also prepared for a day of reckoning. That country had always been on the outskirts of German civilization, but now German patriots and conservatives migrated to Berlin to help their fellow Germans expel the French. There was the philosopher-statesman Stein, the soldier-theorist Gneisenau, administrator-diplomat Hardenberg, and others from various parts of Germany. They agreed with Gneisenau when he declared that "The Revolution has set in action the national energy of the entire French people, putting the different classes on an equal social and fiscal basis. . . . If the other states wish to establish the former balance of power, they must open up and use these same resources. They must take over the results of the Revolution, and so gain the double advantage of being able to place their entire national energies in opposition to the enemy and of escaping from the dangers of a revolution. . . ." [4] The old order had to be abandoned. The French could not be defeated by an indifferent people with an old-fashioned army composed of noble officers and serf soldiers.

Reforms were inaugurated in 1807 under the direction of Stein and Hardenberg. Serfdom was abolished. The freedman was permitted to go where he pleased and do what he pleased, but he was not automatically relieved of all obligations. Only by surrendering from a third to a half of the land he worked did he receive the remainder as his private property free from all dues. The result was that the estates of the junkers re-

[4] *Ibid.*, page 407.

489

mained large and the peasants often became no more than day laborers. At the same time, the division of society into estates was abolished. Nobles were permitted to engage in trade and the middle class in their chosen occupations. The bureaucracy was revamped and made more efficient, towns were given more self-government, incompetent army officers were discharged and sometimes replaced by members of the middle class. Napoleon had limited the army to 42,000 men, but the Prussians secretly trained that number, then transferred them to the reserves, and trained 42,000 more. By 1812, they had an available force of 150,000 men.

There were rumblings in other parts of Germany. Belgians, Dutch, and especially Swedes began to question the value of their French ties. Kings and conservatives were promising reforms nearly as revolutionary as those introduced by the French, and people were beginning to think more of their national ties than of the cosmopolitanism of the Grand Empire. At this point, French defeats in Russia and Spain touched off a general war that brought about the downfall of Napoleon.

MOSCOW, LEIPZIG, AND WATERLOO

Napoleon was not content with the role of Charlemagne. In 1812, he began to dream, or rather to renew his dreams, of an eastern empire worthy of a Caesar or an Alexander. His designs conflicted with the Russian desire to expand southward at the expense of the Ottoman Empire. His creation of a grand duchy of Poland at the expense of Prussia and Austria threatened Russia's share in the partitions of Poland. His demand that Tsar Alexander I (1801-1825) accept the Continental System increased the tension between France and Russia. Both rulers prepared for war.

In 1812, Napoleon began the long march into Russia. He had 600,000 French and allied troops, one of the largest forces ever assembled before 1914. Indeed, the very size of his army proved a disadvantage because of the difficulty of moving supplies. The outnumbered Russians retreated, destroying everything before the advancing enemy. Disease and hunger took a heavy toll, but Napoleon pressed on towards Moscow hoping to force his enemy into a pitched battle. Finally, in September, the two armies clashed and seventy thousand men fell at Borodino. Napoleon entered Moscow the following week, but he had no sooner arrived than the city was mysteriously destroyed by fire, leaving him to face a Russian winter without housing and without supplies. Still he hesitated, hoping that the tsar would sue for peace, and it was not until October 19 that he gave the order to retreat along the same route. The Russians proved bolder now. They blocked river passages, attacked foraging troops, and took every advantage of snow and weather. In all, the Grand Army lost a half million men, killed, wounded, captured, deserted, or dead from cold and hunger.

Napoleon did not accompany his troops all the way out of Russia. He rushed ahead to raise a new army because it was obvious that the War

Francisco Goya (1746-1828), from his drawings, THE DISASTERS OF WAR. This highly original painter reacted strongly to the sufferings and cruelty of war. This scene was inspired by the French invasion of Spain in 1808 during the Napoleonic wars. (Prado Museum, Spain)

of Liberation was at hand. Prussia allied itself with Russia and called on all Germans to join in the quest for national independence. Austria hesitated, for that country now feared the Russians as much as the French, but by June, 1813, the four great powers—Russia, Prussia, Austria, and Great Britain—and a host of minor powers joined in an effort to defeat Napoleon.

Although Napoleon won several victories, the Battle of Leipzig in October, 1813, proved decisive. At first, his 170,000 men held their own against 200,000 allies, but the arrival of an additional 100,000 Russians, Prussians, and Swedes turned the tide. Napoleon withdrew into France, followed by the allies.

Meanwhile, French armies were retreating in Spain. Napoleon had placed his brother, Joseph, on the Spanish throne in 1808, but most Spaniards had little love for the secular, materialistic philosophy of the Enlightenment or for the upstart foreigner who was now their king. A rebellion quickly followed, in which the Church and the young army officers provided the backbone of the resistance. Although the Spaniards were at first in no position to fight pitched battles with the French, their country's rugged terrain was admirably suited for guerrilla warfare. From the beginning, they were able to tie down 200,000 French troops. The British sent an army under the future Duke of Wellington to aid them and the Portuguese, who were also fighting the invaders. By 1813, the French army was in full retreat. Joseph Bonaparte was forced to abandon Madrid; and a few weeks after Napoleon himself was defeated at Leipzig, Wellington penetrated into France. Bordeaux and Paris were taken in March, 1814, and Napoleon was forced to abdicate in April. After some hesitation the allies decided to restore the Bourbons. The Count of Provence, brother of Louis XVI, ascended the throne as Louis XVIII, and Napoleon was declared ruler of the island of Elba off the Italian coast near his native Corsica. An emperor who was not content with the role of Charlemagne could never have been satisfied with an island. He landed at Cannes on March 1, 1815, with 1,500 men and marched north towards Paris, proclaiming himself a child of the Revolution and a lover of peace. His veterans of many wars, who had been put on half pay by Louis XVIII, joined his standard. Jacobins, who hated the Bourbons above all else, lent their support, and Louis XVIII was forced to flee. On March 13, the allies declared Napoleon "an Enemy and Disturber of the tranquillity of the World," and on June 18 the opposing armies clashed at Waterloo. As at Leipzig, the timely arrival of reinforcements ensured an allied victory. Wellington was left master of the field, and on June 22 Napoleon once more abdicated.

This time he was safely deposited as a prisoner on the island of St. Helena in the South Atlantic, where he spent his six remaining years fashioning the Napoleonic legend. He depicted himself as a lawgiver devoted to liberty and equality, as a reformer who had saved the Revolution from the reactionary forces within and from the kings without. He had sought to create a European federation of free peoples, but after many glorious victories had been defeated by overwhelming numbers. A modern Prometheus, he was chained to a lonely rock in the Atlantic, but someday another Bonaparte would rise to overthrow the conservatives and materialists and restore the regime of equality and glory. Napoleon, who portrayed himself as the greatest of the enlightened despots, became to the next generation, Napoleon, the greatest of the romantic heroes.

THE PEACE SETTLEMENT

The problems of peace had never been far from the minds of the victorious allies, especially during the last stages of the war. After some debate, they had agreed in the Treaty of Paris of May, 1814, that France should be given its boundaries of 1792, that Britain should restore nearly all the colonies taken during the long wars, and that there should be no war indemnities. There remained, however, the problem of redrawing the map of Europe. To accomplish this task two emperors, four kings, two hereditary princes, and some 215 heads of princely families, accompanied by their ministers, wives, and mistresses gathered at Vienna in September. Much has been written about the gay social life that taxed the Habsburg hosts during the ensuing months, but the ministers of the five great powers remained hard at work. They fashioned one of the most important, most abused, and most lasting treaties in European history.

The British delegation was headed by Lord Castlereagh (1769-1822), a lonely, awkward man little given to social amenities. Nevertheless, he was an able diplomat who saw that British interests lay in a stable, peaceful continent, not territorial aggrandizement. Austrian interests were handled by Prince Metternich (1773-1859), an experienced statesman of great capacity who was to be a powerful force in European diplomacy until 1848. He was conceited, lazy, and, reported a contemporary, "most intolerably loose and giddy with women." He, too, however, stood for stability and order. Tsar Alexander I (1801-1825) of Russia served as his own representative at the conference. He was a strange, unpredictable man who at one moment regarded himself as the military genius who had conquered Napoleon and at another as a Christian liberator sent to restore morality and justice to Europe. He had received an excellent liberal education under the direction of his grandmother, Catherine the Great, and was regarded as a crowned Jacobin by conservative rulers. His zeal for reform, however, was tempered by the power of the Russian nobility, for his father, Paul I, and other predecessors had been murdered in palace revolutions.[5] Prussia was represented by the stupid Frederick William III (1797-1840) and Hardenberg (1750-1822), while the restored Louis XVIII (1814-1824) sent the clever Prince Talleyrand (1754-1838). Talleyrand had been a bishop in 1789 and later found employment under the constitutional monarchy, the

[5] See pages 439-442.

493

The Congress of Vienna. Metternich (standing left of center) gestures while holding the attention of Castelreagh (seated with arm over back of chair). Talleyrand is seated at table (extreme right). Engraving by George E. Perine. (Charles Phelps Cushing)

republic, the Directory, and Napoleon. Always he had been able to anticipate a change in regimes and had shifted sides in time to save his head. His goal at Vienna was to win Bourbon France a respected place in the family of nations.

The great problem before statesmen at Vienna was how to restore social and international stability and at the same time compensate and reward the victors. To ensure social stability, Talleyrand pressed for acceptance of the idea of legitimacy, which required the restoration of the reigning houses of 1789 to their former position. In general, his recommendation was followed. The Bourbons resumed their thrones in Spain and Naples as well as France. The Papal States were returned to the pope, and Sardinia, Tuscany, and Modena were given back to the old dynasties.

Castlereagh and Metternich advocated international stability through a balance of power. The Russians, however, created a serious problem. They regarded themselves as the chief architects of the victory. Their armies had penetrated deep into Europe in pursuit of the French, and one of their generals had boasted that "one does not need to worry much about negotiations when one has 600,000 men under arms." Alexander demanded that an "independent kingdom" of Poland be created with himself as king. This arrangement would have deprived Prussia and Austria of a large part of what they had obtained in the three partitions of that unhappy country, but what was especially disturbing was that it would

494

PRINCE TALLEYRAND, *by Jean Auguste Ingres.* (*Giraudon*)

have upset the balance of power and established Russia permanently in central Europe. Nothing was gained by pointing out to Alexander that he had won Finland and Bessarabia during the past few years. Finally, **Britain, Austria, and France formed an alliance against the Russians.** Faced with this threat, Alexander agreed to accept a smaller Polish kingdom. Prussia was compensated for its loss by receiving part of Saxony, and Austria was given Lombardy and Venetia. Norway was taken from Denmark and given to Sweden to compensate for its loss of Finland. Saxony and Denmark could be despoiled because they had been too loyal to Napoleon and were too weak to protest. In this manner, further Russian advances into Europe would be checked by the powerful Austrian and Prussian states and by a strengthened Sweden.

France seemed harmless enough as long as Louis XVIII could hold his throne, but the possibility of another revolution could not be disregarded. The decision was made to surround France with strong buffer states. The former Dutch republic and the Austrian Netherlands were reunited to form a kingdom under the Prince of Orange. Switzerland was declared to be perpetually neutral, and Sardinia was strengthened by the incorporation of Genoa. If France broke through the Netherlands, it would face a Prussia strengthened by additional Rhineland territories. If it broke through Sar-

495

dinia, it would meet Austria. Thus, Prussia and Austria checked France as they did Russia, and in central Europe they balanced each other.

The Vienna Congress failed to create a united Germany. The dream of the liberal nationalists who had responded to the call for a War of Liberation awakened no response from the monarchs after victory had been won. A united Germany would upset the balance of power. It would mean that a choice between a Habsburg and a Hohenzollern ruler would have to be made and that the other German dynasties would be stripped of their power. The solution adopted was probably the best that could be hoped for under the circumstances. Only thirty-nine German states were recognized, about a tenth of the number that existed in 1789, and a Germanic Confederation was created with a diet under the presidency of Austria. There was no other common institution, although an obligation to act together in case of war was recognized.

Britain, which had so often stood alone against Napoleon, was content with a few colonies. Of those captured from the Dutch when they were allied with France, Britain kept only Ceylon and the Cape of Good Hope. Malta, Heligoland, and a few French West Indian islands were also held. Castlereagh sought and achieved a far more important goal than mere colonies: a continental equilibrium. With the European states so carefully balanced, Britain was not only secure; it could also win future objectives by tipping the scales of the balance one way or the other. The Vienna settlement guaranteed Britain a dominant position during the nineteenth century.

The Vienna diplomats have often been condemned for their work. They denied the nationalistic aspirations of the Germans and Italians by leaving them disunited; they denied liberal aspirations by restoring the old dynasties; they denied self-determination by shifting people from one ruler to another without their consent. Yet there is some truth in the statement of a contemporary defender of the treaty that "The Congress of Vienna was not assembled for the discussion of moral principles, but for great practical purposes, to establish effectual provisions for the general security." In this task, the very absence of popular influence on the deliberations was an advantage. In spite of the fear and hatred inspired by Napoleon, he was not executed. In spite of the many wars caused by the French since 1792, they were not severely punished. Even after Napoleon had escaped from Elba and met defeat at Waterloo, the desire for reprisals was curbed. An indemnity and a brief period of occupation were required, but by 1818 France was a fully accepted member of the family of nations with slightly more territory than in 1789. France had no cause to disrupt the treaty. It ceased to be the threat to European security that it had been since the days of Louis XIV. The Vienna treaty was not seriously altered for over a generation, and a century elapsed before there was another general European war. The democratic statesmen at Versailles in 1919, with all their insistence on nationalism, liberalism, and self-determination, could make no such boast.

EUROPE IN 1815 AFTER
THE CONGRESS OF VIENNA

BOUNDARY OF
GERMAN CONFEDERATION
EUROPEAN NATIONAL
BOUNDARIES

SCALE OF MILES
0 50 100   200   300

12/ The Age of Romanticism, 1815-1850

ROMANTICISM

WHILE the conservative statesmen of Europe were mustering their armed strength to overthrow Napoleon, a new intellectual movement was developing, especially in Germany, to combat the ideas of the Enlightenment. This movement shifted emphasis from the senses as the most important source of knowledge to emotion, feeling, or what may be called inner experience. Since the emotional nature of individuals differs widely, the new movement had a wide variety of manifestations. It is usually referred to as romanticism.

THE ORIGINS AND CHARACTERISTICS OF ROMANTICISM

Romanticism was in part a reaction against the Enlightenment. If the Enlightenment's emphasis on the senses was carried to its logical conclusion, the existence of God and the hope for immortality would have to be denied. Those who stopped short of this extreme found in deism a cold, uninspiring religion. Nature, depicted as a mechanistic order controlled by checks and balances, was hardly a subject to inspire emotion. The Enlightenment had been characterized by a skeptical view of institutions and beliefs. Many began to feel the need to believe, to laugh, and to weep. Necker's daughter, Madame de Staël, revealed the new frame of mind when she wrote, "I do not know exactly what we must believe, but I believe that we must believe! The eighteenth century did nothing but deny. The human spirit lives by its beliefs. Acquire faith through Christianity, or through German philosophy, or merely through enthusiasm, but believe in something."

Romanticism was also in part a natural outgrowth of the emphasis on sensibility that became popular in the late eighteenth century. Rousseau, as we have seen, had taught the cultivation of the heart rather than the mind and had believed that emotions provided a better guide to conduct than reason. In England, Samuel Richardson's (1689-1761) *Pamela*, Thomas Gray's (1716-1771) *Elegy Written in a Country Churchyard*, and Oliver Goldsmith's (1728-1774) *The Deserted Village* glorified sensibility rather than thought.

The intellectual content in romanticism, however, was largely a German contribution, and the Germans replaced the French as the cultural leaders of Europe. The German Immanuel Kant (1724-1804) provided the rational justification for the movement. He wisely refrained from rejecting either the sciences or the scientific method of the Enlightenment. Instead, he argued that their use was limited. The universe did not consist of one world but of two. One was physical. Here, the senses and induction yielded fruit. The other world was spiritual. Here, religion, aesthetics, and ethics had their place, and the tools of the scientists could not be employed to advantage. St. Thomas Aquinas had argued that faith and reason could not conflict because they had a common creator; now Kant created a second world to achieve the same results.

In general, romanticism was characterized by an abandonment of classical form and restraint and a glorification of individualism. The Enlightenment had sought the universal principles of human nature; the romantics concentrated on the emotional differences among individuals and their diverse reactions to various stimuli. They often had a melancholy outlook that had not been characteristic of their predecessors. They believed in the evolution of political and social institutions, which were thought to be organic and to change gradually like other forms of life. A people was assumed to have a distinctive *Geist*, or spirit, that was reflected in its government and its culture. The romantics loved the unfamiliar and exotic, whether located in the past, or some far-off place, or in the supernatural. They also loved nature: woods, streams, and birds became favorite subjects of poets, and novelists found appealing subjects in Indians of the forest and sailors on distant seas. The romantic era witnessed a religious revival that emphasized an appeal to the emotions.

499

THE CLASSICAL REVIVAL

Romanticism never became as dominant as the Renaissance and Baroque styles had become in the earlier periods. Indeed, since the decline of the Rococo, styles have become so numerous that generalizations about art and literature are difficult. In the period under consideration, however, only a renewed interest in classicism seriously competed with the dominant romanticism.

Like romanticism, the classical revival involved an idealized and emotional interest in a past age. Otherwise, the differences between the two movements were pronounced. The classicist emphasized form, order, and proportion and esteemed reason as the surest guide to conduct. Whenever they interfered with a desired emotional response, the romanticist ignored artistic rules, and he esteemed natural feelings as the surest guide to conduct. "It was my heart that counselled me to do it," one of them declared, "and my heart cannot err." His admiration for the standards of the ancient world led the classicist to question the idea of progress. The romanticist's belief in evolution led him to accept the idea of progress, and he saw in the past a means to discover the *Geist* of his particular race rather than a guide for correct artistic taste.

The respect for classical rules had begun to increase once more during the late Baroque period, but the classical revival itself did not get fully under way until near the close of the eighteenth century. This revival was partly a reaction against the lightheartedness of the Rococo and partly the result of increased knowledge of the ancient civilizations. Excavations at Pompeii and elsewhere provided more information concerning the Roman period, but above all it was the efforts of Johann Winckelmann (1717-1768) and others to achieve an understanding of Greek civilization that characterized the classical revival in the romantic period. The ancient Greeks had been imperfectly understood before, and their influence had always been less than the Romans', but now their contributions were emphasized so much that the Neo-Classical movement has often been referred to as a Greek revival.

It is necessary now to see how romanticism and the opposing, less important classical current affected thought and art.

LITERATURE, ART, AND MUSIC

Since poetry is uniquely effective in arousing emotions, the romantic era was marked by an unparalleled flowering of poetic genius. William Wordsworth (1770-1850) and Samuel Coleridge (1772-1834) established the new style in England. Wordsworth's poetry was idealistic, moral, and reflective. His descriptions of his native Lake Country in northern England were exceptionally beautiful. Coleridge was deeply influenced by German philosophy and found his romantic impulses stimulated by the strange

Goethe, from a contemporary engraving. (Courtesy Free Library of Philadelphia)

and the distant. His *Rime of the Ancient Mariner* and *Kubla Khan* achieved a weird, haunting beauty that has rarely been equaled. These two poets were followed by such geniuses as the violent, moody Lord Byron (1788-1824) and the idealistic, rebellious Percy Bysshe Shelley (1792-1822). The new republic of the United States produced a master of horror in the unbalanced Edgar Allan Poe (1809-1849) and a typical sentimentalist in Henry Wadsworth Longfellow (1807-1882).

It is impossible to discuss all the great poets of this period who wrote in other languages, but to mention France's Victor Hugo (1802-1885), Germany's Heinrich Heine (1797-1856), Poland's Adam Mickiewicz (1798-1855), and Russia's Alexander Pushkin (1799-1837) is enough to establish the role of poetry in the age of romanticism. A few secondary poets found their inspiration in classical models.

Johann Wolfgang von Goethe (1749-1832) was unquestionably the greatest literary figure of the age. In his early life, he was a leader of the pre-romantic movement in his native Germany, but the classical conception of beauty and harmony influenced his later writings. His *Faust*, which was written over a period of sixty years, reflects his growing respect for classicism. His outlook, however, remained predominantly romantic, and he never abandoned his belief in evolution, a belief that was sustained by his own scientific investigations and his distrust of human reason.

Drama was also a popular medium among the romanticists. Even Paris' Théâtre Français, the very center of classical influence, was unable to resist the romantic movement. The novel, however, was a more congenial form. Sir Walter Scott (1771-1832), Alexandre Dumas (1802-1870), and Victor Hugo won tremendous popular success with such romantic tales of the past as *Ivanhoe, The Three Musketeers,* and *The Hunchback of Notre Dame.* James Fenimore Cooper (1789-1851) capitalized on the interest in remote places and "noble savages" in *The Last of the Mohicans* and other Indian stories. He was also one of the first novelists of the sea.

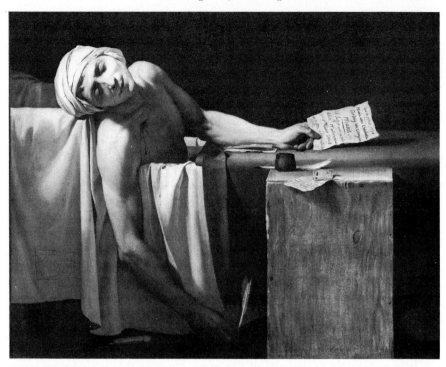

DEATH OF MARAT, *by Jacques-Louis David. Although Marat was assassinated in his bathtub by a young woman, not killed in action during a battle, David imparted a sense of dignity and grandeur to his subject by the stark simplicy of the setting and the classical form of the dying revolutionary. (Alinari-Art Reference Bureau)*

Even François René Chateaubriand (1768-1848), the leading member of the French romantic school, wrote a book about Indians, although this egotistical, dreamy, unstable Breton of an ancient family was more important as an apologist for Catholicism. Interest in the strange and the supernatural was exploited by Emily Brontë (1818-1848) in *Wuthering Heights* and by Mary Wollstonecraft Shelley (1797-1851) in *Frankenstein.*

The classical revival was more evident in painting, sculpture, and architecture than in literature. Jacques-Louis David (1748-1825) abandoned the Rococo style of his masters and emphasized harmony, proportion, and line in accordance with the classical tradition. As an official painter for the French revolutionary government and later for the court of Napoleon, he often preferred contemporary subjects, such as the death of the radical revolutionary leader, Marat, or the coronation of Napoleon, to the subjects of classical antiquity. Although the romantics found his work cold and uninspiring, he succeeded in re-establishing the classical tradition in France. His work was carried on by his pupil, Jean Auguste Ingres (1780-1867).

David and Ingres were vigorously challenged by Ferdinand Eugène Del-

William Turner, THE DOGANA AND SANTA MARIA DELLA SALUTE, *Venice.*
Turner emphasized the dramatic qualities of nature at the expense of
exact, linear drawing. (National Gallery of Art, Washington)

acroix (1798-1863) and other romantics who sought to impart an emotional
quality to their work by using such subjects as old castles, ruins, and cavalry charges. They stressed color more than line and often ignored the
classical rules of harmony and proportion in order to enhance the emotional impact of their work. The romantics' love of nature led to a renewed
interest in landscape painting. In William Turner (1775-1851), England
found an artist who liked to depict the dramatic qualities in nature, such
as a storm at sea or a rugged mountain scene. His contemporary John
Constable (1776-1837) was content to paint commonplace views of nature
exactly as he saw them.

The Neo-Classical tradition prevailed in sculpture, but the Gothic and
Renaissance styles were also imitated, and the emphasis placed by some
sculptors on dramatic scenes and violent movements exemplified the emotionalism of the romantic era.

The tendency of the romantics to imitate past styles was even more
evident in architecture than in sculpture. Churches were often built in the
Gothic style because the medieval period was believed to have been an age
of faith. Palace architects turned to the Renaissance for inspiration, while
those who built opera houses preferred the Baroque because the first operas
had been a product of that age. Public buildings in Washington, D. C.,
were classical, as befitted the admirers of Athenian democracy, and universities turned to the Gothic because the first institutions of higher learning

In WIVENHOE PARK, *Essex, John Constable, unlike Turner, found peace and serenity in nature and sought to paint exactly what he saw. (National Gallery of Art, Washington)*

had been started in the Middle Ages. There were, of course, many exceptions to these rules. The Madeleine Church in Paris and the University of Virginia were classical, but the English, mindful of when representative assemblies began, constructed their parliament buildings in the Perpendicular Gothic style. No new architectural style emerged, and the large number of old styles prevented any one of them from becoming characteristic of the period.

In music, the Neo-Classical revival preceded rather than paralleled the romantic movement. It was marked by greater clarity, harmony, and simplicity than had exemplified the earlier period. The piano slowly replaced the harpsichord as the basic musical instrument, and the symphony became the most popular instrumental form. Austria, with such great composers as Franz Joseph Haydn (1732-1809) and Wolfgang Mozart (1756-1791), was clearly the musical center of Europe. Many great nobles, such as Prince Esterhazy of Hungary who befriended Haydn, had theaters in their palaces and employed musicians, singers, and composers. It was this combination of generous patronage and native genius that made Austria's great achievements in music possible.

Austria maintained its leadership in music after Ludwig van Beethoven (1770-1827) inaugurated the romantic era, even though Beethoven himself scorned the assistance of a patron. The younger generation of romantic composers included Franz Schubert (1797-1828), Felix Mendelssohn (1809-1847), and Robert Schumann (1810-1856). These composers, like other romantics, appealed to the emotions more than to reason. The dramatic and the sentimental were deliberately cultivated, subject matter was often taken from legendary and historical episodes, and folk songs

504

Eugène Delacroix, THE BARRICADE *(July 28, 1830), Paris, Louvre. Compare the heavy dramatics of this painting of the Goddess of Liberty inspiring the combatants with Jacques-Louis David's* DEATH OF MARAT *(p. 502). In the Delacroix painting, the emphasis is on color and action rather than on simplicity and draftsmanship. (Bettmann Archive)*

were much admired. The works of these men were so popular that the romantic style prevailed in music until the close of the nineteenth century.

THE NATURAL AND THE SOCIAL SCIENCES

Rapid progress in the natural sciences continued during the romantic period, although no scientific discoveries were made comparable to those of the sixteenth and seventeenth centuries. Biologists and geologists groped for a theory of evolution. The cell was found to be the basic unit in all plant and animal life, and the atom was found to hold a similar place in the physical world; but it was only after the middle of the century that the full impact of these discoveries was felt.

In the social sciences, a theory of historical evolution became widely accepted after 1800. Most eighteenth-century theorists had followed Locke in the belief that there were natural laws and natural rights, and they had used the contract theory to justify revolution. It was in keeping with these ideas that the Americans and French had overthrown their governments

The Parliament buildings in London were designed in the 1830's by Sir Charles Barry and Augustus W. N. Pugin. (Charles Phelps Cushing)

and prepared new constitutions. Now, the existence of a social contract, natural laws, and natural rights was challenged. The first important theorist to question the political doctrines of the Enlightenment was Edmund Burke (1729-1797). In 1790, he published his *Reflections on the Revolution in France,* in which he foretold the chaos that would result from the efforts of the French reformers to change suddenly the structure of their society and government. "Society is indeed a contract," he declared, "but the state ought not to be considered as nothing better than a partnership agreement in a trade of pepper and coffee, to be taken up for a temporary interest and to be dissolved by the fancy of the parties. . . . It is a partnership in all science, in all art, in every virtue and in all perfection. As the ends of such a partnership cannot be obtained in many generations, it becomes a partnership not only between those who are living, but between those who are living, those who are dead and those who are to be born." Herder and Fichte, as we have seen, developed somewhat similar arguments in Germany to justify the nationalistic uprising that helped to expel the French. With the restoration of the dispossessed dynasties after the downfall of Napoleon, the new theory found supporters in every European country.

The fully developed romantic theory held that there were no universal

Ludwig van Beethoven at the age of forty-two, from a plaster lifemask by Franz Klein. (Beethovenhaus, Bonn)

natural laws or natural rights and that there never had been a formal social contract. Primitive man had been a slave to his passions and fears, and he achieved freedom and rights only when he became a member of a state and society. Individual states and societies evolved through time, just as any other organism. Each had its own *Geist* or spirit that was inherited by one generation and passed on to the next. Therefore, the customs, privileges, and rights of one people differed from those of another. Since there had been no social contract, there could be no claim that a breach of contract justified revolt. To alter suddenly political and social institutions was to abandon the tried and proven ways of the past that would not have evolved if they had not suited the *Volksgeist*. To do so also denied future generations their just inheritance. For a group of men to sit down and prepare a constitution was the height of conceit, for they pitted their knowledge against the wisdom of countless generations. To follow such a course could only lead to disaster, as the tragic events in France showed only too well.

The most important theorist who adopted this approach was Georg Wilhelm Hegel (1770-1831). Hegel took the idea of historical evolution and gave it a controlling force, God, and a final goal, the perfect state. He believed that as the institutions of a society matured and performed their mission, they created opposites or antitheses. Out of the clash between the two opposites a new society or synthesis was created. This synthesis, in turn, created a new opposite, and the whole process was repeated over and over again. The change was not cyclical, however, for there was a steady movement forward in accordance with a divine plan. The ultimate goal was the perfect state in which the interests of the individual and society were the same. Man could then be completely free without danger to the rights of others. Thus, "The state is the divine idea as it exists on earth." Nothing can halt the historical process. Hegel accepted the idea of progress and with other liberals dreamed of a united Germany. His theories influenced Karl Marx more than those of any other man, but they were also adopted by many conservatives who put the state and the existing order before the individual.

The emphasis on evolution made it desirable to define the *Geist* or spirit of a people. To prove whether something was good or bad, it was necessary to discover whether it had evolved down to the present. These were tasks for the historians, and the nineteenth century saw a great historical renaissance. Historical societies were founded by the hundreds to encourage the study of the past, and governments sponsored the publication of huge collections of documents. The decoding of Egyptian hieroglyphics and archeological discoveries stimulated further study of ancient history, but above all it was the study of the Middle Ages that profited by the new approach. The period between the decline of Rome and the Renaissance had been held in contempt by the Enlightenment, but now its art, culture, society, and institutions were subjected to searching inquiry, for it was during this period that the European states began their independent existence. Not content merely to describe political events, historians tried to depict the spirit of a people as it evolved through time. Englishmen found in the evolution of their institutions evidence of special talent for constitutional government. The native genius of the Italian people was given by Jakob Burckhardt (1818-1897) as an explanation of the origins of the Renaissance in that country. There were no longer any universal truths. Every people had its peculiar spirit, and this spirit explained how and why it had evolved to its present state.

THE RELIGIOUS REVIVAL

The romantic movement was accompanied by a widespread religious revival. In Protestant countries, it began so early that it has been considered one of the causes of the romantic movement. Actually, since both the religious revival and romanticism were characterized by an appeal to the emotions, they may be considered different aspects of the same phenomenon. Both found their first home in Germany.

In the late seventeenth century, a reaction set in against the emphasis on theology in the Lutheran church. The leaders of this pietistic movement belittled human reason and insisted on the necessity of emotional religious experience. In general, they emphasized man's natural depravity, his lack of free will, the need for faith, and the imminent coming of the day of judgment. Many were puritanical and condemned dancing, the theater, hunting, and similar pleasures. Although they usually remained loyal to the Lutheran church, their teachings influenced other sects, especially the Moravians.

The Moravians were a Hussite sect that had refused to become reconciled with the Catholic Church. In 1722, some of them immigrated to Germany from Moravia to escape persecution and settled on the estate of the Count of Zinzendorf (1700-1760). Zinzendorf was a well-educated, devout pietist who had already spent much time studying religions in different parts of Europe. He organized the little group of refugees into a militant band of missionaries. Although the Moravians had bishops and practiced infant baptism like the more conservative Protestant churches, they put great stress on the mystical and emotional elements of religion. By the time of Zinzendorf's death, Moravian missionaries were working among the Indians, Eskimos, and slaves in the Americas and in many parts of Asia and Africa. Even more important was their influence on other churches. They were instrumental in touching off a Lutheran revival in the late eighteenth century and deeply affected John Wesley (1703-1791).

John Wesley came of an old English family that had produced several scholars. His father, a conservative Anglican clergyman, had quarreled with his wife, who temporarily left him, and with his parishioners, who burned the rectory. However, John was carefully raised by his mother. He was graduated from Oxford, where he became a lecturer in Greek, and a member of the Anglican clergy. In 1735, he went to Georgia as a missionary, but his insistence that the Anglican ritual be strictly observed brought him many enemies. He even refused communion to Governor Oglethorpe's niece, whom he charged with misconduct. When she sued for libel, Wesley fled back to England.

In London, he came under the influence of some Moravians whose faith had already impressed him. While attending one of their meetings in May, 1738, in which Luther's *Preface to the Epistle to the Romans* was read, he underwent a deep emotional experience. "About a quarter before nine," he writes, "while he [the reader] was describing the change which God works in the heart through faith in Christ, I felt my heart strangely warmed. I felt I did trust in Christ, Christ alone, for salvation; and an assurance was given me that he had taken away *my* sins, even *mine*, and saved *me* from the law of sin and death."

This episode had a profound effect on Wesley and through him on history. He abandoned his earlier emphasis on ritual, organized a Methodist society to assist him, and began to preach to all who would listen whether in a church or in the fields. By declaring that "The fall of man is the very foundation of revealed religion," he threw himself into the teeth of the Enlightenment. "Is man by nature filled with all manner of evil?" he asked. "Is he void of all good? Is he wholly false? Is he totally corrupted? . . . Allow this, and you are so far a Christian. Deny it, and you are but a heathen still." He emphasized the importance of Christ's atonement and man's faith in the process of salvation, but avoided the doctrine of predestination. "Faith is that divine evidence," he said, "whereby the spiritual man discerneth God and the things of God. It is with respect to the spiritual world what sense is to the natural. It is the spiritual sensation of every soul that is born of God. . . . Till you have these internal senses, till the eyes of your understanding are opened, you can have no proper apprehension of divine things, no just idea of them. Nor consequently can you either judge truly or reason justly concerning them; seeing your reason has no ground whereon to stand, no materials to work upon." Thus, he denied that reason or the external senses can be used to understand religion. The internal senses—that is, feeling, emotion, inner experience—and the Bible are man's only guides.

Wesley therefore put great emphasis on both the literal interpretation of the Bible and the emotional aspects of religion. His fundamentalism caused him to reject the Copernican theory and to hold that to give up a belief in witchcraft was to give up the Bible. The emotional fervor of his sermons was exceeded only by that of the itinerant preachers in his movement. One unsympathetic eye witness reported that "The manner of the itinerants' holding forth is generally very boisterous and shocking and adapted, to the best of their skill, to alarm the imagination and to raise a ferment in the passions. . . . The preacher has recourse to frightful representations: that he sees hell-flames flashing in their faces; and that they are now! now! now! dropping into hell! into the bottom of hell! the bottom of hell!"

This judgment of an itinerant's preaching should be tempered with one made by the unsympathetic but impressed Benjamin Franklin. "It was a matter of speculation to me to observe the extraordinary influence of his oratory on his hearers, and how much they admired and respected him, notwithstanding his common abuse of them, by assuring them they were naturally half beasts and half devils. It was wonderful to see the change soon made in the manners of our inhabitants. From being thoughtless or indifferent about religion, it seemed as if all the world were growing religious."

Wesley was not warmly received by the upper classes, who generally agreed with the Duchess of Buckingham that "It is monstrous to be told that you have a heart as sinful as the common wretches that crawl the earth." He carried his message primarily to miners, laborers, and small shopkeepers in the new cities that were springing up everywhere in England. These people were neglected by the Anglican clergy, but their desire for religious experience and need for moral reform can hardly be exaggerated. Many of them lived under the most degrading circumstances, and drunkenness had become a serious social problem.

To reach these people, Wesley rode approximately 5,000 miles a year and preached fifteen sermons a week. He wrote a vast amount of religious literature, which was sold at prices that the poor could afford. A few other Anglican clergymen joined his movement and rendered great assistance. His brother, Charles, wrote about 6,500 hymns and preached ably as well. On the whole, the Anglicans were offended by the emotionalism in his movement. They denied him the use of churches and refused to ordain his lay preachers. At length, Wesley was forced to ordain ministers to carry on his ever-expanding program, but he himself never broke with the Anglican Church. His followers, however, took this step soon after his death.

It is difficult to overemphasize the importance of his work. By his death in 1791, there were 71,000 Methodists in Great Britain and 57,000 in America. So well had he organized the movement that their number tripled in less than another generation. Like the Moravians, the Methodists influenced other churches and Anglican laymen. Wesley's demand for moral reform was most timely, and his insistence that respect be shown for the upper classes and the government is said to have been one of the chief factors that saved England from revolution in the late eighteenth century.

The principal inspirer of the Catholic revival was François René Chateaubriand (1768-1848). In his youth, Chateaubriand had been a student of Voltaire and Rousseau, but in 1802 he published a persuasive defense of Catholicism. He believed that the past glories of the Roman Church, the beauty of its service, and its contributions to civilization all combined to justify its position. It was no longer necessary to defend Catholic dogma from the rationalists. To demonstrate its eternal truths, it was sufficient to describe the emotions of a peasant girl as she stopped to pray at a wayside cross. Catholic revivalist meetings were held, sometimes in the open air.

By 1815, a religious awakening had spread throughout western and central Europe and the United States. It was not as deep as that of the Reformation era, but much of the ground that had been lost during the Enlightenment was regained. Even Tsar Alexander I, who had been educated by the philosophers and who was regarded by conservatives as a crowned Jacobin in 1814, fell under the influence of a religious mystic in the following year.

The generation that reached maturity in 1815 lived in an age deeply influenced by romanticism. Based as it was on emotional experience, romanticism influenced different people in different ways. For some, it justified political and social conservatism at home and the defense of the Vienna settlement in Europe. For others, it justified revolt against the conventions of society and the rule of foreign kings. It is therefore necessary to investigate the forces of conservatism and the forces for change in order to evaluate carefully the role that romanticism played in the evolution of Europe.

THE FORCES OF CONSERVATISM

THE MONARCHS, THE ARISTOCRACY, AND THE CHURCHES

The principal conservative forces in Europe after 1815 were the monarchs, the aristocracy, and the churches. As a whole, the monarchs of the period were no more able or intelligent than those who had confronted the Revolution in 1789. Now, however, they were strengthened by the growing belief that their rule was the lesser of two evils. Republics created in the 1790's had been warlike and unstable. Furthermore, as the Reign of Terror proved only too well, they had shown little respect for normal legal proceedings. Indeed, democracy and despotism were frequently regarded as inseparable. Elective kingship had been tried by Napoleon, and once more there had been wars and a loss of freedom.

Though professing to abhor the despotic tendencies of republican and Napoleonic rule, the monarchs were not slow to appropriate the tools of these regimes. Where centralized administrations had been established, they were maintained; the Napoleonic secret police, the first efficient one in Europe, was everywhere emulated. Even well-known conservatives found that their letters were opened and their conversations reported. Known subversives were in constant danger. Moreover, monarchs who lacked the competence necessary to rule often found capable advisers and administrators.

The European aristocracy as a whole had lost little by the Revolution. They remained large landowners in England and eastern Europe, and land was still the chief source of wealth and power. Even in France and the border regions the nobles who had fled during the Revolution managed to regain about half their confiscated lands, and those aristocrats who had accepted the republic and empire had kept their estates. Among the major powers only Great Britain and France had a commercial or industrial middle class wealthy enough to pose a serious threat, but even in these countries the best positions in the army, the bureaucracy, and the church went to the aristocracy.

The Protestants had suffered little by the Revolution. In most of the countries that had come directly under the sway of France, they had been outlawed minorities until the Revolution had given them legal status approximately equal to that of the Catholics. The Catholic Church had been less fortunate, but it now capitalized on the sympathy that it received for having been persecuted. Its lands had been confiscated, its control over education and marriage broken, and its clergy mistreated. Even the papal states had been incorporated into the Grand Empire. For Catholicism, the decade after 1815 was a period of revival. The papal states were restored by the Vienna settlement. The Jesuit order, which had been destroyed on the request of the enlightened despots, was re-established and welcomed by most Catholic sovereigns. Lay Catholic orders were created to foster the piety of the upper classes. The Inquisition returned to Spain, and the Index once more became a force to control men's minds. Part of the ground lost in education was regained, and although the lands of the Church were seldom restored, governments voted generous grants to support its activities.

The monarchy, the aristocracy, and the churches might seem slender reeds upon which to base the European social order. They had quickly succumbed to the revolutionary forces in 1789, and in some respects they did not completely regain their position in 1815. Four factors, however, made them stronger. In the first place, they were now united. Before the Revolution, the aristocracy had often resisted the monarch, and the monarch had sometimes attacked the wealth and power of the Church. Monarchs and aristocrats alike had occasionally been numbered among the religious skeptics. The Revolution had taught the folly of division. Through conviction or through self-interest, the throne, the altar, and the aristocracy stood side by side for a generation after 1815.

Many people had undergone a change of heart. After over two decades of war, they wanted peace above all else. The monarchy of the old regime seemed far safer than either a republic or a Napoleonic restoration. Not only had the wars caused loss of life and heavy taxation; they had also brought blockades and trade restrictions that had affected the standard of living.

Third, the intellectual outlook changed when romanticism triumphed over the Enlightenment. The divine right monarchy, the privileged aristocracy, and the teachings of the churches no longer had to stand trial before the bar of reason. They could be judged by their emotional worth. An ancient family name, like an old church, was now treated as an object of veneration. The reigning dynasty, the privileged aristocracy, and the church were part of the *Volksgeist*. To destroy them would break the continuity of history and lead to dire results. Thus, the intellectual, who in 1789 had so loudly demanded reform, now threw his support behind the established order more often than not.

Finally, the European monarchs in 1815 were united in their desire to preserve the established order. They were blood relatives, just as before the Revolution, but now some of them recognized that it was not in their interest to take advantage of one another. Instead, they tried to stand together against external aggression and internal revolt. Protestant monarchs were almost as insistent as Catholic monarchs that the pope be restored, so anxious were they to preserve the rights of rulers. To further their cooperation, the great powers established the Concert of Europe.

THE CONCERT OF EUROPE

The Concert of Europe grew out of the Quadruple Alliance made in 1815 between Great Britain, Russia, Prussia, and Austria. This treaty committed the allies to a twenty-year alliance to overthrow Napoleon, to establish and preserve the political divisions of Europe, and to meet periodically to settle disputes. No international court of justice or army was established. In this respect, the Concert of Europe fell short of the projects for perpetual peace developed by the eighteenth-century philosophers, but it was nevertheless a definite improvement over any previous effort at international collaboration to preserve the peace.

In addition to the Quadruple Alliance, Tsar Alexander proposed a Holy Alliance between Christian monarchs in which they promised "to consider themselves all as members of one and the same Christian nation" and to conduct their foreign and domestic affairs in accordance with the principles of the Christian religion. Few European monarchs took Alexander's proposal seriously. Metternich referred to it as "a high sounding Nothing" and Castlereagh as "a piece of sublime mysticism and nonsense." Nevertheless, the tsar, who had come under the influence of religious mystics, was quite sincere, and there was little to be gained by offending him. Only three European monarchs failed to sign the Holy Alliance: George III, who was no longer sane; the sultan of Turkey, who was an infidel; and the pope, who declared that "from time immemorial the papacy has been in possession of Christian truth and needed no new interpretation of it." The Holy Alliance was too vague to be of practical importance, but to discontented people during the next half century it became a symbol of monarchical reaction.

Despite general agreement among the monarchs that it was in their interests to cooperate within the Concert of Europe to preserve the established order, there was disagreement from the beginning over what the established order ought to be. To Castlereagh, the goal of the Concert of Europe was to preserve the balance of power on the continent. A balance of power would leave the British free to exploit their powerful trading position. He was opposed to interference in the internal affairs of other nations and would go no further in this direction than to promise to prevent a Bonaparte restoration in France. Tsar Alexander had the opposite opinion. He pointed out that it was an internal revolution in France that had led to the wars of the republic and the Napoleonic empire. Internal revolutions should therefore be stifled by an international army before they became dangerous to Europe, and lawful monarchs should be restored to power. At first, Metternich wavered between the two positions. He desired a European equilibrium and knew that the intervention of the great powers into the internal affairs of a state might upset the status quo. However, he soon accepted Alexander's view with so much enthusiasm that the Concert of Europe has sometimes been called the Metternich System. His decision was motivated by his fear of nationalism. An avowed advocate of the cosmopolitanism of the Enlightenment, he regarded nationalism as a divisive force that separated one European people from another. Furthermore, Austria itself was a dynastic, not a national, state. A successful nationalistic uprising in one of the Italian states or in Russian Poland could lead to uprisings among the Italian or Polish subjects of the Habsburgs. It was clearly wiser to provide for international cooperation to stifle a revolt before it became a serious threat.

The first meeting of the great powers was held at Aix-la-Chapelle in 1818. France borrowed money in order to pay the indemnity that had been imposed upon her. In return, the other great powers decided to withdraw the army of occupation and to accept France as a participant in the Concert of Europe, but Tsar Alexander's proposals for disarmament and the formation of an international army were rejected. The tsar was also rebuffed when he proposed that Spain be helped to recover its American colonies, which had taken advantage of the Napoleonic wars and their aftermath to assert their independence.[1]

The next meetings of the great powers were held at Troppeau and Laibach in 1820 and 1821. The occasion was a Spanish revolution that had forced a liberal constitution upon the king. The tsar favored armed intervention, but Castlereagh and, at first, Metternich were opposed. However, revolts in Naples and Savoy that threatened Austrian possessions in northern Italy caused Metternich to change his mind. Over British protests, it was finally decided that an Austrian army should restore the rulers of Naples and Savoy to their former position.

The great powers met at Verona in 1822. No action had been taken concerning the rebellion in Spain or in the Spanish colonies, and the Greeks had just revolted against their Turkish masters. The first matter was readily resolved by authorizing the French to send an army into Spain to restore the absolute power of the discredited king. No action was taken to reconquer the Spanish colonies. The British had developed a lively trade with these colonies during the Napoleonic wars and had no desire to see Spanish authority with its inevitable trading restrictions re-established in the New World. Furthermore, they were opposed to the Concert's policy of internal intervention in other countries. The new British foreign minister, George Canning (1770-1827), therefore sought joint action with the United States to prevent any move by Spain against its former colonies in the New World.

President Monroe decided to act alone, however, and in 1823 he announced in the doctrine which bears his name that any effort on the part of the European powers to extend their political system to any portion of the New World would be regarded as dangerous to the United States. France also supported the British position, the former Spanish colonies were not attacked, and the meetings of the rulers and foreign ministers of the great European powers came to an end, although they continued to cooperate on the Eastern question, of which the Greek rebellion was but one aspect.

[1] See page 596.

THE EASTERN QUESTION

The Eastern question plagued European statesmen throughout the period between the Napoleonic wars and World War I. Indeed, their failure to find a satisfactory solution was a major cause of the latter conflict. The question was raised by the decline of the Ottoman Empire, the rise of nationalism among the Balkan peoples, and the conflicting interests of the great powers.

The slow, almost imperceptible decline of the Ottoman Empire that had begun near the close of the sixteenth century continued throughout the eighteenth century after the brief revival under the Kiuprili grand viziers.[2] The shift in trade routes to the Atlantic undermined the Ottoman economy, the sultans continued to be harem-ridden incompetents, and corrupt administrative officials bribed and intrigued when assigned to the capital or carved out semi-autonomous states for themselves when given governorships. Confident of their superiority, the Ottomans ignored the scientific and technological advances of the West and did not even establish a modern army.

The French Revolution inaugurated a long, slow process which led to an awakening of the Christian inhabitants of the Balkans and of the Turks themselves. In the year the Revolution began, Selim III (1789-1807) became sultan and sought to save the Ottoman Empire by Westernization just as Peter the Great had saved Russia a century before. He tried to rid the country of administrative abuses, but the conflicts of the age compelled him to devote much of his reforming energy to war and diplomacy. He attempted to create a Western-style army and imported French officers to train his troops. At the same time, he established permanent embassies in the leading European capitals. These military and diplomatic contacts enabled a small nucleus of Turks to become familiar with the ideologies of the French revolutionary era as well as Western science and technology.

Selim's actions angered the janissaries who were fearful that the effort to build a modern army would cost them their influence. With the co-operation of Moslem religious leaders, they dethroned and strangled him. His death brought the reform movement temporarily to an end, while the failure to create a large modern army enabled the Balkan peoples to revolt and the great powers to interfere in Ottoman affairs.

French revolutionary ideas made greater headway among the inhabitants of the Balkans than among the Turks. The French governed the Ionian islands off the western coast of Greece for a time, and the coastal provinces along the eastern side of the Adriatic Sea were actually incorporated into their empire. There the serfs were emancipated, the Code Napoleon was introduced with its doctrine of equality before the law, and the Serbs, Croats, and Slovenes who inhabited the region acquired a vague idea of a common, south Slav nationality that was reinforced by a literary

[2] See pages 255-259.

revival. Napoleon also consciously appealed to Greek pride in their former greatness; although most Greeks, like the other inhabitants of the Balkans, were illiterate peasants, there was an educated minority whose nationalistic spirit was stimulated by his appeals. These educated Greeks held most of the important posts in the Orthodox Church in the Balkans and served as merchants, money lenders, and tax farmers for the region. The Slavic peasants, whom they oppressed by their exactions, hated them more than the Turks, but they knew and understood the developments in the West. With the exception of those whose interests depended on continued Ottoman supremacy, these educated Greeks took the lead in winning their country's independence.

Of the rest of the Balkan peoples, only the Rumanians began to be indoctrinated with a nationalistic spirit prior to the latter half of the nineteenth century. They fancied themselves descended from the Romans who had conquered their land between A.D. 107 and 274. They spoke a Romance language, studied French literature and thought, and imagined themselves a cultured island in a sea of barbarian Slavs, although for a long time Greek influence remained strong. They inhabited the Turkish-owned principalities of Wallachia and Moldavia, Austrian-held Transylvania, and Russian-held Bessarabia, a situation which meant that they could be united only at the expense of all three of the large eastern multinational empires.

What would have happened if the Turks and Balkan peoples had been left to their own desires will never be known because the great powers were interested in the region. The Russians were inexorably drawn towards intervention whenever a crisis arose. They had a natural desire to protect their fellow Greek Orthodox Christians from persecution by their Moslem overlords, although the Ottomans were generally tolerant of other religions. Their right to protect their co-religionists had been recognized by the sultan in the Treaty of Kuchuk-Kainarji, 1774,[3] but it served more as a pretext than as a cause for intervention. The Russians were anxious to expand along the eastern and western shores of the Black Sea, but, above all, they wanted Constantinople and the Straits. Control of this city and the narrow body of water connecting the Aegean and Black seas would protect the south European part of their empire from attack by the great powers. It would also enable them to draw supplies through the Mediterranean in time of war and to send their own warships into that sea in case of need.

The same factors that made Russia want Constantinople and the Straits made the other great powers anxious to deny them access to the region. Russia's very size frightened foreign diplomats, and they were prepared to do all they could to prevent further growth. Other factors were also important. The British had replaced the French as the principal foreign merchants in the eastern Mediterranean during the Napoleonic wars. In 1783, they had exported only £88,065 worth of goods to the Ottoman

[3] See pages 441-442.

Empire; by 1825, the value of their exports had climbed to £1,079,671 and by 1845 to £7,620,140, an amount which was greater than the value of their exports to France, Italy, Russia, or Austria. They were therefore anxious to preserve the Ottoman Empire in order to protect their export market as well as to halt Russian expansion towards the Mediterranean.

The French and Austrians were also anxious to preserve the Ottoman Empire, at least from the Russians. The French would have liked to regain part of their former east Mediterranean trade, but they sought to do this more by expansion in north Africa or supporting Egyptian independence from the Turks. Certainly they had nothing to gain from Russian expansion. The Austrians already ruled nearly all the Balkan peoples they could hope to assimilate. Rarely did they want more for themselves, but they feared both Russian expansion in the Balkans and the establishment of independent states there that might seek to unite with peoples already in their empire to form nation-states. As a result, in the nineteenth century they usually supported British and French efforts to preserve the Ottoman Empire.

This situation made the Greek uprising in 1821 an international affair. Tsar Alexander was tempted to intervene, but his dedication to the concept of the Concert of Europe was so strong that he restrained himself, and for four years the Greeks were left to their own devices. They regained some islands and part of the Greek mainland from the incompetent Turks, but soon fell to quarreling among themselves. Their revolution had been supported mainly by merchants and intellectuals who had succumbed to the nationalistic fervor of the age and by peasants who wanted Turkish land. The interests of these groups often conflicted with each other, and with those Greeks who had profited from Ottoman rule through their posts in local government in Greece and wanted to maintain their positions when independence was won. Bitter personal animosities developed and Greek began to fight Greek. Under these circumstances, the tide of battle turned in 1825 when the sultan received aid from his powerful Egyptian vassal-state.

At this point, intervention by the great powers could no longer be avoided. Europeans were unwilling to sit idly by while Moslem Turks slaughtered the Christian descendants of the founders of the classical culture they so much admired. Furthermore, Tsar Alexander had died and his successor had determined on war. Great Britain and France decided to intervene as well, partly in response to the popular demand to protect the Greeks but more in an effort to settle the matter before the Russians over-ran the Balkans.

The Turkish and Egyptian fleets were easily defeated by the combined British, French, and Russian fleets at Navarino, and the Russian army moved towards Constantinople. The Turks made peace at Adrianople in

1829. As a result of the war, Greece was recognized as independent, and a few years later a Bavarian prince became king.

Some Rumanian peasants in Wallachia and Moldavia had staged an unsuccessful revolt in 1821 in conjunction with the Greeks, and at Adrianople the two provinces were placed under Russian protection although they remained under Ottoman sovereignty. Henceforth, the governors of the two provinces were Rumanians and the nascent nationalism of the people continued to grow.

The Serbs had revolted against Turkish misrule in 1804 under the leadership of Kara George (1766?-1817), a peasant-born pig merchant. At first he was successful, but Turkish rule was restored a few years later and he was eventually assassinated by the rival Obrenovitch clan. Milos Obrenovitch himself staged a revolt in 1815, and the great powers forced the Ottomans to grant the Serbs autonomy in the Treaty of Adrianople in 1829. Milos became hereditary prince, but the feud between his family and that of Kara George continued. Of the nine Serbian rulers between 1804 and 1945, four were assassinated and four were exiled, an unenviable record even for a Balkan state.

By 1830, when the revolutionary movement in the Balkans quieted, Greece had joined the little mountainous country of Montenegro as an independent state, and Moldavia, Wallachia, and Serbia had become autonomous under Turkish sovereignty. The Concert of Europe had succeeded in preserving most of the Ottoman Empire. To leave no doubt about their dislike of rebellions in spite of the assistance given the Greeks, Austria, Russia, and Prussia made a treaty in 1833 in which they promised to consider sending aid to any sovereign threatened with revolution. Thus, the eastern powers remained a threat to all who sought change, and the British continued to assist them when the European balance of power was threatened. During the revolutions of 1848, Great Britain and Russia cooperated diplomatically to preserve the balance of power, and the Russians aided the Habsburgs by suppressing a rebellion in Hungary.[4] So long as the cooperation between the great powers continued, revolutionary movements in central or eastern Europe had little chance of success.

Their cooperation also preserved the African and Asian territories of the Ottoman Empire. Sultan Mahmud (1808-1839) ruthlessly restored his authority in Asia and rid himself of the corrupt, incompetent janissaries by massacring about 6,000 of them, but he was nearly overthrown by Mehemet Ali (1769-1849), an Albanian adventurer who had set himself up as ruler of Egypt in 1805. With some assistance from the French, Mehemet Ali had introduced cotton culture, built irrigation canals, and developed a modern, efficient army and navy. In 1832 and 1839, he completely defeated the Turkish army; but the English and Russians forced him to disgorge his conquests, and in the end he was only able to establish his

[4] See page 559.

dynasty as hereditary rulers of Egypt under Ottoman suzerainty. In this manner, the theoretical unity of the Ottoman Empire was preserved although Egypt, like some of the Balkan countries, became autonomous.

THE FORCES OF CHANGE

The monarchs, the aristocracies, and the churches depended directly or indirectly on land for a large part of their wealth and power. So long as land was the chief source of wealth, so long as large estates were the rule and the population was concentrated in villages where their influence was strong, the conservatives remained powerful. However, two developments gradually weakened their position. One was the opening of vast tracts of land to small independent farmers in the western United States, parts of the British Empire, and, to a much lesser extent, in Russia and Latin America. The people who settled these lands along the frontiers of Western civilization not only improved their economic lot; they also removed themselves from the effective control of the conservative forces. These new lands became a breeding ground for democracy and eventually influenced the older centers of civilization. The second development was even more important. Beginning in England around 1760, industrialization, which had been progressing slowly for several generations, suddenly began to leap ahead at an accelerated rate. By 1850, a middle class had developed in England that could vie with the landed aristocracy, rural hamlets had become cities, and the typical Englishman was a factory laborer, not a farm tenant. The change came later on the continent; but during the nineteenth century, first Belgium, France, and Germany, and finally Russia felt the effects of industrialization. The rapidly rising middle class, the new urban workers, and the small independent farmers all had political and social programs that furthered the egalitarian revolution begun in the eighteenth century. Between 1815 and 1865, these groups struggled with the conservatives in Europe and Latin America for power and began to assert their control in the United States and some parts of the British Empire.

THE INDUSTRIAL REVOLUTION: ENGLISH ORIGINS

The industrial changes that began to take place in England around 1760 have long been referred to as an industrial revolution. They were characterized by the substitution of steam-power for the power of water, wind, and human exertion; by the use of many labor-saving machines that greatly increased productivity; and by the employment of workers in factories rather than in their homes. Some historians deny the term "revolution" to these developments. They point out that some progress had been made in this direction before 1760 and that even England was far from being completely industrialized in 1850. Indeed, industrial change is

An early industrial application of the steam engine. This is a horizontal model used to operate a grindstone. Patent drawing by Perrier, April 24, 1792. (Bettmann Archive)

still proceeding at a rapid pace. On the other hand, it should be borne in mind that political revolutions rarely bring about fundamental changes overnight. The Glorious Revolution, for example, merely halted James II's efforts to extend royal authority and paved the way for the gradual assumption of power by Parliament, a process that was to go on for a century and a half. The economic developments that began in England about 1760 were equally slow in effecting profound changes, but they were equally revolutionary. In the long run, they changed society fundamentally.

A series of inventions touched off the industrial revolution. The most important of these was the invention by James Watt (1736-1819) of an economical, efficient steam engine, patented in 1769. Numerous attempts had been made to turn steam into a source of power during the seventeenth century in response to the needs of mining and industry. In 1702, Thomas Newcomen had built a steam engine that was successfully used in pumping water out of coal mines. However, the engine wasted so much fuel that only a mine owner, to whom the price of coal had little importance, was willing to use it. Consequently, not until Watt produced his greatly improved engine did the use of steam-power become feasible in industry.

Since water and wind were very limited sources of power, the development of steam-power was extremely important. In itself, however, it was not sufficient to touch off a revolution. To build and operate the new engine, bar iron had to be made in greater quantities and more coal had to be mined. Steam-driven machines had to be invented to replace machines driven by hand. The use of big machines and steam-power meant that neither the guild nor the home was suitable for manufacturing. Factories had to be built and workers brought to them and trained. Transportation had to be improved to convey fuel and raw materials to the factories and deliver the finished product to the market, and capital had to be found to finance all these projects.

Changes in the coal industry were unspectacular but significant. Ways were found to sink shafts deeper, rails were built for coal carts, and ponies were used to pull them. Ventilation was improved, gunpowder was employed for blasting, and safety lamps were invented. The iron industry also profited from numerous improvements. Henry Cort (1740-1800) invented the puddling process, in which pig iron was converted into bar iron through the use of coke, and a rolling mill for the manufacture of iron plates, rails, and girders. Previously, charcoal had been used in the manufacture of iron, but England's forests were nearly exhausted and it had already become necessary to import wood from the Baltic. This situation had permitted France to forge ahead in iron production during the eighteenth century. The substitution of coke for charcoal now permitted England to regain its lead, for that country had a plentiful supply of coal, located near its iron mines.

The cotton textile industry was the first to use steam-power to drive machines. For the most part, the transition from hand-weaving to power-weaving took place between 1767 and 1779. It began with James Hargreaves' invention of the spinning jenny, which could spin five or six and eventually eighty threads at a time. Light, cheap, and easily operated by a woman, the jenny was admirably suited to the domestic system. However, the threads it spun were too weak to be used in the warp or longitudinal fibers of cotton cloth. In 1768, Richard Arkwright invented the water frame. The frame produced strong, coarse thread but was so heavy that it had to be installed in a factory. In 1779, Samuel Crompton combined the features of the jenny and the water frame in a machine called the mule. At first, water-power or horses were used to operate the frame and mule; later, beginning in 1790, steam was substituted.

While the production of thread was becoming industrialized, improvements were being made in weaving. In 1784, a clergyman named Edmund Cartwright invented a loom that could be driven by horses, water, or steam-power. The power loom was not immediately popular. In 1813, there were only 2,400 in Britain, but by 1833 the number had increased to 100,-000. The development of a cheap way to make cotton cloth created a demand for raw cotton, which was met by another invention. In 1792, an American, Eli Whitney, made a cotton gin that separated the seeds from the cotton fiber. The southern part of the United States, which until then had produced little cotton, now abandoned most of its other crops and became the chief supplier of cotton for the new British factories. The need for bleaches and dyes was gradually met by the development of the chemical industry.

Other industries lagged behind cotton textiles. The related clothes-making industry, for example, remained in the hands of tailors throughout the nineteenth century. The construction industry was slow to adopt new labor-saving machines, and the mass-produced or prefabricated house is a recent innovation. However, while most industries lagged behind cotton textiles, there were few that did not profit by the invention of power-driven ma-

Calico printing machine in the early nineteenth century. (Bettmann Archive)

chines and better tools. Even in the manufacture of pottery, where a degree of artistic ability was needed, the steam engine was successfully employed by Josiah Wedgwood (1730-1795), and Wedgwood china became justly famous.

The mechanization of industry necessitated the mass production of machines. This need was met by the use of interchangeable parts. Although the idea of interchangeable parts dates back to the seventeenth century, it was not until the industrial revolution that machine tools were capable of enough precision to make the idea practical. With interchangeable parts, for example, the gunsmith ceased to make the entire gun; rather each part was made by a different worker or workers, who had the necessary tools. This division of labor led to more rapid production and made the replacement of parts easier. Eli Whitney, who invented the cotton gin, helped to introduce the idea of interchangeable parts into the United States.

The industrial revolution could not have taken place if improved transportation facilities had not made it possible to bring coal and raw materials to new factories having steam-operated heavy machinery and to carry away the finished product. The Duke of Bridgewater built a canal from his mines to the nearby industrial city of Manchester where, in 1761, the first load of coal was delivered at half the previous cost. Other canals were built, and freight costs were in some instances reduced to a sixth of their former amount. Highways, which had been impassable to wagon and stage-coach traffic during rainy seasons, also began to be improved about the turn of the century. A Scot, John McAdam (1756-1836), proposed laying a foundation of large rocks, covering it with smaller rocks, and covering these with clay. Macadam roads were crowned on top for drainage, rolled, and gutted. The result was a relatively cheap, durable highway. Wagon transport became practical, and the speed of stagecoach travel increased many times over.

The greatest step in the improvement of transportation was taken when the steam engine was joined to the wagon and the boat. Both of these developments were gradual. By 1767, wagons were being pulled by horses over iron rails. The use of rails reduced friction and overcame the problem of mud, but there were still limits to how much a horse could pull and how fast it could travel. In 1803, a steam carriage was driven through the streets of London, but it was not until 1812 that a steam wagon was put on rails. George Stephenson (1781-1848) made the first practical loco-motive, and by 1829 the usefulness of the new machine had been clearly demonstrated.

In 1785, James Rumsey drove a steamship up the Potomac River at the unbelievable rate of four miles per hour. John Fitch operated another steam-boat on the Delaware River a little later, but it was not until 1807, when Robert Fulton took the *Clermont* from New York up the Hudson River to Albany, that the new invention was accepted as practical. Soon, paddle-wheel steamboats were being employed on all major rivers. In 1838, the Atlantic Ocean was crossed by a steamboat for the first time.

Mass production for a world market and rapid transportation neces-sitated faster communication. This need was only partly met by the use of the steamboat and the locomotive for mail deliveries and the invention of the telegraph. A French physicist named Ampère made use of electro-magnetism to send a message over a wire in 1820, but it was not until 1837 that a satisfactory telegraph was made. In 1844, Washington was connected to Baltimore by wire, in 1851 England was joined to the con-tinent, and in 1861 the Atlantic cable was laid connecting the New World with the Old.

The construction of factories and railroads required capital. The initial capital usually came from the family or partnership that began the enter-prise. Hence, the early factories were small. The owners were able to ex-pand by paying themselves a small salary for their labor and putting all their profits back into the business. If additional capital was needed, a new partner was found—a relative, a friend, even an employee—or the factory was mortgaged. Large-scale financing by the sale of stock was im-possible because at that time liability was complete. If the concern went bankrupt, the stockholders not only lost their investment, but also lost other property, which was taken to repay the creditors in full. Few today would invest in corporation stock if their other assets were put in jeopardy.

A good example of the origin of an industry is provided by the diary of Samuel Walker, who started a steel mill with his brother:

> 1741. In or about October or November of the same year, Saml. and Aaron Walker built an Air Furnace in the old nailer's smithy, on the backside of Saml. Walker's cottage at Grenoside, making some small additions thereto, and another little hutt or two, slating with sods etc., with a small Garth walled in: and after rebuilding the chimney or stacks once, and the furnace once or more, began to proceed a little, Saml. Walker teaching the school at Grenoside, and Aaron Walker making nails and mowing and shearing, etc., part of his time.
>
> 1743. Aaron Walker now began to be pretty much imploy'd, and had 4 shillings a week to live upon. . . .
>
> 1745. This year Saml. Walker, finding business increase, was obliged to give up his school, and built himself a house at the end of the old cottage, then thought he was fixed for life; then we allowed ourselves ten shillings a week each for wages to maintain our families.[5]

In 1746, the Walkers set up a casting house. The money came in part from the concern, which was then valued at £400, in part from their savings, and in part from a third brother and an employee. Although hard work and low salaries continued, the business expanded. In 1757, the Walkers paid themselves their first dividend, and when Samuel Walker died in 1782, the assets of the concern were £128,000. With courage, ingenuity, hard work, and self-denial, he had built a fortune.

If the owners decided to mortgage their factory to raise money for expansion, they usually turned to someone in the neighborhood with funds to invest. Sometimes a landowner or a merchant was found, and in this manner profits that had been made in agriculture and trade helped finance new industry. The only chartered joint stock bank in England before 1825 was the Bank of England itself, and it did not make loans to manufacturers. However, small local banks that were organized as partnerships with full liability did render some assistance. The Bank of England helped the local banks, and its notes made the currency more flexible. Nevertheless, there was a lack of capital for industrial expansion until the early decades of the nineteenth century. Only for projects that benefited the public and also required large initial outlays of capital—such as building canals, turnpikes, and railroads—did Parliament pass special acts permitting the formation of joint stock companies with limited liability. Manufacturers were fortunate in that there were no individual or corporation income taxes to reduce their earnings for future investment. Not until the second quarter of the nineteenth century, when the possibility of large industrial profits was more fully recognized, did it become easier for industrialists to borrow from landowners, merchants, and banks.

Industrialization demanded power-driven machines, iron, coal, raw

[5] Quoted in Thomas S. Ashton, *The Industrial Revolution, 1760-1830* (London: Oxford U. Press, 1948), pp. 95-96.

materials, and capital. It also required labor. While there was no scarcity of people, there was a serious lack of engineers and machinists, and the supply of unskilled labor was inadequate where it was most needed. The new factories were necessarily constructed in areas having coal and iron —that is, in southern Scotland, southern Wales, and especially in central England, including western Yorkshire, Stafford, and Lancashire. Since these were among the more thinly populated areas in 1750, there was an initial scarcity of labor. At the same time, southern England, with its commercial towns and handcraft industries, was becoming overpopulated, and the rural areas as a whole were producing more people than could be absorbed by the farms. As a result, workers migrated from the south and from the farms to the new industrial cities. Unhappily, the craftsman was often unwilling to abandon his trade for unskilled jobs in industry, the domestic weaver did not want to leave her family, and the agricultural worker was unhappy when subjected to factory discipline. At first, therefore, from one-half to two-thirds of the factory employees were children, apprenticed to learn a trade. After the Napoleonic wars, when the supply of unskilled labor became adequate, the proportion of children to adults in the factories began to decline, even though children could be paid lower wages.

A profitable market for manufactured goods was another prerequisite to industrialization. In this respect, too, conditions became more favorable after 1750. The European population had begun to increase more rapidly and had more money to buy goods. The British colonies in the New World provided an ever-expanding market, and even after the United States had won its independence, the flow of goods from England did not cease. When the Napoleonic wars isolated continental Europe from world markets for over a decade, Britain seized this opportunity to become the chief supplier of manufactured goods to the New World. The British profited especially by the chance to deal directly with the Spanish colonies without interference from the mother country. Since it was easy to undersell products made by handcraftsmen in the colonies, the early industrialists often made large profits. Only when factories became so numerous that they competed with each other did the efficient, adequately financed manufacturer experience difficulty.

THE INDUSTRIAL REVOLUTION: RESULTS

By 1850, the industrial revolution had already produced significant results. The most obvious change was that England had become urbanized. In 1750, London had been the only city with over 50,000 inhabitants. Liverpool, Manchester, and Birmingham had less than 15,000 each. By 1800, the population of these last three cities stood at 82,000, 77,000, and 71,000, respectively. By 1850, it had grown to 397,000, 303,000, and 242,000. Over 20 per cent of the English people lived in cities of 100,000 or more, and over half the population dwelt in populous towns. Cities and towns were connected by a network of turnpikes, canals, and 6,600 miles of railroad which brought them food and raw materials and carried off their manufactured products. Lands were enclosed at a faster rate, and the improved agricultural methods were adopted more widely in response to growing markets in the cities. Nevertheless, the population increased so rapidly that England had become an importer rather than an exporter of food. To bring in supplies and to carry away manufactured goods, the tonnage of its merchant marine had increased over fivefold. A new industrial middle class had come into being. Combined with those who had become wealthy in commerce and banking, they were in a position to wrest political power gradually from the large landowners.

The industrial revolution also created a huge urban labor population. Much has been written about their sufferings. Factories were hot and damp, ventilation was poor, and sanitation was primitive. Although women and children made up a large part of the labor force, the work day began at dawn six days a week and continued until dark. Living conditions varied. When a factory was built in a hamlet, the owners usually constructed homes for the adult workers that were not uncomfortable for that day. When they built in a city, however, they generally left the workers to their own devices, and many had to inhabit crowded, unsanitary apartments. Over 10 per cent of the population in some industrial cities lived in cellars. The cities themselves were smoky, dirty, and drab. They lacked public recreational facilities and most other attractions now associated with urban life.

But before condemning the industrial revolution because of the suffering of the laborer, we should remember that men, women, and children had worked long hours when they lived on the farms and that their rural cottages had lacked even the most basic comforts. Furthermore, the wages of urban workers rose 43 per cent between 1790 and 1831, an increase that more than compensated for an 11 per cent rise in the cost of living. Unquestionably, there were two groups that suffered acutely as a result of the industrial revolution. One group comprised the textile workers in the domestic system who tried to compete with the power machines. Between 1814 and 1829, machine competition brought down the price paid for hand-woven calico from 6½ shillings to just over one shilling, even though the domestic system survived for another generation. The other group consisted of the workers who were laid off during periods when industrial activity was slack. Depressions in the past had rendered few agricultural workers jobless.

It is also of interest to speculate on what would have happened if there had been no industrial revolution, in view of the rapid increase in population. This increase was not a direct result of industrialization. It resulted from the simple fact that between 1740 and 1840 the annual birth rate increased slightly while the death rate per 1,000 declined from 33 to 23 because of dietary improvements and an absence of plagues. During these years, the population in England and Wales increased from about 6,000,000 to 15,900,000. The agricultural population grew slowly until about 1830, in spite of the enclosures, and the farms were unable to absorb more than a small fraction of this increase. Without industrialization, where would the worker have found employment? It is possible that the English standard of living would have declined until the population growth was checked by misery and actual famine, a process that has repeatedly occurred in Asia. Ireland furnishes a good example of what happens when the population increases without industrialization. Its population increased from 5,200,000 in 1800 to 8,200,000 in 1840, but in 1845 failures in the potato crop brought misery and famine. Many died, others emigrated. By 1920, the population had fallen to half the 1840 figure. Thus, even in the short run, the laborers themselves benefited from industrialization, although less selfish employers and a more sympathetic government could have made their lot easier. In the long run, the benefits of industrialization have been obvious. The West owes its high standard of living today to the increased productivity of labor, and this increase had been very slow until the introduction of steam-driven machinery.

THE SPREAD OF THE INDUSTRIAL REVOLUTION

Prior to 1850, industrialization proceeded at a slower rate on the European continent and in the United States than in England. The British had more capital available to invest in industry because they had profited most from the growth in trade and had made greater use of the new and more profitable agricultural methods. In addition, their banking and currency systems were more satisfactory than elsewhere. English industrialists were subject to fewer restrictions than their counterparts in many continental countries, where the guilds were stronger. It will be remembered that guild regulations were designed to control competition by limiting the number of employees, the use of machinery, and the like. English labor was more mobile, for the guilds were weaker, and, more important, the enclosure movement had freed the surplus rural population to work in the factories. On the continent, where enclosures took place more slowly, a greater part of the growing population was absorbed in the rural economy. In eastern Europe, the survival of serfdom prevented the movement of labor even more effectively. England had a plentiful supply of iron and coal; no continental nation had comparable quantities of a grade that was then usable. Finally, English industrialists had greater incentive. They had the largest colonial market, the largest merchant marine, and the opportunity to profit, at the expense of their rivals, from the continental blockade during the Napoleonic wars. The American industrialists possessed many of the advantages of the British, but they lacked capital and an adequate supply of factory labor. The demand for raw cotton turned the southern United States into a cotton-growing region that used slave labor. The agricultural opportunities in the western United States placed a constant drain on the labor supply concentrated in the northeastern part of the country. What capital existed for large-scale enterprises went largely to canal builders and later to railroad building.

The fact that industrialization proceeded at a slower rate on the continent and in the United States should not be interpreted as meaning that there was no economic progress in these regions. Enclosure continued to take place, especially near large urban markets, and improved agricultural methods were gradually introduced. However, many of the large landowners in France and western Germany used sharecroppers rather than manage their own estates or lease their land to tenant farmers in large enough segments to make the new techniques practical. Furthermore, the French Revolution had left much of the land in the hands of the peasants, but their average holding was only nine acres. The new machinery invented after 1830 could not be economically used on such farms. Indeed, the three-field system with its strip farming and common pasturage was still practiced on most of the continent in 1850.[6]

The population of the continent continued to grow, but not as rapidly as in England. The number of Frenchmen increased from 24,000,000 in 1750 to only 33,400,000 in 1840 and the number of Italians from 16,000,-000 to 22,000,000 during the same years. Russia and the United States were the only important segments of the European civilization that matched or more than matched the English record. However, in both Russia and the United States the increases went to new farmlands as well as to the cities. Few European cities doubled in size between 1800 and 1850, much less rivaled the growth of Liverpool and Manchester. The handful of big cities owed their size more to their status as capitals than to their new industries. Moscow was the only locality on the continent in 1850 with over 200,000 people that was not the seat of a government. The United States possessed two cities, New York and Philadelphia, in this category, and their growth was truly phenomenal. New York went from 64,000 in 1800 to 696,000 in 1850, and Philadelphia increased fivefold during the same period.

Continental Europe lagged behind England in other aspects of industrialization. As late as 1850, Paris still had no railroad connections with southern France. Italy had only 16 rail miles for each million inhabitants, and St. Petersburg was connected with Moscow but not with the rest of the Russian hinterland or central Europe. The Balkans, Spain, Portugal, and Sweden had no railroads at all. Only northern France, the Low Countries, the German-speaking parts of central Europe, and the northeastern United States had adequate networks. France had produced twice as much pig iron as England on the eve of the Revolution, but in 1850 the island kingdom was turning out five times as much as its French rival and handling three times as much foreign trade as well. Steam-driven machines were adopted more slowly on the continent; the domestic system remained strong in France, and the German states kept their guilds.

Yet after it is acknowledged that Great Britain forged far ahead of its

[6] See pages 36-37.

continental rivals in nearly all aspects of industrial civilization between 1800 and 1850, it is nonetheless true that the continental middle class did grow larger, a factory labor population did come into being, production did increase, and cities did grow in size. France's pig iron production increased from 230,000 tons in 1789 to 650,000 in 1850; industrial cities like Lyon grew from 90,000 in 1800 to 177,000 in 1850, and seaports like Bordeaux from 91,000 to 131,000 during the same years. Other countries in western and central Europe made similar records of industrial progress. The middle class, which had been able to challenge the aristocracy in 1789, was in an even stronger position when revolutions broke out in 1830 and 1848. The factory laborers were also becoming a force to be reckoned with.

LIBERALISM

A second force for change during the early nineteenth century was the growth of liberalism. Although partly a new creation, liberalism owed much to the Enlightenment and to romanticism. Because its tenets were especially popular with the middle class, the philosophy of liberalism became increasingly important as the industrial revolution progressed. Its advocates did not belong to a single school of thought, and they disagreed among themselves on many issues. In general, however, they shared the conviction that man should be freed from restraint as much as possible. The radical fringe of the romantic movement carried this belief to extremes. Lord Byron, for example, espoused Rousseau's idea that man was naturally good but had been corrupted by society; it followed that if the existing society were destroyed, man would recover his natural freedom and virtue. In his behavior, Byron defied the social conventions of his day, and in his writings he mercilessly ridiculed accepted beliefs and institutions. Percy Bysshe Shelley also had faith in man's essential goodness and accused both religion and government of destroying human character.

> *Kings, priests and statesmen blast the human flower*
> *Even in its tender bud.*

Most of the liberals, however, accepted the less radical view of the Enlightenment that man was born neither good nor bad but was molded by his environment. The problem was to establish criteria for determining the proper environment. The most influential solution was achieved by a wealthy Englishman named Jeremy Bentham (1748-1832).

Bentham believed that every institution, every law, and every custom should be judged by its utility. If it passed this test, it should be retained; if it failed, it should be abandoned. The utility of an institution, law, or custom depended on whether it promoted "the greatest happiness of the greatest number." By happiness, Bentham meant pleasure, and by unhappiness he meant pain. The individual naturally seeks pleasure and tries to avoid pain, but in the process he sometimes causes others to suffer. The wise legislator tries to reconcile private and public interests so that the individual's quest for happiness adds to the general happiness of society. Whenever he must choose between conflicting interests, his choice will be determined by his obligation to promote "the greatest happiness of the greatest number." Like the romantics, Bentham denied the existence of natural rights or natural laws, but he had none of their respect for tradition. He and his fellow utilitarians decided to work for reforms that would establish a happier and therefore a better society.

Bentham was not content merely to criticize existing society. He spent sixty years of his long life drawing up legislative proposals for reforms. Bentham's concept of utility was coupled with the belief that every man was the best judge of his own interests. Therefore, the utilitarians' legislative proposals were designed to remove restrictions that hampered the individual's freedom of action and expression. Following Adam Smith, the utilitarians attacked efforts to regulate trade. Was not every businessman the best judge of how to make his own profit, and did not the profit of the individual bring profit to society as a whole? They advocated constitutional government and insisted on freedom of religion and expression. They stressed the importance of education. In short, they put emphasis on every aspect of individual liberty and individual initiative; they were the leading exponents of the cult of the individual, or individualism, that became so popular as the century progressed.

Bentham and his immediate followers were more radical than most liberals, but they were so persuasive that their ideas concerning economics, government, and nationalism influenced many English and continental reformers.

Adam Smith and laissez-faire were, of course, the starting points of the liberal economists. They repeated Smith's argument that free trade increased production by creating a worldwide division of labor and at the same time made available articles not produced in the mother country. This was advantageous to every nation and every social class. Free trade gave one nation the opportunity to help another while it helped itself. It drew nations closer together by making them interdependent. It was "a providential doctrine. It teaches us the wisdom of those arrangements by which nations may ultimately, we trust, be led into one great confederation, one brotherhood of communities, rendering and receiving mutual service." It was hoped and believed that the establishment of free trade would bring an end to economic strife and lead to world peace.

The liberals never doubted that the individual was the best judge of his economic interests and that if left alone he would produce wealth and achieve happiness. Their arguments against government interference in economic affairs were strengthened by Thomas Malthus (1766-1834), a clergyman who was neither a utilitarian nor a liberal. In 1798, Malthus published an *Essay on Population* in which he attacked the ideas of human perfectibility and progress so popular in the Enlightenment. His basic argument was that population tends to increase more rapidly than the food supply. In the long run, this imbalance would lead to overpopulation and famine if it were not checked by one of two conditions. Either wars, misery, disease, and hunger would prevent the population from outstripping the food supply, or the birth rate would have to be limited by what Malthus called "moral restraint," that is, by late marriage. Without moral restraint, the population will increase. "The food, therefore, which before supported eleven millions, must now be divided among eleven millions and a half. The poor consequently must live much worse, and many of them be reduced to severe distress. The number of labourers also being above the proportion of work in the market, the price of labour must tend to fall, while the price of provisions would at the same time tend to rise." This situation would demand harder work and would result in more suffering and perhaps death until the food supply was again sufficient for the population.

Most economists had little hope that the workers would ever practice moral restraint. One of them, a successful Jewish stock exchange speculator named David Ricardo (1772-1823), identified an iron law of wages. An increase in population, he believed, must lead to lower wages because of the greater supply of labor. Misery results, but eventually this very misery reduces the population, and wages rise again above the subsistence level. At this point, the population increases again and the cycle is repeated. Thus, the laborers' wages necessarily fluctuate from a point just above to a point just below the amount necessary to purchase their subsistence. To raise wages arbitrarily would accomplish nothing because the number of workers would soon surpass the food supply.

Malthus, Ricardo, and other economists did not wish to condemn labor perpetually to a bare subsistence wage, but they sincerely believed that neither generosity on the part of the employer, nor demands on the part of labor, nor legislation on the part of the state, could improve the workers' condition. Hence, they were opposed to wage and hour laws and other forms of factory legislation. The only remedy was to curb the population by advocating moral restraint or passing legislation designed to accomplish the same result.

If the liberals could offer little hope for the working class as a whole, they could nevertheless promise great rewards for those individual workers who were willing to help themselves. They taught that by hard work and frugality a day laborer could become a factory foreman and eventually a factory owner. In 1859, Dr. Samuel Smiles (1812-1904) published *Self-Help*, in which he taught all the capitalistic virtues. "Many popular books," he declared, "have been written for the purpose of communicating to the public the grand secret of making money. But there is no secret whatever about it, as the proverbs of every nation abundantly testify. 'Many a little makes a meikle.'—'Take care of the pennies and the pounds will take care of themselves.'—'A penny saved is a penny gained.' —'Diligence is the mother of good-luck.'—'No pains no gains.'—'No sweat no sweet.'—'Sloth, the key to poverty.'—'Work, and thou shalt have.'—'He who will not work, neither shall he eat.'—'The world is his, who has patience and industry.'—'It is too late to spare when all is spent.'—'Better go to bed supperless than rise in debt.'—'The morning hour has gold in its mouth.'—'Credit keeps the crown of the causeway.' Such are specimens of the proverbial philosophy, embodying the hoarded experience of many generations, as to the best means of thriving in the world." Smiles sold 150,000 copies of his book by 1889. It was translated into Japanese, Arabic, and Turkish, as well as several European languages and its dictums were inscribed on the walls of the khedive's palace in Egypt. Smiles's writings were not designed to justify capitalistic society, but to express his belief that laborers could deliver themselves from sloth, ignorance, and poverty only by building their characters.

POLITICAL LIBERALISM

The liberals reacted to the bitter experience of France during the republican and Napoleonic regimes by seeking to limit the powers of government. Most of them believed in a constitutional monarchy, partly because they felt that a king would add stability to the government and check popular excesses and partly because most states already had kings and could not hope to get rid of them short of revolution. Hence, few liberals outside Latin America followed the example of the United States and sought freedom in a republic. The liberals did not justify the limitations that they tried to impose on governments by appealing to the natural rights of man. Both the romantics and the utilitarians had forsaken this concept and now stressed the practical and spiritual benefits deriving from individual liberty. Benjamin Constant (1767-1830), a French liberal, declared that "The liberty of the individual is the object of all human association." He went on to define this liberty as "the peaceful enjoyment of private independence; the right to pursue our own ends unimpeded, so long as they do not interfere with the equally legitimate activities of others."

The idea that a man ought to be permitted to do as he pleases so long as he harms no one else was beautifully expressed in 1859 by John Stuart Mill (1806-1873) in an essay entitled *On Liberty*. In this essay, Mill went further than many earlier liberals by recognizing that individual liberty may be infringed not only by governments but also by the people as a whole, who may seek to impose their collective will on minorities. He tried to show "that the sole end for which mankind are warranted, individually or collectively, in interfering with the liberty of action of any of their number, is self-protection. That the only purpose for which power can be rightfully exercised over any member of a civilized community, against his will, is to prevent harm to others. His own good, either physical or moral, is not a sufficient warrant. He cannot rightfully be compelled to do or forbear because it will be better for him to do so, because it will make him happier, because, in the opinions of others, to do so would be wise, or even right. These are good reasons for remonstrating with him, or reasoning with him, or persuading him, or entreating him, but not for compelling him, or visiting him with any evil in case he do otherwise." The role of a government was thus reduced to the related tasks of defending its nationals from foreign attack and preventing its citizens from injuring one another. The typical liberal denied government any right to interfere with the people's freedom of speech, action, and belief or, as we have seen, to make economic regulations or to legislate for social welfare.

Since nearly every country had an established church, the liberals' insistence on religious freedom led to bitter quarrels with the clergy. Even in countries like England where minority faiths were tolerated, their adherents were denied equal political rights. Often, the established churches controlled education, marriage, and divorce, and were supported by taxes collected from nonmembers as well as members. Some exasperated liberals attacked the churches as bitterly as the philosophers of the Enlightenment had, but the majority, though secular-minded, were content to work towards a separation of church and state and complete equality among the various faiths.

The English believed that their institutions guaranteed the basic freedoms and that only reform was necessary. Bentham advocated changes in judicial procedure to ensure greater justice. He sought to put an end to the savage punishments inflicted for minor crimes and, with the aid of other liberals, pressed for the repeal of acts authorizing governmental interference in economic and social affairs. In continental countries lacking the liberal traditions of the English, the liberals agitated for new constitutions that guaranteed the rights of the individual. In these countries, a break with the past was necessary in spite of the romantics' preference for the slow evolution of native institutions. The English system, with its limited monarchy, was most often copied, but the continental countries also influenced one another once they began to establish constitutions of their own.

The liberals agreed that the constitution should guarantee individual freedom and limit the authority of the government, but they divided on the issues of cabinet responsibility and the extent of the suffrage. Over a period of many years, the British had developed a system of government in which the cabinet was responsible to the House of Commons instead of to the king. Some continental liberals advocated a similar plan, but at first many were content to have the legislature control the cabinet indirectly through its control of taxes. Gradually, however, the advantages of controlling the executive branch directly led most liberals to advocate ministerial responsibility, and by the end of the nineteenth century, ministerial responsibility had become almost as much a mark of democracy as universal suffrage.

The utilitarians, because of their belief that a man was the best judge of his own interests and that the purpose of government was to secure "the greatest happiness of the greatest number," were among the earliest advocates of a very generous suffrage. It was necessary only that the people be taught to read first and that they be permitted freedom of discussion. Mill wrote concerning his father, a devoted utilitarian: "So complete was my father's reliance on the influence of reason over the minds of mankind, whenever it is allowed to reach them, that he felt as if all would be gained if the whole population were taught to read, if all sorts of opinions were allowed to be addressed to them by word and in writing, and if by means of the suffrage they could nominate a legislature to give effect to the opinions they adopted. Accordingly, a democratic suffrage was the principal article of his political creed and the most essential security for good government."

During the first half of the nineteenth century, however, most European liberals thought it dangerous to permit the workingman to vote, because of his alleged ignorance and lack of respect for the property of others. They believed that the right to vote and to hold office should be limited to property owners. Benjamin Constant voiced the majority opinion ably when he declared: "Those whom poverty keeps in eternal dependence are no more enlightened on public affairs than children, nor are they more interested than foreigners in national prosperity, of which they do not understand the bases and of which they enjoy the advantages only indirectly. Property alone, by giving sufficient leisure, renders a man capable of exercising his political rights." Only in the United States, where the plentiful supply of cheap land made the ownership of property commonplace, was a union between liberalism and democracy quickly effected.

The liberals should not be accused of hypocrisy because they refused to support legislation to help the working classes and because they wanted to limit the vote to propertied people. They believed that all men were created equal, not that all men were equal. A determined man, they were convinced, could rise in the economic and hence in the political and social order. If the state lent a helping hand, it would destroy the individual's initiative. Indeed, it was only when man was left free to choose between right and wrong, to struggle unaided for advancement or to sink in poverty that he had the opportunity to develop his individuality and became "a noble and beautiful object of contemplation." Mill declared that "The human faculties of perception, judgement, discriminative feeling, mental activity, and even moral preference are exercised only in making a choice." To this Dr. Samuel Smiles could add: "The spirit of self-help is the root of all genuine growth in the individual; and, exhibited in the lives of many, it constitutes the true source of national vigor and strength."

NATIONALISM

The third force for change in the nineteenth century was nationalism. Nationalism was rejected by the Vienna peace conference in 1815, but it became increasingly important during the first half of the nineteenth century because its cultural manifestations were allied to romanticism and its political manifestations were allied to liberalism. Both romanticism and nationalism appealed to the emotions, and both involved an effort to discover and re-establish the traditional culture of a people. Some peoples, such as the Welsh, Irish, Croats, Bulgars, and Ukrainians, had lost all knowledge of their past and all sense of differing from the dominant nationality in their geographical areas. Even their written languages had to be resurrected by philologists; dictionaries had to be compiled, and grammars written. Other peoples, such as the English, French, and Germans, who had enjoyed a continuous history since the medieval period, had no need to rediscover their national language, but in other respects their cultural activities resembled those of nationalities that were only beginning to be aware of themselves.

Historians published great collections of documents and wrote long accounts of their countries' past. Where written records failed, myths and ballads were collected to reveal national character. The search for folklore was best exemplified by the efforts of Jacob Grimm (1785-1863) to gather together the fairy tales that Germans had passed on from one generation to another. To aid in this work, scholarly societies were founded, newspapers and magazines were published in the native languages, and schools were established to teach pupils their cultural heritage. Poets, novelists, and composers based many of their works on historical and legendary subjects. In this way, the romantic's love of the past combined with the nationalist's search for traditions, culture, and the spirit of a people.

The cultural awakening of a nationality usually preceded the desire for political unity and independence. This political phase did not reach explosive proportions among the English and French, who had long had independent national states, or among the Welsh and Scots, whose native Gaelic revival did not lead to independence movements. As a rule, however, cultural nationalism developed into political nationalism. Disunited peoples, like the Germans or the Italians, demanded national unity; and subject peoples, like the various branches of the Slavic family, demanded independence. In its demand for unity and independence, nationalism found a firm ally in liberalism during the first half of the nineteenth century.

The liberal believed that freedom could be achieved only by those nationalities who governed themselves. Each people should therefore have its own country, and no state should attempt to rule other peoples. The tie between nationality, liberty, and government was aptly stated by J. S. Mill when he wrote that "it is in general a necessary condition of free institu-

536

tions that the boundaries of governments should coincide in the main with those of nationalities," and by Jeremy Bentham when he insisted that England and France surrender their colonies to give subject peoples a chance to develop their own states.

The most famous of the liberal nationalists was Giuseppe Mazzini (1805-1872). In 1831, he founded Young Italy, an association of young men dedicated to the establishment of a free, united republic of Italy. Soon, there were 60,000 members. Mazzini believed that "The nation is the God-appointed instrument for the welfare of the human race, and in this alone its moral essence lies. . . . Fatherlands are but the workshops of humanity." Each nation had the duty to train its members "in the light of the moral law" so that they could make their unique contribution to mankind as a whole. Mazzini, like other liberal nationalists, rejected the idea that the Italians should ever rule other peoples. Indeed, he organized a Young Europe movement and was instrumental in establishing a Young Poland, a Young Hungary, a Young Germany, and a Young Ireland, to agitate for the independence or unity of these peoples. By his death in 1872 these goals had been partly achieved.

THE PROTEST OF LABOR AND UTOPIAN SOCIALISM

Another group desiring change was composed of industrial workers and those who sympathized with their cause. At first, the most vocal members of this group were workers employed under the old domestic system whose hand-made goods were being undersold by machine-made products. In anger and desperation, they rioted and smashed machines, but they were savagely punished by the authorities. Soon, it was the workers in the new factories themselves who began to protest. Although their living and working conditions were in most cases no worse than they had been before the introduction of the factory system, these conditions were nevertheless oppressive, and the workers could claim with justice that they were not receiving their share of the fruits of industrialization. At first, their protests were disorganized, confused, and sometimes violent. James Stephens, a former Methodist minister who founded a sect of his own, took up the cause of the English laborer. "If they [the mill owners] do not reform," he declared in 1838, "they shall have the revolution they so much dread. We shall destroy their abodes of guilt. . . . If they do not learn to act as the law prescribes and as God ordains, so that every man shall by his labour find comfortable food and clothing . . . we have sworn by God, by heaven, and by hell, that we shall wrap in one awful sheet of devouring flame the manufactories of the cotton tyrants and the palaces of those who raised them by rapine and murder." Becoming more defiant, he exclaimed: "If the musket and the pistol, the sword and the pike are of no avail, let the women take the scissors, the child, the pin or the needle. If all fails, the firebrand—ay, the firebrand, the firebrand, I repeat." But there was no revolution, and the preachers of violence only frightened the government into taking repressive measures. Help was to come from three other sources.

The first and most obvious source was the labor union. The guild had filled the function of the labor union during the Middle Ages, and the workers in the domestic system had been so scattered that it was difficult for them to organize. Consequently, the few labor unions that existed in 1815 were small, weak, secret organizations, outlawed in nearly every country. The industrial revolution, however, caused a dramatic increase in the number of industrial laborers and, equally important, brought them together in one place where they could organize. Most of the early trade unions failed because of opposition from governments and employers, but new ones were invariably organized, and eventually they made themselves heard.

Secondly, help came from landed aristocrats who transferred their traditional paternalistic interest in the rural poor to the inhabitants of the new cities. As a group, they disapproved of the upstart factory owners and were not attracted by the laissez-faire doctrines of the liberals. As members of legislatures and friends and advisers of rulers, they were in a powerful position to lend assistance. What factory legislation was passed over the opposition of the liberals was due largely to their efforts.

The third source of assistance was a small group of radical intellectuals who were aptly called utopian socialists. The utopian socialists accepted the majority opinion of their day that man was not by nature evil and was capable of a higher moral development within the proper environment. This environment, they agreed, was not being provided by the present economic system, which brought great wealth to a few and left the remainder of the inhabitants in relative misery. They recommended the social ownership of industry, accompanied by a more equitable distribution of income. To secure these ends, the utopian socialists used persuasion rather than force. They hoped to convince men of wealth and influence of the justice of their cause. They wrote books and established small model communities to demonstrate the practicality of their theories.

The specific teachings of individual utopian socialists varied greatly. Count Henry of Saint-Simon (1760-1825) was a member of one of the most distinguished families of France. He early determined on a glorious career and each morning was awakened by his valet with: "Arise, Monsieur le Comte, you have grand deeds to perform." The deeds he turned to were in the field of social reform. He and his disciples thought that everyone should work and that the reward should be in proportion to the quantity and quality of the work performed. They advocated the common ownership of property and the abolition of inherited privileges and wealth. Under the leadership of industrialists, philosophers, and social scientists, society would be planned and regulated for the benefit of mankind.

Charles Fourier (1772-1837) was of middle-class extraction. He advo-

538

cated the establishment of communities, or phalanxes, of from 400 to 2,000 persons who would live together in one large building and work at some occupation that suited their taste. To secure financial backing for his program, Fourier announced that he would be at home at noon each day to receive philanthropists. For twelve years, he kept the appointment, but no millionaire appeared. However, some Americans were more interested than the practical French. They established thirty-four communities, all of which failed. The most famous of these was the Brook Farm Community near Boston, which counted among its friends and supporters many of the leading New England intellectuals and Horace Greeley, editor of the *New York Tribune* and later Democratic candidate for the presidency.

Robert Owen (1771-1858), the son of a day laborer, represented a third type of utopian socialist. At ten, he was apprenticed to a clothier; by dint of hard work and study, he became the superintendent of a large cotton mill by the time he was nineteen. In 1800, he took over the management of a cotton mill in New Lanark, Scotland. New Lanark was an unattractive mill town with its full share of vice and misery. Owen built decent houses for the workers, established stores where they could purchase supplies at cost, provided a system of education for them, encouraged their moral development, and even paid them when the mill temporarily closed during a depression. The result was a model community for the workers, substantial profits for the owners, and world fame for the experiment. In 1817, Owen undertook to reform society as a whole, and for the next four decades he made one proposal after another to improve working conditions. He suggested the establishment of community-owned villages in every parish, where the inhabitants would engage in agriculture and industry. He advocated the abolition of private property, the formation of trade unions and cooperatives, and a host of other changes, but his proposals were out of touch with the ideas of his day. When the American Ralph Waldo Emerson asked him, "How many men possessed of your views, who will remain after you, are going to put them in practice?" Owen could only reply, "Not one."

In spite of their impractical programs, which could not be realized so long as most men remained more devoted to their individual interests than to the interests of society, the utopian socialists were not without importance. Their criticism laid the groundwork for later theories of economic planning and for later attacks on capitalism that were to have far-reaching effects. During the first half of the nineteenth century, however, most working people preferred to follow the middle-class liberals.

REPUBLICANISM

A minority of the European liberals and a majority of the socialists and other advocates of state intervention preferred the republican form of government. This was especially true in France, where a strong republican tradition survived among the radical intellectuals and the Paris populace. These Frenchmen dreamed of a return to the glorious days of Danton and Robespierre when the people controlled, or seemed to control, the destiny of the nation. Nearly all republicans advocated universal suffrage. This fact, along with their admiration of the Jacobins, caused them to be among the most feared advocates of change.

13/ Reaction, Revolution, and Reform, 1815-1850/65

THE conservative forces were very strong in Europe in 1815, but the forces of the egalitarian revolution gathered strength with each passing year. There were widespread revolutions in Europe in 1830 and 1848 and local revolts in other years. Compared with their counterparts of the late eighteenth century, the revolutionaries of this period were more strongly motivated by the desire for national unity, they spoke more of the rights of nationalities and less of the rights of men, and yet in most respects their egalitarianism was more pronounced. Their efforts were usually unsuccessful. Italy and Germany were not united, and Austria, Russia, the United States, and Brazil overcame nationalist or, at least, separatist movements within their boundaries, movements that were supported by the majority in the regions concerned. Some progress, however, was made towards liberalism, nationalism, and democracy in a number of countries during those years. The Latin Americans won their independence from Spain and Portugal, and, most important, the reformers managed to rid the Western world of the twin curses of slavery and serfdom.

FRANCE

THE RESTORATION

After the allies had toppled the Napoleonic empire, they were faced with the task of establishing a new government for that often misguided country. After some justifiable hesitation, they agreed to restore the Bourbons, and the fat, lazy, gouty count of Provence was brought to Paris as King Louis XVIII. Louis XVIII had been more fortunate than his brother, Louis XVI, and had escaped from France in 1791 only to spend twenty-three years in exile in Russia, Poland, and England, scorned and neglected by friend and foe alike. Now, almost sixty, he was called upon to assume the throne of his ancestors.

But was it the throne of his ancestors? Louis XVI had ruled one France, subdivided, it is true, into provinces and social classes but united in objectives, outlook, and loyalty. Louis XVIII found himself king of two Frances: the old France with its ancient families whose members flocked back to Paris with him after years in exile, and the new France of the Revolution with its Jacobins, liberal bourgeoisie, and Napoleonic nobles. Louis realized that the new France was by far the larger and that there would be no stable government as long as the country remained divided. "I will never be king of two peoples," he declared, "and to the ultimate fusion of these all the efforts of my government are directed." This meant that there could be no return to the old regime's system of government. A regime more like England's was clearly in order.

To implement his ideas, Louis issued in 1814 on his authority a hastily prepared constitution or charter. This charter created a bicameral legislature; one chamber consisted of peers chosen by the king and the other of deputies selected by a very restricted suffrage designed to vest power in the nobility and upper middle class. The chambers were to vote taxes and to approve laws, but the king retained the right to name his ministers, through whom he maintained considerable influence over the army, diplomacy, and administration.

The importance of Louis' failure to make his ministers responsible to the legislature should not be exaggerated. Ministerial responsibility was not yet formally accepted in Great Britain, but Parliament's control over taxation led to its gradual development. The same development could occur in France. Indeed, Louis XVIII nearly always saw to it that his ministers commanded the support of a majority in the legislature. The decision to maintain Napoleon's concordat with the pope and his legal codes gave the French religious toleration, equality before the law, and fair trials. Even freedom of the press was promised. The centralized administration of the empire was kept to ensure uniformity and efficiency of government, and the revolutionary land settlement was preserved with its many peasant and middle-class proprietors. In short, the most constructive work of the Revolution and Napoleon was maintained. If Louis XVIII and his successors kept the initial settlement and if the two Frances became reconciled, there was no reason why a liberal and, finally, a democratic monarchy could not evolve.

Until 1820, there seemed at least a chance that this evolution might take place. Louis and his ministers governed with moderation. They even did their best to restrain the old France from avenging itself on the new when the latter rejoined Napoleon after his escape from Elba in 1815 to conduct the ill-fated Waterloo campaign, but they were only partially successful. Fanatical royalists, especially in southern France, slaughtered revolutionaries and Bonapartists. The division grew wider, and royalists became less willing than ever to accept the moderate policies of their king. They bitterly resented the failure to restore their confiscated lands and found Louis XVIII's court a far cry from the Versailles that they vaguely remembered. Louis was dependent on the legislature for his income and could not reproduce the splendor of his ancestors. He established the court in Paris at the Tuileries, where he made his appearance in the morning at 10:00 and retired at 8:30 in the evening after eating a 6 o'clock dinner. Such a routine was well suited for an old man whose recreational needs did not go beyond occasional discussions of art and letters, but it was hardly adequate to restore the old court. More serious, the king was unable to reward his aristocratic friends as his ancestors had done. He had no lands and few profitable offices to bestow. Even the Church was less attractive, because high clerical posts had ceased to be lucrative when the state confiscated Church lands and assumed the obligation of paying the clergy. As a result, few nobles came to court. Most of them divided their time between their town houses and their estates, sulking over their losses and eagerly awaiting an opportunity to regain their former position.

What few concessions Louis did make to the old France were resented by the new. He replaced the revolutionary tricolor of such glorious memories with the white flag of his Bourbon ancestors. To ornament his court, he revived a few companies of the guard in which nearly every private was a noble, a fact that disgusted Napoleon's officers, many of whom had to be put on half pay. More serious, most of the prerevolutionary nobility refused to mix on equal terms with the nobles created by Napoleon. They never lost an opportunity to show their scorn for newly-acquired titles.

A turn for the worse took place in 1820 when a radical assassinated the duke of Berry. As the son of the count of Artois, the king's brother, Berry had seemed certain to come to the throne because Louis had no children. Only the birth shortly thereafter of Berry's posthumous son, later known as the Count of Chambord, prevented the French Bourbon line from becoming extinct. Nevertheless, the ultra-royalists of old France were furious. Louis was now too old and tired to check their excesses. The electorate was altered in such a way as to favor the landed aristocracy at the expense of the middle class, and liberty of the press was curtailed. Then, in 1824, his death removed the last restraining influence and Artois became King Charles X.

Charles was more energetic and attractive than his brother, and he was determined to go as far as he could in restoring the old regime. "I would rather chop wood," he declared, "than reign after the fashion of the King of England." He began by having himself crowned at Rheims with all the ritual and splendor of the past. The holy oil used to anoint the king had been destroyed during the Revolution, but a few drops were "miraculously" found. All that was lacking was a devout and loyal people to be impressed by the ceremony.

But the ultra-royalists rejoiced; at last they had a king after their own hearts, although there were limits on how far even they dared to go. Instead of restoring the land confiscated during the Revolution, they voted an indemnity to compensate dispossessed aristocrats. This was to be financed by reducing the interest rates on the national debt from 5 to 3 per cent. In the long run, the measure was wise since it confirmed forever the Revolutionary land settlement, but the immediate result was to weaken the monarchy by further alienating the middle class, who resented seeing their income from government bonds reduced to benefit the old nobility.

The union between the throne and the altar was strengthened. Sacrilege was made punishable by death, and clerical influence over education was increased. Again, the liberal middle class, who still saw religion through the eyes of Voltaire, was offended. When the National Guard, largely a middle-class militia, voiced its disapproval of the government, it was disbanded.

Opposition became so strong that the liberals were able to win the elections in 1827, despite the suffrage that favored the landed aristocracy. For two years, Charles X experimented with a liberal ministry in order to keep the support of the legislature, but he soon tired of compromise. In August, 1829, he violated the principles of ministerial responsibility by making an ultraconservative aristocrat, the Prince of Polignac, his chief minister. The Chamber of Deputies protested, but Charles countered by dissolving it and ordering new elections to take place in May of the following year. Once more, the liberals triumphed. Charles determined on a coup d'état, because he believed that "concessions" had ruined Louis XVI. "I have either got to mount a horse or a death-cart," he declared. On July 26, he issued four ordinances dissolving the chamber, reducing the electorate to ensure the triumph of the ultra-royalists, imposing censorship of the press, and ordering new elections. The charter had become meaningless. Liberal monarchists determined to defend it, and radical republicans were ready to exploit the confusion. Paris rose once more in revolt; barricades were raised; royalist troops were unable to retake the city; and Charles, remembering the fate of his brother, fled to England.

THE BOURGEOIS MONARCHY

The Bourbon monarchy had been overthrown so suddenly that no one was in a position to name its successor. The upper middle class desired little more than a king who would respect the charter. They selected Louis

Philippe, Duke of Orléans and relative of Charles X, as their candidate. Others, including the aging Lafayette, who had assumed command of a reconstituted national guard, preferred a republic. Young, able Adolphe Thiers (1797-1877) mediated between these two factions. He pointed out to Lafayette that the radical wing of the republican movement was dreaming of a new Jacobin regime. Did he, Lafayette, desire to further their design? The "hero of two worlds" remembered that he, too, had been forced to flee from France when the Revolution of 1789 had moved too far to the left. He became convinced, and on July 31 he embraced Louis Philippe on a balcony of the Hôtel de Ville at Paris. The crowd roared its approval, and a new dynasty was born. The disgruntled Jacobins could only withdraw to plot and wait.

Louis Philippe was then fifty-seven years old. His father had catered to the liberals during the old regime and had voted for the execution of Louis XVI, but he had been beheaded in 1793 during the most radical stage of the Revolution. Louis Philippe himself had escaped after serving in the army of the republic. He had taught mathematics for a while, wandered through the United States, and lived in several European countries until the fall of Napoleon. On his return to Paris, he had renewed his contacts with the liberal and upper middle class elements of society. Bankers, industrialists, merchants, and intellectuals were welcomed at the Palais Royal where he resided, and he himself cultivated the virtues and assumed the prejudices of his guests. He was a staunch family man, and his children were sent to the schools of the well-to-do, not to private tutors, like most princes. He and his wife appreciated the value of thrift; no couple could have been further removed from the extravagances of Versailles. He gave the impression of preferring the business suit to the uniform, the handshake to the kissing of hands, and a stroll through the streets with his umbrella to a ride in a splendid carriage. He welcomed the tricolor of the Revolution, and the white flag of the Bourbons was abandoned forever. In short, he stood for a liberal, national, bourgeois monarchy—at least so the people of Paris and France believed.

On the whole, Louis Philippe justified expectations. The four ordinances of July 26 were revoked, and the charter was reinstated with minor changes. The divine right theory of Charles X was abandoned in favor of the theory of a contract between the king and the people. The financial qualifications for voting were reduced to permit about 200,000 persons to ballot in a nation of over 30,000,000, just enough to transfer political control of the Chamber from the landed aristocracy to the upper middle class. The National Guard was reorganized, and its members were required to purchase their own equipment, a provision that excluded the workers from membership. Thus, although the aristocracy remained very important, political power passed to the king and the upper middle class, and military power to the middle class as a whole. The Paris workers made an attempt to overthrow the new regime in 1832 and the Lyon workers in 1834, but the loyalty of the middle class to Louis Philippe ensured the failure of both revolts. An uprising favoring a Bourbon restoration was also suppressed.

Perhaps the greatest threat to the new dynasty during its early years came from abroad, for it was quite possible that the great powers would restore the legitimate dynasty as they had done when Napoleon returned from Elba in 1815. There was little doubt that the conservative eastern monarchs wanted to intervene, but they were quickly occupied nearer home by Italians and Poles who hoped that the events in Paris in July, 1830, were but the first step towards the overthrow of conservatism in Europe. They revolted in the expectation of French aid; but instead of being saved by France, they saved Louis Philippe by occupying the Russian and Austrian armies until he had become firmly established. Great Britain was willing to see a more liberal regime established in France, provided that country made no effort to expand its boundaries. This effort Louis Philippe was soon tempted to make.

The Belgians, it will be remembered, had been united with the Dutch in 1815 and placed under the rule of William I of the House of Orange. The marriage had not been a happy one. The Belgians were Catholics; the Dutch were Protestants. The Belgians were manufacturers; the Dutch were traders. Instead of trying to reconcile the differences between his subjects, William I constantly favored his fellow Dutchmen. As a result, the Belgians, following the example of the French, revolted in September, declared themselves independent in October, and elected the second son of Louis Philippe as their king a few months later. Louis Philippe was tempted. The acquisition of Belgium would increase the prestige of his house in Europe. More important, it would increase his own popularity in France, for it would be regarded as the first step towards regaining the natural frontier of the Rhine. The British, however, looked on the establishment of French influence in Belgium as a threat to their security. Louis Philippe hesitated, then refused to permit his son to accept the throne. Leopold of Saxe-Coburg was selected as king.

Louis Philippe gave the French bourgeoisie peace and order, but he also had to provide prosperity if he were to maintain his throne. Fortunately for him, the industrial revolution was just beginning in France, and there were ample opportunities for the bourgeoisie to increase its wealth. Between 1830 and 1848, the number of steam engines in the country rose from 600 to 4,853; coal consumption increased rapidly; and the construction of railroads began in earnest. The workers here, as elsewhere, did not share in the new prosperity, nor did they have effective legal means of getting consideration for their wants. Labor unions and strikes were forbidden; to the liberal bourgeoisie, these restrictions were not contrary to liberty but were essential to freedom of contract.

For years all went well. The upper middle class and the king shared in the control of the government. In the Protestant historian, François Guizot (1787-1874), they found a suitable minister. By appointing deputies to government posts, awarding them contracts, and granting similar favors, Guizot was able to keep the support of a majority in the Chamber. There were scandals when some high officials accepted bribes, but as long as the rich were becoming richer, the authorities would see no danger. For the poor little was done beyond the establishment of primary schools in every commune. These were set up to teach the advantages of law, order, and the existing regime, not to educate the masses to participate effectively in the government. Neither Louis Philippe, Guizot, nor most of the upper middle class would consider extending the suffrage.

The opposition party in the Chamber was usually headed by Adolphe Thiers (1797-1877). Thiers, like Guizot, was a historian who would rather make history than write it. He wanted a stronger, more nationalistic foreign policy. More important, he advocated ministerial responsibility and a limited extension of the suffrage. Louis Philippe's failure to recognize that the government had to change with the changing economic and social structure was to cost him his throne.

THE REVOLUTION OF 1848

The lower middle class and the small peasant proprietors remained content as long as they were prosperous, and the workers remained quiet as long as they had jobs. However, a severe industrial and agricultural depression began in France in 1846. There were widespread crop failures, and the price of wheat rose 250 per cent. In their distress, the lower middle class turned once more towards the republicans, the workers gave a sympathetic ear to the socialists, and the peasants saw less reason to support the existing regime. Intellectuals who had formerly supported the monarchy as part of the romantic credo now began to defend the common man and to toy with democratic and socialist ideas. Scandals in high places and the government's refusal to extend the suffrage or to institute other political reforms especially angered the disfranchised element of the middle class. Louis Philippe lacked glamor, and the people as a whole were bored with his colorless regime. Even most of the landed nobility and the clergy had not yet become reconciled to his rule; they did not regard him as a staunch Catholic or their legitimate king. Truly, the government rested on a slender reed, although most of its opponents thought more in terms of reform than revolution.

When Louis Philippe refused to make concessions, part of the upper middle class under Thiers' leadership joined with the republicans and socialists to agitate for the dismissal of Guizot and the extension of the suffrage. A big banquet in honor of George Washington's birthday was scheduled for February 22, 1848. As the speeches on such an occasion were likely to be republican in nature, the government forbade the banquet. Thiers, and even the socialist leader, Louis Blanc, thought that resistance was useless, but a large, curious crowd gathered on the appointed day in the hope of excitement. There were minor fights with the police, and some barricades were raised across the streets. The government became frightened and called out the National Guard, but the typical guardsman was a member of the lower middle class and could not vote. He, too, demanded reform. Shaken at last, Louis Philippe dismissed Guizot, but regular army troops stupidly fired on the crowd. The Parisians, now thoroughly angered, began to raise barricades in earnest. The republicans and socialists saw that their hour had come, although liberal monarchists like Thiers were vainly trying to stabilize the situation. The populace stormed the Palais Royal and the Chamber of Deputies. Louis Philippe fled to England, leaving the republicans and socialists, who were as surprised at the suddenness of their success as anyone else, in control of Paris. Once more, the Parisian populace had dictated the fall of a dynasty.

The destruction of the Orléanist monarchy proved far easier than the establishment of an alternative form of government. Thiers and the liberal monarchists were temporarily discredited because of their willingness to support Louis Philippe after he had dismissed Guizot, and it was left to the republicans and the socialists to divide the spoils. A provisional government was established which proclaimed a republic and ordered that deputies be chosen by universal manhood suffrage to prepare a new constitution. Furthermore, the National Guard was expanded to include all citizens, an action that gave arms to the Paris workers.

Meanwhile, the depression that had begun in 1846 continued. The socialists, led by Louis Blanc, demanded that the Paris working day be limited to ten hours and that the government provide jobs for the unemployed. Some bourgeois republicans accepted the idea, and a public works program, known as the National Workshops, was established to provide employment. This program was badly administered, although the charge that its bourgeois director purposely bungled in order to discredit the plan has never been proven. All that can be said is that laborers were not required to work hard and were often given useless tasks. The cost of the program became increasingly heavy and contributed to the necessity to raise direct taxes.

The peasant proprietors and the urban middle class who dominated the provinces were furious. In the elections to the 900-man assembly that was convened to prepare a constitution, they voted for republicans or monarchists and less than a hundred radical republicans and socialists were able to win seats. On June 21, the new assembly closed the workshops. The workers raised barricades hoping to start another revolution, but the middle-class republicans proved to be of sterner stuff than the Bourbons in 1830 or the Orléanists four months before. The regular army and the loyal part of the National Guard were instructed to restore order, but only after several thousand workers had met their death were they able to suppress the insurrection. As a result of the June Days, the upper classes became more fearful of the Paris populace and the workers became more hostile to those in power. Nevertheless, a constitution was completed by November that reflected the aspirations of the age of the egalitarian revolutions by providing for a president with wide powers and a unicameral legislature, both chosen by universal manhood suffrage. Elections were held in December, and when the ballots were counted, it was discovered that Louis Napoleon Bonaparte had received 75 per cent of the votes for the presidency.

LOUIS NAPOLEON

Louis Napoleon was the son of Louis Bonaparte, one of Napoleon Bonaparte's younger brothers. Louis Bonaparte had served briefly as King of Holland, but the downfall of Napoleon had doomed his seven-year-old son to a life of exile. Death gradually extinguished the senior members of the Bonaparte line, so that by the time Louis Napoleon was elected president he was also the claimant of the imperial throne. Once in 1836 and again in 1840, he had tried to seize power, but both efforts had quickly ended in failure. After the first occasion, the government had contemptuously released him, and after the second, he had been so carelessly guarded that he had easily escaped.

Perhaps the reason that few took Louis Napoleon seriously during these years was that he seemed so little like his uncle. He was obviously no general, as his ridiculous rebellions proved. About the only evidence of generalship, planning, or administrative ability that he had shown was his decision to include a tame eagle, the symbol of the imperial crown, in his second attempt. During his captivity, it is true, he had written on such subjects as national defense, the advantages of having a popularly elected ruler, and the means of eliminating poverty, but these works were not taken seriously. Few suspected that they contained the seeds of future imperial policy. The revolutionaries of 1848 had not felt that he was enough of a threat to the new republic to be stopped from entering the country and winning a seat in the assembly to prepare the constitution. Yet, in the presidential elections this man was given three out of every four of the ballots cast.

Undoubtedly, the principal reason for Louis Napoleon's overwhelming victory was that he bore the name of Bonaparte. The romantic age had made his illustrious uncle one of its greatest heroes, while the sufferings caused by his selfish ambition had been forgotten. "Why shouldn't I vote for this gentleman," an old veteran declared as he prepared to ballot for Louis Napoleon, "I, whose nose was frozen near Moscow!" To the ignorant peasants who made up the majority of the voters, the name of Napoleon was the only familiar one on the ballot. To the middle class, it stood for law, order, and economic progress. To Catholics, it meant better treatment for their Church than they could hope to obtain from the secular republicans. To nationalists, it symbolized the glories that had been France's.

Sincere republicans were so divided among themselves that to many Louis Napoleon was the least objectionable candidate.

Once established in the presidency, Louis Napoleon began to show that he had considerable talents as a politician and intriguer. He courted the favor of the masses by making numerous public appearances, he ensured his control over the cabinet and the prefects who governed the departments, and he won the loyalty of the army whose officer corps had little use for a republican regime. Disaffected generals were removed, loyal officers were promoted, double rations of brandy and extra pay were given to the enlisted men. The name of Napoleon could be counted upon to do the rest.

Meanwhile, the newly elected and conservative legislature was hanging itself. The suffrage was altered to disfranchise three million of the nine million voters and ensure the dominance of the middle class. The influence of the Catholic Church in education was greatly increased, to the horror of the secular-minded; and a restoration of the Bourbon or Orléanist dynasty appeared increasingly probable, to the dismay of the republicans.

Until the summer of 1851, Louis Napoleon cooperated with the legislature, although he sincerely disapproved of some of its measures. Only when the conservative majority in that body refused to support a constitutional amendment to permit him to have a second term did he decide on a coup d'état. On the night of December 1-2, 1851, thousands of his opponents were arrested, and orders were issued re-establishing universal manhood suffrage. The French people were then asked to vote on whether they wished to maintain Louis Napoleon's authority and to give him the power to make a new constitution. The actions of the conservative legislature had enabled him to pose as the defender of democracy and the republic. The stunned people responded, with some persuasion, by giving their approval in a vote of 7,500,000 to 640,000. In December of the following year, the empire was declared re-established, and Louis Napoleon became Emperor Napoleon III. Once more, the republican road had led to a dictatorship in which equality was preserved but liberty was lost.

CENTRAL EUROPE

ITALY IN 1815

Italy, the land that had produced the intellectual, political, and economic changes which began the transition from medieval to modern times, was one of the most backward countries in Europe in 1815. The favorable beginning that the Italians had made in trade and industry had not been followed by further advances. Their cities had ceased to grow, and in 1815 the typical Italian was a poverty-stricken, ignorant peasant. Where there was wealth and culture, the inspiration was largely due to French rather than to Italian influence.

Nowhere was the backwardness of Italy more apparent than in its political structure. Little real progress had been made towards territorial unity since the dawn of the sixteenth century, in spite of the dreams of a few intellectuals. Napoleon had temporarily reduced the multitude of tiny Italian states to two, without counting the generous slice of the peninsula that he had added to France, but the Treaty of Vienna had turned back the clock. Nine states were created, or rather re-created, varying in size from the relatively important kingdoms of Sardinia (including Savoy and Piedmont on the mainland), the two Sicilies, and the Papal States, to a handful of small duchies such as Tuscany, Parma, and Modena, and finally to the tiny republic of San Marino. In addition, two of the most advanced Italian provinces, Venetia and Lombardy, were assigned to Austria.

Nowhere outside France had the reforms of the Revolutionary and Napoleonic period penetrated more deeply than in Italy, for the entire peninsula had been under the control of the French. As a result, nowhere was the reaction carried further after the restoration of the deposed monarchs. Few of these monarchs shared Louis Philippe's willingness to compromise. Out went French innovations including, in some instances, the Code Napoleon, street lights, and French palace furniture. Only with difficulty were the bridges preserved that Napoleon had built over the Po River.

The reactionary forces were stronger in Italy than elsewhere and therefore attempted to restore more of the old regime. In addition to the princes and most of the clergy and nobility, the reactionaries could rely for support on the papacy and Austria. The pope, Pius VII (1800-1823), had the power and authority common to all temporal rulers; as head of the Church, he could also direct the thinking of devout Catholics in Italy and obtain aid from Catholic sympathizers in other countries. That he had every intention of making full use of his spiritual authority was indicated by his decision to reinstitute the Jesuit order, the Inquisition, and the Index. Ecclesiastics resumed the principal role in the government of his temporal domain. Austria was an even stronger pillar of the reactionaries. Its acquisition of Lombardy and Venetia gave that country an interest in Italian affairs. To protect its own domain, Austria was determined to quell every liberal or national manifestation on the peninsula.

THE REVOLUTIONARY MOVEMENT

The very extent of the reaction ensured the growth of an opposition. This opposition took the form of secret societies, of which the Carbonari, or Charcoal Burners, were the most important. Inspired by liberal and humanitarian sentiments, the Carbonari modeled themselves after the Masons, from whom they borrowed much of their elaborate ritual. During the Napoleonic period, they had plotted against their French oppressors, but after 1815 their conspiracies were directed against the reigning Italian dynasties, the Austrians, and the pope.

Much of the Carbonari's strength lay in the army. In 1820, a military uprising took place in Naples which forced the incompetent reactionary, Ferdinand I (1751-1825), to grant a constitution. However, as we have seen, Metternich, backed by Russia and Prussia, sent troops into Italy to put down the insurrection.[1] In 1821, there was a similar uprising in the kingdom of Sardinia. Victor Emmanuel I (1802-1821) was forced to abdicate; and the regent, Charles Albert, granted a liberal constitution, but royalists and Austrians defeated the revolutionaries near Novara. Charles Felix (1821-1831), Victor Emmanuel's younger brother, was placed on the throne as an absolute monarch.

The success of the French revolutionaries in July, 1830, inspired the secret societies to foment uprisings in Parma, Modena, and the papal states, but once more aid from Austria gave victory to the conservative forces. Clearly, the ill-planned conspiracies of the secret societies could never free the Italian people from the yoke of their oppressors. A new approach and greater popular support were needed.

The revolutionary forces needed a wider following than could be admitted to secret societies. They needed a more definite program and a more dedicated outlook, a *risorgimento* (resurrection) of the Italian spirit. The most famous leader of the spiritual renewal was the nationalist Giuseppe Mazzini.[2] In 1831, he organized the Young Italy movement, dedicated to the furtherance of spiritual and moral improvement, progress, and, more specifically, the unification of Italy through the combined efforts of its people. Mazzini had little ability as a conspirator, and the numerous uprisings that he led ended in complete failure; but he had the gift of inspiring others to dedicate themselves to moral renewal and to Italy. Romanticism began to influence Italian literature at about this time. The romantics, by appealing to Italy's past greatness, constantly reminded their readers of its present degradation and exhorted them to make their land once more the center of European culture and achievement.

The desire to industrialize also spurred efforts to achieve unity. Italy was economically backward, but there were some economic leaders who wanted to construct railroads, build factories, and practice scientific agriculture. Their efforts were blocked by the political disunity of their country. It was hard to build a railroad when it had to pass through so many countries. It was difficult to establish big industries with access to raw materials and large markets when each tiny state had high tariff barriers. Even those who attended meetings of societies dedicated to the promotion of scientific agriculture strayed in their conversation from the virtues of the potato to the need for unity.

The great difficulty was that no general agreement could be reached on the methods for achieving unity or the nature of the new Italy. Mazzini and his followers dreamed of a democratic republic. To implement

[1] See page 515.
[2] See page 537.

their plan, it was necessary to destroy the temporal power of the pope, overthrow the reigning dynasties, and drive out the Austrians. All this, Mazzini insisted, must be accomplished by a rejuvenated Italian people without outside aid. Others were more moderate. They feared democracy and had no special desire for a republic. Many hoped to establish an Italian, or at least a north Italian, kingdom under the leadership of the house of Savoy, the rulers of northwest Italy and the island of Sardinia. The house of Savoy was among the oldest in Italy, and in Charles Albert (1831-1849) it boasted a man with liberal sentiments. Had he not granted a constitution in 1821 during the period of his brief regency? Other moderates dreamed of a federal Italy under the presidency of the pope. Their program had the advantage of making revolution unnecessary. All that was needed was to persuade the princes. Perhaps even Austria need not be expelled.

The cause of a federal Italy received impetus in 1846 when the reforming Pius IX (1846-1878) became pope. Liberals everywhere took heart. There were riots in Milan in January, 1848, and a revolution broke out in Sicily at about the same time. The kings of the two Sicilies and Sardinia, the pope, and the Duke of Tuscany granted constitutions during February and March as a result of liberal urging. The peninsula was already afire when the news arrived of the February Revolution in France and the March uprisings in Austria.[3] The patriots determined to profit by the Habsburg preoccupation with internal troubles, and Milan and Venice revolted. Sardinia, the papal states, and the two Sicilies sent troops to aid the rebels. For a time, it seemed as though Austria would be driven out of Italy, but diplomatic pressure led the pope to withdraw his troops and a counter-revolution in the two Sicilies caused that country to follow suit. The Sardinian troops under Charles Albert proved no match for the Austrian veterans, led by old Marshal Radetsky who had won distinction in the Napoleonic wars. At Custozza and later at Novara, they were completely defeated. "All is lost, even honor," Charles Albert cried, and he abdicated in favor of his son Victor Emmanuel II (1849-1878). Within five months, he was dead, and Austria had restored its authority in northern Italy.

Meanwhile, Pius IX had become so alarmed at the demands of the radicals that he had abandoned his reform program and fled from Rome. Mazzini immediately proclaimed a republic, but Louis Napoleon, who had just become president of France, seized the opportunity to win favor with French Catholics by dispatching an army to restore the pope. At first, volunteer red-shirted troops led by the fiery, patriotic Giuseppe Garibaldi (1807-1882) were able to hold their own, but French reinforcements finally carried the day. Rome fell, the reactionary forces triumphed, but Garibaldi and Mazzini escaped to fight again on other fields. The revolution of 1848 had failed, but several lessons had been learned. The pope had become too conservative to be acceptable to the liberal advocates of Italian unity. The republicans were militarily too weak to succeed if they continued to act

[3] See pages 547-548, 556-557.

alone. Only Sardinia, through the heroic but unsuccessful efforts of Charles Albert, had gained in stature. Sardinia had maintained its constitution after the reactionaries returned to power elsewhere in Italy. It was to this little kingdom that most patriots now turned, but another decade passed before they began to achieve any success.

THE GERMANIC CONFEDERATION AND THE HABSBURG EMPIRE

The Treaty of Vienna recognized the existence of thirty-nine sovereign states in the territories that had once belonged to the Holy Roman Empire. Two of them, Austria and Prussia, were great powers; four, Bavaria, Saxony, Hanover, and Wurttemberg, were kingdoms of secondary importance; and the remainder were a curious assortment of grand duchies, duchies, principalities, and free cities that varied in size from Schaumburg-Lippe with eight square miles to Baden with 5,800 square miles. These states were joined together in a loose Germanic Confederation designed more to protect its members from foreign invasion and domestic insurrection than to satisfy the nationalistic aspirations of the people. The Confederation had no real executive or judiciary, and important actions could be undertaken in the diet only with the consent of all the member-states. Foreign kings still ruled the kingdom of Hanover and the duchies of Luxembourg and Holstein. At the same time, two members, Austria and Prussia, controlled huge areas outside the Confederation that were inhabited by Slavs, Italians, and other peoples. Such a hodgepodge seemed a poor reward indeed for the nationalists who had courageously assisted the rulers' efforts to expel Napoleon during the War of Liberation. Nor were the liberals more satisfied. Only a handful of princes granted constitutions, and these constitutions called for estates-generals in which each class of society was represented rather than for modern parliaments in which the middle class exercised greater influence.

Fortunately for the conservatives, the industrial revolution had not yet begun to penetrate Germany, so that the small dissatisfied portion of the middle class consisted primarily of college professors, students, and professional people. In 1815, students at the University of Jena organized the *Burschenschaft*, a society dedicated to improving the virtues of German youths and to fostering the development of nationalism. They chose as their colors, red, black, and gold and as their motto, "Honor, Liberty, Fatherland." Other universities followed suit, and many professors lent their support. In 1817, they held a general assembly at Wartburg to celebrate the 300th anniversary of Luther's break with Rome and the victory over Napoleon I at Leipzig. The meeting itself was harmless enough, but a few extremists aped Luther's burning of the papal bull by consigning the works of certain conservative anti-nationalists to the flames. One author thus treated was later murdered by a demented student.

This was too much. The German princes, abetted by Austria's Metter-

554

nich, pushed the Carlsbad Decrees through the diet. These decrees provided for the censorship of the press and of the classroom throughout Germany. The *Burschenschaften* were dissolved, liberal professors were imprisoned, and the secret police redoubled its vigilance. For nearly three decades, Metternich was able to impose his ideas on Germany as well as on the rest of Europe. There were minor uprisings, especially in 1830, but on the whole the established order was unshaken.

Metternich hoped to act with Russia and Prussia through the Congress system to hold the revolutionary activity of the liberals and nationalists in check, but he was too wise a man to believe that the status quo could be maintained forever. He was willing to see the Germanic Confederation strengthened to give partial satisfaction to the nationalists, provided it remained under Austrian leadership. But the Germanic Confederation could be strengthened only at the expense of the lesser princes who clung desperately to their petty rights. Since these princes could be dispossessed only by force and the Habsburgs, in their respect for tradition, were unwilling to go to this length, nothing was done.

Within the Habsburg empire, too, precious time passed and little was accomplished. Metternich knew full well that the Habsburg monarchy was a dynastic state held together only by the person of the emperor, the loyalty of a few magnates, an oft-defeated army, and an efficient if unimaginative bureaucracy. He hoped to satisfy the inhabitants of this multinational state by reviving their provincial estates and respecting their ancient traditions. He even patronized a Czech literary revival, but to no avail. The estates and the literary revival both served to spread nationalistic feeling among the subject races. Part of Metternich's failure must be attributed to the persistent refusal of Emperor Francis I (1792-1835) to establish an estates-general to which the provincial estates would send deputies. By this means, Metternich had hoped to broaden the horizons of the people and to make them appreciate the role of the dynasty and the empire. Thus, in spite of his subtle genius, Austria stood still while the forces of liberalism and nationalism slowly strengthened. In 1847, the aged statesman sadly declared, "I am an old doctor; I can distinguish a passing illness from a mortal ailment. We are in the throes of the latter." Within six months, the fastidious courtier had to flee from Vienna.

For a time, Prussia offered no more satisfaction to the liberal nationalists than Austria. Frederick William III (1797-1840) gradually dismissed the ministers who had instituted reforms during the Napoleonic period,[4] and the constitution he so often promised during those trying days was never forthcoming. Prussia did take one significant step towards securing German unity during Frederick William's reign. In 1819, the tariffs between the various Prussian provinces were removed, and a *Zollverein,* or customs union, began to be formed with neighboring Germanic states. The *Zollverein* called for the abolition of duties between the member-states

[4] See pages 489-490.

and the establishment of a low uniform tariff against outsiders. By 1844, nearly all of Germany outside of Austria had joined. In this manner, Germany achieved economic unity at a time when no real progress was being made towards political unity. The *Zollverein* made possible the more rapid development of industry and transportation since goods could flow back and forth easily, but the great period of industrial progress was reserved for the second half of the century. The *Zollverein* also caused some to look towards Prussia, not Austria, as the state most likely to bring about a united and liberal Germany.

The prestige of Prussia in the eyes of the liberal nationalists increased further when Frederick William IV (1840-1861) came to the throne in 1840. Frederick William began his reign by relaxing censorship, only to restore it after he became convinced that his generosity was being abused. In 1847, he summoned a united Landtag, or parliament, representing the entire kingdom and made proposals for the strengthening of the Confederation, but once again he ended by quarreling with the liberal nationalists. The basic difficulty was that Frederick William was a dreamy romantic. His conception of liberty, like Montesquieu's, was essentially that of recognized historic privileges enjoyed by this or that group or class, and his conception of a united Germany was that of a revived and divinely ordained Holy Roman Empire with all its pomp and pageantry. The liberal nationalists also respected the past, but they emphasized the liberties enjoyed centuries before by the Teutonic tribes and saw in contemporary British institutions the logical form into which their own state would have evolved had it been as free from outside interference as that of their island cousins. It was to the constitutional monarchy of the British, therefore, that they looked for a model. Frederick William's actions aroused enough hope to keep Prussia in the forefront, but not enough to oust Austria from leadership in Germany. Indeed, Frederick William's respect for tradition was so sincere that he always accepted the Habsburgs as the preeminent German house. In March, 1848, the storm broke.

THE REVOLUTION OF 1848

There had been rumblings before. Frederick William's quarrel with the liberal nationalists was an ominous sign, as was a nationalistic uprising in Austrian Poland in 1846 that had had to be vigorously suppressed. The liberals had won a majority in the Hungarian lower house the following year and were demanding that their country be transformed into a parliamentary monarchy with a responsible ministry. Manorial dues and unpaid labor services were to be abolished with compensation for the landlords; and equality before the law and freedom of speech, press, and religion were to be guaranteed. It was in this already tense situation that news arrived of the February Revolution in Paris.

The early disturbances in central Europe were minor, but the riots became more serious as the news from France flowed eastward. By the end of March, Prague, Budapest, and Vienna were in an uproar, Metternich had been forced to flee, and the emperor had felt compelled to accede to the Hungarian demands. April and May saw Bohemia, Austria, and other Habsburg lands insisting on greater autonomy and constitutions. The imperial family abandoned Vienna for the safer, quieter Innsbruck. The Habsburg position was further complicated by rebellions in Lombardy and Venetia. On March 22, Sardinia embarked on a crusade to drive out the Austrians and unite Italy. The future of the Habsburg monarchy seemed bleak indeed.

The news from Germany was also far from reassuring. On March 15, there were riots in Berlin. Barricades were raised, troops were sent in, and there was some bloodshed. However, Frederick William suddenly withdrew his forces from the city rather than incur further loss of life. He sought to placate popular demands by abolishing censorship of the press, summoning another united Landtag, and promising to work for a united Germany. Half prisoner of the mob, half willing captive of the popular enthusiasm, he paraded through the streets of Berlin wearing the black, red, and gold tricolor of the *Burschenschaften* that had become the symbol of a united Germany. The lesser German princes followed the same course. They acceded to popular demands for liberal reforms and agreed to work for unification, but at the same time kept their armies and bureaucracies intact. They even permitted deputies to be chosen by universal manhood suffrage to participate in a parliament at Frankfurt to prepare the constitution for a new united German state.

Although the Frankfurt Parliament has become one of the most maligned bodies in history, its faults were the faults of its age and its failures were largely the result of the difficult problems it faced. An unusually brilliant array of deputies was chosen. Nearly half were lawyers, judges, and government officials, and a fifth were college professors, teachers, writers, and ministers. Their weakness was not a lack of intellectual originality or practical experience in government; it was their assumption that the princes, like themselves, were men of good will and that the demands of the working classes were to be feared rather than satisfied.

The Parliament began its work by suspending the diet of the Confederation and appointing Archduke John, the most liberal of the Habsburgs, imperial regent. Cabinet officials were also named, but no army or bureaucracy was created. Then the Parliament turned to the task of preparing a constitution. Almost immediately, several problems arose. Some deputies wanted decentralized government; others favored centralization. Some wanted a monarchy; others, a minority, favored a republic. More serious still was the problem of where the boundaries of the new state should be drawn. The majority at first wanted to include all the lands that had been a part of the Germanic Confederation. If this, the *grossdeutsch* solution, were adopted, the Habsburg empire would have to be divided, for neither its north Italian territories nor Hungary were included in the Confederation. It would also ensure the imperial throne for a Habsburg. This consideration, along with the fact that Hungary was already being administered separately, led many to hope for Habsburg cooperation. The second, or *kleindeutsch,* solution called for the exclusion of all the Habsburg lands. Its adoption would make the Prussian king the logical choice for emperor, but at the same time leave many Germans outside the empire. It was not an easy choice, and Germans have fluctuated from one solution to another from that day to this.

Events outside of Frankfurt determined the outcome of the debate. The inhabitants of Bohemia were the first to awaken the deputies to the complexity of their task. They refused to send representatives to Frankfurt on the grounds that their country was Czech, not German. Instead, they summoned a Pan-Slav Congress to prepare a constitution for Bohemia in which a personal tie with the Habsburgs was recognized but any connection with the proposed German empire was denied. The surprised and exasperated deputies hardly knew what to do. They sincerely believed that every nationality should have its own country. But a nationality to them was more than a group of people with a common language; it embraced those with a common heritage as well, and Bohemia had for centuries been associated with Germany. Its king had even been one of the electors in the Holy Roman Empire, and it now lay within the boundaries of the Confederation. Indeed, over a third of the inhabitants of Bohemia were Germans, and they made up the bulk of the upper classes. Few nationalists of that day were so democratic that they were willing to equate the half articulate desires of a Czech peasant with the aspirations of a German nobleman or wealthy Prague merchant. The Frankfurt deputies therefore insisted that Bohemia was a part of the new Germany, and they took a similar position with respect to the equally complex problems of Prussian Poland and the Danish king's designs on the duchy of Schleswig. But since they had no army, these problems were ultimately resolved by the princes, especially the Habsburgs.

At first, the Habsburgs had bent before the revolutionary onslaught. In June, however, the tide began to turn. Rioting Czechs in Prague accidentally killed the Princess Windischgrätz, wife of the Austrian commander. That angry old soldier bombarded the city, crushed the revolution, and established martial law in Bohemia. He then marched to Vienna, where he easily overcame the revolutionaries. The army in Italy proved equally efficient and loyal. A victory at Custozza restored Lombardy to the Habsburgs, and gradually the peninsula returned to normal.[5]

Another weakness appeared in the rebels' armor. The Magyars had been loud in their demands for self-government, but they steadfastly refused to make similar concessions to the other inhabitants of Hungary, who made up half the population. These peoples, for the most part Slavs,

[5] See pages 553-554.

now rallied to the side of the emperor. Under the leadership of the able Croat, Jellachich, and assisted by Windischgrätz, they invaded Hungary. In December, the feeble-minded, epileptic Ferdinand abdicated to make room for the eighteen-year-old Francis Joseph I (1848-1916). With a loyal army, a determined monarch, and an excellent opportunity to divide and conquer, the government's forces gradually drove back the rebels. In June, a tsarist offer of assistance was accepted, and by August, 1849, the combined Russian and Austrian troops had crushed the rebellion in Hungary.

Meanwhile, a group of liberal Germans and Czechs had met at Kremsier and prepared a constitution that called for a decentralized Habsburg empire in which the historic provinces and the racial minorities within them were to receive recognition. The victorious Habsburgs imprudently rejected these proposals, which might have satisfied the more moderate liberal nationalists indefinitely, and created instead a centralized bureaucratic state in which the German influence predominated. Their monarchy returned to its pre-1848 characteristics, except that Hungary ceased to be treated as a separate unit and that the serfs, who had been freed at the height of the revolution, were not restored to bondage.

The bulk of the deputies at the Frankfurt Parliament had cheered the Habsburg victories because they saw in the Slavic drive towards freedom a disrupting force in their new empire, but now they discovered their error. The Habsburgs had no intention of dividing their lands in order to place their German subjects in the new state, and the Frankfurt deputies were unwilling to consider incorporating the entire Austrian empire because to do so would destroy the predominantly German character of their creation. Austria withdrew its deputies from Frankfurt, leaving those who remained no choice but to accept the *kleindeutsch* solution. In March, 1849, they elected Frederick William emperor and issued a constitution calling for a federal state with a bicameral parliament, the lower house to be chosen by universal manhood suffrage, and a responsible ministry. This liberal document was to inspire future German constitutional efforts, but it was never put into effect because Frederick William declined to "pick up a crown from the gutter."

The Prussian king took this action only after some hesitation. He longed for the imperial crown, but he disliked having it offered by the people rather than his fellow princes. His conservative advisers were opposed to Prussia's being swallowed by a liberal Germany, and it was becoming increasingly evident that Austria would not peaceably acquiesce in an extension of Hohenzollern power. The last proved all too true, for the following year Austria, supported by Russia, forced Frederick William to suspend his efforts to persuade the German princes to accept a united Germany under his leadership. Meanwhile, the Frankfurt assembly had been dissolved and the diet restored.

The only lasting gain from the revolution was made by the peasants in the Habsburg empire who were freed from unpaid labor services and other dues in return for compensating the lord of the manor, a concession that the nobles had been eager to make because they had come to the conclusion that it would be more profitable to farm capitalistically using paid laborers.

In other respects, the revolution in central Europe had failed. The liberals had been too humane to seize power by force. When the princes, backed by their loyal armies, turned against the Frankfurt Parliament, the deputies had no recourse but to submit or to raise a popular rebellion. The latter alternative was unacceptable to the majority, in part because they feared the radicalism of the masses, in part because they respected the historic rights of the princes, and in part because they abhorred violence and bloodshed. Had their task been less difficult or had Germany then been predominantly urban, middle class, and liberal rather than rural, agricultural, and conservative, they might have succeeded even with their gentle methods; but the glory of uniting the fatherland was to go to those who did not hesitate to use force and whose success was to make a deep impression on the minds of future generations of Germans.

GREAT BRITAIN AND ITS EMPIRE

The egalitarian movement made more gains in the British Empire, the United States, Russia, and Latin America than it did in France and central Europe. These four countries or regions had one characteristic in common—vast underdeveloped areas waiting for exploitation. They were, or they could have been, lands of opportunity, lands where ability, ingenuity, and initiative could bring wealth and social position. But they also had marked differences. In the British Empire and especially in the United States, the forces of conservatism were either weak or willing to compromise, while in Russia and Latin America they were strong and obstinate. Then, too, in those parts of the British Empire and the United States where there was rapid industrialization, the forces for change were strong, while in Russia and Latin America, where industrial progress was slow, the opportunity to exploit the machine did not equal the opportunity to exploit the land. Only in the British Empire and the nonslave area of the United States could the individual achieve his full economic potential; only there could the bourgeoisie acquire wealth almost unhindered by the state or by privileged social classes; only there could individualism, liberalism, and even democracy flourish. Nevertheless, in Russia and Latin America, the groundwork was laid for future progress, although these areas remained relatively backward.

THE CROWN AND THE ARISTOCRACY

In 1815, the British crown was still an important factor in the government because it controlled patronage. This patronage was derived from the civil list, the power of appointment, and the right to create peers and knights. Few ambitious men dared risk royal displeasure. The existence of depopulated boroughs which elected deputies to the Commons was also a factor in the survival of royal power, because it enabled the king and his supporters easily to influence the composition of that house. The House of Lords was even more subject to royal influence because the king could strengthen his supporters there whenever he desired by creating new peers. Finally, the tendency of the aristocracy to separate itself into small factions rather than to divide into well-organized, well-disciplined political parties made it possible for the king to bargain with various groups rather than face united opposition. In 1788, Pitt's supporters in the Commons were divided into 52 Pittites, 15 East Indians, 10 Scots, 9 followers of Lord Shelbourne and 9 of Lonsdale, 108 independents, and 185 of "the party of the crown." His majority depended more on the independents and "the party of the crown" than on his own followers, and in 1801, when the king disapproved of his Irish policy, Pitt had no choice but to resign.

On the other hand, the landed aristocracy were equally powerful. They controlled local government and held nearly all the seats in Parliament. In the long run, the king could not hope to govern without considerable support from this class. In short, the relation between the crown and the aristocracy in 1815 was much as it had been in 1715, except that the aristocratic cabinet had a greater sense of solidarity and acted with more initiative. This development was caused by George I and George II's infrequent attendance at cabinet meetings and George III's insanity, which was recurrent after 1788 and permanent after 1811. The way had thus been left clear for men like Walpole and the two Pitts to raise the office of prime minister to a position of leadership in the cabinet and the cabinet to a more independent position with regard to the crown.

Actually, there was very little conflict between the crown and the aristocracy after the overthrow of the French monarchy in 1792. The dangers of presenting a disunited front before the people were all too obvious. Radical leaders, fired by the French example, were beginning to form left-wing societies, organize labor unions, hold mass meetings, advocate universal suffrage, and use the dread word, "republic." Before such threats, king and aristocrat joined in a policy of repression. Pitt's reform program was dropped, several leading radicals were tried for treason, habeas corpus was temporarily suspended in 1794, trade unions were outlawed, and suspected societies were suppressed.

The policy of repression did not cease with the overthrow of Napoleon. Indeed, it became more severe because popular unrest increased. The return of peace brought a depression. Government purchases decreased, but continental Europe was in no position to resume the purchase of British manufactured goods. Iron prices dropped from £20 to £8 a ton, industrial products followed suit, workers were laid off, and discharged soldiers and sailors could not find employment. At the same time, poor harvests in 1816 and 1819 drove up the price of grain.

The few measures that Parliament passed were designed to help the aristocracy, not the workers. In 1815, a corn law was enacted which virtually prohibited grain imports until domestic wheat reached the very high price of eighty shillings a quarter. This law ensured an ample income for the landed aristocracy, but meant high bread prices for the workers. The income tax was abolished and the currency was deflated, both measures that helped the wealthy creditor class at the expense of the workers. The selfish program of the aristocratic Parliament led to widespread demands for the abolition of the "rotten" boroughs and an extension of the suffrage. Most of the assemblies held by the reformers were peaceful. They spoke of petitions rather than revolution, but a riot did break out at Spa Fields, London, in 1816. The government became frightened, habeas corpus was again suspended, and seditious meetings were forbidden. The unrest continued, and in 1819 troops became panicky and attacked a peaceful crowd of from 50,000 to 60,000 persons who had gathered at St. Peter's Field, Manchester, to hear speeches demanding parliamentary reform and repeal of the Corn Law. Eleven persons, including two women, were killed and about 400 were wounded. The magistrates and soldiers responsible for the Peterloo Massacre, as this event was called, were congratulated by the government, and six acts were passed which further curtailed public meetings, forbade the training of persons in the use of arms, empowered magistrates to seize seditious literature, and imposed a tax on newspapers and periodicals. This effort to curb freedom of expression caused extremists to plan to overthrow the government by blowing up the cabinet. The plot was discovered and the conspirators were arrested in Cato Street, London. The Cato Street Conspiracy only served to frighten the authorities more.

Meanwhile, the prestige of the monarchy sank to a new low. In 1820, the mad king, George III, died, and his son, George IV (1820-1830), who had been serving as regent, came to the throne. George IV was a corpulent, self-indulgent man who lolled around in gaudy dressing gowns most of the day and had to wear tight corsets whenever he dressed for state occasions. He enjoyed good literature and had a well-developed aesthetic sense with regard to art and architecture, but neither collecting old masters nor building palaces were hobbies to endear a monarch to his poorer subjects. He had a reputation for immorality that was made worse by his effort to divorce Queen Caroline, a vulgar woman who never washed and rarely changed her clothes. When George had met her for the first time in 1795 after she had been chosen as his bride, he could only gasp: "I am not well, get me a glass of brandy." He went through with the marriage, but quickly deserted his wife for his mistresses. On becoming king, he demanded a divorce. For months, the private life of the royal family was aired before the House of Lords, where the case was tried. The people hated the king so much that Caroline became a heroine who, like them, suffered at the hands of the royal ogre. The fact that her behavior had been as bad as his made little difference. Finally, the king dropped the suit, but only after the monarchy had suffered damage difficult to repair. There was some talk of a republic and widespread demand for Parliamentary reform.

This left the crown and the aristocracy with a choice of trying to withstand the popular tide at the risk of revolution, as their French counterparts did, or of making a few concessions in the hope of satisfying the more moderate reformers. They wisely chose the latter course; beginning in 1822, the cabinet became less conservative and a number of reforms were passed.

THE AGE OF REFORM

The new cabinet, which included George Canning (1770-1827) as foreign minister, William Huskisson (1770-1830) as president of the board of trade, and Robert Peel (1788-1850) as secretary for home affairs, hoped to reduce the popular demand for changes in the electoral procedure of the House of Commons by embarking on a program calculated to convince the moderate liberals that they could get reform legislation under the existing system. Canning took a stronger stand than Castlereagh against international cooperation to reduce rebels in other countries to obedience to their legitimate sovereigns.[6] Huskisson was a staunch advocate of free trade. He reduced the duties on many products imported into England and relaxed the navigation laws so that foreign ships could enter British harbors on the same terms as British ships.

Peel took the lead in bringing about a revision of the criminal code. The death penalty was abolished for about a hundred crimes; prisons were improved by requiring that jailors be paid regular salaries and by putting women prisoners under the care of female wardens. More important, the idea that the purpose of imprisonment was to reform the prisoner rather than to punish him gained partial acceptance and many prisoners were taught reading, writing, and Christian precepts. There was no adequate police force in England at this time, but Peel partially corrected this neglect by establishing a police commissioner for London and its suburbs at Scotland Yard. Finally, the act forbidding the formation of labor unions was repealed in 1825, although the right to strike continued to be denied.

Progress was also made in the direction of religious toleration, but it was the Irish Catholics rather than the spirit of reform that forced the issue. In 1828, rather than risk a rebellion in Ireland, Parliament repealed the Test Act, which forbade Catholics and non-Anglican Protestants to hold public office. In the following year a Catholic Emancipation Act was passed which gave Catholics who met the other qualifications the right to vote and to hold nearly all public offices.

The reform wing of the Tory party was considerably weakened be-

[6] See page 515.

tween 1827 and 1830 by the deaths of Canning and Huskisson, and the conservative wing sought to reassert itself. The election which took place in 1830 following the death of George IV saw a lively contest between the divided Tories and the Whigs, who sought victory by promising Parliamentary electoral reform. Events played into the Whigs' hands, for in July the French overthrew their king in an almost bloodless revolution and established the more liberal monarchy of Louis Philippe. The much stronger British middle class determined to profit by this example. Their support brought about a Whig victory, and the Tory government under the leadership of the duke of Wellington soon decided to resign, thereby ending nearly a half century of almost continual rule.

The Whigs under Earl Grey (1764-1845) were as much landed aristocrats as the Tories, but they believed that if they gave some political recognition to the wealthy middle class that was springing up in the new industrial cities, they could bring the demand for constitutional change to an end. If they had known that their reform bill was to be the first step towards parliamentary democracy, they would have been aghast. The bill that they introduced after being installed in the cabinet met such strong opposition in Parliament that Grey persuaded the new king, William IV (1830-1837), to dissolve it and order new elections. Once more, the electorate showed that it desired reform. The strengthened Whigs pushed a second reform bill through the Commons, only to have it defeated in the House of Lords. Riots broke out in Nottingham, Bristol, Derby, and other places. There was talk of forming a national guard and of starting a run on the bank. Revolution seemed possible. The Whig-controlled Commons would not surrender reform and the Tory-controlled Lords would not accept change. Finally, the king decided to throw in his lot with the reformers. He threatened to create enough liberal peers to ensure passage of a third reform bill through the Lords. The Lords surrendered. By his action, William may have saved the English monarchy, for if he had followed Louis XVI's and Charles X's example of allying the crown with the conservative aristocracy, there would probably have been a revolt sooner or later.

The Reform Bill of 1832 disfranchised fifty-six tiny or rotten boroughs and took away one of the two seats previously assigned to thirty-two small boroughs. Forty-four of these seats were given to twenty-two large towns that had previously been unrepresented, and twenty-one other towns received one representative each. The remaining seats were divided between the English counties, Ireland, and Scotland. This reapportionment gave the new industrial towns some voice in the government, although still not as much as their population entitled them to. At the same time, the boroughs lost the right to determine their own suffrage requirements. Previously, some boroughs had had such a wide suffrage that a few representatives of working-class origin had been elected, while others had allowed only a handful of persons to ballot. Now all householders paying

£10 annual rent were given the vote. The influence of the aristocracy and the laboring classes was thereby weakened in the boroughs to the benefit of the middle class, but in the counties the aristocracy remained as firmly entrenched as before, even though the more prosperous tenants and lease-holders were permitted to vote.

The immediate effect of the bill was not very great. The suffrage was only increased from 435,000 to 652,000 persons, Earl Grey's cabinet was one of the most aristocratic Britain had ever had, and the new Commons that met in 1833 included 217 sons of peers and baronets. In the long run, however, the Reform Bill of 1832 had considerable effect on the position of the crown and the aristocracy. When the rotten boroughs were abolished, the king lost most of the seats that he had controlled in the Commons. As a result, the prime minister ceased to be dependent on royal patronage for a majority in the Commons, and along with the cabinet and members of the lower house, he could become more independent of the crown. The abolition of the rotten boroughs also cost the great nobles part, though not all, of their patronage. Thus, the passage of the Reform Bill of 1832 enabled the cabinet and the Commons to develop gradually the modern British system of government and provided a valuable precedent for future measures extending the suffrage.

Except for one brief interlude, the Whigs remained in power until 1841. They were followed by a five-year Tory ministry headed by Robert Peel. Although conservative by temperament, Peel was a highly intelligent states-man who could change his opinions in answer to changing conditions and who had the courage to take necessary but politically undesirable actions. Under both Whigs and Tories, therefore, the period between 1832 and 1846 saw the enactment of reform legislation that held the wide-spread popular discontent in check and may have saved England from revolutions like those that engulfed Europe in 1848.

In 1835 during the Whig ministry, political reform was extended to the urban communities and a Municipal Corporations Act was passed which established a uniform system of government in nearly all the towns. Some of the smaller localities were dissolved, and 179 new boroughs received charters. This measure reduced corruption, curtailed the power of the urban oligarchies by giving all taxpayers the right to vote in local elections, and achieved a uniformity in municipal government that the French won only by a revolution.

Two years earlier, Parliament had turned its attention to the slavery question. There were then about 750,000 slaves in British West Indian and South African lands. The first step towards eliminating this evil had been taken in 1807 by the passage of a law abolishing the slave trade, but not until 1833 did Parliament free all the slaves. It ruled that children under six were immediately free. Older slaves were to serve an apprentice-ship for seven years in which part of their time was to be spent working for their owners and part for themselves. The slave owners were compensated for their property loss by a grant of £20,000,000. A milestone was peaceably passed that the United States achieved a generation later only by a bloody war.

In spite of the strong attachment to laissez-faire, Parliament turned its attention to laboring conditions in the new industrial plants and passed the first effective child labor act in 1833. This act forbade the employment of children who were under nine years of age in textile factories. Those between nine and thirteen were limited to a nine-hour day, and those between thirteen and eighteen to a twelve-hour day and a sixty-nine hour week, but no limitations were placed on the working hours of those who were over eighteen. A system of inspectors was established to ensure the enforcement of these provisions. In 1846, the working day in factories for boys under eighteen was reduced to ten hours. These measures were voted largely at the insistence of such members of the Tory aristocracy as the earl of Shaftesbury, who had little interest in industrial development but a strongly engrained sense of the responsibilities of the upper classes towards the lower. The measures could never have passed, however, without some middle-class and Whig support.

Working conditions in the mines were worse than in the factories. Six-year-old children were employed underground for twelve hours a day to open and close doors and work in tunnels too small for adults. The Mines Act of 1842 corrected the worst features of this situation by forbidding boys under ten and women to work underground. These acts later formed the basis for far-reaching labor legislation, but at mid-century there were no limitations on the working hours of men, women, or boys over eighteen in factories. To have regulated the working hours of an adult would have been to limit his right to make a free contract for his labor, and few were willing to violate the laws of laissez-faire to this extent.

The strength of the laissez-faire philosophy was evidenced by the passage of a new Poor Law in 1834. An act in Queen Elizabeth I's reign had made each parish financially and administratively responsible for the care of its own poor. This act had remained virtually unchanged. In 1795, the practice had started of giving aid, not only to the disabled and unemployed, but also to agricultural workers who earned less than a subsistence wage. This practice enabled agricultural employers to reduce wages to below the subsistence level without causing their workers to starve, but in doing so, they made it necessary to raise the taxes to support the relief system. This situation, and the belief that giving aid to the unemployed encouraged laziness and increased the number of paupers, led to a demand for change. The Poor Law of 1834 attempted to correct the situation by making paupers so miserable that they would prefer to work. Doles to the sick, aged, unemployed, and underpaid ceased, and those who could not provide for themselves were herded together in workhouses where the ablebodied men were made to work. Living conditions in the workhouses were purposely made uncomfortable to encourage everyone to find gainful employment. The food was poor, heat was limited, husbands were separated from their wives, and even burial in the parish churchyard was denied.

THE CHARTIST MOVEMENT AND THE ANTI-CORN-LAW LEAGUE

While reforms of the 1830's did much for women, children, and slaves, they did little for male industrial workers who labored in the new factories under the most unfortunate conditions. Their lot may have been no worse than that of their farm labor ancestors, but they were determined to improve their position. Although efforts to organize trade unions were conspicuously unsuccessful, the formation of the London Working Men's Association in 1836 to secure "equal political and social rights" for all classes in society gave them new hope. Its leaders had been disappointed that the Reform Bill of 1832 had not extended the suffrage to working men, for they had hoped to secure political equality that could then be used to win economic and social advantages. They therefore demanded a new reform bill to include the six points of a "People's Charter" that they prepared. These points included demands for universal manhood suffrage, the secret ballot, the removal of property qualifications for members of Parliament, and the payment of members of Parliament to ensure that all men could vote without intimidation and afford to serve as representatives. Other points were a demand for equal electoral districts and for annually-elected Parliaments.

The Charter was published in 1838, and in 1839 it was presented to Parliament as a petition. When it was rejected by a vote of almost six to one, there was talk of a general strike and insurrection, but few serious disorders occurred. In 1842, the Chartists once more presented their petition to Parliament. This time they claimed over three million signatures, but the members of that august body were unimpressed. Macaulay, the Whig historian, voiced the fears of most men of property when he declared that "universal suffrage would be fatal to all purposes for which government exists, and for which aristocracies and all other things exist, and that it is utterly incompatible with the very existence of civilization. . . . I will assert that while property is insecure it is not within the power of the finest soil, or the moral or intellectual constitution of any country, to prevent the country sinking into barbarism." The petition was once more rejected by a vote of six to one. A third effort to get Parliament to accept the Charter was made in 1848 after the republicans had overthrown the monarchy in France. The English government was afraid that it would suffer a similar fate, and the aged duke of Wellington pressed thousands of special constables into service, but they were not necessary. For the last time, the Chartists chose to petition, not to revolt, and once more their demands were rejected without receiving serious consideration. Their wild talk and seemingly radical program had only served to frighten the aristocracy and the middle class, while internal quarrels had weakened their activity. The movement itself declined rapidly in the 1850's, but by 1911 the request for annual Parliaments was the only one of its six points that had not been enacted into law.

One factor which weakened the Chartist movement was the formation of a rival organization dedicated to the improvement of the worker's lot. This organization was the Anti-Corn-Law League led by Richard Cobden and John Bright, both textile manufacturers. Great Britain, as we have seen, was moving rapidly in the direction of free trade, but the aristocracy obstinately insisted on maintaining the Corn Law which was designed to ensure a good price on domestic grain by limiting or taxing foreign imports. To Cobden and Bright, the Corn Law served only to enrich the wealthy landowners at the expense of the poor. They argued that if the Corn Laws were repealed, the workers would benefit by a fall in the price of bread. The landed aristocracy countered by charging that the middle-class manufacturers really wanted to reduce the price of bread so that they could pay their workers less. The League, however, managed to persuade many of the Chartists to abandon their demands for political reform and at the same time to convert Robert Peel and enough Tories to bring about the repeal of the Corn Law in 1846.

AN ERA OF STABILITY

After the excitement surrounding the submission of the last Chartist petition in 1848, England settled into a period of stability in which neither revolutionary agitation nor Parliamentary reforms played an important role. There were three sources of stability. First, the industrial revolution and the accompanying boom in railroad building finally led to a period of unexampled prosperity. Most other nations reduced or abolished their tariffs. Great Britain's exports increased almost fourfold between 1850 and 1872, and its imports from other countries grew nearly as rapidly. Industries expanded, the middle class prospered, and even the laborers profited as their real wages increased 18 per cent in two decades. The Malthusians' fear of overpopulation began to subside as it became increasingly evident that industrial production would produce sufficient exports to pay for the necessary food imports. The iron law of wages was also gradually discredited. The agricultural classes did not suffer from the abolition of duties on grain imports. The growth in population and the cost of importing foreign grain kept prices high enough to ensure substantial profits. The result was a decline in the conflict between the employee and employer as well as between the middle class and the aristocracy.

A second cause of the growing stability of the age was the increased prestige of the crown. In 1837, the eighteen-year-old Victoria (1837-1901)

568

succeeded her uncle, William IV, to the throne. She had been raised in seclusion; no adult had been allowed to converse with her unless her mother or governess was present. Nevertheless, Victoria had a natural dignity and a sincere desire to reign well. When it was revealed to her a few years before her coronation that she would some day be queen, she simply said, "I will be good," and this became the motto of her life. At first, she was a gay socialite, but after her marriage to the serious, shy, studious Prince Albert of Saxe-Coburg-Gotha, she became less carefree. They were a devoted couple and their happy married life, large family, and high moral character gave an elevated tone to the court that had been sadly lacking under most of their predecessors. The new court atmosphere was especially welcome because the religious revival led by the Methodists, other nonconformists, and the Anglicans had begun to have a profound effect, and a pious, moral, somewhat prudish complacency replaced the licentious gaiety of the earlier period. At first, the young couple was not popular. Albert was too much a scholar and too little a sportsman to please the aristocracy, and Victoria had as little hesitation in interfering with affairs of state as her ancestors. Gradually, however, they became more popular, and by the time Victoria died in 1901, after enjoying the longest reign in British history, she had become a symbol of her age.

A third cause for the growing British stability was the powerful position of Britain in world affairs. The Vienna settlement had led to a balance of power on the continent. This situation freed Britain from any threat from that quarter, and its powerful navy secured its far-flung colonial and trading interests. Indeed, the British foreign office, for nearly thirty years dominated by the bluff, energetic, aristocratic Lord Palmerston (1784-1865), was able to assume a belligerently nationalistic stance without the dangers that have usually attended such a policy. British citizens were assured the protection of their government wherever they went. Palmerston even sent the British fleet to Greece to secure compensation for a Portuguese money-lender with questionable claims to British citizenship when his house was pillaged in Athens. When the Chinese confiscated British-owned opium in an effort to stop the opium trade, Great Britain went to war. By the terms of the Treaty of Nanking in 1842, Hongkong was ceded by the Chinese, five other Chinese ports were opened to foreign trade, and the confiscated opium was paid for. Furthermore, the opium trade continued.

THE DECLINE OF BRITISH COLONIALISM

During the ninety years following the American war for independence, British liberals fought against efforts to build up a colonial empire by conquering backward peoples. There are several explanations for the desire to abandon the elder Pitt's efforts to spread the British flag throughout the world. The successful revolts of the Spanish, Portuguese, and British colonists in America[7] indicated that when colonial territories became strong and wealthy enough to be of some assistance to the mother country, they went their separate ways. Before that time, they were only an expense and a cause of war.

The mercantilist belief that the colonies were necessary for trade was abandoned for Adam Smith's concept of the advantages of a world-wide division of labor. Great Britain repealed the Navigation Acts and permitted its remaining colonies to trade with whomever they pleased. Other countries did likewise, so that the ownership of a colony no longer entailed a monopoly of its trade. The advantages of trade with, rather than ownership of, a territory were clearly stated by a politician who declared that "In 1844 we exported to the United States produce and manufactures to the value of £8,000,000, an amount equal to the whole of our real export trade to all our colonial dominions, which we govern at a cost of £4,000,000 a year; while the United States costs us for consular and diplomatic services not more than £15,000 a year, and not a ship of war is required to protect our trade with the United States." Indeed, in 1842 colonies were called "the chief cause of wars for the last hundred and fifty years." Increased employment occasioned by the industrial revolution removed much of the demand for colonies to provide homes for the excess population. Finally, the belief of the liberal nationalists that every people had a right to self-government caused them to oppose having colonies when they involved the unwilling subjection of the inhabitants.

The liberals were opposed at home by entrenched interests that profited from colonial civil and military posts and abroad by colonists who sought every opportunity for expansion either to obtain more land for settlement or to secure existing holdings. On the whole, the anti-colonial forces were successful during the ninety years following 1783 in preventing the sudden acquisition of large territories. In the Vienna settlement of 1815, the British returned nearly all the colonies that they had conquered from other states, except for a few trading posts. Later, the China war led only to the acquisition of Hongkong and the opening of several ports, not to the incorporation of large slices of Chinese territory.[8]

CANADA, THE WEST INDIES, AND AUSTRALIA

The liberals were most successful in getting their ideas of colonial self-government put into practice in those places where the bulk of the population was of English descent. Canada, for example, was transformed from a handful of separate colonies, governed much like most of the thirteen colonies that later became the United States, into a united self-governing dominion. Around 1800 Great Britain held the colonies of Newfoundland, Prince Edward Island, Nova Scotia, New Brunswick, On-

[7] See pages 423-426 and 593-599.
[8] See page 569.

tario, and Quebec to the north of the United States. The first five had been settled by Englishmen or by Americans who had sided with the crown during the Revolution and had later migrated in order to remain under the British flag. The sixth, Quebec, had been settled by the French, but as early as 1774 the English had agreed to let them keep their own laws, customs, and religion. Each colony had an elected lower house, an appointed upper house, and a governor who was named by the crown and who exercised considerable executive authority.

The separate Canadian provinces remained loyal during the War of 1812 and gallantly repelled several efforts on the part of the United States to annex them.[9] In 1837, however, a minor rebellion broke out that so alarmed the British that they dispatched the liberal Lord Durham (1792-1840) to the New World. In 1839, he made a very significant report to Parliament in which he recommended that responsible government be established. By responsible government, he meant that the provincial executive should be dependent on the lower elected house, just as the British cabinet had become dependent principally on the Commons. The adoption of this plan would therefore free a colony's internal affairs from the control of the mother country, but leave foreign policy and trade to be directed by Parliament. For a while the British hesitated to act on the Durham report, but in 1846 governors were instructed to act through responsible ministers. Because of this decision they began to occupy a role more like that of the queen in Great Britain than that of a prime minister. Upper and Lower Canada, or Ontario and Quebec as they became known, were united into a single province and given the right to regulate their own trade. In 1867, the Dominion of Canada was formed by adding Nova Scotia, New Brunswick, and later Prince Edward Island, the Hudson Bay Territory, British Columbia, and other provinces. A new state was thereby created that was larger than the United States but whose loyalty to the mother country was assured by the grant of self-government. Similar concessions a century earlier might have maintained the unity of the English-speaking world by making the American War for Independence unnecessary.

The West Indian islands were not so fortunate. The creation of an independent United States ruined their trade patterns, and the discovery of a method of extracting sugar from beets ended much of the European demand for their sugar. At the same time, the gradual adoption of liberal policies of trade by the mother country injured their position. The movement toward free trade took away the guarantee they once had of the exclusive enjoyment of the market within the empire, and the emancipation of the Negro slaves in 1833 cost them part of their labor force. In Jamaica, the Negroes fled to the wilds of the island rather than work for their former masters. They revolted in 1865, and the alarmed government abolished the colonial legislature and ruled henceforth through an ap-

[9] See page 589.

pointed governor and council. Most other West Indian legislatures suffered a similar fate. The history of these islands was a tragic exception to the general growth of prosperity and self-government among the British possessions in North America.

The newer Australian colonies fared much better. At first, the British showed little interest in settling this island continent; but when the United States won its independence, it became necessary to find a new place to dump convicts, and a penal colony was established for this purpose at Sydney, New South Wales, in 1788. Lawlessness marred the early history of the colony, but sheep raising proved so profitable that legitimate settlers followed the convicts. Other colonies were founded, but it was not until the discovery of gold in 1851 that the Australian population grew rapidly. Tasmania and New Zealand were occupied without official encouragement by a curious mixture of the most lawless elements of society, legitimate settlers, and missionaries. Finally, a reluctant home government had to incorporate the islands into the empire to ensure order. These colonies, like those in Canada, were given local self-government, but it was not until a much later date that they achieved dominion status.

INDIA

India and Ireland occupy special places in the history of the British Empire. Unlike Australia or Canada, they both contained native populations that were too large to be absorbed or exterminated. Both engaged in valuable trade with the mother country and provided land or offices for the British aristocracy that they were unwilling to surrender in response to the demands of the liberals at home or the natives abroad. As a result, both were ungenerously treated, and both were trials for the British crown.

The Treaty of Paris in 1763 had destroyed French power in India, but the British East India Company controlled only Bengal and several coastal strips. The remainder of the vast subcontinent remained in the hands of native princes who gave nominal allegiance to a Mongol emperor. These princes recognized the potential British threat and were easily persuaded by the French to attack during the Napoleonic wars. The anticipated French aid did not materialize, the native princes were defeated, and by 1805 the British had taken a third of the peninsula. Growing opposition at home to colonies led to a slowing down of the acquisition of territories, but British colonials made certain that expansion did not entirely cease. By 1857, Burma and a large part of northern India had been conquered, and the remaining princes had become puppet rulers.

Meanwhile, the British had taken steps to reorganize the government of the territory. In 1773, a Regulating Act had been passed which transferred much power from the East India Company to a governor-general responsible to the cabinet at London. A small band of able English officials were appointed to administer the lands directly under the crown, and residents were named to watch over the states still ruled by native princes. To support the civil officials, the British maintained a force of about 250,000 sepoy (native) troops commanded by British officers and about 45,000 European troops who were poorly provided with artillery.

With such a small force, the British could not hope to hold a land of over 200 million people in subjection unless their policies were popular. On the whole, they ruled well, but their annexations of princely territory, their insistence that English be the language in education, and their interference with such Hindu practices as burning widows on their husbands' funeral pyres caused widespread discontent. Many Indians feared that an attempt would be made to force them to accept Christianity or to abandon the caste system, and in 1857 a serious rebellion of the sepoy troops was touched off by the adoption of a rifle that required greased bullets. The Hindus thought that the grease came from cows, which they regarded as sacred animals, and the Moslems thought that it was from pigs, which to them were unclean. Over 400 men, women, and children were massacred at Cawnpore, but the rebellion quickly collapsed because most of the sepoys and Indian princes remained loyal. Nevertheless, Parliament decided to take away the remaining authority of the East India Company, and a viceroy was appointed to perform the duties of the governor-general.

IRELAND

Ireland proved even more troublesome. By the last quarter of the eighteenth century, about 4,500,000 people inhabited the island of whom over 3,000,000 were Catholics. The remainder of the population consisted of about a million Scottish Presbyterians who had settled in the northeast corner of the island in the early seventeenth century and 450,000 Anglo-Irish concentrated in the region around Dublin. The Anglo-Irish, as their name implies, were either inhabitants of Ireland or absentee landowners of English descent and of the Anglican religion. They dominated the local parliament and government of the island, owned above five-sixths of the land, and exploited their tenants. Presbyterians who had the necessary property qualifications were permitted to vote, but they were barred from office for religious reasons until 1780. Catholics could neither vote nor hold office, and they were even forced to pay the tithe to support the unwanted Anglican Church.

It would seem that the Anglo-Irish should have been satisfied with their preferred position, but like the eighteenth-century British North American colonists, they resented the fact that their parliament was subordinate to that of the British. Inspired by the example of the American Revolution and led by the able Henry Grattan (1746-1820) they persuaded the British government to give their parliament independence in 1782 and to accept Ireland as a kingdom of equal status with England but ruled by the same monarch.

At first all went well, and in 1793 Catholic freeholders were given the right to vote, though not to hold office. But the French Revolution inspired a group known as the United Irishmen to seek to establish a republic in which Catholic and Protestant would live together with complete liberty, equality, and fraternity. The authorities acted vigorously to suppress the movement. Its leaders were arrested, and the Protestants in Ulster and the other northeastern counties were disarmed. When rebellion came, the Catholic peasants alone were in a position to act. They knew little about the philosophy of the Enlightenment, but they understood fully that a large part of their meager income went to pay rents to Protestant landlords and the tithe to the Anglican Church. Heedless of the plan to establish a united Irish republic, they butchered landlords and Protestants. When they were defeated in 1799 in spite of receiving some French assistance, they were treated with equal brutality by the Protestant victors. Whatever chance there had been for cooperation between the two religions and nationalities of the island came to an end.

The English decided to try to preserve order and to bind the Irish more closely to them by making Ireland an integral part of Great Britain, just as they had done with Scotland in 1707. The names of the states were changed in 1801 from the kingdom of Great Britain and the kingdom of Ireland to the United Kingdom of Great Britain and Ireland. The Irish parliament was persuaded with the aid of numerous bribes to merge with the English one. Thirty-one Irish peers were admitted to the House of Lords, and 100 Irish representatives were enrolled in the House of Commons. Unfortunately, George III refused either to permit Catholics to serve in Parliament or to free them from paying the tithe to the Anglican Church. As a result, the formation of a single parliament for the two islands did not lead to fair representation of religious and national interests, as many had hoped, and the small Anglo-Irish minority dominated Ireland's representation.

Irish religious and economic discontent continued, and the growth of Irish nationalism under the leadership of Daniel O'Connell (1775-1847) added another cause for discord. In 1828, when O'Connell was elected to Parliament, the British were faced with the difficult choice of either repealing the anti-Catholic law to permit him to take his seat or denying him admission to the Commons and risking rebellion. They chose the former course and the Catholic Emancipation Act of 1829 opened nearly all offices in England and Ireland to Catholics, but the Irish continued to demand independence or home rule.

In 1846, a blight attacked the potato crop in Ireland and ruined three out of four acres. Since about half the people were so poor that they lived almost entirely on potatoes, a serious famine resulted. Relief proved inadequate, and the repeal of the Corn Laws did not lower the price of grain enough for the poor to buy it. About 250,000 people died of starvation or its related effects, and millions emigrated to other parts of the world, especially the United States. By 1851, the population had dropped from 8,200,000 to 6,500,000 and by 1920 only 4,100,000 remained on the unhappy island.

RUSSIA

The forces of change were weaker in Russia than in the other major European states. The country remained predominantly rural, and the gentry continued to be the most important social class. Nevertheless, the older order was slowly undermined. Only the court aristocracy had been interested in Western ideas during the seventeenth and eighteenth centuries, but this circle expanded in the nineteenth century to include some army officers who had become acquainted with the West during the Napoleonic wars, a handful of the more cultured members of the gentry, and part of the slowly growing middle class. Under the impact of the romantic era with its emphasis on the *Geist* of each individual people, a counter-movement developed which opposed Westernization and stoutly defended Slavic culture and institutions. As a result, the Westerners and the Slavophiles frequently clashed, although they were in general agreement that the existing regime should be changed. Sometimes the tsars advocated Westernization, sometimes they tried to maintain the status quo until the defeat in the Crimean War made it obvious that the only alternative to reform was disintegration. The tsars chose the former course, just as Peter the Great had done, and their regime survived until 1917.

ALEXANDER I

Alexander I (1801-1825) was a tall, handsome, blond, blue-eyed youth in his twenty-fourth year when he came to the throne in 1801. His grandmother, Catherine the Great, had taken a keen interest in his education and had secured the Swiss philosopher, Laharpe, as his tutor. Under their joint direction, he became a product of the Enlightenment and an advocate of the Westernization of Russia. He believed in the natural order and the rule of law. A proper society could be created only by the issuance of ordinances that were in accord with the laws of nature. These laws included freedom of speech, freedom of thought, and freedom from the bonds of serfdom. They also involved a respect for law and order as defined in written constitutions. But with all his apparent liberalism, Alexander was a typical enlightened despot who believed that order, good government, and reforms should be handed down from above. He "would have willingly agreed," one of his liberal advisers declared, "that every man

575

should be free, on the condition that he should voluntarily do only what the Emperor wished." Alexander never fully recognized that there was an inherent conflict between constitutional government and absolute monarchy, between the freedom of the people and the will of the tsar. This fact does much to explain his reign.

Alexander was fortunate in having a small group of intimate friends with whom he discussed his plans of reform. On their advice he granted an amnesty to political prisoners and exiles, abolished torture, permitted the sale of foreign books, and relaxed censorship. He dreamed of freeing the serfs, but the opposition of the powerful gentry and other practical difficulties caused him to hesitate. He did seek to ensure better treatment for them, to halt their sale in the open market, and to encourage private individuals to grant them freedom. Nevertheless, he continued the practice of reducing crown peasants to serfdom by giving royal estates to the gentry, and when he freed the serfs in the Baltic provinces, he provided no land for them. This measure created little opposition, since most of the nobles in the north were content to receive complete ownership of the land and to be freed from any responsibility to their former serfs. The result was a large rural proletariat. Alexander also sought to improve the educational system, but there was insufficient money to put his plans fully into effect. Some universities and other schools were established, but Russia remained culturally backward.

Some of Alexander's most interesting plans pointed towards constitutional reform. With the aid of Michael Speransky (1772-1839), he devised a system of government based largely on local and provincial diets and a national representative assembly. Nothing came of it, but lesser reforms involved the creation of Western-style ministries to administer the laws and a council of state to discuss new laws. By these actions, a degree of legality and order was brought into the legislative and administrative system. The adoption of a hereditary rule of succession to the throne by Alexander's father also contributed to this development. Palace revolutions came to an end; and when one of Alexander's successors was murdered, it was not by aristocratic guardsmen but by revolutionaries.

Nevertheless, the story of Alexander's reign was more of reforms postponed than reforms accomplished. This was due in part to determined conservative opposition, especially among the gentry. It is significant that Alexander actually gave constitutions only to his Polish and Finnish subjects. Many reforms cost money, and Alexander was perpetually in debt. Then, too, wars scuttled more than one promising proposal. Alexander annexed the kingdom of Georgia and took several provinces from Persia, Finland from Sweden, and Bessarabia from the Ottomans after long but successful encounters. At the same time, Russians pressed southward along the American Pacific coast from Alaska to northern California. Alexander's greatest triumph was over Napoleon I. As a result, in 1815 he became King of Poland and the arbitrator of Europe. Never be-

Alexander I, from a contemporary portrait.
(Bettmann Archive)

fore had Russia been so much a part of the European family of nations. For a brief period, Alexander was the hope of liberal Europe, but his outlook on life—and his policies—began to change.

The death and destruction that attended Napoleon's Moscow campaign had turned the tsar's thoughts towards religion. "The fire of Moscow lit up my soul," he declared, "then I got to know God and became another man." In 1814, he came under the influence of a mystic and from that time his loyalties were more to the religious revival that was sweeping the Western world than to the Enlightenment. Uprisings in Europe, the mutiny of a favorite regiment, and, still more, the failure of the Poles to appreciate the constitutional monarchy that he had created for them drove him into the hands of Metternich. Gradually, at home and abroad, he became an instrument of repression rather than emancipation. Censorship and the secret police were revived. Alexander also created military colonies consisting of men, women, and children from selected villages who divided their time between drilling and farming, at little cost to the government. In 1825, he died by the Sea of Azov, but his strange behavior has led some to believe that an empty coffin was returned to the capital and that the devout tsar ended his days as a monk in Siberia.

NICHOLAS I

Alexander's sudden death left the government in confusion. Since he had no children, it was naturally assumed that his brother, Constantine, would ascend the throne. Constantine, however, had renounced his claim when he had married a commoner, a fact that was known only to a few high officials. As a result, when the news of Alexander's death reached

577

St. Petersburg in early December, Nicholas, a third brother, proclaimed Constantine tsar. Only when a message arrived from Constantine, who was at Warsaw, that he once more renounced the throne did Nicholas accept the crown. This delay led many to suppose that Nicholas had usurped the throne, and the misunderstanding gave discontented persons an opportunity to revolt.

Some members of the officer corps had been indoctrinated with liberal ideas during their long stay in central and western Europe at the time of the Napoleonic wars. These officers formed tiny secret societies dedicated to the task of reforming their own country. A Southern Society was organized at Kiev that favored a republic and talked of freeing the serfs and dividing the land. The less radical but poorly organized leaders of a Northern Society with headquarters at St. Petersburg were in a more favorable position to act when news arrived of Alexander's death. They sought the establishment of a constitutional monarchy and the abolition of serfdom, but they bungled badly once they began to act. On December 26, they marched their troops into the square before the palace and exhorted them to yell, "Long live Constantine and the Constitution." Most of the enlisted men thought that Constitution was Constantine's wife, but they courageously refused to disband until persuaded by a few rounds of artillery. The rebellion of the Decembrists, as they were called, ended in complete failure, but their uprising marked the halfway point between the old palace revolutions and the popular uprisings that were to come.

Nicholas I (1825-1855) possessed Alexander's good looks and his determination to be a good ruler, but he was so much younger that he had never known Catherine the Great nor had he been taught by Laharpe. As a result of his conservative education, he had neither Alexander's inquiring mind nor his desire to flirt with new ideas. He strongly opposed revolutionary changes, but he did improve the lot of the crown peasants and even provided a few schools for them. It was more difficult to help the serfs because of the opposition of the all-powerful gentry, but he did have inventories made in some places to determine their obligations and he tried to prevent them from having to perform more services than they owed. The gentry's power to punish the serfs was also checked, and their obligations towards their subordinates were stressed. To improve his control over the gentry and to make local government more effective, Nicholas strengthened the bureaucracy and brought it more directly under the supervision of the central government. The gentry were pressed into service like the junker aristocracy of the Prussian kings. Since neither the officials nor the people always knew what the law was, Nicholas had Speransky codify the existing laws and publish them in a series of forty-five volumes.

Nicholas strengthened the political police, rigorously censored the press, and carefully prevented any unorthodox ideas from creeping into the universities. The Poles especially suffered at his hands. Prior to 1830,

Nicholas I, from a contemporary portrait. (Brown Brothers)

they had been relatively well treated, but in that year they revolted. The Russian garrison was driven out, and Nicholas was deposed from the Polish throne. Within a year, Russian troops had regained control, and the Polish constitution, diet, and special privileges were abrogated. Russian institutions were introduced, the Russian language was taught even in primary schools, and the Polish universities were closed. Poland was reduced to the status of a province, but in spite of Nicholas' efforts, Polish nationalism continued to exist.

Nicholas was not successful in his foreign policy. Early in his reign, he managed to win concessions from Persia and to take more land from the Ottoman Turks. His primary aim, however, was to maintain the status quo in Europe in cooperation with Austria and Prussia. This policy failed when Austria refused to support him in the Crimean War, and he died a broken man amidst the Russian defeat.[10] Under the impact of this reversal, his repressive system began to crumble at home and abroad and his successor had no choice but to make changes.

THE REFORMS OF ALEXANDER II

Alexander II (1855-1881) inherited from his father one of the largest empires the world had ever known. It included nearly all the lands of the present-day Soviet Union except for a few provinces along the southern border, as well as Finland, Poland, and Alaska. Like the Habsburg monarchy, it was a multinational state, but few of the subject peoples were

10 See pages 605-606.

579

then conscious of their origins or caused difficulty on this account. The center of the empire was still west of the Ural Mountains, for the prevalence of serfdom had prevented free immigration to the eastern frontier. Indeed, as we have seen, the very presence of unoccupied land on the frontier had been instrumental in binding the once free peasants to the soil to prevent the depopulation of old Russia. Thus, millions of square miles in Siberia were virtually uninhabited or else occupied by primitive, nomadic people. Nevertheless, the Russian population nearly doubled during the first half of the nineteenth century, and by 1851 it stood at 67,000,000, almost twice that of France, the nearest European competitor.

The rapid population growth was accompanied by very slow industrialization and urbanization. Only a few cities, like Moscow and St. Petersburg kept pace with the Western European metropolises. Nevertheless, industry did begin to move into the Ural Mountains at this time. The number of factories employing more than fifteen workers increased from 1,200 in 1800 to 2,818 in 1860; some machines were imported, and others were manufactured in Russia; foreign trade increased three- or four-fold; and Moscow and St. Petersburg were linked together by a railroad in 1851. There were significant accomplishments, but compared with Western Europe, Russia was falling steadily behind. In 1851, only 7.8 per cent of the population lived in towns, a smaller percentage than in many parts of Europe during the thirteenth century.

Agriculture responded to the stimulus of the slowly growing urban market, and the production of potatoes and wine increased rapidly. On the whole, however, serf labor proved inadequate to the needs of scientific and capitalistic agriculture. The gentry were unable to accommodate themselves to changing conditions, and the majority fell into debt in spite of their efforts to extract all they could from the serfs. The serfs were reduced to abject misery. One scholar has actually counted 1,467 uprisings between 1801 and 1861, and others have increased this estimate. Under such miserable conditions, the number of serfs increased slowly, if at all, in spite of the rapid growth in other segments of the population. Nevertheless, there were still 52,000,000 serfs and crown peasants in Russia in 1861.

Since most of the people lived in the country, local rural administration was extremely important. Catherine the Great had divided the country into provinces and districts that were governed by appointed officials and the elected representatives of the gentry. Below the provinces and districts were the landed estates. These were controlled by officials if they belonged to the crown and by a gentleman if he were the owner. The estate, in turn, was divided into *mirs*. The *mir* was rather like the medieval manor. Its members had a collective responsibility to pay taxes and dues and to perform required services, but they had a collective right to the pastures and woods. Land was periodically divided between the various heads of families who were given several strips in

Alexander II, from a contemporary portrait. (Brown Brothers)

each field in order to ensure a fair distribution of the good and bad soil. Scientific agriculture could not be practiced under such circumstances even if the inhabitants of the *mir* had had the necessary knowledge. The lot of these inhabitants had been growing steadily worse since the sixteenth century. Because of the population increase, there was insufficient land for them in central European Russia, but, as serfs, they were not permitted to move to the frontier. They could be bought, sold, and mortgaged like any other piece of property. In short, they lived in poverty and had few more rights than slaves.

Although the elders of the *mirs* ruled on most matters, ultimate police and administrative authority rested with the gentleman owner of the estate. Thus, the gentry largely controlled their *mirs*, their estates, and the districts, and they were quite influential in the provincial government as well. No far-reaching reform could be effective unless they gave some support. Most of the gentry were themselves poor and ignorant. Rich or poor, they were likely to be in debt because they lived beyond their means. Nearly two-thirds of their land and many of their serfs were mortgaged when Alexander became tsar.

Under such circumstances, it is not surprising that elementary education was largely limited to the sons of the gentry and the clergy. Eighty per cent of the bureaucracy was without formal education, and only 3,000 persons attended the universities. What could be called an intelligentsia was extremely small, but this handful of men exercised considerable influence.

There were two main schools of thought in Russia around 1855, both of which derived much of their original inspiration from the West. One school, the Westerners, wanted Russia to become a part of Western civilization. They talked of constitutional monarchies, parliaments, and individual rights, including freedom of speech, trial by jury, the abolition of serfdom, laissez-faire economics, and the secularization of society.

581

The second school, the Slavophiles, derived their basic ideas from the romantic rather than the liberal tradition, from Hegel and Fichte rather than Voltaire and Mill. They saw in Russia a distinctive civilization that must not be polluted by ideas from the West. They stressed Russia's past glories, present mission, and future greatness and held that Russians had their own peculiar characteristics and native genius. They conceived of the state as governed by a benevolent autocrat and the people as guided by the Greek Orthodox Church, but at the same time they advocated freedom of thought and speech and the emancipation of the serf. They singled out the *mir* as being a distinctive Russian institution that must be defended at all costs, for in it resided the *Geist* of the people.

Alexander himself was not a formal member of either school of thought. Like his father, he was an honest conservative determined to rule benevolently and justly. However, defeat in the Crimean War brought home to him the necessity for changes if his empire were to survive. The war had revealed amazing stupidity, ignorance, and inefficiency in the Russian officer corps and bureaucracy. Clearly, the military, administrative, and educational systems must be altered. The war had also shown that though the serf made a brave soldier, he had neither the initiative nor the intelligence of the Western European enlisted man. The serf must be made free and the economic, social basis of the country must be altered. It was this task that Alexander first set for himself.

Alexander proceeded cautiously but firmly. The position of the gentry was too powerful for him to act unless he could persuade some of them to accept change. To get popular support, he relaxed censorship of the press and of the universities. Committees of the gentry were formed on his initiative throughout the provinces to discuss emancipation. He emphasized constantly that it was "better to abolish serfdom from above than to wait till it begins to abolish itself from below." Reluctantly, under pressure from the tsar and public opinion, most of the gentry accepted the necessity of emancipation; still more reluctantly, they accepted the fact that the serf must have part of the land. In March, 1861, Alexander issued his Edict of Emancipation. By its terms, the serfs were given their freedom and permitted to retain about half of the cultivated land. The gentry was generously compensated by the state through the sale of treasury bonds, and the state in turn was to be compensated by the freedmen in installments paid over a period of forty-nine years. The land was not turned over to the individual peasants, but ownership was usually vested in the *mir*. The older communal system of agriculture was continued, including the periodic redistribution of the land, but the elders of the *mir* now had full responsibility to see that the taxes were paid and order enforced. They could even levy money for religious education and other local needs. No one could leave the *mir* without their permission.

Alexander has often been criticized because he did not give the peasants more land, because he did not turn it over to individual heads of families, and because for years the economic position of the peasants did not improve. Yet when the magnitude of his task is considered, when the power of the gentry (who had murdered his grandfather and great-grand-father when they hinted at lesser reforms) is remembered, when the value of the *mir* as a guide and protector for the ignorant freedman is ac-knowledged, the extent of his achievement may be realized. During his reign, three fourths of the population of the country were freed and given a degree of economic and social security. At the same time, the basis for breaking the power of the gentry was laid, because the *mir* replaced the gentry as the basic unit of rural government.

Local government was changed to stimulate more popular initiative. In 1864, a decree was issued establishing *zemstvo* assemblies in the dis-tricts and provinces. The district *zemstvos* were composed of deputies elected by the gentry, townsmen, and peasants voting separately in an elaborate system of indirect suffrage. The townsmen and the peasants were thus assured a voice, although the gentry received more district *zemstvo* seats than their numbers warranted. They also held about three-fourths of the seats in the provincial *zemstvos* because the other two classes could rarely spare the time or the money to serve so far from home. On the other hand, the more reactionary members of the gentry were not likely to be chosen, because the district *zemstvo*, where the gentry was a minority, served as the electoral unit for the provincial assembly. The *zemstvos* were charged with matters related to education, health, roads, and public welfare. They had the power to tax to support their program.

Municipal government was reformed in a similar manner. Town coun-cils elected by the propertied classes were created with powers and duties comparable to those of the *zemstvo*. In this manner, the Russian people were given some experience in self-government, but at the same time the tsar did not abandon control. The organs of the central government remained in his hands, and he directed the military and the police at all levels of government.

Other reforms saw the judiciary separated from the administrative branch of the government. Judges were made irremovable, except by court action, trials were held by judges in public, rather than by administrators in secret, juries were used for serious criminal cases, and judicial proce-dures were modernized. A legal profession was born, and although Rus-sian justice remained inferior to that of the West in some respects, a great step forward had been taken.

A fourth series of reforms concerned the army. The old military sys-tem of noble officers and serf soldiers had proven inadequate in the Cri-mean War. In its place was substituted a system of universal military training which included all classes. The length of service was reduced from twenty-five to six years, and schools were established to ensure better-trained officers.

Alexander's accomplishments were great, but not great enough to remove demand for more. To get support for his initial reforms, he had had to encourage the development of liberal opinion, but when he felt that he had gone far enough, he found that he was unable to halt the demand for change. In 1863, the Poles revolted once more, and privileges he had given them at the beginning of the reign had to be revoked. In Russia proper, Alexander felt it necessary to curtail freedom of the press and to interfere in education. This only served to increase discontent. Some opponents of the government were liberals who sought a parliament and other constitutional reforms. Some were radicals who sought to overthrow the social order, often by terroristic methods. Several attempts were made on Alexander's life. Finally, in 1880, he decided to try to satisfy the liberal critics of his regime. Censorship was once more relaxed and plans were laid to have the *zemstvo* elect representatives to sit with the council of state to discuss new laws. It was not a parliament, but it was a definite step in that direction. Fearful that this measure would satisfy the liberals, the radicals redoubled their efforts. On March 13, 1881, a bomb was thrown at Alexander's feet. Torn to pieces, the tsar could only gasp, "Home to the palace to die there." One of Russia's best chances for orderly constitutional development came to an end.

THE UNITED STATES

The new republic of the United States did not escape the forces which were operating in Europe, but the forces that made for conservatism were weaker than in the Old World while the forces for change were stronger. There was no king, no titled aristocracy, not even a bishop at first, to stand in defense of the old order, and the Concert of Europe that checked the aspirations of the rebellious people in Europe did not operate on the western shores of the Atlantic Ocean. It is true that there was an aristocracy of wealth, but it consisted of untitled merchants and bankers, the revolutionary element in central and western Europe, and of large landowners, a class that was frequently rebellious in Hungary and Poland. Thus, even the more conservative inhabitants in the United States were liberal by European standards, a situation that permitted the new nation to be in the forefront of the egalitarian movement of the age.

THE GOVERNMENT OF THE NEW REPUBLIC

The Declaration of Independence made it necessary to create new state constitutions to replace the old colonial charters and a national government to replace the British imperial system. The provisions in the new state constitutions varied, but in general they abolished primogeniture, which provided that landed property should be inherited by the eldest son, and entail, which prevented the owner from selling the land or giving it away. The legal means which a few American families had used to maintain their dominant position generation after generation were thereby destroyed. Churches were disestablished, except in New England where the Congregational (Puritan) church managed to maintain its position for another generation, and the payment of tithes ceased to be required by law. The American tradition of separation of church and state was thereby born. In a reaction against the power wielded by colonial governors, chief executives of the states were not given wide authority and the legislatures were strengthened. Suffrage depended on the ownership of property, but the amount required was not large, and about 120,000 men out of a total population of about 3,000,000 met the test, a generous percentage compared to what was permitted in France or England. These constitutions generally contained a bill of rights to protect the individual from infringements on his liberties by the state.

The organization of the central government also reflected the reaction against the British imperial system. The states were no more willing to permit a federal American authority to levy taxes or regulate trade than they were to permit the British king or Parliament. The Articles of Confederation, which served as the first United States constitution, gave both these powers to the individual states and provided for neither a federal executive nor a federal judiciary. The federal government acted upon separate states which it could not coerce; it could not act upon the people. The result was judicial, financial, and commercial disorder at home and a weak foreign policy abroad. The British could not be expelled from the Great Lakes region, and the Spanish could not be persuaded to open their port of New Orleans to American settlers in the West. This situation led to a movement supported by the more conservative, propertied people to modify the constitution. A constitutional convention was held in Philadelphia in 1787, and a new constitution was adopted the following year.

The new Constitution corrected the most glaring weaknesses of the old. A president with broad powers and a federal judiciary were provided, and the authority to tax and to levy import but not export duties was granted. In order to check the democratic forces, a variety of complex methods was established for electing public officials, but the suffrage was far broader than in any of the European monarchies. At the same time the acceptance of Montesquieu's system of a division of powers among the executive, legislative, and judicial branches of the government and the approval of a bill of rights safeguarded the essential liberties from the powerful president and from the people. As a result, although the new Constitution marked a turn towards conservatism, it was a very liberal document by the standards of the day.

Many problems of government were not decided by the new Constitution. Should the president or cabinet officials appear before Congress to ex-

plain and defend their proposals? Did the Supreme Court have the power
to declare acts of Congress unconstitutional? Such questions were answered
through precedents that were soon established, and not by the Constitution. Even points of etiquette had to be solved. Some wanted to emphasize republican simplicity, others desired to imitate the wigged British
judges, and Vice President Adams insisted on referring to Washington's

inaugural address as "His Most Gracious Speech." Fortunately, the new nation was blessed with a large number of remarkable men, and most problems were quickly solved.

One important development took place in the early days that was neither anticipated in the Constitution nor desired by the first president— the formation of political parties. Washington, who was aware of the British experience, looked on parties as selfish quarreling factions. He chose the ablest men he could find for his cabinet without regard to their political beliefs, but it was around two of them, Alexander Hamilton (1757-1804) and Thomas Jefferson (1743-1826), that the first political parties formed. Hamilton was sympathetic with the banking-commercial interests of the northeast upon whose support he was convinced the success of the new government depended. As secretary of the treasury, he proposed that the federal government pay the national debt in full and assume the debts incurred by the states during the Revolutionary War. This measure played into the hands of well-to-do speculators who had bought bonds from patriotic investors at greatly reduced prices, but it also firmly established the credit of the government. Hamilton believed that only a strong government could curb the democratic and, to him, lawless, uncouth element in American society. He therefore insisted that the central government claim every power not expressly denied it by the Constitution. He specifically took this stand in reference to his proposal to create a Bank of the United States modeled after the highly effective Bank of England. He disapproved of the experiments of the French Revolution, and when some farmers in western Pennsylvania challenged the power of the federal government to collect an excise tax on whisky, he persuaded Washington to call out the militia in four states to restore order. It was largely through his efforts that a fiscally sound and politically stable government was created. Around him and his program the Federalist party was formed.

Hamilton's great rival, Jefferson, was an idealist more than a man of practical affairs. He emphasized liberty, not authority; the farmer, not the merchant; the natural virtues of the common man, not the necessity to appeal to his innate greed; and the superiority of a democratic republic, not the rule of an oligarchy. As a result, he supported the rights of the states and the people against the extension of the power of the federal government, the development of an agrarian West against the urban East, and revolutionary France against monarchical Britain. Around him and his program, the original Republican party was formed.

At first, victory went to the Federalists, but the expansion of the West and the growth of democracy brought the Republicans ever-increasing strength. The Federalist party declined rapidly after its unpatriotic behavior during the War of 1812 with Britain. By 1821, there was only one political party, but soon the Republicans began to quarrel among themselves. Part of the trouble was due to personal rivalries and part was due to conflicting principles. The democratic, agrarian and urban-worker factions joined

Andrew Jackson to form the Democratic party, while industrialists, bankers, and many large landowners formed the Whig party under the leadership of Henry Clay and Daniel Webster. The Whig party eventually disintegrated like its Federalist predecessor, with many of its members going over to a Republican party that was formed in the 1850's. Since that time the Democratic and Republican parties have vied for power. Rarely has a third party received a large number of votes.

A second important development not anticipated by the Constitution was the role assumed by the Supreme Court. The founding fathers had done little more than to define the types of cases which were to come before federal courts and to insist that judges remain in office during good behavior. Nothing was said about the right of the Supreme Court to declare acts of Congress unconstitutional, although the idea of the sovereignty of law was far older than that of the sovereignty of a legislature or the people. Nevertheless, after the appointment of John Marshall (1755-1835) as chief justice in 1801, the decisions of the court were bold and significant. During the thirty-four years that Marshall served in this capacity, he wrote 519 of the 1,106 opinions that were given. So great was his influence over the other justices that only eight times did he find it necessary to dissent from the majority. Marshall was a Federalist. Like Hamilton, he believed in a strong central government with wide powers. Nevertheless, upholding the principle of judicial review, he did not hesitate to declare void Congressional acts that specifically violated the Constitution. State laws that contravened federal statutes were ruled invalid on several occasions. Equally important were his numerous decisions in defense of the sanctity of property and the inviolability of contracts.

THE EXPANSION OF THE NEW REPUBLIC

Perhaps the outstanding characteristic of the newly-launched republic was that it was a land of economic opportunity. The population increased rapidly because of large families and an ever-growing number of immigrants from Europe. By 1860, the number of inhabitants nearly equaled that of France or the British Isles. Most of the increase went to the cities, where industries were being rapidly developed. Only six cities had had over 8,000 people in 1790, but two generations later localities several times that size were commonplace, and New York and Philadelphia were numbered among the great metropolises of the world. Numerically less significant, but of considerable importance, was the growth in the agricultural population made possible by territorial expansion.

At one time, it was doubtful whether the United States could hold the large expanse of territory given it by the Treaty of Paris in 1783. The British remained in the Great Lakes region despite the treaty, and settlers in the Ohio and Mississippi river valleys flirted with Spain, because the Spanish held New Orleans, the port through which their goods had to flow to reach eastern and European markets. Washington was finally able to persuade the British to withdraw into Canada and the Spanish to open the mouth of the Mississippi to Americans. In 1800, however, Spain ceded Louisiana to Napoleon.

Napoleon could not be frightened into making concessions, but he needed money and he knew that he could not protect his new possession from the British fleet. As a result, he suddenly decided to sell Louisiana to the United States for about $12,000,000. In return for this small sum, the new republic was able almost to double its size. In 1819, it rounded off its southeastern boundary by the purchase of Florida from Spain.

Meanwhile, westerners accused the British of stirring up the Indians. Recognizing in Canada a likely area for further expansion, western Congressmen persuaded the United States to take advantage of Britain's preoccupation with Napoleon and declare war. The excuse was Britain's violation of American rights on the seas, but the real motive was to put an end to British dealings with the Indians by taking Canada. The Americans were unsuccessful in their aggressive designs, but the British were content to make peace on a basis of the status quo. Thereafter, the young republic might bully Mexico and Spain, but it was willing to compromise on boundary disputes with the more powerful Great Britain. In 1846, when Oregon was divided along the 49th parallel, the northern boundary of the United States was completed. Texas was annexed at its own request in 1845, and in 1848 the United States took California and adjacent lands to the east from Mexico after a brief war. The purchase of an additional strip of land from Mexico in 1853 gave the republic its present southern boundary. Within three generations of its birth, the United States had grown as large as the continent of Europe.

Wars and purchases from foreign countries were but one aspect of the American expansion. Indians, relatively few in number, inhabited the forests, plains, and mountains of the broad continent. Often they were unwilling to recognize the American conquests and purchases because they thought that they, not the French, the Spanish, or the Mexicans, owned the lands through which they wandered. Sometimes they were persuaded to sell their land; sometimes they gave way peaceably before superior force; and sometimes they fought back savagely. But the white man moved relentlessly forward. In the end, the Indians were either confined to reservations or exterminated.

The Americans were remarkably successful colonizers, largely because of a policy established during the days of the discredited Confederation. By the terms of the Northwest Ordinance of 1787, the land north of the Ohio and east of the Mississippi rivers was divided into from three to five territories. Each territory was to be admitted to the union on an equal footing with the original thirteen states whenever it had 60,000 inhabitants. This principle was extended as the United States expanded, so that California today is an equal state, not a colony of New York or Virginia. Without this generous policy, the inhabitants of the West would undoubtedly have broken away from the seaboard states, just as these states had broken away from the British Empire, because of their colonial status. To speed the settlement of the West and to satisfy the demands of farmers, public land was sold at ever-decreasing prices until 1862, when the federal government offered to give 160 acres of land to anyone who would reside on it for five years.

THE AMERICAN CHARACTER

The lack of conservative checks and the numerous opportunities that lay within the grasp of those Americans who went to the new industrial cities or followed the westward tide had a profound effect on the American outlook and character. Economic opportunity bred initiative and individualism; success brought a welcome to the best social circles far more rapidly than in Europe because there was no firmly entrenched hereditary aristocracy.

Democracy was furthered in part by the relative equality of opportunity and in part by the existence of the West. The earliest inhabitants of a territory were for the most part men of very modest means. When they prepared the new state constitutions at the time of admission to the Union, they naturally failed to include the conservative features that remained in those of the original thirteen states. Religious and property qualifications for voting were swept away, universal manhood suffrage became the general rule, and many appointive offices were made elective. Even state judges were chosen by the people, a thing that would have horrified the authors of the federal Constitution. These changes in the West touched off demands for greater democracy in the thirteen original states, and between 1830 and 1850 many of them prepared new constitutions. The federal government also underwent changes. Parties began to choose their candidates for office in conventions rather than in caucuses composed of a few leaders, and the president came to be chosen for all practical purposes by the people. The word "democratic," which was still a term of reproach in 1790, was chosen as the name of a political party a generation later.

A relatively high percentage of Americans became property owners. Lands jointly owned like the common pastures in the manorial system or the Russian *mir* were virtually unknown. This led to an unusual emphasis on the sanctity of property that has implanted a bourgeois character on the country. The Supreme Court, as we have seen, vigorously supported this development.

Numerous economic opportunities and the position in society granted to the successful led Americans, more than other people, to believe that the acquisition of wealth was a major aim in life. Plentiful goods became both a mark of success and a necessity for happiness. Cultural pursuits were regarded with a degree of suspicion in the eastern states while the frontier community was often anti-intellectual.

The opportunities found in America and the optimistic spirit that prevailed quickly won the loyalty of European immigrants to the new nation, whether they settled in the eastern towns or moved on to the western frontier. Native Americans were also captivated by the progress of their country and came to believe that they were destined to rule the entire continent. In the early days of the republic, men had thought of themselves as Virginians or New Yorkers, but those who moved westward cut their old ties and chose their country as their primary loyalty, not their newly adopted state. Thanks to opportunity, immigration, and the westward movement, nationalism developed more rapidly in the United States than in Europe, and provincialism was more easily overcome.

THE SOUTH AND ITS STRUGGLE FOR INDEPENDENCE

One section in the United States, the South, largely escaped these developments. The ultimate cause of its unique position was geographical. Only in the South was the climate favorable for growing cotton. This fact made little difference before 1800, and the social structure and intellectual outlook of this section did not differ greatly from the structure and outlook of the North. Indeed, nationalism found more adherents in the South than in New England around 1810. Only when the industrial revolution created a tremendous demand for cotton in Britain and Eli Whitney's invention of the cotton gin in 1793 made its cultivation practical did the South start on its separate way. More and more landowners abandoned their other crops for cotton. By 1820, 80,000 tons were being grown; by 1860, nearly 1,150,000 tons. The increase in cotton production depended on the use of slaves, and slavery became acceptable in Southern eyes. North and South grew further apart.

During the formative period of the republic, slavery had been generally decried. Jefferson, a Virginian, had included a clause prohibiting it in his Northwest Ordinance of 1787, and the Constitution permitted the abolition of the slave trade after twenty years. During the first half of the nineteenth century, Northern opinion became increasingly convinced that slavery was a moral evil, and the slaves north of the Mason-Dixon Line were freed by the individual states. Southerners, however, even before the advent of cotton, hesitated to advocate emancipation because the number of Negroes was already so large that the expense of compensating the owners would be great and the social problems that would be created seemed insurmountable. A society was formed to send the Negroes back to Africa, and in the 1820's there was a strong demand for the abolition of the "peculiar institution" in Virginia, but the growth of cotton culture soon made slavery seem an economic necessity. Southerners, especially in the deep

591

South, came to justify slavery. What had earlier been considered an evil that could not be eradicated now became a virtue that must be defended. Thus, the South slowly separated itself from the moral standards of the North and the civilized world.

The existence of slavery checked the growth of democracy in the South. Only a few could afford a plantation with a large number of slaves, and that few dominated political and social life. European immigrants avoided this region, where the governing class was a landed aristocracy not unlike the one that they were trying to escape and where they would have to compete with slave labor. They preferred to work in the factories in the Northern cities or to stake out a small farm in the West. Thus, Southern industry lagged far behind that of the North. In 1790, Charleston had been the fourth largest city in the country, with more inhabitants than Baltimore. It grew, but by 1850 Baltimore was four times its size, and there were new cities in the West that had become as large.

The absence of a large number of European immigrants also left local inhabitants free to perpetuate state loyalties and checked the development of nationalism. Thus, out of the climate came the cotton culture and the slave economy, and out of these developed the characteristics which separated the South from the rest of the nation.

From the earliest days of the republic, there had been quarrels between sections over the slavery question, over the protective tariff, which Northern industrialists demanded and Southern importers of European goods decried, and over states' rights. On each occasion, able statesmen had arisen to effect a compromise, but each compromise made future compromise more difficult and an eventual break seemed inevitable.

The rapid growth of the North made Southerners fearful of what the future held in store. At first, they dominated national politics because of support from the agrarian West, and in only twelve of its first sixty years did the republic have a president from the North. After 1850, however, the West began to shift towards the North, with which it had developed an economic link through the construction of canals and railroads and a moral link in a common love of the nation and a common abhorrence of slavery. In 1860, East and West joined in electing a Republican, Abraham Lincoln, as President. With the Republicans, a party had come into power that was dedicated to supporting the economic program of the industrial East and the free-soil program of the agrarian West. To the die-hard Southerner who loved his state, or at best his section, more than his country, the time had come to leave the Union.

Even before Lincoln was inaugurated, the states of the deep South had begun to secede from the Union and form the Confederate States of America. There were efforts at compromise, but neither Lincoln nor the overconfident leaders of the deep South were willing to bargain seriously. The question was whether the President could muster enough support in the North for his plan to reconquer the recalcitrant states. This issue was settled by the Southerners themselves when they fired on Fort Sumter on April 12, 1861. The North rallied to the flag, and war had come.

The South had no chance of victory unless outside help were obtained or the North tired of the war before achieving success. Industry, wealth, and sheer numbers were too weighted on the Northern side. For a time, intervention by the British and French appeared possible. The English aristocracy felt kinship with its Southern counterpart, and Napoleon III was eager to divide the United States, but Lincoln won wide support from world opinion by issuing a proclamation emancipating the slaves. British workers would rather see their cotton mills idle than fight a war to perpetuate the evil of slavery, and Napoleon III dared not act alone. The other chance for Southern success, that the North would tire of the war, also proved illusory. Lincoln's greatest gift was his ability to win public support for his policies, and his greatest determination was to use all his talents to preserve the Union. Despite defeat after defeat inflicted on the federal troops in Virginia through the superior generalship of Robert E. Lee and Stonewall Jackson, Lincoln was able to put new armies in the field. The South could find no replacements for its losses, and in the western theater of operations its troops were constantly driven back. Finally, at Appomattox in April, 1865, Lee was forced to surrender his remaining troops to the superior forces of General U. S. Grant.

National unity had triumphed over the separatist forces of states' rights, and the slaves, like the Russian serfs, had been emancipated. But beneath the surface, American statesmanship had failed. Unity had been achieved at a tremendous cost in lives and property, and one section of the country had been left embittered. The emancipation program had been achieved without compensation to the slave owners and without providing land, livelihood, or education for the freedmen. To the United States belongs the questionable distinction of being the only important country that did not, or could not, free its slaves peaceably.

LATIN AMERICA

Many parallels may be drawn between the historical development of the English and Spanish settlements in America. Both areas were large and well endowed with natural resources. Both were first settled by Asiatic peoples many thousands of years ago, both began to be visited by courageous, greedy, devout Europeans during the Renaissance, and independent states were established in both during the late eighteenth and early nineteenth centuries. Yet the differences are nearly as striking as the parallels, for in Latin America the forces of conservatism were nearly as strong as the forces of change.

COLONIAL LATIN AMERICA

The British established no prelates in their colonies; but a hierarchy of Catholic archbishops, bishops, and abbots came to Latin America. They taught and protected the Indians, but they also defended the established order. Spanish and Portuguese kings made large land grants to the Church, explorers, officials, and favorites, and these lands became the basis of an agricultural system of huge estates. The large, half-civilized Indian population generally served as the labor force. Where there were insufficient Indians or where they were exterminated, as in the West Indies and Brazil, Negro slaves were imported from Africa. The small white landholder who dominated North America except in its southernmost portion was an exception in Latin America. He could not compete with the Indian-Negro labor force, and the rugged mountains and hot jungles were less suitable for small farms than the plains and more temperate climate to the north. The Latin American aristocrat scorned trade and industry, like his European counterpart, and made little effort to develop the mineral resources of his homeland, other than gold and silver. Thus, Latin America had neither the large middle class nor the European farmers who led the British settlements so rapidly toward democracy. Instead, there was a landed aristocracy and an ecclesiastical hierarchy that had little desire for change.

Nevertheless, the colonial Latin American economy did expand. New land was brought under cultivation, the population grew rapidly, and trade between Spain and its colonies increased from 171,900,000 francs in 1753 to 638,500,000 in 1800. These developments were largely brought about by the *creoles* and the *mestizos*, the two classes that took the lead in fomenting change.

The creole was a pure-blooded European of the second generation or more. It might be supposed that an early comer to a new land who belonged to the dominant race would be in an advantageous position, but the Spanish made a practice of naming only citizens born in Spain to the important administrative and ecclesiastical posts. To them went the most extensive land grants and other favors. The creoles, loving titles, honors, and position, chafed under this injustice. They were often well-to-do landowners, but they also turned to mining and trade, where they were restricted by mercantile regulations that became another grievance.

The mestizo was of mixed European and Indian descent. He was a small businessman, an artisan in a town, or small farmer. Economically, he was better off than the Indian, but he was no more accepted by his mother's forbears than his father's. Sometimes able and energetic, he was anxious to improve his status and remove the stigma attached to his birth. The lot of the Indians and the Negroes was far worse, but they were usually too docile to play a revolutionary part. Tupac Amaru, descendant of the Inca rulers, did raise a serious revolt in 1780, only to be torn to

UNITED
STATES
OF
AMERICA

ST. LOUIS

VICEROYALTY OF NEW SPAIN

NEW ORLEANS

GULF OF MEXICO

TROPIC OF CANCER

ATLANTIC

CUBA

HAITI

PUERTO RICO

SANTIAGO

PORT
AU PRINCE

SANTO
DOMINGO

SAN
JUAN

MEXICO CITY

HONDURAS

JAMAICA

OCEAN

CARIBBEAN SEA

SAN JOSE

CARACAS

ORINOCO R.

PARAMARIBO

STABROEK

CAYENNE

VICEROYALTY OF NEW GRANADA

BOGOTA

GUIANA

QUITO

JAPURA R.

PUTUMAYO R.

NEGRO R.

JAPURA R.

MARANON R.

HUALLAGA R.

AMAZON R.

MADEIRA R.

PURUS R.

VICEROYALTY OF PERU

LIMA

VICEROYALTY OF BRAZIL

LA PAZ

CHUQUISACA

PACIFIC

TROPIC OF CAPRICORN

OCEAN

VICEROYALTY OF LA PLATA

ASUNCION

PARAGUAY R.

RIO DE JANEIRO

VALPARAISO

SANTIAGO

BUENOS AIRES

PARANA R.

URUGUAY R.

MONTEVIDEO

PATAGONIA

COLONIAL LATIN AMERICA
1790

BRITISH POSSESSIONS

FRENCH POSSESSIONS

SPANISH POSSESSIONS

PORTUGUESE POSSESSIONS

DUTCH POSSESSIONS

0   250   500   1000

SCALE OF MILES

pieces by the revengeful Spaniards, and the Negro Toussaint L'Ouverture, also a descendant of kings, led a slave insurrection that brought Haiti its independence in 1804, but only after he had died in a French prison.

But the desire for change was not enough. The educated creoles needed an ideological justification. They found it in the doctrines of the Enlightenment, in the example of the American and French revolutionaries, and finally in the still more recent liberalism. An opportunity was also necessary, and this was provided by Napoleon when he took possession of Spain and Portugal in 1807. The Portuguese royal family fled to Brazil, but Charles IV of Spain abdicated, and Joseph Bonaparte, not Charles's son, Ferdinand, was made king. Immediately, in one Spanish colony after another there were revolts in support of Ferdinand's claims. The conservatives were sincere in their desire to preserve the rights of their Bourbon king, but many creoles and mestizos were republicans who used Ferdinand's name as a shield to hide their ultimate purpose. As a result, the rebels were too much at cross purposes to hold their own; only in the Rio de la Plata (Argentina) were they successful.

THE HEIRS OF SPAIN

The Allied victory over Napoleon brought satisfaction to the upper-class conservatives in Spanish America, for Ferdinand was restored to the throne. The liberals, however, reacted quite differently since Ferdinand was totally unwilling to make concessions. In 1816, they revolted once more, this time against the very monarch whom they had supported against the Bonapartes several years before. They were successful for a number of reasons. Their aim was clear: to throw off the yoke of Spain. Their armies were more experienced; European soldiers and sailors of fortune who before had been engaged in the Napoleonic wars lent their assistance, and capable leaders appeared, like José de San Martín (1778-1850) in the south and Simón Bolívar (1783-1830) in the north. Both Great Britain and the United States gave diplomatic support, and by 1825 all that remained of the once mighty Spanish empire in the New World were a few West Indian islands.

At this point, the parallel development of the British and Spanish colonies ceased. The British colonies, as we know, formed a federal but united country. The bonds of union between the former colonies were strengthened by the adoption of a new constitution in 1789 and sealed forever by the unsuccessful bid of the southern states for independence between 1861 and 1865. The Spanish colonists, on the other hand, were never able to establish a united country. The four great viceroyalties into which the old empire was divided never joined together. Indeed, they showed a decided tendency to disintegrate as one subordinate jurisdiction after another proclaimed its independence. The viceroyalty of New

596

Simón Bolívar from a contemporary painting. (Bettmann Archive)

Spain became the independent state of Mexico in 1821, but Central America proclaimed its independence from the new state two years later and Texas followed suit in 1836. To make matters worse, Central America broke up into five separate states in 1838. The viceroyalty of New Granada also began as a single state but quickly separated into Colombia, Venezuela, and Ecuador. Much later, in 1903, Panama won its independence from Colombia. The viceroyalty of Rio de la Plata broke up into Argentina, Paraguay, Chile, Uruguay, and Bolivia. Only the relatively small viceroyalty of Peru managed to remain more or less intact.

Several factors explain this development. The area involved—from 6,000,000 to 7,000,000 square miles—was so huge that it would have been difficult to govern from a single capital. Even Bolívar, who recognized the advantages of unity, thought in terms of five or six independent states leagued together in a confederacy. In addition, Spanish America was subdivided by the Andes Mountains, a range so high that the very passes were 12,000 or more feet above sea level. Lesser ranges and jungles added to the geographical factors making for disunity. Even the Spanish had found it necessary to detach districts from the viceroyalties that were autonomous, and these districts became the nucleus of some of the separate states after the war for independence. Another cause for the break-up of the viceroyalties was the ambitious and quarrelsome character of many early leaders, who would rather establish themselves as independent rulers of small states than take orders from a rival who had claims to govern the area where they held power.

There is no need to pursue the individual histories of the former Spanish colonies. Mexico and Haiti experimented briefly with monarchy, but the remainder immediately established republics. These republics had constitutions which guaranteed the usual freedoms, except, in some instances,

597

freedom of religion. In practice, however, they quickly fell into the hands of strong men, who ruled as arbitrarily as the viceroys had done. Revolutions changed presidents as often as ballot boxes did.

The tumultuous history of the Spanish American republics must be attributed in part to the lack of experience in self-government. Even the creoles had been denied important administrative posts by the Spanish, and there had been no colonial legislatures. The Catholic Church and the large landowners were important and often anti-liberal forces in most countries, but even the idealist could reasonably doubt whether an overwhelmingly illiterate, racially mixed population could wisely choose its political leaders. As a result, both conservative and reformer were likely to seize and maintain power by force when other means failed. Often the issue at stake was only whether one faction or another would enjoy the profits of power, but there were also more serious issues. Conservatives sought to protect the huge estates of private individuals and of the Catholic Church and opposed giving legal equality to other religions. Liberals urged that the church and state be separated and religious toleration decreed. Sometimes reformers sought to confiscate the large individual and clerical estates and divide them among poor farmers. On the whole, however, land reforms made little progress, although slavery ceased to exist.

THE HEIR OF PORTUGAL

The Portuguese empire in the New World underwent a somewhat different experience. When it became known in 1807 that Napoleon planned to invade Portugal, the Portuguese royal family fled to Brazil, where it established the seat of its government. Even after Napoleon was overthrown, King John VI preferred to remain in Rio de Janeiro. In 1820, the neglected Portuguese revolted, established a constitutional monarchy, restored Brazil to its former colonial status, and told John to return to Lisbon. After some hesitation he complied, leaving his son, Peter, in Rio as regent. The Brazilians had enjoyed being the center of an empire for too long to accept a colonial status again, and Peter quickly saw that he would have to put himself at the head of the revolutionary forces or else abandon the country. He chose the former course, and in 1822 Brazil declared itself independent with Peter as its constitutional monarch. Peter acted vigorously to prevent Brazil's provinces from breaking away and forming separate states, but he soon lost popularity and in 1831 was forced to abdicate in favor of his youthful son. A regency followed which was marked by separatist movements and revolts, but in 1840 Peter II was declared of age.

The young monarch inherited the largest and most difficult country to govern in America; in many ways, it was also the most backward. Nearly half the 4,000,000 inhabitants were Negro or mulatto slaves, one tenth were freedmen, and another tenth were Indians living for the most part in a tribal state. Only a fifth of the population was white, and even they were frequently illiterate. Not over 5 or 6 per cent of the inhabitants could read or write. Fortunately, Peter was a man of unusual ability and sincerely dedicated to improving the condition of his subjects. He was an advocate of religious toleration and did not interfere with the freedom of the press even when he himself was attacked, a concession that few presidents of Latin America's so-called republics would have made. He encouraged education and fostered cultural development. Economic matters claimed his attention. Rubber and coffee began to be developed into major industries, and railroads were built. Perhaps his greatest contribution was the emancipation of the slaves by stages between 1871 and 1888. The population of Brazil more than tripled during his long reign. In spite of his reforms, or rather because of them, Peter was deposed in 1889. He had offended the Catholic Church by his toleration of Protestants, the land-owners by his freeing of the slaves, the military by his peaceful policies and his desire to keep them out of politics, and strangely enough the intellectuals, who had become doctrinaire republicans. But his work was partly done. The republican regimes that followed could not be called stable or democratic, but the country's economic development continued at an accelerated rate.

CONCLUSIONS

Around the middle of the nineteenth century, the age of the egalitarian revolutions came to an end. Beginning with the American Revolution, or even earlier if some minor uprisings are counted, the standards of rebellion had been raised time and again in the name of liberty, equality, and the right of a people to govern themselves. As a result of these rebellions, nearly all the colonies in the New World had won their independence, established more egalitarian forms of government, and eventually liberated their slaves. On the European continent, the emancipation of the serfs was the only important gain. Romanticism still challenged some of the basic tenets of the Enlightenment; industrialization was proceeding rapidly only in Great Britain, and the forces of conservatism everywhere held sway. Few in 1850 could have believed that the triumph of the Western world was only a generation or two away.

PART **V**

THE TRIUMPH OF
WESTERN CIVILIZATION

NEW WORLD	EUROPE	AFRO-ASIA
	1830-1854, Comte founds positivism	
	1846, Repeal of Corn Law in England marks victory for middle class and laissez-faire	
	1848, *Communist Manifesto*	
	1848-1916, Francis Joseph emperor of Austria-Hungary	
	c.1850-c.1914, "Age of Materialism"; realism in art and literature; Social Darwinism; great improvements in transportation and communication; rapid industrial expansion; growth of democracy; formation of labor unions; rise of nationalism in eastern Europe	**1850-1866,** Taiping rebellion
	1853-1856, Crimean War	
		c.1854, End of Japanese isolation
	1857, Flaubert's *Madame Bovary*	**1857,** End of British East India Company; India incorporated into British Empire
	1859, Darwin's *Origin of Species*	
	1859-1860, Kingdom of Italy formed	
1861-1865, American Civil War	**1861,** Emancipation of serfs in Russia	
	1862-1890, Ministry of Bismarck	
	1864, First International	
1865-1877, Period of Reconstruction		
1866, Cable laid between U.S. and Europe	**1866,** Seven Weeks War	
1867, Canada achieves dominion status; U.S. purchases Alaska	**1867,** Marx's *Das Kapital*	
	1867, Dual Monarchy of Austria and Hungary created	

NEW WORLD	EUROPE	AFRO-ASIA
	1867-1894, Gladstone leader of Liberal party	
	1867, Trade Union congresses begin	
1868-1870, Constiutional amendments in U.S. to guarantee voting and property rights	1868, Gladstone's first ministry	1868, Beginning of Meiji Era in Japan; rapid industrial growth and partial Westernization
		1869, Opening of Suez Canal; Stanley begins African exploration
	1870, Vatican Council proclaims doctrine of papal infallibility	
	1870-1871, Franco-Prussian War; Germany united	
	1874-1880, Disraeli Prime Minister	
c.1875-1917, Era of big business and reform in U.S.	c.1875, Revival of imperialism	c.1875, Revival of imperialism
c.1880, Increase in European immigration; "yellow press"	c.1880, Increase in European emigration	c.1880, Increase in European immigration
1881, American Federation of Labor founded		
	1883-1887, Nietzsche's most important work	
		1885, Indian National Congress organized
		1885-1898, Partition of Africa
	1888-1918, William II of Germany	
1889-1890, U.S. frontier declared closed		c.1889-c.1931, Growth of democracy in Japan
	1894-1918, Reign of Nicholas II of Russia	1894-1895, Sino-Japanese War
	1897-1906, Dreyfus affair	
1898, U.S. war with Spain; U.S. becomes world power		
		1899, "Open Door" policy in China
		1899-1902, Boer War
	1900, Labor party formed	
1901, Roosevelt Corollary	1902, Entente Cordiale	
1903, Ford begins mass-production of automobile		
		1904-1905, Russo-Japanese War
	1905, Revolution in Russia	
	1905-1914, Liberals institute welfare legislation and Parliamentary reform in England	
	1907, Triple Entente	
		1908, Young Turk rebellion
		1910, Union of South Africa formed
		1911-1912, Chinese Revolution; Manchus abdicate and Sun Yat-sen forms republic in South China
1913-1921, Woodrow Wilson President		
1917, U.S. enters World War I	1914-1918, First World War	
1918, Fourteen Points	1918, Treaty of Brest-Litovsk	
	1919, Peace Treaties	
1920, Women granted suffrage in U.S.	1920, League of Nations	

THE romantic era during the first half of the nineteenth century proved to be only a temporary setback to the spread of ideas and values espoused during the Enlightenment and, in some cases, during the more remote Renaissance. The second half of the nineteenth century witnessed the triumph of the empirical over the emotional. Materialism was once more emphasized in thought and naturalism in art. The conception that men were shaped by their environment and the hope that they could achieve perfection by manipulating that environment received a tremendous sanction from the Darwinian theory of evolution and from the growing influence of Marxian socialist thought.

The ideas of romanticism lingered on, but music was the only art in which their influence was decisive, and nationalism was the only important movement that drew its inspiration from them. Conservatives ceased trying to maintain the status quo and sought to remain in power by recasting themselves in a popular image. Germany and Italy were united by kings advised by noble ministers, not by popular uprisings as Mazzini had dreamed. In their hands nationalism itself became a conservative force that worked for the preservation of time-tested political and social institutions supposed to reflect the *Geist* of the people.

In spite of the tendency for nationalists and conservatives to draw together in some countries, rapid industrialization so strengthened the middle class that by 1914 it was ascendant, or seemed destined to be ascendant, everywhere. With the growing influence of this class, the egalitarian aspirations of the preceding period were largely achieved without violence. Among these aspirations were liberalism, with its constitutional guarantees of free speech, equality before the law, and trial by jury, and democracy with its ministerial responsibility and extended suffrage.

The victory of modern Western civilization was not limited to Europe and the Americas; emigrants, missionaries, and a revived imperialism carried it to Africa and much of Asia. Those non-European countries that managed to maintain their political independence did so at the cost of partially Westernizing on their own initiative. It is true that there were danger signals here and there. Liberalism came under attack from several directions, and there was a growing cult of violence that made some question the innate goodness of man. But, taken as a whole, the dreams of the philosophers of the Enlightenment seemed about to be fulfilled. Even World War I could be interpreted as an unpleasant but necessary experience in a movement to achieve liberty, equality, democracy, and self-determination for all people.

14/ Nationalism, Materialism, and Liberalism

T HE Revolution of 1848 proved to be a turning point in European history. During the decades that followed, nationalism triumphed in central Europe, materialism triumphed in the arts and sciences, and liberalism reached its peak, only to be threatened by new social and economic forces.

THE UNIFICATION OF ITALY AND OF GERMANY

The unification of Italy and of Germany could not take place so long as most of the great powers cooperated to maintain the status quo, as the events surrounding the Revolution of 1848 clearly showed.[1] Although the uprisings of that year accomplished nothing directly for the cause of nationalism, they assisted the unification movement indirectly by forcing

[1] See pages 547-550 and 556-560.

Metternich, the leading figure in the Concert of Europe, from office in Austria. In other countries as well, new leaders began to appear who were too young to remember the Napoleonic wars and who were willing to lie, deceive, and regard treaties as scraps of paper to be unilaterally destroyed when national interests were at stake. Among these new leaders was Napoleon III.

Between 1815 and 1848 the French kings had avoided foreign adventures that might upset the status quo, but Napoleon III was ever ready to fish in troubled international waters in the hope of increasing France's prestige abroad and winning support at home. He was a sincere friend of the nationalistic aspirations of disunited peoples and correctly foretold that nationalism was the wave of the future. By allying his dynasty with such a movement he hoped to ensure it a prominent place in the new era. At times he dreamed of an international congress that would redraw the map of Europe along nationalistic lines. At times he gave diplomatic and even military support to nationalistic movements, but his activities would probably not have led to the unification of Italy or Germany had not the Crimean War made the Concert of Europe ineffective.

THE CRIMEAN WAR

Napoleon had hardly come to power before he began to support Catholic priests in their quarrel with the Greek Orthodox clergy over who should control the holy sites in Palestine. In 1852 the sultan, persuaded by the presence of a French fleet, gave in to his overtures. Napoleon won a smile from French Catholics, but he infuriated the Russians, who sent a mission to Constantinople to secure recognition of their claim to protect Greek Orthodox Christians. When the Ottomans refused, the Russians decided to apply pressure, as the French had done, and sent troops into Moldavia and Wallachia, two Danubian principalities that were nominally under Turkish sovereignty. The great powers worked out a compromise, but the Ottomans, confident of eventual support, declared war on Russia in October, 1853.

At this point the Concert of Europe began to fall apart. The British press and public opinion were strongly pro-Turkish, and the long period of peace had engendered a desire for excitement that could be satisfied only by a foreign war. The British cabinet was too weak and divided to take firm action. Spurred on by public opinion and perhaps misunderstanding the Russian intentions, they declared war in March, 1854. The French followed suit because Napoleon III, mindful of the fact that British hostility had done much to topple the first empire, was determined to use this opportunity to win Britain's friendship. Sardinia later joined the conflict in the hope of winning British and French support for the cause of Italian unity.

The fighting centered on the Crimean Peninsula, where the allies finally took Sebastopol after a long siege. At this point the Austrians threatened to enter the war, in part because of British and French hints that active participation was necessary to keep them from aiding Sardinian efforts to unite Italy and in part because they felt that the Russians threatened their own interests in the Balkans. Faced with a military defeat and the prospect of a new enemy, the Russians sued for peace.

By the terms of the Treaty of Paris, 1856, the Russians suffered minor territorial losses and gave up claims to protect Christians in the Ottoman Empire. They also agreed to the neutralization of the Black Sea and the closing of the Dardanelles and the Bosporus to warships, provisions which prevented future advances directly to the south and in the Balkans. Moldavia and Wallachia were temporarily left under Turkish sovereignty, but they were united shortly thereafter; and in 1866 the new land was recognized as an independent state under the name of Rumania.

On the surface the Concert of Europe was restored, but genuine cooperation between the great powers ceased. The Russians, who had helped the Austrians to suppress the Magyars in 1849, now despised them for their ingratitude and became willing to countenance changes in Europe. They wanted to upset the status quo in order to regain what they had lost. English military leadership in the war had been so inept and the English people were so obviously cured of their desire for foreign adventure that the island kingdom ceased to carry as much weight in world affairs. Of the remaining great powers, both France and Prussia were willing to alter the Vienna settlement of 1815, and Austria alone could do nothing. Thus, the real significance of the Crimean War was that it cleared the way for the triumph of the forces of change in central and eastern Europe.

THE UNIFICATION OF ITALY

The Italians were the first to profit by the breakdown of the Concert of Europe. The failure of the Revolution of 1848 had discredited the republicans and had transformed Pope Pius IX into a conservative.[2] It had also focused the patriots' attention on Sardinia, although it was doubtful that this little state could provide the necessary leadership until King Victor Emmanuel named Count Camillo di Cavour (1810-1861) premier in 1852.

Cavour was a liberal, well-traveled nobleman with a great admiration for the English. He liked their parliamentary system, their economic philosophy of laissez-faire, and their industrial and agricultural techniques. Before becoming premier, he had introduced scientific farming on his estates and sponsored it elsewhere. He had also been an active leader in the effort to promote banks, railroads, and industry. In 1847, he had founded a liberal nationalistic newspaper, *Il Risorgimento*, which had helped to center attention on Sardinia, on the house of Savoy, and on himself.

Cavour was no radical. Indeed, he was no democrat. He accepted the Sardinian constitution, whose upper house was appointed for life by the

[2] See pages 556-560.

king and whose chamber of deputies was elected by limited suffrage. Was this not a close replica of the English Parliament after the Reform Bill of 1832? He governed with the help of the middle-of-the-road parties in the Chamber of Deputies. With their aid, he lowered tariffs, reorganized governmental finances and the army, and enacted legislation favorable to banks, railroads, and industry.

Cavour's reforms were not only intended to strengthen Sardinia; they also were designed to win the applause of Italians in other parts of the peninsula and above all to earn the sympathy of the French and English. The events of 1848 had shown clearly that French military help was needed to drive the Austrians out of Italy. English diplomatic support was needed to keep other powers from coming to Austria's aid. To secure the friendship of these states, Cavour had dispatched 17,000 Sardinian troops to aid them in the Crimean War. At the Paris peace conference he not only presented the Italian cause but made the acquaintance of Napoleon III.

Napoleon was deeply conscious of the Italian origins of his house and during his years in exile had actually joined the Carbonari and participated in the revolution of 1830. His Italian sympathies were buttressed by the belief that a short, successful Italian war would enhance his prestige in France. As a result, it was not difficult for Cavour to win from him a promise of assistance. At Plombières in 1858, the two wily statesmen agreed to create an Italian federation under the presidency of the pope. This federation was to consist of the two Sicilies, Rome, a new kingdom of central Italy centered on Tuscany, and an upper Italian kingdom centered on Sardinia but including the Austrian territories of Lombardy and Venetia, part of the papal states, and several smaller states. Obviously these changes could be brought about only by war, but Napoleon promised assistance, provided Cavour made Austria seem the aggressor. In return, Sardinia was to cede Nice and Savoy to France.

Cavour had no intention of accepting the presidency of the pope or the creation of a kingdom of central Italy in spite of what he had told Napoleon. He had to agree to these proposals in order to get a guarantee of French assistance. By one action after another, he provoked Austria, and in April, 1859, Emperor Francis Joseph foolishly gave his troops orders to march. In doing so, he seemed to be the aggressor; the French dispatched the promised aid, and at Magenta and Solferino the Austrians were defeated. At this point, there was a sudden turn of events that seemed certain to dash all of Cavour's hopes. Without consulting his ally, Napoleon made a peace with Austria at Villafranca in which only Lombardy was given to Sardinia.

Napoleon's decision to abandon the original, more ambitious scheme resulted from several considerations. The Austrian army had fought well and was lodged in a strong defensive position. A single defeat might cost him his throne. French Catholics were opposed to the dismemberment of the papal states, and French patriots foresaw a threat if a strong upper Italian

UNIFICATION OF ITALY

1859	JOINED BY PLEBISCITE TO SARDINIA
1860	JOINED BY REVOLUTION AND PLEBISCITE WITH SARDINIA TO FORM KINGDOM OF ITALY
1866, 1870	JOINED WITH KINGDOM OF ITALY
------	BOUNDARY OF THE KINGDOM OF ITALY 1866-1919

kingdom were created next to France. Furthermore, Prussia was mobilizing with the apparent intention of coming to the aid of Austria. Napoleon was unwilling to risk fighting simultaneously on the Rhine and Italy, and he acted accordingly.

Cavour was furious, but just when it seemed that his policy had failed, nationalists seized control of Parma, Modena, Tuscany, and part of the papal states. In a plebiscite, they voted to join Sardinia; and Napoleon, in return for Nice and Savoy, agreed to the annexations. But the two Sicilies, the bulk of the papal states, and Venetia remained outside the new Italian state.

At this point, the revolutionary spirit of the nationalists once more came to the rescue. Garibaldi set out for Sicily with about a thousand red-shirted patriots. His troops were greatly outnumbered by those of the Bourbon king, but for once his maxim "Fortune favors the bold" proved correct. He was welcomed by most of the inhabitants. Sicily and then Naples

Giuseppe Garibaldi. (Courtesy Free Library of Philadelphia)

fell before his furious onslaught, and the last of the Bourbon rulers in Italy, deserted by his subjects, fled to Rome.

Meanwhile, Cavour had maintained an officially correct attitude in order not to offend neutral opinion, while at the same time giving undercover assistance to Garibaldi. However, the rapid course of events soon forced him to show his hand. Garibaldi was a republican, not a monarchist, and he was becoming more famous than King Victor Emmanuel. Equally dangerous, he had begun with typical irresponsibility to move on Rome. If Rome were attacked, Napoleon seemed certain to intervene, in deference to Catholic opinion at home, on the side of the pope. To prevent this, Cavour marched southward through the papal states in order to put his troops between Garibaldi and Rome. There was a moment of uncertainty, but Garibaldi, still republican at heart, was persuaded to surrender his power to Victor Emmanuel although he refused all titles and public honors. Victor Emmanuel was proclaimed King of Italy on March 17, 1861, but Cavour died a few months later, leaving Rome and Venetia still outside the new kingdom.

Thus far the French army had been the greatest military factor in the steps taken towards Italian unity, but the Prussian army now assumed this role. In 1866, Italy joined Prussia in a war against Austria. The Italian troops were defeated, but a Prussian victory brought Venetia to the new kingdom. In 1870, war broke out between Prussia and France, and Napoleon had to withdraw his troops from Rome. The Italians annexed the city, and the pope shut himself up in the Vatican palace, declaring that he was a prisoner. There he and his successors remained until 1929, when a settlement was made with the none-too-devout dictator, Benito Mussolini.

Mazzini and Garibaldi had provided the inspiration and Cavour the

609

diplomatic skill that had brought about the geographical unity of Italy. To less able men was left the equally difficult task of making the young kingdom a truly united modern state. The upper classes enjoyed a common language and culture, but the lower classes in each of the former states had their own dialects. Seventy-eight per cent of the population was illiterate. The customs, laws, and traditions; the weights, measures, and coinage of each of the former states were different. There were no railroads connecting the various parts of the country and few natural resources to support badly needed industries.

Faced with such tremendous problems, there is little wonder that the Italians had few conspicuous successes. They borrowed their constitution from Sardinia and their administrative system from the French. The country was divided into fifty-three departments, each under a prefect who was directly responsible to the central government. A common army and navy, a single legal code, and a uniform system of weights and measures were established. But despite every effort, Italy remained weak, poor, and divided. Differences between the northern Italian and the more backward southern Italian have not been erased even to this day. Thus, Italy emerged in 1870 as a geographically united state with claims to the status of a great power but with internal weaknesses that made that claim ineffective.

THE UNIFICATION OF GERMANY

The decade following the Revolution of 1848 was one of reaction in nearly all the central European states. Austria led the way, and conservative forces were strong in Prussia as well. Nevertheless, the latter state remained the hope of most of the liberal nationalists because it had appeared more inclined to support German unification than Austria, and it had emerged from the Revolution with a constitution that called for a two-house legislature. The upper house was the bulwark of the privileged, but the lower house was elected by an unusual type of universal manhood suffrage. Those who paid the top third of the taxes elected one-third the deputies, those who paid the next third of the taxes elected a second third, and the remaining 83 per cent of the population elected the last third. The result was that the aristocracy and middle class controlled the lower house, but the fact that the lower classes had any voice at all appeared radical at that time. In contemporary Britain, they could not vote, and in the second French empire elections were manipulated to such a degree that balloting was almost meaningless. The Prussian Landtag, or parliament, could vote taxes and laws, but the ministers were responsible to the king, who could issue ordinances on his own authority when the Landtag was not in session. This constitution remained in effect until 1918.

Other factors also kept Prussia high in liberal favor. A group of very able historians had become fascinated with the policies and accomplishments of the Hohenzollern dynasty which they incorrectly assumed were

THE FORMATION OF THE GERMAN EMPIRE

– – –	BOUNDARY OF THE GERMAN CONFEDERATION OF 1815	
———	BOUNDARY OF THE GERMAN EMPIRE 1871–1918	
	KINGDOM OF PRUSSIA BEFORE 1866	
	ANNEXED BY PRUSSIA 1866	
1867	ENTERED NORTH GERMAN CONFEDERATION	
1871	ENTERED GERMAN EMPIRE AS MEMBER STATE	
	ALSACE–LORRAINE ANNEXED	

SCALE OF MILES
0 50 100 200 300

designed to lead to German unification. Their work did much to popularize the family at the expense of the reactionary Habsburgs. Then, too, the *Zollverein* bound the smaller states close to Prussia, although most of the German princes continued to prefer the Habsburgs to the Hohenzollerns until after 1866.

In 1858, Frederick William was declared insane, and his sixty-one-year-old brother, William became regent and finally king. William (1861-1888) was conservative, but he was an honest, conscientious man with the mental stability that his brother lacked. When Italian successes in 1859-1860 fanned liberal hopes, a National Union society was formed to achieve a united Germany. Most of its leaders looked to Prussia, but their hopes were suddenly crushed by William's army reform program.

Liberals and conservatives agreed that the army must be strengthened if Prussia were to remain a great power, but William wanted a professional army, officered by the junkers, that would be trustworthy in the face of foreign attack and domestic insurrection. The liberals wanted to place greater reliance on reserves that were officered in part by the middle class. Such an army, to William, was a "band of uncouth individuals" that was unlikely to support the crown if the uprisings of 1848 were repeated. A long struggle followed. Each new election increased the liberal and progressive strength in the lower house. William considered abdicating, but as a last resort he named the forty-seven-year-old Count Otto von Bismarck (1815-1898) chancellor.

Bismarck was a tall, erect, broad-shouldered, energetic man. He had served as the Prussian representative to the Confederation's diet, where he had come to the conclusion that war with Austria was inevitable, and as ambassador to France and Russia, where he formed ties that were later to be useful to him. The policy he followed during his twenty-eight years in office was based on three loyalties that guided his whole life. His first loyalty was to the Hohenzollern dynasty. "I am first and foremost a royalist," he wrote; "everything else comes after that." His second loyalty was to his class. "I was born and raised as an aristocrat," he declared; and while he was often contemptuous of the narrow stupidity of his fellow junkers, he never ceased to defend what he conceived to be their true interests. His third loyalty was to his church. He was a sincere Lutheran who never freed himself from a deep-seated suspicion of Catholicism.

These loyalties all pointed toward the same policy. Bismarck believed that the forces of nationalism would sooner or later lead to German unity. If this were accomplished through the efforts of a Hohenzollern king assisted by his loyal junkers, both the dynasty and the class could have a prominent place in the new Germany. If it were accomplished by the Habsburgs, the Hohenzollerns would be little more than great nobles, and the Catholic religion of Austria and south Germany would predominate. If it were accomplished by a popular uprising, both dynasties and the junkers would be thrown out. As a result, Bismarck early adopted the *Kleindeutsch* solution to be achieved by Prussian efforts.[3] Only in this manner could he assure the future of king, class, and church.

Since it was clear that Austria could never be persuaded to permit Prussia to unify Germany, war was necessary. "Not through speeches and majority decisions are the great questions of the day decided," he declared, "that was the great mistake of 1848 and 1849—but through blood and iron." To prepare Prussia for the test to come, he threw himself behind William's plans. When the lower house refused to vote money for the army, he went ahead and collected the necessary taxes anyway. This action forfeited the good will of the liberals, but, as in 1848, they hesitated to lead the lower classes in a bloody revolt. When the Schleswig-Holstein question

[3] See pages 556-559.

came to the fore in 1864, the army under the able Helmuth von Moltke (1800-1891) was ready.

The Schleswig-Holstein question was an extremely complicated one. Lord Palmerston, long-time British foreign minister, had once declared that only three men had ever understood it; one had died, one had gone crazy, and the third, himself, had forgotten all about it. Suffice it to say that the two duchies had been recognized as inseparable since 1460, but one, Holstein, was in the Germanic Confederation, and the other was not. Both were ruled by the King of Denmark. Holstein was entirely German, and Schleswig was partly so. Hence, German national feeling was inflamed when the Danish king arbitrarily incorporated Schleswig into Denmark. Bismarck saw his opportunity and, in conjunction with Austria, attacked the Danes. The war was relatively bloodless, and by October the Danes were willing to surrender both duchies.

Then followed two years of haggling between the victorious powers over what should be done with the spoils of war. While Bismarck goaded Austria into attacking him, he sought to isolate his intended victim. Russia had nursed a grievance against Austria since the Crimean War, when the Habsburgs had leaned towards France and Great Britain rather than toward their former ally, this despite Russian aid in quelling the Hungarian rebellion in 1849. Prussia had been more friendly, and in 1863 Bismarck was most sympathetic when the Poles had revolted against the tsar. Clearly, Russia would not again impose the status quo on its western neighbor. France was lured into neutrality with a vague promise of some Rhineland provinces, and Italy became an active ally in return for the promise of Venetia. Only in Germany itself did Bismarck's diplomacy fail. The diet sided with Austria, and the bulk of the German princes lent the Habsburgs military support when hostilities commenced in June, 1866.

The war was amazingly brief. The Austrians defeated the Italians, but the Prussians quickly overcame the Habsburgs' German allies and at Königgrätz won a decisive victory over Austria itself. The Prussian victories were due in part to the army reform, in part to Moltke's intelligent use of railroads, and in part to the adoption of the breech-loading rifle that could be fired from a prone position rather than from the standing position required by Austria's old muzzle-loaders.

The peace ending the Seven Weeks War, as this conflict was called, marked the end of the Germanic Confederation. Austria was excluded from Germany, and the territory of its allies north of the Main River was incorporated into Prussia along with Schleswig and Holstein. With the remaining northern German states, Bismarck formed the North German Confederation. He took nothing from Austria, and the southern German states were left completely free because he did not want to drive them into the arms of France. Italy did get previously promised Venetia, but this was Austria's only territorial loss.

Napoleon III was shocked. He had counted on a long war in which both sides became exhausted. At that point, he planned to impose a peace that was favorable to France and included the acquisition of some Rhineland provinces. To his postwar requests for compensation in the Rhineland, Belgium, or Luxembourg, however, Bismarck turned a deaf ear because he no longer needed French neutrality. Napoleon's demands served only to drive the frightened southern German states into a defensive alliance with Prussia and to make Britain, ever anxious to keep Belgium out of the hands of a strong power, doubly suspicious of France. Napoleon sought an alliance with the Habsburgs; but Francis Joseph held back, in part because of internal difficulties, in part because Russia's close ties with Prussia made him doubly fearful of a new war, and in part because he had been so leniently treated by his recent enemy. Napoleon then turned to Italy for support, but its price was the withdrawal of French protection of Rome, and this the emperor of Catholic France could not do. So Napoleon remained isolated while his astute opponent looked for means to goad him into war, for Bismarck well knew that further progress towards unification could be achieved only by "blood and iron." France could not permit a united Germany to be formed that would be a constant threat to its security, and the particularistic inhabitants of the southern German states would not join with Prussia unless their patriotism was fired by a victorious war in the defense of the fatherland.

Bismarck did not have long to wait. In 1868, the Spanish overthrew their worthless, immoral queen. After some debate, the vacant throne was offered to Leopold of Hohenzollern-Sigmaringen, a distant relative of the Prussian ruling family. Leopold refused, but Bismarck pulled various strings; the offer was renewed, and this time Leopold accepted. The French reacted as Bismarck intended. There were cries that to put a Hohenzollern on the Spanish throne was to recreate the empire of Charles V. King William himself had no desire for war, and to Bismarck's dismay he hinted to his cousin that he would like him to reject the Spanish offer once more. This the Hohenzollern-Sigmaringen family did, but Napoleon refused to let the affair die because he needed a greater diplomatic triumph to strengthen his position at home. On July 12, 1870, the French ambassador was instructed to extract a promise that never in the future would Leopold be permitted to become a candidate. On the morning of the 13th, the ambassador sought an early audience with William who was then vacationing at Ems, but he was put off until later in the day. Rudely, he waylaid the king in a garden, but the venerable old man refused his request, saying that "You are asking a promise without limit of time and for all conditions."

Bismarck was sulking with Moltke and the war minister when he received the royal dispatch from Ems telling him what had occurred. He saw his chance. Quickly he stripped from the account of the meeting all the niceties and extra words. What was left was a factually correct statement that made the French ambassador seem ruder than he was and made William's unwillingness to be further committed seem like a curt refusal. "This,"

Bismarck gleefully declared, "will have the effect of a red cloth upon the Gallic bull." And he released the condensed version to the newspapers.

The French responded as anticipated. Extremists demanded war; Napoleon's advisers were anxious for an opportunity to humiliate Prussia, and the sickly emperor himself was finally persuaded that the prestige of the monarchy could be maintained only by war. Without waiting to hear their ambassador's account of his meeting with the Prussian king, without an ally, the French acted on the blind faith that "the army is ready down to the last gaiter button." The first official document the Prussians received after the Ems episode was a declaration of hostilities. World opinion sided with the Prussians, and a wave of nationalistic feeling swept over Germany. The southern German states joined with Prussia, and three armies swept into France. One French army was bottled up in Metz, and another was captured at Sedan. Napoleon was taken prisoner, Paris capitulated in January, 1871, and the Peace of Frankfurt ending the war was signed in May.

By the terms of the treaty, France ceded Alsace and part of Lorraine. These provinces had once been part of the Holy Roman Empire and were still predominantly German in language and culture. However, the bulk of the inhabitants preferred to remain with France. In addition, an indemnity of $1,000,000,000 was demanded. Until it was paid, there was to be an army of occupation. These terms were less harsh than those the first Napoleon had meted out to Prussia two generations before, but they were severe enough to prevent friendly relations between the two countries from that day. The Prussians missed no opportunity to humiliate their opponents. As a crowning blow it was in the Hall of Mirrors of the palace of Versailles that had reflected the glories of Louis XIV that William I was proclaimed German emperor. The southern German states had consented to join with Prussia, and German unity had been achieved.

Bismarck could look on his work with satisfaction. Germany had been united by the Hohenzollerns, the junkers, and the Lutherans. The future of the three seemed assured, for it was Germany that had been merged into Prussia, not Prussia into Germany.

The liberal nationalists were also exultant. Their dream had been "Unity! Freedom!" The first had been achieved, and the second seemed within their grasp. Yet unconsciously many of them had turned from their goal. The brilliant triumphs of the Hohenzollerns had taught them too much respect for authority and power. The Prussian Landtag had passed a bill of indemnity after the Seven Weeks War which said in effect that Bismarck had been justified in collecting taxes without its consent because of the victory he had won. One old liberal wrote: "I cannot shake off the impression of the hour. I am no devotee of Mars; I feel more attached to the goddess of beauty and the mother of graces than to the powerful god of war, but the trophies of war exercise a magic charm even upon the child of peace. One's view is involuntarily chained and one's spirit goes along with

AUSTRIA – HUNGARY

AUSTRIAN EMPIRE

KINGDOM OF HUNGARY

OCCUPIED BY AUSTRIA 1878
ANNEXED 1908

SCALE OF MILES

0 25 50   100   150

KINGDOM OF PRUSSIA

RUSSIAN EMPIRE

AUSTRIAN EMPIRE

GALICIA

RUTHENIA

BUKOVINA

DNIESTER R.

BLACK SEA

RUMANIA

DANUBE R.

TURKEY

BULGARIA

TRANSYLVANIA

ALUTA R.

THEISS R.

MAROS R.

MORAVA R.

KINGDOM

OF

HUNGARY

BANAT

SERBIA

DANUBE R.

BUDAPEST

MORAVIA

PRAGUE

BOHEMIA

VIENNA

AUSTRIA

DRAVA R.

CROATIA – SLAVONIA

BOSNIA-
HERZEGOVINA

MONTENEGRO

ALBANIA

DALMATIA

ADRIATIC SEA

CARNIOLA

TYROL

SWITZERLAND

ITALY

CORSICA

SARDINIA

45°

15°

10°

the boundless rows of men who acclaim the god of the moment—success."

Germany had been seduced by victory itself. Prior to 1860 the typical German had been thought of as a kindly, impractical man—a lover of good books, good music, and good beer. Thereafter, the world saw him as an energetic, efficient, practical man who would stop at nothing to achieve his ends. Neither picture was completely accurate, but the failure of the Frankfurt liberals in 1848 and the success of Bismarck's policy of "blood and iron" did have a profound effect on the German mind.

THE DUAL MONARCHY

Meanwhile, a settlement was being made in the remainder of central Europe. With the Habsburgs' victory in 1849, centralized, autocratic government had been restored, and even Hungary had lost its privileged position. This system, which had been resisted by liberal Germans and minority races alike, was discredited by the defeat inflicted by the French and Italians in 1859. A new solution had to be found, and in February, 1861, a parliament was established with a nominated House of Lords and an elected House of Representatives chosen by a complicated formula designed to give control to the German middle class. This satisfied the Germans, but the Magyars remained discontented. Only when the government's weakness was again revealed, this time by the Prussians during the Seven Weeks War, did Francis Joseph make further concessions. The result was the creation of the dual monarchy of Austria-Hungary in 1867.

By the terms of the compromise, the Magyars got nearly all they had sought during the revolution of 1848. Hungary was made an autonomous kingdom consisting of the ancient lands of the crown of Saint Stephen, and the subject peoples in this area were placed under its control. There was to be a parliament and a responsible ministry that met in the capital, Budapest. A second parliament for the remainder of the empire sat at Vienna. Here the Germans predominated, but the Slavic races were given some recognition. Each state was to handle its internal affairs, but they maintained a united front before Europe by having a common emperor, common ministries of foreign affairs and war, and a tariff union. Deputations between the two parliaments met annually to decide matters of common interest. This solution satisfied the Germans, the Magyars, and Francis Joseph, who retained considerable influence over foreign affairs and the army, to him the true marks of sovereignty. Only the Slavs who made up over half the population remained dissatisfied, and their dissatisfaction was eventually to destroy the dual monarchy that had neglected their nationalistic aspirations.

CONCLUSIONS

By 1871 the Germans, Italians, and Magyars had fulfilled their nationalistic dreams; of the major continental European peoples, only the

617

Slavs of eastern Europe still had no country that they could call their own. These great changes, which had taken place in little more than a decade, had not been accomplished by romantic, liberal idealists like Mazzini, but by aristocratic realists who had not hesitated to employ lies and deceit to secure their aims. "If we did for ourselves what we do for Italy," Cavour declared, "we would be great rascals." National interests became an acceptable reason for ignoring international obligations, and the law of the jungle replaced the Concert of Europe.

Statesmen were not alone in embracing the new policy of realism, or *Realpolitik* as it was often called. Ordinary citizens became ashamed of what they now regarded as their impractical idealism of the pre-1848 era and awarded their accolades to those leaders whose policies brought the desired results regardless of the means that were used. In this manner the world of diplomacy became realistic and practical during the very years when an age of materialism was replacing an age of romanticism in thought and aesthetics.

THE AGE OF MATERIALISM

Science and psychology contributed heavily toward making the last half of the nineteenth century an age of materialism. They also provided scientific evidence in support of two convictions of the Enlightenment: that man was molded by his environment and that progress toward human perfection was possible. Of the sciences, biology loomed as the most important; and of the biologists, Charles Darwin stood above the others, as Copernicus and Newton had stood above their colleagues during earlier ages.

DARWIN AND EVOLUTION

Charles Darwin was born in Shrewsbury, England, in 1809. His academic record at the local school was far from enviable, but he went on to Edinburgh to read medicine and from there to Cambridge to study for the ministry. He devoted more of his time to biology and geology than to any other academic pursuit; what had been a hobby became a vocation. He abandoned his intention of becoming a clergyman and in 1831 accepted an appointment as naturalist on *H.M.S. Beagle,* which was dispatched to survey the land masses of much of the Southern Hemisphere. For five years, he traveled in South American and Pacific waters studying geological formations and especially the structure of various forms of animal life. Upon his return, he published several books describing his specific discoveries, and in 1859 his revolutionary work, *The Origin of Species,* appeared. In it he showed that man and other forms of animal life "are descended from at the most only four or five progenitors, and plants from an equal or lesser number." He held forth the possibility that all plant and animal life had a common ancestor.

The idea of evolution was not new. Historians, philosophers, and political theorists had put great emphasis on the evolution of society and institutions during the romantic period. Some biologists, including Dar-

*Charles Darwin at about
seventy years of age by
John Collier. (National
Portrait Gallery, London)*

win's grandfather, had discussed the possibility of changing plant and animal life, but their theories had not been accepted for four reasons. First, the earth was not generally considered to be old enough to permit biological evolution; second, plant and animal life were not thought to be composed of the same basic substance; third, no one had explained how new species could originate even if all life were composed of the same substance; and fourth, insufficient empirical evidence had been presented to support such a belief.

Darwin was fortunate in that the first and second obstacles had been removed by the time he published his book. For several generations, some geologists had been arguing that the surface of the earth was constantly changing and that it could not have reached its present form unless it had been created before 4004 B.C., the date of creation preferred by most theologians. In 1830, Sir Charles Lyell began to publish his three-volume *Principles of Geology,* which offered so much evidence of the great antiquity of the earth and of the gradual evolution of its surface that these ideas became generally accepted by scientists. A few years later, two Germans showed that all plant and animal life was composed of cells. The difference between a man and a tree resulted from different combinations of slightly different types of cells. They could, therefore, have had a common ancestor.

Darwin's contribution was to show how these cells developed into different forms of life. He got his inspiration from Malthus' argument that a

620

man reproduces himself more rapidly than his food supply increases. "Many more individuals of each species are born than can possibly survive"; Darwin declared, "and as, consequently, there is a frequently recurring struggle for existence, it follows that any being, if it vary however slightly in any manner of life, will have a better chance of surviving, and thus be *naturally selected.*" How came one being to vary slightly from another? Darwin's answer was chance inheritance. Two animals born to the same parents will vary slightly. One may be colored a little differently so that it can hide better from the enemies of that species, or it may be able to move a little faster, resist cold a little better, or possess some other advantage that enables it to survive while the other perishes. The survivor passes on to its offspring the fortunate characteristic that enabled it to live, and thus, Darwin believed, new species gradually came into being just as the earth's surface slowly changed through endless time.

Darwin's empirical proof was not absolutely complete, but he offered so much evidence that within a decade his theory had been accepted by most biologists and was being applied by some historians, sociologists, philosophers, and others to their respective fields of scholarship.

There was, however, resistance. Religious fundamentalists were horrified to find scientists discrediting the Biblical account of the creation. Others were more upset to find man treated as an animal. Copernicus had shown that the earth was not the center of a universe created for man; now Darwin was indicating that even on his tiny planet man was but another species that had evolved from lower forms of life and would in the remote future be a different sort of animal. Still others were upset to find the older conception of a harmonious, mechanical universe being cast aside for an organic, changing universe based on the struggle for survival. Nevertheless, in time, the opponents of the Darwinian theory became reconciled. Some agreed with Darwin when he quoted a theologian as saying that "he has gradually learnt to see that it is just as noble a conception of the Deity to believe that He created a few original forms capable of self-development into other and needful forms, as to believe that He required a fresh act of creation to supply voids caused by the action of His laws." Or with Darwin himself when he declared, "For my part I would as soon be descended from that heroic little monkey who braved his dreaded enemy in order to save the life of his keeper, or from that old baboon, who, descending from the mountains, carried away in triumph his young comrade from a crowd of astonished dogs—as from a savage who delights to torture his enemies, offers up bloody sacrifices, practices infanticide without remorse, treats his wives like slaves, knows no decency, and is haunted by the grossest superstitions."

The overall effect of the Darwinian theory was to add scientific proof for three beliefs that had been held by many since the Enlightenment. One was that man was molded by his environment, for it was the environment that determined which of a slightly different progeny would survive. A second belief was in progress and human perfectibility. If man had come from a primitive organism to his present state, he would in the distant future, Darwin believed, "be a far more perfect creature than he now is." A third belief was in the inductive method, for it had been through the use of this tool that Darwin had arrived at his great discovery. The speculation of the romantics and their emphasis on "inner truths" were largely abandoned for the gathering, weighing, and measuring of material things.

PSYCHOLOGY AND MEDICINE

The three beliefs which had been aided by the theory of evolution were furthered by developments in other sciences. Psychology, for example, had been a field reserved for deductive philosophical speculation, but in 1873 a German, Wilhelm Wundt (1832-1920), published his *Principles of Physiological Psychology* in which he insisted that the human mind must be studied by the same laboratory methods as physiology. A Russian, Ivan Pavlov (1849-1936), won the Nobel prize in 1904 for experiments on conditioned reflexes. He found that saliva would come to a dog's mouth when it heard a tuning fork, provided the fork had been sounded on previous occasions when the animal had been given meat. If the dog's reaction was conditioned by its environment, might not man's be? The behavioristic school of psychology was developed largely by an American, J. B. Watson (1878-1958), to investigate this problem. Evidence was produced indicating that a new-born baby had few responses and that conditioned reflexes were built up as it grew older. Thus, environment becomes the controlling influence on man's actions. If subjected to the proper stimuli from earliest childhood, man could become a happier, better being. Psychology, like biology, pointed to the possibility of progress and human perfection.

In medicine, the discovery of the germ theory of disease, the use of antiseptics, and the growth of sanitation made longer, healthier, and presumably happier lives possible. In 1854 Louis Pasteur (1822-1895) began studies in France which led to his discovery that fermentation was not caused by spontaneous growth, as had been supposed, but by tiny bacteria. If bacteria could cause beer or wine to ferment, might not other germs cause disease in plants and animals? Pasteur and Robert Koch (1843-1910) carried on a series of independent experiments in which they proved that germs were responsible for anthrax, rabies, tuberculosis, and cholera. Other scientists identified the diphtheria and typhoid germs. When a germ was discovered, it was generally possible to develop an inoculation that would protect the human being and the animal from its ravages. Joseph Lister (1827-1912) was led by Pasteur's experiments to believe that all diseases were caused by germs. To prevent germs from entering the human body during surgery, he began to wash his instruments in carbolic acid, with epoch-making results. In Vienna, the use of disinfectants cut the deaths

622

of mothers from infection in childbirth from one in six to one in a hundred. Anesthetics came into use around 1850 and added to the patients' comfort. Where life could not be protected by inoculation, or the germ killed by disinfectants, the carrier of the germ was sought. Malaria and yellow fever were found to be carried by the mosquito, and Koch showed that the bubonic plague was transmitted by fleas from rats. Formerly nuisances to be politely ignored, mosquitoes, rats, and fleas became enemies to be destroyed. Sewage, garbage disposal, and a good water supply became the concern of progressive municipal governments. Between 1890 and 1910, the number of deaths per 1,000 people in England and Wales was cut by a third, and over ten years was added to life expectancy in civilized countries. For the first time, inhabitants of cities, now sanitary and provided with good hospitals and doctors, could hope for healthier, longer lives than the inhabitants of the country.

CHEMISTRY AND PHYSICS

While biologists after 1850 were showing how living organisms evolved, while psychologists were explaining the functioning of the mind and medical scientists were utilizing the germ theory of disease, chemists were explaining the nature of matter. Their synthesis, like that of the biologists, was based on two earlier discoveries. One was Lavoisier's dictum that matter was immortal; it could be neither created nor destroyed. The other was John Dalton's (1766-1844) research during the early nineteenth century on the atom. Dalton noted that if he combined five parts of carbon by weight with one of hydrogen, an entirely new substance, ethylene gas, was produced. Regardless of how large or how small a unit he used, he got the same results. He gave the smallest conceivable unit of carbon and of hydrogen the old Greek name of *atom.*

Scientists began to speculate that the universe might be composed of the atoms of these and a few other basic *elements,* which sometimes occurred in their natural state and sometimes combined in *compounds* such as ethylene gas. Chemists during the last half of the nineteenth century undertook the task of gathering evidence to support this theory. This work led to an important discovery in 1869 by a Russian, Dmitri Mendeleev (1834-1907), who found that if he arranged the known elements in a table in order of their atomic weights, beginning with hydrogen, every eighth element possessed somewhat similar characteristics. When a gap appeared in his table, he predicted that an unknown element must exist with an atomic weight which would justify its inclusion. He was right, and before his death the missing elements had been found. Chemists now felt that they could assert with confidence that the earth consisted of the atoms of ninety-two elements. Meanwhile, the technique of spectrum analysis had been developed, which enabled scientists to determine the elements in a source of light, and it was found that the sun was composed of the same substances as the earth. It followed that the atoms of ninety-two elements composed the universe.

A theoretical basis had been laid for the development of industrial chemistry. Ways were found to produce and use such little-known elements as aluminum, chromium, and tungsten. Other elements were combined to produce countless new compounds and mixtures. Coal, for example, was found to yield a variety of substances, from the dyes so necessary for the textile industry to quinine so useful against malaria. Chemistry became so highly diversified that it was subdivided into an organic and an inorganic branch; various sub-fields also developed. Industries began to employ chemists to carry on research, and by 1914 the industrial laboratory had begun to make significant contributions to science.

Physics also moved forward, although the greatest developments in this field were not to come until the end of the century. Just before 1850, the law of the conservation of energy was formulated. This law stated that energy could be neither created nor destroyed. Energy could be transformed into motion, and, it was soon discovered, motion could be transformed into energy. This law brought to an end useless speculation concerning the possibility of a perpetual motion machine and led to the development of two new sources of power. In 1819, Hans Oersted (1777-1851) had demonstrated that magnetism, and through it, motion, could be produced by electricity. Twelve years later, Michael Faraday (1791-1867) reversed the experiment by inducing an electric current with a magnet; this experiment led to the invention of the electric dynamo. Electricity could now be used to produce motion, and motion to produce electricity.

INVENTIONS

The practical value of these discoveries can hardly be overestimated. Communication literally became as swift as lightning with the invention of the telegraph by Samuel Morse (1791-1872). Washington and New York were connected by a cable in 1844, France and England in 1851, and the New and the Old World in 1866. Ten years later, Alexander Graham Bell (1847-1922) invented the telephone. The first electric train was made in 1851, but some years elapsed before one was constructed that could be operated economically. The first incandescent electric lamp was made in 1840, but it was not perfected until 1879. The same year saw the first street car appear in Germany. One of the greatest triumphs was achieved by Guglielmo Marconi (1874-1937) in 1895, when he transmitted a message for a mile on electromagnetic waves. Wireless telegraphy had come into being. Often a number of years elapsed between an invention and its widespread use, but by 1877 electricity was in such demand that Niagara Falls was harnessed to produce power.

Another new source of power appeared in 1876 as a result of the research of Nikolaus Otto (1832-1891) on the internal combustion machine. Eleven years later a German, Gottlieb Daimler (1834-1900), made the first successful automobile, and in 1903 Henry Ford began to mass-produce the new vehicle. That same year, the Wright brothers used a gasoline motor to propel the first airplane. Only the invention of the steam turbine in 1884 enabled that once pre-eminent source of power to hold its own.

The number of important inventions that appeared are legion. Thomas Edison (1847-1931) alone patented over a thousand, including the phonograph in 1877, the first motion picture machine in 1887, and sound moving pictures in 1904. Never before had scientific knowledge of the material world advanced so rapidly. Not without justice the last half of the nineteenth century has been called an age of materialism.

SOCIAL DARWINISM

The scientific discoveries had a powerful impact on thought. Had not scientists revealed the secrets of nature, how the atom was the basic unit of the universe, how all plant and animal life evolved from tiny cells, and how the human mind was conditioned by its environment? Since these discoveries had led to many useful inventions in the technological world, ought they not be of equal value if applied to society? Many thought so, and materialism replaced romanticism as the dominant theme among intellectuals.

Many thinkers were influenced by Darwin's theory of evolution. Of these, none was more prominent than Herbert Spencer (1820-1903). Spencer had become indoctrinated with the idea of evolution even before Darwin published his findings, and he took as his life's work the application of evolution to society. Societies, he thought, were organisms which had developed through various stages as a result of their struggle with their environment. The earliest societies were primitive, warlike, military organizations, but as their members became more industrious and developed various techniques, they became less violent. At some future date when industrialization was complete, there would be universal peace and material well-being. The state was not to aid the individual in achieving this goal. Its single role was to protect its citizens from physical violence, Progress can be achieved only by allowing the strong and able to move forward and letting the weak fall by the wayside, just as it was through the free operation of the "survival of the fittest" that primitive organisms had evolved into man. "Pervading all Nature we may see at work a stern discipline which is a little cruel that it may be very kind," he declared. "It seems hard that an unskillfulness which with all his efforts he cannot overcome, should entail hunger upon the artizan. It seems hard that a labourer incapacitated by sickness from competing with his stronger fellows should have to bear the resulting privations. It seems hard that widows and orphans should be left to struggle for life or death. Nevertheless, when regarded not separately but in connexion with the interests of universal humanity, these harsh fatalities are seen to be full of beneficence—the same beneficence which brings to early graves the children of diseased parents, and singles out the intemperate and the debilitated as the victims of an epidemic."

Spencer's justification of rugged individualism and laissez-faire found an immediate response in the business world. The iron law of wages was abandoned as a justification for the miserable condition of the workingman. If he were able and energetic, he would rise. If he were stupid and indolent, it was necessary for the progress of society to leave him in squalor. Andrew Carnegie (1835-1919) found the contrast between the palace of the millionaire and the cottage of the laborer better than "universal squalor." Competition between businesses was equally important. Through it, inefficient organizations were weeded out and low-priced industrial goods were produced. "It is to this law [of competition] that we owe our wonderful material development, which brings improved conditions in its train." While this law "may be sometimes hard for the individual, it is best for the race, because it insures the survival of the fittest in every department."

John D. Rockefeller (1839-1937) also found the Darwinian theory useful in justifying his own ruthless competitive activities. In an address to a Sunday school class, he declared that "The growth of a large business is merely a survival of the fittest. . . . The American Beauty rose can be produced in the splendor and fragrance which brings cheer to its beholder only by sacrificing the early buds which grow up around it. This is not an evil tendency in business. It is merely the working-out of a law of nature and a law of God."

It would be unjust to accuse Carnegie and Rockefeller of insisting that the doctrine of the "survival of the fittest" be applied to the business world solely to justify their own acquisition of wealth. Both gave away huge sums, and Carnegie declared on many occasions that "the man who dies thus rich dies disgraced." They sincerely believed that progress depended on weeding out the unfit, and their gifts were designed to help people help themselves, not to help those who could or would not.

Industrialists were not alone in finding "truth" in the new biological discoveries. Woodrow Wilson applied the theory to the state and to international relations. The checks and balances in the American Constitution reflected its authors' concern with the checks and balances of the mechanistic, Newtonian conception of the universe, but society was an organism and, he suggested, "what we have been witnessing for the past hundred years is the transformation from a Newtonian constitution into a Darwinian constitution." Likewise the concept of the balance of power must give way before a new system governing the relations between states. Wilson's own answer to these trends was to emphasize Presidential leadership at home and the League of Nations abroad.

Socialists who interpreted history in terms of the class struggle pointed to the certain eventual triumph of the workingman as proof of his superiority. Racists were equally eager. White southerners were using biology to prove their superiority over the Negro slave, even before the Civil War. Englishmen, Americans, and Germans spoke of the admirable characteristics of the Teuton, and Russians put their faith in the Slav. At best, this development was only a continuation of the romantic conception that each people had its own particular Geist; at worst, it bred conflict between races to see which was the more fit. The noted English scientist Karl Pearson (1857-1936) declared that a race must be "kept up to a high pitch of external efficiency by contest, chiefly by way of war with inferior races, and with equal races by the struggle for trade routes and for the sources of raw material and of food supply. This is the natural history view of mankind." Walter Bagehot (1826-1877), a constitutional historian, believed that "Those nations which are the strongest tend to prevail, and in certain marked peculiarities the strongest are the best." Or in the words of a German general, "War gives a biologically just decision."

In this manner, the harmonious conception of the universe gave way to one that was characterized by a perpetual conflict for survival. Yet we must not exaggerate the degree in which Darwinism was applied to society. This tendency—Social Darwinism, it is called—was denied by Darwin himself, and his great supporter Thomas Huxley (1825-1895) never tired of pointing out the basic fallacy of the so-called ethics of evolution. "Fittest," he declared,

> has a connotation of "best"; and about "best" there hangs a moral flavour. In cosmic nature, however, what is "fittest" depends upon conditions. Long since, I ventured to point out that if our hemisphere were to cool again, the survival of the fittest might bring about, in the vegetable kingdom, a population of more and more stunted and humbler and humbler organisms, until the "fittest" that survived might be nothing but lichens, diatoms, and such microscopic organisms as those which give red snow its colour; while, if it became hotter, the pleasant valleys of the Thames and Iris might be uninhabitable by any animated beings save those that flourish in a tropical jungle. They, as the "fittest," the best adapted to the changed conditions, would survive.

COMTE AND POSITIVISM

The scientific and materialistic interests of the age were clearly reflected by the popularity of positivism, a philosophical system which recognized only positive facts and observed phenomena as valid. The leading figure in the movement was Auguste Comte (1798-1857), whose work provided the connecting link between the philosophers of the Enlightenment, who believed that man could be made better and happier by being subjected to the proper environment, and the social scientists of the late nineteenth century, who sought to discover exactly what the proper environment was.

Comte believed that the evolution of the human mind went through

627

three stages in accordance with definite scientific laws. The first and most primitive stage was the theological, in which man gave supernatural explanations to phenomena. The second stage was the metaphysical, in which man sought to answer questions concerning the ultimate origins and nature of things through the use of deductive reasoning. The third and final stage was the positive, in which man explained observed phenomena through inductive reasoning. Thus, man progressed through history from seeking knowledge from religion, to seeking knowledge from philosophy, and finally to seeking knowledge from science. The development of science also proceeded in accordance with a definite pattern, beginning with mathematics and progressing through astronomy, physics, chemistry, and biology to sociology, which was more complex and more important than its predecessors.

Comte has often been called the father of sociology, but the social system he constructed won few adherents because his belief in a planned, authoritarian society ran counter to the liberalism of his age. Furthermore, he prepared a precise description of a religion of humanity which included a calendar of saints and a hierarchy of sacraments that seemed to many the product of a deranged mind rather than of scientific thought. Nevertheless, the emphases of the positive movement—on the role of the scientist and industrialist in society, on practical rather than theoretical problems, and on the inductive method—became characteristic of most of late nineteenth-century social thought. Following Comte's suggestion, sociologists, anthropologists, historians, and other social scientists became more "scientifically" minded and devoted their energies to gathering empirical data to explain the origin and evolution of the species.

JAMES AND NIETZSCHE

Some philosophers, like the American William James (1842-1910), accepted the materialistic, environmental character of their age, but revolted against the emphasis on organic evolution and the belief that there were no truths that could not be demonstrated by laboratory experiments. Rather the practical-minded James declared that the testing ground of truth must be experience. "An idea is 'true' so long as to believe it is profitable to our lives. . . . We cannot reject any hypothesis if consequences useful to life flow from it." Religion, morality, any doctrine then, may be accepted as true if it brings happiness. Thus, pragmatism, as the new philosophy was called, found a place for God and ethics in a materialistic, skeptical world.

Other philosophers, a minority, revolted against the smug materialism and determinism of their age. The German-born Friedrich Nietzsche (1844-1900) wrote of supermen who rejected Christianity because the virtues it taught were those of weaklings, and attacked the growing industrial democracy, statism, and nationalism because they were the means whereby "cattle become masters." He longed for the emergence of men with a "will to power," the will to endure torture and inflict pain, but with "that enormous *energy of greatness* which can model the man of the future. . . ." These half-mad, half-prophetic utterances were a connecting link between the dreams of the romantics and the irrational cult of violence that was to come.

LITERATURE

Literature and art reflected the scientific achievements of the age, the growth of materialism, the spread of democracy, and the increased literacy. The influence of these forces on artistic expression was not altogether fortunate. The increased literacy made it possible for writers to reach a wider audience, but only if a way was found to produce reading material cheap enough for the underpaid masses to buy. The French solved the problem during the 1830's by publishing novels in serial form in newspapers; the English, by printing them in installments. Both ventures were financially successful, but their effect on style was questionable. To ensure the purchase of tomorrow's paper or the next installment, each issue of a novel had to suggest that something interesting or amusing was about to take place. This made the careful delineation of characters and the slow construction of a moving, but realistic, climax difficult. Indeed, authors frequently began to publish their stories before they had an exact idea how they were to end or what characters would be introduced. The inevitable result was faulty construction. A master of the dramatic like Alexander Dumas (1803-1870) was able to use the new medium with conspicuous success. Indeed, he became so popular that he hired hack writers who wrote the greater part of many of his books. Charles Dickens (1812-1870) proved that the serial form of publication was also adaptable to humor when he began in 1837 to tell the story of Mr. Pickwick and his club. The serial form could not, however, be adapted to original thought, aesthetic expression, or the subtle treatment of important problems.

This situation raised the problem of whether the artist should write or paint for the masses or whether he should abandon hope for a wider public and devote himself to art for art's sake. Prior to the eighteenth century, this had not been an important problem because the artist was so completely dependent on the patron that he had no choice but to consider the patron's wishes. Then, too, the patron was generally a man of culture so that there was little reason for his taste and that of the artist to conflict. By the eighteenth century, it had become possible for an author to achieve financial independence by appealing to the rising middle class, but once again there had been a unity of interest and culture. This unity gradually ceased during the nineteenth century.

As the middle class achieved their goals during the course of the nineteenth century, they became less interested in literature as a means of raising problems or of pointing to the need of reform, and more interested in reading books that enabled them to escape from their humdrum existence in the new industrial society. The working classes, who had begun to capture the attention of both writer and artist, lacked the money, education, and taste to support their would-be benefactors. They too sought a means of escape.

The escape literature took several forms. In it, the romantic tradition has remained strong until this day. The novel that carries the reader through a series of adventures in the past or in some far-off place has never ceased to be popular. Alexander Dumas has had a steady line of successors until our day. Some have been writers of modest ability, but others like Henryk Sienkiewicz (1846-1916), who thrilled his readers by his tales of the heroic deeds of the Poles during their period of greatness or who was able to appeal to Christians everywhere in his *Quo Vadis,* were men of genuine talent. The popularity of stories of far-off places is exemplified by Rudyard Kipling's (1865-1936) accounts of life in India.

Science, detective, and humorous stories also reached a wide public. Sir Arthur Conan Doyle (1859-1930) created Sherlock Holmes, the great detective, who pitted his exceptional capacity to reason inductively against criminals who were almost, but not quite, as clever. Jules Verne (1828-1905) capitalized on the interest in science to write science fiction, while Dickens, with his appeal to humor, has had a steady line of successors down to the present time.

This type of writing, however, appealed to few of the really great writers, and by 1850 they had had enough of romanticism. They no longer wanted to assist people to escape from life; they wanted to describe their lives, to discuss their problems, and to show the workings of their minds. In short, they wanted to be natural, to depict life as it really was. Thus, naturalism replaced romanticism as the intellectual's preferred form of literature.

The new naturalistic or realistic literature dealt principally with two topics, the problems of society and the problems of the human mind. Since the novel was the best medium for dealing with both, it became the most characteristic form of literature. Poetry, whose emotional potentialities had made it such an ideal vehicle for the romantics, fell into disuse. Charles Dickens, one of the first realists, kept much of the romantics' appeal to the dramatic and sentimental, as his *Oliver Twist* shows, but at the same time he exposed the treatment of foundlings, the life in the slums, and the cruel folly of imprisonment for debt. His critics called him vulgar, but he was one of the few writers of great talent who could appeal to the masses. Victor Hugo (1802-1885), who had been in the forefront of the romantics, produced *Les Miserables* in 1862, in which he dealt with the problems of poverty and the inhumane administration of justice, while Harriet Beecher Stowe (1811-1896) attacked slavery in *Uncle Tom's Cabin.*

These early realists often retained much of the sentimentality of the romantics, but the second generation dropped the moral overtones of their predecessors and began to deal with the less attractive aspects of contemporary society in a blunter fashion. Prostitution and drunkenness were described in almost unnecessary detail. Émile Zola (1840-1902) wrote twenty volumes dealing with a degenerate French family in which he tried to demonstrate the influence of heredity on human character. Guy de Maupassant (1850-1893) described lower middle-class life in a somber, realistic fashion. Thomas Hardy (1840-1928) preferred to tell of man's struggle for existence in a chaotic world ruled by chance. Upton Sinclair (1878-   ) exposed the hardship of the day laborers and the irresponsible behavior of the Chicago beef trust. The Norwegian Henrik Ibsen (1828-1906) used drama as a means to attack the vices and hypocrisy of modern society, and George Bernard Shaw (1856-1950) was equally devastating in his use of comedy to achieve the same end.

The first great naturalistic novel was Gustave Flaubert's (1821-1880) *Madame Bovary*, a portrait of a woman so revealing that author and publisher were haled into court on charges of immorality. This action only gave the book greater notoriety than it would ordinarily have achieved, as has so often been the case, and one psychological novel has followed another from that day. Nearly all of them have attacked middle-class intellectual, aesthetic, and moral standards, just as the social novelists attacked middle-class society and capitalism.

One of the outstanding features of the literature of the last half of the nineteenth century was the important role played by Russia. Russian novelists assumed a leading position in European culture for the first time. Living in a pre-industrial society, they were far less conscious of a conflict between social classes than their western counterparts, for as Dostoevski said: "We have no class interests, because strictly speaking we have no classes and because the Russian soul is wider than class differences, class interests and class law." It was the soul, then, that they sought to penetrate, but they did so in relation to Russian society. What internal forces led the individual to revolt against society? Was he justified, or did his action bring only ruin? In answering these questions, they pointed to the loneliness and isolation of the individual who had freed himself from social bonds. Yet despite the dark violence and seemingly unhappy endings, one was left with the feeling that human suffering was not altogether meaningless and in vain.

The two greatest Russian novelists of this period were Feodor Dostoevski (1821-1881) and Count Leo Tolstoi (1828-1910). Dostoevski led as miserable a life as any of his characters. A youthful radical, he was condemned to death when he was twenty-eight but had his sentence changed to exile in Siberia. Years later, he returned to St. Petersburg, a poverty-striken epileptic. Gradually, he came to feel that is was only through suffer-

Feodor Dostoevski from a painting by Vasily Perov. (Charles Phelps Cushing)

ing and mystical faith that the soul of man can be purified. His best known works, *Crime and Punishment* and *The Brothers Karamazov*, express these views.

Fate was kinder to Tolstoi; yet his outlook was similar to Dostoevski's in many ways. From *War and Peace*, where he described the forces unleashed by Napoleon's invasion of Russia, he turned to man's inner struggles in *Anna Karenina*. Anna, who violates the laws of society, commits suicide, but Levin, who conquers his desire to revolt, survives. Thus, Tolstoi condemned individualism with its desire to break the bonds of society. He gave away his property and spent his last years in peasant's garb preaching a moral, religious revival and providing a living example of his belief that a simple, natural way of life brings one closer to the secret of goodness and happiness.

ART

The artist's fate in the nineteenth century was much like that of the writer. He could please the public by continuing to paint in the romantic or classical tradition, doing portraits, and copying the old masters, or he could adopt the slogan of "art for art's sake," paint what he pleased, and live in penury. Paris became the favorite home of artists who defied middle-class tastes, middle-class morals, and middle-class social conventions. It is

632

Leo Tolstoi in his study at Yasnaya Polyana. (Bettmann Archive)

difficult to say whether their behavior or their art irritated the public more.

The first artists to defy the accepted standards were the naturalists, or realists as they were sometimes called. Like their literary counterparts, they were determined to depict man and nature as they really were. A nude swimmer was to look like a woman, not a nymph. The common man was the only fit subject for a portrait. Dancers, laundresses, wrestlers, and peasants replaced goddesses, kings, warriors, and saints as subjects. Gustave Courbet (1819-1877) and Honoré Daumier (1808-1879) became the leaders of the movement in Paris. Jean François Millet (1814-1875) turned his attention to the struggles of the peasant.

Yet even this realism did not seem real enough. A group of painters led by Édouard Manet (1832-1883), Claude Monet (1840-1926), and Auguste Renoir (1841-1919) sought to reduce their paintings to ultimate reality. In the work of these three innovators, only the immediate impressions of the artist were depicted. Since this impression depended entirely on the light they received from the object, they put great emphasis on light. Light, they learned from scientists, consisted of primary colors; therefore, they used primary colors almost exclusively. Many significant details were omitted because correct form and detail can be seen only after prolonged observation. Indeed, dabs of color were often substituted for linear drawing. Only if the observer stood at the proper distance did some paintings have any recognizable shape. Literary and historical subjects ceased to be painted because the artist did not see them. The classical rules of harmony and proportion were abandoned because they made subjects seem posed in an unnatural manner, and deep-seated passion passed from the realm of art because painters sought only to catch a fleeting moment.

633

Claude Monet, THE BANKS OF THE SEINE AT VENTEUIL. Monet's desire to paint his first, immediate impression made speed necessary. He used rapid brush strokes, took no time to match colors, and ignored details— but the overall effect was pleasing. Compare with Constable's landscape (on page 504). (National Gallery of Art, Chester Dale Collection)

The Impressionists held their first collective exhibition in 1874, but for a generation they were severely criticized by the classically oriented and academically trained art public. One well-known critic declared in 1876 that "An exhibition has just been opened at Durand-Ruel which allegedly contains paintings. I enter and my horrified eyes behold something terrible. Five or six lunatics, among them a woman, have joined together and exhibited their works. I have seen people rock with laughter in front of these pictures, but my heart bled when I saw them. These would-be artists called themselves revolutionaries, 'Impressionists.' They take a piece of canvas, colour and brush, daub a few patches of colour on them at random, and sign the whole thing with their name. It is a delusion of the same kind as if the inmates of Bedlam picked up stones from the wayside and imagined they had found diamonds."

In spite of this and other criticism, these artists won many adherents, and Impressionism became the last universally accepted European style in painting. It was also the last style that adhered, albeit in an original fashion, to the Renaissance theory that things should be painted as they really are in nature.

The architects and sculptors of the last half of the nineteenth century

634

Auguste Renoir, A GIRL WITH A WATERING CAN. *Renoir applied the Impressionists' principles to portraits and achieved a "realistic" picture without clearly defined lines or attention to detail. Compare with Jan van Eyck on frontispiece. (National Gallery of Art, Chester Dale Collection)*

were more conservative than the artists. For the most part, they were content to imitate earlier styles. Composers generally preferred to work under the inspiration of the romantic or classical tradition. Of the romantics the most important composer was Richard Wagner (1813-1883), who transformed early German legends into opera. Of the classicists, Johannes Brahms (1833-1897) and Richard Strauss (1864-1949) were outstanding. Only in Claude Debussy (1862-1918) did the world of music produce a rebel. He sought to apply the ideas of the Impressionist painters to music and achieved considerable success.

THE TRIUMPH OF LIBERALISM

The unification of Italy and of Germany, the accompanying establishment of constitutional government, and the growing power of the middle class assured the liberals and nationalists that their dreams were being realized. By 1871, every European country had a constitutional form of government except Russia, the Ottoman Empire, and tiny Montenegro, and there were signs that these three states would eventually come within the fold. Parliaments and consent to taxation were the rule. In some places kings still exercised considerable authority; in others they had been reduced to figureheads, and actual power was wielded by parliaments through responsible ministers. In either case, the fundamental human rights were preserved. Freedom of religion, freedom of the press, freedom of speech, and the right to a fair trial were commonplace. Each of the major nationalities was united, but the Jews, Irish, and a number of east European peoples remained subject to foreign domination. Free trade, or at least a low tariff for revenue purposes only, was the rule in Europe, although in the New World the United States was perverse enough to keep its duties almost prohibitively high. Money flowed so freely that the Russians were able to borrow in England during the Crimean War. Its exchange was facilitated by the adoption of the gold standard by civilized countries. Man had the same privileges as his wares. He could go from country to country without restrictions, without a passport.

INDUSTRIALIZATION AND URBANIZATION

The rapid economic expansion of the first half of the century continued at an accelerated rate. The industrial revolution, which had been centered in England prior to 1850, spread to central and eastern Europe and to the New World. Between 1870 and 1900, world industrial production increased fourfold and the capital investment of the industrial powers threefold. The United States and Germany equaled or surpassed Great Britain in most phases of industrial production by 1910. Coal production, for example, stood at 81 million tons in Great Britain, 13 million in the

United States, and 12 million in Germany in 1860. By 1910, the figures were 268 million, 455 million, and 152 million, respectively. Britain nearly doubled its output of pig iron during the same period, but Germany surpassed Britain by multiplying its output almost tenfold. In one type of production after another, new inventions, new techniques, and new factories increased the production of goods at a fantastic rate. Western civilization ceased to be predominantly agricultural and became predominantly industrial.

Transportation made equally rapid strides. Western and central Europe and the United States constructed adequate railroad networks. North America was spanned by several transcontinental lines, and in 1905 the Russians completed a railroad across Siberia. Locomotives became more powerful, and their speed was doubled. The invention of the internal combustion machine provided new means of transportation, and by 1914 the truck, car, and airplane gave promise that they would someday rival the railroad. Between 1850 and 1910, ocean tonnage increased twelvefold for Great Britain and over thirtyfold for Germany. The speed of ships was increased, and travel time was further reduced by the completion of the Suez Canal in 1869 and the Panama Canal in 1914. No longer were the long voyages around Africa and South America necessary. Communication by wire and wireless made possible the instantaneous exchange of information and ideas. Never had there been such rapid material progress.

In highly industrial countries the agricultural population actually began to decline because machines reduced the need for farm laborers and improved transportation brought in food from abroad to feed the urban population. Cities, however, grew quite rapidly. The population of greater London stood at 6.6 million in 1900, and the population of Paris and New York reached more than half that number. Cities of over 100,000 persons became so commonplace by 1910 that outside of the Slavic lands there were few countries in Europe in which more than 10 per cent of the inhabitants did not live in urban centers of that size or larger. Germany, which had only eight cities with over 100,000 inhabitants in 1870, boasted forty-one in 1900.

This population increase was brought about in spite of a fall in the birth rate that was partly caused by urbanization itself. In an agricultural or an early industrial economy, large families had been an economic asset because the children worked. In a more developed industrial society, children were excluded from the factories and became a heavy financial drain. Then, too, parents were anxious to keep their families small in order to provide educational and other advantages for their children. Knowledge of birth-control methods became more widespread. As a result, the birth rate in England and Wales fell from 37 per 1,000 in 1840 to 27 in 1910. Other industrial countries experienced a similar phenomenon, but the overall population continued to increase quite rapidly because of the declining

An American railroad scene in the first decade after the Civil War:
LIGHTNING EXPRESS TRAINS LEAVE A JUNCTION. (*Library of Congress*)

death rate. Between 1830 and 1900, the European population increased from 266 million to 401 million and at the same time provided about 30 million emigrants for other parts of the world. This migration, plus the natural increase of the previous inhabitants, caused the population of the United States, Canada, and Australia to triple during the half century and that of Latin America to double.

Industrialization and urbanization caused the middle class to grow larger and more powerful. In advanced countries, it surpassed the landed aristocracy in wealth by a wide margin. Here conservative landowners ceased to be a serious check to middle-class aspirations, unless they found allies elsewhere. The church as a conservative force also grew weaker. The triumphs of science shook the faith of educated people in revealed religion, while members of the lower classes often broke with their ancestral church when they migrated to the cities. Catholic and Protestant clergymen alike were slow to establish parishes in the new urban centers. Monarchs, so happy to rely on their nobles and their bishops for support in 1815, began to show a surprising willingness to make a compromise peace with the middle class.

THE GROWTH OF DEMOCRACY AND EDUCATION

Some middle-class aspirations began to change. As late as 1840, most European middle-class liberals were opposed to universal manhood suffrage, and only a handful of radicals desired to give women the right to

638

The first Ford assembly line, 1913. The adoption of the assembly-line technique greatly increased the rate of production. Note two men ready to place seat into back of car from ramp. (Bettmann Archive)

vote. After 1870, however, many liberals and some conservatives vied for the honor of increasing the suffrage, and by 1914 universal manhood suffrage was no longer the exception. During the same period, public voice voting was abandoned, and the secret ballot was adopted to ensure that the enfranchised workers were not unduly influenced by their landlords or employers. The cause of democracy was also furthered by the efforts made in many countries to reduce the power of the hereditary house in the legislature and to establish the principle of ministerial responsibility to the lower house. In regard to these two issues, the march of democracy often proceeded at a snail's pace, but the debates that centered around them colored the political history of most Western countries and, after World War I, ended in victory for the liberals.

Women also had to wait until after 1918 to receive equal rights, but a strong feminist movement developed after 1870 that paved the way for eventual victory. Neither conservative nor liberal was enthusiastic about woman suffrage. The conservative thought that a woman's place was in the home, and secular-minded liberals feared that the more devout nature of the gentler sex would lead them to favor the clergy at the ballot box. However, the mass movement to the cities broke family ties. New industries provided respectable employment for women as secretaries; new hospitals employed them as nurses, and new schools as teachers. Once women escaped the home and were able to earn a living, their eventual participation in politics was assured.

The great expansion of the electorate made necessary the establishment of adequate public school systems. "We must educate masters" became the cry. To this the practical-minded, patriotic middle class added that the growing complexity of industry required educated workers. Schools were necessary to indoctrinate children with patriotism as well as the traditional virtues that had once been taught by the family and the Church before their role was weakened. Beginning around 1870, one European country after another created free public schools and passed laws requiring attendance. Vast sums were spent to build schools and pay teachers. By 1900, the literacy of the adult population in Great Britain had risen from 66 to 95 per cent, in France from 60 to 95 per cent, and in Belgium from 55 to 86 per cent. Only in the more backward countries of eastern Europe, Italy, and the Iberian Peninsula did a majority of the population remain illiterate. At the same time, new universities were created and old universities were expanded. Never before had a civilization put so much emphasis on education.

It is true that the mass of mankind did not always put this new literacy to the best use, a fact illustrated by the type of newspaper that became the vogue. Until around 1880, the approximately six thousand newspapers in Europe consisted of several pages of news, for the most part related to diplomacy or politics. They were too sophisticated, too dull, and too expensive for the new reading public. Publishers like Joseph Pulitzer (1847-1911) and William Randolph Hearst (1863-1951) in the United States and the Harmsworth brothers in Great Britain saw their opportunity and created the sensationalist "yellow press." Their papers emphasized stories of crime, sex, and adventure, which they advertised on their front pages with provocative headlines. Technological improvements and advertising reduced the price of a newspaper to a penny. The circulation of papers like the *Daily Mail* and the *Daily Express* of London soared to a million, and at the same time the number of newspapers doubled.

Distressing as this development must have been to many, most of the middle-class liberals were optimistic in 1914. They had won, or seemed about to win, control of most European governments. With their new power they could improve the environment and educate mankind; given the proper environment and education, they believed, men would be better and happier. Progress toward perfection could be realized.

THREATS TO LIBERALISM

There were, however, six threats to liberalism that largely grew out of the activities of the middle class itself. One was the development of joint stock companies with limited liability, which made possible the growth of huge industrial combinations that stifled competition. Others included a movement away from laissez-faire, the growth of labor unions, the emergence of Marxism, Christian Socialism, anarchism, and syndicalism, the advent of a new type of nationalism, and the growing cult of violence.

JOINT-STOCK COMPANIES AND COMBINATIONS

The typical industrial enterprise prior to 1850 had been individually owned or else held in partnership. Only for large expensive projects like canal and railroad building had joint-stock companies with limited liability been formed, with specific approval of the government. The advantages of this system were too obvious to be missed by the industrialist.

Individually owned concerns and partnerships could obtain only a limited amount of capital for their enterprises, for no one would buy stock in a firm they could not control, if failure meant the loss of their other property to pay the creditors. With limited liability, however, only the amount invested in the stock was lost. On this basis, there were many investors. Then, too, incorporation gave legal identity to an enterprise and with it all the rights and privileges guaranteed to the individual. For a time, the difficulty in getting special acts passed to incorporate an enterprise held the movement towards the formation of joint-stock companies in check, but between 1855 and 1870, Great Britain, France, Germany, and other countries removed this requirement for special legislative acts. The amassing of large-scale capital for industrial enterprises became possible, and the big limited liability company replaced the small individually owned concern as the typical industrial unit. A similar movement took place at the same time in banking. Banks became larger and obtained the capital to make huge loans to industry.

Ignorance, speculation, fraud, and the hazards of the business profession caused many of the early corporations to fail. One-third of the 20,500 British companies registered between 1856 and 1883 collapsed within five years. Those that survived often grew larger by ruthlessly destroyed their competitors. As a justification, some businessmen argued that economic, like biological, progress depended on free operation of the law of the survival of the fittest. Others believed that competition was wasteful and sought to make agreements with their competitors. These agreements were of three basic types. In some, competitors agreed to restrict production, divide markets, and fix prices. These arrangements in the United States were generally temporary and were known as *pools*. In Germany, where they were called *cartels*, they were organized on a more permanent basis, although the member corporations retained their managerial and financial independence. Some cartels, such as the dynamite industry, were organized on an international basis.

Holding companies and *trusts* were quite similar to each other, just as were pools and cartels. A holding company was one which owned enough stock in several other companies to control their policies. A trust was formed when the stockholders of various companies gave their stock to a group of trustees in return for certificates which entitled them to a share in the net earnings. The trustees, however, controlled the activities of the companies concerned.

The third type of combination was the *merger*. Here, two or more companies were simply merged into one with a single management and a single group of owners.

Some industrial combinations were horizontal; that is, they consisted of companies doing the same kind of work. The Rhenish-Westphalian Coal Syndicate, for example, was a cartel of coal-mining concerns. Other industrial combinations consisted of concerns doing different but related work. An example would be a steel company that owned a coal mine or a chain store that manufactured its own preserves and jellies.

In some respects combinations were beneficial. The very fact that they were large meant that they were less subject to business fluctuations and could provide more stable prices and more secure positions for their employees. They could also undertake projects too large to be handled by small firms with limited capital. Then, too, they could establish scientific laboratories to search for new products and find better ways to make old ones. By the greater use of machinery, they increased productivity. In this manner, combinations made possible the production of better and less expensive products.

In other ways, however, large combinations were harmful. They provided means whereby a few men could wield such power that they could virtually control the business life of a nation. In 1913, a committee of the House of Representatives reported that John D. Rockefeller, J. P. Morgan, and their respective business associates held 341 directorships in 112 corporations whose total resources came to over twenty-two billion dollars, a sum larger than the assessed valuation of all the property in the United States west of the Mississippi River. Wealth, like power, became concentrated in fewer hands. In 1893, 9 per cent of the families in the United States owned 71 per cent of the wealth; and by 1911, 1 per cent of the adult population of England and Wales possessed 70 per cent of all private property.

The powerful position of the leaders of big business enabled them to stifle competition in many areas and to reduce opportunities for newcomers to go into business for themselves. At one time, it had taken only a few hundred dollars, then a few thousand, and now often many millions in capital to purchase the necessary plant, machinery, and raw materials to compete in such fields as steel, oil, or public utilities. The young man who followed Dr. Smiles' program of "self-help" might hope for promotion within a big industry, but his opportunities of obtaining ownership were slim indeed. The typical member of the middle class became a salaried worker rather than a small independent businessman. Laissez-faire and individual initiative were stifled more by the giant corporations than by the state. The older economic liberalism was threatened by the very industrial combinations it had created.

THE MOVEMENT AWAY FROM LAISSEZ-FAIRE

At the same time, the big continental industrialists began to lose faith in free trade. Their misgivings arose from a variety of causes, of which British competition was the most important. During a depression which began in 1873, British industrialists dumped their surplus products on the foreign market at prices lower than the weaker continental industries could stand. The reaction of the European businessman may readily be imagined, and he was clever enough to win some support from labor by pointing out that it might be necessary to cut wages in order to meet British prices without risk of bankruptcy. Nationalists were won over by the argument that a strong nation must be economically self-sufficient and economic self-sufficiency could be achieved only by protecting infant industries behind a tariff wall.

The traditional ideas of laissez-faire were so strong that, perhaps even with nationalist and labor support, the demands of the European industrialists would not have led to higher tariffs if many farmers had not joined in their effort. Until the 1870's, the European farmer had been in an enviable position because urbanization was creating what appeared to be an inexhaustible market for his goods, but now railroads or steamships tapped the Russian Ukraine and the plains of the American Midwest where wheat could be raised more cheaply than in Europe. The world price of wheat went down, and the aristocratic landowner and the peasant joined in the cry for protection. Between 1876 and 1880, Russia, Spain, Italy, and Germany raised their tariffs. Only the older industrial nations, such as Britain and Belgium, or the mercantile states, such as the Netherlands, held to the theories of Adam Smith. A movement away from a world-wide division of labor had begun. More serious to the cause of liberalism, the big industrialists who were already separated from the bulk of the middle class by their greater wealth began to associate more and more with the old aristocracy. In Great Britain, they joined the same political party; and in Germany, they formed separate but often allied parties.

The less fortunate members of the middle class also began to abandon their adherence to laissez-faire. They did not do so because they had lost their desire to be free, but rather because they had come to the conclusion that big business was more of a threat to their liberty than the state. "American enterprise is not free," Woodrow Wilson declared in his presidential campaign in 1912; "the man with only a little capital is finding it harder to get into the field, more and more impossible to compete with the big fellow. Why? Because the laws of this country do not prevent the strong from crushing the weak. . . . What this country needs above everything else is a body of laws which will look after the men who are on the make rather than the men who are already made." The result was a raft of legislation in every country designed either to prevent the formation of new combinations or to regulate their actions in the public interest. In some places, taxes were passed, designed to halt the concentration of wealth in the hands of a few, not merely to raise revenue. Just as the upper-middle class began to unite or cooperate with the conservative land-owners, so the lower middle class began to unite or cooperate with the workers in many countries. Thus, by 1914 the once powerful middle class was beginning to divide into several segments, each of which abandoned the old or classical concept of liberalism in one respect or another. Only a small group of middle-class liberals remained loyal to their traditional position, and the word "liberal" itself began to be applied to those who ad-vocated state intervention to protect the people from big business in-terests.

LABOR UNIONS

The third threat to liberalism came from labor. This was not because the living standards of laborers were becoming worse, for their real wages rose sharply during the last half of the nineteenth century. In 1900, the typical worker could buy about a third more than his father could in 1850. Rather it was because the conditions of labor were still unsatisfactory. A reduction of the work week to sixty hours was more an objective to be sought than a reality in most countries. The greater use of machinery had increased the danger of working in certain industries, and the new as-sembly line techniques had increased the monotony. Furthermore, al-though the industrial revolution was bringing the workers a higher stand-ard of living, they believed that business leaders were getting far more than their share of the profits. To strengthen their bargaining position, they formed labor unions and often adopted one of the new social ideolo-gies dedicated to improving their lot.

Labor discontent was but one factor that led to the growth of unions. The industrialization that made the middle class grow so large also in-creased the number of workers and brought them close together so that it became physically possible for them to organize. The acceptance of joint-stock companies and later combinations discredited the old liberal argu-ment that a laborer should bargain individually with his employer. Collec-tive bargaining by labor came only after the collectivization of industry by business had begun. This situation, plus the establishment of universal suffrage, led to the repeal of anti-labor union laws in most countries be-tween 1864 and 1890. Union membership in Great Britain and Northern Ireland increased from 1,600,000 to over four million between 1892 and 1913 and that of Germany from about 350,000 to 3,000,000 during the same years.

644

The first successful unions were organizations of skilled workers on a craft basis. The local union of a given craft then joined with other local unions in the same trade to form a national union in which considerable authority remained at the local level. The British Amalgamated Society of Engineers, which was founded in 1851, became the model for similar organizations of carpenters, miners, tailors, and other crafts. The next step was to secure cooperation between the various national unions. This was achieved in Great Britain by the Trade Union Congresses which began to be held in 1868, in the United States by the formation of the American Federation of Labor in 1881, and in most other countries by similar organizations before the outbreak of the First World War.

Unskilled labor organized more slowly until the last decade of the nineteenth century. Earlier unions of unskilled laborers had been unsuccessful because of poor leadership, the ignorance of the prospective members, and above all because their wages were so low that they could neither pay substantial dues nor long survive if they went on strike. In 1889, the London dock workers struck to secure a minimum wage of sixpence an hour and other minor concessions. The dock companies contemptuously refused to negotiate, and within two weeks the workers were on the verge of surrender because of hunger. However, at the critical moment, the Brisbane wharf laborers voted to send assistance. Other Australians followed suit; British public opinion fell in behind the strikers; and the dock companies, recoiling in surprise, surrendered. The dock workers' victory inspired other non-skilled workers to unite. Unions of railway workers, gas workers, and textile workers were organized in Great Britain and elsewhere that were open to all employees in a given industry regardless of their particular job.

On the whole, the craft unions accepted the capitalistic system. They were content to try to obtain higher wages, shorter hours, and better working conditions for their members. A large part of the dues they collected went to support insurance benefits and strike relief. In England and especially in Germany, they formed cooperatives which enabled their members to buy goods at low prices. The industrial unions were more radical. They sometimes talked of revolution and tended to espouse one of the new anti-capitalistic social creeds.

MARXIAN SOCIALISM

The most important of the new anti-capitalistic creeds was Marxism. Karl Marx was born in western Germany at Trier in 1818. Both of his parents were Jewish, but they embraced Christianity when Karl was six. He studied at the universities of Bonn and Berlin and received his doctor of philosophy degree in 1841 when he was only twenty-three. Shortly thereafter, he married the cultured and nobly-born Jenny von Westphalen, but neither her parents nor his own had sufficient influence to secure a university position for him, for he was already too radical to find favor in the pre-1848 era. As a result, Marx left Germany, dabbled in newspaper work, studied socialist literature, and on the eve of the Revolution of 1848 published the *Communist Manifesto* in collaboration with his longtime friend Friedrich Engels (1820-1895). The German uprisings a few months later led to his return to the Rhineland, where he edited a radical newspaper that did much to convince the middle class that the aristocracy was less to be feared than the masses. After the defeat of the Revolution, he withdrew to London, where he spent nearly all the remainder of his life, living in poverty but going daily to the British Museum to gather material for his monumental three-volume work, *Das Kapital.* The first volume appeared in 1867, and the other two were completed after his death in 1883 by the loyal Engels.

During his university days, Marx had become enamored of Hegelian philosophy. Hegel, it will be remembered, had argued that as the institutions of a society mature and perform their mission they create opposites or antitheses.[4] Out of the clash between the two opposites a new society or synthesis is created. This synthesis, in turn, creates a new opposite, and the whole process is repeated over and over again. As a result of this process, society moves forward, guided by a divine plan until perfection is achieved. Marx accepted Hegel's theory of progress, with one fundamental difference. To Hegel, God had been the controlling force; to Marx, "the mode of production conditions the general character of the social, political and intellectual processes of life." The material, not the ideological, determines the course of history.

Marx believed that the feudal age had been based on agriculture and that out of it had developed its antithesis, urban industry and the bourgeoisie. The bourgeoisie of his day were in the process of overthrowing the feudal aristocracy. Where they had already succeeded, the ideas of liberalism, or as he put it "naked, shameless, direct, brutal exploitation," had replaced "the most heavenly ecstasies of religious fervor, of chivalrous enthusiasm, of philistine sentimentalism" of the earlier age.

The bourgeoisie themselves, however, were their own "gravediggers." They had unified the state, a step which made future revolutions easier. They had brought the workers together to labor in factories, but by doing so they had enabled their antithesis to get together and organize. By concentrating the ownership of capital in a few hands, they were making it impossible for the lower middle class to compete; they were driving them into the ranks of labor. Thus, their numbers grew smaller and smaller while the proletariat—those who owned no means of production—grew larger and larger. The bourgeoisie could not even control the means of production which had given rise to their class. They overproduced, bringing on an economic crisis, and recovery was achieved only by finding new

[4] See page 507.

646

Karl Marx at the age of fifty-eight.
(Wide World)

markets in other parts of the world. Again they overproduced, again there was a crash, and again recovery was achieved only by the opening of new markets. This process was repeated over and over again, but each new crisis was worse than the one before. Finally, there would be one gigantic crash, there would be no new markets in the world to open, the bourgeoisie intellectuals would desert their class and provide leadership for the proletariat, a revolution would take place, and a dictatorship of the proletariat would begin.

At this point Marx became vague, but he apparently envisioned that the bourgeoisie would be destroyed by having the means of production taken away from them. The opposition between manual and intellectual labor would terminate, and a classless society would emerge. Only after this has happened and "after labor has become not only a means of life, but also the highest want in life, when, with the development of all the faculties of the individual, the productive forces have correspondingly increased, and all the springs of social wealth flow more abundantly—only then may the limited horizon of capitalist right be left behind entirely, and society inscribe on its banners: 'From everyone according to his faculties to everyone according to his needs.' " Only then will man become so faultless that he will work for the common good, not his own gain; only then can the state "wither away."

Thus, Marx accepted most of the basic ideas of the Enlightenment. He was a materialist who believed in the ideas of progress and human perfectibility. He thought, as did most economists of his day, that labor gave an object its value. The unique aspect of his doctrine was his insistence that the proceeds of labor should therefore go to the laborers, not to the bourgeoisie, whom he accused of getting all the benefits of the increased productivity brought about by technological improvements. Even here, Marx was motivated by the humanitarianism of the Enlightenment. He was a product, if a perverse one, of his age; there was nothing Russian in his outlook or thought. Indeed, like most Germans, he looked upon the Slav with contempt.

The impact of Marx's doctrines was immense. The earlier Utopian socialist movements died and in their place arose the new "scientific socialism," "scientific" because had not Marx demonstrated the truth of his teachings by the inductive method? "Just as Darwin discovered the law of the evolution of organic nature," Engels wrote, "so Marx discovered the evolutionary law of human history. . . ." This law gave the laboring masses the hope, nay the promise, that one day they would receive social justice. They flocked to the Marxist labor unions, and by 1914 a Marxist-oriented political party had become the largest in Germany.

REVISIONISM AND CHRISTIAN SOCIALISM

Soon after his death, however, Marx's theories began to be questioned by many of his socialist followers. Eduard Bernstein (1850-1932) pointed out in 1899 that some of his predictions had not come true. The capitalistic system had not collapsed, nor did its collapse appear imminent. The middle class was growing larger, not smaller, and, most important of all, the lot of the working classes was improving with increased productivity and the growth of democracy. Bernstein therefore abandoned the emphasis on the class struggle and began to insist on the need for the workers to cooperate with other progressive forces to secure reform. Revolution was not necessary; by a slow evolutionary process, the workers could eventually achieve their goal. Marx himself had recognized before his death that a revolution might not be needed in those countries that had universal suffrage, but some of his followers were more orthodox than their master and a vigorous debate broke out between them and the revisionist or evolutionary socialists, as Bernstein and his supporters were called. On the surface, the orthodox Marxists were still in the lead in 1914, but in fact most socialist parties had become convinced that their ends could be achieved by peaceful reform.

The preference for social reform over revolution is also illustrated by the Christian Socialist movement in both Catholic and Protestant churches which eventually weakened the historic tie between the clergy and the forces of conservatism. Prior to the last quarter of the nineteenth century, the Catholic Church had continued its policy of resisting every hint of modernism. In 1864, Pope Pius IX (1846-1878) had issued a *Syllabus of the Principal Errors of Our Time* in which he declared that "it is an error to believe that the Roman Pontiff can and ought to reconcile himself to, and agree with, progress, liberalism, and contemporary civilization." He censured among other things nationalism, socialism, religious toleration, and lay-controlled education. In 1870, the Vatican Council, the first general Church council since the Reformation, had proclaimed that the pope, by virtue of his apostolic power, was infallible when he spoke *ex cathedra* on matters of faith and morals. It was at this moment, and not during the Middle Ages, that the Roman pontiff won his final triumph over the bishops and council of the Church.

In 1878, however, the sixty-seven-year-old Joachim Pecci became Pope Leo XIII (1878-1903) and inaugurated a newer, more positive approach. He encouraged the study of Saint Thomas Aquinas, as a means of reconciling the seeming conflict between faith and reason, and of history as a means of showing the contributions the Catholic Church had made towards the progress of civilization. Democracy he found as acceptable to Christianity as monarchy, and in the encyclical *Rerum novarum* he upheld the individual's right to own private property and condemned Marxism but at the same time insisted that employers had a moral responsibility to improve the lot of the workers. By his actions, he strengthened a group of socially-minded Catholics in Germany, France, and elsewhere. Catholic labor unions and moderate Christian Socialist parties dedicated to reform by peaceful evolution began to appear in various countries.

A similar move developed more slowly in Protestant circles, where capitalism had won firmer roots, but as early as 1848 a small group of Englishmen had proclaimed themselves Christian Socialists and argued that their creed of cooperation was more Christian than the capitalistic creed of competition.

ANARCHISM AND SYNDICALISM

In the less democratic or more backward countries like Russia and Spain, revolutionary violence remained the only means of securing reforms. Here anarchism and syndicalism vied with Marxian socialism. Anarchism was an extreme form of liberalism. Its adherents carried the liberal's dictum that the government that governed least governed best to the logical extreme that there should be no government at all. Man, they firmly believed, was inherently good but was corrupted by the state and society. Destroy these two and he would be good again. Some anarchists were essentially philosophers who had no intention of harming anyone, but others, like the Russian Michael Bakunin (1814-1876), believed that a small group of highly trained, dedicated revolutionaries could commit so much violence that the state and society would collapse. Bakunin devoted his life to revolutionary activities, and during the quarter of a century following his death, a Russian tsar, an Austrian empress, an Italian king, and one president each from France and the United States were assassinated by anarchists.

The anarchists were nevertheless more a nuisance than a serious threat to the social structure, except in those localities where they infiltrated the labor union movement and encouraged the development of syndicalism. The syndicate was a union of workingmen in the same or similar trades. Unlike other unions, however, its primary motive was not to get higher wages or better working conditions for its members, but to overthrow the state. Syndicalist theorists like Georges Sorel (1847-1922) put great emphasis on the class struggle and advocated frequent strikes to develop the workers' class consciousness. Non-striking syndicates were to lend financial support to those on strike to strengthen the spirit of co-operation. As this spirit developed, the strikes would become larger and the workers more class conscious until finally there would be a general strike, bourgeois society would collapse, and the state would disappear, leaving the syndicate the only organization. Man would be free from compulsion, but he would rather work for the common good than remain indolent. Until the successful strike, violence, the destruction of machinery, indeed anything that would disrupt the capitalistic system and develop the worker's class consciousness, were the orders of the day. This radical movement won control of France's largest labor union, the *Confédération Générale du Travail*, and was influential in the union movement in Italy, Spain, and a few other countries.

THE INTERNATIONAL WORKING MEN'S ASSOCIATION

An effort was made to secure cooperation between the various labor reform movements by forming the International Working Men's Association (or First International) in London in 1864. Present at the first meeting were nationalists like Mazzini, anarchists like Bakunin, socialists like Marx, and some relatively conservative labor union leaders. Quarrels, as might be expected from such a heterogeneous group, were frequent. Most of the union leaders and Mazzini withdrew after Marx and others had endorsed the Parisian uprising of 1871. This left the field free for Marx and Bakunin to compete for control. Marx finally won, but the movement had become so discredited that it collapsed in 1876.

In 1889 the Second International was established. It was a loosely organized federal group consisting of representatives from the socialist parties of various countries. Congresses were frequently held, but they served more to frighten conservatives and nationalists than to bind the workers of the world together. When war came in 1914, German and French socialists alike forgot Marx's dictum that a worker had no country, and jumped to the flag.

The laborer, because of his unions, the threat of the new ideologies, and above all his recently acquired right to vote, was greatly benefited by social legislation, especially after 1900. Beginning with Germany in the 1880's, country after country passed acts regulating or forbidding woman and child labor and limiting the working hours of adult males. Sickness insurance, health insurance, workingmen's compensation acts, and the like became commonplace. It was these acts that won the loyalty of most socialists by 1914, but at the same time they marked a further departure from laissez-faire.

INTEGRAL NATIONALISM

Another threat to liberalism came from the development of a new type of nationalism. Nationalism during the first half of the nineteenth century had been allied with romanticism and liberalism. States, it had been believed, should be established along racial lines and no one race should try to rule another. They were not to compete with one another for power, but rather each was to make its unique contribution to civilization. The conservative had opposed nationalism because it threatened the dynastic state, just as he had opposed liberalism because it threatened his power.

The emergence of integral nationalism during the last quarter of the century brought about a profound change in social-intellectual alignments, and nationalism and conservatism often became allies. The integral nationalists, in the words of one of their number, believed in "the exclusive pursuit of national policies, the absolute maintenance of national integrity, and the steady increase in national power—for a nation declines when it loses military might. . . . A true nationalist places his country above everything; he therefore conceives, treats, and resolves all pending questions in their relation to the national interest." Where this happened, nationalism ceased to be a liberalizing force and became a totalitarian force that compelled one to consider every act in regard to the effect it would have on national destiny. For a diplomat to advocate compromise with a foreign government, for a racial minority to ask for autonomy, for a laborer to strike in time of emergency was considered treasonable. To prevent this from happening, public schools were used to teach loyalty to the nation. Minority races were discouraged in the use of their mother tongue, and attempts were made to persuade them to adopt the culture of the dominant race. The Germans, who had lately been seeking unity for themselves, tried to Germanize the Poles and French in their territory. Russians treated the Poles and Magyars treated the Slavs in like manner.

Several factors led to this development. Industrialization caused the people of a nation to draw closer together. They began to live in cities rather than in villages or scattered farms. Social and business contacts increased, and labor unions were organized along national lines. Contacts with foreigners increased less rapidly. This was especially true after 1875 when economic rivalries became more intense, tariffs were raised, and imperialism was revived.[5]

Wars that led to German and Italian unification had taught that success was not to be achieved by the romantic dreams of an idealistic Mazzini, but by the "blood and iron" policies of a realistic Bismarck. They bred a

[5] See pages 704-728.

martial ardor that was further inflamed by the growth of compulsory military training, the advent of cheap sensational newspapers, and the application of the biological concept of the "survival of the fittest" to the relations between states and races. The Englishman, German, or Russian was led to believe that the very existence of his race as an independent entity proved its superiority over the other races in his state. At the same time, growing competition between states made him feel that every minority race must be incorporated culturally into the state whether it willed or not. The inauguration of universal compulsory education provided the means to achieve this cultural integration and also to make the members of the leading race in the state more conscious of their national identity. Conservatives were especially vociferous in their adoption of the new integral nationalism because it gave them a popular platform which would draw votes in the newly democratized countries, and it was a weapon they could hurl at the socialists who denied that the worker had any country.

THE CULT OF VIOLENCE

Perhaps the most serious threat to liberalism came, not from those who attacked its principles, but from those who abandoned its methods. Once a national state had been formed and a constitutional framework had been established, the nineteenth-century liberals had been willing to listen to the voices of reason and compromise. They had respected the opinions of others and after 1850 had sought to achieve their goals through legal means. As the twentieth century dawned, however, an unwillingness to compromise and an impatience with the slow rate of legislative reform appeared, and there was an alarming tendency to turn towards direct action outside the law. Some used force when persuasion failed, and others regarded violence as a mark of virtue.

The cult of violence reached its greatest proportions in the pre-war years in left-wing and labor movements. Anarchists sought to disrupt society through the assassination of judiciously selected persons; syndicalists wrecked factories and talked of the myth of the general strike; Marxists plotted a class revolution; and even responsible labor unions sought to win their objectives through paralyzing general strikes. The aristocracy and middle class were only slightly less affected. Army officers balked at carrying out orders of civilian governments; France, Germany, and unmilitaristic Great Britain had trouble on this score. Businessmen went beyond the limits of the law in their efforts to destroy competitors or to frighten away union organizers. Even women did not escape the cult of violence, and in staid England, suffragettes indulged in vandalism, assault, and exhibitionism. They broke window panes, went on hunger strikes when arrested, and renewed their activities when the bewildered authorities released them. Perhaps the cult of violence may be explained by the prevalence of Social Darwinism with its doctrine of the survival of the fittest, perhaps it is inherent in human nature, but whatever its origin it took the international violence in World War I to bring the wave of internal violence to a temporary end.

CONCLUSIONS

Despite the growth of combinations, the movement away from laissez-faire, the rising threat from labor and socialism, the growing popularity of integral nationalism, and the cult of violence, the middle class and liberalism were still triumphant when war came in 1914. There were still fields of industry which one could enter as an independent businessman, and there were still many opportunities for promotion in big industry for the able man with initiative. Laissez-faire was only partially abandoned, and many new restrictions were designed more to protect the freedom of the individual than to destroy it. The rising demands of labor were not intended to halt material progress, but to spread material gains among a larger percentage of the population—and the older liberal nationalism remained strong enough to combat the newer integral nationalism in most countries.

15/ The Growth of Democracy

B Y 1871 the great historic races in western and central Europe had
achieved unity and independence, and the major internal issues
centered on the degree of democracy to be permitted and the extent
of social reform. The problems concerning democracy were whether suffrage
should be extended, whether the popularly elected lower house of the legislature should have greater authority than the more aristocratic upper house,
and whether the cabinet should be responsible to the king or the legislature.
These issues were most often resolved in favor of greater democracy, although in a few countries progress in this direction was barely perceptible. Social legislation to benefit industrial workers was enacted everywhere. In some instances, the initiative was taken by the representatives of
the expanded electorate; in other instances, it came from conservative ministers of the crown. Russia and the American republics experienced similar movements in varying degrees.

GREAT BRITAIN

During the half century before the outbreak of war in 1914, democracy was increased in Great Britain by extending the suffrage and by other constitutional changes. The crown interfered less and less with the government, and the House of Lords was stripped of most of its powers. It is true that the growing complexity of government made it necessary for the cabinet to prepare important bills and that party discipline became so exacting that the members of the Commons rarely voted contrary to the wishes of their party leaders. Nevertheless, by 1911, Britain was a genuine democracy. All but one of the demands of the Chartists were realized. The same period saw part of the upper-middle class desert the Liberal party and join the aristocratic conservatives. The old laissez-faire liberalism was abandoned to make way for a new liberalism that involved government action to secure social reform. Political parties had to change their philosophies and platforms to meet the new conditions. These developments were complicated by an everpresent Irish question.

DISRAELI AND GLADSTONE

The Tory party, or Conservative party as it was now called, was the first to undergo revision. The Conservatives had been seriously divided in 1846, when Peel had persuaded some of them to vote for the repeal of the Corn Law. The majority, under the leadership of Benjamin Disraeli (1804-1881), insisted on tariffs to protect the interests of the landed gentry who dominated the party. A Jew who had been baptized, Disraeli was an eccentric man of modest means whose family had not come to England until 1748. He had studied law, written several novels, and finally entered politics. He undoubtedly possessed intellectual powers of a high order, but his ambition, his contempt for his enemies, and his disdain for his supporters led many to believe he lacked sincerity. One opponent declared that he was "without principle, without feeling, without regard to anything, human or divine, beyond his own personal ambition. He has dragged, and will continue to drag everything that is good, safe, venerable, and solid through the dust and dirt of his own objects." Nevertheless, it was Disraeli who became the accepted leader of the conservative landed gentry, the friend of Queen Victoria, the reorganizer of the Conservative party, and one of the principal founders of the modern British Empire.

During the two decades following the repeal of the Corn Law, the Whigs, now rechristened the Liberals, were in power most of the time, but in 1866 the Conservatives assumed office with Disraeli as the real, though not the titular, head of the government. To strengthen his party's position in the Commons, Disraeli persuaded titled conservatives to mix with the wealthy middle-class members of Parliament who were especially anxious to be accepted by the old aristocracy. Eventually, a Primrose League was

Benjamin Disraeli from a painting by Sir John E. Millais. (National Portrait Gallery)

formed to facilitate this plan. To win the confidence of laborers, Disraeli sponsored an extension in the suffrage to give them a vote and a program of social reform. That it was the landed aristocracy who first abandoned the doctrine of laissez-faire and used the state to help the poor is not surprising. This class had a traditionally paternalistic attitude towards the poor and less of a stake in the new industry than the Liberal party with its larger middle-class component. The first result of Disraeli's new program was the Reform Bill of 1867, which gave the ballot to nearly all the adult male inhabitants of the towns and extended the suffrage in the countryside. The number of voters was increased from about one million to two million, a fact which caused even the sponsors of the bill to call it "a leap in the dark." Furthermore, the seats in the Commons were redistributed to remove some of the inequities uncorrected by the Reform Bill of 1832.

The great increase in the size of the electorate reduced the role of personal influence and outright bribery that had characterized the earlier history of the elections to the Commons. Political parties had to be better organized to manipulate the electorate, and party discipline had to be enforced. Prior to 1832, a large portion of the members of the Commons had owed their election to the patronage of the crown or some great noble; factions had been more important than parties; and the composition of the cabinet had reflected the desires of the king as much as those of the Parliament. The Reform Bill of 1832 had dealt an important blow to this system, but it was the Reform Bill of 1867 that brought it to an end.

After 1867, there was no longer any doubt that Great Britain would become a parliamentary democracy with a cabinet system of government. The old parties and factions joined together to form two major political parties, each with a recognized national leader, a national platform, and a national organization. After an election had been held, the leader of the party that won the largest number of seats in the Commons was asked by the crown to form a cabinet. This cabinet was responsible to the Commons in that it had to resign if one of its proposals was rejected. Rejections were rare because they necessitated a new election in which the members had to undergo the expense of another campaign and the risk of losing their seats. In practice, therefore, the cabinet directed the executive branch of the government and proposed legislation that was nearly always accepted by the Commons.

Before the development of a rather rigid two-party system in which each party had a recognized leader, the kings had enjoyed some latitude in the selection of a prime minister and a cabinet, although since the Revolution of 1688 they had tried to have a cabinet that was acceptable to a majority in Parliament. The role of the crown in choosing the cabinet had steadily declined since the late eighteenth century, and after 1867 it disappeared almost completely, except when factional strife or the presence of a small third party prevented a single party from commanding a majority in the Commons. In this manner, the role of the monarch was reduced under normal circumstances to presiding at formal functions and to giving encouragement and warning to public officials.

To the surprise and disappointment of the Conservatives, the industrial workers voted for the Liberals in 1868, and Disraeli was forced from office before he had an opportunity to pass social measures. His great antagonist, William Gladstone (1809-1898), became prime minister. Gladstone was the son of a wealthy merchant. He had received an aristocratic education at Eton and Oxford and had entered Parliament at an early age, where he had supported Peel in the move to repeal the Corn Law. Since this hurt his chances for advancement in the Tory party, he decided to join the Liberals. He was a staunch defender of the principles of civil, religious, and economic liberty; a hard, methodical worker; and a brilliant orator. Indeed, in every respect he was an opponent worthy of Disraeli.

Gladstone's first ministry (1868-1874) was one of the most important in British history. He sought to pacify the Irish by enacting a series of measures. The Anglican Church in Ireland was disestablished, and Catholics were relieved from the obligation of paying the tithe for its support. A land act was passed providing that evicted tenants be compensated for improvements they had made and for the inconveniences of moving. The law also enabled tenants to borrow money from the government to buy land.

At home, the extension of the suffrage in 1867 had given votes to many illiterate persons and made doubly necessary the improvement of public education. In 1870, a measure was passed establishing new schools and providing additional support for those already in existence.

657

In a few years, the number of children in schools doubled and illiteracy became less common. In 1871, Oxford and Cambridge fellowships and professorships were opened to non-Anglicans for the first time. To improve the efficiency of the government, Gladstone reduced the role of influence and money in appointments. Competitive examinations were established to determine who would be named to most positions, and the centuries-old practice of purchasing commissions and promotions in the army was abandoned. Finally, to protect the new voters from being unduly influenced by their employers and landlords, voting by voice was abandoned and the secret ballot was adopted.

In spite of his many accomplishments, Gladstone was decisively defeated in the elections of 1874. Each of his reforms had hurt a special interest, and his pacific foreign policy during the years the Italians and Germans were winning unity and glory angered British nationalists. He had even agreed to submit to international arbitration an American claim for compensation for damage done by the Confederate cruiser *Alabama*, which had been built in England. An adverse decision cost $15,500,000 and further loss of pride.

Disraeli returned to office determined to revive British prestige abroad, to expand the British Empire, and to prove that the conservative aristocracy was the natural protector of the workingman. He played a prominent part in the affairs of eastern Europe, purchased the Khedive of Egypt's shares in the Suez Canal in order to give Britain some influence over that vital trade artery, and made Victoria Empress of India. The new title was attacked by the liberals as being "un-English," but it pleased the lonely Queen. More important, the very title indicated that India was a country federated with the crown and not just another colony. It pleased the Indians and reduced their opposition to being a part of the British Empire.

Disraeli's efforts in the domestic sphere were equally important. The urban workers wanted, he declared, "better, healthier, more humanizing conditions in their own daily life. They wanted sanitary and commodious homes; they wanted regulations of their occupations so as to minimize risk to life and health; and to prevent excessive toil for their women and children; they wanted freedom of contract and equality before the law with their employers; they wanted encouragement and security for their savings; they wanted easy access to light and air and all the beneficent influences of nature." During Disraeli's ministry, the first serious attempt was made to clear the slums, despite the protests of middle-class landlords. A Public Health Act was passed which led to much needed improvements in sanitation. The enclosure movement was halted, and public lands were turned into playgrounds and parks. Shipowners were required to discard unseaworthy vessels and to treat sailors decently. More important, governmental opposition to trade unions was reduced, and an act was passed which had the effect of legalizing collective bargaining.

Despite these significant achievements, Disraeli was defeated by Gladstone in 1880, largely because the economy had taken a temporary turn for the worse during his administration. Within two years he was dead, but his efforts had borne some fruits. During the next twenty-five years, the Conservatives were predominantly in power.

Gladstone's second ministry (1880-1885) saw further advances towards democracy. The franchise was extended in 1884 to include rural workers, thereby adding two million voters to the electorate. The following year the medieval system of representation by boroughs and counties was abandoned, and single-member constituencies with approximately equal populations were established almost everywhere. Suffrage of male adults had become virtually universal, and the vote of an inhabitant of one locality carried no more weight than the vote of the inhabitant of another. These acts brought to completion the constructive phase of the Liberals' domestic program. They had come to accept a broad, democratic suffrage, but were not ready to abandon laissez-faire. As a result, they were unwilling to pass social legislation to benefit the workingman and did little more than to try to solve the Irish problem.

The Irish had become more troublesome to their British masters than ever. In addition to their chronic economic complaints, they had become increasingly nationalistic. Under the leadership of Charles Stewart Parnell (1846-1891), they determined to force the English to re-establish a parliament in Ireland and give them home rule. Parnell was a brilliant orator, but it was not by persuasion that he hoped to secure his ends. He advised the Irish members of Parliament to do everything in their power to make the English want to get rid of them. They were to disrupt the proceedings of the Commons by making unnecessary speeches and amending every bill; they were to avoid polite social contacts with the English outside its halls.

In 1881 Gladstone made a final attempt to win Irish loyalty by economic concessions. Under his leadership, Parliament passed an act which departed from the laissez-faire ideals of the Liberals to the extent of fixing rents at a fair rate, but Irish nationalism was too strong to permit satisfaction short of home rule. Gladstone shared the generous attitude of most Liberals towards the aspirations of subject peoples, and during his third ministry he tried to push through Parliament a bill creating an Irish parliament to control domestic affairs, but retaining military and trade matters for the British Parliament. His efforts brought only a split in his party and a defeat at the polls. When Gladstone came to power for the last time in 1892, he made another attempt to give Ireland home rule, but the conservative House of Lords rejected the measure. The Liberals renewed the attempt in 1912, but the Lords succeeded in delaying the bill until the outbreak of war in 1914 forced a further suspension.

659

THE LIBERAL AND LABOR PARTIES

Meanwhile, the gradual desertion of the wealthier members of the middle class from the Liberal party and their growing influence among the Conservatives led to the abandonment of Disraeli's policy of befriending the workingman. Under the Conservative, Lord Salisbury (1830-1903), there were few domestic reforms beyond the creation of elective councils in every county to perform the administrative duties that during the less complex earlier period had been done by the justices of the peace. Foreign policy and imperialism held the Conservatives' attention. What talk there was of abandoning laissez-faire came from those who wanted a protective tariff, not from leaders desirous of protecting the rights of workingmen.

Rejected by both major parties, representatives from the labor unions joined with a group of intellectuals known as the Fabian Socialists to form a Labor party in 1900. The Fabian Socialists included such men as George Bernard Shaw, H. G. Wells, and Sidney and Beatrice Webb, who became famous as writers, historians, and reformers. Their program called for getting the workingman to use his newly-won vote to capture the Commons and enact legislation that would improve the lot of labor. Much of the socialism they advocated was to be applied at the municipal level and did not go beyond providing the services now furnished by most well-run European or American cities.

At first, the Labor party made little progress, but two events gave it impetus. In 1901, the House of Lords, acting as the highest court in the land, ruled in the Taff Vale case that labor unions were subject to injunctions and could be sued for damage done by their members. This decision made the strike, the only economic weapon of labor, a virtual impossibility and caused unions to throw more effort into the new party in the hope of using it to get favorable legislation. The second event which furthered the growth of the Labor party was a decline in the economic status of the workingman. Between 1873 and 1900, the real wages of workers had risen over 40 per cent, but after 1900, foreign competition became so intense that British manufacturers had to cut prices. Real wages fell 10 per cent by 1914, and workers became more determined to use the power of the ballot to alleviate their lot. The result was that the English and Irish Laborites won about fifty seats in the Commons in 1906.

The Liberals, who won control of the Commons in that year, saw that they would have to provide a program of social reform or they would eventually lose their remaining support from the working classes. As a result, they abandoned laissez-faire and voted a series of major measures through Parliament. The Taff Vale decision was reversed in 1906, and unions were given the right to picket. A Workingman's Compensation Act required the employer to compensate employees injured while at work. An Old Age Pension Act provided a small income for those over seventy, minimum wage rates were established, and steps were taken to improve the housing of workers. Most important of all, a National Insurance Act provided sickness and unemployment insurance for the poorer workers.

Part of the costs of the National Insurance was borne by the employer and employee, but part was assumed by the government. This obligation, added to the costs of the other social measures and of growing naval expenditures, made new taxes necessary. To get funds, it was decided to increase the taxes of the rich. The clever, energetic Welsh Chancellor of the Exchequer, David Lloyd George (1863-1945), prepared a budget calling for higher income and inheritance taxes and for a 20 per cent levy on the increased value of land, a proposal which hit those aristocrats who had made fortunes by selling their land at inflated prices near rapidly growing cities.

The budget passed the Commons in 1909 but was rejected by the Lords. It was unprecedented for the Lords to refuse to accept a money bill passed by the Commons, but that aristocratic body not unnaturally considered Lloyd George's proposals as class legislation. New elections were ordered and the Liberals were returned to power. The conservative House of Lords accepted defeat and passed the budget bill, but this was not enough. The Liberals and their Irish allies were tired of having the Lords block their desires. They passed an act which denied the right of the Lords to veto money bills and left them only the power to delay for two years other measures passed by three successive sessions of the Commons. Needless to say, the Lords also rejected this bill, but the new king, George V (1910-1936), resolved the ensuing constitutional crisis by promising to create enough Liberal peers to ensure the bill's passage. The Lords surrendered as they had done in 1832, and the Parliament Bill became law in 1911. Another important step towards democracy had been taken.

Indeed, the dreams of the Chartists, dreams that had once seemed so radical, were on the verge of being realized. In 1911, salaries were voted for the members of the Commons, permitting poorer persons to serve, and in 1918 universal suffrage of adult males became a law. Even women, whom the Chartists had neglected, were given the right to vote if they were over thirty. In 1928, the age limit was reduced to twenty-one, the same as for men. Of the Chartists' six demands, only annual Parliaments were not realized, but the Act of 1911 had reduced the maximum life of a Parliament from seven to five years.

Legally, Great Britain had almost become a complete democracy, but the system of rigidly disciplined political parties mitigated the effect of universal suffrage, the secret ballot, and ministerial responsibility. Furthermore, the influence of the aristocracy remained strong. The diplomatic service and the army continued to be their favorite preserve, and because of their willingness to compromise with changing times and to recast themselves in a more popular image by taking the lead in imperialism and some aspects of social reform, the Conservative party remained one of the two largest in the nation. A grandson of the Duke of Marlborough guided

Britain to victory in World War II, and the Earl of Home abandoned his title to serve as prime minister in 1963.

FRANCE

France appeared headed for democracy in 1848 when Louis Philippe was overthrown and a republic was established, but the Bonaparte restoration temporarily reversed this trend. By 1869, however, the Second Empire had become a liberal constitutional monarchy; by the early twentieth century French institutions were as democratic as those of England, and the influence of the Church and the aristocracy had been reduced to a minimum.

THE SECOND EMPIRE

Napoleon III had always had faith in his own and his family's destiny. It was this faith and the nostalgic desire to recreate the glorious romantic empire of his uncle that had given him the courage to act in his youth in spite of the great odds that were against him. It is therefore not surprising that the Second Empire was very much like the first. The Emperor assumed control over the army, diplomacy, and administration. A council of state chosen by the Emperor was re-created to recommend legislation, and a legislative assembly was re-created to approve but not to initiate legislation. This assembly was chosen by universal manhood suffrage, but a system of official candidates and governmental pressure prevented the free choice of its members. Other aspects of the First Empire, the Code Napoleon, the centralized administration, the fiscal system, and the concordat with the pope, had, of course, been kept by the various regimes after 1815 and did not need to be re-established. The first Napoleon had sought to achieve the amalgamation of the old pre-revolutionary aristocracy and the new one he created from the rising middle class. His nephew had a more difficult task, for since 1800 the urban workers and the peasants had become so important that they had to be included in any reconciliation between the forces of conservatism and the forces of change. To unite the old France and the new, Napoleon III had to effect a compromise between authority and democracy, between Catholicism and nationalism, between economic liberalism and the workers' welfare. By 1869, it appeared possible that he had succeeded, but a year later military defeat toppled the regime.

Napoleon was fortunate that his reign coincided with the rapid expansion of French industry and transportation. He did what he could to stimulate this development and to make the middle class believe that it was a natural accompaniment of the imperial regime. Government subsidies were furnished to help finance a joint-stock bank known as the *Crédit Mobilier,* which loaned large sums to railroads and other big enterprises. Between 1851 and 1858, the number of railroad miles increased over fourfold, and the following year a French company began to construct the Suez Canal. The full extent of French economic and technological progress was demonstrated by the Paris International Exposition in 1855. Five years later, Napoleon felt that French industry was so nearly ready to compete with British industry that he made a free trade treaty with that country to the discomfiture of many industrialists.

Napoleon also embarked on a huge public works program to help business and improve the standard of living. Most conspicuous was the rebuilding of Paris. The old city walls and the narrow, winding streets lined with medieval houses were cleared away to make room for the broad boulevards, beautiful public buildings, and well-built apartments that characterize Paris today. Before this building program began, the well-to-do often resided on the lower floors of a building, those of moderate income inhabited the middle floors, and the poor lived on the top floors. The new apartments were so expensive, however, that the workers moved to the suburbs, while the installation of elevators made the well-to-do willing to inhabit the upper floors. This led to social segregation. The central quarters of Paris became overwhelmingly middle class, and many of the suburbs became proletarian. The removal of radical elements of the population from the center of the city and the construction of wide boulevards that could easily be swept by artillery or cleared by cavalry charges reduced the possibility of successful uprisings. Since these changes were made, the Paris populace has not been able to change the form of government as it had so often done before, except in time of national military disaster.

Napoleon did not neglect the workers, in whom he was sincerely interested. Public hospitals and asylums were constructed, labor unions were tolerated for the first time since 1791, and conciliation boards composed of employers and employees were established to settle wage disputes. Wages rose, and the French workers probably suffered less than their British counterparts during the transformation into an industrial economy.

A bank was established to make loans to people in the provinces to enable them to make improvements. Swamps were drained, and the advent of railroads began to affect the rural economy by removing part of the sharp difference between town and country, although the typical French peasant remained quite conservative. Rural France, where Catholicism was strong, was gratified by Napoleon's decision to maintain clerical influence in education and to protect the pope from the threat of Italian nationalists who were seeking to unify their country.

For the French people as a whole, Napoleon offered national self-satisfaction. Paris once more became the capital of Europe. Here peace conferences and international expositions were held. Here his beautiful wife, the Empress Eugénie, and his glittering court established the social and fashion capital of the world.

Napoleon sought to recapture the military glory of the First Empire as well. In 1854, he led France into a successful war with Russia in the Crimea.[1] The Moscow campaign of 1812 was avenged, and the Russo-Austrian cooperation to prevent the triumph of liberalism and nationalism was brought to an end. In 1859, he embarked on a war against Austria to help Sardinia unite north Italy. French arms were once more victorious, but more of Italy became united than Napoleon had intended. Most of the papal states were lost to the new kingdom of Italy, and the remainder appeared threatened.[2] The staunch Catholic frowned and the taxpayer grumbled, but Napoleon remained convinced that the path of glory led to popularity. He engaged in imperialistic adventures in Algeria, Indo-China, Syria, and above all Mexico, where he sought to establish the Habsburg Maximilian on the throne during the American Civil War. The northern victory in 1865 enabled the United States to force a French withdrawal two years later, and Maximilian was captured and shot by irate Mexicans.

As one foreign policy failure followed another and as the costs of belligerency increased, opposition to the Emperor grew. It was then that Napoleon, now sick and tired, showed his political wisdom. Instead of continuing the repressive policies he had adopted when he seized power, he gradually abandoned them and permitted increased popular control over the government. Censorship of the press was halted, public assemblies were permitted, and in 1869 the ministers were made responsible to the legislature rather than to the Emperor. The legislature received the power to propose and debate bills, and the empire became a liberal constitutional monarchy. Napoleon was the only French ruler during the century flexible enough to change with changing conditions. Like the English kings, he slowly surrendered his power to keep his throne. He made orderly progress possible. Had he been given more time, he might have done much to unite the new and the old France, but his defeat and capture by the Prussians in 1870 brought the Second Empire to an abrupt end.

THE ESTABLISHMENT OF THE THIRD REPUBLIC

The republican-minded Parisians capitalized on Napoleon's defeat to force the legislative assembly to create a government of national defense to continue the war with Prussia. The new government did surprisingly well, since by all the laws of war France was already defeated. Paris heroically resisted the besieging Germans, and Léon Gambetta (1838-1882) made a spectacular escape from that beleaguered city in a balloon to raise

[1] See pages 605-606.
[2] See pages 607-609.

troops for its rescue. But it was all to no avail. By the end of January, 1871, Paris had been forced to surrender, and Gambetta's hastily-assembled forces were defeated.

It was amid these defeats and the persistent republican clamor for war that elections to the new national assembly were held. The results were surprising, at least to the Parisians. Only 200 of the deputies elected were republicans. Of the remaining 430, thirty favored a return to the Bona-partist regime, and the others were about evenly divided between those who advocated a Bourbon and those who advocated an Orléanist restora-tion. The vote probably reflected the constitutional outlook of Frenchmen far less than their attitude towards the war. Rural France recognized de-feat and voted for the advocates of peace. Urban France, still much less numerous, voted for the advocates of war.

Still, a monarchical restoration appeared a distinct possibility. The aged Thiers, who had played such a prominent role in the establishment of the Orléanist monarchy in 1830, assumed the role of chief executive in the new government, peace was made with the Germans, and the National As-sembly voted to transfer the capital to Versailles, twelve miles from the Paris populace.

Radical Parisians were angered and alarmed. If the rest of France had resisted as heroically as they had done, would Alsace and part of Lorraine have to be ceded, would an indemnity have to be paid, would the hated Ger-mans have to be permitted to march through their city? To these questions they gave a resounding "No!" The monarchists had betrayed France and were using the national defeat as an opportunity to put another king on the throne and to enact measures that put economic hardships on the workers. Another Parisian uprising seemed so likely that Thiers sent troops to re-move two hundred cannons from the city. The Parisians resisted, there was bloodshed, and the troops withdrew.

Paris was in a state of rebellion. A municipal council known as the Commune was elected to govern the city, and once more the question was raised of whether Paris or the rest of the nation would determine the fate of France. The supporters of the Commune were members of the lower middle and working classes. Some were mild republicans, some were radi-cal Jacobins, some were Utopian socialists, anarchists, or even Marxists. On the whole, their egalitarian, patriotic, anti-rural, anti-clerical, and anti-monarchical temper reflected the Jacobin spirit of 1793 far more than the Marxian theory of class struggle or even the Utopian socialists' desire for economic and social reform.

Unhappily for the Commune, Thiers had a stronger character than Charles X or Louis Philippe. Regular troops numbering 130,000 were launched against the city, and in one bloody week nearly 20,000 persons were slain—a few by the Communards, who murdered the Archbishop of Paris, and many by the government's troops, who executed prisoners with little or no trial. Much blood had been shed, but order was restored.

The problem of establishing a new government proved more difficult than that of quieting the rebellion. A majority of the assembly wanted a monarchy, but who was to be king? About two hundred deputies supported the Count of Chambord, a grandson of Charles X, but an equal number favored the Count of Paris, grandson of Louis Philippe. After much debate, the Orléanists agreed to support the claim of the childless Chambord in return for recognition of the Count of Paris as his successor. Thiers was ousted from the presidency, and Marshal MacMahon (1808-1893) was appointed in his place. Thiers had secured the withdrawal of German troops from French soil, but he was no longer considered trustworthy by the monarchist majority in the assembly because he had come to the conclusion that a republic "is the government that divides us least."

The way now seemed clear for a Bourbon restoration, but at the last moment the monarchists' plan failed because Chambord issued a manifesto which revealed that he thought in terms of the restoration monarchy if not that of the old regime. He even refused to accept the tricolor of the revolution and insisted on the white flag of the Bourbons. He would never, he declared, "abandon the flag of Henry IV." Even the royalists recognized that few Frenchmen were willing to turn back the pages of history that far. Indeed, many of them wanted a king on the English model, who would serve as head of state but who would not interfere directly with the government. There was nothing for them to do but to wait for the obstinate Chambord's death. To put the Count of Paris on the throne before then would violate the laws of succession.

Meanwhile, it was necessary to improvise a government. Early in 1875, the National Assembly passed three laws designed to establish a government which many deputies hoped would last only until Chambord's death. It was, however, destined to survive for sixty-five years. There was to be a president chosen by a bicameral legislature for a term of seven years; the upper house or Senate was to be elected by municipal and departmental officials, and the lower house or Chamber of Deputies by universal manhood suffrage. The powers of the president were not defined because it was hoped that his place would soon be taken by a king. France, as Gambetta's newspaper put it, had "entered the republic backwards."

The first test of the new constitution was soon to come. In the elections of 1876, the system of indirect suffrage enabled the monarchists to obtain control of the Senate, but the republicans won over two-thirds of the seats in the popularly elected Chamber of Deputies. The majority of Frenchmen had clearly been converted to republicanism. This shift in sentiment was due to the widespread desire for peace and stability. The republic, which in 1871 had been associated with the continuation of the war with Germany and the Jacobin radicalism of the past, had proved itself capable of bringing the war to an end, defeating the Paris Commune, and operating an efficient, conservative administration that even refused to have an income tax. Then too, in the hurried, confused elections of 1871, the inhabitants of the small towns and villages had usually voted for the most important man they knew, the local aristocrat, but in 1876 there was more time for republican candidates to make themselves known.

For a time, MacMahon tried to function with republican ministers; but it soon became obvious that the monarchical cause was growing weaker, and he decided to strike while there was still a chance of victory. In May, 1877, he dismissed the republican ministers and named the royalist Duke of Broglie to head the cabinet. When the Chamber refused a vote of confidence to the new minister, MacMahon dissolved the legislature and called for new elections. Pressure was applied on the electorate to vote for the government's candidates, but the republicans carried the Chamber. MacMahon's only remaining weapon was the army, but he was too scrupulous to unleash it on the people. In January, 1879, he resigned when the republicans captured control of the Senate, and the sly, conservative, avaricious Jules Grévy (1813-1891) was elected president in his stead.

MacMahon's defeat not only preserved the republic; it marked the victory of the legislature over the executive. From that time, no president of the Third Republic tried to dismiss a minister, and the cabinet was recognized as responsible to the legislature. If defeated in either house, the cabinet had to resign, but new elections were not held. This system prevented the development of well-disciplined political parties because legislators could vote against their leaders in the cabinet without running the risk of having to stand for re-election themselves. In addition, the political campaign embittered French politics for a generation. It separated the moderate royalists from the moderate republicans at a time when they were beginning to cooperate, and it ensured future attacks on the Catholic Church because the Church had supported the monarchists in the critical period of the 1870's.

During the twenty years that followed MacMahon's resignation, various coalitions of moderate republicans controlled the republic. With the exception of Gambetta, they were colorless men with little vision. Their firm bourgeois, liberal orientation caused them to reject any thought of the government's sponsoring a program of social reform or of attempting to speed the nation's economic growth through industrial modernization. They made no effort to strengthen the executive branch of the government and expended their political energies quarreling among themselves and attacking the Catholic Church because its monarchical leanings endangered their position and its religious doctrines ran counter to the scientism and materialism of the age. Gambetta was the only important exception to this rule. He did his best to strengthen the government's authority, unite the republican factions, and reconcile them with monarchists, Catholics, and laborers. His efforts came to nothing. He died young, and powerful enemies of the republic developed on the right and left.

THE ATTACKS ON THE REPUBLIC

MacMahon's defeat weakened the position of the extreme conservatives who at that time were generally royalists. To them, the republic was the enemy of the king, their church, and their class. In numbers they could no longer match the republicans, but they included in 1879 the bulk of the aristocracy and the clergy, both still powerful in the countryside. Gradually, they were joined by that part of the upper-middle class that opposed the corruption of the republic at home and its weakness abroad. Above all, the devout were displeased with the anti-Catholic attitude of the republican leaders. For a generation, most conservatives were monarchists, but gradually, as World War I drew near, some of them began to believe that conservative, nationalist, and religious values could be best preserved by a republic.

Meanwhile, an enemy had been developing on the left. In 1871, the bulk of the urban laborers had asked only for a republic, but the bloody suppression of the Paris Commune by Thiers had taught them that a republic in the hands of determined conservatives could be more repressive than a monarchy. Most of them abandoned the idea of a Jacobin republic and began to search for other means to gain their desires. For a generation, the French labor movement was weak because so many of its potential leaders had been destroyed in the Paris uprising. Largely through the efforts of Jules Guesde (1845-1922) and Jean Jaurès (1859-1914), labor unions and socialism did develop, but part of the movement's strength was dissipated by division within its ranks. Some became evolutionary socialists who willingly cooperated with middle-class reformers, some were Marxists, and still others were syndicalists. Of the three groups, only the evolutionary socialists supported the republic, and they merged with the larger Marxist party in 1905. Thus, there were those on both the right and the left who did not accept the existing form of government.

This situation plagued most of the history of the Third Republic. Only if those who believed in the republican form of government stood together could a majority in the legislature be counted upon. But some republicans were conservative, some were liberal, some were Catholic, and more were anti-Catholic. To these legitimate differences of opinion were added the lack of party discipline and personal rivalries and jealousies. Together, they led to the growth of a multitude of political parties. No one party ever received a majority of the votes. All ministries had to be coalitions in order to muster sufficient support in the legislature, but government by coalition is notoriously weak. The withdrawal of a single party might mean a government defeat, the resignation of the cabinet, and inevitably the formation of a new, slightly different coalition. Between 1871 and 1914, France underwent fifty cabinet changes, while Great Britain with its disciplined two-party system underwent only nine. This situation did not destroy continuity in the government because the bureaucracy remained unchanged

668

and the same officials often served in first one and then another cabinet. It did mean, however, that a ministry had difficulty achieving genuine changes or taking strong action if the republic were threatened.

The dangerous position of the republic was revealed in 1885, when the monarchists more than doubled their strength in the legislature and the left made substantial gains. General Boulanger (1837-1891) was the first to try to profit from the increased anti-republican sentiment. As minister of war, he had won tremendous popularity with the army by improving its weapons, lodging, and rations; with the nationalists by such dangerous acts as threatening Germany and by such innocuous measures as painting the tricolor on sentinel boxes; and with the masses by military parades and numerous public appearances on his black horse. To the monarchists, Bonapartists, and radicals he appeared as a savior. At the same time, the republic was beset by scandals. President Grévy had to resign when his son-in-law was discovered selling the Legion of Honor and other favors. By January, 1889, victory appeared to be in Boulanger's hands, but at the critical moment he lost his nerve and, thoroughly discredited, fled to Brussels where he committed suicide on his mistress' grave.

The Boulanger affair had hardly subsided when the Panama scandal broke. Since the French had won international acclaim by constructing the Suez Canal, there was a ready response when Ferdinand de Lesseps (1805-1894), the engineer of that project, appealed for funds to support a canal across Panama. Everyone knew that De Lesseps was old in years, but his feat of marrying at sixty-four and having twelve children led many to believe that he was still young in mind and body. Unfortunately, he was not. A combination of engineering mistakes and yellow fever slowed the work on the canal. It became necessary to bribe government officials and newspaper editors to stop investigations and unfavorable publicity. In 1889 the company went bankrupt in spite of these efforts and many lost large sums, though only a handful of the guilty were punished. The once proud boast of a "republic of virtue" became a farce.

Several of the leading figures in the Panama scandal had been Jewish, and this led to a marked increase in anti-Semitic propaganda by nationalists and racists. They were joined in 1897 by some monarchists, clergymen, and army officers. Three years earlier Alfred Dreyfus (1859-1935), a Jewish captain, had been sentenced to Devil's Island for selling military secrets to a foreign power, but now new evidence was uncovered indicating that he was innocent. The army, idol of the nationalists and stronghold of the monarchists, refused to order a new trial, either because senior officers still believed that Dreyfus was guilty or because they wanted to avoid admitting that they had made a mistake. The republicans insisted, and crisis followed crisis amid suicide, forgery, and scandal. In 1899, Dreyfus received a presidential pardon, and in 1906 he was reinstated in the army. The whole affair now seems to have a comic opera quality, but it was nevertheless important. The moderate republicans who had controlled the republic since 1879 lost control of the government because of their failure to take a firm stand, and a group of more radical republicans came to power determined to break the monarchical stronghold in the army and the Church.

The victory of the republic over the aristocratically controlled army and the Church may be attributed largely to social, economic, and intellectual changes that had been taking place in France during the previous generation. The aristocracy had lost control over the government when Mac-Mahon resigned in 1879. Many nobles continued to serve in the Church, army, and diplomatic corps, but even in these preserves their position was weakening, and in 1889 only four of the eighty-six archbishops and bishops were of noble birth. In England, the aristocracy managed to retain considerable influence by allying itself to the wealthy middle class. In France, the past struggles between the aristocracy and the middle class made such a union more difficult to achieve, and, even if it had taken place, the upper-middle class was not strong enough to enable the aristocracy to stem the democratic tide. Control of the government therefore passed quickly from the aristocracy to the lower-middle class, which consisted of shop-keepers, white collar workers, minor civil servants, and school teachers.

The failure of France to develop a large, wealthy middle class was related to its slow economic growth in comparison to other industrial countries. Industrial production increased threefold between 1870 and 1914, but this was accomplished with a minimum of industrial concentration. Trusts and cartels were exceptional and the typical French business continued to be the small family concern. As late as 1914, a third of the industrial workers of France were employed by concerns with ten or less employees.

The failure of the French middle class to keep pace with that of other industrial countries is probably to be explained more by its psychological outlook than by lack of opportunity. Since the Renaissance, the members of this class had generally invested their money in places that yielded secure incomes. Those who owned their own businesses preferred to keep them small, if to enlarge them meant borrowing money or sharing control with other stockholders. The French middle-class ideal was a genteel, cultured life with good food, good wine, and ample leisure. The rough-and-tumble existence of aggressive businessmen in other countries seemed ungentlemanly to them. Foreign competition would probably have forced them to abandon their complacent attitude if a tariff had not been established in 1892 that ensured the domestic market for them. Thus, although some members of the upper-middle class cooperated with the aristocracy and returned to the fold of the Catholic Church, they were not strong enough to stem the popular tide.

At the same time, the aristocracy and the clergy were losing their hold on the peasant. In 1882, a bill had been passed establishing public primary and secondary schools throughout the country in which there was to be no religious instruction. Previously, nearly half the boys and nearly all the girls who received educations had attended parochial schools and many of the peasants were illiterate. As result of the new bill, a state-employed teacher, who was generally a secular-minded republican drawn from the lower-middle class, joined the curé and the aristocrat as the third educated man in the village. Soon he won the allegiance of his pupils and many of their parents from the royalist aristocrat and the priest. The close tie between the Church and the peasant that had plagued the republicans of 1793 waned perceptibly.

The peasants shared most of the prejudices of the lower-middle class. Many were small property owners with limited economic vision and an inherent conservatism that caused them to oppose expensive governmental social reforms and to farm their holdings in the traditional manner. They were much more reluctant to migrate to the cities than their British counterparts, and the rural population continued to increase until 1890. This meant that the already small peasant holdings became smaller still, although birth control was used to limit the size of families, a practice which caused the French population to increase by only three million between 1871 and 1914 while that of the other great powers forged far ahead. Probably foreign competition would have led to the consolidation of the small farms and the use of more scientific methods if the tariff of 1892 that saved French industry had not also applied to agricultural products. As late as 1914, 44 per cent of the French population still resided on farms.

The peasants' acceptance of the secular republic was one of the principal factors that enabled the lower-middle-class republicans to attack the army and the Church, and, through them, the aristocracy. It also enabled them to hold working-class legislation to a minimum and to handle strikes with dispatch. Between 1892 and 1911, laws were passed protecting women and children in industry, establishing a ten-hour day, and providing for workingmen's compensation and old age pensions, but most industrial countries went much further. France's slow progress may be attributed to lower-middle-class and peasant dislike of government interference and to the relatively weak position of French labor unions, occasioned in part by the lack of large industrial plants.

Direct action by labor brought no better results, and a strike by railroad workers in 1910 was met by drafting the disgruntled workers into the army and ordering them to run the trains or face a court-martial. They chose to do the former and the prime minister, Aristide Briand (1862-1932), onetime advocate of the general strike, was credited with a signal victory. By 1914, the republic—democratic, secular, but strong—was ready to withstand defeats that would have toppled any other French regime since the downfall of the old monarchy.

CENTRAL EUROPE

THE CONSTITUTION OF THE GERMAN EMPIRE

The constitution of the new German empire which emerged in 1871 out of the Franco-Prussian War was unique. Unlike the British constitution, it was written, but unlike that of the United States and other European countries, it was not the product of a constituent assembly in which a group of deputies met to create a new system of government. The German constitution was based on that of the North German Confederation, which had been prepared under Bismarck's direction, and on separate treaties with the southern German states. It did not provide for a rational, coherent system of government like those prepared by constituent assemblies, but rather reflected Bismarck's plan for the future empire, mixed with the practical expediency that always marked his program. It therefore had enough democratic features to win the support of all but seven members of the lower house of the new legislature, but at the same time reserved a powerful position for the Hohenzollern emperor and the aristocracy. The imperial government was given the necessary authority to ensure it a powerful voice in European affairs, but enough rights were preserved for the once independent member-states to satisfy the desires of most of those who still felt strong loyalty to their native Bavaria, Württemberg, or Prussia.

The constitution provided that the Prussian kings would be hereditary German emperors. The emperor's powers were roughly comparable to those of the president of the United States in that he was the head of the executive branch of the government. He commanded the army and navy, declared war with the consent of the upper house, planned and regulated diplomatic matters, and directed the internal administration of the government. The emperor acted through a chancellor and various subordinate ministers who were responsible to him, not the legislature. There was some debate over whether he had a veto over legislation, but he had two decided advantages over the president of the United States—he did not have to stand election every four years, and as king of Prussia he wielded considerable power in that all-important state.

The legislature consisted of two houses: an upper house, or Bundesrat, representing the member states and a lower house, or Reichstag, representing the people. Unlike the Senate of the United States, the amount of representation in the Bundesrat that was given to the twenty-five states in the empire varied somewhat in accordance with their importance. Prussia was granted seventeen of the fifty-eight seats, Bavaria six, and the smallest states only one each. However, since Prussia made up over half the empire, there was ample justification for its predominance. The Bundesrat was chosen by the member-states and therefore became the preserve of the princely families of the separate states. The Reichstag was the national and democratic feature of the new constitution. Its seats were apportioned in accordance with population, except that no provision was made for a redistribution of seats to keep pace with the movement towards the cities, and its members were elected by universal manhood suffrage. The powers of the Reichstag were less than in many legislative assemblies because the ministers were not responsible to it; but its control over taxation gave it the same weapon that the English House of Commons had used so effectively, and the chancellors found it expedient to adopt policies that ensured the support of a majority of its membership.

The rights reserved for the member-states varied according to their size and location; states in south Germany were nearly autonomous in internal affairs. Bavaria even maintained its own post office and controlled its army in time of peace. All the member-states kept their kings, grand dukes, dukes, and princes. Thus, the new German empire was conservative and federal, but as years went by there were demands for more democracy, and it is the failure of these demands to bear fruit, rather than the initial conservatism of the constitution, that should be stressed.

Much of the blame for the failure of democracy to develop more fully must be placed on the army and Bismarck. The army regarded itself as the bulwark of the monarchy and the aristocracy against what it considered the radicalism of the middle and lower classes. Its leaders sought to escape the control of the war minister, the only military official subject to questioning by the democratically elected lower house, and to operate under a military cabinet and general staff that acknowledged only the authority of the Emperor. Bismarck himself had difficulty in limiting the independence of the generals; and later chancellors were even less successful. The army gradually became independent of the Reichstag, the chancellor, and the other civilian agencies of government. In addition to freeing the army from civilian control, military leaders took steps to ensure their subordinates' loyalty to the Emperor. As long as there were enough junkers to fill the officer corps, this was not difficult, but the increasing size of the army made it necessary to commission members of the middle class. Great care was taken to select only sons of "honourable *bourgeois* families in whom the love for King and Fatherland, a warm heart for the soldier's calling, and Christian morality are planted and nurtured." In short, officers of bourgeois origin were to have a "nobility of temperament" if not of birth. They were to be as loyal to the monarchy, as brave, and, unhappily, as arrogant as the sons of the most ancient families.

BISMARCK

Bismarck had no more love for liberalism or democracy than the junker army officers, but he was an intelligent conservative. He saw the wisdom of formulating a program that was acceptable to a majority of the people so long as it did not mean a surrender of any significant power on the part of his king or his junker class. He began his chancellorship of the new empire by working in conjunction with the large, well-to-do middle-class National Liberal party. The National Liberals admired his achievements so much that at first they were willing to forgive him for his unwillingness to surrender real power to them. With their aid and that of several minor parties, Bismarck received the necessary support in the Reichstag to enact his tax program. With their aid, he also attacked the Catholic Church.

Catholicism was suspect in the 1870's because of Pius IX's *Syllabus of Errors,* which criticized most aspects of contemporary secular thought, and because of the recent proclamation of the dogma of papal infallibility.[3] By organizing the Center party in 1870, the German Catholics aroused still more suspicion. The program of this party seemed to threaten the new empire by its insistence that the rights of the Church be preserved. It stood for political decentralization and parochial schools and opposed civil marriages. The party was especially large in south Germany, where there were strong historic ties with France and Austria. This was enough to make the National Liberals want to attack. Bismarck was equally suspicious of Catholics and thought that an anti-Catholic crusade might strengthen his foreign policy by winning the approval of anti-papal Russia and Italy. The result was the *Kulturkampf*—the struggle for civilization. The imperial government expelled the Jesuits and made civil marriages obligatory. The Prussian state government went further. In May, 1873, it issued a series of measures which removed the education, appointment, and discipline of the clergy from the hands of the Catholic Church and gave these tasks to the state. The Catholic clergy refused to comply; a number, including two archbishops, were thrown into prison. Diplomatic relations between the papacy and Germany were broken off, and the pope declared that the Prussian laws were null and void because they "contradict the divine institution of the church."

An impasse had been reached; then, in 1878-1879, Bismarck suddenly changed his policy. The attack on the Catholic Church, the alliance with the National Liberals, and the policies of laissez-faire were terminated; he began to operate with the aid of conservatives and the brunt of his wrath was turned against the socialists. There were several causes for this revolutionary shift. In the first place, it was becoming apparent that the Catholics were winning the *Kulturkampf.* The Center party was growing larger, and many Lutherans, including Bismarck, had begun to fear that the anti-Catholic feeling that had been stimulated might turn into a general anti-clerical, anti-religious movement. Bismarck was not one to support lost causes or to endanger the Lutheran church. Happily for him, reconciliation with the Vatican was made easier by the death of Pius IX and the election of the somewhat more liberal and much more diplomatic Leo XIII (1878-1903).

The second cause of Bismarck's shift in policy was the left-wing Social Democratic Workingman's party, which had been formed in 1869. Two

[3] See pages 648-649.

years after its formation it had polled 124,000 votes and sent two deputies to the Reichstag; in 1877, it won 493,000 votes and elected twelve deputies. Here was a far greater danger than the Catholics could ever be. At this time, the Social Democrats were only partly Marxist, but they were radical enough to be anti-capitalistic, anti-nationalistic, and anti-monarchical. To Bismarck, neither the Emperor, the junkers, nor the new nation would long be safe if the growth of this party was not halted.

The third cause was that the National Liberals had ceased to be compliant allies. They insisted that three of their number become ministers, and this step in the direction of ministerial responsibility was unacceptable to both Bismarck and the Emperor. Instead, Bismarck decided to try to split the middle class by uniting its wealthier members with the conservative landed interests in a common program. Upon this coalition, he depended until the end of his ministry.

This coalition, which would have been impossible a decade earlier, was the result of foreign competition. Both the junker aristocrat and the peasant proprietor were beginning to suffer from the competition of foreign wheat brought into Germany by newly constructed railroads. The industrial middle class was equally loud in its complaints about the influx of British manufactured goods since the beginning of the depression in 1873. What could be more natural than a bargain between the government, the agricultural, and the industrial interests in which the common bond would be a protective tariff and the hatred of socialism? The wealthier part of the middle class was willing to desert its advocacy of economic liberalism in such a good cause. Its tie with the junkers was often strengthened by intermarriage. Newly rich industrialists thereby won social prestige, and none-too-wealthy junkers obtained money. In this manner, the German middle class became divided like its English and French counterparts, and the National Liberal party became smaller.

The new policy called for peace with the Catholic Church and a protective tariff, both of which were achieved in 1879. It also called for measures to combat the rise of the Social Democrats. Here Bismarck once more displayed his genius. He saw that repressive measures would not be enough and that a constructive effort would have to be made to win the allegiance of the working class. To halt the spread of socialist propaganda, public meetings and the publication of literature by groups aiming at "the overthrow of the existing order of state or society" were forbidden, but the old liberal tradition was so strong in the Reichstag that Bismarck could not get it to agree to prevent the Social Democrats from running candidates for office or to limit their freedom of debate in the legislature.

The constructive part of Bismarck's program deserves special mention because it was the first large-scale effort on the part of the state to intervene in the economic order on behalf of the workingman. In 1883, a Sickness Insurance Law was passed to provide support for the sick. The costs were to be shared by the workers and the employers. The following year an Accident Insurance Law was enacted to provide support for those who were injured while working. This time the full burden was placed on the employer. An act setting up old age and disability insurance to which the state also contributed followed in 1889, but in spite of these measures, socialism and the Social Democratic party continued to grow. In 1890, it polled over 1,400,000 votes, more than any other party.

Bismarck thought his policy of winning the loyalty of the masses had failed. The rapid industrialization that was taking place in Germany meant that the number of workers and presumably the number of Social Democrats would continue to grow. Someday they might actually capture control of the Reichstag. The monarchy, the aristocracy, and the Church were doomed unless a new course was charted. The iron chancellor decided on more repressive measures—how repressive we do not know, for in March, 1890, he was dismissed from office.

Undoubtedly the principal reason for Bismarck's dismissal grew out of the death of the ninety-one-year-old Emperor, William I, in 1888. William's son, Frederick, ruled only a few months before dying of cancer, and his grandson, William II, assumed the crown. William II (1888-1918) was then not quite thirty and Bismarck was seventy-three. It was too much to expect the crusty old man, who had guided the state so brilliantly for over a quarter of a century, to show the proper deference towards his new sovereign. It was useless to hope that the young Emperor, vain, romantic, and ambitious, would long be content to accept the tutelage of the old statesman. There were questions of policy, too. William opposed further repressive measures against the Social Democrats and was critical of Bismarck's foreign policy. For two years the two strong wills clashed before the dismissal came.

WILLIAM II

William II was not stupid, but he was intellectually unstable. Although not unattractive, he was given to vainglorious speeches in which he made tactless remarks. What other civilized ruler in his day would have told a group of young recruits, "When your emperor commands you to do so you must shoot at your fathers and mothers" or would publicly express the opinion that "There is only one master in the empire and that is I, and I will tolerate no other"? He had no use for the constitution, which he proudly proclaimed he had never read. "The soldiers and the army, and not the decisions of parliaments forged the German empire," he declared. These pronouncements resulted more from personal insecurity than from aggressiveness, for William had an almost pathetic desire to be popular. It was this trait that made him unwilling to repress the Social Democrats, and what little progress Germany made towards genuine democracy took place during his reign.

With the aid of first one chancellor and then another, William set

The Kaiser drops the pilot: a PUNCH
cartoon on the dismissal of Bismarck.
(Bettmann Archive)

about to renew Bismarck's efforts to win the workers. The anti-socialist laws were dropped. Industrial courts were established to adjust wage disputes, factory inspection was improved, the working hours of all persons, especially women and children, were limited, and the benefits of Bismarck's insurance system were extended to cover many not formerly included. Germany was fast becoming the first welfare state. At the same time, the rapid industrialization which was taking place brought increased rewards to capital and labor alike. The per capita income increased from 450 marks in 1896 to 645 marks in 1913. Yet, on the surface, William's efforts were to no avail. The Social Democratic party adopted a firmer Marxist stand in 1891, and it was supported by an ever-increasing number of voters. In 1912, it attracted 30 per cent of the electorate, over twice as many as any other party. But the efforts of Bismarck and William to win the workers did not end in failure. In deed, if not in word, the Social Democratic party was becoming revisionist. Its members were learning that they could obtain social justice from the monarchy without revolutionary violence. In 1914, they were ready to cooperate loyally with the bourgeoisie and the nobility in the defense of their country.

The majority in the Reichstag, though proud of the rapidly growing industrial and military might of the empire and happy at their ever-expanding wealth, did not cease its efforts to make the government more democratic. The chancellors always tried to have the bulk of the deputies support their policies, and ministerial responsibility was a probable development. Salaries were voted the members of the Reichstag in 1906, five years before the British House of Commons passed a similar measure to enable the poor to serve in the legislature. Through its control of the purse strings, the Reichstag sought to control the army. In 1902, it won a notable victory by forcing the reduction of the required term of military service from three to two years. Nevertheless, the army remained a largely independent agency. In 1913, it refused to punish a junior officer for his arrogant treatment of a civilian in Saverne, Alsace, and a vote of 293 to 55 in the Reichstag condemning this position brought no change of heart. In France, the "honor" of the army had been successfully attacked in the defense of Captain Dreyfus; in Germany, it was the civilian forces that met defeat.

Yet when all is considered, the years 1870-1914 were happy ones for the Germans. In less than half a century they had transformed a mass of quarreling agricultural states into the greatest industrial and military power on the continent. Surely the industrialization that had done so much to break the power of conservatism in Western Europe would in time perform the same service for them. Perhaps it would have done so had war not come so soon.

AUSTRIA-HUNGARY

Austria-Hungary was the last of the dynastic states. Its emperor, Francis Joseph (1848-1916), was already a gray-haired, venerable ruler when the German empire was formed, but he was to guide the destinies of his multinational state and his house well into World War I. Francis Joseph was neither a wise nor an astute statesman. A Cavour or a Bismarck could fool him with ease, but at home he was a master of the art of divide and rule. His long tenure in office made him a veritable institution, and he became the most important link in the chain which held the empire together.

When Hungary was given equal status with the Austrian provinces in 1867, it was presumed that the Germans and the Magyars would be the dominant races. Since the Germans made up only 35 per cent of the population of the Austrian provinces and the Magyars only 48 per cent of Hungary, the development of any sort of democracy was difficult. By giving the Poles and Croats special status and by counting the Jews as Germans or Magyars, the two privileged races constituted a bare majority of the population. Since all Germans and Magyars were not in agreement as to politics, a restricted suffrage which excluded the lower classes, for the most part members of one of the numerous Slavic peoples, was necessary. When the Germans or Magyars sought to reduce the role of the emperor in the government, they were in a vulnerable position. Francis Joseph had only

Francis Joseph. (Wide World)

to threaten to give special privileges to the Czechs or to some other national group, or to extend the suffrage, to bring them to their knees.

When the growing industrialization in Austria proper and Bohemia brought the development of both Christian and Marxist Socialist parties, Francis Joseph was not very perturbed. The introduction of the idea of a class struggle might mitigate the more centrifugal struggle between the nationalities. After all, the socialists, like the Habsburgs, professed to belong to no country. In 1907, universal manhood suffrage was introduced in the Austrian provinces; with it came the increased power of the socialist parties and social legislation comparable to that found in other countries. No party, or coalition of parties, could muster a majority in the legislature, and Francis Joseph was left with the happy necessity of ruling by decree. Universal suffrage had not really made Austria more democratic, but it had made the task of divide and rule easier and it had made the lower classes more content.

The Magyars opposed the introduction of universal manhood suffrage into Hungary because they were only a minority of the inhabitants. To be successful, however, they had to buy the Emperor's support by agreeing to abandon their demands to tamper with the army, long an imperial preserve. As a result, Hungary remained an agricultural state guided by a gentry that controlled the countryside and dominated the civil service.

On the surface, Francis Joseph was in a far stronger position in 1907 than he had been when he had come to the throne in 1848 or at any other time in his career, but there were limits to how long his divide and rule tactics could succeed. Many Magyars wanted complete independence; many Austrian Germans wanted union with Germany. More serious, the Czechs and the southern Slavs were beginning to despair of achieving equality. Time and again their hopes had been raised by the Emperor only to have them dashed when he made a new deal with his German or Magyar subjects. By 1914, many awaited only the opportunity to proclaim their independence. They plotted with the Serbs and the Russians. Francis Joseph was wise enough to see this, but he was not wise enough to provide a solution. The empire was about to crumble; only some untoward event could save it from destruction.

ITALY

Italians and non-Italians alike are apt to consider the period to 1870 as one of great achievement but to regard the following half-century as one of failure. There is some justification for this feeling; neither the idealist Mazzini, the statesman Cavour, nor the soldier Garibaldi was to find a successor. Yet when one takes into consideration the problems faced by the newly united kingdom, the post-Risorgimento generation of Italians should not be too severely condemned. There were practical reasons, in addition to their own failings, that prevented Italy from assuming as important a position in world affairs as the newly united Germany.

The inhabitants of both countries suffered from lack of experience in self-government, and in both there were pronounced sectional differences. However, in Italy the Catholic question assumed more serious proportions. Pope Pius IX refused to accept any compromise offer from Italy after the seizure of Rome and shut himself up in the Vatican, declaring that he was a prisoner. Catholics were forbidden to participate in the Italian government. Each individual had to decide between his church and his country. Thus, to sectional differences, was added a religious cleavage that further weakened the state.

More serious still was Italy's economic backwardness. The basic ingredients of the new industrial age were iron and coal. Germany possessed both in abundance, but the Italians had neither. The growing complexity of the industrial system made a modest amount of education on the part of the workers desirable, but three-fourths of the Italian population were illiterate.

Allowing for these handicaps, Italian accomplishments were not meager. An effort was made to establish compulsory education, and by 1913 the number of illiterate persons had been reduced to less than 38 per cent. Slowly, an intelligent, capable group of industrial workers came into being. No alternative was found to importing the iron necessary for railroads and machines, but steps were taken to harness the numerous mountain streams to produce electricity as a substitute for coal. By 1905 Milan had become the greatest silk manufacturing city in the world, and there was considerable progress in other light industries. An adequate system of railroads and a large merchant marine were also constructed.

While the educational and economic opportunities of the Italian people were being improved, progress was made in the direction of democracy. In

1881 the suffrage was increased to include two million persons, over three times as many as before. Universal manhood suffrage was achieved in 1913, and at the same time salaries were established for the members of parliament.

Near the turn of the century, the labor movement became better organized and more radical. This led initially to repressive measures, but the socialist movement was strengthened by some middle-class support. After 1900 reform replaced repression. Accident, sickness, and old age insurance was established, and working conditions, especially for women and children, were regulated.

Hence, something was accomplished, but more might have been done if a large army had not been maintained, a navy developed, and colonial adventures attempted. The parliament and the bureaucracy were riddled with graft, corruption, favoritism, and inefficiency. Many were disappointed that unity had not brought greater advances and became contemptuous of the petty squabbles between officials and of the slow process of constitutional government.

THE SMALLER STATES

Most of the smaller states followed the lead of great powers towards democracy and social reform. A constitutional monarchy was established in Belgium when it broke away from the Netherlands during the Revolution of 1830. The little state industrialized nearly as rapidly as Great Britain; and with industrial expansion came universal manhood suffrage in 1893, old age pensions in 1900, workmen's compensation for accidents in 1903, and other pieces of factory legislation. The Netherlands continued to stress trade rather than industry and the absence of a large number of factory workers may explain why democracy developed more slowly than in Belgium, but by 1917 universal manhood suffrage was established.

In 1815 the Congress of Vienna laid down the principle that Switzerland would be perpetually neutral, but until 1848 the country was less a state than a group of autonomous cantons. In that year, after a brief, successful war with seven conservative Catholic cantons, the more liberal Protestant cantons established a new constitution which strengthened the federal structure but still left the individual cantons some conrol over their internal affairs. During the nineteenth century, Switzerland led the European states in the march towards democracy. All male citizens could participate in legislation in some of the smaller cantons. Initiative and referendum were practiced in the larger cantons and in the federal government where there were elected legislators. Switzerland became a haven of liberty, and exiled radicals like Russia's Lenin made their headquarters there.

The Danish king retained considerable power during the nineteenth century, and even the more liberal constitution of 1866 gave him the authority to appoint part of the members of the upper house. This did not prevent some social and factory legislation from being passed in the 1890's, but it was not until 1915 that the king lost the right to make appointments to the upper house and the upper house itself lost the power to block measures passed by the lower house. In that same year all adult male citizens and most women were given the right to vote.

Norway had been taken from Denmark and given to Sweden by the Congress of Vienna, but the new union was not a happy one. Sweden was still an aristocratic agricultural state in 1814 in which the king exerted considerable authority. It was not until 1864 that the Swedes replaced their medieval four-house diet with a modern bicameral legislature. Industrialization began soon thereafter, and with industrialization came factory legislation and, in 1898, universal manhood suffrage. The Norwegians, on the other hand, were a democratic, seafaring people who accepted the union only when invaded by a Swedish army and even then managed to keep a separate one-house legislature. Norwegian nationalism increased during the latter part of the nineteenth century, and there were frequent quarrels with the Swedes over conflicting economic interests. Finally, in 1905 they persuaded the Swedish king to abdicate and chose a Danish prince to be their sovereign. Two years later Norway became the first country to give women the right to vote. Compulsory education and social insurance were also enacted.

Spain and Portugal were economically backward states in which the kings, the aristocracy, and the Catholic Church suppressed liberal movements. Both countries were plagued by civil wars brought on by rival claimants to the throne and by occasional uprisings against the repressive regimes. Spain actually experimented with a republican form of government in 1873, but the Bourbons were restored the following year. The country became a little more stable in 1876 after a new constitution was adopted, which provided for a bicameral legislature and ministerial responsibility on the English model. However, the suffrage was limited and the crown managed to exercise a strong influence on the government. The Portuguese ousted their dictatorial king in 1910 and established a democratic republic which tried to reduce clerical influence by separating church and state and barring religious instruction from the public schools.

Five kingdoms and one principality were established in the Balkans between 1799 and 1913.[4] All of them had parliaments, and in four the suffrage was increased and institutions were made more democratic in the decades before 1914. However, the kings generally retained more authority than in the West, and the actual functioning of democratic institutions left much to be desired. Since they were backward agricultural states, there was no strong demand for social or factory legislation and little was passed. In spite of these reservations, the Balkans, like the rest of Europe, appeared to be moving towards greater democracy in 1914.

[4] For the emergence of the new Balkan states see pages 519, 558-559, 747-760.

The Growth of Democracy

RUSSIA

Russia, as might be expected, remained less liberal and less democratic than the other major European states, but even here there were signs of progress, especially after 1905.

The successor to Alexander II, the tsar-liberator and tsar-reformer, was his son, Alexander III (1881-1894), a big, powerful, dull man whose chief merits were his courage and his desire to be a good ruler. His conception of the good ruler did not entail a surrender of the ruler's authority or of his responsibility to govern, but it did include an obligation to improve the lot of the peasants and, to a lesser extent, the factory laborers. He reduced the amount of the installments the peasants had to pay for the land they received upon emancipation and substituted a tax on bonds and inheritances, which fell on the well-to-do, for a poll tax which had burdened the poor. Between 1881 and 1886, laws were passed to prohibit the employment of children under twelve in factories and to limit the working hours of those under fifteen.

Alexander III gave serious consideration to his father's plan of having the *zemstvo* elect representatives to sit with the council of state to discuss new laws. Unfortunately, this plan, which might have proved the first step towards the formation of a parliament, was never put into effect, largely because of the influence of Constantine Pobedonostsev (1827-1907), procurator of the holy synod. Pobedonostsev was more than an ordinary reactionary. He was a philosopher, law professor, and Slavophile, who believed that there was a spirit peculiar to the Russian people that must be preserved at all costs. Western ideas of constitutionalism, liberalism, democracy, separation of the church and state, and freedom of speech were rigorously suppressed. Religious and national minorities were persecuted. Jews especially were mistreated, and many left Russia for the United States or elsewhere. The number of pupils in the secondary schools and the universities increased, but the Orthodox Church assumed a larger role in the former, and freedom of discussion was limited in the latter. Reliance was placed on the gentry, and its role in the *zemstvo* was increased at the expense of the lower classes. This was a foolish move because the abolition of serfdom had so weakened the gentry that it was no longer a sufficient bulwark to preserve the crown and because the gentry as a whole was less conservative than the government. Perhaps the gravest mistake of all was Alexander's decision to make Pobedonostsev tutor of his son and successor, Nicholas II (1894-1918).

Nicholas inherited his father's dull mind but not his strength of character. He had difficulty saying no to anyone and was swayed by whomever he was with at the moment. Only a good liberal education could have made him a tolerable ruler. Needless to say, Pobedonostsev taught him to be an autocrat and used his influence to ensure the continuation of Alexander's policies. Nicholas' most redeeming feature was his devotion to his wife and children. The Empress Alexandra was an unintelligent, narrow-minded, devout German princess who ruled her husband with an iron hand. She was dedicated to her five children and determined that her only son, Alexis, should one day receive a crown as autocratic as that of his father. Unhappily, the young prince had inherited hemophilia through his mother from his grandmother, Queen Victoria of England. His life was in constant danger. When doctors could do nothing, the distraught mother sought divine aid in the form of religious mysticism, with the result that the royal family became too deeply involved in its own personal tragedy to realize that Pobedonostsev's reactionary policies were becoming increasingly unrealistic.

INDUSTRIALIZATION, PEASANTS, AND POLITICAL PARTIES

Three related movements were taking place that called for a change in policy: the beginning of industrialization, the increasing dissatisfaction on the part of the peasants, and the growth of political parties. Industrialization was brought about by the importation of foreign techniques, the desire for gain, and the emancipation of the serfs that released an adequate free, as opposed to a serf, labor force. Between 1860 and 1890, progress was steady, but not spectacular. Annual coal production increased from 329,000 tons to over 5,000,000 tons, and the iron and steel output quadrupled. The great period of expansion, however, began around 1890. Sergius Witte (1849-1914), the able finance minister, borrowed heavily from abroad to get funds to construct a railroad system, largely state-owned, that included a line across Siberia to the Pacific Coast. Iron, coal, oil, and textile industries moved forward rapidly in spite of occasional depressions. The production of farm machinery quadrupled between 1900 and 1912 and equal strides were made in other fields. By 1914, Russia had a middle class and an urban labor force of considerable importance, although it was still, relatively speaking, an industrially backward agricultural nation.

The importance of agriculture in Russia caused the worldwide decline of farm prices to be especially serious. The peasants' position was particularly unfortunate because they lacked the capital, the know-how, and the acreage to farm scientifically. The collectivist *mir*, with its outmoded three-field system and its scattered strips, still dominated the rural scene. Equally important, much of rural Russia had become over-populated. The peasants had been given barely enough land in 1861, and the constant increase in the population meant that holdings farmed by each peasant became smaller every time the *mir* redivided the land. The peasant, who was inclined to blame all his troubles on his lack of land, was envious of the estates of the gentry.

The growth of political parties, or, more accurately, of schools of

684

thought, was certain to lead to trouble. One party or school was composed of conservatives like Pobedonostsev who stood firmly behind the existing autocratic regime. A second group was composed of liberals, drawn especially from the gentry in the *zemstvo* and the professional and industrial middle class. The left wing of this group, led by the historian Paul Miliukov (1859-1943), advocated revolutionary changes. It stood for parliamentary government with ministerial responsibility, universal suffrage, and the secret ballot and recommended sweeping legislation designed to bring social betterment. The right wing advocated a slower, evolutionary change with the establishment of a conservative, but constitutional, regime and the rule of law. The two wings of the movement divided in 1905, the left-wing members becoming known as the Constitutional Democrats or "cadets" and the right-wing members as the Octobrists.

More dangerous was the Social Revolutionary party. The Social Revolutionaries owed their origin to a populist movement in the 1860's. The populists were Slavophiles who believed that there was something peculiar in the Russian spirit that must be preserved, but they found it, not in an autocratic tsar, but in the village *mir* where the "real" Russian still resided uncorrupted. They distrusted Western capitalism and liberalism and directed their efforts towards founding a revolutionary movement among the peasants designed to turn all the land over to the *mirs* for their use. In 1879 the movement divided. One group, the People's Will, advocated assassination as the means of achieving its goal. The other adopted more legitimate revolutionary methods. It was the People's Will that murdered Alexander II in 1881. Police and popular reaction was so violent that the movement temporarily declined, only to be revived at the turn of the century as the Social Revolutionary party. The Social Revolutionaries were essentially agrarian reformers, and the urban workers were given only a secondary position in their thinking. Assassination continued to be the weapon of a minority whom the police regarded as more dangerous and more radical than the Marxists.

THE MARXISTS

The first Russian Marxist organization was formed by a group of exiles in Switzerland in 1883. They attacked the Populist-Social Revolutionary thesis that it was possible to base the revolution on the peasants and to move from an agricultural economy directly into socialism without experiencing industrialization. At first, few listened to their arguments, but as time passed the growth of a factory system in Russia seemed to bear out Marx's analysis, and an increasing number of the younger radicals began to join their movement. Among the new converts was Vladimir Ilyich Ulyanov (1870-1924), better known to history as Nicolai Lenin.

Lenin's father had been born into the middle class, educated at a university, and elevated to the nobility in return for his services as a bureaucrat. Lenin was therefore raised in comfortable and intellectual surroundings. He responded to his many advantages by standing at the top of his class in secondary school. However, two catastrophes struck the Ulyanov family in 1886-1887. Lenin's father died, and his brother was executed for his implication in a plot to murder the Tsar. From that time, the youthful Lenin found obstacles placed in his career. As the brother of a would-be assassin, he was kept under police surveillance and expelled from a university. He was fortunate to be permitted to take a bar examination, which he passed in 1892 after an exceptionally brief period of individual study. The following year he became a convert to socialism, motivated by hatred of the government and the society that had murdered his brother and blocked his career, the apparent logic of Marx's arguments, and a sincere desire to help the workers among whom he now began to live. In 1897 he was exiled to Siberia for three years because of his revolutionary activity, but the energetic young man availed himself of this opportunity to write *The Development of Capitalism in Russia,* in which he attacked the populist agrarian approach by showing that Russia was moving towards capitalism. When he was released in 1900, he settled in western Europe where he remained until 1917, except for a two-year span beginning in 1905 when he returned to Russia to participate in revolutionary activity.

During these years, Lenin continued his theoretical studies and fought for leadership of the newly formed Russian Social Democratic party. Two basic issues divided the Russian Social Democrats. Lenin and his followers argued that the workers would develop only a trade-union consciousness if left to their own devices. It was necessary to have a highly trained, disciplined party to direct them towards a revolutionary movement. Since democracy depended on everyone's having full information, a condition impossible in a revolutionary party, dictatorial control must be exercised from the top. The anti-Lenin wing of the party, on the other hand, had more faith in the workers and wanted a large, democratically-functioning party.

The second dividing issue grew out of Lenin's analysis of the capitalistic system. After 1871, he argued, capitalism had entered upon a monopolistic and imperialistic phase which prolonged its life but at the same time marked its end as a progressive force. A successful blow in any one country would topple the system. It was therefore not necessary for a backward country like Russia to be captured by the bourgeoisie before communism could take over. The workers, aided by the peasants, could topple the regime as it then stood and establish a dictatorship of the proletariat which in time would liquidate the feudal and bourgeoisie classes and pave the way for communism. The anti-Lenin faction believed that the bourgeoisie would have to capture control of Russia first and establish a bourgeois state and society. They were, therefore, temporarily willing

686

to help the bourgeoisie against the monarchy in order to speed the historical process.

The two wings of the party became clearly defined during the London conference of 1903. A small majority sided with Lenin and took the name of Bolshevik or majority party. The anti-Lenin group was called the Menshevik or minority party, even though it quickly became the larger group. This division within the Russian Social Democrats was to last until the overthrow of the monarchy.

THE REVOLUTION OF 1905 AND THE REFORMS OF STOLYPIN

By 1904, industrialization, peasant discontent, and political parties had developed to the point that only a spark was needed to overthrow the autocratic rule of the Tsar. This spark was provided by the Russian defeat in the Russo-Japanese War of 1904-1905. Even while the war was still in progress, the ruthless minister of the interior was assassinated; and representatives of the *zemstvo* met in St. Petersburg and formulated a program demanding freedom of thought and expression, equality before the law, and a parliament. In January, 1905, troops foolishly fired on workers peaceably demonstrating in the square before the winter palace in St. Petersburg, killing several hundred. The workers, who had formerly blamed their troubles on the bureaucracy, now began to criticize the Tsar. In St. Petersburg and other cities, they organized *soviets* or councils composed of one delegate for every 500 workers. The Social Revolutionaries formed a Peasants Union in July, 1905. Thus, the liberal members of the gentry and middle class in the *zemstvo* congress, the workers in the soviets, and the peasants in the Union joined in demanding reform, and a series of minor strikes culminated in a general strike in October.

Amidst all this confusion, the Tsar half-heartedly gave vague promises of reforms he never intended to keep, but finally he felt compelled to issue the October Manifesto, in which he promised civil liberties and a representative legislature based on a democratic franchise. By this move, the Tsar divided the opposition. The socialists pressed for a complete political and social revolution, but most noble and middle-class liberals became frightened by the radicalism of their allies and decided to accept the manifesto. Nevertheless, the first and second Dumas, or parliaments, convoked as a result of the October Manifesto, were dissolved because of their radical tendencies. In June, 1907, the suffrage was drastically reduced in such a manner as to favor the gentry, and a third Duma was elected that was sufficiently conservative to cooperate with the government. The cadets and socialists were alienated by this arbitrary act, but an interesting experiment in constitutionalism was inaugurated that carried some promise of success.

Under the post-1905 regime, the Tsar kept control of the army, diplomacy, and the executive branch of the government, but the Duma was given considerable, but not complete, control over legislation and taxation. The ministers, though responsible to the Tsar, therefore found it advisable to cooperate with the Duma whenever possible. Between 1906 and 1911, the chief minister was Peter Stolypin (1863-1911), an able, energetic man who had little sympathy with constitutionalism but who realized that the monarchy would have to get the support of some class other than the declining gentry if it were to survive.

Stolypin made every effort to stamp out revolutionary activity, but at the same time he inaugurated reforms designed to win the loyalty of the abler, more energetic peasants. Peasants who so desired were given the right to consolidate their strips of land in the *mir* and to claim their share of the common land. The results were comparable to the enclosure movement in Western Europe. Individual ownership of the land began to replace collective ownership, and compact farms where a more scientific agriculture could be practiced began to replace the open fields. By 1916 about a fourth of the peasants in European Russia had taken advantage of this opportunity. It was upon this new class of small peasant proprietors that Stolypin fastened the hopes of monarchy.

The departure of the ablest peasants from the *mir* left those who remained without leaders and without an adequate supply of land. Stolypin tried to assist them by providing loans from a state bank for the purchase of crown or gentry lands and by settling inhabitants of the overcrowded provinces in European Russia on farms in Siberia. By 1914, the peasants owned 75 per cent of the arable land in the country, but their insatiable thirst remained unquenched. Additional concessions were made to them in 1905 by abandoning the remaining payments due for the land turned over to the *mir* upon emancipation in 1861 and by furnishing agricultural experts to teach more advanced farming techniques.

Continued industrialization provided profits for the middle class and jobs for the urban workers. Labor unions were permitted, health and accident insurance inaugurated, and wages raised. Steps were taken towards the establishment of universal primary education by 1922, and both the number of universities and the size of their enrollments increased. Censorship was relaxed, although not abolished, and freedom of religion was permitted. Russia remained far from free or democratic and there was still widespread discontent, but enough was accomplished during the decade following the Revolution of 1905 to give middle-class liberals the hope that even Russia would someday join the family of free Western nations.

Indeed, Stolypin's success was so great that he became a target of both the reactionaries, who were horrified at the changes he was making, and the revolutionaries, who feared that he was winning the loyalty of the peasants. The result was his assassination in 1911 by an agent of one or possibly both of these groups. Had he lived, the course of Russian history might have been vastly different.

THE AMERICAS

The United States continued to be a land of progress after 1865. The industrial revolution began in earnest in the Northeast, and the West was rapidly settled. After a generation of corruption, a period of political, social, and economic reforms began. By 1914, the republic, whose capital had been burned by a small British army a century before, had become one of the most powerful nations in the world.

THE PROBLEM OF THE SOUTH

One section, the South, was not a part of the general movement. Its cities and farms had been laid waste by the Union armies. A quarter of a million of its young men had died in uniform, and hundreds of thousands had been crippled. In Mississippi alone, there were ten thousand orphans. Since the Negro slaves had been freed, a new labor force had to be found, but there was no money to pay hired hands. The freedman was at more of a disadvantage than his master. He had no land to cultivate, no trade to practice, and no village *mir* to guide him. Congress did establish a Freedmen's Bureau in 1865 to provide assistance, but though it was effective in preventing starvation, no federal agency at that time was capable of coping effectively with the problem of turning four million former slaves into useful citizens with respected, secure places in society. Out of the rubble a new or, to be more accurate, a somewhat different South slowly emerged.

The planter had land, but no labor or capital. The freedman, after the first flush of liberty, was willing to work, but had no land. It was inevitable that they would come together. The planter divided his plantation into small farms and the freedmen worked them on a sharecrop basis. Many of the poorer whites also became sharecroppers. To get the capital for tools and seed, owner and tenant mortgaged their prospective crop to the local merchant. The merchant, in turn, was indebted to a northern bank or wholesale company. Lack of capital and the risks involved made the interest rates high. By harvest time, the planter and freedman often owed the value of the entire crop to the merchant, and the merchant sent the money to the northern creditor. There was nothing to do but borrow again. Cotton was regarded as the most marketable crop. For this reason, merchants generally insisted that all the land be placed in cotton when they made advances. More than ever before, the South became a one-crop region. Overproduction was the obvious result, and the price of cotton gradually fell from fifteen cents a pound in 1869 to four and one-half cents in 1894. To add to the region's problems, northern-controlled railroad companies charged discriminatory rates, thereby exacting still more capital from the stricken region.

The federal government provided no assistance since southerners were no longer influential in the councils of the nation. The southern historian C. Vann Woodward observes, "For almost fifty of the seventy-two years between the inauguration of Washington and that of Lincoln, southern men held the presidency, and for sixty of those years a southern chief justice presided over the Supreme Court." But, as a result of the war, between 1861 and 1912, no southerner, except Andrew Johnson, served as president or vice-president, and no southerner achieved so much as the nomination of a major party for either office. "Of the 133 cabinet members appointed during the period, only fourteen were from the South, and of the thirty-one justices of the Supreme Court, only seven." Northerners supported by allies in the West were thus in firm control, and they used their power for their own benefit. Tariffs were raised higher and higher to protect northern industry, and the South had to pay unnecessarily high prices for its manufactured goods. Little of the money voted for internal improvements was spent in the most backward region in the country.

Lincoln had not intended to treat the South harshly. The southern states, he theorized, had never had the right to leave the Union. Therefore, they should be allowed to re-establish their state governments and send representatives to Congress as soon as 10 per cent of the electorate had taken an oath of allegiance to the Union. Unfortunately, Lincoln was assassinated at the close of the war, and his successor, Andrew Johnson, had neither the prestige nor the tact to win acceptance for this generous plan. Control of the nation fell to a group of radical Republicans in Congress who were motivated by the desire to protect the Negro freedmen from their former masters and to protect their party, their offices, and their policies from a possible southern Democratic, pro-free-trade revival.

The reconstituted southern state governments played into the radicals' hands by adopting Black Codes designed to prevent Negroes from voting, holding office, and serving on juries. Some states even forbade them to work as skilled laborers to prevent competition with white workers. The Negro was left with a choice of becoming a sharecropper, an unskilled laborer, or a vagrant. If he chose the last course, he was often placed in a chain gang and contracted to a planter to pay for his upkeep. Clearly, the southerners would never willingly permit the Negro to be more than a second-class citizen. Emancipation guaranteed by the Thirteenth Amendment was as far as they would go.

It was therefore with some justification that the radical Republicans rejected the Lincoln-Johnson plan of reconstruction and established military rule in the South. They encouraged Negroes and poor whites to get control of the state governments and forced the adoption of the Fourteenth Amendment to the Constitution, which declared that no state shall "deprive any person of life, liberty, or property, without due process of law," as well as the Fifteenth Amendment, which provided that the right to vote shall not be abridged because of "race, color, or previous condition of servitude."

The inevitable southern reaction was violence. Hooded bands such as the Ku Klux Klan terrorized Negroes, and race relations became worse. By 1877 the North was ready to abandon the Negro to his fate. The idealistic radical Republican leaders had died, and their successors decided it was to their advantage to buy the support of southern white conservatives by withdrawing federal troops and accepting white supremacy. The bitter experience of reconstruction had made the South solidly Democratic, but from that day the northern Republican and the conservative southern Democrat have frequently cooperated in the halls of Congress. To ensure their control over their own states, upper-class southerners raised the race issue with tragic success, and an economically logical alliance between the poor white and Negro tenant farmers was prevented. By 1900 the Negro was rigorously segregated from his fellow white citizen and by one means or another denied the right to vote.

THE NORTH AND WEST

Meanwhile, the northern economy, protected and encouraged by a friendly national legislature, was expanding at a fantastic rate. The government contributed generously in land and loans to railroad construction; and between 1873 and 1893, 100,000 miles of track were laid. East and West were linked by one line after another. The iron and steel industry boomed, as did oil, the various branches of the electrical industry, and many others. The need for large amounts of capital to finance these enterprises led to the gradual replacement of the individually-owned concern by the limited liability joint-stock company, often backed by powerful banks. By 1900 the United States had some of the largest and wealthiest corporations in the world, and these businesses were wielding tremendous influence over the political and social, as well as the economic, life of the nation.

The West experienced equally rapid changes. At the end of the Mexican War, the frontier had been only a few hundred miles west of the Mississippi River. The vast plains that separated the frontier from the Rocky Mountains and the Pacific coast did not seem fit for farmers. It contained no wood for houses, fences, or fuel, and the heavy sod and scarcity of rainfall made farming by accustomed methods difficult. The pioneer farmer temporarily halted his westward advance and his place was taken by the miner who searched for gold and other metals in the Sierra Nevada and Rocky mountains. California and Nevada had enough population to achieve statehood a generation before some territories farther east.

The miner was followed by the cattleman. Texas, especially, became famous for its huge cattle ranches and hard-riding cowboys. Unfenced grasslands provided free forage, and to make a handsome profit, it was only necessary to undertake the long drive to the newly-constructed railroad in Kansas, where the beef was shipped to Chicago and points east. All went well until around 1885, when the range became overcrowded, beef prices declined, and the farmer began to fence off the range.

The appearance of the farmer on the great plains was made possible by a number of discoveries and developments. Barbed wire fences were invented that compensated for the absence of wood, an efficient iron plow was developed that could cope with the hard soil, techniques of dry farming were discovered that compensated for the lack of rainfall, a tougher wheat was found that could withstand the rigorous climate, and railroads were constructed that could transport coal for fuel and other needed products. Small tracts of land were given to settlers who would occupy them, and larger farms were sold by the governments for a few cents an acre. Settlers now swarmed all over the great plains. The remaining Indian tribes were obliterated or confined to reservations. In 1889-1890, six states were admitted to the Union, leaving only Utah, Oklahoma, Arizona, and New Mexico as territories. The frontier was declared closed, and the nation had been settled within three centuries of the landing at Jamestown.

Industrialization and the settling of the West brought social problems. Eastern cities like New York grew at a fantastic rate, those in the Midwest like Chicago sprang from nothing to metropolises, and those in the Far West followed suit. In 1840 less than 8 per cent of the population had lived in towns of over eight thousand inhabitants; in 1900, one-third did. This growth was accompanied by little planning. Huge slums came into being that were most often inhabited by recent immigrants from Europe and Negroes from the South. Sanitation was often bad, public parks inadequate or nonexistent, and zoning regulations almost unknown. Low wages, long working hours, and poor living conditions were the lot of the workers in the new industrial centers. Even the small independent businessman had difficulties. Large corporations ruthlessly sought to force him into bankruptcy. Rockefeller's oil company could compel railroads to give rebates on transportation charges, a smaller company could not; it could afford to sell its product at a loss in order to capture a market, a smaller company had no such opportunity. Once a local monopoly was achieved, prices were apt to skyrocket and the consumer suffered. After a brief period of prosperity, the farmer ran into difficulty. Prices on the world market declined, but costs remained high. The railroad company had a natural monopoly in nearly every rural community, and it often charged high rates for its services.

THE REFORM MOVEMENT

Gradually the laborer, the farmer, the debtor, the small businessman, and the consumer began to demand reforms. At first they made little progress. Big business wielded powerful influence in city, state, and national government, and it used its power to maintain the policy of laissez-faire.

The political machines had learned how to turn out the vote, and the reformers had not. Graft and corruption were deeply embedded in every branch of the government. U. S. Grant's two administrations were noted for their corruption, and Boss Tweed and his gang managed to cheat New York City of more than a hundred million dollars in a period of several years. If the reformers did get control of a city or state, they were apt to find their efforts blocked by the courts, which barred much social legislation on the grounds that it violated liberty of contract or that it was contrary to the Fourteenth Amendment's provision that a person (a corporation was legally a person) could not be deprived of his property without due process of law.

There were reformers in both political parties, but in neither could they win control. By 1876 the Democratic party had once more become as strong as the Republican, but even this situation did not lead to competition for votes by offering reforms. Few issues divided the candidates except the desire for the same office. Few factors affected the party workers except the hope for the rewards of victory. Between 1873 and 1896, only one presidential candidate, Samuel J. Tilden (1814-1886), managed to get over 50 per cent of the vote; he got 51 per cent, but lost the election in the electoral college. Grover Cleveland (1837-1908) also had the unhappy experience of winning the popular vote and losing in the electoral college in 1888, but on two other occasions he was more fortunate. Except for his two victories, all presidential elections between 1860 and 1912 were won by Republicans.

The reformers made little progress at the national level prior to 1901. They could point to the Pendleton Act of 1883, which established a civil service and marked the beginning of an attempt to end the spoils system, to the Interstate Commerce Act of 1887 which forbade rebates and other railroad abuses, and to the Sherman Anti-Trust Act of 1890 which outlawed business combinations in restraint of trade. However, since neither the Interstate Commerce Act nor the Sherman Anti-Trust Act was enforced, they accomplished little.

The failure of the reformers to make a better showing when working within the framework of the two major parties led to several third-party movements. One was dedicated to prohibition, another was socialistic, and still another wanted to increase the amount of currency in circulation by accepting greenbacks (paper money) as legal tender without backing by gold. The most important third-party movement during the period was that of the Populist or Peoples party, which polled over a million popular votes in 1892 and captured 22 votes in the electoral college. The Peoples party grew out of farmers' organizations in the Midwest and South. It advocated unlimited coinage of silver to ease the currency shortage, a graduated income tax, and federal ownership of railroads and public utilities. So great was the Peoples party's success in 1892 that its leaders talked of victory in 1896, but in that year the eloquent William Jennings Bryan

(1860-1925) captured the Democratic nomination and persuaded his party to accept the unlimited coinage of silver. With a major party adopting the reform program, third-party movements ceased to be significant. Bryan lost the election, but Theodore Roosevelt (1858-1919) brought victory to the Republican reformers when he took office in 1901, and Woodrow Wilson's (1856-1924) triumph in 1912 marked the beginning of eight years of Democratic reform administration.

The Roosevelt-Wilson era saw many reforms effected at the national, state, and local level. Some were designed to give the people more control over the government; others were essentially for social betterment. City after city was recaptured from the control of corrupt or inefficient political machines and turned over to expert commissioners or managers without party affiliations. The direct primary was instituted in many states to replace the party convention as a means of choosing candidates for office. Initiative, referendum, and recall—measures to enable the people to initiate legislation, approve legislation passed by legislatures, and to recall unwanted public officials—were instituted in many states, especially in the West. The Seventeenth Amendment providing for direct election of senators was passed in 1913, and the Nineteenth Amendment giving women the right to vote was adopted in 1920.

Reform city administrations attempted to reduce the size of the slums, to build parks, playgrounds, and hospitals, to improve sanitation, and to plan for future growth. Reformed state administrations passed acts limiting, regulating, or prohibiting woman and child labor in factories. They established accident insurance systems to protect workers and provided better care for the aged and destitute.

Theodore Roosevelt strengthened the Interstate Commerce Commission and made a halfhearted effort to prevent the worst abuses of the giant corporations. He was also the first president to try to get a "square deal" for labor. However, his domestic program is best known for the establishment of a conservation program to prevent further waste of natural resources and for a Pure Food and Drug Act to protect the consumer from the worst abuses of the meat, drug, and food industries. Roosevelt's Republican successor accomplished little, but it was near the close of his administration that the Sixteenth Amendment authorizing Congress to levy an income tax was adopted. However, corporate and individual income taxes remained relatively low until World War II.

In 1913 Woodrow Wilson began his first and most successful term in the White House. He never escaped his Virginia-born conservatism, but by a curious twist of fate this made him a reformer. The giant corporations had destroyed the opportunity for a man to go into business for himself and terminated the old close employer-employee relationship. The corporation, not the people, was the dominant influence over the government. The "New Freedom" Wilson advocated was a freedom from the

694

power of corporations, not a freedom from the power of the government.[5] Roosevelt had distinguished between the corporation that recognized a responsibility to the public and the corporation that abused its power. To Wilson, however, size itself was an evil because it thwarted the efforts of the individual to create a new business. He hoped to free man from the giant corporation just as Thomas Jefferson had hoped to free him from the state.

Wilson was an ardent admirer of the British system of government. He used the presidency as a sort of prime ministership and applied the necessary pressure to get his measures through Congress. At no previous time had the executive exerted so much influence over the legislature, but he produced results. His Clayton Anti-Trust Act would have been a reasonably effective weapon against the abuses of large corporations if it had been enforced by his successors. Tariffs were reduced by over 26 per cent, and measures were passed to help the farmer and the worker. Wilson's greatest success was the Federal Reserve Act which finally gave the United States an adequate banking system with a flexible currency. Unhappily, Wilson was forced to turn his attention to foreign affairs in 1914, and his second administration saw few domestic accomplishments. Nevertheless, during the preceding decade the United States had made notable strides towards democracy and some in social legislation, though many European nations remained far in advance in accident, sickness, and other workers' welfare measures.

BRITISH NORTH AMERICA

The development of Canada after achieving dominion status in 1867 was similar to that of the United States. Immigrants, 287,000 in 1910 alone, flocked in from Europe and elsewhere to make possible the growth of large cities and the settlement of the West. A transcontinental railway was completed in 1887, territories were transformed into provinces when the population warranted, and there were the usual Indian wars. In 1869-1870 and again in 1885, Louis Riel (1844-1885), a man of mixed Indian, French, and Irish descent, led a half-breed Indian attempt to halt the westward advance, but his forces were as easily disposed of as the Indians south of the border. From its formation, the Canadian government had been democratic, and this tendency was confirmed in 1918 by the adoption of woman suffrage.

The neighboring dominion of Newfoundland was constantly in financial difficulties. In 1895-1896 there was an unsuccessful move to incorporate it into Canada, but it was not until 1949 that this was accomplished. Britain retained Jamaica and several other territories in the Caribbean region, but their relative importance within the Empire continued to decline.

[5] See page 643.

LATIN AMERICA

Latin America remained one of the most backward areas of the Western world. The forces of conservatism, represented by an untitled landed aristocracy and the Catholic Church, successfully delayed the onslaught of materialism, equalitarianism, and democracy. Family ties remained strong, society remained stable, and traditions remained respected. There was a wide gap between the incomes of the different classes. The poor were miserably poor, but the rich could afford a life of ease and culture. Racial differences added to the social problems. Some countries, such as Argentina, Uruguay, and Costa Rica, were predominantly white; others, like Haiti, Panama, Honduras, and Brazil, had large numbers of Negroes and mulattoes, while in still others the Indians and mestizos were in a majority. Generally, the white and near white made up the upper classes, while the Indians and Negroes composed the lower orders of society. Thus, a racial distinction added to the social distinction, although the white Latin American was far less color-conscious than his Anglo-Saxon neighbor to the north. Most countries passed laws establishing free compulsory education, but they were seldom enforced. Where the whites were predominant, about a fifth of the population remained illiterate; where the Negroes and Indians were in a majority, four-fifths of the inhabitants often could not read or write. Yet despite these facts, there was progress.

The population increased rapidly, although the death rate remained high. The value of foreign trade tripled between 1885 and 1913. Mexico, Cuba, and the nontropical South American countries enjoyed economic progress, but, unfortunately, most tropical countries became dependent on the export of one or two commodities, such as bananas or coffee. A crop failure or a collapse in the world market brought disaster. Then too, much of the large-scale enterprise, whether mining or bananas, was controlled by foreign capital, a fact which led to considerable friction with the great powers and occasionally to their intervention. Politically speaking, Latin America remained a land of liberal constitutions that were ignored and of dictators who seized power and ruled for the benefit of a class or faction. However, by 1914 there was hope that genuine democracy would develop in some countries, especially those with temperate climates, progressive economies, and a large number of white people. Costa Rica and Chile were reasonably democratic and stable, Ecuador became so after 1895, and Uruguay after 1907. Argentina established universal manhood suffrage and the secret ballot in 1912, and Panama and Cuba got off to a good start a few years earlier under the auspices of the United States. The Mexicans overthrew Porfirio Diaz (1830-1915) in 1911 after he had enjoyed the fruits of thirty-five years of dictatorship. A period of revolution and counter-revolution followed, but the way was cleared for social reform and increased popular control over the government.

CONCLUSIONS

In Great Britain, France, and the United States where the forces of conservatism were weak and the forces of change were strong, there was considerable progress towards democracy and some social legislation. In Germany, Russia, and Latin America where the forces of conservatism were strong, progress towards democracy was much less significant, but in Germany there was more social legislation than in the more democratic states. In Germany, Hungary, and Russia the aristocracy managed to retain its position of leadership, although its position was weakening. In France the aristocracy succumbed in the 1870's and in Great Britain its position was dealt a severe blow just before World War I, although it continued to exercise a larger influence than its numbers warranted. In spite of varying degrees of change, however, the aristocracy had waned or was waning everywhere in 1914, the middle class was becoming ascendant, and the continued growth of democracy accompanied by social legislation seemed assured.

16/ The Expansion of the Western Civilization

WESTERN civilization had begun to expand with the explorations of the fifteenth century, but as late as 1870 it had not completely penetrated the American or Australian continents, and in Africa and Asia little beyond a few trading posts had succumbed to its advances. The generation before World War I saw civilization spread into the heartland of the Americas and Australia, Africa divided among the European powers, and much of Asia and the Moslem world transformed, or beginning to be transformed, under European influence. These startling developments were caused by three events: (1) the rapid increase in the European population and the migration of settlers and missionaries to other parts of the world, (2) the revival of imperialism, and (3) the copying of Western techniques by non-European peoples, often in order to preserve their independence.

POPULATION GROWTH AND MIGRATION

POPULATION GROWTH

Much has been said about the rapid growth in the population of the European continent after 1700. The population of Asia increased during the same period, but less rapidly because of a failure to make comparable improvements in agriculture and medicine. Disease, wars, and the slave trade caused the population of Africa to remain static or perhaps even to decrease until near the close of the nineteenth century. Only the population of the Americas and Oceania-Australia grew more rapidly, and they owed part of their rapid progress to the migration from Europe. As a result, while Europeans and those of European descent constituted only a fifth of the world population in 1650 and slightly more than that in 1750, they grew to over a fourth by 1850 and to over a third by 1950. By sheer weight of numbers, the European civilization became important.

ESTIMATED POPULATION OF THE WORLD*

	1650	1750	1850	1900	1950
	MILLIONS				
Europe	100	140	266	401	540
United States & Canada	1	1	26	81	160
Total "Europeans"	101	141	292	482	700
Latin America	12	11	33	63	145
Oceania-Australasia	2	2	2	6	12
Africa	100	95	95	120	175
Asia	330	479	749	937	1,200
Grand Total	545	728	1,171	1,608	2,232
	PERCENTAGES				
Europe	18.3	19.2	22.7	24.9	24.3
United States & Canada	.2	.1	2.3	5.1	7.2
Total "Europeans"	18.5	19.3	25.0	30.0	31.5
Latin America	2.2	1.5	2.8	3.9	6.5
Oceania-Australasia	.4	.3	.2	.4	.5
Africa	18.3	13.1	8.1	7.4	7.8
Asia	60.6	65.8	63.9	58.3	53.7
Grand Total	100.0	100.0	100.0	100.0	100.0

* Figures are from R. R. Palmer, *A History of the Modern World* (New York: Alfred A. Knopf, Inc., 1956), p. 560 and A. M. Carr-Saunders, *World Population* (Oxford University at the Clarendon Press, 1936), p. 42. For dates after 1850, the population of Australasia and a part of that of Latin America were of European descent. There were, therefore, about 750,000,000 "Europeans" in 1950.

THE MIGRATION

Increasing numbers, however, provided only a small part of the explanation for the growing predominance of the European civilization. More significant was the fact that the Europeans did not remain at home. From the time of the Portuguese settlement in North Africa in 1415 and of Columbus' unsuccessful attempt to start a colony in the West Indies in 1492, there had been a steady migration of Europeans from the mother continent. However, only a trickle departed, for the most part from Spain, Germany, and the British Isles, prior to 1800. Emigration increased thereafter, but as late as 1880 the average number of annual departures from Europe numbered only 300,000. At this point, there was a marked upturn, and during the years 1906-1910 an average of 1,400,000 Europeans, largely from Italy and eastern Europe as well as the British Isles and Spain, emigrated each year. Between 1846 and 1932, about 60,000,000 people left Europe. A little over half went to the United States, but large numbers also found their way to Canada, Argentina, Brazil, Australia, and Siberia. Only a handful went to Africa and other parts of Asia.

MIGRATION FROM EUROPE*
1846-1932

FROM

Great Britain and Ireland	18,000,000
Italy	10,100,000
Russia†	9,200,000
Austria-Hungary	5,200,000
Germany	4,900,000
Spain	4,700,000
Portugal	1,800,000
Sweden	1,200,000
Norway	850,000
Poland‡	640,000
France	520,000
Denmark	390,000
Finland	370,000
Switzerland	330,000
Holland	220,000
Belgium	190,000
Total	58,610,000

* Palmer, p. 564 and Carr-Saunders, pp. 49 and 56.
† Including seven million from European to Asiatic Russia up to 1914 only. It is thought that three million went from European to Asiatic parts of the U.S.S.R. between 1926 and 1939. Subsequent movement is unknown.
‡ 1920-32 only.

The fundamental cause of this great migration was economic. There was a period in most European countries when the rural areas became overpopulated, partly due to the fact that industrialization did not proceed fast enough to provide employment. It was at this point that emigration most often reached its peak. When industrialization did take place, farmers moved to the factory towns in their own country. For this reason, most of the potential rural emigrants from England and Scotland were absorbed by industrial expansion between 1850 and 1900. However, emigration reached a new peak around 1910 when factories could no longer provide sufficient employment. Mining and forestry began to absorb the excess population in Norway and Sweden in the 1870's, and industrialization had a similar effect on Germany about the same time. Opportunities at home developed much later for the Italian, Greek, and Slav, with the result that the great period of their migration came when emigration from Western and central Europe was waning.

IMMIGRATION INTO OTHER COUNTRIES FROM EUROPE*

TO	
United States	34,000,000
Asiatic Russia (to 1914 only)	7,000,000
Argentina	6,400,000
Canada	5,200,000
Brazil	4,400,000
Australia	2,900,000
British West Indies	1,600,000
Cuba	860,000
South Africa	852,000
Uruguay	713,000
New Zealand	594,000

* Palmer, p. 566. Carr-Saunders, p. 49.

Overpopulation was not the only factor necessary for migration. It was also necessary to have the freedom, desire, and means to move. Before emancipation, serfdom prevented migration of the unneeded peasant population from parts of central and eastern Europe. The desire to move was awakened in villagers who received information about opportunities in other parts of the world. Sometimes word was spread by the agents of railroad companies seeking unskilled labor to build the great transcontinental lines in the Americas; sometimes it resulted from increased public education provided by the establishment of schools in rural areas; sometimes it came from an adventurous friend or relative who had gone abroad and reported on the opportunities he found. This last factor was especially important and largely accounts for the tendency of ethnic groups to settle together in the New World. Irishmen flocked to Boston and Chicago, Germans and Scandinavians went to the northern Midwest, while by 1910 Italians made up a third of the population of the Brazilian state of São Paulo. The transportation revolution with its railroads and steamships was of the utmost importance in providing the means to move. Low fares were provided by raw cotton and timber ships returning to the

Americas for new cargoes and by the development of Greek steamship lines.

In addition to the "push" factors that drove the excess rural population from their homes, there were certain "pull" factors that attracted them to other parts of the world. The great, sparsely-occupied grasslands of the American and Canadian Midwest, Australia, Argentina, and Siberia naturally attracted those people who generally knew only the life and trade of the farmer. The majority of emigrants, however, found employment in industries and mines. For this reason, migration to a particular country was greater during periods of industrial expansion than during temporary recessions. In general, the pull factors in the last half of the nineteenth century were almost entirely economic. The desire for religious freedom, so important during the Reformation era, was almost entirely removed by growing toleration, and only Russian Jews emigrated to escape persecution.

One result of the migration was that the sparsely-occupied grasslands of the world became thoroughly Europeanized. Even those parts of Latin America which remained dominantly Indian or Negro in race became European in language, religion, and culture. The limited European migration to Africa and to non-Russian Asia prevented these areas from becoming as Europeanized, although missionary activity and imperialism had a far-reaching influence there.

A second result of the migration was the significant shift in the numerical position of the individual European ethnic groups. During the Middle Ages and the Renaissance, the French had been the most numerous European people, with the possible exception of the Germans. During the nineteenth century, however, the population of France itself grew relatively slowly and only a handful of Frenchmen went overseas. On the other hand, the number of Russians increased rapidly. Most of their growth was absorbed by European Russia itself, but about seven million migrated to Asiatic Russia prior to 1914. Even more striking was the increase in the number of the English-speaking people. They grew from about 4.5 million persons in 1500 to 129 million in 1900 and 200 million in 1940, exclusive of English-speaking natives in colonies. During the Renaissance, the French had outnumbered the English four to one. By 1900, the English-speaking people outnumbered the French three to one, and they ruled the largest and most populous colonial empire in the world. The influence of English culture and institutions in the world was therefore greater than that of any other part of the Western world.

THE SIBERIAN MIGRATION

Hardly less important to the expansion of Western civilization was the Russian migration into Siberia, a region of five million square miles stretching across the northern third of Asia.

The Russian conquest of Siberia really began during the reign of Ivan the Terrible when Ermak led a band of less than a thousand cossacks against the Khan of Siber, or Siberia, a small independent Tartar state east of the Ural Mountains. Ermak himself was killed in 1585, but the superiority of Russian troops and equipment gave them victory. Other cossack adventurers penetrated farther to the east, and by 1639 one of them had reached the Pacific Ocean. Expansion to the south was halted by the Chinese in 1689, but elsewhere the land was inhabited by backward Asiatic peoples who could offer no effective resistance and Siberia became a Russian province.

Before the emancipation of the serfs in 1861, few Russians migrated to Siberia, and in all the vast province there were only three million persons, about a fourth of whom were natives. The Russians who migrated were either political exiles or runaway serfs who wanted to escape the overcrowded conditions of European Russia, where the land they worked was inadequate, and establish themselves as free, independent farmers with enough land to support their families. The failure of the gentry to migrate and the more democratic character of any frontier community prevented serfdom from spreading east of the Ural Mountains.

It is true that even after emancipation the peasant could not legally leave the *mir* without permission, but some met the required conditions and others continued to flee to the east. When Stolypin made it easier for the peasants to depart from the *mir* and encouraged the development of independent farmers, the migration was speeded.[1] The completion of the first large section of the Trans-Siberian railway in 1896 and of additional sections soon thereafter facilitated their movement. As a result, the number of Siberian immigrants increased from an average of 8,000 per year during the first half of the nineteenth century, to 25,000 per year following the emancipation, to a peak of 229,000 per year during the first decade of the twentieth century. In all, about 7,000,000 Russians settled in Siberia between 1801 and 1914 and, by the latter date, 90 per cent of the inhabitants were Slavs, not Asiatics.

In the middle quarters of the nineteenth century, the Russians added over a million square miles to their Asian empire by obtaining the district north of the Amur River from China and conquering several native states east of the Caspian Sea. The former was quickly incorporated into Western civilization and the latter was gradually assimilated. Under the Communists, the economic exploitation and settlement of the vast Asian empire has been speeded and an area almost twice the size of Europe has been brought within the sphere of Western civilization.

MISSIONARY ACTIVITY

The incorporation of the Americas, Australia, and northern Asia into the Western world was of major importance, but it was accomplished

[1] See page 687.

with relatively little difficulty because most parts of these continents were thinly inhabited by backward peoples who had been exposed to the superior European culture a long time before their final absorption. The situation was somewhat different in Africa and quite different in southern Asia. Africa was much more thickly populated, and only minor contacts had been made with the natives prior to 1875 except in the coastal region. Southern Asia was very thickly populated in several areas and boasted civilizations that the natives regarded as superior to the European.

The situation might well have delayed Westernization had it not been for a revival of missionary activity during the latter part of the nineteenth century. It is difficult to explain why the increasingly materialistic European civilization began to take so much interest in missionary work. Improved communications undoubtedly made it possible to interest people, and millions were persuaded to contribute. Transportation and technological changes made the lot of the missionary easier. The encouragement by Western governments, the friendly attitude of some of the native states, and the increasing trade between the continents also contributed. But still more was due to the work of such men as Cardinal Charles Lavigerie (1825-1892), who founded the missionary order of the White Fathers, and to the writings of missionary-explorers like David Livingstone (1813-1873). Whatever the reasons, by 1900 61,000 priests and clergymen, lay brothers and laymen, nuns and Protestant women, had migrated to Africa, Asia, and Oceania to engage in missionary activity.

The principal goal of these missionaries was conversion. They were not, however, content only to baptize, as so many of their predecessors had been. Catholic and Protestant alike insisted on long periods of pre-baptismal instruction before the administration of that rite. This reduced the number of converts, but it meant that those baptized understood something of Christianity and European culture. In all, about ten million persons were added to the Christian faith by 1900 in Asia and Africa. Even those native religions that successfully resisted these missionary efforts often adopted a large part of Christian ethics and ideals.

Religious instruction was only one means through which missionaries spread the Western civilization. They reduced many languages to the written form, opened schools, and taught the natives to read. Soon natives were being sent to study at Oxford, Cambridge, and other centers of learning. European medical, technological, and scientific discoveries were introduced into the most backward areas. By 1914, many of the inhabitants of Africa and Asia had adopted much of the Western civilization.

IMPERIALISM

The last quarter of the nineteenth century saw a marked revival of imperialism. Between 1775 and 1875, the European states had lost many more square miles of colonial territory than they had won, and colonies had come to be regarded as expensive, useless luxuries.[2] Then there was a sudden change in attitude. The old liberal-nationalist dictum—that every people had the right to govern themselves—was forgotten, or shoved aside on the ground that it applied only to those who were as highly civilized as the imperialists. Four-fifths of Africa was taken over by the European states between 1875 and 1900, and parts of Asia were turned into colonies or spheres of influence. Great Britain added 4,500,000 square miles to its empire; France, 3,500,000; Germany, 1,000,000; Belgium, 900,000; Russia, 500,000; Italy, 185,000; and the United States, 125,000. A fourth of the population of the world lived in colonies and many more in spheres of influence.

CAUSES OF REVIVAL OF IMPERIALISM

The causes of the revival of imperialism are difficult to ascertain. Some historians attribute it to the industrialization of Europe and the United States. They argue that by the 1870's when the industrial output of Germany, the United States, France, and other states began to rival that of Great Britain, a fierce competition for markets ensued which led the new industrial powers to raise tariff barriers to ensure their domestic market for their own producers. These tariffs furthered the growth of giant corporations and cartels which in turn increased productive capacity and provided additional capital for investment. The home markets ceased to be adequate, and although trade with free backward countries helped, other industrial powers competed for these markets. Only when political control was established over these backward countries, was the entire market assured. This situation resulted in a frenzied competition for colonies.

Industrial goods, these historians believe, were but one type of product Europe had for export. Capital also became a surplus in economically advanced countries, and local interest rates fell, but money invested in the more backward countries where capital was scarce still brought large returns. "The same capital which will earn 3 or 4 per cent in agricultural improvement in France," a contemporary economist declared, "will bring 10, 15, 20 per cent in an agricultural enterprise in the United States, Canada, La Plata, Australia or New Zealand."

Then, too, there was a growing demand for tropical and subtropical products such as cotton, rubber, coffee, tea, and fruit, and for natural resources not found in the mother country, such as tin, phosphate, and, at a later date, oil. With political control over one of the backward regions that produced these products, the physical safety of those who migrated and the economic security of those who invested only their money could be better assured. Furthermore, political control enabled an imperialistic

2 See pages 569-570.

power to compel unwilling natives to produce the goods it wanted and enabled it to deny these products to rival states.

Marxist historians also relate imperialism to industrialization, but they interpret it as a sign of weakness rather than as a dynamic phase of capitalism. Marx, himself, had not specifically foretold the coming of imperialism, but he had indicated that each time there was an economic depression brought on by overproduction, industrialists would seek markets further away from home. Recovery would follow as would renewed depressions until, when there were no more new markets in the world to exploit, there would be no way for the capitalistic system to recover. It was at this point that the revolution would come and the proletariat would assume dictatorial powers.

Lenin, who wrote *Imperialism the Highest Stage of World Capitalism* in 1916 after the Western powers had absorbed most of the non-Western world, was in a better position to evaluate imperialism. He took most of his data from bourgeois historians and interpreted it along the lines vaguely suggested by Marx. To Lenin, imperialism began when the concentration of capital and industry had become monopolistic in a particular country, thereby bringing capitalist free competition to an end. Colonies became necessary to provide markets for the excess capital and industrial goods as well as to provide raw materials. This absence of free competition and the exploitation of small weak nations caused Lenin to define imperialism as "parasitic or decaying capitalism" that occurred when capitalism was about to pass to "a higher system."

The casual student can find circumstantial evidence to support the economic interpretation, whether it be of the capitalistic or Marxist variety. Tariffs were raised after 1875, giant corporations and cartels developed, an excess of industrial goods was produced, competition for overseas markets took place, and some European countries had an excess of capital which they invested abroad to get larger returns. However, close inspection reveals many limitations in the economic approach.

Some states like the United States and Russia were still debtor nations at the time they became imperialistic. Others, like France, preferred to invest their money in Russia and eastern Europe rather than in their colonies. As for the need for markets, the industrial states traded far more with each other despite the tariffs than they did with their colonies. Political control over a backward country was not always necessary before one could buy its products. As a result, while there was some trade and investment in backward countries, there was nothing in the economic system after 1875 that made it necessary for a state to acquire these countries to absorb its excess manufactured goods and capital or to obtain raw materials. The economic factor was important primarily because the people of that day thought it was important and because nations acted to protect the lives and capital of businessmen who did invest in backward countries.

The Expansion of the Western Civilization

The revival of imperialism was as much a product of nationalism, altruism, political expediency, and propaganda as of the changing economic system. Its causes may be best explained by examining the typical steps that led to the acquisition of a colony. Let us assume the existence of backward Hulaland in some remote part of the world. It is visited by a missionary or explorer who, after several years of steadfast work and exciting adventure, returns to his own country, publishes a book, and makes a series of speeches describing what he found. Whether a missionary or explorer, our traveler is apt to exaggerate, perhaps unconsciously, the importance of Hulaland; the missionary so that he can raise more money to support the continuance of his work, and the explorer to achieve greater fame. The new "yellow press" is in search of sensational news; in the absence of a war or a local crime, what could be of greater interest to its literate but none-too-sophisticated readers than the adventures of the self-sacrificing missionary or the bold explorer in far-off, strange Hulaland? Hulaland becomes well-known. Other missionaries and explorers go there. So do those in search of profit. They remember that the explorer had described vast forests of rubber trees in Hulaland and that the missionary in his address to their church had pointed out in horror that the natives wore no clothes. Would it not be profitable to get the right to exploit the resources of Hulaland and at the same time sell the natives clothes and other European products in return for their labor? A company is formed and an agent is sent to Hulaland who makes a treaty with the local king. The king in his ignorance of Western values and Western ways is persuaded to give the company sole rights of economic exploitation in return for a few relatively worthless products of Western civilization. Exploitation begins and the natives become restless. The missionaries are interfering with certain tribal customs, the company's representatives are treating the natives contemptuously and trying to make them work. Whatever the cause, a white man is murdered or the company's property is damaged or confiscated by the now less naïve king of Hulaland.

Immediately there is a loud cry at home. The "yellow press" demands that citizens and property be protected. Religious and reforming groups point out that if Hulaland became a colony, the natives could be more easily converted to Christianity, cruel and immoral practices could be outlawed, the slave trade stopped, medicine introduced, and schools and hospitals built. In short, the inhabitants of Hulaland could be given all the advantages of European civilization. It is not a right, it is a duty, to take up "the white man's burden" and civilize the barbarians. Colonial officials and diplomats see in the acquisition of Hulaland an opportunity for fame and advancement, army officers dream of the glory and promotions that could be won in a war with the natives, naval officers point out that Hulaland has a good harbor that could be used as a naval base and coaling station for merchant ships. Nationalists hold that Hulaland would be a good place for their fellow citizens to emigrate; too many are being lost to the fatherland by going to the United States and Argentina. Furthermore, Hulaland would be the first line of defense in case of war, it would assure an adequate rubber supply, and it would add to the prestige of the country. Social Darwinists point out that the law of "the survival of the fittest" determines the fate of nations as of species. A virile nation expands; only an old, tired organism ceases to grow. Thus, those who want their fellow citizens protected at any cost, those who hope for profit, those who wish to help the natives, and those who dream of national greatness unite in the demand for the acquisition of Hulaland, and this cry is relayed to the people by the "yellow press" in search of every opportunity to create excitement. Bold indeed was a politician who stood in their way.

Troops are sent to Hulaland to restore order, and the natives are easily defeated. The imperialists demand that Hulaland be turned into a colony. The anti-imperialists painfully realize that if troops are withdrawn, the white man and his property will be left at the mercy of the revengeful natives. In these circumstances, there is but one logical step; Hulaland is made a colony. Other nations become jealous. They form colonial societies dedicated to the dissemination of propaganda supporting an imperialistic policy, in part to secure the economic advantages presumably won by the new owners of Hulaland, in part because of a sense of rivalry, and in part because of the fear that if colonies are really as important as everyone says, the failure to acquire any would endanger their country. Once imperialism and imperialistic rivalries begin, they cannot be stopped until the backward nations of the world have been divided among the stronger states.

THE BEGINNING OF IMPERIALISM IN AFRICA

Africa in 1875 was still the least known of the inhabited continents, despite the fact that at one point it is only a few miles from Europe. The explanations for this strange fact were largely geographical. The most obvious point of entry into Africa for Europeans was North Africa, but mountains and desert made deep penetration into the continent difficult from that side. Neither the east nor the west coast had many good harbors, and in addition there were often mountain ranges that paralleled the sea. Even the rivers did not provide much assistance, for though the Nile and Congo were among the largest in the world, they divided into a number of streams when they reached their deltas, none of which were deep enough for large vessels. If the interior of the continent were reached, deserts, jungles, and mountains made movement difficult in many places.

A second factor that slowed the European penetration into Africa was the existence of relatively strong native states in many parts of the continent. The original inhabitants of North Africa were probably of the white race, and those south of the Sahara Desert were of two different branches of the Negroid race. One branch included the short Pygmy, Bushman, and Hottentot, and the other the taller Bantu tribes. Migrations and intermarriage led to considerable mixing of the races, although the deserts which separated the dominantly white from the dominantly black regions prevented the development of a single mixed race.

One of the earliest civilizations began in the predominantly white Nile Valley of Egypt. Negroes and mulattoes played a part in its development and were instrumental in passing many discoveries to the Negroes farther south. Egypt, however, was more easily accessible from Asia than Africa and therefore succumbed to one invasion after another from that quarter. The Arabian conquest between 640 A.D. and 710 A.D. brought the Moslem religion to North Africa, and the Turkish conquest shortly after 1500 brought the same region into the Ottoman Empire. Thus, Europeans were confronted across the Mediterranean by a powerful state. Only as they became stronger and the Ottoman Empire became weaker could they hope to penetrate beyond a few coastal cities.

The predominantly Negro part of Africa never developed a civilization as advanced as that of Egypt, but this point should not be overly stressed. Ethiopia became Christian during the early part of the fourth century, long before most of Europe; and several other empires developed, especially in West Africa in the vicinity of the Niger River. Among them were the Ghana empire with its capital at Kumbi and the Songhai empire which included the fabulous city of Tombouctou. These empires rose, lasted for centuries, and fell like those of the ancient Near East. They enjoyed trade relations with the Arabs and in several instances were visited by Christians. They were not powerful by Western standards of the seventeenth and eighteenth centuries, but with the aid of natural geographic barriers they were in a position to discourage invasion.

When the new imperialistic age began around 1875, the Ottoman Empire still held most of north Africa, although the local governors profited by the weakness of the parent state and acted in a very independent manner. The French held the Algerian coast which they had seized in 1830, and an independent sultan ruled Morocco. The French, British, Spanish, and Portuguese held strips along the west coast that had once been centers of a profitable slave trade but were then regarded of little value.

The Portuguese held a long strip along the east coast known as Mozambique. Only in Cape Colony, at the southern tip of the continent where the natives were very backward and geography and climate were more kind, had the Europeans progressed very far inland. The British had seized this strategic location from the Dutch during the Napoleonic wars, but trouble had soon followed. Missionaries protested against the way the Dutch (Boers) treated the natives. There was friction between the incoming English settlers and the Boers who were already there. Matters came to a head in 1833, when slavery was abolished in the British Empire. About ten thousand Boer farmers and cattlemen left the British colony and moved inland beyond the Orange and the Vaal rivers where they eventually created two independent republics known as the Orange Free State and Transvaal.

The bulk of the interior of Africa remained in the hands of the native states, some of which were relatively advanced kingdoms and others primitive tribal organizations.

The man most responsible for changing this situation was neither an imperialistic statesman nor a capitalistic mogul; he was David Livingstone (1813-1873). Livingstone was born in Scotland, where he studied theology and earned a degree in medicine. In 1840 he sailed for Africa under the auspices of the London Missionary Society. Most of his remaining thirty-three years were spent exploring the "dark continent." His various expeditions carried him from Cape Town north almost to the Equator and from the Atlantic to the Indian Ocean. Early in his labors, he was horrified at the expanding slave trade that was carried on largely by Arabs. He believed that this "open, running sore of the world" could be healed only by the presence of Europeans. In his explorations, he sought possible routes and opportunities for colonists; in his writings, he sought to inform people of what he found. His example inspired other missionaries and explorers to come to Africa and gave a powerful impulse to the idealistic aspect of imperialism, the impulse to spread the white man's civilization to the backward parts of the world.

Among the most famous explorers Livingstone brought to Africa was Henry M. Stanley (1841-1904). In 1869 Stanley was commissioned by the sensationalist *New York Herald* newspaper to find Livingstone who was believed to be lost in the Lake Tanganyika region. A bold, determined man, Stanley succeeded, and the account of his adventures, vividly told in newspaper and book, stimulated further interest in Africa. In 1874-1877 he returned to Africa and explored the Congo River Basin. Hardly had he emerged from the jungle, the sole white survivor of the expedition, than he was accosted by agents of King Leopold II (1865-1909) of Belgium.

A year or so before, Leopold had founded an International Association for the Exploration and Civilization of Central Africa, to whose members he had declared, "To open to civilization the only part of our globe where it has not yet penetrated, to pierce the darkness which envelops whole populations, is a crusade, if I may say so, a crusade worthy of this century of progress." Beneath this cosmopolitan, altruistic façade lay the desire for personal profit. Stanley was employed to return to the Congo under the auspices of a special section of the Association to make treaties with the natives and to search for means of economic exploitation. Britain, Portugal, and other states caught the fever. Disputes followed that led to the Berlin Conference of 1885, which attempted to regulate imperialistic adventures in Africa. The result was the erection of a Congo Free State under Leopold's sovereignty but with freedom of navigation and freedom of trade guaranteed to the white man and the abolition of slavery and the slave trade guaranteed to the Negro. It was further decided that in the future no state was to appropriate African territory without giving prior notice to other states, that actual occupation was necessary to justify claims, and that disputes would be arbitrated.

The crafty Leopold had won a kingdom of over 900,000 square miles. Part of the land was reserved as his private domain and part was granted to concessionaires in whose enterprises he owned large blocks of stock. The natives, who were among the more backward in Africa, did not want to work; they were therefore taxed in rubber and ivory. If they did not pay, force was employed. The results were $20,000,000 in Leopold's pockets, badly mistreated natives, and, eventually, criticism from missionaries and other groups. Leopold recognized that this situation could not continue, and in 1908 he turned the Congo Free State over to a reluctant Belgian government in return for a handsome compensation. Reforms were slowly introduced, and by 1914 the natives had begun to experience some of the more genuine blessings of Western civilization. In this manner, the missionary explorer, Livingstone, had led to the journalistic explorer, Stanley, who had led to the businessman king, Leopold, whose actions had led to the annexation of a colony by a European state. The only unusual features in the pattern of imperialism were that Leopold happened to be a king and that the Belgians were not interested in colonies.

IMPERIALISTIC RIVALRIES IN AFRICA

Leopold's initial success touched off competition to appropriate Africa. Companies were formed to exploit this or that locality. Agents went from one tribal chief to another and persuaded them to recognize their country as a protector and to give their company certain concessions, including mineral rights, in return for a few presents. The tribal rulers agreed, not understanding that they were signing away their independence. After Lo Bengula, a strong south African king, discovered what he had inadvertently surrendered, he informed Queen Victoria, "Some time ago a party of men came into my country, the principal one appearing to be a man called Rudd. They asked me for a place to dig gold and said they would give me certain things for the right to do so. I told them to bring what they would and I would show them what I would give. A document was written and presented to me for signature. I asked what it contained and was told that in it were my words and the words of those men. I put my hand to it. About three months afterwards I heard from other sources that I had given by that document the right to all the minerals of my country." But it was too late. Lo Bengula's country became Rhodesia and his lands were exploited by Cecil Rhodes' British South African Company.

Under the auspices of the Society for German Colonization, the energetic Karl Peters made treaties with a dozen credulous native rulers and won German East Africa for his country and his company. German Southwest Africa, Cameroon, and Togo fell to the same power, but the dream of uniting these territories was thwarted by the advance of the British from the south. The Portuguese expanded their coastal holdings from Angola and Mozambique inland. The Italians appropriated Somaliland and Eritrea but ran into trouble when they tried to round out their African empire by annexing Abyssinia (Ethiopia). They made the usual treaty with the deceived Emperor Menelik (1889-1913), but their calculations went awry. Menelik was an unusually able ruler, his ancient Christian empire with its written language and longtime contacts with Egypt was more advanced than that of most African states, and, more important, the French supplied arms and officers to train his troops. The result was that on March 1, 1896, Menelik with a large army virtually destroyed a much smaller Italian force of 6,000 men. The rivalry between the great powers had preserved at least one native state from annihilation.

The French wanted to block the Italian advance into Abyssinia, having designs on that country themselves. During the previous fifteen years, they had expanded their holdings in Algeria eastward to take Tunis, southward across the Sahara, and through Tombouctou to the Gulf of Guinea. Now they were seeking to connect this vast territory in northwest Africa with their small holdings around Obok on the Aden Gulf. To do so, they would have to control the upper reaches of the Nile in the Sudan and keep Abyssinia out of unfriendly hands. The assistance given Menelik was the first step in this policy. The second was to dispatch Captain Marchand from the French Congo with a force of less than two dozen white men and about two hundred natives to march three thousand miles through the tropics to reach the Nile River. Here they were to be met by a joint Abyssinian-French force coming from the east. Africa would be cut in two. It took two years for Marchand to accomplish his amazing mission, but on July 10, 1898, he arrived at Fashoda. Unhappily for the intrepid explorer, Lord Kitchener (1850-1916) reached Fashoda on September 19 with a British army. The French were about to experience a defeat similar to the Italians' because at this point their plans clashed with British-African ambitions.

The most important architect of the British-African empire was Cecil Rhodes (1835-1902). Rhodes was born in England but went to South Africa in 1870 for his health. Diamonds were discovered at Kimberley shortly after his arrival. He joined in the digging, and in a few years had established an important mining company. By 1890 this company had grown into a giant concern that controlled 90 per cent of the world's production of diamonds by merging with or swallowing its rivals. To Rhodes, wealth was only a means to an end, not the end itself. Early in his South African days, he had caught the vision of empire. South Africa with its healthful climate and vast wealth should become a united federal dominion in the British Empire. This meant that the two Boer republics must be incorporated and tribal lands in the interior removed from the control of the natives. As his ideas matured, he sought to extend British control north-

COLONIZATION IN AFRICA—1914
(EUROPEAN POSSESSIONS)

BRITISH	ITALIAN	FRENCH
GERMAN	SPANISH	PORTUGUESE
BELGIAN		

0 100 300 500 700 900
SCALE OF MILES

ward into the central part of the continent with the hope that one day Egypt itself would be reached. Thus, the British holdings would stretch from north to south from the Cape to Cairo. A railroad and telegraph line would be built to connect the two. As an ultimate dream, he looked to the domination of the world by the Anglo-Saxon race. To expand British holdings in Africa, he used his money and influence during his life; to further the cooperation between Englishmen and Americans, he devoted his immense wealth after his death to the scholarship fund which bears his name.

Rhodes' first task was to get Bechuanaland. If the Boers or Germans got there first, the Cape Colony would be boxed in without opportunity for further expansion. As a result of pressures he brought to bear, the usual treaties were made with the native chiefs and in 1885 Bechuanaland was organized as a territory. Farther to the north lay the domain of King Lo Bengula. Once more there was a treaty. Rhodes' South African Company was given the mining rights, and 440,000 more square miles, known as Rhodesia, were eventually added to the British Empire. Other British imperialists added Nyasaland, British East Africa, and Uganda to the British crown. All that was needed to extend the British lands from the Cape to the Equator was a strip along Lake Tanganyika between the Congo Free State and German East Africa.

Rhodes also played an important part in the internal developments in South Africa. He hoped that the two Boer republics would willingly join in a federal dominion with the British colonists, but they refused. Relations with the Boers became worse, especially after the discovery of gold in Transvaal in 1886. Thousands of Britishers flocked to Johannesburg where they were given a cold welcome by the Boer farmers who regarded them as intruders. In 1894 Rhodes, who had become prime minister of the Cape Colony, visited President Kruger of the Transvaal in the hope of persuading him to join a customs union with the British colonies in the area. Kruger's obstinate refusal caused Rhodes to become involved in an attempt led by Dr. Jameson to seize Transvaal in 1895. The raid failed, but relations deteriorated so seriously that war was formally declared in 1899.

The Boers' willingness to fight was based on the presumption that other imperialistic powers would come to their aid in order to block British expansion in south Africa. They were disappointed, but for one year their armies withstood the might of the British Empire and for eighteen more months they employed guerrilla tactics to the discomfiture of their enemies. It took 300,000 British soldiers to bring 50,000 Boer farmers to terms.

During the war the British had treated the Boers cruelly, but when peace had been restored they were generous. The two republics were annexed, but after several years they were granted representative institutions with responsible government. In 1910 the Boers joined willingly with the British in forming the Union of South Africa. Britain had another self-governing dominion, but Louis Botha, one-time Boer general, became its first prime minister.

Meanwhile, the British were making progress in North Africa. North Africa had been a nominal part of the Ottoman Empire when the new age of imperialism began, but the governors of much of this region had become virtually independent rulers. This was especially true of Egypt, where Mohammed Ali (1769-1849), an illiterate Albanian merchant, had seized power and been recognized by the sultan as governor in 1805. Mohammed Ali proved a strong, ruthless ruler who took the initial steps to Westernize his domain. His efficient army made him a power in the eastern Mediterranean. He intervened in the Greek rebellion of the 1820's and added Crete, Syria, and the Sudan to his territory. Later, Crete and Syria were lost, but Mohammed Ali won European recognition for his family as hereditary governors of Egypt. Most of his · successors were anxious to adopt Western ideas. The European-educated Ismail (1863-1879) carried on big public works and primary education programs, but his various projects and his extravagances ran him deeply in debt to European bankers. In 1875, he had to sell his shares of Suez Canal stock to the British, and the following year the British and French began to exercise control over the country's finances to assure that payments would be made to the creditors. This led to an Egyptian nationalistic uprising in 1881. The French refused to act, but Egypt and the Suez Canal were so essential to British interests in India and the whole of the East that Gladstone ordered armed intervention. Gladstone, who was sincerely opposed to imperialism, promised to withdraw as soon as order was restored.

Intervention, however, proved easier than withdrawal. Order was restored, and the government was efficiently managed by the able Lord Cromer (1841-1917), but it was obvious that the angered native nationalists would respect neither European lives, property, nor the Suez Canal once they were freed from the presence of British troops. The sincerity of the British desire to keep their involvement in Egypt to a minimum is indicated by the decision to withdraw Egyptian troops from the Sudan, where a Moslem prophet or mahdi, Mohammed Ahmed, had seized control of most of the countryside. Even when General "Chinese" (Charles George) Gordon (1833-1885), who was sent into the Sudan to implement the retreat, was surrounded at Khartoum and his small army massacred, no attempt was made to "restore order." Only when the British became aware of the French desire to cut across Africa from east to west did they decide to act.[3] It was one thing to let the semi-civilized natives rule the Sudan, and another to let the French, who could control the flow of the vital waters of the Nile River, into the region. In 1896, Lord Kitchener began the slow reconquest of the region. On September 2, 1898, he won a great victory over the Sudanese at Omdurman; seventeen days later his army made contact with the little band under Captain Marchand at Fashoda. The French drive from east to west had met the British drive from Cape to Cairo.

For a time, it looked as though the two powers would fight for control of the headwaters of the Nile, but in the end the French withdrew. Their country was then torn with dissension over the Dreyfus case, and some of their leaders were becoming increasingly certain that Germany, not Britain, was their real enemy. Only acquisition of the Lake Tanganyika region remained to make Cecil Rhodes' African dream come true.

By 1914 only Abyssinia and Liberia remained independent, the first

[3] See page 712.

because the French had blocked Italian expansion there and the second because the United States exercised a protective influence, for it had been to Liberia that many freed American Negroes had gone before the Civil War.

Who had profited from this generation of African imperialism? The Leopolds and Rhodes, yes, but not the countless unknowns who had invested in unsuccessful African companies. Was it the European states? Again, no; they had spent fortunes to pay the troops to fight and the officials to administer. Africa had provided Europe with diamonds, gold, rubber, cotton, and other products and it had bought manufactured goods, but the value of this trade was small compared with Europe's total commerce.

The real significance of African imperialism was the effect it had had on the native. The Europeans had taken his best land and had often confined him to reservations. They had taught him the vices and brought him the diseases of civilized society. They needed his labor to exploit the mines, farms, and forests that had once been his and had secured it by imposing taxes that he could not pay unless he accepted their employment, by inflicting cruel punishments, or by bribing his tribal chief to compel him to labor. On the other hand, the Europeans had brought to an end the numerous tribal wars, the barbaric native customs, and the slave trade. They had introduced the religious and ethical beliefs of Western civilization, and its science, medicine, and technologies. That the good outweighed the bad is best evidenced by the fact that the African population had been static for centuries before the age of imperialism because misery and the slave trade had checked the growth that normally accompanies a high birth rate. Despite the cruel aspects of European imperialism, the overall misery of the natives was so reduced that the population nearly doubled in the two generations that followed the domination of the continent.

AMERICAN IMPERIALISM

In a sense, the Americas have always been associated with imperialism. Columbus was a fifteenth-century Stanley, and Queen Isabella of Castile played a role comparable to King Leopold of Belgium. Jamestown was a Cape Town, and the idea of Manifest Destiny parallels Cecil Rhodes' Cape to Cairo dream. The Indian was the counterpart of the Negro. In the United States, he fared less well than the Negro because he was unnecessary to the white man's plans of exploitation. Later, in Mexico and Peru he achieved the position that the Africans are now seeking. However, historians do not usually employ the term imperialism to describe designs on neighboring territory. Neither the French desire to retake Alsace-Lorraine nor the United States' expansion at the expense of the Indians and Mexicans are normally classified as imperialistic. The winning of the West so absorbed the energies of the United States that few wished to acquire noncontiguous territory prior to the 1880's. Alaska was purchased in 1867 and an occasional feint was made at the West Indian islands, but until the frontier was about to close, the United States made no concerted effort to get colonies. The other American countries were similarly occupied for a varying number of years, but even after their hinterland had been occupied, they lacked the military and industrial strength to move beyond their contiguous territory. Indeed, their task was often to ward off the colonial aspirations of the European powers and the United States. Thus, the United States was the only New World nation to become an imperialistic power.

The decision of the United States to become imperialistic was based on much the same premises as those of other powers. Some wished to spread the benefits of the American civilization to other peoples, others believed that the Anglo-Saxon "is divinely commissioned to be his brother's keeper." Some talked of tropical products and foreign markets, others argued that colonies with naval bases could be the first line of defense. Many had no real reason at all beyond a desire for excitement, war, and conquest.

The Samoan Islands were the United States' first important overseas colony. In 1878, the young republic was granted the right to use the fine harbor at Pago Pago by the trusting natives. Eleven years later the United States and Germany divided the islands in the best imperialistic fashion. The Hawaiian Islands suffered a similar fate. Pearl Harbor was made a naval station in 1887, and American settlers obtained control of most of the sugar production. The government itself soon fell into their hands, and when Queen Liliuokalani sought to reassert her authority, they revolted with the assistance of the American minister and the marines. Success was quickly achieved and the triumphant whites petitioned the United States to be annexed. The anti-imperialistic Democratic president, Grover Cleveland, refused to act, but in 1898 after he had been succeeded by the less squeamish Republican, William McKinley, Hawaii was annexed amid a wave of nationalism inspired by the Spanish-American War.

The Spanish-American War was one of the least justifiable conflicts of the imperialistic generation. Theoretically, it was fought to aid the badly treated Cubans win their independence and to punish the Spanish for blowing up the battleship *Maine*. These explanations are not entirely satisfactory because the United States' interest in the Spanish colonies was not altogether altruistic. One of Cuba's greatest problems after the war was to maintain its independence from the United States; and the Philippine Islanders, who suddenly found themselves under American rule as a result of the war, fought more courageously against their new masters for independence than ever the Cubans had against their former ones. As for the battleship *Maine*, it is still not known why it sank, but one thing seems certain: the Spanish government was not directly responsible. The last thing it wanted was a war with the far more powerful United States.

The underlying causes of the Cuban revolt were political and economic. Administrative reforms that included a greater degree of self-government had been promised the inhabitants in 1878, but had not been forthcoming. Then, too, there was a collapse in the sugar market. Foreign capital, largely American, had moved into Cuba during the decade prior to the war to increase sugar production. At that time, the United States had no duty on sugar, and Europe provided a ready market. However, in 1894 the United States put a 40 per cent tariff on sugar to protect domestic producers, and increased sugar beet production elsewhere reduced the world price from eight to two cents a pound. The resulting hardship led to the outbreak of guerrilla warfare. Cuban bands armed by American sympathizers burned the plantations of loyalists by night and hid in the hills by day. The exasperated Spanish finally decided that the only way to restore order was to herd all suspected persons into concentration camps.

At this point the American "yellow press" intervened. Many Americans naïvely believed the stories of Spanish cruelty embroidered by cynical journalists. The desire to aid the Cubans and to experience the excitement of a war caused many to talk of intervention. More rational considerations also played a part, and there were those who spoke of the need for West Indian bases to protect a proposed Panama or Nicaraguan canal, of the obligation to protect American property in Cuba, and of the economic advantages of colonies. The *Washington Post* accurately put its finger on the pulse of the nation when it declared, "A new consciousness seems to have come upon us—the consciousness of strength—and with it a new appetite, the yearning to show our strength. . . . Ambition, interest, land hunger, pride, the mere joy of fighting, whatever it may be, we are animated by a new sensation. We are face to face with a strange destiny. The taste of Empire is in the mouth of the people even as the taste of blood in the jungle. It means an Imperial policy, the Republic, renascent, taking her place with the armed nations." In such a climate of opinion there is little wonder that the explosion of February 15, 1898, that sank the battleship *Maine* in the Havana harbor with a loss of 260 lives led to war.

The Spanish government knew that it was no match for the United States and on April 9 accepted every American demand, but the aggressive Teddy Roosevelt declared that "the blood of the murdered men of the *Maine* calls not for indemnity but for the full measure of atonement, which can only come by driving the Spaniards from the New World." On April 11, President McKinley, who had been aptly labeled by the Spanish ambassador as a "spineless politician," gave way to popular demand and sent a war message to Congress.

"It wasn't much of a war," Theodore Roosevelt later admitted. Admiral Dewey sank the outmoded Spanish fleet in Manila Bay without the loss of an American life, and an incredibly badly planned expedition was landed in Cuba. Teddy Roosevelt and his "Rough Riders" were without their horses, and the army was clothed in winter uniforms to fight a summer campaign in the tropics. Happily for the vigorous young republic, Spanish incompetence proved equal to the occasion, and after ten weeks of actual fighting, the war was brought to a successful conclusion. Only 289 American lives were lost in battle and thirteen times as many from disease. By the terms of the Treaty of Paris, Spain withdrew from Cuba and ceded Puerto Rico, Guam, and the Philippine Islands. Overnight the United States had become a world power with possessions lying on the other side of the globe. No longer could it confine its interests to the Western hemisphere. The world's problems were now its own.

The first task was to establish effective control over the new empire. At the war's end, the Philippine Islands were largely in the hands of the native leader, Emilio Aguinaldo (1870?-1964), who had long sought independence from the Spanish. Aguinaldo had hoped that the United States, who had just fought a war ostensibly to win Cuban independence, would not deny the Philippines a similar privilege. He was mistaken. McKinley decided that the United States had no recourse but "to educate the Filipinos and uplift and Christianize them." Since the Filipinos had been Roman Catholics for centuries, it is not surprising that Aguinaldo did not accept this line of reasoning. For three years, he and his followers fought for their freedom. Only by the use of 60,000 troops and the concentration camps the Spanish had so lately been condemned for employing were the islands brought firmly under the American flag. Even the Cubans found their newly won independence restricted by a provision that the United States could intervene at its discretion in their internal affairs "for the protection of life, property, and individual liberty."

Happily, the idealism engendered by its own war for independence soon asserted itself and the United States became a model colonial power. Hawaii was given full territorial status in 1900, and statehood in 1959. The Philippines were authorized to elect the lower house of a legislature in 1907, given virtual control over their domestic affairs in 1916, and complete independence in 1946. Puerto Rico was also given a territorial government; only in the smaller islands were the inhabitants left without reasonable rights of self-government. In addition, Americans brought in sanitation and medical and educational improvements, as well as capital for industry, farming, and railroad building. In the long run, the American colonial territories probably profited more by the arrangement than the mother country.

The Spanish-American War did not bring American imperialism to an end. In 1901, the bellicose Theodore Roosevelt became president. His most notable achievements in the field of imperialistic diplomacy were the acquisition of the Panama Canal Zone and the establishment of the Roosevelt Corollary to the Monroe Doctrine. The need for a canal across Central America had long been evident, and when the republic of Colombia refused Roosevelt's offer to purchase a six-mile strip across Panama, he felt justified in taking action. Tacit approval was given for a Panamanian insurrection, and American warships were placed in those waters to prevent Colombia from sending troops to repress the rebellion. The revolt broke out on November 3, 1903, the United States accorded diplomatic recognition to Panama on November 6, and on November 18 the new republic turned the Canal Zone over to the United States. Construction was quickly begun.

The prospect that it would soon have a canal of great strategic and commercial importance across Panama made the United States much more interested in the Caribbean region. The republics in this area were as disorderly and as disinclined to pay their debts as Egypt had been, but the occupation of one of them by a great power to "restore order" or to collect debts due its citizens would pose a threat to the United States and violate the Monroe Doctrine. On the other hand, it was unthinkable for the United States to prevent other powers from intervening if these republics violated the rights of their citizens. To Roosevelt the obvious solution was for the United States to exercise "an international police power" to protect the citizens of all the imperialistic states. In pursuance of this corollary to the Monroe Doctrine, the United States intervened in the Dominican Republic, Cuba, Honduras, and Haiti within the next ten years to restore order or to collect debts.

Roosevelt's policy probably preserved the independence of several of these states, but United States' interference, often to protect investments of its own citizens, was not popular in Latin America and has become known as "dollar diplomacy." When Woodrow Wilson became president in 1913, he determined to alter this policy, but he soon found that the choice lay between permitting violence and disorders in the Caribbean states or actively intervening. Haiti, the Dominican Republic, and Cuba felt his heavy hand, and the United States narrowly missed going to war with Mexico. Wilson did not act to protect the American dollar as his predecessors had done, but he was too much of a moralist to stand aside while the Haitians or Mexicans murdered their presidents. As a result, his moralism led him down the same path as dollar diplomacy. Then, too, the need for more naval bases in the Caribbean Sea caused him to purchase the Virgin Islands from Denmark in 1917.

IMPERIALISM IN ASIA: GENERAL CONSIDERATIONS

Asia, like Africa, began to succumb to the forces of Westernization during the latter part of the nineteenth century. Before that time, its very distance from Europe had done much to protect it from outside influences; and its vast size, high mountains, large deserts, tropical jungles, and frozen wastes had made penetration into the interior difficult. India and the East Indies had been too divided politically to stop European advances during the seventeenth and eighteenth centuries, but China and Japan had successfully enforced a policy of isolation. The Chinese halted the

OVERSEAS TERRITORIES 1900

SPANISH TER.
GERMAN TER.
U.S. TER.
BRITISH TER.
FRENCH TER.
RUSSIAN TER.
PORTUGUESE TER.
ITALIAN TER.
BELGIAN TER.
NETHERLANDS TER.
TURKISH TER.

Russian penetration north of the Amur Valley in 1689, and during the reign of Ch'ien Lung (1736-1795) they held a territory larger and more populous than all of Europe.

Three events brought Asia within the grasp of Europe during the latter part of the nineteenth century. They were (1) the industrial revolution, (2) the revolution in transportation and communication, and (3) the opening of the Suez Canal in 1869. The Suez Canal shortened the distance to Asia by four or five thousand miles, the steamship increased the speed of travel and the size of cargoes, and the industrial revolution made it possible for the Europeans to produce manufactured goods cheaper than the handcraft industries of Asia. In the eighteenth century, the English had bought textiles in India; in the nineteenth, the Indians bought textiles in Britain. These developments also increased the military superiority of the Europeans and made it logistically possible for them to conduct big campaigns anywhere on the globe. By the latter half of the nineteenth century, there was no doubt that Europeans had the capacity to make large inroads into Asia. They also had the desire, for the forces that led to imperialism in Africa operated in Asia. The inevitable result was the incorporation of much of Asia into the European sphere of influence.

INDIA

The English, who took the lead in bringing Western influence into Asia, already had sizable holdings there when the revival of imperialism began. India, the heart of the nascent empire, had been taken from the East India Company in 1857 as a result of the Sepoy Mutiny.[4] To rule the populous territory, a secretary of state for India was appointed who resided in London and was a member of the cabinet. This secretary functioned through a viceroy stationed in India. The viceroy, with the aid of a small nominated legislative and an executive council, made the laws and administered the central government. That part of India directly under the British crown was divided into districts of about two thousand square miles and one million people each for purposes of local administration. Each district was placed under the care of an official of the small, highly trained, efficient Indian Civil Service. None of the important officials were elected and few were of Indian descent. The government of India was therefore a foreign, efficient, paternalistic, and undemocratic regime.

About 40 per cent of India remained in the hands of over 500 different Indian princes who ruled states that varied in size from Hyderabad with 82,000 square miles to Bilbari with less than two square miles. The British appointed residents to watch over the activities of these princes, but they did not interfere unless the princes behaved in an uncivilized or barbarous manner. The princes were left free to squander the wealth they received from their poverty-stricken subjects. In return, they usually co-

[4] See page 573.

operated loyally with the British. Before World War I, the people had little influence over the government above the municipal and village level.

British rule undoubtedly brought many benefits to the Indians. Among the greatest was unity. By the mid-nineteenth century, the huge subcontinent had become divided into many independent states, but the conquerors abolished internal wars and restored theoretical unity by proclaiming Victoria empress in 1877. Princes who failed to cooperate and rulers of border states who caused trouble found their territories incorporated. Between 1881 and 1901, 223,000 square miles were added to India. In 1911 George V was actually crowned emperor in the historic capital of Delhi.

The British also brought Western technology. By 1914 they had invested over two billion dollars in Indian railroads, banks, mines, and industry. India had the best railroad network in Asia with more miles of track than Great Britain and nearly as many as in the entire Russian empire. Western medical knowledge and hospitals saved countless lives, and many cruel native customs were eliminated. Western ideas made inroads, especially among the Indian upper classes, through high schools and colleges constructed in India, through training given well-to-do Indians in Europe, and through the activities of Christian missionaries who brought about seven million persons into their churches. The educated Indian learned to appreciate the advantages of self-government and came to be deeply influenced by feelings of nationalism.

Despite the advantages brought by English rule, the Indian people remained poor. In 1901 their per capita income was less than $10 per year and two-thirds of the population were undernourished. This situation was in part the result of the nature of Indian society and culture and in part the result of British policy. Nearly 90 per cent of the population lived in villages where the average holding was only five acres and the agricultural practices were most primitive. As a result, yields per acre did not increase as rapidly as the population, which climbed from 150,000,000 in 1850 to 303,000,000 in 1911. Only famine, disease, and misery, not voluntary birth control, kept the increase from being greater. In 1891 the life expectancy in India was still less than 26 years.

The most obvious way for the Indians to improve their diet was to eat more meat, but the Hindus, who made up two-thirds of the population, believed that all life was sacred, from the rodents who destroyed their crops to the cows who wandered through their villages. As a result, a third of the world's cattle dwelt in India, but, like the people, they were too numerous to be properly nourished. These underfed animals could not even supply an adequate amount of milk. The rigid caste system was also a barrier to economic progress. It was a determining factor in a man's choice of his vocation, his friends, and his wife. The orthodox Hindu would not eat food prepared by a lowly untouchable. Since no man could rise above his caste, the social structure was regarded as permanent and unchanging.

The Indians, however, blamed the British for most of their troubles. They complained that British manufactured goods destroyed the native handcraft industries and that inadequate amounts were spent to build factories in India that would compete with British producers. They complained that Indian wealth was siphoned off to buy British goods, to pay interest on British loans, to pay high salaries to British officials, and to support an unnecessarily large army. The British, they charged, were concentrating on providing advanced education for a few Indians and were leaving 90 per cent of the population illiterate. Furthermore, they made English the language of instruction and the humanities the basic ingredient in the curriculum, rather than science, agriculture, and other much-needed practical subjects.

Out of this situation, Indian nationalism arose. The nationalists agreed that the government of India must be wrested from the British and devoted to the betterment of the Indian people, but at this point they separated into opposing camps. The Moslems, who made up a fourth of the population, were bitterly opposed to the Hindu majority, as were the Sikhs, Christians, and other smaller minorities. Some dreamed of restoring an idealized version of an earlier Indian society and culture, others were content to adopt the ideas of the West. Of the latter, some were for laissez-faire and some were socialistic. There were those who wanted to destroy the caste system, and those who wanted it retained. Small wonder British officials came to believe that only their presence kept the natives from tearing each other to pieces. Nevertheless, a moderate Indian National Congress was organized in 1885 that wielded an ever-increasing influence. The Japanese victory over Russia in 1905 gave heart to the colored peoples throughout the world.[5] Some Indians became more violent and all became more demanding, but modest British concessions kept the Indians loyal during World War I.

THE BRITISH AND THEIR RIVALS IN ASIA

The British had always regarded India as a great source of national wealth, although the poverty-stricken Indians bought fewer British products in 1911 than the nineteen million prosperous inhabitants of the predominantly white dominions. Partly to protect their "lifeline" to India, they had bought Suez Canal stock and later occupied Egypt. Partly to protect India from the Russians, they expanded elsewhere in Asia. The Russians did not seek overseas colonies. Instead, they preferred to occupy contiguous territory by pressing southward along the shores of the Caspian and Aral seas in search of a warm water outlet on the Indian Ocean. When they annexed territory adjoining Persia in 1884, a race began between them and the English to win banking, railroad, and oil concessions from the Persians. For a time war seemed possible.

[5] See page 738.

Russian pressure on Persia was accompanied by similar moves in the direction of Afghanistan, where there were mountain passes leading to India. In 1878, a Russian mission to Kabul negotiated a treaty with the ruler of that state. The British immediately dispatched an army which overran the country and forced its ruler to conduct his foreign policy through the Indian government. The Russians renewed their efforts to expand in this direction around 1900 and at about the same time began to negotiate with neighboring Tibet. Tibet was a vassal state of China, but neither this fact nor the rights of the Dalai Lama, who was both the religious and political leader of the country, disturbed the Russians or British. Once more the British dispatched an army, this time to Lhasa, to ensure that Russia did not establish itself in a neighboring state to India. Thus, by 1907 the two powers were clashing in Persia, Afghanistan, and Tibet, just as the British and French African interests had clashed in the Sudan. The results were much the same. Peace was preferred to war. It was agreed in 1907 that Tibet should be left for the Tibetans and Chinese, that the Russians should stay out of Afghanistan, and that Persia should be divided into spheres of influence. The northern third was to go to Russia, the southern third to Britain, and the remainder was to be left open to nationals of both countries. The Russians had been kept from the Indian Ocean and the mountain passes leading to India; the "lifeline" to India and India itself were secure.

Some Persians, meanwhile, had come under the influence of Western ideas. They started a revolution designed to break the autocratic power of the shah, establish a parliament, and introduce reforms. The Russians and British, now allies, blocked this effort because, if Persia reformed, there would no longer be an excuse to treat it as a backward protectorate. Seldom has imperialism appeared less altruistic.

To the east of India, it was the aspirations of the French that caused the British concern. As early as 1858, the French had used the murder of a Spanish missionary as the excuse to send an expedition against Annam, a tributary state of China. The inevitable result was the establishment of a French colony in the Saigon area. With this toehold, the French advanced northward, especially after the imperialistic age had begun. Between 1883 and 1885, a war was fought with China to terminate its claims and in 1887 Annam and several other states were organized into the colony of Indo-China.

Meanwhile, the French had been seeking to expand westward towards India by getting territory from Siam and establishing friendly relations with Burma. Interest in Burma, especially, was regarded by the British as a threat, and they quickly settled the matter by annexing that state. This brought them into a head-long collision with the French in Siam in 1893. In the end, the able Siamese king preserved the independence of most of his country by playing the rivals against each other. At the same time, he introduced a modernization program that made his country more advanced than most of the neighboring lands that had become European colonies.

South of Siam was the Malay Peninsula and a large group of islands that stretched eastward for nearly 3,000 miles, known as the Malay Archipelago. Here the Dutch loomed as British rivals. They had established trading posts on many of the islands and had blocked British efforts to establish colonies during the seventeenth and eighteenth centuries. In keeping with the ideas of the time, however, they had not generally occupied a significant area of the interior of these islands. The British renewed their interest in the region during the Napoleonic wars, but their conquests were restored to the Dutch by the Treaty of Vienna in 1815. Four years later, however, an Englishman founded the strategically located city of Singapore, thereby laying the groundwork for future expansion in the region. As elsewhere, the last half of the nineteenth century proved to be the period of rapid European expansion. By this time, the Dutch were too weak to block all their rivals. The British advanced northward from Singapore to occupy the Malay states and took the northern part of Borneo and the southern section of New Guinea as well. Another section of New Guinea fell to the Germans, but most of the remaining islands, in all comprising some 735,000 square miles, fell to the Dutch.

In the eighteenth century, the Dutch had exploited the islands by demanding tribute from the native chiefs, but after a revolt had forced them to conquer the interior of Java in 1825-1830, they introduced a system of forced labor that brought them sizable returns. In 1860, slavery was abolished, and beginning in 1870 the amount of forced labor required was reduced, although it was not until 1917 that it was abandoned in the production of coffee. The Dutch can claim credit for introducing Western medicine into the islands and for adding tea, tobacco, palm oil, and quinine to their exports, but they made little effort to educate the natives prior to the twentieth century. Unlike the British, they preserved the native languages and cultures. This fact, plus the strong Moslem beliefs of the bulk of the people, caused Europeanization to proceed at a slower rate than in many other places. Nevertheless, the Dutch were eventually troubled by the growth of nationalism and the desire for self-government on the part of the natives.

AUSTRALIA AND NEW ZEALAND

South of the Malay Archipelago lay Australia. When the various colonies on this continent had been given self-government in 1850, they had each proceeded to adopt different tariff laws and to lay railway track of different widths. The resulting confusion and the growing fear of aggression as a result of the imperialistic behavior of the great powers led to a desire for federal union. In 1901, the British freely gave Australia dominion status. The new commonwealth adopted a constitution like that of the

United States, with a senate to represent the member states and a house of representatives to represent the people. One notable exception was the adoption of the British system of ministerial responsibility to parliament. In 1907 the neighboring islands of New Zealand were also given dominion status.

Australia and New Zealand were unusual in two respects. In the first place, they were completely European, since their inhabitants came almost entirely from the mother continent. The aborigines, never numerous, were almost completely exterminated, and rigid laws were passed limiting immigration from the Orient. In the second place, they were both very democratic. Even women were given the right to vote in New Zealand in 1893 and in Australia in 1902. Both adopted the social reform programs supported in part by income taxes that became characteristic of the European states in the early twentieth century. Indeed, New Zealand achieved a world-wide reputation for its experiments in this field. The two dominions grew rapidly in population, Australia going from 1,200,000 in 1860 to 5,400,000 in 1920 and New Zealand from 500,000 to 1,200,000 during the same period.

By 1914 the Indian Ocean had become a British lake. The tiny island kingdom controlled most of the east African coast, India, Burma, Malaya, Australia, and New Zealand and held a sphere of influence in Persia. The few other powers, like the Portuguese, the Italians, and the Dutch, who owned colonies on the "lake" were too weak to challenge Britain's supremacy. The Russians had been kept from the "lake's" shores and the French had too little territory in the region to be a serious threat. Contact was maintained by the "lifeline" through the Suez Canal, which in the years just before 1914 carried more than twelve million net tons of British shipping annually.

Although the British had won an empire consisting of about a fourth of the land surface and a fourth of the population of the world, they had not yet developed an imperial theory. The relationship between the self-governing dominions and the crown had purposely been left vague. This void was partially filled by Joseph Chamberlain (1836-1914). Chamberlain made a fortune as a Birmingham manufacturer, became famous as its reforming mayor, and served in several Liberal cabinets. However, like so many other big industrialists, he abandoned the Liberal party and laissez-faire, cooperated with the Conservatives, and advocated imperialism. To be secure and profitable, Chamberlain believed, the Empire must be made "self-sustaining and self-protecting." As colonial secretary between 1895 and 1903, he advocated that the Empire be bound together economically by a system of preferential tariffs designed to exclude trade with outsiders and to encourage trade between its various parts. Defense was to be coordinated and its cost shared. Chamberlain's proposals were not then accepted, more because England itself was not yet ready to abandon the principles of free trade, even in return for closer ties with its Empire, than because of the independent behavior of the dominions. Chamberlain was disappointed, but he had not failed. Sentiment for the Empire grew stronger as a result of his efforts, a degree of naval cooperation was achieved, the dominions supported the mother country during World War I, and after the war imperial preference was actually adopted.[6]

THE FAR EAST

Three important non-European states came under the influence of Western civilization without becoming colonies of one of the great powers. They were China, Japan, and the Ottoman Empire. The Japanese adopted Western techniques so rapidly and efficiently that they were actually able to expand their territory during the age of imperialism. The Chinese and Ottomans at first resisted Western ideas and then adopted them so slowly that they were lucky to maintain their independence. Both lost substantial amounts of territory and had to concede spheres of influence. We will treat China and Japan at this point, but will postpone dealing with the Ottoman Empire until the next chapter since its troubles were so intimately related to the origins of World War I.

THE CHINESE EMPIRE

One need not be surprised that at first the Chinese saw no advantage in adopting Western culture and techniques. Theirs was the oldest and most populous empire in the world. For centuries, they had influenced Europe more than Europe had influenced them. The printing press that the Europeans used to disseminate information about the Far East, the compass that guided them to China's shores, and the gunpowder that they employed to defeat the armies of Manchu emperors were probably Chinese inventions. During the eighteenth century, the Chinese system of government was admired by the French philosophers and Chinese gardens were imitated everywhere in Europe. Chinese silks, both ancient and modern, were sought by Europeans; and the word "china" itself has become synonymous with fine porcelain. Little wonder the Chinese regarded their state as the "Celestial Empire," the "Middle Kingdom"; to them it was the center of the world. The ambassadors of a Tartar prince, of an Indo-Chinese monarch, or, for that matter, of the British king were expected to kneel and touch their heads to the floor three times when they were admitted into the presence of the Chinese emperor.

The Chinese assumed that the European could produce nothing that they would want to buy. "We possess all things," the powerful Emperor Ch'ien Lung informed Britain's George III. "I set no value on objects strange or ingenious, and have expounded my wishes in detail and have

[6] See pages 905-906.

commanded your tribute envoys to leave in peace on their homeward journey. It behooves you, O King, to respect my sentiments and to display greater loyalty in the future. . . ." Then, perhaps thinking that he had been too harsh, Ch'ien Lung dispatched another message: "I do not forget the lonely remoteness of your island, cut off from the world by intervening wastes of sea, nor do I overlook your excusable ignorance of the usages of our Celestial Empire. I have consequently commanded my ministers to enlighten your ambassador on the subject. . . ." This correspondence took place less than two centuries ago!

Nevertheless, the Europeans were permitted to engage in trade with the Chinese at Canton. If Chinese merchants showed no interest in British manufactured goods, they were willing to accept gold and opium in return for their silk and tea. By 1839 nearly 30,000 chests of opium were being brought to China from India each year despite an imperial edict of 1800 forbidding this trade. Suddenly, the Emperor decided to enforce the law. The opium was seized, and the British merchants engaged in the trade were temporarily imprisoned. Britain's response was the Opium War, which was not a war to make the Chinese use opium, but to compel them to abandon their pretensions of exclusiveness and superiority, to force them to respect the lives and property of Europeans, to remove trade restrictions, and to permit Westerners to be tried by European rather than Chinese law. The outcome of the war was never in doubt. One port after another fell to the British. The Chinese sued for peace and in a series of treaties signed between 1842 and 1844 an indemnity was paid, Hong Kong was ceded, and five ports, including Shanghai, were opened to foreigners. Foreigners in these ports were to be tried by their own laws and their consuls were to be treated by the Chinese as equals.

The British victory revealed the weakness of the Manchu emperors to their subjects. The rural inhabitants of south China, who suffered from a lack of land, heavy taxes, and absentee landlordism, rose in revolt in 1850 under the leadership of Hung Hsiu-ch'uan (1812?-1864). Hung had three times failed to pass the examinations required of prospective Chinese bureaucrats and during his period of disappointment had read some missionary tracts from which he learned a little of Christianity. Hung's rebellion had all the elements of a social and religious crusade. The land was to be divided among the peasants. He himself claimed to be Jesus' divine younger brother and to rule over T'ai-p'ing T'ien-kuo (The Celestial Kingdom of Peace). For sixteen years the T'ai-p'ing rebellion raged and estimates of the loss of life reach thirty million. In 1860 the British and French profited by the confusion to attack the Emperor, seize Peking, burn the fabulous imperial summer palace, and compel the Chinese to ratify a new peace treaty. This treaty imposed an indemnity, opened eleven more ports to European trade, gave Christian missionaries freedom to proselytize in the interior, established custom duties to be administered by Westerners, and legalized the opium trade.

The introduction of Western civilization into China began in earnest. Merchants poured into the international settlements of Shanghai and the other treaty ports. Religious, medical, and educational missionaries came in great numbers. Denominational schools and colleges were established. Between 1872 and 1881, 150 Chinese students were sent to study in the United States and Europe. Diplomatic missions went abroad and marveled at the streets of London where it "rained all day, yet there is no mud." But unhappily for the Chinese, the Westernizing movement was reversed when the government fell into the hands of Tzu Hsi, one-time concubine and now dowager empress, who directed the government as regent or as the power behind the throne from 1862 until her death in 1908. She was a clever, unscrupulous, indomitable woman, but she hated all things Western and hoped to save China by restoring the efficiency of the old Chinese administration.

For a time, it looked as though Tzu Hsi and the host of able Chinese officials who rallied to her call might save the dynasty and the empire, but in 1894 Japan provoked a quarrel over Korea. The Chinese army and navy were destroyed, and by the terms of the Treaty of Shimonoseki the following year, Korea was recognized as independent, and Formosa, the Pescadores Islands, and the Liaotung Peninsula were ceded to the victors. Russia, Germany, and France forced Japan to return the Liaotung Peninsula, but a mad scramble then ensued among the European powers for Chinese territory. Russia obtained the right to build a railway across Manchuria and received the southern tip of the Liaotung Peninsula that it had just denied to the Japanese; the Germans and British occupied part of the neighboring Shantung Peninsula; and the French demanded a 99-year lease on Kwangchow. The United States became fearful that China would be divided among the great powers and its own profitable trade curtailed. At the urging of the American secretary of state, an "open door" policy was established to ensure that every nation had an equal right to trade with China regardless of the concessions.

The defeat by Japan was even more galling to Chinese pride than the defeats by the Western powers because the Japanese had always been regarded as a backward, uncultured people. For a brief period in 1898, Chinese reformers got control of the government and issued many decrees leading towards Westernization, but the old Empress quickly reasserted her authority and made one last effort to save China by an appeal to the past rather than to the future. Orders were sent out to provincial officials to revive the ancient local militia to protect Chinese soil. Unfortunately, brigands and desperate poverty-stricken men joined in large numbers. They assumed the picturesque name of the "Fists of Righteous Harmony," the "Boxers" to the less subtle, more abrupt Western mind. The Boxers became convinced that the Western powers were about to divide their country and attacked all things Western. Missionaries and Chinese Christians were slain, and the German minister was murdered. English, French, German, Russian, Japanese, and American troops were rushed to China; once more Peking was taken and a heavy indemnity imposed.

Even the dowager Empress and the illiterate peasants now knew that the only alternatives were Westernization or destruction. Steps were taken to Westernize the army, revamp the fiscal and administrative system, and prepare a new legal code. Railroads and telegraph lines were constructed, and the British were persuaded to reduce the amount of opium they imported from India. Schools and colleges were opened in China where a Western curriculum was taught, and thousands were sent abroad to study. The old system of appointing to important posts only those who had passed an examination in the Chinese classics was abandoned and training in Western political science, economics, and similar subjects became the preferred avenue to advancement. A parliamentary form of government was promised, and to prepare the people for this step, provincial assemblies were created.

Unfortunately, both the Emperor and the old dowager Empress died in November, 1908. The throne went to P'u Yi, a child in his third year, and the actual government was given to a regent who slowed the progress of reform. This was unwise, for the Manchus were still regarded as an alien dynasty by the Chinese, especially in the south, and recent events had already thoroughly discredited their rule. An almost bloodless revolution began in 1911, and on February 12, 1912, the Manchus abdicated to make way for the creation of a republic.

THE CHINESE REPUBLIC

Two men now vied for leadership. One was Dr. Sun Yat-sen (1866-1925), who had received an Anglo-American education in medicine. He became involved in a revolutionary plot in 1895 and spent most of his time from then until 1911 living in exile in the United States and Europe. He emerged as the leader of the Kuomintang (National People's Party) and the controlling force in south China. Sun was thoroughly acquainted with Western ideas and could speak as eloquently in English as in Chinese. His program consisted of the three people's principles: democracy, nationalism, and livelihood. By democracy, he meant the Western concept of the sovereignty of the people, but until the masses could be educated, he believed in adhering to the old Chinese concept that government should be in the hands of the educated and the able. In nationalism, he hoped to find a force that would bind the vast Chinese population together so that they could better resist outside aggression. By livelihood, he meant the improvement of the economic lot of the people by a program of land reform and industrialization under the auspices of the state, not of individuals who sought private gain. The Kuomintang advocated a parliament with a responsible ministry and a president with few powers.

Sun's rival was General Yuan Shik-k'ai (1859-1916), one of the ablest

EXPANSION OF RUSSIA AND ENGLAND AND
SPHERES OF INFLUENCE (1914)

BRITISH COLONIES   ACQUIRED 1533 TO 1588
BRITISH PROTECTORATES   ACQUIRED TO 1689
BRITISH SPHERE OF INFLU. SPHERES OF INFLUENCE
RUSSIA 1533   GREATEST EXTENT OF EMP.

SCALE OF MILES
0 100 200   400   600

officials of the Manchu dynasty. Yuan was a leading advocate of adopting Western military and scientific techniques and had already taken steps to modernize the army, but he was a political and social conservative who neither believed in democracy nor wished to confiscate the landlords' estates. It was into his hands that the Manchus had placed the government when they abdicated, and it was in him that the army, the old bureaucracy, and most foreign governments put their trust. He emerged in control of north China and was elected first president of the new republic in 1913. Once installed in office, Yuan purged parliament of its Kuomintang members and established himself as emperor in 1915. Republican-inspired revolutions broke out, but Yuan settled the matter by dying in 1916.

The central government now collapsed. North China fell into the hands of war lords who ruled their respective territories by military force, extracted taxes from the peasants, and fought their neighbors when they pleased. The Kuomintang, under the leadership of Dr. Sun, gradually established control over south China with the aid of Russian Communist advisers. Sun died in 1925 and his place was assumed by the able General Chiang Kai-shek (1887-   ). In 1927 Chiang expelled the Communists and left-wing members from the Kuomintang, and the following year troops of the south China regime advanced northward and entered Peking. After years of civil war China proper was once more politically united, in theory at least.

Under these circumstances the European powers abandoned their control over the Chinese customs, and steps were taken to end eventually the special privileges their nationals enjoyed in China. The first or military phase of the reconstruction that Dr. Sun had outlined years before had come to an end. The second phase, one of political tutelage in which a dictatorial government would teach the people the duties and responsibilities of citizenship, was about to begin. The Kuomintang accomplished much in these years, but at the cost of alienating the Communists and left-wing reformers and of compromising with the warlords and vested economic interests. Still, had there been time, China could have become a democratic state enjoying the economic advantages made possible by the adoption of Western techniques. Another fourth of the world's population was being brought under the influence of Western civilization.

JAPAN: THE PERIOD OF ISOLATION

The Japanese reaction to the impact of Western civilization was quite different from the Chinese. They had no comparable imperial tradition. Tribute had not been brought to their rulers by the fawning ambassadors of neighboring states, and their religious and cultural ideas had been largely borrowed from abroad. There was no reason for them to have that overwhelming sense of superiority that made it so difficult for the Chinese to realize that they must imitate the West if they were to survive. This is

733

not to say that the Japanese were an uncivilized people. They had their cities and towns, their theaters and novels; but if they had achieved their present position by adapting the Chinese culture to their needs, why could they not now adapt the Western civilization to their native culture with equal success? The way was clear for more rapid innovations in Japan.

Portuguese merchants had reached Japan in 1542 or 1543 and in 1549 the great Jesuit missionary, Saint Francis Xavier, had introduced Catholicism. At first, both the merchant and the priest had been welcomed. The Japanese wanted the trade of the merchants, and it is estimated that 300,000 had accepted baptism from the priests by 1617. This promising beginning was brought to an abrupt halt around 1640; Christianity was stamped out, and all the European traders except a few Dutch were expelled. This drastic change in policy resulted from the authorities' conviction that Christianity was a subversive influence. The priests were considered quarrelsome and intolerant, their converts backed the losing side in several political uprisings, and it was feared that the European states might use their nationals and the converts as a means to occupy the islands. From 1640 to 1854 Japan kept its doors closed to the outside world. Its only foreign contacts were through a few Dutch and Chinese merchants who were permitted to reside under strict supervision at Nagasaki. Through the Dutch, some Japanese scholars kept informed concerning Western scientific and political developments, but the West knew almost nothing of Japan.

The period of Japanese isolation was one of peace. The emperor, who was believed to be a direct descendant of the sun goddess, was maintained in political seclusion at Kyoto, and actual power was wielded by the shogun, who throughout the period was a member of the Tokugawa clan. The shogun was a military chief. Beneath him were the daimyo, or great lords, and lower still were the samurai, or knights. As in European feudalism, the system was bound together by ties of mutual loyalty and respect. The Tokugawa shoguns established themselves at Yedo (Tokyo), which within two centuries grew from a village to a city of a million inhabitants. To tame the daimyo and samurai and to keep them out of politics, the shoguns encouraged the study of Confucian ethics, literature, and history. This led to the development of a high ethical code governing the conduct of the warrior that may be compared with chivalry. It also paved the way for a restoration of royal authority, because Confucius had taught loyalty to a monarch, and historical research had revealed that the emperor had formerly ruled. It also helped bring about a revival of Shintoism, the ancient religion of Japan based on the worship of the emperor as a deity.

The social classes in Japan were rigidly separated. The daimyo and samurai could be soldiers, scholars, administrators, or courtiers, or they could reside on their estates, but they could perform no physical labor. The peasant who worked the land and the merchant who plied his trade were of a definitely inferior class. They were governed by different codes

734

of laws and subject to different systems of taxation. Even their clothing was regulated; only the samurai had the right to carry two swords and this became the mark of his class. Since the daimyo and samurai had a social position to maintain and limited opportunities to increase their incomes, they frequently became indebted. The merchants, on the other hand, were often men of wealth. By the dawn of the nineteenth century, the system showed signs of weakening. Wealthy merchants had begun to buy their way into the ranks of the samurai, and the daimyo had begun to ignore the authority of the shogun. This was the Japan that the American Commodore Perry (1794-1858) found when he docked in Tokyo Bay in the summer of 1853.

Perry had been instructed to persuade the Japanese to treat shipwrecked sailors better, to permit American vessels to purchase coal, and to allow American merchants to trade in at least one port. His requests ushered in a fifteen-year period of Japanese indecision. The shogun was well enough informed concerning Western military strength to know that the courageous samurai, even when wielding both swords at once, were no match for rifles and artillery. A few modern weapons were owned by the Japanese, but not enough to affect the outcome. On the other hand, the great majority of the Japanese people wanted to adhere to the time-honored policy of isolation, and the shogun knew that he was no more able to compel the daimyo and samurai to obey his decrees than he was to repel the Americans. He therefore took the unprecedented step of asking the emperor to consent to the American request in the hope of thereby strengthening his position. The emperor agreed, and during the years that followed the Americans extended their commercial rights in Japan and the British, Dutch, Russians, and other powers won similar privileges. Western nations were given extraterritorial authority over their citizens who were to be tried in their own courts for crimes committed on Japanese soil rather than in those of Japan. Japanese tariffs were regulated by the United States and several European powers.

These concessions raised a storm of protest in Japan. The emperor reversed his earlier consent to the treaties and became the center of the resistance to the Tokugawa shogunate. Confucian and historical studies and the revival of Shintoism had done much to increase his prestige, and the shogun's initial appeal to him in the matter of the American treaty proposals was interpreted as an admission of his superiority. There were armed clashes between the supporters of the shogun and the anti-Tokugawa, anti-foreign elements. Semi-independent daimyo fired on American and European vessels, but the Western powers retaliated by shelling Japanese strong points and extracting still more concessions. It looked as though Japan would follow the way of China. However, the shogun died in 1866 and the emperor the following year, thus paving the way for change. With little opposition from the discouraged, discredited Tokugawa clan, imperial authority was restored on January 3, 1868, in the person of the fourteen-year-old Mutsuhito, son of the late emperor. Nearly seven centuries of feudalism came abruptly to an end. The Meiji Era (Enlightened Government) began.

THE MEIJI ERA

The reign of Mutsuhito (1867-1912) was one of the most remarkable in history. In little more than a generation, Japan was transformed from a weak, decentralized, backward nation into a world power which, on the surface at least, was thoroughly Westernized. During the years immediately before the fall of the shogunate, the advocates of an imperial restoration had become convinced that Japan could survive only by Westernization. They therefore abandoned their former anti-Western position and threw themselves wholeheartedly into their new task. Thousands of Japanese students were sent abroad to study the natural and social sciences of the West; French and German officers were brought to Japan to train a new Westernized army, British officers came to advise the navy, and American educators arrived to help revamp the educational system. Engineers and scientists were summoned to introduce the industrial revolution and to build railroad and telegraph lines. Where the old order stood in the way, it was abolished. The daimyo surrendered their fiefs to the emperor, and the samurai were forbidden to wear two swords. In return for the loss of their fiefs and privileges, daimyo and samurai were given partial financial compensation and the latter were permitted to engage in trade. The peasants bore the brunt of the costs; 70 per cent of their income was given to the government in taxes.

The results were startling. In 1872 universal military training was introduced to facilitate the creation of a modern peacetime army of 240,000 men, and the following year construction was begun on two warships for the navy. To speed modernization, most of the early military and naval equipment was purchased abroad. Small handcraft industries were replaced by modern factories using steam power, railroads were constructed, and steamship tonnage increased from 15,000 tons in 1893 to 1,522,000 tons in 1905. The population grew rapidly and thousands left the countryside for the industrialized cities. Family and clan life was partially disrupted. By 1930 a fifth of the population was engaged in manufacturing, and only one-half remained in agriculture. A new nobility consisting of princes, marquises, counts, viscounts, and barons was formed to take the place of the old. So much progress was made in education that by 1923, 99 per cent of the population was literate, a record that could be equaled by few other states in the world. Japan was everywhere regarded as the finest pupil of the teachers of Western civilization.

These changes were brought about largely by the samurai "of the robe," members of the warrior class who had administered the fiefs of the daimyo. These experienced, able, farsighted men had been the real governing force in the old Japan, and as administrators their position was assured in the new. They did not accomplish their task without difficulty. In 1877 many of the samurai of the sword rebelled, but they were crushed by the new modern army. Thereafter, there was no question of whether Japan would be militarily or economically European; the big problem was whether a Western-styled democracy or a strong monarchy in which an aristocracy and the military were powerful would emerge to direct the state.

Many Japanese who studied abroad or at home became indoctrinated with the concepts of Western democracy as well as the techniques of Western science. They sought to fashion their own government after that of states like Great Britain, and their efforts bore some fruit in 1889 when the constitution was promulgated. Under the new constitution the emperor was given control over the executive branch of the government, including the army, navy, and diplomatic corps, as well as emergency legislative powers. The cabinet was made responsible to him and not to the bicameral legislature consisting of a house of lords and a house of representatives elected by a relatively small number of persons who paid substantial taxes. The liberal element was disappointed that greater democracy was not accorded, and in spite of its efforts a responsible ministry had not been achieved by World War II. On the other hand, the liberals were successful in getting the suffrage extended in 1900, 1919, and finally in 1925, when all males over twenty-five were given the ballot.

When everything is considered, the Japanese made reasonable progress towards democracy until about 1931, and they would have gone further if certain obstacles had not stood in their way. The first was the lack of previous experience in the use of democratic institutions. A second was the emperor, who was not only the head of state in the Western sense, but also the descendant of the sun goddess according to the ever-growing Shinto religion. He did not actually govern, but acted on the advice of a handful of conservative advisers. Blame for mistakes was placed on these advisers, not the crown. Third, the warlike ardor of the samurai did not die. Those who could, became officers in the new army and navy; those for whom there were no positions (the samurai had made up about 5 per cent of the population) became disaffected elements in the population. The clan spirit remained a divisive factor. The Satsuma won control of the navy, the Choshu controlled the army, while several families became the controlling force in industry. Thus, cliques were formed that were capable of dominating the government. In the crises which took place between 1871 and 1885, the civilian forces managed to hold back the military expansionists who advocated a war with China, but in 1894 they were unsuccessful. China, as we have seen, was easily defeated, to everyone's surprise, by the modernized Japanese military forces, and Japan emerged with substantial additions in territory. The military's prestige at home was heightened, and during the patriotic fervor that had accompanied the outbreak of war, it decreed that

737

only officers of the rank of lieutenant general or higher could serve as ministers of war or of the navy. Since these officers were still subject to the orders of the general staff, from that time it was impossible to form a cabinet that was opposed by the military. The general staff had won a veto over the civilian government.

The remarkable development of Japanese military power and the rapid Westernization of its institutions made it both unwise and unnecessary for the United States and the European powers to retain their extraterritorial claims in the face of ever-growing opposition. They therefore abandoned their special status between 1894 and 1899, and Japan emerged free from the imperialistic claims of the Western powers except for some regulations on its customs. It was not until the Russo-Japanese War of 1904-1905, however, that the full extent of Japanese military power was recognized.

THE RUSSO-JAPANESE WAR

The Russians, as we have seen, had forced Japan to disgorge the Liaotung Peninsula at the close of the Sino-Japanese War in 1895 and then had proceeded to get part of it from the Chinese, as well as special concessions in Manchuria. The Japanese were furious and in 1902 concluded a defensive alliance with the British to check Russian expansion in the Far East. Unintimidated, the Russians began to intrigue in Korea, which the Japanese had come to regard as their special preserve. On February 4, 1904, the Japanese navy attacked the Russians at Port Arthur without waiting for a formal declaration of war. The Russian army was defeated in a huge battle at Mukden and its navy was destroyed in the battle of Tsushima. By the terms of the Treaty of Portsmouth of September, 1905, Japan was given the southern half of Sakhalin island, was recognized as having a permanent interest in Korea which Japan annexed in 1910, and was given the Russian holdings in the Liaotung Peninsula. Several years later, Japan and Russia agreed to divide Manchuria into spheres of influence.

The Japanese victory had far-reaching significance. It not only marked Japan's emergence as a world power, but also provided a lesson to the other colored peoples of the world. By Europeanization, they could become strong nations, free from the imperialistic intervention and exploitation of other states. The Russian defeat, as we have seen, touched off the Revolution of 1905, which led to the establishment of a less autocratic system of government and eventually to the Revolution of 1917. It also convinced the Russians that they could not advance further in the Far East. This led them to reach an agreement with the British over the Middle East in 1907 and to turn their attention to the Balkans.[7] Their intrigues here were a factor leading directly to World War I.

Victory did nothing to abate Japanese expansive tendencies. They

[7] See page 725.

EXPANSION OF RUSSIA IN ASIA

	RUSSIA IN 1533
	ACQUIRED TO 1598
	ACQUIRED TO 1689
	MAXIMUM EXPANSION OF EMPIRE
	SPHERES OF INFLUENCE
+++	TRANSIBERIAN RAILROAD IN 1914

SCALE OF MILES
0 100 200 300 400 500

profited from World War I by seizing the German concessions in China and their islands in the Pacific. They then turned on China with additional demands and finally tried to take advantage of the Russian Revolution to expand into Siberia. During the 1920's, however, the civilian element in the population managed to check the militaristic expansionists and in 1926 an informed scholar could write that "In the course of time, there can be little doubt, the liberals will triumph, the Japanese Government will be made genuinely responsible to the people, and the militarists will be forced into the background."

CONCLUSIONS

By 1914, only the most remote corners of the world still escaped the influence of Western civilization. The Americas, Australia, and Siberia had been brought within the fold largely by the migrations of European peoples. The activities of missionaries and imperialistic nations had brought Western civilization to Asia and Africa, while here and there a people became partially Westernized in order to maintain their independence. The sharp demarcations that had formerly differentiated the civilizations and cultures of the world were fading. There was one accepted science and technology, that of Western civilization. There was one market, the world market. There was one source of raw materials, the world. The Ukrainian wheat crop had more effect on the price that the American farmer could get for his grain than the crop in northern France had had on the prices in southern France two centuries before, for modern transportation and communication bound the world closer together economically than the provinces of individual countries had been bound in former years. It is true that the colored races of the world adopted the cultural aspects of Western civilization more slowly than its science and technology, but still, in 1914, the world appeared to be moving towards prosperity and happiness, just as the leaders of the Enlightenment had dreamed and the nineteenth-century liberals had predicted. It was in this predominantly optimistic world that war came in 1914.

17/ World War I

THE wars between 1859 and 1871 had led to the unification of Italy and of Germany, but as long as three conservative multinational empires continued to exist in eastern Europe, the subject peoples of this region could not hope to achieve national self-determination. Of the three, Russia was the strongest and successfully held the Poles and other minorities in subjection until 1917 when the monarchy was overthrown in an internal revolt that followed military defeat. The Ottoman Empire was the weakest, and nearly all the inhabitants of its Balkan territory became independent during the century following the Vienna settlement of 1815. Among them were the Serbs who dreamed of becoming the nucleus of a unified state including all the Serbs, or even all the Slavs who lived south of the Danube River, just as Sardinia had become the nucleus for a united kingdom of Italy. To secure this objective, it was necessary to disrupt the Austro-Hungarian Empire. Faced with the possible dismemberment of their country, the leaders of this multinational state sought a military solution. For a number of complex and often obscure reasons many other states decided to enter the conflict and turned what had been intended as a local military action into a long world war. To understand their motives it is necessary to consider not only the minority problem in eastern Europe, but also several general factors that may have influenced them to enter the war. It will also be necessary to examine the alliance system and the series of crises that preceded the conflict.

As a result of the war, the multinational empires crumbled and new nation-states appeared in eastern Europe and the Arab world. Liberty, equality, and national self-determination were almost fully achieved, and a League of Nations was organized to maintain peace. Western civilization was triumphant, but the war had other unanticipated results that threatened the goals of liberalism and helped to usher in the twentieth-century crisis.

THE ORIGINS OF THE WAR

GENERAL CONSIDERATIONS

At one time many Americans thought that the war had been caused by kings who were willing to sacrifice the lives of their subjects to win a few square miles of territory or to satisfy their pride. This was a doubtful position to take. The monarchs had cooperated in maintaining peace after 1815, and by the time of the war the growth of democracy had removed much of their power. Some kings still had enough influence in 1914 to make critical mistakes, but the growth of democracy was as much a factor in causing the war as their continued presence on the European scene.

Once the directors of foreign policy became subject to popularly elected parliaments, they had to consider the desires of the people. In no nation had a majority of the inhabitants ever been well informed about foreign policy or the techniques of diplomacy. Often the people's aspirations were unobtainable by peaceful means, and their emotions were easily aroused by the cheap, sensational newspapers that began to be published near the close of the nineteenth century. Poorly informed "yellow journalists" magnified every quarrel between states in order to attract more readers. The excitement they generated by their irresponsible demands for national aggrandizement increased the diplomats' difficulties in making the compromises necessary for the preservation of peace. A diplomat who went to an international conference and came back with less than the press expected was likely to find his party voted out of office by an aroused electorate.

On the other hand, diplomats were not simply the tools of the newspapers. By the use of the "leak" to the press, they were often able to rally public opinion behind their policies. Many European newspapers accepted money from their own and foreign governments in return for favorable editorials and articles. A large number of French newspapers, for example, received bribes from the Russian ambassador at Paris. Since the newspapers were as much tools of the diplomats as the diplomats were their servants, they were not an important cause of the war. Furthermore, although the people and the press sometimes advocated war with a smaller state or a backward country, they rarely desired to fight nations with comparable strength. Neither the existence of kings, the advance of democracy, nor the new "yellow press" were major factors in causing the war.

The disruption of the Concert of Europe during the Crimean War was certainly one of the most important indirect causes of World War I, just as it was of the wars that unified Italy and Germany. So long as the great powers cooperated, no major war could take place. After 1871, Bismarck attempted to revive the old alliance of the eastern emperors, and congresses of the great powers settled many disputes that might have led to war. The loss of Alsace-Lorraine, however, made it difficult for the French to cooperate with the Germans, and the policy of realism, which came into vogue as a result of the methods of Bismarck and Cavour, poisoned international relations by destroying the mutual trust that had formerly existed.[1] As a result, cooperation among the eastern powers degenerated into an alliance between Germany and Austria-Hungary while a second alliance was built around Russia and France.

The alliance systems made compromise more difficult to achieve than during the days of the Concert of Europe. Both alliances were defensive, not offensive, but they both contained secret clauses that were often arrived at by secret negotiations. This secrecy, accompanied by the general acceptance of the idea that it was a diplomat's duty to lie and deceive when his country's vital interests were at stake, created a climate of fear and uncertainty that may have contributed to the war. Properly handled, the alliances provided means whereby peaceful nations could restrain their more quarrelsome partners. It was due to a failure of diplomacy that the reverse happened in 1914 and those powers which recoiled from war were dragged on by those who thought that armed conflict had become necessary. Perhaps the alliance systems broadened the scope of the war once it had begun, but in the final analysis it was their interests, not their treaties, that caused nations to join the original combatants in 1914.

Economic and imperialistic rivalries have often been considered one of the principal causes of the war. The Austro-Russian clash in the Balkans was certainly a major factor, as will be shown below, but in most respects economic and imperialistic considerations were of minor importance. The British were jealous of the rapid German economic growth. In 1815 they produced six times as much iron as Germany, but by 1910 German production was half again as large as theirs. Their foreign trade was increasing, but Germany's was growing faster. Everywhere, German merchants

[1] See pages 617-618.

were winning business from their British counterparts. Yet Germany itself was one of Britain's best customers and, in any case, it was not the British who started the war. Indeed, the United States' industrial capacity was increasing even more rapidly than Germany's, and Japan was becoming a serious competitor; yet both powers were British allies during the war. Economic rivalry, however, was one of the factors that caused the English to join the anti-German alliance system. As for imperialism, it undoubtedly led to many disputes and created tension, but the most frequent imperialistic quarrels were between Britain, France, and Russia, all allies in World War I. Furthermore, by 1914 Africa and Asia had been largely divided and the outstanding colonial disputes settled.

Arms races and militarism have also been blamed for causing the war. The size of the standing armies of the great powers grew from 2,473,000 in 1870 to 4,416,000 in 1914, and their naval tonnage from 1,813,000 to 8,065,000 during the same years. However, the growth of armaments was as much the result of international tensions as the cause of them. Militarism, that is, the unwarranted influence of the military in the diplomatic and internal affairs of a state, was a more serious matter. At certain critical junctures in the negotiations prior to the declaration of war in 1914, both the German and the Russian chiefs of staff took actions that were detrimental to the cause of peace, while military planning affected the diplomacy of all the states.

Some historians have sought for subtle, indirect causes of the war and have found them in the cult of violence associated with Social Darwinism.[2] There was, indeed, an increased tendency to try to settle problems by direct action rather than by reason and compromise within the framework of the law. In the realm of labor disputes, this meant the general strike; in the realm of international disputes, it meant war. In this regard, it must be remembered that there had not been a bloody European war since the time of Napoleon I and that the brief conflicts connected with the unification of Italy and of Germany had satisfied the nationalistic aspirations of the peoples concerned. This outcome seemed to justify the expectation that international violence could solve problems.

Internal disputes in many states had become so serious that some historians have suggested that those in power looked on war as a possible escape from their dilemma. The labor movement had become increasingly violent from Great Britain to Russia, and the Marxist Social Democrats had grown to be the largest party in Germany by 1914. Nationalistic problems in Austria-Hungary defied solution, and the English were facing an uprising in their failure to solve the Irish problem. Russia was in the throes of major political and social changes, and the discontent of its subject nationalities was mounting. These circumstances may have made some government leaders, especially conservative ones, more willing to gamble on a successful war that might unite their people than they would

[2] See pages 652-653.

have been under normal conditions. However, neither the influence of the cult of violence nor the serious internal dissensions can be specifically documented as causes of the war, except for the role that the internal nationalistic problems played in determining Austro-Hungarian policy.

Indeed, nationalism was one of the most important causes of the war. Just as the wars of the 1859-1871 period may be attributed largely to the desire of the German and Italian peoples to create nation-states, so World War I may be attributed largely to the desire of the non-Russian Slavic people for self-determination and to the efforts of the multinational empires to maintain their territorial integrity. The diplomats were able to solve most of their other problems peaceably, but in the clash between nationalism and multinational empires they were never able to do more than postpone the day of reckoning. The story of the origins of World War I, therefore, is primarily the story of rising nationalism, dying empires, and ineffectual diplomacy.

THE PROBLEM OF NATIONALISM IN EASTERN EUROPE

Nationalism was the basic problem in eastern Europe although religious, social, and economic factors added complexity to the already confused situation. Subject races made up a majority of the inhabitants in each of the multinational empires, and as these people became conscious of their nationality, they began to agitate for autonomy, if not independence.

Of the three empires, the Russians proved best able to cope with the situation during the nineteenth century. Their subject nationalities included the White Russians and Ukrainians who had been part of Kievan Russia but whose ethnic and linguistic difference from the Great Russians who inhabited Muscovy had solidified during the late Middle Ages when they had become a part of the Polish-Lithuanian state.[3] By 1815, however, the Great Russians of Muscovy had expanded so far to the west that they ruled the Ukrainians, White Russians, and most of the Poles, who were fellow Slavs, as well as the Lithuanians and Letts, who were members of the Baltic branch of the Indo-European linguistic family, and the Finns and Estonians, who belonged to the Finno-Ugrian linguistic family.[4] Their expansion to the south and east had also brought a number of other peoples within their vast empire.

All these peoples were considered as part of the empire and were administered without consideration of their nationalistic susceptibilities, with the exception of the Finns and Poles. Their special treatment resulted from the fact that the tsar ruled the former as a constitutional grand duke and the latter as constitutional king because of the terms under which Poland had been acquired during the Napoleonic wars. The

[3] See page 323.
[4] See page 13.

745

arrangement worked very well in Finland during the nineteenth century, for the Finns had had no strong nationalistic traditions and had been ruled by the Swedes before the tsar had become grand duke of their autonomous duchy.

Autonomy, however, was not enough to satisfy the Poles, who remembered the day when a great Polish kingdom had included Lithuania, White Russia, and the Ukraine and had threatened to engulf Moscow itself. They regarded themselves as culturally superior to the Russians, and their devotion to the Roman Catholic Church divided them further from their Greek Orthodox neighbors. Their first opportunity to revolt came in 1830 when the toppling of the Bourbon monarchy in France gave rise to the vain hope that the French would once more overthrow the conservative powers. As an autonomous kingdom, Poland had its own army, but it proved no match for the Russians. The Poles were further hampered by the lack of interest shown by the serfs. Nationalism had not reached the peasants, who were as likely to oppose the gentry class as they were to oppose the tsar. As a result, the patriotic gentry, supported by the clergy, went down to defeat, and by the close of 1831 the tsar's authority was restored. The Polish constitution was revoked, and Poland was made an indivisible part of the Russian empire. Polish universities were closed, and the Russian language was used in the secondary schools. The estates of the rebels were confiscated, as were the lands of the Catholic Church, whose clergy began to be paid by the state. In White Russia and the Ukraine, where the gentry had often been Poles, the policy of Russification was carried further. So thorough was their work that the Revolution of 1848 did not cause serious nationalistic problems in Russia.

At first, Alexander II (1855-1881) treated the Poles more leniently, but the strongly nationalistic gentry profited by the general relaxation and revolted in 1863. After the Russians had restored order, they worked with increased vigor to Russify the inhabitants. The newly emancipated Polish serfs were given more land and were allowed to make smaller redemption payments than their Russian counterparts in order to win their support against the often rebellious gentry. By 1870 it looked as though the Russians might have solved their minority problem.

A generation later it was evident that this prospect had failed to materialize, and Russia was in the throes of nationalistic agitation that involved not only the Poles, but all the east European minorities. There were several causes of this increased nationalism. One was the growth of literary societies and similar organizations among the Ukrainians and other peoples, societies that cultivated a nationalistic spirit. These groups were aided by the beginnings of industrialization in eastern Europe, for industrialization brought an educated, nationalistic middle class into being. Furthermore, in eastern Europe nationalism had begun to seep down into the ranks of the peasantry, especially in the Ukraine where the landlord was often a Russian. Falling grain prices resulting from the opening of the Amer-

746

ican Midwest and from improved transportation added economic hardships that were translated into nationalistic agitation. A sympathetic government might have handled the situation without excessive difficulty, but the Russians themselves moved towards conservative integral nationalism that called for the complete Russification of all inhabitants of their empire. Even the autonomous Finns were not excluded. As a result, Russian nationalism began to clash violently with that of the minorities at the close of the nineteenth century. Although this clash was not an important factor in causing World War I, it strongly influenced the events which followed the conflict.

The Austro-Hungarian empire included many minority groups, most of which were Slavs. The grant of autonomy to the Magyars in 1867 had satisfied the most unruly Habsburg subjects, but north of Hungary there were Czechs, Slovaks, Poles, and Ukrainians. The Austrians treated minority races with greater consideration than the Russians did, but the highly developed, nationally-conscious Czechs were disgruntled because of the Habsburg refusal to grant them the autonomy enjoyed by the Magyars. The Poles were favorably treated by the Habsburgs and directed most of their resentment against the Russians who ruled the bulk of their former state, but it was obvious that their loyalty was to a unified, independent Polish state, not to the Habsburg monarchy.

In the south the situation was even more dangerous. The Slavs dreamed of a south or Yugoslav state whose status in the Habsburg monarchy would be equal to that of Hungary. Most of them resided in the Hungarian part of the Dual Monarchy when the Magyars adopted a policy of Magyarization comparable to the Russification practiced by the tsarist regime. In the east there were Rumanians who agitated for autonomy and occasionally dreamed of joining the Rumanian kingdom that had been formed shortly after the Crimean War.

None of the Balkan peoples were as highly developed economically as the Czechs or Poles, nor were they as nationalistically conscious until the late nineteenth century, but they were potentially more dangerous because in Greece, Montenegro, Serbia, and Rumania they had autonomous or independent states. If ultranationalists won control of one or more of these states, they might provoke a war in the hope of uniting with their fellow nationals who still resided in the Austro-Hungarian or Ottoman empires. The nationalists first stripped the weaker Ottomans of nearly all of their remaining European possessions; then in 1914 they turned on the stronger Habsburgs.

THE OTTOMAN EMPIRE

In 1871 when the Italians and Germans had completed their wars of unification, millions of Greeks, Bulgarians, Albanians, Serbs, and Macedonians still resided within the Ottoman Empire. The nationalistic intensity among the Greeks, Serbs, and Rumanians had increased since earlier in the century; and the Bulgarians and Albanians were beginning to be aware of their distinctive cultures. The Macedonians lagged behind the other Slavic peoples and paid for their tardiness by being claimed by the Serbs, Bulgars, and Greeks.

Only a strong, reformed, and intelligent Ottoman government could hope to deal with this situation. Selim III's efforts to modernize the Ottoman Empire during the era of the French Revolution had finally awakened a few Turks to the rapid transformation that the West had undergone, and repeated defeats convinced others that the survival of the Empire was contingent upon reform.[5] The sultans, however, were generally drunken, harem-ridden weaklings who were incapable of the ruthless energy necessary to transform the Ottoman Empire into a modern state. Among them were the kindly, extravagant, drunken Abdul Mejid (1839-1861) and the handsome, gracious Abdul Aziz (1861-1876), who enjoyed his predecessors' recreational pursuits but who was deposed and either committed suicide or was murdered. Murad V had spent so much time in drunken seclusion in the harem-filled prison or "cage" in which Ottoman princes were kept until called upon to rule that he was too insane to be tolerated even by the Turks. He was deposed after a three-month reign and Abdul Hamid II (1876-1909), his cowardly, cruel, crafty brother, became sultan. For years he played one faction against another both at home and abroad only to be deposed in the end. His successor, the sixty-four-year-old Mohammed V (1909-1918), had had little difficulty imitating the mannerisms of an idiot to avoid extermination by his predecessor while he found solace in the "cage," shut off even from newspapers. The last sultan was Mohammed VI (1918-1922), who was deposed like six of his eight immediate predecessors. Such were the descendants of Suleiman the Magnificent! Little wonder reforms were not fully implemented, officials plundered the inhabitants, and military forces remained backward.

Since the reign of Selim III there had been a small but ever-growing number of Turks who recognized that the survival of the empire depended on Westernization. Occasionally, with the assistance of the British, who wanted to preserve the Ottoman Empire, they persuaded the sultan to enact reform edicts, but no amount of logic or eloquence could give the sultans the energy to transform Ottoman society and institutions.

As far back as 1839 an edict had been issued guaranteeing life, liberty, and property to all subjects "of whatever religion or sect they may be. . . ." Other reform decrees followed, but for the most part they remained dead letters. The Crimean War, however, once more revealed to the Turks the strength of the European states and their own weakness. A group of leaders emerged who were determined to modernize the empire along Western lines as the Japanese were to do a generation later. With the encouragement of the great powers, a far-reaching ordinance was is-

[5] See pages 516-520.

sued in 1856 which reaffirmed the provisions of the 1839 edict and more clearly enunciated the principle of equality before the law regardless of religious affiliation. Christians became eligible to hold any office and to serve in the army, torture was abolished, and the authority of the ecclesiastical hierarchy in the Orthodox and other non-Moslem churches was weakened by making their governing bodies synods that included laymen as well as clergymen. It was hoped that by minimizing clerical control, the barriers that had separated various religious denominations would disappear and the idea of a common Ottoman citizenship would develop. In this the reformers were disappointed, for nationalism, not loyalty to the Ottoman Empire, replaced the old allegiances the people had given to their respective churches.

The reform legislation was not fully enforced, but for twenty years following the Crimean War Western ideas circulated freely in the Ottoman Empire. American missionaries started Robert College in 1860, and nine years later a university was founded in Constantinople. A literary revival began, Western books were translated, and newspapers played an active role.

Thus far the reform movement had been carried out by all-powerful ministers of an autocratic sultan. Their work had removed the capacity of groups such as the provincial governors, janissaries, and ecclesiastical officials to check the autocracy of the central government, but to many it was desirable to create new institutions to take their place. Under the impact of Western liberalism, a group of reforming ministers persuaded Abdul Hamid II to agree to proclaim a Western-style constitution guaranteeing all the essential liberties and providing for parliamentary government before they made him sultan. The first elections in Islamic history were held, and in March, 1877, the parliament began its deliberations. As soon as Abdul Hamid was firmly on the throne, however, he dismissed his liberal ministers, terminated parliament, and governed as autocratically as any of his predecessors. He did not even have the virtue of being a reformer; a thorough reactionary, he cunningly sought to restore and retain the old order by playing one faction against another. But even before he came to the throne, it was apparent that the reformers had failed; in 1875 an insurrection broke out in the Balkans, and Serbia and Montenegro soon came to the aid of the rebels.

THE BALKANS

There were several causes of the Balkan insurrection. By 1875 over half the annual income of the Ottoman Empire had to be surrendered to international bankers who had loaned the spendthrift government money since the Crimean War. This meant higher taxes which the inhabitants could ill afford to pay, especially because of the general European depression that began in 1873 and local crop failures. The revolt first broke out

749

in the western provinces of Bosnia and Herzegovina where the Serbian nobility had become Moslems centuries before and exploited their Christian and Moslem peasantry without discrimination. For once the Turkish army proved equal to the occasion. The Serbs were thoroughly defeated, and over 12,000 Bulgarians were slaughtered by irregular troops because of a minor peasant uprising in which a few peaceable Turks had been murdered. Once more the great powers were faced with the decision of whether to intervene to save their fellow Christians from Turkish atrocities.

At first the Russian and the Austrian governments exercised considerable restraint, but in both countries there were those who wanted to profit from the Balkan revolt. Some Austro-Hungarian statesmen hoped to annex Bosnia and Herzegovina and combine them with Slavic provinces within their empire to form a south Slav kingdom whose status would be equal to that of Hungary and Austria. They also believed that the provinces were essential for the defense of their Adriatic coast. On the other hand, they were opposed to the creation of a large Balkan state that might some day be a threat.

In Russia the Pan-Slavic movement was becoming increasingly important. Its origins lay in Slavophile theories which taught that Russian society, institutions, and culture were superior to those of the West and should be carefully preserved. Pan-Slavism was an extension of this concept to include all Slavic peoples. A Slavic Ethnic Congress had been held in 1867 and among the members of the movement was Count Nicholas Ignatiev, the Russian ambassador at Constantinople between 1864 and 1877. He and other Pan-Slavists dreamed of freeing the Slavs from Ottoman and Austro-Hungarian domination and forming a great Slavic confederation with its headquarters at Constantinople.

The official tsarist policy was opposed to the Pan-Slavic position, and the inhabitants of the Balkans wanted independence, not a disguised form of Russian domination. Nevertheless, the Pan-Slavic movement added to the popular demand in Russia for intervention to protect Orthodox Christians in the Balkans and to expand towards Constantinople and the Straits. As a result, when a Constantinople conference to settle the Balkan question failed because of Turkish intransigence, which the British supported to prevent an expansion of Russian influence, Russia declared war.[6] In March, 1878, after less than a year of fighting, the Russians dictated the peace of San Stefano, which called for the creation of a large Bulgarian state with access to the Aegean Sea. It was presumed that the new state would be a Russian satellite and that the next mouthful of the Russian bear would be Constantinople and the Straits. Great Britain and Austria-Hungary disliked these prospects, and Bismarck summoned a congress to meet at

[6] For an account of the objectives of the great powers in the Balkans see pages 755-760.

Berlin during the summer of 1878 to find a peaceful solution to the dispute.

The Balkans, Bismarck declared, "involved no German interest which would be worth the bones of a single Pomeranian grenadier." He could, therefore, act as an "honest broker" in an effort to effect a compromise. In the end he was successful. Bulgaria was divided into three parts, each of which remained under Ottoman sovereignty. Northern Bulgaria, however, was made autonomous with an elected prince, southern Bulgaria including the Aegean coast was returned to the Turks, while central Bulgaria was administered by a Christian governor. Serbia and Rumania became independent, and Russian gains were limited to southern Bessarabia, which had belonged to Rumania, and some small provinces in Asia Minor. As compensation, the great powers helped themselves to parts of the Ottoman Empire. Austria-Hungary took Bosnia and Herzegovina to administer and was given the right to garrison Novi Bazar, a small strip of land located between Serbia and Montenegro. This enabled them to prevent the unification of these Serb-speaking states. The British occupied Cyprus and the French were offered Tunis, which they took three years later. The Italian representative returned with "clean hands," but when he got home he was attacked because they were also empty. Bismarck asked for and received nothing.

The Berlin Congress had prevented a war between the great powers, but it had done nothing permanently for the cause of peace. The Balkan peoples felt that their aspirations had been denied. The Bulgarians had hoped for a large, united state; the Greeks had hoped to expand their kingdom; the Rumanians were embittered by the loss of Bessarabia although they received a Black Sea coastal province as compensation; and the Serbs were embittered at seeing their plans for an enlarged Serbian state blocked by the Austrians in Novi Bazar, Bosnia, and Herzegovina. As they were not yet in a position to attack Austria-Hungary, they and the other Balkan peoples waited for an opportunity to despoil what remained of the Ottoman Empire in Europe. The Russians were also angry at having to surrender so much of their conquests, but to understand the implications of their disappointment, it is necessary to consider the diplomatic situation in Europe as a whole.

THE BISMARCKIAN SYSTEM

The leading figure on the diplomatic scene between 1871 and 1890 was Otto von Bismarck. One would think that the man who had guided Prussia into three wars between 1864 and 1871 in order to create the German empire would be a detriment to the cause of peace. Nothing could have been further from the truth, however, for Bismarck knew that the emergence of Germany as a united state had upset the balance of power established in the Vienna settlement of 1815. If Germany used its power aggressively, as France had done under Louis XIV and during the Revolutionary-Napoleonic period, coalitions would be formed to humble it. Only by talking and acting as though Germany was a contented nation could Bismarck hope to maintain what he had won. Indeed, his professions were sincere, for Germany could not grow further without weakening the dominant position of Prussia, the junkers, and the Lutherans, all so dear to him.[7]

Bismarck saw that France would be Germany's most implacable foe. The defeated Danes were too weak to count. The defeated Austrians had been treated kindly; blood ties bound the two peoples together, as the monarchical principle did the two rulers. But defeated France was not likely to forget the loss of Alsace-Lorraine. Alone the French were no threat because German industrial and population growth were more rapid; only if they found allies were they dangerous. To prevent this, Bismarck decided to make as many friends as he could for Germany and at the same time to keep France isolated. In 1872 he took the initiative in forming the Three Emperors' League, consisting of Russia, Austria-Hungary, and Germany, to which Italy lent its support the following year. This league was purely defensive in nature. Like the Concert of Europe before the Crimean War, it was designed to maintain the status quo. Since the British preferred to remain free from entangling alliances, France was isolated.

The weakness in the system lay in the Austro-Russian rivalry in the Balkans. Many considerations, as we have seen, tempted the Russians to expand in this region, while the nationality problem within the Austro-Hungarian empire made its statesmen fearful of changes in the existing situation, whether they led to stronger Balkan states or the expansion of Russian power. Bismarck had managed to prevent a war between his two allies in 1878, but the infuriated Russians blamed him for their failure to make greater gains at the Berlin Congress. Alarmed, Bismarck made a secret defensive alliance with Austria-Hungary in 1879. In 1882 the Italians, who felt too weak to stand alone, asked to join, and the Triple Alliance was born. Meanwhile, Bismarck had mollified the Russians and the Three Emperors' League was renewed. Britain remained friendly, France remained isolated, Germany remained secure.

During the imperialistic scramble of the 1880's Bismarck encouraged the Russians to expand in Asia in the hope that they would forget about the Balkans, and the French in Africa in the expectation that they would embroil themselves with the British and perhaps forget Alsace-Lorraine. He took very few colonies for fear of offending the island kingdom. However, the troubled Balkans continued to threaten his alliance system.

In 1885 the northern and central portions of Bulgaria united without great power sanction. The Russians opposed this move because northern Bulgaria had not become their satellite as they had anticipated and had even preferred Austrian railroad construction plans in the Balkans to their own. This was an age when both Russia and Austria-Hungary were trying

[7] See page 612.

to exploit the Balkans economically just as the other powers were seeking investments and markets in the colonial sphere. The Austro-Hungarians had already signed political and commercial treaties with Serbia and Rumania; if an enlarged Bulgaria was drawn within their net, there would be little left in the Balkans for Russia. The English supported an enlarged Bulgaria because it would be better able to check the Russians. In the midst of this dispute, the Serbs attacked Bulgaria in the hope of gaining additional territory, but they were quickly defeated and only Austro-Hungarian support saved them from invasion.

Bismarck managed to save his alliance system in this confused situation by reminding Austria-Hungary that Germany was obliged to give military support to them only if they were attacked. Publicly he supported the Tsar's Bulgarian aspirations, but privately he encouraged the formation of a Mediterranean Agreement between Great Britain, Italy, and Austria-Hungary to prevent Russia from unilaterally changing the status quo in the Balkans. This opposition prevented the Russians from doing anything and the Balkans momentarily became quiet again. However, the Russians and the Austro-Hungarians had become so distrustful of each other that they refused to renew the Three Emperors' League in 1887. Faced with this situation, Bismarck retained the alliance with Austria-Hungary and Italy, and made a Reinsurance Treaty with Russia which assured that country's neutrality in case Germany was attacked by France and promised German neutrality in the event Austria-Hungary attacked Russia. In this devious manner Bismarck managed to retain the friendship of both his quarreling allies until he was dismissed by William II in 1890.[8]

THE FORMATION OF THE TRIPLE ENTENTE

During the years that followed, the young kaiser and his advisers made three mistakes Bismarck would never have made. They permitted the Reinsurance Treaty with Russia to lapse because they thought that it conflicted with their alliance with Austria-Hungary. They built a large navy, which frightened Great Britain, and they became loud in their demands for colonies, which offended all the powers. When not given their way immediately, they blustered, fumed, and threatened. By 1907 they had driven Russia and Britain into the arms of France, and Italy was giving indications that it might desert the Triple Alliance. It was Germany and Austria-Hungary who were isolated when war began in 1914.

When Germany refused to renew the Reinsurance Treaty, Russia found itself as isolated as France. It was but natural that the two powers should gravitate towards each other because of their common fear of Germany and their common imperialistic rivalry with Great Britain. From the moment they made a secret defensive alliance in 1894, it became necessary in event of war for Germany to fight on two fronts. Instead of becoming

[8] See page 676.

ATROPOS.   LACHESIS.   CLOTHO.

In Greek mythology three daughters of Zeus control human destiny. Clotho spins the thread of life; Lachesis measures its length, and Atropos cuts the thread. To a PUNCH *cartoonist on October 27, 1888, the fate of Europe likewise rested in the hands of the Three Sisters. (Bettmann Archive)*

cautious, the Germans made greater nuisances of themselves. They helped block an Anglo-Belgium Congo agreement in 1894, sympathized publicly with the Boers during their conflict with the British, and began their construction of a huge navy. Despite their behavior, the British felt so threatened by Russia and France that between 1898 and 1901 they carried on serious negotiations for a German alliance. Once more the Germans bungled by not offering reasonable terms, and in 1904 the British made an alliance with Japan to block Russian advances in the Far East.

Meanwhile, the British and French settled their outstanding colonial difficulties. The French recognized the paramount British interests in Egypt and the Sudan after the Fashoda incident, and the British promised to support the French in a move to take Morocco.[9] These agreements, known as the Entente Cordiale, were made in 1902 and marked the beginning of closer cooperation between the two countries. The French then set about trying to bring their British and Russian friends together. The Japanese victory in 1905 removed much of the British fear of Russia and made the Russians themselves desirous of an additional ally. In 1907 when the two powers settled their differences in Persia, Tibet, and Afghanistan,[10] the Triple Entente was born.

[9] See pages 712, 715.
[10] See page 725.

The French also drew the Italians into their net by agreeing to support their plan to annex Tripoli. In return they won Italian support in their quest for Morocco. In 1902 each power agreed to remain neutral if the other were attacked or unduly provoked. Italy had all but deserted the Triple Alliance, and France, seventeen years after Bismarck's dismissal, was allied with Russia and Britain, who in turn had an alliance with Japan. It remained to be seen whether the two defensive alliance systems could live in peace together.

Germany felt encircled. Several courses of action were open to it. Germany could either conciliate the British by halting its naval building program, win back Russia by an offer of a defensive alliance, or try to split the Entente apart by threats and blustering. Talks with the British were renewed on several occasions, and efforts were made to draw Russia and even France into a continental alliance, but all too much energy was devoted to threats and blustering.

Between 1904 and 1906 the Germans attempted to break the encirclement. France, as we have seen, had won promises of British and Italian support for its scheme to annex Morocco. The German chancellor, Bernhard von Bülow (1849-1929), decided to block this move. Russia was then involved in the struggle with Japan, and Britain, he thought, would recoil from the threat of war. France would then realize how useless the Entente was and would accept a settlement with Germany. The natural results of this program were that Britain and France drew closer together, and military conversations were begun between the two powers. In an ensuing international conference at Algeciras in 1906, Austria-Hungary was the only great power that supported Germany. Even Italy voted with the Entente to keep Morocco independent, but to give France police powers within the country. The French had called the Germans' bluff; the Germans had decided not to fight.

THE BALKANS AGAIN

Meanwhile, two events were taking place in the Balkans that led to a series of crises in that troubled region. The first occurred in 1903 when a group of army officers murdered the unpopular Alexander I (1889-1903) of Serbia. Alexander was a member of the Obrenovich dynasty which had traditionally maintained close political and economic ties with Austria-Hungary. The man chosen as his successor was Peter I (1903-1921) of the rival Karageorgevich clan that had been feuding with the Obrenovich family since the dawn of the nineteenth century.[11]

Peter was not an absolute monarch. For generations Serbia's elected assembly had served as window dressing to royal autocracy, but in 1903 liberty and democracy became more nearly established facts. Nevertheless, Peter still possessed considerable authority and the policy he chose to

[11] See page 519.

755

"Damned!" a PUNCH *cartoonist has the Kaiser exclaim. "I thought it was paper and now I see it was really stone." (Bettmann Archive)*

pursue was one that attracted wide support from Serbian nationalists. He reversed the policy of friendship with the Habsburgs, sought new markets for Serbian pigs and other agricultural commodities to reduce his country's economic dependence on Austria-Hungary, purchased arms from France instead of his northern neighbor, and lent a sympathetic ear to those who dreamed of a large Serbian south Slav state.

The second event was the Young Turk revolution of 1908. The Young Turks were a revolutionary organization that included intellectuals and army officers. Its members agreed on two things: the desire to preserve the Ottoman Empire and the necessity to remove the autocratic, cruel Abdul Hamid II from authority. This done, a series of revolutions and counterrevolutions followed in which a faction became predominant who believed that the Empire could be saved only if a genuine Ottoman nationality was created. To it, all citizens regardless of their language or religion would give their loyalty, but within the new state they would all be equal. To create this nationality, local autonomy must cease and a centralized state be formed in which everyone would have the same language and laws. Western science and technology were to be accepted and Western dress and social customs adopted. These Young Turks hoped to achieve the same success as the Japanese, whose decision to Westernize had just enabled them to defeat the Russians. Unfortunately for them, their emphasis on Ottoman nationality was opposed by other national groups within the Empire and their supporters abroad. Also, the confusion that accom-

TERRITORIAL CHANGES IN
THE BALKANS 1856-1914

AUSTRIAN EMPIRE

RUSSIA

KINGDOM

OF

HUNGARY

BOSNIA-HERZEGOVINA
ANNEXED 1908

SERBIA

RUMANIA
INDEPENDENT 1878

BESSARABIA TO RUSSIA 1812

DOBRUDJA TO RUMANIA 1878

TO RUMANIA 1913

MONTENEGRO

TO SERBIA 1878

BULGARIA
INDEPENDENT 1908

EASTERN RUMELIA
TO BULGARIA 1885

TO SERBIA 1912-13

ADRIATIC SEA

ITALY

ALBANIA
INDEPENDENT 1912-13

TO GREECE 1913

TO BULGARIA 1913

TURKEY

TO GREECE 1881

AEGEAN SEA

ISLANDS TO GREECE 1913

IONIAN SEA

GREECE INDEPENDENT 1830

DODECANESE IS. TO ITALY 1912

OCCUPIED BY AUSTRIA 1878	TO GREECE 1880-1913
MONTENEGRO 1878-1913	TO SERBIA 1878-1913
TO RUMANIA 1878-1913	BULGARIA 1914

- - - BOUNDARY OF THE OTTOMAN EMPIRE IN 1815

0   50   100   200   300
SCALE OF MILES

CRETE
AUTONOMOUS 1898
UNITED TO GREECE 1908-13

MEDITERRANEAN SEA

panied their assumption of power encouraged the Russians and Austro-Hungarians to seek profit from the occasion.

A few weeks before the Young Turk revolution, Alexander Izvolsky (1856-1919), the Russian foreign minister, had suggested to his Austro-Hungarian counterpart that Russia would consent to the annexation of Bosnia-Herzegovina in return for support in opening the Straits to Russian warships so that they could enter the Mediterranean Sea. When news arrived of the Young Turk revolt, the Austro-Hungarians decided that the time was ripe and announced the annexation of the province. The day before, as a result of their prompting, Bulgaria had declared its independence from Turkey, and its ruler, Prince Ferdinand of the German house of Saxe-Coburg, assumed the proud title of tsar, in memory of an almost forgotten medieval Bulgarian empire. Within a few months of coming to power, the Young Turks had seen their country stripped of two territories. More serious were the other repercussions from these unilateral acts.

The Austro-Hungarians had hoped that by annexing Bosnia-Herzegovina they would end Serbia's dream of incorporating the province into an enlarged Serbian state, but their action had the opposite effect. An aroused Serbia demanded part of the province, and when the Russians discovered that the other powers were unwilling to open the Straits to their warships, they lent their support. For a time war seemed probable. The Germans were afraid not to assist their one faithful ally and gave Russia to understand that an attack on Austria would mean war with Germany. When the British and French proved less firm in supporting their ally, Russia and Serbia had no recourse but to accept the annexations. By leading Germany to the brink of war, Bülow had won a diplomatic victory, but beneath the surface he had made implacable foes in both countries. Izvolsky spent his not inconsiderable talents in the years that followed plotting his revenge on the Austro-Hungarians who, he believed, had tricked him. When the conflict began in 1914, Izvolsky proudly proclaimed, "This is *my* war, *my* war."

In 1911 the French began to take the long-awaited step of incorporating Morocco into their north African empire. The Germans dispatched a gunboat to Agadir on the Moroccan coast, probably in the hope of frightening the French into giving them compensation. The French stood firm and the British indicated that they would support their ally. This time Germany backed down in return for a few face-saving square miles in the French Congo. France had at last won Morocco, and, as a result of the crisis, the ties of the Entente were drawn closer together.

Hardly had the Moroccan crisis been settled than the Italians decided that they had better take Tripoli from the Ottoman Empire before the French forgot that this was the reward assigned them in return for their diplomatic support. As the Young Turks had not yet had time to consolidate their position, this was not a difficult task, but it touched off new troubles in the Balkans. Immediately after the Bosnian crisis, the Russians and Serbs had begun to work for the creation of a Balkan League to block Austrian ambitions. For a time they had little success because of the rivalries between the prospective members, but the spectacle of the Italians defeating the Turks in Tripoli suggested that the time was ripe to take what remained of the Ottoman Empire in Europe. The Young Turk policy of trying to turn their European subjects into Ottoman citizens helped lead to a revolt in Albania and gave impetus to the decision to act. As a result, a Balkan League consisting of Serbia, Bulgaria, Montenegro, and Greece was

758

THE BALKAN BOILING POT *as seen by a* PUNCH *cartoonist, October 2, 1912. (Bettmann Archive)*

formed in 1912, but it was directed against the Ottoman Empire, not the Austrians as the Russians had intended.

In the war which began in October, 1912, the outnumbered, disorganized Turks were easily defeated and forced to disgorge all their European territory except Constantinople and its environs. At this point the victors began to quarrel over the spoils. Serbia and Greece had hoped to divide Albania between them, but the Albanians wanted independence and

759

the Austrians supported their aspirations to prevent an enlarged, and therefore more dangerous, Serbia. When the great powers agreed that Albania should be independent, the Serbs demanded some of the territory that had been assigned to Bulgaria. The Bulgarians refused and a second war broke out in which Greece, Montenegro, Rumania, and the Ottoman Empire joined the Serbs. Bulgaria was defeated and stripped of part of its previous gains.

The two Balkan wars left the inhabitants of that region embittered. The Turks and Bulgarians were unreconciled to their losses, and the Serbs were angrier than ever at the Austro-Hungarians because they had prevented them from getting part of Albania with access to the Adriatic Sea. More serious was the effect the wars had on the relations between the great powers. While the fighting was taking place, the Austrians had supported the Albanians and Bulgarians because they wanted to prevent an enlarged Serbia, and the Russians had supported the Serbs. The Germans and British had restrained their allies and had prevented the outbreak of a general European war.

For years first one alliance system and then the other had won diplomatic victories by threatening war. Each time the other side had backed down, but suppose both sides, half bluffing, threatened war at the same time? Would either accept the loss of prestige that would come with a withdrawal of its demands? Could Russia again fail to support Serbia fully without losing face in the Balkans? Could the English and French once more restrain Russia without losing their ally? Could Germany fail to give unqualified support to Austria-Hungary, the only ally remaining from the Bismarck system of alliances? It was the diplomats' negative answers to these questions that caused Europe to bungle into war.

THE COMING OF WAR

On June 28, 1914, Archduke Francis Ferdinand and his wife were assassinated at Sarajevo by a Serb. Sarajevo was in recently annexed Bosnia, and the assassin, like so many of his fellow Serbs, was an Austro-Hungarian citizen. It was, however, more than an internal matter because the Archduke had been heir to the Habsburg throne and at one time had been associated with the idea of transforming the Dual Monarchy into a triple monarchy in which the Slavs would have equal status with the Germans and Magyars. If adopted, this policy might satisfy the Slavs within the empire, thereby reducing Serbia's chances of creating a south Slav state. For this reason, many believed, the Archduke had been the target of an assassin's bullet.

Big as Austria-Hungary was in comparison with Serbia, it felt threatened because half its population was Slavic. Leopold von Berchtold (1863-1942), the foreign minister, decided that Serbia must be crushed. The Germans agreed because they believed that if the Russians were threatened with war, they would not support Serbia, and they feared that failure to act would condemn their only trustworthy ally to eventual destruction. On July 23 the Austro-Hungarians sent an ultimatum to Belgrade that they knew would be unacceptable. The Serbs' reply on July 25 was conciliatory, but those parts of the ultimatum affecting their sovereignty were rejected. Even before it was delivered, they began to mobilize, convinced that the long anticipated conflict was at hand. Three days later Austria-Hungary declared war.

In the meantime the German chancellor, Theobald von Bethmann-Hollweg (1856-1921), had become thoroughly frightened because he began to realize that Russia and France could not be bluffed. He had been willing to have Austria-Hungary fight a preventive war with Serbia to save itself from possible destruction, but he was altogether unwilling to become involved in a general European conflict. He belatedly tried to restrain Austria, but a Russian decision to mobilize gave him little time for negotiations because of the German military campaign plan.

Since the formation of the Franco-Russian alliance, Germany had been faced with the possibility of war on two fronts. The Russian army was larger than the combined Austro-Hungarian and German forces in 1914, and France itself had a larger army than Germany. Confronted by this situation, the German staff had formulated the Schlieffen Plan, which required the Austro-Hungarian army and a small German force to hold back Russia while the main German army swept through Belgium and encircled Paris. Once France was out of the war, the main army was to turn on Russia. Time was of the utmost importance, because if Russia completed its mobilization before Austria-Hungary did, the eastern front would collapse before the French were defeated. Strategically, the Schlieffen Plan may have had its merits. The problem was that the German general staff had no other plans; and this one, which was not used as planned, did not meet the political needs of the summer of 1914.

While Bethmann-Hollweg urged the Austro-Hungarians to hold back, the German chief of staff, Helmuth von Moltke (1848-1916), pleaded with them to mobilize so that the Russian army would not be able to strike first. Under these circumstances the confused Austro-Hungarians could not be restrained, and after Russia rejected a final German appeal to halt its mobilization, Germany declared war. At this point the Germans ought to have left a small force to guard strongly fortified Alsace-Lorraine from a possible French attack and tried to defeat Russia, but there was no plan. The French would almost certainly have entered the war anyway because they had promised the Russians their full support, but the Schlieffen Plan made it necessary for the Germans to strike at France first, passing through neutral Belgium to outflank the strong fortifications the French had built along the German border. The attack on Belgium brought a united Britain into the war and made Germany appear guilty in the eyes of the United States and most other peoples of the world.

EUROPE IN 1914

EUROPEAN ALLIED
STATES OF WWI

CENTRAL POWERS OF WWI

NEUTRAL STATES

SCALE OF MILES
0 100 200 300 400 500

Who was really to blame for the war? No government had sought it; no people wanted it. Serbian officials had plotted to destroy the Austro-Hungarian empire, and some of them knew in advance of the plan to assassinate the Archduke but did not give adequate warning. Austria-Hungary suspected this and had determined on the destruction of Serbia.

762

Its provocation was greater than that which led the British to attack the Boers, the United States to attack Spain, or any of the other powers to attack the backward Asian or African peoples, but as the consequences were more serious, Austria-Hungary bears a heavy burden of responsibility. The Russians had encouraged Serbian aspirations and had mobilized to frighten Austria-Hungary. They ought to have halted when requested by Germany because mobilization was as serious a step as a formal declaration of war. The German sins were those of stupidity. Bismarck had used alliances to hold his allies in check, and he would never have permitted Austria-Hungary to act unilaterally during the early days of the crisis, or the German general staff to dictate foreign policy during the critical stage. The French wanted Alsace-Lorraine, but their crime was mainly that of not holding Russia back. It has been suggested that if the British had clearly stated in the beginning that they would stand by France and Russia, Germany would have been more cautious. This is true, but only Parliament had the authority to make such a declaration. The foreign minister hesitated to request that it do so in spite of secret military commitments to France until the German invasion of neutral Belgium united the British people behind the war. Whoever was at fault, it was the people who suffered. By the middle of August, all the major European powers were at war except Italy.

THE WAR

THE STALEMATE

The European wars between 1854 and 1870 had been short, with one or two important battles deciding the issue. It was presumed by both sides that the conflict of 1914 would be similar. Indeed, the diplomats would have been less willing to resort to war had they envisaged the years of carnage that were to follow. This was especially true of the Central Powers, who doubted whether they could win a long war. If the Allies could withstand the initial onslaught, their chances would be good. They had twice the manpower of the Central Powers, they could establish a naval blockade which in time would create serious supply problems, and they could probably persuade Austria-Hungary's numerous Slavic peoples to rebel. The Central Powers had only the advantages of interior lines of communication and superior military organization. Neither side had many generals with above-average ability. Indeed, Moltke's bungling during the first month of the war cost Germany its best opportunity to emerge victorious, while the offensive-minded French generals threw hundreds of thousands of lives away on assaults that had no chance of success.

During the night of August 4, the German army swept into Belgium. Brussels was taken on the twentieth, and the forward echelons of the

German army came within twenty miles of Paris during the first week of September. Victory might well have been theirs had Moltke not weakened the main effort by detaching troops to block the French thrust into Lorraine and to check the unexpectedly rapid Russian advance on the eastern front. As a result, a gap developed between the first and second German armies from which the French were quick to profit. They counterattacked and between September 5 and September 12 in the first Battle of the Marne the Germans were compelled to assume defensive positions. The Allies were unable to dislodge them and by the close of the year the western front had stabilized. Networks of trenches had been constructed that were protected by barbed wire fences and murderous machine-gun fire. It was not to be the anticipated war of movement in the west; it was to be a war of position which cost hundreds of thousands of casualties to advance a few miles.

The eastern front also stabilized near the end of 1914, although it was too long for as powerful a system of defenses to develop as in the west. The Austro-Hungarians had been defeated by the Russians and had even failed in their effort to overrun Serbia, but the Germans compensated for these setbacks after they recalled Paul von Hindenburg (1847-1934) from retirement and gave him as chief of staff, Erich von Ludendorff (1865-1937). The two generals surrounded and destroyed one Russian army at Tannenberg, taking over 100,000 prisoners between August 26–30, and the following month captured 125,000 more Russians in the battle of the Masurian Lakes. In spite of these successes, however, they were unable to follow up their advantage before the approach of winter.

THE SEARCH FOR ALLIES

As the prospects of a stalemate increased, the contestants sought additional allies by appealing to the nationalistic aspirations of the various peoples of Europe. During the fall of 1914 the Central Powers won the Ottoman Empire to their side. German soldiers had been active in training the Turkish army, and German bankers and engineers had been constructing railroads in the Empire. More important to the Ottoman leadership, however, was their desire to regain Egypt from Britain, and territories in the Caucasus Mountains from Russia. The Ottomans proved unable to take the Suez Canal, much less advance into Egypt, and they made no progress against the Russians before the Revolution in 1917. Their efforts tied down some allied troops, but their greatest contribution was in preventing badly needed supplies from reaching Russia by closing the Straits. The allied fleet tried to force a passage in March, 1915, but abandoned the effort at the moment when the Ottomans were about to exhaust their ammunition supply. In April they disembarked troops on the Gallipoli Peninsula in the hope of seizing Constantinople and the Straits by land, but poor leadership and inferior numbers led to a costly defeat.

The allied failure to secure the Straits and Russian defeats in 1915 convinced the Bulgarians that victory would go to the Central Powers. They were disgruntled at their defeat in the Second Balkan War and entered the conflict in the fall of 1915 when the Germans promised them a larger share of Serbian territory than the Allies could afford to offer, since they were presumably fighting to protect that little Slav state. With Bulgarian assistance the Central Powers were able to overrun Serbia and establish a direct line of communications between Berlin, Vienna, Constantinople, and Asia Minor. They had no further diplomatic successes, however, since the Allies could outbid them by offering prospective supporters territories from the multinational Ottoman and Austro-Hungarian empires.

Japan quickly entered the war on the allied side in the expectation of winning Germany's holdings in the Far East. The Italians refused to come to the aid of the Germans and Austro-Hungarians on the grounds that they were not fighting a defensive war as stipulated in the terms of the Triple Alliance. Actually, the Italians had decided to wait and see who would bid most for their assistance. Since most of what they wanted belonged to Austria-Hungary, the Allies could afford to be more generous. In April, 1915, Italy signed a secret treaty with the Allies in which it agreed to enter the war in return for Trentino, Trieste, and part of the Dalmatian Coast, areas inhabited largely by Italians or historically connected with the former Venetian republic. Rumania agreed to join the Allies in 1916 in return for Transylvania and Bukovina, both Habsburg territories in which many of the inhabitants spoke Rumanian. The Greeks thought that they could best satisfy their nationalistic aspirations at the expense of Bulgaria and the Ottoman Empire, but their king, whose wife was the Kaiser's sister, kept the country neutral until a British threat to bombard Athens in June, 1917, forced his abdication.

Appeals were also made by both sides to the subject nationalities in the multinational empires. Here, as elsewhere, the Central Powers found that they could offer less than their foes. Their most obvious opportunity was to appeal to Polish aspirations, although both Germany and Austria-Hungary ruled parts of the former Kingdom of Poland. In November, 1916, they announced the creation of an independent Polish state and called for volunteers to fight the Russians. The Tsar countered with talk of Polish autonomy, but the Russian record in Poland inspired little confidence, and the Central Powers might have won considerable support from this quarter if their own motives had not become suspect. The German general staff was anxious to incorporate into Germany some Russian-held Polish territory and was therefore very vague concerning the boundaries of the new state. As a result, the Poles made no prolonged effort to aid either contestant.

After the Russian monarchy collapsed in 1917, other subject nationalities from Finland to the Ukraine proclaimed their independence. The expansionist ambitions of the German officer corps alienated some of these

*Hindenburg, Kaiser Wilhelm, and Ludendorff at German General Head-
quarters in 1917. (Ewing Galloway)*

peoples, although the Finns momentarily elected a German prince as king.
In the end, the confusion on the eastern front was too great for the
Central Powers to profit much from the emerging national states and the
war ended before order could be restored.

The Allies were more fortunate. The Slavic citizens of the Austro-
Hungarian Empire seized upon the war as an opportunity to achieve their
nationalistic aspirations, and the Habsburg government had to establish a
virtual military dictatorship to ensure their obedience. Thousands were
arrested and civilian hostages were actually taken in an effort to prevent
disloyal actions by other members of their families. On the front, Czech
and Serb troops proved untrustworthy. About 300,000 Czechs surrendered to the Russians at the earliest opportunity. Once in allied hands,
they often formed units to fight for their independence under the direction
of a Czechoslovak National Committee that was established in exile. The

766

south Slavs also formed a government in exile and made preparation for the creation of a united south or Yugoslav state. Emperor Francis Joseph died in 1916, and his successor, Emperor Charles I (1916-1919), relaxed the dictatorial regime the following year and summoned the Austrian parliament to meet. By this act he provided a forum in which the subject nationalities could publicly express their aspirations. By 1918 the Austro-Hungarian monarchy was collapsing as much from internal nationalistic agitation as from military defeat.

The Ottoman Empire also provided the Allies with an opportune field to exploit the ambitions of discontented nationalities. In 1915 the Armenians, who occupied the northeastern portion of the Empire, proclaimed their independence and assisted the Russians in that region. The Turks ruthlessly deported the Armenians from areas near strategic military installations and about 500,000 perished. The Arabs proved of greater assistance to the allied cause. In 1916, Sharif Husayn (1856-1931), the governor of Hijaz in western Arabia, raised the banners of revolt in return for a British promise of an independent Arab state. Stimulated by the famed liaison officer, Colonel T. E. Lawrence, the Arabs conquered vast stretches of the Ottoman Empire.

To ensure that the profits of war would be great enough to prevent desertions from their ranks, the Allies made several secret treaties dividing the Ottoman Empire. The hard-pressed Russians, who appeared most likely to be tempted by German offers of peace, were promised long-coveted Constantinople and the Straits. The British, French, and Italians were given administrative rights or spheres of influence in most of what remained of the Empire including areas that had been promised the Arabs. To win international Jewish support, the British promised to create an independent state for them in Palestine, although it had been assigned to the Arabs. So desperate were the Allies that they gave little thought to their perfidy and none to the troubles it might cause after the war.

THE WAR CONTINUES

In 1915 the Germans decided to make their main effort against Russia rather than France. This decision was taken because of the strength of the allied position in the west and the imminent collapse of Austria-Hungary unless Russian troops were driven from its soil. The offensive that was launched in May all but knocked Russia out of the war. Within two months, troops of the Central Powers advanced a hundred miles, and by the middle of September they had seized Poland and Lithuania. The Russians fought well, but they suffered from lack of artillery and munitions as well as poor leadership. In September the Tsar himself took personal command in the hope of reviving the spirit of his army.

The Allies tried to take advantage of the German preoccupation with the east and launched huge offensives in the west during the spring and fall of 1915. Officers, trained in the traditions of the wars of 1859-1871 when troops moved rapidly and the outcome was often decided in a matter of months, proved unable to devise tactics to meet the new situation in which the trench and machine gun had once more made defense triumphant. They hurled their troops towards the German lines behind rolling artillery barrages just as they would have done years before. The French suffered 1,430,000 casualties in 1915, but at no point could they or their British allies advance more than three miles. The tragic folly of the French military leaders lent justification to Clemenceau's famous statement that "war is too important to be left to the generals."

By 1916 Russia appeared so weak that the Germans decided to renew their efforts on the western front, where many believed the final decision on the outcome of the war would be made. The Allies also planned a great offensive in this region, supported by lesser offensives along the Italian, Russian, Rumanian, and Arabic fronts. The Germans launched their attack first. For five months the battle raged before Verdun. The French held the city, but at a cost of 350,000 men. The allied offensive in the Somme was even more bloody. At a cost of 600,000 men an advance of seven miles was achieved. Tanks were employed for the first time by the British, but their tactical use was so little understood that they did not greatly affect the outcome. Other fronts saw the Russians regaining a few of their territorial losses, the Italians holding their own, the Rumanians being defeated, and the Arabs successfully revolting against their Ottoman masters. When the year ended, the Germans occupied a large amount of allied territory, but the outcome of the war was uncertain. It seemed doubtful whether a breakthrough could be accomplished on any front. As a result, there was talk of peace negotiations and an increased interest in naval warfare. The latter was the immediate cause of American intervention.

THE AMERICAN INTERVENTION

When war came to Europe in 1914, the overwhelming desire of the American people was to remain spectators. President Wilson's appeal to remain "impartial in thought as well as in action" met with general approval. However, it was one thing to talk of neutrality and another thing to practice it. A few Americans, especially those of German and Irish descent, favored the Central Powers, but from the beginning the great majority hoped for an allied victory. The Central Powers were generally regarded as the aggressors because they had declared war first and because they had attacked Belgium in violation of a treaty. Allied propaganda cleverly exploited this and other themes while German counterefforts were clumsy. Then, too, the American people had the same language and literature as the British, and many of their institutions were of British origin. It was widely believed that the Allies represented the cause of democracy and the Central Powers absolute monarchy, although the presence of tsarist Russia in the allied camp caused some embarrassment on this score. In any event, most Americans including President Wilson were favorably disposed to the Allies in 1914 and drew close to them as the war progressed.

The initial problem which confronted Americans was that of the rights of neutrals on the high seas. The British used their naval superiority to bottle up the German surface fleet in the North Sea and to try to cut off German imports from neutral countries. In carrying out this policy, they paid scant attention to international law. They arbitrarily defined as contraband not only war materials, but all articles of importance including food. Furthermore, their insistence that neutral ships be searched for contraband in ports rather than on the high seas caused long delays. They limited American trade to Denmark, the Netherlands, and other neutral countries that might re-export American goods to the Central Powers and in 1916 blacklisted American companies suspected of dealing with Germany.

Wilson protested against this disregard of neutral rights, but he, and especially the American ambassador in London, were so pro-British that there was no effort at retaliation. Indeed, Wilson gradually convinced himself that American security depended on the triumph of the Western democracies. Furthermore, despite restrictions and hazards, American trade with the Allies increased fourfold during the first two years of the war. In 1914 the country had been in the midst of a depression, but by 1916 the economy was booming. When the Allies ran out of capital, American bankers made loans to enable them to continue to buy. In this manner, economic and cultural ties drew the United States nearer to the Allies.

The reverse was true with the Central Powers. The German surface fleet was bottled up in the North Sea, but their submarines escaped to prey on allied merchant vessels. It was dangerous for submarines to give warning before attacking because they could be easily sunk by armed merchant vessels, nor could they pick up the passengers and crew after a successful attack because they had no room for them. Thus the blockade the Germans set up around the British Isles violated international law just as did the British blockade of Germany. Both countries justified their actions on the grounds of necessity, but British methods caused only inconvenience; German methods caused loss of life. On May 7, 1915, the British passenger liner, *Lusitania,* was sunk by a submarine with a loss of 128 Americans. The Germans had published warnings in the New York papers to prevent passengers from traveling on the liner, which also carried munitions, but Wilson lodged a strong protest. The Germans, anxious to avoid war, agreed not to sink liners in the future without making provisions for the safety of the passengers, provided the United States held the British equally accountable for their violations of international law. This Wilson did not do. Trade with the Allies increased, but trade with the Central Powers virtually ceased because of the British blockade.

Wilson became increasingly fearful that the United States would be-

NORWAY

SWEDEN

GREAT BRITAIN

DENMARK

RUSSIA

NETHS

GERMAN EMPIRE

BEL

PARIS •LORRAINE
ALSACE

FRANCE

AUSTRIA-HUNGARY

SWITZ

MILAN

SPAIN

ITALY

RUMANIA

MONT. SERBIA
BULGARIA

ALBANIA

BLACK SEA

DARDANELLES

GREECE

OTTOMAN EMPIRE

PE

CASPIAN SE

MEDITERRANEAN SEA

ARABIA

EGYPT

① ② ③ ④ ⑤ ⑥

FINLAND

EASTERN FRONT 1914-1918

〰〰〰 DEEPEST AUSTRO-GERMAN PENETRATION 1918

------ FARTHEST RUSSIAN ADVANCE 1914

—— FARTHEST RUSSIAN ADVANCE 1916

········ FARTHEST RUMANIAN ADVANCE 1916

0 50 100   200   300

SWEDEN

BALTIC SEA

PSKOV

GERMAN

BERLIN

EMPIRE •WARSAW

•PRAGUE

MOHILEV

RUSSIA

AUSTRIA

VIENNA

HUNGARY

BUDAPEST

SERBIA ALBANIA

RUMANIA

BULGARIA

BLACK SEA

TURKEY

①

NORTH SEA

BELGIUM

LIEGE

CAMBRIA

PARIS

WESTERN FRONT 1914-1918

〰〰〰 DEEPEST GER. PENETR. SEPT. 1914 (SCHLIEFFEN PLAN)

—— ALLIED OFFENSIVE FALL 1918

—— GER. OFFENSIVE SUMMER 1918

0 10 20 30 40 50

②

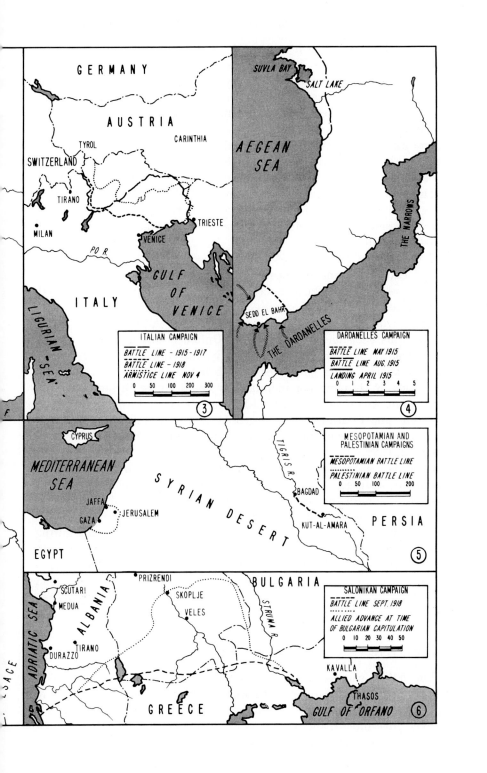

GERMANY

AUSTRIA

SWITZERLAND

TYROL
CARINTHIA

TIRANO

MILAN

TRIESTE

PO R.

VENICE

ITALY

GULF
OF
VENICE

LIGURIAN
SEA

SUVLA BAY
SALT LAKE

AEGEAN
SEA

THE NARROWS

SEDD EL BAHR

THE DARDANELLES

ITALIAN CAMPAIGN

BATTLE LINE - 1915-1917

BATTLE LINE - 1918

ARMISTICE LINE NOV 4

0   50   100   200   300

③

DARDANELLES CAMPAIGN

BATTLE LINE MAY 1915

BATTLE LINE AUG. 1915

LANDING APRIL 1915

0   1   2   3   4   5

④

CYPRUS

MEDITERRANEAN
SEA

JAFFA

GAZA   JERUSALEM

EGYPT

SYRIAN   DESERT

TIGRIS R.

BAGDAD

KUT-AL-AMARA

PERSIA

**MESOPOTAMIAN AND
PALESTINIAN CAMPAIGNS**

MESOPOTAMIAN BATTLE LINE

PALESTINIAN BATTLE LINE

0   50   100   200

⑤

PRIZRENDI

BULGARIA

SCUTARI

MEDUA

ALBANIA

SKOPLJE

VELES

STRUMA R.

SALONIKAN CAMPAIGN

ADRIATIC SEA

TIRANO
DURAZZO

KAVALLA

BATTLE LINE SEPT. 1918

ALLIED ADVANCE AT TIME
OF BULGARIAN CAPITULATION

0   10   20   30   40   50

THASOS

GREECE

GULF OF ORFANO

⑥

come involved in the war if it continued. In 1915 and again early in 1916 he made efforts to mediate, but the Allies, still hopeful of victory, rejected his proposals. In 1916 Bethmann-Hollweg and a majority in the Reichstag took steps to secure a negotiated peace, but the conservative German officers hampered their efforts because they believed that only large territorial annexations would silence the popular demand for political and social reforms. When Wilson asked both sides to state their terms for peace, the Allies demanded that their adversaries abandon all their conquests and that the map of Europe be redrawn in accordance with nationalities. This would mean the destruction of the Habsburg and the Ottoman empires. Although the German demands were more moderate, these too involved some concessions. Neither side was willing to accept Wilson's call for "peace without victory."

Indeed, as the sufferings of the war grew more intense, more determined leaders became the heads of government, the influence of the military increased, and the chances for a negotiated peace diminished. This was especially true in Germany, where on January 8, 1917, the military won permission to renew submarine warfare. Although they anticipated that this decision would bring the United States into the war, the Germans also recognized that, economically, the Americans were already in the war against them. Moreover, they believed that if they could sink 600,000 tons of shipping per month, they could starve Britain into submission before American military aid became effective. To delay American intervention, the Central Powers urged Mexico and Japan to attack the United States. Faced with this situation, Wilson asked Congress to declare war in April, 1917.

For a time it seemed the German gamble would succeed. In April, May, and June, an average of 700,000 tons per month of allied shipping was sent to the bottom of the sea. At one time Britain's supply of grain would last for only six more weeks, but improved anti-submarine methods and the adoption of the convoy system reduced losses sharply, and during the last year of the war sinkings posed no serious threat. Neither Japan nor Mexico attacked the United States; by March, 1918, there were 300,000 American troops in France, and by the end of the war, over 2,000,000 had crossed the Atlantic. The Germans had miscalculated, and their miscalculation had destroyed their last opportunity to win the war.

THE DEFEAT OF THE CENTRAL POWERS

While Wilson was weighing what action to take in view of the German decision to renew submarine warfare, workers were rioting and troops were mutinying in St. Petersburg. On March 12, 1917, the Duma established a provisional government, and three days later the Tsar abdicated.[12] Although

[12] For Russian Revolution see pages 825-833.

they remained in the war nominally for nearly a year, the Russians became so embroiled in revolutions and counter-revolutions that their participation ceased to be a major factor. In November, the Bolsheviks under Lenin emerged in control of the capital, and in March of the following year they signed the Treaty of Brest-Litovsk with Germany. Finland, Poland, the Ukraine, and the Baltic provinces were recognized as independent, and several provinces east of the Black Sea were ceded to the Ottoman Empire. The Ukrainians promised to send grain to Austria-Hungary, and some troops were freed to fight on the western front.

Meanwhile, the Germans had turned on Italy, and during the fall of 1917 the Italians were nearly driven out of the war. Ludendorff, who had emerged as the most influential German general, felt free to plan a last great offensive on the western front. In March, 1918, he struck in the direction of Arras and Amiens. In two weeks the Germans advanced forty miles, only to be halted. In April they launched a drive near Ypres but were stopped once more. In May they drove towards Soissons and Rheims. A fourth drive was halted in early June near Château-Thierry in an engagement that saw American troops playing a leading role for the first time. The great spring offensive had failed. Ludendorff made a last desperate effort to win victory around the middle of July. The Marne River was crossed, but the French and Americans held. On July 18 Marshal Foch, who had been named commander-in-chief of the allied armies, counterattacked. The Germans were driven back and the second Battle of the Marne, like the first, ended in an allied victory. Henceforth, the Germans were forced to retreat slowly along the western front.

Once the United States entered the war, Wilson abandoned his objective of "peace without victory" because he had become convinced that a permanent peace could not be established unless the economic causes of war were removed, the boundaries of Europe redrawn in accordance with the principles of national self-determination, the governments put into the hands of the people, and a league of nations created to guarantee that the rule of law, not the rule of the jungle, would govern the conduct of states. In keeping with these ideas, he formulated fourteen points which he presented to Congress on January 8, 1918.

The first five points dealt with the presumed causes of war. Secret treaties and secret diplomacy were to be outlawed, armaments reduced, economic barriers removed as far as possible, and freedom of the seas guaranteed in peace and war. Furthermore, an impartial adjustment of colonial claims was to take place in which the interests of the native populations were given equal weight with those of the colonial powers.

The next eight points dealt with territorial settlements. The Central Powers were required to evacuate all the allied territory, Alsace-Lorraine was to be returned to France, and the various nationalities in the Austro-Hungarian and Ottoman empires were to be given autonomy. The Italian-

Austrian frontier was to be drawn along clearly recognizable lines of nationality, and Serbia was to be given secure access to the sea. No mention was made of the subject nationalities in Russia, the third multinational empire, except that an independent Poland was to be created with access to the sea.

The fourteenth point was designed to prevent future wars and to provide a means of settling international disputes justly. It called for a general association of nations for the purpose of affording mutual guarantees of political independence and territorial integrity to great and small states alike.

This program was a far cry from being "a peace without victory." It gave France Alsace-Lorraine, created an independent Poland, and destroyed the multinational Austro-Hungarian and Ottoman empires. On the other hand, it was also a far cry from the secret treaties the Allies had prepared to divide the spoils of war. Wilson's appeal lay in the fact that his program was not predicated upon territorial aggrandizement, but upon ideals long dear to Western civilization. He talked of economic freedom, nationalism, self-determination, and democracy. He promised perpetual peace, not a new balance of power to be disrupted by future wars. He became both a hero and a sage to war-weary Europe. Frenchman and German, Italian and Austrian, were drawn to this new type of statesman, who advocated international cooperation instead of international rivalry.

As the Allies began to win victories in the Ottoman Empire and the Balkans, as the subject peoples of the Austro-Hungarian Empire began to revolt, and as the Allies relentlessly pushed forward along the western front in August and September, 1918, the German will to resist weakened. Why continue to fight for a victory that could not be won, when such a peace was offered? But even before the German people were ready to take matters into their own hands, the generals knew they were defeated. On September 29, the panic-stricken Ludendorff asked the government to start peace negotiations before the army collapsed completely.

The liberal Prince Max of Baden (1867-1929) was named chancellor on October 4 and, with the support of the left-wing and center political parties, asked for an armistice based upon the Fourteen Points. After some debate, the Allies notified the Germans of their acceptance with reservations concerning the freedom of the seas and the extent of the reparations expected. Austria-Hungary had already been informed that its subject peoples would be granted independence rather than autonomy if they desired. Upon these terms the Germans agreed to make peace and an armistice was signed which required them to withdraw their troops to the east of the Rhine River and surrender a large number of trains, trucks, and ships to the Allies. The Allies were given bridgeheads over the Rhine River and continued to blockade Germany despite the suffering it inflicted upon non-combatants.

The Germans accepted this severe armistice because they had no choice, although they knew that its terms would prevent them from renewing the war if the Allies violated the principles set down in the Fourteen Points. The fleet had mutinied on November 3 and a revolt had broken out in Munich. The Kaiser abdicated, largely as a result of American pressure, and on November 11 the armistice went into effect in the west. Bulgaria, the Ottoman Empire, and Austria-Hungary had already laid down their arms. Peace had returned to Europe.

THE RESULTS OF THE WAR

ON THE BATTLEFIELD

What were the results of the war, the most terrible the world had ever known? Some were all too obvious. Ten million men had been killed and twice that number wounded. If these losses had been spread equally among the various age groups and between the sexes, they would not have been as serious, but they were taken almost entirely from the male youth upon whom each nation depended for its fathers of families and for its productive capacity. France, with 1,385,000 dead and over three million wounded out of a population of about 39,000,000, has never fully recovered. Russia and Germany suffered heavier numerical losses, but their larger populations mitigated the results.

The soldier who did return from the trenches was not always the same man who had gone to war. Often he had difficulty adjusting himself to the humdrum existence of civilian life and looked back to the days when he and his comrades made decisions daily that involved life or death. To such men the slow, halting procedures of parliamentary democracy seemed inadequate to meet a crisis, and political leaders who attempted to guide the state through compromises appeared worthy of only contempt. At home, as on the battlefield, they admired the man who could make quick, bold decisions, and they were not squeamish if brutality accompanied his acts. Thus, the war helped breed a new race of men whose ideals and aspirations differed from those of their forefathers in the age of the egalitarian revolutions. Their willingness to reject their heritage was one of the causes of the twentieth-century crisis.[13]

The static nature of the conflict had limited the physical destruction of the war to relatively small areas, but these areas were completely wrecked. Once again France, with its northeast in ruins, was among the heaviest sufferers. It has been estimated that the war cost $350,000,000,-000, and all the major participants emerged with astronomical debts which called for large interest payments and heavy taxes.

[13] See pages 797-1062.

775

ON THE HOMEFRONT

Although the destruction in life and property occasioned the most concern in 1918, there were more far-reaching developments on the homefront. The old order had been weakened. The emperors of Russia, Germany, and Austria-Hungary were no more. With them had gone most of the old aristocracy of central and eastern Europe. That portion of the middle class which depended upon income from bonds, insurance, or other investment had been seriously weakened by inflation. As a result, the very classes that had provided a stabilizing if undemocratic influence throughout the nineteenth century were no longer in a position to stem the popular tide.

To many, including President Wilson, this was desirable progress towards a new capitalistic, democratic order, but unconsciously the essential supports for capitalism and democracy had also been weakened. The war had forced governments to take extraordinary measures. Freedom of the press and freedom of speech had been rigidly curtailed in every country. Troop movements, of course, had to be kept secret, but once censorship bureaus were established, they were often used to hide blunders and to prevent criticism. Equally serious was the development of a vast system of official propaganda. To keep the soldiers willing to fight at the front and the civilians willing to make sacrifices at home, it had been necessary to inspire hatred of the enemy and a deadly fear of the consequences of defeat. Even American scholars, far removed from the horrors of war, had lost their scientific objectivity and had depicted the Kaiser as an autocratic ogre and the Germans as Huns. The culture that Americans had once so admired that thousands had flocked to Berlin, Heidelberg, and other universities was now thought to be barbaric and depraved. The German language virtually ceased to be taught in American high schools.

At first, all elements of society had pledged their support to the governments of their respective states. Those few who criticized the war effort, advocated peace, or refused to fight found themselves in serious difficulty with their fellow citizens, if not their governments. As the war went on and failure followed failure, criticism of the governments became widespread, but this did not lead to greater freedom. Indeed, to most people the answer to defeat or the failure to win quick victory was to give exceptional powers to a strong, able leader who promised results. By the war's end, the British had found David Lloyd George, the French Georges Clemenceau, and Germans General Ludendorff. Imperial Russia was less fortunate in its search for a leader; it ceased to exist. As a result, people became accustomed to abandoning their essential freedoms and to putting their trust in leaders when faced with serious difficulties. At the same time, would-be leaders like Adolf Hitler learned the value of propaganda as a weapon to delude and indoctrinate.

Capitalism and laissez-faire economics were also undermined in every country. Military demands for arms and munitions greatly exceeded industry's ordinary capacity. In 1914 daily production of shells in France did not exceed daily expenditure by a single army corps. Logistical support in Russia broke down so completely by the end of 1914 that infantry had to attack at night with bayonets because there were no shells to fire artillery preparations and no rifle ammunition. By 1915 some Russian regiments had rifles for only two-thirds of their men. Under such circumstances, munitions ministers were appointed with wide powers to marshal the forces of industry. Soon shortages developed in food, clothing, fuel, and other materials; more ministers were appointed to direct this or that aspect of the economy, and rationing was introduced. Conscription was enacted to supply the manpower needs of the military, and efforts were made to direct workers towards essential industries. Since imports had to be paid for, they were carefully limited to essentials, and exports were manipulated to increase the gold reserve. Even the profit motive was frowned upon. Workers were expected to labor without seeking wage increases, industries were expected to function with small margins of profit, and prices were often controlled. In this manner a planned economy emerged in which hatred of the enemy and loyalty to one's own country were supposed to replace the quest for profit as the motivating force for human effort. As a recompense, a greatly accelerated rate of production was achieved; only Russia collapsed because of lack of supplies.

Economic planning was carried further in Germany than elsewhere because the allied blockade shut off the normal sources of supply. Here the brilliant industrialist, Walther Rathenau (1867-1922), became head of a War Raw Materials Department and operated the nation's economy as a huge trust or combine. An Imperial Grain Office and Central Purchasing Company soon followed. Every effort was made to see that raw materials reached the factories at the proper time. When an essential article could not be produced in large enough quantities, a substitute was sought. Nitrates for explosives had come from Chile before the war, but scientists found ways to extract nitrogen from manure and finally from the air. Margarine replaced butter, an artificial coffee was produced, and chestnuts were made into flour. Synthetic rubber was used, and garbage was turned into animal feed. Wooden shoes replaced shoes made of leather. Where the original could not be produced in sufficient quantities or a substitute found, rationing was resorted to. Only the magnificent achievements of Rathenau and his associates enabled Germany to remain in the war.

Even the United States, where the traditions of individual freedom were strong, became involved in the general trend. A War Industries Board under Bernard Baruch (1870-1965) directed the American industrial effort. A Food Administration under Herbert Hoover (1874-1964) sought to conserve the supply of food. There were meatless days and wheatless days. Prohibition was inaugurated to save grain. A Railroad Administration operated the nation's railroads, and a Committee on Public Information was formed to feed Americans patriotic propaganda. An Espionage Act and a Sedition Act were passed providing heavy punishments for anyone who impeded the war effort or criticized the government severely. Over 1,500 persons, for the most part loyal Americans, suffered under the provisions of these acts.

The family, the very basis of civilized society, was altered. Ties between parents and children, husbands and wives, were weakened as some entered the military service and others sought employment in distant essential industries. Women, who had previously led sheltered lives in their homes, found their services demanded elsewhere as the manpower shortage became acute. In Great Britain alone, over 800,000 women accepted employment. With employment came financial independence and with financial independence a more equal status in the home. Marriage began to be transformed into an association of equals.

The war also had a profound effect on the position of Europe in the world. When British, French, and German factories turned to the production of war goods, the United States, Japan, and other countries not deeply involved in the conflict began to capture their markets and some of the more backward countries took steps to develop their own industries. By the war's end, the European states had lost much of their foreign market, and little of it was ever regained. To pay for the war, Europeans had to sell part of their foreign investments and to borrow from abroad. The United States emerged as a creditor nation and New York replaced London as the financial capital of the world.

But these changes were not immediately apparent. Few in 1918 failed to believe that the war had made the world safe for democracy, that capitalism and human freedom were on the rise, and that European ascendancy was unchallenged except by the United States. It was with confidence in the future that the victorious powers sat down to prepare the peace treaties.

AT THE CONFERENCE TABLE: PERSONALITIES AND PRINCIPLES

Not since 1815 had the diplomats redrawn the map of Europe, but those who congregated at Paris and Versailles in 1919 had little in common with their illustrious predecessors save their assigned task. At Vienna the crowned heads of Europe had gathered with a host of noble advisers, and a peace was prepared on the basis of legitimacy, compensations, and the balance of power. The peacemakers of 1919 were untitled politicians responsible to democratic electorates, and their advisers were experts drawn from professional diplomatic corps or academic life. The principles which governed the Vienna treaty were anathema to men like Woodrow Wilson, who refused even to use a book describing the procedures followed in 1815 as a guide. Yet in one respect the peacemakers adopted a similar course.

778

The representatives of the lesser states in both instances were assigned minor roles; it was the representatives of the great participating powers who made the major decisions.

Certainly the most important participant was Woodrow Wilson. The United States had come late into the war, but the very fact that it was fresh as well as powerful put Wilson in a strong position, for he was dealing with heads of states whose people were exhausted by over four years of conflict. Wilson's personal prestige was also high when the deliberations began. His idealistic slogans of a "war to end wars," a war "to make the world safe for democracy," and a "peace without victory" had captured the minds of Europeans as well as Americans. Unfortunately, Wilson was not a tactful diplomat. He was convinced of his own and America's moral superiority, and had no appreciation of the historical forces that had molded Europe or of the complexity of the problems before him. When confronted with opposition, he often compromised when he ought to have held firm, and took an obstinate, self-righteous stand when compromise was in order. Yet with all his faults, the peace treaties of 1919 would probably have been worse had he never lived.

France was represented by its prime minister, Georges Clemenceau (1841-1929). Clemenceau was old enough to have been a prominent figure during the Franco-Prussian War and from that time he had been motivated by hatred and fear of Germany. Before 1914 he had used his newspaper to espouse radical causes, expose scandals, defend Captain Dreyfus, and above all to attack the government for its failure to prepare for war. During the war he had constantly agitated for more guns and ammunition and had constantly railed against pacificism and defeatism. In the dark days of November, 1917, when he was called to office, he turned his indomitable will and fiery patriotism to the task of winning victory. His was the Jacobin spirit of 1793. Now 78, he entered the peace conference determined to shackle Germany so that it would never again be a threat to France.

The British David Lloyd George (1863-1945) had a far more flexible character. He had begun life as a poor Welshman and had achieved prominence as a courageous left-wing politician.[14] In 1915 he became minister of munitions; he displayed so much energy and ability that he was made prime minister in December, 1916. Although he had campaigned for re-election on an anti-German policy in December, 1918, he generally supported Wilson in his efforts to check the French desire for a harsh peace.

The least important member of the Big Four was Italy's Vittorio Orlando (1860-1952). Orlando had neither Wilson's idealism, Clemenceau's drive, nor Lloyd George's adaptability. He was just another politician, but one motivated by the desire to win all that Italy had been promised in the secret treaties.

Russia, in the throes of a Communist revolution, was not invited to attend, and Austria-Hungary had ceased to exist. Germany was also con-

14 See page 661.

779

spicuous by its absence. Although peace treaties in the past had always been made by representatives of the victorious and defeated powers deliberating together, the Allies decided to exclude Germany so that it could not exploit differences that arose between the victors as Talleyrand had done in 1815.[15] The complexity of the problem led them to decide to prepare separate treaties for Germany, Austria, Hungary, Bulgaria, and the Ottoman Empire.

The Central Powers had surrendered on the assumption that Wilson's Fourteen Points would be the basis of the treaty, and Germany had been given a specific promise to this effect. These points, as we have seen, made nationalism the principal criterion for drawing boundaries. At first glance this would seem a simple and just solution, but the European population was so intermixed that no exact ethnic boundaries could be drawn. It was equally difficult to let the people concerned decide. If they voted by province, a large minority might be left disgruntled. If they voted by village, the exact boundary would be difficult to draw because of overlapping ethnic groups. Furthermore, many persons held that historic, strategic, and economic considerations could not be entirely ignored. The Allies turned these difficulties to their advantage. Where plebiscites were held, they were usually conducted so as to favor the Allies; where strategic, economic, or historic considerations were preferred to ethnic ones, the result was usually detrimental to the defeated powers. Secret treaties between the Allies dividing the anticipated spoils of victory added to the dilemma. To those like the Italians who had entered the war only to gain territory, these treaties were as binding as the agreement with Germany to establish a peace based on the Fourteen Points. Finally, France and the new states that emerged out of Austria-Hungary were fearful of a German or a Habsburg revival and demanded that special measures be taken for their security. Under such circumstances it is surprising that the treaty-makers adhered to the Fourteen Points as well as they did.

THE TREATY OF VERSAILLES

By the terms of the Treaty of Versailles, Germany surrendered Alsace-Lorraine to France, as was anticipated in the Fourteen Points. Clemenceau had also demanded the Saar Basin, where there were rich coal mines, and control over the west bank of the Rhine, but Wilson refused to turn so many Germans over to France. It was decided to hold a plebiscite in fifteen years to determine the fate of the Saar and to limit French occupation of the left bank of the Rhine to the same length of time. Three hundred and eighty-four square miles were surrendered to Belgium, and part of Schleswig was turned over to Denmark after a plebiscite. It was the eastern boundary that most angered the Germans. Poland's promised access to the sea turned out to be a corridor leading to the Baltic which separated Ger-

[15] See page 493.

The Big Four in Paris. Left to right: David Lloyd George of England, Vittorio Orlando of Italy, Georges Clemenceau of France, and Woodrow Wilson of the United States. (Wide World)

many from East Prussia. No plebiscite was held there or in Posen to the south. A majority of the inhabitants of Upper Silesia voted to remain with Germany, but the ballots were counted by village, and part of the province was turned over to Poland. The predominantly German cities of Danzig and Memel were also ceded. Danzig became a free city, and Memel was seized by the newly created state of Lithuania in 1923. In all, Germany lost 13 per cent of its European territory, including the great mining areas of Alsace-Lorraine and Silesia.

Germany was even less fortunate in the colonial settlement. It was stripped of all its colonies, but the Allies refrained from incorporating them directly because one of the Fourteen Points had promised that colonial claims would be impartially adjusted and the interests of the population considered. Instead, Germany's colonies were made mandates and placed in the care of more advanced nations, whose duty it was to guide them towards a higher stage of civilization and eventual self-government. This plan pleased Wilson, who was a strong believer in the evolutionary nature of the state and society and who readily agreed that colonial peoples were generally not yet capable of handling their own affairs. The moral flavor of the mandate system was somewhat weakened by the fact that Britain and France were given nearly all of Germany's African colonies and that Japan took its holdings in the north Pacific and China, in spite of strong protests from the Chinese, who had entered the war on the allied side.

To remove any future threat of German aggression, the German army was limited to 100,000 men, and its navy was sharply restricted in size and denied submarines. Furthermore, Germany was forbidden to fortify the right bank of the Rhine River, thereby leaving France free to invade at will. As a further guarantee to France, the United States and Great Britain promised to come to France's aid if Germany attacked, but Congress later refused to ratify this treaty.

By the terms of the armistice, Germany was expected to pay compensation for "all damage done to the civilian population of the Allies and their property." This already tremendous sum was doubled by adding the cost of pensions given to allied soldiers. The total amount claimed by the Allies reached fantastic proportions. Both France and Belgium asked for sums greater than their total wealth in 1914. Even the Allies realized that Germany could never pay the total claim, and in the end it was decided to establish a Reparations Commission to determine the amount and method of payment. In addition, Germany was required to make payments in kind. Although Germany's people were hungry as a result of the allied blockade, it was required to surrender a large amount of livestock. Although some of its best coal fields had been given to France and Poland, Germany was required to give the victors forty million tons of coal annually for the next ten years. Virtually Germany's entire merchant marine was surrendered, and it was required to build 200,000 ships' tonnage annually for five years for the Allies.

Partly to justify these heavy reparations, the Allies stipulated in Article 231 of the treaty that the war had been "imposed upon them by the aggression of Germany and her allies." This War Guilt Clause was poor history and poor diplomacy; it poisoned the atmosphere of Europe for years to come. The treaty also made provisions for the trial of the Kaiser and other "war criminals." Happily, the Dutch, with whom William II had found asylum, refused to surrender him and only a dozen lesser figures were ever brought to trial. The treaty also called for the creation of a League of Nations, but Germany was not permitted to join.

The newly established German republic protested strongly against the treaty. Its representatives pointed out that it violated the terms of the armistice, but the Allies refused to make significant modifications. A renewal of the war was impossible because by the terms of the armistice they had had to give the Allies large quantities of guns, airplanes, and railroad equipment as well as bridgeheads over the Rhine. In July, 1919, the helpless democratic parties in the National Assembly voted to accept the treaty.

THE OTHER PEACE TREATIES

Austria-Hungary had gradually disintegrated during the last years of the war. Two university professors, Thomas Masaryk (1850-1937) and Eduard Beneš (1884-1948), had organized a Czech army among the prisoners taken by the Allies and gained recognition for a new Czech-Slovak republic prior to the armistice. During the same period, the Serbs, Croats, and Montenegrins had agreed on the formation of a Yugoslav kingdom under the Serbian royal dynasty, and Austria and Hungary had grown further apart. Emperor Charles encouraged the imperial bureaucracy to assist in these changes, and he himself retired to Switzerland where he hopefully awaited a recall to the throne of one of his former territories. In this manner, the historic Habsburg monarchy quietly disappeared; it remained for the peacemakers of 1919 to redraw the boundaries of central Europe.

The Germans in Austria established a republic and claimed that since they were as much a new state as Czechoslovakia, they should not be penalized as a defeated nation. The Allies paid scant attention to this argument; by the terms of the Treaty of St. Germain, Italy was given the region south of the Brenner Pass as promised in the secret treaties. Two hundred and fifty thousand Germans were thereby turned over to Italy, in spite of the stipulation in the Fourteen Points that boundaries would be drawn along clearly recognizable lines of nationality. Ethnic considerations were also overlooked when the Germans in the Sudetenland and Moravia were given to Czechoslovakia on the ground that they had been part of the historic crown of Bohemia. In all, Austria lost three-fourths of its former territory and four of the ten million Germans who had once lived within its boundaries. In addition, Austria was required to disarm and to pay reparations. The Allies even denied Austria the right to have submarines, a strange precaution since it no longer had a sea coast. Of a once great empire, little remained beyond the city of Vienna and some Alpine scenery. The new republic hoped to join Germany, but once more the Allies denied the right of self-determination. France was fearful that such a union would make Germany stronger.

Hungary fared no better. Its leaders first followed the Czech example and asked that its boundaries conform to the historic crown of Hungary; when this was denied, they begged in vain for a plebiscite. By the terms of the Treaty of Trianon, Hungary lost all but 28 per cent of its territory and 3,500,000 Magyars, many of whom could have easily been included within its boundaries. Again there were reparations and arms limitations.

Czechoslovakia profited most by the demise of the Habsburg Empire, for the entire country was carved from the former monarchy. Poland was given Galicia; Rumania, Transylvania; Yugoslavia, Slavonia, Croatia, Bosnia, and Herzegovina; and Italy, Trentino and Trieste—less than it had been promised in the secret treaties. By the terms of the Treaty of

THE DISSOLUTION OF THE
AUSTRO-HUNGARIAN EMPIRE
--- BOUNDARY OF AUSTRO-HUNGARY 1914

TO ITALY
TO YUGOSLAVIA
TO POLAND
TO RUMANIA
TO CZECHOSLOVAKIA

SCALE OF MILES
0 25 50   100   150

RUSSIA

POLAND

WARSAW

DNIESTER R.

GALICIA

RUTHENIA

CZECHOSLOVAKIA

MORAVIA

BOHEMIA

PRAGUE

DANUBE R.

VIENNA

AUSTRIA

BUDAPEST

HUNGARY

TISZA R.

TRANSYLVANIA

MAROS R.

RUMANIA

BANAT

BUCHAREST

DANUBE R.

BLACK
SEA

TURKEY

BULGARIA

BELGRADE

DRAVA R.

CROATIA-SLAVONIA

YUGOSLAVIA

BOSNIA-
HERZEGOVINA

TRIESTE

TRENTINO

ADRIATIC SEA

ITALY

GERMANY

SWITZERLAND

45°

15°

10°

Neuilly, Bulgaria was cut off from the Aegean Sea, to the profit of Greece, and had to make small territorial concessions to Yugoslavia. Rumania profited by the confusion in Russia to get Bessarabia, where many Rumanian-speaking people lived. Where once the multinational Habsburg and Ottoman empires had held sway, there were now nine states, none of whom were economically self-sufficient or capable of defending themselves. Even the problem of nationalism had not been completely solved, for Czechoslovakia, Rumania, and Yugoslavia were left with serious minority problems.

The collapse of the Russian Empire permitted many of the subject nationalities in eastern Europe to create independent states. Finland, Estonia, Latvia, and Lithuania had all proclaimed their independence after the abdication of the Tsar and managed to maintain their position thereafter, in spite of Bolshevik efforts to regain possession. An independent Polish republic was likewise created. Its southern and western boundaries were established by the peacemakers in France, but the Russian Revolution and the absence of Russian diplomats at the peace conference made it difficult to settle on an eastern frontier. The diplomats attempted to resolve the matter by preparing the Curzon Line, which gave Poland only those regions in the east which were predominantly Polish. This the new republic refused to accept, and between 1919 and 1920 a war was fought with the Bolsheviks. In the end the Poles, with French technical assistance, were successful, and in the Treaty of Riga, 1921, they were awarded additional territory at Russia's expense. Their boundaries were still short of those before the first partition of 1772, but nevertheless their country was now the sixth largest in Europe. As a result, over a fifth of the population was non-Polish; from being an abused nationality, the Poles had become the abusers. The Russians lost more square miles of territory as a result of the war than any other people, although they stood first in the number of casualties suffered in the allied cause. As might have been anticipated, they regarded their losses as temporary and eagerly awaited an opportunity to regain their former position.

The peace settlement with the former Ottoman Empire was also achieved only after another war. Turkish resistance had collapsed in October, 1918, but it was not until 1920 that the Allies imposed the Treaty of Sèvres on the helpless, incompetent sultan. By its terms, all claims to non-Turkish territory had to be renounced. Armenia and Hijaz were recognized as independent. Palestine, Transjordan, and Iraq were made British mandates, and Syria a French mandate. Thrace was given to Greece, and eastern Anatolia, where there were a large number of Greeks, was turned over to Greece to be administered. Egypt was recognized as a British protectorate, and the Italians obtained some islands in the Aegean Sea. There was no longer a tsarist Russia to claim Constantinople and the Straits; even so, little remained of the Ottoman Empire that had besieged Vienna 237 years before.

785

At this point there was a startling reversal of fortune. Mustapha Kemal Pasha (1881-1938), an ardent Young Turk nationalist and Westernizer, began to organize a movement to keep all of Anatolia under Turkish sovereignty. When the sultan, backed by the Allies, ignored his proposals, he adopted an independent course. A distinguished general, he raised an army which reconquered Armenia, drove the Greek army from Anatolia, deposed the sultan, and established a republic. The Allies were too tired of war to resist so determined a leader. By the terms of the Treaty of Lausanne, eastern Thrace was returned and Turkey's control of all of Anatolia was recognized. The Straits were demilitarized and opened to all ships in time of peace. It was also agreed that the 400,000 Turks living in the Balkans would be returned to Turkey and the 1,300,000 Greeks whose ancestors had settled in Anatolia 2,500 years before would be sent back to Greece. These dispossessed people suffered greatly, but there was one beneficial result: there was no longer a nationality problem to poison the relations between the states. The weak, divided Ottoman Empire had been replaced by a republic that exerted a stabilizing influence over the entire region.

How wise were the peacemakers of the 1919 era as compared with those of 1815? The latter had treated their defeated foe generously. France, who was far more responsible for the wars between 1792 and 1815 than Germany was for the conflict between 1914 and 1918, had been permitted to participate in the peace conference, had been given a slight increase in territory, and had quickly resumed its place among the great powers. The restored Bourbons and most of their subjects had no desire to alter forcibly the terms of the treaty. The Germans, on the other hand, had been handed a dictated peace which violated the terms of the armistice. They had been severely punished, and their new republic was not admitted to the League of Nations. It is not surprising that every German became dedicated to the task of altering the Versailles settlement. The question was whether they would use peaceful means to achieve their ends. In justice to the allied statesmen, they were not free agents. As representatives of democracies, they were responsible to the people, and while the people wanted peace without victory in November, 1918, they wanted to see their enemies punished once the war had definitely come to an end.

The peacemakers of 1815 had sought a balance of power, but by ignoring the question of nationality they had paved the way for the wars of German and Italian unification. The peacemakers of 1919 had sought to determine boundaries by nationalities. In spite of the exceptions they made to benefit their allies at the expense of their foes, the map of Europe in 1919 reflected nationalities and the desires of the people better than any of its predecessors. But the peacemakers of 1919 ignored the question of the balance of power, and by creating a host of small states in eastern Europe, they invited aggressive moves by the Germans and Russians. The peace of 1815 lasted nearly a half century without a major modification

TERRITORIAL CHANGES AFTER W.W. I
TERRITORY LOST IN WORLD WAR I BY

RUSSIA
GERMANY
AUSTRIA-HUNGARY
BULGARIA

SCALE OF MILES
0 50 100 200 300 400

ATLANTIC OCEAN

GREAT BRITAIN
LONDON

NORTH SEA

NORWAY
OSLO

SWEDEN
STOCKHOLM

FINLAND

LENINGRAD

RUSSIA

MOSCOW

BALTIC SEA

DENMARK
COPENHAGEN

ESTONIA
LATVIA
LITHUANIA
MEMEL
DANZIG

EAST PRUSSIA

POSEN R.
WARSAW
VISTULA
PINSK

KIEV

BUG R.

DNIESTER R.

BESSARABIA

BLACK SEA

THE NETHERLANDS
AMSTERDAM
HAMBURG
BERLIN

GERMANY

ODER R.

SILESIA

CURZON LINE 1919-1920

SAN R.

CZECHOSLOVAKIA
PRAGUE

RUMANIA
BUCHAREST

DANUBE R.

BULGARIA
SOPHIA

CONSTANTINOPLE

BRUSSELS
BEL.

PARIS

FRANCE

LOIRE R.

RHINE R.

DANUBE R.
MUNICH

ALSACE

BERN
SWITZ.

RHONE R.

AUSTRIA
VIENNA

HUNGARY
BUDAPEST

YUGOSLAVIA
BELGRADE

ITALY

ROME

DANUBE R.

SPAIN
MADRID

PORTUGAL
LISBON

50°
40°

30°
20°
0°
10°
20°

and a full century without a world war. The peace of 1919 was already largely altered when war again came to Europe in 1939. Yet the peace-makers of 1919 should not be blamed too harshly. Had the League of Nations corrected the wrongs perpetrated by the treaties, had it become an effective agent of collective security, had the Wilsonian program been truly fulfilled during the following years, there need have been no World War II.

POSTWAR PROBLEMS

The desire for peace was almost universal in 1919, but many states had policies that made the abolition of war difficult. The French were obsessed by fear of a German revival, because in spite of its losses, Germany had a larger population and a greater industrial potential. The French therefore sought every means to keep Germany in the weakened position in which it had been placed by the Versailles treaty. The defeated states with equal logic bent their efforts towards securing a revision of the peace settlement which they regarded as unjust and degrading.

Had the Allies continued to cooperate, this situation might not have been dangerous, but the British gradually awoke to the fact that they had destroyed the balance of power in Europe that had been so advantageous to them between 1815 and 1914. They began to look favorably on a mild German revival as a check on France, with whom they were having some quarrels in the colonial sphere, and as a bulwark against Communist Russia in central and eastern Europe. The Italians' position was much the same. Their growth since 1859 had been due less to their own power than to the fact that there had been a balance of power in Europe. By selling their support to one side and then another, they had been able to achieve their present position. They were still far from content, however, because the peace treaties had failed to give them all they had been promised. As there was no opportunity for further growth so long as France dominated the continent, a mild German revival was also acceptable to them.

The United States withdrew from the continent after the war, thoroughly disillusioned by the secret treaties and what was regarded as the grasping, selfish behavior of all Europeans. The Senate refused to ratify the peace treaties or to join the League of Nations, so determined were Americans to avoid further foreign commitments that might involve them in war. A sympathy for Germany developed in some circles that was quickly augmented by the revelations of American historians studying unpublished German diplomatic documents. Germany, it was now found, had not premeditatedly caused the war. Such influence as the United States consented to wield in Europe was therefore dedicated to achieving a mild improvement in the German position.

THE LEAGUE OF NATIONS

Wilson had recognized that there were unwise provisions in the peace treaties and that new causes for conflicts between nations would arise. To solve these problems, he had secured the consent of the allied states to the creation of a League of Nations. Often he had made concessions during peace negotiations that he thought unwise but necessary if the League was to win general acceptance; he had hoped that the League, once established, would rectify the injustices.

The League was not the first international organization for preserving peace. After the Treaty of Utrecht, 1713, the great powers had cooperated for a time with beneficial results, and the eighteenth-century philosophers had never wearied of drawing up plans for international organizations to preserve the peace.[16] After the Napoleonic Wars, the Concert of Europe had functioned effectively as an international organization for a number of years, and the representatives of the great powers did not cease to meet together to settle their differences until the debacle of 1914. The laws of war had been defined by the Hague Peace Conference of 1899, and a permanent court of arbitration had been established. Nations were not compelled to submit their disputes to the court, but the means were available to settle quarrels peaceably if the contesting parties so desired. What was unique about the League of Nations was its size, scope, and ambitions.

The League had an Assembly in which all the member-states were represented. The Assembly was essentially a debating forum where any matter "affecting the peace of the world" could be discussed. Important decisions were actually made by the Council. The Council consisted of representatives of the great powers and from four to eleven minor states elected periodically by the Assembly. Unanimity was required except in procedural matters. A Secretariat was also created. It consisted of over 500 secretaries, translators, and administrators to handle matters related to the functioning of the League. A Permanent Court of Arbitration was maintained, and a Permanent Court of International Justice was created to settle disputes between states on the basis of international law. In the first two decades of its existence, it rendered thirty-two judgments. The Court was equally active in giving advisory decisions at the request of the Assembly or the Council. The League also had a number of commissions which did everything from fighting diseases, combating the opium trade, and studying the currency problem to supervising the disarmament of the Central Powers and administering the Saar Basin. An International Labor Organization was formed to improve the conditions of working people, and a number of other international organizations were started for everyone from art dealers to poultry owners. These commissions and

[16] See pages 418-419 and 397.

*Humanity accuses the United States Senate of murdering the Versailles
treaty. From the New York* WORLD, *March 22, 1920. (Bettmann Archive)*

international organizations alone did enough good to justify the relatively
small costs of the League, but they were not enough to secure the peace
of the world. And this was the League's main purpose.

The League had a capital, Geneva, Switzerland; it had executive, legislative, and judicial organs, but it was not a world government. Like the
American Articles of Confederation, it acted upon the member-states,
not the people. States were not compelled to settle their disputes in its
courts, and only economic sanctions could be imposed to halt aggression.
This was adequate if every nation complied, for no nation was completely self-sufficient, but unanimity was difficult to achieve. The United
States refused to join the League for fear of being drawn into another
conflict; Great Britain and some other powers failed to cooperate fully for
various reasons; and Germany and Russia were not at first permitted to

790

join. The French, on the other hand, wanted to strengthen the League and use it as an instrument for their own security. They advocated the creation of an international army, but this proposal was rejected and the League remained impotent when confronted by a large, determined aggressor. It did, however, render sixty-six political decisions between 1920 and 1939, some of which prevented wars, and by its very existence it caused some states to refrain from aggressive action.

This was not enough for France. Neither Clemenceau nor his successors put much faith in such an organization. They would have been content with a joint Anglo-American pledge of aid in case of German aggression. This Wilson had promised in return for France's surrender of its claims to the left bank of the Rhine. When the pledge became a dead letter because of the United States' Senate's refusal to ratify the treaty, the French felt justified in providing for their own security through three means. First, they maintained a huge army with trained reserves that could easily crush the Germans, whose 100,000 men were not allowed airplanes, tanks, heavy artillery, or trained reserves. Second, they created a new alliance system. As Russia was no longer strong or respectable, they turned to the Poles, who also feared a German revival. Czechoslovakia, Rumania, and Yugoslavia had profited greatly from the war and were fearful of a Habsburg restoration. They formed the Little Entente after the war, and France became their sponsor. These states were not great powers, but they each had armies larger than Germany's and their aid would make the Germans once more fight on two fronts. Third, the French did all they could to prevent a German revival. The Versailles treaty was made a sacred document that could not be altered, and the League of Nations was made an instrument to preserve the status quo just as the Concert of Europe had become.

To combat the French predominance, the Italians looked across the Adriatic Sea and sought friendship with Austria, Hungary, and Bulgaria, their enemies several years before but now their means to rival French influence in the Danube Basin. More serious, the allied decision to exclude the Soviet Union from the peace conference and the League of Nations made it seek the friendship of that other power which had been ostracized from the family of nations. In 1922 the Soviet Union and Germany signed a treaty at Rapallo initiating close political and economic ties. Once more, Europe was haunted by the specter of rival alliance systems, but the French, instead of relenting in the hope of winning German friendship, decided to insist that reparations be collected, not only to solve their own financial problems, but also to check Germany's economic revival.

On May 1, 1921, the Allies had announced that the Germans owed $33,000,000,000, exclusive of the Belgian war debt which they were also to pay. A schedule of payments was established and an interest rate of 5 per cent on the balance due was required. The only way the Germans could get the gold or credits to pay such a sum was to export substantially more than they imported. This they were prevented from doing because of tariff barriers and competition from other countries. The value of the German mark declined rapidly; the Germans defaulted in their payments, and on January 11, 1923, French and Belgian troops, mindful of the Rapallo Treaty, occupied the highly industrialized Ruhr Valley over British and American protests. The French goal was to extract reparations and to encourage the Rhineland Germans to set up a separate state. They were met, not by an army, but by the passive resistance of the people. The Ruhr industries ceased to operate, the mark fell precipitously, and the French franc declined as it became increasingly evident that substantial reparations would not be collected.

THE PERIOD OF COOPERATION

In August, 1923, Gustav Stresemann (1878-1929) became chancellor of Germany and embarked on a policy of cooperation. Every reasonable effort was made to meet treaty obligations in the hope that eventually the Allies would accept Germany back into the family of nations and remove the treaty's most objectionable features. Passive resistance was abandoned, and a settlement prepared by the British and Americans known as the Dawes Plan was accepted by all concerned. Troops were withdrawn from the Ruhr Valley, a $200,000,000 loan was made to Germany to enable it to establish a new sound currency, and reparation payments were reduced and made to vary with Germany's prosperity. No time limit was set on the number of payments. In 1929 the Young Plan provided that they would be terminated in 1988, nearly three generations after the war.

One reason the Allies were so insistent on reparations which they, or at least their economists, knew the Germans could not pay was that the United States refused to cancel the war debts they owed it. France, Great Britain, and other states depended on reparations for the funds to pay installments on American loans. If one were reduced or cancelled, so must the other be. Only if the United States reduced its tariffs and bought more goods than it sold, could they repay their loans without receiving reparations. This the Republican administration in Washington never seriously considered doing. What happened after 1924 was that American bankers loaned Germany money, the Germans paid reparations to the Allies, and the Allies paid their debts to the United States. When the Great Depression caused the American loans to cease, reparations and debt payments also stopped. The Germans could have paid something, but they could not have paid all that was demanded. Not feeling responsible for the war, they saw no reason why they should bear its cost. The whole reparations war-debt question served only to poison international relations for a number of years. Fortunately, with the advent of Stresemann and the Dawes Plan a willingness to compromise returned to the world. Indeed, a period was inaugurated when it looked as though the dream of perpetual peace, security, and prosperity might be achieved.

Aristide Briand (1862-1932), who became foreign minister in April, 1925, reversed French policy in regard to Germany. It was through his efforts and those of Stresemann that the old enemies achieved a partial reconciliation. In a conference held at Locarno in October of that year, Germany, France, and Belgium agreed to accept their present boundaries. Disputes that arose were to be arbitrated, and Great Britain and Italy promised to come to the aid of the injured party if the agreement were violated. France, at last, was given the security it sought, and Germany was invited to join the League of Nations and given a permanent seat in the Council in return for accepting the loss of Alsace-Lorraine. An attempt was also made at Locarno to establish Germany's eastern frontier in the same manner, but no German statesman would ever accept the separation of East Prussia from Germany, nor was Britain willing to act as guarantor. Stresemann did agree not to seek to change the eastern frontier by force, and arbitration treaties were signed with Poland and Czechoslovakia. France promised to come to the aid of both these states in event of German aggression.

Other nonaggression and arbitration pacts followed. As a friendly gesture, Briand suggested in 1927 that the United States and France make such an agreement. Frank Kellogg (1856-1937), the American secretary of state, countered with the suggestion that the nations of the world should be asked to renounce war as an instrument of national policy and to promise to settle their disputes by peaceful means. Sixty-three states, including Japan, Soviet Russia, and the other major powers, signed the pact. Some states expressly reserved the right to fight in self-defense, but at the time this did not seem very important, for how could there be another war if everyone had promised not to be an aggressor?

Armaments were widely regarded during this period as being an important cause of war. Wilson had advocated disarmament in his Fourteen Points, and in 1919 the Allies had told the Germans that they would reduce the size of their armed forces also. Actual disarmament, however, proved difficult to achieve because each nation thought that its security depended on its being stronger than its neighbor. The Washington Conference of 1921-1922 did succeed in preventing a naval race between the recent allies. A ratio of 5-5-3-1.67-1.67 was established on the tonnage of capital ships of Great Britain, the United States, Japan, France, and Italy, respectively. Agreement could not be reached concerning smaller vessels of 10,000 tons or less at this time or on the size of land forces at later conferences, but in 1930 the naval limitations were extended to cover cruisers and submarines.

Thus, a decade after the armistice, the Great War seemed a horrible nightmare, a temporary step backward in man's progress towards happiness and perfection. Such a mistake could not happen again! The men of 1928 believed that the principal causes of war had been removed by redrawing the map of Europe approximately in accordance with nationality, giving the people control of their governments, and outlawing secret negotiations and secret treaties. States had promised to settle their disputes peaceably, a League of Nations had been created with some coercive powers, naval armaments had been limited, and plans were constantly being offered to reduce the size of armies. France and Germany, those historic enemies, were now cooperating. There was even talk of a European Union by no less a figure than Aristide Briand. The triumph of Western civilization seemed almost complete. But the hopes of the men of 1928 were soon to be dashed, and talk of ethical progress was soon to be relegated to the naïve. The twentieth-century crisis was at hand.

PART **VI**

THE TWENTIETH-CENTURY CRISIS

AMERICA	EUROPE	AFRO-ASIA
	c.1860-c.1930, Mendel and others found science of genetics	
.1890-1966, Improvements in medicine decrease mortality rate; industrialization and urbanization accelerate; vast improvements in transportation and communication	**c.1890-1966,** Improvements in medicine decrease mortality rate; industrialization and urbanization accelerate; vast improvements in transportation and communication	
	c.1895-c.1930, Einstein and others revolutionize physics	
	c.1900-c.1939, Freud undermines optimistic view of man	
	1914-1918, World War I	
	1917, Russian Revolution begins	
	1918-1924, Lenin establishes communist state in Russia	**1918-1940,** Revolt against European imperialism gains momentum in Asia and North Africa
	1918-1933, Weimar Republic	
1920-1930, Period of political scandal and lawlessness; business plays dominant role in government		**1920,** Gandhi becomes leader of Congress party
	1922, Liberal party begins decline in Britain; Mussolini becomes dictator	
	1923, Inflation in Germany	
	1925, Locarno conference	
		1927, Communists expelled from Kuomintang
1929, Wall Street Crash	**1929,** Great Depression begins; Stalin becomes dictator	
		1932, Sino-Japanese war begins
1933-1937, Period of New Deal legislation	**1933,** Hitler becomes dictator	
	1935, Italy attacks Ethiopia	
	1936-1939, Spanish Civil War	
		1937, British partition Palestine

AMERICA	EUROPE	AFRO-ASIA
	1938, Hitler seizes Austria, occupies Sudetenland	
	1939, Hitler attacks Poland; Britain and France declare war on Germany	
	1940, Paris falls; Battle of Britain begins	
1941, Japanese attack Pearl Harbor; U.S. declares war on Axis	1941, Hitler invades Russia	1941, Japanese attack Pearl Harbor
	1942-1943, Turning point of World War II; U.S. takes offensive in Pacific; Allies take North Africa; Russians counterattack; Teheran conference	1942, Battle of Midway
1943-1944, U.S. retakes strategic Pacific islands; recovers Philippines		1943-1944, U.S. retakes strategic Pacific islands; recovers Philippines
	1944, Allies land at Normandy	
	1944-1945, Formation of U.N.	
	1944-1948, Eastern Europe comes under communist control	
	1945, Yalta conference; surrender of Germany	1945, Atomic bomb dropped on Hiroshima and Nagasaki; Japan surrenders to U.S.
	1945-1953, Stalin rebuilds Russian industrial capacity	1945-1966, Revolt against colonialism spreads
1947, Marshall Plan begins; Churchill's "Iron Curtain" speech	1947, Beginning of Marshall Plan and of rapid European recovery	1947, Partition of Indian subcontinent
		1947-1950, Communists drive Nationalists out of China; Mao transforms China into communist state
		1948-1964, Nehru leads Congress party
	1949, Russia explodes its first atomic bomb	
1950-1953, Korean War		1950-1953, Korean War
1952-1960, Eisenhower administration		
	1953, Death of Stalin	
		1954, Nasser becomes dictator; Arab nationalism increases; French withdraw from Indo-China
	1957, Formation of EEC	
	1957-1964, Khrushchev era	
1959, Castro becomes dictator	1958, Russians launch first earth satellite; beginning of Fifth Republic under DeGaulle	1958, Chinese Communists begin "Great Leap Forward"
1960-1963, Kennedy administration		1960, Seventeen African colonies become independent
1961, Alliance for Progress and Latin Free Trade Association formed	1961, Berlin Wall	1960-1964, Continual fighting in the Congo
1962, Cuban missile crisis		
1962-1964, Reapportionment decisions of Supreme Court		
1963, Assassination of Kennedy		
1964, Civil Rights Bill; election of Johnson		1964, Federation of Malaysia formed

THE course of Western civilization from the late seventeenth century had evolved along relatively consistent lines except for the romantic interlude. We have seen how the middle class and the ideals of liberty, social equality, and nationalism became ascendant in many Western countries, how most people believed that progress towards happiness and human perfection was possible because man was molded by his environment, and how they admitted the existence of only a mechanistic, material world which could be experienced.

Four revolutions took place during the first half of the twentieth century that altered this course and led to a new crisis in Western civilization. One revolution was in aesthetics and reversed the emphasis on naturalism and classicism that had generally dominated the artistic world since the Renaissance. A second revolution was in science and shook the very foundations of thought. The reality of material things was challenged by the new physics, and the omnipotence of the environment was challenged by new discoveries in genetics and psychology. The distinctions between energy and matter and between animate and inanimate objects became blurred. Some intellectuals who comprehended these discoveries lost faith in progress. They faltered, and failed to provide leadership for the masses of mankind. The masses, separated from their leaders and bewildered by war and depression, sought new prophets. Too often they found them in dedicated communist or fascist demagogues who turned their fears into hatreds and their hopes into violent deeds.

Out of this chaos two more revolutions brought the Communists to power in Russia and the Fascists to power in Italy, Germany, and other states. Both threatened the political, social, and economic bases of the Western democracies. Torture once more became a weapon of the police, and slave labor returned on a larger, more violent scale than ever before in Europe. A second world war ensued in which the Communists and the Western democracies destroyed the fascist states, only to confront each other in a "cold war" in which both sides sought the allegiance of the underdeveloped countries that were emerging in Asia, Africa, and Latin America. Whether the current crisis marks the end of modern Western civilization or whether it marks a momentary confusion before our civilization moves forward to new triumphs, only time can tell.

797

18/ The Revolutions, I

THE scientific and intellectual revolutions of the seventeenth century had profoundly affected nearly every form of human activity. They were primarily responsible for defining the objectives sought during the age of egalitarian revolutions, and they had also helped lead to such momentous changes in agriculture and industry that a far higher standard of living was achieved by the Western world than by any other civilization.

By the early twentieth century, it was apparent that a new scientific revolution was taking place. This scientific revolution promises to be even more significant than its predecessor, although it is still too early to predict exactly what its ultimate impact will be on society and thought. It has already led to far-reaching technological developments that enable the average citizen today to live in luxury scarcely dreamed of several generations ago, but by providing atomic energy, rapid transportation, and mass communication, it has created conditions which threaten life and liberty as never before. Today, man is learning how to change one element into another and to create new forms of life. He is mastering the universe, but his survival depends on whether he can master himself.

THE SCIENTIFIC REVOLUTION

THE NEW PHYSICS

Beginning in 1893, the University of Chicago catalogue stated that " . . . it seems probable that most of the grand underlying principles [in the physical sciences] have been firmly established and that further advances are to be sought chiefly in the rigorous application of these principles to all the phenomena which come under our notice." This statement was probably not written by the ordinary academic administrator, but by Professor Albert A. Michelson (1852-1931), a distinguished scientist who had just completed a very delicate experiment with what seemed to be negative results. It had been believed that space was composed of a weightless, transparent substance called ether, which carried light and through which the earth moved in its orbit around the sun. As it was most improbable that ether would move in the same direction and at the same speed as the earth, light transmitted in the direction ether was moving should travel faster than light transmitted against the ether current, just as a swimmer goes faster downstream than upstream. By measuring the speed of light transmitted in different directions, Michelson hoped to find the direction and speed of the ether current. To his surprise, he discovered that light traveled at the same velocity in all directions. The fact that the speed of light did not vary with the motion of its source or of the observer defied the conception held by Galileo, Newton, and the classical physics of absolute time and absolute motion. In the attempt to resolve this dilemma, a scientific revolution was born.

The man who resolved the difficulty was a young German scientist named Albert Einstein (1879-1955). In 1905 he published his doctoral dissertation on the theory of relativity. Five years later, the University of Chicago recognized the impending revolution by dropping the statement quoted above from its catalogue, and by 1949 light, motion, gravity, and electromagnetism had been brought into a single system. Traditional physics had been abandoned, and physicists appeared to be nearing a new synthesis, the first since that of Sir Isaac Newton.

The methods Einstein used are too complex to be explained adequately in a history text, but the conclusions he reached must be considered. Time and space, he found, are not absolute, but relative. They are interwoven into what he called a time-space continuum. Time, in short, is a sort of fourth dimension. If a spaceship traveling at 99 per cent of the speed of light went to the star Procyon and returned, the time of flight measured by an earth calendar would be twenty-one years, but the clock on the space-

Albert Einstein. (Courtesy Yerkes Observatory)

ship would indicate only a three-year lapse of time and the space traveler would have aged by only three years. Voyages to the most distant points of the universe are therefore theoretically possible. A space traveler would age only 27.5 years in a voyage to the Andromeda galaxy, but when he returned to the earth, he would be fortunate indeed if the nation that sent him still existed or even if the homo sapiens still dominated our globe, for three million earth years would have elapsed.

In a paper entitled "Direct Contact among Galactic Civilizations by Relativistic Interstellar Space Flight," Harvard astronomer Carl Sagan declared, "Allowing for a modicum of scientific and technological progress within the next few centuries I believe that interstellar space flight at relativistic velocities to the farthest reaches of our galaxy is a feasible objective for humanity." The reverse is also true. There is no reason why advanced civilizations in other parts of the universe could not send expeditions to the earth. Indeed, one may be on the way now.

Space, or mass—the capacity to occupy space—is likewise relative. As a traveler approached the speed of light in his voyage, his spaceship would shorten in the direction of his motion, and if the speed of light were achieved, it would be transformed into energy. The historic distinction between mass (matter) and energy is destroyed in accordance with the equation $E = mc^2$. In this equation E represents energy, m the mass of an object, and c the velocity of light. Since the speed of light is about 186,000 miles per second, c^2 is a tremendous number, 34,596,000,000 to be explicit. A pound of coal burned the ordinary way will not run a locomotive very long, but a pound of coal transformed into energy by moving at the speed of light would provide 11,400,000 kilowatt hours of electricity, enough to last the entire United States for several weeks. Einstein's formula thus provided the theoretical basis for the construction of the atomic bomb and for an almost unlimited supply of energy that could be turned to constructive purposes.

In developing the equations for his theory, Einstein made use of a new type of mathematics formulated during the nineteenth century. Euclid had based his geometry upon certain postulates which he had regarded as self-evident truths. Upon these postulates, the theorems of the traditional geometry and related subjects had been constructed. Included were the postulates that the shortest distance between any two points was in a straight line and that a straight line may be extended without limit in either direction. But suppose the shortest distance between two points was a curved line; or that if a straight line were extended without limit in either direction, it would bend back and form a circle? Upon such postulates a system of non-Euclidean geometry had been developed, and Einstein, by accepting them, found it necessary to reconstruct the theories of the universe.

To Einstein, the universe is not infinite in its extent, as had been thought for nearly four centuries, but rather it is finite, as most ancient and medieval astronomers had believed. This does not mean that a space traveler moving at 99 per cent of the speed of light would ever come to the "end" of the universe, for space is curved and he would bend back upon himself. Just as an airplane could fly around the earth indefinitely without changing its direction or coming to an "end," so a space traveler would never come to an "end" of his journey. He might see the same things twice just as our airplane pilot, but it has been estimated that it would take him over 3,000,000,000,000,000,000,000 earth-measured years before he returned to his starting point for the first time. It is fortunate indeed that time would be almost meaningless to a traveler at that rate of speed.

The fact that the universe was depicted as being finite once more did not mean that man was returned to the exalted place he had enjoyed in the scheme of things prior to the Copernican Revolution. The universe, as the illustration of the space traveler in the preceding paragraph shows, remained boundless. Indeed, astronomers are constantly increasing their estimates of its extent; one theory holds that our finite, boundless universe is now expanding at a rate of about 60,000 miles per second. The earth as it is now depicted is but a tiny part of a solar system which is part of the galaxy or star cluster we call the Milky Way. The Milky Way is about 100,000 light years (a light year is the distance light travels in one year, or about 6,000,000,000,000 miles) in diameter. It has been estimated that there is enough material in the universe to form 100 billion stars with an average mass equal to that of the sun. The telescope has located galaxies 2 billion light years away. The light which we now receive from these galaxies had traveled three-fourths the distance to the earth by the time the earliest known fossils in any rocks were formed. Other galaxies are known to lie beyond these. Although higher forms of life probably do not exist anywhere in our solar system except on the earth, it is quite possible that there are millions of other planets in the universe with life as advanced as man or more advanced. Only the optimist would arbitrarily give man the highest place in the order of things.

Momentous as were Einstein's theories concerning the universe, they were no more important than the discoveries that were being made at the same time concerning the nature of the matter that composed it. We have seen how, during the nineteenth century, chemists had come to believe that the earth consisted of ninety-two elements.[1] Elements could be combined to form compounds and mixtures, but they were considered indestructible. Most scientists believed that atoms were the smallest particle into which an element could be divided.

These theories began to be disrupted in 1895 when Wilhelm Röntgen of Munich discovered X-rays by passing electricity through a tube from which most of the gases had been taken. These X-rays attracted considerable attention because they would pass through opaque material. The following year, Henri Becquerel (1852-1908) made the still more disturbing discovery that uranium spontaneously gave off rays that would penetrate black paper, metal, and other substances. Other elements such as radium were also discovered to emit waves. In 1897 a British scientist, Joseph J. Thomson (1856-1940), made the upsetting suggestion that these rays were not a form of energy, but rather were tiny particles of matter. Max Planck (1858-1947) concurred and in 1900 published his quantum theory, in which he argued that the emission of these particles took place in spurts or jumps and not in a steady stream. In a remarkable feat of theoretical physics, he provided an equation to express this phenomenon. But if particles from uranium and other radioactive elements could pass through matter, could matter be solid? Then, when Pierre and Marie Curie found that radium gave off energy and theorized that it could transform itself into other elements, the distinction that had always been made between matter and energy became questionable. Furthermore, if the atoms of one element could transform themselves into the atoms of another element, how could the composition of the universe be explained?

The atom became the subject of many studies directed towards finding the answer to these questions. By 1911 Lord Ernest Rutherford (1871-1937) was able to offer evidence that the atom consisted of a positive nucleus surrounded by negative electrons. Other discoveries followed, and our current conception of the atom, the basic entity of the universe, took form.

The atom, as science now sees it, is essentially electrical. It consists primarily of a nucleus and one or more negatively charged electrons. The nucleus itself consists of one or more positively charged particles called protons and generally one or more uncharged neutrons. Nearly all the

[1] See pages 623-624.

weight of the atom lies in the nucleus, around which the tiny electrons revolve at a high rate of speed. Atoms vary in size, but they may be thought of as being about one 200 millionth of an inch in diameter. The nucleus occupies about one ten thousandth of this distance. The remainder of the atom consists of empty space, except for the electrons and other tiny particles. If the proton in the nucleus of the atom were the size of a baseball, the electron represented on the same scale would be about a quarter of a mile away. In between there would be nothing. This means that the book you are now holding is not a solid, hard mass as your senses tell you; rather it is almost entirely empty space. A more disturbing thought is that you yourself are composed of atoms and are therefore not what you see and feel yourself to be, but really almost entirely empty space. This explains why the radioactive particles can pass through what was thought to be solid matter.

The implications of these discoveries are immense. One element can be changed into another by altering the number of protons and electrons. Radioactive atoms transform themselves spontaneously; uranium eventually turns into lead. Nonradioactive substances may be transformed by man, either by bombarding the nucleus of an atom with particles from radioactive substances or by using special atom-smashing machines. Man can thus alter the basic components of the universe. By destroying atoms, he can release a tremendous amount of energy, as Einstein showed in his equation $E = mc^2$. Energy and matter become one. Man has found a new, almost unlimited source of power which he may use to make bombs with immense destructive capacity that might destroy life on the earth, or to harness any type of power plant. Since all plant and animal life is composed of atoms, both medicine and agriculture may be revolutionized. Of equal importance is the influence Einstein's theories and the new knowledge of atomic structure may have on the scientific method and our concept of reality.

THE SCIENTIFIC METHOD

The scientific-philosophical method advocated by Newton and Locke and generally accepted by scholars during the eighteenth and nineteenth centuries was based primarily on the inductive method. Data gathered by the senses lay at the base of the ideas that existed in one's mind and of the discoveries of the scientists. Newton, it is true, had a place in his system for hypothesis and for mathematical logic, but he insisted that every hypothesis be checked by experiment. His followers had been vehement in their attacks on the mathematical deductive science of the Cartesians because of the scant attention they paid to observation and experiment. But were not these new great discoveries being made by those who were willing to ignore the common experiences of the everyday world? Einstein talked of a boundless, finite universe, of straight lines that bent, and of a fourth dimension. Time and space ceased to be absolutes; matter and energy ceased to be distinguishable. Since neither man nor matter existed in their observed form, could our senses any longer be taken as our guide?

Some empiricists sought to escape their dilemma by denying the validity of the new discoveries, just as they had denied the Copernican theory because of the rape it committed on their senses. One physicist declared,

> Einstein's "great idea" requires us to surrender our common sense for the sake of an arbitrary dictum of his which he and his followers have raised to a fetish. It is preposterous, and to my way of thinking so inherently idiotic that I cannot understand anyone wasting his breath in giving utterance to such a view. If I had first heard this opinion uttered at a scientific meeting by some scientific nonentity, I should have longed to have got up and said that in my opinion such a view was simply a bit of perverse imbecility.

Other scientists sought escape by refusing to believe that the new theories did more than slightly modify previous thought. When the ideas of relativity and the quantum theory have been thoroughly assimilated, these scientists wrote, "future students of present-day writings on their philosophical implications may wonder what all the fuss was about!"

Powerful voices were heard against these points of view. Astronomer Sir Arthur Eddington (1882-1944) maintained that "there is nothing in the whole system of laws of physics that cannot be deduced unambiguously from epistemological considerations." Or again: "An intelligence unacquainted with our universe . . . should be able to attain all the knowledge of physics that we have attained by experiment." In short, to Eddington mathematical deductive logic unaided by observation or experiment could construct our whole physical theory. Descartes had gone no further. Indeed, Eddington has been accused of advocating a return to the scientific methodology of the Middle Ages.

Chemistry professor Donald H. Andrews (1898-   ) questioned the reality of matter. "Today we can prove that the atom is not a hard, round 'billiard ball,' for we can see inside it and explore it in great detail. And we find that . . . the atom is mostly an empty hole; and since everything material is made of atoms, all things around us . . . are also mostly empty holes.

> We can see still further what this means in the following way. Suppose it is possible to construct an atomic press in which these holes are squeezed out, like squeezing out the holes of a sponge. If my body were compressed down in such a press to the point where it was pure solid matter and no holes, I would be smaller than the tiniest speck of dust which you could see lying on a sheet of paper. . . .
>
> Now, if the atom is really mostly empty space filled with a little electricity and only a tiny speck of matter at its center, we have to revive our ideas about what is real. It is clear that we can no longer take our senses as our guides. . . .
>
> It is the Spirit which is real, and not matter. . . . We live and move

804

in the midst of an invisible world of the Spirit. Thence we came and thither we go.[2]

Andrews carries us back to a system of thought comparable to Neo-Platonic mysticism.

Max Planck, Nobel prize-winning physicist and discoverer of the quantum theory, did not go quite so far. Like Kant, he suggested the existence of two worlds. To him the world revealed by scientific discoveries is the *real world.* "The immediately experienced sense impressions, the primordial sources of scientific activity, have dropped totally out of the world picture, in which sight, hearing, and touch no longer play a part." There is, however, another world, the world of our senses, the world of experience.

What will be the outcome of the debate among scientists and philosophers concerning the significance of the new discoveries is not yet known, but it does seem certain that the dependence on the senses and inductive reasoning that has been so characteristic since the Enlightenment has been shaken. If our environment is not what it seems to be, can it be the all-important molding force of our character? The discoveries in physics raise this question; those in biology and psychology suggest a negative answer.

THE ATTACK ON ENVIRONMENT: HEREDITY

Around 1900 the omnipotent position environment had held for two centuries came under attack. This attack was occasioned primarily by the discovery of new information concerning the laws of heredity and the functioning of the human mind.

In popular parlance, a person might be said to be of "good stock" or one race might be said to be superior to another, but prior to 1900 the idea of heredity was rarely raised by well-informed persons to challenge the position of environment. Indeed, the growth of democracy reduced talk of "good stock" to the level of social snobbery, and environmental conditions were generally considered to be a determining factor of racial character. Nearly all the early advocates of the theory of evolution, including Darwin himself, thought that natural selection was made largely by environmental conditions and that acquired characteristics could be inherited. Thus, the acceptance of the theory of evolution gave additional strength to the already powerful position of the environment as a causative force and made progress toward perfection seem highly probable.

In 1869 Francis Galton published a study showing that brilliant parents were more likely to have brilliant children and imbecilic parents were more likely to have imbecilic children than the mass of mankind. Despite the sensational character of some of his statistics, additional evidence was necessary to support his thesis that intelligence was primarily a product of heredity. After all, the environment of children of brilliant

[2] *Christian Science Sentinel*, LII (May 20, 1950), p. 878.

parents might be presumed to be better than that of children of imbeciles.

The credit for firmly establishing the role of heredity belongs to an Augustinian monk named Gregor Mendel (1822-1884) who carried on a series of experiments with peas in his monastery's garden in Austria between 1854 and 1863. In these experiments, he bred peas with tall and short vines, red and white flowers, and green and yellow seeds. He found that there was no blending of characteristics as Darwin had imagined, but that characteristics were inherited as units. Characteristics in one parent might be recessive, that is, not apparent in the first generation, but apparent in the second. Nevertheless, heredity was an orderly process that could be predicted with almost mathematical precision. Mendel published his findings in the transactions of an obscure natural history society in 1866, but they were overlooked until 1900, when they were discovered by the Dutch biologist Hugo de Vries (1848-1935) and others.

The carriers of the inheritance characteristics were called genes, which were found to reside in cell structures called chromosomes. The life expectancy of a gene has been estimated at 2,500,000 years, but as a person has about 20,000 genes, one gene changes or mutates on an average of every 125 years. These mutations may be recessive or they may be of minor significance, but sometimes important mutations occur. De Vries noted that a black sheep born in a white flock would transmit its blackness to its descendants. The possibility that the evolution of the species is to be explained by these mutations, rather than gradual change caused by chance variation and environmental selection, immediately became apparent. This hypothesis was reinforced by the realization that acquired characteristics could not be inherited because the genes would be unaffected. Today, there are still scientists who believe in micro or gradual evolution, but few deny the powerful role played by heredity.

These discoveries were of both social and philosophical significance. The principles of heredity, or genetics as the new science was called, were applied to domestic plant and animal life. Through scientific breeding, chickens laid more eggs than before, cattle gave more milk, and sheep provided more meat. Hybrid corn likewise proved invaluable. Knowledge about mutations was used to produce a seedless grape, a shortlegged sheep that could not jump over fences, and other varieties of plants and animals that had not formerly existed. In 1929 the American geneticist, H. J. Muller, found that he could produce mutations in flies with X-rays. An infinite number of useful possibilities were thereby opened, but a danger also. If X-rays produced mutations, so did other radioactive materials, such as those from atomic bombs. A person might escape every apparent effect of an atomic blast, but if it caused a gene to mutate, his descendants would be affected. Mutations in human beings are nearly always degenerative and therefore undesirable. A degenerative mutation is passed on for generations.

Other problems raised by the new science of genetics are of equal importance. Man's physical characteristics, intelligence, and innate drives or urges have been shown to depend on heredity. This does not mean that environment is of no importance. Identical twins have the same genes, but if the first is well fed and well educated while the second is poorly fed and poorly educated, the first will grow into a bigger man with a higher I.Q. Heredity, however, places a definite limit on how big, how strong, and how intelligent a person may become, regardless of how favorable the environment may be. Heredity, in short, is undemocratic.

By the process of natural selection, the bearers of undesirable genes have been weeded out in the past, and human civilization has marched forward. Today, with the growth of humanitarianism and social consciousness the weakling and the moron survive, beget children, and pass their genes on to future generations. Many studies were made showing that people in the higher walk of life, who presumably had the best genes, were producing fewer children, while the lower classes continued to have as large families as before. During the first four decades of the twentieth century, there was a decided tendency in many Western countries for college graduates to have two or three children, while those who did not get beyond primary school had six or eight. To many it seemed as though Western civilization must decline if in the future the abler people were a tiny minority. Man, it was pointed out, was the only useful animal that was not scientifically bred. He mated as freely and unintelligently as the scrawny beasts that had wandered over the unclosed commons during the Middle Ages. What intelligent modern farmer would allow a sickly bull to run free in his herd?

The science of eugenics was established to study the problem of heredity and the improvement of mankind. Two related solutions present themselves. One is to decrease the number of children begotten by undesirable parents, and the other is to increase the number begotten by desirable parents. Neither can readily be accomplished in a free democratic society. Only the German Nazis have sought to apply the principles of eugenics on a large scale. Their goal was to preserve a "superior" race rather than a superior class; their barbaric behavior will be described later. Man's ability to alter the genetics of living things may have been greatly enhanced by the discovery of DNA (deoxyribonucleic acid) and RNA (ribonucleic acid). DNA is the principal constituent of chromosomes and is believed to be the substance that stores all genetic information; RNA is thought to be the substance that transmits DNA's information to the cell and thus to the entire organism. DNA and RNA were first identified in 1909 and 1929, respectively, by the Russian-American chemist Phoebus Levene.

THE ATTACK ON ENVIRONMENT: FREUD

The development of a new field in psychology by Sigmund Freud (1856-1939) provided a second blow to those who insisted on the omnipotent influence of environment. Freud was born in Freiberg in Moravia, but his

*Sigmund Freud at the age of eighty.
(Wide World)*

parents moved to Vienna in 1860 where he spent nearly his entire life. Freud was educated as a physician, but early developed an interest in the study of hysteria. Hysteria at this time was treated by hypnotizing patients and then guiding them back through their past in the hope of discovering the cause of the trouble. Patients under hypnosis, Freud noted, recalled events which they had either forgotten or else had pressed from their conscious minds. This indicated to him the existence of an unconscious mind, a discovery that became the basis of his later ideas. Hypnotism, however, failed to provide permanent cures, and Freud decided to gather the necessary information by encouraging patients to relax and talk freely about themselves. He also put considerable emphasis on the interpretation of dreams as a means to discover what lay in the unconscious. Gradually, he emerged with a theory explaining the psychical apparatus of the human mind.

The oldest mental apparatus he called the *id*. "It contains everything that is inherited, that is present at birth, that is . . . the instincts. . . ." A second mental apparatus is the *ego*. The ego is related to that part of the brain which receives sensory perception and controls voluntary movement. It "pursues pleasure and seeks to avoid unpleasure." The third mental apparatus was the *superego*. It consists of traits and social connections learned in childhood primarily as a result of parental influence. Thus, ". . . the id and the superego have one thing in common: they both represent the influences of the past (the id the influence of heredity, the superego essentially the influence of what is taken over from other people), whereas the ego is principally determined by the individual's own experience, that is to say by accidental and current events." Our mental health depends on the interaction of these three apparatuses. Too great a conflict between the id and the superego, for example, may cause a mental breakdown.

The Enlightenment had recognized the existence of the ego and, in a sense, the superego. What Freud had added was the id. Man's mind was not like a blank sheet of paper at birth, as Locke had said. It was motivated by powerful innate forces. Man could not, therefore, be completely molded by his environment, although the environment was also a powerful determinant of human behavior. Nor did Freud share what had been the prevailing optimistic view of man. The id contained not only a sex instinct, which he emphasized, but also a destructive instinct. This meant that ". . . men are not gentle, friendly creatures wishing for love, who simply defend themselves when attacked, but that a powerful measure of desire for aggression has to be reckoned as part of their instinctual endowment. The result is that their neighbour is to them not only a possible helper or sexual object, but also a temptation to them to gratify their aggressiveness on him, to exploit his capacity for work without recompense, to use him sexually without his consent, to seize his possessions, to humiliate him, to cause him pain, to torture and to kill him."

Many of Freud's writings were based more on deductive reasoning and bold flights of the imagination than on empirical observation, but by World War I his basic conclusion that man was governed in part by an id or unconscious mind was becoming increasingly accepted and belief in the progress of man towards happiness and perfection was further shaken.

OTHER SCIENTIFIC AND TECHNOLOGICAL ADVANCES

The advances in chemistry were scarcely less revolutionary than those in physics, genetics, and psychology, and they were of equal practical importance. Chemists learned to produce materials of almost any needed weight, durability, or color. One has only to think of the textile industry, where wool, cotton, and linen were largely replaced by such newly created fibers as rayon, dacron, and nylon.

Biologists and chemists devoted much of their time to medical research. In conjunction with other specialists, they made a number of important discoveries. By 1912 the existence of hitherto unknown substances essential for proper nutrition was suspected. These substances, called vitamins, were later isolated from raw foods and are now easily produced to supplement diets. The study of glands led to the discovery that they secreted hormones necessary for life. Diabetes was controlled in 1921 when a method was found to get insulin from the pancreas. Research on the secretions of the pituitary gland and on sex hormones led to a growing understanding of the human body and the functioning of the sexual process. Much has been revealed during the last few decades concerning the origins of life and the relation between organic and inorganic substances. Eggs have been fertilized by inorganic materials, and viruses have been found that reproduce themselves like living organisms but have other properties associated only with inanimate objects. The sharp dividing line that had once existed between living matter and matter that had never lived was thereby removed, just as the division between energy and matter was being taken away. These viruses caused many diseases, for which no adequate remedies have been discovered.

The improvements in medical science caused life expectancy to increase rapidly. An Englishwoman born in 1895 had a life expectancy of 48 years, but one born in 1930 could anticipate a life of 63 years, and one born in 1950, 72 years. In the Western world, the decreasing death rate did not lead to as rapid an increase in population during the twentieth century as it had during the nineteenth, because families became smaller. The number of Frenchmen was almost stationary, and the population of Europe as a whole grew significantly only because of the relatively high birth rate in Russia and other Slavic countries. The population of Asia and Africa, however, grew more rapidly than ever and the relative number of non-Western people in the world began to increase.

The slackening birth rate in industrial countries did not halt the movement from the country towards the cities. Metropolitan London had a larger population in 1950 than England, Scotland, and Wales had had together in 1800, and metropolitan New York contained over four times as many people as the entire United States in 1790. The geographical area of cities increased even more rapidly than their population as improved transportation enabled upper and middle income groups to reside in suburban residential districts. Everywhere, rich farmland was being turned into well-kept lawns, but these changes did not threaten to exhaust the food supply because of the great improvement in agricultural techniques. During the Middle Ages, 90 per cent of the population had to live in the country to produce enough food for 10 per cent to live in towns, but despite their efforts many were undernourished and famines were frequent. Today 10 per cent of the population of the United States produces more food than the remainder can eat or can sell abroad, despite the fact that the federal government pays farmers to plant fewer acres.

The farmer's ability to increase his production has been more than matched by growth in industry. Large corporations established laboratories which employed scientists to search for improvements in their products; national governments, universities, and foundations sponsored research in the more theoretical aspects of science. A host of labor-saving devices were invented. Heat in houses turned on automatically, elevators ran when a button was pressed, garage doors opened when an electric eye announced an approaching car, and electronic calculators made computations in a matter of seconds that a skilled mathematician could not perform in a year. The time was coming when man could provide admirably for his needs with a few hours of labor. The age of automation was at hand.

Some of the most obvious miracles accomplished in recent years have been in the fields of transportation and communication. The radio, telephone, and automobile became part of the equipment of every family with a moderate income. The year 1927 was especially noteworthy. Transatlantic telephone service was opened, Charles A. Lindbergh flew his monoplane nonstop from New York to Paris, and the first television signals were transmitted. In 1939 regular commercial flights began between the United States and Europe. Today there are few spots in the world so remote that they cannot be reached in two days. In 1953 New York was "closer" to Tokyo than it was to Philadelphia 125 years before, and television brought the coronation of Queen Elizabeth II to the homes of her subjects throughout the world. Today manmade satellites are orbiting around the earth and interplanetary space travel appears certain in the near future.

SCIENCE AND TOTALITARIANISM

The great scientific and technological advances of the twentieth century have also brought dangers with them that our forefathers never encountered. No country is so far removed from its neighbors that it cannot be overwhelmed by a sudden atomic attack, and an atomic war could destroy life on the globe.

Not only have foreign powers become more dangerous, but the state, which had ceased to be feared by liberals when it fell into the hands of the people, now looms as a far more dangerous threat to human liberty than the most powerful monarchies of the past. A would-be dictator can sway thousands upon thousands of people at one time with the techniques of mass psychology by employing loud-speaker systems, radio, and television. Once in power, he can utilize large bureaucracies equipped with modern machines to regulate every act of the people, outlaw opposition political parties, and prohibit criticism in the press. A man might talk to one friend and then another about a revolt, but before he has enough accomplices to act he is arrested by the secret police. Only more or less spontaneous revolts are possible and these are quickly suppressed by troops with tanks and machine guns. Once established, the totalitarian state is almost impossible to destroy without help from abroad or a struggle for power between would-be heads of state.

THOUGHT

Philosophers had been so closely allied with scientists since the days of Descartes that they naturally felt challenged by the discoveries in physics, biology, psychology, and other fields. Some philosophers refused to accept the validity of the new discoveries where they affected cherished preconceived ideas, or insisted that they were of only minor significance. The former, the refusal to accept the new discoveries, was limited largely to Marxist thought. Marxists have to defend the role of environment, for their theory depends upon its omnipotence. In 1928 T. D. Lysenko (1898-   ), a worker in an agricultural research station in the Soviet Ukraine, published a paper in which he argued that wheat plants could be given special chemical treatments that would enable their seeds to grow farther north. This was directly contrary to the findings of the geneticists that acquired characteristics could not be inherited, but it was in keeping with the Marxist theory that materialistic environmental forces control destiny. Lysenko was given a powerful position in Soviet science, and in the 1940's Russian geneticists critical of his view were purged or forced to recant. Unhappily for the Russian people, Lysenko was more a political than a scientific success. The special cold weather wheat was not found, but only after years of prominence was Lysenko discredited.

Doctrinaire democrats have not been so foolish, but they have generally refused to consider that genetics may justify the existence of an elite or that there may be violent, irrational forces inherent in human nature that make moral progress difficult, if not impossible. Where they have faced these issues, they have tried to solve them by arguing that the non-environmental forces are of minor importance. In this, they have the support of the behaviorist school of psychology and the pragmatist school of philosophy, both still very powerful in the United States.[3]

A second approach to the problems posed by the scientific discoveries is to try to re-establish the nineteenth-century materialistic philosophy on a more modern base. A leading role in this movement is played by Earl Bertrand Russell (1872-   ) and the philosophical school of logical analysis of which he is the leading member. This school advocates the use of the logical and analytic methods of science and mathematics in the hope that, in the words of Russell, "The habit of careful veracity acquired in the practice of this philosophical method can be extended to the whole sphere of human activity, producing, wherever it exists, a lessening of fanaticism with an increasing capacity of sympathy and mutual understanding." This approach admittedly offers no hope for the discovery of ultimate truths or even of resolving questions of value. "Science alone," Russell admits, "cannot prove that it is bad to enjoy the infliction of cruelty. Whatever can be known, can be known by means of science; but things which are legitimately matters of feeling lie outside its prov-

[3] See pages 622 and 628.

ince." But it was in these very areas that man felt the greatest need for guidance. Most great thinkers, especially in continental Europe, therefore refused to revive the materialism of the nineteenth century and returned to an idealist position comparable to that of Kant.

The neo-idealists accepted the existence of a material world, but held that ultimate reality lay in the world of the idea or the spirit. There was much in the new scientific discoveries which could be construed to support this position, as we have seen, but many leading thinkers actually adopted the neo-idealistic position before the new science emerged and many continued to be unaware of the implications of these discoveries until years after they had been made. An idealistic position readily makes a place for religious and ethical truths and can be used to justify tradition. Its re-emergence at the dawn of the twentieth century therefore marked a conservative revival comparable to that which had appeared a century earlier in the guise of romanticism. Indeed, there were romantic elements in the new movement, for it gave ample space to the role of emotion, feeling, and intuition. The French Henri Bergson (1859-1941), for example, saw the world as consisting of life and matter. In life there was a will to action, an *élan vital* or vital impulse that drives man forward under the guidance of intuition towards "the life of the spirit."

The growing influence of the neo-idealistic movement paved the way for a religious revival. One leading thinker after another returned to the fold of the church during the twentieth century as a result of intellectual conviction. The horror of war and sufferings that took place during the depression brought others. Today a higher percentage of the population of the United States are church members than ever before.

Catholics have sought an answer to the confusing problems of the day by turning back to St. Thomas Aquinas. In a far-reaching neo-scholastic movement, scholars like Étienne Gilson and Jacques Maritain, himself a convert, are insisting on the complementary role faith and reason must play to guide man in his conduct on earth and towards the hereafter. Protestants under the leadership of Karl Barth are likewise turning to the past, not, of course, to Aquinas, but to Luther, Calvin, and the early Protestant reformers. These neo-orthodox theologians emphasize the sinful nature of man, the need for faith, and the righteousness of God. They never tire of insisting that "man is made to serve *God* and not God to serve man."

Two additional twentieth-century tendencies must be mentioned. One is a belief in action, however irrational, as opposed to inaction, however reasonable. Philosophically, it can be traced back to the Social Darwinist concept of the struggle for survival, to Nietzsche's "will to power," to Bergson's *élan vital*, and to others who have justified violence or preferred the will to the intellect. Politically and socially, it can be traced to nationalistic disappointments and economic depressions. Psychologically, it may be taken as empirical proof of Freud's theory of the destructive instinct in man's unconscious mind. These irrational forces played a large part in the fascist revolutions that will be discussed in the next chapter.

The second tendency is one of extreme pessimism. Just after the close of World War I, Oswald Spengler (1880-1936) published *The Decline of the West,* in which he tried to prove that Western civilization was coming to an end. Several years later, Arnold Toynbee (1889-   ) began to issue his multivolume *A Study of History,* in which he hints at a somewhat similar conclusion. Still others decry what they consider our dehumanized, mechanical society or point to the possible destruction, not of Western civilization alone, but of life on this earth by an atomic war between the United States and the Soviet Union.

THE AESTHETIC REVOLUTION

The scientific revolution was paralleled by an aesthetic revolution that began in the closing years of the nineteenth century. The nature of the aesthetic revolution varied somewhat from one art to another, but in general it involved the abandoning of the Renaissance tradition that had dominated aesthetic conceptions for five centuries except for the brief Mannerist and Romantic periods. Since the Renaissance was characterized by an effort to depict nature as it really was and by a slightly contrary effort to idealize nature to make it conform to the classical concepts of balance, order, and form, the aesthetic revolt in most forms of art involved a rejection of this naturalism and classicism. It was deeply influenced by the new sciences, especially psychology, and by the tragic events of the twentieth century.

As popular tastes remained traditional, artists and writers continued to be faced with a choice of trying to appeal to a wide public or adopting the slogan of "art for art's sake" and joining the aesthetic revolt. It took eight million copies printed in thirty languages to satisfy the popular demand for Margaret Mitchell's historical novel *Gone With the Wind* (1936) during its first thirteen years, while Thomas Mann's penetrating *Magic Mountain* (1924), which dealt with fundamental, contemporary problems, has found relatively few readers. The official Soviet Russian interpretation of Western art and literature was that it was bourgeois and decadent. Decadent it may well be, but bourgeois it certainly was not. Social novelists like Sinclair Lewis never tired of criticizing middle-class morals, standards, and ways of life. When a Thomas Mann or a John Galsworthy dealt at all sympathetically with a bourgeois family, it was to trace its slow decline. Artists were equally scornful of middle-class tastes and continued to paint as they pleased, even though a life of poverty was the usual reward of their independence. Thus, the middle class, which had done the most to make the dreams of the Enlightenment a reality, found itself deserted by its intellectual and cultural leaders at the very time the revolutionary crisis in the political sphere was reached.

PAINTING

The painters revolted from the Renaissance tradition more completely than any other type of artist. "Modern Art," the name assigned to their movement, became even less naturalistic than medieval painting. Modern Art was born in the late nineteenth century when three painters, Cézanne, Van Gogh, and Gauguin, abandoned the teachings of the Impressionists, who had tried to paint nature as man sees it, and had developed separate styles of their own. These painters were quite different in many respects, but when their works were exhibited together in London in 1911, they were given the name of Post-Impressionists.

Paul Cézanne (1839-1906) was a native of Provence, where he spent most of his life. During his Paris days he came under the influence of the Impressionists, but he soon realized that their sacrifice of linear drawing to bright color caused their paintings to lack form and depth. He admired the harmony and symmetry of the high Renaissance painters and the solidity and volume of the Baroque painters. Unlike the Impressionists, he believed that ". . . balance and symmetry are perpetual characteristics of the visual world." On the other hand, he saw that the old masters had achieved the sense of solidity and volume by an unnatural darkening around an object and by the use of light and shade. In short, they achieved an overall natural effect by painting in accordance to rules rather than from nature. Cézanne set out to develop a method in which the strong, intense colors of the Impressionists could be maintained because they were part of nature, but at the same time the harmony, symmetry, solidity, and volume of the old masters could be re-established.

In his effort to combine the type of reality the Impressionists achieved by painting their momentary impression from nature with the type of reality the old masters achieved by carefully following predetermined rules, Cézanne became one of the fathers of Modern Art. He was not completely successful and his paintings never ceased to be experimental, but he came close enough to achieving the impossible to become one of the greatest painters of all time. He owed his success in part to the use of thickly applied bright colors and to altering the direction of his brush stroke and in part to his willingness to distort figures whenever necessary to create the desired effect.

Cézanne was outwardly a serene artist with an independent income. In contrast, Vincent van Gogh (1853-1890) was an emotionally distraught, poverty-stricken man. He was born in the Netherlands and served for a time as a lay preacher among the Belgian coal miners. Eventually he wandered to Paris where he became acquainted with the Impressionists, and

Paul Cézanne, LANDSCAPE IN PROVENCE. *Compare with the landscapes of Constable on page 504 and Monet on page 634. (National Gallery of Art, Chester Dale Collection)*

to Provence where his unstable, emotional mind gave way. After a brief period of recurring insanity, he shot himself.

Like Cézanne, Van Gogh admired the bright, pure colors of the Impressionists, but he believed that in their effort to impart a fleeting moment of nature they deprived art of its emotional content. He continued to use bright colors, but the ones he chose were designed to express his emotions more than to imitate the natural color of the object. He applied his paint in thick layers and much of his own emotional intensity was revealed by the clear outlines of his brush strokes. In this, he and other modern artists were markedly different from Van Eyck and the artists of the northern Renaissance who obliterated all sign of the brush stroke to make the objects they painted look more natural. Van Gogh also found that he could express his emotions by distorting the shape of objects, and, like Cézanne, he did not hesitate to do so.

Paul Gauguin (1848-1903) decided on painting as a career later in life than most artists. Not until 1875 did he begin to paint as a hobby, but he soon became so enthusiastic that in 1881 he resigned his position at a

816

Vincent van Gogh, SELF-PORTRAIT. *Van Gogh achieved emotional intensity while using the color and most of the techniques of the Impressionists. (National Gallery of Art, Washington, Samuel H. Kress Collection)*

bank, deserted his wife and four children, and made a conspicuously unsuccessful attempt to earn a living as an artist. For a time he resided in Brittany because it was cheaper than Paris, but in 1891 he fled to Tahiti to escape the artificialities of European society and to be "without money troubles." For a time Gauguin was influenced by the Impressionists, but

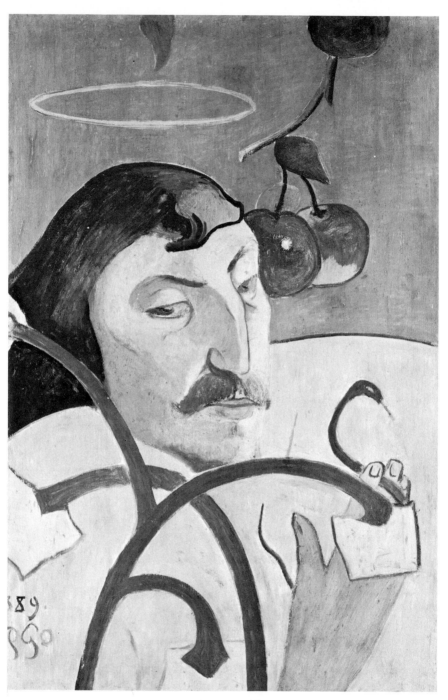

*Paul Gauguin, SELF-PORTRAIT. On a canvas of red and orange, the artist
painted his head beneath a halo. Compare his self-portrait with Van
Gogh's on page 817. (National Gallery of Art, Chester Dale Collection)*

he soon began to criticize their empirical approach. "They heed only the eye," he declared, "and neglect the mysterious centers of thought, so falling into merely scientific reasoning." He sought to recapture the spirit of the Tahitian natives. His lines and forms were simple, like those of native art, and he used the strong colors of the Impressionists in larger patches than they would have done. He distorted nature when he desired, and he painted flat two-dimensional figures.

Cézanne, Van Gogh, and Gauguin became the founders of Modern Art because of their willingness to abandon the effort to paint nature exactly as they saw it in return for other values. Their distortions of nature were relatively mild in comparison to what was to come. When they painted a man, it was recognizable as a man; when they painted a tree, it was recognizable as a tree. Indeed, their violation of the natural went no further than that of the Mannerists, but their successors chose to continue to experiment with new forms rather than to return to the Renaissance tradition as the successors of the Mannerists had done. The result was the emergence of many different styles in the twentieth century, most of which were short-lived, though a few, perhaps, were of lasting importance.

One group of artists became known as the Expressionists because they sought to use their art to express their feelings. They derived much of their inspiration from Van Gogh, but they were also influenced by wars, violence, depressions, and other tragedies of their age. Their works frequently dealt with death, poverty, and misery; and they imparted a sense of human suffering by exaggerating features to the point of caricature.

Another school known as the Cubists was deeply indebted to Cézanne's interest in solidity and form. Their work often lacked perspective and the objects they painted were distorted to assume the shapes of cubes, cones, and cylinders. Pablo Picasso (1881-   ), the most famous artist of the mid-twentieth century, first achieved recognition as a Cubist, but he has since experimented with several other styles of art.

Many objects the Cubists put in their paintings were recognizable as existing in nature although they were distorted and arranged in unnatural fashions. Their movement led to abstract art, in which all interest in painting natural objects was abandoned and the artist arranged lines and colors as his inspiration dictated. At this point, the world of sensuous experience disappeared as completely from painting as it did from physical science. Neither the abstract artist nor the atomic physicist viewed the world from the standpoint of sensuous experience.

The Primitivism advocated by Gauguin has probably received a wider following than any other form of Modern Art because it did not involve complicated artistic theories or such a complete denial of sensuous experience as to make the objects painted unrecognizable. Elaborate training was not necessary; indeed it almost seemed as though a painter like Henri Rousseau (1844-1910), who had few technical qualifications, had a positive advantage, since the aim of the Primitives was to recapture the

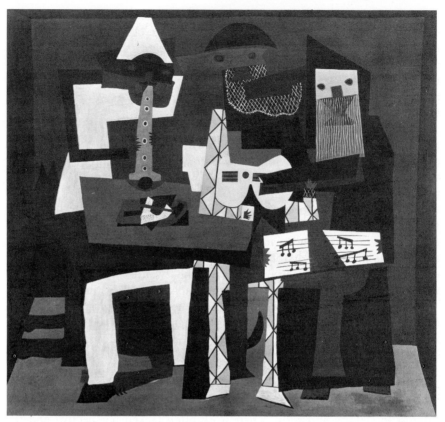

Pablo Picasso, THREE MUSICIANS. *When Cézanne told Picasso to visualize nature in terms of cubes, cylinders, and other geometric figures, his advice was followed literally. Compare with Cézanne's landscape on page 816. (Museum of Modern Art)*

unsophisticated simplicity of the savage or child. Primitivism also led to a fuller appreciation of early Medieval and African art.

One final group of artists, the Surrealists, must be mentioned. They sought a reality beyond the material, sensible world, and, inspired by the Freudian concept of the unconscious mind, they found it in the world of dreams. Salvador Dali (1905-   ), the foremost Surrealist, is an excellent draftsman who paints individual objects with the greatest care, but his paintings as a whole deny the reality of nature. They include a watch that is melting over the edge of a table and a dog whose body consists of a human head and a bowl of fruit. Such combinations may, of course, be possible in dreams, but they are difficult to evaluate objectively. All that can be said with certainty is that the artist, like the physical scientist and the Freudian psychologist, has abandoned the world of sensory experience in the search of a more "real" world that can only be ascertained by other means.

Salvador Dali, THE PERSISTENCE OF MEMORY. *The idea of painting these soft, melting watches came to Dali after eating a piece of over-ripe Camenbert cheese. The relationship between the cheese, the watches, and the weird landscape is understandable only in the world of the unconscious mind, which forms a connection among the strange, unpredictable forms. Here the watches express the flexibility of time and the weird landscape reflects the eternity and depth of space. (Museum of Modern Art)*

SCULPTURE, MUSIC, AND ARCHITECTURE

Twentieth-century sculpture also reflected the revolution in aesthetics. Few artistic mediums had adhered more loyally to the Renaissance tradition, but today there are schools of sculpture that roughly parallel those in painting. The sculptor no longer feels obligated to copy nature or to follow the rules of proportion, but rather carves his stone into something that barely resembles an object in the sensory world.

The desire to experiment with new forms was also present in music. However, since composers had rarely attempted to imitate the sounds of nature, there was no need for the revolt in music to take the form of an attack on naturalism. Rather, the avant-garde composers rejected the classicism and romanticism of the nineteenth century and even the more recent Impressionism of Claude Debussy. Arnold Schönberg (1874-1951) and his pupil Alban Berg (1885-1935) tried to substitute atonality for the tonality that had dominated music for several centuries. So far

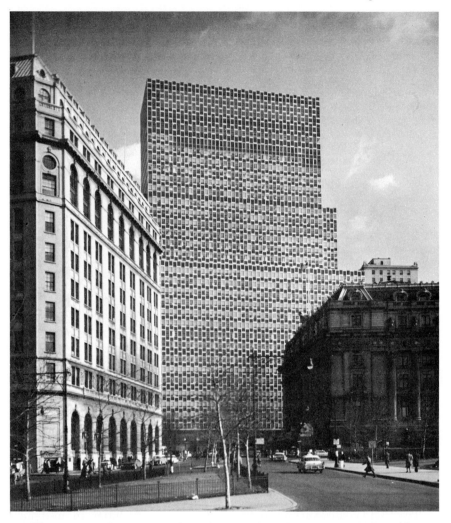

The contrast between modern functional architecture and the older styles is clearly revealed in this view of Broadway, New York City. For another example of functional architecture, see the United Nations Building on page 975. (H. Armstrong Roberts)

they have not been very successful, and the majority of composers have held to the traditional styles.

The aesthetic revolt in architecture was quite different from that in other mediums. Instead of denying nature, modern architects emphasized the material out of which a building was made and the practical purpose it was to serve. Perhaps for this reason they have won a wider following than the rebels in any other art. The principal characteristic of the new architecture was functionalism; that is, buildings were designed to reflect the purpose they were to serve. Useless ornamentation was therefore

822

The use of glass walls and the union of interiors and exteriors in one architectural unit has even been applied to apartment buildings as in Marina City, Chicago. (H. Armstrong Roberts)

removed to make buildings stand out boldly in their stark simplicity. Architects of the modern or functional school make use of the new materials provided by industrial advances. Prestressed steel, high pressure concrete, glass block, and chromium have come into common use. Utility, efficiency, economy, and comfort are stressed. In place of closed-in box-

823

like rooms, entire walls are made of glass to give a feeling of spaciousness and to join the garden and the room in a single architectural unit. Not since the Renaissance has there been a comparable revolution in architecture, and the innovations of that day were less original. The outstanding exponent of the new style in the United States was Frank Lloyd Wright (1869-1959).

LITERATURE AND THE CINEMA

During the first decade after World War I, writers like Ernest Hemingway and Erich Remarque dwelt on the meaninglessness and brutality of war or else decried the failure to achieve the goals for which the war had been fought. The Great Depression of 1929 and the rise of the fascist states awakened some intellectuals to the fact that a reformed capitalism combined with the philosophy inherited from the Enlightenment was less objectionable than the alternatives. Writers began to take a more positive position. Many wrote of the sufferings of the poorer people, but took hope in the efforts to improve their lot. Others recounted the horrors of dictatorship, but found satisfaction in the courageous way the Spanish loyalists resisted the advance of Fascist troops. A touch of the old idealism returned, not of the immature, naïve sort that characterized the beginnings of World War I, but of a more considered, determined, less optimistic variety. Writers today are perhaps less despairing than they were a generation ago.

The late nineteenth-century interest in the psychological novel has continued; here authors borrowed heavily from the research of Sigmund Freud, who has influenced literature more than any other scientist. Freud himself made psychoanalytical studies of Leonardo da Vinci and Dostoevsky. Other nonfiction writers followed his lead and made comparable contributions. Writers of fiction owed Freud a more considerable debt. Some like Thomas Mann acknowledged Freud's contribution to their understanding of the human mind; others like D. H. Lawrence attacked Freud's conclusions, but nevertheless accepted the role of the unconscious. Among the important writers who dealt with the unconscious were F. Scott Fitzgerald, Aldous Huxley, Eugene O'Neill, and Sherwood Anderson. Freudianism gave birth to the "stream of consciousness" technique in literature, of which James Joyce's *Ulysses* is the most famous example.

Other literary movements may be compared with the revolt against nature in art. Some writers have tried to impart a mystical, dreamlike quality to their work and displayed more interest in the sound of words and the use of symbols than in depicting man and nature as they really are. Others, like the Rumanian playwright Eugène Ionesco turned to Surrealism.

By the 1930's the film industry had perfected its techniques to the point that the cinema assumed an artistic importance rivaling that of literature and surpassing that of most other arts. By far the most widely viewed films were those made in the United States to cater to the same tastes as the popular forms of escape literature, but French, Italian, Japanese, and Swedish producers have shown a willingness to experiment artistically.

It is, of course, too early to tell what direction civilization will take because of the scientific and aesthetic revolutions. In many respects both revolutions point in the same direction. Both reject the material world as comprehended by the senses and in so doing reverse the leading trend in science and art since the Renaissance. Both question the dominant role of the environment upon which theories of human equality and perfectibility have been based and emphasize the parts played by heredity and instincts residing in the unconscious mind. Yet it would be dangerous to assume that materialism will easily surrender to a new form of idealism, for today in both the Western democracies and the Communist states the mass of the people and their governments still think in the same terms as before the revolutions in science and aesthetics began.

THE RUSSIAN REVOLUTION

The third great twentieth-century revolution took place in Russia. In many respects the Russian Revolution that began in 1917 and the French Revolution that began in 1789 were similar. Both came to countries which during the preceding decades had enjoyed increasing wealth, but whose people were temporarily suffering hardships. Both came to countries with well-meaning, incompetent kings, who had domineering, intriguing wives and inefficient, corrupt bureaucracies. In both countries, the overthrow of the monarchy came about largely as a result of military defeat. In both, the control of the government fell into more and more radical hands during the early years, and in both there was eventually a conservative reaction.

However, the parallels should not be pushed too far. The French Revolution was started by the aristocracy, but it was essentially a middle-class movement. Its goals included political and economic liberty. The Russian Revolution was started by the middle class, but it was essentially a workingman's movement. Economic liberty was denied in theory and political liberty in practice. In some respects the French leaders were doctrinaire, but only after their movement had begun did any of them plot to overthrow governments and none of them except Napoleon had a very clear idea of what to do after power was achieved. The Russian leaders were professional revolutionaries who had studied with care the upheavals of the past and had elaborate theories of how and when power was to be achieved and what was to be done to maintain control when success was won. The period of the New Economic Policy may have been a conservative reaction comparable to the Directory, and Stalin, like Napoleon, may have been both the savior and the destroyer of the revolution, but the Romanovs are further from a restoration than the Bourbons were at any time during the revolution. In short, the Communists have been able to establish a stable government that has already lasted twice as long as the first French republic and empire and has withstood one world war.

THE MARCH REVOLUTION

The underlying cause of the Russian Revolution may be found in the rapid economic, social, and intellectual changes that were taking place in a relatively static political-administrative framework. During the generation before the revolution began, industrialization and railroad building had proceeded rapidly and the middle class had grown in size and economic importance. Under the impetus of Stolypin's reforms the peasants were leaving the *mir* to become workers in the new industrial cities or independent farmers, although their hunger for land remained unsatisfied. Literacy was improving at all levels and a system of universal primary education was projected for 1922. Intellectual life at the university level was as creative as anywhere else in Europe. Russian historians, mathematicians, and natural scientists compared favorably with those of other countries and their novelists had no peers.

The political-administrative framework of the government was relatively static. Some of the great gains won in the revolution of 1905 were actually restricted; even the existence of the Duma, or Parliament, was not secure. In 1907 the Tsar arbitrarily changed the electorate in order to obtain a more pliant assembly, and there was no assurance that he would not abolish the institution altogether if it suited his purpose. The court and gentry exercised a disproportionate influence on the government, and except for a few wealthy capitalists, middle-class interests were not favored. Officials were generally incompetent reactionaries who resisted, rather than encouraged, the changes that were taking place around them. If the peasants acquired more land or the urban workers improved their lot after Stolypin's death in 1911, they did so over the opposition of the administration rather than with its encouragement. Under such circumstances men, who in Western Europe would have been reforming administrators, became revolutionaries and slowly won the support of the rural and urban masses for drastic changes.

Perhaps if war had not come, the tsarist regime could have reformed itself before it was too late, but military defeats between 1914 and 1917 revealed the full extent of the bankruptcy of the government and became the immediate cause of the revolution. Over half the 15,500,000 men who were called to arms were killed, wounded, or captured. Millions of civilians died, vast quantities of property were destroyed, but these tremendous losses did not lead to victories. There had been little besides defeats. On the

Nicholas II with Empress Alexandra and family. (Brown Brothers)

home front, shortages had quickly developed because of military demands and the breakdown of transportation facilities. The villages, which were largely self-sufficient, did not fare too badly, but the railroads were unable to carry a sufficient supply of food to the cities. Prices rose far more rapidly than wages, and the suffering of the poorer people was intense.

Defeat and privation alone were not enough to cause revolution. The Belgians suffered both, but the war cemented the loyalty of the people to their able, patriotic king. Tsar Nicholas was patriotic, but not even his warmest sympathizers would call him able. His blunders and those of the bureaucracy responsible to him were blamed for most of the catastrophes. His wife, a German princess, was unjustly regarded as pro-German, and the same may be said of some of his ministers.

The royal couple's only son was a victim of hemophilia. The medical profession could offer no cure, but in 1905 the Empress Alexandra met "a man of God," Gregory Novykh (1871?-1916), better known by his nickname, Rasputin, the licentious one. Rasputin was a notoriously immoral, half-literate Siberian peasant who was associated with one of Russia's many religious sects. He developed a reputation as a faith healer and was credited by the Empress with stopping the bleeding of her son. Whether this was accomplished by hypnotism or drugs, or whether it resulted from sheer chance, cannot be said, but once Rasputin had convinced the royal couple that he could preserve the life of the young prince, they refused to believe ill of him. Rasputin exercised little influence prior to 1911, but during the war he was a dominant factor in the government. He had no policy and did not seek office for himself, but he saw to it that his friends and supporters were given high places in the government. None of his protégés were men of ability. Nearly all were corrupt, immoral, and inefficient, and one was probably insane. Russian defeats were blamed on them and through them on the Tsar.

The situation became so bad that several courtiers, including relatives of the Tsar, plotted to murder Rasputin in the hope of saving the monarchy. In December, 1916, they gave their unsuspecting victim a large quantity of poison without effect. He was wounded several times by gunfire, but still he did not die. Finally his enemies exterminated the strange man by shoving him under the ice of the Neva River, but it was too late. The imperial regime had become so associated with incompetence, corruption, suffering, and defeat that even royalists began to favor a change. A strike broke out in St. Petersburg on March 8, 1917. Troops sent to quell the disturbance went over to the strikers. The Duma, which had been highly critical of the conduct of the war, was dissolved by the Tsar. Its members refused to depart, but instead formed a provisional government on March 12. The Tsar accepted the advice of his generals and abdicated three days later. The Romanov dynasty had come to an end after a rule of three centuries. The revolution had begun.

The provisional government was not radical, at least by Western standards. Prince Lvov (1861-1925), a Constitutional Democrat, or "Cadet", became prime minister and Paul Miliukov (1859-1943) of the same party was made minister of foreign affairs. Alexander Kerensky (1881-   ), a Social Revolutionary, was the only member of the cabinet from a workers' or peasants' party. The program of the provisional government was as liberal and nationalist as one would expect of a middle-class regime. Civil liberties were proclaimed, and equality before the law was established. Political prisoners were released; Bolsheviks, Mensheviks, and Social Revolutionaries swarmed into the capital from Siberia, from jail, and from abroad. The war was continued because the middle-class leaders were too honest to desert their allies and too nationalistic to abandon the opportunity to obtain Constantinople and the Straits, both promised by one of the secret treaties.

The Allies were pleased at the turn of events, for they expected the new government to pursue the war more efficiently and more vigorously than the old, but they were sadly mistaken. A change in regime in itself brought

Lenin, left, and Stalin in 1922. (Sovfoto)

neither food to the cities nor supplies to the troops, but only increased confusion and disorder. In the country the peasants began to appropriate the large estates. As a class, they already owned most of the land, but their individual holdings were small. The government was willing to satisfy the peasants' land hunger by giving them the estates of the crown and the monasteries, but it insisted that this not be done until after the constituent assembly had met and prepared a new constitution. The peasants did not understand the niceties of constitution-making and soon fell prey to revolutionary propaganda.

The towns proved equally difficult to control. The workers had organized *soviets* (councils) composed of elected deputies at the same time the provisional government had been formed. The St. Petersburg soviet was especially important. It, and not the provisional government, controlled the city. Leadership in the soviet rested in the hands of Mensheviks and Social Revolutionaries who refused to cooperate with the middle-class government, but at the same time made no effort to seize power. To the Mensheviks, as good Marxists, the March uprising was only a bourgeois revolution that had to destroy the feudal regime before it would be possible to have a

829

successful workers' revolt. They did fear that the generals might lead the army in a counter-revolution; to reduce this possibility they issued Order No. 1, which set up elective committees in the army units to choose officers and to see that orders of the provisional government that countered those of the soviet were not obeyed. The result was utter confusion in the military forces. Many peasant soldiers began to desert and go home in the hope of getting land.

The situation went from bad to worse. The provisional government could not act because it controlled neither the countryside, the towns, nor the army, and the soviets would not act positively because in accordance with Marxist theory the time was not ripe. The peasants were left without land, the towns without food, and the troops without supplies. Soldier, worker, and peasant began to demand peace. This was the situation on April 16, when Lenin, Zinoviev, and other Bolshevik leaders arrived at St. Petersburg.

Lenin had been living in exile in Switzerland when the revolution had begun. He had immediately sought to return to his native land and won the assistance of the Germans, who took him and his followers through Germany in a closely guarded train. They rightly suspected that the Bolsheviks would stir up trouble and weaken Russia's war effort; they little suspected the far-reaching results of their action.

At first the Bolsheviks were one of the smaller parties in the soviet, but Lenin gave them the sense of direction and purpose that was lacking elsewhere. The able Leon Trotsky (1877-1940) arrived from the United States at about this time, and Stalin (1879-1953) had already come to the capital from Siberia. With these able lieutenants, Lenin began to make headway with the argument that the bourgeois capitalistic revolution need not be completed before the workers seized power in conjunction with the poor peasantry. The provisional government was to be overthrown and all power transferred to the soviets. Peace was to be made with the Central Powers and land given to the peasants. In the face of the rapidly deteriorating situation, Lenin was slowly able to rally additional support with his positive program and his popular slogans of "all power to the soviets" and "peace, land, and bread."

In May, Miliukov was dropped from the government, Kerensky was made war minister, and several Social Revolutionary and Menshevik leaders joined the cabinet. The revolution had taken its first step towards the left, but the middle-class parties were still dominant and it was hoped that more could be accomplished now that the two largest radical parties were represented in the government. A general peace with no annexations and no indemnities was advocated, but to secure such a peace it was necessary to revamp the army. Kerensky proved to be a fiery orator. He went among the troops crying: "I summon you forward, to the struggle for freedom, not to a feast, but to death. We, revolutionaries, have the right to death." Such a prospect would have discouraged many soldiers, but Kerensky's grandil-

Leon Trotsky at the age of thirty-five.
(Bettmann Archive)

oquent phrases inspired the troops to launch an offensive in late June that quickly failed. The Bolsheviks participated in an uprising in St. Petersburg in July, but it was also unsuccessful. Trotsky was imprisoned and Lenin fled to Finland. Kerensky, who was the most dynamic figure in Lvov's cabinet, now became prime minister, but it was soon apparent that he was no more able to control the soviets than his predecessor. The city masses, through the soviets, could influence the provisional government just as the Paris populace had dictated to the various assemblies during the French Revolution.

In September peasant-born General Kornilov (1870-1918) began to march his troops to St. Petersburg with the intention of strengthening the provisional government by breaking the power of the soviets. Perhaps through a misunderstanding, Kerensky took alarm and sought support from the extreme left by pardoning the Bolsheviks. In the end, Kornilov's troops refused to obey him, but the harm had been done. Lenin, Trotsky, Stalin, and others were free once more to make converts among the workers.

THE BOLSHEVIK VICTORY

Meanwhile, the situation had continued to deteriorate. The army had collapsed as a result of repeated defeats, revolutionary propaganda, and confusion. The authority of the central government in the provinces had come to an end. Minority races from the Finns in the north to the Ukrainians in the south had declared themselves independent. In Russia proper, peasants were seizing land and demanding legal title for what they had taken. Bread was scarcer and more expensive than ever before in the cities. It is not surprising that the Bolsheviks with their positive program of "peace, land, and bread" began to make more rapid progress. In the early fall they finally achieved a majority in the St. Petersburg soviet. On November 6, with the assistance of part of the local army and navy garrisons, they seized control of the city. Kerensky escaped, but on the following day the All-Russian Congress of Soviets met, approved the coup, and established a Council of People's Commissars headed by Lenin to govern the state. The day Karl Marx had dreamed of had arrived. A dictatorship of the proletariat had been established, not in an advanced industrial state as anticipated, but in backward Russia.

The Bolsheviks, or Communists as they began to call themselves during this period, had achieved power more easily than they had anticipated, but like their predecessors they found that it was easier to seize power than to exercise it. They still had little strength outside the towns and the army. In the elections held late in November for the long-awaited constituent assembly, they received less than a fourth of the vote. An electoral defeat did not bother Lenin—he closed the assembly the day after it opened—but it did indicate that the Communists had not yet sold their program to the people, although they had made considerable progress.

Undaunted, Lenin and his associates set out to implement their program. Peace negotiations were begun with the Germans and ended with the Russian acceptance of the disastrous Peace of Brest-Litovsk, which stripped Russia of over a third of its population and nearly all its coal mines and oil fields.[4] Even the Communists hesitated to betray national interests, but Lenin realized that only with peace could their position in Russia be consolidated. Besides, he anticipated a world revolution shortly, after which national boundaries would be meaningless.

On the home front, opposition parties were outlawed and their leaders arrested. Banks, industries, and land were declared to be the property of the state. Workers were given an eight-hour day and their committees assumed the role of managers of the factories. The church was separated from the state and its property was confiscated. Poor peasants were encouraged to attack rich peasants, but instead they were more inclined to turn on the Communists. When these measures failed to produce an adequate supply of food or industrial goods, troops were sent into the countryside to seize food for the urban population, and a system of compulsory labor was inaugurated.

Under these circumstances, monarchists, Octobrists, "Cadets," Social Revolutionaries, and Mensheviks began to gather their forces to try to overthrow their oppressors. In this they were assisted by the independence movements among the subject peoples who occupied the frontier prov-

[4] See page 773.

inces all around the country. Help also came from the Allies. British, French, American, and Japanese troops were sent to Russia with a rather vague idea that they might be able to restore the eastern front, to keep military supplies from falling into the hands of the Germans, and possibly to overthrow the Communist regime. Some Czech troops who were already in Russia were especially effective.

For more than three years the civil war raged. At times victory seemed to be almost within the grasp of the White Russians, as the counter-revolutionaries were called, but poor leadership, quarrels between the widely divergent factions within their movement, and the failure of the Allies to give sufficient aid told against them. The Communists established a reign of terror. Members of the aristocracy and middle class were slaughtered wherever they were found. Among the victims were the Tsar and his family. Trotsky as war commissar organized an effective Red Army by compelling nearly fifty thousand tsarist officers to train and command his troops. Loyalty was ensured by holding their families as hostages and by assigning party members to army units to watch their movements and to indoctrinate the soldiers. Campaigns were fought against the Finns, Poles, Ukrainians, and the inhabitants of the Baltic and Caucasian provinces as well as the White Russians, and in 1921 the Communists emerged victorious in most localities. The Finns, Poles, and Baltic peoples did establish their independence, but separatist movements in the Ukraine, White Russia, Georgia, Armenia, Azerbaijan, and Siberia were crushed, and the Allies withdrew their troops after having done very little fighting.

LENIN'S RUSSIA

The Communists were the victors, but Russia lay in ruins. Industrial production stood at 13 per cent of the pre-war level; there was an inadequate supply of fuel for cooking and of power to operate the city trolleys. Famine conditions existed because of severe droughts in 1920-1921, the breakdown of the transportation system, and the Communist economic system. Millions died of starvation and misery. People left the cities by the thousands, hoping to find food in the agricultural districts. The population of St. Petersburg dropped to less than a third its former level. There was growing unrest among the workers, a naval garrison near St. Petersburg revolted, and there were peasant uprisings in many localities.

Lenin was among the first to realize that the Communist system was not working as planned. In theory, the peasants were to produce the food, take what they needed, and send the surplus to the cities. The urban workers were to produce the manufactured goods, take what they needed, and send the remainder to the country. The exchange was to be based on barter carried on under the direction of the government. The difficulty was that the worker-controlled factories could not produce much without the guidance of experienced management, especially in a war-torn nation; the peasants were unwilling to part with the food they produced without receiving something in return; and the merchants who had formerly distributed goods had ceased to exist because they were considered a nonproductive, bourgeois class. What food the cities obtained was usually brought there by troops sent out to confiscate it from the peasants. The peasants retaliated by eating what they could and hiding or actually destroying the remainder.

In 1921 Lenin won approval from the Congress of the Communist party for a New Economic Policy (NEP). Pure communism, he declared, could not be established in Russia before the revolution had spread to other countries. It was therefore necessary to compromise with the peasantry and base the economy on worker-peasant cooperation. In effect, the NEP was a tactical retreat, a return to a modified capitalistic system. The peasants were permitted to own the land and to sell their products for money; in return, they were expected to pay a tax in kind based on the amount they produced. Industries employing less than twenty persons were returned to private ownership. Larger industries, banks, and railroads remained in the hands of the government, but they were more effectively managed. The control of factories of a given type was placed in the hands of a board that was expected to operate them efficiently and profitably. Government-owned though it was, Russian big industry began to resemble that of Germany and other countries with well-organized systems of cartels or trusts. Gradually the Russian economy revived. By 1926 the national income had reached the 1913 level and opposition to the new regime lessened.

Meanwhile, steps had been taken to organize the state. In 1918 a constitution was adopted which provided for a suffrage based on class rather than territory. The bourgeoisie was disenfranchised and the vote of an urban worker, who was likely to be favorably disposed to communism, was given five times the weight of that of a peasant. Voting was in public and freedom of speech was promised only to the workers. Under these conditions, the local soviets elected representatives to provincial congresses of soviets, and the provincial congresses chose representatives to the All-Russian Congress of Soviets, which served as the law-making body. The Congress in turn elected a Central Executive Committee and the Council of the People's Commissars, which functioned something like the cabinet of a Western state, with the commissars being the ministers. The constitution was not democratic in the usual sense of the word and was not designed to be. It represented the dictatorship of the proletariat phase in the communist theory of the evolution of the state. Power was expressly stated to belong exclusively "to the toiling masses."

In 1922 a new constitution was adopted that was almost identical to the old except that provision was made for the various nationalities. By this time the Communists had reasserted control over the Ukraine, White Russia, and Transcaucasia, where soviet states had been organized like that of Russia. To satisfy the numerous smaller racial groups, autonomous republics and autonomous regions were established within the republics. Inhabitants were not only permitted, but encouraged to use their native language and wear their native costumes. These republics were bound together in the Union of Soviet Socialist Republics which, like the Russian Soviet Republic, had its Congress of Soviets, Central Executive Committee, and Council of the People's Commissars. The Central Executive Committee was divided into a Council of the Union and a Council of Nationalities, which was composed of five deputies from each republic and autonomous republic and one from each autonomous region. This complex system was relatively successful in dealing with the 180 different nationalities in the Soviet state, although it must be remembered that the historically conscious races were either small or closely related to the Russians. It was intended to incorporate other parts of the world into the Soviet Union as the Communist revolution spread. There were four Soviet republics in 1922; there are fifteen now.

Neither the constitution of 1918 nor that of 1922 mentioned the role of the Communist party. This omission was important because it was the party which made the theoretically decentralized Soviet Union a centralized state. The Communist party recognized no national allegiance. It operated in all the republics and autonomous regions where its members took the lead formulating and executing policy. Only the dedicated communist was permitted to join, and there were periodic purges to get rid of lax, incompetent, or disobedient members. As late as 1934, there were only two million members and the number has only quadrupled since that day. The party itself was theoretically governed by the Party Congress which met annually during the early years, but effective control was at first given to a large Central Committee and then, by 1925, to small subcommittees of the Central Committee. The policy-making subcommittee was known as the Politburo. It usually consisted of five to ten members and was the real governing force in the party. The Orgburo was a subcommittee which assigned persons to carry out the Politburo's decisions. A Secretariat was established to administer and coordinate the various committees and subcommittees. Thus, a decision of the Politburo was transferred by the Orgburo with the aid of the Secretariat down to the smallest party cells in the various republics and autonomous regions. There loyal party members exercised their power and talents of leadership by persuading the noncommunist members of the local soviets and other government units to carry out the decision. These local soviets, as we have seen, chose the Congress of Soviets by a system of indirect suffrage. Thus, the chain went from Politburo to local cell, to local soviet, and back to the Congress of Soviets, theoretically the ultimate authority in the state. Since only one party was permitted and the press was censored, this complex system was less inclined to break down than one might suspect. In any case, there were always the secret political police, known variously as Cheka, OGPU,

NKVP, and MVD, and the Red Army to take care of any individual or group that refused to implement party decisions.

Soviet foreign policy was also dualistic. A foreign commissar resided in Moscow, the new capital, and ambassadors, consuls, and other diplomatic officials were sent to foreign countries where they dressed the same way and performed the same duties as their counterparts in Western states. But at the same time there was also the Communist party organ, the Comintern, which organized Communist parties in other countries as a prelude to the coming revolution. Thus, the foreign commissar might sign a treaty with Germany, as he did in 1922, at the same time the Comintern was planning to overthrow the German state, as it did both before and after the treaty.[5] The ultimate communist goal, world revolution, was never abandoned, but often during the 1920's and 1930's the Soviet Union's official foreign policy was friendly and cooperative. Neither Lenin nor Stalin wanted to invite a capitalistic coalition to attack their new state.

The Communists separated the church from the state, dissolved the monasteries, and confiscated church property, but they did not carry their attack to extremes. Lenin was an atheist, but he knew that the church still had a powerful hold on the people and saw no reason to add to his troubles by vigorous anti-religious acts. Indeed as an economic determinist, he expected the people to abandon their religious faith gradually as the dictatorship of the proletariat changed the economic base of society. Therefore, the church doors were left open, although Communists were not to attend. The Orthodox clergy revived the office of patriarch and functioned with a reasonable degree of freedom except for those of its number who criticized the Communist regime. Most of the older people remained faithful to the church, but many of the younger generation escaped its influence, largely because the clergy lost all power to educate or proselytize.

The Communists were bolder in altering existing family relations which they regarded as bourgeois. Women were declared equal to men, marriage could be accomplished by writing a note to the proper authority, and divorce was as easily achieved at the request of either husband or wife. State nurseries were established to care for the children of working mothers, and abortions were legalized to benefit those who did not care to have children. Nor did the Communists neglect education and culture. Education, they realized, had a powerful propaganda value and they sought to reduce illiteracy, but progress during the 1920's was not very rapid. Soviet educational theory, borrowed as it largely was from the American, John Dewey, was quite progressive during this period. Democracy was practiced more fully in the classroom than in the state and little effort was made to compel students to learn difficult subjects that did not interest them. University faculties were purged of outspoken critics of communism and those that remained were often the least able. Lenin recognized the im-

[5] See pages 791 and 863.

portance of culture and the creative artists' need for freedom. He resisted the efforts of some party members to establish an official style of painting or literature; only artists who became involved in anti-Communist politics found themselves in difficulty. Because of the favorable climate of the 1920's, many of the artists who had fled during the revolution returned to Russia, among them Count Alexis Tolstoi.

In 1924 Lenin died. He was unquestionably the greatest revolutionary of all time. As a communist theorist, he rivaled Marx himself, but he was also a man of action. In six years he had taken a small party which had only 23,000 members in 1917 and had led it to a dominant position in the largest country in the world. By his action he had altered the course of the Russian Revolution and, through it, of history. He was often ruthless in his measures, yet within the councils of the party, he not only permitted debate, but was occasionally out-voted. He knew when to compromise and, unlike many men in a position of power, he was willing to acknowledge his mistakes. Power to him was not a way to wealth, but a means to establish a world communist state; it was to achieve this goal that he had set himself in his youth, and he had never permitted the desire for security or comfort to turn him from his course.

Lenin did not name a successor, but he did prepare a will shortly before his death in which he pointed out the strengths and weaknesses of the leading members of the party. Later, just before he was incapacitated by a stroke, he added as a postscript: "I propose to the comrades to find a way to remove Stalin from that position (Secretary of the Communist Party) and appoint to it another man. . . more patient, more loyal, more polite and more attentive to comrades, less capricious. . . ." But he did not live to take this step and Stalin became his successor.

STALIN

Stalin was a Georgian who spoke Russian with an accent. He was born in a little town in the Caucasus Mountains on December 21, 1879. His father was a violent, drunken man who practiced the trade of cobbler; his mother was a pious woman of serf extraction who wanted her son to be a priest. He entered a seminary, but was expelled in 1899. Two years later he published a Marxist essay, and in 1902 he was arrested for the first time. Between then and the Revolution, he spent most of his time in prison, generally in Siberia. However, during intermittent periods of freedom he raised party funds by robbing banks, met Lenin, became editor of the party newspaper, *Pravda,* and substituted Stalin, man of steel, for his family name of Dzhugashvili. Stalin proved himself a good party worker during the Revolution, although he was not regarded by his colleagues as particularly intelligent. He was one of the original five members of the Politburo and also served as Secretary of the Communist party. This last office was contemptuously regarded as an administrative position by his rivals, but Stalin used it to appoint loyal supporters to key positions in the party and the government. The secret police, the Red Army, and the labor unions were gradually brought under his control.

During the years immediately following Lenin's death, there was a struggle for power. Gradually, by playing one rival faction against another and making full use of his control of party machinery, Stalin emerged with dictatorial powers. The principal cause of the struggle was a clash in personalities, but there were also differences in policy, despite agreement that the ultimate goal was world communism. Trotsky held that the dictatorship of the proletariat could not establish socialism in one country, especially in an industrially backward one like Russia, where the bulk of the inhabitants were peasants who preferred the private ownership of property. He therefore advocated that greater emphasis be placed on seizing power in Germany and other countries. Gregory Zinoviev (1883-1936) and Leo Kamenev (1883-1936), two other members of the Politburo, were more concerned about the return of capitalism to Russia under the NEP and believed that, if necessary, Russia alone should move rapidly towards socialism. Nikolai Bukharin (1888-1938), also a member of the Politburo, thought that the NEP had proved a success and that they should creep towards socialism at "a snail's pace." Stalin first allied himself with Zinoviev and Kamenev to defeat Trotsky, then with Bukharin and the right wing of the Party to defeat his late partners. Finally, in 1929 he removed Bukharin from the Polituro and emerged as dictator of Russia.

Stalin had shifted his ideological stand in the struggle for power several times, but his ultimate position was that socialism could be established in one country. He wanted to abandon the NEP and collectivize industry and agriculture because as a Communist he believed that men's ideas and characters would change only if private ownership of the means of production ceased. Furthermore, he thought collectivization would lead to increased production and that Russia would then become a powerful state, capable of serving as a base for the world revolution. It was with these ideas in mind that Stalin inaugurated the first Five-Year Plan in 1928.

THE FIVE-YEAR PLANS

The first Five-Year Plan called for tripling production in heavy industry, doubling it in light industry, and increasing it by 50 per cent in agriculture within five years. This was to be accomplished by collectivizing agriculture and constructing factories with modern labor-saving machinery.

As late as 1917, only 10 per cent of the peasants had profited by Stolypin's reforms to divide the *mir* into individual farms, but half the remainder were engaged in the complicated process of doing so. During the Revolution, they had rapidly broken up the *mir* and seized the remaining non-peasant land. In 1927 only 4 per cent of the peasants were without land or livestock, and only 5 per cent were classified as *kulaks*, "rich" peasants with property worth over $800 who hired the labor of others fifty or more days a year. With this near equality in income, there was little class antagonism in rural Russia, but Stalin now set out to liquidate the *kulaks* and abolish the remaining farmers' privilege of engaging in agriculture individually. The peasants fought when they could, and when they were outnumbered they destroyed their buildings, livestock, and grain rather than surrender them to the government. Between a third and a half of the livestock in the nation was slaughtered, and famine ensued which took many lives. In all, about five million peasants died as a result of collectivization and another five million were made slave laborers. Not until 1937 did Soviet agricultural production reach its pre-1928 levels, but the face of rural Russia had been changed. About a hundred million people were transferred from individual farms to collectivized farms.

The peasants' resistance was not entirely in vain. Each peasant household on a collective farm was permitted to have a small plot of land to raise vegetables and some livestock which could be consumed or sold. The bulk of the land was cultivated as one big farm. Machine tractor stations were established in strategic locations that rented tractors and modern farm machinery to the collective farms, furnished experts to advise on scientific farming methods, and used party members to spy on peasant activities. The produce of the collective farms was divided among the peasants according to the amount and type of work they did, after the bulk of it had been taken by the government for taxes, loans, and the use of the machinery. Collectivization was not an unmitigated evil. The small peasant proprietor under the old system had had neither the necessary capital, technical information, nor acreage to farm scientifically. In the long run, agricultural production increased slightly, and between 1926 and 1939 twenty million peasants were freed to move to cities, where they provided an industrial labor force.

The industrial phase of the Five-Year Plan called for the nationalization of the small, privately-owned businesses and the construction of large factories to produce machinery for other factories and the collectivized farms. Consumer products were given a very low priority in the early five-year plans; but the people were promised that once the coal mines, steel plants, and machine-making factories were constructed, their new industrial power would be directed more towards producing the things they wanted. Just as the first British industrialists had taken only a minimum of their profits for their own use and put the greater part back into their businesses, so now the Russian people set about to produce a great quantity of goods that would be used to produce more goods. Only when they had become a great industrial power did they anticipate enjoying the profits of their labor. Russia, like England, succeeded in becoming an industrial nation without borrowing substantial amounts from abroad.

Farm houses and private plots on a collective farm, USSR. (Sovfoto)

The first Five-Year Plan was followed by a second and then a third. Announced goals were not always achieved, but by 1938 iron and steel production had been increased fourfold and coal nearly as much. Railroad mileage had nearly doubled and more trains and farm tractors were being produced than in any other country in the world. Many of the new industries were constructed east of the Ural Mountains, where coal and iron were available and where the arms of capitalistic powers could not hope to reach in event of war.

This progress was not achieved by the application of the Communist slogan of "from each according to his abilities; to each according to his needs." That happy state was reserved for the highest stage of communism, when man had become so unselfish that he would work as hard for the common good as for his own economic well-being. During the dictatorship of the proletariat phase in the Marxist theory of evolution, the criterion was "from each according to his abilities; to each according to his deeds." The manager of a plant was paid more than the foreman, the foreman more than a skilled laborer, and the skilled laborer more than the unskilled one. There was a greater difference between the pay received by a Soviet private and a Soviet general than between the pay of an American private and an American general; the difference in pay between a college instructor and a distinguished professor was greater in the Soviet Union than it was in the United States. All salaries were very low by American standards except in the field of education. This was especially true of the managers of the new large factories, who received much less than the presidents of big American corporations, but the fact remains that Soviet Russia relies until this day on the capitalistic incentive system to spur the people to greater effort.

Indeed, in some respects Soviet Russia carried the incentive system further than capitalistic countries, where labor was paid by the hour rather than by the accomplishment. Early in the period of the five-year plans, payment by piece work was introduced; that is, a bricklayer was paid by the number of bricks he laid and not by the number of hours he spent at work. This sort of system has been vigorously resisted by labor unions in Western countries, but in the Soviet Union unions were too weak to offer resistance. In 1935, Alexei Stakhanov dug 102 tons of coal in a single shift. This fantastic feat of endurance and organization was followed by others, and the Stakhanovite movement was launched. Champion workers were feted, decorated, and well paid, and they were given wide publicity and special favors. The Soviet youth was encouraged to aspire to become a coal digging king, not a home run king, and the Soviet newspapers were read as anxiously by those who wanted to learn whether the steel quota or the tractor quota was being met as American newspapers are by those who want to see how their favorite baseball team fared the preceding day. In this manner, the government sought to instill the spirit of competition and the desire for achievement in all phases of Soviet economic life. There were those who resisted, those who complained, and those who were incompetent, but they were quickly silenced. There was only one employer in the Soviet Union; he who failed in one job was not likely to be given another chance; he who resisted, whether peasant or urban worker, was sent to a slave labor camp. It has been estimated that as many as twelve million persons were so confined in 1938, a very large percentage of the total labor force.

The real distinction between the Russian and the capitalist economic systems lay not in the presence or absence of economic incentive, but rather in ownership, control, and planning. The means of production, as distinguished from personal property, were owned by the Soviet state. Savings could be put in state banks or used to buy government bonds, but there were no industrial stocks or bonds to be purchased. Production was not geared to what factory management thought could be sold, but to what an over-all planning committee in Moscow thought was needed to achieve the goals of the five-year plans. The Soviet economy then was a planned economy like that of wartime Germany, rather than a free economy operating under the impetus of consumer needs. The early Soviet planners made countless mistakes. Factories were built for which there were no machines, machines were sent to localities where the factories had not yet been constructed. Tractors were made that could not run, and good equipment was allowed to rust by workers who did not understand its use. But as the planners became more experienced and as more technicians were trained, the number of mistakes diminished. If the Soviet economic system were a failure, our own system would not be competing with it today.

OTHER ASPECTS OF THE STALINIST ERA

The revolution Stalin began in the economic fields was paralleled by comparable changes in other areas. The relative freedom that had been previously allowed to the intelligentsia was sharply curtailed. Soviet literature and art were expected to reflect the teachings of the Communist party. Soviet history was to emphasize economic causation and to portray as heroes those who furthered the cause of the revolution. The lax days of progressive education were brought to an end. The curriculum was revised to include a heavy emphasis on science, and competition between students was introduced by the return to a discriminating grading system. Only those who were loyal and who excelled were permitted to enter the advanced educational institutions, graduation from which assured a relatively comfortable livelihood. Family position undoubtedly helped, but the Soviet Union came nearer advancing the able, energetic child and holding back the dull, lazy one, than any other country. Social science and humanistic subjects were used to indoctrinate students with Marxist ideas, and natural science was largely devoted to training technicians to achieve the goals of the five-year plans. Religion, the great rival of the Communist ideology, was intermittently attacked with vigor. By 1937 no more than 40 per cent of the population would admit to religious beliefs. Marriage was discovered to be a necessary institution, not just a bourgeois means of exploitation, and divorce was made more difficult to obtain than in most Protestant countries. Abortions were outlawed, and large families were encouraged in order to swell the labor force.

The 1930's also saw a partial abandonment of the generous treatment previously given to national minorities. The study of Russian was made compulsory in the Ukraine, anti-Semitism began to appear for the first time since tsarist days, and there were some difficulties with other peoples, but on the whole the Soviet record remained fairly satisfactory. Russian nationalism itself was more emphasized. Ivan the Terrible and Peter the Great, who had expanded the territorial boundaries of the state and had wrought social changes by ruthless methods, became heroes. Thus, Stalin's system of government penetrated every walk of life, and every human activity was bent towards achieving the goals he had set. The army stood ready to impose his will, the secret police arrested all who were suspected of opposition, and children were encouraged to inform on their parents.

These economic changes warranted a new constitution, Stalin declared, because they had led to the extinction of the bourgeoisie and the *kulaks*. Only the workers, the peasants, and the intellectuals remained and the distinction between these classes was being erased. As a result, a new constitution was promulgated in 1936 that theoretically recognized these changes. Elections were to be held by direct, universal suffrage, with a peasant's vote being given equal weight to that of a worker. The right to work, to sickness and old age insurance, and to free education were guaranteed, as were the democratic freedoms of speech, of conscience, and of the press. The home and the privacy of correspondence were declared inviolate, and no person was to be arrested "except by decision of a court or with the sanction of a procurator." This document, Stalin insisted, was "the only thoroughly democratic constitution in the world."

Undoubtedly, the new constitution proved an effective propaganda weapon in a world where there were millions of unemployed and where fascist dictatorships were admittedly taking away the liberties of the people, but in fact the totalitarian nature of the Soviet regime remained unaltered. Only the Communist party was permitted to operate. "The party is part of the class, its vanguard section," Stalin reasoned.

> Several parties and consequently freedom of parties can only exist in a society where antagonistic classes exist whose interests are hostile and irreconcilable, where there are capitalists and workers, landlords and peasants, kulaks and poor peasants.
> But in the U.S.S.R. there are no longer such classes. . . . Consequently there are no grounds for the existence of several parties, and therefore, for the existence of freedom of such parties. . . .

How effective one party rule can be is revealed by an official candidate's ability to get 99 or 100 per cent of the vote. Indeed, opposition candidates are not allowed.

How effective the guarantees of individual freedom were is revealed by the purges that began a few months before the adoption of the constitution and continued until 1938. In August, 1936, sixteen prominent Bolsheviks, including Zinoviev and Kamenev, were tried publicly for being Trotskyists, confessed, and were executed. In January, 1937, seventeen more Communist leaders were put on trial, but this time only thirteen were executed. In June, Marshal Tukhachevesky and seven generals were accused of conspiring with the Germans and Japanese and were executed. Others followed, among them Bukharin. Many were sent to slave labor camps, driven to suicide, shot without trial, or simply murdered. Of the last the most prominent was Trotsky, who was assassinated in Mexico presumably on Stalin's order. How many lost their lives in the purges and why Stalin decided to destroy his comrades is unknown. Perhaps he was motivated by fear of them, perhaps he wanted to destroy all those in prominent positions who remembered the old days with Lenin, perhaps he only wished to instill fear in any possible opponent and to be sure that those in a position of power were young men who owed their position to him. The public confessions of the prisoners were probably the result of torture and "brain washing," not of guilt.

These purges once more awakened the people of other countries to the violence and injustices of the Soviet regime, but they did not completely obscure its genuine accomplishments. In about two decades the Communists had transformed Russia from a socially stratified, economically backward state into a great industrial power in which those who served loyally and ably were given the highest rewards, not those of aristocratic birth. Few found much in Russia worthy of admiration before the Revolution, but by 1938 the Soviet Union had become, in the minds of many inhabitants of backward countries, a beacon to guide them towards a better life. They only awaited an opportunity, like that provided by the weakening of the old order in World War II, to move towards its light.

19/ The Revolutions, II

THE fascist revolutions were the second type of political upheaval that threatened the position of the democracies. During the years between the wars, Spain, Portugal, and nearly all the central and east European states established some sort of dictatorship. By 1939 only ten of the twenty-seven European states could be classified as democracies. Many Latin American and Asiatic countries were also ruled by dictators.

There were some similarities between communism and fascism. Both were the result of mass movements that achieved power by violence, clever propaganda, and revolution. Once in power, both communists and fascists created totalitarian states. Every aspect of the people's lives was regulated. Individual interests were made to bow before those of the state or party through the use of force and through an appeal to the ideal of service or duty to a cause that was made to appear worthy of every sacrifice. Without this idealism, neither communism nor fascism would have been a serious threat. Both permitted only one political party to function and denied freedom of speech and of the press. Both thought that capitalism was doomed and rejected laissez-faire in favor of a regulated economy. Both used the secret police, the army, and terrorism, along with persuasion, idealism, and propaganda to remain in power.

The differences between communism and fascism were equally striking. Communism was a product of the materialism, optimism, empiricism, and cosmopolitanism of the Enlightenment. Fascism was a product of the revolt against the Enlightenment; it decried the materialism of the people, said little about the perfectibility of man, theoretically rejected empiricism, and emphasized nationalism. Communists advocated equalitarianism and looked forward to an era of perpetual peace in a Communist world. Fascists proudly proclaimed the "fruitful inequality of mankind," put great emphasis on the development of an élite, and regarded the sacrifices involved in war as positive benefits to building human character. The role of the leader, *Il Duce, Der Führer,* or what have you, in a fascist state was fundamental in both theory and practice; leadership played a much less important role in Communist theory, and collegiate government was acceptable. Communism was a highly doctrinaire philosophy in which the development of theory preceded actions. Fascism was a doctrine of action in which goals were only vaguely suggested and often changed. In it, theoretical justification followed the act. Communism was a dictatorship of the proletariat aided by a few intellectuals; fascism was a dictatorship of the middle class aided by the army, aristocracy, and a few laborers. Communism denied the right of individuals to own the means of production. Fascism protected property rights, but planned and regulated the economy.

Since there was no uniform doctrine of fascism, its nature varied from state to state. Most fascist states cooperated closely with the Catholic Church, but the Nazi Germans persecuted the clergy. Some put little emphasis on race, but the Germans displayed a fanatical belief in the superiority of the Aryans and tried to exterminate those peoples whom they regarded as inferior. As a result, it will be necessary to examine the fascists in each of the important states to see how and why they came to power and what they did when they won control of the government. However, first it will be helpful to consider some of the reasons why so many democracies succumbed to totalitarianism.

THE GREAT DEPRESSION

CAUSES

The most important single cause of the rise of fascism was the Great Depression. The war had produced a business boom, and all the participating nations had suffered from manpower shortages, but wartime demands ended in 1918 and by 1920 civilian shortages had been rectified and millions of discharged soldiers were unable to find employment. A depression ensued which contributed to the establishment of an authoritarian regime in Italy and the formation of fascist parties in other countries. However, by 1924 the immediate postwar economic problems appeared solved, and within the next two years major European countries regained their pre-war levels of production.

Beneath the surface all was not well because world prosperity depended on the purchasing power of the consumer and the confidence of the investor and creditor. The first was gradually undermined during the 1920's, and the second suddenly disappeared during the financial crash of 1929. These economic problems were common to all countries, but they may be best explained by describing them in the United States since the crash of the New York stock market was the immediate cause of the collapse elsewhere.

After a brief period of postwar economic dislocation, the American people embarked on what appeared to be an unrivaled period of prosperity. This prosperity, however, was limited to relatively few people and to the automobile, radio, and related industries. New agricultural techniques had greatly increased productive capacity, but people ate no more, either because they were already adequately fed, or, as in the case of the people of Asia, because they lacked the purchasing power. The prices of farm products declined until a point was reached in 1930 when they were as low as they had been at the beginning of the sixteenth-century price revolution. The net income of the American farmer had dropped to a fourth of its 1920 level by 1932. As a result, the farmer bought less farm machinery, fewer clothes, and learned to make his Model T Ford last a few more years.

The industrial worker did not earn enough to offset this decline. His productive capacity increased 43 per cent between 1919 and 1929, but most of the benefits of his labor went to relatively few people. In 1929, over two-fifths of American families had annual incomes of less than $1,500. The 24,000 most wealthy families received over three times as much as the 5,800,000 poorest families. If the well-to-do had spent all they made, there might have been less serious economic consequences, but much of their income was reinvested in industry. Consequently, the industrial capacity of the country continued to grow at a time when its consumptive capacity was limited. The result was overproduction in industry as well as in agriculture.

The form most of this investment took was the purchase of stock on the New York Stock Exchange. Those who lacked the money to buy all they wanted, borrowed, and many persons owed eight or ten times their original capital. The prices of stock rose. At first this only increased the speculative fever, as many hoped to make quick fortunes by buying low and selling high, rather than waiting for the slow accumulation of dividends. Wise investors, who saw this and saw also that big inventories were being accumulated because the people were not able to buy all that was produced, began to sell. Others recognized the downward trend and followed suit. A panic developed in October, 1929. So much stock was offered for sale that prices dropped 40 per cent in a single month, at a cost to investors of $32,000,000,000. By 1932, fifty key industrial stocks whose average value had been 252 three years before were selling at an average value of 61.

The stock market crash led creditors to lose confidence, and they recalled their loans. Industries tried to pay by selling their inventories at reduced prices. Individuals had to surrender their homes and other properties. Prices declined, but still few could buy. Companies curtailed their production because inventories were not cleared. In doing so, they laid off employees and thereby reduced consumer purchasing power still more. Thus, a chain reaction began in the United States that ended in twelve million unemployed people, five thousand closed banks, and numerous business bankruptcies by 1932.

The depression was not limited to the United States, because the problem of overproduction and underconsumption existed in Europe as well. Only a slight push was needed to start the European economy on the downward trend. This push was provided when New York bankers recalled their loans to Germany and other countries to meet the withdrawals of their depositors. The Germany economy, which had become dependent on these loans, was thrown into a tailspin. At the same time, American purchases from abroad declined. In 1931 a great Vienna bank upon which much of central Europe depended closed its doors. The price of a world economy was a world depression. Production in Europe declined to 72 per cent of its 1929 level, unemployment spread, one country after another went off the gold standard, and international trade fell to one-third its former value.

THE ATTACK ON DEPRESSIONS

At this time several methods were advocated to combat depressions. The approach of the laissez-faire economists was to reduce government expenses in order to keep the budget balanced in spite of lower tax revenue. This ensured a sound currency and prevented inflation. Businesses cut costs on their own initiative by lowering wages, laying off needless workers, and making other economies. These economists believed that, when prices fell sufficiently, people would begin to buy again and recovery would begin. To ensure the domestic market they began to advocate a protective tariff after the movement away from free trade began around 1875.[1] This method had eventually led to recovery from all the nineteenth-century depressions and to the one that began just after World War I. Under these circum-

[1] See page 643.

The Great Depression in the United States: a breadline in New York City, the unemployed in Central Park, the jobless gathered before a radio shop, and from a loudspeaker the reassuring voice of President Franklin D. Roosevelt in 1933. (Charles Phelps Cushing)

stances, it was quite natural that the democracies first turned to it to combat the Great Depression of 1929.

A second method of combating depressions involved vigorous government action. In Soviet Russia this took the form of the state's owning the means of production and deciding what was to be produced. Russia was the one European country that had no agricultural or industrial surplus in the 1930's and no unemployment problems. This was one reason why communism became more popular among workers and intellectuals during the Great Depression, although it was as logical to attribute the absence of surpluses to the inefficiencies of the system as to the virtues of state ownership of the means of production.

In fascist states the ownership of agriculture and industry was left in private hands, but the governments profited from the wartime experience with planned economies. They allocated raw materials and decided what was to be made. Wages were controlled, but roads were built, marshes drained, apartments constructed, new sources of power developed, armaments produced, and armies enlarged. These measures were designed to provide employment, to increase military strength, and to make the nation as self-sufficient as possible. Such a program was expensive, but the fascist states were so powerful that they could compel their own citizens to accept their currency. They cut imports to a minimum by high tariffs and outright refusal to permit the purchase of many foreign products. If there was a necessary article that could not be produced at home, it was usually purchased abroad on a bilateral basis. That is, a German importer was not permitted to buy where he wished, but he had to purchase from a country that had agreed to take a comparable amount of German goods. Actual barter was sometimes adopted. This system avoided the necessity to export gold or to have gold backing for the national currency. The German economy recovered in the 1930's when treated in this manner, but Italy and the other fascist states were less successful.

Several democracies, including the United States, tried to combat the depression by increased government action, especially after they found that the methods of the laissez-faire economists did not bring quick results, but they did not go as far as the fascist states. Their goal was to put more money into the hands of producers and consumers so that the former could afford to manufacture goods and the latter to buy them. This policy was inflationary, and as the price of goods rose, foreign sales were reduced. Efforts were made to counter this by going off the gold standard, that is, by increasing the amount of paper money in circulation in relation to the amount of gold the country held, and by refusing to exchange gold for paper money. The effect of this policy was to raise domestic prices in terms of paper money, but to decrease the price of goods sold abroad in terms of gold. The advantages gained in the international market proved temporary, however, because other countries followed suit in order to compete. The obvious result was international monetary confusion. At this point the disadvantages of having a world economy, but only a national polity, were revealed. As early as July, 1931, President Hoover had made a statesmanlike proposal for a moratorium on international debts and reparations to enable countries to stabilize their currencies. All but token payments on World War I debts and reparations ceased from that time, but at this point international cooperation stopped. Sixty-four countries sent representatives to London during the summer of 1933 to try to re-establish trade and industry by reducing tariffs, restoring an international monetary standard, and removing restrictions on foreign loans, but nothing was accomplished because most nations preferred to try to solve their problems individually.

LORD KEYNES

The above rather haphazard, inconsistent approach had been used by some of the democracies for several years when the brilliant English economist, John Maynard Keynes (1883-1946), published his persuasive book, *The General Theory of Employment, Interest, and Money* in 1936. This work provided the theoretical justification for increased governmental influence in the capitalistic system and led to a revolution in capitalistic economic thought, although it came too late to have much practical effect prior to the outbreak of World War II in 1939.

The nineteenth-century liberals had divorced economics from government. Economic matters were to be left alone so that natural self-regulatory laws could operate, and the government's role was limited to that of protecting its citizens from violence at home and attack from abroad. It was Lord Keynes' mission to renew the tie between economic matters and governmental action, but he did so in a way different from mercantilists, fascists, and socialists. His goal was to find a cure for the economic problems posed by the postwar era and the depression; he did not wish to destroy the capitalistic system or to interfere with the freedom of the individual.

Keynes pointed out that in liberal economic thought production and prices depended on the law of supply and demand as they were related to gold. The quantity of gold, however, varied with the discovery and operation of gold mines, and not with the needs of the economy. Thus, both the discovery of precious metals in the New World in the sixteenth century and the failure to discover important new gold mines between the California strike of 1849 and the Klondike strike of 1896 had been the result of chance; yet both had affected the economy: the sixteenth-century discovery of precious metals by causing a rapid rise in prices, and the late nineteenth-century failure to make any significant discovery of gold by causing a slow decline in prices. What Keynes proposed was that gold and currency be divorced and that the quantity of money in circulation vary with the needs of the economy rather than the supply of gold. If business was optimistically investing at a rate that threatened to produce an inflationary boom to be followed by the inevitable bust, it should be checked by reducing the quantity of money available. If business was sluggish, it should be stimulated by increasing the amount of money available to the producer and consumer.

There were several ways in which this could be accomplished. By raising the interest rate, a too rapid economic expansion could be checked; by lowering it, a stagnant economy could be stimulated. A public works program and deficit financing could cure widespread unemployment and a depressed economy, while a booming economy could be checked by heavy taxation. It was important to distinguish between the uses put to money by the rich and the poor. The rich save and invest part of their earnings; the poor have to spend all they make. Therefore, if the economy is suffering from overproduction, it is best to put more money into the hands of the poor consumers. If there is need for money to encourage industrial expansion, it is wiser to cater to the interests of the well-to-do. Thus, by manipulating currency, credit, taxes, and government spending, the state can regulate the economy, prevent the boom and bust cycle, provide for social justice, and at the same time keep the production and sale of goods free from direct control by the state.

THE RISE OF FASCISM

Unfortunately, Lord Keynes' theories about how to combat a depression did not become generally known until many states had succumbed to the rise of fascism. In the 1920's the typical European still believed in the self-evident truths that had become popular in the age of the egalitarian revolutions. Included among them were not only liberty and equality, but also several cherished economic doctrines. Since the days of Adam Smith, production had been regarded as the source of wealth and it had been assumed that problems concerning price and distribution would take care of themselves through a self-regulating economic law of supply and demand. When the Great Depression came in 1929, these assumptions were suddenly revealed to be unrealistic. Factories closed when there were millions who needed manufactured goods; farm produce remained unsold while millions more went hungry. Everywhere unemployment was a chronic problem. To many the old laissez-faire doctrines seemed bankrupted. To their willingness to abandon their economic freedom in return for economic security, they half-unconsciously coupled a willingness to surrender the other truths they had regarded as self-evident since the age of the egalitarian revolutions.

In their willingness to surrender their liberty, many people were undoubtedly motivated by wartime experiences on the home front. During the war even the most liberal democracies had engaged in economic planning and regulation, compelled people to serve in the army and often in critical industries, censored the press, issued official propaganda, and stifled serious dissent. As bankruptcies became more frequent and unemployment grew, the Great Depression became as serious a crisis as the war itself and seemed to call for drastic action. At this point the intellectuals, who had been in the forefront of the battle for liberty, democracy, and national self-determination, faltered. Some turned to communism or socialism. Others, confused by the seemingly unsolvable problems of their day, became disenchanted with the materialistic Western civilization and sought a new set of values and a new type of solution for the issues that confronted them. Too often they thought they found them in fascism with its emphasis on action rather than reason, violence rather than legality, and courage rather than mercy.

Factory laborers often became Communists, but members of middle-class origin who had lost their property and their positions were too conscious of their social status and too nationalistic to join an international workingman's movement. They, and those ex-soldiers who had been unable to accustom themselves to civilian life, became the nucleus of the fascist movement. As the threat of communism seemed to grow, the upper-middle class and the remnants of the aristocracy often joined them, and together they tried to create fascist states.

Those countries in which liberal, democratic traditions were strong and the people were experienced in the art of self-government resisted the fascist threat. Where these traditions were not firmly implanted and this experience was lacking, the fascists were often successful. This was especially true in economically backward countries, or in countries where there was a serious minority problem, bitterness at the outcome of World War I, or fear of a foreign power. As the situation varied from one country to another, it will be necessary to consider each in turn to see how they confronted the immediate postwar problems and what actions they took when the Great Depression came.

ITALY

MUSSOLINI AND THE FASCIST REVOLT

The founder and leader of Italian fascism was Benito Mussolini. Mussolini was born in a small Italian village in 1883. His father served both as the local blacksmith and as the local socialist leader. Radicalism was more plentiful in the household than the conveniences of life, but in spite of poverty, young Mussolini managed to get an education and became an elementary school teacher in 1902. After one year of teaching, he fled to Switzerland to avoid army service. Here he earned his living as a bricklayer, but found time to mingle with socialists, anarchists, and syndicalists, to attend lectures at the University of Lausanne, and to learn several foreign languages.

In 1904 Mussolini returned to Italy where he rose rapidly in the socialist hierarchy. By 1910 he was editor of the principal Socialist newspaper and a leader of the militant wing of the party. He had nothing but contempt for the gentle methods of the revisionist socialist leaders, for the most part middle-class university graduates who had never done a day's manual labor. He himself was a powerful man who liked to display his athletic ability and engage in street brawls. He was, however, no ordinary ruffian, for he was self-confident, industrious, well-informed, intelligent, and studious. His dark sunken eyes, expressive face, animated voice, and unfailing sense of the dramatic made him an inspiring speaker. Above all, he understood human nature. He knew how to command and how to lead. Even during his days of power, he worked in the fields with the peasants and mixed with the common soldiers on maneuvers. He did not seek material gain like so many Italian politicians. His great desire was for power; he had the will and the courage to achieve it.

The outbreak of World War I produced a crisis in Mussolini's career. As a socialist, he was obligated to work to keep Italy out of this nationalistic, bourgeois conflict, but at heart he was more a man of action than a doctrinaire Marxist. In October, 1914, he advocated intervention on the allied side, in November he was expelled from the Socialist party, and in December he founded his own newspaper with funds probably provided by the French. Mussolini's editorial efforts were partly responsible for Italy's decision to accept allied promises of additional territory in return for entering the war in May, 1915. Soon thereafter, Mussolini abandoned his desk and took up the life of a soldier, but in January, 1917, he had to return to civilian life, claiming to have received forty wounds. He had known poverty, and he had known war. He had espoused the cause of the common man, and he had espoused the cause of his country. Few men were better situated to profit from the position in which Italy now found itself.

The war had caused a rapid rise in prices; industrial profits were large, but wages lagged. Socialist-led workers, therefore, began to demand welfare legislation and higher wages. Industrialists were unwilling to vote taxes to support the first or to reduce their profits in order to increase wages. Strikes and violence were the result. Agricultural laborers had a similar grievance against their landlords and actually began to appropriate some large estates for their own use.

The returning soldier was an equally serious problem. The civilian economy was unable to absorb him, and he was often psychologically unable to return to his former life. War has a curious fascination. Its discomforts and boredom are soon forgotten; remembered are the comradeship that is bred by life under difficult conditions, the acts of personal sacrifice, and the unrecorded deeds of heroism. In every country returning veterans formed organizations to work for their own and what they conceived to be their country's welfare, to enable them to meet and recount their past experiences, and to sponsor patriotic parades in which they once again marched in uniform. Where the economy was sound and the democratic tradition strong, such activities were not a serious threat. Italy, however, was poor. The soldier who had gone to war amid the plaudits of those who remained behind, returned, not to a hero's welcome, but to a society that showed little appreciation for his sufferings. No government in 1918 made a serious effort to re-establish its soldiers in civilian life. Many in Italy went jobless; veterans' organizations, instead of serving as recreational activities, became the former soldiers' only occupation. Quickly they were transformed into private armies composed largely of unemployed or underpaid ex-soldiers who came originally from the lower-middle and working classes. These men, trained in violence against a foreign foe, now turned against their countrymen.

If the government had been strong, it could have quickly suppressed any violence, but it was not. Italy had numerous political parties, none of which had a large following throughout the country. The historic differences between the north and south made united action difficult. As a result, no Italian party could hope to obtain the support of a majority of the nation. Every cabinet was a coalition. To suggest reform or to enforce law and order was sure to trample on someone's interests; a party would with-

Benito Mussolini—Il Duce—in a fiery attitude as he addressed 25,000 of his followers in Rome on October 16, 1932. The occasion was the tenth anniversary of the Fascist march on Rome. (Wide World)

draw from the coalition, the cabinet would fall, there would be a scramble for office, and a new coalition would be formed. Only by the careful award of favors, the occasional practice of graft and corruption, and the avoidance of strong measures could a prime minister hope to remain in office long. Under these circumstances, many sincere idealists wanted to adopt a new form of government in which the interests of the nation, rather than the interests of the politicians, would be served.

To make matters worse, Italy was a disappointed nation. The Allies had promised much in return for its entry into the war in 1915, but at the peace conference Wilson limited Italy's conquests to only 9,000 square miles of territory in return for its 600,000 dead and 1,000,000 wounded. Not a single German colony was given to Italy as a mandate. Nationalists blamed these failures on the government. The fiery poet, Gabriele d'Annunzio (1863-1938), raised an army of ex-soldiers and seized Fiume, which the Italians had claimed. He was soon dislodged, but Fiume eventually became an Italian city.

On March 23, 1919, before D'Annunzio had shown the world what could be done with a private army, Mussolini founded the Fascist movement in Milan. The term fascism or *fasces* refers to the group of rods containing an ax that was carried by a Roman magistrate as a symbol of his authority. The original fascists were radicals who wished to improve the laborers' lot and to defend Italy's national interests. They organized their bands into centuries and legions and revived the Roman salute. Many such fascists were ex-soldiers who thought little of committing acts of violence to gain their ends. From the standpoint of economic policy, their natural allies were the socialists, but Mussolini was distrusted by his former colleagues. Indeed, his Fascists, clad in black-shirted uniforms, took special pleasure in using physical force against their socialist rivals, whom they regarded as unpatriotic.

Under normal circumstances, such acts would win few supporters, but events in Russia after the end of the war made conservatives especially fearful of a communist revolution. Italian workers led by socialists frequently went on strikes and in some instances seized control of factories, as the Bolsheviks had done in Russia several years before. The government did not act vigorously to protect property rights and, to make matters worse, the Socialists emerged as the largest single party in parliament in 1919. Slowly conservatives began to believe that Mussolini might be of use to them, and Mussolini, in turn, spoke less of his radical economic program, declared the Fascists were saving Italy from Bolshevism, and announced his willingness to support the monarchy. In the elections of 1921, the Fascists, who cooperated closely with the nationalists, won only thirty-five seats, but in 1919 they had gained none.

In October, 1922, the Fascists struck. From every part of Italy their troops began to march on Rome. By the 28th, 8,000 had reached the city and two days later there were from 50,000 to 60,000. On the 31st, King Victor Emmanuel III summoned Mussolini to form a cabinet. The Fascists had triumphed. Why? Not because they had won popular support, not because the regular army was unable to disperse their ill-armed bands, but because the king, the army, the nationalists, and the upper-middle class were either active supporters or passive observers of the movement.

Victor Emmanuel III (1900-1947) was a weak-willed king with a domineering, autocratic wife. He knew the army liked the belligerent nationalism of the Fascists, that many members of the upper-middle class looked on them as a bulwark against communism and socialism, and that his cousin hoped to be placed on the throne in his stead if he refused to cooperate. The cabinet voted to declare martial law on October 27, but several military leaders advised the King not to sign the decree and the prime minister, who expected to be included in the new ministry, did not press him to do so. Victor Emmanuel, therefore, refused to support the cabinet and no effort was made to halt the Fascists.

Mussolini was now prime minister, but he was not yet a dictator. Only by including nationalists and conservatives in his cabinet could he get the support of a majority in parliament. Most Italian politicians did not feel threatened because they predicted that Mussolini's cabinet, like others, would fall in a year. They were wrong, but Mussolini made few immediate changes in the system of government, and for more than a year he was content to strengthen his hold over local government officials and the police. The Fascist bands were formally organized into a militia, and by April, 1924, he felt strong enough to hold elections. Every form of political pressure was used; where pressure was not enough, Fascist squads used force against the opposition. The result was foredoomed. Sixty-five per cent of the voters declared their support for the Fascists.

Meanwhile, the behavior of the Fascists had frightened many, and it had become obvious they were no ordinary political party. The courageous socialist leader, Giacomo Matteotti, who had already published a book exposing the violent methods of the Fascists, rose in parliament and attacked their behavior during the elections. When he had finished, he informed his friends: "Now you can prepare my funeral oration." Ten days later, on June 10, his body was found in an alley behind the parliament building.

There was an immediate uproar. The press, which was still free, demanded justice. Many non-Fascist deputies withdrew from parliament and swore to remain away until the guilty were punished. Count Campello, a friend of the king, confronted him with documentary evidence implicating Mussolini in the plot. The weakling king stammered, "I am not a judge; these things ought not to be told to me. . . ." The murderers were tried, found guilty, but released from prison two months later when the crisis had passed. From that time until the eve of his dismissal from office in 1943, Mussolini's authority was not seriously challenged. Censorship of the press was established, freedom of speech was curtailed, and an elaborate system of propaganda was inaugurated to win support for the new regime. Those who were opposed were soon silenced by the secret police, except for a few scholars like the historian Benedetto Croce, whose fame was so great that he was allowed to remain in Naples unmolested.

THE FASCIST CREED AND THE FASCIST STATE

It was one thing to become a dictator and another to decide what to do with power once it had been achieved. The Marxists had an elaborate theory telling them when the revolution would come, how power could be seized, and, more vaguely, what was then to be done to achieve the ultimate goal, world communism. The Fascists had no such guide for their conduct. "Fascism was not the nursling of a doctrine worked out beforehand with detailed elaboration," Mussolini declared; "it was born of the need for action and it was itself from the beginning practical rather than theoretical. . . ." This emphasis on action, if need be, on violent action, was characteristic of much of the thought of the time. Nietzsche had praised the "will to power"; Bergson, the *élan vital*, and Sorel the noble sentiments evoked by a general strike.[2] All had pointed to the ennobling qualities of action, and action was the one thing in which Mussolini always believed.

Related to this worship of action was what little else the creed of fascism contained. War was praised, for it "alone brings up to its highest ten-

[2] See pages 650 and 813.

sion all human energy and puts the stamp of nobility upon the peoples who have the courage to meet it. All other trials are substitutes, which never really put men into the position where they have to make the great decision—the alternative of life or death." Materialism, both in its Marxist and capitalistic form, was rejected. "Fascism denies the validity of the equation, well-being = happiness, which would reduce men to the level of animals, caring for one thing only—to be fat and well-fed. . . ." There was neither a class war nor economic determinism, and capitalism was considered a decadent economic system. Egalitarian democracy was rejected because of its devitalizing effect, and the "immutable, beneficial, and fruitful inequality of mankind" was affirmed.

Liberalism was scorned; borrowing from Hegel and his intellectual heirs, Mussolini emphasized the role of the state. "The State, as conceived of and as created by Fascism," he wrote, "is a spiritual and moral fact in itself, since its political, juridical, and economic organization of the nation is a concrete thing and such an organization must be in its origins and development a manifestation of the spirit. The State is the guarantor of security both internal and external, but it is also the custodian and transmitter of the spirit of the people, as it had grown up through the centuries in language, in customs, and in faith. And the State is not only a living reality of the present, it is also linked with the past and above all with the future, and thus transcending the brief limits of individual life, it represents the immanent spirit of the nation." Such a state must be totalitarian because it "absorbs within itself, in order to transform and invigorate them, all the energy, all the interests, all the hopes of a people." Irrational, yes; destructive of human liberty, yes; but the Fascist doctrine, by appealing to the spirit of self-sacrifice and to the need for moral vigor, had qualities that could and did inspire loyalty. Mussolini's popularity increased, rather than waned, until he led his people into World War II.

The Fascist doctrine described above was not in itself sufficient to form the basis of a political or economic system. Indeed, the expansion of the initial doctrine of action outlined in the preceding paragraph into a creed was not achieved until long after Mussolini had come to power. The lack of a rigid theory left Mussolini free to inaugurate a system that was both opportunist and practical. He did not change the Italian constitution fundamentally. The king remained as a figurehead, and respect for the crown and the royal family was carefully nurtured. The cabinet, headed by Mussolini, continued to function, as did the two houses of parliament. However, the senators had always been appointed and the lower house was controlled by the Fascist party, offering a list of 400 candidates which the people voted to accept or reject, no rival parties or candidates being permitted. Actually, there was little need for so much care, for Mussolini could issue decrees that had the force of law. The judiciary and the local government remained about as before, except that anti-Fascists were dismissed.

The Fascist party was the real policy-making body in Italy, just as the Communist party was in Russia. At its head stood Mussolini, *Il Duce*, the leader. Below him in descending order were a Grand Council consisting of about thirty members which made policy under his direction, ninety-two provincial directories, and about ten thousand local party headquarters. Through these channels the chain of command went from Mussolini down to the smallest communes. In addition, the party sponsored youth organizations which indoctrinated children from the time they were six, university student societies, teacher associations, and elaborate programs providing athletic and cultural activities for the working class.

The economic reorganization was of greater interest. The medieval guild had long interested some idealists who liked the way master and journeyman had worked together, presumably without strikes or quarrels. The medieval system of representation by estates or classes seemed to some more logical than the modern system of representation by geographical districts. Out of this admiration of the past emerged the corporative theory of the state and society which the Fascists gradually put into effect in Italy and in varying forms in other countries.

A revival of the guild system in an industrial world was obviously impossible. Instead, six (later four) national confederations, one each for those employed in industry, agriculture, commerce, banking and insurance, maritime and air transport, and land transport and inland navigation, were established for employees, and another six (later four) were established for employers in the same fields. A thirteenth confederation was formed for professional people and artists, who presumably were neither employers nor employees. Beneath each of the national confederations there were federations, provincial groups, and finally local syndicates consisting of the employers or employees in a given occupation in a relatively small area. Each of the local syndicates theoretically elected its own officials, but in practice the government was the determining factor in appointments from the lowest to the highest level. Strikes were forbidden. Disputes between employers and employees were settled by arbitration between their respective syndicates or federations. If agreement could not be reached, the case was turned over to a special labor court where judges handed down decisions that were binding on both parties. There is something to be said for the substitution of labor courts for strikes. The strike awards the decision to the strongest, after considerable losses in production, and it is no more likely to lead to a just decision than a medieval trial by combat. On the other hand, it is difficult to establish what capital's, management's, and labor's just shares are and to find judges who are truly impartial in such matters. In Italy hundreds of thousands of cases were arbitrated or brought to the labor courts. On a numerical count, the employees were awarded more decisions, but the employers won most of the important cases, and the real wages of the Italian worker declined about 10 per cent under the Fascist regime.

Italian production was also organized vertically. Twenty-two corporations were established in 1934, largely on a basis of cycles of production. One, for example, was the corporation for fruit. It included those who raised the fruit, picked it, transported it, and sold it in retail stores. Both employers and employees were represented in each corporation in equal numbers. Also represented were members of the Fascist party and other groups who were to look after the public's interest, that is, to prevent employee and employer from agreeing to raise prices, wages, and profits at the expense of the consumer. The twenty-two corporation councils were joined together in a National Council of Corporations, which was guided by a Central Corporative Committee and placed under a cabinet official. Mussolini himself assumed the cabinet post and the office of president of each of the twenty-two corporations. The corporations were used to bring employers and employees together and to plan and direct the economy, but it cannot be said that they played an important role. Nevertheless, in 1938 the Chamber of Deputies was abolished and a Chamber of Fasces and Corporations composed of the members of the National Council of Corporations and the Grand and National councils of the Fascist party was established in its place. Geographical representation ceased, and the corporative state was at last fully established.

The Italian state was both totalitarian and corporate. Freedom of speech and freedom of the press were curtailed. Anti-Fascist organizations were prohibited, and secret police spied on everyone's activities. Efforts were made to Italianize the Austrian Germans south of the Brenner Pass who had been ceded as a result of World War I. Yet compared to Stalin's and Hitler's dictatorships, Mussolini's dictatorship was mild. He could be ruthless, but he had no desire to exterminate any race or class. In 1938 laws were issued curtailing the rights of Jews, perhaps at Hitler's request, but they were never fully enforced. Public education was improved in many respects, although freedom of inquiry was restricted. University professors were required to take a loyalty oath, and secondary schools taught patriotism, Fascism, and admiration of *Il Duce*.

Mussolini's most famous triumph was reaching an agreement with the pope. It will be remembered that when the Italian government seized Rome in 1870 the pope had shut himself up in the Vatican and declared that he was a prisoner. There he had remained, although the tension between church and state had relaxed. When Pius XI became pope in 1922, he began to make a series of concordats with various states defining the position of the Church. In 1929, he signed the Lateran Treaty with Mussolini in which he was given St. Peter's basilica, the Vatican palace, and Castle Gandolfo, a summer residence, in full sovereignty. These 108.7 acres made him once more an independent temporal ruler. In addition, the papacy received $87,500,000 in compensation for the property confiscated during the period of unification. The clergy was to be paid by the state, religious instruction given in the public schools by priests, and

Catholicism recognized as the official religion. The pope had gained much, but at the cost of giving indirect support to the Fascist regime; this support, of course, was what Mussolini wanted.

Mussolini's economic policy changed abruptly during the period of his rise to power. His early followers had been drawn from the lower-middle and working classes; in them, his radical talk of minimum wage laws and extraordinary taxes on capital struck a responsive cord. But when the aristocracy and upper-middle class began to take an interest in his movement because of its stand against communism and socialism, he became more conservative. The workers' interests became secondary, and the dictatorship he established was essentially one of the middle class to which the aristocracy and army lent support. The split which had begun to develop between the upper- and lower-middle classes around the turn of the century was erased,[3] and Mussolini's economic policies benefited this class more than the workers.

Mussolini claimed that he saved Italy from communism, although the possibility of a communist seizure of power had largely passed before he took office. Nevertheless, many believed him. He provided employers with a docile labor force that could not strike, raised tariffs to ensure them the domestic market, and granted them financial aid during the depression. The worker, on the other hand, suffered a decline in real wages, and during the depression over a million were unemployed. Enough of Mussolini's youthful sympathy for labor did survive for him to strengthen social insurance and enlarge the public works programs. Some slums were cleared and better housing provided for the poor.

Italy was far from being economically self-sufficient. Mussolini tried to compensate for its lack of coal by developing hydroelectric power. He reclaimed land, drained the Pontine marshes, and encouraged scientific agriculture in an effort to produce more food. On the whole, he was only moderately successful. Many said that at least he made the trains run on time. It was rumored, however, that this was not accomplished by greater efficiency, but by adopting less ambitious schedules.

Mussolini's desire to make Italy a great, economically self-sufficient nation led him to embark on a policy of colonial expansion. The army and navy were expanded, and there was much talk of the morally invigorating character of war. Ethiopia and Albania were seized, and the hope that the Adriatic and Mediterranean would once more become Italian seas as they had been in Roman times was frequently expressed. A policy of encouraging large families and discouraging emigration was adopted to provide numerical support for these ambitions and settlers for the colonies. Thus Italy, like the defeated Central Powers, was a revisionist state, in that it wanted to alter the terms of the peace treaties of 1919. It was not surprising, therefore, that Mussolini eventually became Hitler's ally. This alliance brought his own and his country's ruin. In April, 1945, the once

[3] See pages 643-644.

mighty dictator was caught while trying to escape to Switzerland. After a mock trial, he was shot by left-wing partisans whom he had deserted so many years before. In life he had been the first great Fascist revolutionary and had provided the inspiration for others to follow, not the least of whom was Adolf Hitler. In death he marked the virtual eclipse of one of the great twentieth-century revolutions.

GERMANY

THE ESTABLISHMENT OF THE WEIMAR REPUBLIC

In 1918 Germany became a republic. This decision was not undertaken with the enthusiasm that greeted the establishment of the French republic in 1792. Even a majority of the socialists would have preferred to have kept the monarchy in 1918 if it had been practical, and those members of the middle class who came to accept the republic did so only because there was no alternative. The army, the aristocracy, and the more conservative wing of the middle class never abandoned their desire for a Hohenzollern restoration, while many radicals looked to Soviet Russia as a model and refused to participate in the framing of the new constitution. The German republic was a product of circumstances; when the circumstances changed, the republic ceased to exist.

Events moved too swiftly during the fall of 1918 for people to understand what was taking place. The average German during that spring and summer had still expected victory. Russia had been brought to its knees, and everywhere along the western front German troops were deep in allied territory. Ludendorff's recommendation on September 29 that armistice negotiations be commenced caught even the leaders of the government by surprise. In the hope of securing better terms from the Allies, it was decided to democratize the government. The liberal Prince Max of Baden was named head of the cabinet, ministerial responsibility to the Reichstag was established, the various states, including Prussia, were made democratic, and other reforms were introduced. Quietly, as a result of this "revolution from above," Germany was transformed into a liberal, democratic monarchy like Great Britain. These changes, plus the abdication of the Kaiser and the rejection of the unpopular crown prince's claims to succeed, would have satisfied most Germans whether conservative or liberal. The Kaiser refused to abdicate, however, and the situation became worse. The sailors mutinied, soldiers and workers established councils on the model of the Russian soviets, and Kurt Eisner, a left-wing socialist, proclaimed a republic in Bavaria. On November 9, Prince Max announced the abdication of the Kaiser without his permission, but it was too late. Left-wing elements had obtained control and Prince Max surrendered the government to Friedrich Ebert (1871-1925), one-time saddle maker and now leader of the Social Democratic party. Ebert himself was not opposed to a continuation of the monarchy, but fear that radicals would get control of the masses if drastic changes were not announced led to the proclamation of a republic immediately after the Kaiser's abdication. Two days later the armistice was signed.

The sequence of events had been important. Only after the generals had realized that defeat was inevitable had internal uprisings or armistice negotiations begun, but to a casual observer the left-wing revolts seem to have forced the Kaiser to abdicate and the army to surrender when it was still on foreign soil. This gave rise to the legend that the allied victory and the republic were the premeditated result of a socialist-democratic "stab in the back."

The chances of forming a strong republic were reduced still further by a series of rebellions during the winter of 1918-1919 and by the terms of the Treaty of Versailles. When the Social Democrats took power, they were not a united party. The majority followed Ebert in his desire to proceed in a constitutional, democratic manner, but on the extreme left the Spartacists, a group led by Rosa Luxemburg and Karl Liebknecht, wanted to establish a dictatorship of the proletariat as Lenin had just done. A third faction, the Independent Socialists, advocated a social revolution, but not a reign of terror. They insisted that considerable authority be given to the workers' and soldiers' councils which were springing up all over Germany.

The Reichstag was not allowed to reconvene after the end of the war, and in December the First Congress of German Soviets met in Berlin. The Social Democrats won the Congress' consent to convene a national assembly at Weimar. The Spartacists refused to participate, became affiliated with the Russian Communists, and between December and June led a series of insurrections and strikes designed to overthrow the government. On January 5, they tried to seize Berlin, but Ebert and the Social Democrats were more fortunate than Russia's Kerensky. With the aid of the regular army and private armies composed of volunteer soldiers (*Freikorps*), the rebellion was crushed. Rosa Luxemburg and Karl Liebknecht were killed, but the cry of "all power to the soviets" was raised in other parts of Germany. In Bavaria, Eisner was assassinated by a conservative, but on April 9 the Communists proclaimed a soviet republic. Once more the army and *Freikorps* suppressed the uprising. The Social Democrats had prevented Germany from falling into the hands of the Communists, but they had restored order only by appealing to the army and *Freikorps*. How real the Communist threat had been is difficult to say, but it should be remembered that Lenin had come to power under similar circumstances. From this time, among the aristocracy and the middle class, the fear of Bolshevism grew.

In January, 1919, the Socialist government held elections to the national assembly. All men and women over twenty were allowed to vote, but to their disappointment the Social Democrats failed to win a majority and had to govern with the predominantly middle-class Catholic Center and Democratic parties. It was the members of this coalition who were given the distasteful assignment of accepting the Versailles treaty. They protested vigorously and signed only after the army had told them that further resistance was impossible. Nevertheless, the Versailles treaty was added to the "stab in the back" on the list of charges against Germany's most democratic parties. Had the Allies been wise, they would have encouraged their development by giving them more generous terms.

The Weimar national assembly also prepared the constitution for the new republic. It provided for a president to be elected for a term of seven years, an upper house (Reichsrat) to represent the states, and a lower house (Reichstag) chosen by universal suffrage to represent the people. A system of proportional representation was established which gave seats in the Reichstag to political parties in accordance with the percentage of the total vote they received rather than in accordance with the number of geographical areas they carried. This was very democratic, but it helped to prevent the development of a two-party system by enabling small political parties to play important roles in the Reichstag. The president was a figurehead except in time of emergency, when he could rule by decree. The privileges enjoyed by the state governments in the old empire were reduced, and an exhaustive bill of rights was included. Few constitutions have ever been so democratic or so perverted from their original intent.

THE WEIMAR REPUBLIC

The mild, humane, and orderly behavior of the Social Democrats and their allies deserves special comment. No social class was disfranchised, no property was confiscated, the former reigning families were even allowed to retain most of their land. The civil servants of the empire were given comparable positions under the republic. The judges remained unchanged, as did the teachers and the officer corps. Respect for position continued, and egalitarian modes of address such as "citizen," "comrade," or just plain "mister" were not adopted. The count continued to be called "count" and the professor, "professor." There was much to be said for this mildness, but there were also disadvantages. Army officers and bureaucrats were loyal to Germany, not to the republic. Judges punished left-wing agitators more severely than right-wing nationalists with whom they often sympathized. Educators continued to instruct the youth in nationalist and monarchical traditions and made no effort to stimulate enthusiasm for the republic. Thus, the republic never had the full loyalty of its officials or won the full devotion of the people. It is surprising that it survived the attacks leveled against it as long as it did.

In March, 1920, Dr. Wolfgang Kapp seized control of Berlin with the aid of segments of the regular army, and proclaimed the Weimar constitution null and void. The labor unions remained loyal, however, and ordered a general strike. In less than a week, Kapp and his supporters were forced to flee. That same month witnessed an unsuccessful Communist uprising in the Ruhr valley. The two years that followed saw the assassination of several leaders of the Weimar Republic by rabid nationalists. Included was the able Jewish industrialist and statesman, Walter Rathenau, whose economic planning had contributed more to Germany's war effort than the strategy of any of its generals. The year 1923 was marked by a Communist uprising in Saxony, separatist movements in the Rhineland and Bavaria, and an equally unsuccessful "Beer Hall Putsch" in Munich in which a relatively unknown agitator named Adolf Hitler and the famous Field Marshal Ludendorff attempted to overthrow the government.

Rebellion was but one problem the new republic faced. Neither the wartime imperial government nor its successor had dared to tax heavily enough to meet expenses. Loans were solicited and paper money, insufficiently backed by gold, was printed to meet expenses. The situation became especially serious in 1923 when the French and Belgians decided to occupy the Ruhr valley because Germany had defaulted in its reparation payments.[4] Incapable of offering military resistance, Germany went on a national sit-down strike. Workers and employers refused to operate the Ruhr industries, and the government provided financial support by running the printing presses day and night. The result was inflation. In 1914, 4.2 marks purchased an American dollar, in 1919 it took 8.9, on November 1, 1923, 130,000,000,000, and on November 20, 4,200,000,000,000.

At this point, the government called a halt. Passive resistance ceased, a new *Rentenmark* was issued that was worth 1,000,000,000,000 of the old marks, and the Dawes Plan was accepted, which reduced reparation payments, provided for an American loan, and led to the withdrawal of French troops. The situation had been stabilized but only after tremendous losses. Bank deposits, private pension funds, life insurance policies, government and corporation bonds, and similar types of savings and investments had become worthless. A person with a trillion dollars in the bank in 1914 had only one dollar's purchasing power on November 20, 1923. The old, the widowed, and the orphaned were left with nothing. Members of the middle class who had relied largely on their investments now had only their salaries. "The intellectual and productive middle class," Stresemann later declared, "which was traditionally the backbone of the country, has been paid for the utter sacrifice of itself to the state during the war by being deprived of all its property and by being proletarianized." There were, of course, those who profited. The government emerged relatively free of domestic debt. Clever businessmen borrowed money and bought property during the early stages of inflation and then paid off their debts with ease during the period of runaway inflation.

The existence of profiteers further angered the mass of the German people. In addition to the "stab in the back" and the Treaty of Versailles,

[4] See page 792.

the Weimar Republic was charged with the inflation. The growing disillusionment was clearly revealed by the elections of May, 1924. The pro-republican coalition of the Socialist, Center, and Democratic parties who had received over three-fourths of the votes in 1919 won less than 40 per cent of the ballots. Many workers had grown tired of the mild democratic policies of the Socialists, and 3,700,000 had voted for the Communists. On the right, the anti-democratic Nationalist party which drew its support primarily from the old aristocracy and industrialists emerged as the second largest in the country, and Hitler's National Socialists polled more votes than the Democratic party, despite the fiasco of the Munich uprising six months before. The following year Field Marshal Paul von Hindenburg, a known monarchist, ran for the presidency with the support of the conservative Nationalists and won. Fortunately the middle-class People's party led by the able Gustav Stresemann (1878-1929) had come to the conclusion several years before that a republic was the only possible form of government under the existing circumstances and had joined the Weimar coalition. Even with its aid and that of several minor parties, the republican forces barely controlled the Reichstag.

The six-year period ushered in by the currency stabilization and the Dawes Plan were happy ones for Germans. American loans stimulated industrial development. New factories were built, and cartels were formed. The I. G. Farben concern was organized in 1925 and became one of the largest industrial empires in the world with 900 firms under its control. Du Pont, Standard Oil, and Royal Dutch Shell were among the hundreds of foreign corporations with Farben ties. Foreign trade increased rapidly, and a superb merchant fleet was constructed. By 1928 the national income was half again as large as in 1913. The workers benefited, though far less than the industrialists. Real wages rose only 6 per cent, but slums were cleared, low-cost housing was built, and unemployment insurance was established. Swimming pools, stadiums, and athletic fields were built by many municipalities, a program for land redistribution provided farms for 50,000 settlers, but the more ambitious parts of the Socialist program were not enacted because middle-class parties always dominated the coalitions that governed Germany; this in part explains why more radical parties captured a large part of the younger generation of workers.

THE DEPRESSION

October, 1929, was a fateful month for Germany. Gustav Stresemann died, and the New York stock market crashed. Stresemann had won for Germany a respected place in the family of nations,[5] and he had kept his conservative People's party loyal to the Weimar coalition. Both as a diplomat and as a party leader, he was missed, for no one else proved capable of coping with the growing German impatience with the conciliatory foreign

[5] See pages 792-793.

policy and with the Wall Street crash which brought to an end the brief period of German prosperity. By 1930 there were over three million unemployed persons in Germany, and by 1932 the figure passed six million, a third of the entire labor force. Heinrich Brüning (1885-   ), a devout, determined, conservative Catholic, had become chancellor in March, 1930, before the economic effects of the stock market crash had been felt in Germany. The conservative-moderate coalition he headed held the support of a bare majority of the Reichstag, so that there was no great surprise when his budget bill was defeated in July. Instead of resigning, Brüning persuaded President von Hindenburg to authorize the measure by decree. The constitution provided for presidential decrees during times of emergency, and this authority had been used 131 times during the first six hectic years of the republic. Nevertheless, the Reichstag protested. Brüning arranged for new elections in the belief that public opinion was shifting in his direction.

By September when the elections were held, the depression had become severe and the public did not react as Brüning expected. The Communists increased their vote from 3,263,000 in 1928 to 4,600,000, and the once insignificant National Socialist vote grew from 810,000 to 6,410,000. The seriousness of Brüning's defeat and of the crisis that paralyzed the Reichstag is clearly revealed by the following table:

PARTY REPRESENTATION IN THE REICHSTAG

	May 1928	September 1930	July 1932	November 1932	March 1933
Conservative					
Nationalists	78	41	37	51	52
People's	45	30	7	11	2
Economic	23	23	2	1	0
Other Parties	23	53	9	12	7
Total	169	147	55	75	61
Moderate					
Center	61	68	75	70	74
Bavarian People's	17	19	22	20	18
Democrats	25	15	4	2	5
Total	103	102	101	92	97
Left					
Social Democrats	153	143	133	121	120
Totalitarian					
Communists	54	77	89	100	81
National Socialists	12	108	230	196	288
Total	66	185	319	296	369
Total Reichstag					
Deputies	491	577	608	584	647

Between 1928 and 1930, a coalition of the conservative and moderate parties could control the Reichstag. The difficulty was to get them to agree, as Brüning had discovered. After September, 1930, the two totalitarian parties were so strong that a Reichstag majority could be produced only if the moderate parties could persuade the Social Democrats and several of the conservative parties composed of industrialists and landed aristocrats to agree on a common policy, a near impossibility. There were only two alternatives. One was to continue to rule by decree. The other was to permit one of the totalitarian parties to participate in the government. For over two years Hindenburg chose the former course; then on January 30, 1933, he appointed Adolf Hitler chancellor.

ADOLF HITLER

Adolf Hitler was born in Braunau, Austria, on April 20, 1889. He came from peasant stock, but his father had worked his way into the lower-middle class by becoming a minor customs official, a position of which he was inordinately proud. The young Hitler graduated from elementary school, but never received a certificate for completing secondary school. He went to Vienna in 1903 with the intention of studying painting, but the Academy of Fine Arts refused to accept him and the School of Architecture had an equally low opinion of his talents. Hitler never desired regular employment, but he managed to eke out a bare existence in Vienna and later in Munich by painting designs on postcards. Economically, he sank into the proletariat, but he had his father's pride of being middle class. He scorned the Austrian Social Democrats and held democracy in contempt. Having little to be proud of save his German heritage, he despised the Jews, whom he accused of leading a world conspiracy to destroy all things German. With typical inconsistency, he blamed the Jews for monopolistic capitalism, which pressed the lower-middle class down into the ranks of the proletariat, and for Marxian Socialism, which pointed to the destruction of capitalism and the eventual triumph of the day laborer.

When it came, the war was a welcome relief. "For me these hours came as a deliverance from the distress that had weighed upon me during the days of my youth," he later wrote. "I am not ashamed to acknowledge today that I was carried away by the enthusiasm of the moment and that I sank down on my knees and thanked Heaven out of the fulness of my heart for the favour of having been permitted to live in such a time." He joined a Bavarian infantry regiment and was soon at the front. In December, 1914, he received the Iron Cross, Second Class; in October, 1916, he was wounded in the leg; in August, 1918, he was awarded an Iron Cross, First Class, an exceptional honor for an enlisted man, and in October, 1918, he was hospitalized because of temporary blindness resulting from a British gas attack. He never rose beyond the rank of corporal, probably because his superiors distrusted his obvious lack of balance and his eccentricity, but he always looked back happily on his army days. As a civilian, he had had neither family, position, nor prospects; as a soldier, he had comradeship, status, and a sense of belonging. Often he later referred to "the stupendous impression produced upon me by the war—the greatest of all experiences. For, that individual interest—the interest of one's own ego—could be subordinated to the common interest—that the great, heroic struggle of our people demonstrated in overwhelming fashion."

Peace brought a return to the old uncertain existence, but gradually Hitler found himself. He became associated with a group known as the German Workers' party founded by a Munich locksmith named Anton Drexler. In 1920 he began to devote himself fully to politics, and the Drexler group changed its name to the National Socialist German Workers' party. Within one year Hitler was its leader, and within three he made his Munich attempt to imitate Mussolini's march on Rome, but the "Beer Hall Putsch" was a complete failure because the army remained loyal to the government. Hitler was sentenced to five years in prison, where he devoted his time to writing *Mein Kampf*, in which he described his ideas, methods, and goals. He was released in 1925 and immediately set to work rebuilding his party. Within five years it became the second largest in Germany; within seven years it became the largest.

The nature and success of the Nazi movement were largely due to Hitler. During the 1920's he catered to people like himself: frustrated intellectuals and ne'er-do-wells, ex-soldiers who were unable or unwilling to settle down to the dull drudgery of civilian life, members of the lower-middle class who were being pressed down into the proletariat by the loss of their savings during the period of inflation and by the growing power of big business, and unemployed or underpaid artisans who were conscious of their superiority over unskilled laborers. In England these groups, with the possible exception of the ex-soldiers, found their way into the Labor party, but on the continent they were generally too class-conscious and too nationalistic to join the Marxist working-class parties. It was they who made up most of the early membership of the Nazi movement.

Hitler was well qualified to lead this sort of people. They were confused and suffering, but lacked the education and intelligence to recognize the real causes of their difficulties. What they wanted was a self-confident leader to tell them who was to blame for their difficulties and how Germany and the world could be altered to provide a better life for themselves and their children. This role Hitler happily accepted, and although he was momentarily indecisive during several critical periods of his career, he always assumed an air of confidence in public.

Hitler was totally without moral scruples, and much of his success lay in the inability of others to believe that a man could be so dishonest. The bare boldness of his lies and the effrontery of his charges left his opponents too stupefied to take action. He believed in a crude Social Darwinism and saw in the struggle for survival the means whereby the elite of his new order would be selected. He coupled this idea of an élite, which he identified more as his Nazi followers than as the whole German people, with a crude conception of the laws of heredity and the science of eugenics. His goal was to establish a master race that would dominate central and eastern Europe, exterminating the lesser races or reducing them to the status of slave laborers. Hitler could be crafty and calculating, but he was essentially a nationalistic, emotional, romantic dreamer. He would work himself into a rage; yell, scream, beat his fists on the table, and then suddenly revert to his normal manner. During his years of success, he became convinced that his intuition was sparked by divine guidance. He publicly declared that "I go the way that Providence dictates with the assurance of a sleepwalker." Often he confided that he was the greatest German who ever lived.

He was a master propagandist. If emotion could conquer his own capacity to reason, he knew that it could conquer others as well. "To be a leader, means to be able to move masses," he declared. "Since the masses have only a poor acquaintance with abstract ideas, their reactions lie more in the domain of the feelings, where the roots of their positive as well as their negative attitudes are implanted. . . . The driving force which has brought about the most tremendous revolutions on this earth has never been a body of scientific teaching which has gained power over the masses but always a devotion which has inspired them, and often a kind of hysteria which has urged them into action. Whoever wishes to win over the masses must know the key that will open the door to their hearts. It is not objectivity, which is a feckless attitude, but a determined will, backed up by power where necessary." [6]

The key Hitler found to the hearts of the masses lay in their desire to know how they had fallen into their present predicament and how to escape from it. He did not offer an elaborate intellectual explanation because "the receptive powers of the masses are very restricted, and their understanding is feeble. On the other hand they quickly forget. Such being the case, all effective propaganda must be confined to a few bare necessities and then must be expressed in a few stereotyped formulas." "Only constant repetition will finally succeed in imprinting an idea on the memory of a crowd." The ideas Hitler chose were few and they were certainly repeated enough. The army was winning the war when it was "stabbed in the back" by the socialists. Versailles was a dictated peace that must not be tolerated. The Germans were a superior race, but were the victims of a Jewish conspiracy. If the Versailles treaty were overthrown and the power of the Jews broken, Germans would once more be powerful and wealthy. They would stand as a bulwark against the Bolsheviks, whom Hitler hated almost as much as the Jews.

Circumstantial evidence made it possible to persuade Germans to believe that the socialists had betrayed the army in 1918, and they never doubted that Versailles was a dictated, unjust peace. As for the Jews, there had always been anti-Semitism in Germany, although perhaps no more so

[6] Quoted by Alan Bullock, *Hitler, A Study in Tyranny* (London: Odhams, ed. of 1955), pp. 44-45.

than in France and other countries. Indeed, many of the Nazis' ideas concerning the Jews came from an Englishman, Houston Stewart Chamberlain. What Germany had that other countries lacked was a clever propagandist like Hitler who fanned the sparks of anti-Semitism into a burning flame. Hitler could correctly claim that many Communists were Jews, including Marx and Trotsky at the international level and Luxemburg and Eisner in contemporary Germany. He could correctly point to Jews who had made fortunes during the period of inflation. It did not matter to him that other Jews had been victims of Bolshevism and inflation or that Gentiles had also joined the Communist party and had profited from the inflation. It would confuse his audience to present both sides of the question. Where there were no facts to support his charges, he told lies, not little lies, but big lies because "in the primitive simplicity of their minds they [the masses] more readily fall victims to the big lie than the small lie, since they themselves often tell small lies in little matters, but would be ashamed to resort to large-scale falsehoods." Thus, the Germans who had offered a haven in the 1920's for Jews mistreated in other countries became their persecutors during the 1930's.

The positive ingredients in the Nazi program were nationalism and social reform, the two most powerful forces during the late nineteenth and twentieth centuries. Any party that could convince the people that it could achieve these two goals was sure to win wide popularity. Hitler was never very clear about how he intended to rearm, overthrow the Versailles treaty, and bring all Germany under one flag, but he never missed an opportunity to criticize Stresemann or anyone else who was willing to compromise short of the ultimate goal. Even vaguer was Hitler's position with regard to social reform. Many of his followers were genuine left-wingers who wanted to abolish capitalism, nationalize the key industries, and tax the rich heavily to pay for generous social benefits. Others whose support he wanted were social conservatives. However, the technique of the "big lie" need not be precise. All that Hitler sought was to convince anyone that somehow through him lay the road to national aggrandizement and prosperity.

Hitler was not only a great speaker; he was a great showman. The annual party rallies at Nuremberg were magnificent displays, with their marching troops, martial music, waving banners, and blazing torches. A sense of unity and power, a feeling of loyalty to the leader and party, and a desire for honor and glory were instilled in the onlookers. Hitler himself was always deeply affected, as were foreign witnesses. It was not only before the loudspeakers of a stadium or the microphone of a radio that he excelled. He spoke again and again in the smaller towns; no hamlet was so insignificant that it was not regularly visited by the Nazis.

To help him in his work he organized his own private army. Certain army officers had formed volunteer *Freikorps* regiments in 1918 to suppress socialist uprisings and to prevent the dismemberment of Germany.

The Communist, Social Democrat, and Conservative parties all had their bands. What was unique about Hitler's troops was their size and organization. His movement had hardly begun before he formed with the aid of Ernst Röhm (1887-1934), a regular army officer, the S.A. (*Sturmabteilung*) or Storm Troops. By 1932 they numbered 300,000 men and included a motor corps and an officers training school. The brown-shirted S.A. was difficult for even Hitler to control and he later organized the S.S. (*Schutzstaffel*) or Élite Guard that was sworn to complete obedience. Its members wore black shirts and were commanded by a one-time poultry farm manager, Heinrich Himmler (1900-1945). Hitler used these troops to participate in the party rallies, break up rival demonstrations, beat up opponents, and protect himself from assault. After 1923 he did not look on them as a means of seizing power. His one effort to use force at Munich had failed, and thereafter he was determined to win power by legal means.

Hitler, of course, had able lieutenants. Besides Röhm and Himmler, they included the crippled, contemptible Dr. Paul Goebbels (1897-1945), who was responsible for propaganda; Rudolf Hess (1894-   ), who helped him write *Mein Kampf* and later made a spectacular solitary flight to England during the war in the hope of negotiating peace; Gregor Strasser (1892-1934), an efficient party organizer and leader of the left wing of the movement; Alfred Rosenberg (1893-1946), an embittered, blond intellectual who preached an anti-Bolshevik, anti-Christian crusade; Hermann Göring (1893-1946), a World War I ace and future air marshal who loved art, gaudy uniforms, and princely living; and many others, not one of whom, with the possible exception of Strasser, was completely normal. Yet with these people, his constant harping on nationalistic disappointments, and his promises of better things to come, Adolf Hitler built a party that received the second largest number of votes in September, 1930.

THE CHANCELLORSHIP

Chancellor Brüning recognized the threat to his position, although no more than anyone else did he foresee the full danger of a Hitler triumph. He sought to combat the depression in the traditional laissez-faire manner by cutting government expenses and by reducing salaries, wages, and prices in the hope of capturing more of what remained of world trade. Increased unemployment made it necessary to reduce unemployment benefits in order to keep expenses within bounds. Deficit financing and a large public works program were not adopted, because of their inflationary effect, and taxes were kept high. This policy pleased neither the industrialists nor the workers, both of whom would have preferred a policy that reflected their own interests exclusively. To combat Hitler in the field of foreign policy, Brüning tried to get reparations reduced, establish a customs union with Austria, and increase the size of the army, but the French blocked his efforts and Hitler continued to profit from nationalistic dissatisfaction.

Brüning could remain in power only so long as he was supported by President Hindenburg and not actively opposed by the army and the Social Democrats. With the army leaders he felt secure. The war minister, General Wilhelm Groener (1867-1939), was an exceptionally able, loyal officer who held the Nazis in contempt. Hindenburg was an aged monarchist with scant understanding of the problems of his day, but he was an honorable man, loyal to his oath to the republic and most unfavorably impressed with the antics of ex-corporal Adolf Hitler. He therefore decreed that part of Brüning's program that the Reichstag would not approve. The Reichstag did have the right to reject a presidential decree, but here the dilemma of the Social Democrats worked to Brüning's advantage. They opposed his policies and would not vote for them, but they were afraid to join the other opposition parties and vote against them in the Reichstag for fear that it would drive Hindenburg into the arms of the ultra-conservatives or Hitler. During the presidential elections of March, 1932, the Social Democrats joined the middle-of-the-road parties and supported Hindenburg, who had become the mainstay of the republic. It took two ballots before the old field marshal triumphed over his principal rival, Adolf Hitler, who had made effective use of the S.A. and S.S.

One might ask why Brüning had permitted the S.A. and S.S. to exist. He saw the danger, as did Groener, but he hesitated to act because since 1923 Hitler had been careful to follow a legal course. If he outlawed the Nazi military forces, would he not also have to treat the unarmed Social Democrats' *Reichsbanner* and the conservative parties' *Stahlhelm* in the same manner? The question of the *Stahlhelm* was especially touchy because Hindenburg was interested in it. Furthermore, if the S.A. and S.S. were outlawed, they might revolt. They were more numerous than the regular army, and there would be much bloodshed. Indeed, would the army fire on Germans who advocated a patriotic program and indoctrinated the youth of the nation with a martial spirit? Many junior officers were known to be affected by the Nazis' promises of military expansion and the long-awaited promotions it would bring. One reason Brüning and Groener sought allied permission to enlarge the armed forces was to mitigate the appeal of the Nazi program to the army. Despite these dangers, Brüning and Groener finally decided to get Hindenburg to sign a presidential decree dissolving the S.A. and S.S. on the grounds that "These organizations form a private army whose very existence constitutes a state within the State, and represent a permanent source of trouble for the civil population."

Their triumph was shortlived. First Groener and then, on May 30, 1932, Brüning were compelled to resign. Their defeat was engineered by the politically minded General Kurt von Schleicher (1882-1934). Schleicher's immediate goal was to establish a stable government free from petty party politics; his ultimate goal was probably· to reestablish the monarchy. He therefore persuaded the army generals to refuse to continue to support Brüning and Groener. This was not difficult, because Brüning was planning to divide some junker estates into small farms for the peasantry and Groener was disliked for having insisted that the Kaiser abdicate in 1918 and that the Versailles treaty be accepted because resistance was impossible. This done, Schleicher easily persuaded Hindenburg, who was tired of what he called "Bolshevist wage laws and Bolshevist colonization schemes," to drop his loyal chancellor and appoint Franz von Papen (1879-   ), a Westphalian nobleman whose only claims to distinction were his social charm, which he had utilized at various diplomatic posts, and his excellent horsemanship. Schleicher and Papen hoped eventually to split the Nazi party and with a splinter group to form the basis of a new coalition in the Reichstag. Meanwhile, they tried to purchase nominal Nazi support by lifting the ban on the S.A. and S.S. and ordering new elections.

The results of the election could have been anticipated in view of the increasing unemployment, Hitler's clever propaganda, and the renewed activities of the S.A. and S.S. There were 461 riots in Prussia alone between June 1 and July 20, 1932, in which 86 people were killed, but the Nazis won 37.4 per cent of the vote and 230 seats in the Reichstag. Most of their strength had been obtained at the expense of the conservative parties. Clearly the upper-middle class was beginning to join the movement.

The dapper chancellor was unperturbed. When Hitler refused to be content with the office of vice-chancellor, he obtained a decree from Hindenburg dissolving the Reichstag the day it met and ordering new elections. He believed that the Nazis had reached the peak of their popularity and calculated that their party treasury was nearly empty. In both surmises he was correct. Goebbels continually noted in his diary that the "scarcity of money has become chronic," and in the November elections the Nazis won two million fewer votes than in July.

Papen was delighted. If Hitler would not now accept a secondary position in his cabinet (and the Nazi chief again refused), he would bring him to his knees by holding still another election. Meanwhile, he talked of governing the country by dictatorship. At this point, General Schleicher betrayed Papen as he had betrayed Groener. He was motivated in part by jealousy, in part by concern over the rise of communism, and in part by the army's dislike of having to enforce a dictatorship. He told Hindenburg that Papen no longer had the support of the army. Hindenburg regretfully abandoned his chancellor, and on December 2 Schleicher himself assumed that post.

Schleicher hoped to'detach Gregor Strasser and other Nazis from Hitler, but he failed. He attempted to win Social Democratic support by promising social reforms, but only succeeded in alienating the conservatives. He had even less support in the Reichstag than Papen and when he advocated a presidential dictatorship in January, 1933, Hindenburg refused. For several years Germany had been the scene of continual violence and there appeared to be a strong possibility that the Nazis would attempt to seize power if they were denied office much longer. Under these circumstances the old man finally came to the conclusion that the only way to avoid civil war was to appoint Hitler chancellor. Ironically, Hitler was the only man who could hope to command the support of a majority in the Reichstag, and this he attempted to do in coalition with the conservative Nationalist party.

Hindenburg would not have appointed Hitler chancellor if he had not been persuaded by Papen, and Papen would not have acted as he did if he had not felt sure that he could control Hitler. Papen and his fellow conservatives regarded Hitler as an ignorant fool who could be directed along the course they desired, a course that would lead to the restoration of the monarchy, the expansion of the army, and the sacrifice of the laborers' rights to the industrialists. To assure that Hitler did not stray from the outlined course, Papen assumed the posts of vice-chancellor of Germany and minister-president of Prussia, a state which made up two-thirds of the country. Other than the chancellorship only two of the eleven cabinet posts were given to Nazis; one was the ministry of the interior and one was without portfolio. The army and the bureaucracy were outside Hitler's grasp, and the president would never side with him against the conservative program which could of itself win few votes. Papen had united Hitler's lower-middle class and working-class following with the upper-middle class and aristocracy.

THE CONSOLIDATION OF POWER

These chains would have bound an ordinary man, but not Adolf Hitler. His first task was to get rid of the rival parties and establish control over the bureaucracy. The initial step was taken by ordering new elections in March. This time he had money supplied by the industrialists who had decided to support him, an enlarged S.A. and S.S., and the power of the state behind him. No stone was left unturned to ensure a majority. Even fortune played into his hands. A demented youth set fire to the Reichstag. Hitler blamed the deed on the Communists and, perhaps sincerely believing that a Bolshevik uprising was about to take place, persuaded Hindenburg to issue an emergency decree suspending constitutional guarantees of freedom of speech and freedom of the press. Yet despite their violence and the widespread fear of a Communist uprising, the Nazis received only 43.9 per cent of the vote.

With his Nationalist allies, Hitler barely controlled the Reichstag, but on March 23 he persuaded that assembly to pass an enabling act which gave him power to make laws, to initiate constitutional amendments, and to conclude treaties during the next four years without its consent. As this act altered the constitution, it had to be passed by a two-thirds vote. Hitler disposed of the eighty-one Communist deputies by refusing to allow them to be seated on the grounds that they had plotted a "blood bath." The Catholic Center party was persuaded to support the measure by generous promises and veiled threats. The president, army, and conservatives were brought into line by a magnificently staged ceremony at Potsdam in which Hitler intimated that a monarchical restoration was in store. Catholic and conservative alike were also influenced by fear of communism, belief that parliamentary democracy could not function in Germany, and confidence that Hitler would not go to extremes. Only the Social Democrats opposed the enabling act. By a vote of 411 to 94, the Reichstag abdicated its authority. Germany became a dictatorship through constitutional procedure. It was only then that the revolution really began.

During the months that followed, Hitler used his authority to dissolve the rival political parties and ban all private armies other than his own. Anti-Nazi officials were discharged, and the judiciary was gradually brought under control. The power of the separate states was greatly diminished, and Germany became a centralized national state controlled from Berlin. As President Hindenburg was known to be dying, only the army and the left-wing element within his own party stood in Hitler's path toward absolute, total power.

At first Hitler hesitated. Indeed, he was caught between two fires. The left wing of his party wanted a genuine social revolution, including the destruction of the capitalistic system. They were dismayed by his new alliance with the conservatives and in Röhm, the S.A. chief, they had a powerful spokesman. His S.A. now numbered several million men and included aviation, intelligence, engineer, and medical units as well as the older motor corps. He hoped to make this force the nucleus of the army expansion and was angered by Hitler's refusal to override the officer corps' opposition to this plan. "Adolf is a swine [he swore]. He will give us all away. He only associates with the reactionaries now. His old friends aren't good enough for him. Getting matey with the East Prussian generals. They're his cronies now. . . . Adolf knows exactly what I want. I've told him often enough. Not a second edition of the old imperial army. Are we revolutionaries or aren't we? *Allons,, enfants de la patrie!* If we are, then something new must arise out of our *élan,* like the mass armies of the French revolution." [7]

The officers, on the other hand, had no use for Röhm or his undisciplined S.A. ruffians and had no intention of including them in their planned expansion. Conservatives thought it was time to tame Hitler's radical following. ". . . He who threatens to employ the guillotine," Papen declared in a speech, "may be its first victim. . . . There is much talk of the coming socialization," he continued. "Have we gone through the anti-Marxist revolution in order to carry out a Marxist programme? . . .

[7] Quoted by Gordon A. Craig, *The Politics of the Prussian Army, 1670-1945* (Oxford: Oxford University Press, 1955), p. 475.

It is time to join together in fraternal friendship and respect for all our fellow countrymen, to avoid disturbing the labours of serious men and to silence fanatics."

Clearly, Hitler had to make a choice between his old and his new allies. Two factors determined the decision he was to take. Hindenburg was dying, and he needed army support to assume the office of president. Röhm was certainly not a cowed, obedient servant, and Hitler may have believed that he was plotting with Schleicher and Strasser. When Hitler finally made up his mind, he struck during the night of June 29-30 with his devoted S.S. Röhm and other S.A. leaders were seized and shot. When Schleicher answered the doorbell, he was felled with his wife by a shower of bullets. Another general and Strasser met the same fate. Several Catholic conservative leaders who had criticized Hitler were also disposed of; only Hindenburg's affection for Papen prevented his inclusion on the list. In the blood purge, old scores were paid off, some Jews were murdered for amusement, and there were cases of mistaken identity. A Dr. Schmidt was seized in the presence of his family by the S.S. When they belatedly found that they had the wrong Schmidt, they thoughtfully returned his body with a sum of money to his widow and three children. Hitler admitted that seventy-seven persons were killed, but there were probably more. His justification was that he had acted to block a coup d'état. "If anyone reproaches me and asks why I did not resort to the regular courts of justice," he told the Reichstag, "then all I can say to him is this: in this hour I was responsible for the fate of the German people, and thereby I became the supreme Justiciar of the German people. . . ."

The Germans as a whole accepted this explanation. They knew enough of Röhm and the S.A. leaders to suspect the worst of them. Only Hindenburg and the army could have acted; the former accepted Hitler's explanation, and the officers were so pleased to be free of Röhm and the S.A. that they asked few questions. On August 1, the eighty-seven-year-old Hindenburg died; Hitler assumed the office of president with the approval of a popular plebiscite; and the officers and men of the army swore to serve Adolf Hitler, "Führer of the German Reich and People," rather than the "people and the fatherland." The oath was of importance, because many officers would rather permit Hitler to commit the most fiendish crimes than break their word.

Hitler proceeded more slowly against the officer corps. He had, at first at least, a German corporal's respect for his superior officers, and he thought that he would win their support, or at least break their power, by his program of military expansion. He had withdrawn from the world disarmament conference in October, 1933, and had begun to re-arm in defiance of the Versailles treaty. During the first four years of expansion, it was necessary to increase the officer strength over sixfold. The new officers were generally Nazis or Nazi sympathizers and the new enlisted men were drawn from Hitler's youth movement, or at least were well-indoctrinated by Nazi propaganda. Thus, the old officer corps soon found itself a small minority uncertain whether their junior officers and troops would support them if they moved against Hitler. Of their own number, some were not above seeking the promotions made possible by military expansion and acceptance of the new regime. The majority, however, were horrified at Nazi brutality and opposed to its anti-Christian policy.

The senior officers, of course, were drawn almost entirely from the old officer corps. They tried to block what they regarded as Hitler's too rapid military expansion, and they tried to dissuade him from reoccupying the Rhineland because it might lead to war. When Hitler reached the conclusion near the end of 1937 that the present army leadership would not support his plans to dominate Europe, he acted in characteristic fashion. Field Marshal von Blomberg, the minister of defense, was encouraged to marry a woman with a questionable background. When it was revealed after the wedding that she had a police record, the officer corps itself insisted that he resign. General Werner von Fritsch, the commander-in-chief, was accused of immorality and relieved of his command pending an investigation. He was, of course, found innocent, but by then Hitler himself had assumed the post of defense minister and had appointed a more pliable general in Fritsch's stead. Sixteen other generals were retired and forty-four were reassigned. There were rumors of reprisals, but the officers were confused by Hitler's diabolical tactics and hesitant to break their oath of allegiance to him. When Hitler prepared to move against Czechoslovakia, the chief of general staff, Ludwig Beck, made an effort to muster sufficient support to halt him. When he failed, Beck resigned and there was no one left to stand in Hitler's way when he plunged the world into war on September 1, 1939.

THE NAZI STATE

Hitler did not wait for the complete subjection of the officer corps before he established a totalitarian state. No opposition was tolerated. The Nazi party was the only party. Like the Communist and Fascist parties, its governmental activities paralleled those of the regular bureaucracy. There was, unhappily, this difference; the German bureaucracy was more efficient than that in other nations, although it was gradually corrupted under Nazi influence. Opponents of the regime had no way to reach the public because the radio and the press were denied them, while under the direction of Dr. Goebbels the official propaganda reached every home. The educational system was used to indoctrinate the youth of the nation, uncooperative professors were discharged, and books by Jewish authors were burned. Enemies of the regime were sought out by the Gestapo (secret police) and the S.S.

Hitler never established a corporative system, but the old labor unions

A Nazi rally at Nuremberg on September 6, 1934. (Wide World)

were abolished, strikes were forbidden, and special courts were established to settle wage disputes. The economy was carefully planned and regulated to make Germany as self-sufficient as possible and to support the program of military expansion. The gross national product and the national income were doubled in four years, but foreign trade was often negotiated on a barter basis, especially with southeastern Europe, because of the currency shortage. Some industrialists regretted the bargain they had made with Hitler, but most of them enjoyed their docile labor force and their profits.

The workers, too, found much in Hitler's economic system that they could support. Military expansion and a huge public works program reduced unemployment from six million in 1932 to less than one million in 1936, at a time when the democracies were still plagued with the depression. The *Autobahnen*, the first great superhighway system, were constructed, and homes with gardens were built for workers, over 300,000 in 1937 alone. Vacation trips, athletic events, and excursions were arranged for their amusement, and plans were made to produce the currently popular *Volkswagen*, a car that they could purchase with their modest wages.

The peasants were especially favored because of the Nazis' fantastic *Blut und Boden* (blood and soil) theory. "Only the fruits of the German earth—clod earth—can create German blood," a Nazi wrote. "Through them only are transmitted to the blood, and thence to the body and the soul, those delicate vibrations which determine the German type. The type is unique the whole world over because there is but one German soil on the earth." The superior race thus sprang from the superior soil, and those closest to it were especially favored. One law enacted on the basis of this theory forbade peasants with estates of less than 309 acres to sell or mortgage their farms and required that they leave them to a single son. In this manner, the tie with the blood-giving soil would be preserved. Owners of these hereditary peasant farms were even given official titles.

The theory of *Blut und Boden* was the root of the ideological differences between the Nazi and the Italian Fascist states. The Nazis were deeply conscious of blood and race. They, the Aryans, were the racial élite; the Slavs were inferior; and the Jews were the authors of all that was contemptible and hateful. Through a gross perversion of the science of eugenics, they determined to "purify" their nation. At first Hitler was content to drive the Jews from Germany by business and professional boycotts and by withdrawing their rights of citizenship. In 1938 he burned their synagogues and confined them to concentration camps, and in 1942 he began systematically to exterminate all of them that he could find.

Hatred of the Jews caused the Nazis to attack the Old Testament. Some of them claimed that Jesus was really an Aryan; others rejected the New Testament as well as the Old and tried to restore the ancient Nordic Gods, Woden and Thor. The new German Faith Movement did not win many converts, but Hitler managed to exercise considerable control over the Protestant churches. The pope negotiated a concordat with him in 1933 as he had done with Mussolini. In return for special privileges, the Catholic clergy was to refrain from political activity, but as the evil character of the Nazi regime became more evident, many courageous ministers and priests opposed it, at the price of confinement in concentration camps.

It is difficult to understand why more voices were not raised against this tyranny since most Germans were decent, well-intentioned people. Fear was part of the answer. No private individual could hope to start a successful revolution, and to protest was to court death. But the principal explanation of the lack of more outspoken opposition to Hitler is more subtle. Few people knew that the Jews were actually being exterminated. The majority thought that they were only being persecuted, imprisoned, and exiled. This was harsh, but the Jews were different from themselves, and the authorities said that they were dangerous to the state. Perhaps some of them were, the Germans thought, and they did nothing. It is well to remember that after the attack on Pearl Harbor over 100,000 American citizens of Japanese descent were confined without trial in complete disregard of their constitutional rights because it was believed that a few of them *might* be traitors. This action was well-publicized in the newspapers, but few of the free and presumably liberty-loving American people attempted to aid their fellow citizens.

To most Germans, the pre-war Hitler state was not a barbarous tyranny but the wave of the future. They saw that in only six years Hitler had

880

transformed the seemingly inept, faction-ridden Weimar Republic into a powerful, prosperous, disciplined state. It was true that he had censored the press, dissolved labor unions and rival political parties, and silenced opponents in the churches, army, bureaucracy, judiciary, and his own party, but this seemed a small price to pay for full employment at home and the restoration of Germany's position abroad. They themselves had no desire to do the things that they were forbidden to do and believed that the few who did were stupid, stubborn, or disloyal. As a recent investigator has found, *They Thought They Were Free.*[8]

THE SMALLER EUROPEAN STATES

The unhappy fate of democracy in Italy and Germany after 1918 was duplicated in many smaller European states. They will be treated briefly under three headings: (1) Danubian Europe and Greece, (2) the Baltic states and Poland, and (3) the Iberian Peninsula.

DANUBIAN EUROPE AND GREECE

The eight states lying in the Danube Basin and the Balkans had been part of the polyglot Habsburg or Ottoman empires in 1815. The peace treaties of 1919 presumably established the boundaries of these states as nearly as possible along ethnic lines. Where parliamentary government had existed at the end of the war, it was maintained. Where it had not existed, it was established. Universal manhood suffrage, proportional representation, and ministerial responsibility to parliament were the rule. Elaborate bills of rights were included in the constitutions to protect individuals from their government, and independent judiciaries were established. With liberty, democracy, and national self-determination, it was hopefully assumed in 1919 that peace, happiness, and prosperity would be the lot of this once strife-torn, poor, unhappy region. Seldom has optimism been less justified. By March, 1939, the Danubian states had ceased to be democratic, and their inhabitants were still poorly housed and poorly fed.

There was a multitude of causes for the failure of democracy in this region. Democratic and parliamentary traditions were not strong, the surviving kings still exercised considerable power especially in the army, and the standards of education and literacy were generally low. The threat of communists, socialists, and agrarian reformers frightened still powerful reactionary elements. Certain countries, such as Yugoslavia, Czechoslovakia, and Rumania, contained large, disaffected national minorities to whom they were unwilling to grant provincial autonomy. Religious differ-

[8] Milton Mayer, *They Thought They Were Free: The Germans, 1933-1945* (Chicago: University of Chicago Press, 1955).

ences often coincided with racial and class distinctions. There were Roman Catholics, members of the Greek Orthodox church, Protestants, Moslems, and Jews in the region.

The dissolution of the multinational empires weakened the economy. Six of the states had backward, agricultural economies. A third of the inhabitants of a seventh, Austria, lived in Vienna, which had once been the capital of a great empire, the center of its banking, and the home of the central offices of its big industries. Many of these people were now without employment, for the small Austrian hinterland could not support what had been one of the greatest bureaucratic, cultural, and economic centers of Europe. Czechoslovakia, the eighth state, was alone in having a reasonably balanced economy, for it contained 75 per cent of the industries of the old Habsburg Empire as well as an ample amount of agriculture.

Only by a policy of free trade could the region as a whole have developed a self-sufficient economy, but the new states' jealousy of each other led them to raise protective tariffs in an unsuccessful effort to encourage the growth of their own industry. Reparation payments further weakened Austria, Hungary, and Bulgaria. Czechoslovakia and the Balkan countries embarked on a program of breaking up the large estates to provide small farms for the peasants. This action may have been socially desirable, but small farmers did not have the knowledge, capital, or acreage to farm scientifically. Production per acre was only a fifth of what it was in the Netherlands. Furthermore, many of the large estates belonged to Germans or Magyars who bitterly resented the loss of their hereditary lands for which they received little compensation. Population pressures developed because the birth rate remained high but the death rate declined. The decision of the United States and some of the Commonwealth countries to reduce immigration removed this means of escape. By 1930 from 50 to 60 per cent of the agricultural population in the Balkans was unneeded to farm the land. As a result, poverty and unemployment were common even before the Great Depression began.

In Austria the Social Democrats controlled Vienna, but the more conservative Christian Socialist and Agrarian parties dominated the rural areas. Both socialists and conservatives had private armies. For a long time, Austria sought to escape from its economic difficulties by effecting an economic union with Germany, but France blocked this move in 1931 and helped cause the collapse of a great Viennese bank by withdrawing its funds. Economic conditions worsened during the depression and an Austrian National Socialist party that was affiliated with Hitler became most troublesome. In 1933 the short, energetic Engelbert Dollfuss (1892-1934) became chancellor at the head of a Christian Socialist-Agrarian party coalition. He was opposed to union with Germany and desirous of establishing a fascist dictatorship on the Italian model. All opposition parties were abolished. The Social Democrats went on strike, but Dollfuss silenced their opposition by ordering his private army to bombard their homes.

882

The Nazis proved tougher. In July, 1934, they attempted to seize power with Hitler's backing and Dollfuss was assassinated, but strong Italian opposition caused Hitler to refrain from taking over at this time. Kurt von Schuschnigg (1897-   ) became chancellor and continued Dollfuss' dictatorial policies. To most Austrians, Hitler's seizure of their little state in March, 1938, meant only the exchange of a mild dictatorship for a more ruthless one.

Hungary remained a democracy for a much shorter period of time. In 1919 Bela Kun (1886-193?) established a soviet republic, but a Rumanian army drove him out and a conservative regime under Admiral Horthy (1868-1957) came to power. Horthy declared that Hungary was a kingdom and sought to bring about a Habsburg restoration, which the neighboring states would not permit. As a result, landlocked Hungary became a kingdom without a king with an admiral without a navy as regent. The depression was followed by the formation of several fascist groups, but the Magyar landed aristocracy remained in control as they had nearly always been in the past. They did not formally outlaw opposition parties or establish an authoritarian state. It was enough to have their tenants vote orally in their presence, to establish close ties with Hitler in 1933, and to prove their racial purity by passing anti-Semitic laws. When it was discovered that one anti-Semitic premier had a Jewish grandfather, he was forced to resign.

The new Yugoslav kingdom was the product of a union between several closely related Slavic races under the Serbian royal family. In addition to the kingdoms of Serbia and Montenegro, the new state consisted of provinces which had been integral parts of the Austro-Hungarian and Ottoman empires, and Croatia which had been a quasi-autonomous province of the Hungarian half of the dual monarchy. Under such circumstances the background and traditions of the people were quite different. The Croats and Slovenes were generally Roman Catholics while the Serbs were members of the Greek Orthodox church, and there was a large Moslem minority. Literacy varied from over 90 per cent in Slovenia to less than 20 per cent in Bosnia-Herzegovina and Macedonia.

The formidable task of ruling the new state was aggravated by Serbian insistence on a highly centralized government which could be dominated from Belgrade. The non-Serbian inhabitants favored a federal structure. This preference was particularly strong among the Croats, who insisted on autonomy, if not complete independence. A bitter quarrel developed in which one Croat leader was murdered while he was making a speech in parliament. By 1929 a complete impasse was reached and King Alexander (1921-1934), who controlled the army and exercised considerable influence in the government, suppressed the Croats and established a royal dictatorship. Croat revolutionaries evened the score by assassinating him five years later, but by 1939 the international situation had become so threatening that the Croats were given autonomy in the hope that this concession would ensure their loyalty if difficulties arose with Germany. Other groups immediately demanded similar concessions, but the Germans attacked in April, 1941, before any definite decision was taken.

Few nations seemingly profited as much from the war as Rumania. Bulgaria, Austria-Hungary, and Russia ceded territory that enabled its area to increase from 53,489 to 122,282 square miles and its population from 7,516,000 to 17,594,000. In many respects these gains proved to be doubtful blessings, however, because they created a serious minority problem. Furthermore, the newly acquired provinces wanted a federal state, but the old kingdom imposed a centralized regime. The Rumanian government carried out extensive land reforms in order to prevent the peasants from joining the Communist movement in neighboring Russia. About 1,400,000 peasants were given land, but this was not enough to solve the problem of overpopulation, land hunger, and poverty in the countryside.

Rumanian institutions were outwardly democratic in the 1920's, but the Liberal party remained in power because of intrigues, bribes, favors, and fraudulent elections. There were high hopes for improvement when the Peasants' party managed to win the elections in 1928, but the depression soon followed, agricultural prices fell more rapidly than industrial prices, and economic conditions in the predominantly agrarian country worsened. Under these circumstances King Carol (1930-1940) was able to play one faction against another and assume more and more power. He subsidized a nascent fascist movement in the hope that it would enable him to strengthen his position. The minority problem became more troublesome and an anti-Semitic policy was adopted. Finally, in 1938, after one political leader after another had proved his incapacity to govern, Carol abolished the old constitution and established a royal dictatorship. Political parties were suppressed and leaders of the fascist movement were shot "while attempting to escape." The day of reckoning came in 1940 when Russia, Hungary, and Bulgaria demanded that most of the territory they had lost in World War I be returned. Carol meekly surrendered and, thoroughly discredited, fled the country.

Bulgarian politics were dominated in the immediate postwar years by Alexander Stambolisky (1879-1923), an able peasant party leader. Unfortunately, the Communist movement was stronger in Bulgaria than in most Balkan countries and a Macedonian organization dedicated to winning independence for Macedonia or uniting it with Bulgaria was very active. This Macedonian faction, aided by other Stambolisky opponents, overthrew the government and assassinated the peasant leader in 1923. A Communist uprising and numerous assassinations followed. On one occasion when the Sofia cathedral was filled with mourners attending the funeral of an assassinated general, the Communists exploded a bomb killing 123 persons and injuring many others. In 1934 a group of reformers and army officers joined together to establish a dictatorship, but within a year the able king, Boris III (1918-1943), managed to win control of the government. He allowed parliament to serve as a consultative body, but refused to permit candidates to run as members of political parties. A Macedonian terroristic organization was suppressed, but the government itself generally refrained from the brutal tactics of the fascist states.

Albania was a backward, mountainous country with a semi-tribal social structure and a predominantly Moslem population. In 1928 Ahmed Bey Zogu made himself King Zog I and began to modernize his country using dictatorial methods and Italian economic assistance. The Italians, not content with increasing their control over the country's economy, landed troops there in 1939. Zog fled, and Victor Emmanuel III assumed the title of King of Albania.

Greece, too, had a troubled history. Failure to make good its claims to the eastern shores of the Aegean Sea at the expense of the Turks led to the establishment of a republic in 1923 and to the influx of about 1,400,-000 Greek refugees, for the most part from Turkey where their ancestors had lived for several thousand years.[9] The problem of resettling these dispossessed persons was an immense burden for a small, poor, overpopulated state to bear. Some of them eventually became communists and others contributed to the violence and rebellions that characterized Greek politics in the inter-war years. Time and again there were coups led by patriotic, though misguided, army officers who were disgusted at the factionalism and corruption in Greek politics. The depression was especially severe in Greece because many of its agricultural exports, including olives, currants, and tobacco, were in the luxury class. Income from the tourist trade and the merchant fleet, upon which the Greeks had normally depended, also declined more rapidly than income from most other economic activities. When the republican leaders proved incapable of coping with the situation, the monarchy was restored in the person of George II (1935-1947). After vainly trying to reconcile the various political factions, he came to the conclusion that Greece could not be governed in a parliamentary fashion, and cooperated with the brilliant general, John Metaxas (1871-1941), in establishing a dictatorship. Metaxas strove to improve Greece's economic position, but he won little popular support and suppressed every form of opposition to his rule.

In spite of its balanced economy and the exceptionally able leadership of Thomas Masaryk (1850-1937) and Edward Beneš (1884-1948), Czechoslovakia also had difficulties. Most of them resulted from the demands of the large Slovak, Ruthenian, Magyar, and German minorities for autonomy. The Czechs, however, insisted on maintaining a centralized state. The situation worsened during the 1930's, because the depression led to widespread unemployment, and Hitler, on coming to power, supported the demands of the Sudeten German minority. It became almost impossible to get a parliamentary majority for any legislation, and the cabinet was forced to govern by decree. Parliament was not abolished, however, and only the extremist groups found their liberties in any way curtailed. Dur-

---

[9] See page 786.

ing the fall and winter of 1938-1939 Germany annexed the Sudenten-land and established a protectorate over Bohemia and Moravia. Slovakia became a theoretically independent one-party state. The last of the Danubian states had succumbed to dictatorship, but in this instance only as a result of outside force.

THE BALTIC STATES AND POLAND

The three Baltic states of Lithuania, Latvia, and Estonia had much in common. They all achieved their independence at the close of World War I and established democratic republics with universal suffrage, responsible ministries, bills of rights, and even initiative and referendum. Nevertheless, by 1934 they all had authoritarian regimes.

Their difficulties arose from political inexperience, economic backwardness, and external threats. They had been part of the Russian empire, and now almost completely blocked their former master from the Baltic Sea. For economic and military as well as ideological reasons, Soviet Russia was determined to reassert control. Over half the land in the three republics was held in large estates, for the most part owned by German barons. This land was converted into small peasant farms, which reduced productivity and infuriated the Baltic barons, who received little compensation. Hence the relations between these states and Germany were unfriendly, especially after the rise of Hitler. They were backward industrially and depended almost entirely on their agricultural and timber exports to buy what they needed. The prices of these products fell especially low during periods of depression. Army officers and other conservative nationalists seized control of Lithuania, the most backward of the three, in 1923 and established a dictatorship. Economic unrest brought on by the Great Depression caused conservatives to overthrow the democratic regimes in Estonia and Latvia in 1934. In 1939 Germany took Memel from Lithuania, and the Soviet Union won the right to establish military posts in the three republics as a prelude to incorporating them into the Soviet Union.

The Poles were no more fortunate than their smaller neighbors. They began in 1918 with one handicap which most of the other newly created estates escaped, a great historic past. They determined to restore Poland to its boundaries of 1772, that is, before the first partition. This brought them into conflict with all their neighbors: the Russians, the Germans, the Czechs, and the Lithuanians. They came surprisingly near achieving success, but at the cost of making powerful enemies and creating internal difficulties including disastrous inflation. Germany was completely unreconciled to the existence of the Polish corridor separating it from East Prussia, and Soviet Russia awaited only the opportunity to win back the territory inhabited by White Russians and Ukrainians which the Poles had seized during the Revolution. This successful policy of expan-

886

sion also meant that a third of the population belonged to minority races. The Poles themselves were divided into every type of conservative, moderate, and left-wing group. A combination of racial minorities, internal divisions, and political inexperience caused them to form eighty different political parties and made the normal functioning of a cabinet system of government difficult. In spite of rich coal mines and some industry, Poland remained a poor, backward, predominantly agricultural country. Three per cent of the landowners owned half the land, but progress toward dividing these estates among the four million landless peasants was slow because the owners were Poles, not Germans as in the Baltic states and Czechoslovakia.

The Polish constitution which was adopted in 1921 was democratic, but external threats and internal divisions led the war hero, General Joseph Pilsudski (1867-1935), to seize power in 1926. Left-wing groups were suppressed and the powers of the president were increased. In 1935 a new constitution was issued which further strengthened the government, but Poland never became fully totalitarian: opposition parties were permitted to operate, albeit under great handicaps, and the press was allowed to criticize the government. The Poles made a friendship pact with the Nazis in 1934 and did not hesitate to profit from Germany's demands on Czechoslovakia in 1939 by taking Teschen, but that same year they once more lost their own independence to their overly powerful German and Russian neighbors.

THE IBERIAN PENINSULA

The dawn of the twentieth century found the Iberian Peninsula controlled by the same sort of people who had controlled it two centuries before. A Bourbon sat on the throne of Spain and a Braganza on the throne of Portugal. The aristocracy and the Catholic Church owned most of the land and controlled both governments. Only the interests of the wealthiest members of the middle class were given due consideration. The majority of the people lived in poverty, in ignorance, and without an effective voice in their government. Both countries had suffered during the nineteenth century from warring royalist factions; during the twentieth century, they continued to suffer, but the disputants assumed a more modern guise.

The Portuguese overthrew their monarchy in 1910 and immediately set out to weaken the influence of the Catholic Church. Participation in World War I weakened the already poor, backward economy, and social unrest was often translated into revolt. Between 1910 and 1926 there were sixteen revolutions and about forty governments. In the latter year, General Antonio Carmona succeeded in establishing a dictatorship, but he was gradually replaced by Antonio de Oliveira Salazar (1889-   ) under whose direction Portugal became a modified corporative state in 1933. Salazar, a devout, unselfish, economics professor, was able to improve Portuguese conditions somewhat, but on the whole his arbitrary rule favored the conservatives.

Alfonso XIII (1886-1931) of Spain was literally born a king, his father having died shortly before his birth. In addition to the usual troubles that had plagued his predecessors, he was faced with industrial growth, especially in Catalonia, that led to the rise of socialism, anarchism, syndicalism, and all the other isms of an industrial society. Furthermore, Catalonia began to demand autonomy, if not actual independence, from the more conservative central government at Madrid. In 1921 a Spanish army was defeated and nearly destroyed by rebels in Morocco. The military, who expected parliamentary investigators to reveal their corruption and inefficiency, seized power under the leadership of Primo de Rivera (1870-1930). Alfonso, who was tired of quarreling political parties and implicated in the defeat, was a party to this act, and for seven years Rivera ruled Spain as Mussolini ruled Italy. His regime became increasingly unpopular, especially after the beginning of the depression, and in 1930 Alfonso forced him to resign. It was too late, however, to save his throne, for in April of the following year Alfonso was compelled to abdicate. Europe was at last free of the Bourbons, although perhaps not forever, for a restoration in Spain is still quite possible.

A democratic republic was established and the new prime minister, Manuel Azaña (1880-1940), immediately attacked the powerful position of the Catholic Church and landowners. The Church was separated from the state, secular schools were established, and the Jesuits were dissolved. Church and noble estates began to be divided among the peasants, and Catalonia was given a wide measure of autonomy, but before Azaña could proceed far with his proposed reforms, he was defeated at the polls. Undiscouraged, he organized a popular front consisting of Catalan nationalists, republicans, socialists, syndicalists, communists, and other left-wing groups, won the elections of 1936 by a decisive majority, and resumed the reform program.

At this point the army, dominated by aristocratic, Catholic army officers, revolted. For nearly three years, a bloody civil war ensued in which Italy and Germany gave considerable aid to the conservative rebel forces, led by General Francisco Franco (1892-   ), and Russia lent some support to the republican regime. Finally on March 28, 1939, Madrid surrendered and Franco was victorious. Spain had joined the ranks of the fascist states at a cost of from one to two million lives. The landowners and the Catholic Church resumed their former privileges, and working-class reform movements were effectively suppressed.

By the time war came in 1939 the Iberian Peninsula and nearly all of central and eastern Europe had succumbed to the fascist or communist revolutions. The post-World War I era that had begun with so much hope had not been characterized by the growth of liberty and democracy; rather, a new trend seemed to have begun which rejected most of the goals of the age of the egalitarian revolutions and revealed that the political, social, economic, and intellectual frameworks of European civilization were gravely imperilled. The twentieth-century crisis was fully revealed.

20/ The Surviving Democracies

ALL Europe did not succumb to the blandishments of would-be dictators between the two wars. In the western part of the continent, where the conservative forces had first given way before the onslaught of the liberal middle class and where the democratic heritage was strongest, free institutions were preserved. There were totalitarian parties, both fascist and communist, that became dangerous in several countries, but in most cases they were not serious threats. No state, however, escaped the problems connected with the war, the return to peace, and the Great Depression.

FRANCE

France emerged from the war as the strongest power on the continent. For more than four years the Third Republic had withstood the heaviest assault ever launched against a French regime. It had proved its mettle, and it might reasonably have expected to be free from the challenges of the left and right that had so plagued its early years. But beneath the surface all was not well. The French knew that without British, Russian, and American assistance they would not have defeated Germany. Now neither the Americans nor the British would ratify the pledges their representatives had made at the Versailles peace conference to defend France's eastern frontier, and a Communist Russia was unacceptable as an ally. The war had given France Alsace and Lorraine and had stripped Germany of these and other provinces, but Germany's population and industrial potential remained greater than those of France. Hence, victory brought the French no feeling of self-confidence. Their only hope seemed to be to keep Germany disarmed and economically weak, but by the time Hitler came to power they could not muster the will to maintain such a policy.

POSTWAR PROBLEMS

It was the loss of their sense of *élan vital,* the vital drive about which their popular philosopher Henri Bergson[1] was still lecturing, that so marked the postwar French. Part of their *élan vital* had been literally killed by the war. Over half of the men who were between the ages of twenty and thirty-two in 1914 died on the battlefield, and many who survived were hopeless cripples. Yet the trouble lay deeper than the loss of the youth upon which every nation depends, inasmuch as their places were partly filled by immigration from other countries. Germany's losses had been greater on a numerical though not on a percentage basis, but Hitler was able to inspire a sense of national purpose in the German people although no enthusiasm for war. Perhaps the answer is that Germany in defeat had a leader and a motive, the recovery of its losses. France in victory had neither. The sense of *élan vital* died as the conviction grew that sacrifices sustained with so much courage for over four years had brought nothing. Old problems remained unsolved, and new ones had been added.

The multitude of political parties that had plagued pre-war France persisted. Ministries were difficult to form and still more difficult to maintain. The average life of a postwar cabinet was only six months. Under these circumstances, the bureaucracy might be able to function, but necessary, unpopular changes could not be made. There was talk of constitutional reforms. Some wanted to do away with the Senate; others wanted a strong American-type president. How much chance these proposals had of being accepted is indicated by the type of president the legislature chose. Two strong men of national stature, Clemenceau and Briand, sought the office in the 1920's, but neither was elected. Instead, the legislature chose in succession Deschanel, who went insane in a few months; Millerand, who was forced to resign because he tried to strengthen the role

[1] See page 813.

of the president; and Doumer, who was assassinated. Only Doumergue and Lebrun were innocuous enough to complete their seven-year terms. The few great leaders France had were rarely permitted to hold important offices. Part of the objection to a powerful executive came from Louis Napoleon's nineteenth-century conversion of his strong presidency into a monarchy, but part came from the deputies' love of party politics and the spoils of office. A "Republic of Pals" one observer called the French system, and he was near the truth.

Sometimes the evils of the system were mitigated by several parties' agreeing to operate together as a bloc. There was a conservative nationalist bloc which included Clemenceau, Poincaré, Millerand, and Briand. A slightly left-of-center bloc was headed by Édouard Herriot, and finally in 1936 a left-wing bloc known as the popular front was led by Léon Blum (1872-1950). These blocs were never very strong, and they were constantly disintegrating. When they did so in time of emergency, it was necessary to give the prime minister authority to issue decrees without parliamentary consent. This happened once in 1926 and six times in the troubled, depression-ridden 1930's. Thus, the French were moving towards the abandonment of parliamentary government before they met their crushing defeat in 1940.

The first postwar task the French faced was the restoration of war-devastated areas. Fortunately, they were limited to the ten northeastern departments, but in this region hundreds of thousands of homes and factories had been destroyed. The transportation system was in chaos, and much of the farm land had turned to waste. Sparing no expense, the French government restored the war-devastated areas by 1926. The unusual energy with which the French proceeded was based on the assumption that German reparations would be forthcoming to cover the cost. When the Germans proved unable or unwilling to pay, French finances were imperiled.[2] The war itself had caused a huge debt, because taxes had not been significantly increased, and now reconstruction costs were added to the total. The taxpayers, of course, wanted to shift the burden to the Germans, and the nationalist bloc headed by Poincaré was ever anxious to weaken France's hated adversary. For these reasons, troops were sent into the Ruhr Valley in January, 1923, to compel the Germans to pay. This action failed, as we have seen, and the more conciliatory left-of-center bloc came to power and established better relations with Germany, but the new government could not solve the financial problem. The franc, which had been worth twenty cents in 1914, dropped to two cents. Poincaré was returned to office in 1926 and given the power to issue emergency decrees, which enabled him to effect economies, raise taxes, and balance the budget. Confidence in the franc was restored, and its value was stabilized at about four cents.

By stabilizing the franc at one-fifth its former value, the government

[2] See pages 791-792.

had in effect repudiated four-fifths of the national debt, thereby freeing itself from its most pressing financial difficulties. At the same time, it had relieved the wealthy classes' fear of catastrophic inflation such as the Germans had suffered. Yet the fact remained that the owners of government and corporation bonds, insurance policies, and the like suffered heavily. Many of these same people, for the most part members of the middle class and peasants, had also bought Russian bonds in the pre-war era as part of France's policy of strengthening its tsarist ally. The Bolsheviks, on coming to power, had cancelled the debt leaving the French with nothing to show for their investment. As a result, the French middle class was severely hurt, although not so badly as its German counterpart, by the financial effects of the war and its aftermath. Many persons were embittered by their losses, and there was a revived royalist and a new fascist movement. However, the majority of the middle class remained loyal to the republican form of government.

The one important gain France obtained from the war was the return of Alsace and Lorraine, and yet these two provinces also brought difficulties. The economies and transportation systems of the provinces were tied to Germany's, and their workers benefited from the superior German social insurance system. Special concessions solved these issues, but the questions of language, religion, and local autonomy were less easily settled because the government insisted on treating the inhabitants like other Frenchmen. Although 88 per cent of the population were German-speaking, French was made the language of instruction in the schools. Even at the great University of Strasbourg, the courses in the German language and literature had to be taught in French. Towns and streets were given French names, and all instructions and signs were changed to conform. This was both irritating and inconvenient. Furthermore, the inhabitants of the two provinces who had been permitted a considerable amount of local autonomy by their German masters now found themselves governed as three departments in the centralized French state. German-speaking officials were dismissed, and in their place Frenchmen were appointed who could not always speak the language of most of the inhabitants. The clergies of the various churches were also unhappy. Their salaries had been paid by the German state, and they had been permitted to give religious instruction in state-supported Catholic, Protestant, and Jewish schools. Now they were faced with the French laws separating church and state.

These difficulties led the inhabitants of Alsace-Lorraine to demand local autonomy, but timely concessions on the part of the French and the rise of Hitler caused them to reconsider. By 1939 most of the people of the provinces were reconciled to French rule, although they still wanted to be left alone. The lot of the inhabitants of these disputed frontier provinces was always difficult, but they did have one advantage. They emerged on the winning side of every war and never had to pay reparations.

The church-state problem had flared up again over Alsace and Lorraine, but on the whole the postwar period saw a remarkable improvement in the relations between the two institutions. The pope withdrew the support that the Church had given to royalists and conservatives since the founding of the republic and further pleased republican opinion by canonizing Joan of Arc. Socially conscious young priests began to move among the workers, where they encouraged the establishment of Catholic trade unions and aided in such movements as the Boy Scouts. Conservatives were horrified, but they could do nothing. The Church, the republic, and the movement towards social reform were drawing together. The state even relented and returned some of the church property it had seized before the war. Yet the left-wing parties still refused to advocate female suffrage because they were afraid that priests would take advantage of the devout nature of women and induce them to vote conservative.

Although the French workers had expected major concessions in return for their loyalty during the war, all they were given after the armistice was an eight-hour day with Saturday afternoons and Sundays free. This was not enough, and many began to turn to communism. In 1922, the *Confédération Générale du Travail* (C.G.T.) split; the larger section adopted a moderate labor program, but the smaller one was organized as a Communist trade union. The fate of the Socialist party was also revealing. At the party congress in Tours in 1920, the majority of the Socialists affiliated themselves with the Communist Third International and took with them the great party newspaper, *L'Humanité*. The remnant became primarily a party of white collar workers and civil servants, which continued to call itself Socialist and, under the leadership of Léon Blum (1872-1950), soon became one of the largest parties in France. The Communists, on the other hand, made deep inroads into the ranks of the workers and even made notable progress among the traditionally conservative and devout peasants. It became increasingly clear that they, and not the Socialists, were the real threat to the capitalistic system.

THE DEPRESSION

For a long time, France seemed immune to the Great Depression. The French economy had revived slowly after the war, and by 1929 industrial production was 40 per cent above pre-war levels. Agriculture was 10 per cent higher, and foreign trade was up 66 per cent. These gains resulted more from the addition of Alsace and Lorraine and the construction of modern factories in the northeast to replace those destroyed by the war than from any change in business methods. In spite of the efforts of a few businessmen to organize trusts and cartels and to adopt large-scale production techniques, France remained primarily a country of small manufacturers and shopkeepers.[3] This situation made the French less dependent on a mass market than most industrial nations, and their conservative

[3] See page 670.

business practices meant that few companies were heavily in debt for new plants and machinery. Furthermore, the balance that still existed between agriculture and industry made large imports unnecessary for an adequate standard of living; this, in turn, made large exports unnecessary to pay for imported goods. As a result, prosperity in France continued through 1931; and because of a favorable balance of foreign trade, gold flowed into France from more highly industrialized, economically depressed nations.

No country, however, can be entirely self-sufficient, and to pay for necessary imports the French had relied on the sale of luxury goods, such as perfume and dresses, and on the tourist trade. As other countries sank deeper into the depression, the luxury trade and tourist travel sharply declined. French prices on more stable exports were too high to compete in the international market because the government did not follow other countries in devaluing the currency. Germany added another blow by ceasing reparations payments. By 1932, France was clearly in the throes of the depression, and the government was perilously in debt. To combat this situation, it was decided to follow the traditional practice of trying to balance the budget by discharging some government employees and by reducing the salaries of those who remained. The powerful French bureaucracy was incensed, and the unemployed were not satisfied by such measures. However, the numerous political parties in the Chamber of Deputies could not agree on any other course. As a result, in a period of only nineteen months, there were six cabinets.

The French people were irritated to see so much squabbling in a time of crisis and were further incensed by a scandal like those which had plagued the republic during its early days. In December, 1933, it was revealed that a certain Serge Stavisky had been involved in the issuance of about $25,000,000 worth of bonds on behalf of Bayonne. As Bayonne was a small town, it was difficult to see why so much money was needed, why so many insurance companies purchased the bonds, and why the charges brought against Stavisky for other activities in 1927 had been postponed nineteen times. Right-wing papers were quick to point out that one of the prosecuting attorneys who should have brought Stavisky to trial was the premier's brother-in-law and that the minister of finance had encouraged the skeptical insurance companies to buy the bonds. Meanwhile, Stavisky had disappeared, only to be found dead, by suicide said the police, by murder to keep him from talking said the rightist press. Two months later, a high legal official who presumably knew about the case was found dead, whether by suicide or murder was disputed. In all about seventeen deputies may have been involved in the scandal.

Rightists paraded the streets yelling, "Out with the thieves." Among them were several uniformed groups that resembled the fascists, the most important of which was the *Croix de Feu,* headed by Colonel de la Rocque. The *Croix de Feu* had originally been an organization of veterans who had been decorated for gallantry, but it had been expanded to include over 700,000 men. On February 6, 1934, there was a serious riot in the Place de la Concorde across the river from the Chamber of Deputies. The republic seemed to be in danger, and a supposedly strong-man ministry was formed under former president Gaston Doumergue. Neither Doumergue nor his immediate successors could find sufficient support to alter the constitution or to solve the problems of the depression. Fortunately, Colonel de la Rocque was more a patriotic, conservative royalist than an admirer of Hitler's techniques, and his movement was more a protest against the weakness and dishonesty of the republican officials than an effort to seize power by brute force. Since genuine fascist organizations were small, there was probably very little danger of a rightist coup.

Nevertheless, the left had seen enough of Mussolini and Hitler to feel threatened. German Communists had stupidly refused to cooperate with the republican forces in their country. French Communists decided not to make the same mistake. For the first time, they decided to support the bourgeois Radical Socialist and Socialist parties in a popular front to prevent the triumph of fascism. In May, 1936, the popular front emerged victorious in the elections, and Léon Blum, a well-known Socialist leader, became prime minister. The Communists would not go so far as to accept cabinet posts, but their seventy-two deputies supported the coalition and their labor union was reunited with the larger C.G.T.

During the year that followed, the popular front attacked the depression by trying to increase consumer purchasing power and by trying to improve the lot of the workers rather than by reducing wages and prices. A big public works program was inaugurated to provide employment, and liberal credit was provided for industry. Labor disputes were to be settled by arbitration rather than by strikes. Workers were given a 12 to 15 per cent raise, a long-demanded forty-hour work week, fifteen days of vacation with pay each year, and a 40 per cent reduction in railway fares. Farmers were guaranteed artificially high prices for part of their wheat crop, arms factories were nationalized, and the power of the two hundred men who controlled the Bank of France, and with it much of the country's finance, was sharply curtailed.

Unhappily for Blum, his inflationary program wiped out the workers' raise in wages and at the same time reduced sales abroad. The government itself was hopelessly in debt, and private investors had as little interest in lending money to support even a very moderate socialist program as they had in coming to the aid of Louis XVI in 1789. The result was that Blum had to devalue the franc by another 25 per cent in order to make French prices competitive on the world market and to ask for emergency powers in fiscal matters. The Chamber of Deputies agreed, but the more conservative Senate, which anticipated a heavy tax on the well-to-do, refused on June 19, 1937, and Blum was forced to resign.

During the next ten months, all was confusion. Franco was clearly winning in Spain, Hitler was growing more threatening, and cabinets were changing rapidly. There were three different cabinets during this period, but none existed at the moment that Hitler occupied Austria. Finally in April, 1938, Édouard Daladier (1884-   ) became prime minister and was given the power to issue decrees. His government favored a return to laissez-faire in the hope of restoring the confidence of the business community. He devalued the franc once more and abandoned part of Blum's social reforms. The forty-hour week was modified to speed production. A retaliatory workers' strike was abruptly halted. A belated effort was made to prepare for the coming war. When Russia and Germany announced their pact in August, 1939, Daladier suppressed the Communist paper, *L'Humanité*. Despite these efforts which led to a 15 per cent increase in production and the stabilization of the franc, France entered the World War II a few days later, psychologically and materially unprepared for the ordeal.

THE SMALLER EUROPEAN STATES

Eight of the smaller European states managed to maintain their free institutions throughout the inter-war period. It is noteworthy that of these eight, only three had been involved in any way in World War I and only two contained more than one large language group.

THE LOW COUNTRIES

During the nineteenth century the Grand Duchy of Luxembourg belonged to the King of the Netherlands, but it was also a part of the Germanic Confederation and included in the *Zollverein*. It was not absorbed into Bismarckian Germany because of its neutral status and Dutch connection, but in 1890 this tie was cut when Wilhelmina inherited the Dutch throne. Luxembourg's laws of succession at that time permitted only a man to rule, and a member of a collateral line of the Dutch royal house became grand duke of the little independent state of 999 square miles. In 1919, Luxembourg cut its tariff ties with Germany and concluded a tariff and monetary union with Belgium.

Both Luxembourg and Belgium had been invaded by the German armies in 1914. Luxembourg, with an army of less than 200 men, offered no resistance and escaped damage from the war. Belgians, on the other hand, fought courageously under the leadership of King Albert I (1909-1934), and their country suffered more heavily from the war in proportion to its size than France. In addition, they were plagued by a serious minority problem. The Dutch escaped direct involvement in the war and suffered only shipping and trading losses. They had no ethnic issue, but the rapid increase in the number of Roman Catholics created a religious problem.

897

In spite of these potential sources of trouble, none of the Low Countries had serious difficulty in retaining a democratic form of government.

By 1926, Belgium's industries and mines were restored with modern equipment. All men and some women were given the right to vote in 1919, and the educational system was improved. The minority problem was temporarily mitigated by making Flemish (Dutch-related) and Walloon (French-related) the official languages in the areas where they were spoken. A small Fascist party did develop in the Flemish section during the 1920's and later in the Walloon section after the advent of the depression, but it was denied the use of the radio. In July, 1934, Fascist military units and parades were made illegal, and two years later the Fascist leader was arrested. These stern measures were effective. In 1938 the Fascist party polled only 5 per cent of the vote. The Belgians did not, however, escape all difficulties. Extraordinary powers had to be granted the government in 1932 to cope with the budget deficit and the depression, and during the two years before the outbreak of war one cabinet crisis followed another as in France. Some Belgians in 1939 were skeptical of the advantages of the parliamentary system of government and doubtful about the wisdom of resisting the Germans in 1914.

The Dutch, who had escaped World War I and had no ethnic problem, fared very well during the 1920's, but the depression dealt them a severe blow as it did all nations dependent largely on foreign trade. A National Socialist party grew rapidly. However, in 1934 the government was given emergency powers to fight both the depression and political extremism. The first was accomplished by a large public works program, a tariff against foreign agricultural products, and a limitation on internal agricultural production. Measures were passed against the National Socialists, who were forbidden to hold office. In the elections of 1937, the National Socialist vote declined sharply. Thus, by granting emergency powers to the government and by curtailing freedom of speech and assembly, the inhabitants of the Low Countries managed to control extremist groups and maintain most of their basic liberties.

SWITZERLAND

The Swiss also preserved their traditional democratic way of life without serious difficulty. This was especially noteworthy because there were three major language groups in the country, two of which—German and Italian—were used by the inhabitants of neighboring totalitarian states who might be expected to encourage fascist movements. Furthermore, the depression dealt Switzerland a severe blow because of its dependence on foreign and tourist trade. A National Socialist organization was established for resident German citizens, but the Swiss outlawed the party in 1936. Neither nazism nor communism made significant progress, while the threat of invasion from Germany or Italy was checked by the obvious willingness of the citizenry to fight for their mountainous, easily defended land. Switzerland maintained no standing army, but nearly all male citizens between the ages of twenty and forty-eight served in the national militia and kept their rifles and uniforms in their homes. Under such circumstances even Hitler thought it wiser to exclude the German-speaking Swiss cantons from his dream of a great empire that would include all the German-speaking people of Europe.

THE SCANDINAVIAN COUNTRIES

At this time Norway, Sweden, and Denmark were the most trouble-free countries in Europe. Nearly all the inhabitants of each country spoke the same language and went to the same church (Lutheran), if they attended at all. They were far enough from the center of European activity to have escaped most wars and to have been free to develop without major internal or external problems. During the last generation or two they have become noted for their broad schemes of social and medical insurance, their public housing projects, and their numerous cooperatives. In some areas, state and private corporations have competed; in others they have jointly provided the capital for various projects. Scandinavia saw little of the rivalry between government and free enterprise so prevalent in the United States.

Political democracy arrived relatively late in these countries. Yet by 1919 members of both sexes had won the right to vote in all three countries, and although the kings retained important theoretical powers, they ceased to use them. The depression brought economic hardship to Scandinavia, but this was met by an expansion of governmental activity in the economic sphere and by greater cooperation between the three countries. Neither the fascists nor the communists were able to win significant followings.

The Finns were in a less fortunate position. They had been part of Russia until 1917, when they profited by the revolution to proclaim their independence. It took nearly two years of fighting under the leadership of Baron Carl Mannerheim (1867-1951) to establish peace with the Soviet Union, and this colossal neighbor has never ceased to be a threat. The communist element in Finland was regarded, therefore, as doubly dangerous. In 1930 and 1932, the communist threat gave rise to a nationalistic-fascist type of organization that attempted to seize power. The government acted strongly against both the left and the right, and the two extremist parties together never polled as much as 20 per cent of the vote. The Finns have displayed an exceptional talent for democratic government and have transformed a weak economy into a relatively strong one. Also, significantly, they alone, of all the countries to whom the United States loaned money during the war period, never defaulted in a payment.

899

GREAT BRITAIN AND THE DOMINIONS

The British towns and countryside almost totally escaped the destruction of war, and Britain suffered only half as many casualties as France. Nevertheless, British postwar economic problems were very serious. The depression was little short of catastrophic to Britain. Both communist and fascist movements developed, but neither became a serious threat to its parliamentary institutions.

POSTWAR PROBLEMS

Few Britons anticipated unusual difficulties at the war's end. Lloyd George, the prime minister, pledged himself during the elections of December, 1918, to make Britain a "fit country for heroes to live in." With this promise and with suggestions that the Kaiser be hanged and that everything be taken from Germany "that you can squeeze out of a lemon and a bit more," the coalition that had governed Britain during the last years of the war was returned to power. There were, of course, some immediate problems. Order had to be restored on the continent, the army had to be demobilized, and the soldiers had to be found jobs. There were several mutinies, as well as alarming reports of soldiers' councils being established in Egypt. Strikes and talks of strikes were frequent, especially in the coal industry, but on the whole the economy boomed as people sought to buy the articles they had been denied during the war years. The boom provided employment for the discharged soldier, and by October, 1919, there were less than a half million persons seeking jobs. Wages went up rapidly, but prices rose faster still.

By 1921, the postwar boom began to come to an end. Overseas trade dropped by over one-half between 1920 and 1922. Industrial production and mining declined rapidly, wages fell, and the number who received employment insurance passed the 2,000,000 mark in March, 1921. Britons began to awaken to the fact that they had lost their once enviable economic position and that henceforth a million or more persons would be out of work even in normal years.

There were several reasons for this situation. Since the United Kingdom was a relatively small island inhabited by over 40,000,000 people, food and raw materials had to be imported in large quantities. Before the war these imports had been paid for by almost equally large exports, interest received from foreign loans, and payments for shipping and other services performed. During the war, however, Japan had taken much of Britain's Asiatic market; by 1934, Japan's trade with India had increased ninefold, while sales to that country from Britain's textile industry had dropped to one-fifth of their former value. In Latin America, the United States had profited from British preoccupation with the war to take many of Britain's pre-war customers. In addition, when the underdeveloped nations, such as China, India, and the Latin American countries, had found themselves cut off from their usual source of manufactured goods during the war, they had begun to establish their own industries. After the war, these industries were generally protected by high tariffs.

Germany had been one of Britain's best customers, but the severity of the peace treaty made it impossible for the Germans to buy as much after the war as before. This was one reason why the British soon tried to reduce the reparations payments and to restore German prosperity.

Coal had been one of Britain's largest exports. After the war, however, ships and industries began to convert to oil. Another reason for the declining market was that British goods cost more than those produced by countries which had industrialized more recently. Many of the British factories were equipped with antiquated machinery; their new competitors had more efficient plants. British coal mines had become especially inefficient because of the failure to make full use of labor-saving machinery and because they had been used so long that mine shafts had to burrow deep into the ground. Many Europeans found it cheaper to buy American coal despite the higher transportation cost.

The loss of many foreign markets dealt a heavy blow to the huge British merchant marine. Ships were idle in the harbors, and the shipyards that had worked with such feverish energy several years before to turn out transports faster than the German submarines could sink them were now without orders. The British had foolishly required the Germans to surrender part of their merchant marine to them as a requirement of the peace treaty. Now they were no longer needed and served only to postpone the day when orders would again come to the shipyards. Meanwhile, over a third of the workers in the shipbuilding industry were unemployed.

Although Britain continued to draw large sums from foreign investments, it was necessary now to make payments to the United States on the loans made during the war. The sum that remained, and it was considerable, did little more than compensate for the foreign trade deficit even in the 1920's. In addition, the government was saddled with a huge domestic debt requiring interest payments that came to a total higher than Lloyd George's famous budget of 1909, which had so shocked Conservatives.[4] Accordingly, postwar Britain had to accustom itself to heavy taxes, a modest standard of living, and widespread unemployment; that is, unless some means could be found to alleviate the situation.

Government and business applied the same solution: they both tried to reduce expenses. Governmental economy caused very little comment, but the coal mine owners' decision to cut wages by as much as 49 per cent in some localities provoked the threat of a general strike. Army leaves were cancelled, and the reserves were called up. Then on "Black Friday," April 14, 1921, the day before the strike was to begin, the miners were deserted by the other unions, and they were forced to accept a heavy wage cut. Failure

[4] See page 661.

to take a united stand proved costly to labor, for wages were later reduced in other industries. By 1925 union membership had dropped by 3,000,000 persons. Those who had jobs found their wage gains during the war years wiped out; those without jobs received unemployment insurance. This insurance was to have been paid for only fifteen weeks per year, but the continued economic slump caused the government to extend it indefinitely. This process of handing out a sum sufficient for bare subsistence to unemployed workers, known as the "dole," was characteristic of British life for many years to come.

PARTY POLITICS

Meanwhile, the members of Lloyd George's coalition government of Liberals and Conservatives were becoming restive. Although an able, energetic administrator with proven ability, Lloyd George was also autocratic in his methods and had nearly involved Britain in a war with Turkey.[5] In the elections of November, 1922, the Conservatives were returned to power. The Liberal party fared badly. One wing followed Lloyd George and supported the wartime coalition; the other remained loyal to its nominal leader, Lord Asquith, who had had nothing to do with the coalition and would have nothing to do with Lloyd George. Divided, the Liberal party fell. Its two wings together received fewer votes than the Labor party, which profited from the general economic discontent to elect 142 men to Parliament. From this time, the Liberal party declined and at best held the balance of power between the Conservatives and Laborites, who henceforth were the principal contenders for power.

Victory in 1922 brought the Conservatives only problems. Unemployment continued high, and no solution seemed forthcoming. Finally, the prime minister, Stanley Baldwin (1867-1947), decided to abandon Britain's historic free trade policy and to establish a protective tariff. Other nations were shutting out British goods with high tariffs; why should not Britain reply in kind and ensure the domestic market for its own producers? Before abandoning Britain's historic free trade position, he decided to appeal to the country. The elections of 1923 reflected the growing dissatisfaction. The Conservatives won only 258 seats. The reunited Liberal party stood by its traditional position in favor of free trade and won 158 seats. The Labor party likewise opposed the tariff and profited by the popular discontent to win 191 seats. As no party held a majority, the Liberals had a choice of forming a coalition with the Conservatives, who wanted laissez-faire at home and protection from abroad, or the Laborites, who wanted a socialized domestic economy and free trade. The country held its breath. Some Conservatives predicted that property would be confiscated and capitalism terminated if they were removed from office, but the Liberals chose the Labor party notwithstanding. Neville Chamberlain (1869-

[5] See pages 785-786.

1940), future Conservative prime minister, sagely observed that there was nothing to fear. Labor in a coalition government "would be too weak to do much harm but not too weak to get discredited." He was right.

The new Labor prime minister was Ramsay MacDonald (1866-1937), the son of a Scottish day laborer and himself a one-time clerk, teacher, journalist, and student of socialism. His cabinet included several peers, but most of its members were drawn from the lower walks of life. One of them later wrote that as he and his colleagues waited to be received by the King in the palace, "I could not help marveling at the strange turn of Fortune's wheel, which had brought MacDonald, the starveling clerk, Thomas the engine-driver, Henderson the foundry labourer and Clynes the millhand, to this pinnacle." Neither could others, and they saw to it that the Laborites were not long in power.

MacDonald made no attempt to socialize the country. He was dependent on the votes of the Liberal party to remain in power, and he knew that its members would never agree to such a program. The only domestic legislation of importance during his ministry provided a government subsidy to encourage building low-cost houses. MacDonald's main objective was "to gain the confidence of the country," which he seemed to feel could best be accomplished by doing nothing beyond insisting that his ministers wear evening clothes when the occasion demanded. Some owned none, but three suits were bought and the ministers took turns using them.

In foreign policy, MacDonald was much more active. He was instrumental in securing the acceptance of the Dawes Plan by Germany and France, and he embarked on a program of friendship with Russia. Recognition was granted to the Soviet regime, and there was talk of a loan in return for Russian trade. This was too much for the Liberals, who also had other minor grievances. MacDonald had to resign after only nine months in office.

During the elections of October, 1924, a letter was published which encouraged British workers to support the Russian trade treaty and to work for a communist revolution. Whether Zinoviev, the head of the Communist Third International, wrote the letter as was charged has never been determined, but the timing of its publication and its contents could not have been better calculated to bring advantage to the Conservative party. A red scare swept across Britain, and Liberals deserted their party en masse because of its previous support of the Labor government. Some Liberal leaders, including Winston Churchill, joined the Conservatives at this time. The Conservative party won 415 seats and the Liberals dropped to 42. The Labor party retained the loyalty of its following, despite the disappointment that more had not been accomplished in the way of domestic reform. It polled more votes than in the preceding year but won only 152 seats. Baldwin returned to the post of prime minister, an office which he held for the next five years.

Baldwin was a genial man of modest ability who rarely took any action unless compelled. The one noteworthy domestic event of his ministry was the general strike of May, 1926. In 1925 the coal mine owners announced that a wage cut of from 13 to 48 per cent was necessary to reduce the costs of production. The miners, of course, threatened to strike, and they were promised support by other unions. Baldwin granted a temporary government subsidy to keep wages at the current rate while an investigating commission sought a solution. The commission recommended that the coal industry be reorganized to make it more efficient and that wages be reduced, but both the mine owners and the workers refused to accept these proposals. Baldwin's efforts at a compromise failed, and when the government subsidy was discontinued, the miners struck with the support of the railway, iron, steel, and building trades. The government acted with vigor. Some 226,000 special constables were sworn in to help maintain order and deliver food shipments that had been halted by the railroad workers. After nine days, the unity of the labor movement dissolved. Everyone except the mine union leaders called off the strike. The miners kept up their resistance for another seven months, but in the end they had to accept a longer working day at lower wages.

Despite Baldwin's desire to be neutral, most of the actions of his government had favored the mine owners; and he had moved vigorously to break the general strike. Several times the king, George V (1910-1936), had had to caution the overly belligerent government to avoid possible violence. When the strike was over, the Conservatives passed a Trade Disputes and Trade Union Act which outlawed general strikes and other forms of sympathy strikes but left the workers of an individual industry free to strike to secure direct benefits for themselves. This act was bitterly resented by the unions and the Labor party, but they did not muster strength to repeal it until 1946.

THE DEPRESSION

The elections of 1929 brought a Labor ministry into office a few months before the crash on the New York stock market. The Labor party won 287 seats to the Conservatives' 261. Once more the 59 Liberal members of Parliament held the balance of power, and once more they threw their support behind MacDonald. As a result, it was the Labor party that initially had to cope with the depression. British exports fell from £839,000,000 in 1929 to £461,000,000 in 1931. Industries had to discharge employees, and the number of insured workers who were unemployed grew from a little over 1,000,000 in 1929 to 2,707,000 in June, 1931. This increased the cost of unemployment benefits at a time when governmental income was falling. The budget could not be balanced in 1931 and would be even harder to balance in 1932 if something were not done. The Bank of England was saved only by timely aid from New York and Paris bankers, who hinted that there would be no further assistance without governmental economy and a balanced budget.

One would think that a Labor party would try to solve British economic problems by going off the gold standard and by initiating a huge public works program to provide employment. This policy could have been financed by additional taxes on the wealthy, borrowing if possible, and printing more paper money. However, the Liberals on whom the Laborites depended would not have supported such a program, and MacDonald accepted the orthodox recommendations of his economic advisers. He attempted to balance the budget by economies, which included a cut in the benefits paid to the unemployed. A large percentage of his party refused to accept this solution. On August 24, 1931, his cabinet resigned.

Instead of asking a Conservative-Liberal coalition to assume control, the King called on MacDonald to form a national government including all three parties to deal with the emergency. The new cabinet, which included four Laborites, four Conservatives, and two Liberals, cut the wages of civil servants as well as payments to the unemployed. However, worsening economic conditions forced the cabinet to abandon the gold standard in September anyway. MacDonald and the handful of Laborites who had followed him were ejected from their party for what was regarded as their great betrayal. In the elections that followed, the coalition won an overwhelming victory, but as nearly all of its support came from the Conservatives, the members of this party, not MacDonald, dominated the government. Indeed, in June, 1935, he resigned because of ill health, and Baldwin once more became prime minister. In 1937, Baldwin in turn gave way in favor of his Chancellor of the Exchequer, Neville Chamberlain. Not until 1945 did Labor return to power.

The national coalition's, or more aptly the Conservatives', solution to the depression was essentially to wait for better times. Its leaders were anxious to straighten out the international debt-reparations tangle and to have worldwide disarmament, because the first would aid in solving the currency problem and the second would help balance the budget. Beyond this, they were content to revive the tariff issue. In 1932 an act was passed levying duties of from 10 to 20 per cent on most articles in order to reserve the domestic market for British producers. Thus, the upper middle class which now controlled the Conservative party dealt another blow to nineteenth-century liberalism by abandoning its historic position in favor of free trade. The Labor party was aided by a remnant of the once-powerful Liberal party that voted against the measure.

The Conservatives hoped to work out a system of free trade, or at least one of preferential tariffs, within the empire in order to increase the flow of goods. A conference was held with representatives of the dominions at Ottawa during the summer of 1932, but agreement was difficult to reach. The plan called for the dominions to buy British manufactured goods and for the British to buy their agricultural products and raw materials. The difficulty was caused by the desire of British agriculture to be protected from dominion competition; at the same time, the infant dominion industries had no desire to compete freely with their British counterparts. In the end, preferential rates were instituted, which meant that a lower duty on Canadian wheat was paid in Britain than on American wheat and, in return, less was paid on British textiles entering Canada than on American textiles. The result was an increase in trade between Great Britain and the dominions.

Compared with the activities of other governments, these were mild measures, but the economic conditions of the country began to improve slowly in 1933. By 1937, production was 24 per cent higher than in 1929, and the working force that was unemployed was reduced from 22 to 12 per cent. Some industries continued to lag, and many depressed areas remained, but Great Britain recovered as rapidly from the depression with a balanced budget and almost no public works program as the United States did with an unbalanced budget and a public works program. The principal reason for British recovery was probably increased consumption. The cost of living fell more rapidly than wages, and this led to greater buying. The housing industry was especially active. The government's encouragement of lower interest rates and its decision to rearm in the face of the growing power of the aggressive fascist states also helped.

In January, 1936, the popular, dependable George V died and was succeeded by his bachelor son, Edward VIII. Edward had been a gay, popular, self-willed prince who had mixed with company not normally invited to court. Among his acquaintances was Mrs. Wallis Warfield Simpson, an American woman then in the process of obtaining her second divorce. In October, 1936, he announced his intention to marry her. However, the cabinet and the Archbishop of Canterbury opposed the marriage, and in this decision they were supported by the dominions. Edward was left with the choice of abandoning his throne or abandoning Mrs. Simpson. He chose the former course and abdicated in December. His brother ascended the throne as George VI (1936-1952). The episode might have weakened the crown, but Baldwin had acted with decision and finesse. There was hardly a ripple of discord, and only Ireland profited by the situation to weaken its ties with the British Empire.

IRELAND

The British were on the verge of giving the Irish home rule when the outbreak of war in 1914 postponed their plans.[6] Both Irish Catholic and Irish Protestant leaders agreed to wait for peace, but their policy of moderation, trust, and patience was rejected by the radical Catholics who wanted a completely independent, united Ireland and who saw in Britain's preoc-

[6] See page 659.

cupation with the Germans the best opportunity to obtain their desires. They organized the Sinn Fein (Ourselves Alone) movement; the Germans promised arms; and on Easter Sunday, 1916, a serious rebellion broke out in Dublin. Fortunately for the British, they were able to prevent the German arms from reaching their destination, and after nearly a week's fighting order was restored. Few had supported the insurrection, but the British decision to execute fifteen of the leading rebels made them heroes and caused most Irishmen outside the Protestant north to support the Sinn Fein movement.

In 1917, a Sinn Fein convention met in Dublin, prepared a constitution, and elected an American-born Irishman, Eamon de Valera (1882-   ), president. The British, of course, did not recognize this act, but in the elections of December, 1918, Sinn Fein won seventy-three of the 105 Irish seats in the British Parliament. Those who were elected refused to go to London. Instead they established their own parliament and declared Ireland independent. A period of many months followed, in which the Sinn Fein army and the British fought. Although it was less a war of pitched battles than one of assassination, the toll in lives was high. In December, 1920, the British passed an act giving both northern and southern Ireland parliaments, but providing that they keep their present representation in the British Parliament as well. Predominantly Protestant northern Ireland accepted this proposal and is still governed under its provisions. Predominantly Catholic southern Ireland refused, and the following year was granted full dominion status as the Irish Free State. Even this did not satisfy the minority, led by De Valera, who were opposed to the requirement that an oath of loyalty to the crown be taken and to the separation of the island into two states. De Valera resigned from the presidency and started a revolt against the Irish majority. Not until 1927 did he consent to take his seat in Parliament, and even then he did not disband his army.

The depression brought hardships to Ireland which enabled De Valera to defeat the moderates in the elections of 1932. As president he tried to abolish the oath of allegiance to the British crown and took advantage of Edward VIII's abdication to remove direct mention of the crown in the new Constitution of 1936-1937. Southern Ireland became the "sovereign, democratic state" of Eire, and only the vaguest ties with Great Britain were maintained. The Irish were not only unwilling to participate in World War II; they also refused to let the British use the naval bases in southern Ireland which had been turned over to them in 1938.

THE DOMINIONS

The British relations with their dominions were much happier, although they had been behaving in an increasingly independent manner for years. In 1919 the dominions signed the peace treaties and joined the League of Nations as individual states. Soon thereafter, they began to exchange ambassadors with foreign powers. The British made no effort to check this development. Instead, in 1926 they defined the dominions as "autonomous communities within the British Empire, equal in status, in no way subordinate one to another in any aspect of their domestic or external affairs, though united by a common allegiance to the Crown and freely associated as members of the British Commonwealth of Nations." This definition contained nothing new. Indeed it was too vague to be much of a definition at all. The situation was slightly clarified by the Statute of Westminster, 1931, in which the British Parliament specifically declared that its acts did not apply to the dominions except at their request.

By refraining from attempts at compulsion, the British actually encouraged the development of ties of loyalty and sentiment. The United Kingdom and the dominions shared the same king, who was represented in the dominions by a governor-general. Appeals could still be made to the British Privy Council, and changes in a dominion's constitution had to be approved by Parliament. Otherwise, the dominions were completely sovereign. Only Eire and the Union of South Africa, where the Boers were anti-British, had any desire for greater independence. Common problems were dealt with by frequent Imperial conferences and by high commissioners sent by Britain to the dominions and by the dominions to Britain.

All the dominions were largely agricultural and, therefore, suffered heavily during the depression. As a general rule, they attempted to stimulate recovery by raising tariffs, buying excess farm produce, and establishing public works programs. New Zealand also nationalized banking and brought the railroads under government control.

Canada was faced with quarrels between the French Catholics of Quebec and the English Protestant majority in the other provinces. The Union of South Africa had a serious racial problem. The large Negro population was very backward, and the Boers, who made up the majority of the white population, were very race-conscious. Few Negroes were allowed to vote. In Cape Province where they were permitted to do so, they could only choose three non-Negroes to represent them in the dominion parliament. The Boers were anti-British, and there was some sentiment for leaving the British Empire. Except for the Union of South Africa, however, the dominions remained free, democratic states without strong fascist or communist parties or without undue racial consciousness.

THE AMERICAS

THE UNITED STATES IN THE 1920'S

The United States emerged from the war into a position of world leadership. Escaping the years of grueling warfare that had exhausted friend and foe alike, the nation still stood, in November, 1918, fresh, well-armed, and powerful. Only 50,000 American soldiers had been killed in battle; yet the United States could with justification claim to have been the deciding factor in the war. While other nations were sinking deep into debt and losing overseas markets, the United States was capturing their customers and becoming a creditor rather than a debtor nation. So much power and wealth helped in the assumption of a dominant role at the peace conference and thereafter in world affairs.

Wilson tried to play the role at Versailles that fate appeared to have assigned to him, but on his return to the United States he found little enthusiasm for his accomplishments. German-Americans thought the treaty was too severe. Irish-Americans complained at his not supporting the cause of Ireland's independence. Italian-Americans thought that Italy had received too little. Pro-Chinese Americans thought that China, not Japan, should have received the former German concessions in that country. In point of fact, however, the territorial provisions of the treaty caused less opposition than the clause creating the League of Nations. A spirited debate ensued as to whether the United States should accept the world leadership to which its wealth and power entitled it or whether it should reject the proffered mantle and refuse to join the League or to work actively for world justice and world peace.

Three different positions were taken by Americans. Some were isolationists and felt that membership in the League would involve the United States in wars in which it had no interest. A second group loyally accepted Wilson's internationalism and idealism because they believed that the League of Nations was essential to the preservation of peace. In between, a host of people would have supported the League only if certain reservations were permitted. If Wilson had accepted this position, he could have won the necessary two-thirds vote in the Senate for ratification; but he believed that to do so would weaken the League. In spite of a speaking tour that wrecked his health and eventually caused his death, he could not muster sufficient support to get the treaty ratified by the Senate. The League became the principal issue in the election of 1920. The Democratic presidential team of Ohio's Governor James M. Cox and Assistant Secretary of the Navy Franklin D. Roosevelt supported the League, while the Republicans led by Ohio's Senator Warren G. Harding (1865-1923) catered to the isolationists and to those who wanted to join the League with reservations. This ambiguous stand pleased most of the voters, who had tired of Wilsonian idealism and were already beginning to regard the European intervention as a mistake. Of the 26,000,000 voters, 16,000,000 chose Harding to go to the White House. The Senate never ratified the treaty, and Congress was content to pass a resolution stating that the war had come to an end.

If Harding's victory in 1920 marked the American refusal to accept world leadership, it also marked the end of a phase in domestic history. The previous generation had staunchly advocated reform. The progressive movement had been powerful in both parties, and much had been accomplished at the national, state, and local level. The new era turned its back on reform and embarked on another course often called "normalcy." Actually, the term was a misnomer. The dominant characteristics of the 1920's were comparable only to those of the post-Civil War years.

Harding's nomination and election to the presidency in itself marked the change. Theodore Roosevelt and Woodrow Wilson had been great leaders who took decided stands on important issues. Harding was a genial small-town editor, who had been elected to the Senate in 1914, his first important office. He had neither political principles, programs, nor pretensions. But he looked like a president, and he had played too insignificant a role in American life to have made many enemies. His very nomination was a result of backstage manipulation by a group of Republican politicians in a smoke-filled room in a convention hotel, and a number of dishonest deals took place during his term of office. Indeed, the Harding administration rivals that of Grant as the most corrupt in American history.

The most famous scandal was the Teapot Dome case. Secretary of the Interior Fall persuaded Secretary of the Navy Denby to transfer Navy-controlled government oil reserves at Teapot Dome, Wyoming, and in California to his department. Then he leased one reserve to Harry F. Sinclair's oil company and the other to E. L. Doheny's Pan-American Petroleum Company without competitive bidding. In return, he received $408,000. When exposed, after Harding's death, both Fall and Denby were forced to resign, and Fall was fined and briefly imprisoned.

Charles R. Forbes, Director of the Veteran's Bureau, squandered or stole from $200,000,000 to $250,000,000. He accepted kickbacks and paid outrageous prices for federal purchases, but he was sentenced to only a brief prison term and a small fine. The Attorney General made "extras" by selling pardons and liquor permits, and the alien property custodian sold German chemical patents. Harding himself does not appear to have been involved in the dishonest activities of his friends and appointees, and he died suddenly in August, 1923, before the scandals of his administration were revealed. His death was officially attributed to ptomaine poisoning, but a rumor soon began to spread that his wife had poisoned him to save him from the pending disgrace and/or to quiet her own jealousy, for he was not a faithful husband. These suspicions were probably unfounded, but that they should have been voiced at all is indicative of the character of the period.

Harding was succeeded by Vice President Calvin Coolidge (1872-1933), an honest, frugal, colorless New Englander whose silence became proverbial. He made no particular effort to punish the wrongdoers in the previous administration, but his own appointees were honest men who did not bring additional scandal to the Republican regime. Indeed, the public showed little concern about the corruption of the Harding era and had no hesitation in 1924 in giving Coolidge four more years in the White House in his own right. At the end of this term he simply announced, "I do not choose to run for President in 1928." No one expected him to say more, and the Republicans nominated and elected Herbert Hoover.

In addition to scandal and to Presidents without stature, the 1920's were characterized by widespread intolerance. Anyone who was not a native American or at least of northern European stock was likely to be considered inferior. Immigration, especially from southern Europe and Asia, was rigidly limited by Congressional acts. The Ku Klux Klan was revived and chose as its enemies not only Negroes, but also Catholics, Jews, and all things foreign or different. The movement was by no means limited to the South. The Klan operated in Pennsylvania, Massachusetts, Indiana, California, and many other states. In all, 6,000,000 Americans joined to ride around in nightshirts, burn crosses, and beat Negroes, union organizers, and others whom they disliked. In their 1924 convention, the Democrats had difficulty deciding whether to condemn the Klan. Fortunately, the Klan began to decline soon thereafter, but for a time it was more widespread than the somewhat similar Nazi movement in Germany.

Alien ideas were as much feared as alien people. Schools were to teach Americanism. Radical labor unions were outlawed in many states. Aliens with unorthodox ideas were deported, especially immediately after the end of the war. Moderate socialism was confused in the public mind with Bolshevism. The New York state legislature went so far as to expel five legally elected Socialists from its midst. Because of the practice of sending time bombs through the mail, anarchism became a source of legitimate concern. In a famous court case, Italian anarchists Nicola Sacco and Bartolomeo Vanzetti were convicted of murder more on the ground of their political creed than on evidence produced at the trial. Intellectuals throughout the country protested the conviction on the grounds that the trial was unfair and tried unsuccessfully to save the lives of the two men. Religious fundamentalists joined the political and economic orthodoxy and persuaded the state of Tennessee to outlaw the teaching of the Darwinian theory. This led to the famous Scopes trial, in which a high-school teacher was prosecuted for ignoring the act. No less a person than William Jennings Bryan (1860-1925) testified for the state, and young Scopes was found guilty by the court but not by public opinion.

Lack of respect for the law was another characteristic of the age. During the war, the manufacture of alcoholic beverages had been outlawed to preserve grain, and in January, 1919, this law was made part of the Constitution by the ratification of the Eighteenth Amendment. There had been strong prohibition forces in many states prior to the war, but why the American people voted for the Eighteenth Amendment is difficult to explain, for it soon became obvious that few were willing to alter the customs of a lifetime. The saloon disappeared only to be replaced by the speakeasy. Wine and milder whiskeys were replaced by bathtub gin. The cocktail party and the bootlegger became familiar aspects of the American scene. Al Capone and other gangsters made fortunes on crime and vice, as normally law-abiding citizens violated the prohibition act daily. Over 500,000 arrests were made between 1920 and 1930 without effect. The law was unenforceable, and it apparently bred more crime than the saloon ever did. The manufacture of fast automobiles and the enactment of speed limits and traffic regulations soon provided another kind of law that respectable citizens had no compunction about disregarding.

Government scandals and gangsters captured most of the newspaper headlines, but undoubtedly the outstanding characteristic of the 1920's was the role played by business. At no time had the pursuit of wealth been more respectable or the businessman given a higher place in the community. The Chamber of Commerce and the National Association of Manufacturers extolled his virtues; newspapers, politicians, and clergymen added their assent. One executive wrote a popular book describing Christ as the world's best businessman because of His advertising and selling ability. Few denied that the nation owed its prosperity to the businessman.

Certainly the government subscribed to this view and did all in its power to aid him. Tariffs were raised higher to protect him from foreign competition. Andrew Mellon (1855-1937) used his influence as Secretary of the Treasury between 1921 and 1932 to get the excess profits tax repealed and the income tax reduced so that the rich would have the money to establish new industries and enlarge old ones. Anti-trust laws were forgotten, and the Commerce Department under Herbert Hoover actually assisted in limiting and controlling competition by getting over 400 industries to establish trade associations which pooled purchases, exchanged information, and developed codes of fair business practices. The automobile industry was aided by a huge highway building program, and the merchant marine and airlines were given direct or indirect federal subsidies. The Interstate Commerce Commission, which had been formed to prevent railroad abuses, was now used to reduce competition. As a result of the government's policy of favoring business, wealth was concentrated in fewer hands. By 1933, 53 per cent of the corporate wealth of the country was owned by 594 corporations, and smaller businesses were being swallowed up daily. Of the 200 firms established to make automobiles, only forty-four still survived in 1927, and soon three were to account for nearly all the cars manufactured in the country.

Labor received no aid from the government. Even the conservative unions on whom Wilson's administration had smiled received no encouragement. Federal and state troops and court injunctions were employed by the government to break strikes. Even without federal and state intervention, the unions were no match for the big industries, and membership dropped from 5,110,000 to 4,330,000 between 1920 and 1929. The real wages of workers nevertheless improved, although their share in industrial profits declined. About a million persons were unemployed, and some with jobs received low wages. Workers in the southern textile industry earned about ten dollars for a sixty-hour week. Women and children were permitted to work as long in some states.

The fate of the farmer caused more concern, because his vote determined the outcome of the elections in many states, but no effective means were found to give him aid. His basic problem continued to be that he bought in a protected national market but had to sell in an unprotected world market. This meant that though the price of his purchases was unnaturally high, the price of his product was subject to foreign competition and sank steadily. In the South alone there were 500,000 farm families whose annual crops were worth less than $400. Only the large landowners and those engaged in fruit growing or dairying could make reasonable profits.

HOOVER AND THE DEPRESSION

The troubles of the laborer and the farmer did not weaken the optimism of most Americans when they went to the polls in 1928 and elected Herbert Hoover (1874-1964). Although born poor and soon orphaned, Hoover managed to get a college education and to make a fortune as a mining engineer because of his energy and ability. During and after the war, he gained a worldwide reputation for his administration of an American-sponsored relief program in European countries, and as Secretary of Commerce under Harding and Coolidge he outshone most of his fellow cabinet officials. Hoover himself had achieved wealth and position by rugged individualism, and to him this was the outstanding American characteristic, the one which had made the country great. He was no Social Darwinist, however, for competition between companies seemed wasteful to his ordered mind; and as Secretary of Commerce he had encouraged cooperation among businesses. To him, it was permissible for the government to help industry but not to engage in industry. If this policy were followed, he sincerely believed that "poverty will be banished from this nation."

It was Hoover's unhappy fate to have been President for less than eight months when the stock market collapsed. At first, it was anticipated that the stock market decline and the depression would be short-lived. Optimists pointed out that the United States still had the same mines, factories, and farms as before. Prosperity must surely be around the corner, they thought, but as inventories continued to accumulate, prices to decline except in those areas where virtual monopolies kept them steady, businesses and banks to fail, and workers to be laid off, it became obvious that something serious was wrong with the economy. Between 1928 and 1932 the national income declined from $83,326,000,000 to $39,963,000,000, and the number of unemployed increased to 12,000,000.

Most actions taken by the Hoover administration to combat the depression were in keeping with Republican tradition. Tariffs, of course, were raised still higher despite the protest of over 1,000 economists. This led other countries to retaliate, and American exports dropped from $5,241,-000,000 in 1929 to $1,611,000,000 in 1932. To prevent more bankruptcies and to make more money available for business expansion, the Federal Reserve Board took steps to reduce interest rates. By January, 1932, the situation had become so serious that the Reconstruction Finance Corporation was established to lend money to banks, railroads, and other institutions that were threatened with bankruptcy. At the same time, Federal Land Banks were established to loan money to farmers threatened with foreclosure. Some grain and cotton were purchased in an effort to prevent their prices from dropping further, but the government was no more able to sell these crops than the farmer. Its warehouses filled, and prices continued to fall. Hoover went further than any of his American predecessors in using the government to combat depressions, but there were limits. He would not engage in public works to provide jobs for the unemployed, for relief to him was a local matter. The role of the government was to help people help themselves. It could lend, but it could not give money or provide employment. He believed that if industry were persuaded to increase production, more jobs would be provided and purchasing power would grow. For this reason, he expected the benefits of the Reconstruction Finance Corporation to trickle down to the people. Before there was time to test his theory fully, he was defeated at the polls by Franklin D. Roosevelt (1882-1945).

ROOSEVELT AND THE NEW DEAL

Roosevelt was born in 1882. As a youth, he had everything Hoover had not: wealth, family, and social position. Yet in a different way his life reflected as much courage and rugged individualism as his predecessor's. After serving as Assistant Secretary of the Navy under Wilson, he had been chosen Democratic candidate for the Vice-Presidency in 1920. A brilliant political career seemed opened to him, but the following year he was stricken with infantile paralysis. Although he never recovered the use of his legs, he returned to politics in 1928 and won the governorship of New York despite the Republican landslide of that year. This made him an obvious candidate for the Presidency in 1932, and he easily defeated the then unpopular Hoover by a vote of 22,821,857 to 15,761,841.

Roosevelt had imagination and a willingness to experiment with new ideas provided by a "brain trust" composed largely of college professors, but he lacked intellectual consistency and administrative efficiency. He tried first one thing and then another to lift the United States out of the depression. In the beginning, he advocated industrial combinations; later he returned to the Wilsonian concept that big business in itself was an evil. Agencies were created whose duties and functions conflicted with those of existing agencies. In general, his cure for the depression was "pump-priming." Just as it was sometimes necessary to put a little water into a pump to get a lot more to come out, so it was sometimes necessary for the government to put money into the economy, more than it collected in taxes, to get the economy to produce in larger quantities. Once the economy was healthy again, Roosevelt assumed that the budget would be balanced and that the deficit accrued during the "pump-priming" period could be repaid. Some of the "pump-priming" dollars went to industry, but some also went to the farmer and consumer to increase purchasing power. Many aspects of the New Deal, as his program was called, were only enlargements of the Republican program; others were completely new.

When Roosevelt took office on March 6, 1933, the nation was in the midst of a banking crisis. Frightened depositors everywhere were trying to withdraw their money, thereby endangering even the soundest banks. Roosevelt acted quickly. He declared a bank holiday and made a radio speech to calm the people. Such popular comedians as Amos and Andy devoted their fifteen-minute program to explaining that there was no cause for alarm. Within a week, when the sound banks began to reopen, the hysteria had passed. A few months later the Federal Deposit Insurance Corporation was established to insure bank deposits up to $5,000. Banking activities were regulated. The public no longer had to fear the loss of savings, an important consideration since in 1931 alone no fewer than 2,294 banks had failed. At about the same time, the Securities and Exchange Commission was established to supervise the stock market and to prevent the abuses that had led to the crash of 1929. Both these measures created a greater sense of security, but they did not in themselves promote recovery.

To promote recovery, Roosevelt took the United States off the gold standard and induced currency inflation in the expectation that higher prices would strengthen the economy. In the early stages of the New Deal, great hopes were also placed in the National Industrial Recovery Act (NIRA), which provided that industries of a given type would draw up codes regulating wages, prices, and working hours. Anti-trust laws were ignored in the writing of the new codes, and these codes were enforced by the government. By fixing a relatively high wage scale, it was hoped to increase consumer purchasing power; by establishing high minimum prices, it was hoped to assure business profits. The NIRA was definitely a step away from the idea of competition and toward economic planning of the type used during the war. It was not instituted over the protests of business, but with its consent. The codes were in many ways similar to those prepared voluntarily by businessmen under Hoover's auspices when he was Secretary of Commerce. However, as most of the codes were badly drawn and poorly enforced, business leaders complained. In some cases, prices were fixed so high that purchases declined. As a result, the Supreme

Court's 1935 decision that the NIRA was unconstitutional came as a welcome relief to both government and business. Neither the inflation induced by currency manipulation nor the NIRA had produced recovery.

Other New Deal measures were more beneficial to business. The activities of the Reconstruction Finance Corporation were expanded and reciprocal trade treaties calling for tariff reductions were made with twenty-six countries. Exports to these countries increased twice as fast as to those with whom no treaties had been made.

The New Deal attempted to improve the lot of labor, just as it tried to help industry and banking. This program was motivated by both humanitarian considerations and the desire to increase consumer purchasing power. It operated in a number of areas. The growth of labor unions was encouraged. The codes drawn up under the NIRA called for collective bargaining, and this policy was continued by the Wagner Labor Act after the NIRA was declared unconstitutional. When the American Federation of Labor (AF of L) failed to take full advantage of this opportunity because of the desire of most of its leaders to limit membership to skilled laborers, John L. Lewis of the United Mine Workers and others formed the Committee on Industrial Organization (CIO), which was organized on an industry-wide basis without regard to the worker's trade. It was conspicuously successful in organizing the steel and automobile industry. By 1940 both the AF of L and the CIO had memberships of about 4,000,000.

Through their activities, labor unions increased the class-consciousness of the workers, and strikes became much more frequent. In the past, corporations had relied largely on the support of federal and state governments and the courts to defeat the strikers, but now that the weight of the federal government was thrown on the other side, they relied more on force than previously. Spies were hired to watch workers, and "private detectives" were hired to beat up union organizers. Henry Ford kept an army of 800 men to prevent the unionization of his company; and such well-known firms as General Motors, U. S. Steel, and Montgomery Ward employed private detectives. The steel companies spent nearly $500,000 for tear gas and arms during a seven-month period in 1937. Yet in spite of all such efforts, unions were organized in most large industries; and higher wages, shorter working hours, and better working conditions were won. The New Deal aided in this process by passing laws establishing a minimum wage of twenty-five cents per hour and a maximum work week of forty-four hours. Later acts raised the minimum on wages and reduced the work week to forty hours.

The New Deal also tried to assist those without jobs. Agencies were established, such as the Public Works Administration (PWA), the Works Progress Administration (WPA), and the Civilian Conservation Corps (CCC). The PWA contracted with private corporations to build schools, parks, hospitals, and other buildings useful to the public. It was designed to help industry as well as to provide employment. Many of the activities carried on by the WPA overlapped with those of the PWA, for it also constructed useful buildings, but the former's main aim was to provide employment. Among those aided were artists, musicians, and actors. The CCC provided jobs for unemployed young men living for the most part in city slums. Most of their work was devoted to improving public parks and forests and to constructing recreational facilities.

A third way the New Deal tried to relieve the unemployed was by the passage of the Social Security Act. It provided assistance for widows, orphans, and retired persons, as well as the unemployed. Similar measures had been enacted by the European states between 1878 and 1914, but the United States did not follow the lead of other countries on social legislation until this time.

The New Deal sought to assist the farmer by reducing agricultural production in the hopes of bringing higher prices. Under the provisions of the Agricultural Adjustment Act (AAA), farmers were paid to reduce their acreage in certain crops and to slaughter excess livestock. In 1936 the AAA was declared unconstitutional, but another act was passed designed to achieve a similar purpose. Farm income increased, but it never achieved the desired level. The program was expensive, and the public was distressed to see 6,000,000 pigs slaughtered and crop acreage reduced at the taxpayer's expense when millions of people were underfed. Seed and tools were provided for poor farmers, special efforts were made to help tenants, and government loans were offered to those who were about to lose their land by foreclosure. No other administration had ever tried to do so much for the farmers. Their position improved, but the basic problem could only be solved by finding markets for all farm produce.

Other New Deal legislation included the passage of the Twenty-First Amendment, which repealed prohibition, and the establishment of the Tennessee Valley Authority (TVA). The TVA was given sweeping authority to do everything from generating and selling electric power to advancing the economic and social welfare of the people of the Tennessee Valley. A big dam had been built at Muscle Shoals in 1918 as a part of the war effort, and other dams were now added to prevent floods and produce power. Cheap electricity was brought to many homes. Industries settled in the region to receive the benefits of low-cost power. Private utility companies complained, but there was little doubt that the region profited greatly from the Authority.

In his efforts to re-establish the national economy, Roosevelt also rebuilt the Democratic party. Prior to 1932 it had been based on the old alliance between the solid South and the Northern city machines that was rarely strong enough to win a national election. Roosevelt strengthened this coalition in the North by winning the support of most laborers and Negroes who benefited from his program. Even the traditionally Republican midwestern farmer began to give the Democrats a large number of votes. A past master of politics with great leadership ability, Roosevelt managed to break the two-term tradition and be elected to the presidency four times. Yet there were limits beyond which even he could not go. In 1937, after the conservative Supreme Court had declared many of the New Deal's legislative acts unconstitutional, he asked Congress to increase the number of judges to fifteen so that he could appoint some liberals. There was an immediate outcry that constitutional liberties were threatened, and Congress rejected his proposal.

The impact of Roosevelt and the New Deal is difficult to evaluate. As an economic program, its design was to save capitalism by introducing a moderate amount of federal control and planning. The power of big corporations actually increased during this period, and the national income grew from $39,963,000,000 in 1932 to $71,513,000,000 in 1937. Part of this gain was offset by higher prices, but there was no doubt that big government spending had produced partial economic recovery. It was equally clear that "pump-priming," the basic economic doctrine of the New Deal, had failed, because in 1937 when the federal budget was cut, the economy began to decline. It did not continue to give forth as a pump does after it has ceased to be primed. Only the great spending brought on by World War II restored full employment and prosperity.

Two of the attacks most frequently made on the New Deal were that it increased the national debt and that it taught the people to look to the government for assistance whenever they were in trouble. Both charges were obviously correct, but in justice it should be remembered that the federal deficit during the last year of Hoover's administration was at about the same level as the average under Roosevelt between 1933 and 1940. In a single year (1958) under Eisenhower, when the economy was far stronger than in the 1930's, the deficit was nearly as great as during Roosevelt's first four years in office. The New Deal may have taught the mass of the American people to look to the government for aid, but business leaders had already been doing so for years with considerable success.

It was also charged that New Deal legislation was illogical and inconsistent and that its administration was inefficient. Again the point must be ceded, but it should be remembered that with all its mistakes the New Deal sponsored more acts of permanent value than any other regime in American history. Such measures as the regularization of the stock exchange, the insurance of bank deposits, and the Social Security program are almost universally regarded as beneficial. They were preserved and expanded by Eisenhower's Republican administration.

The English experience suggests that recovery might have come as rapidly without the New Deal.[7] But if the government had done nothing to inspire hope, it is equally possible that the American people, like so many

[7] See page 906.

Europeans, would have followed a demagogue who offered to lead them to a promised land. There were those in the United States who aspired to this role. Father Coughlin and Gerald L. K. Smith preached fascist doctrines. Huey Long established a dictatorship in Louisiana. The Communist and Socialist parties tripled their combined vote between the elections of 1928 and those of 1932. Public opinion in 1933 would have supported more radical measures than Roosevelt proposed, and it is fortunate that he found a way to bring hope to many people with only minor infringements on human liberty.

LATIN AMERICA

Latin America continued its economic development during the first postwar decade. As investments from foreign countries, especially the United States, stimulated mining and industry, European immigration provided workers of greater skill than the typical natives. The war created a demand for raw materials, which led to a great increase in exports, and provided an opportunity for infant industries in several countries to grow stronger because of reduced European competition. This strengthened the middle class and helped free democratic governments to replace more authoritarian regimes. Although labor unions were weak and socialism was almost nonexistent prior to the Great Depression, some states enacted welfare legislation. Included were minimum wage, maximum working hour, and child labor laws.

The Great Depression reversed this trend. The value of Latin American exports dropped from $3,000,000,000 to $1,000,000,00 between 1928 and 1932. This dealt a severe blow to the entire economy. Every country except Venezuela and Argentina defaulted in their foreign interest payments, and there was widespread unemployment with attending political repercussions. The Latin American people, most of whom had had scant experience in self-government, began to look once more to dictators, and during 1930 and 1931 there were revolts in eleven of the twenty republics. Other uprisings followed. By 1940 few governments could boast democratic regimes. As in previous eras, some revolts were the products of factionalism and personal rivalries, while others resulted from the efforts of conservatives to preserve their economic and social privileges. New types of leaders, however, also appeared who rose to power through their demagogic nationalism and their demands for radical social reform. Some, like Cuba's Fulgencio Batista, Argentina's Juan Perón, and, to a lesser extent, Brazil's Getulio Vargas, may be compared with European fascists. The communist movement grew, but it did not become a serious threat until after World War II. Fortunate indeed was a state like Mexico which was able to carry out a radical social and economic reform program without undue violence or loss of liberty.

THE REVOLT OF ASIA AND AFRICA

The expansion of European civilization in Africa and Asia, which had increased rapidly during the last quarter of the nineteenth century because of migrating Europeans, imperialism, and the efforts of the natives themselves, continued after World War I, with one very notable difference as far as the people of Asia and North Africa were concerned. The imperialistic feature of the European advance was not only unwelcome; it was resisted with increasing determination and effectiveness. On the other hand, science, technology, and other aspects of Western culture continued to be desired. Indeed, the natives' adoption of nationalism, a Western contribution to the world, made them more anxious for independence, and their adoption of the new technologies enabled them to insist that their desires be considered.

To colonial peoples, imperialism meant economic, political, and social domination. They believed that their persons and their natural resources were exploited for the benefit of foreign capitalists who generally lived thousands of miles away, that new native industries were not developed unless desired by the mother country, and that any effort to improve their lot was secondary to the desire for profit. Virtually every important office in a colony was held by a European. Only minor positions were entrusted to natives. If a native population were so fortunate as to be given a legislature, it found its powers limited and its membership largely appointed. As a result, both political and economic decisions were made by outsiders. The social aspects of imperialism were equally resented. Europeans, even missionaries, were rarely willing to treat the natives as equals or to learn their language. In cities where Africans or Asians had lived for thousands of years, there were now parks, restaurants, clubs, and theaters reserved for Europeans which natives could not enter except in a servant's capacity. Proud peoples with ancient cultures were infuriated at finding themselves segregated by their new masters.

The colonials' attitude was stimulated by the example of the Japanese, who had proved that if a non-Western people quickly adopted Western technology, they could defeat a major European power like Russia. It was furthered by World War I, which led imperialistic states to make concessions to colonies in return for loyalty and at the same time reduced their ability to compel obedience. It was inflamed by Wilson's Fourteen Points, which promised nationalism and self-determination, and by the Russian Communists, who denounced imperialism as an aspect of capitalism, and bent every effort to stir up natives against their European masters. As a result, World War I ushered in a period of revolt in Asia and North Africa. The less advanced central and south African natives caused the Europeans little trouble at this time; their awakening was delayed until World War II.

HEIRS OF THE OTTOMAN EMPIRE: TURKEY

The Turks were the most direct and important heirs of the Ottoman Empire. Under the leadership of Mustapha Kemal Pasha, they had been among the first to reverse the peace treaties of 1919 by force, and Turkey had emerged in 1923 as an independent republic with Kemal as president.[8] The Constitution of 1924 declared that all people were equal before the law and guaranteed freedom of speech, the press, and other civil liberties. Initially, legislative powers were invested in a parliament elected by universal manhood suffrage, but in 1934 women were also given the right to vote. Despite these democratic and liberal provisions, Kemal wielded dictatorial authority throughout the remainder of his life. However, he used his power to institute reforms, not to bring profit to himself or to a selfish clique. Only one political party was initially permitted, but Kemal was so determined to make Turkey like the Western states that in 1929 he encouraged the formation of an opposition party. Although it was soon disbanded, independent deputies continued to serve in parliament.

Kemal classified his program under six headings: republicanism, secularism, populism, nationalism, statism, and reformism. The first, republicanism, was achieved mainly by the Constitution of 1924, which was followed by a new legal code based on Western models to replace the old codes that were heavily influenced by the Moslem religion.

Secularization was more difficult to achieve because the Moslem religion influenced many aspects of life. However, the office of caliph, or head of the Moslem church, was abolished in 1924, and the Western calendar was adopted, with Sunday as the day of rest in lieu of the Moslem holy day of Friday. Men were forbidden to wear the fez, and women were discouraged from wearing the veil. Polygamy was outlawed, a less radical innovation than one would think, for few men had been able to support more than one wife. Schools were removed from the jurisdiction of the church. By 1939 religion played no greater role in secular affairs in Turkey than it did in a Western state.

By populism Kemal meant that all privileges claimed by groups, classes, families, and individuals were abolished; and political equality and uniformity were to be achieved. Universal free education was inaugurated in an effort to reduce illiteracy, which stood at 80 per cent when Kemal came to power. To speed the educational process, the complicated Arabic script was abandoned in favor of Latin characters, and a strictly phonetic system of spelling was adopted. Adult education was also encouraged as were various cultural activities.

The heart of the Young Turk movement was nationalism, and every effort was made to instill a sense of pride and unity in the Turkish people. Histories were composed extolling the Turkish past. Arabic words were re-

[8] See page 786.

Kemal Pasha (Ataturk). (Wide World)

moved from the written language. The term statism referred primarily to the government's broad activities in the economic life of the nation. Banking, railroads, and public utilities were largely government-owned; and beginning with the Five-Year Plan of 1933, many factories were built under government auspices because private enterprise was moving too slowly. Scientific agricultural methods were encouraged; government aid was provided to keep the prices of farm products from falling.

By reformism Kemal meant that Turkey should never be content with the status quo and that the betterment of the people should be a constant process. He tried to stamp out the graft and corruption that had been so commonplace under the Ottoman Empire. He encouraged women to enter the professions. Disgusted at the well-to-do Turks' aversion to physical exercise, he encouraged sports.

By 1938 when Kemal died, Turkey was a relatively stable sovereign state. The controls the Western powers had exercised over the former Ottoman Empire had been removed, and the internal economy had been strengthened. When it was decided that Turks should have family names like Europeans, parliament chose for Kemal that of *Ataturk*, "father of the Turks." It was a well-deserved title, for Kemal Ataturk, as he is most often called, was the founder of his country and its most popular hero.

THE ARABS AND THE JEWS

Most of the non-Turkish parts of the Ottoman Empire had been inhabited by Arabs. The Arabs had had little national consciousness prior to 1880, but during the decade before World War I it grew rapidly. At first, the Arabs co-operated with the Young Turks against the sultan and envisaged a dual Turko-Arab empire on the model of the Austro-Hungarian

922

state. When it became apparent that the Young Turks were going to insist on a unified, centralized state, the Arabs withdrew their support. The Ottoman decision to enter the war in 1914 provided the Arabs with the opportunity to revolt and win their independence in alliance with the British. Leadership in this direction was assumed by Sharif Husayn (1856-1931), who was fortunate in possessing three able sons and the governorship of Hijaz, where the holy cities of Mecca and Medina were located.

In 1916 Husayn agreed to lead an Arab revolt against the Ottoman Empire in return for British recognition of an Arab state at the end of the war. This state was to include all the land between Turkey and Egypt except for Aden, Kuwait, and Muscat, which were then owned by the British or were under their protection, and the Mediterranean coast line northwest of Damascus. Shortly thereafter, the British and French made a secret agreement to divide approximately this same territory between themselves. To further complicate the situation, Lord Balfour issued his famous declaration in 1917 promising to give Palestine to the Jews as a national homeland. In doing so, the British once more broke their pledge to the Arabs. Nevertheless, the Arabs rendered valuable assistance during the war and confidently expected that in the peace treaty they would be awarded their promised independence.

Instead, the peace treaty recognized only the independence of the Arab states on the Arabian peninsula. The more advanced peoples of the Tigris and Euphrates Valley and the Mediterranean coastal belt were assigned to Britain and France as mandates of the League of Nations to be prepared for a higher state of civilization and eventual self-government. The Arabs were bitterly disappointed at what they considered British treachery, and the region was in a turmoil during much of the period between the wars.

The French received Syria as their share of the booty, but by the time their troops arrived, the Syrians had already declared their independence and elected Faysal, a son of Husayn, king. The French quickly deposed him and established their own regime. Lebanon, the western portion of the mandate, was made into a separate province because the majority of its inhabitants were Christians. The Lebanese were fairly well treated, but the French high commissioner of Syria was so arrogant and tactless that he soon drove some of the natives to revolt. Twice the French shelled Damascus, and once they were faced with a general strike. In 1930 they agreed to recognize both Syria and Lebanon as independent states within three years, but when war came in 1939, final action had not been taken.

The British took as mandates Iraq, Transjordan, and Palestine. They placed Faysal, whom the French had just expelled from Syria, on the throne of Iraq as a constitutional monarch. Their choice proved satisfactory, and in 1932 Iraq became an independent state and was admitted to the League of Nations. In withdrawing from Iraq, however, the British were careful to see that their economic interests, especially in oil, were protected. With nine-tenths of the population illiterate, the Iraqis had difficulty functioning as a Western-style constitutional monarchy, and power naturally fell into the hands of the upper classes. The death of Faysal in 1933 led to increased instability. For a brief period in 1936, a military dictatorship was established, but the monarchy survived under Faysal's less capable descendants.

Abdullah, another son of Husayn, was established on the throne of the desert kingdom of Transjordan. Transjordan was quickly recognized as an independent state, but British influence remained very strong. Britain granted Abdullah a subsidy and aided in the formation of an Arab Legion which became the finest army in the Near East.

The most controversial postwar problems in the Near East were connected with Palestine. The Balfour Declaration of 1917 had resulted from the British desire to please the Zionists and to establish a friendly state near the Suez Canal. The Zionist movement was both nationalist and religious. It was led by Jews who were anxious to have a homeland where they could escape from the Gentile's feeling of superiority as well as actual persecution. The movement began during the latter part of the nineteenth century and quickly enlisted the support of such influential Jews as the Rothschilds, the famous scientist Dr. Chaim Weizmann, and United States Supreme Court Justices Brandeis and Frankfurter.

In his 1917 declaration, Lord Balfour declared that "His Majesty's Government views with favour the establishment in Palestine of a national home for the Jewish people and will use their best endeavours to facilitate the achievement of this object, it being clearly understood that nothing shall be done which may prejudice the civil and religious rights of existing non-Jewish communities in Palestine or the rights and political status enjoyed by Jews in any other country." In answer to Husayn's immediate protest, the British assured him that nothing would be done to compromise "the political and economic freedom of the Arab population." These assurances, plus the clause in Balfour's original declaration protecting the rights of the existing population, reassured the Arabs. Initially, they had no objection to a moderate Jewish immigration into Palestine so long as the essentially Arabic character of the state was maintained.

At this time there were about 550,000 Moslems, 70,000 Christians, and only 50,000 Jews in Palestine. Furthermore, most of the Christians and Jews were Arabic in language and culture. Immediately after the end of the war, the Zionists began to encourage large-scale immigration into Palestine in the hope of quickly establishing a Jewish majority. Only after this had been achieved did the Zionists want an independent state. Most of the land was then owned by absentee Arab landlords and farmed by tenants, but the Jews began to purchase large tracts with the aid of contributions from wealthy Zionists throughout the world. On becoming owners, they ejected the tenants whose families had lived there for centuries and established Jewish farming communities in their stead. With adequate capital, scientific knowledge, and ability, the Jews were able to increase agricultural output and at the same time to construct beautiful modern cities like Tel Aviv.

As a result, Arab tenant farmers were faced with eviction and Arab aristocrats were faced with a neighboring, advanced outpost of Western civilization that was certain to undermine their privileged position and way of life. This situation caused Arabs of all classes to protest against the influx of Jews and to demand immediate self-government, a proposal the Jews vehemently rejected so long as they remained a minority. Other Arab and Moslem people lent their support. The British found themselves caught between the powerful political pressure of the Jews at home and the demands of their numerous Arab and Moslem colonial population abroad. There were many bloody episodes, and compromise appeared impossible. In 1937 the British decided to partition the disputed country. Part of Palestine was to be made into a Jewish state, part was to be incorporated into Transjordan, and a small section including Jerusalem was to remain a British mandate. The Jews complained about the boundaries assigned to them, and the Arabs rejected the whole scheme, as nearly half the inhabitants of the proposed Jewish state were their fellow nationals. When war came in 1939, the matter was still unresolved. The Jewish population had swelled to nearly half a million, but the Arabs still numbered more than a million.

Meanwhile, important changes were taking place on the Arabian Peninsula. It had been assumed that Husayn would emerge at the end of the war as the most important ruler of this region, and Hijaz became one of the original members of the League of Nations. Husayn, however, was confronted by the rising power of Ibn Saud (1901-1953), a member of the fanatical, fundamentalist Wahhabi sect of the Moslem religion, who was then consolidating his control over the nomadic tribes of central Arabia. In 1924 Ibn Saud forced Husayn to abdicate after a brief war. The years that followed saw his strength increase, and even the British made no effort to extract special privileges from him. In 1933 he granted an oil concession to two American companies in order to get financial resources for a modest reform program that consisted of improving transportation and communication facilities and settling nomadic tribesmen on farms. The emergence of Ibn Saud and his new state of Saudi Arabia caused further disunity among the Arab rulers, because Faysal of Iraq and Abdullah of Transjordan were angered at the deposition of their father, Husayn, by a member of a different Moslem sect. From that time, united Arab action against the Jews or anyone else became almost impossible to achieve.

Egypt was still a nominal part of the Ottoman Empire in 1914, but the British used the war as an opportunity to break the formal tie and establish a protectorate. They were soon confronted by a fanatical nationalist movement led by the Wafd party. The British had no objection to declaring Egypt independent, but they insisted that they continue to occupy a special position in the country because of the vital importance of the Suez

Canal to their Empire. As a result, the quarreling continued after Egypt became an independent, constitutional monarchy in 1922. Finally in 1936-1937 the opposing sides came to terms. Great Britain agreed to limit its military forces to the vicinity of the Suez Canal and to permit its citizens living in Egypt to be subject to Egyptian law in twelve years.

AFRICA

The Europeanization of Africa continued during the inter-war period, and in the northern part of the continent especially there were growing demands from the natives for an increased role in the government. In Ethiopia, Haile Selassie I established himself as emperor in 1930 and attempted to modernize his state. Unfortunately, his work was cut short in 1935 when the Italians attacked his country and forced him to flee after a brief war.[9]

The French incorporated northern Algeria into European France by dividing it into departments, granting citizenship to many inhabitants, and permitting them to elect deputies to the legislature at Paris. Elsewhere, neither the French nor the British went further towards granting the Africans self-government than to create councils or colonial assemblies of limited authority in which most of the native members were appointed. The natives were not yet strong enough to resist, and the Moroccans were the only inhabitants of Africa whose aspirations for independence caused much trouble.

IRAN, AFGHANISTAN, AND SIAM

Persia, or Iran as it came to be called during the inter-war period, had been divided into spheres of influence by Russia and Great Britain. After World War I, the British tried to strengthen their position, but in 1921 a patriotic, able, uneducated army officer named Reza Kahn seized power and within four years made himself shah. He took Kemal Ataturk as his model and began to Westernize his state along the same lines as Turkey. Both the British and the Russians were persuaded to surrender privileges which compromised Iranian sovereignty. The power of the clergy was weakened, and their property was confiscated to provide funds to support secular schools and hospitals. New secularized law codes were prepared, and women were unveiled. To help the economic development of his country, Shah Reza built roads and railroads and established state-operated industries. Oil concessions brought considerable revenue, but the agricultural problem was not effectively handled. Most of the land was owned by absentee landlords who were unwilling to make the necessary initial expenditures to farm scientifically. As a result, although Shah Reza accomplished much, more remained to be done when he was deposed in 1941 by

[9] See pages 936-937.

the British and Russians, who were alarmed at his pro-German attitude and anxious to use his country as a supply route. Although autocratic and often mistaken, Shah Reza was one of Asia's greatest Westernizers.

Amanullah of Afghanistan was less fortunate. He came to power in 1919, won British recognition of his country's complete independence in 1921, and embarked on a program of rapid Westernization. Conservative and religious leaders became so incensed that they revolted and deposed Amanullah in 1929. A period of civil war followed from which Mohammed Nadir Shah emerged victorious and continued Amanullah's Westernizing policy but at a far more moderate rate.

Siam took advantage of World War I and the years immediately following to get rid of the extra-territorial privileges held by European states. Continued contact with the West had led to the growth of liberal sentiment. In 1932 the liberals seized power and transformed the absolute monarchy into a constitutional monarchy with a parliament elected by universal suffrage. Despite counter-revolutionary activity, pro-Western liberals generally dominated the country from that time until World War II.

INDIA

Despite the existence of a strong nationalist movement, India remained loyal to the British during World War I. Over a million troops and laborers were supplied to the Allies, and nearly 75,000 Indians were killed. In return, the British passed the Government of India Act in 1919 which created a legislature for all of India except the states ruled by native princes. The British, however, retained considerable authority because the viceroy appointed twenty-seven of the sixty members of the upper house and had the power to issue decrees when he thought it necessary. Legislatures with more elected members were also created at the provincial level, but as a precaution the British reserved control of the judiciary and financial administration for themselves and surrendered to the Indians only such secondary matters as sanitation, education, and agriculture. The Indians were bitterly disappointed, and the National Congress rejected the system entirely. At this point, a new leader emerged—one quite different from any of the other apostles or opponents of Westernization. His name was Mohandas K. Gandhi (1869-1948), later known as Mahatma, the Holy One.

Gandhi was a high-caste Hindu who had been educated, like so many young men of his social position, in England. He settled in South Africa to practice law, and there he became the leader of the Indian minority who were being mistreated by the racially conscious Boers. In 1914 he returned to India and within six years emerged as an outstanding leader of the Congress party.

Gandhi was a deeply spiritual man who was repelled by the materialism and violence that characterized Western civilization. He abandoned European clothing for the traditional Indian costume and even attended a

London conference clad in a loincloth. India should have home rule, he declared, but it must be achieved without violence. He established a boycott against British goods that created havoc with the mother-country's exports, especially in textiles. When imprisoned, as he frequently was, he went on hunger strikes until the British released him, alarmed at the Hindu reaction in the event of his death. On one occasion, he led a pilgrimage to the sea on foot where he extracted salt in defiance of a British monopoly on that essential substance. The British knew how to cope with an armed insurrection, but they never devised a method of dealing with the deep spiritual force represented by this Asiatic mystic. In the end, they were to bow before his superior will.

Gandhi preached friendship between Hindu and Moslem and between the high-caste Hindu and the untouchable. Industrialism he came to abhor. In its place, he advocated a return to the handcraft industries and spinning wheels of an earlier day. Some of his followers, such as Jawaharlal Nehru (1889-1964), rejected his more impractical teachings; others could not resist committing acts of violence. Yet Gandhi emerged as the greatest religious teacher of the century, if not of modern history.

By 1929 the British were ready to grant India dominion status, but the Hindus and the Moslems, the higher castes and the lower castes, could reach no agreement on the kind of government to be established. To many, anarchy appeared the only alternative to foreign rule. Although in 1935 the British extended the power of the provincial assemblies, World War II came and still India had not achieved dominion status.

The French in Indo-China and the Dutch in the East Indies were also faced with nationalist movements, but they were not so well-organized or dangerous as the one in India. Both colonial powers established legislatures composed largely of appointed members that were allowed to exercise limited powers. These assemblies provided some, but not nearly enough, experience in parliamentary procedures and self-government.

Thus, the post-World War I era saw the Asiatic and African peoples attempt to assert their independence, but they were still too weak and the Europeans too strong for them to accomplish much. Only after they had had more time to develop their strength and the Europeans had further weakened themselves by fighting another war, could the revolt of Asia and Africa achieve success.

THE CHANGING WORLD

The world in 1939 seemed different from the world of ten years before. In the twenties, a strong belief prevailed that the principal causes of war had been removed and that the existence of a League of Nations ensured collective security. Liberty and democracy had been obtained by the inhabitants of nearly all the advanced states, and there was reason to hope that most other countries would soon follow this example. The marriage between science, technology, industry, and agriculture had given promise only of future wealth, not of eventual atomic destruction. It is true that the scientific and aesthetic revolutions had begun about a generation before, but few recognized that they threatened the materialism or egalitarianism that, except for the romantic interlude, had generally characterized Western thought since the Enlightenment. Few realized that these revolutionary trends were also challenging the faith of Western man in the decisive influence of environment on human possibilities, a faith that had justified dreams of human progress and perfection. It was equally true that the Communists had seized control of Russia, but the first Five-Year Plan which had begun the year before had not progressed far enough to suggest that a Marxist economic system could compete successfully with capitalism, nor had the full brutality of the Stalinist regime been revealed. Fascism seemed a minor threat, although Italy had already succumbed to Mussolini's wiles. Most people ignored the fact that Mussolini boldly proclaimed "the fruitful inequality of mankind," and most outsiders assumed that his bombastic utterances concerning the moral virtues of war were intended for domestic consumption only.

By 1939 all of this had changed. The Great Depression had turned millions away from capitalism and democracy. In one European country after another, fascist revolutions had taken place, and fascist-like states were beginning to appear in Latin America. The colonial peoples in Asia were becoming restive, and those in Africa would soon follow their example. It was doubtful how long the democracies could continue to hold them in subjection, weakened as they were by the Great Depression and the communist and fascist threats. Even an impartial observer might well agree with the fascist theorists who confidently proclaimed that liberalism, capitalism, and democracy had lost their dynamic power and that the future of the world lay with authoritarianism. It was perhaps fortunate that the mantle of fascist leadership fell on an incautious man like Adolf Hitler, who stupidly sought to destroy simultaneously both the democratic and the communist worlds. A wiser leader would have brought the Russians to their knees, and with the food, oil, and raw materials of eastern Europe at his disposal, turned upon the West. Had Hitler done so, the predictions of the fascist theorists might have proved correct.

21/ The Struggle for World Supremacy

SCIENTIFICALLY and economically, there was one world in the 1930's; politically, there were many; and ideologically, there were three. The Japanese, Russians, and Americans shared the same science. This science had made neighbors of the most remote peoples because messages could be sent thousands of miles in a matter of seconds and travelers could reach any point in the world in a few days. The spread of the Great Depression to all inhabited portions of the globe was a clear demonstration that a world economy had come into being. However, the possibility of world government was as distant as ever. In spite of the League of Nations, international politics was based on a multitude of nation-states, each of which demanded the first loyalty of its citizens and preached one of three ways of life: the democratic way, which was inherited directly from the Enlightenment; the communist way, which denied the individualism of the Enlightenment but accepted its materialism and its faith in human progress; and the fascist way, which rejected all the Enlightenment's principal tenets and dreamed of a new order with a new set of values.

None of the exponents of these three ideologies were content with the status quo. The democracies longed for the day when the whole world would accept their creed, but they sought to convert by example rather than by force. In 1939 they seemed hardly able to hold their own. The communists and fascists also looked forward to the time when their ideological system would receive world acceptance, but they hoped to achieve this end by internal revolutions and, especially in the case of the fascists, by foreign conquests.

The conflict of 1914-1918 was called a world war because nations from all parts of the globe were involved, but it began as a defensive struggle between two alliance systems with roughly comparable ideologies and at no time was more than the hegemony of Europe at stake. World War II began when the fascists attacked in an effort to win hegemony on three continents. Their defeat left the communists and the democracies alone to vie for supremacy.

THE FAILURE OF COLLECTIVE SECURITY

The story of the origins of World War II is the story of the failure of collective security. If the League of Nations had functioned properly and if the various nonaggression pacts and treaties of alliance had been supported, there would probably have been no war. Unfortunately, the fascist states were dissatisfied. Italy dreamed of a Mediterranean and North African empire. Germany had a vision of regaining its losses of 1918 and of expanding into eastern Europe. Japan saw itself establishing a hegemony in the Far East. The democracies were divided. France feared Germany and was willing to block its expansion if supported by the British. The British regarded Italian Mediterranean ambitions as a threat to their communications with their Indian Ocean empire and were willing to take a firm stand against them if supported by the other democracies. To France, Italy was a potential ally against Germany and therefore a prize to be courted. To the British, many of the German demands were just and only French intransigence prevented a settlement. Japanese ambitions were frowned upon, but few thought that the Far East was worth a war. Besides, Japanese, German, and Italian claims to be bulwarks against communism brought them wide support among conservatives, while liberals were more concerned with combating the depression than with halting aggression. Soviet Russia dreamed of a communist world, but for the moment it was too weak to take action. Thus, the fascist states sought actively to prevent the League from functioning as an instrument for collective security and ignored the nonaggression pacts they had signed with other nations, while the democracies were too divided to take effective countermeasures.

THE SINO-JAPANESE WAR

The Sino-Japanese war, which began in Manchuria on September 19, 1931, reversed a decade-old Japanese trend towards liberalism and democracy. Under the direction of their liberal foreign minister, Baron Kijuro Shidehara (1872-1951), they had respected the sovereignty and territorial integrity of China in the 1920's and had sought the friendship of the Chinese people without, however, surrendering their own economic interests in that country. Unfortunately, the position of Shidehara and the liberal prime minister, Yuko Hamaguchi (1870-1931), was insecure and in spite of the overall strengthening of the liberal position during the 1920's, there were periods when imperialist reactionaries like Baron Gi-ichi Tanaka (1863-1929) were in power. Furthermore, political parties were poorly developed and cabinet crises were frequent. Between 1920 and 1932, there were eleven prime ministers, three of whom were assassinated.

The reversal of this faltering liberal trend around 1931 was caused by Japan's perilous economic situation, the powerful position of the military, and developments in China. At this time 65,000,000 Japanese were crowded into about 150,000 square miles, and the population was growing at a rate of 1,000,000 per year. Neither the quantity of Japanese arable land nor their natural resources could support such a large population even at their low standard of living. As a result, they believed that the only solution to their economic problems lay in a large, ever-expanding volume of trade and the exploitation of Manchuria. When the Great Depression dealt a serious blow to their trade and the Chinese threatened their interests in Manchuria and their markets in China, they felt compelled to take strong action.

It will be remembered that in 1927 Chiang Kai-shek and the conservatives broke with the Communists and other radical reformers in the Kuomintang but continued their policy of trying to bring all Chinese territory under their rule.[1] In 1928, they took Peking and began to cast covetous eyes on Manchuria, where both Russia and Japan had special interests. When Manchuria's warlord, Chang Tso-lin (1873-1928), showed signs of favoring the Kuomintang, he was assassinated, probably on orders of Japanese army officers. His son and successor, Chang Hsueh-liang (1898-   ), was a more ardent nationalist. He brought Manchuria closer to the Kuomintang, and even the liberal Japanese were disturbed. In China proper, the Kuomintang was raising tariffs to protect Chinese industries and taking steps to end the special privileges that foreigners held in their country. No one denied that Manchuria was under Chinese sovereignty, but its economic development had been brought about largely by Russia and Japan. Since the loss of access to Manchuria's 380,000 square miles of fertile land, coal, iron, and forests would be a severe blow to the Japanese econ-

[1] See page 733.

omy, there was a growing demand to prevent the Chinese from asserting their sovereignty.

If the Japanese liberals had been in firm control, some sort of compromise might have been reached, but army officers were independent of the civil government and responsible to the Emperor alone.[2] They were determined to bring Manchuria firmly within the Japanese orbit, and they found factions at home to support their position. From the close of World War I, fascist-like societies had been formed in Japan which sought to check the growth of communism and socialism and to promote the imperial greatness of the country. These superpatriots were often anti-big business as well as anti-liberal. They were fond of contrasting the greed of capitalists and the bickering of the members of parliament with the simple stalwart virtues of the soldier and farmer. To these forces must be added the powerful Japanese military tradition and the growing popularity of Shintoism or emperor worship. Assassination of liberal ministers by reactionary militarists became commonplace. In November, 1930, Prime Minister Hamaguchi was shot, and in May, 1932, Prime Minister Inukai (1855-1932) met a similar fate. During the time interval between these murders the military took matters into its own hands in Manchuria.

On the night of September 18, 1931, the Japanese army, on its own initiative, seized the city of Mukden, ostensibly to prevent the Chinese from blowing up the railroad tracks but in fact as the first step toward the seizure of eastern Manchuria. The Chinese, who were not yet in a position to resist, quickly withdrew, leaving the Japanese in control of the valuable province. Reaction in Japan at this easy victory was enthusiastic, and the liberal, peaceful policy of Shidehara was discredited. From this time, the militarists were ascendant. In February, 1932, Manchuria, or Manchukuo as the Japanese renamed the province, was declared a sovereign state. A little later Henry Pu Yi, the last Manchu ruler of China, was made emperor to strengthen the fiction of independence.

The Chinese took the only recourse open to them. They appealed to the League of Nations. The League appointed the Lytton Commission to investigate, but by the time it made its report the Japanese were in firm control of Manchuria and refused to withdraw as requested. Because of its dependence on trade, Japan was vulnerable to economic sanctions, but neither the League nor the United States was willing to adopt such a plan for fear that it might lead to war. Instead, the United States declared that it would never recognize the conquest of territory in defiance of international treaties. The Japanese showed their contempt for this policy by seizing part of northern China and by withdrawing from the League. Nevertheless, they did not press their conquests further and from 1933 to 1937 were content to follow a policy of peaceful expansion.

[2] See pages 737-738.

Public opinion in China was unwilling to accept this loss of territory. There were growing demands that Chiang Kai-shek stop fighting the Communists and form a united front with them against the Japanese aggressor. In 1936, General Chang Hsueh-liang, a former Manchurian warlord, kidnapped Chiang Kai-shek. What happened thereafter is not known, but two weeks later Chiang was released and an uncomfortable alliance was soon formed between the Kuomintang and the Communists to resist the Japanese. A second, more violent stage of the war was about to begin.

Meanwhile, the Japanese had provided Manchuria with the most efficient, orderly government that province had ever known and had taken steps to integrate its economy with that of Japan. Some Japanese business leaders who had formerly favored liberal parliamentary government in opposition to the militarists now began to reconsider their stand. Manchuria itself offered vast opportunities for economic exploitation, while further expansion into China and southeastern Asia would provide the markets, minerals, and raw materials necessary to make Japan a great industrial nation. A "co-prosperity in greater east Asia" program was prepared that attracted some, although not universal, support from business interests. With the aid of these converts, the militarists gradually transformed Japan into a fascist-like dictatorship.

In July, 1937, the military took advantage of a clash with Chinese troops to renew the war. This time the more united Chinese were determined to resist. Despite the loss of Shanghai and Nanking in 1937 and Canton and Hankow the following year, Chiang continued to fight. It soon became evident that while the Japanese could capture the major cities and hold the principal railroad lines, they lacked the strength to control the countryside where Communist guerrillas were especially effective or to advance into western China. Again the League took no action. The United States sold goods to both contestants but showed its sympathy for the Chinese by providing financial aid. Russia and Great Britain felt that Japanese expansion threatened their interests and lent some assistance to China, but the Sino-Japanese conflict had become a stalemate when the outbreak of war in Europe provided the Japanese with a perfect opportunity to expand elsewhere.

HITLER'S FOREIGN POLICY

The war that began in Europe in 1939 was the direct result of Hitler's policy. There is no problem of determining who the aggressor was, as there is in the conflict that began in 1914. It is rather necessary to see what Hitler was trying to accomplish and how he managed to transform Germany into a military power capable of dominating the European continent.

Hitler's program was outlined in *Mein Kampf*, which he wrote in 1924. Publicly he repudiated it at times for diplomatic reasons, but privately he never wavered from his original goal. As an Austrian, he believed that Bismarck had only partially united the German people. Therefore, "To demand that the 1914 frontiers of Germany should be restored is a political absurdity. . . . The confines of the Reich as they existed in 1914 were thoroughly illogical, because they were not really complete, in the sense of including all the members of the German nation." The Germans in Austria and Czechoslovakia must be incorporated as well as those lost to the fatherland as a result of the Versailles treaty. Thus, the boundaries of the old Holy Roman Empire more nearly fit Hitler's dreams than those of Hohenzollern Germany. Even this was not enough, however, because he wanted to provide raw materials and living room for the large, rapidly growing German population, not by obtaining colonies in far-off corners of the earth but by renewing the historic German expansion to the east at the expense of the Slavs. He hoped to bring western Russia, including the Ukraine, and the new states in eastern Europe within the German sphere of influence and to reduce the inhabitants to the status of uneducated slave laborers.

Hitler recognized that war with France and Russia would be necessary to secure these objectives, but he hoped that he could win Italian support. He saw no conflict between Great Britain's interests and his own and hoped that war with that power could be avoided. The great German error in 1914 was to become involved in a war on two fronts, and this mistake must not be repeated. Russia or France must be isolated and destroyed. Only then would it be safe to turn on the remaining enemy.

When Hitler became chancellor in January, 1933, he immediately began preparations to secure these objectives. He had no interest in Germany's domestic affairs, except increasing national strength and for anti-Semitic legislation. He devoted nearly all his time to the army and diplomacy. By the terms of the Versailles treaty, Germany had been limited to an army of 100,000 men and denied the right to have an air force. As rearmament obviously had to precede military expansion, Hitler secretly went to work on this task immediately. He was one of the few leaders who recognized that the era of trench warfare was past and that the next war would be one of movement, in which airplanes, parachute troops, armored divisions, and motorized units would play a leading role. His conservative generals balked at many of these ideas and at the speed with which he sought to expand the armed forces, but in the end he prevailed.

During these early days Hitler played his hand cautiously, for until his army was rebuilt the French alone could have crushed him. He was careful to speak of his desire for peace and to make only those demands which would appear just in many foreign eyes. In July, 1934, he declined to back a Nazi revolt in Austria when Mussolini began to mobilize troops along the Italian side of the Brenner Pass[3] to prevent any German move to acquire the little country. In January, 1935, the plebiscite in the Saar Basin was held in accordance with the provisions of the Versailles treaty, and the

[3] See pages 882-883.

German inhabitants of the region voted overwhelmingly to be returned to Germany. With this matter settled, Hitler felt strong enough to repudiate the disarmament clauses of the Versailles treaty, but in doing so he cleverly pointed out that it had originally been planned for all the powers to disarm and not Germany alone. At the same time, he left the door open for further negotiations. The British were wary of French military predominance on the continent and thought that there was some justice to Hitler's position. Several months later they agreed to let Germany construct a navy up to 35 per cent of their own sea strength. In doing so they unilaterally condoned the abandonment of provisions of the Versailles treaty. The French were not so complacent. They strengthened their ties with Czechoslovakia and Italy and made a five-year alliance with Russia. Further German moves appeared halted by this threat of a war on two fronts. Nevertheless, it was at this point that Mussolini began to precipitate crises.

THE ETHIOPIAN CRISIS AND THE SPANISH CIVIL WAR

Mussolini had long planned to develop an East African empire as part of his larger project of Italian predominance in the Mediterranean Basin. The one remaining independent country in this part of Africa was Ethiopia, the kingdom which had administered a severe defeat to the Italians at Adowa in 1896.[4] It was not hard for Mussolini to create sentiment in Italy for revenge and to find an excuse to attack Ethiopia in October, 1935. Somewhat to his surprise, British public opinion insisted that their country persuade the League to take action to halt aggression. Economic sanctions were imposed, but the British and French governments were careful to exclude coal and oil from the list of items which were not to be sold to Italy and to leave the Suez Canal open to Italian ships. The French were primarily responsible for the failure to take measures which would have forced Italy to give up its plans of conquest. The French feared the revival of German power and were anxious to maintain Italian support. The results were disastrous. Italy completed the conquest of Ethiopia during the spring of 1936, and the very fact that the League had seemingly tried and failed to prevent aggression rendered it, henceforth, virtually useless as an instrument of collective security. The way seemed clear for other nations which were anxious to alter the status quo in Europe.

One reason for the League's failure to act vigorously was the dubious role of the United States. Roosevelt and the liberal Democrats had abandoned Wilson's internationalism and adopted a policy of isolationism in response to the desires of a large majority of the American people. The belief was widely held that profit-hungry bankers and munitions makers had drawn public officials into a policy that led to World War I. To prevent a recurrence of this situation, a Neutrality Act was passed in 1935

[4] See page 712.

936

which forbade the sale of war materials to belligerents. Oil was not among the forbidden products, and League members used this as an excuse for not including this important item in their sanctions. Another weakness of the Neutrality Act was that it failed to differentiate between the aggressor and the defender. As a result, the United States refused to sell arms to Italy, which already had what it needed, and to Ethiopia, which was seriously handicapped by the lack of modern weapons. Nevertheless, the Neutrality Act was strengthened in 1936 and 1937 to prohibit loans to belligerents and to deny them raw materials of any type unless they were paid for in cash and transported in their own vessels. The Chinese wisely refused to declare war when attacked by Japan in 1937 in order to continue to be eligible for American trade. Thus, the United States, which had done so much to convince Europe of the value of collective security in 1918, refused to provide effective leadership when there was need in spite of sincere sympathy for the Chinese and Ethiopians. When one considers the vulnerable position of Italy and Japan, it is difficult to believe that they could have continued their aggressive policies if the League had imposed severe economic sanctions under joint British-American sponsorship. Failure to do so opened the way for further moves by the dissatisfied powers.

Hitler watched the democracies' preoccupation with Italy with interest. In March, 1936, he judged the time opportune to violate the treaties of Versailles and Locarno by sending troops into the Rhineland. His excuse was that the Franco-Soviet treaty made it necessary for Germany to fortify its western frontier. It was a bold move, because the French army was still much stronger than Germany's, but Hitler correctly judged that France was too divided to act alone and that the British would convince themselves that it was only just that the Germans should be permitted to fortify part of their own country. The Poles offered to move with the French against Hitler, but to the German generals' amazement, the French did nothing more than protest. Their failure to act was critical; for once the Germans fortified their western frontier, they were relatively free to act against the small east European states.

In July, 1936, the fascist revolt began in Spain.[5] Mussolini backed Franco by keeping an army of from 60,000 to 100,000 men in Spain in the belief that a fascist victory would strengthen his hold on the Mediterranean. Hitler also sent aid, although in much smaller quantities. He saw the advantage of surrounding France with fascist states and was anxious to get access to Spanish raw materials and to test his new military equipment under battle conditions. The League of Nations adopted a policy of non-intervention which prohibited sending military supplies to either side. The fascist states ignored these provisions, but the democracies did not. As a result, Franco continued to receive a large amount of foreign assistance, while the legally elected Spanish republic had to be content with the trickle of military aid Russia managed to get to it and with some 40,000

[5] See page 888.

volunteers from various parts of the world who were anxious to strike a blow against fascism.

Mussolini's invasion of Ethiopia and his large-scale intervention in Spain isolated him from Britain and France and made him susceptible to a German offer of closer co-operation. For more than a year he and Hitler had won conspicuous successes by taking turns upsetting treaty provisions and committing acts of aggression. At Hitler's suggestion, they formalized this arrangement by signing a pact in October, 1936, in which Italy took the Mediterranean and Germany took eastern Europe as spheres of expansion. In November, Japan signed an Anti-Comintern Pact with Hitler designed to prevent the spread of communism. Later, Italy joined the pact, and the Rome-Berlin-Tokyo axis was born. The tie was not a close one, and the allies did not always communicate before they committed acts of aggression. However, even a modest amount of co-operation between the great fascist states posed a serious threat to the democracies and Soviet Russia.

THE ROAD TO MUNICH

On the surface, the year 1937 was a relatively quiet one. Neville Chamberlain replaced Stanley Baldwin as prime minister of Great Britain and began a policy of actively working for peace instead of waiting for serious trouble to occur. It consisted of giving the dissatisfied powers what they wanted if their demands seemed at all reasonable. This policy of appeasement, as it was later called, offered a genuine possibility of winning Italy away from Germany, but it played into Hitler's hands in every other respect. All that he had done thus far could be justified in the name of Germany's right to have the army, navy, and frontier fortifications necessary for self-defense, and his immediate territorial demands in Austria and the Sudetenland could be reconciled with the idea that boundaries should be drawn in accordance with ethnic considerations. There was no chance, however, of ever satisfying all of Hitler's territorial demands, and Chamberlain's greatest error was the failure to realize this fact. In the end, the policy of appeasement weakened the democracies and strengthened Hitler at home and abroad. War became more certain than ever, and the chances for a victory by the democracies were diminished.

During this period, Hitler's public utterances pointed to his desire for peace, and his demands were kept within the bounds of reason. However, on November 5, 1937, he met secretly with a small group of officers and revealed his intention of seizing Austria and Czechoslovakia before the democracies could rearm. The generals balked because they felt that such a move would mean war with France and Great Britain. This opposition only led Hitler to replace his army commanders a few months later by men more willing to obey his orders and to make an irresponsible "yes man," Joachim von Ribbentrop (1893-1946), foreign minister.

After consolidating his position at home, Hitler seized Austria in March, 1938. The French, who had so often blocked this move before Hitler came to power, were at that moment in the midst of a cabinet crisis and took no counteraction. The Italians, who had saved Austria in 1934, were now deeply involved in Spain. Mussolini was irritated, but he refrained from breaking the Rome-Berlin tie. Chamberlain did nothing on the grounds that the Austrians were Germans, and he carried his policy of appeasement to the point of recognizing the Italian conquest of Ethiopia. Hitler had once more been successful. On March 14, the once-ignored Viennese painter presided over a reception in the palace of the Habsburgs in Vienna.

The seizure of Austria was of far-reaching importance because it opened the way for German political and economic penetration into the whole Danube Basin. Nearly all of the states in this region had become fascist. While they still desired to keep their political independence, they leaned more toward co-operation with the Germans than toward maintaining their earlier connections with the now thoroughly discredited France. Furthermore, by taking Austria, Hitler obtained another avenue through which he could invade Czechoslovakia.

The Czechs were still in a strong position. They had thirty-five good divisions and one of the largest armament industries in Europe. France was obligated by treaty to come to their assistance if they were attacked. Russia had agreed to add its support if the French honored their pledge. No treaty existed with Great Britain, but British obligations under the League covenant and recent close ties with France indicated probable support from this power also. Nevertheless, Hitler immediately set about making plans to annex all or part of Czechoslovakia. In May, the German threat became so serious that the Czechs partially mobilized, and France and Russia promised support. Hitler backed down, but in his fury at being balked, he ordered plans to be laid for an invasion on October 1. Meanwhile, he directed the Nazi leader of the Sudetenland Germans to demand large concessions from the Czechs. Each time the Czechs granted these demands, additional claims were made. By September, the situation had become so serious that Chamberlain made two trips to Germany only to learn that Hitler would no longer be content with autonomy for the Sudetenland Germans. He insisted on annexations as the price of peace. On September 25, the British cabinet decided to reject these terms, and on the following day they notified the French that they would stand by them and the Czechs.

The German generals were appalled at the prospect of war against Great Britain and France. Some of them plotted to remove Hitler if he ordered the attack. The German people were equally opposed to war, but throughout the crisis Hitler remained inflexible. It was only on the urging of Mussolini that he agreed to meet Chamberlain and Daladier of France in a four-power conference at Munich on September 29 in a final effort to avoid war. Here the British and French agreed that the Czechs would immediately surrender over 10,000 square miles of territory inhabited primarily by Germans. In return, Hitler promised to follow a peaceful policy in the future. He was disappointed at not being able to use his new army and at getting only part of Czechoslovakia but had no intention of being thwarted in the long run. Chamberlain returned to England proudly proclaiming that he had brought "peace in our time." Daladier was more skeptical, but divided France was unwilling to act without Britain. Although the Russians were ready to stand by their ally, the Czechs rejected their offer because it was doubtful whether permission could have been secured for Russian troops to march through Poland or Rumania. Even if they could pass through these two countries, the Russians were not regarded as a match for the Germans. The Czechs, therefore, acquiesced, and on October 1, German troops occupied the Sudetenland. Poland and Hungary took part of what remained. The surviving fragment of the Czechoslovakian state was to last only a few months more.

With the advantages of hindsight, the Franco-British policy seems stupid as well as cowardly and dishonorable. Each time they gave in to Hitler's demands, the allied powers weakened the opposition to him in Germany and at the same time lost an ally. Yet it should be remembered that the diplomats of 1914 were blamed for not getting their allies to make concessions. Until his seizure of Bohemia in March, 1939, Hitler had acted only to secure territory whose inhabitants were predominantly German. To many, the British were guilty only of persuading the French and Czechs to be reasonable and conciliatory. If the Germans had been as active in holding back Austria-Hungary or if the French had restrained the Russians in 1914, there would have been no World War I. Chamberlain's error was in not recognizing the true nature of the Nazi regime. Hitler would be satisfied with nothing less than the domination of central and eastern Europe, and he was willing, even anxious, to fight a war to achieve this goal. His pledges to the contrary were worthless. Superior force was the only law he recognized, and during the last two years of his life he refused to bow before even this. Had Britain and France made half the concessions to Stresemann and Brüning, who had followed the path of peaceful persuasion, that they later made to Hitler, who threatened the use of force, the Nazis might never have come to power. Once in power, however, the only solution to the Nazi menace was to contain it with an overwhelming force or to destroy it.

Chamberlain finally came to this point of view in March, 1939, when Hitler violated the pledges he had made at Munich by turning Bohemia into a protectorate, taking Memel from Lithuania, and making demands on Poland. The following month Italy invaded Albania; and in May, Hitler and Mussolini made a "pact of steel" tying themselves closer together. Western and central Europe was at length divided into two camps, one democratic and one fascist. Soviet Russia held the balance of power. On Stalin's decision the fate of Europe depended.

THE NAZI-SOVIET PACT AND THE OUTBREAK OF WAR

To the Communists, fascism was a decadent form of capitalism, and as a result they had stood idly by while the Fascists seized control of Italy and the east European states. The Nazi triumph in Germany soon awakened them to their danger, for Hitler brutally suppressed the Communist party in Germany and talked of attacking Russia. Stalin, therefore, directed Communists in other countries to cooperate with bourgeois parties in popular fronts to prevent any more fascist victories. In September, 1934, Russia joined the League of Nations. As a member of the League, the Russians were stalwart champions of collective security. To Stalin, the Anglo-French Munich decision not to defend Czechoslovakia's western frontier could only be explained by their desire to turn Germany eastward so that it would attack Russia. The fact that neither the Czechs nor their Russian allies had been invited to the Munich Conference added substance to this view. It followed, therefore, that Stalin sought to reverse the direction of the Nazi attack. If war was to come, he would rather have the democracies and fascist states fight each other with Russia standing on the sidelines than have the fascist states attack Russia while the democracies sat idly by. Nevertheless, during the spring and summer of 1939 he permitted negotiations to take place with the democracies to see whether they would be willing to pay his price for a grand alliance to halt the fascist peril. To Stalin, Russian security required promises by the democracies to defend all the east European states. The British and French readily promised to defend Poland, Rumania, and Greece if they were attacked. Beyond this they would not go. Many of the east European states were more afraid of the Communists than of the Nazis, and they resisted any alliance that might lead to their occupation by Russian troops in order to defend them against the Germans. Soon Stalin abandoned hope of reaching agreement with the West. Pro-Western Foreign Minister Maxim Litvinov (1876-1951) was dismissed, and the hard-headed Vyacheslav Molotov (1890-   ) was appointed in his place.

Meanwhile, Hitler had begun to look with favor on a Russian alliance. At first he had toyed with the idea of an alliance with Poland against Russia, but the Poles, who were anxious to remain independent of both their powerful neighbors, rejected his suggestion. The Anglo-French decision to defend Poland infuriated Hitler, and on April 3, he ordered the army to be prepared to attack on September 1. On May 23, he informed his leading admirals and generals that the war might lead to a conflict with Great Britain and France but that he would try to isolate Poland before destroying it. When his efforts to shake the British in their determination to stand firm failed, he took the next obvious course. Secret negotiations were opened with Russia. On August 23, 1939, Molotov and Ribbentrop signed a nonaggression pact in which each country promised to remain neutral in case the other became involved in war. In a secret protocol, eastern Europe was divided into two spheres of influence. Western Poland and Lithuania were to go to Germany, while eastern Poland, Finland, Estonia, Latvia, and Bessarabia, a Rumanian province, were assigned to Russia.

In signing the pact Hitler sacrificed a great deal from an ideological standpoint. He had always painted the Nazi as the bulwark against bolshevism and "Asiatic barbarism," and his Japanese and Italian allies in the Anti-Comintern Pact were horrified. His gains, however, were great. He had spared Germany from the strategic danger of fighting on two fronts. The pact might cause Great Britain and France to hesitate to honor their pledge to defend Poland. If they did decide to fight, he could destroy Poland, leave his eastern front to be held by a few troops, and attack in the west before the democracies were prepared to act. His ultimate objective of conquering a large amount of Russian territory to provide raw materials and living room for the Germans was not abandoned; it was merely postponed until he could defeat his enemies in the west.

Stalin was equally pleased with the pact, although he had no illusions about Hitler's long-range plans. By its terms Russia regained most of the territory it had lost during World War I and the Revolution. These gains made Leningrad and other Russian centers easier to defend when the German attack did come. Furthermore, for the time being, the fascist states and the democracies would fight each other while the communists peacefully prepared for the struggle for world supremacy that ultimately seemed certain to come. Stalin may have anticipated a stalemate in the west as in 1914. After the antagonists had exhausted each other in such a long-drawn struggle, central and western Europe would be ripe for communist expansion.

For a few days after the announcement of the Nazi-Soviet pact, Hitler hesitated. The German people and many of his top advisers were opposed to war. Mussolini did his best to effect a compromise and made it clear that Italy was not prepared to fight despite the "pact of steel." Finally, Hitler decided to attack, but he did so with the hope that Great Britain and France would agree to make peace after he had destroyed the Polish state. To convince the German people and the outside world that the Poles were the aggressors, he had some criminals dressed in Polish uniforms shot just inside German territory on August 31. Newspaper correspondents were shown the corpses and witnessed other staged "incidents." Then, on the morning of September 1, German troops invaded Poland in "retaliation." Two days later Great Britain and France declared war. The struggle for world supremacy had begun.

THE WAR

THE EARLY NAZI TRIUMPHS

No one thought that the Poles could defend their country indefinitely, but the world was surprised by the rapid advance of the German armies. Largely at Hitler's insistence, his generals had abandoned the position warfare of 1914-18 in favor of a war of movement. The air force was used to destroy enemy air strength and to bomb strategic objectives. Tanks were massed together in *Panzer* divisions and used to break through the enemy lines, by-pass strong points, and move far to the rear where they disrupted communications and, with the aid of infantry divisions who followed closely on their heels, eventually surrounded large elements of the opposing army in giant pincers. In the Polish campaign the Germans used fifty-six divisions to the Poles' thirty, but more significant was the presence of nine *Panzer* divisions whose speed and power could not be matched by the Poles' old-fashioned cavalry divisions. The German armor broke through and surrounded the Polish army west of Warsaw. Then, in a second giant pincer, Warsaw and the remaining Polish forces were taken. By September 27, the defeat of Poland was accomplished. A nation of 150,-000 square miles and 35,000,000 people had been conquered in less than four weeks. It was indeed *Blitzkrieg* or lightning war.

On September 17, the Russians began to occupy the portion of Poland assigned to them. Mutual assistance pacts were made with Latvia, Estonia, and Lithuania, which were now also assigned to the Russian sphere of influence. In these pacts, the Baltic states permitted the Russians to establish military bases inside their territory. When Finland refused to cede an ice-free port the Russians considered essential for the defense of Leningrad, Stalin ordered his army to attack. From November, 1939, until March, 1940, the Finns resisted, but with the coming of spring they were overwhelmed and had to surrender more territory than the Russians had originally demanded. Thus, Stalin profited as much as Hitler had during the first months of war.

Hitler had originally intended to try to make peace with the democracies after the defeat of Poland, but he was so elated at his easy victory that he determined to attack in the west early in November. Only half-hearted peace gestures were made, and these were designed more to satisfy the German people who wanted peace than to persuade the democracies to come to terms. Hitler's generals were so disturbed at the thought of turning the inactive western front into an active theater of war that they once more talked of deposing him. In the end, they failed to act, but excuses were found to postpone the attack time and again.

Meanwhile, Hitler became engrossed in planning an attack on Denmark and Norway. These countries would provide valuable air and naval bases in the war against Britain. Furthermore, it was known that the British were considering coming to Finland's aid in its war against Russia. This would probably involve their occupation of Norway, which in turn would enable them to halt Swedish iron ore shipments to Germany. Hitler as usual decided to strike first. Without warning, German sea- and air-borne troops began to seize key points in both Denmark and Norway on April 9, 1940. Several German ships were lost, and an Anglo-French expedition was dispatched to aid the Norwegians, but by the end of the month resistance was limited to a few localities. Hitler was once more free to turn his attention to the western front.

His generals had planned to repeat the strategy of 1914. The main effort was to consist of a great sweeping movement through the Low Countries into France. Hitler, however, rejected this plan because the French anticipated an attack from this direction and because the canal-riddled countryside was unsuitable for tank operations. Instead, he adopted the plan of one of his junior generals and made the main effort a drive through the Ardennes to Sedan and thence across the splendid tank country of northern France to the English Channel. This drive was to be commanded by the able Karl von Rundstedt. The right flank under Fedor von Bock was to move simultaneously into the Low Countries, while the left flank was to be kept relatively quiet.

The attack began on May 10. Bock dropped parachutists on key forts and used them to capture bridges and other objectives. So rapidly did the Germans move that the Dutch never had time to open their dykes to halt their advance. On the fifth day of the battle, the Netherlands surrendered, and on May 26, the Belgians followed suit. Even more spectacular was Rundstedt's advance. After crossing the rugged Ardennes with relative ease, he dashed across France, seized Abbeville on May 20, and the channel port of Boulogne on May 26. The allied armies were cut in two, and Dunkirk was the only remaining port from which the armies in the north could be evacuated. Here the Germans halted. The generals wanted to press on and take Dunkirk, but Hitler was fearful that if given a moment's respite the French would be able to re-form their lines to the south of the Somme River. This delay gave the British the opportunity to reach Dunkirk first, and 335,000 men were evacuated in an amazing operation in which every available private yacht in Britain was used to assist the navy.

The Germans now turned to the south, and the French retreated rapidly. Paris fell on June 13, and, on June 17, the aged Marshal Philippe Pétain, who had replaced Paul Reynaud (1878-   ) as prime minister the day before, asked for an armistice. Winston Churchill, who had replaced Chamberlain as prime minister in May, tried to convince the French to carry on the war from North Africa and the British Isles, but they refused because they thought that the English would soon surrender, and they did not want to place their entire country at the mercy of German troops. On June 22, they signed the armistice in the same railroad car at Compiègne where the Germans had surrendered in 1918. According to the armistice terms, northern and western France were to be occupied by the Germans, but about two-fifths of the country with its new capital at Vichy was left under French control. Here Pétain set up a conservative, mildly authoritarian regime that collaborated with the Germans yet at the same time avoided aiding them directly in the war and minimized their brutality to the French people. In six weeks, the Germans had defeated armies as large as their own and had forced the Netherlands, Belgium, and France to surrender. Their own

Adolf Hitler performed this joyous dance at Compiègne in 1940 after dictating armistice terms to conquered France. It was at the same site that Germany signed what Hitler considered humiliating armistice terms on November 11, 1918, ending World War I. (Wide World)

losses had been slight. Even Napoleon had not won such quick and decisive victories. Mussolini was so impressed that, on June 10, he finally entered the war in order to share in the spoils of victory.

It has long been a favorite pastime to try to explain why France fell so rapidly before the German onslaught in 1940 after having resisted so heroically between 1914 and 1918. Some historians have found the explanation in the ideological disunity which plagued the French people. There were fascists and neo-monarchists on the right who had little use for the republic and who were especially fearful that Blum and the popular front would someday resume the reins of government. Communists, equally alienated from the Republic, were following the temporary Stalinist line of friendship with the Germans. Nevertheless, the Third Republic had nearly always been plagued by enemies on the right and the left. Few

945

from either extreme were traitors: many fought valiantly in the army and the resistance movement.

Others have attributed the rapid French defeat to the loss of *élan vital*. So many young men had been killed or crippled in World War I that the French felt that a repetition of such a holocaust must be avoided at all costs. They had attempted to act almost alone against Germany when the French army had occupied the Ruhr in 1923, but this experiment had been economically so disastrous that they never dared to repeat it. For a decade thereafter, they had relied on their alliances with the small east European states. However, when the Germans re-armed and fortified the Rhineland, these alliances became inadequate unless the British also gave their support. As a result, the French always deferred to the British before taking any action, suspecting, indeed perhaps hoping, that Chamberlain would advise appeasement.

Neither of these interpretations ought to be entirely discounted, but they overlook the obvious cause of the French debacle, military defeat. Most experts in 1940 compared the French army favorably with that of Germany in terms of equipment and training, and only the German air force was clearly superior in numbers. The difference between the two lay in strategy. The Germans planned a war of movement in which tanks were brought together in armored divisions to strike on a small front with overwhelming force. They were supported by air-force bombers, gliders, and parachute troops. The French thought in terms of the trench warfare of 1914, and their tanks were scattered among the infantry divisions. As a result, when the Germans made their breakthrough, the French had no armored divisions to throw into the gap until their lines could be re-formed. Infantry divisions could not move rapidly enough to close a gap, and individually they had too few tanks to halt a German armored division. Once the Germans broke through, they could not be stopped until they reached a geographical barrier such as the English Channel or until they had covered such a great distance that they ran out of supplies and their equipment wore out, as was to happen in the Russian campaign; that is, unless they met a superior armored force.

Therefore, the principal explanation of the French defeat lies in their inability to move rapidly enough to re-form their lines after the initial German penetration. When they began to retreat, roads became clogged with refugees fleeing from the Germans, troop units lost contact with each other, and events moved so rapidly that there was no time to formulate new plans of defense, much less to put them into action. Had it not been for the English Channel, Great Britain would almost certainly have been overrun in a matter of weeks. Conversely, had the Loire River been so wide and swift that it could not be bridged, it is quite possible that the French lines could have re-formed south of it and Paul Reynaud, the French prime minister, who was a man of courage and confidence, might have become a French Churchill.

By 1940, technology had developed to the point that large states like France and Germany could destroy each other in a matter of weeks, just as the tiny Italian city-states could reduce each other in a short time during the Renaissance. By 1960, technology had reached the point that still larger states like the United States and Russia, who were separated by a wide expanse of water, could probably perform the same feat.

THE SURVIVAL OF BRITAIN

Hitler was naturally elated at his easy victory. He waited anxiously for a British offer of peace and was prepared to deal generously with the island empire, but he reckoned without Winston Churchill (1874-1965). This direct descendant of the John Churchill, Duke of Marlborough, who had fought so brilliantly to prevent Louis XIV from dominating the continent, had no intention of permitting an upstart corporal to do so now. A great man by any standards, he reached unbelievable heights in the throes of defeat. The British army had been saved at Dunkirk, but its armament had been lost. Only twenty-five tanks had been brought back from Europe. Half-armed and alone, the British confronted the greatest military power the world had yet seen. Churchill felt ready to meet the challenge. In a series of fiery speeches, he inspired the British people with his determination to resist and his hope for eventual victory.

To get weapons, Churchill appealed to President Roosevelt, who had become aware of the Nazi threat several years before and was now more international in outlook than most of the American people. Roosevelt replied with a promise of 500,000 rifles, 80,000 machine guns, 900 field guns, and an adequate amount of ammunition, which had all been stored in grease since World War I. In September, 1940, fifty U. S. destroyers were turned over to the British in return for naval bases in the West Indies, and in March, 1941, the Lend-Lease Act was passed which authorized American aid to Britain and other countries whose survival was essential to American security. Thus, the United States became "the arsenal of democracy," building weapons for the British as well as its own expanding armed forces. In his determination to defend the island kingdom, Churchill ordered that the French fleet at Oran be sunk to prevent it from falling into German hands. Now certain of controlling the sea, the British awaited the Nazi onslaught.

It is not certain how seriously Hitler considered the possibility of invading the British Isles. An effort was made to plan a channel crossing, but the army and navy could not agree on the number of troops or the width of the invasion front. In truth, the Germans lacked the transports and naval strength to invade unless their air force could defeat the British air arm and prevent their fleet from blocking the channel. A cross-channel invasion even under these circumstances was dangerous, and it is not surprising that Hitler preferred to try to compel the British to make peace by

947

submarine warfare and aerial bombardment. Over 7,000,000 tons of shipping were sunk by July, 1941, but the Germans did not have enough submarines to impose an effective blockade. During the late summer and fall, numerous heavy bombing raids were sent against London and other cities; but German air force losses were two or three times as great as their adversary's. The development of radar detecting devices by the British and of superior armament for their planes gave their air force a decisive edge over that of the Germans. In November, Hitler called off the attack, thus losing the Battle of Britain. Since summer, he had been engrossed in a new project—the invasion of Russia.

THE BALKANS, NORTH AFRICA, AND RUSSIA

Hitler had always regarded his treaty with Stalin as a temporary arrangement because his ultimate goal was to expand to the east. Stalin had infuriated him by demanding in June that Rumania surrender northern Bukovina as well as Bessarabia and again in August by incorporating the Baltic states into the Soviet Union. Clearly there was not room for two such aggressive powers in eastern Europe. In deciding to attack Russia, Hitler violated his own rule against fighting a war on two fronts. He probably felt that the British were no more able to launch a cross-channel invasion than he was and were therefore not dangerous. If he defeated the Russians, the British would be discouraged and at the same time Germany would get access to the raw materials necessary for survival in case the war and naval blockade continued.

The German military leaders did not share Hitler's optimistic belief that Russia could be defeated in six months, and they were anxious not to embark on new ventures until the British threat had been completely eliminated. Admiral Raeder, the naval commander, suggested that Gibraltar and the Canary Islands be seized to prevent the Allies from sending troops to North Africa and to enable the Germans to seize Egypt, the Suez Canal, and the Near East. This would have dealt a vital blow to British lines of communication, brought Germany valuable oil and other resources, and at the same time protected southern Europe from invasion. The last was an important consideration because a small number of Frenchmen had refused to accept Pétain's surrender and had fled to London, where, under the leadership of General Charles de Gaulle (1890-   ), they continued the war. France's North African territories were at the moment loyal to Pétain's Vichy regime, but the possibility existed that they might join De Gaulle and the British at an opportune moment. Furthermore, it seemed likely that the United States would become a more active participant. In this event, an Anglo-American-French invasion of Europe from North Africa was a distinct possibility.

Hitler saw merit in Raeder's plan, but he was unwilling to abandon his attack on Russia. Instead, he sought to persuade Vichy France and Spain to enter the war and, in conjunction with the Italians, ensure Axis control of the Mediterranean. Franco and Pétain procrastinated and finally refused, the former because he was not certain that the Germans would eventually win and the latter because he did not wish to fight his one-time British ally. Mussolini, however, was anxious to use this opportunity to expand his Mediterranean empire. In August his troops took British Somaliland; in September, they began to invade Egypt in the hope of taking the Suez Canal and uniting Libya with Italian East Africa (formerly Ethiopia); and in October, they invaded Greece from Albania.

Unhappily for the Axis, the Greeks not only ably defended their own country but in December invaded Albania and took 28,000 Italian prisoners. The British initially retreated in North Africa; but, in December, they counterattacked and drove back a much larger Italian army a distance of 500 miles, taking 130,000 prisoners. During the spring of 1941, they conquered nearly all of Italian East Africa. Clearly the Germans themselves would have to intervene to save the Balkans and North Africa.

Hitler had already brought Hungary and Rumania into his network of alliances preparatory to his invasion of Russia, and in March, 1941, he added Bulgaria and Yugoslavia to the list of his allies. A military coup in Belgrade caused the Yugoslavs to reverse their position. Infuriated, Hitler postponed his attack on Russia and, on April 6, hurled his troops into Yugoslavia and Greece. Before the end of the month, both countries were compelled to capitulate, and a 60,000-man British expeditionary force in Greece was forced to evacuate. In May, German parachutists paved the way for a seaborne landing on Crete, and once more the British had to withdraw. Equally spectacular were German successes in North Africa, where in April the dashing General Erwin Rommel (1891-1944) drove the British back into Egypt. By June, Hitler felt that his southern flank was sufficiently secure for him to launch his long-intended invasion of Russia.

Without warning, without even informing his Italian and Japanese allies, Hitler sent three army groups into Russia on June 22, 1941. His excuse was that the Russians were about to attack Germany and that the British continued to resist only because they hoped for eventual Russian aid. In fact, Stalin was perfectly content to see the democratic and fascist states destroy each other and may have been taken by surprise by the German onslaught, despite warnings from the British and Americans. For a time, Hitler's confidence appeared justified. Field Marshal Bock's army group captured nearly 300,000 men near Minsk during the first two weeks of the campaign and pleaded for permission to press on to Moscow, but Hitler refused. Instead, he dispatched part of Bock's armor to the south to assist Rundstedt's army group in the Ukraine. At Kiev, they surrounded and captured 600,000 troops in September. By the end of October, nearly all of the Ukraine had been conquered, and the Germans were in the Crimea. Meanwhile, Field Marshal Leeb, who commanded the northern army group, besieged Leningrad, assisted by the Finns who had re-entered the war in the hope of regaining their lost territory. Hitler was now able to return Bock's armor to him, and on October 2, he resumed the march on Moscow. At first, the German army moved rapidly forward, but the Nazi attack foundered in the snow in the very suburbs of the Russian capital. Hitler's decisions to conquer the Balkans before invading Russia and to attack along a more than thousand-mile front rather than let Bock take Moscow without interruption may have cost Germany the war. In addition to its obvious psychological effect, the capture of Moscow would have deprived the Russians of a great railroad and industrial center. Whether the Russians would have continued to resist after the loss of their capital is an open question. As it was, the Germans faced the prospect of wintering in Russia without adequate winter clothing; Hitler had been so confident of an early victory that he had supplied enough winter uniforms for an army of occupation only. Indeed, in September, he had actually reduced arms production. The generals wanted to withdraw, but Hitler refused. He relieved his commander-in-chief and his three army group commanders, and the Germans withdrew only a few miles, despite Russian counterattacks and extreme cold which killed thousands.

In the spring of 1942, Hitler renewed the offensive. This time he knew that the Germans were too weak to attack on all fronts, and the main effort was directed towards taking the Caucasian oil fields. Again, great victories were won. In September, the Germans laid siege to Stalingrad, an important city on the Volga River. Around its fate the outcome of the war seemed to hang.

THE "NEW ORDER" IN EASTERN EUROPE

Faulty strategy was only part of the explanation for the German failure to defeat the Russians during 1941 and 1942. Many of the people of the Soviet Union, especially the Ukrainians and other national minorities, welcomed the German troops as deliverers from Russian oppression. Everywhere there were some who hoped that the Germans would abolish the collective farms and restore the traditional position of the Christian churches. But Hitler scorned their aid when it might have been a decisive factor and began to impose the "New Order" in eastern Europe. In the "New Order" there was no more room for Christianity than in the Soviet regime, and whether the Slavic peoples had individual farms or not was a minor matter. The role of the Slav was to be a slave laborer. Some were used to dig trenches in Russia under the direction of the S.S. troops, who were told to be indifferent when men and women died at their arduous tasks. Others were sent back to Germany to work in the factories and farms. By the end of the war, there were nearly 5,000,000 slave laborers in Germany, for the most part from Slavic countries. No education was provided for their children, so that future generations would be too stupid to cause much trouble.

Jews, Communists, and other undesirables were exterminated. Men, women, and children were stripped naked and made to stand before pits, where they were mowed down by machine gun fire; then another row was lined up and told to shove into the pit those of their predecessors who had thoughtlessly fallen in the wrong direction. The machine guns burst forth once more and the whole process was repeated. Others were brought to places that looked like public baths, told to undress, promised a cup of coffee when they had washed, and then sent into shower rooms that spurted forth poisonous gas rather than water. The gold in the teeth of the dead was extracted by S.S. dentists, the bodies were cremated, and the ashes often sold as fertilizer. Rather than bring the "selectees" to the huge extermination camps such as the one at Auschwitz in Poland, the Nazis sometimes sent mobile gas units consisting of enclosed trucks from one locality to another. Other prisoners were used as human guinea pigs for "scientific" experiments. How many people died will never be known, but at Auschwitz alone about 2,500,000 persons were killed between 1942 and 1944, and the total number liquidated to "improve" the European racial stock must have approached 7,000,000. The Jew virtually ceased to exist in central and eastern Europe. Of the few who survived, many had been sterilized so that they could be used as slave laborers without endangering the racial purity of the master race.

In 1940, Hitler and Himmler began trying to create a superior race by killing Germans who were incurably sick or mentally deficient. The news leaked out, and outraged public opinion caused them to curtail this program the following year. The effort to keep the extermination of the Jews secret was more successful, although those living near the concentration camps must have known of the massacres. The policy of extermination was adopted only after the war began and was carried out on verbal orders by the most depraved members of the S.S. Under such circumstances, the initial welcome accorded the German invaders in Russia soon turned to hatred. When Hitler finally agreed to the formation of some anti-Communist Russian divisions, it was too late. After the defeat of the Axis, the generals who had consented to lead this force were turned over to Stalin by the British and Americans. They were, of course, executed.

One should not overemphasize the willingness of the inhabitants of Soviet Russia to welcome the Germans. From the first, the majority were loyal to the existing regime, and their numbers increased both because of Hitler's folly and Stalin's clever policy. The Russian dictator did not emphasize that this was a struggle to save communism, since few Russians were willing to die for such a cause. Instead, he depicted himself as a great nationalist leader and asked the people to fight to save their country. The conflict became known as the "Second Great Fatherland War." The "First Great Fatherland War" had turned back Napoleon's invasion of Russia. Tsars and aristocratic generals of the past who had won great victories were praised, and every effort was made to associate their deeds and sacrifices with the present crisis. As a further popular move, the anti-Christian crusade was halted, and the Orthodox church was permitted to elect a patriarch, the first since 1925. What could not be accomplished by persuasion was done by emphasizing the cruel treatment meted out to Russians who fell into Nazi hands. Stalin's assumption of the nationalist's role delighted the democracies, and to give further credibility to this point of view he abolished the Comintern in 1943. From the start, the Americans made the Russians eligible for lend-lease. Over 16,000,000 tons of goods were sent to them with a value of $11,000,000,000.

The result was that the Russians continued to resist despite the loss of over 3,000,000 men in 1941 alone. Replacements were readily found by an all-encompassing conscription. Even women served, and, in all, nearly 20,000,000 persons were in the armed forces. Noncombatants who were fourteen years of age and above worked in essential industries seventy-seven hours a week without vacations. Most of the old industrial sections of Russia were captured, but just before the outbreak of war the Russians had begun to move many factories eastward into the Ural Mountain region where they escaped the advancing German army. Despite these preparations, Hitler was still at the height of his power in the fall of 1942. He and his satellites controlled the land from the Atlantic Ocean almost to the Caspian Sea and from the Baltic to the Mediterranean. Only neutral Switzerland managed to escape his influence. Outside this great area, he held Norway to the north and extensive lands in North Africa. It was the greatest empire Europe had ever known.

THE JAPANESE CONQUEST

During 1940, the Japanese watched European developments with interest. The German victories opened the way for expansion in Southeast Asia at the expense of the conquered French and Dutch and the imperiled British. One would think that Hitler would have tried to persuade the Japanese to attack Russia in conjunction with his own onslaught, but instead he told them nothing of his plans and pleaded with them to seize Britain's Far Eastern possessions in the hope that this would compel the island kingdom to make peace, or at least to divert its energies from Europe. Germany, Hitler believed, could easily defeat Russia during the summer and fall of 1941. Since the Japanese themselves were far more interested in winning the natural resources, raw materials, and markets of Southeast Asia than they were in taking part of Siberia, they settled their differences with Russia during 1939 and 1940 and turned their attention to the south. The British were persuaded to close the Burma road temporarily, over which Chiang got most of his supplies, and after the fall of France northern Indo-China was occupied. These actions provoked strong American protests accompanied by economic sanctions. It soon became clear to the Japanese that they would either have to abandon hopes for an expanded empire, reach a compromise with the United States, or attack the strongest power in the Western Hemisphere.

At first the peace party was ascendant, and negotiations were carried on throughout most of 1941. Agreement could not be reached because the United States was unwilling to recognize any of the Japanese gains

953

in China on one hand, and there was no hope that the peace party could pursuade the militarists to abandon their Chinese conquests on the other. When it became apparent in October that negotiations were making no progress, General Tojo, an ardent advocate of war, was elevated to the premiership. On November 5, the Japanese imperial conference decided to attack the United States if their diplomatic efforts were not successful by November 25; still the United States refused to yield. Early in the morning of December 7, the Japanese launched a surprise air and submarine attack against the U. S. Pacific fleet at Pearl Harbor. Five battleships and three cruisers were sunk or seriously damaged, and most of the remaining ships in the fleet suffered injury. In addition, the army lost one-half of its planes on the island of Oahu. The United States and Great Britain declared war on Japan, while Germany and Italy declared war on the United States. The struggle for European superiority had become a struggle for world supremacy.

The Japanese never had any intention of attacking the continental United States or of making a serious effort to take India, because they knew that their resources were limited. Their aim was to capture the Pacific islands within a 3,000-mile radius of their homeland to serve as a defense against future counterattack and to carve out an empire in Southeast Asia before the Americans could recover from the attack on Pearl Harbor. They hoped to consolidate their gains and defend them so vehemently that the United States would eventually desist and make a compromise peace. Their error, like that of the Germans, was to underestimate the determination of the democracies. Both Great Britain and the United States had been slow to react against the fascist threat, but, once aroused, they were unwilling to accept any sort of compromise peace. The only chance the fascists had of winning the war had been for the Japanese to settle peaceably their differences with the United States and to strike at Russia in Siberia. Perhaps they would have done so if they had delayed making a decision for a few more months, for while they were attacking at Pearl Harbor, the Russians were beginning their great winter offensive. The possibility of a German defeat in Russia became apparent for the first time. This meant that eventually the Japanese would have to face Russia as well as the democracies; under these circumstances defeat was certain. They acted, however, before the outcome of the war in Europe was assured and were to pay a severe penalty for their haste.

During the first months of the war, all went well for the Japanese. They had intended to destroy the bombers at Clark Field in the Philippine Islands before the Americans there learned of the Pearl Harbor attack. Bad weather delayed the assault, but when they finally struck around noon on December 8, they found the American bombers lined up on the field preparing for a raid on Formosa the following day. In a matter of minutes, the American air force was as easily wiped out as the American Pacific fleet had been at Pearl Harbor the day before.

The chances of defending the Philippines were severely jeopardized by these two defeats, but the American commander, General Douglas Mac-Arthur (1880-1964), still had over 30,000 regular army American and Philippine soldiers as well as 110,000 poorly equipped, poorly trained Philippine troops. Against this force, the Japanese initially sent only two reinforced divisions numbering 43,000 men. The long-rehearsed plan for the defense of the Philippines had been for the troops on the large island of Luzon to retreat to the Bataan Peninsula along one side of Manila Bay to make a stand until help could arrive, but MacArthur decided instead to drive the small Japanese force back into the sea. His decision to advance to the landing beaches meant that supplies were sent forward rather than to Bataan. Unfortunately, his troops proved unequal to the task assigned to them, and they fell back so rapidly before the Japanese onslaught that large quantities of valuable supplies were lost. Little time remained to move stores from other parts of the Philippines to Bataan. As a result, when MacArthur finally took up defensive positions on Bataan early in January, he had to put his men on half rations. This weakened them physically and made them more susceptible to malaria. The Japanese suffered as heavily from lack of supplies and sickness, but by April 9 they were able to force the 78,000 remaining Bataan defenders to surrender. Shortly before, MacArthur had obeyed President Roosevelt's order to leave the Philippines in order to take command of the allied forces in the southwest Pacific.

The next Japanese objective was Corregidor and several other fortified islands in Manila Bay. After a long artillery and air bombardment, 2,000 Japanese troops attempted to land on the island just before midnight on May 5. The 11,000-man American garrison destroyed about half this force before it reached shore, but, knowing that eventual defeat was certain, they surrendered the following morning. In six months, the Japanese had destroyed the American Pacific fleet at Pearl Harbor and the air force at Clark Field, defeated and captured an army three times as large as their own, and conquered a group of islands containing 115,000 square miles and 17,000,000 people.

Even more remarkable were the Japanese advances at the expense of the British and Dutch. Two British battleships were sunk on December 10 in an air attack. Hong Kong was taken on Christmas, and an invasion of the Malay Peninsula and Dutch East Indies was launched. In February, 1942, the large British garrison at Singapore surrendered after offering very little resistance. In March, Java and Burma were taken. By the spring of 1942, little remained in allied hands north of Australia except part of New Guinea. In less than six months the Japanese had conquered nearly all their desired empire, become the new rulers of over 100,000,000 people, and taken 250,000 prisoners of war at a cost of only 15,000 men and fewer ships than they were able to capture. It remained to be seen whether they could round out their outer rim of defense and hold their gains until the democracies grew tired of the struggle.

THE TIDE TURNS

The world did not have long to wait before receiving an answer. On May 4, 1942, two American aircraft carriers and other vessels encountered a Japanese fleet convoying troops to take Port Moresby in New Guinea and part of the Solomon Islands in an effort to cut supply lines between the United States and Australia. A hard-fought battle followed in the Coral Sea between New Guinea and the Solomon Islands in which carrier-based planes and anti-aircraft batteries played leading roles. By May 8, the Japanese were forced to turn back after both combatants had suffered heavy losses. Allied troops also halted a Japanese attempt to take Port Moresby by advancing over the New Guinea mountains, and the remaining threat to Australia's vital supply lines was ended when U.S. marines seized Guadalcanal in the southern Solomons during the late summer.

In June, 1942, the decisive battle of the Pacific war was fought near Midway Island, which the Japanese hoped to capture to buttress their outer rim of defense and to serve as a base for a possible attack on the Hawaiian Islands. Two hundred ships, including eleven battleships and four aircraft carriers, were thrown into the action. The outnumbered Americans refused to close with the enemy but seized every opportunity to destroy their opponents with carrier- and land-based planes. When the battle ended, the Japanese losses included their four carriers and 322 planes. This defeat terminated their capacity for expansion by sea; and, since their submarine fleet was very small, the Japanese were unable to prevent the Americans from moving men and equipment to Australia and other Pacific bases preparatory to assuming the offensive.

Meanwhile, America's vast productive capacity was beginning to have its effect in other theaters of operation. The United States had begun to re-arm in earnest after the fall of France, when half-armed Britain and the Atlantic Ocean had become the only barriers to prevent direct confrontation with the German aggressors. During the spring and summer of 1940, the National Guard had been called to active duty, the first peacetime conscription act had been passed, the rapid expansion of the navy had begun, and Roosevelt had called for the production of "at least 50,000 planes a year." The Lend-Lease Act of March, 1941, had made American supplies and equipment available to any anti-Axis country in return for "payment in kind or property or any other direct or indirect benefit which the President deems satisfactory." At first the threatened British had been the primary beneficiaries of this act, but by September, 1942, thirty-five nations had received American assistance, and by the end of the war the Soviet Union had been sent \$4,750,000,000 worth of supplies. In all, about 300,000 planes and 87,000 tanks had been manufactured for American and allied use.

There was little advantage in making the United States the "arsenal of democracy" if the German submarines were to be permitted to send its consignments to Britain and the Soviet Union to the bottom of the sea. To prevent this, Roosevelt ordered the American fleet to convoy merchant ships across the Atlantic, and the American army to send troops to Greenland, Iceland, and Ireland. Prior to the Japanese attack on Pearl Harbor, the American navy had become engaged in an undeclared war in the Atlantic Ocean in which both German submarines and U.S. destroyers had been sunk or damaged. In 1942, the Allies lost 8,330,000 tons of shipping; but, aided by radar detecting devices and small carrier escorts to provide detection and bombing from the air, efficient convoys gradually reduced the submarine menace. By November, 1942, cargo ship construction was exceeding losses, and the battle of the Atlantic was clearly won. Only 4,329,000 tons of shipping were sunk in 1943, and by May of that year German U-boat losses were exceeding construction.

Not enough men and material could be transported to the British Isles in time to launch an attack across the English Channel in 1942 or 1943, but the democracies were able to resume the offensive in North Africa. In June, 1942, the brilliant Rommel had advanced to El Alamein, a point only sixty miles from Alexandria. If attacks by the British Mediterranean fleet and Malta-based aircraft had not depleted the paltry supply of oil, tanks, and troops that Hitler tried to send him, the Nile delta and the Suez Canal might have been his. By October the democracies had won the battle of supplies, and General Bernard Montgomery counterattacked with superior forces. Rommel's troops were hurled back. At the same time, an Anglo-American force under the command of General Dwight D. Eisenhower landed in Morocco and Algeria. Caught between two forces, Rommel made a stand in Tunisia, but by the middle of May, 1943, all North Africa was in allied hands. The Mediterranean was open to their shipping, and they had only to choose at what point on the poorly defended southern shores of Europe they would invade.

The tide of battle turned on the Russian front during the late fall and early winter of 1942. In August, the advancing German army had reached Stalingrad on the west bank of the Volga River, and a battle of attrition followed that rivaled the slaughter at Verdun in 1916. The city was coveted by both forces because of its strategic value and because it bore Stalin's name. By early November it was almost entirely in German hands, but on the twentieth of that month, the Russians counterattacked. Rumanian satellite troops on the German left flank broke, and the Russians succeeded in surrounding the German Sixth Army of 300,000 in the city. Instead of ordering his troops to break out of the Russian ring, Hitler instructed them to defend their position "until the last man." Obediently, the Germans fought on without adequate supplies and without hope of rescue. Finally, early in February, 1943, to Hitler's disgust 123,000 survivors surrendered. The Russian losses in this one battle exceeded those of the United States in the entire war, but the German advance had finally been halted. Aided by

957

American trucks, planes, and food, the Russians continued their drive westward, and by the spring of 1943 they had recaptured the ground lost in 1942.

Thus by the winter of 1942-43, the tide of battle had turned on every front, and the Axis troops were hopelessly outnumbered in men and material on the land, on the sea, and in the air. Hitler's days were clearly numbered.

ALLIED STRATEGY AND PEACE PLANS

While the war was in progress, the allied leaders found it necessary to have frequent conferences to decide on military objectives and to discuss the new world order to be established after victory had been won. Difficulties arose during these meetings that became more serious as the defeat of the Axis grew imminent, although only after complete victory had been won and the necessity to co-operate had been removed, did the Allies discover the magnitude of their disagreements. That there should be disputes was not surprising, because only chance had made Soviet Russia the ally of the democracies. When war began, the Russians had co-operated with Germany, and early in 1940 they had nearly become involved in a war with the British and French who were on the verge of coming to the aid of the Finns. Only Hitler's foolish decision to attack Russia in 1941 had brought that country into alliance with the democracies, and the desire to destroy the Nazi regime was the only bond which held the coalition together.

In the early days of the alliance, Stalin was suspicious but somewhat co-operative. He was fighting for survival and avoided disputes with the democracies that might cause them to reduce their aid to him. As he became more confident of his ability to turn back the German onslaught, his objectives became more ambitious. He began to work toward bringing the small east European countries under Russian influence, if not toward actually incorporating them into the Soviet Union. In Asia, his objectives are more difficult to determine, although it is clear that he wanted the Japanese to surrender their gains made during the Russo-Japanese War of 1905. In addition, he undoubtedly anticipated a period of confusion following the war, just as after World War I, in which there would be opportunities for Communists to seize power in other states on both continents.

Roosevelt and the American people were much more idealistic. They had disliked Stalin and communism prior to 1941, but when the Russians became their allies, they were swept by enthusiasm for the gallant stand made against a common foe. The old suspicions and fears were forgotten. They convinced themselves that Stalin was only another nationalist, whose territorial ambitions were no greater than the tsars'. In his hands, they believed, communism had ceased to be a world threat. The hope of the postwar world lay in the continued co-operation of the great powers, and this could be achieved only through friendship with the Russians and through timely concessions that would mitigate their suspicions of the West. Roosevelt displayed more sympathy for Russian security needs than for those of Western Europe. Yet many of the concessions he made were granted at a time when he had no alternative because of the position and power of the Russian army. To Roosevelt's trust of Russian intentions, therefore, must be added the mistake of refusing to connect military and political objectives. The President desired freedom for Poland and the Balkan states, but he did not realize that these objectives could be obtained only if the states were occupied by American armies at the end of the war.

Churchill made fewer mistakes, especially after he recognized Stalin's true intentions. He foresaw that an increase of Russian influence in eastern Europe could not be avoided, but he wanted to limit that influence as much as possible. His unwillingness to trust Stalin fully led him to advocate an Anglo-American invasion of the Balkans that would remove any need for Russian armies to enter this region. He was more sympathetic than the United States with the aspirations of De Gaulle and the Free French, for he believed that De Gaulle would contribute to the revival of France after the war and therefore help to restore the balance of power in Europe. He opposed Roosevelt's anticolonialism and told him frankly that "we mean to hold our own. I have not become the King's First Minister in order to preside over the liquidation of the British Empire." This well-known position made his ideas suspect to Roosevelt, who remarked to his son that "I see no reason for putting the lives of American soldiers in jeopardy in order to protect real or fancied British interests on the European continent." Unfortunately, at times Roosevelt seemed more suspicious of Churchill's motives than Stalin's. Without support, Churchill was unable to make the moves on the continent which might have limited Russian influence in eastern Europe.

The first of the wartime meetings between Roosevelt and Churchill took place in August, 1941, before the United States had become a formal participant in the struggle. As a result of their discussion, they issued the Atlantic Charter stating the policies "on which they based their hopes for a better future for the world." In their eight-point program, they declared that they sought no aggrandizement and that there ought to be no territorial changes "that do not accord with the freely expressed wishes of the peoples concerned." People would choose "the form of government under which they wished to live. . . ." Nations were to cooperate to increase the prosperity of the world. The Nazi tyranny was to be destroyed, after which there was to be an abandonment of the use of force and general disarmament pending the establishment of a "permanent system of general security."

These vague statements, so reminiscent of the philosophy underlying Wilson's Fourteen Points, were augmented by the United Nations Declaration of January 1, 1942. In it the various powers fighting the fascist states, including the United States, promised to wage war with all their resources and not to make a separate "armistice or peace." Thus the democratic and

Communist states pledged themselves to crush jointly the third and rival system of government. In keeping with this decision, Roosevelt and Churchill decided that the Germans were the principal enemy and that therefore the bulk of the allied resources should be devoted to defeating them before a major effort was made against Japan. Militarily, this was a sound decision, but if Roosevelt had been a Machiavellian statesman he might well have permitted Russia and Germany to exhaust each other while the United States devoted most of its initial effort to defeating the Japanese. Most Americans would have preferred that priority be given to the war against Japan, because of the treacherous attack on Pearl Harbor, and Churchill feared that Roosevelt would insist on an early victory in the east. Great Britain's security was so closely related to the defeat of Hitler that Churchill sought to avoid any diversions in the Pacific until this had been accomplished.

Stalin evidently suspected that the democracies were permitting the Russians to bear the brunt of Hitler's attack. Since he himself had sat quietly by in 1940 while the Germans destroyed the democratic armies on the western front, he might well anticipate that the democracies would use his own strategy. He therefore demanded that the democracies open a second front in Europe in 1942 in order to compel the Germans to relax pressure on the eastern front. The democracies still lacked the strength to do this, but as a substitute they launched the campaign which drove the Axis out of North Africa. In January, 1943, Roosevelt and Churchill met at Casablanca, where they decided on a policy of unconditional surrender, partly to avoid a repetition of the German complaint after World War I that the Allies had not honored the terms of the armistice and partly to convince Stalin and occupied Europe that they would fight until victory had been won. Plans for a cross-channel invasion had to be postponed until the spring of 1944 due to lack of men and equipment, but Churchill argued that meanwhile an attack on "the soft under-belly of Europe," the Mediterranean coast, could be launched. The Americans were reluctant, but, on July 10, Eisenhower landed in Sicily. By the 22nd, the island was half conquered, and three days later Mussolini was suddenly arrested on order of King Victor Emmanuel. Stalin had not obtained his second front in France, but the first Axis state was about to be removed from the war.

The Italians had long been critical of Mussolini's conduct of the war. They thought, correctly, that he had come so much under Hitler's influence that Italian interests were being sacrificed to achieve German ends. Defeats in North Africa and Sicily, along with heavy bombing raids and the imminent prospect of invasion, had led to sharp criticism by the Fascist Grand Council on July 24 and to the king's action on the following day. Marshal Badoglio (1871-1956) was appointed to take Mussolini's place. He immediately dissolved the Fascist party and secretly asked for armistice terms. Here was a wonderful opportunity for the Allies in the west. A quick surrender, accompanied by the rapid movement of allied troops through Italy, might have brought them to the Alps before the Germans had time to act, but the concept of unconditional surrender now arose to plague them. For five weeks they negotiated while the suspicious Germans prepared for action. In the end, the Italians surrendered unconditionally, but with the understanding that in return they would receive better terms. The Germans promptly seized Rome and rescued Mussolini, who established a Fascist republic in northern Italy. Instead of taking advantage of their control of the seas and invading near Rome, the Allies stupidly landed their armies south of Naples. As a result, they had to drive up the entire length of the narrow, mountainous peninsula, a task which was not completed until the war's end.

Meanwhile, the heads of state continued to discuss war strategy and peace plans. During the fall of 1943, Roosevelt, Stalin, and Churchill met together for the first time at Teheran in Iran. On their way there, Roosevelt and Churchill met Chiang Kai-shek at Cairo, where they decided that Japan should be stripped of all its gains since 1914. Korea was to be made independent and China was to recover Manchuria, Formosa, and the Pescadores island group between Formosa and China. In this manner, Japan, the only Asiatic nation capable of halting Russian expansion in the Far East, was to be reduced to a few rocky islands to benefit China. If China had been strong, this would not have upset the balance of power in that part of the world; but these concessions were made to China because it was weak. They were given in the hope of inspiring greater military effort. China's failure to revive under the leadership of Chiang Kai-shek left a vacuum in the Far East that has since been filled by the advancing forces of communism. Stalin dropped a few hints at Teheran concerning Russia's territorial ambitions in the Far East, but he indicated that in return he would attack Japan soon after the defeat of Germany. The democracies enthusiastically approved of this intent, because Russian assistance would make the Japanese defeat much easier to accomplish.

At Teheran the Allies devoted most of their time to European problems. Churchill argued for an invasion of the Balkans from the Aegean and Adriatic seas, but Stalin announced his preference for a cross-channel invasion, whether for military reasons or to keep the democracies out of the Balkans is not known. Military considerations led Roosevelt to agree with Stalin, and it was decided that the cross-channel invasion should take place in May, 1944. At the proper moment, part of the allied army in Italy would be used to land in southern France, not the Balkans as Churchill desired. Stalin made known his desire to keep the territory he had received at the expense of Finland, Poland, and the Baltic states during the period of his alliance with Hitler, but he gave no inkling of the full extent of his ambitions, either because he did not feel that the time was ripe or because at this point he did not anticipate being in a position in which he could hope for more.

Roosevelt devoted considerable energy to winning Stalin's friendship.

Stalin, Roosevelt, and Churchill at the Teheran Conference. (Wide World)

His personal charm had been a strong asset on the American political scene, and he assumed that it would be equally persuasive in foreign affairs. At first Stalin was coldly distant, but on the third day of the conference, Roosevelt later informed a cabinet member, "I began to tease Churchill about his Britishness, about John Bull, about his cigars, about his habits. It began to register with Stalin. Winston got red and scowled, and the more he did so, the more Stalin smiled. Finally Stalin broke out into a deep, hearty guffaw and for the first time in three days I saw light. I kept it up until Stalin was laughing with me and it was then that I called him 'Uncle Joe'. . . . From that time on our relations were personal. . . . The ice was broken and we talked like men and brothers." [6] One wonders whether it was Roosevelt's humor or the revelation that he could be separated from Churchill's more realistic policies that brought signs of amusement to the Communist dictator's face.

LIBERATION OF FRANCE

The closing months of 1942 had seen the tide of the war change. On every front, the Axis advance was halted. The year 1943 marked some

[6] Quoted by Chester Wilmot, *The Struggle for Europe* (New York: Harper, 1952), p. 141.

allied gains, but it was essentially a year of preparation. The huge American industrial system was geared fully to the war. Equipment and men swarmed into England until the island seemed like an armed camp. The greatly enlarged British and American air forces carried out huge bombing raids on German cities in the hope of destroying their industrial potential. In this, they were disappointed, for although their cities were reduced to ruins, the Germans managed to increase their armament output until near the close of 1944. Their achievement was due to Albert Speer, a brilliant young architect who was named Minister of Arms and Munitions in February, 1942, and to their determination not to permit allied bombings to deter them from their work. Their courage and Speer's planning and co-ordination made it possible nearly to quadruple production of ammunition, artillery, and tanks between 1941 and 1943 and to more than double the production of airplanes. Oil was the only serious shortage that developed. Neither the oft-bombed Rumanian oil fields nor the synthetic German plants could produce enough to meet the military's minimum needs. However, allied production grew more rapidly and when the battle of Normandy began in June, 1944, the Allies had complete control of the air and the sea; and their ground forces were many times more numerous and better equipped than their German counterparts. Partly as a result of American aid, even the Russians had more and better armaments than the Germans, as well as three times as many men along the eastern front.

It was with confidence, therefore, that General Eisenhower, who had been named commander of the cross-channel invasion, launched his troops against the coast of Normandy early on June 6, 1944. Eighty warships blasted enemy positions and the air force flew over 10,000 sorties against ground targets. Airborne divisions were dropped behind the enemy lines and 4,000 ships bore the British and American armies to the beachheads. Despite the magnitude of the operation, the Germans were surprised by the landing and the invaders suffered only 10,000 casualties during the first day. Slowly they pressed inland while more and more troops were poured ashore. By the end of June, about 1,000,000 men had been landed in Normandy. The beachhead was secure, and the greatest seaborne invasion in history was a success.

For a time the Germans were able to contain the beachhead, but on July 25 General Omar Bradley's First Army launched an assault. The German lines were breached to permit General George Patton's Third Army to break through near Saint-Lô and race southward. One corps turned westward into Brittany to take Brest; the remainder of the army turned eastward toward Le Mans and then northward in the direction of Falaise in an effort to surround the German army which had been containing the allied beachhead. Only a rapid withdrawal could save the Germans, but Hitler, as usual, refused to authorize a retreat. As a result, two-thirds of the German Seventh Army was killed or captured. The allied armies raced onward to Paris and the Seine River, which they reached during the latter part of

August. The German commander in the west, Günther von Kluge, committed suicide after writing a letter to Hitler advising him to make peace.

A great debate now developed among the allied leaders. Eisenhower wanted to continue the attack on a broad front by bringing the armies landed in Normandy and those from Italy that were coming ashore in southern France into a common line along the Rhine River. Montgomery advocated attacking in a huge mass along a narrow front in the direction of Brussels and the industrial Ruhr Valley. Patton pleaded for the logistical support to enable him to seize Frankfurt in a rapid drive through the Vosges Mountains. Each commander felt sure that his plan would bring victory that year, and the debate over who was right is likely to last for a long time. Suffice it to say that Montgomery's plan was somewhat similar to the one Hitler rejected when he launched his assault in the west in 1940. The rivers in the Low Countries were so wide that crossings were quite difficult. Eisenhower's plan was similar to the one Hitler used so unsuccessfully against the Russians in 1941. The Allies, like the Germans at that time, lacked the great numerical superiority necessary to attack successfully on such a broad front.

The route Patton had chosen came closer to the one the Germans had used so successfully against the French. Perhaps with his exceptional ability to move troops rapidly, he could have made his plan work. Whatever the merits of Patton's and Montgomery's proposals, Eisenhower adopted his own plan. Patton drove his army to the east until he ran out of gas, a delay which enabled the Germans to re-form their battle line around Metz. Montgomery, constantly complaining about lack of supplies, launched a much larger attack at Arnhem in the northeast, but the rivers and the Germans proved too much for him. By the middle of September the allied armies had ground to a halt. France and most of the Low Countries had been liberated in a summer's campaign. Yet Germany had scarcely been penetrated.

The halting of the allied offensive in the west was accomplished only by Hitler's decision to use his reserves on this front. This enabled the Russian armies, which had been pressing forward all summer, to continue their drive. Poland and the Baltic states were reconquered and Rumania, Bulgaria, and Finland were compelled to surrender during the late summer. Yugoslavia was freed largely through the efforts of communist guerrillas led by Marshal Tito. Budapest was besieged, and Germany was penetrated during the fall.

THE LAST DAYS OF HITLER

There had always been some who opposed the Nazi regime in Germany. Here and there groups of Germans drew together and plotted to overthrow the hated tyranny and save the fatherland from further destruction. Outstanding among them was General Ludwig Beck,[7] who had resigned as chief of the general staff in 1938 rather than participate in a war he regarded as unjust and immoral. He and his associates devoted their efforts to winning support among the officers' corps, for the army alone had the power to act in a totalitarian state. A few generals such as Rommel recognized a higher moral law than their oath of allegiance to Hitler and wanted to seize the tyrant and bring him to trial,[8] but the majority remained true to their word and would not act until freed from their pledge by Hitler's death. It was decided, therefore, to assassinate Hitler, seize power, and make peace. One attempt after another failed. Finally the successful allied landing in Normandy brought renewed efforts.

On July 20, 1944, Colonel Count von Stauffenberg attended a conference with Hitler. After a few minutes he excused himself to use the telephone, leaving a time bomb concealed in his brief case under the conference table. At the moment of the explosion, Stauffenberg rushed off to give the signal for the revolt. A few seconds later Hitler staggered forth dazed but only slightly wounded. Had the meeting been held in the usual bunker rather than in a wooden building, he would surely have been killed. The underground attempted to seize the principal European cities anyway. At Paris they were successful, but at Berlin they failed. When the generals learned that Hitler was still alive, they refused to march. Rommel, who had commanded Army Group B in the west, might have acted, but at the moment he lay in a hospital, the victim of an allied air attack. Hitler's revenge was severe. Beck and Rommel were told to commit suicide. Hitler did not want the German people to learn that such respected figures were implicated in a plot against his life. Rommel complied to save his family from destruction, and Hitler carried the tragic farce to the point of ordering a state funeral for the greatest of German war heroes. Thousands were executed and still more were sent to the concentration camps. The underground was broken, and the war went on.

Hitler himself had never abandoned his faith in victory, and he took his miraculous escape as proof that he had divine protection for his mission. During the fall of 1944, he placed his hopes in a counterattack to be launched in the Ardennes, where he had won his greatest victory in 1940. Over twenty divisions were massed for the drive that had Antwerp as its ultimate objective. Hitler's generals knew that they had no chance of success, but on December 16 they attacked anyway. The thinly held American line broke at the center, but on both sides of the assault area it held firm. The Germans were restricted to a deep narrow penetration during the initial days of the assault. Once the Allies had recovered from the initial shock, Patton's Third Army turned northward and the British-American forces in the north turned southward to close the bulge the

[7] See page 878.
[8] See page 877.

German penetration had made in their lines. During the winter months the snow-covered hills and forests of the Ardennes were the scene of some of the most bitter fighting of the war, but in the end superior numbers and equipment once more had their effect. Before spring the American line was restored, and the Allies were ready to take advantage of the fine spring weather to drive into the heart of Germany.

Still Hitler did not despair. More and more he placed his hope in secret weapons that German scientists had invented. A new submarine was being developed which he felt sure would enable Germany to blockade the British Isles, jet planes were being built to regain control of the skies, and rockets were invented to bomb Britain into submission. But always it was a question of too little and too late. The few thousand rockets the Germans had time to produce and fire served more as a prelude of things to come than as a decisive factor in the war. Actually it was the Allies who won the war in science. The invention of radar had enabled the British to detect air raids in time to send fighter planes to protect their shores and to locate submarines before they launched their torpedoes. The Americans invented a proximity fuse which exploded anti-aircraft shells if they passed near enough to a plane to destroy it. They also devised artillery shells that exploded at the height above the ground where they would take the heaviest toll. The atom bomb, also developed by the United States, was the greatest wartime scientific achievement. It was developed at a cost of $2,000,000,000 by a host of scientists, some of whom were men like Albert Einstein who had had to flee from Germany to escape Nazi persecution. Hitler put no such concerted effort into science and this was one more cause of his defeat.

As spring drew near in 1945, the defeats on the eastern and western fronts multiplied. Hitler withdrew to a bomb-proof concrete bunker beside the chancery in Berlin. His left arm and left leg had begun to tremble. One doctor thought he had Parkinson's disease, but he never submitted to a medical examination. Instead he put his faith in a quack doctor who kept him full of drugs. His skin became discolored. His mind became more and more unbalanced. He lost all sense of restraint, and his destructive instinct was given full play. Generals were forbidden to retreat. When their armies were cut off, they were told to fight until the death. Army after army that could have been preserved for a final stand in Germany was surrounded and destroyed. If a general refused to obey or if he acted on his own initiative at the front, his courage was impugned and he was relieved of command. When the Anglo-American armies began to penetrate Germany, Hitler ordered the destruction of all property before it fell into the enemy's hands. Speer remonstrated against this "scorched earth" policy and pointed out that even after defeat some Germans must live on, but Hitler declared, "If the war is lost, the nation also will perish. This fate is inevitable. There is no need to consider the basis even of a most primitive existence any longer. On the contrary, it is better to destroy even that, and to destroy it ourselves. The nation has proved itself weak, and the future belongs solely to the stronger eastern nations. Besides, those who remain after the battle are of little value; for the good have fallen." Wisely, Speer did not obey his orders and some German cities and fields were preserved for those who survived.

The allied advance continued. In early March the Anglo-American army crossed the Rhine River at many points, and the Russians soon established a bridgehead over the Oder. April saw the final conquest of Austria, Italy, and the Ruhr Valley.

Still Hitler ordered the German people to fight on. For months he had made no public appearances, but his propaganda minister, Paul Goebbels, had never ceased to point out that the allied unconditional surrender policy meant the destruction of Germany unless, as he promised, Hitler could perform some last-minute miracle. Horoscopes were cast which indicated that the situation would change after the middle of April, and Hitler took comfort in the thought that Frederick the Great was on the verge of suicide when the sudden death of Empress Elizabeth removed Russia from the war and permitted Prussia to survive.[9] The news of Roosevelt's death reached Berlin on April 13. For a brief moment Hitler thought that his passing was the needed miracle, but the American army continued its advance.

Of all the things that gave Hitler hope during the last year of his life the most important was his belief that the democracies would not destroy Germany for fear of a Russian take-over in central Europe. War between the two was certain, he predicted, and he grasped at every difference between the Communists and the democracies as proof of his contention. Distrust did begin to form, but it did not become a military factor until after the downfall of the Nazi regime. Eisenhower refused to follow Churchill's suggestion to take Berlin and Prague, as he could easily have done. Instead he held his troops in the north along the Elbe River while his southern forces took Bavaria to prevent a last desperate stand in that mountainous region. Russian and American soldiers met at the Elbe on April 25. The Americans had permitted the Russians to occupy Czechoslovakia and eastern Germany.

When the hope of allied discord vanished and the Russians were fighting their way into Berlin, Hitler at length turned his thoughts towards death. He left a political testament in which he blamed the war on international Jewry and the defeat on the officers' corps. He married Eva Braun, his mistress, who had voluntarily joined him in Berlin to share his fate, and said farewell to the few who remained with him in the bunker. On April 30, one day after news had come that Mussolini had been captured and executed by Communist guerrillas, Hitler and Eva Braun retired to their suite. A few minutes later they were found dead, Eva from poison and Hitler from a bullet wound through the mouth. After supervising their cremation, the faithful Goebbels poisoned his five children and shot

[9] See page 420.

his wife and himself. A week later the empire that was to last a thousand years came to an end.

THE DEFEAT OF JAPAN

Meanwhile, the democracies had not been idle in the Far East. MacArthur may be justly criticized for his failure to prepare the Philippine army better for war, and it is surprising that he escaped censure for his handling of the Philippine campaign, but when he assumed the offensive in the Pacific, he displayed a strategic and tactical skill rare in the annals of American military history. The Japanese had about 3,000,-000 ground troops, for the most part located on the Asiatic mainland. The democracies never mustered nearly so large a force; but, by combined air, sea, and amphibious operations, MacArthur bypassed strongly held Japanese islands and attacked weaker positions that could be used as bases for further advances. At the same time, of course, he cut the lines of communication between Japan and the bypassed islands from which essential supplies were drawn. In this manner MacArthur finally won islands from which Japan could be easily bombed and blockaded by aircraft, surface vessels, and submarines. In the end he forced the Japanese to surrender without having to engage more than a small fraction of the enemy army or to conquer more than a small percentage of their vast empire.

MacArthur's first step was to drive the Japanese out of New Guinea and the Admiralty Islands, while Admiral Nimitz took the Gilbert Islands, Eniwetok in the Marshalls, and Saipan in the Marianas between the fall of 1943 and the summer of 1944. Tojo's militaristic cabinet was forced to resign, but its successor continued the war with no better results. By the fall of 1944, the Americans had bypassed many Japanese held positions, and MacArthur had landed troops on Leyte Island in the Philippines, near which the Americans had emerged victorious in the biggest naval battle of the war. Thereafter the Japanese were unable to challenge them on the seas.

In the year 1945, the war in the Pacific drew to a close. The struggle for Iwo Jima and Okinawa, which took place during the late winter and early spring, was extremely bloody, but the conquest of these islands enabled the Americans to cut the lines of communication between Japan and China and gave them air bases within a few hundred miles of the principal Japanese cities. There followed the greatest air offensive in history. Thousands of tons of bombs were dropped every month. After the German surrender in May, the Japanese Supreme War Council sought to end the war, but the allied unconditional surrender policy enabled the extremists to win enough support to continue the struggle. On August 6, long after they knew that the Japanese were considering surrender, the Americans dropped an atomic bomb on Hiroshima killing over 70,000 persons. On August 8, the Russians declared war, and on August 9 a second atomic bomb leveled most

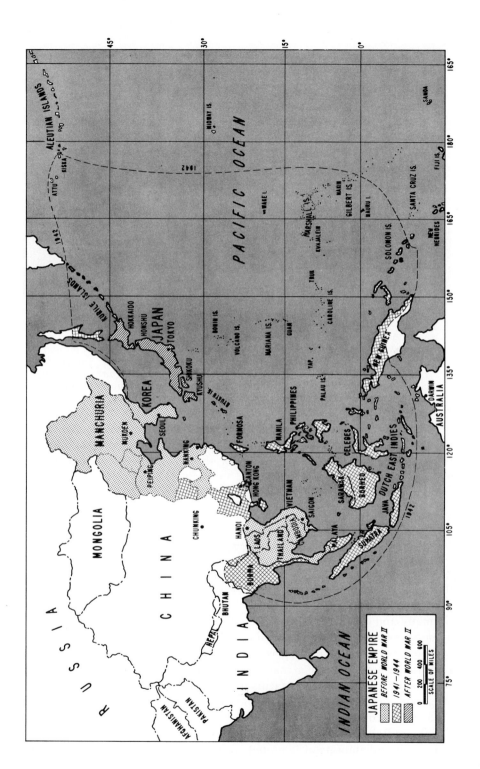

JAPANESE EMPIRE

BEFORE WORLD WAR II

1941–1944

AFTER WORLD WAR II

SCALE OF MILES

0   200   400   600

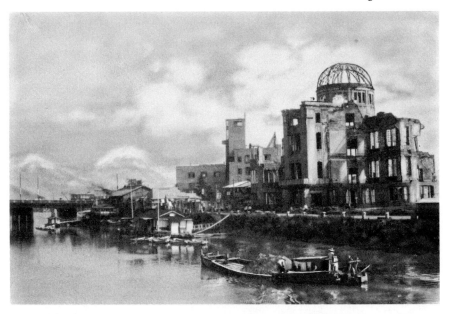

The Industrial Exhibition Hall, Hiroshima, Japan, a charred reminder at ground-zero of the world's first atom bomb explosion of August 6, 1945. This gutted remnant of a once sprawling building that covered a city block before the bomb exploded is preserved as a monument for the people of Hiroshima. (Courtesy John Bernheim)

of Nagasaki to the ground. The Emperor now took the unusual step of advising the Japanese Supreme War Council to surrender provided the imperial institution was preserved. On August 14, the war in the Pacific came to an end.

THE RESULTS OF THE WAR AND THE EARLY PEACE SETTLEMENTS

The results of World War II were similar to those of World War I except that they were more severe in every respect. In both conflicts, there was a heavy loss of life, but in World War II the civilian population, especially in Germany and eastern Europe, suffered more. In this second conflict, about 35,000,000 combatants and noncombatants were killed. In both wars, there was heavy destruction of property. In the earlier war, however, the destruction was limited to a few areas; this time, there were bomb-cratered cities, wrecked bridges, and ruined farms in most of Europe and the Far East. So desperate was the plight of the people in the war-torn areas that the United States and other more fortunate countries established the United Nations Relief and Rehabilitation Administration in November, 1943, to provide relief for the inhabitants of liberated countries, whether friend or foe, communist or democratic. Through UNRRA and other agencies, the United States gave about $11,000,000,000 to Western Europe alone by 1947 to prevent hunger, cold, and disease, while the inhabitants cleared away the wreckage and began to produce again.

In both wars there was the same impetus toward state control of the economy because the regulation of industry became mandatory in every country deeply involved in the conflict. Here again, World War II had more far-reaching results than its predecessor, for the governments of Eastern Europe assumed ownership of the means of production, and many large industries were nationalized in Western Europe. Today no important country is without its corps of economists and statisticians who advise governmental leaders on economic policy.

World War II, even more than World War I, accelerated the process of freeing women from the home. In some countries they were drafted into the armed forces and into industry; in others they volunteered their services by the millions. The old social order was weakened in Europe and the Far East, and the way was opened for greater democracy and social reform than ever before.

In some notable respects, however, the results of the two wars were different. After World War I, a single ideological position—liberal democracy—had overshadowed its rivals; but after the second conflict, two ideologies of equal strength—democracy and communism—emerged from the ruins to compete for world supremacy. As in 1814, the end of the war found Russia deep in central Europe, and the democratic alliance that was eventually organized because of this situation did no more than halt further communist advances. The division of Europe into two ideological camps delayed the signing of peace treaties with Japan and Austria until years after the war, and the victorious powers have still not been able to decide on the ultimate fate of Germany. No great peace conference like that held at Vienna in 1815 and at Versailles in 1919 has yet taken place. Peace was made in a reasonable period of time only with those states that fell under the military control of one great power or the other.

THE PEACE TERMS

Throughout the war allied statesmen had discussed the peace settlement, and at Cairo, Teheran, and other places a few general agreements had been made. But it was not until Roosevelt, Churchill, and Stalin met at Yalta in February, 1945, that much of a specific nature was accomplished. By this time all or nearly all of eastern Europe had been, or was about to be, liberated by the Russians; and it was obvious that the democracies would have to make substantial concessions to them in view of their failure to invade the Balkans or to advance farther eastward. The only alternative was to threaten to use force, but the war-weary democracies were unwilling to risk a new conflict. It is not surprising, then, that Roosevelt and Churchill could do nothing to alter the situation in eastern Europe. They did well, in fact, to get Stalin to agree that interim governmental authorities would be established in liberated countries that were "broadly representative of all democratic elements in the population and pledged to the earliest possible establishment through free elections of governments responsive to the will of the people." The Curzon Line, which the peacemakers of 1919 had intended to be the boundary between Poland and Russia, became the new boundary between the two countries.[10] This gave the White Russian and Ukrainian territory which Poland had seized after World War I back to the Soviet Union and made the Poles, in whose defense the democracies had entered the war, one of the heaviest sufferers at the conference table, although it was tentatively decided to compensate them in the west at the expense of Germany. Germany itself was to be divided temporarily into zones of occupation controlled by the three great powers and France, which was given a voice at Churchill's insistence. It was also agreed that a new world organization would replace the discredited League of Nations.

The charge has often been made that Roosevelt gave concessions to Russia at Yalta in regard to the Far East that led to the triumph of communism in China. At that time, it seemed likely that the Japanese would fight for several more years, and the Americans were most anxious to obtain Russian military aid as well as permission to establish air bases in Siberia. Stalin granted these requests, but in return he demanded that Japan cede the southern half of Sakhalin Island and the Kurile Islands to Russia and that the privileges the tsars had exercised in Manchuria before their defeat in 1905 be restored to Russia. Dairen was to be made a free port; Port Arthur was to be leased to Russia as a naval base; and the Manchurian railroads were to be operated by a joint Soviet-Chinese company. These concessions put Manchuria in the Russian sphere of influence, but they were to take effect only with the concurrence of Chiang Kai-shek and in themselves they do not explain why the Chinese soon abandoned Chiang for the Communists.[11]

The next meeting between the leaders of the great powers was at Potsdam in the summer of 1945, just after the fall of Hitler. Roosevelt had died in April, and Truman represented the United States. It was followed by a series of conferences between the foreign ministers of the various states, leading up to a Paris peace conference during the spring and summer of 1946. In these conferences no decision was reached with regard to the future of Germany and Austria, but it was decided that Ethiopia would once more be an independent state and that Italy's African empire would temporarily remain under British rule. In addition, Italy was to yield land along the northern shores of the Adriatic Sea to Yugoslavia and the Dodecanese

[10] See page 785.
[11] See pages 986-988.

Islands in the eastern Mediterranean to Greece. Poland assumed control, but not sovereignty in Western eyes, of that part of Germany which lay to the east of the Oder River except for northern East Prussia, which was annexed by Russia. Bulgaria received part of Dobruja from Rumania, and there were other minor changes in the Balkans, although in most places the 1919 boundaries were restored. The biggest gains were made by the Russians, who profited at the expense of all their western neighbors. Reparations were demanded of the defeated nations, but the victors remembered the lessons learned by the peacemakers of 1919 and asked for relatively small amounts that could be paid in a reasonable time. Italy was assessed only $360,000,000, and Bulgaria escaped with $70,000,000, none of which was paid.

The ethnic boundaries of Europe conformed approximately, or were soon made to conform, to the new political boundaries. The Poles protested bitterly against the loss of their pre-1939 territory to the east of the Curzon Line, but this region was inhabited by Ukrainians and White Russians. The Baltic states were incorporated into the Soviet Union without the Allies' permission but as federated republics with a theoretical degree of autonomy. The 13,000,000 Germans who lived in Czechoslovakia or to the east of the Oder River were abruptly expelled from the homes where they and their ancestors had lived for centuries. This cruel act had the merit of removing the minority problems that had beset Czechoslovakia and Poland during the inter-war period.

The question was not so much whether there were several unjust provisions in the treaties, but whether the Russians would adhere to their promise to permit free elections in eastern Europe. If they did, the idealistic promises of freedom, democracy, and self-determination contained in the Atlantic Charter would be approximately realized. If they did not, the peoples of eastern Europe would once more find themselves in the hands of ruthless dictators. There was evidence by the war's end that Stalin had no intention of honoring his pledge, but the Americans withdrew their armies about 120 miles along a three or four hundred mile front to permit the Russians to move into the occupation zone in Germany assigned to them at the Potsdam Conference. Churchill urged that American troops be kept in east Germany, "until we are satisfied about Poland, and also about the temporary character of the Russian occupation of Germany, and the conditions to be established in the Russianized or Russian controlled countries in the Danube Valley, particularly Austria and Czechoslovakia, and the Balkans." President Truman, new and insecure in his office, refused to alter his predecessor's policies, and the Russians were permitted to move farther into central Europe. At the same time, the Americans demobilized their armed forces as rapidly as possible, an act which would leave them nearly helpless if Stalin decided to transform eastern Europe into communist satellite states.

973

THE UNITED NATIONS

The concessions that Roosevelt made to the Russians were designed to remove the suspicion with which the Communists had regarded the West, especially since the betrayal of Czechoslovakia at Munich in 1938. The President believed that peace would be assured only if East and West learned to cooperate. To aid in developing a cooperative spirit and to settle future differences, he early advocated the creation of a new international organization. The old League of Nations was so discredited that it was abandoned, although the new association of nations was to bear many resemblances to it. Roosevelt discussed the matter with Churchill and Stalin during their various meetings, and many of the details were worked out at the Dumbarton Oaks Conference near Washington during the late summer of 1944. The actual charter was not prepared until the San Francisco Conference during the spring of the following year. Only those nations that were at war with the Axis were invited to attend, and the new organization was called the United Nations, the name of the victorious coalition. Peace-loving neutral nations like Sweden had to wait until a later date to become members of the new international society to prevent war, and some of the defeated states have not yet been permitted to join.

The old League of Nations Assembly was transformed into the General Assembly. In it all the member-nations were represented, but it was intended to be a forum for debate more than an organ for action, although it has become increasingly important since 1950. The League's Council became the Security Council. It consisted of eleven members. Five—Great Britain, Russia, the United States, France, and China—were permanent because of their status as great powers in fact, or through courtesy as in the case of France and China. The six remaining members were elected by the General Assembly for two-year terms. The Security Council was empowered to take "such action by air, sea, or land forces as may be necessary to maintain or restore international peace and security." Member-states were obligated to furnish troops and other forms of assistance at its request. Thus, the United Nations was given greater power of coercion than the old League, but it was plagued by a similar difficulty, for a negative vote by one of the permanent members prevented action. This veto power had been demanded as much by Great Britain and the United States as by the Soviet Union, but since the Russians have been most often outvoted, it is they who have used it extensively. The Security Council's power to act against an aggressor was therefore limited to minor states that did not have close ties with the communist or democratic world.

A new International Court of Justice was established to settle disputes between states at their request and to render advisory opinions. A Secretariat headed by a Secretary-General was formed to handle administrative matters. It became much more prominent than the League's Secretariat largely because of the ability of its first two secretary-generals, Trygve Lie

974

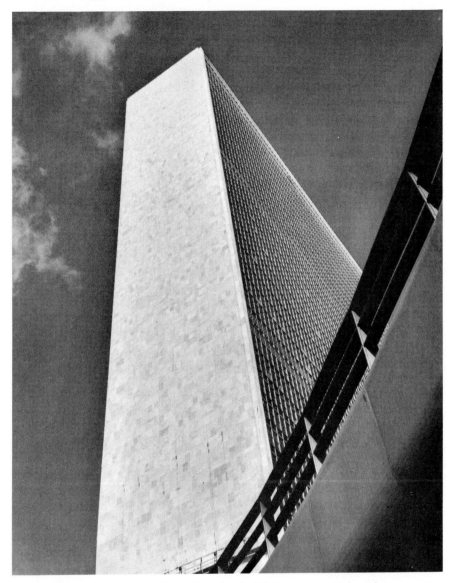

The United Nations Building, New York. (H. Armstrong Roberts)

of Norway and Dag Hammarskjöld of Sweden. The United Nations was given an even larger number of commissions and specialized agencies than the League. They included agencies to deal with everything from human rights, the status of women, and the sale of narcotics to a Food and Agriculture Organization, an International Bank for Reconstruction and Development, and the United Nations Educational, Scientific and Cultural Organization. Even if the United Nations is unable to find a peaceful solution to

975

the struggle for world supremacy, these agencies and commissions alone are useful enough to warrant its continuation.

WESTERN EUROPE IN THE CONTEMPORARY WORLD

Perhaps the most far-reaching result of the war was the new position of Western Europe. For centuries the inhabitants of the western half of the peninsular continent had taken the lead in science and art, in industry and trade, in government and international affairs. The superiority of their armies and navies had enabled them to spread their civilization to many parts of the world through force of arms, while the inhabitants of other portions of the globe had Westernized in order to enjoy a higher standard of living and to maintain their independence. Western Europeans had been the aggressors. Through their ideas and their deeds, they had affected other peoples more than the activities of other peoples had influenced them.

After World War II, all this changed. Two super-powers, the United States and Soviet Russia, now dwarfed the individual Western European nations. No other state could compare with them in science, industry, or military might. Even in the cultural sphere the Western Europeans had difficulty competing; for both the United States and Russia produced great artists, and the former had the wealth to attract the leading European performers across the Atlantic to its opera and its stage. For a generation or more, Western European industrialists had admired American business techniques and Western European workers had been interested in the Russian communist experiment, but now the impact of the two super-states began to affect nearly every aspect of life. Bubble gum was sold in vending machines in railroad stations in Paris, and Coca-Cola was advertised amid the vineyards of Burgundy. The inhabitants of the underdeveloped countries ceased to look to Western Europe as a model and, after asserting their independence, chose the United States or Russia as their guide. In short, Western Europe ceased to act upon other portions of the world and was itself acted upon by the two super-powers. Because of this dramatic change, we must begin our investigation of the postwar era with the activities of the two super-powers, not, as previously, with developments in Western Europe.

22/ The Expansion of Communism and the American Reaction

WORLD War II did not bring the struggle for world supremacy to an end. It only narrowed the contestants to two, for the few remaining fascist states were too weak to play significant roles. The communists had gained most from the war. Only Soviet Russia had espoused the doctrines of Marx before 1940; but a few years after the end of the war China and Eastern Europe joined the communist ranks; and Western Europe, Africa, Latin America and the rest of Asia were penetrated by the communist movement. Russia itself, which had been regarded as weaker than Germany, Great Britain, or France before the war, became the second most powerful nation in the world. The Americans responded vigorously to this threat. Putting their own house in order, they became a living proof that, with a few controls, a capitalistic, democratic state could provide ever-increasing prosperity and social justice for its citizens. At the same time, they rebuilt their armed forces to ward off actual

977

communist aggression and sought to raise the standard of living in the underdeveloped countries of the world.

THE EXPANSION OF COMMUNISM

Many observers in 1945 predicted that communist influence would spread into eastern and central Europe, but few, if any, thought that Russia would recover so rapidly from the war and become one of the greatest industrial and scientific powers on earth. Without this internal growth, the communist gains in Europe could not have been consolidated and preserved. With the possible exception of Germany, Russia suffered the heaviest losses from the war. Estimates of the total loss of life, military and civilian, from all causes related to the war run as high as 20,000,000. Over 1,700 cities and towns and over 70,000 villages were destroyed. In the large area of European Russia occupied by the Germans, the transportation system had been wrecked and the factories had been destroyed. Industrial output of consumer goods in 1945 was only three-fifths of what it had been before the war. The number of hogs dropped to less than half the pre-war figure, and as late as 1948 there were still 17,000,000 fewer cattle than in 1928. Only in heavy industries were production levels as high as before the Nazi onslaught.

THE RECOVERY OF RUSSIA

If Stalin had been less firmly in control, the miserably housed, miserably fed, and miserably clothed Russian people might have rioted or revolted, but no serious disturbance took place even though Stalin made few efforts to cater to the immediate needs of the Russian populace. Instead of concentrating on the production of consumer goods, Stalin started in 1946 a new series of five-year plans that were designed to repair war damage and to develop heavy industry. The steel that was produced was used primarily to build more steel plants, factories, and tractors. Little of it went for automobiles or even bicycles. In the short run, this meant that Russian laborers continued to work over a hundred hours to earn enough money to buy a pair of shoes. In the long run, it meant that Russia might eventually have an industrial capacity equal to that of the United States. Only then was the emphasis to be shifted to consumer goods. To achieve production goals, a forty-eight hour work week was maintained until 1956, when it was reduced to forty-six hours. Thus, the Russians worked eight hours a week longer to manufacture articles that were used to make more products than the Americans worked to manufacture articles that they used. Understandably the Russian economy moved forward at a more rapid rate than that of the United States. By 1955, the output in heavy industry was nearly four times what it was in 1940, despite the war-time losses. One must not, however, overemphasize the Soviet achievement, for the United States remained ahead in production. If use of power is taken as an indication of industrial modernization, it is interesting to note that power equivalent to 8.25 tons of coal was used by the average American in 1955; while the average Russian used only 2.02 tons. The Russian figure, however, compared favorably with that of Western Europe and was about ten times that of non-Russian Asia and Africa.

The Soviet regime also gave considerable attention to agriculture but with far less success. At first, relatively small collective farms worked by small groups were emphasized, but so little progress was made that in 1950 Nikita Khrushchev (1894-   ), a one-time coal miner who had just finished conducting a purge in the Ukraine, was put in charge of the agricultural program. He enlarged the collective farms and cultivated them with factory-size labor groups, but without success. In 1952 agricultural production was only 10 per cent higher than in 1940, but the population to be fed had grown considerably. Khrushchev, therefore, turned more attention to bringing new land under cultivation. Between 1953 and 1957, 86,000,000 acres, largely in central Asia, were farmed for the first time. The planting of corn was encouraged, but again without achieving substantial success. The basic trouble with the Soviet agricultural program was that although most of the able, energetic farmers disliked the collectives, the Communist hierarchy insisted on keeping the collective farms and anticipated the day when even the small individual garden plots could be abolished.

The Communists continued to stress education after the war, and a somewhat higher percentage of the national income was devoted to this purpose than in the United States. Especially significant was the large number of engineers and scientists graduated from the universities who became largely responsible for industrial development and rapid progress in nuclear and rocket studies. The Russians exploded their first atomic bomb in September, 1949, years before most Americans thought it would be possible. In August, 1953, they tested their first hydrogen bomb. Other triumphs followed and it became quite clear that in some fields Soviet science was at least equal to that of the United States. The democracies could no longer afford to be complacent.

The marked Russian advances in science were not equaled by comparable advances in other fields. History and the social sciences continued to be taught with a strong Marxist bias, and writers and artists were subjected to strong restraints. Travel between communist and non-communist countries was severely limited, and the millions of Russians who had been slave laborers or prisoners of war in Germany were treated with suspicion. Many did not want to return to Russia, but they were compelled to do so by the American army. Once in Russia they were often made slave laborers, or even executed if they were regarded as having been pro-German. Minority national groups suspected of disloyalty were deported to Siberia. The Jews, who had once been well treated, were now persecuted because of their presumed international outlook. Thus, an Iron Curtain was drawn between East and West which prevented the circulation of people as well as ideas. Apparently, Russian leaders believed that only in this way could they persuade their people to continue to accept a very low standard of living and stringent controls while the nation grew strong in science and in heavy industry. It was not until after Stalin's death in 1953 that the Iron Curtain began to be raised slightly.

THE EXPANSION OF COMMUNISM IN EUROPE: GENERAL CONSIDERATIONS

As a result of the war, Estonia, Latvia, Lithuania, and parts of Finland, Poland, Czechoslovakia, Germany, Rumania, and Hungary were incorporated into the Soviet Union. The inhabitants of these regions were quickly brought within the Communist economic system. Those who had the misfortune to be aristocrats, members of the middle class, socialists, or democrats were put into slave labor camps. Industry was nationalized, and farms were collectivized.

This much had been anticipated, but during the immediate postwar years Communists took over Poland, Hungary, Czechoslovakia, Yugoslavia, Albania, Rumania, and Bulgaria, and many other countries were threatened with similar internal revolutions. Five factors contributed to this development. One was the chaos in which much of the world found itself as a result of the war. Widespread poverty caused many to look to the followers of Marx, who promised an infallible cure for all economic difficulties. Secondly, the old order, that is, the middle class and the remnants of the aristocracy, appeared to be crumbling. The frequent association of these classes with fascism before the downfall of Hitler discredited them in the eyes of the victors and opened the way to dominance for the working-class and peasant parties whose records were more favorable. A third factor that facilitated the spread of communism was the prestige Russia won by its heroic stand against Hitler and its successful postwar accomplishments in the fields of science and industry. Certainly, however, the most important factor in the extension of communism was the presence of Russian armies in central and eastern Europe. Conservatives and democrats alike saw little use in risking their lives by speaking out against the expansion of communism when they knew that troops were available to establish and preserve a pro-Russian regime. Finally, the democracies themselves were militarily, materially, and morally weak. The United States demobilized its army immediately after the end of the war. The European democracies were temporarily paralyzed by heavy war losses and were more interested in trying to regain their old standard of living than in playing the game of power politics. Morally, there was at first the same unwillingness to risk war in the cause of freedom and justice that had led to the attempts to appease Hitler. Two world wars had left the democracies with the feeling that a third must be avoided. Only when they became convinced that the Russians could not be appeased were they finally willing to take a firm stand.

The Russians desired expansion both to increase their security and to spread communism. It is difficult to separate these two motives. The *Communist Manifesto* had ended with a summons to the working men of all nations to unite. This ultimate goal of world communism was never lost sight of by Lenin and his successors. At the same time, these men believed that Russia was encircled by unfriendly European capitalistic states with backward Asiatic colonial dependencies. Only by expansion could the communist heartland in Russia be secured. When the Russians thought that the capitalistic states were weak, as in 1918 and 1945, they tried to expand. When they met with strong resistance, as in the 1920's and 1950's, they talked of "socialism in one country" and "peaceful coexistence." They regarded an eventual struggle between capitalism and communism as probable, but since they believed that capitalism was decadent and that their own system was growing stronger, they saw no reason to provoke major wars. They contented themselves with trying to spread communism by encouraging revolutions.

The actual transformation of eastern Europe into communist states was generally accomplished in two stages. The first stage was marked by the establishment of coalition governments, in which the Communists were a minority. Other co-operating groups were the liberal middle-class, socialist, and peasants' parties. The old conservative parties ceased to exist because their members had either made peace with the new regime, fled before the advancing Russian troops, or been executed for real or fancied fascist leanings. In this period, such posts as president, prime minister, and foreign minister that carried great prestige were generally held by non-Communists. The Communists were content to provide the minister of the interior, through whom they could control the police, and the minister of justice, through whom they could protect those who attacked their opponents and punish those who attacked or were charged with attacking their comrades. They also took care to see that their supporters received key positions in the army. Once in control of the police, the judiciary, and the army, the Communists ushered in the second stage either by suddenly seizing power or by gradually winning control of, or suppressing, the non-Communist parties. At this point, freedom of speech, of the press, and of elections was denied. Those who desired to resist were cowed by the presence of the Russian army. By the spring of 1948, eastern Europe was firmly under communist control.

During the first stage of the communist takeover, a planned economy was inaugurated to promote recovery. Large industries were nationalized, but smaller ones were permitted to function freely. Farms owned by Germans in Poland and Czechoslovakia, and the large estates throughout eastern Europe, were turned over to the landless peasants, so that eastern

EXPANSION OF COMMUNISM
AND GROWTH OF U.S.S.R.

- COMMUNIST AFTER W.W.II
- TERRITORIAL GAINS OF U.S.S.R.
- --- PRE-W.W.II RUSSIAN BORDER
- ······ PRE-W.W.II POLISH BORDER

0 50 100   200   300
SCALE OF MILES

BERLIN OCCUPATION ZONES

Europe was transformed into a region of small farms. During the second stage, five-year plans on the Russian model were imposed. The small industries were nationalized, and large collective farms equipped with machines were established. There was resistance, as there had been in Russia, but the opposition was ineffective.

THE INDIVIDUAL STATES

Only a very small percentage of the east European peoples were Communists in 1945, but their attitude towards the Russians varied greatly from one state to another. To the Poles, Russia was a historic enemy that had seized the eastern portion of their country in alliance with the Germans in 1939. To the Czechs, Russia was the one great power that had stood by them during the Munich crisis of 1938 when the democracies had betrayed them into the hands of Hitler. They were willing to admit Communists into the government, and they looked upon themselves as the bridge between East and West. Despite the similar results, therefore, there were marked differences in the history of the extension of communist power in the various east European states.

After the Poles had been defeated by the Germans and Russians in 1939, they established a government in exile in London and organized a widespread resistance movement against the two invaders of their country. Hitler's attack on Russia in 1941 suddenly made Stalin a potential ally and led the British and Americans to try to effect a reconciliation. The Poles, however, were unwilling to accept the Curzon Line as the boundary with the Soviet Union, and Stalin was unwilling to see an unfriendly regime established so near to his country. As a result, he organized and recognized a pro-communist Polish group, which ultimately placed its headquarters at Lublin, as the official government even though it had little popular following. At the same time, he made every effort to destroy opponents of communism. Strong circumstantial evidence indicates that the Russians massacred thousands of Polish officers in 1940. In the summer of 1944, the anti-communist Polish underground army tried to seize Warsaw. For sixty-three days it fought the Germans before the surviving remnant was forced to surrender. All this time the Russian army stood outside the city and made no effort to assist, although Soviet spokesmen had urged the Poles to try to seize the city.

At the Yalta Conference, the best that Roosevelt and Churchill could achieve was a promise from Stalin that the Lublin group would be expanded to include a few members of the Polish government in London and that free elections would be held later.[1] From the start, the Communists interfered with rival political parties. Stanislaw Mikolajczyk, the Peasants' party leader who had been premier of the government in exile in London and who undoubtedly had the support of a great majority of his countrymen, found his

[1] See pages 971-972.

political meetings broken up and thousands of his followers jailed by the Communist-dominated police. Under these conditions, it was not surprising that the Communists were able to claim a victory in the elections. In October, 1947, Mikolajczyk abandoned the unequal struggle and fled from Poland, leaving that unhappy country firmly in Communist hands.

Ex-President Beneš headed the Czechoslovakian government in exile. Since he had always been friendly to the Russians, they permitted him, after the German withdrawal, to establish a coalition government, which included Communists. Free elections were held in May, 1946, in which the Communists won 38 per cent of the votes, twice as many as any other party. Klement Gottwald, a Communist, became head of a coalition cabinet. Until the summer of 1947, the coalition functioned satisfactorily despite some friction, but thereafter the Communists became more openly undemocratic. The minister of the interior was found to be appointing an exceptionally large number of Communists to the police force as a preliminary move to ensure victory in the elections scheduled for the summer of 1948. When Gottwald refused to act, most of the democratic members of the cabinet resigned in the expectation that Beneš would ask a non-Communist to form a new coalition cabinet which would exclude the Communists and that the democratic parties would win the elections. Communist workers paraded in the streets, and toughs beat up opposition leaders. The army proclaimed its neutrality, and the Communist-controlled radio and press defended the action of their leaders. Sick and tired, Beneš gave way as he had done earlier before the threats of Hitler, and Gottwald was permitted to form a new Communist-dominated cabinet. Jan Masaryk, son of Czechoslovakia's first president and a world-renowned democrat, remained as foreign minister, but on March 10, 1948, he fell from a window to his death. The official explanation of his mishap was suicide, but foul play seems more likely. Under these circumstances, the Communists won an overwhelming victory in the elections in May. Beneš resigned and died a few months later. Czechoslovakia, the most democratic of the east European countries, was firmly in the hands of the Communists.

Young King Michael of Rumania had courageously overthrown the fascist regime in his country, formed a coalition government that included the Communists, and declared war on Germany in August, 1944. Russian troops entered Rumania to help drive out the Germans and then remained to insist that the Communists be given a greater voice in the government. By the end of 1947, the popular Michael had joined the ranks of the kings in exile, and Rumania had fallen completely under Communist control. The presence of Russian troops proved equally decisive in the Communist triumph in Bulgaria and Hungary at about the same time.

Only in Albania and Yugoslavia were the Communists able to come to power without the sheltering influence of the Russian army. Their success in Albania may be explained by the backward state of the country and the lack of serious opposition. In Yugoslavia, Joseph Broz (1892-   ), better known as Marshal Tito, and a strong nationalistic Communist movement proved the deciding factors. In the early days of the German occupation, the principal resistance leader had been the pro-Western monarchist, Colonel Drazka Mikailovich, but Tito soon mustered a larger, more warlike following. When Mikailovich saw that the Germans were certain to be defeated and that opposition to the Germans only caused them to butcher Yugoslav patriots, he began to devote most of his energies to fighting his Communist rival, who he thought was the greater threat to his country's future. Unfortunately for him, the British, who were at the moment more interested in defeating the Germans than in the character of the postwar Yugoslav government, decided to send supplies to the aggressive Tito. Tito was thus able to emerge as master of the country when the Germans were driven out, and the equally patriotic Mikailovich was tried and executed for treason.

In Eastern Europe, only Finland and Greece managed to escape communist domination. The Finns' well-proven fighting ability was enough to convince the Russians that the costs of conquest would be greater than the fruits of victory. The Greeks owe their present position in the democratic ranks to the British decision to intervene in 1944. Stalin stood aside while the British won some initial victories, because he had agreed to permit Greece to fall into their sphere of influence in return for comparable concessions in Rumania and Bulgaria. Yugoslav, Bulgarian, and Greek Communists, however, kept up the fight, and the war-weary British had to withdraw. At this point, the Americans took their place. Money was provided to equip the Greek army and to modernize industry. Military and economic experts were dispatched to give technical advice. As a result the Communist rebellion was suppressed, and industrial and agricultural production soared well beyond pre-war levels. The Communists continued to poll some votes, but the monarchy was restored and a relatively stable cabinet system of government established.

For a brief period, central and western Europe seemed nearly as threatened by the communist specter as eastern Europe. The Germans, who had so long served as a check on Russia's expansive tendencies towards the west, were prostrate. In nearly every country, bridges and factories had been destroyed and cities laid in ruins. The transportation system was not even adequate to bring food to the urban centers, and these centers were for the moment incapable of producing the railroads and engines necessary for its repair. Many members of the upper classes had lost their influence because they were tainted by collaboration with fascism, while the Communist party was in a position to capitalize on the revived patriotism because its members had made use of their training in subversive activities to play leading parts in the resistance movement. Postwar problems and patriotism thereby combined to give the Communists a wider following than ever before. In conjunction with Socialists and other left-wing parties, they formed blocs similar to the popular fronts of the 1930's, except that this

985

time they were willing—even anxious—for their members to accept cabinet posts. Labor unions fell largely into their control. In 1946, France, Italy, and Belgium seemed almost as close to becoming Communist as some of the countries of eastern Europe. Indeed, the absence of the Russian army may have been the most decisive factor in saving them from the fate of Poland and Hungary.

Capitalism seemed everywhere abandoned. Together, the Socialist and Communist parties, both Marxist, came close to receiving a majority of the votes in several countries. The Catholic Church, once the citadel of conservatism, now supported political parties that were socialistic in a non-Marxian sense. Advocates of nationalization of key industries and economic planning were almost everywhere in the majority. The welfare state in which every adult was guaranteed a job when he was well, free medical aid when he was sick, a pension when he retired, and a special family allowance if he had many children became the acknowledged goal of most people. The old laissez-faire liberalism did indeed seem dead. The future seemed to lie with communism or socialism.

THE EXPANSION OF COMMUNISM IN ASIA

The communist advances in Asia were as important as in Europe. In less than five years after the war, China, with over one-fifth of the population of the globe, was brought within the communist orbit, and notable progress was made elsewhere. Many of the same factors that had worked for communist advances in Europe did likewise in Asia. Poverty was acute, and Russian economic advances pointed to a possible cure for the sufferings of the masses. The old order was often discredited, and the Japanese, who had halted Russian advances for decades, had been crushed by the triumphant Americans. Roosevelt had incorrectly assumed that Chiang Kai-shek and the Kuomintang would emerge from the war in firm control of China and in a position to replace Japan in its historic role of checking the Russians. At Roosevelt's insistence, China had been recognized as a great power and given a permanent seat in the Security Council of the United Nations.

The events leading to the Communist triumph in China may be described in terms of the mistakes made by Chiang Kai-shek and the Kuomintang party and in terms of the astute policy followed by the Communist leader, Mao Tse-tung (1893-   ). After overthrowing the monarchy, Dr. Sun Yat-sen and the Kuomintang had set out to achieve three objectives: democracy, nationalism, and livelihood (economic betterment). The second, nationalism, was largely obtained by the defeat of the Japanese in 1945 and the removal of most of the special privileges enjoyed by Europeans in China; but the other two, democracy and livelihood, seemed further than ever from attainment. Sun had recognized that the Chinese people were too poor and ignorant to permit the immediate establishment of a

986

democratic form of government, and he had anticipated a period of tutelage in which the Kuomintang would educate the masses and improve their economic lot. Unfortunately, after Sun's death the Kuomintang was reluctant to move towards democracy. Its leaders, who were often men of means, were still more reluctant to introduce economic reforms that would threaten their privileged position. This was especially true after 1927, when Chiang expelled the Communists and became too dependent on the landlord-merchant class to institute economic reforms or enforce honesty in government.[2] Gradually, the Kuomintang changed from a revolutionary party dedicated to improving the lot of the masses to a conservative oligarchy dedicated to maintaining the status quo. The few reforms that were enacted, such as a measure limiting the landlord's share of the tenant farmer's sales to 37.5 per cent, were not enforced. Corruption and inefficiency became as characteristic of the Kuomintang regime as it had been of the emperors. The long Japanese war permitted the warlords to act with greater independence and led to rampant inflation. All these developments made the lot of the masses worse and led to the triumph of Mao Tse-tung.

Mao was a university librarian when he joined the Communist party in 1921. He quickly saw that China was not sufficiently industrialized for a revolutionary program to be based successfully on the proletariat. He therefore turned his attention to the peasantry, and by advocating agrarian reform he won their support. With this support he built a well-trained, indoctrinated army and sought political power. In 1935 Mao established his regime in the northwest provinces of China where he introduced moderate agrarian reforms based more on rent and credit control than confiscation of the landlords' property. Other political parties were permitted to operate; free elections were held; and dishonest, incompetent officials were removed from office. To many, the Communists appeared to be the true successors of Sun Yat-sen, and the Kuomintang seemed to have betrayed his cause. Western observers, including some American State Department officials and newspaper men, began to regard the Chinese Communists as agrarian reformers. Mao's ultimate objective, however, never changed although even Stalin appeared to doubt his orthodoxy, or at least his capacity to win. Between 1937 and 1941, Stalin gave military assistance to the Kuomintang; and in 1945, when Chiang recognized the concessions Roosevelt had granted Russia at Yalta, Stalin again accepted the Kuomintang as China's legal government. Russian troops were withdrawn from Manchuria, taking with them all the factory machinery that they could move. Clearly they did not plan to return soon, although they did retire in a way that facilitated the occupation of most of Manchuria by Mao's army. Thus, by 1946 Mao was well entrenched in the north and enjoying considerable popular support in all parts of China.

Between 1945 and 1947, General George C. Marshall headed an American mission to arrange a compromise between the Communists and the

[2] See page 733.

987

Kuomintang. Mutual suspicion and confidence of victory by the members of both parties led to the failure of his mission. Late in 1946, Chiang decided to embark in a war against the Communists. His armies outnumbered their opponents three to one. Thirty-nine of his divisions were American-trained and largely American-equipped. The Communists had received little aid from Russia, and the Russians had promised not to interfere. Understandably, Chiang felt confident. His regime, however, had lost popular support. Many of his generals were as corrupt and inefficient as his bureaucracy. By mid-1947, his attack had been halted, and the Communists had begun to march southward. Peking and Tientsin fell in January, 1949, and Shanghai was taken that spring with scarcely a blow offered in its defense. By 1950 only Formosa and some neighboring islands remained in Chiang's hands. During the last year of the war, neither he nor his followers exhibited a will to resist.

The loss of China led to bitter attacks against Truman's Asiatic policy in the United States.[3] Most critics failed to see the obvious, namely, that Chiang was defeated because he had lost the confidence of the Chinese people. On the other hand, State Department officials misjudged the character of the Chinese Communist movement, and the cooperation they sought to achieve between Mao and Chiang had no chance of success. Only large-scale American military and economic assistance could have saved Chiang, and this the majority of the American people were unwilling to provide until it was too late. Failure to act more boldly, however, may have been a costly mistake, because if Chiang's control over part of China could have been maintained, the Korean War would probably not have taken place, and the rest of Asia would now be more secure from communism.

At first the Chinese proceeded gradually with the nationalization of the means of production; but after the adoption of the first five-year plan in 1953, they accelerated the process. The plan called for doubling the industrial output and improving transportation facilities at the expense of consumer goods. A 23 per cent increase in agricultural productivity was also sought. To achieve this goal, 125,000,000 rural households were organized into 750,000 collective farms, agricultural techniques were improved, wastelands were cultivated, and extensive irrigation projects were undertaken. As a result, the gross national product increased at a rate of at least 7 or 8 per cent annually, or about four times as fast as that of India and faster than anywhere else in Asia except Japan.

The success of the first five-year plan caused the Communists to throw caution to the winds and embark on a "great leap forward" in 1958. This time more attention was paid to agriculture, because there was a limited amount of arable land in China. The already huge population had increased by 65,000,000 during the first five-year plan and was expected to reach the billion mark in the 1980's. To secure the desired goals, the collective farms were consolidated into 26,000 communes of about 5,000 fami-

[3] See page 1000.

The Big Three of the People's Republic of China in 1947: left to right, Chou En-lai, Mao Tse-tung, and Chu Teh. (Charles Phelps Cushing)

lies each. Each commune was organized along military lines, which sent companies of workers out to farm, to work in rural industries, or to engage in other activities. Communal living, like collective labor, was practiced as far as possible. Meals were eaten in mess halls, and nurseries were provided for children so that the women could work beside the men. In short, family life, which traditionally had been so powerful in China, was to come to an end, and communal life, which was heralded as the first step from socialism to communism, was to take its place.

It is still too early to evaluate the Chinese experiment. The initial Communist claims after the inauguration of the "great leap forward" were fantastic, but considerable progress does appear to have been made during the first two years of the program. In 1960-1962, however, natural calamities led to bad harvests; the effort to develop small rural iron and steel industries admittedly failed; and industrial output fell to the 1957 or 1958 level. Since 1962 the Chinese have been unable to restore their earlier rate of economic growth, but if they do succeed in industrializing, a tremendous impetus will be given to the expansion of communism among the Asiatic people, to whom poverty has been a way of life for centuries.

Once in power Mao began to transform China into a totalitarian state closely modeled after Russia. The warlords who had plagued so many regimes were reduced to obedience. Opposition in China proper was vigorously suppressed, and even far-off, autonomous Tibet was reduced to the stature of a province. Education was improved to train technicians and to indoctrinate the people, taxes were collected more efficiently, inflation was better controlled than ever before, and in October, 1964, the Chinese joined the nuclear powers by exploding an atomic bomb.

The communists' second largest postwar territorial gain in Asia was made at the expense of Korea. The World War II victors had decided that Korea should be given its independence "in due course," but meanwhile they had divided the country into zones of occupation. Russia assumed responsibility for the land north of the 38th parallel, and the United States served in the same capacity in the land to the south. The United States permitted Syngman Rhee (1875-1965), an aged, conservative nationalist, to organize a republic in its zone, and the Russians established a communist state in theirs. Both powers withdrew their troops in 1948-1949, but neither they nor the Koreans could agree on any of the proposed plans of unification.

Even in areas far removed from the Russian armies, the communists made advances. The poverty and ignorance of backward peoples of the world played into their hands. Nearly everywhere, poor tenant farmers readily listened to communist proposals that their landlords be dispossessed for their benefit. The democracies, with their belief in property rights, had difficulty offering comparable expectations. As the chief imperial powers, they were constantly charged with economic exploitation. Their medical science kept many from dying, but the resulting population growth negated part of their efforts to improve the standard of living because increased productivity had to be used to feed additional mouths. Too often the democracies delayed so long in granting independence to their colonies that the communists were able to capitalize on the natives' desire for independence. There were communist-led revolts in Burma, Malaya, the Philippines, Indo-China, where they achieved partial success, and many other places. The Arab world, Africa, and Latin America became subject to increased communist activity. Thus, the revolt against imperialism that had begun years before became involved in the struggle for world supremacy.

THE RISE OF KHRUSHCHEV

Stalin died during the first week of March, 1953, at a moment when he seemed to be planning a new purge of the top leaders in his government. The circumstances that surrounded his death and the simultaneous disappearance of some of his closest associates suggest the possibility that he was murdered before he had a chance to murder fellow Communists. Whatever the cause of his death, an era had come to an end, and the world waited with interest to see how a Communist dictatorship would govern itself after the dictator was gone.

Georgy Malenkov (1902-   ) was the most likely heir, and he immediately became both senior party secretary and chairman of the Council of Ministers. He had spent most of his career as a Communist party official, but he was thought to draw the bulk of his support from the bureaucracy. It seemed obvious that Stalin had intended him to be his successor, although there were signs that he was losing favor the month before the dictator died. Of nearly equal importance were Lavrenty Beria (1899-1953), chief of the secret police, who had almost certainly been on Stalin's list of those to be purged, and Vyacheslav Molotov (1890-   ), long-time foreign minister

Joseph Stalin's funeral: front to rear, left, Malenkov, Vasily Stalin (son of Joseph Stalin), Molotov, Bulganin, Kaganovich, and Shvernik. Beria leads pallbearers on the right. (Sovfoto)

and the only one of the three who displayed any grief at Stalin's funeral. There was apparently a strong desire for collective leadership rather than one-man rule. To satisfy this desire, Malenkov was quickly forced to surrender the senior party secretaryship to Khrushchev, a significant defeat because it was the power that the dead dictator had wielded through this post that had enabled him to triumph over Trotsky years before.

For four years after Stalin's death, there was a period of collective leadership that was made necessary by the inability of any member of the Soviet hierarchy to assume a dominant position, but it was also facilitated by the XIX Communist party Congress which had met in 1952. Under Stalin's direction this Congress had increased the size of the Central Committee, the Politburo which became known as the Presidium, and the Secretariat. As a result, the new Soviet leaders inherited a system of party control that was somewhat more broadly based than before. Some of these institutions were later reduced in size, but decisions began to be made by balloting rather than by one man as in Stalin's day.

During the period of collective leadership, each of the potential leaders tried to strengthen his position. Malenkov courted favor with the bureaucracy, which included the managerial class in industry as well as those who held administrative posts, by promising more consumer goods. Beria, of all people, attacked police methods and talked of the need to have a new criminal code and to protect the rights of citizens. Khrushchev quietly strengthened his hold over the Communist party and noisily spoke of plans to increase agricultural production.

There was a general relaxation of tension in the communist world, but not in the Soviet hierarchy. The first to fall was Beria, who may have been murdered when he tried to take power during a meeting of the Presidium in the summer of 1953. Whatever the occasion, he and his principal followers were liquidated. The power of the secret police was lessened, and its control was entrusted to a committee rather than to an individual.

Gradually, Khrushchev emerged as the most powerful figure in the Soviet regime. In February, 1955, he forced Malenkov to resign as chairman of the Council of Ministers, but he was not then strong enough to remove him from the Presidium. Nicholas Bulganin (1895-   ) was elevated from the defense ministry to the chairmanship, and an army hero, Marshal Georgy Zhukov (1894-   ), was given the defense department. The following year Khrushchev took one of the most curious steps in his rise to power by bitterly denouncing Stalin and the "cult of personality" he had fostered at the expense of collective leadership. At the same time, Khrushchev defended the basic objectives of the Communist party. Probably he was seeking the support of those who had hated the Stalinist regime and suspected that rule by the Communist party which he now headed would inevitably involve dictatorship. At any rate Khrushchev stigmatized Malenkov and his other opponents as "anti-party" men.

The crisis came in June, 1957, over a question of economic organization. Malenkov actually won by a seven to four vote in the Presidium, but Khrushchev carried the matter to the Central Committee of the party where he was victorious. Malenkov and Molotov were immediately removed from office; and Bulganin, who had sided with them, was ousted the following year. Khrushchev's victory seems to have been achieved in part because of the assistance he received from Zhukov, but once the "anti-party" element was disposed of he demoted the marshal. In this manner, he and the Communist party reduced the possibility that the army and bureaucracy, where a large, educated élite class had come into being, would contend for power. Either because he was more humane than Stalin or because he was not strong enough to do otherwise, Khrushchev gave the defeated leaders minor government posts, generally in Siberia.

992

This 53-foot statue of Stalin stands on a structure 110 feet high situated on a hill overlooking the city of Erevan, capital of the Armenian S.S.R. Constructed immediately after World War II when most of the Russian people were living in misery, it provides a conspicuous example of the "cult of personality" which Stalin fostered at the expense of collective leadership.

THE KHRUSHCHEV ERA

During the Malenkov era, the Soviet Union had relaxed its control over scientific and cultural pursuits and had encouraged the east European states to follow its example. Some Stalinists were removed from office, the production of consumer goods was emphasized, and more intellectual liberty was permitted. In foreign policy, tensions were relaxed, and the Korean and Indo-Chinese wars were brought to an end.[4]

When Khrushchev emerged as the leading Communist in 1955, there was a visible tightening of the reins of government at home and an attempt was made to exert leadership over the worldwide communist movement. On the other hand, no effort was made to return to the brutal methods of Stalin, whom Khrushchev continued to denounce to show how different he was from his hated predecessor. The secret police was less in evidence and the concentration camps were almost emptied. A degree of liberty was permitted, cultural exchanges with foreign countries were encouraged, foreign tourists were allowed to travel in Russia, and a few Russian scholars were allowed to go abroad for professional purposes. However, there was a definite limit to this freedom, and when Boris Pasternak (1890-1960) was offered the Nobel Prize in 1958 for *Doctor Zhivago*, a novel which was critical of communism, he was advised to reject the honor.

The Communist party continued to dominate the government. When Khrushchev came to power, it consisted of about 7,000,000 members, or 3 per cent of the population. As few Communists were old enough to remember the tsarist regime or had traveled abroad except with the armed forces, they knew no other life and were probably content to follow the directions of the party leaders. They and the educated non-party technicians were the élite of Russian society and were given special privileges to ensure their loyalty. Included were radios, refrigerators, comfortable living accommodations, and a number of other things available to the skilled laborers in the United States. In Soviet Russia, however, such possessions set them apart from the toiling masses whose lot was not greatly improved by the growth of Soviet heavy industry. In this manner, the Soviet Union is producing a bureaucratic and professional class whose aspirations may in some respects be comparable to those of the middle class in Western states. What ultimate effect the existence of such a class will have on the communist experiment is impossible to say, but to date there is no avowed deviation from Marxist-Leninist ideology.

The periodic elections that were held in Soviet Russia provided no indication of the real opinions of the inhabitants because only the names of the official candidates appeared on the ballot. Over 99 per cent of the population dutifully voted, but they had a choice of putting the ballot directly into the box to signify approval or of retiring to a booth and scratching out the

[4] See pages 1006-1007 and 1039-1040.

Nikita S. Khrushchev addressing the Central Committee of the Communist party in November, 1962, before he was deposed as premier. Front row, left to right: Aleksei Kosygin, who was to succeed Khrushchev as premier; Leonid Brezhnev, who was to replace Khrushchev as first secretary of the party; Khrushchev himself; Koslov; and Suslov. (Sovfoto)

name of the candidate, an action the authorities might interpret as an indication of disloyalty. As a result, approval of the official candidates was virtually unanimous.

Khrushchev continued Stalin's emphasis on the development of heavy industry and gave only slightly more attention to consumer goods, although some concessions to popular demand may be seen in an expanded apartment construction program and in the continued effort to produce more food. Both agricultural and industrial production plans have been changed frequently in recent years, which suggests that they have not been completely successful. However, the Russians achieved world leadership in space research. By 1957, they had intercontinental ballistic missiles that promised to antiquate the American strategic air force. In 1958, they launched the first earth satellite; in 1959, they shot a rocket around the moon to photograph the other side; and in 1961, they sent Major Yuri Gagarin on a manned space flight around the earth. These triumphs increased Russian prestige throughout the world, but they did not prevent difficulties with other communist-controlled states.

The establishment of communism in eastern Europe in the late 1940's did little to solve the problems of the inhabitants of that region. The chronic overpopulation in rural areas continued, the collectivization of

995

agriculture was unpopular, and the productivity of workers remained low despite more rapid industrialization. The result was continued poverty that was aggravated by the Russian practice of subordinating the eastern Europeans' interests to their own. This situation, coupled with the continuance of strong national feelings, caused widespread discontent. During Stalin's lifetime, local Communist leaders who protested against Russian exploitation or who tried to follow their own course were removed from office and often executed. The one exception to this rule was Yugoslavia's Tito. Stalin tried to remove him from power in 1948 because of the independent stand he had taken in several matters, but the absence of Russian troops in Yugoslavia and Tito's firm control over the party, bureaucracy, and military forces of his country enabled him to maintain his position.

On coming to power Khrushchev denounced the strict regimentation of the eastern European states as Stalinist in the hope of quieting popular discontent there and opening the way for renewed cooperation with Tito. In regard to Tito, he was partly successful, for although the Yugoslavian leader made it clear that he had no intention of surrendering his independent status, ties between Yugoslavia and other communist states were strengthened.

Khrushchev, however, could do nothing to quiet popular discontent. There were serious riots among workers in East Germany, Czechoslovakia, and other countries. The Poles and Hungarians were especially anxious to take a more independent, nationalist course. In October, 1956, Wladislaw Gomulka (1905-   ), a Communist with well-known Titoist tendencies, won control of Poland with the backing of the communist labor unions. Aided by Catholic leaders who saw that a moderate, nationalistic Communist prime minister was the best that Poland could hope for, he prevented violent anti-Russian demonstrations and was allowed to remain in power.

The story in Hungary was more tragic. There Imre Nagy, another nationalist-minded Communist, was raised to power at about the same time as Gomulka as a result of huge demonstrations in Budapest organized by university students and workers. For a few days, it seemed that the popular demand for free speech and free elections might be fulfilled. Hungarian leaders officially expressed their desire to abandon the Soviet camp and assume a neutral position in the struggle for world supremacy. This was unacceptable to Russia, and on November 4, 1956, the Soviet army struck. Thousands were killed in the streets; additional thousands fled to the West. Nagy was arrested treacherously, and the ironclad Soviet regime was imposed once more. Khrushchev had retained control over eastern Europe, but the spectacle of workers protesting in Poznan, Warsaw, Budapest, and elsewhere cannot have made a government that claimed to rely on the proletariat feel more secure.

More serious from the standpoint of the strength and unity of the communist movement was the quarrel that began in 1957 between Khrushchev and Mao. Personal and national rivalries were undoubtedly factors in the

996

dispute, but the debate centered on the interpretation of communist dogma. To Khrushchev war between the communist and capitalist states was not inevitable; indeed the development of nuclear weapons made it imperative that armed conflict be avoided. International tensions should be relaxed a little, and a period of peaceful coexistence should be inaugurated. This did not mean that Khrushchev had abandoned the goal of world communism; rather he hoped to achieve it through the supposed superiority of the communist economic system. By 1970, he promised that Russian per capita production would exceed that of the United States. As the communist economy grew stronger and the capitalistic economy weaker, a bloodless victory would be achieved.

To Mao and his fellow Chinese this was revisionism, and like the revisionism of the late nineteenth century it would turn Marxism into an evolutionary reform movement. The Chinese believed that wars with the imperialistic powers were inevitable and that there was no need to fear the United States, a country they described as a "paper tiger." Indeed, violent revolutions should be promoted throughout the world, regardless of the hazards.

In 1960 the quarrel became so bitter that the Russians unilaterally broke a 1957 treaty in which they had promised to provide Peking with assistance in building atomic bombs. By 1964 a point had been reached in which a permanent split in the communist movement appeared probable, with party members in other countries having to choose between one or the other of the two camps. This opportunity to choose enabled communist states such as Rumania to play China off against the Soviet Union and thereby adopt a slightly more independent course.

Seriously concerned by this state of affairs, the Central Committee of the Soviet Union's Communist party voted in October, 1964, to oust Khrushchev. Other factors, such as his failure to solve the agricultural problem and his crude behavior, contributed to his fall, as did the perennial struggle for power in the Kremlin. Indeed, one of the charges brought against Khrushchev was that he was reviving the "cult of personality" with himself as the central figure, and the most obvious result of his fall was a return to collective leadership as in the months immediately after Stalin's death. Khrushchev's posts of chairman of the Council of Ministers and senior secretary of the Communist party were given to Aleksei Kosygin and Leonid Brezhnev rather than to a single man. Efforts were made to prevent a complete break with Communist China, but for the time being, at least, few other major changes in policy were anticipated.

In spite of continued problems the Russians have achieved a great deal. In two decades they have recovered from the war, increased their productive capacity, developed a nuclear capability, taken an early lead in space research, and, most difficult of all, changed their leadership without civil war. If the unity of the communist movement was threatened, it was only because that movement had spread so far and achieved such great successes.

997

THE AMERICAN REACTION

At the end of the war, the United States was the most powerful nation the world had ever seen. Its industrial might was fully geared to war production, and no other country could challenge its position in the air or on the seas. In the field of scientific warfare, Americans alone had the capacity to make atomic bombs, although for the moment none were in stock. Russia's armies were superior in number, but they were inferior in equipment. As a result, the United States could have imposed its will on the Soviet Union in 1945 if it had kept its military forces intact and had been willing to risk war. However, nothing was further from the typical American's mind. He had learned to admire the Russians during the war and had been persuaded that co-operation with the Communists after the war was possible. He wanted to disband the armed forces, reconvert factories to produce for civilian needs, and return to "normalcy." Only when Russia's expansionist policies became so obvious that they could no longer be denied was the American citizen willing to accept the responsibilities that went with world leadership and to support an aggressive foreign policy.

THE DOMESTIC SCENE: TRUMAN

The task of leading the United States during the postwar era fell to Harry S. Truman (1884-   ). Truman had served in the Senate for ten years before becoming Vice President in January, 1945, and President in April when Roosevelt died after a long period of declining health. He had few apparent qualifications for this office. Neither his formal education nor his experience suggested that he could cope with the difficult problems before the nation. He seemed more like the average American than the successor of the almost legendary Roosevelt. Indeed, in some respects he was a little less than average because of an unfortunate tendency to indulge in petty personal disputes with those who displeased him and to defend his friends blindly at the cost of lowering the dignity of his office and the effectiveness of his leadership. Nevertheless, his understanding of American history and traditions, his deep compassion for those in difficulty, whether farmer, laborer, or Negro, and his great courage enabled him to deal satisfactorily with the many serious problems that confronted his administration. During his years in the White House, the New Deal was revived and expanded, civil rights were strengthened, and foreign policy was reoriented to halt the advance of communism and to induce prosperity in other parts of the world.

The two most important domestic issues which confronted the nation in 1945 involved reconversion to a civilian economy and the role the government should play in internal affairs. The mighty American military machine was rapidly dismantled as a result of popular demand to bring the soldiers back from the far corners of the world. By midsummer of 1946, there were only 1,500,000 men in the army. Truman's request for legislation to establish universal military training aroused little support. In 1950, the American army was limited to 600,000 men.

The returning veterans were treated far better than their World War I counterparts. Both parties joined in passing a Servicemen's Readjustment Act which provided educational opportunities and numerous other benefits to help veterans resume their places in society. In 1950, its cost exceeded nine billion dollars, more than the entire annual budget during the New Deal era, but the results were beneficial both to the veterans themselves and to the economy as a whole. Without some form of assistance, millions of veterans might not have been able to find suitable employment, and widespread unemployment might have led to a depression.

The transition from price control and rationing to a free economy was handled much less effectively. Truman was willing to end rationing as fast as possible, but he was anxious to keep wage and price controls until industry was able to meet long-denied consumer demands. When the Congress passed a weaker price control bill than he desired, he angrily vetoed it; and effective price controls came to an end on July 1, 1946.

At the same time, laborers, who found that their take-home pay was less because of a reduction in overtime work, demanded raises to compensate. Business leaders refused, and there was a series of strikes in the most important industries. Labor unions had become so strong under the New Deal that they were able to win most of their demands. On the other hand, scarcity and near monopolistic conditions permitted basic industries to raise prices as fast as desired. The result was a wage-price spiral in which both industry and labor profited at the expense of those with relatively fixed incomes. Price and wage controls had prevented the cost of living from increasing significantly during the height of the war, but the removal of controls was followed by a price rise of over 25 per cent in two years. Farmers were especially hurt by the increased cost of industrial goods, for after the restoration of peace, prices on their products began to decline because of increased agricultural production in Europe. Despite these difficulties, however, the United States rapidly converted to a peacetime economy without experiencing the widespread unemployment or the return of the depression that many had predicted.

During the immediate postwar period, several important nonpartisan pieces of legislation were passed. One act created the Atomic Energy Commission, which preserved the governmental monopoly in the production of fissionable materials. A second act called for a Department of Defense to reduce the jealous competition and wasteful duplication that had characterized the armed services when they had each maintained separate departments. Most important of all was the establishment of a nonpartisan Council of Economic Advisers to study the economy and to advise the President and the Congress. Those appointed to the council were economists, not politicians, who sought to guide the economy through the control of credit and interest rates accompanied by increased government spending during periods of recession, as Lord Keynes had advocated. The results

999

have been spectacularly successful, and during the two decades following the war the United States has enjoyed a remarkable period of economic growth and prosperity. There is hope that capitalistic society has finally found a cure for the boom and bust cycle that had so plagued it in the past and on which the communists have counted so heavily to help bring about world revolution.

More controversial was the question of whether the New Deal legislation should be left intact or whether the government should enact further measures. Truman took a strong stand in favor of the latter course. Hardly had the Japanese surrendered before he sent to the Congress his "Fair Deal" program. It called for raising minimum wages from forty to sixty-five cents an hour, full employment, and an expansion of Social Security. Slums were to be cleared, natural resources were to be protected, and public works like the St. Lawrence Seaway were to be authorized. Federal aid to education and a health insurance program were also requested. A new approach to the problem of farm surpluses was offered, and a strong civil rights program was advocated.

Unfortunately for Truman, the Republicans recaptured control of the Congress in 1946 and refused to enact his program. He got partial revenge by winning a second term in the presidential election of 1948; but during the four years that followed, a coalition of Republicans and conservative southern Democrats blocked most of the Fair Deal program. Little besides the extension of Social Security, a higher minimum wage law, and a modest slum clearance and federal housing law was passed.

By this time, the seriousness of the Russian threat was generally recognized. Some Republicans, like Senator Joseph McCarthy (1908-1957) of Wisconsin, sought to explain American setbacks by declaring that numerous Communists were high in the councils of the Democratic regime. He produced no evidence to substantiate his wild charges, but enough espionage activity was uncovered by competent investigators to cause grave concern. Several instances of corruption and many cases of unethical conduct were also found. The press and the Republicans began to talk of little save the "mess in Washington." These circumstances, taken with the Korean War, made probable a Republican victory in the election of 1952. To remove any doubt, the Republicans passed over the old party stalwart, Senator Robert A. Taft, and nominated popular General Dwight D. Eisenhower. They were not disappointed. Eisenhower won a sweeping victory over the Democratic candidate, Adlai E. Stevenson (1900-1965), and the Republicans captured control of both houses of Congress by narrow margins.

EISENHOWER, KENNEDY, AND JOHNSON

Neither the Democratic forecasts of doom nor the Republican forecasts of foreign and domestic triumphs were confirmed by the eight-year Eisenhower regime. Eisenhower described himself as a moderate Republican. As one, he preserved nearly all the New Deal and Fair Deal social legislation. Indeed, in several areas he made notable additions to the earlier programs. Social Security was expanded, and some federal aid was provided for education. A ten-year highway building program was inaugurated whose estimated cost of twenty-five billion dollars dwarfed all of Roosevelt's and Truman's projects. Federal aid was granted to support scientific research, and a civil rights bill was passed to protect Negro voting. By clever manipulation of currency and credit controls, taxes, and government spending as suggested in the Keynesian theory, the boom and bust cycle that had so plagued the American economy was avoided.

On the other hand, the business leaders Eisenhower summoned to Washington to advise him added little to the efficiency of the government. Taxes were reduced slightly, primarily to the benefit of corporations and the well-to-do, but several serious budget deficits followed. The total deficit of Eisenhower's eight years in the White House was far greater than Truman's, in spite of several decades of Republican protests against excess spending. The farm problem remained unsolved despite huge federal expenditures, and questionable concessions were made to private power and oil interests. More serious, insufficient effort was made to meet the Russian challenge in the fields of education, space science, and foreign affairs.

The feeling that the United States was not moving forward fast enough coupled with the campaign mistakes of Vice-President Richard Nixon (1913-   ), the Republican standard-bearer, enabled the Democrats to win the election of November, 1960. The new president, John F. Kennedy (1917-1963), was the youngest man ever elected to occupy the White House and the first of the Roman Catholic faith. His brilliant mind and the high cultural tone that he and his wife set for the Washington scene quickly endeared him to intellectuals, while his youthful vigor made him popular with most other Americans, although the presumption and powerful ambition that he and his brothers occasionally displayed alienated some people. He was successful in reducing tariffs and in obtaining increased sums for national defense and foreign aid, but many of his more controversial proposals had not passed Congress when he was assassinated in November, 1963, by a mentally unbalanced ex-marine with Communist connections.

The Vice President, Lyndon B. Johnson (1908-   ), immediately assumed the presidency and proceeded to carry out many of the unfinished aspects of the Kennedy program. He lacked his predecessor's intellectual attainments, but this was compensated for by his great gifts as a politician. To a surprising degree, he managed to win the confidence of management and labor, as well as white Southerners and Negroes. As a result, he was able to get a strong civil rights bill passed guaranteeing Negroes the use of hotels and other public accommodations and providing for fair employment practices. Federal aid to education was increased, and less controversial legislation was enacted reducing corporate and personal income taxes in the hope of stimulating more rapid economic growth. His success ensured his

Renewed ties between the Bonn government in Germany and the West were symbolized by Chancellor Adenauer's visit to Washington in 1961. He is greeted here by President John F. Kennedy in the White House. (Wide World)

nomination by the Democrats to run for another term and led to an overwhelming victory over his conservative Republican opponent in November, 1964.

In retrospect, the critical period of the postwar era was in the Truman administration. His decision to consolidate and slowly expand New Deal social and economic legislation was carried on by his successors whether Republican or Democrat. By the middle of the century, the economy had become "mixed" in the sense that neither business nor labor, banking nor agriculture was dominant. It was a free-enterprise economy in that private persons owned and operated most of the means of production. It was a welfare state in that many services were performed by federal and state governments. It was a planned economy in that elaborate statistics were gathered and interpreted by expert economists who advised the government on when and how to stimulate or check the economy as Lord Keynes had suggested between the two wars.

THE SUPREME COURT

Outside the realm of economics, American society was probably shaped more by the Supreme Court than by either the President or Congress. In 1953, President Eisenhower appointed the California governor, Earl Warren (1891-   ), Chief Justice of the Supreme Court. Warren and his associates abandoned the belief of most of their predecessors that judges should interpret the law in accordance with the intent of the lawmakers and adopted the loose-construction theory that it should be interpreted in the light of current concepts of justice. Using this approach they handed down a series of decisions whose importance has been equaled only by those issued during the tenure of John Marshall.[5] In general, the Supreme Court acted to ensure liberty, equality, and democracy for all citizens.

The most important single decision resulted from the *Brown versus Board of Education of Topeka* case in which it was decreed in 1954 that public school segregation was unconstitutional even when "separate but equal" facilities were provided. Non-Southern and border states that had practiced some segregation immediately moved to comply with the ruling, but many Southern states vigorously resisted. Within ten years, however, Negroes had won admission to public schools in every state in the Union. Some Southern private colleges and universities voluntarily admitted Negroes, Emory and Tulane even going to the extent of getting state laws in Georgia and Louisiana annulled to enable them to take this step. Desegregation proceeded more slowly at primary and secondary school levels in the South, but repeated Supreme Court decisions backed by the authority of the executive branch of the government gave promise that eventual success would be achieved. De facto segregation in many Northern cities also came under attack from the strong Negro movement, and educators are now seeking solutions to this difficult problem.

The Supreme Court furthered the cause of democratic government in several decisions between 1962 and 1964 requiring that seats in both houses of state legislatures be apportioned in accordance with the distribution of the population. In the typical state, there were rapidly growing cities and depopulated rural counties, but the rural legislators had refused to redraw electoral districts to conform to the changing population pattern. As a result, a rural vote might carry ten, twenty, or forty times as much weight as an urban vote. To date the Supreme Court has handed down decisions in only a few specific cases, but when it has acted, it has provoked a political revolution in the state concerned. In 1964, the Supreme Court also ruled that congressional districts had to be substantially equal in population. As a result of these decisions, the influence of rural areas has been reduced, and the cause of democracy and probably better government has been furthered.

A third type of Supreme Court decision has dealt with liberties. These

[5] See page 588.

Action by the Congress and the Supreme Court improving the status of Negroes in the United States resulted largely from the efforts of the Rev. Dr. Martin Luther King, winner of a Nobel Peace Prize, and other Negro leaders. Here Dr. King addresses a crowd of 70,000 at a rally in Chicago's Soldier's Field in June, 1964. (Wide World)

decisions have protected the accused in cases resulting from the efforts of state and federal governments to tighten their loyalty programs. In 1957, the Court ruled that the defendant was entitled to see FBI reports used in his trial, to the discomfiture of that agency, which wanted to keep its sources of information secret. Most controversial of all was the 1963 decision banning state and local regulations requiring that the Lord's Prayer or the Bible be read in public schools.

THE REACTION TO THE RUSSIAN THREAT

When Truman entered the White House, his first reaction was to continue Roosevelt's policy of cooperation with Russia. He began to demobilize American military forces as rapidly as possible, and in November, 1945, he recommended that the United Nations create an International Atomic Development Authority. The Authority, it was hoped, would supervise the development of atomic energy for peaceful purposes and inspect countries throughout the world to see that no atomic bombs were made. The Russians, however, refused to accept this plan, and the international control of atomic energy remains a dream that must eventually be realized if mankind is to survive.

As one instance of Russian intransigence followed another, Truman turned more and more towards a "get tough" policy. The threat created by the presence of Russian troops in Iran at the close of the war was checked by the determined stand taken by the United Nations under American leadership. In the early spring of 1946, the Russians began to withdraw their forces, leaving Iran with both its territorial integrity and its independence.

Indeed, once Truman awakened to the Soviet threat, he tried to move more rapidly than public opinion would permit. In March, 1946, he arranged for Winston Churchill to make a speech at Fulton, Missouri, in which he referred to the "iron curtain" that had descended between democratic and communist Europe. Strength, Churchill declared, was the only thing the Russians respected. Most Americans reacted adversely to this speech, and many protested violently when Truman tried to slow the rate of military demobilization. Slowly, the American people began to awaken to the dangers which threatened the democracies. They continued to refuse to vote sufficient taxes to support an adequate military force or to inaugurate universal military training, but within a few months they were willing to accept most of Truman's program for halting the expansion of communism.

Truman's program was based on the idea of containment. If Russian expansion could be permanently halted, it was hoped that sooner or later there would be internal trouble in the Soviet Union. Perhaps the Soviet system would gradually change and Soviet policies would become less aggressive. Perhaps the younger generation of Communists would lose revolutionary fervor and look forward to a comfortable "middle-class" existence. Perhaps the regime would topple in the struggle for power that would almost certainly follow Stalin's death. The proletariat, it was hoped, would be its own gravedigger, just as Marx had predicted that the bourgeoisie would be. Thus, the United States assumed that time was on its side, just as the Russian Communists had always assumed that it was on theirs. So long as both sides believed this, there was little possibility for a third world war unless someone bungled. Rather it was to be a competition for men's minds, a competition between economic systems to see which could best provide for the material needs of mankind, a "cold war" in which there would be constant international tensions but only minor wars.

To contain Russia indefinitely the United States would have to assume world leadership. It would have to restore economic and political stability to Europe and lead it towards greater unity, raise the standard of living in the underdeveloped parts of the world, and provide military support for those nations threatened by the communists. This, Truman declared on March 12, 1947, the United States was prepared to do. The immediate occasion for the announcement of the Truman Doctrine was the pressure that the Soviet Union was placing on Greece and Turkey, but the concept was soon expanded into a Europe-wide program.

In June, 1947, General George C. Marshall, then Secretary of State, made use of the opportunity offered by a Harvard University commencement address to promise American aid to the associated European states in rebuilding their economy. The Russians refused to participate or to permit their satellites to do so, but sixteen Western nations formed the Organization for European Economic Cooperation to plan how the proffered American assistance could be used to make Europe once more economically self-supporting. Congress, motivated by the belief that only an economically stable Europe could halt communism's westward advance, voted about thirteen billion dollars over a period of four years. The plan was conspicuously successful, and within two years of its inauguration the recipients were producing 25 per cent more than before and were preparing for greater efforts at cooperation.[6]

In the spring of 1949, the United States joined eleven European nations in forming the North Atlantic Treaty Organization. NATO provided for joint action by the member-states if one of them was attacked. A joint system of defense was established with headquarters of the supreme command at Paris, and plans were laid for rearming Germany. The United States not only provided the commander for the international force but also contributed funds to strengthen the armies of its allies. Within three years, Truman had awakened to the communist threat and had persuaded the American people to establish an expensive but enlightened program to restore the European economy and to rearm Europe to make it militarily secure. In foreign policy, as in domestic policy, the critical decisions in the postwar era were made in his administration.

THE KOREAN WAR

Hardly had Europe begun to free itself from the immediate Communist threat than trouble broke out in the Far East. On June 24, 1950, the surprised world learned that a well-trained North Korean army had invaded South Korea. Truman acted swiftly. Without difficulty, in view of the absence of the Russian delegate, he persuaded the Security Council to ask members of the United Nations to give military aid to the embattled South Koreans, and General MacArthur was appointed commander-in-chief of an international army which was drawn from fifteen nations.

At first the news from the front was disheartening. The smaller United Nations army was thrown back precipitously until only the area around the port of Pusan remained in its hands. Meanwhile, MacArthur had received reinforcements from the United States, and on September 15, he took ad-

[6] See pages 1011-1013.

vantage of his control of the sea to land troops at Inchon, halfway up the Korean Peninsula. In an effort to escape capture, the North Koreans had to retreat even more rapidly than they had advanced. With little opposition, the United Nations' forces swept past the 38th parallel which had divided the two Koreas. Unity, it seemed, was about to be achieved by force of arms.

The Communists, however, were no more ready to accept a loss of territory than the democracies had been. China warned that it would intervene if the 38th parallel were crossed, but MacArthur scoffed at the threat and failed to take proper precautions as his army sped toward the Chinese border. As a result, his troops were caught off balance and defeated when the Chinese launched their attack in November. Seoul, the South Korean capital, had to be abandoned again; but by January, 1951, the front had become stabilized, and in March the United Nations' forces drove forward to the 38th parallel again.

At this point a great debate arose. MacArthur publicly insisted that North Korea be conquered and that Chinese bases in Manchuria be bombed. He also wanted to blockade the Chinese coast and support an invasion of China itself by Chiang Kai-shek's forces on Formosa. This desire to win total victory awakened a wide response in the United States, but more cautious counsel prevailed. Russia was probably no more willing to sit idle while its Chinese ally was defeated than the Chinese had been to permit the defeat of North Korea. This was especially true at this time when the split between the two communist powers was years away. Furthermore, an attack on China would have alienated India and other neutralists in Asia and would have found no support among the European democracies, which had just begun to rearm under the provisions of NATO. In short, MacArthur's proposals would almost certainly have led the United States, with little or no support from other countries, into a conflict with China, leaving Russia free to conquer Europe after available American troops had been committed in Asia. MacArthur was relieved of his command when he showed no disposition to obey civilian authority, and armistice negotiations were begun at Russia's suggestion. For two years, representatives of both sides wrangled at the conference table; but in July, 1953, as a result of American threats to renew the war and the more conciliatory policy adopted by the men who replaced Stalin upon his death, the Communists came to terms. Korea remained divided almost where it had been before.

On the surface, nothing had been accomplished to compensate for the 150,000 American casualties, but the war had finally awakened the democracies to the communist threat. The United States once more had a powerful army, and steps were being taken to speed the rearmament of Europe. The Russians had learned that the United States would fight to prevent the advance of communism and in the future were less willing to countenance open aggression. Truman and his advisers must be blamed for not making clear in the beginning that the United States would defend Korea, but they deserve credit for not permitting public opinion to panic them into a major war.

THE POLICY OF CONTAINMENT IN ASIA

The invasion of South Korea and the communist penetration into other parts of Asia awakened the United States to the need for establishing a more dynamic policy in the region. In 1950, Truman inaugurated a program to provide underdeveloped countries with technical and financial assistance which, in the long run, might substantially raise the standard of living of the Asiatic people. However, there would be no time for this to happen unless the military defenses in Asia were bolstered.

Truman took the first step in this direction by signing a peace treaty in 1951 with Japan and by trying to persuade the Japanese people to rearm to protect themselves. The Japanese were happy to be recognized as fully sovereign once more, but they displayed little enthusiasm for the idea of rearmament. They had even included in their new postwar constitution a provision renouncing war and forbidding the maintenance of "land, sea, or air forces." Most Japanese had had enough of war and did not want to become involved in a struggle between the United States and Russia. To change the constitution and build a large armed force might lead to a revival of militarism and would certainly be costly to the taxpayer. As a result, although the Japanese did decide to rearm somewhat, they were no longer a match for the Russians or even the Chinese.

When Eisenhower became President, he organized the Southeast Asia Treaty Organization, which included Australia, New Zealand, the Philippines, Thailand, and Pakistan as well as Great Britain, France, and the United States, which still had interests in the region. SEATO never became more than a pale imitation of NATO, however, because most Asiatic nations preferred to remain neutral and those that did join were too weak to halt the communist tide.

The situation in the Middle East was equally grave. When the Russians began to take an intense interest in this region around 1955, the United States countered by bringing Turkey, Iraq, Iran, and Pakistan together in the Baghdad Pact, but it was doubtful if all of these states could crush a communist revolt, much less halt a Russian thrust to the south. In 1957, Eisenhower persuaded Congress to authorize economic and military aid to assist the countries of this region to resist communism, an act which may have slowed the Russians' aggressive designs.

By this time the communist threat had become more serious in Africa and Latin America. The English and French gave a considerable amount of assistance to the emerging African nations, and Eisenhower laid plans for extending American economic aid to Latin America. After his inauguration in January, 1961, Kennedy stepped up economic aid to underdeveloped countries throughout the world and began a special ten-year twenty-billion-dollar program known as the Alliance for Progress for the economic and social improvement of Latin America. In addition, he organized the Peace Corps to provide educational and technical services in underdeveloped countries where there was a scarcity of trained personnel.

The Expansion of Communism and the American Reaction

The communist gains during and immediately after the war had led to a strong although belated American reaction. In the years that followed there was fierce competition between the democratic and communist systems for man's allegiance in every part of the world. It is now necessary to study individual countries to see how Russians and Chinese tried to continue the expansion of communism by propaganda, internal rebellions, and threats of war and how the United States sought to counteract their efforts by promoting economic progress and democratic institutions.

23/ The Developed
and Underdeveloped Countries

I N the competition for world leadership the United States and the communist powers have sought to persuade other countries of the world to accept their opposing ways of life. Broadly speaking, the reception accorded each has depended largely on whether the country concerned is developed or underdeveloped. A developed country is one having adequate transportation and communication systems, banking facilities, sources of power, and industrial establishments; its governmental officials are reasonably honest and efficient and a high percentage of its inhabitants are literate; and its population includes scientists and technicians, bankers and executives, skilled laborers, and competent farmers.

Marx had thought that the more industrialized a country became the riper it would be for communism, but events after 1945 proved that he was completely wrong. The developed, industrialized countries quickly showed a preference for the democratic way of life, but communism has had strong appeal in the underdeveloped countries, where there is widespread poverty and ignorance and where there has been a lack of trained leaders and skilled laborers to develop industry and to govern efficiently. The fact that most of the underdeveloped countries are colonies, or former colonies, of the democracies enabled the communists to play on the anti-imperialistic sentiment of the inhabitants to win converts to their cause.

THE DEVELOPED COUNTRIES

The American hope of preventing central and western Europe from falling into communist hands depended on how successfully three goals were achieved. One goal was the transformation of the relatively small, quarreling European states into one political, economic, and military unit. Collectively, Europe might check the Russian expansion; disunited, it could not hope to do so. The second goal was the restoration of German industrial and military power, a necessary preliminary for the establishment of a prosperous and secure Europe. The third goal was reviving the European economy and raising the standard of living in order to restore political health and to eliminate all chance of a successful communist revolt in any of the European states. To achieve these goals the Americans promoted the economic recovery of Europe through the Marshall Plan, helped organize NATO to defend the European democracies in case of a Russian attack,[1] encouraged the movement toward European unity, and spearheaded the drive to rebuild Germany. The United States also undertook to revive the Japanese economy and to teach their former enemies the functions of democracy.

The intelligent and generous efforts of the United States, coupled with the ability and energy of the inhabitants of the developed countries, produced astonishing results. The European and Japanese economies became more prosperous than ever before. The advance of communism was halted as was the trend towards democratic socialism, so apparent during the first few postwar years. Even more important, by cleansing the developed countries of fascism, World War II appears to have created the conditions necessary to a healthier society in Europe. The old aristocracy of birth has almost completely disappeared, and the new aristocracy of wealth is far wiser than before. Democracy and equality have become generally accepted, imperialism has become an almost extinct and largely forgotten phenomenon, and the cult of violence has been replaced by the cult of reasonableness and moderation. It is one of the ironies of history that the years after World War I, which were entered upon with so much hope, should have ended in depression, dictatorship, and war, while the years after World War II, which were entered upon with so much misgiving, have borne better fruit than anyone dared to hope.

[1] See page 1006.

TOWARD EUROPEAN UNITY

World War II and the events that immediately followed made it obvious to most observers that the individual European states would be too weak, henceforth, to play a prominent role in world affairs. The alternative to domination by Russia or the United States was to join in a common program.

The first experiment in this direction was the OEEC (Organization for European Economic Cooperation), which had been organized to decide how American aid provided under the Marshall Plan should be spent. It was followed by the inauguration of the Benelux Union on January 1, 1948. This Union, which consisted of Belgium, the Netherlands, and Luxembourg, provided for a common tariff on imports from the outside world and for the gradual establishment of a free-trade area within its boundaries. A committee of ministers and an Inter-Parliamentary Advisory Council composed of members of the three states were set up to implement the agreement. By 1958, considerable progress had been made despite many problems.

In 1949, ten western European nations, later joined by six more, established the Council of Europe with headquarters at Strasbourg, France. The Council consisted of a Committee of Ministers and a Consultative Assembly, to which the member-states sent representatives who varied in number according to their population. The members of the Assembly voted as they saw fit, not as they were directed by their mother country. In this respect, the Council was well in advance of the United Nations, but to date the member-states have been unwilling to surrender any of their sovereignty. The Council serves only in an advisory capacity, and its significance lies more in the fact that it might eventually lead to a closer union than in its present importance.

The European states proved more venturesome in their experiments in economic cooperation. The OEEC was continued after 1952, although the American economic assistance which had brought it into being officially ceased. It attempted to get member-states to reduce tariffs and remove currency restrictions that hindered the flow of trade. More significantly, six members of the OEEC—France, Italy, the Benelux countries, and the newly organized German Federal Republic—formed a European Coal and Steel Community in 1951. The ECSC was to bring about increased production of coal and steel by integrating economically the production of these vital materials in the member-states. This time the participants sacrificed a degree of sovereignty by providing for an international council, assembly, and court with authority to act.

The ECSC worked so well that in 1957 the member-states agreed to pool their resources in the development of atomic energy and to establish a European Economic Community. The European Economic Community, or Common Market as it has often been called, provided that in a period of from twelve to fifteen years trade barriers between the member-states would be removed and a common tariff would be established on imports from the outside world. An integrated economy consisting of 170,000,000 people would come into being. In short, just as the United States Constitution of 1789 removed all barriers against the movement of goods and people from one state to another, so the Common Market was to remove these barriers between its members. Industries located in these states, which had not experienced competition from abroad since tariffs began to be raised around 1875, were compelled to achieve greater efficiency if they wanted to survive. At the same time, labor was permitted to go where it was needed, and hundreds of thousands of unemployed Italians migrated into France and Germany where there was a shortage of labor.

The results were conspicuously successful, and the timetable has been speeded up so that the transition period is now scheduled to end in 1966. A common agricultural policy, designed to enable Europe to produce farm surpluses in all its products except feed grains by 1970, was established in 1962.

The British initially refused to join the Common Market and organized the less ambitious European Free Trade Association in 1960, which included Austria, Denmark, Norway, Sweden, Portugal, and Switzerland. The rapid progress of the Common Market, however, soon caused them to reconsider, and they applied for admission in 1962. In January, 1963, France unilaterally blocked their entry, ostensibly because their dominions and colonies made them too "insular and maritime" to be integrated into Europe. More likely the real reason was that British entrance would prevent France from playing the dominant role in the new Europe. Other member-states were disheartened by the French attitude, and it remains to be seen whether the objectives of the Common Market have been imperiled. One hopeful sign is the admission of Greece and Turkey to associate membership in 1962 and 1963 respectively.

The stimulating effect produced by the Marshall Plan in 1947 and the cooperative efforts of the Europeans themselves led to a rapid economic recovery. By 1950, pre-war production levels had been reached, and, by 1960, industrial production in most countries was two or even three times as high as it had been in 1948. Unemployment was no longer a problem in many states and per capita income moved rapidly forward.[2]

THE REVIVAL OF WEST GERMANY

The revival of Germany was essential for the economic rehabilitation and political security of Europe, but it took the democracies several years to realize this fact. During these years, their German policy differed little from that of the Soviet Union. Both envisioned a demilitarized, decentralized, agricultural state. German heavy industry was to be dismantled and given

[2] See page 1034.

EUROPE IN 1965

- **NORTH ATLANTIC TREATY ORGANIZATION (NATO)**
- **SOVIET RUSSIA AND OTHER COMMUNIST STATES**
- ■ **MEMBERS OF THE COMMON MARKET**
- ▲ **MEMBERS OF THE OUTER SEVEN**

0   100   200   300   400   500
SCALE OF MILES

N DVINA

STONIA

VIA

ANIA

DUNA

SOVIET UNION

BUG

DNIEPER

DON

VOLGA

DNIESTER

PRUT

MANIA

DANUBE

CASPIAN SEA

ULGARIA

BLACK   SEA

TURKEY

TIGRIS

IRAN

DODECANESE IS.

CYPRUS
BR.

SYRIA

EUPHRATES

IRAQ

LEBANON

to Russia and other states as reparations, and the Nazi leaders were to be tried and punished. Actual control of Germany was to be administered by an Allied Control Council consisting of representatives of Russia, Great Britain, France, and the United States, each of whom was responsible for an occupation zone. The Poles, who had been charged with the administration of that part of Germany east of the Oder-Neisse river line, were not represented.

Little difficulty was experienced in bringing twenty-two leading Nazis to trial before an international military tribunal at Nuremberg, for Communist and democrat had a common hatred of the Hitler regime. Whether it was just for the victors to try and punish the leaders of a defeated state is open to question, especially since no effort was made to apprehend those "war criminals" who had served in the armies of the victorious powers. Twelve of the defendants were sentenced to death, and seven more were given prison terms. In addition, each of the occupying powers was to punish the less important Nazis in its zone. The idealistic Americans went to absurd lengths. Insufficient effort was made to distinguish between those who were personally responsible for crimes and those who became Nazis through lack of understanding or force of circumstance. Questionnaires were filled out by over 13,000,000 persons and over 600,000 were punished. In this respect, even the Russians were more generous to their foes.

Soon the occupying powers quarreled over the remaining aspects of their occupation policy. The Russian zone was largely agricultural and could produce enough food for its people, but the democracies controlled the heavily industrialized western portion of the country that had long depended on the sale of manufactured goods to buy the necessary food for its inhabitants. The dismantling of these industries would leave many of the existing inhabitants without means of support. To make matters worse, the Poles and Czechs expelled about 12,000,000 Germans who inhabited their territories, nearly all of whom settled in the zones controlled by the democracies. The result was that the democracies soon realized that they would either have to reverse their stand against German heavy industry or expend huge sums for relief in their zones.

Two other factors pointed to a change in democratic policy. It soon became apparent that the prosperity of Western Europe depended on the economic revival of Germany. Equally important, only with a strong, united, industrial Germany could the European democracies hope to halt the spread of communism to the shores of the Atlantic. The Russians, on the other hand, having been quick to see that a weak, divided, agricultural Germany played into their hands, resisted every Western effort to make a change. The result was that during the summer of 1947 the United States and Great Britain abandoned the policy of keeping German industrial production at a low level, although the dismantling of German industry did not cease for another two years. During the spring of 1948, an important conference was held at London in which the democracies agreed to create a German federal state consisting of their occupation zones. At about the same time, they introduced much-needed currency reforms. The Russians, angered by these unilateral actions, imposed an economic blockade on Berlin. As Berlin was completely surrounded by the Russian zone, the communists had high hopes of forcing the democracies to reverse their stand or to withdraw from Berlin, where they each had an occupation zone. The democracies proved equal to the threat. For nearly a year they flew supplies to Berlin in a spectacular demonstration of air power.

Meanwhile, the democracies proceeded with plans to unite their zones politically and economically. In May, 1949, a German Federal Republic was established in western Germany. Its constitution provided for a president who was little more than a figurehead and a cabinet, headed by a chancellor, that was responsible to a popularly elected lower house. The upper house, which was composed of representatives from the member-states, was given few powers. Some safeguards were written into the constitution to prevent the constant rise and fall of cabinets that had plagued the Weimar Republic, but the real reasons for the stability of the new German republic were the emergence of what came close to being a two-party system and the leadership of an iron-willed chancellor, Konrad Adenauer (1876-   ). Fourteen parties entered the field in 1957, but only four of them won enough votes to receive seats in the lower house and Adenauer's Christian Democratic Union received a majority of the total electorate, the first time in German history any party had ever achieved such wide support in a free election.

Adenauer was a devoted adherent to the idea of co-operation among the Western European states. His determined leadership, joined with the democracies' growing fear of Russian aggression, led to a diplomatic revolution. The Germans replaced the Russians as the Western democracies' principal allies. They were persuaded somewhat against their will to rearm and enter NATO. With greater enthusiasm, they joined the ECSC, the OEEC, the Council of Europe, and the other international organs that were slowly merging Western Europe into a unit. By 1960, Germany was once more a great industrial power capable of contributing significantly to a general European economic revival, and its new army was an important factor in the defense of Western Europe against communist expansion.

Germany's economic revival has been one of the most remarkable achievements of the postwar period. This revival was accomplished under the most difficult circumstances within the framework of a capitalistic system. The ruling Christian Democratic Union was an outgrowth of the old Catholic Center party that had been expanded after the war to include Protestants. Its original platform had included demands for the nationalization of the coal mines, heavy taxes, and a controlled economy; but in 1950 Ludwig Erhard (1897-   ), the minister of economics, won party acceptance for his "social market economy" which permitted employers to search for profits without government interference except where regulation was necessary to ensure social justice. Areas where there were critical shortages, as in housing, remained subject to government action; and industry was advised to share profits with labor. However, plans for nationalization were dropped; indeed, the Volkswagen plant was denationalized.

Although the Federal Republic was only half the size of Bismarck's Germany, employment was found for 12,000,000 German refugees from eastern Europe in rebuilt factories. By 1955, industrial production was three times greater than it had been in 1948. Exports exceeded imports, and the German mark was one of the most stable currencies in Europe. This achievement enabled the Christian Democratic Union to defeat the Social Democratic party in each election, although its margin of victory was so slight that it governed in coalition with several minor parties. Under the impact of its success, the Social Democrats themselves abandoned their demands for nationalization.

If the health of the German economy was beyond dispute, the health of German democracy was open to question. In an era of economic progress, neo-Nazi organizations won little support, but Adenauer himself displayed such an authoritarian temperament that it was difficult for his cabinet and his party to function as they should. It was encouraging that they grew restive in spite of the great services that Adenauer had rendered. When several members of a magazine staff were arrested in 1962 for criticizing the army, there was a wide outcry. Adenauer survived the storm for the moment, but in the fall of 1963 he surrendered the chancellorship to the popular Erhard, although he continued to play an important role in party politics.

The greatest problem the Germans faced was reunification. When the democracies permitted the Federal Republic to be formed, the Russians responded by organizing their zone into a Communist state with its capital in a Berlin suburb. Called the German Democratic Republic, it adopted, under the leadership of Walter Ulbricht (1893-   ), policies like those of the eastern European satellites, with their five-year plans, collective farms, and curtailment of individual freedom. There was little economic progress, and hundreds of thousands of East Germans fled to West Germany until the Berlin wall was erected in 1961 to prevent further defections. In spite of this evidence of widespread discontent, there is little prospect of a successful uprising against the Communist government of East Germany. The presence of a Russian army removes any possibility of an internal revolt that would lead to eventual union with the Federal Republic. The possibility remains that the Federal Republic will eventually break its close ties with Western Europe and adopt a neutral position in the struggle for world supremacy in order to gain Russian consent to reunification. This step would deal a severe blow to the prospects for a gradual merging of Western Europe into a single economic and political unit, and would give the communists an immense advantage in the battle for Europe and the world.

THE FOURTH FRENCH REPUBLIC

Few people in Western Europe suffered as much material damage from the war as the French, and none suffered as great a blow to their pride. France, a great power, had collapsed almost as rapidly before the German onslaught as Poland. Only the refusal of General Charles de Gaulle and his little band to admit defeat and the heroic resistance movement, which had defied the Germans at every opportunity, offered solace. It was but natural that in the fall of 1944, when Hitler's armies had been driven almost entirely from France, De Gaulle should become the head of the provisional government and that resistance leaders, among whom were Communists, should be given posts of importance. Quickly the banks, coal mines, insurance companies, and public utilities were nationalized as well as some large corporations, such as the Renault automobile manufacturers. By 1950, nearly a third of the productive capacity of France was state-owned and a large amount of welfare legislation had been passed.

In one way only did the advocates of laissez-faire win a victory. Despite serious shortages of food and coal in Paris and elsewhere, no serious effort was made to curb inflation or enforce rationing. Prices skyrocketed. The rich bought what they needed in the flourishing black market, and the poor were left cold and hungry. The franc, which had been pegged at fifty to an American dollar at the end of the war, declined so rapidly that in 1959 the unofficial exchange rate was approximately 500 to a dollar, despite the decline of the purchasing power of a dollar in the United States. The French middle class was sorely hit, and the working classes suffered from lagging wages in the price spiral.

One mistake De Gaulle did not make. As soon as he came to power, he insisted that the resistance forces be absorbed into a regular army equipped by the Allies. This enabled France to regain its status as a great power with a voice in the occupation of Germany. At the same time, it removed the threat created by the Communists' private resistance army. As a result, the Communists quickly lost the military capacity to seize power and the general strikes they called in 1947 and 1948 did not create a situation in which they could get control of the government as they had hoped.

The old political parties were quickly revived, and one important new one, the MRP (*Mouvement Républicain Populaire*) was added to the list. The MRP, organized by Georges Bidault under Catholic auspices, advocated moderate reforms. In the elections to choose a National Assembly in October, 1945, the new party won 142 seats, a remarkable feat; but the Communists won 146 seats and the Socialists 133. The old conservative parties were generally ignored by the voters. Clearly France had moved far to the left.

The first important dispute after the elections was between De Gaulle and the left-wing parties over the amount of money that should be devoted to the military. De Gaulle resigned in disgust in January, 1946, when it became evident that the politicians preferred to spend money on social reforms rather than national greatness. A second quarrel developed over the nature of the government. The French were almost unanimous in the opinion that they should not revive the Third Republic, but they could not agree on the constitution of a Fourth Republic. De Gaulle wanted a strong president and a bicameral legislature after the American model. The Communists wanted the president to be a mere figurehead, with nearly all authority residing in a single chamber. De Gaulle desired a strong France, free from the frequent cabinet crises which had paralyzed the Third Republic. The Communists knew that they could never elect one of their number president, and they saw that the powers De Gaulle wanted to give that office could be used to check their aspirations. If there were a powerful chamber instead of a strong president, the house might be controlled if the Communists could effect an alliance with the Socialists. If not, the government's work could be disrupted; bickering parties and falling cabinets would have the effect of discrediting parliamentary democracy. However, De Gaulle and his supporters mustered enough strength to defeat the Communist constitutional proposals, but not enough to have their own program accepted by the voters. In the end, the constitution adopted for the Fourth Republic was much like that of the Third, except that the old Senate was transformed into an Advisory Council. The president remained a figurehead, and cabinets rose and fell in accordance with the whim of a host of rival political parties in the Assembly. In a period of a little over ten years, there were nineteen cabinets.

If the Socialists and MRP had united and won scattered support from other parties, they probably could have controlled the Assembly and provided France with a stable government. The social programs of the two parties did not differ greatly, but the old issue of church and state came to the fore once more. The MRP wanted the state to give support to the hard-pressed Catholic schools, but the secular-minded Socialists refused to consider such a move. Fortunately, the Socialists were equally suspicious of the Communists, who were then drawing from 25 to 30 per cent of the popular vote. The result was that one fragile coalition of parties followed another, and no concerted effort was made to halt the inflation spiral or to deal effectively with the colonial problem which was growing increasingly serious. In 1947, De Gaulle launched the RPF (*Rassemblement du Peuple Français*), a movement designed to cut across party loyalties and unite the people behind a vaguely defined program for strengthening France politically, economically, and socially. The RPF won considerable support from the MRP and the right-wing parties, but little from the left. It quickly became just one more political party, and De Gaulle himself disowned it in 1953 when several of its members accepted cabinet posts.

Despite the political confusion and persistent inflation, there was economic progress. In 1947, the first four-year Monnet Plan was adopted to increase production in the basic industries. Other four-year plans followed, facilitated by American economic aid which enabled the French to buy much-needed machinery from abroad. Strikes became less serious when the communist control over labor was weakened by the formation of a splinter union. By 1955, France was producing half again as much as in 1938. This was achieved in part by a longer work week, but more by a 37 per cent rise in the average productivity of labor. The result was a 29 per cent increase in the standard of living during the same period, despite the losses suffered during the war. Progress in agriculture was somewhat disappointing, although the movement towards larger farms and increased use of machinery gave promise for the future. France greatly needed an accelerated home building program, but that this might come with continued economic progress was suggested by the fact that after nearly a century of virtual stagnation the French population began to grow once more, primarily because of a significant increase in the birth rate. By 1962, the population was 8.8 per cent larger than in 1954.

Pierre Mendès-France became prime minister in 1954 with the avowed mission of speeding France's economic transformation from a land of small shopkeepers to one of big industries and chain stores. First, however, he had to extricate France from a costly civil war in Indo-China[3] and give Tunisia and Morocco independence to avoid similiar difficulties there. This achieved, he found himself voted out of office by those who had been happy to see some of France's colonial difficulties solved but who feared dynamic changes in the economy.

The power of the shopkeepers in France was further revealed at the same time by the Poujade movement. Pierre Poujade was a small-town tobacconist who correctly pointed out that little shops like his own would go bankrupt if they had to pay taxes, but instead of trying to enlarge his business, he advocated meeting the emergency by not paying taxes. The movement caught on like wildfire, and the Poujadistes captured 3,000,000 votes in the 1956 elections. This electoral expression was probably the last echo of the past, for industrialization accelerated, and the Poujade movement began to decline almost immediately.

Colonial problems also plagued postwar France. Indo-China, Lebanon, Syria, and all its North African territories except Algeria were abandoned because of pressure from the natives. The desire to hold Algeria at all costs was motivated by the fact that over one-tenth of its population was French. These colonists were anxious to retain their ties with the mother country and were fearful that if Algeria became independent they would lose their privileged status. French reluctance to grant full independence was increased by the discovery of oil and other natural resources. Thus, while willing to integrate Algeria into France by making its inhabitants French citizens and by dividing the country into departments with representation in the Paris legislature, France refused to grant the colony independence. The result was that the revolt in Indo-China had not ended before a serious uprising broke out in Algeria. More and more men and money that were sorely needed in France were poured into the rebellious land.

To eliminate the costly warfare, the Paris government offered greater

[3] See pages 1039-1040.

and greater concessions to the Algerians. Nothing short of independence, however, was acceptable to the rebels. The French colonists and the conservative, nationalist officers' corps began to suspect that sooner or later Paris would grant even this. Extreme right-wing leaders, some of whom were for De Gaulle and some of whom were surviving supporters of the Vichy regime, joined the army and colonists. On May 13, 1958, they seized power in Algeria, then in Corsica, and finally began to threaten France itself. A conservative revolution appeared in the making. To save the republican form of government and to avoid civil war, the Paris legislature called upon Charles de Gaulle to assume once more the role of his country's savior. For a period of six months, he was given dictatorial powers with the mission of drafting a new constitution to be approved by popular referendum.

THE FIFTH REPUBLIC

De Gaulle acted swiftly. The army trusted him because of his patriotism; the republicans trusted him because they had no choice. By September, 1958, he had prepared a new constitution which was ratified by an overwhelming majority of the French people. The shortlived Fourth Republic was declared at an end, and in the Fifth Republic the president was given the powers De Gaulle had long desired him to have. The president was to serve for seven years, to control the executive branch of the government, to name the prime minister, and to dissolve the National Assembly when he desired. In an emergency, he could assume dictatorial powers. Even the President of the United States did not enjoy a comparable position in his own country.

In the elections that followed the creation of the Fifth Republic, the left-wing political parties were severely defeated and a newly formed Gaullist party known as the UNR won 212 seats. This dramatic movement to the right was achieved as much by the abandonment of proportional representation as by an actual change in voter sentiment. In the elections of 1962, the Communists and Socialists won an increased number of seats, but the Gaullist UNR and its allies won an absolute majority in the assembly, the first political party ever to do so. At the same time, the French people agreed to a constitutional amendment calling for popular election of the president rather than by an electoral college. This action further freed the president from dependency on political parties and strengthened his ties with the people.

A power-hungry demagogue could easily use the new constitution as a stepping stone towards a permanent dictatorship in the manner of Napoleon III. De Gaulle would not stoop to this, but among his followers there were men like those who had supported the fascist dictators before the war. Whether the French can remain free under these circumstances will depend upon what happens when De Gaulle ceases to be president, but for the first time since the days of Napoleon III, France has a government capable of taking necessary but unpopular actions.

De Gaulle immediately set about trying to solve France's colonial and domestic problems. The constitution of 1958 gave overseas territories other than Algeria the option of becoming completely independent or of joining the French Community. Only Guinea chose independence at this time. The president of France was to serve as the president of the Community, but there was to be a council and a senate consisting of governmental officials of the member-states. By 1960 the independence movement had become so strong in the former colonies that the constitution was amended to permit states to become completely independent but still remain a part of the Community. Even with this concession, some of the former colonies decided on a complete break.

The institutional organs of the Community are becoming less and less active, but France has maintained close ties with its former colonies through a generous program of economic and technical assistance. The Community may never achieve the co-operative spirit that characterizes the British Commonwealth of Nations, but at least it has enabled France to get rid of its former colonies without new Indo-Chinas or Algerias.

The Algerian problem, however, proved far more difficult to solve. The army, French colonists, and others whose revolt had brought De Gaulle to power had assumed that he would act vigorously to suppress the Algerian nationalist movement. Instead he hesitated, and then, apparently realizing that the French must make a choice between draining their energies in an Algerian war and building a powerful country based on European France, he chose the latter course and began to negotiate with the rebels. Riots in Algeria, threatened army coups, and assassination attempts could no more deter this inflexible man once he had reached a decision than the fall of France in 1940 could make him admit defeat. An agreement was reached with the rebels in March, 1962, and Algeria became independent in July. By the terms of the agreement, Europeans who remained in Algeria were to have full rights and France was to retain its position in the Sahara. In return, France was to give Algeria economic and technical assistance.

Nearly all the French colonists decided to return to France, a wise decision, as it soon became apparent that the Algerian government of Ahmed ben Bella had no intention of respecting their rights. Their departure left the country in confusion since they alone had the technical skill to make the economy function. Unperturbed, Ben Bella rooted out native opposition and established a left-wing dictatorship.

Meanwhile, De Gaulle had been trying to solve France's domestic problems. When he came to power, he found the budget unbalanced and the gold reserve dangerously low because high prices prevented the French from selling as much abroad as they bought. It had long been recognized that an austerity program was necessary, but De Gaulle was the first statesman with the courage and the power to put one into effect. Taxes were raised, and government expenses were cut in order to balance the budget. Even veterans' pensions and subsidies to keep down the costs of food did not escape. To increase foreign trade, wages and prices were controlled, and the franc was devalued. Strikes and threats of strikes by farmers, miners, and industrial workers were frequent. At the same time, efforts were made to increase the French businessman's competitive spirit.

Despite complaints, the program was successful. The budget was approximately balanced, and the balance of trade was redressed, making the franc one of the strongest currencies in the world. The gross national product increased 5.5 per cent in 1962, and wages rose nearly 10 per cent. Many problems remain, but the Gaullist regime has accelerated the movement towards a more competitive and efficient economy.

Part of the criticism of De Gaulle stemmed from his determination that France should head a group of European states capable of acting separately from the United States. This ambition made it necessary to spend large sums to develop a nuclear striking force that many thought could have been more wisely employed to secure the educational and social betterment of the people. His desire for French predominance also helps to explain his attempt to exclude the British from the Common Market. Thus far, De Gaulle's continental policy has been moderately successful, but its success has owed much to Adenauer's willingness to co-operate for the sake of a Franco-German rapprochement. Whether this policy will continue now that Erhard has replaced Adenauer as Chancellor is problematical. Momentarily, at least, De Gaulle has gone far towards restoring France to the position it held in Western Europe in the 1920's. It is very doubtful, however, that France can fully regain its former position in Europe, because of its lack of size, population, and industrial capacity relative to Russia and the United States, which now plays an active role in continental affairs.

THE REVIVAL OF ITALY

The possibility of a Communist triumph in Italy after the war appeared more real than in France, although at first the Communists polled a smaller percentage of the votes. The long period of Fascist rule had destroyed democratic institutions, and most conservatives had become so discredited that they had difficulty winning popular support. Italy's standard of living was lower than France's. Italy lacked the natural resources to develop great industrial strength, and its soil was too poor to support a flourishing agriculture. At the turn of the century, a third of the natural population increase had emigrated to foreign countries. This had helped to reduce the unemployment problem and to pay for the imports of those who remained, for the emigrants sent money home to their relatives. By 1950, most foreign countries had, like the United States, restricted immigration for several decades, and second-generation Italians abroad were less generous to their relatives than the first generation. As a result, much of the ever-increasing Italian population joined the ranks of the unemployed. The man without a job or with one that paid too little to support his family was likely to sympathize with the Communists. The Communists controlled the largest labor union and made notable gains in rural areas among the poor peasants. Many who remained faithful to the Catholic Church began to vote for the Communists on election day. A further reason for the seriousness of the Communist threat in Italy was that close ties were established early with the Socialist party.

When Mussolini was forced to resign in July, 1943, he was replaced by Marshal Badoglio. Badoglio had had close Fascist ties, but he saw clearly that the defeat of the Axis was inevitable. He was willing, therefore, to bring men of different political outlooks into his cabinet. Even Palmiro Togliatti, the Communist leader, was given a post. Badoglio led Italy into the war on the allied side in October, 1943. Yet despite the valuable services the Italians performed thereafter, they were treated as enemies at the 1946 Paris peace conference, where they were forced to cede territory to Yugoslavia, surrender their colonies, and pay reparations.

While the victors were deciding what penalties to inflict on the Italians because of the Fascists' activities, the inhabitants of the boot-shaped peninsula were making an important decision themselves. In June, 1946, they voted 12,717,932 to 10,719,284 to abolish the monarchy, and at the same time they chose a constituent assembly to prepare a new constitution. The Christian Democrats, a moderately reformist Catholic party like the French MRP, emerged as the largest party, but the Socialists and the Communists together won more seats. A coalition which included the Communists had to be established with Alcide de Gasperi (1881-1954), the able Christian Democrat leader, as prime minister. The new constitution prepared by the assembly declared Italy to be a republic with a president who was given few powers as the head of state. Executive authority was placed in a cabinet responsible to a bicameral legislature. The concordat Mussolini had made with the papacy remained in effect, and the Church became an active supporter of the Christian Democrat party in its struggle against the Communists.

The late winter and early spring of 1948 proved to be the most critical period in Italy's struggle against communism. The Americans poured in economic aid, and the Catholic Church used all its persuasive powers. In April when the ballots were counted, it was found that De Gasperi's Christian Democrat party had won nearly half of the popular votes and over half of the seats in the legislature. The Communists and their left-wing Socialist allies received nearly a third of the votes, but Italy was guaranteed five years of stable government.

On the whole, the Christian Democrats used their power wisely. They tried to improve the lot of the poor Italian farmers, especially in southern Italy, by engaging in reclamation projects and by undertaking a modest program of turning large estates into small farms. There was some increase in the use of farm machinery and fertilizer. Vegetables and other intensive crops were substituted to some extent for the traditional wheat, but Italian agriculture as a whole has remained very backward.

Fortunately, Italian industry began to move forward rapidly after the formation of the European Economic Community in 1957. By 1960, it could be officially announced that industrial production was increasing 11 per cent annually, faster than in any other Western European country. Even this unparalled progress was insufficient to take care of Italy's needs because of chronic unemployment in the south. There was considerable migration from this region to northern Italy and other Common Market countries, but only part of those who moved could be absorbed into the labor force because so many were unskilled. At the same time, even the best-paid workers were discontented with their wages. The Communist and left-wing Socialist parties increased their strength slightly, and the ruling Christian Democrats were dismayed to see their own position deteriorate to the advantage of monarchist and neo-Fascist groups. By 1960, the Christian Democrats had either to rely on the support of the extreme right or to persuade the Socialists to desert their Communist allies. The left wing of the Christian Democrat party sought Socialist support by nationalizing electricity, enacting welfare legislation, and decentralizing the government during 1962, despite opposition within their own party. In return, the Socialists finally agreed to enter the government near the close of the following year.

It is still too early to evaluate the significance of the Christian Democrat-Socialist alliance. In most elections the Communists had polled about 25 per cent of the vote and the Socialists 15 per cent. Together they represented too large a part of the population to be ignored; but if the Christian Democratic alliance with the Socialists were stable, the Communists would be weakened, and democratic government would proceed more effectively. On the other hand, the threat of nationalization and costly social reforms slowed the flow of foreign capital into Italy and caused many well-to-do Italians to deposit their funds abroad. The result was a decline in the amount of money available to continue the expansion of the economy, an expansion that might in the long run do more for the worker and, through him, for democracy than any program of nationalization and social reform.

Whatever the outcome in the economic sphere, postwar Italy has made a remarkable comeback. Also noteworthy have been the advances made in every aspect of culture from painting to literature, from motion pictures to dress designing. For the first time since the seventeenth century, Italy is in the forefront of the artistic and intellectual world.

THE SMALLER STATES

The small Western European democracies have warded off internal communist threats despite economic difficulties. The Dutch and Norwegians had lost a large percentage of their merchant marine during the war and had suffered severe internal damages. In addition, the Dutch lost valuable colonies in the East Indies after a brief civil war.[4] Nevertheless, the economies of the two nations revived slowly. Denmark, which emerged from the war with less damage than Norway and the Netherlands, recovered without too much difficulty. Sweden and Switzerland, which had been subjected to no more than the usual inconveniences suffered by neutrals during and immediately after a large war, became more prosperous than ever before.

Belgium, however, had serious internal political problems. Here Communists were stronger than in the other small democracies, and cooperation between the Catholic and Socialist parties was necessary to ensure stable government. Unfortunately, they quarreled over the question of state aid to parochial schools and over the position of King Leopold III (1934-1951). Leopold had offended the Socialists by his unilateral decision to surrender to Germany in 1940 and by his authoritarian character. He had affronted conservatives by marrying a commoner. Only the Catholic party wanted to see him return to the throne. After years of wrangling Leopold abdicated in 1951 in favor of his son, Baudouin I. In the other small democracies, monarchy remained popular. Only in Italy and the communist-controlled Balkans did kings fail to maintain their crowns after World War II.

Fascism, like democracy, had shown a tendency to accommodate itself to royalty. In 1947, Franco declared that Spain was a kingdom and took steps to see that the monarchy would be restored upon his death. Immediately after the war it had seemed probable that the Franco regime itself would fall. The victorious powers refused to admit Spain to the United Nations, and many of them were reluctant to resume diplomatic or trade relations. The Spanish economy suffered, but the growing differences between the democracies and Russia led to a relaxation of tension. The West feared that the alternative to Franco was not a democratic republic, but a communist state. Portugal has likewise remained a mild dictatorship since the war.

THE BRITISH RECOVERY

World War II multiplied the problems Great Britain had to face. Between 1919 and 1939 the island kingdom had difficulty paying for food and raw materials imports to support its ever-growing population, but now matters were much worse. The German air force had damaged over 3,000,000 pieces of property, and their submarines had sunk over half the British merchant marine. British mines and industries were more antiquated than ever. Their foreign investments had shrunk. Their colonies were successfully demanding independence. American and other non-European countries had increased their industrial strength and, in many

[4] See pages 1042-1043.

cases, their merchant marine. The result was that British export trade sank to 30 per cent of its pre-war figure, but large imports were necessary to recoup wartime losses. Under these circumstances, few economists saw much chance of an economic revival in Britain.

With their customary courage in adversity, the British quickly set about accomplishing the impossible. The first task was to determine who would lead them in their economic struggle. Winston Churchill had won immense prestige through his leadership in what at one time had seemed the hopeless struggle against the Germans, but the overwhelming majority of the British people had far less faith in the old aristocrat and his Conservative party when it came to economic and social issues. In the elections of July, 1945, the Labor party won 393 seats in the House of Commons to 189 obtained by the Conservatives and twelve by the virtually defunct Liberals. For the first time the Labor party ruled the state without having to depend on another party for support. Clement Attlee (1883-), a long-time Fabian Socialist, became prime minister.

The Laborites' program had two purposes: (1) to restore the economy and (2) to create a socialized welfare state. To secure the first objective, Labor adopted an austerity program designed to control nonessential imports. Rationing was continued, and domestic agriculture was encouraged in order to decrease food imports. Foreign commitments were reduced, and many colonies were given dominion status or independence. Trade treaties were negotiated; the pound was devalued; and imperial commercial ties were strengthened to increase imports. The dollars the British earned, borrowed, or received in aid from the Americans were used to purchase machines and equipment in the United States to modernize industries. Through stern self-denial and hard work, the country slowly regained its feet and employment was available for virtually everyone for the first peaceful years since before 1914.

More spectacular was Labor's socialization program. The Bank of England and the coal, electricity, railroad, iron, steel, and trucking industries were nationalized. In all, about one-fifth of British industry was taken over by the government, always with compensation given to the owners. An ambitious housing program was undertaken, and social services were greatly extended. Old age and unemployment insurance programs were completely overhauled, and a National Health Service Act was passed to provide free medical service. Doctors under the plan were paid a fixed salary by the state and an additional sum that varied with the number of their patients. Patients were left free to choose their doctor. Educational opportunities were improved. Particularly noteworthy was the construction of new universities and the generous scholarship programs for needy students. Oxford and Cambridge ceased to be preserves for the aristocracy and the middle class. By 1951, 73 per cent of the students in universities were receiving aid from the government.

On the whole, the nationalization of industry led neither to the glorious progress predicted by Labor nor to the dire consequences predicted by the Conservatives. Perhaps the economic consequences of transferring large industries that were virtual monopolies from the ownership of thousands of stockholders to the ownership of millions of voters are of little importance. In either case, a small group of men actually manage the industry, and labor problems remain much as they were before. There is little doubt that the program of social services, especially the free medical service, has been immensely popular.

The cost of the nationalization and social service program was met by high income and corporate taxes. A married man who earned £85,000 a year was left only £6,000 after taxation. Few British aristocrats could afford to maintain their stately ancestral houses. Some were sold to institutions or given to the National Trust, an institution which assumed the care of properties of particularly significant historical and cultural interest. Others were kept up by opening them to tourists. There was a touch of tragedy in this, but for the first time in generations there was full employment. Of the national income, 48 per cent went for wages in 1948 as opposed to 39 per cent in 1938. Medical care and social security were available to everyone, and city slums were rapidly disappearing.

In 1951 the Conservatives won a victory at the polls by a narrow margin, and Winston Churchill resumed his post as prime minister. In the campaign, he and his fellow Conservatives had accepted the welfare state, but they had promised to manage it more efficiently. They had also opposed nationalization, but once in office they denationalized only the iron and steel industries and part of the trucking industry. Sparked by a group of young Conservative intellectuals, the new government put its emphasis on greater production and foreign trade. Both goals were realized, although the rate of increase in industrial production was slower than in most continental countries. Rationing was ended in 1954. Taxes were reduced on several occasions, and greater economic freedom was permitted, although government planning and controls were practiced in the Keynesian manner. Social services were improved, and in the decade before 1959 real wages increased 16 per cent.

Their successes enabled the Conservatives to increase their lead in every subsequent election until 1964, in spite of Churchill's retirement and the blundering Suez policy of his successor, Sir Anthony Eden (1897-   ). Harold Macmillan (1894-   ) took the reins of government in 1957 and carried his party to new successes until ill health and scandals involving several members of his government led to his resignation in 1963 and the return of the Labor party to power the following year.

The long series of Conservative victories forced the Labor party to reconsider its position. With the Conservative decision to accept the idea of a welfare state, Labor had been left only with slogans of nationalization and full employment to attract voters. The first was no longer popular with the white collar workers whose votes were needed to win elections, and the latter ceased to be an issue once it was achieved and the chronic unemployment of the 1920's and 1930's was forgotten. As a result, the Labor party abandoned most of its demands for further nationalization. The platforms of the two parties, one of them still the preserve of the aristocracy and the other filled with labor leaders, became almost indistinguishable. Between them, in the postwar years, they had accomplished a near miracle. England had become more prosperous than ever before, in spite of war losses and the dissolution of its Empire.

JAPAN

Japan was the most important non-European industrialized nation, with the exception of the United States. Like the British, the Japanese inhabited heavily populated islands that made a huge export trade necessary for survival. Like the British, they had suffered heavily from wartime bombing. Like the British, they had lost their merchant marine, their overseas investments, and their colonial empire. The chances of an economic revival, therefore, seemed slim when the Americans began their occupation in 1945 and introduced the Japanese to political and social democracy.

The new Japanese constitution was similar to that of Great Britain in many respects. The emperor became little more than a figurehead, and Shintoism was abolished. Sovereignty was vested in the people and expressed through a parliament to which the cabinet was responsible. For a time the presence of numerous political parties made for cabinet instability, but in 1954-1955 there was a widespread political realignment from which two important parties emerged. A bill of rights was included in the constitution which guaranteed freedom of the press as well as other liberties. Complete social equality was decreed, and women were given the right to vote. War and the maintenance of an armed force were initially outlawed, but these provisions were later rather reluctantly removed at the Americans' suggestion as a result of the communist threat in Asia.

To build a large middle class, which was regarded as necessary for vigorous democracy, and to achieve greater economic justice, the American occupation forces redistributed the land and tried to break up the great business concentrations. Landlords were forced to surrender their holdings, and 3,000,000 of Japan's 3,800,000 tenant farmers became independent landowners. No communist state could boast a more thorough agricultural revolution. Japanese commerce, banking, and industry had been operated by huge family-controlled holding companies, one of which employed 2,000,000 persons. Since these cartels were held to be partly responsible for Japanese imperialism, an attempt was made by the American occupation forces to destroy them. These efforts accomplished little, and were undone by the Japanese when they resumed control of their own affairs in 1951.

In spite of all the difficulties that confronted them, the Japanese have experienced an industrial revival since the war. Their annual economic growth reached 9.3 per cent between 1953 and 1958. Yet they have difficulty selling enough abroad to feed a soaring population that is expected to pass the 100,000,000 mark in the 1960's. Their vulnerable economic position and their new-found pacifism make it questionable whether they will prove an effective barrier to the expansion of communism in the Far East.

THE UNDERDEVELOPED COUNTRIES

The inhabitants of the underdeveloped countries have thought more in terms of improving their standard of living and winning their independence, if not already won, than in terms of the struggle for world supremacy. However, the rivalry between the Western democracies and the communist states has played into their hands, because each bloc has vied with the other in providing economic assistance, technical aid, and diplomatic support. The frequent communist charge that the democracies are imperialistic has been a factor in leading them to grant independence to their colonies, and it has caused the United States to side against its Dutch and Portuguese allies on colonial issues.

THE REVOLT AGAINST IMPERIALISM

By 1945, the situation was favorable for the inhabitants of the underdeveloped regions of the world to revolt against imperialism. World War II had gravely weakened the European colonial powers, and the many defeats they had suffered at the hands of the Japanese had discredited them in the eyes of Asiatics. Only with extensive military and economic assistance from the United States could they hope to regain their former position in Asia, but this was one form of aid that the Americans denied their European allies.

Then, too, the colonial people in Asia and Africa were in a stronger position to assert their independence. Whatever their remaining shortcomings, they were better informed in Western science and technology than ever before. Furthermore, many natives had become indoctrinated with the alien creeds of nationalism, democracy, and communism and had dedicated their lives to bringing these supposed blessings to their people. Under these circumstances, whenever the European states were confronted with determined native opposition, they had little choice but to make the best terms they could.

The Western nations adopted four different approaches toward their colonial territories after World War II. Sometimes they continued to rule them with governors and other officials, giving very little authority to the natives. This was especially true in the case of islands too small to hope for independence and territories where unenlightened colonial administrators had done so little to introduce Western ideas that the native population had not fully awakened to the possibility of self-government. Portuguese possessions in Africa were examples of this situation until the second postwar decade, when storm clouds first began to appear.

The second approach the Western nations sometimes adopted was to attempt to satisfy colonial peoples by giving them full citizenship with the right to elect representatives to the legislature of the mother country. This practice of complete incorporation of a colonial territory was adopted by the United States when it admitted Alaska and Hawaii into the Union as states. Denmark made a somewhat similar arrangement with Greenland in 1953, and France created sixteen departments in Algeria, the islands of the Indian Ocean, and the Americas, whose inhabitants sent representatives to Paris. This approach was a conspicuous failure in Algeria, but it has generally succeeded where there was no strong native national movement.

A third approach was to grant autonomy to the local inhabitants, and to maintain some sort of direction over foreign policy, trade, and defense. This direction may be barely perceptible, as in the case of the British Commonwealth of Nations where ties of sentiment, influenced by occasional imperial conferences, are all that hold the dominions together. Or they may be somewhat more formal, as in the case of the French Community established in 1958, which provided for executive, legislative, and judicial organs of government. By 1960, the independence movement had become so strong in the former French colonies that these institutions were abandoned, and the French Community became a loose, ill-defined association like the British Commonwealth. The Dutch have made somewhat similar arrangements to govern their territories in South America and the West Indies.

The fourth approach to colonial territories was to grant them complete independence. The United States, Great Britain, France, the Netherlands, Denmark, and Spain have all surrendered colonies since the outbreak of World War II.

The transfer of sovereignty by a European state to a colonial people was accompanied by many problems. In the first place, the inhabitants of a territory often quarreled so bitterly among themselves because of different religious or social allegiances that the mother country hesitated to withdraw for fear that civil strife would break out. Then, too, white settlers who had generally occupied preferred positions in the colonies did all they could to prevent the natives from assuming power. When a European state granted a territory an independent or semi-independent status, it generally included in the arrangement safeguards to protect its economic investments and often the privilege of maintaining military bases. Indeed, Great Britain and France are now investing more money in many of their former colonies than they were a generation ago. Thus, political independence has not brought an end to all the economic aspects of imperialism.

The Developed and Underdeveloped Countries

Underdeveloped countries that were independent before World War II, but had been subject to economic penetration by the imperialistic powers, must also be considered in the current revolt against imperialism. The Arab states, for example, have been loud in their demands for a greater portion of the revenue derived from the oil concessions in their territory, and Latin Americans have frequently protested against the important role American capital is playing in their countries, although they are anxious for more economic aid.

ECONOMIC PROBLEMS

Since World War II it has been easier for a colony to win its independence than to improve the standard of living of its inhabitants once it has become free. Even the older underdeveloped countries have experienced considerable difficulty in achieving rapid economic gains. The reason for slow progress may be found in the basic characteristics of an underdeveloped country. By definition, such a country lacks transportation and communication systems, sources of power, factories, or banking facilities. A high percentage of the inhabitants are illiterate, the number of skilled workers is small, and there are few institutions of higher learning. As a result, progress in one direction is dependent on progress in another. It is necessary to have an adequate transportation system to have factories, and it is necessary to have factories to build a transportation system. For both, managers, engineers, and skilled workers are essential, but it is obligatory to have schools and teachers to train this personnel.

Foreign aid and technical assistance can help overcome some of these handicaps in time, but to use aid effectively the underdeveloped country must have a reasonably honest, efficient bureaucracy that is sincerely interested in the welfare of the people. Too often this has not been the case, and American assistance has done more to enrich the faction in power than to improve the economic position of the inhabitants as a whole. Sometimes the social changes that must precede economic improvement are blocked by native aristocracies. Customs, taboos, and ignorance often cause further difficulties. The rapid population increase in crowded countries, for example, must be checked, or it will offset increased production. In spite of new factories, the annual per capita income of the people of India increased from $62 to only $73 between 1953 and 1962 while that of Pakistan actually declined from $78 to $74.

Since 1947 the underdeveloped countries have generally allied themselves with the Western democracies or adopted a neutralist position; but if they do not begin to move forward more rapidly, they will be increasingly tempted to try the communist experiment or, as some have already done, to establish non-communist dictatorships with partially socialized economies. The great strides the Russians have taken during the last generation and the industrial progress now being made in eastern Europe encourage other countries to follow their example. It is true that the democracies achieved material wealth under the capitalistic system and that they are still making praiseworthy progress, but it took them generations to achieve their present position. Few inhabitants in the underdeveloped countries want to wait so long.

The table below indicates the estimated average annual rates of growth of the per capita gross national product at constant market prices between 1951 and 1959 and the estimated per capita gross domestic product expressed in current U.S. dollars for most nations of the world. It should be noted that highly developed countries, such as the United States, are growing at a very slow percentage rate, but that the output per person increased $611 between 1953 and 1962, a far greater amount than the total per capita domestic product of most of the underdeveloped countries, many of whom are growing at a rate of only a few dollars per person per year. As a result, the rise in their standard of living is hardly perceptible.

ECONOMIC DEVELOPMENT: 1951-1962

	AVERAGE ANNUAL RATE OF GROWTH	PER CAPITA GROSS DOMESTIC PRODUCT EXPRESSED IN U. S. DOLLARS			INCREASE
	1951-59	1953	1958	1962	1953-62
Developed States:					
Australia	—	993	1211	1416	423
Austria	5.6	407	656	871	464
Belgium	2.0	852	1029	1215	363
Canada	1.0	1521	1767	1807	286
Denmark	2.8	791	975	1390	599
Finland	3.0	687	750	1047	360
France	3.3	866	1113	1300	434
Germany, Federal Rep. of	6.1	619	931	1349	730
Israel	4.9	361	579	823	462
Italy	5.2	353	490	688	335
Japan	7.2	189	284	504	315
Netherlands	3.3	530	767	1003	473
Norway	2.2	794	1035	1316	522
Sweden	2.8	981	1313	1703	722
Switzerland	2.7	1097	1316	1740	643
United Kingdom	2.1	810	1078	1288	478
United States	1.1	2080	2324	2691	611
Communist States:					
Bulgaria	7.1	—	—	—	—
Czechoslovakia	6.6	—	—	—	—
Hungary	4.9	—	—	—	—
Poland	6.0	—	—	—	—
Rumania	7.5	—	—	—	—
Yugoslavia	8.0	—	—	—	—

	AVERAGE ANNUAL RATE OF GROWTH	PER CAPITA GROSS DOMESTIC PRODUCT EXPRESSED IN U. S. DOLLARS			INCREASE
	1951-59	1953	1958	1962	1953-62
Underdeveloped States:					
Africa					
Algeria	4.8	180	220	—	—
Angola	—	—	60	—	—
Cameroon	—	—	88	—	—
Congo (Leopoldville)	2.6	81	87	—	—
Ethiopia	—	—	41	—	—
Ghana	—	—	154	193	—
Guinea	—	—	94	—	—
Kenya	—	—	76	79	—
Liberia	—	—	122	—	—
Libya	—	—	127	185	—
Madagascar	—	—	87	—	—
Morocco	—	—	159	150	—
Mozambique	—	—	45	—	—
Nigeria	0.3	74	79	82(1961)	8
Fed. of Rhodesia and Nyasaland	0.9	—	134	147	—
South Africa	—	317	386	435	118
Sudan	—	—	82	94(1961)	—
Tanganyika	—	—	52	60	—
Tunisia	—	140	147	—	—
United Arab Republic	—	95	116	—	—
Underdeveloped States:					
Asia					
Afghanistan	—	—	54	—	—
Burma	4.2	47	51	52(1961)	5
Cambodia	1.5	—	91	—	—
Ceylon	0.5	114	122	129	15
China (Taiwan)	3.7	—	115	—	—
Cyprus	2.0	332	403	432	100
India	1.6	62	67	73(1961)	11
Indonesia	2.1	—	69	—	—
Iran	—	—	159	—	—
Iraq	—	157	215	259(1961)	102
Korea	2.6	—	105	—	—
Laos	—	—	80	—	—
Lebanon	—	246	262	—	—
Pakistan	—0.2	78	63	74(1961)	—4
Philippines	2.2	—	191	—	—
Saudi Arabia	—	—	175	—	—
Syria	—2.9	144	138	149(1961)	5
Thailand	1.8	—	78	93(1961)	—
Turkey	3.2	159	201	211	52
Vietnam, Republic of	—	—	88	—	—
Underdeveloped States:					
Europe					
Greece	5.5	190	310	394	204
Ireland	1.0	410	474	641	231

	AVERAGE ANNUAL RATE OF GROWTH	PER CAPITA GROSS DOMESTIC PRODUCT EXPRESSED IN U. S. DOLLARS			INCREASE
	1951-59	1953	1958	1962	1953-62
Portugal	3.3	176	218	279	103
Spain	3.9	—	322	—	—
Underdeveloped States:					
Latin America					
Argentina	—0.1	—	474	—	—
Bolivia	—	—	104	—	—
Brazil	3.2	—	250	—	—
Chile	1.0	—	409	—	—
Colombia	2.4	—	301	—	—
Cuba	—	333	370	—	—
Ecuador	1.7	159	179	178	19
El Salvador	2.0	—	198	193	—
Guatamala	2.0	138	164	162	24
Honduras	1.2	185	192	202	17
Mexico	1.9	222	288	356	134
Panama	1.7	313	348	413	100
Paraguay	—0.4	—	111	—	—
Peru	0.8	142	148	—	—
Puerto Rico	4.2	405	581	825	420
Uruguay	—	—	450	—	—
Venezuela	4.6	716	975	901	185

DATA: *United Nations Compendium of Social Statistics: 1963* (New York, 1963), pp. 566-68; and *United Nations Yearbook of National Accounts Statistics: 1963* (New York, 1964), pp. 321-324.

THE FATE OF THE BRITISH ASIAN EMPIRE

Great Britain had the most farflung possessions in Asia at the outbreak of World War II. British concessions to the anti-imperialistic crusade, therefore, had to be the greatest. As early as 1929, Britain had been willing to grant India dominion status, but it refrained from doing so because the Hindus and the Moslems as well as the higher castes and lower castes were unable to agree on what kind of government to establish.[5] Native agitation became more intense during World War II, and at the end of that conflict the British decided to withdraw whatever the cost. Since the Hindus and Moslems could still reach no agreement, the vast subcontinent was divided in 1947 into two states, India and Pakistan.

India was by far the largest of the new states. It consisted of 1,266,900 square miles and in 1960 contained about 400,000,000 people, of whom about 10 per cent were Moslem. Pakistan consisted of two widely separated areas. It was only one-fourth as large as India and had barely one-fifth the population. Many of its inhabitants were Hindus. The result was that the Hindus persecuted the Moslem minority in India, and the Moslems persecuted the Hindu minority in Pakistan. In addition, the two states quarreled

[5] See page 928.

over the possession of Kashmir, a northern province of the old India. About 12,000,000 persons became refugees; 200,000 died from violence and still more from the hardship of being forced from their homes. The price of independence was disunity and fratricidal struggle, as the British had so long predicted.

Fortunately, India had able leaders. Mahatma Gandhi pleaded passionately for better treatment of Moslem and other minority groups, but on January 30, 1948, he was assassinated by a Hindu fanatic. His death accomplished what he had not been able to do in life, for shocked Hindus and Moslems began to make a more serious effort to settle their differences. The question of Kashmir remains unresolved, but riots and bloodshed have nearly ceased.

The death of Gandhi left Jawaharlal Nehru (1889-1964) undisputed leader of the Congress party and of the new India. Nehru possessed many of Gandhi's spiritual and moral qualities and was a determined opponent of war and violence. A non-Marxian socialist, he advocated social and economic progress aided by science and big industry. The India he and others created possessed a democratic constitution with a bill of rights and guarantees of equality before the law regardless of race, religion, or caste. The princely states which had enjoyed a special status under the British were dissolved, and efforts were made to improve the lot of women.

Nehru's great popularity ensured a stable government, but in the long run only substantial economic progress could ensure India's future. Indian leaders were well aware of this, and they realized that they faced a Herculean task. The illiteracy rate was high. The mass of the people were poor and underfed, and an average population growth of over 5,000,000 a year consumed much of the increased national output. Land was divided among the peasants, and a series of five-year plans was inaugurated to increase agricultural output, build dams for power and irrigation, develop industry, and improve transportation and social services. Some progress was made, but it is still not certain that democratic India, with its emphasis on consumer goods and its respect for human rights, can develop economically as rapidly as Communist China, where the emphasis is put on heavy industry and the individual is ruthlessly disregarded. Upon the outcome of this contest the fate of Asia may well depend.

Nehru tried to occupy a central position in the struggle for world supremacy. He steadfastly refused to join anti-Russian alliances, and sought instead to serve as a bridge between the democratic and communist worlds. His leadership was accepted by many Asian nations, and this did much to enhance his prestige at home and abroad. For a time his policy seemed successful. However, in 1959, Communist China occupied territory claimed by India after having cruelly suppressed an uprising in Tibet. The situation worsened in 1962 when the Chinese renewed their advance. Nehru declared that a state of emergency existed in October, and his appeal for arms was answered by both the United States and Russia. When he died

Jawaharlal Nehru and Mohandas Gandhi at the opening meeting of the All-India Congress Committee in Bombay, July 6, 1946. (Wide World)

in 1964, he left to his successor, Lal Bahadur Shastri, the problem of settling this quarrel as well as the long-standing dispute with Pakistan over Kashmir.

Pakistan's problems were worse than those of India. Its people were more backward. There were quarrels between the eastern and western provinces, and no leader of Nehru's stature emerged. Nevertheless, despite its stormy political history, Pakistan now appears to be moving slowly forward under the direction of a five-year plan. Pakistan joined the West in its effort to halt the advances of communism. But when the United States gave arms to India without insisting that Nehru negotiate seriously about Kashmir, Pakistan established friendlier relations with Communist China.

After driving the British out of Burma, the Japanese granted the former colony its independence in 1943. The British sought to reassert control after the end of the war, but in January, 1948, they somewhat reluctantly withdrew, leaving Burma an independent state. The Burmese had considerable difficulty suppressing the communists within their borders after the war. Still, they maintained a neutralist attitude in the struggle for world supremacy. Numerous problems beset the new state, and the quarreling political parties accomplished little. This situation led General Ne Win to seize power in 1962 and establish a thoroughly socialistic state, but one in which the Burmese culture and Buddhist religion played important roles.

The British granted the island of Ceylon dominion status in 1948. In their foreign policy the Ceylonese have also adopted a neutralist position in the struggle between the democracies and the communist states. In their domestic policy they have taken a socialist course and have nationalized many industries, sometimes without compensation to the owners. Although nominally democratic, the government has sometimes violated civil liberties. The island is troubled by a minority problem as well as by economic difficulties, and there have been several attempted coups. Little has been done to relieve the situation, although the recent discovery of iron ore gives hope for future industrial growth.

Malaya was given dominion status in 1957 after a communist uprising had been suppressed and the Chinese and Malays who inhabited the peninsula had reached an agreement on the government. This proved to be the first step towards the formation of the Federation of Malaysia in 1963, which also included the former British colonies of North Borneo, Sarawak, and, until 1965, Singapore. Defense and internal security were responsibilities of the Federation, but a wide degree of self-government was reserved for the member-states. The new Federation was challenged by the Philippines and Indonesia, which had claims to North Borneo and Sarawak. Indonesia even started a small guerrilla war over the issue, but under the astute leadership of Prime Minister Tunku Abdul Rahman, a Cambridge University graduate, the new Federation has a fair chance of success.

Today little remains of the once vast British territories in the Far East, except a few scattered islands such as Hong Kong. Yet recent changes should be considered more a tribute to the years of British rule than an indication of failure. Of the five new states, Burma alone has refused to retain any ties with the Commonwealth. British-educated and British-trained native leaders are today endeavoring to bring social and economic progress to the people, often using democratic processes in spite of almost insurmountable difficulties. British motives were often selfish, but on the whole the native population has profited from their rule.

THE PHILIPPINES, INDO-CHINA, AND INDONESIA

The same statements may be made in regard to the United States. The Philippines were granted their long-promised independence on July 4, 1946. At first, little of the moral fervor or impetus to reform that has so characterized most of the new British dominions appeared, but in 1953 Raymon Magsaysay (1907-1957) was elected president after having acquired popularity by vigorously suppressing a long-troublesome communist revolt. He reduced corruption in government, increased economic productivity 30 per cent in three years, and began to divide large estates among the peasants. He was a firm friend of the United States, and his accidental death in 1957 was a damaging blow to the American position in the Far East. Since 1957, evidence of governmental corruption has reappeared; but economic progress has continued at a slower rate, and the close ties with the United States have been maintained.

The postwar French relations with Indo-China were less happy. The French had conferred cultural and economic benefits upon the people and had let the eastern state of the confederation, Vietnam, keep its emperor and the western states of Laos and Cambodia their kings, but they had discouraged nationalist movements. The inevitable result was that the communists won the support of most nationalists; and when the desperate French decided to release the reins of government, able, honest pro-Western native officials were difficult to find.

In 1946, the nationalists under the able leadership of communist Ho Chi-minh (1892-   ) embarked on a long and costly war to drive the French from Vietnam. Finally, the capture of a French army of 15,000 men at Dienbienphu in 1954 made the Paris government realize that a greater effort was required to regain its former possession than it was worth, even though the United States offered limited military assistance. A compromise peace resulted in which North Vietnam was surrendered to Ho. The latter immediately began to turn his country into a communist state. A number of expropriated landlords and Catholics fled to South Vietnam to add to the problems of that already overburdened state.

Fortunately, Ngo Dinh Diem, an anti-communist, nationalist leader, managed to get rid of most of what remained of French influence in South Vietnam, to depose the puppet emperor, and with American aid to organize the country's defenses against communist guerrilla troops supplied from North Vietnam. Diem was an able, determined Roman Catholic, but his authoritarian temperament, and that of members of his family to whom he gave important government posts, alienated many people. His enemies charged that his regime was inefficient and corrupt, but above all else he was accused of persecuting the Buddhists who made up the majority of the population. No real proof of religious persecution was ever presented, but several Buddhist monks dramatized their cause by publicly incinerating themselves. To the Western mind this was convincing evidence, and, possibly with American acquiescence, Diem was overthrown and slain in a military coup on November 1, 1963. Victory over the communist guerrillas had seemed imminent during that spring and summer; but after Diem's death the situation deteriorated rapidly, and in 1965 the United States was forced to intervene on a large scale to avoid the loss of all of South Vietnam.

Cambodia and Laos also became independent kingdoms when the French left in 1954. It was understood that both countries would remain neutral. Neither the United States nor the communists, however, were willing to leave Laos to its own devices because of its strategic location between pro-Western Thailand and South Vietnam and Communist China and North Vietnam. After several years of effort, Prince Souvanna Phuma managed to bring communist, neutralist, and pro-Western leaders together in a coalition government in 1958, but two years later he was forced into exile by pro-American forces generously aided by the Eisenhower administration. The communists immediately stepped up aid to their own Laotian leader, Prince Souvanna Vong, who slowly extended his hold over the country. Both Eisenhower and Kennedy then sought to re-establish the neutralist coalition government under Souvanna Phuma. This was finally

ASIA—1965

SCALE OF MILES 0 200 400 600 800 1000

achieved in 1962. At the same time, the Western and communist powers agreed to respect Laotian neutrality. Nevertheless, the fighting has continued, and the future of this small but strategically important country remains in doubt.

Partly because the Western position has been deteriorating, neutralist Cambodia has drawn steadily closer to the communist camp. The Cambodians even refused to accept further American economic aid in 1963 but continued to receive assistance from the Chinese. If these three former French territories fall into communist hands, pro-Western Thailand will be seriously threatened. Indeed, there are growing signs that the United States will be faced with the choice of large-scale intervention in South Vietnam and Laos or the loss of all of Southeast Asia.

The Dutch repeated many of the mistakes of the French in their dealings with their colonies. They neither prepared the inhabitants of their East Indian islands properly for self-government nor co-operated with moderate nationalist elements. As a result, the strongly nationalistic Achmed Sukarno (1902-   ) won a wide following and established control over Java and Sumatra with Japanese consent during the war. The Dutch refused to make adequate concessions after the war and launched several attacks to regain their position. In 1949, they were forced to recognize the independence of Indonesia. They hoped that an imperial tie could be maintained, but in 1956 Sukarno severed all connections with them and the following year seized their property.

In recent years Sukarno's regime has become increasingly dictatorial. In May, 1963, he was made president and prime minister for life after having threatened the existence of political parties and newspapers that were not "constructive," that is, that criticized his regime. Already a host of organizations from the Rotary Club to the Girl Scouts have been prohibited on the grounds that they are undemocratic. The Communist party has fared better. Its 2,000,000 members make it the largest one in the world with the exception of those of the Soviet Union and China. Several of its members have held cabinet posts, but Sukarno himself has adopted a neutralist position in the struggle for world supremacy and has accepted a large amount of aid from both the Soviet Union and the United States.

Serious economic problems beset the new state. The per capita income is about $100 a year, and the rapid growth of the population, which reached about 100,000,000 in 1964, negates what increased production has been achieved. Since Dutch and Chinese businesses have been confiscated, the old economic leaders have been removed. However, there is a lack of trained Indonesians to replace them in spite of great improvements in the educational system. Most industry has been nationalized, and large estates have been divided among the peasants.

Sukarno's ambitious foreign policy has also retarded the economy. He determined to incorporate the Netherlands' portion of New Guinea into his sprawling island state, although he had no conceivable claim to it except that, like the rest of Indonesia, it belonged to the Dutch. When the Dutch refused to surrender the island, Sukarno built up an army of 300,000 men by milking his economy and receiving Russian aid. There was some actual fighting; but when the United States refused to permit the Dutch to reinforce New Guinea, they abandoned the island. Indonesia assumed control in 1963 with a promise to hold a plebiscite there by 1969 to determine its final disposition. Sukarno immediately turned his attention to trying to prevent the formation of the Federation of Malaysia because it would block his design to incorporate North Borneo and Sarawak. Demands for Portuguese Timor may be anticipated in the future. Perhaps the American policy of territorial appeasement and extensive economic aid will keep Indonesia out of the communist ranks as long as Sukarno is in power, but thereafter Indonesia's future will be very uncertain.

IRAN, TURKEY, AND CYPRUS

Iran was the first state to be seriously threatened by the communists. The Russians had occupied the northern province of Azerbaijan during the war to expedite the flow of supplies from the democracies and to forestall German penetration into the country. Instead of withdrawing six months after the return of peace as promised, Russia organized a revolution there and refused to permit Iranian troops to reassert control. Pro-communist demonstrations were held in Teheran. The United Nations, strongly backed by President Truman, forced the Russians to withdraw their troops in 1946, but local communist leaders continued to seek popular support.

An opportunity presented itself in 1950 when a dispute broke out between the British-controlled Anglo-Iranian Oil Company and the Iranian government. The Iranians, disappointed that anticipated American aid had not been forthcoming, decided to seek a larger share of the revenue derived from their own oil fields to strengthen their economy. When the British proved reluctant to make significant concessions, Mohammed Mosaddeq (1880-   ), an ambitious demagogue, seized the occasion to demand the nationalization of the oil company's properties. Aided by the strong nationalistic and anti-imperialistic attitude of the Iranian people, he rose to the premiership in 1951 and acted quickly on his nationalization scheme. The British withdrew, leaving the Iranians without the technicians to produce oil and without the facilities to market it if they were able to reinstitute production. The loss of oil revenue was a severe blow to the Iranian economy. As many of Mosaddeq's followers began to desert him, he came to rely more and more on the communists and other fanatical groups who were always ready to organize demonstrations in Teheran on his behalf. Once more, the warm-water ports on the Indian Ocean and the vast oil supply in the region seemed within the communist grasp.

Suddenly, in August, 1953, the shah, Mohammed Reza, dismissed Mosaddeq and made one of his own supporters prime minister. Orderly government was restored; an advantageous agreement was reached with British oil interests; and today, oil revenue is financing an ambitious program to build dams for irrigation and power, improve agriculture, and develop the other resources of the country. The shah has taken the lead in dividing large estates, including those of the crown, among poor farmers. He also has pressed a reform program that includes more equal rights for women and profit-sharing for industrial and commercial laborers. Serious riots were instigated by conservatives in 1963, and a communist threat persists; nevertheless, the rapid progress being made in Iran gives hope for the future.

Turkey had profited from World War I to throw off the imperialistic yoke, but the post-World War II era has not been free of problems. Little progress had been made towards democracy. The economy was still backward by European standards. Furthermore, the Russians hopefully awaited an opportunity to seize the Straits. In an effort to move towards democracy, President Inönü (1884-   ) relaxed censorship restrictions and permitted the opposition Democratic party to be formed in 1946. The result was a Democratic victory in 1950. Unhappily, the Democratic party has proved less devoted to the principles of democracy than its predecessor. Once in power it restored censorship and tampered with the ballot box in the elections of 1957. In 1960, the military overthrew the government, and Inönü once more became prime minister.

In 1947 the United States promised to protect Turkish territorial integrity and began to pour economic and military aid into the country. This led to a business boom, high prices, and, in 1954, to an inevitable crisis in foreign trade. Turkey was strategically too important in the struggle for world supremacy for the United States to permit its economic collapse, and in 1958 funds from Washington were again made available. Industry, more under the auspices of private enterprise than before the war, and agriculture made slow advances in spite of political instability; and land was distributed among the poor farmers as in so many other countries in Asia.

The Mediterranean island of Cyprus was elevated to dominion status in 1960. The British had long desired to give the Cypriots independence, but the inhabitants themselves had not previously been able to reach an agreement. The Greeks, who made up about 80 per cent of the population, wanted union with Greece, while the Turks, who made up most of the remainder, demanded partition. Greek terroristic activity in which the island's archbishop, Makarios (1913-   ), participated finally led the British to propose a bizarre constitutional arrangement in which the Greek and Turkish communities looked after many of their own affairs. Both the president, who was to be a Greek, and the vice president, who was to be a Turk, were to have veto powers. This system of government proved unsuccessful, and the struggle between the Greek and Turkish communities was renewed near the close of 1963. United Nations' troops had to be dispatched in 1964 to restore order. Turkey and Greece, though NATO allies, considered intervention to protect their countrymen, and the possibility of war could not be overlooked.

The Developed and Underdeveloped Countries

PALESTINE AND THE ARAB WORLD

The situation in the Arab world was complicated by the presence of Jews in Palestine. The British had held trouble in check before the war by limiting Jewish immigration, but now there were nearly a million Jewish refugees in central and eastern Europe who did not desire to return to their former homes where 5,000,000 of their brethren had been slain by the Nazis. Their plight provoked widespread sympathy, and when the British sought to escape responsibility by turning the matter over to the United Nations in 1947, that organization decreed that Palestine be partitioned and that an independent Jewish state be established. The Arabs not unnaturally refused to accept a solution that created a Jewish state in their midst, nearly half of whose population consisted of their fellow Arabs. A war ensued which resulted in an Israeli victory, and nearly as many Arabs were deprived of their homes as there had been Jewish refugees in Europe. An armistice negotiated by the United Nations in 1948 brought an unstable peace.

Once Israel became independent, the immigration barriers were removed, and thousands of Jews emigrated from Europe and elsewhere. By 1958, the population of the tiny 8,000-square-mile state had passed 2,000,000, and more emigrants were on the way. Only by industrialization and the use of the most advanced agricultural methods could the Jews hope to support so large a population. Aided by individual gifts, loans, and grants from the United States, they have made considerable progress, although the fact that in 1962 the value of their imports was still over twice that of their exports indicates how much more needed to be accomplished before the economy was self-supporting.

Meanwhile, some economic and social progress was being made in the Arab world. Most people in this region had to depend on agriculture for a livelihood as the natural resources necessary for large-scale industrial development were missing. Lack of rainfall made intelligent farming methods and irrigation necessary, but intelligent farming required an educated population and irrigation required the construction of expensive dams. These needs in turn presented difficult problems. At present the literacy rate in Arab countries varies from 50 per cent to only 3 per cent, and the per capita income is about $100 per year. The discovery of oil in some of these states provided a possible source of revenue to pay for the necessary education and irrigation projects. However, much of the income from this source has gone into profits for foreign oil companies and luxurious living for native rulers. Those Arab states in which the native leaders were anxious to improve the lot of the people were often, unhappily, the ones in which little or no oil has been found.

The presence of large deposits of oil upon which Europe has come to depend and the strategic location of the region have made it a bitter battleground in the struggle for world supremacy in which Arab aspirations were not necessarily of primary importance to the main contenders. These aspirations consisted of political independence and the severance of all imperialistic ties, to which goals the more enlightened Arabs added the social progress of the people. In 1945, the Arab states formed a league to further their designs, but for years rivalries between the native rulers prevented successful co-operation. Nevertheless, progress towards political independence was made after World War II. France freed Syria, Lebanon, Tunisia, and Morocco. Great Britain made Sudan independent and withdrew from Egypt and several other already nominally independent Arab states. The former Italian territory of Libya was freed. Spain turned most of its African territory over to the new state of Morocco. France belatedly recognized the independence of Algeria. Except for several small areas in southern Arabia, all the Arab peoples are now independent. Recently they have insisted that the oil companies give them a larger percentage of income, and it is to be hoped that social progress will follow.

A relatively well-educated citizenry and a large population have made Egypt the most important Arab state. During the immediate postwar period, the immoral, corrupt King Farouk (1937-1952) and his like-minded advisers played one faction against another to remain in power, but they were thoroughly discredited by their defeat in the Palestine War in 1948. The army officers, far from accepting any blame for the course of events, plotted to seize power. A small group of them formed a Revolutionary Command Council which masterminded a rebellion in 1952 that led to Farouk's deposition and the establishment of a republic. By the end of 1954, Lieutenant Colonel Gamal Abd al-Nasser (1918-   ), a leading member of the Council, had established himself as president, prime minister, and virtual dictator of the new state.

Nasser was both a patriot and a reformer. His policy abroad has been directed towards ridding the Arab world of British influence and uniting it under Egyptian leadership. At home he has advocated social and economic reforms. In pursuit of this policy, he secured the withdrawal of British troops from the Suez Canal, but in return he had to recognize Britain's right to re-enter in case of emergency and to give Sudan, which Egypt had partly owned, its independence. For adopting this reasonable attitude, he was led to expect American aid in building a huge dam in the Nile River at Aswan and in strengthening his army. The Aswan dam provided the most logical means of improving the lot of the Egyptian people, because it would increase the amount of arable land by 30 per cent and at the same time produce an untold amount of electric power. Nasser needed military aid to support his ambitious foreign policy and to placate the officers' corps upon whose support his regime was largely dependent.

When Eisenhower refused to offer a significant amount of aid, Nasser turned to the Russians who arranged for large shipments of military supplies from Czechoslovakia in 1955. This act caused the Eisenhower administration to reconsider, and early in 1956 arrangements were made to construct the Aswan dam. At this point, Nasser began to play the communist world against the democratic world in the hope of getting better terms from both. Angered, the United States cancelled the proffered aid.

Nasser's situation was now desperate. He had encouraged the Egyptian people to expect too much from the Aswan dam to discard the project safely. In July, 1956, he boldly nationalized the Suez Canal Company in defiance of his international agreements and announced that he would use its revenue to build the dam. The British and French who owned most of the canal stock were furious. Sir Anthony Eden, the British prime minister, warned Eisenhower that if Nasser was not compelled to rescind this act, his prestige in the Arab world would become so great that pro-Western regimes in Saudi Arabia, Jordan, Syria, and Iraq would be overthrown by young army officers seeking Arab unity. With control over the oil resources of the region and the Suez Canal, which carried 100,000,000 tons of cargo a year, he would have Western Europe at his mercy. In spite of these warnings, the United States refused to countenance the use of force.

Meanwhile, Israel had become increasingly concerned at the build-up of Egyptian forces near its borders and, perhaps in collusion with the English and French, decided to strike first. On October 29, 1956, the superb Israeli army swept into the Sinai peninsula and routed the larger Egyptian forces in a campaign that took place in a hundred hours. On October 31, the English and French intervened, ostensibly to protect the Suez Canal. The United States, caught by surprise, strongly supported the United Nations' demand for a cease-fire, and the Russians, seeing an opportunity to win favor with the Arabs, spoke of sending "volunteers" to aid the Egyptians. Faced with a possible war with Russia without the support of their American ally, the British and French had no recourse but to withdraw from the Suez Canal. The threat of war subsided, but Nasser was left stronger than before. He still had the canal, and he had gained additional prestige by flouting the British and French.

Just as Eden had predicted, Nasser set about trying to undermine the pro-Western Arab governments. He used the powerful radio at Cairo and his well-organized propaganda staff to agitate for Arab unity under his leadership. Revolts and assassinations were resorted to when rulers did not act as desired. In February, 1958, Syria voluntarily joined Egypt to form the United Arab Republic, and shortly thereafter Yemen took a similar step. A few months later Nasser supporters launched a revolt against the conservative, pro-Western Christian ruling faction in Lebanon, and the pro-Western king of Iraq was assassinated when army officers seized power. A prime minister favorable to Nasser was appointed in Saudi Arabia, and the position of the young king of Jordan was extremely precarious. To stabilize the situation, the United States and Great Britain rushed troops to Lebanon and Jordan respectively, but in spite of their successful efforts the Arab world seemed to be falling into Nasser's hands. Or perhaps it was the communists' hands, for though Nasser tried to suppress communism in Egypt, many feared that the communists would profit from the confusion. In 1959, Iraq abandoned the Baghdad Pact which had been designed to prevent Russia from expanding in the Middle East.[6]

At this point other factors intervened to prevent either a Nasser or a communist triumph. The Arab nationalist movement was essentially middle class, although it was dedicated to social reform. Its leaders had been willing enough to accept Soviet diplomatic aid in getting the imperialistic powers out of the Middle East and North Africa and Soviet economic aid in achieving material progress, but they had no wish to become captive to any international movement, especially one that denied the right to private property. As a result, the Arabs themselves suppressed communist activity more vigorously than before. Even Abdul Karim Kassem (1914-1963), the new ruler of Iraq who depended heavily on native communist support, sought to check their growth.

On the other hand, Arab unity proved far more difficult to achieve than had been anticipated once the European imperialistic powers had been removed from the scene because of the rivalry that developed between the leaders of the movement. Both Nasser and Kassem believed in Arab unity, but both chose to rule their respective states rather than enter a union that was headed by the other. Their personal quarrel found some support among their countrymen because of the historic rivalry between the Nile and the Tigris and Euphrates river civilizations and between Cairo and Baghdad for the control of the Middle East. The split between these two leaders enabled the traditional monarchical governments of Saudi Arabia, Jordan, Libya, and Yemen to escape, at least momentarily, the turbulence of the nationalist movement. In 1961, Syria and Yemen broke away from the Nasser-dominated United Arab Republic, and Kuwait, a former British protectorate, was recognized as an independent Arab state in spite of Iraq's desire to annex the oil-rich sheikdom.

At least one factor that had caused the middle-class and military nationalist leaders in Syria, Iraq, and other Arab states to hesitate to unite with Egypt was Nasser's socialist program. Foreign investments were welcomed in Egypt as a means to develop the economy; but some Egyptian-owned industry was nationalized, wages and social benefits were increased, and large estates were divided among the peasants. By 1960, Egyptian industrial production was more than twice what it had been when the monarchy was overthrown in 1952. The rate of growth was increasing. A 17.3 per cent increase took place in 1960, and the great Aswan dam was slowly being built with Soviet aid. This progress naturally strengthened Nasser's position and gave an impetus to Arab socialism, which he saw as conforming to early Islamic practices.

Meanwhile, an Arab socialist party known as the *Baath* had been developing in other countries independent of Nasser. In February, 1963, the *Baath* party overthrew Kassem in Iraq, and the following month it seized control of Syria. As the *Baath* party strongly supported the Arab nationalist

[6] See page 1008.

movement and as its economic-social philosophy was similar to Nasser's, unity seemed closer than ever before. Once more, however, Nasser's desire to dominate the union caused the other states to hesitate, and in Syria some of his supporters were executed for trying to seize the government. Tempers cooled a little, and on May 26, 1964, Iraq and the United Arab Republic, as Egypt still called itself, agreed once more to seek a basis for unity.

The enmity between Nasser and the traditional monarchies continued. In September, 1962, pro-Nasser army officers overthrew the king of Yemen and established a republic. The tribes rallied to the royal cause and with aid from Saudi Arabia seemed on the verge of regaining control when Nasser dispatched over 40,000 troops to assist the rebels. Sporadic fighting continued for several years, but during the summer of 1965 both Nasser and Saudia Arabia agreed to adopt a more neutral attitude so that a plebiscite could be held in Yemen to decide the future of the country. Even if peace is restored, however, the Arab nationalist dream of a state stretching from the Persian Gulf across North Africa to the Atlantic Ocean still appears far from realization.

THE EMERGENCE OF AFRICA

In 1945, there were only four independent states in Africa: Ethiopia, which had just been freed after a brief period of Italian rule, Egypt, Liberia, and the Union of South Africa, which enjoyed only dominion status. The remainder of the large continent consisted of colonies whose inhabitants, unlike those of Asia, made few demands for independence. By the close of 1963, there were thirty-five independent African states, seventeen of which became independent in 1960. A continent of colonies had become a continent of free states. Of the European colonial powers only Portugal was not preparing its remaining important colonies for independence.

This dramatic change was initiated by the decision the English and French made soon after the war to give their African colonies self-government as soon as they were ready. The English hoped that their colonies would accept dominion status, and the French anticipated that they would remain within the French Community. Once African leaders awakened to the possibility of ridding themselves of the colonial status, however, they vied with one another in their demands for more complete and more rapid independence. In the end, few British colonies in Africa voted to join the British Commonwealth of Nations, and the French colonies that remained in the French Community reduced it to an informal association that would not infringe on their independence. Italy lost its African colonies as a result of the war, and Belgium followed the example of the great powers in surrendering the Congo. When one considers the years of agitation that took place in the Asiatic colonies before the great powers granted them independence, the generosity with which the less advanced African colonies were treated may be taken as evidence of how bankrupt imperialism had become after World War II.

It is customary today to attribute the native emancipation movement to African nationalism. It would be more accurate, however, to speak in terms of anti-colonialism. African leaders disliked being governed by colonial officials and having their economies run by European businessmen for the advantage of Europeans. They wanted to direct their own affairs. Contact with the Europeans had shown them the advantages Westernization could bring, and they thought that they could provide their people with these benefits more rapidly than the colonial powers were doing. Above all else, they wanted to be treated as equals, a courtesy that only the French had habitually accorded them. Whenever an issue involving colonialism has come up before the United Nations, the African delegates have reacted with more emotion than reason.

Nationalism, on the other hand, can scarcely be said to have existed in the new African states located south of the Sahara Desert at the moment they became independent. When the Europeans began to expand in this region after 1875, African society had been organized on a tribal rather than a national basis. Lines separating native ethnic groups were not considered or even known when the Europeans delineated the boundaries of the individual colonies. The typical colony, therefore, contained several tribes, each with its native language and customs. This tribal organization had often been preserved by the colonial officials because it was easier and less expensive to govern through the native chiefs than to hire Europeans to do the task. European parliaments, political parties, and other similar institutions were not introduced until after World War II. As a result, when independence came, the loyalty of most Africans still centered in their tribe, not in the European-constructed colony that now became a sovereign state. Only those natives who had left their tribes to work in the new cities or to receive a good education had broader outlooks, and these favored few often thought as much in terms of a larger Pan-African loyalty as in terms of loyalty to a state. It was usually they, and not the tribal chiefs, who took the lead in working for independence, as the chiefs were often content with the preferred position in native society that the Europeans had permitted them.

Both the English and French colonies generally modeled their constitutions after those of their respective mother countries, but the preservation of tribal loyalties often led to an altering of the spirit behind the constitutions. To bind several tribes into a state, many African leaders thought it necessary to build a mass movement whose loyalty centered in themselves as national symbols. Every form of propaganda was utilized for this purpose, and opposition was vigorously suppressed. This situation led to one-party states in Tunisia, Algeria, Mali, Guinea, Tanganyika, Nyasaland, and above all in Ghana, whose president, Kwame Nkrumah (1909-   ), was called "the redeemer" by his followers. As a result, in securing their independence the Africans have often lost their liberty.

Where the tribal structure has been too strong to be broken down, federal governments have been established in which special status has been

The introduction of industry into Africa is illustrated by this African employee in a nail factory. (Courtesy of East African Tourist Travel Association)

assigned to the leading tribes. Nigeria, Kenya, Uganda, and, after a bloody civil war, the Belgian Congo have become federal rather than unitary states for this reason.

A number of problems beset the new African states, but the most universal is the need for better educational facilities. In 1960, 80 per cent of the population was illiterate, and only 16 per cent of the children of school age in tropical Africa were enrolled in public schools, mostly at the primary level. Of the university-age youths, only one in five hundred was attending an institution of higher learning. Many of the new states are making a heroic effort to remedy this situation, but progress is bound to be slow because of the scarcity of teachers and school buildings. It is worthy of note that the situation was far worse in Ethiopia, where less than 4 per cent of the children between five and fourteen attended school, than it was in the former English, French, or Belgian colonies.

This situation has led the new African states to keep many of their former colonial officials as advisers and to welcome investment by European governments and private concerns, a practice which has usually permitted the transition from a colonial to an independent status to be accomplished with relative ease.

The Belgian Congo was the most conspicuous exception to this rule; but here the natives had had little colonial experience in government, and the colonial officials and the native leaders failed to cooperate. The Belgians had adopted a paternalistic attitude towards the Congolese. They had provided them with an unusually good system of primary education and had trained them to be skilled laborers. Congolese cities were neat and clean. Nowhere were there shanty towns like those that grew up around urban centers in the English and French colonies. Not until the 1950's, however, did the Belgians give any thought to providing a system of higher education for the natives or permitting them to hold important government posts. The lack of educated and experienced leaders meant that there was less agitation for independence than in the French and British colonies. It also meant that when independence came the Congolese were not prepared to assume their new responsibilities.

When the Belgians decided in the late 1950's to give the Congo its independence, they worked out a careful plan to provide the natives with more experience in self-government before giving them their freedom. However, native leaders like Joseph Kasavubu and Patrice Lumumba organized political parties and in their efforts to win wide followings insisted on early independence. There were some disturbances in 1959; and the Belgian cabinet, in its anxiety to avoid serious trouble, promised independence in 1960, with the understanding that colonial officials would be retained as advisers, a practice followed elsewhere in Africa. Elections were held that led to Lumumba's becoming prime minister and Kasavubu president.

A few days after independence had been granted, the Congolese army mutinied, deposed its officers who were all Belgians, and committed a number of atrocities. When Lumumba found that he could not control the troops, he joined them in their demand that all Belgians leave the country and asked the United Nations to see that they did so.

The United Nations sent troops, but the departure of most of the Belgians left the political and economic life of the new nation in chaos. Moise Tshombe firmly established himself in Katanga province where his Lunda tribe was strong. Unlike Lumumba, he kept Belgian advisers and used the revenue from the rich mines in his province to pay a small mercenary army. While all else in the Congo was in chaos, law and order prevailed in Katanga; and the economy functioned as usual. Emboldened by his success, Tshombe tried to turn his province into an independent state.

Meanwhile, Kasavubu had deposed Lumumba, and Lumumba had deposed Kasavubu. When the Russians began to aid Lumumba, the Americans began to support Kasavubu in the hope of preventing the communists from establishing a foothold in Africa. Kasavubu managed to get control of Leopoldville, where his Bakongo tribe was strong, but Lumumba supporters held the northeastern provinces. The United Nations Assembly, dominated

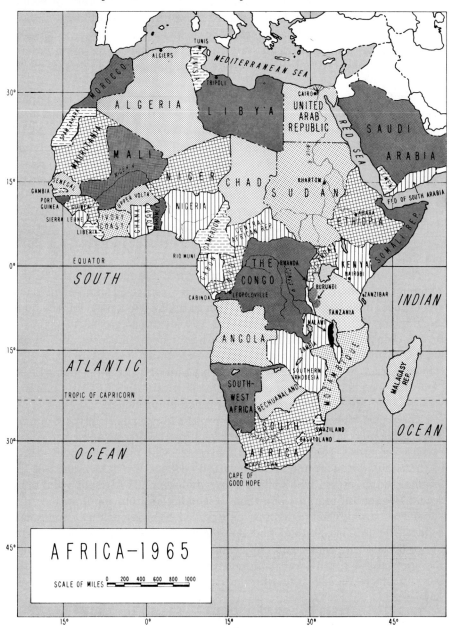

as it was by the Afro-Asian bloc, saw in the presence of Belgians in Katanga a sign of colonialism and insisted that they be driven out, although it was obvious that the Belgians' gravest mistake was in giving the Congo its independence too soon. More fighting followed, but the Katanga separatist movement was brought to an end. By 1964 order still had not been restored, the once prosperous economy had not recovered, and thousands of people had been killed, including Lumumba. Because of this situation the Congolese had rather reluctantly accepted Tshombe as prime minister in spite of the opposition of other African states, and the prospects for more orderly government improved somewhat in spite of communist aid to a rebel movement.

Very few white settlers lived in most of the colonies south of the Sahara at the time they won their independence, so that there was generally little racial difficulty. There were exceptions, however, and in Kenya and Southern Rhodesia the whites who made up a small minority of the population tried to dominate the Negroes by every means at their disposal. In Kenya, a secret Negro society known as the Mau Mau was formed to drive out or exterminate the whites. When the British in desperation decided to give the colony its independence, Negro terroristic activities ceased. Race relations improved after the white settlers accepted the fact that they could not perpetuate their advantageous position, and there is a chance that a multiracial state can develop.

The situation is less fortunate in Southern Rhodesia, where the British could not act unilaterally because it had been a self-governing colony since 1923. The whites controlled the government by having a high income qualification for voting that disfranchised nearly all the Negroes. In 1953, the British combined Southern Rhodesia with Northern Rhodesia and Nyasaland to form a federation, but the racial issue broke it apart in 1963. The following year Northern Rhodesia (Zambia) and Nyasaland (Malawi) became independent Negro-dominated states within the British Commonwealth. The fate of Southern Rhodesia remains uncertain.

The British have been powerless to protect Negro rights in the Union of South Africa because it had become a commonwealth in 1910 before the racial issue arose. The 3,000,000 white people who make up about a fifth of the population were themselves divided between the descendants of the original Dutch settlers who spoke a Dutch dialect called Afrikaans and more recent English immigrants and their descendants. From the first, the Afrikaner was strongly segregationist and denied Negroes political and social rights. The English settlers had no intention of risking white predominance by allowing indiscriminate Negro suffrage, but in the Cape Colony, the one part of the federal dominion they controlled, they permitted the handful of Negroes to vote who had sufficient property to be considered "civilized."

Between the wars the Afrikaners became more nationalistic, and since 1948 they have imposed a rigid segregationalist (apartheid) policy on the entire country. Negroes were denied all political rights even in the Cape Colony. Their movements were restricted, and their economic activities were limited to unskilled work. So rigidly were the races separated that if a Negro sat on a bench in a public park designated for white use, he was subject to a heavy fine, whipping, or imprisonment for a maximum of three years.

South Africa is economically the wealthiest and militarily the most powerful African state south of the Sahara Desert, but how long a small minority of white people can continue to impose its will on the Negro majority in defiance of the newly emerged African states and world opinion remains to be seen. Criticism of the Afrikaners' policies by other British dominions only caused them to withdraw from the British Commonwealth of Nations in 1961 and to establish a completely independent republic.

The Portuguese also have earned the enmity of the new African nations, but for quite different reasons. They were the first European colonists in Africa, and they will be the last to leave. In Angola and Mozambique they have territories twenty times the size of Portugal itself, but since 1951 they have not considered them as colonies but as integral parts of their country. The Portuguese made no distinctions on the basis of color, and Negroes who could pass a rather simple test were accepted as citizens. But since they have made little effort to educate the Negro, only about one out of two hundred has qualified. Furthermore, the Portuguese themselves have few rights, since their government is a fascist dictatorship although a relatively benevolent one. The very backwardness of the inhabitants of Angola and Mozambique has made them slow to demand independence. By 1960, however, they had clearly awakened, and eventually the Portuguese will have to withdraw or face a situation comparable to that of France in Algeria.

The fact that the Africans do not generally feel a strong loyalty to their individual states presents the possibility that larger states will be formed. Proposals for a United States of Africa have not been well received as an immediate goal, but several former colonies have united. Ghana, for example, was formed by the union of British Togoland with the Gold Coast in 1957; and Zanzibar voluntarily joined Tanganyika in 1964, a step that may have saved the island from communism. More ambitious projects are in the offing, so that further changes in the political boundaries of the African states may be expected. Several groups of states have formed common markets on the European model, and there are many joint economic projects. Since 1958 Pan-African conferences have been held to foster co-operation in political, economic, and cultural fields. Such activities justify some optimism about Africa's future as most of the new states are too small to function effectively alone. When one considers the condition of Africa in 1945, it is remarkable how much has already been accomplished. That this has happened is a tribute both to the new African leaders and their former colonial masters.

LATIN AMERICA

World War II brought the Great Depression to a temporary end in Latin America, and the standard of living began to inch forward once more. This economic progress tapered off as the participants in the war regained their normal productivity in peaceful pursuits. From 1956, the situation became especially serious because the price of raw materials which made up most of Latin America's exports began to decline on the world market while the price of the manufactured goods they bought continued to rise. This situation led to an unfavorable balance of trade, one of the factors that caused run-away inflation in Argentina, Brazil, and other countries. A few nations, such as Mexico, managed to continue their economic progress and social reform, but the great majority sank into economic stagnation. Agriculture continued to be inefficient. Industrial and commercial entrepreneurs continued to have retrogressive attitudes, and adequate local markets could not be established because in about three-fourths of the Latin American countries the per capita income was less than $300 a year.

Under these circumstances, rebellions and riots were daily occurrences. Between 1948 and 1958, bandits killed at least 200,000 people in Colombia, a nation of only 14,000,000 inhabitants. Pressing economic problems did lead to one significant change in the nature of the revolutions. In the nineteenth century, revolts had often been caused by quarrels between rival factions, both representing military and conservative interests. More recent revolts have been motivated by clashes between social-economic interests. At first, the radical movements were of native origin and resembled European fascism. Argentina's Juan Peron (1895-   ), for example, was a dashing army colonel who became the idol of the working classes for whose benefit he enacted a broad program of social benefits. His ten-year dictatorship, which began in 1945, was marked by a curtailment of civil liberty, attacks on the Catholic Church, and some of the worst forms of demagoguery the world had seen since the days of Hitler. Finally, he was overthrown by a coup led by military and conservative leaders.

More recently the radical movement has often been inspired by communists who are trying desperately to get a toehold in the New World which they can use for further operations. For a while, it looked as though Guatemala would be the first state to fall into their hands. In 1950 Jacobo Arbenz was elected president of the tiny republic. His policies became increasingly radical. Communists were appointed to key positions in the government. Arms shipments were received from Czechoslovakia. Efforts were made to stir up trouble in neighboring states. Before he had become firmly established, however, a group of Guatemalan exiles invaded from Honduras and with the aid of elements from the army succeeded in overthrowing the regime and establishing a right-wing dictatorship. The communists repeated their efforts to seize the country on several occasions, but their first successful penetration into the Western Hemisphere was in Cuba.

In 1959 a young lawyer named Fidel Castro (1926-   ) managed to overthrow the Batista regime in Cuba after a three-year civil war. His violent, longwinded, half-coherent speeches reminded one of Hitler, but it was the Americans, not the Jews, whom he hated; and he came to regard Communist Russia as his friend, not his enemy. After ridding himself of Batista's followers in a blood bath that far exceeded what was customary in Latin American revolutions, he inaugurated a sweeping land-reform program. Estates with over 995 acres, many of which belonged to Americans, were divided among 300,000 landless peasants. Relations rapidly deteriorated. The United States stopped buying Cuban sugar at more than the market price, and Castro confiscated the remaining American property in Cuba and turned to Russia for economic and military aid. Cuba became a Communist island where revolutionaries were trained to overthrow the governments of the other Latin American states.

When he became president, Kennedy determined to rid the hemisphere of the Cuban menace before Castro succeeded in engineering communist revolutions in other economically depressed countries. Eisenhower had begun to train Cuban exiles to overthrow the Castro regime, and Kennedy authorized an invasion to take place in April, 1961. The expedition was a complete fiasco, and served only to strengthen the ties between Cuba and the Soviet Union. In October, 1962, the United States discovered that the Russians were constructing sites on Cuban soil that were capable of launching nuclear missiles with ranges up to 2,000 miles. The United States reacted so strongly to this threat that the Russians withdrew their offensive missiles and reduced the number of troops they had on the island in return for an American promise not to invade. The episode was heralded as a victory for American diplomacy, but Cuba remained in communist hands. By 1962, Castro had a well-equipped army of 250,000 men, the largest in the Western Hemisphere except for that of the United States; and he continued his efforts to overthrow the governments of other states.

The Castro threat has provided an excuse for conservative military elements in other countries to overthrow constitutional governments because of their real or fancied communist leanings. In 1961-1962 there were successful coups of this sort in Argentina, Peru, Guatemala, Ecuador, the Dominican Republic, and Honduras, while Brazil added itself to the list early in 1964. Castro has not devoted all his efforts to the more conservative Latin American states. Much of his energy has been directed towards trying to overthrow the liberal, reforming Betancourt regime in Venezuela. Thus, a genuine reformer is now likely to be accused of being a communist by the right-wing elements in his country at the same time that he is trying to ward off attacks from Castro's adherents.

This situation has encouraged the United States to try to hasten economic progress while there is still time. Unfortunately, the Alliance for Progress, which was begun in 1961, is moving much more slowly than the Marshall Plan did in Europe. The Latin Americans have been trying to improve their own trading position by creating a Latin American Free Trade Association, which began to operate in 1961. The Association, like the European Common Market, was designed to bring about the complete economic unification of the member-states through a series of gradual stages, but as of 1965 little had been accomplished. The immediate prospects for Latin America are not encouraging, although the progress made by Puerto Rico, Mexico, and Venezuela proves that, where capital is available and where there is intelligent, unselfish leadership, much can be accomplished.

THE SEARCH FOR A PEACEFUL SOLUTION

About 1953 the struggle for world supremacy began to slacken a little. Stalin died, the Korean War came to an end, and the Russians rivalled American military technology by exploding a hydrogen bomb. Both sides became willing to hold diplomatic conferences with the avowed purpose of reaching a peaceful solution, although neither has been willing to make significant concessions.

THE CHANGING RUSSIAN AND AMERICAN ATTITUDES

The Russian attitude towards the struggle for world supremacy began to change for a number of reasons. In the first place, European recovery removed any possibility of peaceful expansion in that direction in the near future. The underdeveloped countries continued to be a fertile ground for communist propaganda, but only a few appeared ready for immediate revolution. The American willingness to fight to save Korea indicated that further advances by armed aggression would be risky. Indeed, it was obvious to almost everyone that Stalin's belligerent behavior had merely compelled the non-communist countries to rearm and draw closer together. Russia had become ringed by a system of defensive alliances sponsored and supported by the United States. Many countries had permitted the United States to establish air bases in strategic localities near the Russian border. If tensions were relaxed, the non-communist states might begin to quarrel again. Time, the Russians were convinced, was on their side. Why risk the horrors of a nuclear war?

Then, too, all was not well in the communist world. Industrial progress was remarkable, but every state that practiced collective agriculture was faced with food shortages. There was obviously discontent among the people, who were more interested in a higher standard of living and greater freedom than they were in communism. The Soviet Union itself was the last of the great multinational European empires and its numerous non-Russian inhabitants were restive. They would not be likely to rebel if the world remained at peace; if war came, however, they might welcome an invading army, just as many had welcomed the Germans. More fragile was the Russian hold over the people in the east European satellites. Once more revolt was improbable unless war provided an opportunity to throw off the communist yoke. China completely freed itself from Russian tutelage and sought support from communists in other parts of the world. People everywhere were tired of talk of war; they wanted peace. Mounting evidence pointed to the wisdom of waiting for time to bring about the promised decay of the capitalistic states rather than running the risk of war. Stalin's death was therefore followed by renewed negotiations with the United States, although the communists continued their subversive activities and there was obviously considerable disagreement about foreign policy among the new leaders of the Soviet Union.

The Republicans swept to victory in the Presidential election of 1952 amid charges that the Truman administration had not taken sufficiently strong action to combat the Russian menace and claims that they themselves would be able to free some of the satellites. Yet the force of circumstances gradually led President Eisenhower to seek a relaxation in the struggle for world supremacy. Peace was made in Korea, and Chiang Kaishek was not "unleashed" on the Chinese mainland. North Vietnam was surrendered to the communists without a fight, and no serious effort was made to profit from the struggle for leadership in Moscow that followed Stalin's death or to give more than verbal support to the Hungarian rebels in 1956.

The failure to act aggressively on these occasions may be attributed in part to the desire of the American people for peace and in part to the changing power situation. The Russian army had always been larger than that of the United States, but in the early postwar years American air superiority, coupled with a monopoly on nuclear weapons, had more than compensated. This situation was altered by Russia's explosion of atomic and hydrogen bombs and by its development of intercontinental ballistic missiles. By 1955, it was clear that nuclear war would lead to widespread destruction in the United States, if not complete annihilation. Republican statesmen had often expressed the belief that the threat of "massive retaliation" by the American air force would hold the Russians in check; now the Russians could also threaten "massive retaliation." A nuclear stalemate was reached in which neither side was likely to use its atomic weapons unless someone blundered.

This situation led President Kennedy to build up conventional American armaments as well as to speed the effort to conquer space. In this way, he provided the United States with an alternative to the use of nuclear weapons when communist advances in Southeast Asia or elsewhere created the necessity for military action. Charles de Gaulle became fearful that the United States would not use nuclear weapons to defend Europe because of the probable Russian retaliation on its own cities. As a result, he insisted that France develop its own nuclear deterrent and followed an increasingly independent foreign policy. The democratic allies of the United States, like the communist allies of the Soviet Union, were becoming more independent. Because they could no longer be certain of their numerous allies, the two great powers became more willing to seek a peaceful solution to their differences.

The growing importance of the neutral nations has also had the same effect. In 1954 there were only sixty-three members of the United Nations, but beginning in 1955 the number grew rapidly and by the close of 1963 there were 113. Nearly all this growth resulted from the new states that were created in Africa and Asia. Most of these states adopted a neutral position in the struggle for world supremacy, and, although they had very little military power, they controlled the General Assembly when they voted as a bloc. More important, they occupied many of the strategic parts of the world; and if their plans for economic development were successful, they might one day hold the balance of power between the two opposing camps. These new states have often been aggressive and uncompromising when their own interests were at stake, but they are strongly opposed to belligerent actions by the great powers. To win their friendship the United States and Russia have modified some of their views, expressed a willingness to negotiate, and hesitated to take aggressive actions.

THE RELAXING OF INTERNATIONAL TENSIONS

Since both the democracies and the communist states were more willing to relax international tensions and to inaugurate an era of peaceful coexistence, they might have been expected to make rapid progress at the conference table. This has not been the case, however, because neither side has wanted to make the necessary compromises. A major dispute centers on the question of where the boundary line between the two systems should be drawn. The United States has been reluctant to admit that it has abandoned its goal of securing the liberation of the east European and Chinese peoples, although public officials now rarely speak of the matter and the inhabitants of these countries have lost all hope of throwing off the communist yoke since the American failure to help the Hungarian rebels. The Russians, on the other hand, have no intention of abandoning their hold on their satellites, and they would like to get the democracies out of West Berlin. It is unlikely that Russia will withdraw from East Germany unless the United States removes its troops from Europe and the reunited Germany is neutralized. This would seriously weaken Western Europe's defenses and might wreck the plans for its economic and political unification. Nevertheless, that neutralization remains a possibility was illustrated by the great powers' decision in 1955 to withdraw from Austria with the proviso that it join neither the democratic nor the communist bloc. Ultimately, the German people may press for neutralization. Chancellors Adenauer and Erhard have staunchly opposed this move, but their successors may demand it as the only likely way to achieve reunification.

The second broad area of disagreement centers on the international control of nuclear weapons, outer space, and the reduction in the size of conventional armaments. The Russians and the Americans have agreed that there should be international control of atomic energy, but the Russians have been unwilling to abandon their great-power veto over the authority that would exercise this control and have refused to permit inspection teams in their country. Judging from their experience with the Russians in recent years, the Americans feel that they cannot trust them, on their word alone, to refrain from making nuclear weapons or preparing for a surprise attack.

In 1955, President Eisenhower suggested that aerial photography could be used for inspecting purposes, but the wrangling continued. Both powers suspended nuclear tests in 1958, and, early in 1961, they seemed to be near agreement on a permanent ban, but once more differences arose. The Soviet Union resumed atmospheric testing of nuclear weapons. Included was the detonation of a fifty-megaton bomb (equivalent to 50,000,000 tons of TNT), a far more destructive weapon than any in the American arsenal. Regretfully, the United States began to test again in 1962. The following year the Soviet Union, the United States, and Great Britain agreed not to conduct any further nuclear tests above the ground, but since then little progress has been made towards a complete test ban, and the task of agreeing on one is likely to become more difficult as more nations develop atomic arsenals. If agreement is not reached soon, an irresponsible power is almost certain to develop nuclear weapons, and the cause of world peace will be seriously jeopardized.

Both the United States and Russia were anxious to reduce the size of conventional armaments, the first to permit the reduction of taxes and the second to permit the production of more consumer goods. Once again mutual suspicion and the problem of inspection have prevented agreement. The launching of the first satellite in 1957 also pointed to the need of reaching agreement on the control of outer space.

To carry on these discussions there have been a number of meetings between the heads of state or their foreign ministers. In July, 1955, President Eisenhower met with the British, French, and Russian heads of state at Geneva, but little was accomplished beyond increasing the amount of travel and cultural exchanges between the communist states and the democracies. Quarrels were soon renewed, but as Khrushchev consolidated his position, he made determined efforts to force the democracies to hold new top-level meetings with him. At first Eisenhower was unwilling, but when Khrushchev threatened to prevent the delivery of supplies to West Berlin, he invited the Russian leader to visit the United States in 1959. The following year another meeting between the heads of state was scheduled to take place at Paris, but the disclosure that the United States had been sending high-altitude U-2 planes over the Soviet Union led Khrushchev to refuse to participate. He and Kennedy exchanged views in Vienna in 1961, and there was speculation that Johnson might consult with the new

Soviet leaders in 1965. These conferences reflected the growing realization on both sides of the Iron Curtain that some sort of settlement must be reached or sooner or later the world will blunder into a devastating war.

It is obviously impossible to predict the outcome of the struggle between the communist and democratic states. Whether it will cease gradually without victory for either side or end in triumph for one or the other, either through war or peaceful competition, cannot be foretold. Whether the future lies with the underdeveloped neutral nations of the world no one knows. This much is certain, however: the civilization created in Western Europe by the Italic and Germanic branches of the Indo-European–speaking people will continue to exercise a decisive influence on the history of the world. History records no more remarkable story than how the inhabitants of the western part of a relatively small peninsular continent developed a new science, a new technology, a new culture, and new institutions and spread them to every continent of the globe. By the twentieth century, they had revolutionized a society once ridden with poverty and disease; they had demonstrated that every citizen could enjoy luxuries not even known by the kings of a century ago and enjoy them for more than twice the life span of their ancestors. Most non-Western people still live in poverty, but they are struggling to achieve a better life. Whether they choose the democratic or the communist way, they will be following a route established by the Western world.

Table of Popes, Rulers, and Regimes

[1] Avignonese line of popes during Great Schism.
[2] Elected by the Council at Pisa.
[3] Elected by the Council at Basel.
   Names in italics are not officially regarded as popes.

POPES *(Continued)*

Clement XIV, 1769-74
Pius VI, 1775-99
Pius VII, 1800-23
Leo XII, 1823-29
Pius VIII, 1829-30
Gregory XVI, 1831-46
Pius IX, 1846-78

Leo XIII, 1878-1903
St. Pius X, 1903-14
Benedict XV, 1914-22
Pius XI, 1922-39
Pius XII, 1939-58
John XXIII, 1958-63
Paul VI, 1963-

HOLY ROMAN EMPERORS

Albert I, 1298-1308 (Habsburg)
Henry VII, 1308-13 (Luxemburg)
Louis IV, 1314-47 (Bavaria)
Charles IV, 1347-78 (Luxemburg)
Wenceslas, 1378-1400 (Luxemburg)
Rupert, 1400-10 (Palatinate)
Sigismund, 1410-37 (Luxemburg)
Albert II, 1438-39 (Habsburg)
Frederick III, 1440-93 (Habsburg)
Maximilian I, 1493-1519 (Habsburg)
Charles V, 1519-56 (Habsburg)
Ferdinand I, 1556-64 (Habsburg)
Maximilian II, 1564-76 (Habsburg)
Rudolph II, 1576-1612 (Habsburg)
Matthias, 1612-19 (Habsburg)
Ferdinand II, 1619-37 (Habsburg)
Ferdinand III, 1637-57 (Habsburg)
Leopold I, 1658-1705 (Habsburg)
Joseph I, 1705-11 (Habsburg)
Charles VI, 1711-40 (Habsburg)
Charles VII, 1742-45 (Bavaria)
Francis I, 1745-65 (Lorraine, husband of Maria Theresa who ruled the Austrian lands, 1740-80)
Joseph II, 1765-90 (Habsburg-Lorraine)
Leopold II, 1790-92 (Habsburg-Lorraine)
Francis II, 1792-1806 (Habsburg-Lorraine; became Francis I, Emperor of Austria, in 1806)

EMPERORS OF AUSTRIA (AFTER 1867, AUSTRIA-HUNGARY)

Francis I, 1806-35
Ferdinand I, 1835-48

Francis Joseph, 1848-1916
Charles I, 1916-18

THE HOHENZOLLERNS

Electors of Brandenburg:
 Frederick I, 1417-40
 Frederick II, 1440-70
 Albert Achilles, 1470-86
 John Cicero, 1486-99
 Joachim I, 1499-1535
 Joachim II, 1535-71
 John George, 1571-98
 Joachim Frederick, 1598-1608
 John Sigismund, 1608-1619. Became duke of Prussia in 1618.

Electors of Brandenburg and Dukes of Prussia:
 John Sigismund, 1618-19
 George William, 1619-40
 Frederick William, 1640-88
 Frederick III, 1688-1713. Became Frederick I, king in Prussia
  in 1701.

Kings in Prussia:
 Frederick I, 1701-13
 Frederick William I, 1713-40
 Frederick II, the Great, 1740-86
 Frederick William II, 1786-97
 Frederick William III, 1797-1840
 Frederick William IV, 1840-61
 William I, 1861-88. Became Emperor of Germany in 1871.

Emperors of Germany:
 William I, 1871-88
 Frederick III, 1888
 William II, 1888-1918

Weimar Republic, 1919-33
The Third Reich, 1933-45
Allied Occupation, 1945-49
German Federal Republic and German Democratic Republic, 1949-

RULERS OF ENGLAND (AFTER 1707, GREAT BRITAIN)

House of Plantagenet:	House of Lancaster:
Edward I, 1272-1307	Henry IV, 1399-1413
Edward II, 1307-27	Henry V, 1413-22
Edward III, 1327-77	Henry VI, 1422-61
Richard II, 1377-99	

RULERS OF ENGLAND (*Continued*)

House of York:
Edward IV, 1461-83
Edward V, 1483
Richard III, 1483-85

House of Tudor:
Henry VII, 1485-1509
Henry VIII, 1509-47
Edward VI, 1547-53
Mary I, 1553-58
Elizabeth, 1558-1603

House of Stuart:
James I, 1603-25
Charles I, 1625-49

The Commonwealth, 1649-53

The Protectorate, 1653-60:
Oliver Cromwell, 1653-58
Richard Cromwell, 1658-60

House of Stuart:
Charles II, 1660-85

House of Stuart (*Continued*):
James II, 1685-88
William III, 1689-1702
and
Mary II, 1689-94
Anne, 1702-14

House of Hanover (called Windsor since 1917):
George I, 1714-27
George II, 1727-60
George III, 1760-1820
George IV, 1820-30
William IV, 1830-37
Victoria, 1837-1901
Edward VII, 1901-10
George V, 1910-36
Edward VIII, 1936
George VI, 1936-52
Elizabeth II, 1952-

RULERS AND GOVERNMENTS OF FRANCE

House of Capet:
Philip IV, 1285-1314
Louis X, 1314-16
John I, 1316
Philip V, 1316-22
Charles IV, 1322-28

House of Valois:
Philip VI, 1328-50
John II, 1350-64
Charles V, 1364-80
Charles VI, 1380-1422
Charles VII, 1422-61
Louis XI, 1461-83
Charles VIII, 1483-98
Louis XII, 1498-1515
Francis I, 1515-47
Henry II, 1547-59
Francis II, 1559-60
Charles IX, 1560-74
Henry III, 1574-89

House of Bourbon:
Henry IV, 1589-1610
Louis XIII, 1610-43
Louis XIV, 1643-1715
Louis XV, 1715-74
Louis XVI, 1774-92

First Republic:
Convention, 1792-95
Directory, 1795-99
Consulate, 1799-1804

First Empire:
Napoleon I, 1804-14

House of Bourbon:
Louis XVIII, 1814-24 (Louis XVII, Louis XVI's son, never actually ruled.)
Charles X, 1824-30

FRANCE (*Continued*)

House of Orleans:
    Louis Philippe, 1830-48

Second Republic, 1848-52

Second Empire:
    Napoleon III, 1852-70 (Napoleon II, Napoleon I's son, never actually ruled.)

Third Republic, 1870-1940

Vichy Regime, 1940-44

Provisional Government, 1944-46

Fourth Republic, 1946-58

Fifth Republic, 1958-

RULERS OF SPAIN

The Catholic kings:
    Ferdinand, King of Aragon, 1479-1516
    Isabella, Queen of Castile, 1474-1504
    Joanna, Queen of Castile (insane), 1504-55

House of Habsburg:
    Charles I (Charles V of the Holy Roman Empire), 1516-56
    Philip II, 1556-98
    Philip III, 1598-1621
    Philip IV, 1621-65
    Charles II, 1665-1700

House of Bourbon:
    Philip V, 1700-46
    Ferdinand VI, 1746-59
    Charles III, 1759-88
    Charles IV, 1788-1808

House of Bonaparte:
    Joseph I, 1808-13

House of Bourbon:
    Ferdinand VII, 1813-33
    Isabella II, 1833-68

Provisional Government, 1868-1871

Amadeo I (son of Victor Emmanuel II of Italy), king 1871-73

First Republic, 1873-74

House of Bourbon:
    Alfonso XII, 1875-85
    Alfonso XIII, 1885-1932

Second Republic, 1932-39

Franco Regime, 1939-

SARDINIA AND ITALY SINCE 1796

Kings of Sardinia:
    Victor Emmanuel I, 1802-1821
    Charles Felix, 1821-31
    Charles Albert, 1831-49
    Victor Emmanuel II, 1849-1878 (Became king of Italy in 1861.)

Kings of Italy:
    Victor Emmanuel II, 1861-1878
    Humbert I, 1878-1900
    Victor Emmanuel III, 1900-1946
    Humbert II, 1946

Republic of Italy, 1946-

MUSCOVY AND RUSSIA

Grand Dukes of Muscovy:
Ivan I, 1325-41
Simeon I, 1341-53
Ivan II, 1353-59
Dmitri Donskoi, 1359-89
Basil I, 1389-1425
Basil II, 1425-62
Ivan III, the Great, 1462-1505
Basil III, 1505-33
Ivan II, the Terrible, 1533-84 (Took title of tsar of Russia in 1547.)

Tsars of Russia:
Ivan IV, the Terrible, 1547-84
Theodore I, 1584-98
Boris Godunov, 1598-1605

Time of Troubles, 1604-13

Michael I, 1613-45, of the house of Romanov
Alexis, 1645-76

Theodore II, 1676-82
Ivan V, 1682-89
and
Peter I, the Great, 1682-1725
Catherine I, 1725-27
Peter II, 1727-30
Anna, 1730-40
Ivan VI, 1740-41
Elizabeth, 1741-62
Peter III, 1762
Catherine II, the Great, 1762-96
Paul, 1796-1801
Alexander I, 1801-25
Nicholas I, 1825-55
Alexander II, 1855-81
Alexander III, 1881-94
Nicholas II, 1894-1917

Provisional Government and Communist Revolution, 1917-1922
Union of Soviet Socialist Republics, 1922-

EMPERORS OF JAPAN SINCE 1867

Mutsuhito, 1867-1912
Yoshihito, 1912-26

Hirohito, 1926-

Bibliography

So MANY thousands of history books have been written that no bibliography can list more than a small fraction of the most useful ones. This is especially true when the bibliography is for a textbook that covers as much time and space as a history of the Western world from the Renaissance to the present. Therefore, the first section of this bibliography is devoted to suggesting ways in which students may find and select historical works on a given subject. The second part suggests a small number of books in English on the various topics discussed in the text. Emphasis is placed on those works that have been published too recently to be included in the standard bibliographies and those that are available in paperback editions that students or college libraries may purchase in large enough quantities to be used in conjunction with the course.

There are now many paperback books in print, and the number is rapidly increasing. R. R. Bowker Company, 1180 Avenue of the Americas, New York City, periodically prints a general list of available titles, as well as a more selective one, *Paperbound Book Guide for Colleges*, in which publishers list those of their works that they regard as especially suitable for use in college courses. Most of these books are either standard accounts by contemporary historians or influential works written by historians who lived some time ago, but an increasing number of histories are now being written especially for the paperback market.

Several hardback series are no more expensive than many paperback ones. The *Berkshire Studies in European History* edited by Richard A. Newall and others consists of brief studies of various periods or countries written specially for college students. The *Teach Yourself History Library* edited by A. L. Rowse is intended for laymen. Each volume is a biography of a great man that is designed to reveal various aspects of the age in which he lived. Titles in both of the above series are frequently available in paperback editions. The *Modern Library* and *Everyman* series include inexpensive editions of the great writers and thinkers of the past.

SECTION I   THE SEARCH FOR A GOOD BOOK

The most common ways to find books on a given subject are to consult the card catalogue in the college library and to consult bibliographies. Nearly all the college libraries in the United States list books in their card catalogues under subject matter as well as under author and title. If, for example, one wishes to find a biography of Louis XIV, he can look under "Louis XIV" in the card catalogue to see what works are available in the library. Or, if he is more interested in the general aspects of Louis XIV's reign, he can consult the card catalogue under "France" and the subheading "history" where books on the history of France are listed by period.

A second method of finding a book is to consult bibliographies. The best one-volume bibliography is the *American Historical Association's Guide to Historical Literature* (New York, 1961), edited by George F. Howe and others. The *Guide* suggests books on the nature and purpose of history, the history of every part of the world, and many related subjects. Since there is space to mention only a small fraction of the historical works that have been published, sections of the *Guide* begin with a list of specialized bibliographies on the period or subject that they treat. By consulting the *Guide* and these specialized bibliographies one can usually find books on the subject that has claimed his attention.

Once a scholar has found the names of several books on a subject, he is faced with the problem of deciding which one or ones to read. The mere presence of a book in a college library does not mean that it is good and most certainly does not indicate that it is the best study on the subject. Before making a final selection, it is wise to examine the book. If the title page indicates that it is written by a professor at an academic institution, it is probably a scholarly work, although it may be badly written. Some historical works by persons not connected with academic institutions are excellent, but others are written more to amuse than to inform. The presence of scholarly apparatus such as footnotes and bibliography may indicate whether the author's purpose is serious, but it is by no means an infallible guide. The preface or introduction to a book often provides useful information concerning the author's purpose, and the acknowledgments he makes may indicate the type of person to whom he feels indebted. But before making a final selection, it is wise to consult book reviews by recognized authorities in the field.

Book reviews usually appear in historical journals from about six months to two years after the book is published. The best-known journals that publish book reviews in English on topics in the history of the Western world are *The American Historical Review*, *The Journal of Modern History*, *The English Historical Review*, and *History*, but there are many more specialized historical periodicals that publish valuable reviews. The *Book Review Digest* contains quotations taken from selected reviews and indicates where the complete review may be found.

Many of the most important contributions to historical knowledge are published as articles in periodicals. Since there are hundreds of important historical periodicals, no individual can hope to consult regularly more than a small fraction, and only the largest university libraries can afford to subscribe to all of them. This situation led to the publication of *Historical Abstracts,* a periodical that since 1955 has summarized articles on the period 1775-1945 that have appeared in historical journals throughout the world. It is anticipated that articles on earlier periods of history will eventually be included.

Our knowledge of the past, like our knowledge of nearly every other subject, is constantly being added to and is constantly being reinterpreted. Bibliographies and book reviews provide valuable assistance to scholars who seek to stay abreast of the latest developments in the study of history. In addition, there are several series of publications to aid in this task. The Service Center for Teachers of History of the American Historical Association is publishing a number of inexpensive pamphlets which analyze "significant contributions in recent writing and pertinent trends in historical study." D. C. Heath and Company publishes a paperback series edited by Ralph W. Greenlaw and Dwight E. Lee called *Problems in European Civilization,* another series edited by William T. de Bary and others called *Problems in Asian Civilization,* and another edited by George R. Taylor called *Problems in American Civilization.* These three Heath series consist of selections, on controversial questions, taken from the writings of various historians. Recently, Holt, Rinehart and Winston has inaugurated a similar series, under the editorship of Mortimer Chambers, entitled *European Problem Studies.* Specific note will be taken of some of the individual titles in the above series in the appropriate place in Section II of this bibliography.

SECTION II SUGGESTED WORKS

The place and date of publication for the works cited below are for the hardback volume, but an asterisk is placed beside those that are also available in paperback editions. Two abbreviations are used: "S.C.T.H." indicates that the work cited is a publication of the Service Center for Teachers of History; and "Heath, *Problems*" indicates that the work is one of the Heath *Problems in American, Asian,* or *European Civilization* series. As far as possible, titles have been listed under the chapter and section of the text to which they relate, but those works which deal with subject matter that pertains to a number of chapters are listed separately below.

GENERAL HISTORIES

The New Cambridge Modern History (Cambridge, 1957 ff.), ed. Sir George
    Clark and others. This multivolume history consists of chapters by leading authorities.
The Rise of Modern Europe* (New York, 1935 ff.), ed. William L. Langer.
    Each volume is written by a different author who seeks to present a synthesis of the period he considers. Good bibliographies.

A General History of Europe (New York, 1961 ff.), ed. Denys Hay. Each volume is by an individual author who employs a topical approach.

The University of Michigan History of the Modern World (Ann Arbor, 1958 ff.), eds. Allan Nevins and Howard M. Ehrmann. Each volume is a predominantly chronological account of a nation or region by an individual author.

The Pelican History of the World * (Harmondsworth, 1950 ff.), ed. J. E. Morpurgo. Each country is treated by a leading authority in a separate volume or volumes.

Lewis C. B. Seaman, *From Vienna to Versailles* (London, 1955). A provocative interpretation of European history between 1815 and 1919.

HISTORIES OF EUROPEAN COUNTRIES AND REGIONS

The Oxford History of England (Oxford, 1934 ff.), 14 vols., ed. Sir George Clark. Each volume is organized topically. Generally dull but authoritative.

The Pelican History of England *(Harmondsworth, 1950-55), 8 vols. Short, well-written volumes that reflect the latest historical thinking.

George D. H. Cole and Raymond Postgate, *The British People, 1746-1946* (New York, 2nd ed., 1947).

William H. B. Court, *A Concise Economic History of Britain, from 1750 to Recent Times** (Cambridge, 1954).

Anthony Wood, *Nineteenth-Century Britain, 1815-1914* (London, 1960).

Gordon Wright, *France in Modern Times: 1760 to the Present* (Chicago, 1960). A well-written, authoritative history. Contains chapters describing the different interpretations of each period.

Alfred Cobban, *A History of Modern France** (Harmondsworth, Revised ed., 1962), 2 vols. The second volume covering the period 1800-1940 will be expanded into a two-volume work.

Denis W. Brogan, *The French Nation from Napoleon to Petain, 1814-1940** (London, 1957).

John P. T. Bury, *France, 1814-1940** (London, 1949).

John B. Wolf, *France, 1815 to the Present* * (New York, 1940).

Shepard B. Clough, *France: A History of National Economics, 1789-1939* (New York, 1939).

Adrien Dansette, *Religious History of Modern France* (New York, 1961), 2 vols., tr. by J. Dingle.

Janet P. Trevelyan, *A Short History of the Italian People, from the Barbarian Invasions to the Present Day* (London, 4th ed., 1956).

Charles F. Delzell, *Italy in Modern Times: An Introduction to the Historical Literature in English** (Washington, 1965). S.C.T.H.

René Albrecht-Carrié, *Italy from Napoleon to Mussolini** (New York, 1950).

Denis Mack Smith, *Italy: A Modern History* (Ann Arbor, 1959).

Selected Bibliography

Arturo C. Jemolo, *Church and State in Italy, 1850-1950* (Oxford, 1960), tr. by D. Moore.

Hajo Holborn, *A History of Modern Germany* (New York, 1959 ff.). Two of the projected three volumes have been published.

John E. Rodes, *Germany: A History* (New York, 1964).

Marshall Dill, *Germany: A Modern History* (Ann Arbor, 1961).

Ernest J. Passant, *A Short History of Germany, 1815-1945** (Cambridge, 1959).

Alan J. P. Taylor, *The Course of German History: A Survey of the Development of Germany since 1815** (New York, 1946).

Leonard Krieger, *The German Idea of Freedom* (Boston, 1957). An excellent study of the German conception of freedom from the 18th century.

Gordon Craig, *The Politics of the Prussian Army 1640-1945* (New York, 1956).

Alan J. P. Taylor, *The Habsburg Monarchy, 1809-1918** (London, New ed., 1948).

Robert A. Kann, *A Study in Austrian Intellectual History: From Late Baroque to Romanticism* (London, 1960).

William C. Atkinson, *A History of Spain and Portugal** (Harmondsworth, 1960).

Harold V. Livermore, *A History of Spain* (London, 1958). A sound but overly factual political history.

Rhea M. Smith, *Spain* (Ann Arbor, 1965).

Ingvar Andersson, *A History of Sweden* (London, 1956), tr. by C. Hannay.

Richard V. Burks, *Some Elements of East European History** (Washington, 1961). S.C.T.H.

Oskar Halecki, *Borderlands of Western Civilization: A History of East Central Europe* (New York, 1952). The author stresses the contributions the countries between Germany and Russia have made to Western civilization.

Francis Dvornik, *The Slavs in European History and Civilization* (New Brunswick, 1962).

Leften S. Stavrianos, *The Balkans since 1453* (New York, 1958). An excellent, well-balanced text with a good bibliography.

George Vernadsky, *A History of Russia* (New Haven, 1934 ff.). The most scholarly long history. The four volumes that have been published reach only to the latter part of the 16th century.

Michael T. Florinsky, *Russia: A History and an Interpretation* (New York, 1953), 2 vols.

Anatole G. Mazour, *Rise and Fall of the Romanovs** (Princeton, 1960).

Jerome Blum, *Lord and Peasant in Russia, from the Ninth to the Nineteenth Century** (Princeton, 1960).

Barbara Jelavich, *A Century of Russian Foreign Policy, 1814-1914** (Philadelphia, 1964). Emphasizes the Balkan policy.

Ivo J. Lederer, ed., *Russian Foreign Policy: Essays in Historical Perspective** (New Haven, 1962).

HISTORIES OF THEMES AND TOPICS

The Macmilian Company is publishing a paperback series, under the general editorship of Bruce Mazlish, entitled *Main Themes in European History*. Individual volumes consist of selections by leading authorities in the field concerned. By the close of 1964 titles were available on the history of science, technology, the state, religion, population movements, and imperialism.

Science and Technology

William C. Dampier, *A History of Science and Its Relations with Philosophy and Religion* (Cambridge, 4th ed., 1961).

Charles C. Gillispie, *The Edge of Objectivity: An Essay in the History of Scientific Ideas* (Princeton, 1960).

Thomas S. Kuhn, *The Structure of Scientific Revolutions* * (Chicago, 1964).

Thomas K. Derry and Trevor I. Williams, *A Short History of Technology: From the Earliest Times to A.D. 1900* (New York, 1960).

Charles J. Singer and others, eds., *A History of Technology* (Oxford, 1954-1958), 5 vols.

Intellectual and Religious

Arthur O. Lovejoy, *The Great Chain of Being: A Study of the History of an Idea** (Cambridge, Mass., 1936).

John H. Randall, *The Making of the Modern Mind* (Boston, Rev. ed., 1940).

Crane Brinton, *A History of Western Morals* (New York, 1959).

John B. Bury, *The Idea of Progress** (London, 1920).

Bertrand Russell, *A History of Western Philosophy** (New York, 1945).

Wilhelm Windelband, *A History of Philosophy** (New York, 2nd ed., 1901), tr. by J. H. Tufts. A classic.

George H. Sabine, *A History of Political Theory* (New York, Rev. ed., 1950).

Friedrich Meinecke, *Machiavellism: The Doctrine of Raison d'État and Its Place in Modern History** (New Haven, 1957), tr. by D. Scott.

Peter R. Viereck, *Metapolitics: From the Romantics to Hitler** (New York, 1941).

Guido de Ruggiero, *The History of European Liberalism** (London, 1927), tr. by R. G. Collingwood. A classic.

George D. H. Cole, *A History of Socialist Thought* (London, 1953-60), 5 vols. in 7.

George L. Mosse, *The Culture of Western Europe: The Nineteenth and Twentieth Centuries. An Introduction* (Chicago, 1961).

Selected Bibliography

Franklin L. Baumer, *Religion and the Rise of Skepticism* (New York, 1960).

Adolf von Harnack, *History of Dogma* (London, 1896-99), 7 vols., tr. by N. Buchanan and others.

Philip Hughes, *A Popular History of the Catholic Church** (New York, 1949).

Kenneth S. Latourette, *Christianity in a Revolutionary Age: A History of Christianity in the Nineteenth and Twentieth Centuries* (New York, 1958-62), 5 vols.

Ernst Troeltsch, *The Social Teaching of the Christian Churches** (New York, 1931), tr. by O. Wyon.

Nationalism

Leonard W. Doob, *Patriotism and Nationalism: Their Psychological Foundations* (New Haven, 1964).

Carlton J. H. Hayes, *Nationalism: A Religion* (New York, 1960).

Hans Kohn, *The Idea of Nationalism: A Study in Its Origin and Background** (New York, 2nd printing, 1945).

Boyd C. Shafer, *Nationalism: Myth and Reality* (New York, 1955).

Louis L. Snyder, *The Meaning of Nationalism* (New Brunswick, 1954).

Economic and Social History

The Cambridge Economic History of Europe from the Decline of the Roman Empire (Cambridge, 1941 ff.), eds., John H. Claphan and Eileen Power.

Herbert Heaton, *Economic History of Europe* (New York, Rev. ed., 1948).

B. H. Slicher van Bath, *The Agrarian History of Western Europe, A.D. 500-1850* (New York, 1963), tr. by O. Ordish.

Richard H. Tawney, *Religion and the Rise of Capitalism** (New York, 1926).

War and Diplomacy

René Albrecht-Carrié, *A Diplomatic History of Europe Since the Congress of Vienna* (New York, 1958).

Edward M. Earle, ed., *Makers of Modern Strategy: Military Thought from Machiavelli to Hitler* (Princeton, 1944).

Cyril B. Falls, *The Art of War: From the Age of Napoleon to the Present Day** (London, 1961).

John F. C. Fuller, *A Military History of the Western World* (New York, 1954-56), 3 vols.

Theodore Ropp, *War in the Modern World* * (Durham, 1959).

John U. Nef, *War and Human Progress: An Essay on the Rise of Industrial Civilization** (Cambridge, Mass., 1950).

Joseph J. Mathews, *Reporting the Wars* (Minneapolis, 1957). A study of war news, censorship, and propaganda.

HISTORIES OF ASIA

Woodbridge Bingham, Hilary Conroy, and Frank W. Iklé, *A History of Asia* (Boston, 1964-65), 2 vols.

John K. Fairbank, Edwin O. Reischauer, and Albert M. Craig, *A History of East Asian Civilization* (Boston, 1960-65), 2 vols.

Kenneth W. Morgan, *Asian Religions** (New York, 1964). S.C.T.H.

J. Holland Rose and others, eds., *The Cambridge History of the British Empire* (Cambridge, 1929-59), 8 vols. in 9.

Charles O. Hucker, *Chinese History: A Bibliographic Review* * (Washington, 1958). S.C.T.H.

Raymond S. Dawson, ed., *The Legacy of China* (Oxford, 1964). A study of Chinese contributions to the world.

Luther C. Goodrich, *A Short History of the Chinese People* * (New York, Rev. ed., 1951). The best one-volume work in English.

René Grousset, *The Rise and Splendour of the Chinese Empire* * (London, 1952). A cultural history.

John W. Hall, *Japanese History: New Dimensions of Approach and Understanding** (Washington, 1961). S.C.T.H.

George B. Sansom, *A History of Japan* (Stanford, 1958-63), 3 vols. The best history in English. Stops in 1867.

Richard Storry, *A History of Modern Japan* * (Harmondsworth, 1960).

Robert I. Crane, *The History of India: Its Study and Interpretation** (Washington, 1958). S.C.T.H.

Ramesh C. Majumdar and others, *An Advanced History of India* (London, 1948). The best one-volume study for advanced students.

William H. Moreland and Atul C. Chatterjee, *A Short History of India* (London, 4th ed., 1957).

Roderic H. Davison, *The Near and Middle East: An Introduction to History and Bibliography* * (Washington, 1959). S.C.T.H.

Carl Brockelmann, *History of the Islamic Peoples** (London, 1949). A German authority who concentrates on the medieval period.

Sydney N. Fisher, *The Middle East: A History* (New York, 1959). An American authority who concentrates on the modern period.

Philip K. Hitti, *History of the Arabs, from the Earliest Times to the Present* (London, 7th ed., 1960). Emphasis on political history.

Bernard Lewis, *The Aabs in History** (London, 3rd ed., 1956). Emphasis on Moslem civilization.

Anthony D. Alderson, *The Structure of the Ottoman Dynasty* (Oxford, 1956). A good study of the royal family and the role of the harem.

Niyazi Berkes, *The Development of Secularism in Turkey* (McGill, 1964). A study of Western influence on Turkey during the last two centuries.

Selected Bibliography

HISTORIES OF AFRICA

Philip D. Curtin, *African History* (New York, 1964). S.C.T.H.
Roland Oliver and John D. Fage, *A Short History of Africa* * (Balitmore, 1962).
G. W. Kingsnorth, *Africa South of the Sahara** (Cambridge, 1962).
Donald L. Wiedner, *A History of Africa South of the Sahara** (New York, 1962).
Roland Oliver and Gervase Mathew, eds., *History of East Africa* * (Oxford, 1963 ff.). One of a projected three volumes has been published.
Alfred J. Wills, *An Introduction to the History of Central Africa** (London, 1964).
Robert I. Rotberg, *A Political History of Tropical Africa* (New York, 1965).

GENERAL HISTORIES OF THE UNITED STATES AND CANADA

There are numerous good one- and two-volume histories of the United States as well as many longer works. Of the latter the most up-to-date is *The New American Nation Series** (New York, 1954 ff.), edited by Henry S. Commager and Richard B. Morris.

Harvard Guide to American History (Cambridge, Mass., 1954), ed. by Oscar Handlin. A detailed bibliography for American history.
Ray A. Billington, *The American Frontier* * (Washington, 1958). S.C.T.H.
George R. Taylor, *The Turner Thesis Concerning the Role of the Frontier in American History** (Boston, Rev. ed., 1956). Heath, *Problems.*
Ray A. Billington, *Westward Expansion* (New York, 1949).
Frederick Merk, *Manifest Destiny and Mission in American History: A Reinterpretation* (New York, 1963).
Oscar Handlin, *The Uprooted* *(Boston, 1951). A study of the great American migrations.
David Potter, *People of Plenty: Economic Abundance and the American Character** (Chicago, 1954). An interpretative study that makes use of the new techniques in the social sciences.
Otis A. Singletary, *The South in American History** (Washington, 1957). S.C.T.H.
Merle E. Curti, *The Growth of American Thought* (New York, 2nd ed. 1951).
Ralph H. Gabriel, *The Course of American Democratic Thought* (New York, 2nd ed., 1956).
Richard Hofstadter, *The American Political Tradition and the Men Who Made It** (New York, 1948).
Stow Persons, *American Minds: A History of Ideas* (New York, 1958).
Harold U. Faulkner, *American Economic History* (New York, 7th ed., 1954).

Richard W. Leopold, *The Growth of American Foreign Policy: A History* (New York, 1962).

Donald Creighton, *The Story of Canada* (Boston, 1960).

Robin W. Winks, *Recent Trends and New Literature in Canadian History* (Washington, 1959). S.C.T.H.

HISTORIES OF LATIN AMERICA

Charles Gibson, *The Colonial Period in Latin American History* * (Washington, 1958). S.C.T.H.

Arthur P. Whitaker, *Latin American History Since 1825** (Washington, 1961). S.C.T.H.

Donald M. Dozer, *Latin America: An Interpretative History* (New York, 1962).

Hubert Herring, *A History of Latin America from the Beginnings to the Present* (New York, 2nd ed., 1961).

ART AND MUSIC

Ernst H. Gombrich, *The Story of Art* (London, 8th ed., 1956). Excellent for students who have had no courses in art history.

Horst W. Janson, *History of Art: A Survey of the Major Visual Arts from the Dawn of History to the Present Day* (Englewood Cliffs, 1962). Longer than Gombrich and has a bibliography.

Frederick B. Artz, *From the Renaissance to Romanticism: Trends in Style in Art, Literature, and Music, 1300-1830* (Chicago, 1962).

Arnold Hauser, *The Social History of Art** (New York, ed. of 1957). 2 vols.

Erwin Panofsky, *Meaning in the Visual Arts** (Garden City, 1955).

Henry R. Hitchcock, *Architecture: Nineteenth and Twentieth Centuries* (Baltimore, 2nd ed., 1963).

Nikolaus Pevsner, *An Outline of European Architecture** (Harmondsworth, 7th ed., 1963).

Beekman C. Cannon, Alvin H. Johnson, and William G. Waite, *The Art of Music: A Short History of Musical Styles and Ideas* (New York, 1960). Bibliography.

Paul H. Lang, *Music in Western Civilization* (New York, 1941). Relates music to other aspects of cultural history.

Denis Stevens and Alec Robertson, *The Pelican History of Music** (London, 1960 ff.). One volume to date.

ATLASES

Edward W. Fox, ed., *Atlas of European History* (New York, 1957). Absence of details and superb relief maps make this atlas ideal for freshman use.

Robert R. Palmer, ed., *Atlas of World History* (Chicago, 1957). Carefully designed for college students. Written explanations accompany each map. Contains tables of historical statistics.

William R. Shepherd, *Historical Atlas* (Pikesville, 8th ed., 1956). The best one-volume historical atlas of the world for scholarly purposes.

CHAPTER I HISTORY, GEOGRAPHY, AND PEOPLE

The Nature, Purpose, and Method of History

W. Stull Holt, *The Historical Profession in the United States* * (New York, 1963). S.C.T.H.

Paul L. Ward, *A Style of History for Beginners** (Washington, 1959). S.C.T.H.

Louis R. Gottschalk, *Understanding History: A Primer of Historical Method* (New York, 1950).

Carl G. Gustavson, *A Preface to History** (New York, 1955).

Allan Nevins, *The Gateway to History* * (Boston, 1938).

Jacques Barzun and Henry F. Graff, *The Modern Researcher** (New York, 1957).

Marc Bloch, *The Historian's Craft** (New York, 1953), tr. by. P. Putman.

Herbert J. Muller, *The Uses of the Past* * (New York, 1952).

The Influence of Geography and Climate

Lucien Febvre and Lionel Bataillon, *A Geographical Introduction to History* (London and New York, 1925), tr. by E. G. Mountford and J. H. Paxton.

Ellsworth Huntington, *Mainsprings of Civilization** (New York, 1945). A study of the influence of geography and climate on history.

Roderick Peattie, *Geography in Human Destiny* (New York, 1940).

Norman J. G. Pounds, *An Historical and Political Geography of Europe* (London, 1947).

Derwent S. Whittlesey, *Environmental Foundations of European History* (New York, 1949).

Races and Peoples

Alan H. Brodrick, *Early Man: A Survey of Human Origins* (London, 1948).

Alfred L. Kroeber, *Anthropology: Race, Language, Culture, Psychology, Prehistory* (New York, 2nd ed., 1948).

William C. Boyd, *Genetics and the Races of Man: An Introduction to Modern Physical Anthropology* (Boston, 1950).

CHAPTER II THE DECLINE OF MEDIEVAL CIVILIZATION

The Medieval Civilization

Frederick B. Artz, *The Mind of the Middle Ages*, A.D. 200-1500 (New York, 2nd ed., 1954). A good introduction.

Marshall W. Baldwin, *The Medieval Church** (Ithaca, 1953).

Walter Ullmann, *Medieval Papalism: The Political Theories of the Medieval Canonists* (London, 1949).

Meyrick H. Carré, *Realists and Nominalists* (Oxford, 1946).

Etienne Gilson, *History of Christian Philosophy in the Middle Ages* (New York, 1955). The most authoritative treatment.

Alastair C. Crombie, *Augustine to Galileo: The History of Science, A.D. 400-1650** (London, 1952).

Charles R. Morey, *Mediaeval Art* (New York, 1942). The best general study.

Erwin Panofsky, *Gothic Architecture and Scholasticism** (New York, 1957). Excellent.

Sidney Painter, *The Rise of the Feudal Monarchies** (Ithaca, 1957).

Maude V. Clarke, *The Medieval City State* (London, 1926).

Charles H. McIlwain, *The Growth of Political Thought in the West from the Greeks to the End of the Middle Ages* (New York, 1932).

Henri Pirenne, *Economic and Social History of Medieval Europe** (London, 1936).

Sidney Painter, *Mediaeval Society** (Ithaca, 1957).

Sidney Painter, *French Chivalry: Chivalric Ideas and Practices in Mediaeval France** (Baltimore, 1940).

Eileen Power, *Medieval People** (New York, 1935). Delightful.

John H. Mundy and Peter Riesenberg, *The Medieval Town** (Princeton, 1958).

Nellie Neilson, *Medieval Agrarian Economy* (New York, 1936).

The Late Medieval Civilization

Wallace K. Ferguson, *Europe in Transition, 1300-1520* (Boston, 1962).

Thomas S. R. Boase, *Boniface VIII* (London, 1933).

Alexander C. Flick, *The Decline of the Medieval Church* (London, 1930), 2 vols.

Guillaume Mollat, *The Popes at Avignon, 1305-1378** (London, 1963), tr. by J. Love.

Brian Tierney, *Foundations of the Conciliar Theory: The Contributions of the Medieval Canonists from Gratian to the Great Schism* (Cambridge, 1955).

Walter Ullmann, *The Origins of the Great Schism* (London, 1948).

Kenneth B. McFarlane, *John Wycliffe and the Beginnings of English Non-conformity** (London, 1952). Teach Yourself History Library.

James M. Clark, *The Great German Mystics: Eckhart, Tauler and Suso* (Oxford, 1949).

Heiko A. Oberman, *The Harvest of Medieval Theology: Gabriel Biel and Late Medieval Nominalism* (Cambridge, Mass., 1963).

Albert Hyma, *The Brethren of the Common Life* (Grand Rapids, 1950).

Matthew Spinka, *John Hus and the Czech Reform* (Chicago, 1941).

Selected Bibliography

Edouard Perroy, *The Hundred Years War* * (London, 1951), tr. by W. B. Wells.

Alec R. Myers, *England in the Late Middle Ages** (Harmondsworth, 1952).

Vivian H. H. Green, *The Later Plantagenets: A Survey of English History between 1307 and 1485* (London, 1955).

Lucien Fabre, *Joan of Arc* (New York, 1954), tr. by G. Hopkins.

Geoffrey Barraclough, *The Origins of Modern Germany* * (Oxford, 1946).

Roger B. Merriman, *The Rise of the Spanish Empire in the Old World and the New* (New York, 1918), vol. I.

Frederick G. Heymann, *John Žižka and the Hussite Revolution* (Princeton, 1955).

James W. Thompson, *Economic and Social History of Europe in the Later Middle Ages (1300-1530)* (New York, 1931). Outdated by recent research.

Raymond De Roover, *Money, Banking and Credit in Medieval Bruges* (Cambridge, Mass., 1948).

Benjamin N. Nelson, *The Idea of Usury, from Tribal Brotherhood to Universal Otherhood* (Princeton, 1949).

Charles F. Mullett, *The Bubonic Plague and England* (Lexington, 1956).

George G. Coulton, *The Black Death* (New York, 1930).

Johan Huizinga, *The Waning of the Middle Ages** (London, 1924), tr. by T. Hopman.

Millard Meiss, *Painting in Florence and Siena after the Black Death* * (Princeton, 1951).

PART II   THE RENAISSANCE

Wallace K. Ferguson, *The Renaissance in Historical Thought: Five Centuries of Interpretation* (Boston, 1948). Excellent.

Denys, Hay, *The Renaissance Debate** (New York, 1965). Holt, Rinehart and Winston, *European Problem Studies*.

Karl H. Dannenfeldt, ed., *The Renaissance: Medieval or Modern?* * (Boston, 1959). Heath, *Problems*.

S. Harrison Thomson, *Europe in Renaissance and Reformation* (New York, 1963).

Wallace K. Ferguson, *Europe in Transition, 1300-1520* (Boston, 1962). The best general treatment of the period in spite of an overemphasis on economic-social causation.

Myron P. Gilmore, *The World of Humanism, 1453-1517** (New York, 1952). A good synthesis.

New York Metropolitan Museum of Art, *The Renaissance, a Symposium, February 8-10, 1952** (New York, 1953). Contains essays on the state, economics, science, religion, literature, and art by leading authorities.

Tinsley Helton, ed., *The Renaissance: A Reconsideration of the Theories and Interpretations of the Age** (Madison, 1961). Contains six essays.

William H. Werkmeister, ed., *Facets of the Renaissance** (Los Angeles, 1959). Contains five essays.

The New Cambridge Modern History, Vol. I: *The Renaissance, 1493-1520* (Cambridge, 1957), ed. George R. Potter; and Vol. II: *The Reformation, 1520-1559* (Cambridge, 1958), ed. Geoffrey R. Elton.

Garrett Mattingly, *Renaissance Diplomacy** (London, 1955).

CHAPTER III   THE RENAISSANCE STATE

The Italian Microcosm

Jacob Burckhardt, *The Civilization of the Renaissance in Italy.** This book, first published in 1860, is available in numerous editions. In spite of errors and misinterpretations, it remains essential to the study of the concept of the Renaissance.

Denys Hay, *The Italian Renaissance in Its Historical Background* (Cambridge, 1961). A good synthesis based on the most recent works.

Cecilia M. Ady, *Lorenzo de Medici and Renaissance Italy** (London, 1955).

Gene A. Brucker, *Florentine Politics and Society, 1343-1378* (Princeton, 1962).

Ferdinand Schevill, *History of Florence from the Founding of the City Through the Renaissance** (New York, 1936). Old-fashioned but useful.

De Lamar Jensen, *Machiavelli: Cynic, Patriot, or Political Scientist?** (Boston, 1960). Heath, *Problems.*

John R. Hale, *Machiavelli and Renaissance Italy * (London, 1961).

Federico Chabod, *Machiavelli and the Renaissance** (Cambridge, 1958), tr. by D. Moore.

Felix Gilbert, *Machiavelli and Guicciardini: Politics and History in 16th Century Florence* (Princeton, 1965).

Dorothy Muir, *A History of Milan under the Visconti* (London, 1924).

Cecilia M. Ady, *The Bentivoglio of Bologna: A Study in Despotism* (London, 1937).

The Renaissance Monarchies in the North

Arthur J. Slavin, *The New Monarchies and Representative Assemblies— Medieval Constitutionalism or Modern Absolutism?** (Boston, 1964). Heath, *Problems.*

Richard Vaughan, *Philip the Bold* (Cambridge, Mass., 1962).

Joseph Calmette, *The Golden Age of Burgundy: The Magnificent Dukes and Their Courts* (New York, 1963), tr. by D. Weightman.

John S. C. Bridge, *A History of France from the Death of Louis XI* (Oxford, 1921-36), 5 vols. Stops in 1515.

J. Russell Major, *Representative Institutions in Renaissance France, 1421-1559* (Madison, 1960).

Selected Bibliography

Conyers Read, *The Tudors: Personalities and Practical Politics in Sixteenth Century England* (New York, 1936).

George W. O. Woodward, *A Short History of Sixteenth-Century England* * (New York, 1963).

Geoffrey R. Elton, *England Under the Tudors* (London, 1955).

Geoffrey R. Elton, *The Tudor Revolution in Government: Administrative Changes in the Reign of Henry VIII* * (Cambridge, 1953). Reinterprets early Tudor government.

Walter C. Richardson, *Tudor Chamber Administration, 1485-1547* (Baton Rouge, 1952).

Alfred F. Pollard, *Henry VIII* (London, New York, and Bombay, 1905). Still the best biography.

John H. Elliott, *Imperial Spain, 1469-1716* (London, 1964). The best and most up-to-date survey.

Roger B. Merriman, *The Rise of the Spanish Empire in the Old World and the New* (New York, 1918-34), 4 vols. Outdated but useful.

John Lynch, *Spain Under the Habsburgs:* Vol. I, *Empire and Absolutism, 1516-1598* (Oxford, 1964).

Hajo Holborn, *A History of Modern Germany:* Vol. I, *The Reformation* (New York, 1959).

Karl Brandi, *The Emperor Charles V: The Growth and Destiny of a Man and of a World-Empire* (London, 1939), tr. by C. V. Wedgwood.

CHAPTER IV   THE ECONOMIC REVIVAL, THE DISCOVERIES,
             AND THE ARISTOCRACY

Economic-Social History

John U. Nef, *The Conquest of the Material World: Essays on the Coming of Industrialism* (Chicago, 1964).

Iris Origo, *The Merchant of Prato: Francesco di Marco Datini* (London, 1957). Delightful.

Frederic C. Lane, *Andrea Barbarigo, Merchant of Venice, 1418-1449* (Baltimore, 1944).

Raymond De Roover, *The Rise and Decline of the Medici Bank, 1397-1494* (Cambridge, Mass., 1963).

Lauro Martines, *The Social World of the Florentine Humanists, 1390-1460* (Princeton, 1963).

Jacob Strieder, *Jacob Fugger the Rich* (New York, 1932), tr. by M. L. Hartsough.

Julius Klein, *The Mesta: A Study in Spanish Economic History, 1273-1836* (Cambridge, Mass., 1920).

Earl J. Hamilton, *American Treasure and the Price Revolution in Spain, 1501-1650* (Cambridge, Mass., 1934). A monumental work in spite of the fact that some of Hamilton's conclusions have been recently challenged.

Jack H. Hexter, *Reappraisals in History** (London, 1961). This provocative study seriously undermines the thesis of the following work.

Louis B. Wright, *Middle Class Culture in Elizabethan England* (Chapel Hill, 1935).

William L. Wiley, *The Gentleman of Renaissance France* (Cambridge, Mass., 1954).

The Discoveries

John H. Parry, *The Age of Reconnaissance** (Cleveland, 1963). The best general treatment.

John H. Parry, *The Establishment of the European Hegemony, 1415-1715** (New York, 1961).

Boies Penrose, *Travel and Discovery in the Renaissance, 1420-1620** (Cambridge, Mass., 1952).

Donald F. Lach, *Asia in the Making of Europe.* Vol. I in two books: *The Century of Discovery* (Chicago, 1964).

Ernest S. Dodge, *Northwest by Sea* (New York, 1961). Popular.

Charles E. Nowell, *The Great Discoveries and the First Colonial Empires** (Ithaca, 1953).

Edgar Prestage, *The Portuguese Pioneers* (London, 1933).

Samuel E. Morison, *Admiral of the Ocean Sea: A Life of Christopher Columbus* (Boston, 1942), 2 vols.; and the greatly abridged, *Christopher Columbus, Mariner** (New York, 1956).

Henry H. Hart, *Sea Road to the Indies* (London, 1952). Devoted primarily to Vasco da Gama.

Charles M. Parr, *So Noble A Captain: The Life and Times of Ferdinand Magellan* (New York, 1953).

James A. Williamson, *The Voyages of the Cabots and the English Discovery of North America under Henry VII and Henry VIII* (London, 1929).

James A. Williamson, *The Age of Drake* (London, 1938).

John C. Beaglehole, *The Exploration of the Pacific* (London, 2nd ed., 1947).

Silvio A. Zavala, *The Political Philosophy of the Conquest of America* (Mexico City, 1953), tr. by T. Hall.

Frederick A. Kirkpatrick, *The Spanish Conquistadores* * (London, 2nd ed., 1946).

Paul Horgan, *Conquistadores in North American History** (New York, 1963).

Lesley B. Simpson, *The Encomienda in New Spain: The Beginning of Spanish America* (Berkeley, ed. of 1950).

Henry R. Wagner, *The Rise of Hernando Cortés* (Los Angeles, 1944).

Charles Gibson, *The Aztecs Under Spanish Rule: A History of the Indians of the Valley of Mexico, 1519-1810* (Stanford, 1964). A major contribution.

Selected Bibliography

CHAPTER V   THE CULTURAL AND RELIGIOUS RENAISSANCE

Frederick B. Artz, *From the Renaissance to Romanticism: Trends in Style in Art, Literature, and Music, 1300-1830* (Chicago, 1962).

Wylie Sypher, *Four Stages of Renaissance Style: Transformations in Art and Literature, 1400-1700** (Garden City, N.Y., 1956). A search for a common denominator between artistic and literary styles.

Literature and Thought

William J. Bouwsma, *The Interpretation of Renaissance Humanism** (Washington, 1959). S.C.T.H.

Hiram Haydn, *The Counter-Renaissance** (New York, 1950).

Elmore Harris Harbison, *The Christian Scholar in the Age of the Reformation** (New York, 1956).

Eugene F. Rice, Jr., *The Renaissance Idea of Wisdom* (Cambridge, Mass., 1958).

Ernest H. Wilkins, *A History of Italian Literature* (Cambridge, Mass., 1954).

Paul O. Kristeller, *Renaissance Thought: The Classic, Scholastic, and Humanistic Strains** (New York, 1961) and *Renaissance Thought II: Papers on Humanism and the Arts** (New York, 1965).

*The Renaissance Philosophy of Man** (Chicago, 1948), eds., Ernest Cassirer and others. Selected writings by six thinkers with introductions by leading authorities.

Ernest H. Wilkins, *Life of Petrarch** (Chicago, 1961).

Hans Baron, *The Crisis of the Early Italian Renaissance: Civic Humanism and Republican Liberty in an Age of Classicism and Tyranny* (Princeton, 1955), 2 vols. A major contribution.

Paul O. Kristeller, *The Philosophy of Marsilio Ficino* (New York, 1943), tr. by V. Conant.

Giuseppe Toffanin, *History of Humanism* (New York, 1954).

Roberto Weiss, *Humanism in England During the Fifteenth Century* (Oxford, 2nd ed., 1957).

Douglas Bush, *The Renaissance and English Humanism* (Toronto, 1939).

Johan Huizinga, *Erasmus** (New York, 1924).

Margaret M. Phillips, *Erasmus and the Northern Renaissance** (London, 1949).

Lewis W. Spitz, *The Religious Renaissance of the German Humanists* (Cambridge, Mass., 1963).

Art and Music

Erwin Panofsky, *Studies in Iconology: Humanistic Themes in the Art of the Renaissance** (New York, 1939). Brilliant.

1085

Erwin Panofsky, *Renaissance and Renascences in Western Art* (Stockholm, 1960), 2 vols.

Bernard Berenson, *The Italian Painters of the Renaissance** (New York, 1952). A classic.

Cecil Gould, *An Introduction to Italian Renaissance Painting* (London, 1957).

Ernest T. Dewald, *Italian Painting, 1200-1600* (New York, 1961).

Kenneth M. Clark, *Leonardo da Vinci: An Account of His Development as an Artist** (Cambridge, 2nd ed., 1952).

Otto Benesch, *The Art of the Renaissance in Northern Europe: Its Relation to the Contemporary Spiritual and Intellectual Movements* (Cambridge, Mass., 1945).

Erwin Panofsky, *Early Netherlandish Painting: Its Origins and Character* (Cambridge, Mass., 1953), 2 vols.

Erwin Panofsky, *Albrecht Dürer* (Princeton, 3rd ed., 1948).

Nikolaus Pevsner and Michael Meier, *Grünewald* (New York, 1958).

Horst W. Janson, *The Sculpture of Donatello* (Princeton, 1957), 2 vols.

Charles H. Morgan, *The Life of Michelangelo* (London, 1960).

Rudolf Wittkower, *Architectural Principles in the Age of Humanism* (London, 1949).

Manfred F. Bukofzer, *Studies in Medieval and Renaissance Music* (New York, 1950).

Charles de Tolnay, *The Art and Thought of Michelangelo* (New York, 1964), tr. by N. Buranelli.

The Religious Renaissance

Harold J. Grimm, *The Reformation in Recent Historical Thought** (New York, 1964). S.C.T.H.

Lewis W. Spitz, *The Reformation: Material or Spiritual?** (Boston, 1962). Heath, *Problems.*

Robert W. Green, *Protestantism and Capitalism: The Weber Thesis and Its Critics** (Boston, 1959). Heath, *Problems.*

Owen Chadwick, *The Reformation** (Baltimore, 1964), *The Pelican History of the Church,* vol. III.

Harold J. Grimm, *The Reformation Era, 1500-1650* (New York, 1954).

Elmore Harris Harbison, *The Age of Reformation** (Ithaca, 1955). A brief well-written Protestant interpretation.

Philip Hughes, *A Popular History of the Reformation** (Garden City, 1957). A brief well-written Catholic interpretation.

Arthur C. McGiffert, *Protestant Thought Before Kant** (London, 1936).

Roland H. Bainton, *Here I Stand: A Life of Martin Luther** (New York, 1950). Delightful.

Robert H. Fife, *The Revolt of Martin Luther* (New York, 1957).

Erik H. Erikson, *Young Man Luther: A Study in Psychoanalysis and History** (New York, 1958).

Selected Bibliography

George H. Williams, *The Radical Reformation* (Philadelphia, 1962).

Roland H. Bainton, *Hunted Heretic: The Life and Death of Michael Servetus, 1511-1553** (Boston, 1953).

John T. McNeill, *The History and Character of Calvinism* (New York, 1954).

Albert Marie Schmidt, *John Calvin and the Calvinistic Tradition** (New York, 1960), tr. by R. Wallace.

John E. Neale, *Queen Elizabeth* * (London, 1934).

Conyers Read, *Mr. Secretary Cecil and Queen Elizabeth* (London, 1955).

Philip Hughes, *The Reformation in England* (London, 1950-54), 3 vols. A beautifully written Catholic account.

Frederick M. Powicke, *The Reformation in England* * (London, 1941). A briefer Protestant version.

Francis E. Hutchinson, *Cranmer and the English Reformation** (London, 1951).

Frederic C. Church, *The Italian Reformers, 1534-1564* (New York, 1932).

Norman R. C. Cohn, *The Pursuit of the Millennium* * (London, 1957).

Philip Hughes, *Rome and the Counter-Reformation in England* (London, 1944).

Henri Daniel-Rops, *The Catholic Reformation** (London, 1962), tr. by I. Warrington.

Hubert Jedin, *A History of the Council of Trent* (London, 1957 ff.), tr. by E. Graf, 2 vols. to date.

James Brodrick, *The Origin of the Jesuits* * (New York, 1940), and *The Progress of the Jesuits (1556-79)* (New York, 1947). Catholic accounts.

Paul Van Dyke, *Ignatius Loyola, the Founder of the Jesuits* (New York, 1926). Protestant account.

Joseph Lecler, *Toleration and the Reformation* (New York, 1960), 2 vols., tr. by T. L. Westow.

PART THREE   THE SEVENTEENTH-CENTURY CRISIS

Crisis in Europe: 1560-1660 (London, 1956), ed., Trevor Aston. A collection of articles dealing with the 17th century crisis. Especially valuable for economic and social history.

George N. Clark, *The Seventeenth Century* (Oxford, 2nd ed., 1947). A topical history by a leading authority. Needs revision.

David Ogg, *Europe in the Seventeenth Century** (London, 8th ed., 1960). A narrative political history. Outdated.

The New Cambridge Modern History, Vol. V: *The Ascendancy of France, 1648-88* (Cambridge, 1961), ed., Francis L. Carsten.

The following books in Langer's *Rise of Modern Europe* series are syntheses with good bibliographies.

Carl J. Friedrich, *The Age of the Baroque, 1610-1660** (New York, 1952).

Frederick L. Nussbaum, *The Triumph of Science and Reason, 1660-1685** (New York, 1953).

John B. Wolf, *The Emergence of the Great Powers, 1685-1715** (New York, 1951).

CHAPTER VI   WAR, DEPRESSION, AND COLONIZATION

Wars and Diplomacy

Garrett Mattingly, *Renaissance Diplomacy** (London, 1955).
Garrett Mattingly, *The Armada** (Boston, 1959).
De Lamar Jensen, *Diplomacy and Dogmatism, Bernardino de Mendoza and the French Catholic League* (Cambridge, Mass., 1964).
Theodore K. Rabb, ed., *The Thirty Years' War: Problems of Motive, Extent, and Effect** (Boston, 1964). Heath, *Problems.*
Cicely V. Wedgwood, *The Thirty Years War** (London, 1939).
Michael Roberts, *The Military Revolution, 1560-1660* (Belfast, 1956).
Herbert H. Rowen, *The Ambassador Prepares for War: The Dutch Embassy of Arnauld de Pomponne, 1669-1671* (The Hague, 1957).

Economic and Social History
(See also bibliography under Chapter VII)

Eli F. Heckscher, *Mercantilism* (London, 2nd ed., 1955), 2 vols., tr. by M. Shapiro. A monumental work.
Earl J. Hamilton, *American Treasure and the Price Revolution in Spain, 1501-1650* (Cambridge, Mass., 1934).
George N. Clark, *The Wealth of England from 1490 to 1760* (London, 1946). Good brief summary.
Charles W. Cole, *Colbert and a Century of French Mercantilism* (New York, 1939), 2 vols. Undigested, but full of useful material.
Violet Barbour, *Capitalism in Amsterdam in the Seventeenth Century** (Baltimore, 1950).

The Colonial Empires

Clarence H. Haring, *The Spanish Empire in America** (New York, 1947). The best general survey.
Woodrow W. Borah, *New Spain's Century of Depression* (Berkeley, 1951).
Charles R. Boxer, *The Golden Age of Brazil, 1695-1750: Growing Pains of a Colonial Society* (Berkeley, 1962).
Herbert I. Priestley, *France Overseas through the Old Regime: A Study of European Expansion* (New York, 1939).
Arthur P. Newton, *The European Nations in the West Indies, 1493-1688* (London, 1933).
Louis B. Wright, *New Interpretations of American Colonial History** (Washington, 2nd ed., 1959). S.C.T.H.

Selected Bibliography

Max Savelle, *A History of Colonial America* (New York, Rev. ed., 1964).

Louis B. Wright, *The Cultural Life of the American Colonies, 1607-1763** (New York, 1st ed. 1957). The New American Nation Series.

Clinton L. Rossiter, *The First American Revolution: The American Colonies on the Eve of Independence** (New York, 1956).

Marcus L. Hansen, *Atlantic Migration, 1607-1860** (Cambridge, Mass., 1940).

Mariano Picón-Salas, *A Cultural History of Spanish America from Conquest to Independence** (Berkeley, 1962), tr. by I. A. Leonard.

Bernard H. M. Vlekke, *The Story of the Dutch East Indies* (Cambridge, Mass., 1945).

George Masselman, *The Cradle of Colonialism* (New Haven, 1963). A study of the Dutch in Southeast Asia, 1595-1629.

CHAPTER VII   THE CONSTITUTIONAL CRISIS

The Constitutional Crisis in England

Robert Walcott, *The Tudor-Stuart Period of English History (1485-1714)** (New York, 1964). S.C.T.H.

G. E. Aylmer, *A Short History of Seventeenth-Century England* * (New York, 1963).

Christopher Hill, *Puritanism and Revolution: Studies in Interpretation of the English Revolution of the 17th Century** (London, 1958).

Jack H. Hexter, *Reappraisals in History** (Evanston, 1961). Contains a brilliant discussion concerning the controversy over the role the gentry in the English crisis.

Lawrence Stone, *The Crisis of the Aristocracy 1558-1649* (New York, 1965). An important contribution.

Wallace Notestein, *The English People on the Eve of Colonization, 1603-1630** (New York, 1954). Excellent survey.

Wallace Notestein, *The Winning of the Initiative by the House of Commons* (London, 1924).

David H. Willson, *King James VI & I* * (London, 1956). Splendid biography.

William Haller, *The Rise of Puritanism** (New York, 1938).

William Haller, *Liberty and Reformation in the Puritan Revolution** (New York, 1955).

G. E. Aylmer, *The King's Servants: The Civil Service of Charles I, 1625-1642* (New York, 1961). Contains comparison with continental office-holders.

Margaret A. Judson, *The Crisis of the Constitution: An Essay in Constitutional and Political Thought in England, 1603-1645* (New Brunswick, 1949).

Philip A. M. Taylor, ed., *The Origins of the English Civil War: Conspiracy Crusade, or Class Conflict?** (Boston, 1960). Heath, *Problems*.

1089

Cicely V. Wedgwood, *The Great Rebellion* (London, 1955 ff.), 2 vols. to date.

Gerald M. Straka, ed., *The Revolution of 1688: Whig Triumph or Palace Revolution?** (Boston, 1963). Heath, *Problems.*

David Ogg, *England in the Reign of Charles II* * (Oxford, 1934), 2 vols. Written in the Whig tradition.

David Ogg, *England in the Reigns of James II and William III* (Oxford, 1955).

The Constitutional Crisis in France

John Lough, *An Introduction to Seventeenth Century France* (London, 1954). An excellent summary.

William F. Church, *Constitutional Thought in Sixteenth-Century France* (Cambridge, Mass., 1941). Good for origins of the political theory of royal absolutism.

John E. Neale, *The Age of Catherine de Medici** (London, 1943).

Nicola M. Sutherland, *The French Secretaries of State in the Age of Catherine de Medici* (London, 1962). Essentially a narrative history of the period as seen from the letters of the secretaries.

Cicely V. Wedgwood, *Richelieu and the French Monarchy** (London, 1949). Needs revision.

Carl J. Burckhardt, *Richelieu: His Rise to Power** (New York, 1940), tr. and abridged by E. and W. Muir.

Orest A. Ranum, *Richelieu and the Councillors of Louis XIII: A Study of the Secretaries of State and Superintendents of Finance in the Ministry of Richelieu, 1635-1642* (Oxford, 1963).

William F. Church, *The Greatness of Louis XIV: Myth or Reality?** (Boston, 1959). Heath, *Problems.*

Maurice Ashley, *Louis XIV and the Greatness of France** (London, 1946).

Warren C. Scoville, *The Persecution of Huguenots and French Economic Development, 1680-1720* (Berkeley, 1960). Proves that economic results of Huguenot persecution have been exaggerated.

Lionel Rothkrug, *Opposition to Louis XIV: The Political and Social Origins of the French Enlightment* (Princeton, 1965).

Constitutional Crises in Other Western and Central European States

John C. Rule and John J. TePaske, eds., *The Character of Philip II: The Problem of Moral Judgments in History** (Boston, 1963). Heath, *Problems.*

Roger B. Merriman, *The Rise of the Spanish Empire in the Old World and the New.* Vol. IV: *Philip the Prudent* (New York, 1934). The best history of the reign in English in spite of many shortcomings.

Selected Bibliography

Gregorio Marañón, *Antonio Pérez, "Spanish Traitor"* (London, 1954), tr. by Charles D. Ley.

John H. Elliott, *Imperial Spain, 1469-1716* (London, 1963). The best survey.

John H. Elliott, *The Revolt of the Catalans: A Study in the Decline of Spain, 1598-1640* (Cambridge, 1963). A monumental work.

Pieter Geyl, *The Revolt of the Netherlands (1555-1609)* (London, 2nd ed., 1958). An important work by a great historian.

Pieter Geyl, *The Netherlands in the Seventeenth Century* (London, 1961-1964), 2 vols.

Francis L. Carsten, *The Origins of Prussia* (Oxford, 1954).

Francis L. Carsten, *Princess and Parliaments in Germany, from the Fifteenth to the Eighteenth Century* (Oxford, 1959). Proves that representative institutions were more important in Germany than has generally been supposed.

Sidney B. Fay, *The Rise of Bradenburg-Prussia to 1786* (New York, 1937). Berkshire Series. A useful brief survey.

Michael Roberts, *Gustavus Adolphus: A History of Sweden, 1611-1632* (London, 1953-1958), 2 vols. A splendid study.

The Constitutional Crisis in Eastern Europe

William H. McNeill, *Europe's Steppe Frontier, 1500-1800* (Chicago, 1964). A study of the frontier in southeastern Europe.

The Cambridge History of Poland (Cambridge, 1950), ed., William F. Reddaway and others, Vol. I.

John L. I. Fennell, *Ivan the Great of Moscow* (New York, 1961). Mostly military and diplomatic.

Marc Raeff, ed., *Peter the Great: Reformer or Revolutionary?* * (Boston, 1963). Heath, *Problems.*

Benedict H. Sumner, *Peter the Great and the Emergence of Russia* * (London, 1950). Brief but excellent.

Benedict H. Sumner, *Peter the Great and the Ottoman Empire* (Oxford, 1949).

Jerome Blum, *Lord and Peasant in Russia, from the Ninth to the Nineteenth Century* * (Princeton, 1961).

CHAPTER VIII   SCIENCE, THOUGHT, AND ART

The Scientific Revolution

Herbert Butterfield, *The Origins of Modern Science, 1300-1800* * (New York, ed. of 1957). A delightful introduction.

Alfred R. Hall, *The Scientific Revolution, 1500-1800* * (London, 1954).

Abraham Wolf, *A History of Science, Technology and Philosophy in the*

Sixteenth and Seventeenth Centuries* (London, 2nd ed., 1950). Contains many illustrations and drawings.

Alexandre Koyré, *From the Closed World to the Infinite Universe** (Baltimore, 1957).

Thomas S. Kuhn, *The Copernican Revolution** (Cambridge, Mass., 1957).

Max Caspar, *Kepler* (New York, 1959), tr. by C. D. Hellman.

Giorgio de Santillana, *The Crime of Galileo** (Chicago, 1955).

Joseph F. Scott, *The Scientific Work of René Descartes (1596-1650)* (London, 1952).

Marie Boas, *Robert Boyle and Seventeenth Century Chemistry* (Cambridge, 1958).

Charles Singer, *The Discovery of the Circulation of the Blood* (London, ed. of 1956).

Charles D. O'Malley, *Andreas Versalius of Brussels, 1514-1564* (Berkeley, 1964).

Martha Ornstein, *The Rôle of Scientific Societies in the Seventeenth Century* (Chicago, 3rd ed., 1938).

The Intellectual Revolution

Preserved Smith, *A History of Modern Culture** (New York, 1930-34), 2 vols. More an encyclopedia than an interpretation.

Paul Hazard, *The European Mind, 1680-1715** (London, 1953). A beautifully written classic.

Richard H. Popkin, *The History of Scepticism from Erasmus to Descartes* (Assen, 1960).

Basil Willey, *The Seventeenth Century Background ** (London, 1934). A study of English thought, poetry, and religion.

The Arts

Heinrich Wolfflin, *Principles of Art History: The Problem of the Development of Style in Later Art** (London, 1932), tr. by M. D. Holtinger. Discusses characteristics of Baroque art.

Victor L. Tapie, *The Age of Grandeur: Baroque Art and Architecture** (New York, 1960), tr. by A. R. Williamson. A general survey by a historian.

Anthony Blunt, *Art and Architecture in France, 1500-1700* (London, 1953).

Rudolf Wittkower, *Art and Architecture in Italy, 1600-1750* (Baltimore, 1958).

Rudolf Wittkower, *Gian Lorenzo Bernini: The Sculptor of the Roman Baroque* (London, 1955).

Harold E. Wethey, *El Greco and His School* (Princeton, 1962), 2 vols.

Walter F. Friedlaender, *Caravaggio Studies* (Princeton, 1955).

Manfred F. Bukofzer, *Music in the Baroque Era: From Monteverdi to Bach* (New York, 1947).

Selected Bibliography

Alec Harman and Anthony Milner, *Late Renaissance and Baroque Music (c. 1505-c. 1750)* (London, 1959).

Imbrie Buffum, *Studies in the Baroque from Montaigne to Rotrou* (New Haven, 1957).

PART IV   THE AGE OF THE EGALITARIAN REVOLUTIONS

Peter Amann, *The Eighteenth-Century Revolution: French or Western?** (Boston, 1963). Heath, *Problems.*

Robert R. Palmer, *The Age of the Democratic Revolution* (Princeton, 1959-1964), 2 vols. A major contribution pointing to the similarities between the late 18th-century revolutions.

George F. Rudé, *The Crowd in History: A Study of Popular Disturbances in France and England, 1730-1848** (New York, 1964).

Eric J. Hobsbawm, *The Age of Revolution, Europe 1789-1848** (London, 1962).

CHAPTERS IX AND X   THE ERA OF THE ENLIGHTENMENT

General Works

The three following works in the *Rise of Modern Europe Series* provide good syntheses of the period:

Penfield Roberts, *The Quest for Security, 1715-1740** (New York, 1947).

Walter L. Dorn, *Competition for Empire, 1740-1763** (New York, 1940). Especially good on administrative and military history.

Leo Gershoy, *From Despotism to Revolution, 1763-1789** (New York, 1944).

The New Cambridge Modern History. Vol. VII: *The Old Regime, 1713-1763* (Cambridge, 1957), ed., J. O. Lindsay.

Matthew S. Anderson, *Europe in the Eighteenth Century, 1713-1783* (London, 1961). A topical approach.

Albert Goodwin, ed., *The European Nobility in the Eighteenth Century* (London, 1953).

(For other studies on social, economic, and military history, see the works listed on the individual states.)

Science and Thought

Ernst Cassirer, *The Philosophy of the Enlightenment** (Boston, 1955), tr. by F. C. A. Koelln and J. P. Pettegrove. The best general study.

Abraham Wolf, *A History of Science, Technology, and Philosophy in the Eigheenth Century** (London, 2nd ed., 1952).

Carl Becker, *The Heavenly City of the Eighteenth Century Philosophers** (New Haven, 1932). A delightful, provocative interpretation of the eighteenth-century mind.

Alfred Cobban, *In Search of Humanity: The Role of the Enlightenment in Modern History* (London, 1960).

Lester G. Crocker, *An Age of Crisis: Man and World in Eighteenth Century French Thought* (Baltimore, 1959).

Lester G. Crocker, *Nature and Culture: Ethical Thought in the French Enlightenment* (Baltimore, 1963).

Peter Gay, *The Party of Humanity: Essays in the French Enlightenment* (New York, 1964).

Peter Gay, *Voltaire's Politics: The Poet as Realist** (Princeton, 1959).

Fredrick C. Green, *Jean-Jacques Rousseau* (Cambridge, 1955).

George R. Havens, *The Age of Ideas** (New York, 1955). Popular but sound.

Paul Hazard, *European Thought in the Eighteenth Century, from Montesquieu to Lessing** (New Haven, 1954), tr. by I. L. May.

Frank E. Manuel, *The Eighteenth Century Confronts the Gods* (Cambridge, Mass., 1959).

Kingsley Martin, *The Rise of French Liberal Thought: A Study in Political Ideas, from Bayle to Condorcet** (New York, 2nd ed., 1954).

Arthur M. Wilson, *Diderot: The Testing Years, 1713-1759* (New York, 1957).

Carl B. Cone, *Burke and the Nature of Politics* (Lexington, 1957-64), 2 vols.

Maurice W. Cranston, *John Locke: A Biography* (London, 1957).

Caroline Robbins, *The Eighteenth-Century Commonwealthman: Studies in the Transmission, Development, and Circumstance of English Liberal Thought from the Restoration of Charles II until the War with the Thirteen Colonies* (Cambridge, Mass., 1959).

Robert A. Kann, *A Study in Austrian Intellectual History from Late Baroque to Romanticism* (New York, 1960).

Friedrich O. Hertz, *The Development of the German Public Mind: A Social History of German Political Sentiments, Aspirations, and Ideas.* Vol. II: *The Age of the Enlightenment* (London, 1962).

Literature and Art

Sidney F. Kimball, *The Creation of the Rococo* (Philadelphia, 1943).

Arno Schönberger and Halldor Soehner, *The Rococo Age: Art and Civilization of the Eighteenth Century* (New York, 1960), tr. by D. Woodward.

Georges de Traz, *The Eighteenth Century: Watteau to Tiepolo* (Geneva, 1952), tr. by S. Gilbert.

Nikolaus Pevsner, *Academies of Art: Past and Present* (Cambridge, 1940).

Osvald Sirén, *China and Gardens of Europe of the Eighteenth Century* (New York, 1950).

The Individual States

Edmund S. Morgan, *The American Revolution: A Review of Changing Interpretations** (Washington, 1958). S.C.T.H.

Selected Bibliography

John C. Wahlke, ed., *The Causes of the American Revolution** (Boston, ed. of 1962). Heath, *Problems.*

Edmund S. Morgan, *The Birth of the Republic, 1763-89** (Chicago, 1956).

Lawrence H. Gipson, *The Coming of the Revolution, 1763-1775** (New York, 1954).

John R. Alden, *American Revolution, 1775-1783** (New York, 1954).

John H. Plumb, *The First Four Georges* (London, 1956). Delightful.

John H. Plumb, *England in the Eighteenth Century** (Harmondsworth, 1957).

Thomas S. Ashton, *An Economic History of England: The Eighteenth Century* (London, 1955).

John H. Plumb, *Sir Robert Walpole, The King's Minister* (Boston, 1961).

Earl A. Reitan, *George III—Tyrant or Constitutional Monarch?** (Boston, 1965). Heath, *Problems.*

John S. Watson, *The Reign of George III, 1760-1815* (Oxford, 1960).

Lewis B. Namier, *The Structure of Politics at the Accession of George III ** (London, 2nd ed., 1957). A monumental work.

Lewis B. Namier, *England in the Age of the American Revolution** (London, 1930).

Charles G. Robertson, *Chatham and the British Empire** (London, 1946).

Richard Herr, *The Eighteenth-Century Revolution in Spain* (Princeton, 1958).

Harold M. M. Acton, *The Bourbons of Naples, 1734-1825* (London, 1956). A lively study of the royal family.

James C. Davis, *The Decline of the Venetian Nobility as a Ruling Class* (Baltimore, 1962).

Hajo Holborn, *A History of Modern Germany* (New York, 1964), vol. II.

Walter H. Bruford, *Germany in the Eighteenth Century: The Social Background of the Literary Revival* (Cambridge, 1935).

Hans Rosenberg, *Bureaucracy, Aristocracy, and Autocracy: The Prussian Experience, 1660-1815* (Cambridge, Mass., 1958). Reveals the social consequences of the Prussian administrative system.

George P. Gooch, *Frederick the Great: The Ruler, the Writer, the Man* (New York, 1947).

George P. Gooch, *Marie Theresa, and Other Studies* (London and New York, 1951).

Saul K. Padover, *The Revolutionary Emperor: Joseph the Second, 1741-1790* (New York, 1934).

Robert J. Kerner, *Bohemia in the Eighteenth Century* (New York, 1932).

Robert H. Lord, *The Second Partition of Poland* (Cambridge, Mass., 1915).

Gladys S. Thomson, *Catherine the Great and the Expansion of Russia** (London, 1947).

John Lough, *An Introduction to Eighteenth Century France* (London, 1960). An excellent summary.

Franklin L. Ford, *Robe and Sword: The Regrouping of the French Aristocracy After Louis XIV* (Cambridge, Mass., 1953).

Elinor G. Barber, *The Bourgeoisie in Eighteenth Century France* (Princeton, 1955).

Paul W. Bamford, *Forests and French Sea Power, 1660-1789* (Toronto, 1956).

Robert S. Quimby, *The Background of Napoleonic Warfare: The Theory of Military Tactics in Eighteenth-Century France* (New York, 1957).

CHAPTER XI   THE FRENCH REVOLUTION AND NAPOLEON

The French Revolution, 1789-1799

Stanley J. Idzerda, *The Background of the French Revolution** (Washington, 1959). S.C.T.H.

William F. Church, ed., *The Influence of the Enlightenment on the French Revolution: Creative, Disastrous, or Non-Existent?** (Boston, 1964). Heath, *Problems.*

Ralph W. Greenlaw, ed., *The Economic Origins of the French Revolution: Poverty or Prosperity?** (Boston, 1958). Heath, *Problems.*

Crane Brinton, *A Decade of Revolution, 1789-1799** (New York, 1934).

Georges Lefebvre, *The Coming of the French Revolution, 1789** (Princeton, 1947), tr. by R. R. Palmer.

Georges Lefebvre, *The French Revolution* (New York, 1962-64), 2 vols., tr. by E. M. Evanson and J. H. Hall. The leading authority.

James M. Thompson, *The French Revolution* (Oxford, 1943). Beautifully written.

Alfred Cobban, *The Social Interpretation of the French Revolution* (Cambridge, 1964).

Paul H. Beik, *The French Revolution Seen from the Right: Social Theories in Motion, 1789-1799* (Philadelphia, 1956).

M. J. Sydenham, *The Girondins* (London, 1961).

James M. Thompson, *Robespierre and the French Revolution** (London, 1952).

Robert R. Palmer, *Twelve Who Ruled: The Committee of Public Saftey During the Terror** (Princeton, 1941).

Donald M. Greer, *The Incidence of the Terror During the French Revolution: A Statistical Interpretation* (Cambridge, Mass., 1935).

Other European States

Robert R. Palmer, *The Age of the Democratic Revolutions* (Princeton, 1959-1964), Vol. II.

Arthur Bryant, *The Years of Endurance, 1793-1802* (London, 1942).

Arthur Bryant, *The Years of Victory, 1802-1812* (London, 1944).

Reuben J. Rath, *The Fall of the Napoleonic Kingdom of Italy (1814)* (New York, 1941).

Selected Bibliography

Walter M. Simon, *The Failure of the Prussian Reform Movement, 1807-1819* (Ithaca, 1955).

Ernst Wangermann, *From Joseph II to the Jacobin Trials: Government Policy and Public Opinion in the Habsburg Dominions in the Period of the French Revolution* (London, 1959).

Enno E. Kraehe, *Metternich's German Policy.* Vol. I: *The Contest with Napoleon, 1799-1814* (Princeton, 1963).

Richard Herr, *The Eighteenth-Century Revolution in Spain* (Princeton, 1958).

Napoleon

Pieter Geyl, *Napoleon, For and Against** (New Haven, 1949), tr. by O. Renier. A superb history of the changing interpretations of Napoleon's career.

Geoffrey Brunn, *Europe and the French Imperium, 1799-1814** (New York, 1938).

Felix Markham, *Napoleon and the Awakening of Europe** (London, 1954).

James M. Thompson, *Napoleon Bonaparte, His Rise and Fall* (Oxford, 1952). Inferior to the same author's works on the Revolution.

Harold G. Nicolson, *The Congress of Vienna: A Study in Allied Unity, 1812-1822* (New York, 1946).

CHAPTER XII   THE AGE OF ROMANTICISM, 1815-1850

General Works

Frederick B. Artz, *Reaction and Revolution, 1814-1832** (New York, 1934).

The New Cambridge Modern History. Vol. X: *The Zenith of European Power, 1830-70* (Cambridge, 1960), ed., John P. T. Bury.

Arthur J. May, *The Age of Metternich, 1814-1848** (New York, 1933).

Literature and Art

John B. Halsted, *Romanticism: Problem of Definition, Explanation, and Evaluation** (Boston, 1965), Heath, *Problems.*

Pierre Courthion, *Romanticism* (Geneva, 1961), tr. by S. Gilbert.

Marcel Brion, *Romantic Art* (New York, 1960).

Fritz Novotny, *Painting and Sculpture in Europe, 1780-1880* (Harmondsworth, 1960).

Walter F. Friedlaender, *David to Delacroix* (Cambridge, Mass., 1952), tr. by R. Goldwater.

Alfred Einstein, *Music in the Romantic Era* (New York, 1947).

Walter H. Bruford, *Culture and Society in Classical Weimar, 1775-1806* (Cambridge, 1962).

The Forces of Conservatism

Henry F. Schwartz, ed., *Metternich, the "Coachman of Europe": Statesman or Evil Genius?* * (Boston, 1962). Heath, *Problems.*

Henry A. Kissinger, *A World Restored: Metternich, Castlereagh and the Problems of Peace, 1812-22** (Boston, 1957).

Hans G. Schenk, *The Aftermath of the Napoleonic Wars: The Concert of Europe, An Experiment* (London, 1947).

Ernest L. Woodward, *Three Studies in European Conservatism: Metternich, Guizot, the Catholic Church in the Nineteenth Century* (London, 1929). Excellent.

Alfred Cobban, *Edmund Burke and the Revolt Against the Eighteenth Century: A Study of the Political and Social Thinking of Burke, Wordsworth, Coleridge, and Southey* (London, 2nd ed., 1960).

Carl B. Cone, *Burke and the Nature of Politics* (Lexington, 1957-1964), 2 vols.

Peter Viereck, *Conservatism Revisited: The Revolt Against Revolt, 1815-1949** (New York, 1949).

Golo Mann, *Secretary of Europe: The Life of Friedrich Gentz, Enemy of Napoleon* (New Haven, 1946).

The Eastern Question

Leften S. Stavrianos, *The Balkans Since 1453* (New York, 1958). An excellent textbook.

Anthony D. Alderson, *The Structure of the Ottoman Dynasty* (Oxford, 1956).

John A. R. Marriott, *The Eastern Question* (Oxford, 4th ed., 1940). Needs revision but still useful.

Christopher M. Woodhouse, *The Greek War for Independence: Its Historical Setting* (London, 1952).

The Forces of Change

Eric E. Lampard, *Industrial Revolution: Interpretations and Perspectives** (Washington, 1957). S.C.T.H.

Philip A. M. Taylor, ed., *The Industrial Revolution in Britain: Triumph or Disaster?* * (Boston, 1958). Heath, *Problems.*

Thomas S. Ashton, *The Industrial Revolution, 1760-1830** (London, 1948). An excellent brief account of the early English phase.

William O. Henderson, *Britain and Industrial Europe, 1750-1870* (Liverpool, 1954).

Selected Bibliography

William O. Henderson, *The Industrial Revolution on the Continent: Germany, France, Russia, 1800-1914* (London, 1961). Heavily factual.

Arthur L. Dunham, *The Industrial Revolution in France, 1815-1848* (New York, 1955).

Rondo E. Cameron, *France and the Economic Development of Europe, 1800-1914: Conquests of Peace and Seeds of War* (Princeton, 1961).

Hans Kohn, *Prophets and Peoples: Studies in Nineteenth Century Nationalism* (New York, 1946). For additional works on nationalism, see p. 1075.

Jacob S. Schapiro, *Liberalism and the Challenge of Fascism: Social Forces in England and France, 1815-1870* (New York, 1949).

Frank Manuel, *The New World of Henri Saint-Simon* (Cambridge, Mass., 1956).

CHAPTER XIII   REACTION, REVOLUTION, AND REFORM,
1815-1850/65

The Revolution of 1848

Melvin Kranzberg, ed., *1848, A Turning Point?* * (Boston, 1959). Heath, Problems.

Priscilla Robertson, *Revolutions of 1848: A Social History** (New York, 1960).

France

Frederick B. Artz, *France Under the Bourbon Restoration, 1814-1830* (Cambridge, Mass., 1931).

Paul H. Biek, *Louis Philippe and the July Monarchy* * (Princeton, 1965).

Frederick A. Simpson, *The Rise of Louis Napoleon* (New York and London, 3rd ed., 1950).

Central Europe

Theodore Hamerow, *Restoration, Revolution, Reaction: Economics and Politics in Germany, 1815-1871* (Princeton, 1958).

Richard H. Thomas, *Liberalism, Nationalism, and the German Intellectuals (1822-1847)* (Cambridge, 1951).

William O. Henderson, *The Zollverein* (Cambridge, 1939).

Jerome Blum, *Noble Landowners and Agriculture in Austria, 1815-1848* (Baltimore, 1948).

Reuben J. Rath, *The Viennese Revolution of 1848* (Austin, 1957).

Gwilym O. Griffith, *Mazzini: Prophet of Modern Europe* (London, 1932).

Kent R. Greenfield, *Economics and Liberalism in the Risorgimento: A Study of Nationalism in Lombardy, 1814-1848* (Baltimore, 1934). An excellent study showing the economic base to Italian liberalism and nationalism.

Great Britain

John W. Derry, *A Short History of Nineteenth Century England* * (New York, 1963).

Ernest L. Woodward, *The Age of Reform, 1815-1870* (Oxford, 2nd ed., 1962). An excellent scholarly account.

Norman Gash, *Mr. Secretary Peel: The Life of Sir Robert Peel to 1830* (London, 1961).

Charles R. Fay, *Huskisson and His Age* (London, 1951).

Herbert C. Bell, *Lord Palmerston* (London, 1936), 2 vols.

Cecil Woodham Smith, *The Great Hunger, Ireland 1845-9** (London, 1962).

John L. and Barbara Hammond, *The Age of the Chartists, 1832-1854* (London, 1930). Overly sympathetic but valuable.

Robert B. McDowell, *Public Opinion and Government Policy in Ireland, 1801-1846* (London, 1952).

Bankey B. Misra, *The Central Administration of the East India Company, 1773-1834* (Manchester, 1959).

Penderel Moon, *Warren Hastings and British India** (London, 1947).

Kenneth Ballhatchet, *Social Policy and Social Change in Western India, 1817-1830* (London, 1957).

Russia

Nicholas V. Riasanovsky, *Nicholas I and Official Nationality in Russia, 1825-1855* (Berkeley, 1959).

Sidney Monas, *The Third Section: Police and Society in Russia Under Nicholas I* (Cambridge, Mass., 1961).

Mikhail Zetlin, *The Decembrists* (New York, 1958), tr. by G. Panin.

R. F. Leslie, *Polish Politics and the Revolution of November 1830* (London, 1956).

Werner E. Mosse, *Alexander II and the Modernization of Russia** (London, 1958).

Michael B. Petrovich, *The Emergence of Russian Panslavism, 1856-1870* (New York, 1956).

The United States

Keith B. Berwick, *The Federal Age, 1789-1829** (Washington, 1961). S.C.T.H.

John C. Miller, *The Federalist Era, 1789-1801** (New York, 1st ed., 1960).

Dumas Malone, *Jefferson and His Time* (Boston, 1948 ff.), 3 vols. to date.

Selected Bibliography

George Dangerfield, *The Era of Good Feeling** (New York, 1952).

Charles G. Sellers, *Jacksonian Democracy** (Washington, 1958). S.C.T.H.

Arthur M. Schlesinger, Jr., *The Age of Jackson** (Boston, 1945). A controversial, well-written study emphasizing the role of the eastern working classes in the development of democracy.

Glyndon G. Van Deusen, *The Jacksonian Era, 1828-1848* (New York, 1959).

Clement Eaton, *The Growth of Southern Civilization, 1790-1860* (New York, 1961).

Kenneth M. Stampp, *The Peculiar Institution: Slavery in the Ante-Bellum South** (New York, 1956).

Louis Filler, *The Crusade Against Slavery, 1830-1860** (New York, 1960).

Allan Nevins, *Ordeal of the Union* (New York, 1947), 2 vols.

Leonard H. Bridges, *Civil War and Reconstruction** (Washington, 2nd ed., 1962). S.C.T.H.

Edwin C. Rozwenc, ed., *The Causes of the American Civil War** (Boston, 1961). Heath, *Problems*.

James G. Randall and David Donald, *The Civil War and Reconstruction* (New York, 2nd ed., 1961).

David Donald, *Lincoln Reconsidered: Essays on the Civil War Era** (New York, 1956).

Clement Eaton, *A History of the Southern Confederacy** (New York, 1954).

Latin America

Arthur P. Whitaker, ed., *Latin America and the Enlightenment** (New York, 1942).

R. A. Humphreys and John Lynch, eds., *Origins of the Latin American Revolutions, 1809-1830: European Influences or American Nationalism?** (New York, 1964).

Salvador de Madariaga, *The Fall of the Spanish American Empire** (New York, 1948).

John B. Trend, *Bolivar and the Independence of Spanish America* (London, 1951).

Robert J. Shafer, *The Economic Societies in the Spanish World, 1763-1821* (Syracuse, 1958).

Clarence H. Haring, *Empire in Brazil: A New World Experiment with Monarchy* (Cambridge, Mass., 1958).

PART FIVE   THE TRIUMPH OF WESTERN CIVILIZATION

Robert C. Binkley, *Realism and Nationalism, 1852-1871* (New York, 1935).

Carlton J. H. Hayes, *A Generation of Materialism, 1871-1900* * (New York, 1941).

The New Cambridge Modern History. Vol. XI: *Material Progress and World-Wide Problems, 1870-1898* (Cambridge, 1962), ed. by Francis Hinsley.

Alan J. P. Taylor, *The Struggle for Mastery in Europe, 1848-1918* (Oxford, 1954). A provocative but sometimes unreliable diplomatic history.

CHAPTER XIV   NATIONALISM, MATERIALISM, AND LIBERALISM

The Unification of Italy and Germany

Gavin B. Henderson, *Crimean War Diplomacy and Other Historical Essays* (Glasgow, 1947).

Charles F. Delzell, *The Unification of Italy, 1859-1861: Cavour, Mazzini, or Garibaldi?* * (New York, 1965). Holt, Rinehart and Winston, *European Problem Studies.*

Harold Acton, *The Last Bourbons of Naples (1825-1861)* (New York, 1961).

Raymond Grew, *A Sterner Plan for Italian Unity: The Italian National Society in the Risorgimento* (Princeton, 1963).

Denis Mack Smith, *Garibaldi, A Great Life in Brief* (New York, 1956).

Denis Mack Smith, *Cavour and Garibaldi, 1860: A Study in Political Conflict* (Cambridge, 1954).

Theodore S. Hamerow, ed., *Otto von Bismarck: A Historical Assessment* * (Boston, 1962). Heath, *Problems.*

Otto Pflanze, *Bismarck and the Development of Germany: The Period of Unification, 1815-1871* (Princeton, 1963).

Lawrence D. Steefel, *Bismarck, The Hohenzollern Candidacy, and the Origins of the Franco-German War of 1870* (Cambridge, Mass., 1962).

Erich Eyck, *Bismarck and the German Empire* * (London, 2nd ed., 1958). A summary of a three-volume work in German.

Science and Thought

Gavin R. De Beer, *Charles Darwin** (London, 1958).

Loren C. Eiseley, *Darwin's Century: Evolution and the Men Who Discovered It** (Garden City, 1958).

Charles Gillespie, *Genesis and Geology: A Study in the Relations of Scientific Thought, Natural Theology, and Social Opinion in Great Britain, 1790-1850** (Cambridge, Mass., 1951).

L. Pearce Williams, *Michael Faraday: A Biography* (New York, 1965).

Jacques Barzun, *Darwin, Marx, Wagner: Critique of a Heritage** (Boston, 1941).

Richard Hofstadter, *Social Darwinism in American Thought, 1860-1915** (Philadelphia, 1944).

Alfred G. Meyer, *Marxism Since the Communist Manifesto** (Washington, 1961). S.C.T.H.

George Lichtheim, *Marxism: A Historical and Critical Study** (New York, 1961).

Selected Bibliography

Leopold Labedz, ed., *Revisionism: Essays on the History of Marxist Ideas**
(New York, 1962).

Peter Gay, *The Dilemma of Democratic Socialism: Eduard Bernstein's
Challenge to Marx** (New York, 1952).

Donald G. Charlton, *Positivist Thought in France during the Second Empire,
1852-1870* (Oxford, 1959).

Edward T. Gargan, ed., *Leo XIII and the Modern World* (New York, 1961).

Henry Stuart Hughes, *Consciousness and Society: The Reorientation of
European Social Thought, 1890-1930** (New York, 1958).

Gerhard Masur, *Prophets of Yesterday: Studies in European Culture, 1890-
1914* (New York, 1961).

Economic Developments

Walt W. Rostow, *The Stages of Economic Growth: A Non-Communist Manifesto** (Cambridge, 1960).

George W. Edwards, *The Evolution of Finance Capitalism* (New York,
1938).

Herbert Feis, *Europe, the World's Banker, 1870-1914* (New Haven, 1930).

Art

John K. Rothenstein, *Turner (1775-1851)* (London, 1949).

John Rewald, *The History of Impressionism* (New York, 1946).

Herman J. Wechsler, *French Impressionists** (New York, 1952).

Margaretta Salinger, *Claude Monet, 1840-1926** (New York, 1957).

CHAPTER XV   THE GROWTH OF DEMOCRACY

Great Britain

Thomas L. Jarman, *A Short History of Twentieth Century England: 1868-
1962** (New York, 1963).

William Ashworth, *An Economic History of England, 1870-1939* (London,
1960).

George S. R. Kitson Clark, *The Making of Victorian England* (Cambridge,
Mass., 1962).

Herman Ausubel, *The Late Victorians: A Short History** (New York, 1955).

Asa Briggs, *Victorian People: Some Reassessments of People, Institutions,
Ideas, and Events, 1851-1867** (London, 1954).

Philip M. Magnus, *Gladstone: A Biography** (London, 1954).

John L. Hammond and M. R. D. Foot, *Gladstone and Liberalism* (London,
1952).

George Dangerfield, *The Strange Death of Liberal England* * (New York,
1935).

Thomas Jones, *Lloyd George* (Cambridge, Mass., 1951).

Nicholas Mansergh, *Ireland in the Age of Reform and Revolution: A Commentary on Anglo-Irish Relations and on Political Theories in Ireland, 1840-1921* (London, 1941).

Lewis P. Curtis, Jr., *Coercion and Conciliation in Ireland, 1880-1892: A Study in Conservative Unionism* (Princeton, 1963).

France

Samuel M. Osgood, ed., *Napoleon III: Bubbon, Modern Dictator, or Sphinx?* * (Boston, 1963). Heath, *Problems*.

James M. Thompson, *Louis Napoleon and the Second Empire* (New York, 1954).

George P. Gooch, *The Second Empire* (London, 1960).

Roger L. Williams, *Gaslight and Shadow: The World of Napoleon III, 1851-1870* * (New York, 1957).

David H. Pinkney, *Napoleon III and the Rebuilding of Paris* (Princeton, 1958).

Lynn M. Case, *French Opinion on War and Diplomacy During the Second Empire* (Philadelphia, 1954).

Denis W. Brogan, *The Development of Modern France* (London, 1940). A splendid account.

Jean T. Joughin, *The Paris Commune in French Politics, 1871-1880* (Baltimore, 1955), 2 vols.

Leslie Derfler, ed., *The Dreyfus Affair: Tragedy of Errors?* * (Boston, 1964). Heath, *Problems*.

David Shapiro, ed., *The Right in France, 1890-1919: Three Studies* (Carbondale, Illinois, 1962).

Central Europe

Arthur Rosenberg, *The Birth of the German Republic, 1871-1918* * (New York, 1962), tr. by I. F. D. Morrow.

Erich Eyck, *Bismarck and the German Empire* * (London, 1950).

John A. Nichols, *Germany after Bismarck: The Caprivi Era, 1890-1894* (Cambridge, Mass., 1958).

Carl E. Schorske, *German Social Democracy, 1905-1917: The Development of the Great Schism* (Cambridge, Mass., 1955).

Robert A. Kann, *The Multinational Empire: Nationalism and National Reform in the Habsburg Monarchy, 1848-1918* (New York, 1950), 2 vols.

Josef Redlich, *Emperor Francis Joseph of Austria* (New York, 1929).

Arthur J. May, *The Hapsburg Monarchy, 1867-1914* (Cambridge, Mass., 1951).

Oszkár Jászi, *The Dissolution of the Habsburg Monarchy* * (Chicago, 1929).

Edward Crankshaw, *The Fall of the House of Habsburg* (New York, 1963).

Selected Bibliography

Arthur J. Whyte, *The Evolution of Modern Italy** (Oxford, 1944).

Shepard B. Clough, *The Economic History of Modern Italy* (New York, 1964).

Richard Hostetter, *The Italian Socialist Movement* (Princeton, 1958 ff.). One volume to date. It covers the 1860-1882 period.

A. William Salomone, *Italian Democracy in the Making: The Political Scene in the Giolittian Era, 1900-1914* (Philadelphia, 1945).

John A. Thayer, *Italy and the Great War: Politics and Culture, 1870-1915* (Madison, 1964).

Russia

Arthur E. Adams, ed., *Imperial Russia After 1861—Peaceful Modernization or Revolution?* * (Boston, 1965). Heath, *Problems*.

Hugh Seton-Watson, *The Decline of Imperial Russia, 1855-1914** (New York, 1952).

Theodore Von Laue, *Sergie Witte and the Industrialization of Russia* (New York, 1963).

Richard Hare, *Portraits of Russian Personalities Between Reform and Revolution** (London, 1959).

Hans Kohn, *Pan-Slavism: Its History and Ideology** (Notre Dame, 1953).

George Fischer, *Russian Liberalism: From Gentry to Intelligentsia* (Cambridge, Mass., 1958).

Jacob Walkin, *The Rise of Democracy in Pre-Revolutionary Russia: Political and Social Institutions Under the Last Three Czars* (New York, 1962).

Richard Pipes, ed., *The Russian Intelligentsia* (New York, 1961).

Cyril E. Black, ed., *The Transformation of Russian Society: Aspects of Social Change Since 1861* (Cambridge, Mass., 1960).

Richard D. Charques, *The Twilight of Imperial Russia* (Fair Lawn, 1959).

The Americas

Edwin C. Rozwenc, *Reconstruction in the South** (Boston, 1952). Heath, *Problems*.

John H. Franklin, *Reconstruction: After the Civil War** (Chicago, 1961).

Comer Vann Woodward, *Origins of the New South, 1877-1913* (Baton Rouge, 1951). An excellent synthesis.

Edward C. Kirkland, *Industry Comes of Age: Business, Labor, and Public Policy, 1860-1897* (New York, 1961).

Harold U. Faulkner, *Politics, Reform, and Expansion, 1890-1900** (New York, 1959).

Foster R. Dulles, *America's Rise to World Power, 1898-1954** (New York, 1955).

George E. Mowry, *The Progressive Movement, 1900-1920: Recent Ideas and New Literature** (Washington, 1958). S.C.T.H.

Edwin C. Rozwenc, *Roosevelt, Wilson and the Trusts** (Boston, 1950). Heath, *Problems.*

Eric F. Goldman, *Rendezvous with Destiny: A History of Modern American Reform** (New York, 1952).

Richard Hofstadter, *The Age of Reform: From Bryan to F.D.R.** (New York, 1955).

Arthur S. Link, *American Epoch: A History of the United States Since the 1890's* (New York, 2nd ed., 1963). A textbook of exceptional quality.

George E. Mowry, *The Era of Theodore Roosevelt, 1900-1912** (New York, 1958).

Arthur S. Link, *Woodrow Wilson and the Progressive Era, 1910-1917** (New York, 1954).

Alva C. Wilgus, ed., *South American Dictators During the First Century of Independence* (Washington, 1937).

Alva C. Wilgus, *Argentina, Brazil, and Chile Since Independence* (Washington, 1935).

Robert E. Scott, *Mexican Government in Transition* (Urbana, 1959).

CHAPTER XVI   THE EXPANSION OF WESTERN CIVILIZATION

Population Growth and Migration

Alexander M. Carr-Saunders, *World Population: Past Growth and Present Trends* (Oxford, 1936). Needs revision in the light of recent research.

Herbert Moller, ed., *Population Movements in Modern European History** (New York, 1964).

David J. Dallin, *The Rise of Russia in Asia* (New Haven, 1949).

Donald W. Treadgold, *The Great Siberian Migration: Government and Peasant in Resettlement from Emancipation to the First World War* (Princeton, 1957).

Stephen Neill, *Christian Missions** (Harmondsworth, 1964).

Imperialism

Harrison M. Wright, ed., *The "New Imperialism": Analysis of Late Nineteenth Century Expansion** (Boston, 1961). Heath, *Problems.*

Robin W. Winks, ed., *British Imperialism: Gold, God, Glory** (New York, 1963). Holt, Rinehart and Winston, *European Problem Studies.*

Joseph A. Schumpeter, *Imperialism and the Social Classes** (New York, 1951), tr. by P. M. Sweezy. Analysis by a leading sociologist.

Earle M. Winslow, *The Pattern of Imperialism: A Study in the Theories of Power* (New York, 1948).

Herbert Feis, *Europe, The World's Banker, 1870-1914* (New Haven, 1930).

George H. Nadel and Perry Curtis, eds., *Imperialism and Colonialism** (New York, 1964). A collection of essays.

Selected Bibliography

Ruth Slade, *King Leopold's Congo: Aspects of the Development of Race Relations in the Congo Independent State* (New York, 1962).

Ronald Robinson and John Gallagher, *Africa and the Victorians: The Climax of Imperialism in the Dark Continent* (New York, 1961).

Ronald Robinson and John Gallagher, *Africa and the Victorians: The Official Mind of Imperialism* (London, 1961).

Theodore C. Caldwell, ed., *The Anglo-Boer War: Why Was it Fought? Who Was Responsible?* * (Boston, 1965). Heath, *Problems*.

Leonard M. Thompson, *The Unification of South Africa, 1902-1910* (Oxford, 1960).

Basil Williams, *Botha, Smuts and South Africa* * (London, 1948).

William K. Hancock, *Smuts: The Sanguine Years, 1870-1919* (New York, 1962).

James Duffy, *Portuguese Africa* * (Cambridge, Mass., 1959).

Martin D. Lewis, *The British in India: Imperialism or Trusteeship?* * (Boston, 1962). Heath, *Problems*.

Philip Mason (Philip Woodruff, pseud.), *The Men Who Ruled India* * (London, 1953-54), 2 vols.

Charles H. Heimsath, *Indian Nationalism and Hindu Social Reform* (Princeton, 1964).

Ramesh C. Majumdar, *History of the Freedom Movement in India* (Calcutta, 1962 ff.). One volume to date.

Bernard Semmel, *Imperialism and Social Reform: English Social-Imperial Thought, 1895-1914* (Cambridge, Mass., 1960).

Richard Koebner and Helmut D. Schmidt, *Imperialism: The Story and Significance of a Political Word, 1840-1960* (New York, 1964). Essentially a study of British imperialism.

William L. Langer, *The Diplomacy of Imperialism, 1890-1902* (New York, 1935), 2 vols. The standard work.

Dana G. Munro, *Intervention and Dollar Diplomacy in the Carribbean, 1900-1921* (Princeton, 1964).

Ernest R. May, *Imperial Democracy: The Emergence of America as a Great Power* (New York, 1961).

The Far East

John T. Pratt, *The Expansion of Europe into the Far East* (London, 1947).

Masataka Banno, *China and the West, 1858-1861: The Origins of the Tsungli Yamen* (Cambridge, Mass., 1964).

Mary C. Wright, *The Last Stand of Chinese Conservatism: the T'ung-chih Restoration, 1862-1874* (Stanford, 1957).

Ralph L. Powell, *The Rise of Chinese Military Power, 1895-1912* (Princeton, 1955).

Charles P. Fitzgerald, *Revolution in China* * (London, 1952).

Abbie M. Sharman, *Sun Yat-sen, His Life and its Meaning: A Critical Biography* (New York, 1934).

John K. Fairbank, ed., *Chinese Thought and Institutions* (Chicago, 1957).

George B. Sansom, *Japan: A Short Cultural History* (New York, ed. of 1952). An excellent cultural history of the period prior to the Meiji restoration.

George O. Totten, ed., *Democracy in Prewar Japan: Groundwork or Facade?* * (Boston, 1965). Heath, *Problems.*

Hugh Borton, *Japan's Modern Century* (New York, 1955). A good account of the more recent period.

Marius B. Jansen, *Sakamoto Ryōma and the Meiji Restoration* (Princeton, 1961).

Albert M. Craig, *Chōshū in the Meiji Restoration* (Cambridge, Mass., 1961).

George C. Allen, *A Short Economic History of Modern Japan, 1867-1937* (London, 1946).

CHAPTER XVII   WORLD WAR I

The Balkans and the Ottoman Empire

Leften S. Stavrianos, *The Balkans Since 1453* (New York, 1958).

Roderic H. Davison, *Reform in the Ottoman Empire, 1856-1876* (Princeton, 1963).

Robert Devereux, *The First Ottoman Constitutional Period: A Study of the Midhat Constitution and Parliament* (Baltimore, 1963).

Charles Jelavich, *Tsarist Russia and Balkan Nationalism: Russian Influence in the Internal Affairs of Bulgaria and Serbia, 1879-1886* (Berkeley, 1958).

Rupert Furneaux, *The Breakfast War* (New York, 1960). A study of the siege of Plevna and the Congress of Berlin.

Wayne S. Vucinich, *Serbia Between East and West: The Events of 1903-1908* (Stanford, 1954).

The Origins of the War

Laurence Lafore, *The Long Fuse: An Interpretation of the Origins of World War I* (Philadelphia, 1965).

Dwight E. Lee, ed., *The Outbreak of the First World War: Who Was Responsible?* * (Boston, Rev. ed., 1963). Heath, *Problems.*

Alan J. P. Taylor, *The Struggle for Mastery in Europe, 1848-1918* (Oxford, 1954). Provocative, but not always reliable.

William L. Langer, *European Alliances and Alignments, 1871-1890** (New York, 2nd ed., 1950). A standard work.

Bernadotte E. Schmitt, *Triple Alliance and Triple Entente* (New York, 1934).

Selected Bibliography

Ernst C. Helmreich, *The Diplomacy of the Balkan Wars, 1912-1913* (Cambridge, Mass., 1938).

Sidney B. Fay, *The Origins of the World War* (New York, 1930), 2 vols. Still one of the best accounts. Covers diplomacy from 1871 until the war.

Luigi Albertini, *The Origins of the War of 1914* (London, 1952-57), 3 vols., tr. by I. M. Massey.

The War

Charles R. M. Cruttwell, *A History of the Great War, 1914-1918* (Oxford, 1934).

Cyril Falls, *The Great War** (New York, 1959).

Maurice P. A. Hankey, *The Supreme Command, 1914-1918* (London, 1961), 2 vols.

Frank P. Chambers, *The War Behind the War, 1914-1918: A History of the Political and Civilian Fronts* (London, 1939).

Z. A. B. Zeman, *The Break-up of the Habsburg Empire, 1914-1918: A Study in National and Social Revolution* (London, 1961).

The Results of the War

Ivo J. Lederer, *The Versailles Settlement—Was It Foredoomed to Failure?* (Boston, 1960). Heath, *Problems.*

Ivo J. Lederer, *Yugoslavia at the Paris Peace Conference: A Study in Frontiermaking* (New Haven, 1963).

Armo J. Mayer, *Political Origins of the New Diplomacy, 1917-1918** (New Haven, 1959).

Frank S. Marston, *The Peace Conference of 1919: Organization and Procedure* (New York, 1944).

Harold Nicolson, *Peacemaking 1919* (London, 1933). A readable account by a British diplomat and historian.

Paul Birdsall, *Versailles Twenty Years After* (New York, 1941).

Francis P. Walters, *A History of the League of Nations* (London, 1952), 2 vols.

PART SIX   THE TWENTIETH-CENTURY CRISIS

The New Cambridge Modern History. Vol. XII: *The Era of Violence 1898-1945* (Cambridge, 1960), ed., David Thomson.

Hajo Holborn, *The Political Collapse of Europe* (New York, 1951). A brief interpretative essay.

Carl Landauer, *European Socialism* (Berkeley, 1959), 2 vols.

CHAPTER XVIII   THE REVOLUTIONS, I

The Scientific Revolution

Science became so complex during the scientific revolution that it is difficult for the layman to understand. Excellent non-technical explanations of recent discoveries can be found in the *Science Library Series* published by *Life Magazine*.

Isaac Asimov, *The Intelligent Man's Guide to Science* (New York, 1960), 2 vols.

James H. Jeans, *The Growth of Physical Science** (Cambridge, 2nd ed., 1951). An account by a leading scientist.

Gwyn O. Jones, J. Rotblat, and G. J. Whitrow, *Atoms and the Universe* (London, 1956). Popular.

Edward N. da C. Andrade, *An Approach to Modern Physics** (London, 1956).

Leopold Infeld, *Albert Einstein** (New York, 1953).

Lincoln K. Barnett, *The Universe and Dr. Einstein** (New York, 2nd ed., 1957).

Bertrand Russell, *The A B C of Relativity** (London, 1925).

Richard H. Shryock, *The Development of Modern Medicine: An Interpretation of the Social and Scientific Factors Involved* (New York, Rev. ed., 1947).

Calvin S. Hall, *A Primer of Freudian Psychology** (Cleveland, 1954).

Richard La Piere, *The Freudian Ethic* (New York, 1959). Attacks Freud and his influence on human behavior.

Philip Rieff, *Freud: the Mind of the Moralist** (New York, 1959). A more favorable appraisal.

The Aesthetic Revolution

Bernard S. Myers, *Modern Art in the Making* (New York, 2nd ed., 1959).

Herbert Read, *The Philosophy of Modern Art: Collected Essays** (London, 1952).

Herbert Read, *A Concise History of Modern Painting** (New York, 1959).

Sam Hunter, *Modern French Painting, 1855-1956** (New York, 1956).

Roger Shattuck, *The Banquet Years: The Arts in France, 1885-1918** (London, 1959).

Meyer Schapiro, *Paul Cezanne* (New York, 1952).

Robert Goldwater, *Paul Gauguin* (New York, 1957).

Henry R. Hitchcock, *Architecture: Nineteenth and Twentieth Centuries* (Baltimore, 1958).

Selected Bibliography

Herbert Read, *A Concise History of Modern Sculpture** (New York, 1964).
Edmund Wilson, *Axel's Castle: A Study of the Imaginative Literature of 1870-1930** (New York, 1931).
Henri Peyre, *The Contemporary French Novel* (New York, 1955).

The Russian Revolution and the Soviet Union

George B. Carson, *Russia Since 1917** (Washington, 1962). S.C.T.H.
Arthur E. Adams, ed., *The Russian Revolution and Bolshevik Victory: Why and How?* * (Boston, 1960). Heath, *Problems.*
Victor S. Mamatey, *Soviet Russian Imperialism** (Princeton, 1964).
Hugh Seton-Watson, *From Lenin to Khrushchev: The History of World Communism** (New York, 1960).
Donald W. Treadgold, *Twentieth Century Russia* (Chicago, 2nd ed., 1964).
William H. Chamberlin, *The Russian Revolution, 1917-1921* (New York, 1952), 2 vols.
Michael T. Florinsky, *The End of the Russian Empire** (New Haven, 1931).
Bertram D. Wolfe, *Three Who Made a Revolution: A Biographical History* (New York, 1948). A study of Lenin, Trotsky, and Stalin.
Theodore H. Von Laue, *Why Lenin? Why Stalin? A Reappraisal of the Russian Revolution, 1900-1930** (Philadelphia, 1964).
Edward H. Carr, *A History of Soviet Russia* (New York, 1951 ff.). Five volumes to date.
Isaac Deutscher, *Trotsky** (New York, 1954-63), 3 vols. Pro-Trotsky.
Robert V. Daniels, ed., *The Stalin Revolution: Fulfillment or Betrayal of Communism?* * (Boston, 1965). Heath, *Problems.*
Isaac Deutscher, *Stalin: A Political Biography** (New York, ed. of 1960).
John S. Reshetar, Jr., *A Concise History of the Communist Party of the Soviet Union** (New York, 1960).
Leonard B. Schapiro, *The Communist Party of the Soviet Union** (New York, 1960).
Ernest J. Simmons, ed., *Continuity and Change in Russian and Soviet Thought* (Cambridge, Mass., 1955).
Cyril E. Black, ed., *The Transformation of Russian Society: Aspects of Social Changes Since 1861* (Cambridge, Mass., 1960).
John S. Curtiss, *The Russian Church and the Soviet State, 1917-1950* (Boston, 1953).
George F. Kennan, *Russia and the West Under Lenin and Stalin** (Boston, 1961).
George F. Kennan, *Soviet Foreign Policy, 1917-1941** (Princeton, 1960).
Ivo J. Lederer, ed., *Russian Foreign Policy: Essays in Historical Perspective** (New Haven, 1962).
Kermit E. McKenzie, *Comintern and World Revolution, 1928-1943: The Shaping of Doctrine* (New York, 1964).

CHAPTER XIX   THE REVOLUTIONS, II

The Great Depression

John K. Galbraith, *The Great Crash, 1929** (Boston, 1955).
David A. Shannon, ed., *The Great Depression** (Englewood Cliffs, 1960).
Roy F. Harrod, *The Life of John Maynard Keynes** (London, 1951).

The Fascist Revolutions

Hannah Arendt, *The Origins of Totalitarianism** (New York, 1951).
Carl J. Friedrich, ed., *Totalitarianism** (Cambridge, Mass., 1954). Essays by forty leading authorities.
Eugen J. Weber, *Varieties of Fascism: Doctrines of Revolution in the Twentieth Century** (Princeton, 1964).

Italy

Charles F. Delzell, *Mussolini's Enemies: The Italian Anti-Fascist Resistance* (Princeton, 1961). A prizewinning study.
Richard A. Webster, *The Cross and the Fasces: Christian Democracy and Fascism in Italy* (Stanford, 1960).
Samuel William Halperin, *Mussolini and Italian Fascism** (Princeton, 1964).
Ivone Kirkpatrick, *Mussolini: Study of a Demagogue* (London, 1964).

Germany

Erich Eyck, *A History of the Weimar Republic* (Cambridge, Mass., 1962), 2 vols., tr. by H. P. Hanson and R. G. L. Waite.
Samuel William Halperin, *Germany Tried Democracy** (New York, 1946).
Werner T. Angress, *Stillborn Revolution: The Communist Bid for Power in Germany, 1921-1923* (Princeton, 1963).
Gordon A. Craig, *From Bismarck to Adenauer: Aspects of German Statecraft** (Baltimore, 1958).
Andreas Dorpalen, *Hindenburg and the Weimar Republic* (Princeton, 1964).
Klaus Epstein, *Matthias Erzberger and the Dilemma of German Democracy* (Princeton, 1959).
Harold J. Gordon, Jr., *The Reichswehr and the German Republic, 1919-1926* (Princeton, 1957).
Henry A. Turner, Jr., *Stresemann and the Politics of the Weimar Republic** (Princeton, 1963).

Selected Bibliography

John L. Snell, ed., *The Nazi Revolution: Germany's Guilt or Germany's Fate?* * (Boston, 1959). Heath, *Problems.*

Alan Bullock, *Hitler: A Study in Tyranny** (New York, Completely Revised Edition, 1962). A superb biography that is also one of the best studies of Nazi Germany.

Oron J. Hale, *The Captive Press in the Third Reich* (Princeton, 1964).

Burton H. Klein, *Germany's Economic Preparations for War* (Cambridge, Mass., 1959).

Fritz Stern, *The Politics of Cultural Despair: A Study in the Rise of the Germanic Ideology** (Berkeley, 1961).

The Smaller States

Carlile A. Macartney and Alan W. Palmer, *Independent Eastern Europe: A History* (New York, 1962).

Charles A. Gulick, *Austria from Habsburg to Hitler* (Berkeley, 1948). 2 vols.

Carlile A. Macartney, *October Fifteenth: A History of Modern Hungary, 1929-1945* (Edinburgh, 1956-57), 2 vols.

Jacob B. Hoptner, *Yugoslavia in Crisis, 1934-1941* (New York, 1962).

Robert J. Kerner, ed., *Yugoslavia* (Berkeley, 1949).

Gerald Brenan, *The Spanish Labyrinth: An Account of the Social and Political Background of the Civil War** (Cambridge, 2nd ed., 1950). A History of Spain from the reestablishment of the monarchy in 1874 until the Franco regime.

Gabriel Jackson, *The Spanish Republic and the Civil War, 1931-1939* (Princeton, 1965).

Stanley G. Payne, *Falange: A History of Spanish Fascism* (Stanford, 1961).

CHAPTER XX   THE SURVIVING DEMOCRACIES

Denis W. Brogan, *The Development of Modern France, 1870-1939* (London, 1944).

Richard D. Challener, *The French Theory of the Nation in Arms, 1866-1939* (New York, 1955).

John T. Marcus, *French Socialism in the Crisis Years, 1933-1936: Fascism and the French Left* (New York, 1958).

Eugen J. Weber, *Action Française: Royalism and Reaction in Twentieth-Century France* (Stanford, 1962).

Henry R. Winkler, *Great Britain in the Twentieth Century** (Washington, 1960). S.C.T.H.

William L. McElwee, *Britain's Locust Years, 1918-1940* (London, 1962).

Alfred F. Havighurst, *Twentieth Century Britain* (Evanston, 1962).

Charles L. Mowat, *Britain Between the Wars, 1918-1940* (Chicago, 1955).

George M. Young, *Stanley Baldwin* (London, 1952).

Edgar Holt, *Protest in Arms: The Irish Troubles, 1916-1923* (London, 1960).

Arthur S. Link, *American Epoch: A History of the United States Since the 1890's* (New York, 2nd ed., 1963). An unusually good textbook.

John D. Hicks, *Republican Ascendancy, 1921-1933: An Age of Disillusionment** (Washington, 1960). S.C.T.H.

John D. Hicks, *Republican Ascendancy, 1921-1933* (New York, 1960).

Frank B. Freidel, *The New Deal in Historical Perspective** (Washington, 1959). S.C.T.H.

Frank B. Freidel, *Franklin D. Roosevelt* (Boston, 1952). Three volumes of a projected nine-volume study have been published to date.

William E. Leuchtenburg, *Franklin D. Roosevelt and the New Deal, 1932-1940** (New York, 1963).

Dexter Perkins, *The New Age of Franklin Roosevelt, 1932-1945** (Chicago, 1957).

Arthur M. Schlesinger, Jr., *The Age of Roosevelt* (Boston, 1957 ff.). Three volumes to date; first volume is paperback.

Jan Romein, *The Asian Century: A History of Modern Nationalism in Asia* (Berkeley, 1962), tr. by R. T. Clark.

Zeine N. Zeine, *The Struggle for Arab Independence: Western Diplomacy and the Rise and Fall of Faisal's Kingdom of Syria* (Beirut, 1960).

Niyazi Berkes, *The Development of Secularism in Turkey* (Montreal, 1964).

Amin Banani, *The Modernization of Iran, 1921-1941* (Stanford, 1961).

Ben Halpern, *The Idea of the Jewish State* (Cambridge, Mass., 1961).

CHAPTER XXI   THE STRUGGLE FOR WORLD SUPREMACY

René Albrecht-Carrié, *France, Europe and the Two World Wars* (Geneva, 1960).

Gerhard L. Weinberg, *Germany and the Soviet Union, 1939-1941* (Leiden, 1954).

Gordon A. Craig and Felix Gilbert, eds., *The Diplomats: 1919-1939** (Princeton, 1953).

Hugh Thomas, *The Spanish Civil War** (New York, 1961).

Keith Eubank, *Munich* (Norman, 1963).

John W. Wheeler-Bennett, *Munich: Prologue to Tragedy** (New York, 1948).

John A. Lukacs, *The Great Powers and Eastern Europe* (New York, 1953).

Dorothy Borg, *The United States and the Far Eastern Crisis of 1933-1938: From the Manchurian Incident Through the Initial Stage of the Undeclared Sino-Japanese War* (Cambridge, Mass., 1964).

John L. Snell, ed., *The Outbreak of the Second World War: Design or Blunder?** (Boston, 1962). Heath, *Problems.*

David J. Lu, *From the Marco Polo Bridge to Pearl Harbor: Japan's Entry into World War II* (Washington, 1961).

Louis L. Snyder, *The War: A Concise History, 1939-1945** (New York, 1960).

Chester Wilmot, *The Struggle for Europe** (London, 1952).

Selected Bibliography

Winston S. Churchill, *Second World War** (Boston, 1948-53), 6 vols.

Alexander Werth, *Russia at War, 1941-1945* (New York, 1964).

Ihor Kamenetsky, *Secret Nazi Plans for Eastern Europe: A Study in Lebensraum Policies* (New York, 1961).

Seymour Freidin and William Richardson, eds., *The Fatal Decisions: Six Decisive Battles of the Second World War from the Viewpoint of the Vanquished** (London, 1956).

Correlli Barnett, *The Desert Generals** (London, 2nd ed., 1960).

Kent R. Greenfield, *American Strategy in World War II: A Reconsideration* (Baltimore, 1963).

Samuel E. Morison, *Strategy and Compromise* (Boston, 1958).

A. Russell Buchanan, *The United States and World II** (New York, 1964), 2 vols.

Hugh R. Trevor-Roper, *The Last Days of Hitler** (London, 3rd ed., 1956).

Heinz Schröter, *Stalingrad* (London, 1958), tr. by C. Fitzgibbon.

Robert Aron, *The Vichy Regime, 1940-44* (London, 1958), tr. by H. Hare.

Cornelius Ryan, *The Longest Day: June 6, 1944** (New York, 1959).

Norman Kogan, *Italy and the Allies* (Cambridge, Mass., 1956).

Gerhard Ritter, *The German Resistance: Carl Joerdeler's Struggle Against Tyranny* (London, 1959).

Gerhard L. Weinberg, *Germany and the Soviet Union, 1939-1941* (Leiden, 1954).

John L. Snell, *Illusion and Necessity: The Diplomacy of Global War, 1939-1945** (Boston, 1963).

Herbert Feis, *Churchill, Roosevelt, Stalin: The War They Waged and the Peace They Sought* (Princeton, 1957).

Herbert Feis, *The China Tangle: The American Effort in China from Pearl Harbor to the Marshall Mission** (Princeton, 1953).

Herbert Feis, *Japan Subdued: The Atom Bomb and the End of the War in the Pacific* (Princeton, 1961).

Clark M. Eichelberger, *UN: The First Ten Years* (New York, 1955).

CHAPTER XXII   THE EXPANSION OF COMMUNISM
AND THE AMERICAN REACTION

George F. Kennan, *Russia and the West Under Lenin and Stalin** (Boston, 1961).

John A. Lukacs, *A History of the Cold War** (Garden City, 1961).

Hugh Seton-Watson, *Neither War nor Peace: The Struggle for Power in the Post-War World** (New York, 1960).

Edward Crankshaw, *Khrushchev's Russia** (Baltimore, 1959).

Wolfgang Leonhard, *The Kremlin Since Stalin** (New York, 1962), tr. by E. Wiskemann and M. Jackson.

Alec Nove, *The Soviet Economy: An Introduction** (London, 1961).

Soviet Foreign Relations and World Communism: A Selected, Annotated Bibliography (Princeton, 1964), ed., Thomas T. Hammond.

Robert D. Warth, *Soviet Russia in World Politics* (New York, 1963).

Zbigniew K. Brzezinski, *The Soviet Bloc: Unity and Conflict** (Cambridge, Mass., 1960).

Richard V. Burks, *The Dynamics of Communism in Eastern Europe* (Princeton, 1961).

Edmund O. Stillman, ed., *Bitter Harvest: The Intellectual Revolt Behind the Iron Curtain* (London, 1958).

Morton A. Kaplan, *The Communist Coup in Czechoslovakia* (Princeton, 1960).

Josef Korbel, *The Communist Subversion of Czechoslovakia, 1938-1948* (Princeton, 1959).

Edward Taborsky, *Communism in Czechoslovakia, 1948-1960* (Princeton, 1961).

Ferenc A. Váli, *Rift and Revolt in Hungary: Nationalism Versus Communism* (Cambridge, Mass., 1961).

Richard F. Staar, *Poland, 1944-1962: The Sovietization of a Captive People* (Baton Rouge, 1962).

Allan B. Cole, *Forty Years of Chinese Communism: Selected Readings with Commentary** (Washington, 1962). S.C.T.H.

A. Doak Barnett, *China on the Eve of Communist Takeover** (New York, 1963).

A. Doak Barnett, *Communist China in Perspective** (New York, 1962).

Jerome Ch'em, *Mao and the Chinese Revolution* (Fair Lawn, 1965).

Chalmers A. Johnson, *Peasant Nationalism and Communist Power: The Emergence of Revolutionary China 1937-1945* (Stanford, 1962).

Edward Crankshaw, *The New Cold War: Moscow Vs. Peking** (Baltimore, 1963).

David Floyd, *Mao Against Khrushchev: A Short History of the Sino-Soviet Conflict** (New York, 1964).

Donald S. Zagoria, *The Sino-Soviet Conflict, 1956-1961** (Princeton, 1962).

Walter Z. Laqueur, *The Soviet Union and the Middle East* (New York, 1959).

Zbigniew K. Brzezinski, ed., *Africa and the Communist World* (Stanford, 1963).

Eric F. Goldman, *The Crucial Decade—and After: America 1945-1960** (New York, 1961).

Walter Johnson, *1600 Pennsylvania Avenue: Presidents and the People, 1929-1959** (Boston, 1960).

Marquis Childs, *Eisenhower: Captive Hero. A Critical Study of the General and the President* (New York, 1958).

Alpheus Mason, *The Supreme Court from Taft to Warren** (Baton Rouge, 1958).

Comer Vann Woodward, *The Strange Career of Jim Crow** (New York, Rev. ed., 1957).

J. W. Spanier, *American Foreign Policy Since World War II** (New York, Rev. ed., 1962).

Selected Bibliography

Tang Tsou, *America's Failure in China, 1941-50* (Chicago, 1963).

Carl Berger, *The Korea Knot* (Philadelphia, 1957).

Russell H. Fifield, *Southeast Asia in United States Policy** (New York, 1963).

Robert Leckie, *Conflict: The History of the Korean War, 1950-53** (New York, 1962).

David Rees, *Korea: The Limited War* (New York, 1964).

Jean E. Smith, *The Defense of Berlin* (Baltimore, 1963).

CHAPTER XXIII   THE DEVELOPED AND UNDERDEVELOPED COUNTRIES

Kenneth Lindsay, *European Assemblies: The Experimental Period, 1949-1959* (London, 1960).

Hans A. Schmitt, *The Path to European Union: From the Marshall Plan to the Common Market* (Baton Rouge, 1962).

F. Roy Willis, *France, Germany, and the New Europe, 1945-1963* (Stanford, 1965).

Alfred Grosser, *The Federal Republic of Germany: A Concise History** (New York, 1964), tr. by N. Aldrich.

Karl W. Deutsch and Lewis J. Edinger, *Germany Rejoins the Powers: Mass Opinion, Interest Groups, and Elites in Contemporary German Foreign Policy* (Stanford, 1959).

Kurt L. Shell, *The Transformation of Austrian Socialism* (Albany, 1962).

Edgar S. Furniss, *France, Troubled Ally: De Gaulle's Heritage and Prospects** (New York, 1960).

Alexander Werth, *France, 1940-1955* (London, 1956).

Dorothy M. Pickles, *France, The Fourth Republic** (London, 2nd ed., 1958).

Dorothy M. Pickles, *The Fifth French Republic** (London, 1960).

James H. Meisel, *The Fall of the Republic: Military Revolt in France* (Ann Arbor, 1962).

David Thomson, *Two Frenchmen: Pierre Laval and Charles de Gaulle* (London, 1951).

Keith Hutchison, *The Decline and Fall of British Capitalism* (London, 1951).

Ernest Watkins, *The Cautious Revolution* (London, 1951).

Alan Bullock, *The Life and Times of Ernest Bevan* (London, 1960 ff.). One volume to date.

Sydney F. A. Coles, *Franco of Spain* (London, 1955).

Giuseppe Mammarella, *Italy after Fascism* (Montreal, 1965).

Raymond Aron, *Imperialism and Colonialism* (Leeds, 1959).

Rupert Emerson, *From Empire to Nation: The Rise to Self-Assertion of Asian and African Peoples** (Cambridge, Mass., 1960).

Stewart C. Easton, *The Rise and Fall of Western Colonialism: A Historical Survey from the Early Nineteenth Century to the Present** (New York, 1964).

John Strachey, *The End of Empire** (New York, 1960).

Michael Brecher, *Nehru: A Political Biography** (New York, 1959).

Anthony T. Bouscaren, *The Last of the Mandarins: Diem of Vietnam* (Pittsburgh, 1965).

Manfred Halpern, *The Politics of Social Change in the Middle East and North Africa* (Princeton, 1963).

John C. Campbell, *Defense of the Middle East: Problems of American Policy** (New York, 2nd ed., 1960).

Kemal H. Karpat, *Turkey's Politics: The Transition to a Multi-Party System* (Princeton, 1959).

Charles D. Cremeans, *The Arabs and the World: Nasser's Arab Nationalist Policy** (New York, 1963).

Robert W. Macdonald, *The League of Arab States: A Study in the Dynamics of Regional Organization* (Princeton, 1965).

Richard M. and Joan Brace, *Ordeal in Algeria* (Princeton, 1960).

Michael K. Clark, *Algeria in Turmoil: A History of the Rebellion** (New York, 1959).

Jules Roy, *The War in Algeria* (New York, 1961), tr. by R. Howard.

John Hatch, *A History of Postwar Africa* (New York, 1965).

Peter Judd, ed., *African Independence** (New York, 1963).

Hans Kohn and Wallace Sokolsky, *African Nationalism in the Twentieth Century** (Princeton, 1965).

Crawford Young, *Transitional Politics in the Congo, Decolonization and Independence* (Princeton, 1965).

James Duffy, *Portugal in Africa** (Cambridge, Mass., 1962).

Leopold Marquard, *The Peoples and Policies of South Africa** (Cape Town, 2nd ed., 1960).

Robert J. Alexander, *Communism in Latin America* (New Brunswick, 1957).

James L. Busey, *Latin America: Political Institutions and Processes** (New York, 1964).

Hugh M. Hamill, ed., *Dictatorship in Latin America** (New York, 1965).

Charles O. Porter and Robert J. Alexander, *The Struggle for Democracy in Latin America* (New York, 1961).

James Daniel and John C. Hubbell, *Strike in the West: The Complete Story of the Cuban Crisis* (New York, 1963).

Edwin C. Stein, *Cuba, Castro, and Communism** (New York, 1962).

Index

Index

Index